THE RAY SOCIETY
INSTITUTED 1844

This volume is No 159 of the series

LONDON

1991

To Kathleen
and
to Roberta,
Abigail, Keir, Natalie and Amy

COPEPOD EVOLUTION

By
RONY HUYS
and
GEOFFREY A. BOXSHALL

ISBN 0 903874 21 0

Sold by The Ray Society
c/o The Natural History Museum, Cromwell Road, London SW7 5BD.

Printed and bound by Unwin Brothers Ltd.,
The Gresham Press, Old Woking, Surrey GU22 9LH
A Member of the Martins Printing Group

PREFACE

Students of copepods have traditionally belonged to one of five more or less separate interest groups, i.e. the marine plankton, the freshwater plankton, sediment inhabiting forms, parasites of fishes and associates of invertebrate hosts. Each of these subject areas has remained rather isolated from the others, with little exchange of ideas. The series of International Conferences on Copepoda, now organised under the auspices of the World Association of Copepodologists, has made significant progress in breaking down barriers between the interest groups but studies of copepod systematics in particular have been hindered because these ecological categories do not correspond to taxonomic boundaries. For example, some orders, such as the Cyclopoida, contain representatives belonging to all five. In our opinion a systematic overview that provides order to the immense diversity of copepods is long overdue and we hope that it will greatly facilitate communication between the ecologically based interest groups. The primary aim of this volume is to provide a detailed examination of the phylogenetic relationships between the orders of copepods and, therefore, a reassessment of the major evolutionary trends within the Copepoda. The evolutionary perspective will provide a strong base for comparative biological studies as well as a robust framework for future taxonomic studies.

The need for a new evolutionary overview is enhanced by the discovery of many new and unusual copepods in the last two decades. In particular, the exploration of deep-sea hydrothermal vents and cold seeps, and of anchialine habitats has resulted in the discovery of several new families and the establishment of a new order, the Platycopioida. In addition, an increasing volume of taxonomic work on the deep-sea meiobenthic community, on groundwater forms, and on associates of marine invertebrate hosts has resulted in the creation of numerous new families.

We have not relied on the literature. Instead we have attempted to examine specimens of the most primitive representatives of all orders and describe them by a consistent set of techniques (see Appendix 2). We have also used a consistent nomenclature for the body, the appendages and their component parts. This was necessary in order to facilitate comparison of different types of copepods, and to enable the identification of homologies between parts of the body, the limbs and their setation elements.

In the light of our decision to reexamine and verify every character for every order we became heavily dependent upon the collections of the great museums of the world and their curators, and upon the immense generosity of our fellow copepod specialists the world over. Without their help this project would never have been completed. It is a pleasure to record our gratitude to the following colleagues who lent us material from the collections in their care or from their personal collections: Gazim Abdelhalim (University of Khartoum), Maria Paloma Alvarez (Universidade de São Paulo), Philippe Bodin (Université de Bretagne Occidentale), Ruth Böttger-Schnack (Universität Kiel), Thomas Bowman (Smithsonian Institution), Marit Christiansen (Zoologisk Museum, University of Oslo), August Coomans (Rijksuniversiteit Gent), Roger Cressey (Smithsonian Institution), Danielle Defaye (Muséum National d'Histoire Naturelle), Gregory Deets (University of California, Long Beach), Harold Feinberg (American Museum of Natural History), Frank Ferrari (Smithsonian Oceanographic Sorting Center), Audun Fosshagen (University of Bergen), Mike Gee (Plymouth Marine Laboratory), Mark Grygier (University of the Ryukyus, Japan), Richard Hamond (Holt, Norfolk, U.K.), Gerd Hartmann (Universität Hamburg), Hans-Volkmar Herbst (Krefeld, Germany), Ju-shey Ho (University of California, Long Beach), Arthur Humes (Boston University), Thomas Iliffe (Texas A & M University), Helmut Kunz (Bischmisheim, Germany), Sybille Maas (Rijksuniversiteit Gent), Claude Monniot (Muséum National d'Histoire Naturelle), Susumu Ohtsuka (Hiroshima University), Roy Olerød (Naturhistorisk Riksmuseet, Stockholm), Dirk Platvoet (Instituut voor Taxonomische Zoölogie, Amsterdam), Paula Rothman (Smithsonian Institution), Raymond Rouch (Laboratoire Souterrain du CNRS, Moulis), Michel Segonzac (IFREMER, Brest), Chang-tai Shih (Canadian Museum of Nature, Ottawa), Jan Stock (Instituut voor Taxonomische Zoölogie, Amsterdam), Willem Vervoort (Rijksmuseum van Natuurlijke Historie, Leiden), Endre Willassen (Bergen Museum), Kris Willems (Rijksuniversiteit Gent), Torben Wolff (Zoologisk Museum, Copenhagen), Karel Wouters (Koninklijk Belgisch Instituut voor Natuurwetenschappen, Brussels) and Wolfgang Zeidler (South Australian Museum, Adelaide). In many cases specimens were given to us and we note here our intention to deposit this donated material in the collections of The Natural History Museum, (BM(NH)), so that others can have easy access to it in future.

We are also grateful to Rick Brusca (San Diego Natural History Museum), Ju-shey Ho (University of California, Long Beach), Gordon Paterson (BM(NH)) and Richard Thomas (BM(NH)) for their advice and assistance with using the PAUP programs. We would like to record our special thanks for the generous assistance given by Sheila Halsey (BM(NH)), in the preparation of reference lists, figure legends, organizing material, proof reading and in many other ways. Her help has ensured a more rapid progress towards publication.

We are also pleased to acknowledge the considerable help we have received in the preparation of material for study. Mrs Rita Van Driessche in Gent and Alan Warren and the staff of the Electron Microscopy Unit at the Natural History Museum in London provided valuable assistance with Scanning Electron Microscopy. We would also like to thank David Cooper for preparing the histological sections. Part of this work was carried out under Research Grant 2.0009.81 of the Belgian Fund for Collective Fundamental Research and EEC Science Grant ST2*0443. For their continuing support and for the provision of laboratory and other facilities we are grateful to Professor Carlo Heip (Delta Institute for Hydrobiological Research, Yerseke), Professor August Coomans (Rijksuniversiteit Gent), and to successive Keepers of Zoology, John Peake and Colin Curds, and the Head of Crustacea, Roger Lincoln, at The Natural History Museum, London.

Lastly we both would like to acknowledge the encouragement and understanding we have received from our respective families. They have shared with us the conception, gestation and, finally, the birth of this book. We would not have succeeded without them and it is only fitting that we should dedicate this volume to them.

CONTENTS

Chapter 1

INTRODUCTION TO THE COPEPODS

1.1 COPEPOD HABITATS

Copepods are aquatic crustaceans, the diminutive relatives of the crabs and shrimps. In terms of their size, diversity and abundance they can be regarded as the insects of the seas. Over 10,000 species are currently known but, since the true diversity of the benthic harpacticoids and of the poecilostomatoid and siphonostomatoid associates of marine invertebrates, has yet to be revealed, this number could easily double by the middle of the twenty first century. Copepods have successfully colonised all salinity regimes from freshwater, to marine and hypersaline inland waters and all temperature regimes from subzero polar waters to hot springs (figure 1.1). They also have an immense vertical range occurring from depths of 9995-10002 metres in the Philippine Trench (Wolff, 1960) to an altitude of 5540 metres up in the Himalayan mountains (Löffler, 1968). This vertical range represents about three quarters of the maximum possible range on the Earth's surface, from the deepest point in the Marianas Trench to the peak of Mount Everest (about 20,372 metres).

Marine Plankton: The sheer abundance of copepods in marine plankton secures for them a vital role in the marine economy. Sir Alister Hardy (1970) estimated that the copepods are the most numerous metazoan animals in the world, even outnumbering the insects which have more species but fewer individuals and the nematodes, both of which have had some claim to this position of preeminence. Hardy's estimate is based primarily on the planktonic copepods that inhabit the oceans of the world. The entire oceanic realm, which covers about 71 per cent of the world's surface to an average depth of about 3700 metres, provides an immense volume of water (1347 million cubic kilometres) all of which is home to free-swimming copepods. They are found from the ocean surface to the bottom of the hadal trenches and occur in densities ranging from 70,000 per cubic metre in the shallow waters of the North Sea, down to 100 per cubic metre at depths of 4,000 metres in the North Atlantic and up to 1.5 million per cubic metre in mating swarms in coral reef environments (Hamner & Carleton, 1979). Some species exploit the ephemeral habitat at the ice-water interface of polar and subpolar ice and can reach densities of 12,500 individuals per square metre during the algal blooms of the late spring (Kern & Carey, 1983).

Freshwater Plankton: Copepods are also abundant in freshwater planktonic communities. Members of the families Cyclopidae in the Cyclopoida, Canthocamptidae in the Harpacticoida, and Diaptomidae in the Calanoida are particularly successful in all kinds of freshwater habitats, from the saline lakes in the Antarctic Vestfold Hills (Burton & Hamond, 1981) to the high altitude lakes on the southern slopes of the Himalayan mountains (Löffler, 1968). Occasionally representatives of other families are dominant, such as the temorid *Epischura baikalensis* Sars which comprises up to 96 per cent of the animal plankton of Lake Baikal.

Marine Sediments: Copepods also live in marine sediments, inhabiting the microscopic spaces between the sediment particles. In this meiofaunal community they are typically second in abundance only to nematodes. Meiofaunal copepods tend to become more abundant as the particle size of the sediment increases and in coarse sands they often outnumber the nematodes (Hicks & Coull, 1983). They are found in all sediment types from mud to sand and at all depths from the intertidal zone to the deepest oceanic ooze. The density changes with sediment type and with depth. Typical densities in shallow water ecosystems (down to about 100 metres) are in the order of 200 to 300 individuals per 10 square centimetres of sediment surface but they range from 0

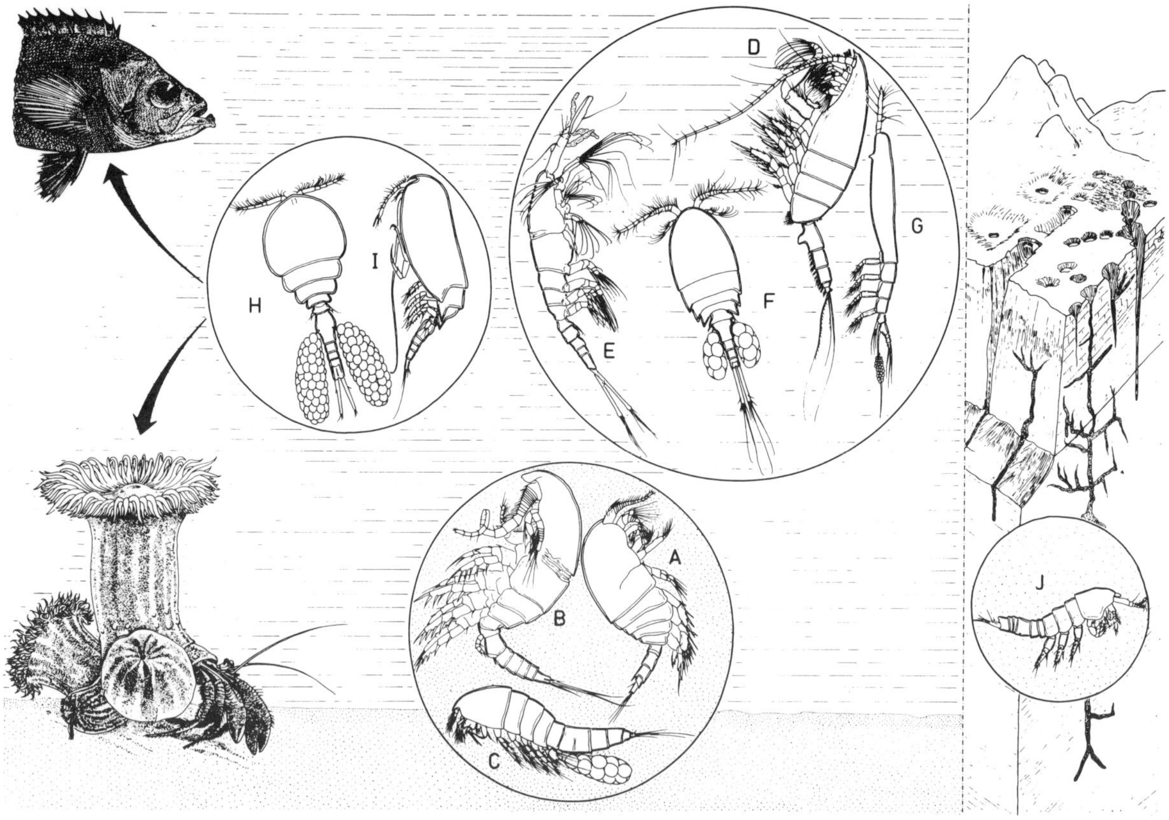

Figure 1.1. Copepod habitats: a schematic representation of the primary habitat of each of the ten copepod orders. **A**. Platycopioida. **B**. Misophrioida. **C**. Harpacticoida. **D**. Calanoida. **E**. Mormonilloida. **F**. Cyclopoida. **G**. Monstrilloida. **H**. Poecilostomatoida. **I**. Siphonostomatoida. **J**. Gelyelloida. [**A-C**, benthic; **D-G**, planktonic; **H** and **I**, associated; **J**, groundwater.]

to over 6,000. Numbers decline with depth and in deep-sea sediments typical densities are 20 to 30 individuals per 10 square centimetres of sediment surface, with a range from 1 to over 400. Meiofaunal specialists usually work with small cores of sediment, hence they calculate densities for columns of sediment beneath a surface area of 10 square centimetres. Typical densities per square metre of surface in shallow waters become 200,000 to 300,000, with a maximum of over 6 million.

Plant Associates: In the marine environment copepods are commonly found on intertidal and subtidal algae and even on some flowering plants, such as the sea grasses (Bell et al., 1984). Some inhabit the sediment and detritus trapped in the interstices of the complex, ramifying holdfast of the alga but many are true phytal copepods and are highly specialised for life on the surface of the fronds. Under reduced silt-clay or detrital loads the dominant and most ubiquitous meiofaunal taxa on marine algae are the harpacticoid copepods. Some harpacticoids belonging to the family Darcythompsoniidae are exclusively associated with the microflora of decaying mangrove leaves (Por, 1984a).

Cryptic Habitats: Other habitats exploited by free living copepods are damp terrestrial situations. Reid (1986) surveyed many of these cryptic habitats. In the organic soil of wet campo marsh in tropical South America Reid found densities ranging from 1,000 to 178,000 per square metre. In the soil of a sedge meadow in the Canadian tundra Bliss et al. (1973) found mean densities of over 6500 copepods per square metre. Copepods are particularly abundant in forest litter, even at high altitude. Sphagnum bogs and terrestrial mosses are also favoured habitats for copepods. They often colonise water tanks in farm and other buildings and are frequently taken in drinking water. A thriving population of freshwater cyclopoids inhabits the water tanks on the roof of the Natural History Museum in London. Copepods have been reported from even more bizarre habitats, such as the pools between the leaves of bromeliads in tropical rainforests. *Phyllognathopus* *viguieri* (Maupas) is commonly found in the liquid retained at the bases of leaves of pineapples in Botanic Gardens (Lowndes, 1931) and in supermarkets in the U.S.A. The cyclopoid *Cryptocyclops anninae* Lowndes was first collected from water contained in empty coconut shells (Lowndes, 1928). Yeatman (1983) also surveyed unusual microhabitats in some South Pacific Islands and reported copepods from taro leaf axils, tree holes, crab burrows and discarded car tyres. They even occur in hot springs, where they are active at water temperatures between 38 and 58 °C (Itô & Burton, 1980).

Subterranean Habitats: They live in groundwater and can regularly be caught in springs, wells and pools in caves. The small order Gelyelloida, comprising just two species, occurs only in subterranean waters in the karstic systems of Switzerland and France. Gelyelloids have been recovered from filtration of subterranean water from boreholes 60 metres below ground level. Two harpacticoid families, the Parastenocarididae and Chappuisiidae, are specialised groundwater inhabitants. Parastenocaridids are widely distributed in groundwater throughout Eurasia, Africa and the Americas. They can occur in oceanic islands, such as the Canary Islands, but are absent from New Zealand. The Chappuisiidae comprises only two species, both found only in groundwaters accompanying the Danube, Elbe, Rhine and Weser rivers and their tributaries, in Central Europe. The cyclopoid family Cyclopidae contains many specialised subterranean species. Lescher-Moutoué (1974a,b) reviewed the taxonomy and biology of the subterranean cyclopids in southern France and recorded forty-one species and subspecies in this region alone.

Deep-sea Vents and Anchialine Caves: In the last two decades much emphasis has been placed on the investigation of the fauna of two particular habitats, anchialine caves and deep-sea hydrothermal vents and cold seeps. These habitats have revealed many interesting new forms of great importance to studies of the evolutionary relationships between the various groups of copepods. The study of anchialine caves has relied primarily on SCUBA diving techniques and has produced many of the most primitive known copepods in the orders Platycopioida, Calanoida and Misophrioida. Access to the fauna of deep-sea vents and cold seeps has been provided mainly by submersibles. Here, many primitive associated copepods belonging to the orders Siphonostomatoida and Poecilostomatoida have been found.

Animal Associates: The abundance and diversity of the free-living forms is only part of the amazing success of the copepods. Nearly half of all known species live in symbiotic relationships with other organisms. They are known to have been living in close association with other phyla at least since the Lower Cretaceous. Copepods parasitise virtually every phylum of animals from sponges and coelenterates to vertebrates including mammals, and they enter into a variety of commensal or other associations with a similar range of hosts (Table 1). Those parasitic on fishes and those living in symbiotic associations with marine invertebrates have been reviewed recently by Kabata (1981) and Gotto (1979) respectively. Most are external parasites, living on the body surface of their hosts but many have colonised more sheltered microhabitats, including the gills, nostrils, mouth and lateral line canals of fishes, the baleen plates of whales, the mantle cavity and gills of molluscs, the brood pouches and gill chambers of other crustaceans, the genital bursa of ophiuroid echinoderms, and the internal canal systems of sponges and coelenterates. Some have even become endoparasites, burrowing into the musculature of their hosts, living within the body cavity, or inhabiting the digestive tract.

Parasitic copepods can occur in very large numbers. Humes (1973) found 17,294 individuals of the siphonostomatoid *Collocherides astroboae* Stock on two shallow-water basket stars in Madagascar. Infestations of over 13,400 individuals of *Ergasilus sieboldi* Nordmann have been reported from the gills of a single host fish (Abdelhalim, 1990). Even restricted microhabitats on a host can carry a substantial population; up to 39 individuals of *Bomolochus confusus* Stock were found in the nostrils of a single cod caught in the North Sea (Boxshall, 1974a). Parasitic and associated copepods occur at all depths, from the intertidal zone to the deep sea, and have been reported in large numbers on the invertebrates of the hydrothermal vent and cold seep communities (Humes, 1988). Humes (1990) found 15,284 females and 8 males of *Stygiopontius quadrispinosus* Humes in a jar containing 210 ml of flocculent material collected from a massive sulphide deposit and a colony of vestimentiferan worms at a depth of 3250 metres on the Gorda Ridge. Parasitic and associated copepods are predominantly marine although a few parasitise freshwater molluscs, fishes and, rarely, amphibians.

Table 1. Copepods as associates of Metazoan phyla

	Calanoida	Harpacticoida	Monstrilloida	Cyclopoida	Poecilostomatoida	Siphonostomatoida
Porifera	–	+	–	+	+	+
Cnidaria	+	+	–	+	+	+
Platyhelminthes	–	+	–	–	+	–
Nemertea	–	–	–	–	+	–
Sipunculida	–	–	–	–	+	–
Vestimentifera	–	–	–	–	–	+
Echiura	–	–	–	–	+	–
Annelida	–	+	+	–	+	+
Mollusca	–	+	+	+	+	+
Arthropoda	–	+	–	–	+	+
Phoronida	–	–	–	–	+	–
Bryozoa	–	+	–	–	–	–
Brachiopoda	–	–	–	–	+	–
Echinodermata	–	+	–	+	+	+
Hemichordata	–	–	–	+	+	–
Chordata						
Urochordata	–	+	–	+	+	+
Vertebrata						
Chondrichthyes	–	–	–	–	+	+
Osteichthyes	–	+	–	+	+	+
Amphibia	–	–	–	+	–	–
Mammalia	–	+	–	–	–	+

In the majority of parasitic copepods it is the adults that are parasitic but the monstrilloids have naupliar stages that are endoparasites of polychaete worms and gastropod molluscs. The adults are free-living but non-feeding members of the marine plankton. The aberrant cyclopoid family Thespesiopsyllidae also has parasitic nauplii and free adults, but the nauplii inhabit the stomach of brittlestars in this case. The siphonostomatoid family Pennellidae exhibits, at least in some genera, a two host life cycle. Larval development through the copepodid stages to maturity occurs on the first host, which may be either a pelagic mollusc (as in *Cardiodectes* Wilson) or a fish (as in *Lernaeocera* de Blainville). After mating on the intermediate host the adult females locate and attach to a final host, on which egg production takes place. These pennellids often exhibit a profound metamorphosis during which the adult female changes shape and increases dramatically in size prior to commencing egg production.

1.2 THE IMPORTANCE OF COPEPODS

Ecological Importance: It would be extremely difficult to overstate the importance of copepods to the marine economy. The abundant calanoid and cyclopoid copepods of the plankton form the first vital link in the food chain that leads from the minute algal cells of the phytoplankton up to the large fishes and mammals. These phytoplankton-feeding copepods are by far the most important primary consumers in marine planktonic communities and, as such, form the base of virtually all pelagic food chains. Copepods are so abundant that even their faecal pellets, which are produced at rates of up to 200 per individual per day, represent an ecologically important energy source for detritus feeders. The flux of faecal pellets to the ocean floor may have a significant impact on nutrient cycling and sedimentation rates.

Most commercially exploited fishes, in temperate waters at least, feed directly on copepods during their larval development and some, such as the herring, continue to feed on copepods as adults. It is not only pelagic fishes that utilise copepods as an important food source. Harpacticoid copepods are the predominant meiofaunal element in the diets of flatfishes and salmonids, which are target species for a rapidly expanding mariculture industry in Europe and North America. Harpacticoids have a high nutritional value and the various life cycle stages of the copepod are intermediate in size between rotifers and brineshrimp nauplii (which are commonly used as live fish food) and, as such, bridge a gap in the size spectrum of available food. These copepods may have an essential role to play in the future development of fish farming (Gee, 1989).

Copepod Pests: Copepods can be important as pest species. The salmon louse *Lepeophtheirus salmonis* Krøyer, for example, can cause devastating economic losses to salmon farmers. These lice breed rapidly in the salmon cages and can kill the fish directly by their feeding activity or indirectly by causing skin lesions that allow microbial diseases to become established. Other copepods are commercially important because they adversely affect the condition of the fish. Kabata (1958) found that heavy infestation by the gill parasite *Lernaeocera* caused a weight loss of up to 28.9 per cent in haddock, *Melanogrammus aeglefinus* (Linn.), caught off Scotland. Mann (1952) reported similar losses caused by the same parasite on other gadid hosts. It has been calculated that weight losses of this magnitude would amount to about two million pounds lost on the total Scottish haddock catch for a given year (Sinderman, 1970). Parasites of commercially important shellfishes, such as *Mytilicola intestinalis* Steuer (European mytilicoliasis) and *M.orientalis* Mori (oriental mytilicoliasis) which parasitise mussels, were also thought to cause considerable loss of weight in infested hosts (Mann, 1951) and thereby reduce their market value but recent work (Gresty, 1990) suggests that the mussel, *Mytilus edulis* Linn. can sustain high infection levels of *M.intestinalis* without suffering any significant adverse effects. Large copepod parasites that live embedded in the flesh of their fish hosts, such as *Sphyrion lumpi* Krøyer, reduce the marketability of the fish by causing problems during filleting. Release of blood from large, engorged females of the endoparasitic philichthyid *Sarcotaces* Olsson also disrupts filleting of its host fish as it stains the flesh.

The harpacticoid copepods *Amenophia orientalis* Ho & Hong and *Parathalestris infestus* Ho & Hong are pests of Wakame, the brown seaweed that is cultivated widely in Korea and Japan as a food crop. These copepods make galls and pinholes in the fronds of the seaweed and reduce its commercial value (Ho & Hong, 1988).

Copepods as Disease Vectors: Copepods are also important as vectors of some human parasites, the most important of these being the guineaworm, *Dracunculus medinensis* Linn., known as the fiery serpent in biblical times. Certain species of freshwater copepods, mainly belonging to the genera *Mesocyclops* Sars and *Thermocyclops* Kiefer, are infested with the larval stages of this nematode in parts of equatorial Africa and the Indian subcontinent. If swallowed in drinking water the guineaworm larva can develop to maturity inside the human body and can cause temporary or permanent disablement, or death. Other human parasites, such as the fish tapeworm *Diphyllobothrium latum* (Linn.), also require a copepod intermediate host in order to complete their life cycles. Freshwater copepods ingest the free swimming coracidium larva of the tapeworm which develops into a procercoid larva. The second intermediate host, a freshwater fish, swallows the infected copepod and the procercoid larva develops into a plerocercoid larva inside the fish. This larva is infective to man and completes its life cycle if eaten in raw or undercooked fish.

Copepods in Biological Control: Some freshwater copepods are the intermediate hosts for *Coelomomyces* Keilin fungus which parasitises larval mosquitoes and can cause high mortalities (Whisler et al., 1974, 1975). The introduction into mosquito breeding sites of infected copepods containing active planonts in the haemocoel, may provide an effective biological control technique for malarial mosquitoes (Toohey et al., 1982). Similarly other copepods, including species of *Mesocyclops*, act as the intermediate host of a sporozoan parasite of mosquitoes that is under investigation as a possible agent of biological control.

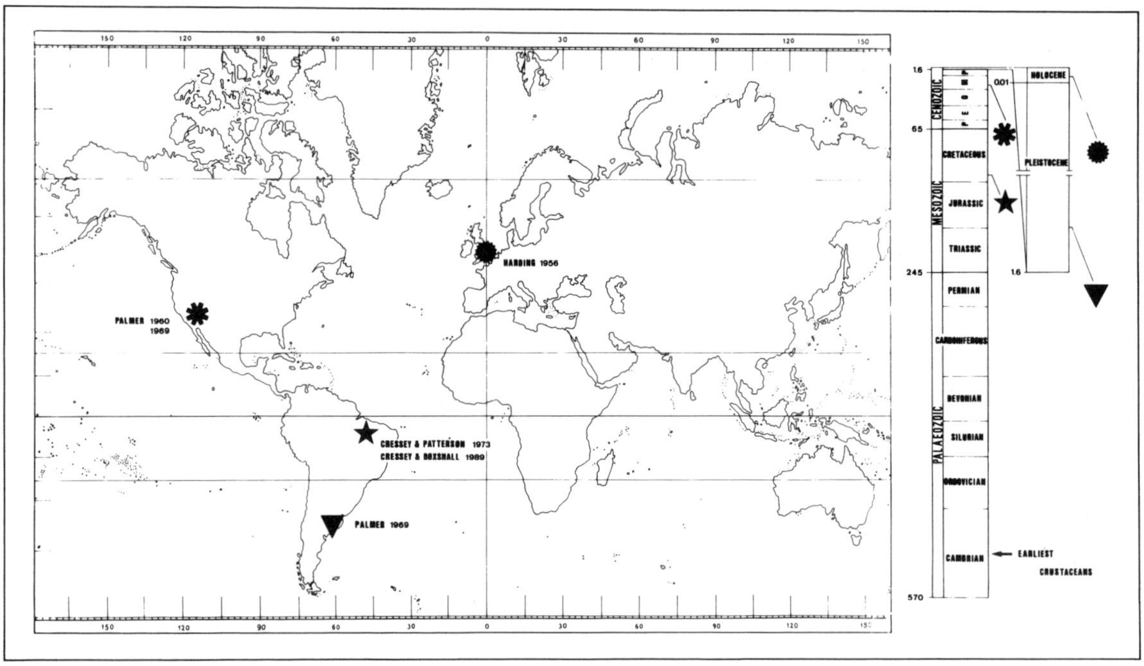

Figure 1.3.1. Localities of all records of fossil and subfossil copepods, with inset geological time scale.

1.3 FOSSIL COPEPODS

Copepods are typically small, fragile organisms that do not fossilise well. Harding (1956) described a harpacticoid copepod, *Enhydrosoma gariene* Gurney, from a neolithic excavation site in Kent in southern England. However, the single male specimen was desiccated rather than fossilised and Harding was able to rehydrate it prior to study. The first true fossils found were the harpacticoids and cyclopoids reported by Palmer (1960, 1969). These were found in North and South America in Miocene and Pleistocene lake deposits associated with Boron minerals. One of these forms was identified as a *Cletocamptus* Schmankewitsch species, the others were classified only to ordinal level. The localities of all records of fossil and subfossil copepods are marked on the map in figure 1.3.1.

The most spectacular fossil copepod is undoubtedly *Kabatarina pattersoni* Cressey & Boxshall, a fish parasite from the Lower Cretaceous (Cressey & Patterson, 1973; Cressey & Boxshall, 1989). Both sexes of this siphonostomatoid parasite were found on the gills of a fossil teleost fish, *Cladocyclus gardneri* Agassiz, preserved in calcareous nodules in the Santana Formation at Serra do Araripe, Brazil. The copepods are preserved in the round, as solid objects and are in remarkable condition, complete with appendages bearing spines, setae and surface ornamentation (figures 1.3.2-4). This discovery considerably extends the known fossil record of the Copepoda, to the Lower Cretaceous (Upper Aptian to Lower Albanian: 110 to 120 my). *Kabatarina* Cressey & Boxshall has been placed in the family Dichelesthiidae, together with the recent genera *Dichelesthium* Hermann and *Anthosoma* Leach (Cressey & Boxshall, 1989).

1.4 COPEPOD CHARACTERISTICS

The name copepod is derived from the Greek words *kope* meaning 'oar' and *podos* meaning 'foot' and literally means 'oar-footed'. This name refers to their broad, paddle-like swimming legs and forms the basis of their common name in other languages, such as the German 'Ruderfusskrebs', the Dutch 'Roeipootkreeft' and the Norwegian 'Hoppekrebs'. They do not have a general common

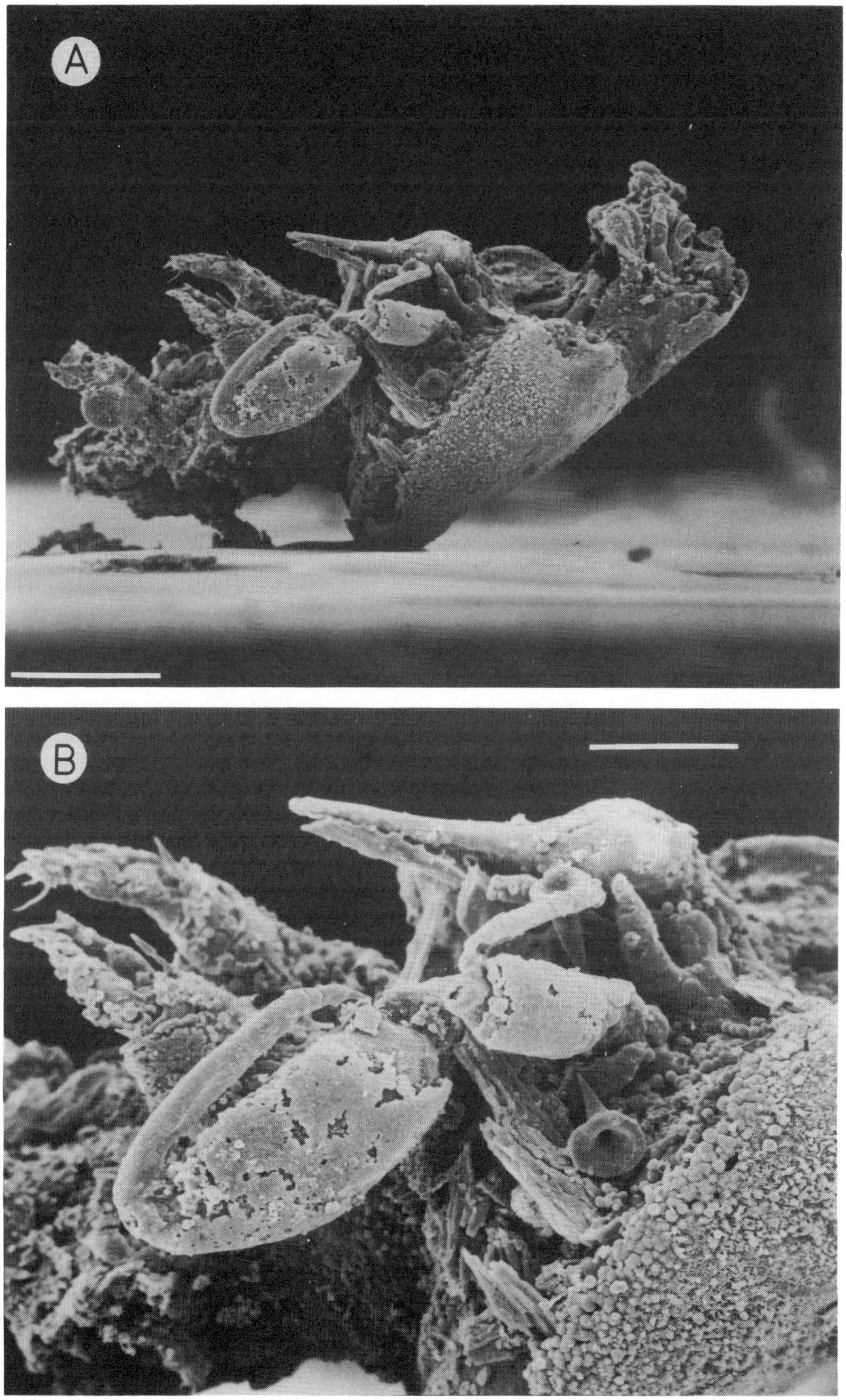

Figure 1.3.2. *Kabatarina pattersoni*, female. [A fossil parasitic copepod from the Lower Cretaceous.] **A.** Cephalothorax, lateral view. **B.** Mouthparts, lateral view. Scale bars A = 100μm, B = 50 μm.

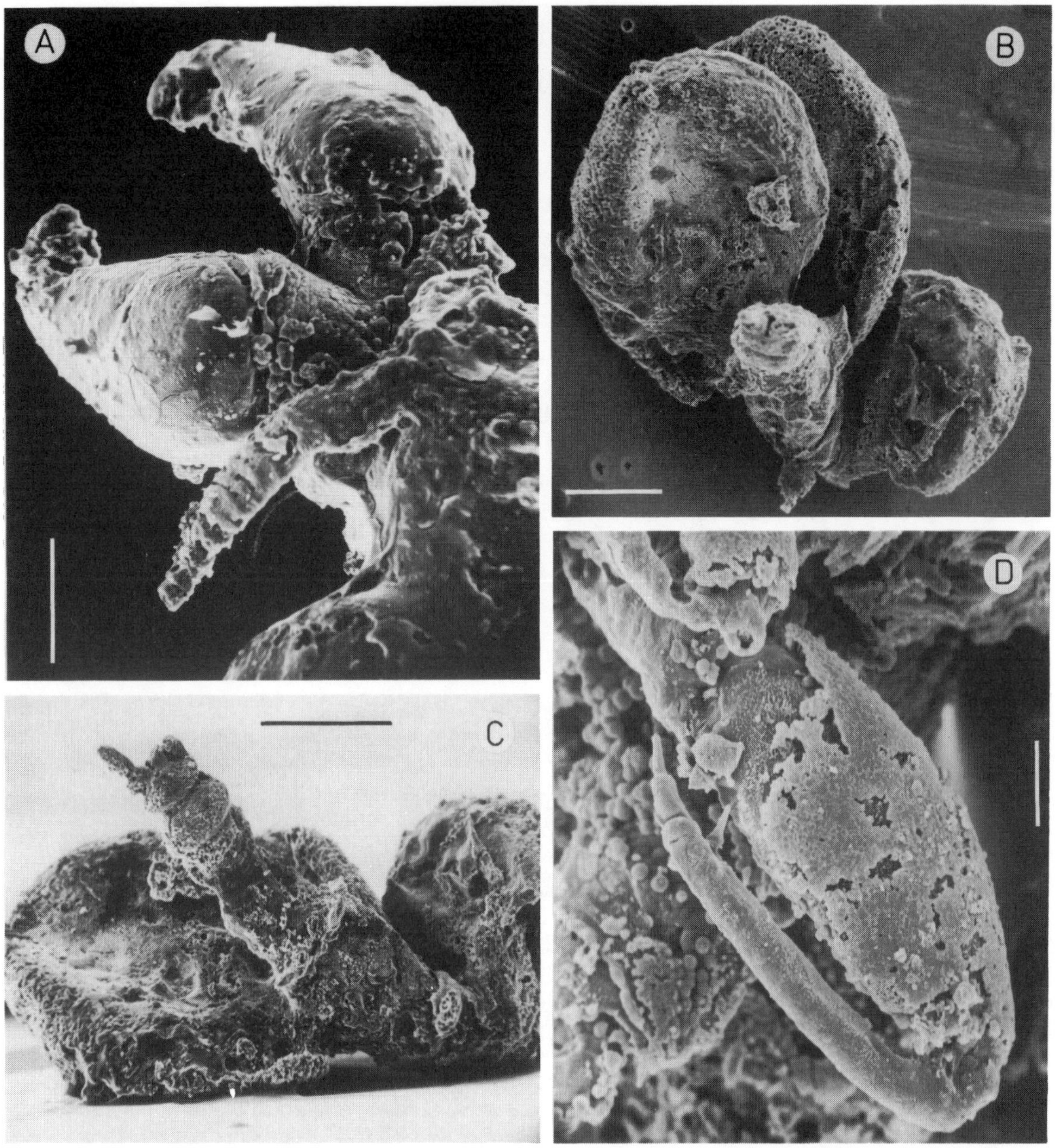

Figure 1.3.3. *Kabatarina pattersoni*, female. **A.** Antennae and proximal part of left antennule in situ, dorso-lateral view. **B.** Elytra of posterior pedigerous somites, posterior view. **C.** Urosome, ventral view. **D.** Maxilliped, ventro-lateral view. Scale bars A = 50μm, B-C = 100μm, D = 20μm.

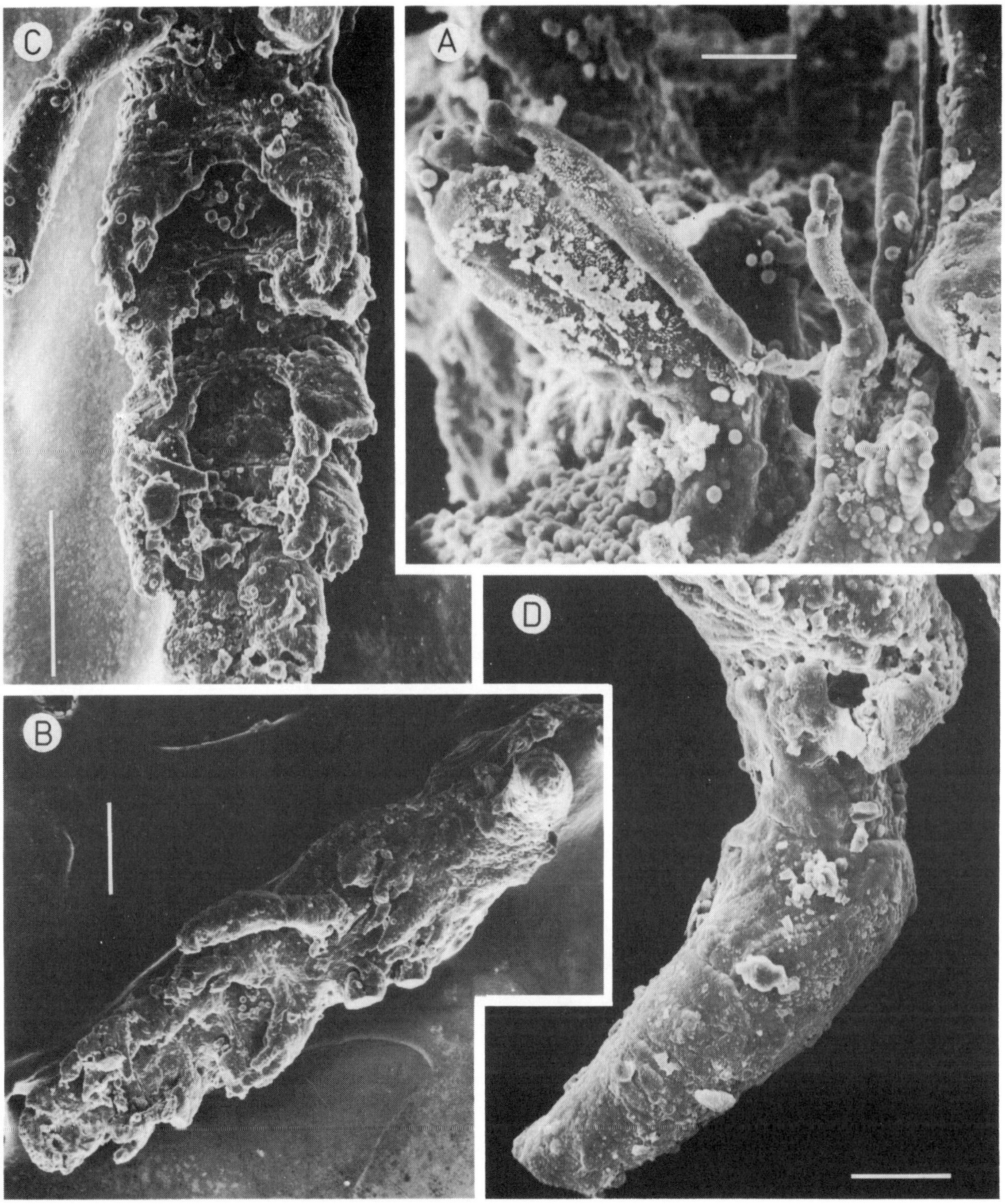

Figure 1.3.4. *Kabatarina pattersoni.* **A.** Female maxilla and maxillule, antero-ventral view. **B.** Male, ventral view. **C.** Male legs 1 to 4, ventral view. **D.** Male antenna, lateral view. Scale bars A = 30μm, B-C = 100μm, D = 40μm.

name in English although a few individual species have such names, the salmon louse (*Lepeophtheirus salmonis*) and the gill maggot (*Salmincola salmoneus* Linn.) of anglers, for example.

Copepods are so diverse that it is difficult to select a typical representative to serve as an introduction to the group as a whole. Instead we present a detailed diagnosis of the subclass Copepoda which, when combined with the plates of basic appendage structure (see section 1.5) and the introductory plate for each order showing the range of gross body forms in that order (see chapter 2), will give a more accurate impression of copepod morphology.

Subclass COPEPODA

The body comprises a cephalosome of 6 somites and a postcephalic trunk of 9 somites plus the anal somite which represents the telson. The cephalosome consists of 5 cephalic somites and the first thoracic somite which bears the maxillipeds. All copepods have the first thoracic somite fully incorporated into the cephalosome. The postcephalic trunk comprises the second to sixth thoracic somites each of which bears a pair of biramous swimming legs, the genital (seventh thoracic) somite which bears the genital opening or openings in both sexes, and 4 postgenital abdominal somites. The abdominal somites are all limbless although the anal somite bears a pair of setiferous caudal rami. In many species the trunk somites are fused to each other or to the cephalosome.

The antennules are uniramous and comprise up to 27 segments. The antennae are typically biramous with a 2-segmented protopod, bearing the exopod, which has up to 9 segments, and the endopod, which has up to 4 segments. In many copepods the antenna is uniramous, with the exopod having been lost. The mouth opening is covered by a posteroventrally-directed labrum. The mandible is typically biramous, with a 2-segmented protopod bearing a large gnathobase on the coxa. The exopod is 5-segmented and the endopod is 2-segmented. In parasitic forms the palp is often reduced, and in some it is missing. Paired paragnaths are present on each side, between the bases of the mandibles and maxillules. The paragnaths are sometimes fused medially to form the labium. The maxillule is biramous and consists of a 3-segmented protopod bearing a well developed praecoxal arthrite, 1 coxal and 2 basal endites, a coxal and/or basal exite, a 1-segmented exopod and 3-segmented endopod. The maxillules are often reduced to a bilobed process and are missing in some forms. The maxilla is uniramous and up to 7-segmented. The protopod comprises praecoxa, coxa and basis. The praecoxa and coxa each typically have 2 endites, the basis has one endite. The endopod consists of 4 small segments and is sometimes lost. The maxilliped is uniramous and comprises praecoxa, coxa, basis and a 6-segmented endopod. The praecoxa has 1 endite, the coxa has 3 endites and the basis is armed with up to 3 setae. The maxilliped is often reduced and sometimes missing.

The first to fifth pairs of swimming legs are typically biramous with a 3-segmented protopod and 3-segmented rami. These legs are often reduced and sometimes missing, especially in parasitic forms. The fifth leg is often modified, by reduction or loss of the endopod or by fusion of the endopod to the basis. The fifth leg is absent in some species. Members of the first to fifth leg pairs are joined medially by a rigid intercoxal sclerite which ensures that both legs of a pair beat simultaneously. The praecoxa of the swimming legs is reduced to a lateral plate at the base of the leg. The sixth legs are reduced, forming the apparatus that closes off the genital openings in both sexes.

Life Cycle: The life cycle primitively includes up to 6 naupliar and metanaupliar stages and 5 copepodid stages prior to the adult. Development is sometimes abbreviated, especially in parasitic forms. Sperm is transferred by means of spermatophores that are placed on the female by the male. The spermatophores discharge the sperm via paired copulatory pores into paired seminal receptacles within the genital somite of the female where they are stored. Eggs are typically carried in paired egg sacs. In some groups there is a single egg sac or a loose egg mass, in others the eggs are released directly and are not carried by the female.

Diagnosis: The ecological adaptability displayed by the copepods is reflected in their morphological plasticity and it is extremely difficult to formulate a rigorous diagnosis of the subclass Copepoda that is both informative yet sufficiently comprehensive to cover the more bizarre parasites as well as the typical free-living forms. In practice recognizing a copepod is relatively straightforward. Virtually all copepods have a phase in their life cycle, either the adult or one of the copepodid stages, in which they possess at least 2 pairs of swimming legs, the members of which are linked by a flat sclerite connecting the coxae. The presence of this intercoxal sclerite joining the members of a leg pair is a unique apomorphy of the Copepoda and forms a true diagnostic character. Manton (1977) identified the presence of the intercoxal sclerite uniting the members of each pair as the key to the achievement of the rapid jumping mode of locomotion in copepods. The only non-parasitic copepods lacking intercoxal sclerites are the 2 species of the stygobiontic genus *Gelyella* Rouch & Lescher-Moutoué (Huys, 1988a; Moeschler & Rouch, 1988) and this is interpreted here as a secondary loss related to the total fusion of the coxae in this genus.

All copepods have a stage exhibiting a cephalosome into which the maxilliped-bearing, first thoracic somite is incorporated. This serves to distinguish between the Copepoda and the other maxillopodan subclasses, such as the barnacles (Thecostraca), fish lice (Branchiura), ostracods and larval tantulocaridans in all of which the first thoracic somite is free and the first thoracopod is a swimming or walking leg, or a cirrus. In adult male Tantulocarida the first thoracopod is not modified as a maxilliped although the first and second pedigerous somites are incorporated into a cephalothorax (Boxshall & Lincoln, 1987). In the Mystacocarida and the fossil Skaracarida the first thoracopod is modified as a maxilliped and plays a role in feeding, as in the Copepoda, but the maxillipedal somite is free. The copepods are the only maxillopodans with the first thoracic somite fully incorporated into the cephalosome. However, a cephalosome of 6 somites is also primitively found in the Remipedia (Yager, 1981; Schram, 1986), so this character is not unique.

The presence of uniramous antennules with up to 27 segments is also a reasonably reliable character although segment numbers are reduced in many groups of copepods. Long, multisegmented antennules are not found in any other maxillopodan groups. Grygier (1987) suggested that the ancestral maxillopodan probably possessed an 8-segmented antennule since this appears to be the basic number for the ostracods, cirripedes and mystacocarids. The multisegmented condition of the copepod antennule may represent an autapomorphy of the subclass. It is interesting to note here that the fossil *Kabatarina* had at least 21 segments in the antennule.

The possession of egg sacs is probably not the ancestral condition of the Copepoda since several important groups lack true egg sacs. However, most of the highly transformed parasitic copepods that lack recognisable appendages and external body segmentation belong to the orders Siphonostomatoida, Poecilostomatoida and Cyclopoida all three of which primitively possessed paired egg sacs. The presence of such paired egg sacs constitutes another extremely useful character in identifying secondarily simplified parasites as copepods. This criterion is not infallible because egg sacs are secondarily lost in some highly derived parasitic genera, such as *Pectenophilus* Nagasawa, an internal parasite of scallops (Nagasawa et al., 1988).

Size: Copepods are typically small. In the marine planktonic forms total body length is usually between 0.5 and 5.0 mm, although the full range is from about 0.2 mm (some species of *Oncaea* Philippi) to about 28 mm (a species of *Valdiviella* Steuer). The benthic harpacticoids fall within the size range 0.2 to 2.5 mm. The real giants amongst the copepods are the parasites. Some of these are also small, including gill parasites such as *Ergasilus* Nordmann and inhabitants of the lateral line canals such as *Colobomatus* Hesse, but many attain considerable size. The largest parasites are members of the siphonostomatoid family Pennellidae. Species of *Pennella* Oken can reach about 250 mm in length and carry linear egg sacs which may exceed 350 mm in length (Wilson, 1917). The large size of these parasites requires a substantial attachment apparatus to prevent their being dislodged from the host. The pennellids and other very large parasites, such as the giant kroyeriid *Kroyeria caseyi* Benz & Deets which attains a length of 65 mm and the sphyriids, are typically mesoparasitic with their anterior ends forming an anchor, deeply embedded in the tissues of the host.

1.5 BASIC APPENDAGE STRUCTURE - TERMINOLOGY

There is no standard terminology that is in universal use for all copepods. Specialists working in the three major fields of copepod research (on the plankton, the meiofauna, or the parasites) tend to have their own terminology, adapted to fit the particular taxa involved. Obviously in an overview such as this book we must adopt a standard terminology to aid comparisons between taxa and to facilitate the identification of homologous structures. We have adopted a terminology that we hope will achieve these objectives and also allow comparisons with other crustacean groups. In the glossary, Appendix 3, we attempt to provide a comprehensive set of cross references between equivalent terms.

The appendages described below are composites, shown in semidiagrammatical form to introduce the fundamental components of each. Full segmentation and setation patterns are given in the illustrations in order to show how the setation formulae are derived for each limb. In many cases these composite limbs combine features that are not found together in any known copepod. For example, a lobate exite on the maxillulary basis is never found on the same appendage as an epipodite on the coxa.

The Antennule

The female antennule (figure 1.5.1) is basically uniramous and 28-segmented. Each original segment is numbered using Roman numerals, I to XXVIII, and actual segment numbers are given using Arabic numerals. Segment I bears 3 setae plus an aesthetasc. Segments II to XXI each possess a trithek comprising a seta on the mid-anteroventral margin and a seta plus an aesthetasc located distally on the anteroventral margin. Segments XXII and XXIII each have just the distal seta and aesthetasc. Segments XXIV to XXVII are each armed with the distal seta and aesthetasc anteroventrally and a seta located distally on the posterior margin. Segment XXVIII bears 4 setae and an aesthetasc.

The male antennule is similar to that of the female except that it is typically geniculate at a position corresponding to the articulation between segments XX and XXI of the female. In male copepods there are typically some segmental fusions associated with the geniculation mechanism and these are indicated using Roman numerals, for example XXI-XXIII denotes a triple segment representing fused segments XXI, XXII and XXIII. Such fusions, in both sexes, are identified by reference to the setation pattern.

The Antenna

The antenna (figure 1.5.2) is basically biramous, consisting of a 2-segmented protopod, a 10-segmented exopod and a 4-segmented endopod. The proximal protopodal segment, the coxa, bears a single medial seta. The distal protopodal segment, the basis, bears 2 medial setae. Each original exopodal segment from the first (I) to the ninth (IX) carries an inner seta; the tenth (X) has 3 apical setae. This corresponds to a setal formula: 1,1,1,1,1,1,1,1,1,3 which is always given in sequence from proximal to distal. Ancestral exopodal segments are numbered using Roman numerals, actual numbers using Arabic numerals. The first endopodal segment has 2 setae, the second 9 setae, and the third and fourth 5 and 2 respectively. The tiny fourth segment is incompletely fused to the third in some calanoids and the setal formula is given as 2,9,5+2. In the majority of copepods the fourth segment is completely incorporated into the third and the setal formula is given as 2,9,7.

The Mandible

The mandible (figure 1.5.3) basically consists of a coxa bearing a large medially directed gnathobase, plus a biramous mandibular palp comprising the basis bearing a 5-segmented exopod and 2-segmented endopod. The coxal gnathobase bears teeth along its distomedial margin and 2 dorsal setae. The basis bears 4 medial setae. Each exopodal segment from the first to the fourth bears 1 inner seta; the fifth has 2 setae. This corresponds to a setal formula: 1,1,1,1,2 which is always given in sequence from proximal to distal. The first endopodal segment has 6 setae, the second 11 setae, corresponding to a setal formula of 6,11.

The Maxillule

The maxillule (figure 1.5.4) is basically biramous and has a 3-segmented protopod consisting of praecoxa, coxa and basis. The praecoxa bears a medial arthrite bearing 16 elements. The coxa

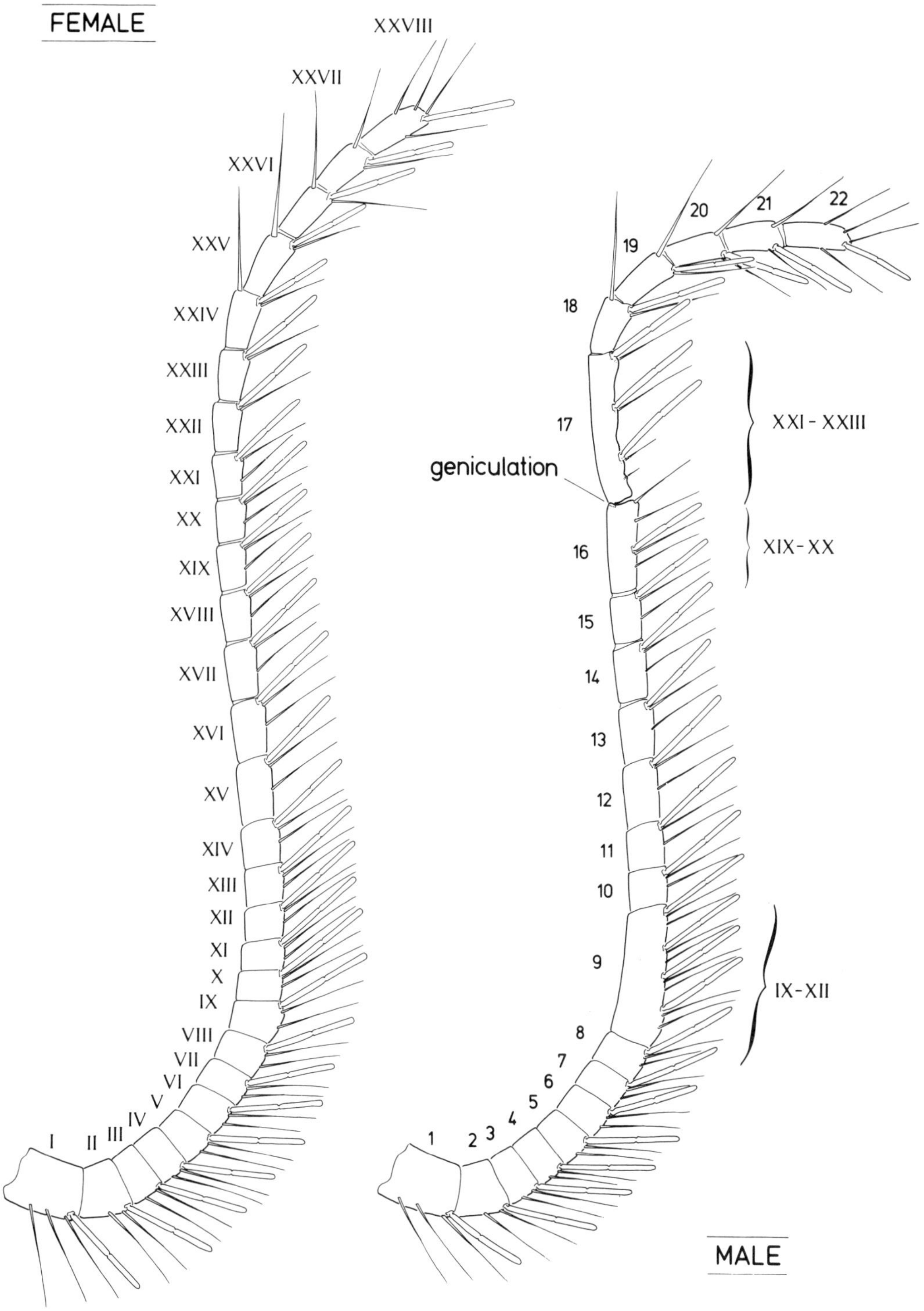

Figure 1.5.1. Basic copepod antennule of female and a male antennule showing fusions.

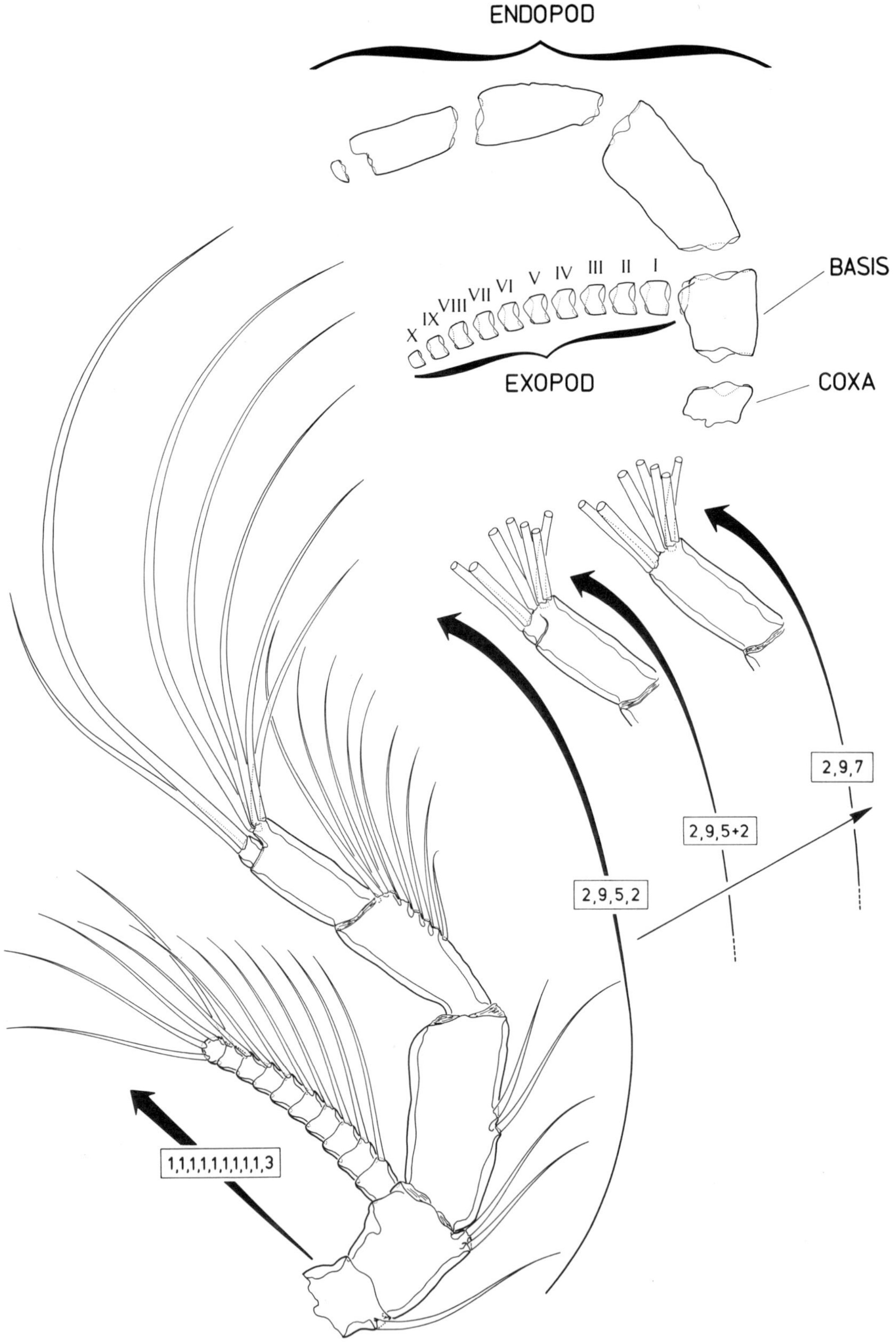

Figure 1.5.2. Basic copepod antenna.

bears a single elongate endite armed with 6 setae and a well developed outer lobe, the epipodite, carrying 9 setae. The basis bears 2 endites, the proximal is well developed and has 4 apical setae, the distal is largely incorporated into the segment and carries 5 setae. The basis also has an outer lobe, the exite, bearing 2 setae. The exopod is 1-segmented and is armed with 11 marginal setae. The endopod is 3-segmented: the first segment bearing 6 setae, the second 4 setae and the third 7 setae, corresponding to a setal formula of 6,4,7. The endopodal segments are often fused but the armature typically remains organised in 3 groups allowing the same tripartite setal formula to be used even though the segments are not distinct.

The Maxilla

The maxilla (figure 1.5.5) is uniramous and 7-segmented, consisting of a praecoxa, coxa, basis and 4-segmented endopod. The praecoxa has 2 endites, the proximal bearing 10 setae, the distal 3 setae. The coxa also has 2 endites, each with 3 setae. The setal formula of the praecoxal and coxal endites is given as 10,3,3,3, passing in sequence from proximal to distal. An outer seta is present on the coxa and probably represents the epipodite. The basis bears a single endite armed with 4 elements, 1 of which typically becomes a claw fused to the endite. The first endopodal segment bears 4 setae, the second 3 setae, the third 2 setae and the fourth 4 setae. This corresponds to a setal formula of 4,3,2,4 in sequence from proximal to distal. In the majority of copepods the first endopodal segment is fused to the basis to form a maxillary allobasis so the setal formula of the free endopod is given separately, as 3,2,4. The armature elements on the basis are identified individually by the letters A to D, and those of the first endopodal segment by Roman numerals I to IV.

The Maxilliped

The maxilliped (figure 1.5.6) is basically uniramous and 9-segmented, consisting of praecoxa, coxa, basis and 6-segmented endopod. The praecoxa has a single endite bearing 1 seta. The coxa has 3 endites, the proximal bearing 2 setae, the middle and distal 4 setae each. The corresponding setal formula for the praecoxal and coxal endites is 1,2,4,4 passing in sequence from proximal to distal. An outer seta is present on the coxa and probably represents the epipodite. The basis has 3 setae on its medial margin. The first endopodal segment bears 2 inner setae. The second and third each have 4 inner setae. The fourth has 3 setae on the inner margin. The fifth has 3 setae on the inner margin plus 1 seta on the outer margin. The sixth segment has 5 setae. The endopodal setation pattern is given by the setal formula: 2,4,4,3,3+1,5 passing from proximal to distal.

The Swimming Legs

The basic copepod swimming leg (figure 1.5.7) consists of a well developed coxa and basis, with the latter bearing two 3-segmented rami. There is a remnant of the praecoxa in the form of a laterally located sclerite at the base of the leg. The members of a leg pair are joined by a median intercoxal sclerite. The coxa bears an inner seta. The basis bears an inner and an outer seta. The first exopodal segment carries 1 (leg 1) or 2 (legs 2 to 5) outer spines and an inner seta. The second segment carries 1 outer spine and 1 inner seta. The third exopodal segment is armed with 3 spines on the outer margin, a terminal spine and either 4 (legs 1 and 5) or 5 (legs 2 to 4) setae on the inner margin. The first endopodal segment has a single seta on the inner margin. The second has 2 inner setae in legs 1 to 4, only 1 seta in leg 5. The third endopodal segment has 1 seta (leg 1) or 2 setae (legs 2 to 5) on the outer margin, 2 on the distal margin and 2 (leg 5), 3 (legs 1 and 4) or 4 (legs 2 and 3) setae on the inner margin. This setation pattern corresponds to the following spine and seta formula:

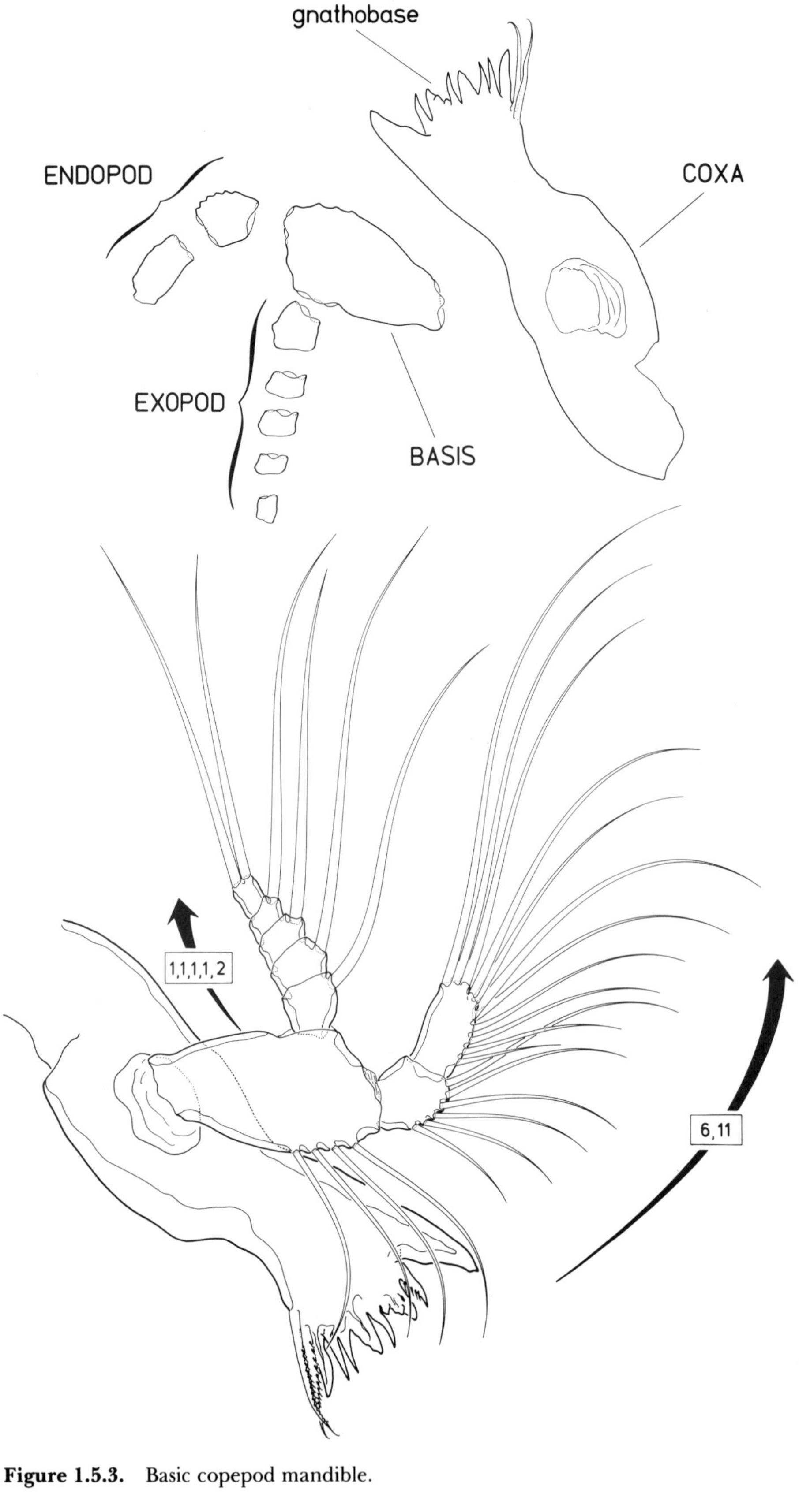

Figure 1.5.3. Basic copepod mandible.

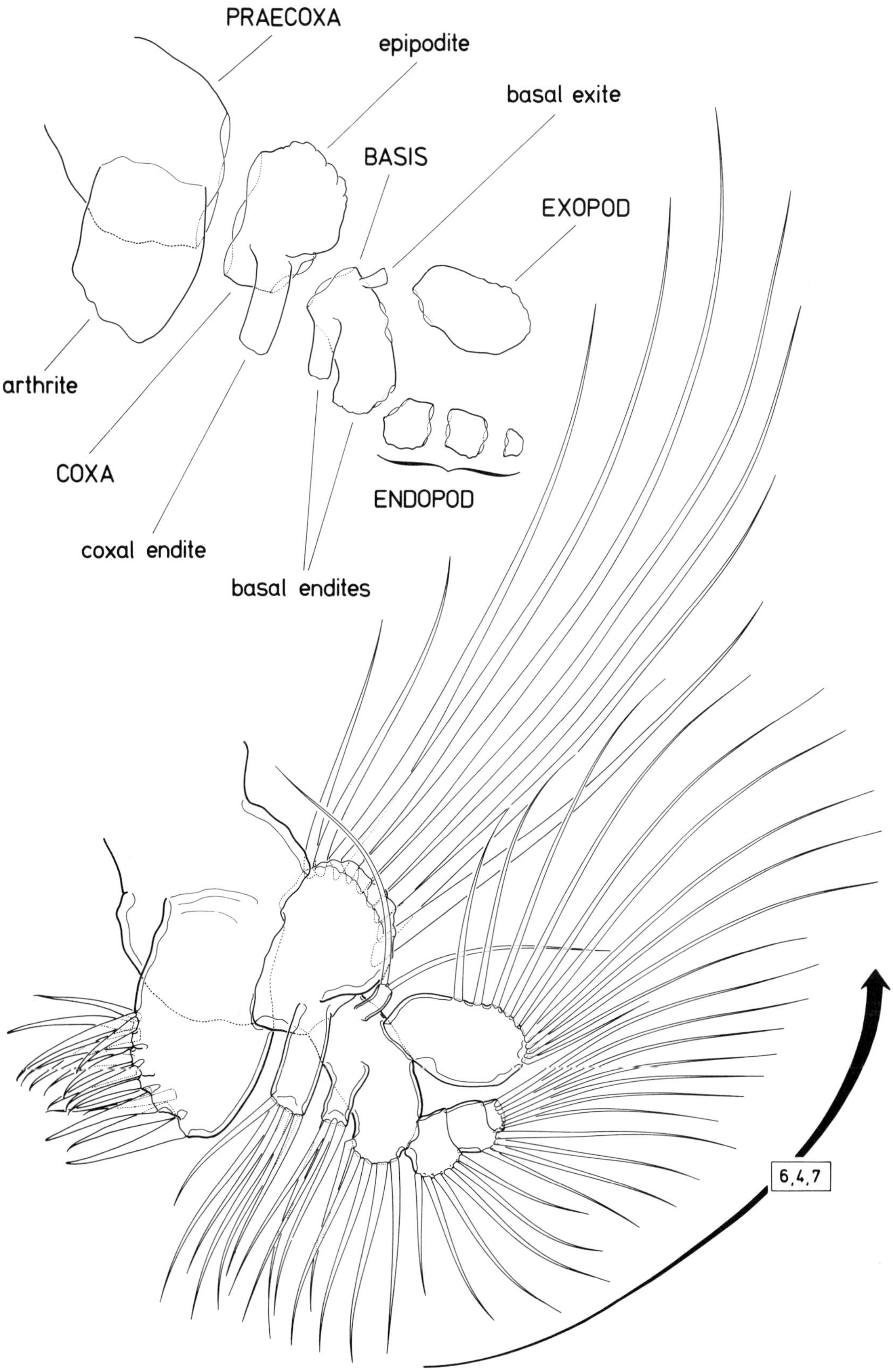

Figure 1.5.4. Basic copepod maxillule.

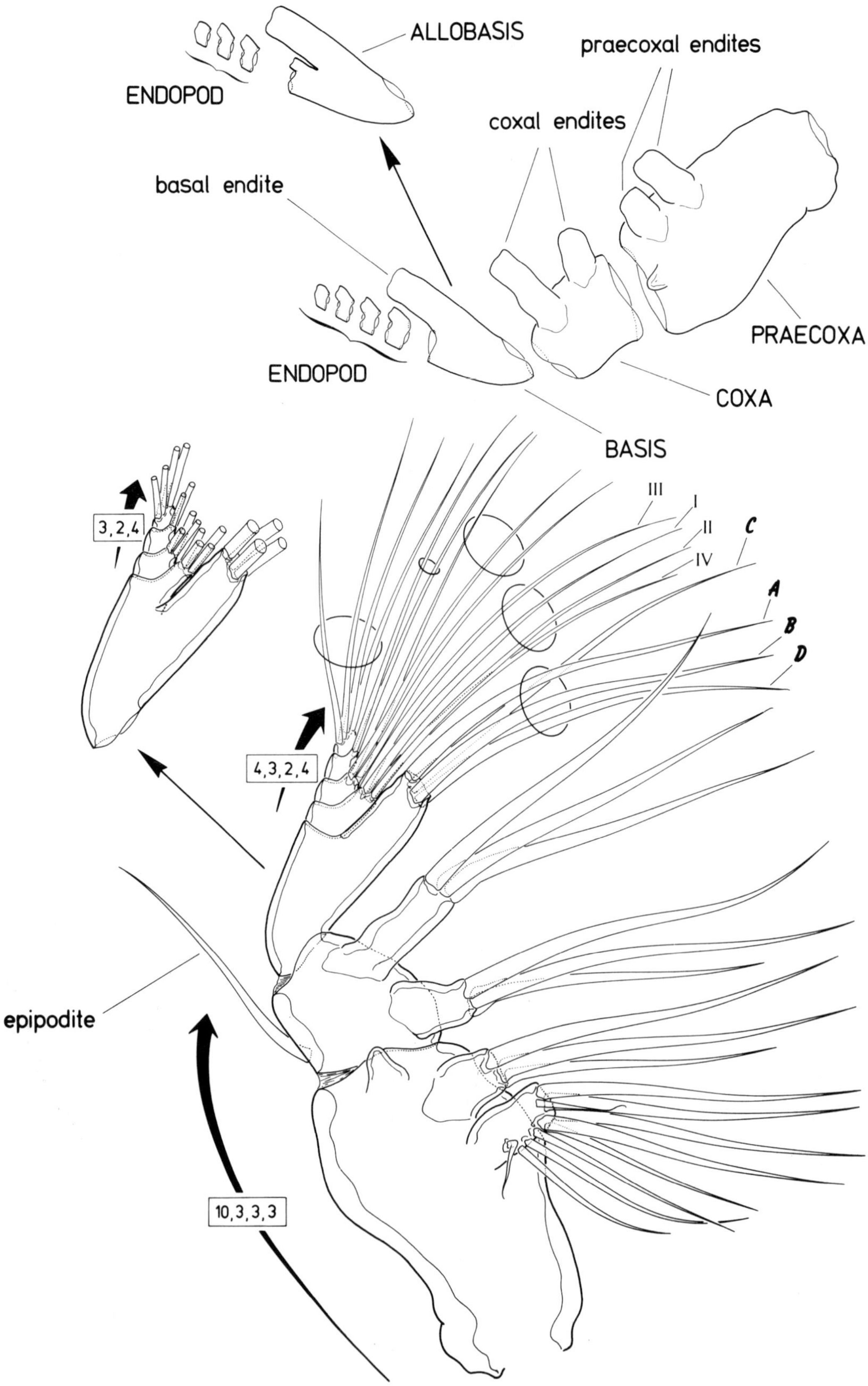

Figure 1.5.5. Basic copepod maxilla (anterior view).

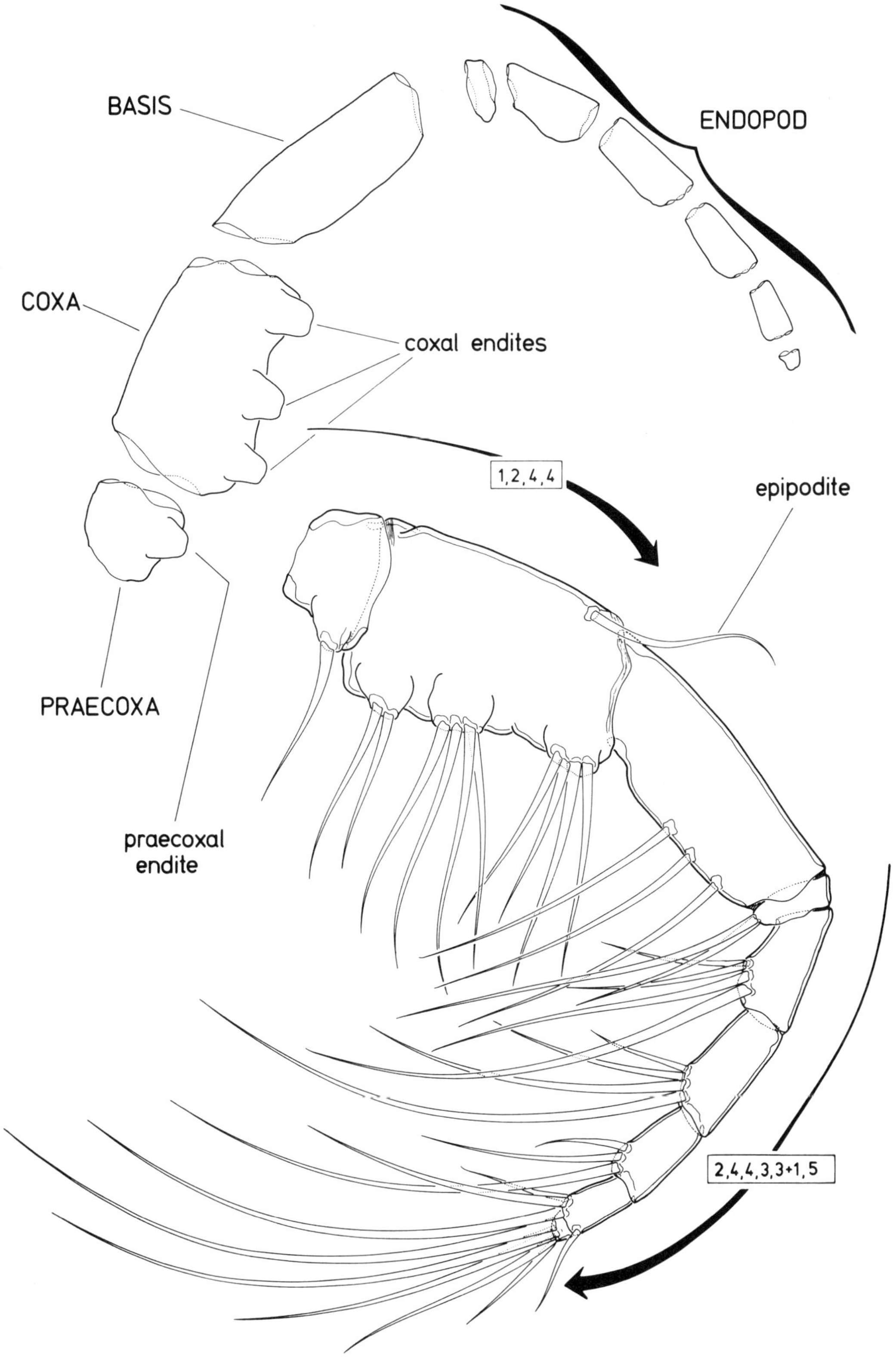

Figure 1.5.6. Basic copepod maxilliped.

	coxa	basis	exopod segment 1 2 3	endopod segment 1 2 3
leg 1	0 – 1	1 – I	I – 1; I – 1; III,I,4	0 – 1; 0 – 2; 1,2,3
leg 2	0 – 1	1 – 1	II – 1; I – 1; III,I,5	0 – 1; 0 – 2; 2,2,4
leg 5	0 – 1	1 – 1	II – 1; I – 1; III,I,5	0 – 1; 0 – 2; 2,2,4
leg 5	0 – 1	1 – 1	II – 1; I – 1; III,I,5	0 – 1; 0 – 2; 2,2,3
leg 5	0 – 1	1 – 1	II – 1; I – 1; III,I,4	0 – 1; 0 – 1; 2,2,2

In the spine and seta formula for the swimming legs devised by Sewell (1949) spines are denoted by Roman numerals, setae by Arabic numerals. The element or elements on the outer margin of any segment are given first, separated by a hyphen from the inner margin element or elements. The armature on the terminal segment of each ramus has three components separated by commas and are given in the sequence: outer margin, distal margin, inner margin. The armature formulae of the segments within a ramus are separated by semicolons. Harpacticoid specialists have traditionally used the setation formula devised by Lang (1934). Both systems are shown on figure 1.5.7 for ease of translation but we have adopted Sewell's system because it has a significantly greater information content.

The setation of the exopod of fifth leg is often considered in detail (figure 1.5.8) and it is necessary to be able to identify each individual armature element on that ramus. These elements are labelled using an alphabetical system, from *a* to *l*, starting with the outer spine (*a*) or spines (a_1 - a_2) of the first exopod segment on the outer margin and progressing distally along the outer margin, round the apex and proximally along the inner margin.

The Caudal Ramus

The caudal rami (figure 1.5.8) are unsegmented, articulating lobes situated on the posterior margin of the anal somite. Each ramus is armed with 7 setae: I - the anterolateral accessory seta, II - the anterolateral seta, III - the posterolateral seta, IV - the outer terminal seta, V - the inner terminal seta, VI - the terminal accessory seta and VII - the dorsal seta. Seta I is always located ventral to seta II. The dorsal seta (seta VII) is typically carried on a biarticulate socle. The large terminal setae (IV and V) have well defined fracture planes.

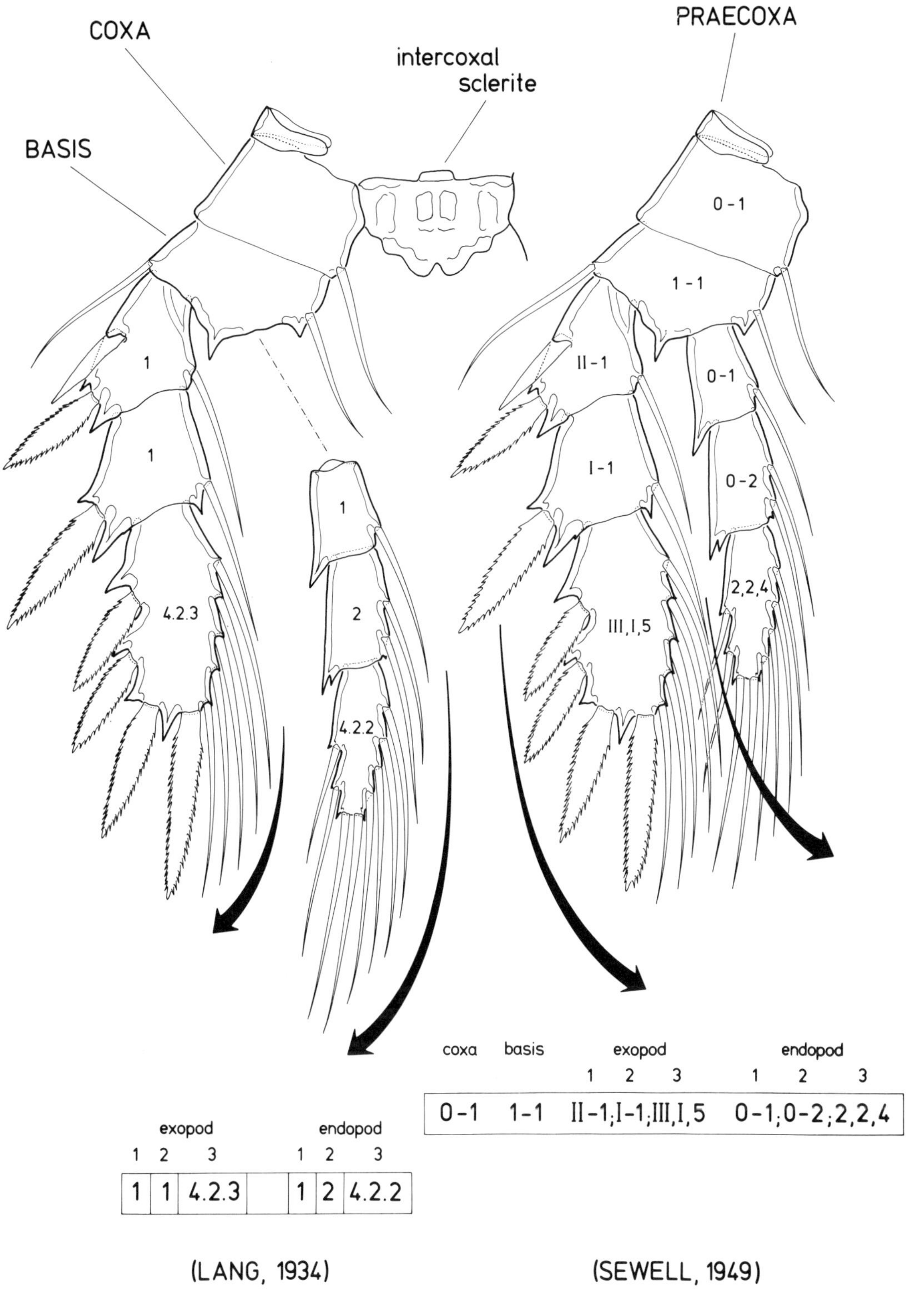

Figure 1.5.7. Basic copepod swimming leg, showing the maximum setation of a second leg.

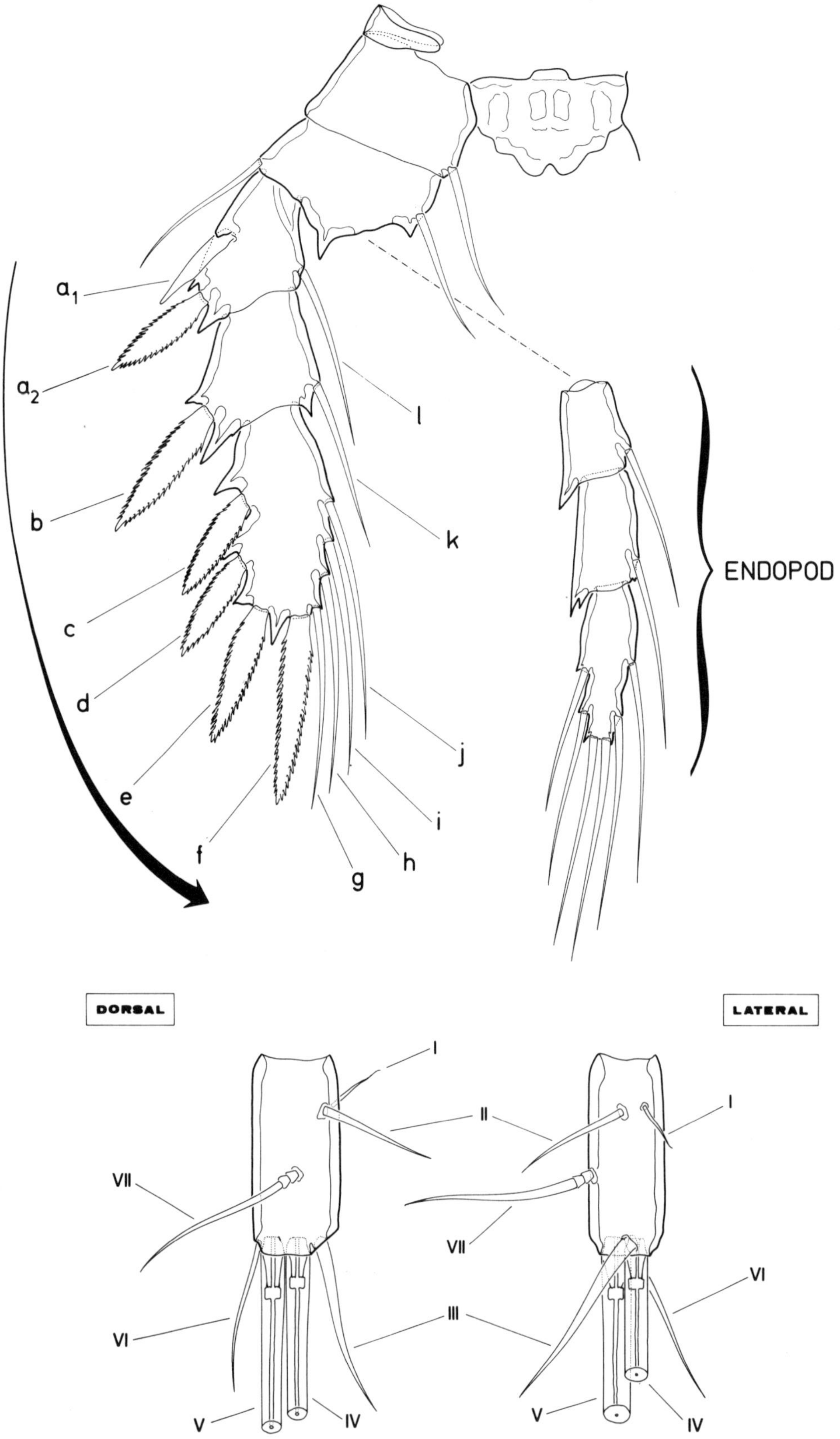

Figure 1.5.8. Basic copepod fifth swimming leg and caudal ramus.

Chapter 2

THE ORDERS OF COPEPODS

It was necessary to examine one or more representatives of every order of copepods in order to standardise our descriptions of segmentation and setation patterns. Specimens of over two hundred species were examined in detail and these included at least one species from every order. A complete list of the material examined in the course of this study is given in Appendix 1. The primary objective of this chapter is to construct a comprehensive list of the most plesiomorphic state exhibited for every character in each order of copepods. Each of the ordinal lists is referred to as the ancestral character set. In the construction of the ancestral character set we have searched for the maximum numbers of segments expressed within each order, for every appendage. As a general rule we have also listed, as the ancestral state, the maximum numbers of setation elements per segment of every appendage. There are a few exceptions to this rule but they are all discussed and justified individually. We have frequently had to deduce the ordinal ancestral state for a particular character by comparison of several taxa because no single modern taxon retains the full ancestral condition. A good example of the way this deduction principle is applied is provided by the harpacticoid mandible. No harpacticoids possess more than 4 segments in the exopod of the mandibular palp, but evidence from the setation pattern of different harpacticoids indicates that the ancestral condition was not 4-segmented. In the Canuellidae some forms have a 4-segmented exopod with a setal formula of 1,1,1,3 whereas members of the Cerviniidae commonly have a 4-segmented exopod with a setal formula of 2,1,1,2 (figure 2.0.1). From comparison of these conditions with the 5-segmented mandibular exopod found in the Calanoida we inferred that in the canuellids segments I, II and III are free but segments IV and V are fused, whereas

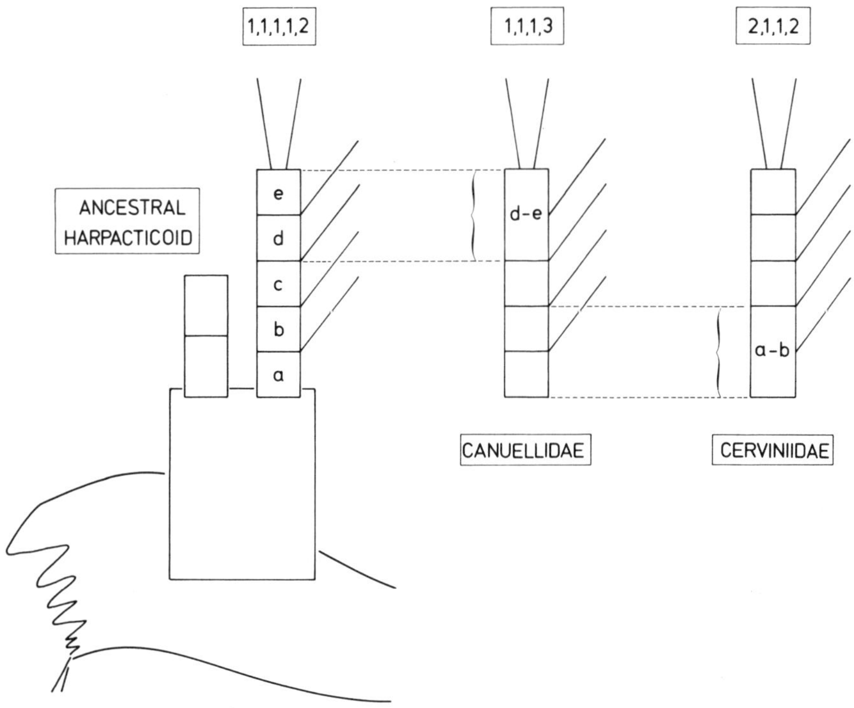

Figure 2.0.1. Schematic comparison of the mandibles of a canuellid harpacticoid and a cerviniid harpacticoid. The different setation patterns indicate that these 4-segmented exopods are derived independently, by distinct segmental fusions, from a common ancestral pattern which is referred to as the ancestral harpacticoid.

in the cerviniids segments III, IV and V are free but I and II are fused. Within the order therefore a total of 5 segments is expressed, with a setal formula of 1,1,1,1,2 and this is designated the ancestral state.

A second and more complicated example is the deduction of the ancestral state of the maxilliped of female Mormonilloida. The maxillipeds of the females of the only two species of *Mormonilla* Giesbrecht differ in segmentation (figure 2.0.2). *M.phasma* Giesbrecht has an unsegmented protopod comprising fused syncoxa and basis, and a 2-segmented endopod whereas *M.minor* Giesbrecht has a compound proximal segment comprising fused syncoxa, basis and first endopodal segment and 3 free endopodal segments. The presence of the single seta distally on the compound proximal segment provides the evidence that the first endopodal segment (segment a) has been incorporated. The ancestral state (in which all segments expressed in both descendants are present) is given as the ancestral mormonilloid and consists of a protopod comprising fused syncoxa and basis, and a 4-segmented endopod. The principal of deduction, as we have applied it, relies heavily on the conservative nature of the setation patterns to identify homologous segments although musculature patterns also provide valuable clues regarding segmental homologies (Boxshall, 1985).

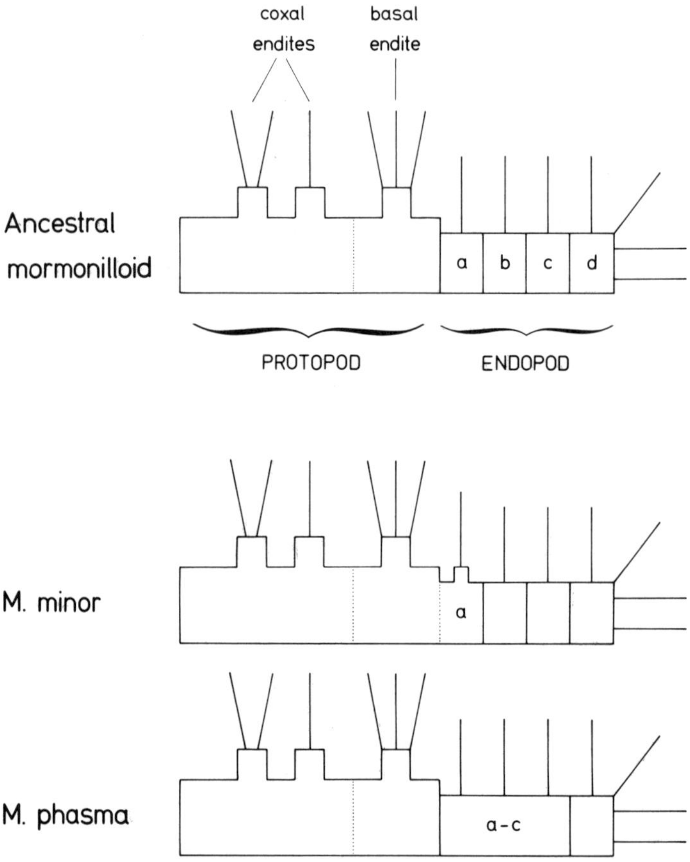

Figure 2.0.2. Schematic comparison of the maxillipeds of female *Mormonilla minor* and *M.phasma*, showing the expressed boundaries between endopodal segments. In *M.minor* the segmental boundaries a-b, b-c and c-d are expressed but in *M.phasma* the only expressed boundaries are basis-a and c-d. Comparison between the two species indicates that, in total, the basis-a, a-b, b-c and c-d boundaries are all expressed and this represents the ancestral mormonilloid condition.

2.1 PLATYCOPIOIDA Fosshagen (in Fosshagen & Iliffe, 1985)

Platycopioids are small, free-living copepods that inhabit the hyperbenthic community in relatively shallow seas (Sars, 1911; Fosshagen, 1972). Species of *Platycopia* Sars have been reported from shallow near-surface waters down to depths of 120 metres in the Atlantic, from Norway, the North Sea, the United States of America, Bahamas and western Africa (figure 2.1.1). The other two genera, *Nanocopia* Fosshagen and *Antrisocopia* Fosshagen, both occur only in anchialine caves on Bermuda (Fosshagen & Iliffe, 1985; 1988). Little is known of their reproductive biology or feeding behaviour.

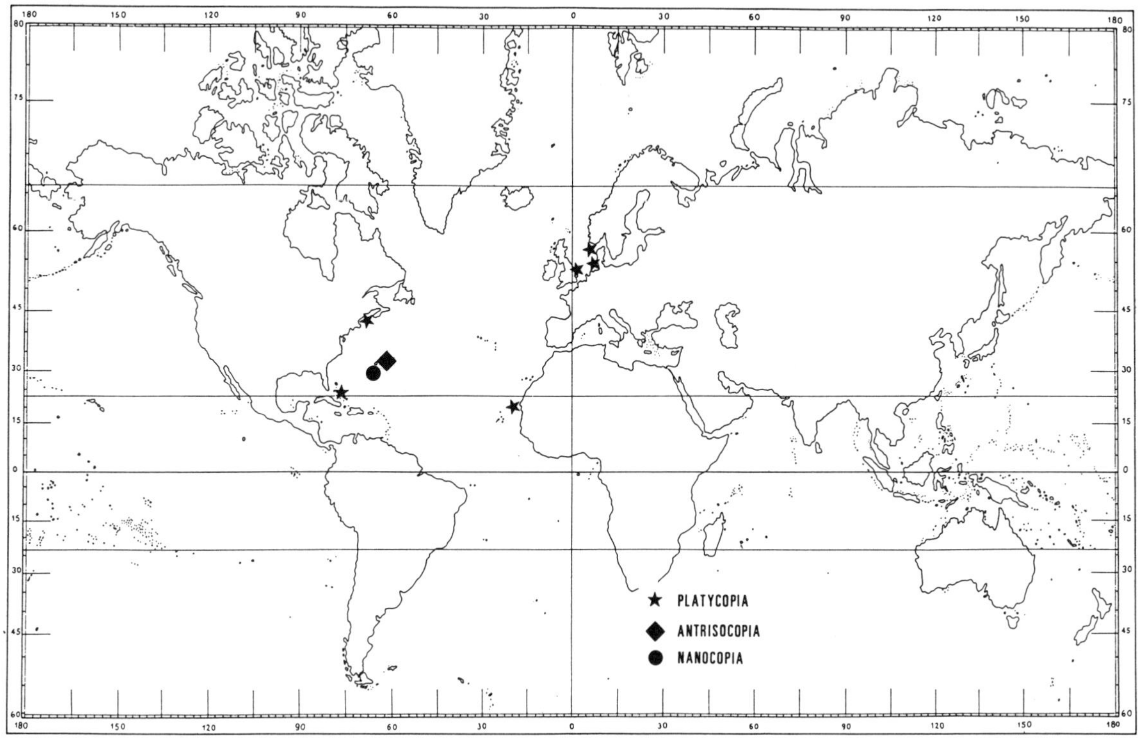

Figure 2.1.1. Geographical distribution of platycopioid genera.

Character set of ancestral platycopioid

Copepoda. Prosome comprising cephalosome and 5 pedigerous somites (figures 2.1.3A and 2.1.9A); boundary between cephalosome and first pedigerous somite lacking arthrodial membrane, nonfunctional; urosome 5-segmented in both sexes. Prosome-urosome articulation between fifth pedigerous and genital somites (gymnoplean position). Genital apertures paired in both sexes, located ventrally at posterior border of genital somite (figure 2.1.11A-B,E). Seminal receptacles paired. Rostrum fused to cephalosome (figure 2.1.10D). Caudal ramus with 7 setae (figure 2.1.3B). Nauplius eye unconfirmed. Antennules 23-segmented in female (figure 2.1.2A), 20-segmented in male (figure 2.1.4); ancestral segment XXVIII free in both sexes; male antennules bilaterally symmetrical, with distal part modified by fusion of ancestral segments XVIII to XX, XXIII to XXIV and XXV to XXVII. Antenna biramous, with indistinctly 9-segmented exopod (figure 2.1.6B) and 3-segmented endopod (figure 2.1.7A); coxa and basis unarmed; endopodal segment 1 unarmed, segment 2 with 3 setae, segment 3 with 7 setae (figure 2.1.7B): exopodal segment 4 representing fused ancestral segments IV and V; setal formula 1,0,0,(1+1),1,1,1,1,3. Labrum tripartite, with long median lobe and bulbous lateral lobes at base (figures 2.1.5B and 2.1.12B). Mandible with large coxal gnathobase and biramous palp (figures 2.1.5A and 2.1.8E-F); exopod 5-segmented (figure 2.1.8F), with setal formula 1,1,1,1,2; endopod 1-segmented, with 6 setae; basis unarmed. Paragnaths separate. Maxillule (figures 2.1.7C and 2.1.8A) with large praecoxal endite bearing 12 elements; coxa with small endite bearing 3 setae, lacking exite (epipodite); basis and rami fused, bearing large basal endite with 3 apical setae and small lobate exite armed with

2 setae (arrowed in figure 2.1.7C): palp with small lobes representing distal basal endite and rami, bearing a total of 8 setae; basal endites widely separated. Maxilla 6-segmented (figure 2.1.9C); praecoxa and coxa each with 2 endites, endite formula 4,1,3,3; allobasis with proximal (basal) endite well developed with 4 setae, distal endite (endopodal) vestigial, represented by single seta; outer coxal seta absent; free endopod indistinctly 3-segmented, setal formula 1,2,3 (figure 2.1.9D). Maxilliped 8-segmented (figure 2.1.7D); syncoxa and basis large; syncoxal formula 0,0,0,2; basis with 2 setae; endopod 6-segmented; setal formula 1,2,2,1,1,4. Intermaxillipedal process (figures 2.1.5C and 2.1.12C) present on midventral surface of cephalosome. Swimming legs 1-5 biramous, members of leg pair joined by intercoxal sclerite (figure 2.1.11C); rami 3-segmented except 2-segmented endopod of first leg (figure 2.1.11D); second to fourth legs bearing inner basal seta but without inner coxal seta (figure 2.1.11C); second to fifth legs each with 2 spines on outer margin of first exopodal segment. Spine and seta formula of legs 1 to 5:

	coxa	basis	exopod segment 1 2 3	endopod segment 1 2 3
leg 1	0 – 0	1 – I	0 – 0; 0 – 0; 0,I,5	0 – 1; 1,2,4
leg 2	0 – 0	1 – 1	II – 1; I – 1; III,I,4	0 – 1; 0 – 1; 2,2,3
leg 3	0 – 0	1 – 1	II – 1; I – 1; III,I,4	0 – 1; 0 – 1; 2,2,3
leg 4	0 – 0	1 – 1	II – 1; I – 1; III,I,4	0 – 1; 0 – 1; 2,2,2
leg 5	0 – 0	0 – 1	II – 1; I – 1; III,I,2	0 – 1; 0 – 1; 1,2,2

Fifth legs the same in both sexes (figure 2.1.8B); praecoxa separate; endopod bearing up to 7 setae, exopod up to 11 spines and setae. Sixth legs represented by tiny setae located at genital apertures in both sexes (figure 2.1.11A-B,E). Eggs not contained in egg sacs.

Remarks

The diagnosis is based on all three known genera, *Platycopia*, *Nanocopia* and *Antrisocopia*. The last genus displays many plesiomorphic character states, particularly in the mandibular palp and fifth legs, although some of its mouthparts are highly specialised (Fosshagen & Iliffe, 1985). The other two genera have retained more generalised mouthparts (Wilson, 1946; Fosshagen, 1972; Andronov, 1985; Fosshagen & Iliffe, 1988). The urosome is 5-segmented, comprising genital and 4 free abdominal somites, in both sexes of all known platycopioids. The caudal rami retain the full complement of 7 setae in *Antrisocopia* (figure 2.1.3B), but in *Platycopia* the dorsal seta (VII) is missing (figure 2.1.10B-C).

Male Antennule: No geniculation mechanism exists in the antennules of male *Platycopia* or *Nanocopia*. However, the antennule of male *Antrisocopia* is an interesting structure since it is modified as a grasping appendage on both sides of the body and is presumably used for holding the female during mating, as in most other copepods. Comparison between the antennules of male *Platycopia* (figure 2.1.2B) and male *Antrisocopia* (figure 2.1.3E) reveals a similar pattern of segmental fusions distally. Using the setation for reference the segmental homologies are identifiable (figure 2.1.4). In the males of both genera the distal fusions are the same: ancestral segments XXIII to XXIV are fused, as are segments XXV to XXVII, and segment XXVIII is free. The geniculation in *Antrisocopia* occurs between segments homologous with ancestral segments XXIV and XXV. This geniculation mechanism is not homologous with that found in the Calanoida and Podoplea, since in these groups the geniculation is located between ancestral segments XX and XXI. The movable, curved spine on the segment proximal to the geniculation in *Antrisocopia* is an integral part of the grasping mechanism. This spine hinges back to form the fixed finger of a chelate apparatus, opposing the movable apical segments. There is no specialisation of the corresponding articulation in male *Platycopia*. There are 3 segments, representing ancestral segments XVII, XIX and XXII (marked by an asterisk in figure 2.1.4), that are unarmed in both sexes of *Platycopia* species and *Antrisocopia*. In males of both genera ancestral segments XVIII to XX are fused, but in *Platycopia* the resulting compound segment also incorporates segment XVII. Excluding ancestral segments I to III (the fate of which is unknown), the first 3 segments (ancestral segments IV to VI) are free in *Antrisocopia*, the next 10 (ancestral VII to XVI) are free in *Platycopia*, and 7 segments are present distal to this in *Antrisocopia*. This produces a total of 20 segments expressed as free segments in male platycopioids.

Female Antennule: The antennules of female platycopioids show considerable fusion between proximal segments (figure 2.1.4) and there is also fusion distally in *Antrisocopia* (figure 2.1.3D) but not in *Platycopia* (figure 2.1.2A). The setation pattern provides no evidence of the fate of the 3 most proximal segments (ancestral segments I to III) in platycopioids. They may be lost or, more likely, incorporated into the proximal segments as asetose elements.

Antenna: The antennae of platycopioids are unusual in that the exopods are considerably larger and better developed than the endopods. All genera retain a separate coxa and basis, both of which are unarmed. In *Platycopia* ancestral exopodal segments I, II and III are separate but IV-V, VI-VII and IX-X are completely fused (figure 2.1.7A) resulting in a 1,0,0,2,2,1,4 formula. The slender antennary exopod of *Antrisocopia* is indistinctly 8-segmented (figure 2.1.6B) and the setation formula is 1,0,1,1,1,1,1,3. In this genus ancestral exopodal segments II-III and IV-V are fully fused, and VI-VII are incompletely fused. Assuming a derivation from an indistinctly 9-segmented condition (with segments IV and V forming a double segment) in the ancestral platycopioid the original armature formula would presumably have been 1,0,0,(1+1),1,1,1,1,3. The antennary endopod has a maximum of 2 free segments expressed (figure 2.1.7B). Endopodal segment 1 appears to be fused with the basis in *Antrisocopia*, forming a somewhat elongate allobasis. No trace of this segment is apparent in other platycopioids. Segment 2 bears 3 setae in *Platycopia* and 2 in *Antrisocopia* and *Nanocopia*. The compound third segment is armed with 7 setae in *Platycopia* and *Antrisocopia*.

Labrum: The tripartite labrum of *Platycopia* appears more or less typical of all platycopioids. In *Nanocopia* it closely resembles that of *Platycopia* (Fosshagen & Iliffe, 1988) but in *Antrisocopia* the central lobe of the labrum is less prominent and the lateral lobes are weakly developed (figure 2.1.8C-D).

Mandible: The mandible comprises a well developed coxal gnathobase plus a biramous palp in all genera. The basis is unarmed. The mandibular exopod of *Antrisocopia* is 5-segmented and retains a 1,1,1,1,2 setal formula. In *Platycopia* this ramus is modified by fusion and may be indistinctly 3- or 4-segmented (figure 2.1.5A). In *Platycopia perplexa* Sars the exopodal formula is 0,2,1,2 indicating the loss of the seta from the proximal segment and the fusion of segments II and III. The 1-segmented endopod bearing 6 setae is found in all genera.

Maxillule: The segmentation of the maxillule is the same in all 3 genera but there is minor variation in precise setal counts (cf. figures 2.1.7C and 2.1.8A). The protopod is clearly 3-segmented, although the basis is fused distally to the rami. The praecoxal arthrite is markedly produced medially and well armed. The coxa lacks any trace of the epipodite and carries 2 or 3 setae on its endite. The basis has a distinct lobate exite bearing 2 setae (arrowed in figure 2.1.7C) in all known platycopioids. The proximal basal endite is elongate, extending mediodistally beyond the apex of the baso-ramal complex. It bears 3 setae. The distal basal endite is weakly defined, being represented by the distalmost lobe bearing 2 setae in *Platycopia* (figure 2.1.7C) and 3 setae in *Antrisocopia* (figure 2.1.8A). The remaining laterodistal part of the palp represents the vestigial rami but the 4 or 5 setae present cannot be identified as originating from either the endopod or the exopod.

Maxilla: The most plesiomorphic condition of the maxilla is found in *Platycopia* (figure 2.1.9C-D). The praecoxa and coxa are separate and have a setal formula of 4,1,3,3 for their endites. The basis and first endopodal segment are fused and armed with 4 and 1 setae respectively. The 3 free endopodal segments have a setal formula of 1,2,3. In *Antrisocopia* this appendage is highly specialised and has reduced segmentation and setation (figure 2.1.3C). The syncoxal armature is reduced to just 2 setae. The free endopod is only 2-segmented, with a setal formula of 2,2.

Maxilliped: The maxilliped of *Platycopia* also exhibits the most plesiomorphic condition within the order. The setation formulae given above in the ancestral character set for the syncoxa (0,0,0,2), basis (2) and endopod (1,2,2,1,1,4) are all found in *P.perplexa* (figure 2.1.7D). In *Antrisocopia* the maxilliped is specialised (figure 2.1.6C). The syncoxa bears a single seta. The basis bears 2 setae but the more distal seta is probably derived from a proximal endopodal segment, now incorporated into the basis. The remaining 5 free endopodal segments have a setal formula of 2,1,1,1,4.

Intermaxillipedal Process: The intermaxillipedal process is a remarkable feature of the Platycopioida. In *Platycopia* it lies in the ventral midline on a median sclerite lying between the bases of the maxillipeds (figure 2.1.12A). It is a rigid, erect process armed with 7 to 8 powerful spinous processes that are anteriorly directed (figure 2.1.12C). At the same location in *Antrisocopia* are a pair of anteriorly directed spines situated on a median sclerite (figure 2.1.6A,D). In *Nanocopia* the intermaxillipedal process is unconfirmed.

Swimming Legs: The first swimming leg has 2-segmented rami in *Antrisocopia* and some *Platycopia* species (figure 2.1.11D) but *Nanocopia* has a 3-segmented exopod, although its endopod is only 1-segmented. The inner coxal seta and the outer seta on the basis are lacking in platycopioids but the inner seta is present (figures 2.1.6A and 2.1.11D). The maximum number of elements on the exopod (I,5) is found in *Platycopia* (figure 2.1.11D) and on the endopod (0-1; 1,2,4) in *Antrisocopia*.

The typical platycopioid swimming leg has a 3-segmented protopod and 3-segmented rami but in *Nanocopia* the endopod is 2-segmented in legs 2 to 5. A vestige of the praecoxa remains as a small laterally located sclerite in legs 2 to 4 (figure 2.1.11C). The typical protopodal armature without an inner coxal seta but with both inner and outer setae on the basis is shown in figure 2.1.11C. Two outer margin spines on the first exopodal segment are found on legs 2 to 5 of *Platycopia* and *Antrisocopia* but only on legs 2 and 3 of *Nanocopia*. The most plesiomorphic spine and setal formula found within the order is that of *Antrisocopia*. It differs from that of *Platycopia* (figure 2.1.11C) only in the retention of 3 setae instead of 2 on the inner margin of the third endopodal segment of legs 2 and 3.

Fifth Legs: In its most plesiomorphic state the fifth leg of platycopioids is similar to swimming legs 2 to 4. The fifth legs of both sexes of *Antrisocopia* (figure 2.1.8B) resemble the fourth legs of *Platycopia* (figure 2.1.11C). An intercoxal sclerite and a sclerite representing the praecoxa are present, and there is no sexual dimorphism in *Antrisocopia*. In *Platycopia* species, however, the male fifth legs are highly transformed, with both rami secondarily modified (figure 2.1.10A).

Differential Diagnosis: The Platycopioida is a distinctive order and its members are easily recognisable by the following combination of characters: gymnoplean-type tagmosis and the presence of 2 spines on the outer margin of the first exopodal segment of at least the second and third swimming legs. They also possess unique apomorphies such as the tripartite labrum. The loss of the inner coxal seta on the swimming legs is also worthy of note. The intermaxillipedal process is well developed in *Platycopia* species but reduced in both *Antrisocopia* and *Nanocopia*. Platycopioids are the only extant copepods that retain a lobate exite on the basis of the maxillule. Although a plesiomorphic character, the basal exite bearing 2 setae is present in all known species and is a reliable diagnostic character.

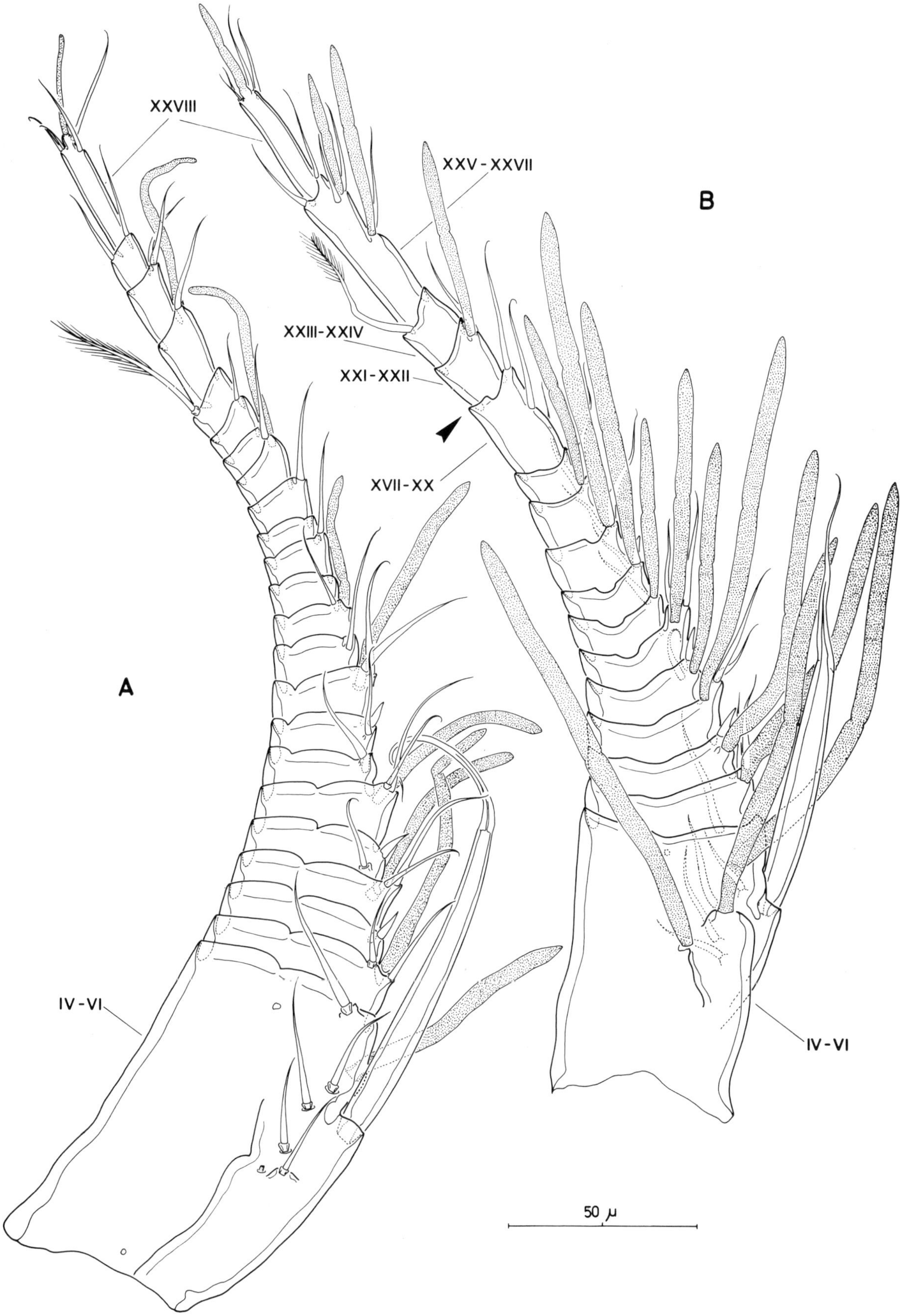

Figure 2.1.2. *Platycopia inornata*. **A.** Female antennule. **B.** Male antennule, with position of neocopepodan geniculation arrowed.

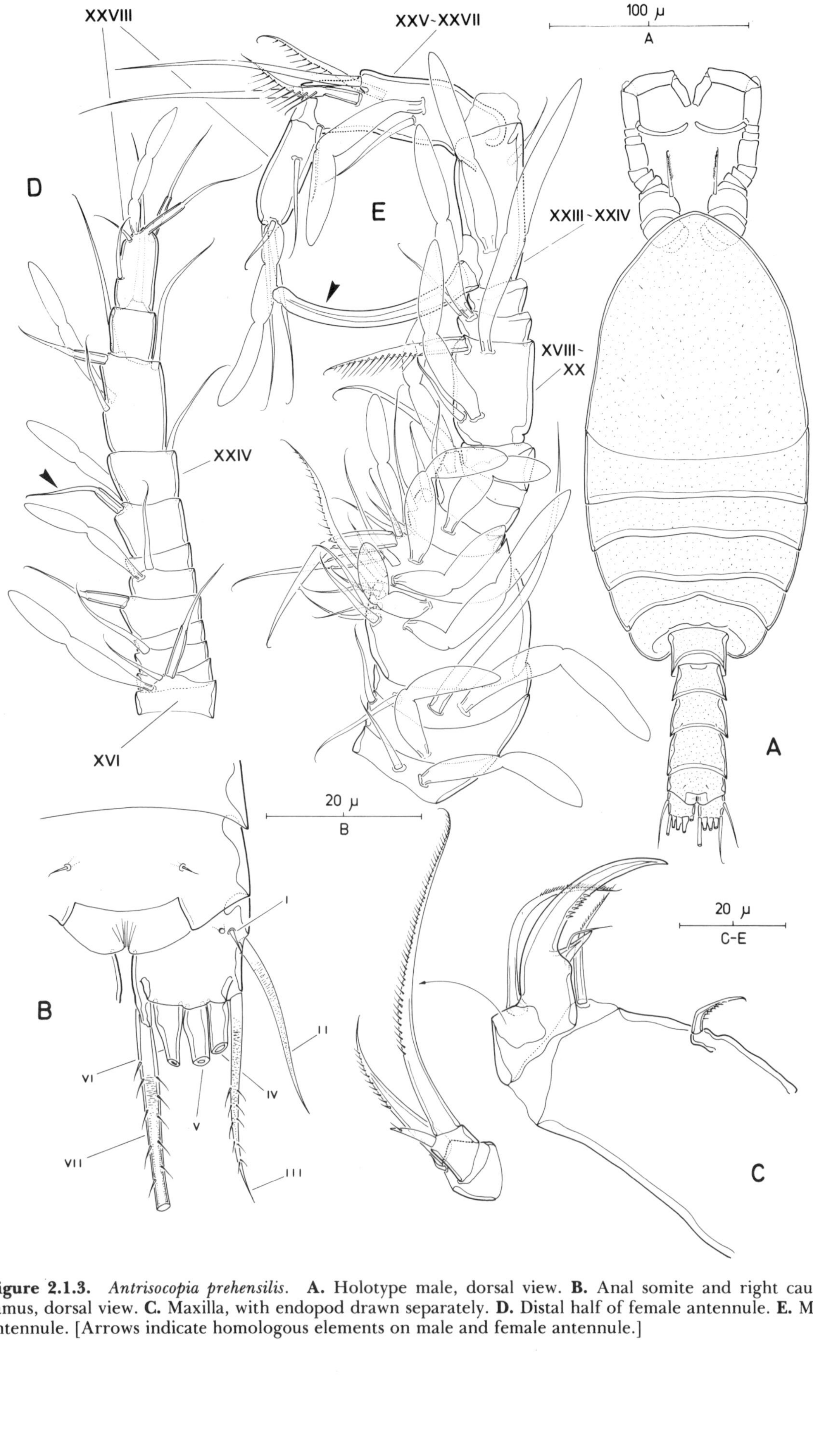

Figure 2.1.3. *Antrisocopia prehensilis.* **A.** Holotype male, dorsal view. **B.** Anal somite and right caudal ramus, dorsal view. **C.** Maxilla, with endopod drawn separately. **D.** Distal half of female antennule. **E.** Male antennule. [Arrows indicate homologous elements on male and female antennule.]

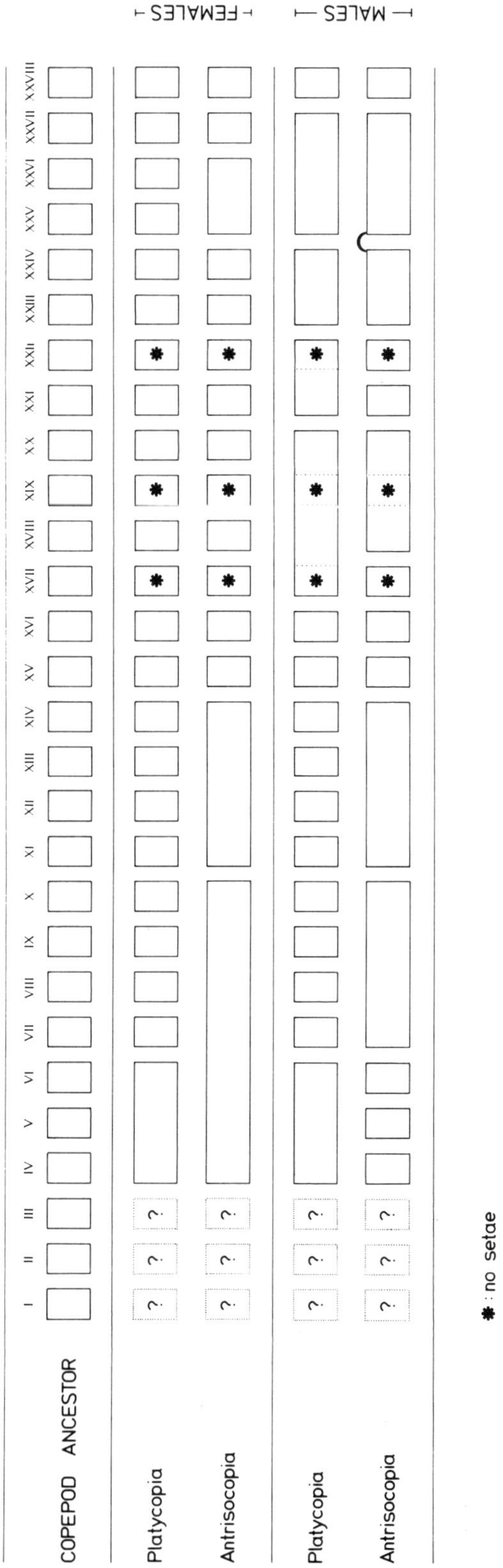

Figure 2.1.4. Schematic comparison of segmental homologies in the antennules of female and male platycopioids.

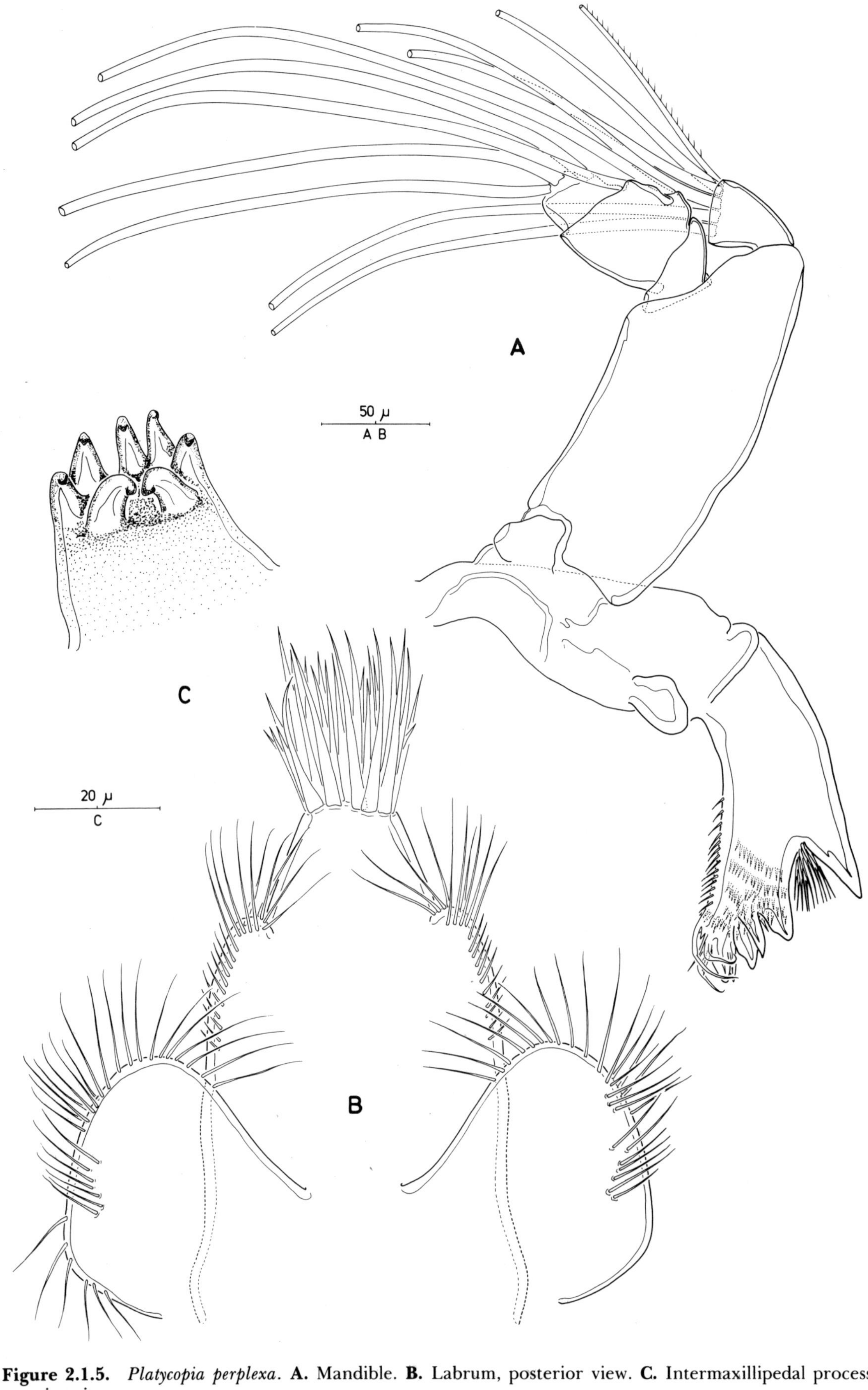

Figure 2.1.5. *Platycopia perplexa*. **A.** Mandible. **B.** Labrum, posterior view. **C.** Intermaxillipedal process, anterior view.

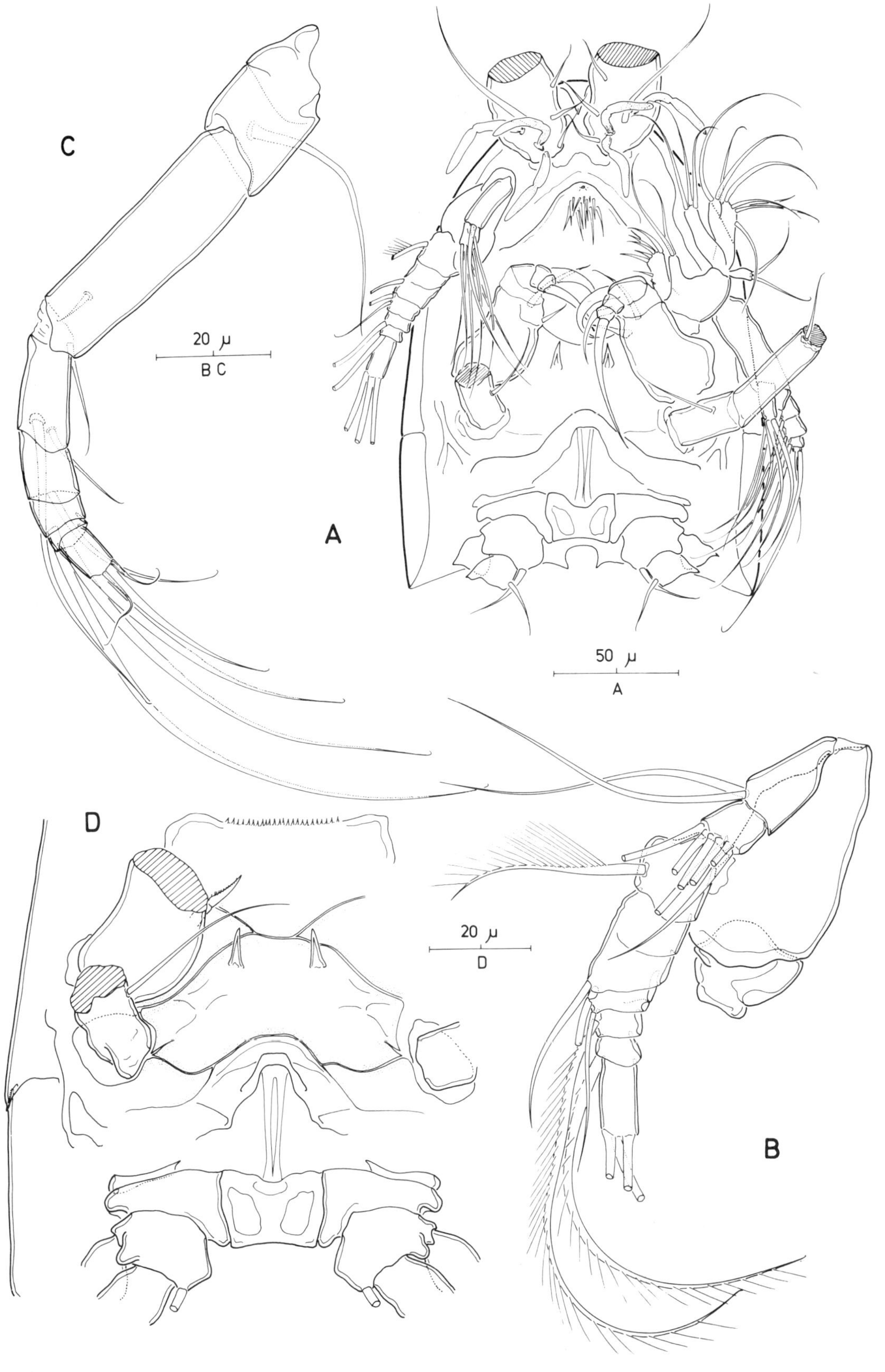

Figure 2.1.6. *Antrisocopia prehensilis*, male. **A.** Cephalosome and first pedigerous somite, ventral view showing arrangement of limbs and position of intermaxillipedal process. **B.** Antenna, drawn in situ. **C.** Maxilliped. **D.** Ventral view of area between maxillipeds, showing position of first legs, maxillipeds, intermaxillipedal process, maxillae and the partial fusion of the epimera of the first pedigerous somite with the cephalosome.

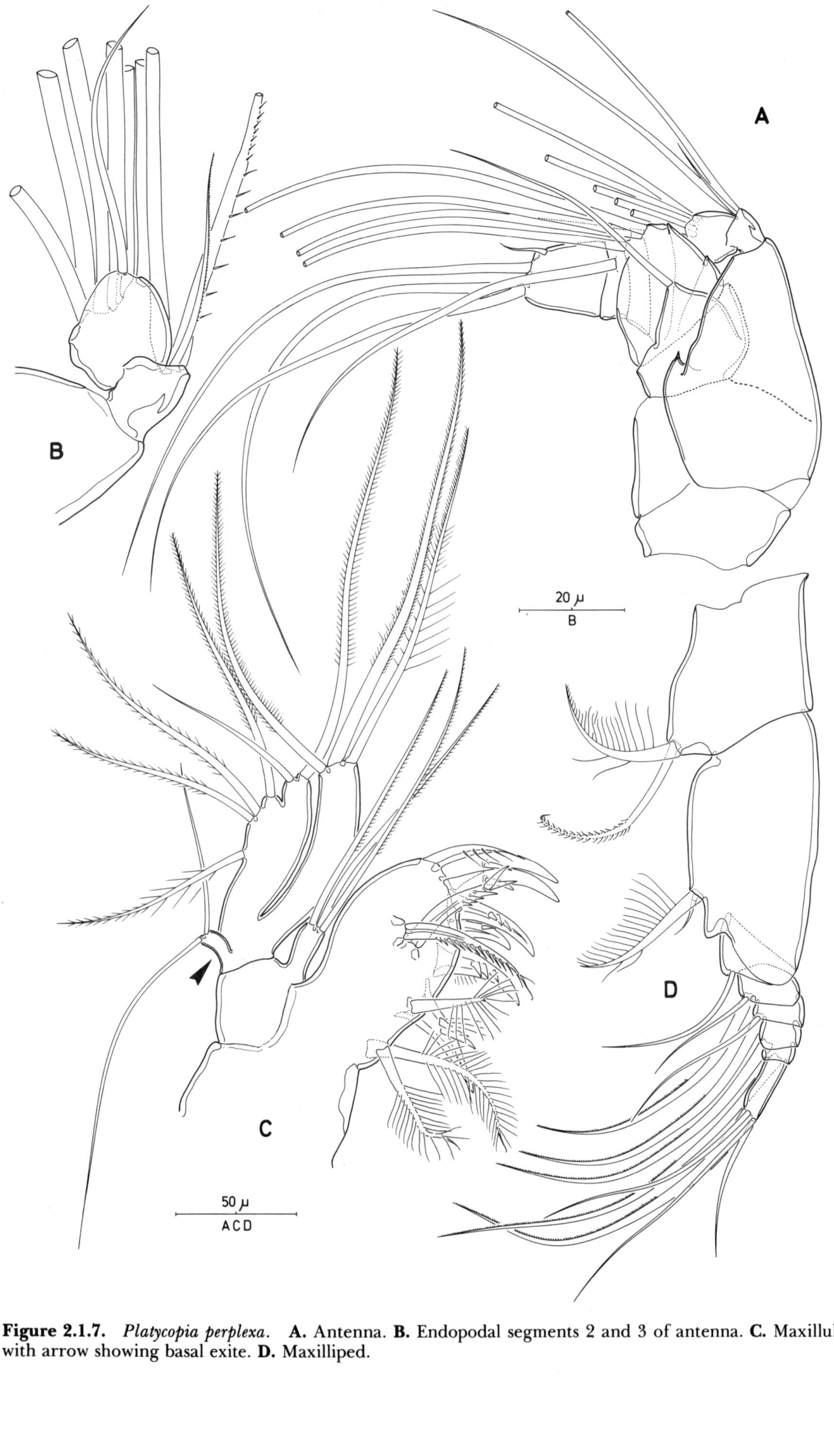

Figure 2.1.7. *Platycopia perplexa.* **A.** Antenna. **B.** Endopodal segments 2 and 3 of antenna. **C.** Maxillule, with arrow showing basal exite. **D.** Maxilliped.

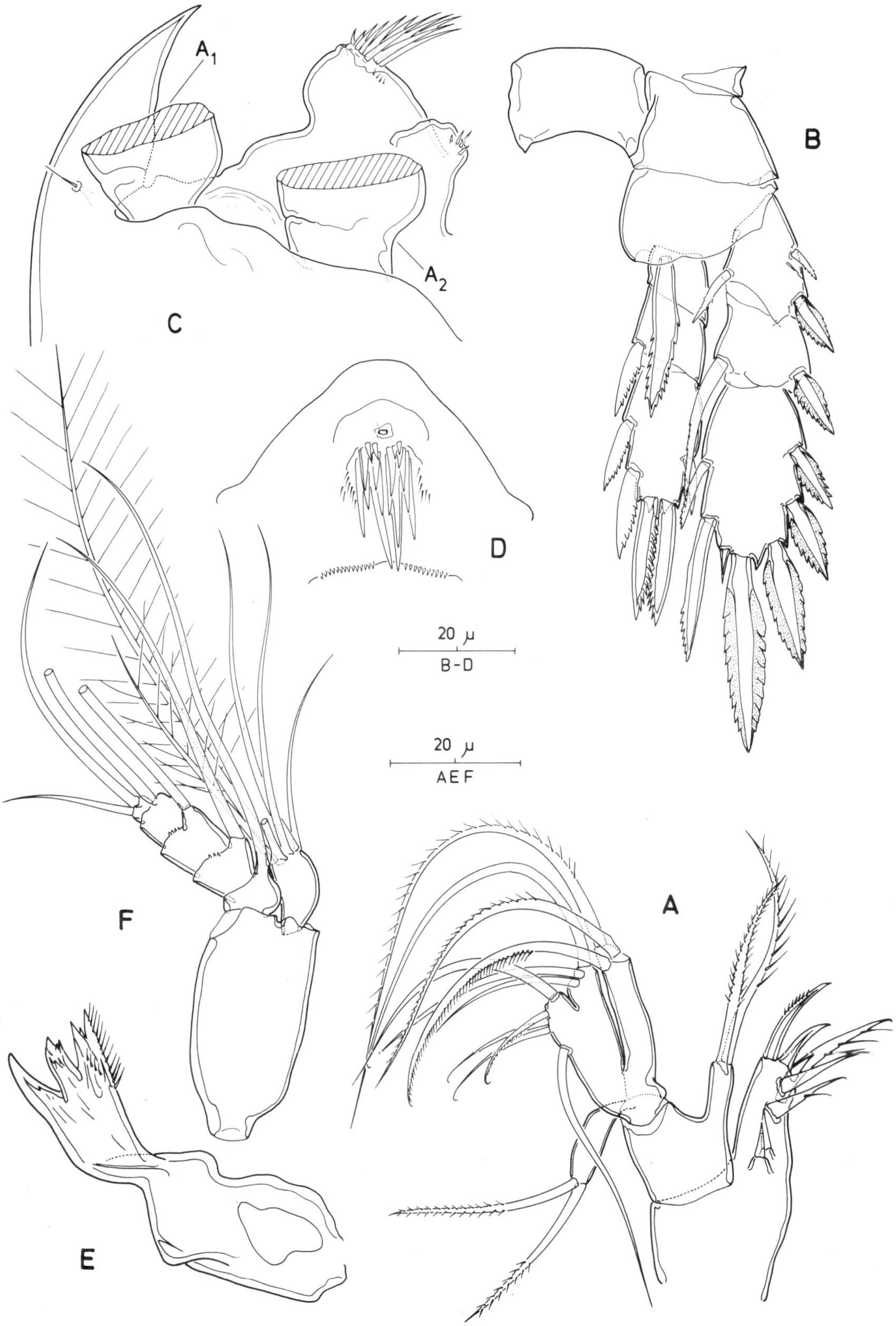

Figure 2.1.8. *Antrisocopia prehensilis*. **A.** Maxillule. **B.** Male fifth leg. **C.** Rostrum and labrum, lateral view with positions of antennule (A1) and antenna (A2) indicated. **D.** Labrum, posterior view of median lobe. **E.** Mandibular gnathobase. **F.** Mandibular palp.

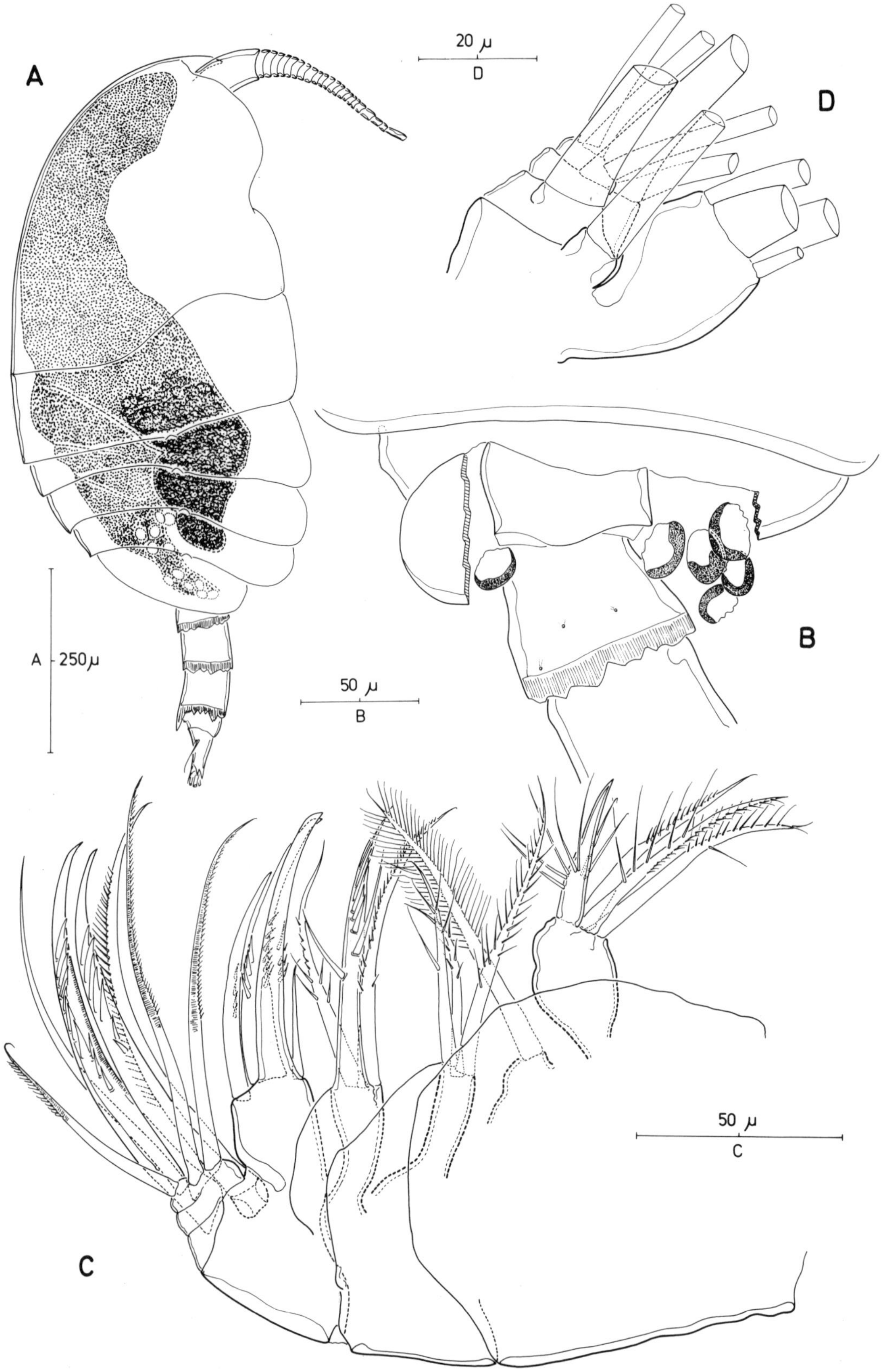

Figure 2.1.9. *Platycopia perplexa*. **A.** Female, lateral view. **B.** Genital and first abdominal somites, lateral view with part of fifth epimera removed. **C.** Maxilla. **D.** Basis and endopod of maxilla.

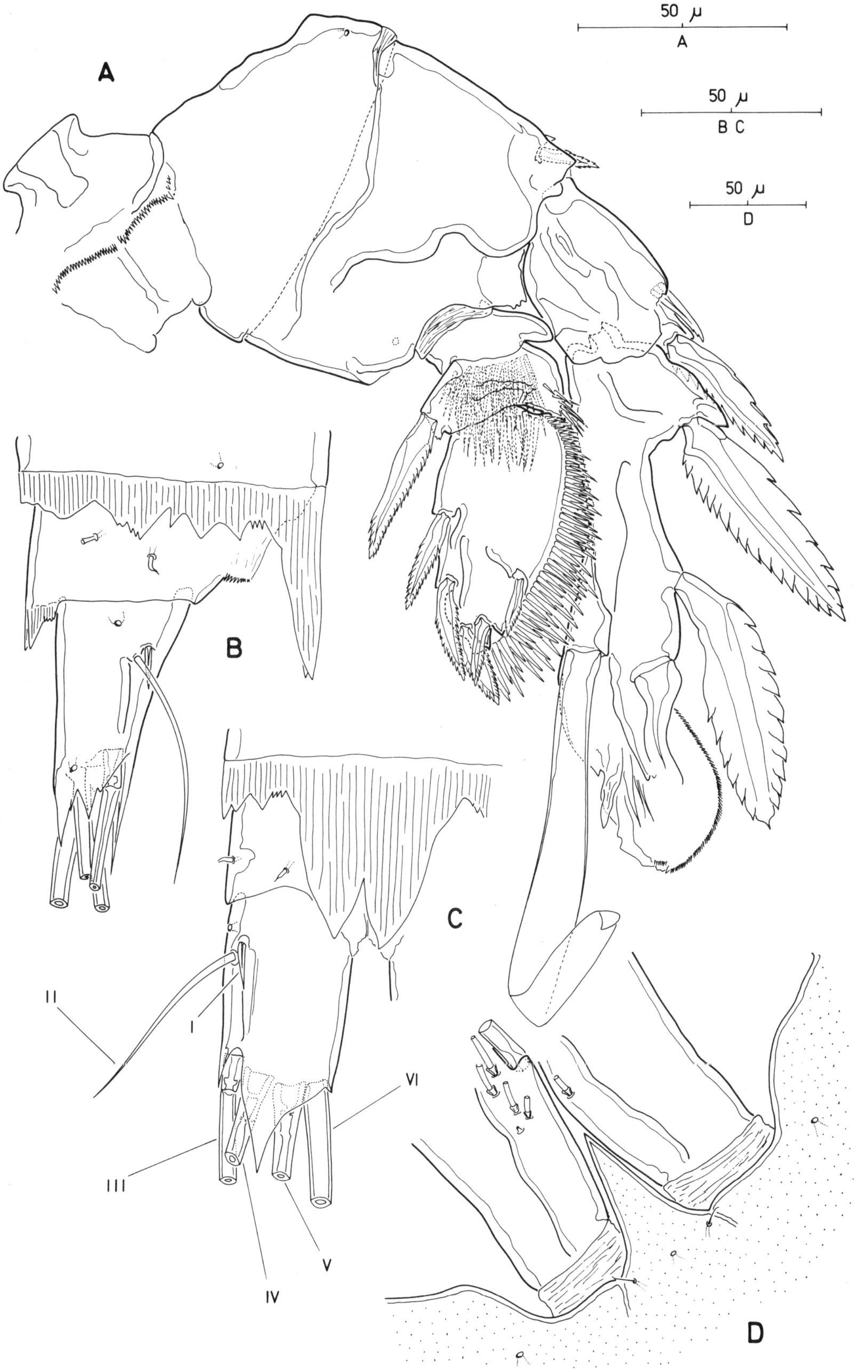

Figure 2.1.10. *Platycopia perplexa*. **A.** Male fifth leg. **B.** Anal somite and caudal ramus, lateral view. **C.** Anal somite and caudal ramus, dorsal view. **D.** Rostral area, frontal view.

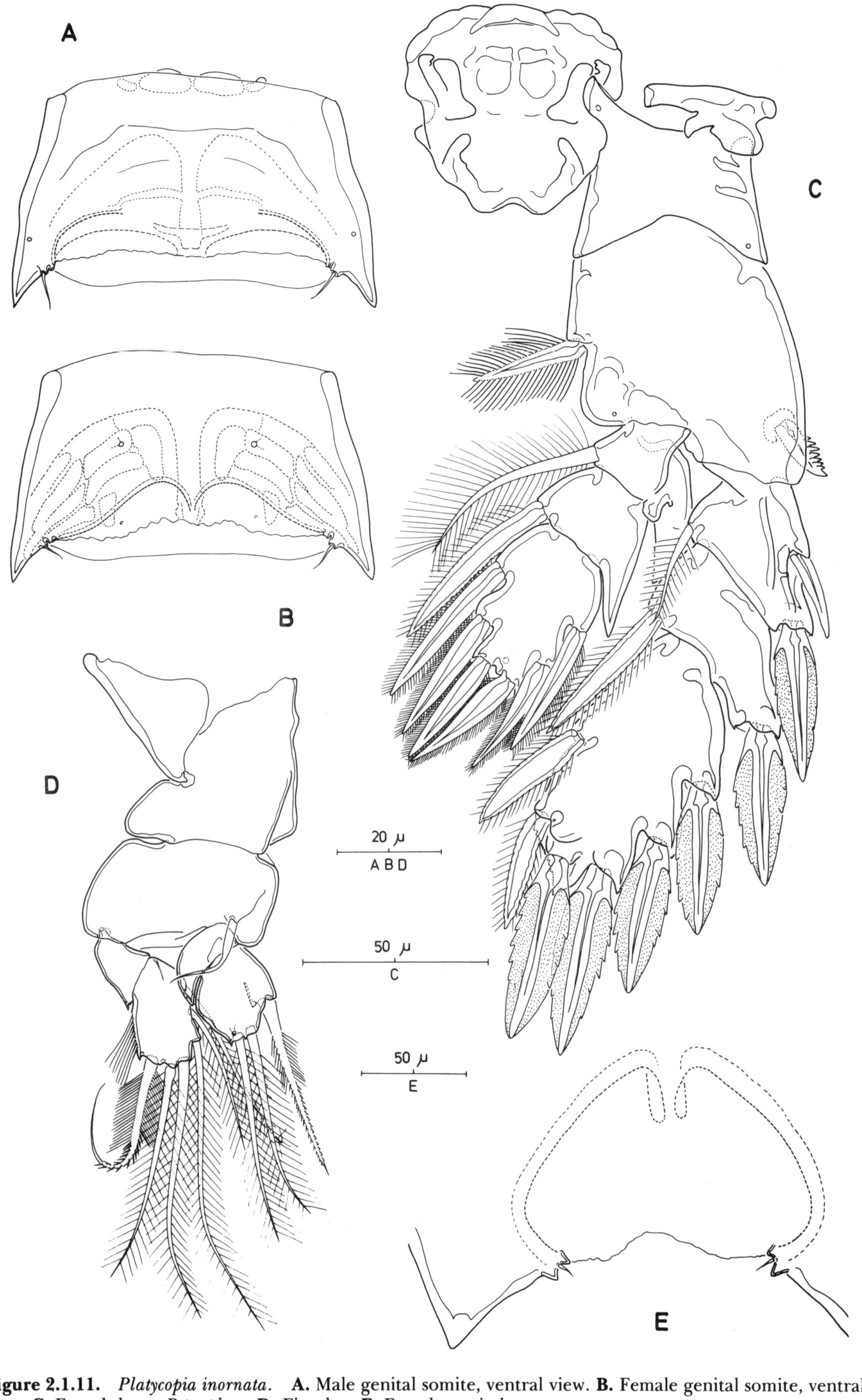

Figure 2.1.11. *Platycopia inornata.* **A.** Male genital somite, ventral view. **B.** Female genital somite, ventral view. **C.** Fourth leg. *P.perplexa.* **D.** First leg. **E.** Female genital apertures.

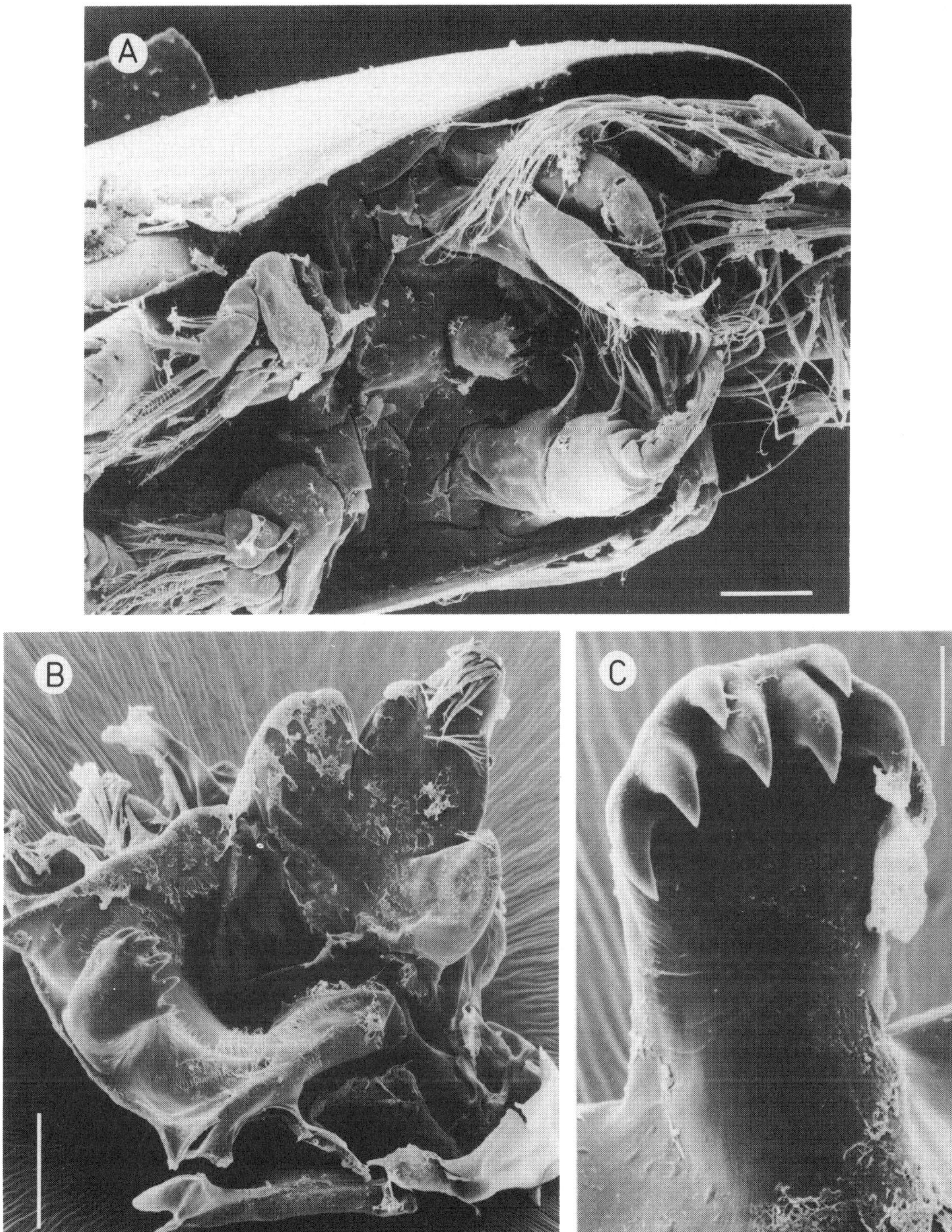

Figure 2.1.12. *Platycopia inornata.* **A.** Cephalosome and first pedigerous somite, ventro-lateral view. **B.** Labrum and intermaxillipedal process, postero-lateral view. **C.** Intermaxillipedal process, anterior view. Scale bars A =50μm, B = 30μm, C = 10μm.

2.2 CALANOIDA Sars 1903

Calanoids are the marine planktonic copepods *par excellence*. They occur at all depths in the water column, from the surface to the abyssal trenches. Most are pelagic, living in the water column away from the influence of the sea bed. Some live in the near-bottom community and a few are more or less benthic. Calanoids are also abundant in the freshwater plankton and in inland saline habitats. They are typical members of the specialised fauna of anchialine habitats. Many are specialist small particle feeders consuming the algal cells of the phytoplankton. Others are predators feeding on a wide variety of animal prey. All calanoids appear to be selective feeders and catch their food particles raptorially. This broad similarity in feeding behaviour is reflected in the basic uniformity of gross morphology in the Calanoida compared to the other large orders. Calanoids have rarely been found in association with other animals. Humes & Smith (1974) reported a species of *Ridgewayia* Thompson & Scott that lived in aggregations closely associated with the sea anemone *Bartholomea annulata* Lesueur in Panama. *Acartia negligens* Dana actively feeds on mucus produced by reef corals and can assimilate up to half of the organic matter present (Richman et al., 1975).

Character set of ancestral calanoid

Copepoda. Prosome comprising cephalosome and 5 free pedigerous somites (figure 2.2.20A); urosome 4-segmented in female (figure 2.2.14D), 5-segmented in male. Prosome-urosome articulation between fifth pedigerous and genital somites (gymnoplean position). Genital double somite present in female, comprising fused genital and first abdominal somites. Genital apertures paired in both sexes, located ventrally about in middle of genital double somite in female (figure 2.2.14D) and at posterior border of genital somite in male. Seminal receptacles paired. Rostrum fused to cephalosome. Caudal ramus with 7 setae (figure 2.2.27G-H). Nauplius eye present. Antennules 27-segmented in female (figure 2.2.2C); apical segment double in both sexes, comprising fused ancestral segments XXVII and XXVIII; geniculate on right side only in male, with fusion of ancestral segments XXI to XXIII and XXIV to XXV distal to the geniculation which is located between segments homologous with XX and XXI of the female (figure 2.2.5A-D). Antenna biramous with a 10-segmented exopod and 4-segmented endopod (figure 2.2.11); coxa with 1 inner seta, basis with 2 inner setae, first to fourth endopodal segments with 2, 9, 5 and 2 setae respectively: exopodal segments with setal formula 1,1,1,1,1,1,1,1,1,3. Labrum an undivided muscular lobe. Mandible with large coxal gnathobase and biramous palp (figure 2.2.17); exopod 5-segmented, setal formula 1,1,1,1,2; endopod 2-segmented, setal formula 4,11; basis bearing 4 setae on inner margin. Paragnaths separate. Maxillule (figure 2.2.19B) with large praecoxal endite bearing 16 elements; coxa with single endite bearing 5 setae, and well developed epipodite bearing 9 setae; basis bearing a single seta on outer margin representing the basal exite, 2 widely separated endites present, proximal endite well developed, with 4 setae; distal endite largely incorporated into segment, represented by 5 setae; exopod 1-segmented with 11 setae (figure 2.2.18B), endopod 3-segmented, setal formula 6,4,7 (figure 2.2.18C). Maxilla (figure 2.2.21) 7-segmented; praecoxa and coxa each with 2 endites, endite formula 10,3,3,3; outer seta on coxa representing epipodite; basis with well developed endite bearing 4 setae; endopod 4-segmented, setal formula 4,3,2,2. Maxilliped 8-segmented, comprising syncoxa, basis and 6-segmented endopod (figure 2.2.23), with proximal endopodal segment incompletely fused to basis; syncoxal formula 1,2,4,4; basis with 3 setae; outer seta on coxa representing epipodite; endopod setal formula 2,4,4,3,3+1,4. Swimming legs 1-5 biramous with 3-segmented rami, members of each leg pair joined by intercoxal sclerite; inner coxal seta and outer seta on basis present in all legs, inner seta on basis of first leg only; first exopodal segment with 1 outer spine. Spine and seta formula for legs 1 to 5:

	coxa	basis	exopod segment 1 2 3	endopod segment 1 2 3
leg 1	0 – 1	1 – I	I – 1; I – 1; II,I,4	0 – 1; 0 – 2; 1,2,3
leg 2	0 – 1	1 – 0	I – 1; I – 1; III,I,5	0 – 1; 0 – 2; 2,2,4
leg 3	0 – 1	1 – 0	I – 1; I – 1; III,I,5	0 – 1; 0 – 2; 2,2,4
leg 4	0 – 1	1 – 0	I – 1; I – 1; III,I,5	0 – 1; 0 – 2; 2,2,3
leg 5	0 – 1	1 – 0	I – 0; I – 1; III,I,4	0 – 1; 0 – 1; 2,2,2

Fifth legs sexually dimorphic; praecoxa present; endopod with 8 setae, exopod with 11 spines and setae. Sixth legs represented by unarmed opercular plates closing off genital openings. Eggs possibly carried in egg sacs.

Remarks

The diagnosis is based largely on the generalised families Calanidae, Augaptilidae, Ridgewayiidae, Pseudocyclopidae, Boholinidae, Stephidae and Epacteriscidae. The basic tagmosis and arrangement of somites is common to most calanoids. Female calanoids primitively have a genital double somite (figures 2.2.27-29) but this character is weak as a diagnostic apomorphy because all copepod orders other than the Platycopioida contain some forms with a genital double somite.

Female Genital System: The presence in the female of a single median gonopore closed off by a common operculum is not diagnostic for the Calanoida since the primitive families Pseudocyclopidae (figures 2.2.14D and 2.2.32A-D), Boholinidae, and at least some members of the family Arietellidae (figure 2.2.29A-E), retain separate paired ventral gonopores in both sexes. The paired sixth legs form the opercula closing off the genital apertures in both sexes and they are unarmed. The loss of the ancestral armature elements from the sixth legs is also an apomorphy of the Calanoida. The asymmetrical 'spines' on the sixth legs of *Parastephos esterlyi* Fleminger shown by Fleminger (1988) resemble the discharged spermatophores of other members of the Stephidae (figure 2.2.33A-B) (Boxshall et al., 1990) and may not be true armature elements.

The different configurations of the female genital system in calanoids can be arranged in a transformation series. The plesiomorphic state is for the entire genital apparatus to be paired, with paired oviducts, seminal receptacles, and genital apertures. Each genital aperture is closed by an unarmed operculum derived from the sixth leg. This is found in the Pseudocyclopidae and Boholinidae (figure 2.2.16).

The genital system of female arietellids displays a modification unique for the Calanoida. In some genera the copulatory pores into which the spermatophores discharge are fused and have migrated across the surface of the genital double somite away from the oviduct openings with their opercular plates derived from the modified sixth legs. *Paramisophria platysoma* Ohtsuka & Mitsuzumi is a profoundly asymmetrical species and the single copulatory pore is found on the left side of the double somite (Ohtsuka & Mitsuzumi, 1990). *Paramisophria cluthae* Scott is also asymmetrical. In this species the pore is connected by paired copulatory ducts to the paired seminal receptacles which lie beneath the paired genital apertures (figure 2.2.29A-B,E). In other arietellids, for example an as yet undescribed new species of *Paramisophria* Scott from Japanese waters, the copulatory pore is median (figure 2.2.29C-D) but the arrangement is otherwise similar. In all calanoids other than these arietellids the copulatory pores or pore remain inside the genital aperture(s) so that spermatophores discharge into and eggs are released out of the common genital aperture (figure 2.2.31A-D).

In *Mesaiokeras* Matthews the opercula are fused to form a common operculum but the genital apertures and seminal receptacles are paired (figure 2.2.28E-F). In *Paracyclopia naessi* Fosshagen (figure 2.2.28C-D) and *Enantiosis cavernicola* Barr (figure 2.2.27F) the gonopores are fused, forming a single common gonopore beneath the common operculum, but the seminal receptacles remain separate. Finally, in *Stephos lucayensis* Fosshagen (figure 2.2.28A-B) only a single seminal receptacle is retained and the gonopores are fused. In this species the common operculum is produced into a posteriorly directed spiniform process. The common genital operculum in diaptomids (figure 2.2.33C-D) shows traces of its derivation from the paired sixth legs but is unarmed, as in all calanoids. Several calanoids exhibit setiform or spiniform structures on the genital double somite of the female. Examination of such processes and outgrowths in *Centropages typicus* Krøyer (figure 2.2.27B-E) reveals that these are derived structures.

Female Antennule: Antennules of 27 segments are found in female *Erebonectes nesioticus* Fosshagen (figures 2.2.2C and 2.2.3B) and in three as yet undescribed new genera of epacteriscids (Barr, pers. comm., Fosshagen, pers. comm.). Most female calanoids exhibit some fusion of the antennulary segments (figure 2.2.9). Typically ancestral segments II to IV are partially or completely fused to form a triple segment, as in *Exumella polyarthra* Fosshagen (figure 2.2.2A) and *Enantiosis cavernicola* (figure 2.2.3A). However, in *Ridgewayia wilsoni* Fosshagen only segments II and III are fused, with IV remaining free (figure 2.2.2B). In *Calanus finmarchicus* (Gunnerus) the female antennule (figure 2.2.7B) exhibits the typical 25-segmented calanoid condition, with the second segment representing a triple segment derived by fusion of II to IV. *Calanus* Leach also shows that the armature of the first antennulary segment of calanoids comprises 3 setae plus an aesthetasc rather than a trithek with 2 setae.

In specialised genera, such as *Placocalanus* Fosshagen (figure 2.2.3C), further fusions have taken place resulting in the formation of a blade-like proximal expansion on the antennule. The antennules of the primitive genus *Pseudocyclops* Brady are highly derived (figure 2.2.8A). There has been some fusion distally and considerable fusion proximally, effectively preventing the precise recognition of segmental homologies.

Disseta palumboi Giesbrecht, a member of the calanoid family Heterorhabdidae, has an unusual setation pattern on the proximal part of the female antennule. Giesbrecht (1892: Taf.29, fig.2) and Sewell (1947: text-fig.48B) both showed an incompletely fused, compound proximal segment bearing 3 groups of armature elements. The first group comprised 1 plumose seta, 1 naked seta and 2 aesthetasc-like elements with rounded tips. The second comprised 1 naked seta and 2 aesthetasc-like elements with rounded tips, and so did the third. The adjacent free segment also carried 1 naked seta and 2 aesthetasc-like elements. The total numbers of elements corresponding to the armature of ancestral segments I to IV are 4, 3, 3 and 3 but each would only have carried 1 aesthetasc. Reexamination of the John Murray Expedition material studied by Sewell revealed that the elements drawn as naked seta are the true aesthetascs and the aesthetasc-like elements are highly modified setae which curve dorsally and are flanged distally.

Male Antennule: In male calanoids the antennule is primitively geniculate on the right side only, the left antennule resembling that of the female. The loss of the left side geniculation in the male is therefore an apomorphy of the Calanoida. This asymmetry is found in the plesiomorphic families Pseudocyclopidae, Boholinidae, Epacteriscidae and Ridgewayiidae as well as in many of the more derived families. The known families exhibiting this asymmetry in male antennules were referred to collectively by Giesbrecht (1892) and Sars (1901-1903) as the section Heterarthrandria. The Heterarthrandria, which is paraphyletic, was abandoned after Andronov's (1974) analysis of calanoid systematics.

Analysis of the segmentation of these geniculate right antennules reveals a common pattern of fusions (figure 2.2.10) associated with the geniculation. In males of the epacteriscid *Enantiosis cavernicola* (figure 2.2.5C-D) and the ridgewayiids *Exumella polyarthra* (figure 2.2.5A-B) and *Ridgewayia wilsoni* (figure 2.2.4C-D) segments XXI to XXIII are fully fused. In another epacteriscid, *Erebonectes nesioticus* segment XXI is only partly fused to the double segment XXII-XXIII (figure 2.2.4A-B). In all calanoid genera with geniculate antennules segments XXII and XXIII are always fused. Segment XXI is fully incorporated into a triple segment (XXI-XXIII) in all genera except *Erebonectes* Fosshagen. Segments XXIV and XXV are fused in all calanoids with geniculate antennules on the right side, including the plesiomorphic genus *Pseudocyclops* (figure 2.2.8B). Proximally, segments II and III are either partly or completely fused in all males examined (figure 2.2.10). Segment IV is free in male *Ridgewayia* but is either partly or fully incorporated into the compound segment II-III in all other calanoids.

The calanoid families placed together by Sars (1901-1903) in a modified concept of the section Amphascandria introduced by Giesbrecht (1892) have symmetrical male antennules without any geniculation but are sexually dimorphic. The male antennules differ from those of their respective females in segmental fusion pattern and in the increased numbers of aesthetascs. Families in this category include the Calanidae and Eucalanidae. In *Eucalanus attenuatus* Dana the male antennules (figure 2.2.7D) carry 2 aesthetascs on virtually every segment (see figure 3.16.1 for detailed count).

Male *Calanus finmarchicus* (figure 2.2.7A) carry 2 aesthetascs on segments 1 (=I-III), 2 (=V), 4 (= VII) and 7 (=XI). We interpret the increase in aesthetasc numbers on male antennules in this group of families as secondary and our interpretation is discussed in detail in chapter 3.16. The Amphascandria is defined on the basis of apomorphic character states and may well be used in any future study of the classification of the Calanoida.

Sars (1901-1903) introduced the Isokerandria as a third section of the Calanoida distinguished from the Heterarthrandria and Amphascandria by the symmetrical male antennules lacking any geniculation, and by the absence of marked sexual dimorphism in either antennule segmentation or armature. This group has no value as a formal taxon and has long been abandoned. Some families placed in it by Sars, the Stephidae for example, display traces of the amphascandrian increase in aesthetasc numbers in the male. The male of *Stephos lucayensis* possesses 3 aesthetascs on the double antennulary segment III-IV, the 2 proximal aesthetascs presumably originally belonging to segment III (figure 2.2.6C). Asymmetry of the male antennules is primitive for the Calanoida, the symmetrical condition exhibited by some forms is secondary. It presumably arises by a heterochronic mechanism such as post-displacement in which the female-like, non-geniculate condition exhibited by the male fifth copepodid is retained in the adult male.

In one group of families, the superfamily Augaptiloidea, it is typically the left antennule that is geniculate, with the right antennule resembling that of the female. Within the Augaptiloidea, however, there are genera with left or right handed species, and even species with left or right handed individuals (Ferrari, 1984). We interpret this as evidence of some kind of genetic switch mechanism controlling the reversal of asymmetry and that left handedness is a derived state. A similar switch between left and right-handedness has occurred within the genus *Spinocalanus* Giesbrecht. The males of most *Spinocalanus* species are characterised by a modification to the left antennule (merging of segments 20 and 21, with alteration of the setal pattern) but males of *S.polaris* Brodsky and *S.similis* Brodsky have this modification on the right antennule (Damkaer, 1975). Dimorphic male asymmetry also occurs within the species *Clausocalanus furcatus* (Brady) which shows a unique concordance between the fifth leg and genital opening (Frost & Fleminger, 1968).

Antenna: The ancestral condition of the calanoid antenna is not retained in any extant genus. The 4-segmented nature of the endopod is best displayed in *Erebonectes* (figure 2.2.11). The first segment is elongate, the second segment partly fused to the third, with the fourth represented by a tiny, laterodistal lobe. In this genus, as in the great majority of calanoids, the second and third endopodal segments are incompletely fused. The fourth segment, which has not hitherto been recognised, bears 2 setae and is demarcated proximally by a hyaline frill. It also carries a muscle insertion (figure 2.2.11D) which provides evidence of its origin as a segment rather than as an outgrowth of the third segment. In many calanoids the fourth segment is reduced, being represented by the common base of its 2 setae (arrowed in figure 2.2.12C), or is fully incorporated into the third segment. The typical configuration of the antennary endopod is found in *Ridgewayia wilsoni* (figure 2.2.13C) and *Pleuromamma xiphias* (Giesbrecht) (figure 2.2.12D) in which the distal section is represented by a bilobed compound segment, with 9 setae on the inner lobe representing the second segment, and 7 on the apical lobe, representing segments 3 and 4. In the plesiomorphic genus *Pseudocyclops* (figure 2.2.14A) however, the second and third segments are completely separate (Sars, 1919-21; Bowman & Gonzales, 1961; Fosshagen, 1968) but there is no trace of a separate fourth segment in *Pseudocyclops*. The setation pattern of 9 on the second segment and 7 on the third presumably indicates that segment 3 (with its 5 original setae) and segment 4 (with 2 setae) are fused.

In many calanoids, such as the Diaptomidae (figure 2.2.30A-B), the antennary exopod is 8-segmented. Vaupel Klein (1982) found evidence of 9 segments in *Euchirella messinensis* (Claus), but according to Park (1986) the exopod was primitively 10-segmented in calanoids. Analysis of the setation of the exopod provides overwhelming evidence supporting the concept of an ancestral 10-segmented exopod and we have adopted this number. Each of the first to ninth segments carried 1 seta and the tenth carried 3 setae. Some of the many fusions found within the Calanoida are shown schematically in figure 2.2.15. Many genera, including *Calanus* (figure 2.2.12E), *Anomalocera* Templeton (figure 2.2.13B), *Rhincalanus* Dana (figure 2.2.13D-E) and *Pseudocyclops* (figure 2.2.14A) retain the ancestral number of setae, although they vary in pattern of segmental fusions.

Labrum and Paragnaths: The labrum in calanoids is typically a simple median lobe (figures 2.2.14B and 2.2.30D). It contains numerous muscles (Boxshall, 1985) and can move slightly in the anteroposterior plane. It is often ornamented with spinule rows both anteriorly and posteriorly and has the opening pore or pores of the labral glands on its posterior surface. The paragnaths are paired lobes although they are often referred to as the divided labium. The paragnaths are typically ornamented with rows of spinules (figures 2.2.14C and 2.2.30D).

Mandible: The ancestral segmentation of the mandible is retained in *Pleuromamma xiphias* (figure 2.2.17B). The coxa bears a well defined gnathobase armed with a row of multicusped blades and a single dorsal seta along its distal margin. The basis bears 4 setae on its medial margin. The endopod is 2-segmented and the exopod is 5-segmented with a 1,1,1,1,2 setal formula. The endopodal setation is reduced in this species but the full setation of 4 and 11 setae on first and second segments respectively is retained in *Ridgewayia wilsoni* (figure 2.2.17A). Vaupel Klein (1985) interpreted the slightly swollen base of the eighth endopodal seta on the mandibular palp in *Euchirella messinensis* Claus as representing a possible third endopodal segment. Using a similar argument he also identified the base of the distalmost seta on the mandibular exopod as a vestigial sixth segment. We have failed to find any evidence to confirm these interpretations and therefore regard both elements as setae with swollen bases. The gnathobase of *Epacteriscus rapax* Fosshagen is highly modified as a scythe-like blade (figure 2.2.17C).

Maxillule: The ancestral segmentation of the maxillule is retained in *Calanus finmarchicus* (figure 2.2.19B) which has a 3-segmented endopod. In many calanoids there is fusion of some of the endopodal segments, as in *P.xiphias* (figure 2.2.18A,C). Maximum setation of the coxal epipodite, basal exite, and exopod (figure 2.2.18B) is retained in both these calanoids. The maximum setation of the praecoxal arthrite (figure 2.2.19A), the coxal and basal endites, and the first endopodal segment (figure 2.2.18C) is found in *P.xiphias*. The maximum setation of the second and third endopodal segments is found in *C.finmarchicus*. Ten setae were recorded on the coxal epipodite of the maxillule of *Stephos exumensis* Fosshagen by Fosshagen (1970; Fig. 5A) but we have been unable to confirm this observation. There is some indication that the maxillulary exopod may have originally been 2-segmented. In *Pseudocyclops bahamensis* Fosshagen there is a partial suture dividing the exopodal setation into a proximal group of 5 and a distal group of 6 setae (figure 2.2.20B).

Maxilla: The presence of 4 endopodal segments on the calanoid maxilla is recorded here. Vaupel Klein (1985) recognised the presence of a compressed but distinct first endopodal segment in *Euchirella messinensis*. This condition is clearly shown in *Pleuromamma xiphias* (figure 2.2.21) but was previously overlooked (Ferrari, 1985). The structure previously referred to as the distal endite on the basis is carried on a distinct segment representing the first endopodal segment (shaded in figure 2.2.21B-C). The three distal segments that have been traditionally referred to as the endopod represent the second to fourth endopodal segments. The hoops of integument representing the actual segments are stippled in the disarticulated endopod illustrated in figure 2.2.21D. The first endopodal segment is partially or completely fused to the basis in most calanoids, such as *C.finmarchicus* (figure 2.2.22C) and *Pseudocyclops bahamensis* (figure 2.2.20C) respectively. When completely fused the resulting compound segment represents an allobasis. The first endopodal segment is sometimes reduced to a lobate endite located distally on the basis, as in *Enantiosis cavernicola* (figure 2.2.22A-B). An outer seta on the coxa of the maxilla (figure 2.2.22C) is present only in the superfamilies Centropagoidea, Megacalanoidea, Eucalanoidea, Ryocalanoidea and Spinocalanoidea. This seta may represent a vestigial exite (epipodite).

Maxilliped: The basic segmentation of the maxilliped is recognisable in most calanoids although the majority retains only 5 free segments in the endopod (figure 2.2.30C). *Ridgewayia wilsoni* displays the 6-segmented endopod condition (figure 2.2.23C). The first endopodal segment is usually either partly (figures 2.2.22D and 2.2.23A-B) or fully incorporated (figure 2.2.24C-E) into the basis. In most cases the 2 setae derived from the first endopodal segment are retained but in highly derived forms such as *Acartia clausi* Giesbrecht (figure 2.2.24E) these are lost. The maximum syncoxal setation of 1,2,4,4, and 3 on the basis is retained in *P.xiphias* and *Erebonectes nesioticus*. Full endopodal setation of 2,4,4,3,3+1,4 is retained in *Ridgewayia wilsoni*. In *Pseudocyclops* (figure 2.2.24C) the endopod is condensed and the first endopodal segment is incorporated into the basis. An outer seta on the maxillipedal syncoxa has been reported in some members of the Metridinidae, such as *P.xiphias* (Ferrari, 1985) and this may represent an exite serially homologous with that on the maxilla.

Swimming Legs: The maximum segmentation and setation of the first to fourth swimming legs is retained in genera such as *Calanus* and *Boholina* Fosshagen.

Fifth Legs: *Calanus*, *Boholina* and other genera, such as *Haloptilus* Giesbrecht and *Epacteriscus* Fosshagen, also retain both 3-segmented rami on the fifth legs (figures 2.2.25A and 2.2.27A). The inner seta of the first exopodal segment is absent in all Calanoida. Calanoids all show some sexual dimorphism in the structure of the fifth legs. At its weakest this dimorphism is expressed as slight differences in proportional lengths of the ramal segments of the fifth legs. More extreme dimorphism is found in many families. The Stephidae, for example, have powerful, asymmetrical fifth legs in the male (figure 2.2.25B) and reduced, peg-like fifth legs in the female (figure 2.2.25D) which are also slightly asymmetrical. Male legs can be modified by extreme elongation, as in *Mesaiokeras nanseni* Matthews (figure 2.2.25C) or be short, squat legs, as in *Pseudocyclops* (figure 2.2.26B). Preliminary analysis of the nature of the sexual dimorphism failed to reveal any homologies that could be used as diagnostic apomorphies for the Calanoida as a whole. The inner coxal seta is retained on the fifth leg in some augaptilids, such as *Haloptilus oxycephalus* (Giesbrecht) (figure 2.2.25A) and some *Euaugaptilus* Sars species, and in *Boholina*. The male fifth legs often lack an intercoxal sclerite as they no longer have the functional requirement to beat in unison.

Eggs: Most calanoids release eggs continuously rather than carry them around in egg sacs or attached egg masses. A few calanoids typically carry their eggs until the nauplii are ready to hatch, including the freshwater family Diaptomidae, the marine family Euchaetidae, and the genera *Pseudocalanus* Boeck and *Eurytemora* Giesbrecht. Examination of the egg mass on the urosome of a female *Eurytemora velox* (Lilljeborg) reveals that the eggs are not enclosed within a membranous sac (figure 2.2.31C-D). It is possible that true egg sacs do not occur within the Calanoida.

Differential Diagnosis: The Calanoida is readily defined by the combination of the gymnoplean-type tagmosis, the presence of only one spine on the outer margin of the first exopodal segment of the second to fifth swimming legs, the presence of a coxal epipodite but not a lobate basal exite on the maxillule, and the presence of a seta on the inner margin of the coxa of the antenna. These are plesiomorphic characters, however, and it is difficult to identify apomorphies of the Calanoida. The presence of a maximum of 2 setae on the terminal (fourth) endopodal segment of the maxilla is an apomorphy of the Calanoida.

The early evolution of the Calanoida is summarised in figure 2.2.16. We interpret the arrangement of the female genital apertures and the segmentation of the antennary endopod as providing evidence of the early divergence of the Pseudocyclopidae from the main calanoid lineage. The Pseudocyclopidae retain full separation of antennary endopodal segments 2 and 3 whereas in all other calanoids these 2 segments are fused. The Pseudocyclopidae, Boholinidae and at least some members of the Arietellidae retained separate genital apertures in the female and each is closed off by its own operculum. The arietellid condition is more derived than that exhibited by the Pseudocyclopidae and Boholinidae because the copulatory pores are fused into a single common pore.

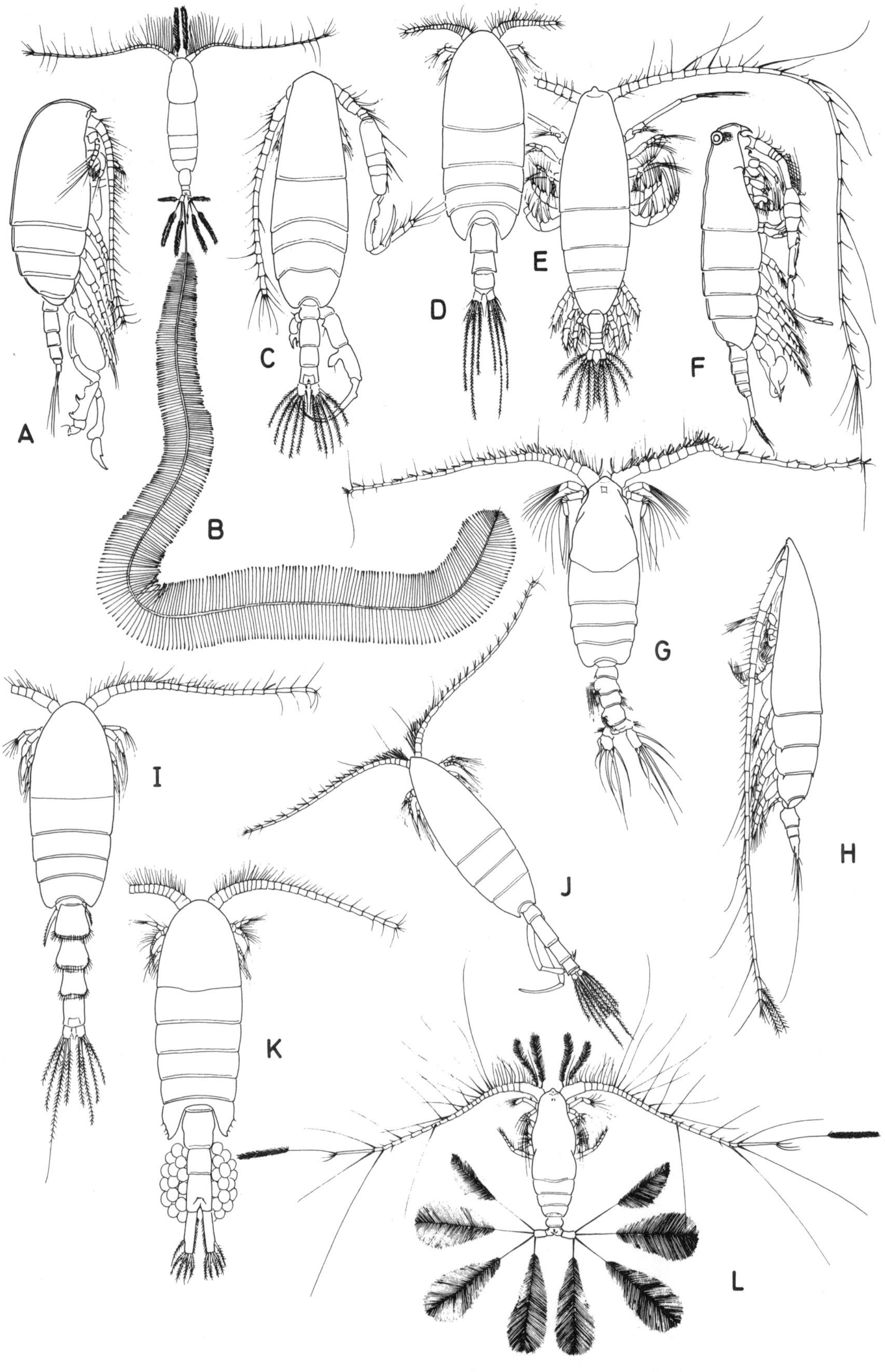

Figure 2.2.1. The diversity of calanoid body form. **A**. Diaixidae. **B**. Calocalanidae. **C**. Acartiidae. **D**. Pseudocyclopidae. **E**. Augaptilidae. **F**. Pontellidae. **G**. Metridinidae. **H**. Eucalanidae. **I**. Stephidae. **J**. Euchaetidae. **K**. Temoridae. **L**. Calocalanidae. The range of gross body morphologies exhibited within the Calanoida is relatively small compared to that found in the other large orders.

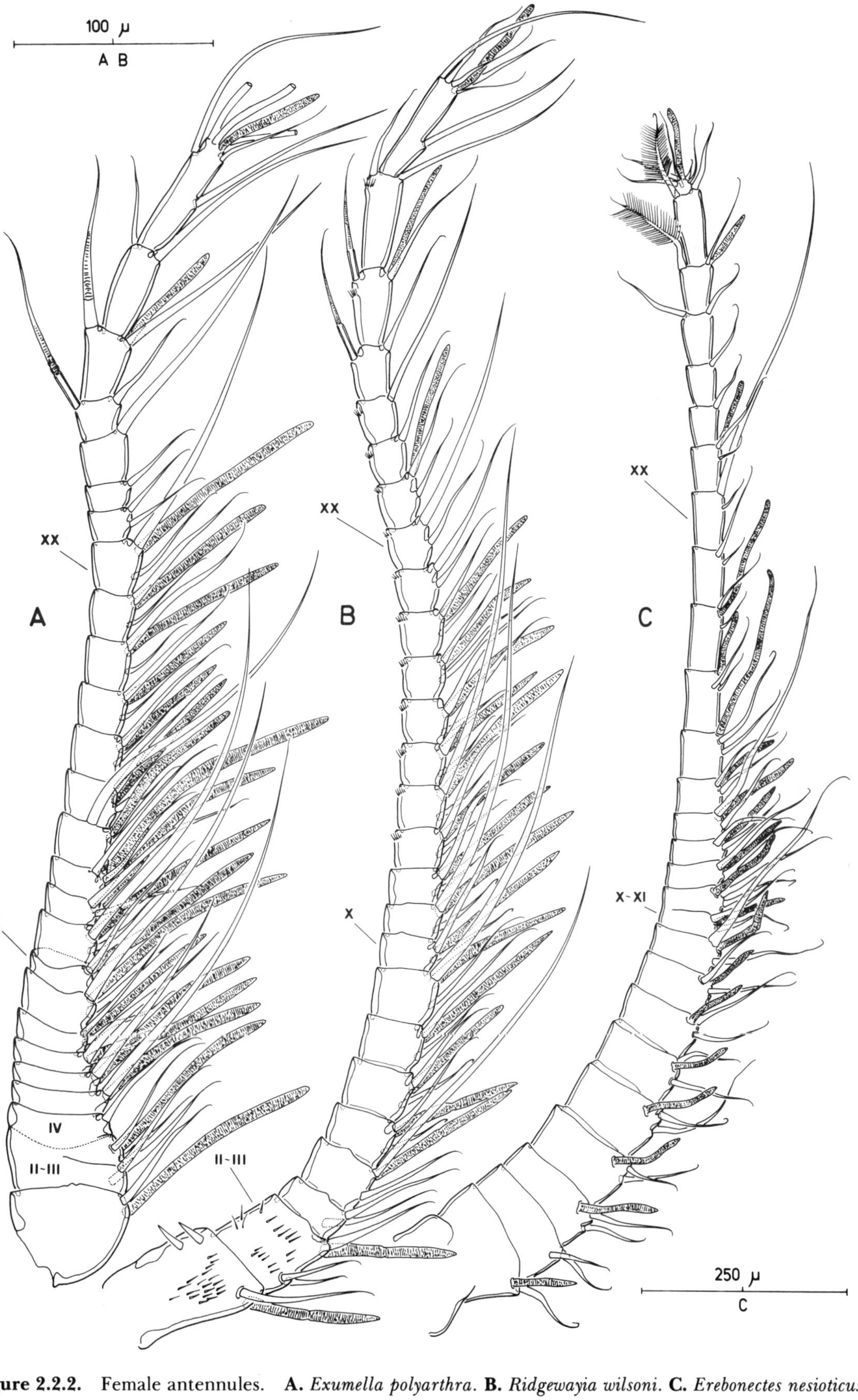

Figure 2.2.2. Female antennules. **A.** *Exumella polyarthra*. **B.** *Ridgewayia wilsoni*. **C.** *Erebonectes nesioticus*.

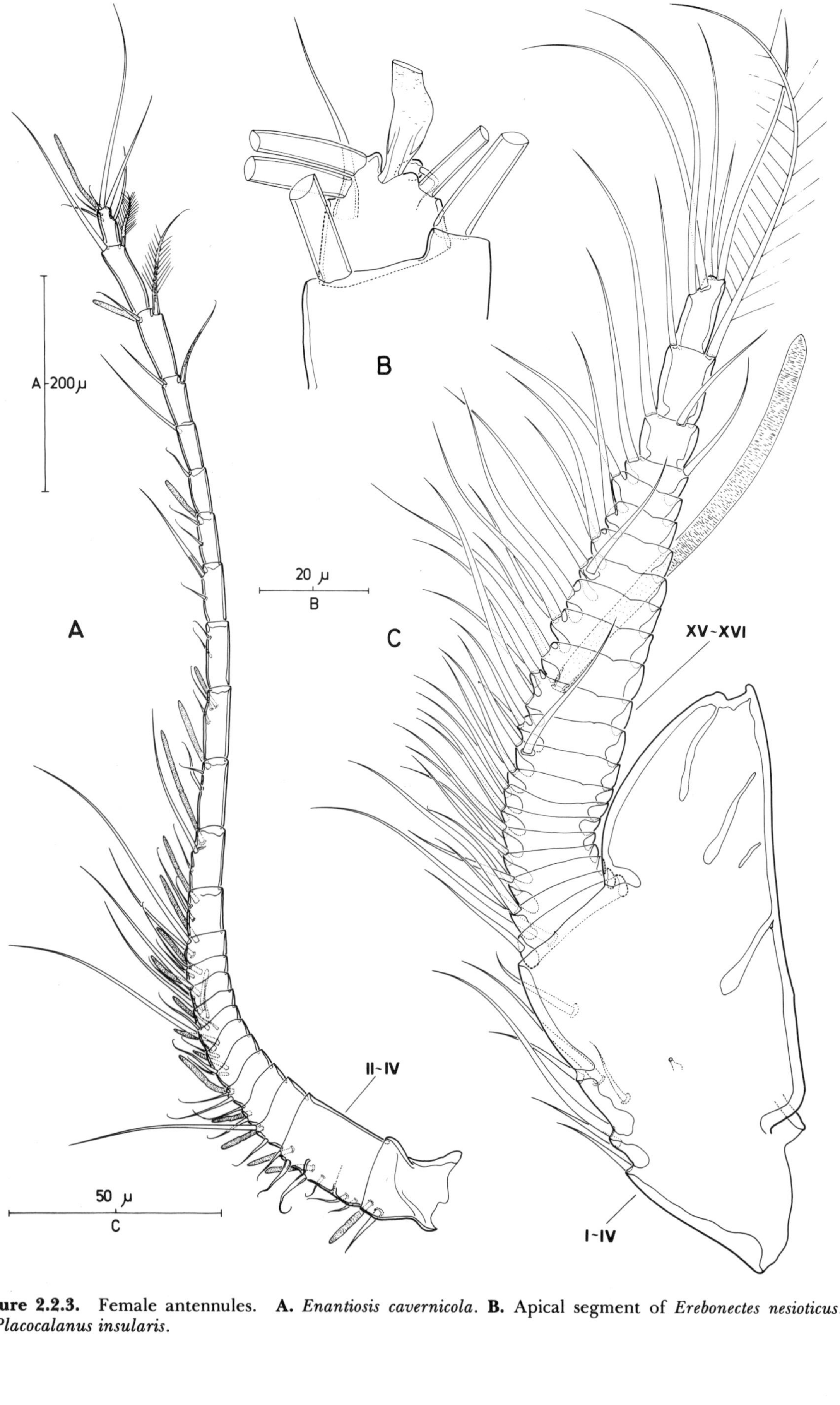

Figure 2.2.3. Female antennules. **A.** *Enantiosis cavernicola*. **B.** Apical segment of *Erebonectes nesioticus*. **C.** *Placocalanus insularis*.

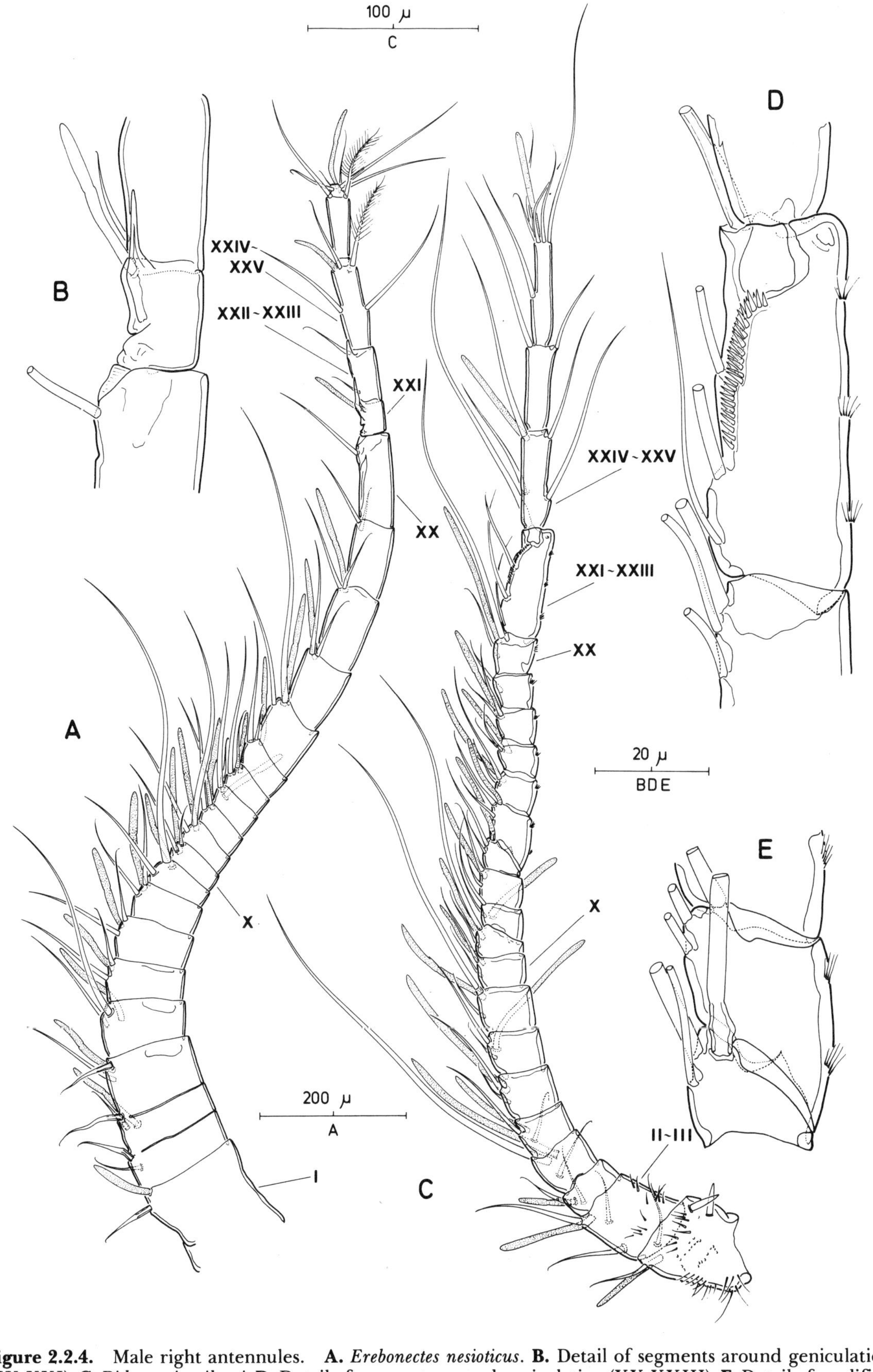

Figure 2.2.4. Male right antennules. **A.** *Erebonectes nesioticus*. **B.** Detail of segments around geniculation (XX-XXI). **C.** *Ridgewayia wilsoni*. **D.** Detail of segments around geniculation (XX-XXIII). **E.** Detail of modified joint between segments XIV and XV.

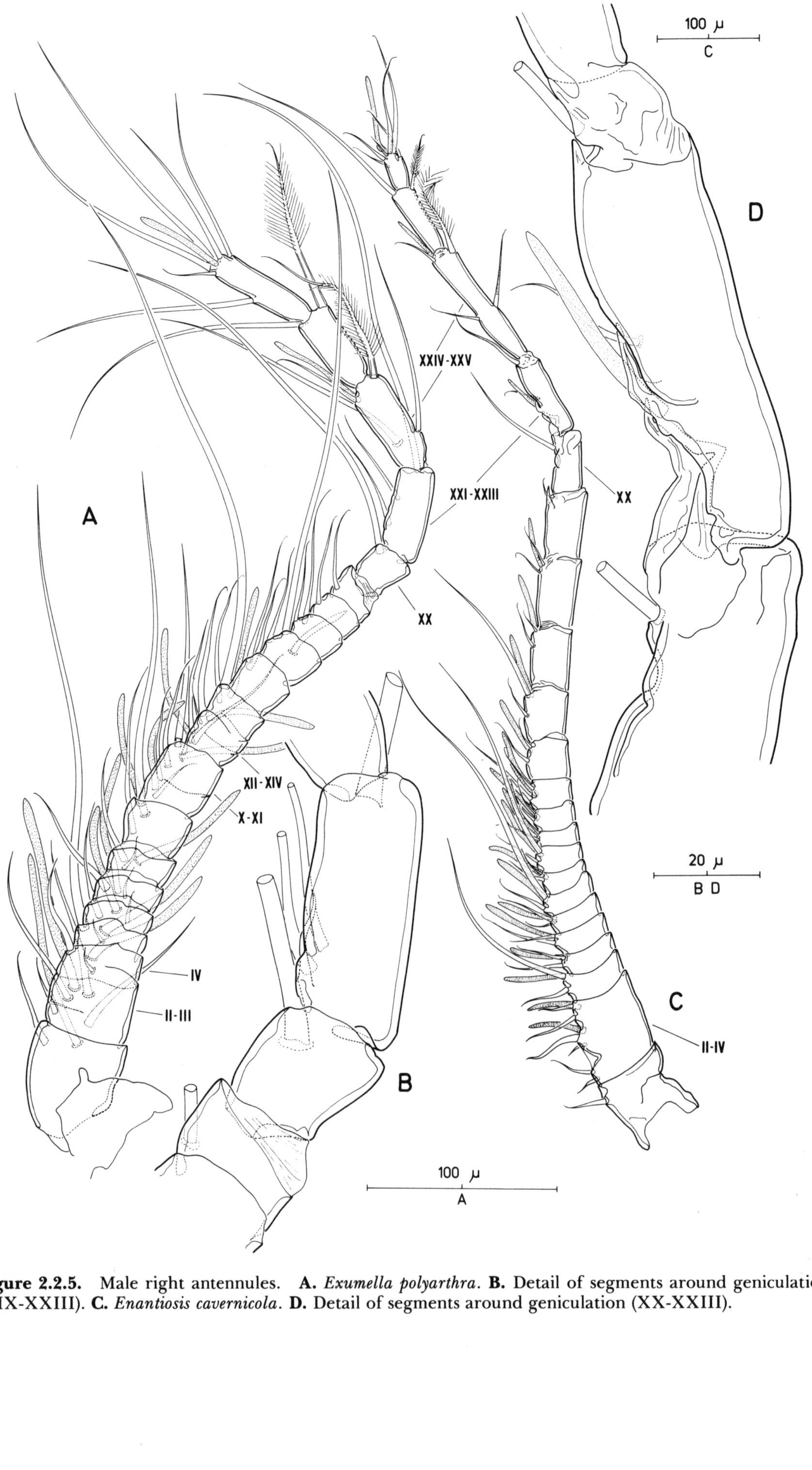

Figure 2.2.5. Male right antennules. **A.** *Exumella polyarthra*. **B.** Detail of segments around geniculation (XIX-XXIII). **C.** *Enantiosis cavernicola*. **D.** Detail of segments around geniculation (XX-XXIII).

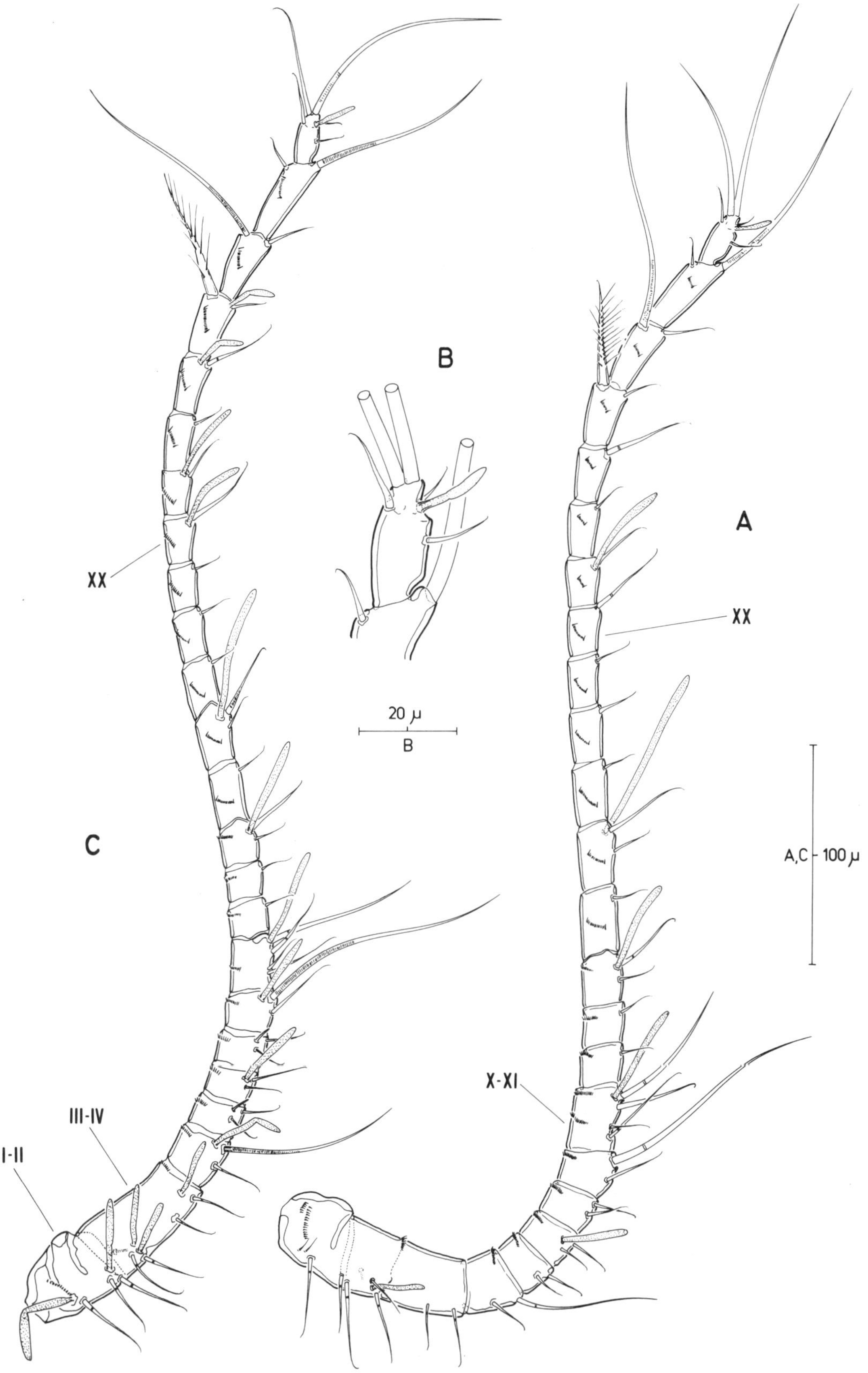

Figure 2.2.6. *Stephos lucayensis*. **A.** Right antennule of female. **B.** Apical segment. **C.** Right antennule of male.

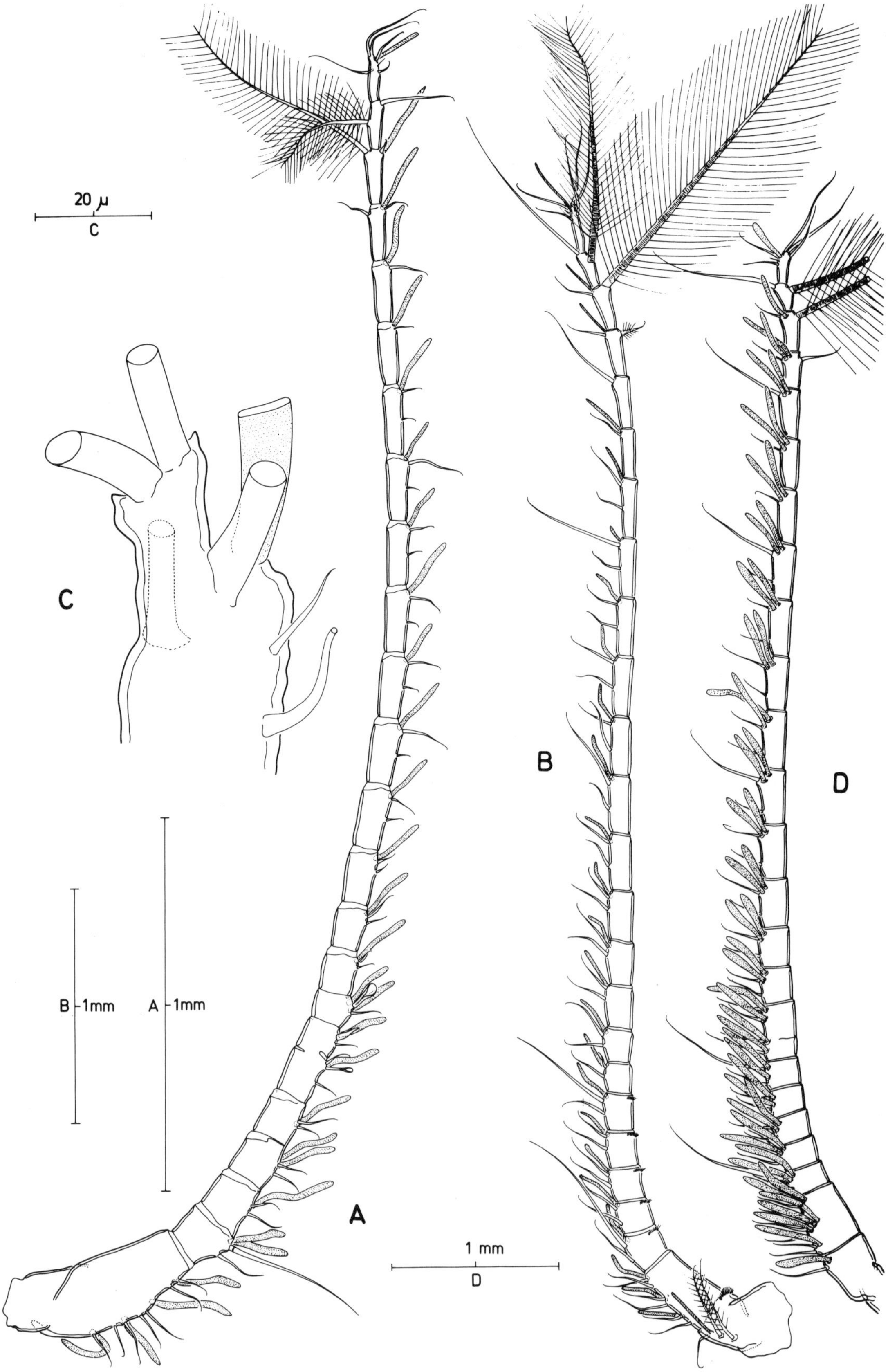

Figure 2.2.7. **A.** *Calanus finmarchicus*, right antennule of male. **B.** Right antennule of female. **C.** Detail of tip of female antennule. **D.** *Eucalanus attenuatus*, right antennule of male.

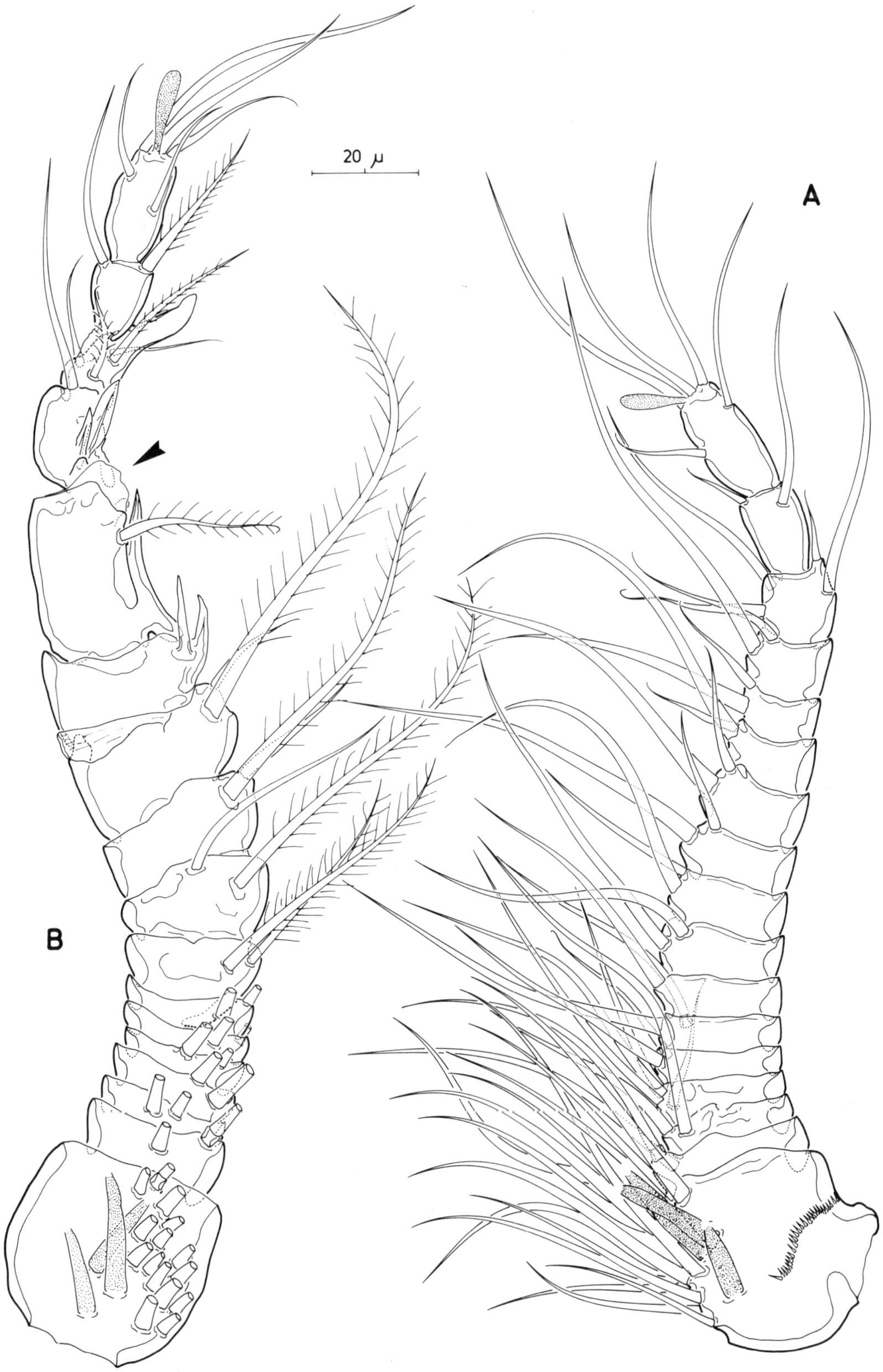

Figure 2.2.8. *Pseudocyclops bahamensis.* **A.** Female antennule. **B.** Male antennule, with neocopepodan geniculation arrowed.

Figure 2.2.9. Schematic comparison of segmental homologies in the antennules of female calanoids.

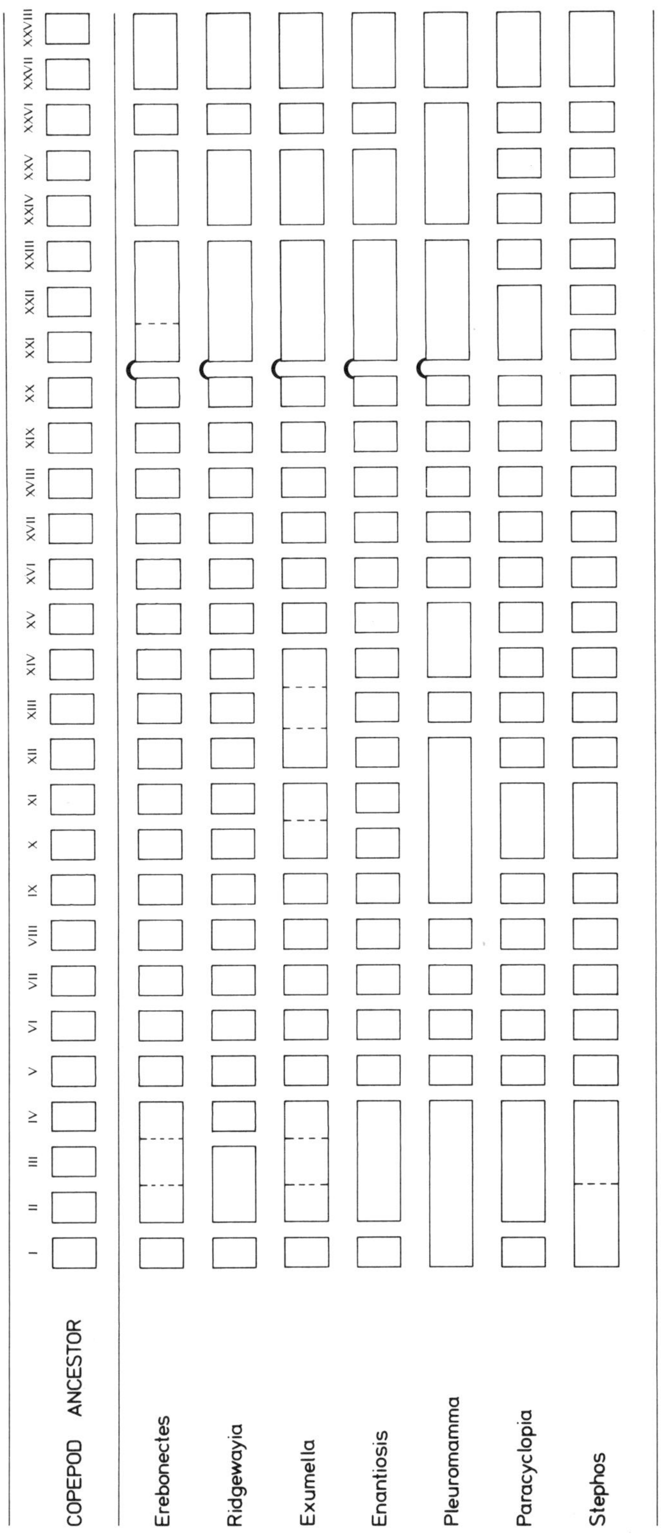

Figure 2.2.10. Schematic comparison of segmental homologies in the antennules of male calanoids.

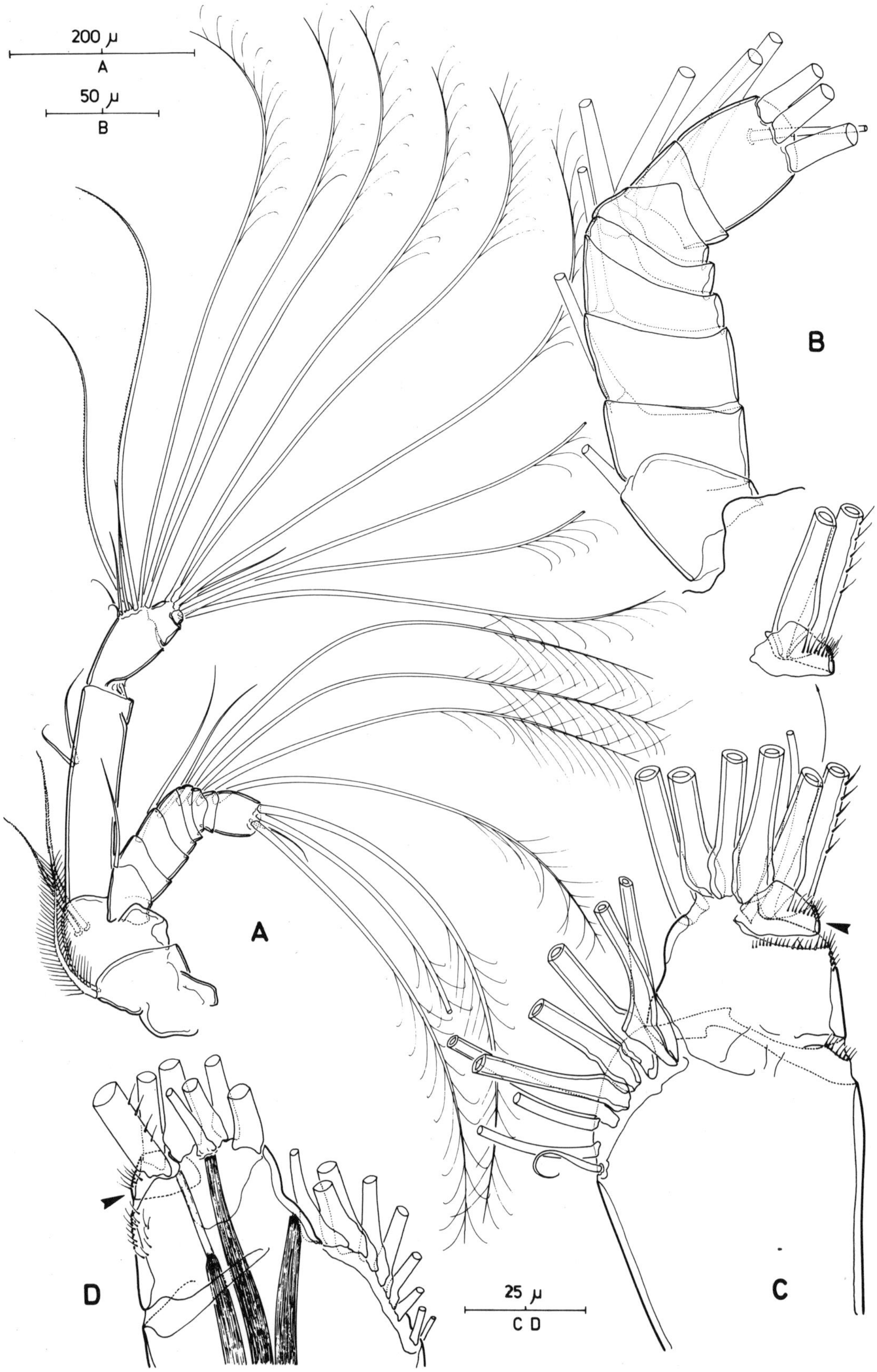

Figure 2.2.11. *Erebonectes nesioticus.* **A.** Antenna. **B.** Antennary exopod. **C.** Apical part of antennary endopod, with inset showing fourth segment (arrowed). **D.** Same, showing musculature.

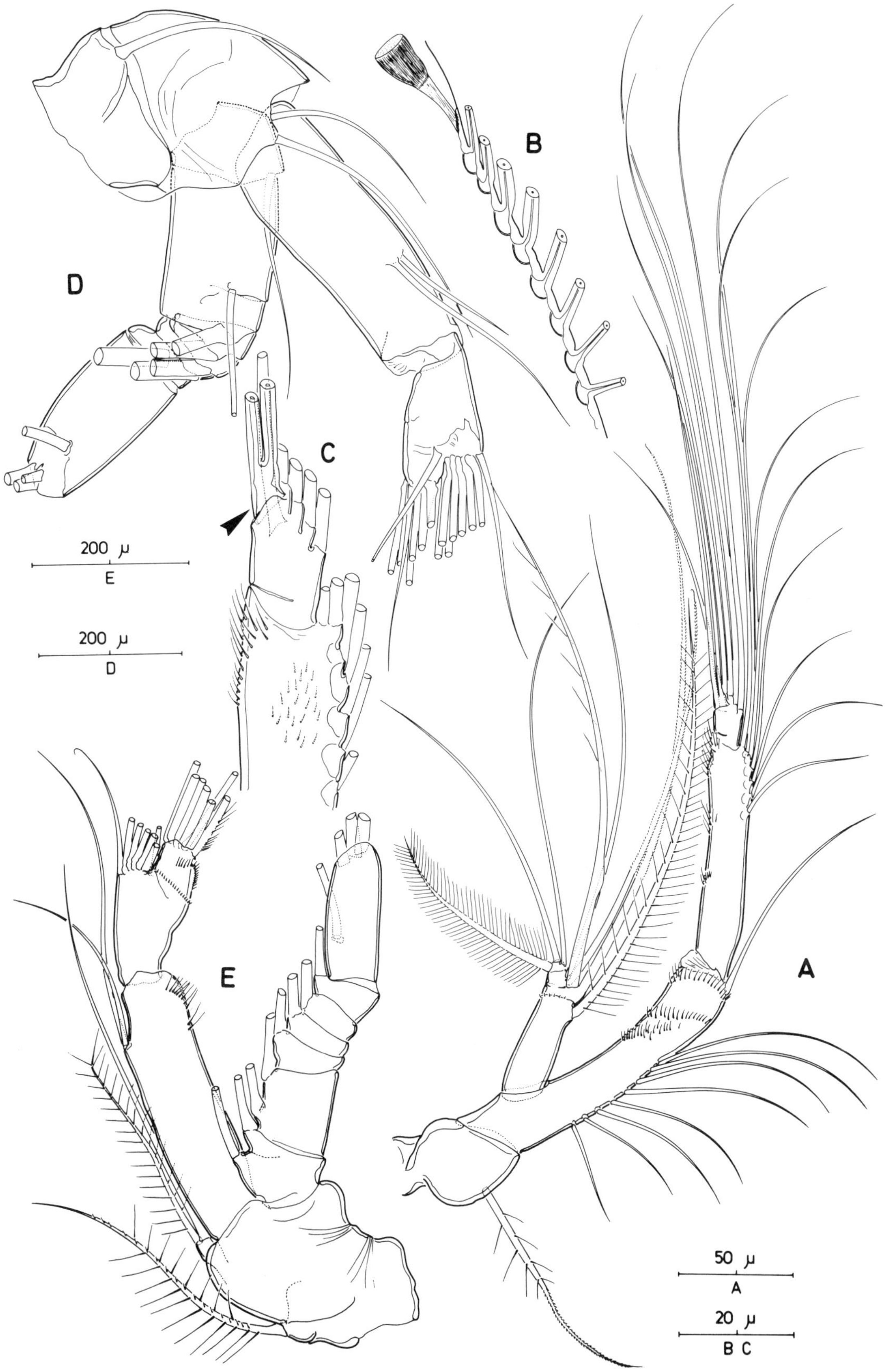

Figure 2.2.12. Antennae. **A.** *Acartia clausi.* **B.** Margin of allobasis, showing muscle and ligaments connecting proximal setae. **C.** Distal tip of endopod with double seta representing fourth segment (arrowed). **D.** *Pleuromamma xiphias.* **E.** *Calanus finmarchicus.*

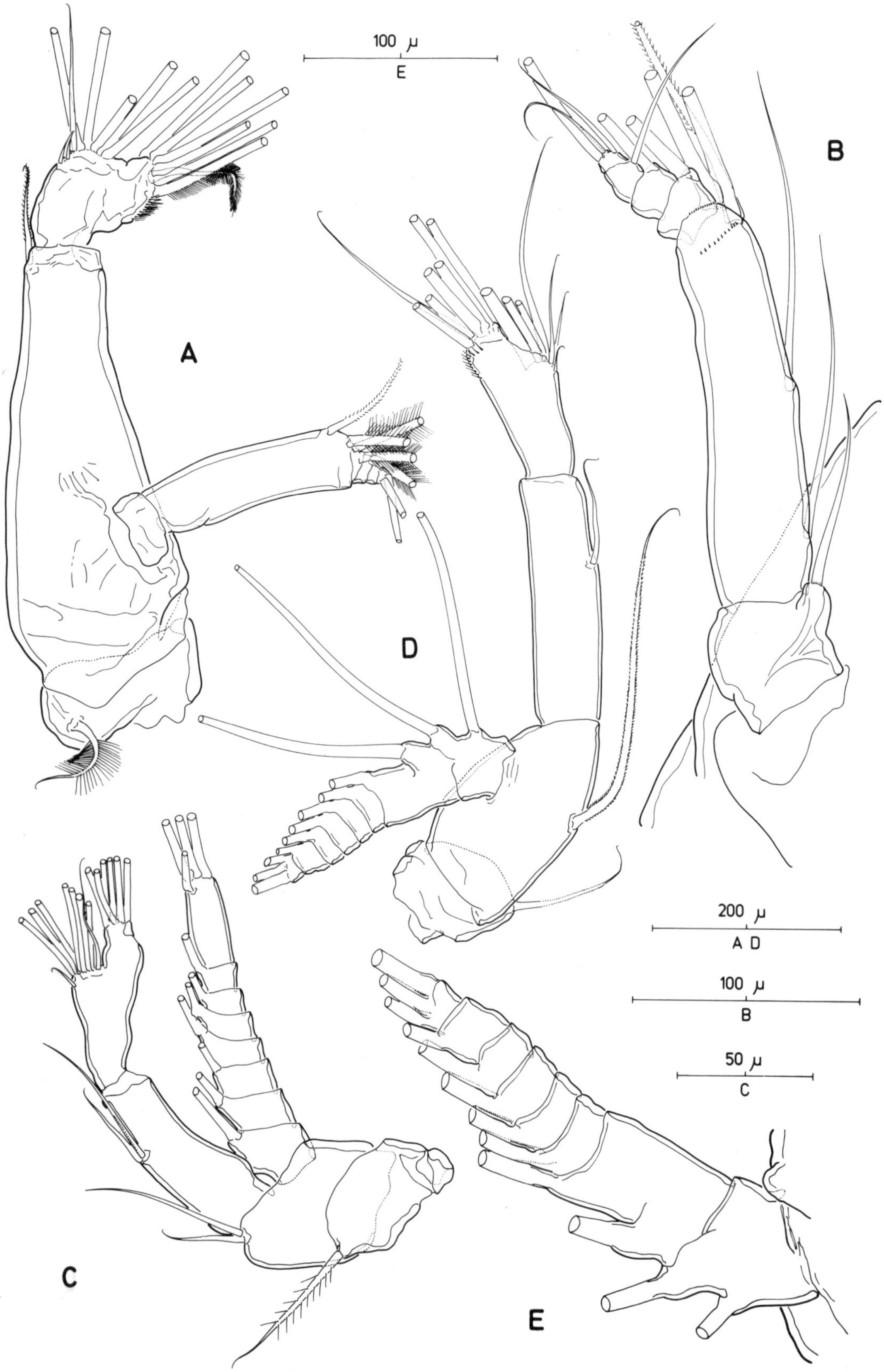

Figure 2.2.13. Antennae. **A.** *Candacia norvegica*. **B.** *Anomalocera patersoni*, exopod. **C.** *Ridgewayia wilsoni*. **D.** *Rhincalanus nasutus*. **E.** Exopod.

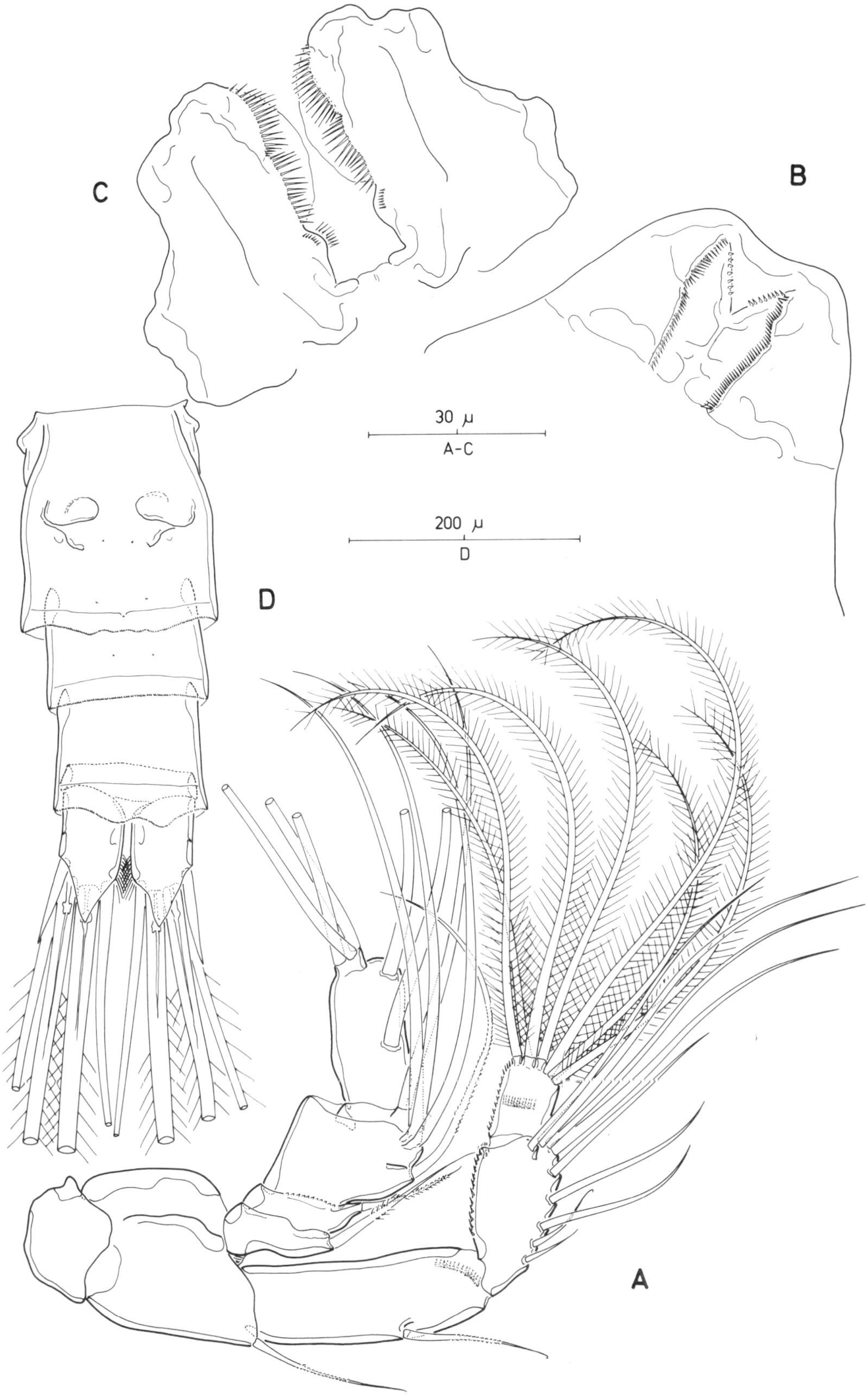

Figure 2.2.14. *Pseudocyclops bahamensis.* **A.** Antenna. **B.** Labrum. **C.** Paragnaths. **D.** Female urosome, ventral view.

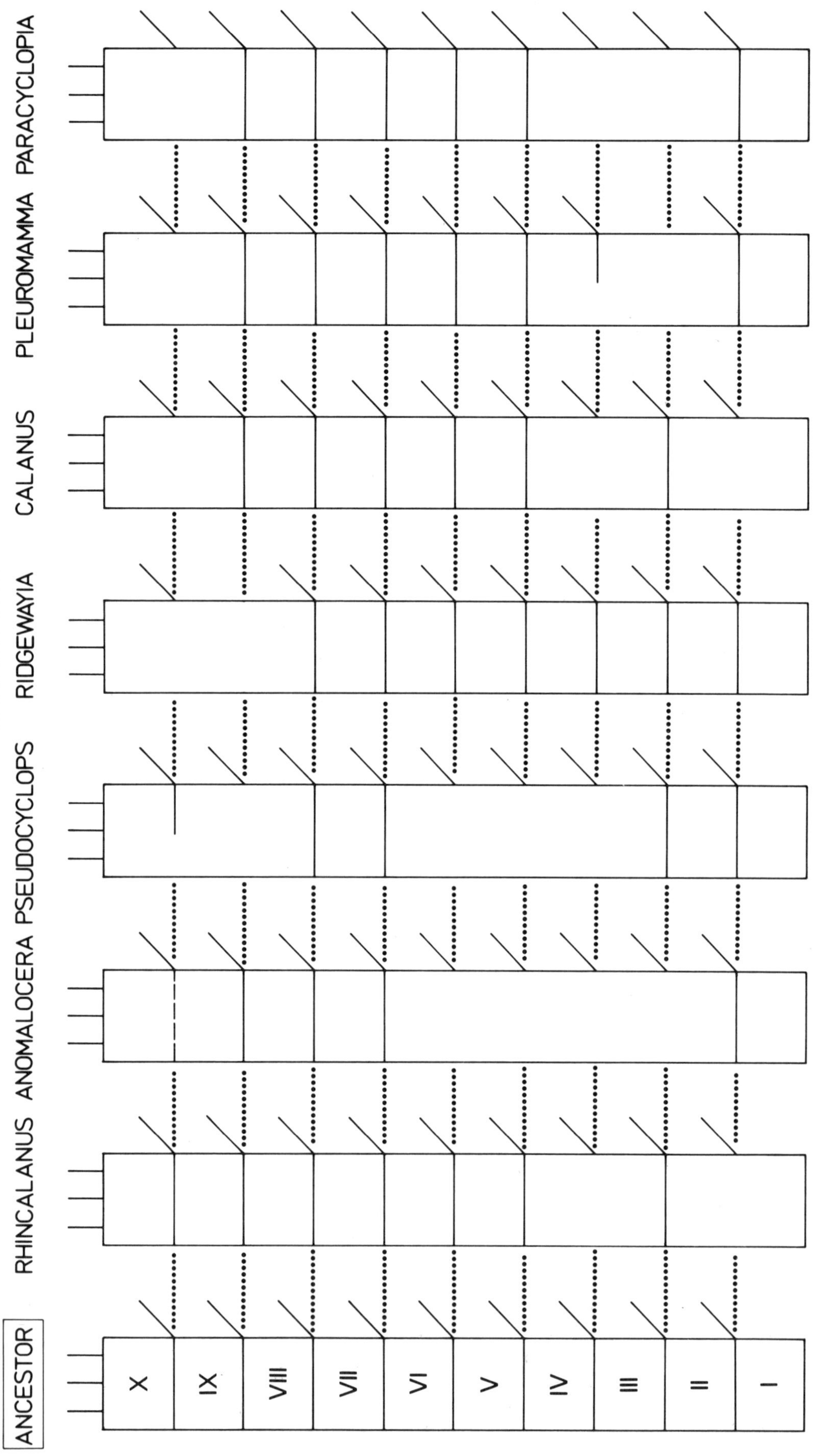

Figure 2.2.15. Schematic representation of segmental homologies between antennary exopods of various calanoid genera.

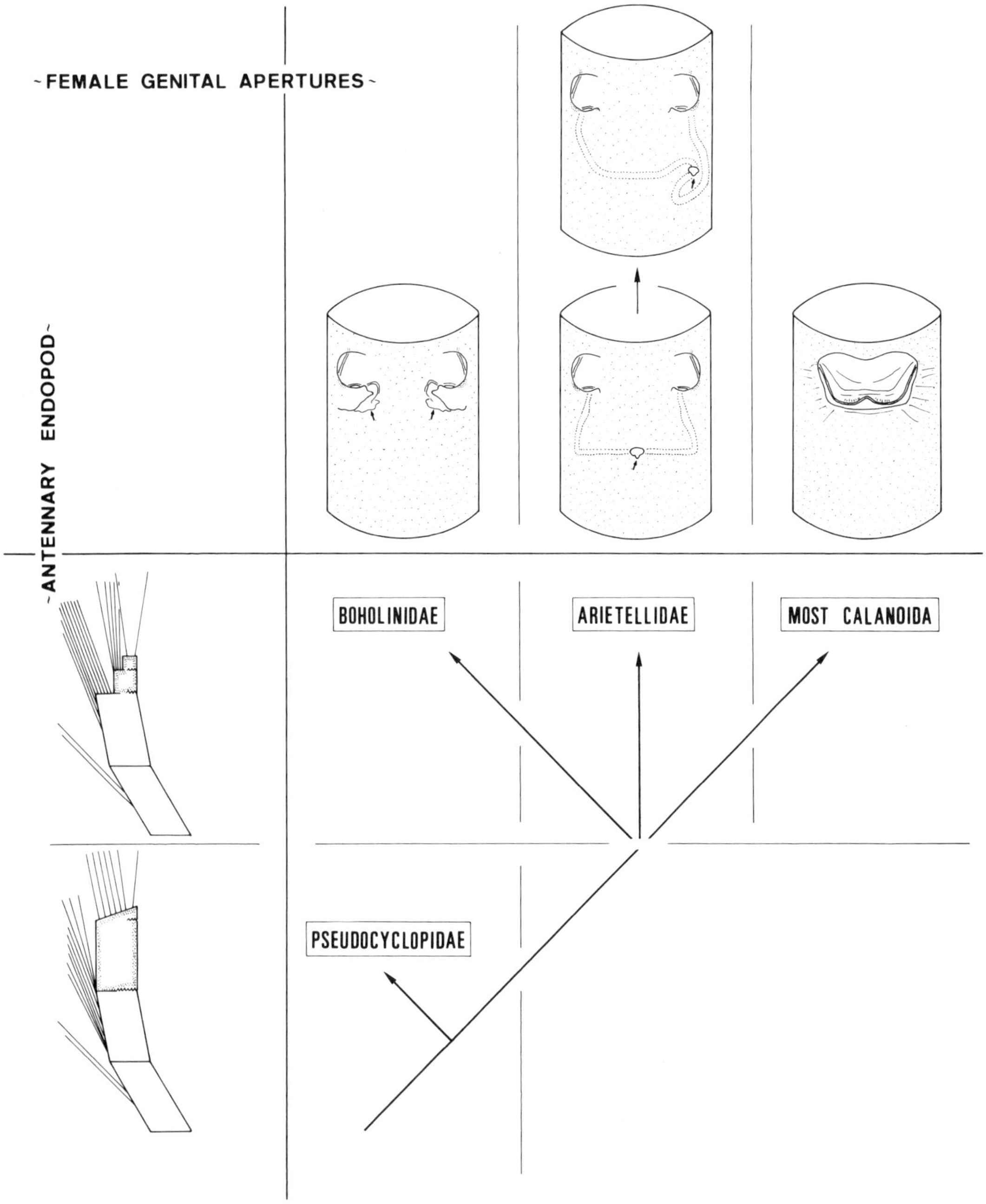

Figure 2.2.16. Early evolutionary changes in segmentation of antennary endopod and in configuration of genital apertures within the Calanoida. [Small arrows indicate positions of copulatory pores.]

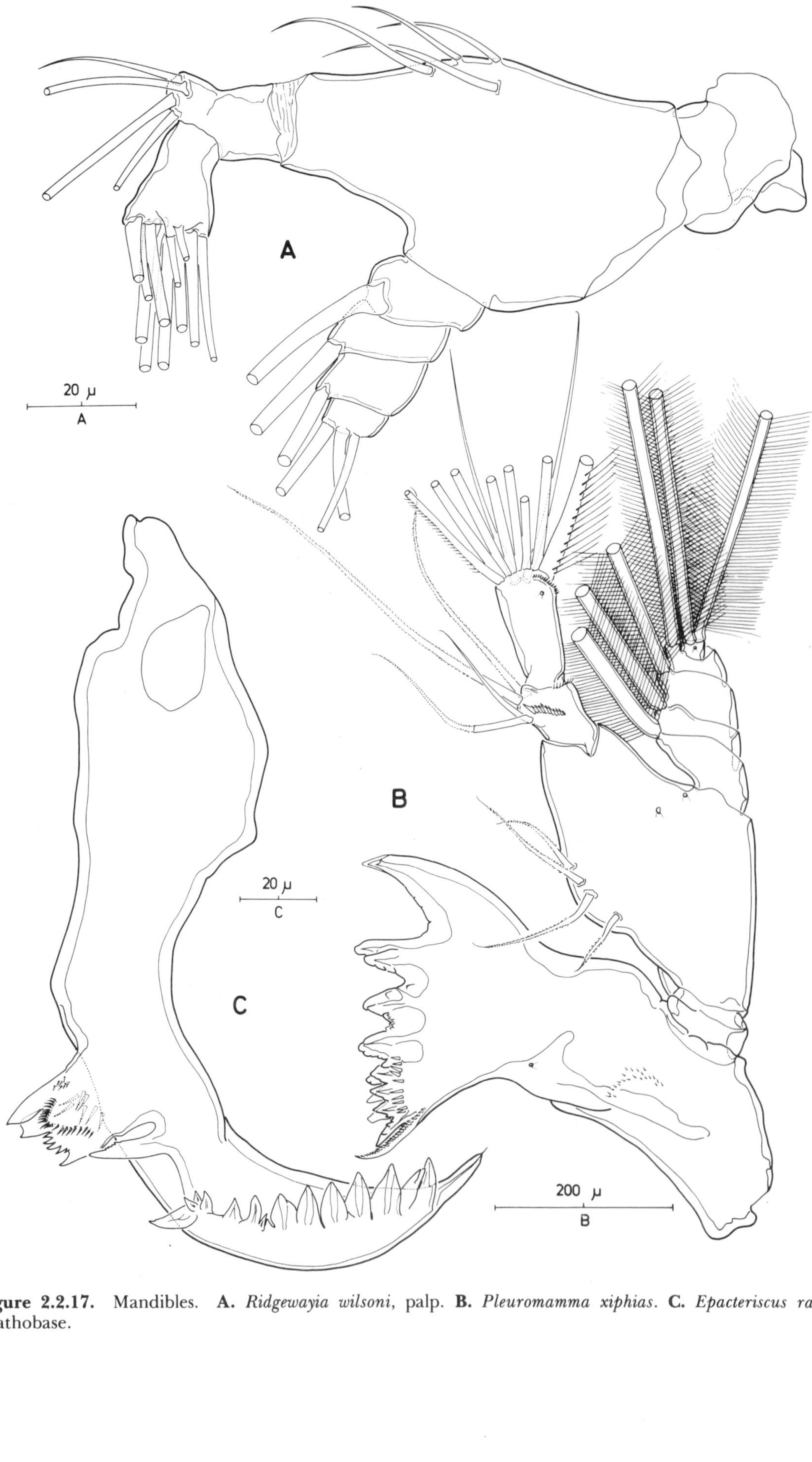

Figure 2.2.17. Mandibles. **A.** *Ridgewayia wilsoni*, palp. **B.** *Pleuromamma xiphias*. **C.** *Epacteriscus rapax*, gnathobase.

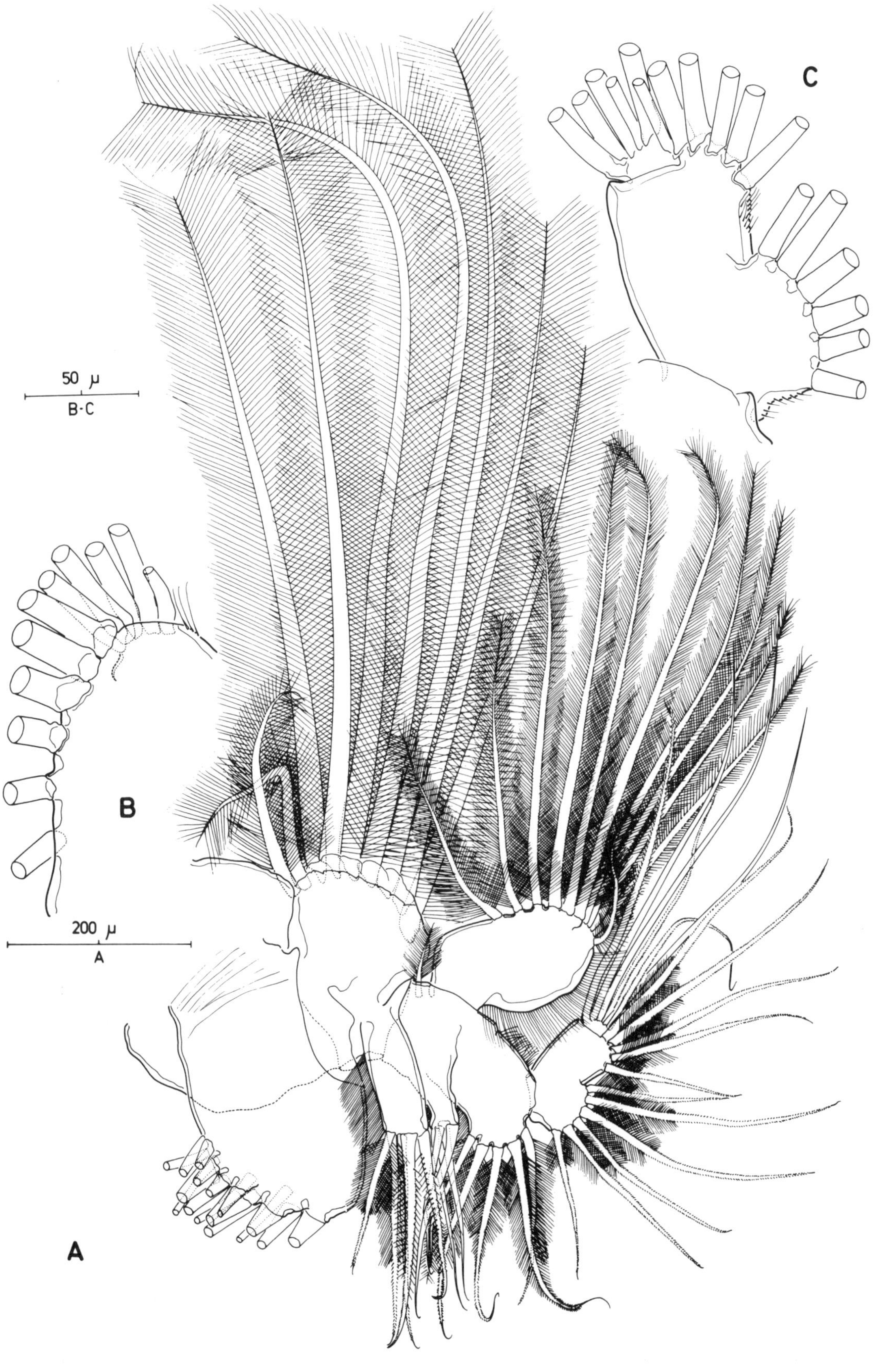

Figure 2.2.18. *Pleuromamma xiphias.* **A.** Maxillule. **B.** Same, exopodal setae. **C.** Same, endopod.

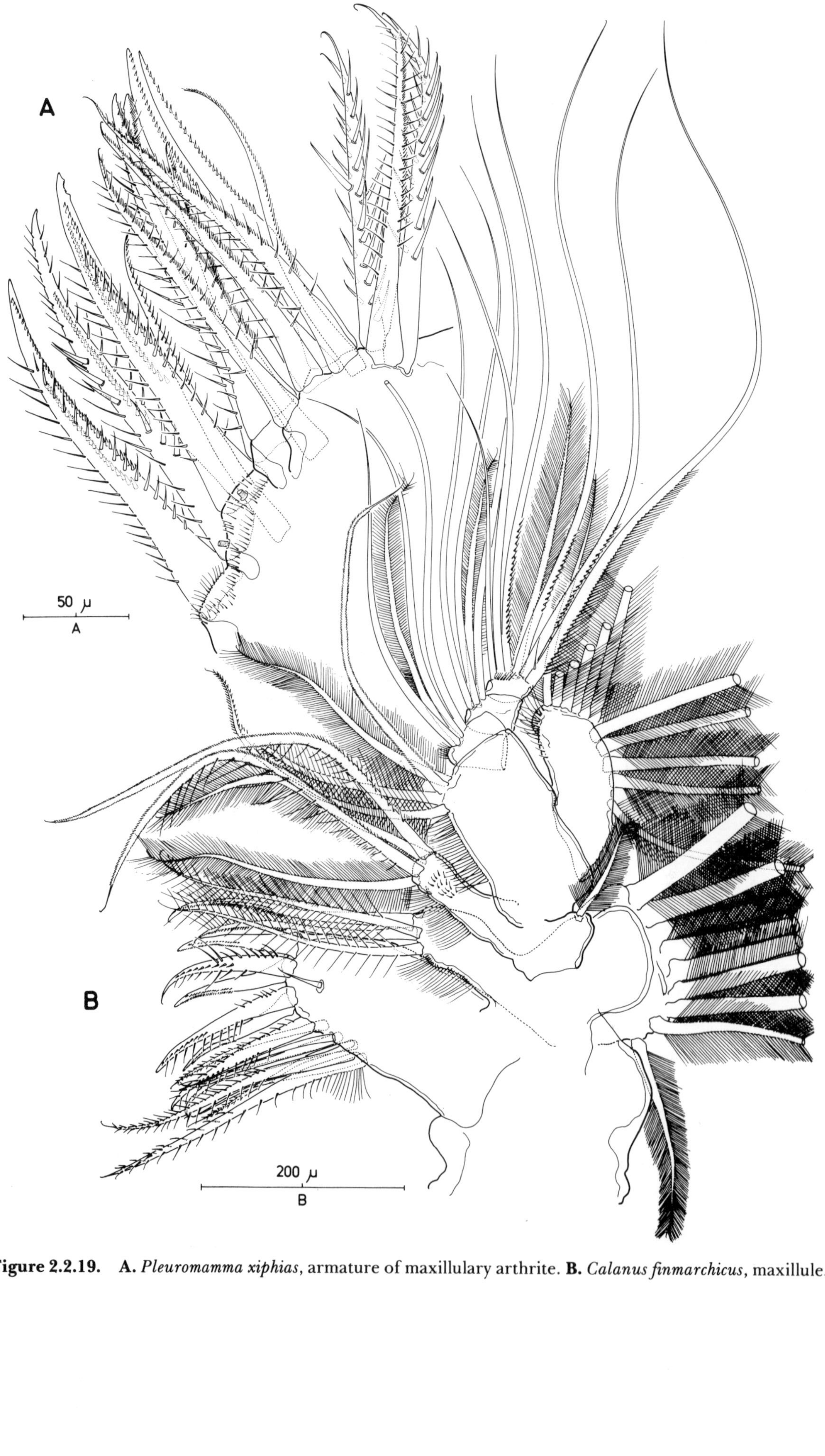

Figure 2.2.19. **A.** *Pleuromamma xiphias*, armature of maxillulary arthrite. **B.** *Calanus finmarchicus*, maxillule.

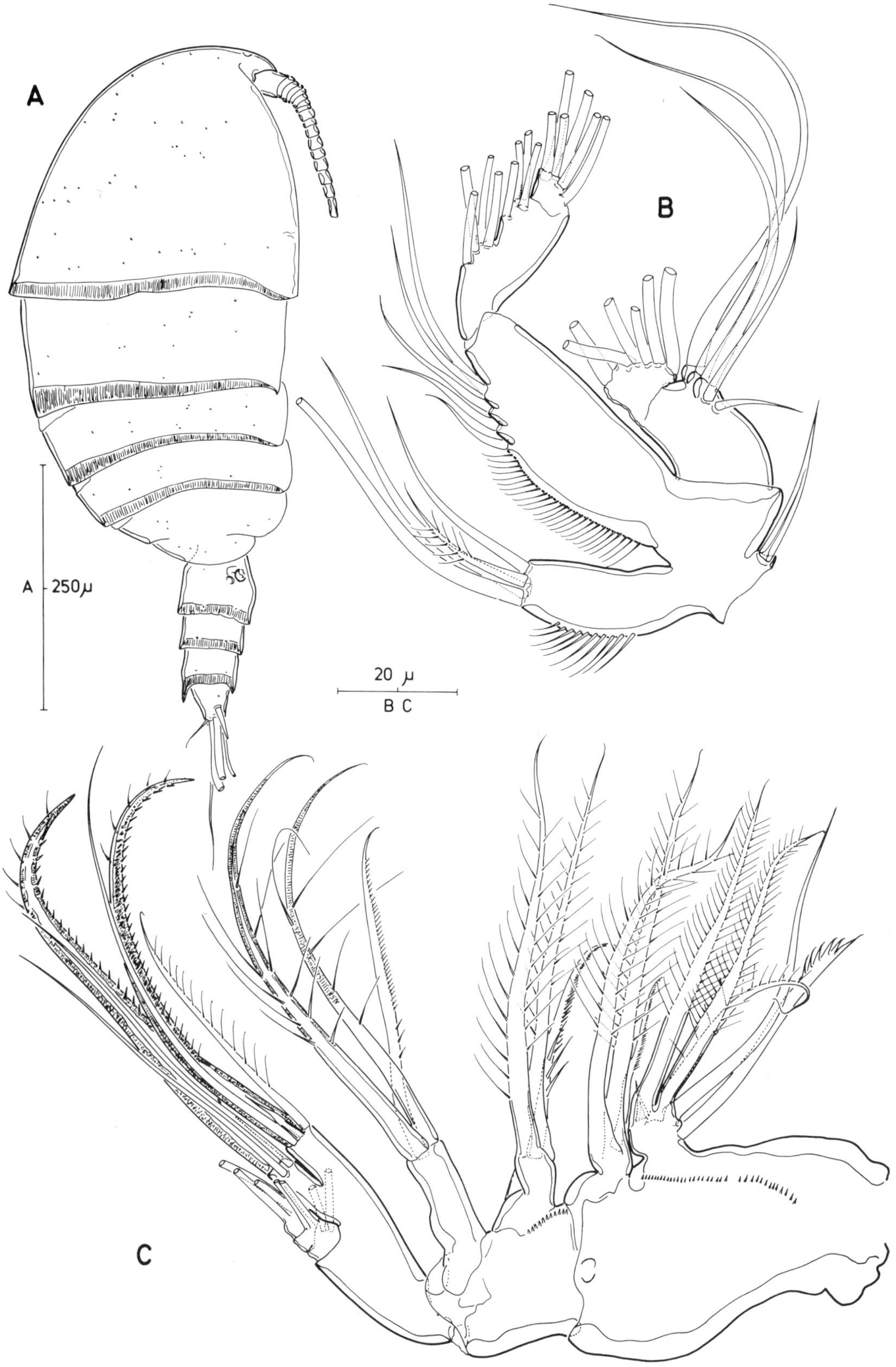

Figure 2.2.20. *Pseudocyclops bahamensis.* **A.** Female, lateral view. **B.** Basis and rami of maxillule. **C.** Maxilla.

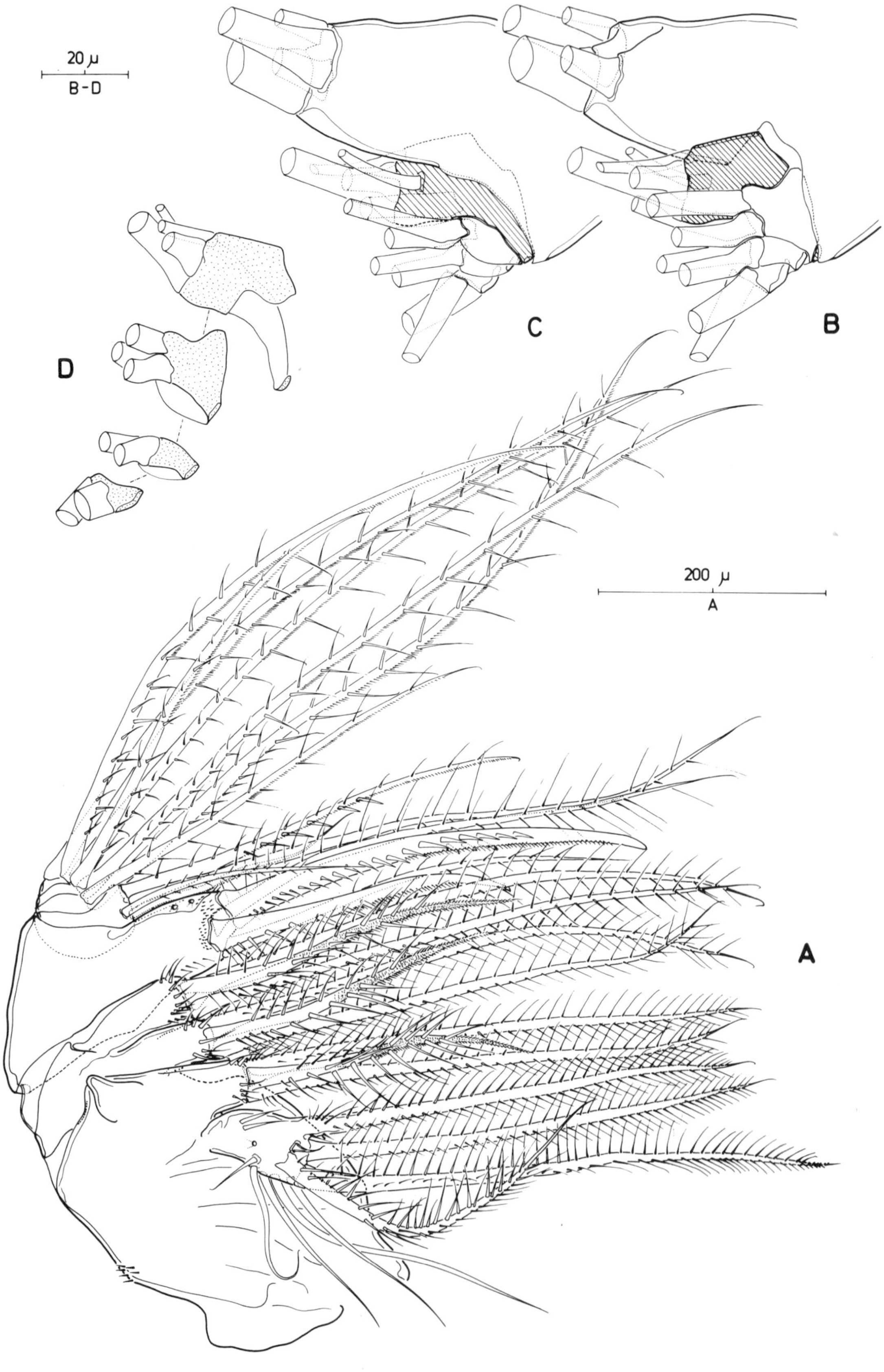

Figure 2.2.21. *Pleuromamma xiphias*, maxilla. **A.** Complete limb. **B.** Basis and endopod, anterior view with first endopodal segment shaded. **C.** Basis and endopod, posterior view. **D.** Endopod, with segments disarticulated.

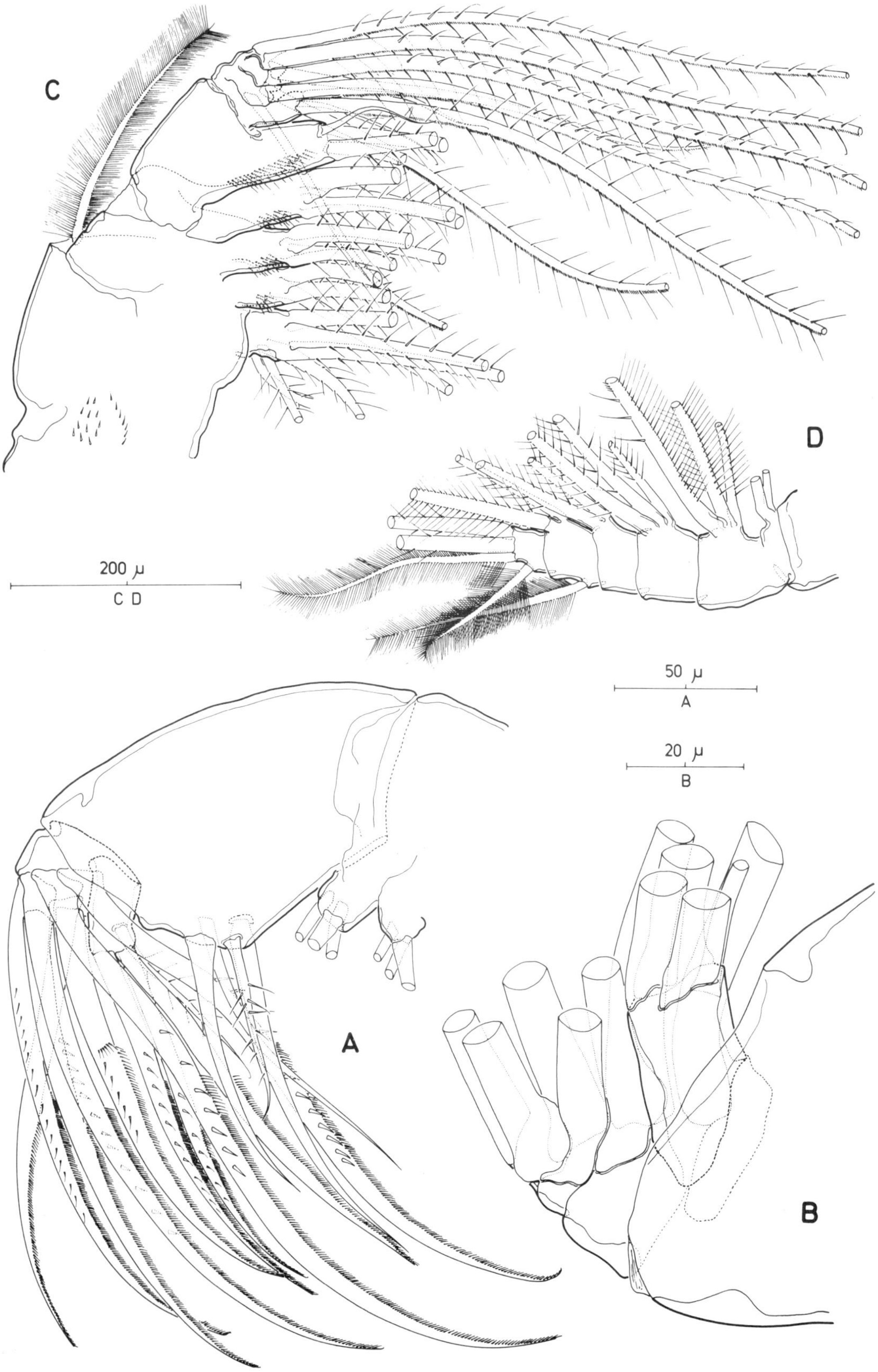

Figure 2.2.22. **A.** *Enantiosis cavernicola*, coxal endites, basis and endopod of maxilla. **B.** Same, showing detail of endopod. **C.** *Calanus finmarchicus*, maxilla. **D.** *Rhincalanus nasutus*, endopod of maxilliped.

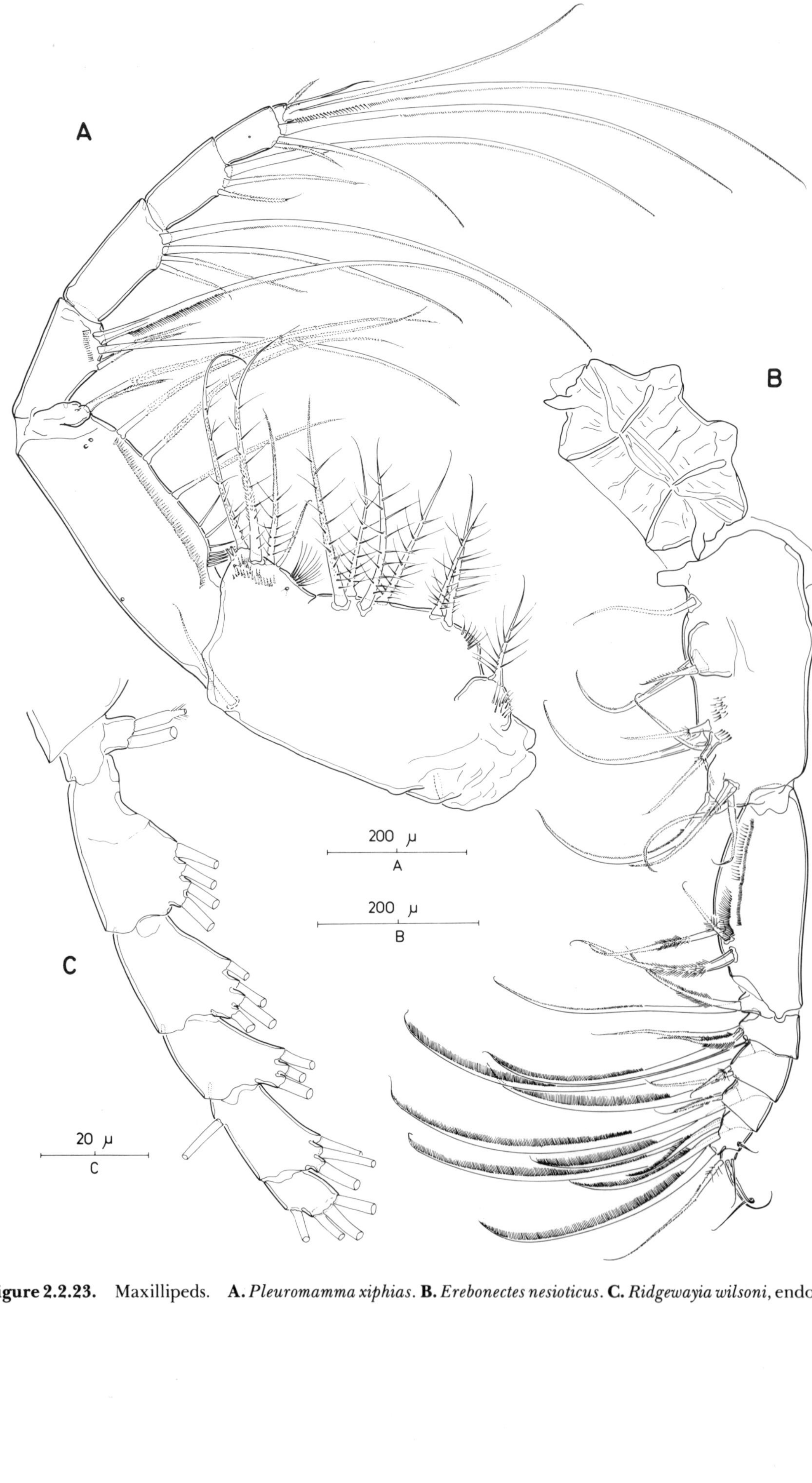

Figure 2.2.23. Maxillipeds. **A.** *Pleuromamma xiphias*. **B.** *Erebonectes nesioticus*. **C.** *Ridgewayia wilsoni*, endopod.

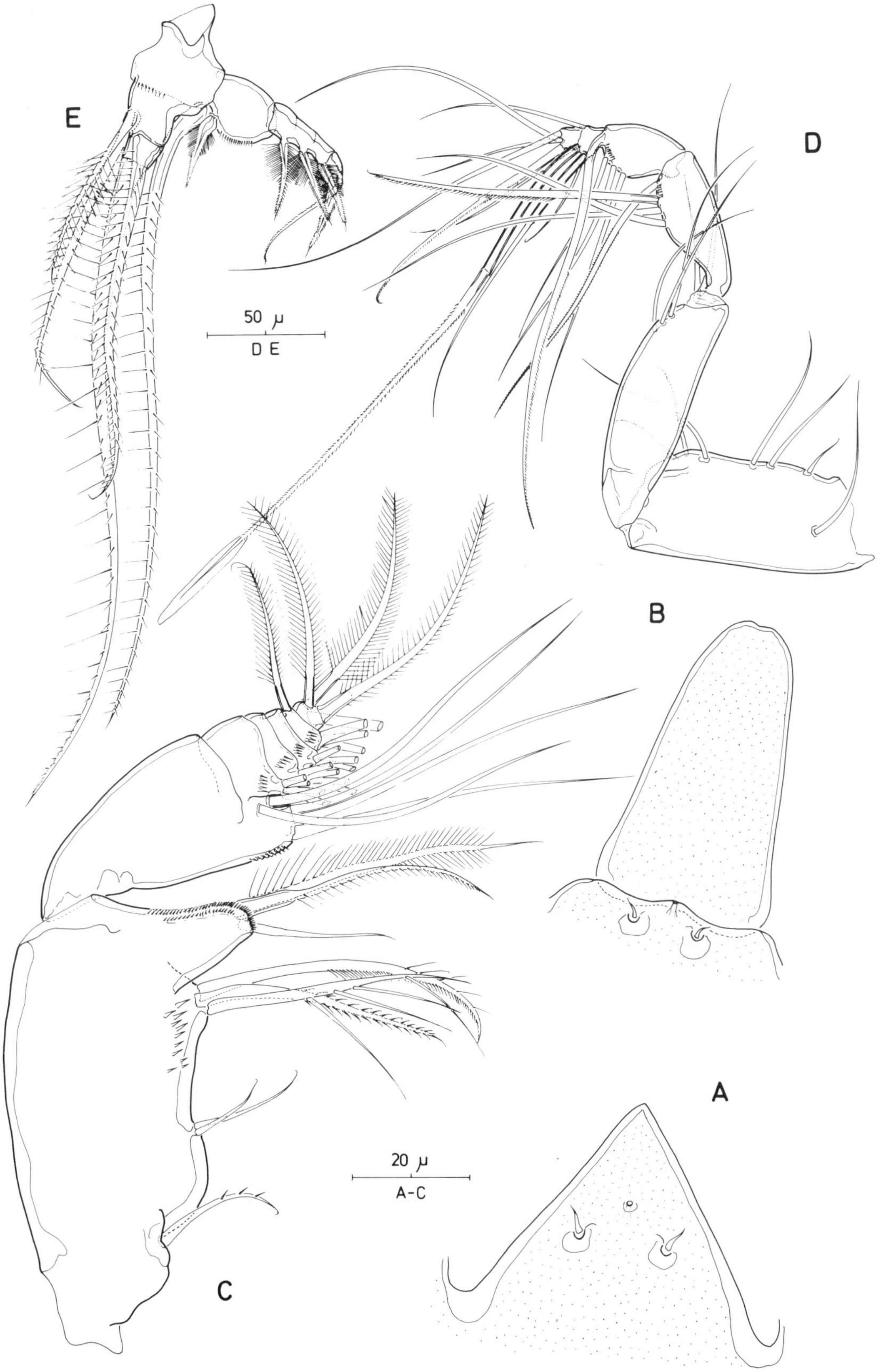

Figure 2.2.24. **A.** *Pseudocyclops bahamensis*, rostrum of female. **B.** Pseudorostrum area of male. **C.** Maxilliped. **D.** *Exumella polyarthra*, maxilliped. **E.** *Acartia clausi*, maxilliped.

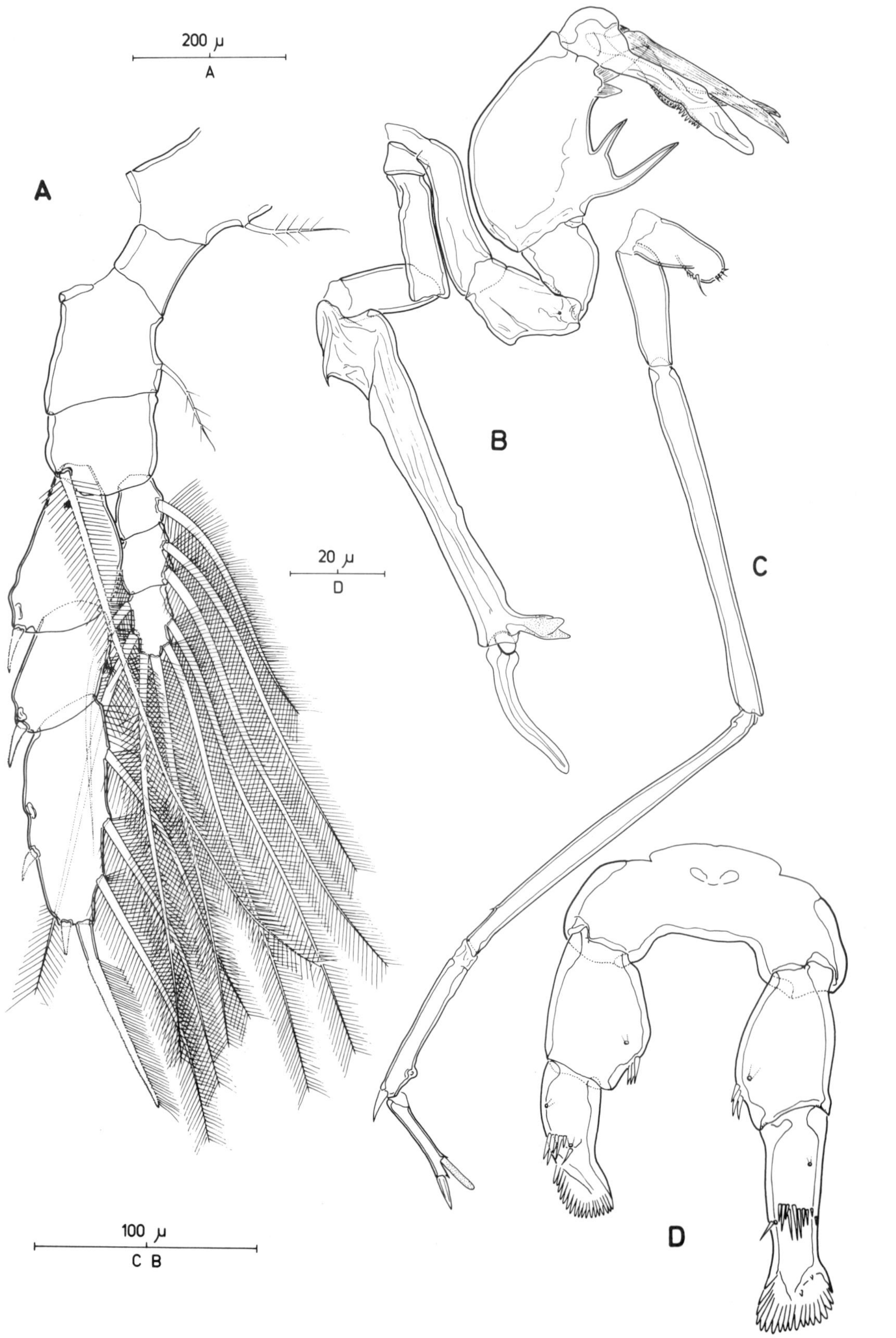

Figure 2.2.25. Fifth legs. **A.** *Haloptilus oxycephalus*, female. **B.** *Stephos lucayensis*, male. **C.** *Mesaiokeras nanseni*, male. **D.** *S.lucayensis*, female.

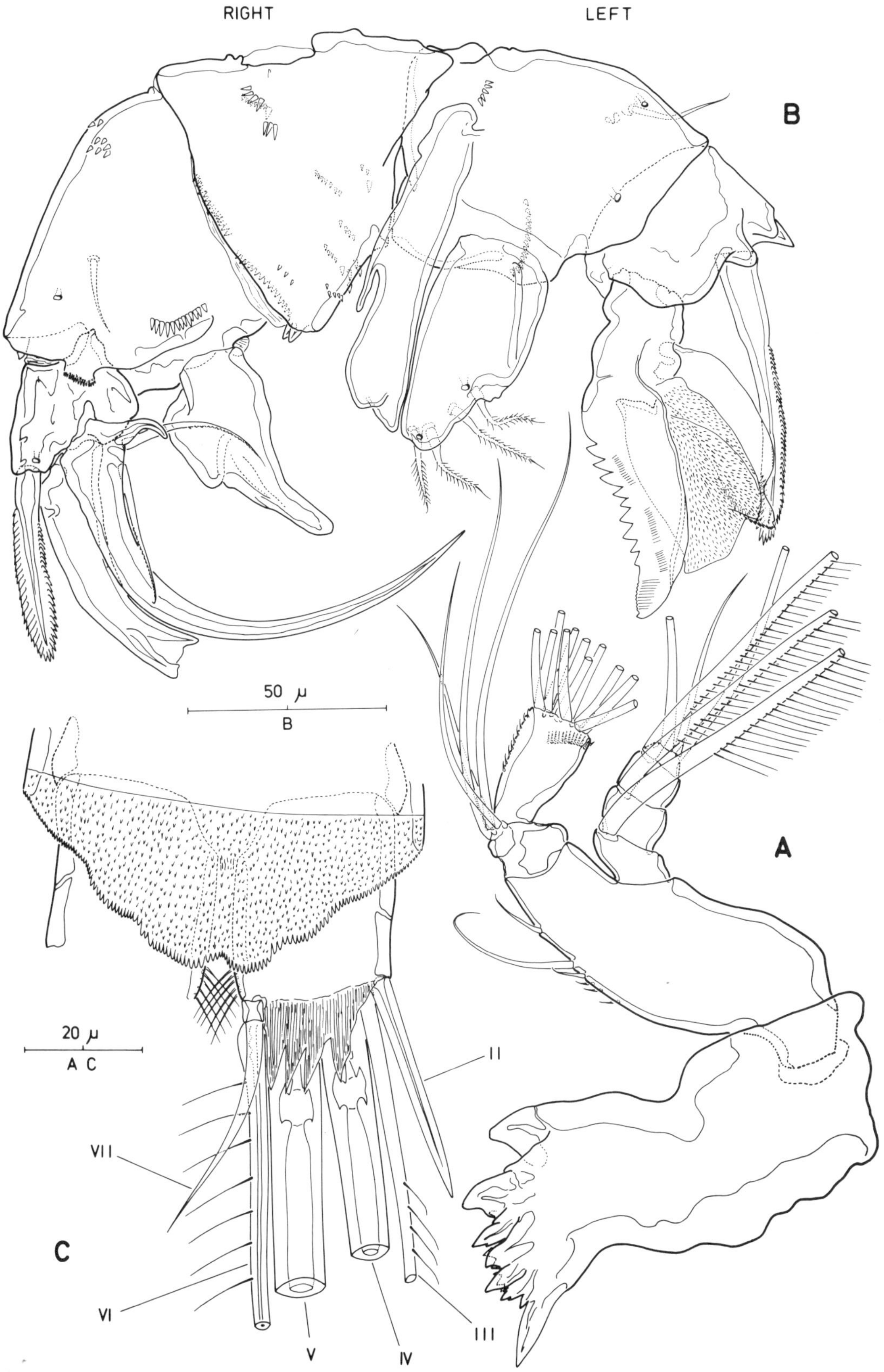

Figure 2.2.26. *Pseudocyclops bahamensis.* **A.** Mandible. **B.** Fifth pair of legs, male. **C.** Pseudoperculum, anal somite and right caudal ramus, dorsal view.

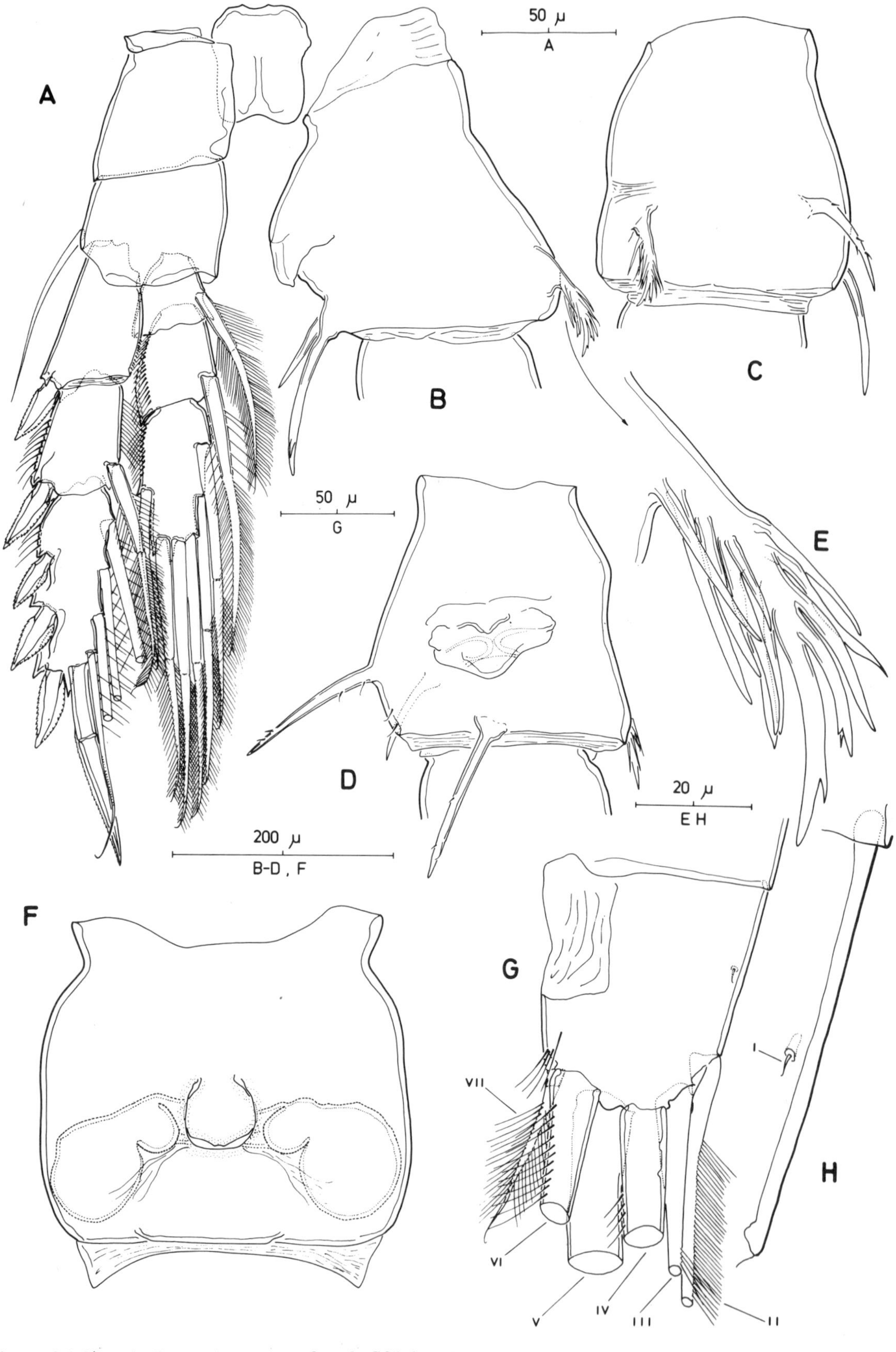

Figure 2.2.27. **A.** *Epacteriscus rapax*, female fifth leg. **B.** *Centropages typicus*, genital double somite of female, lateral view. **C.** Same, dorsal view. **D.** Same, ventral view. **E.** Detail of digitiform process on left side. **F.** *Enantiosis cavernicola*, genital double somite of female, ventral view. **G.** *Erebonectes nesioticus*, left caudal ramus, ventral view. **H.** Detail of seta I on outer margin of ramus.

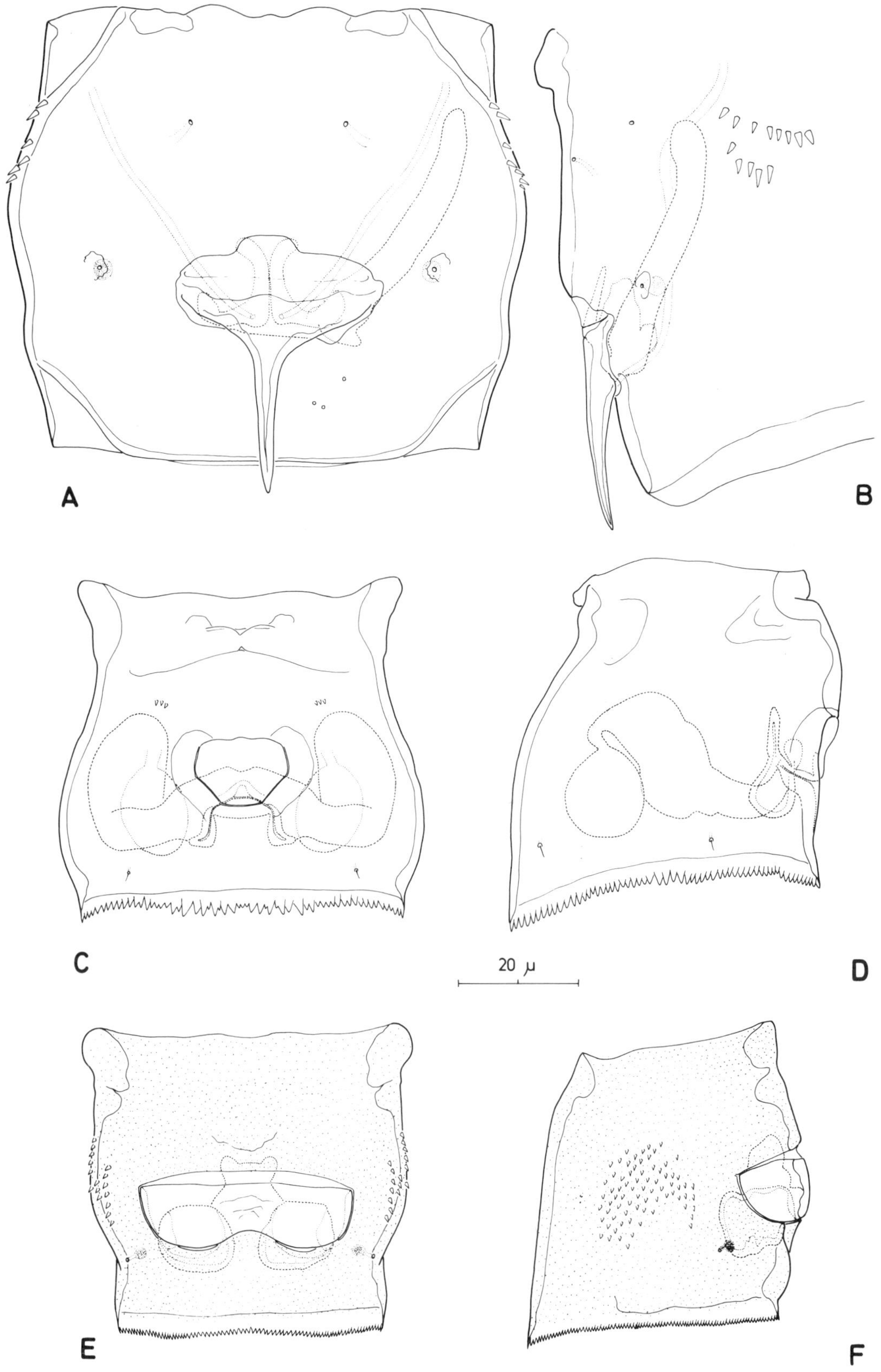

Figure 2.2.28. Female genital double somites. **A.** *Stephos lucayensis*, ventral view. **B.** Lateral view. **C.** *Paracyclopia naessi*, ventral view. **D.** Lateral view. **E.** *Mesaiokeras nanseni*, ventral view. **F.** Lateral view.

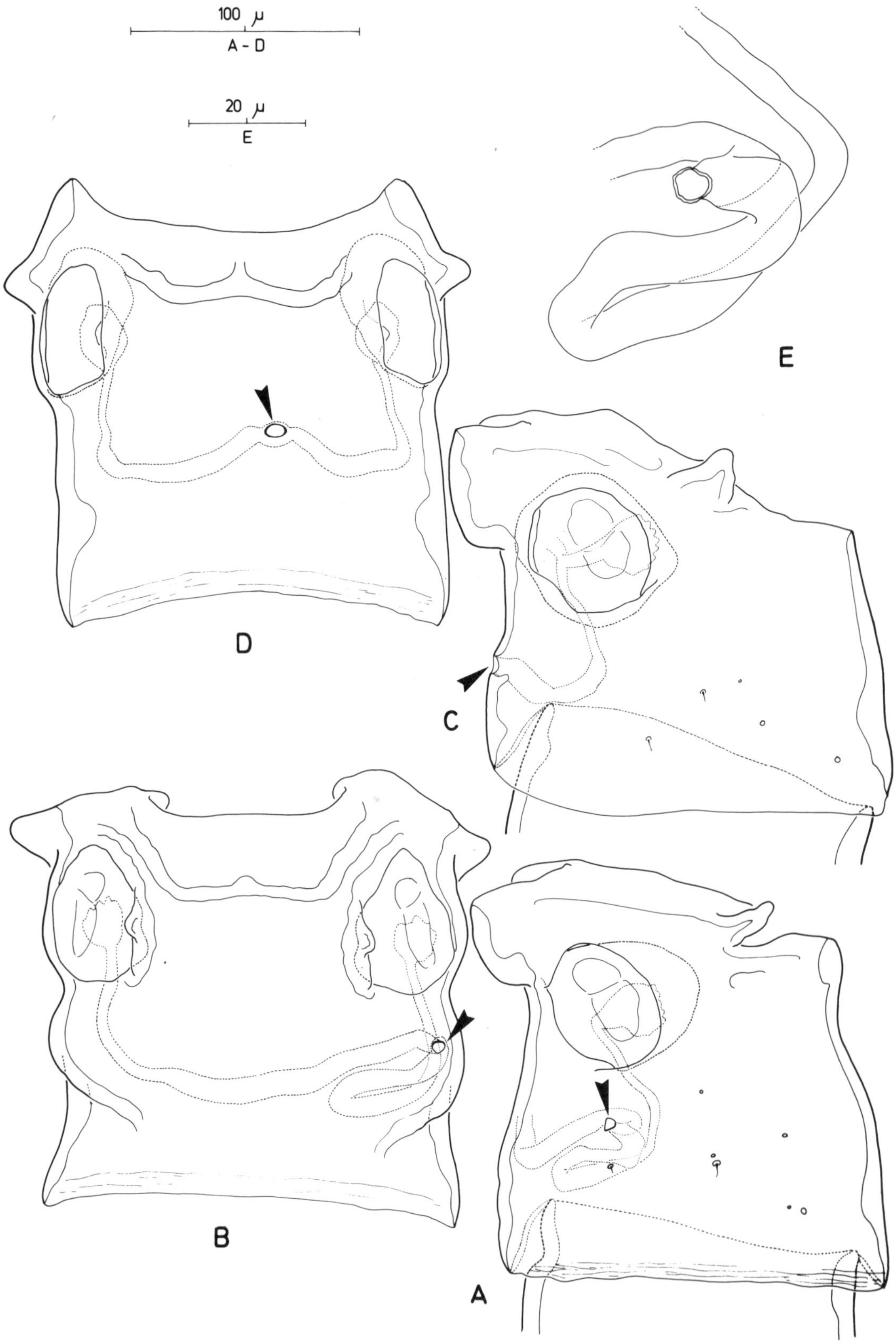

Figure 2.2.29. **A.** *Paramisophria cluthae*, lateral view of female genital double somite. **B.** Ventral view. **C.** *Paramisophria* species 1 from Okinawa, lateral view of female genital double somite. **D.** Ventral view. **E.** *P.cluthae*, detail of copulatory pore and ducts. [Arrows indicate copulatory pores.]

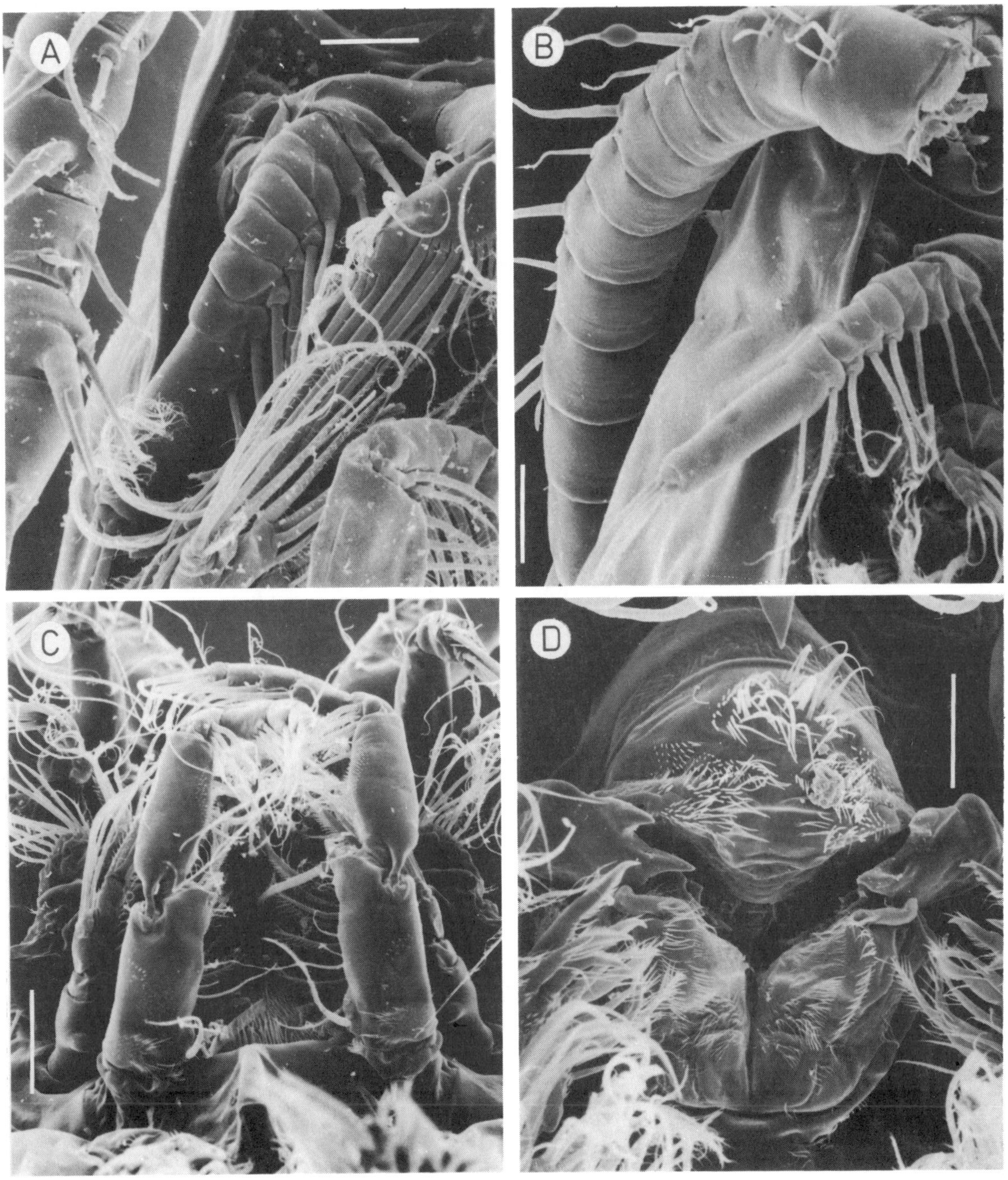

Figure 2.2.30. **A.** Male *Tropodiaptomus*, antennary exopod. **B.** Female *Tropodiaptomus*, antennary exopod. **C.** *Stephos canariensis*, maxillipeds. **D.** *Pseudocyclops* sp., labrum and paragnaths. Scale bars A,C = 40μm, B = 50μm, D = 30μm.

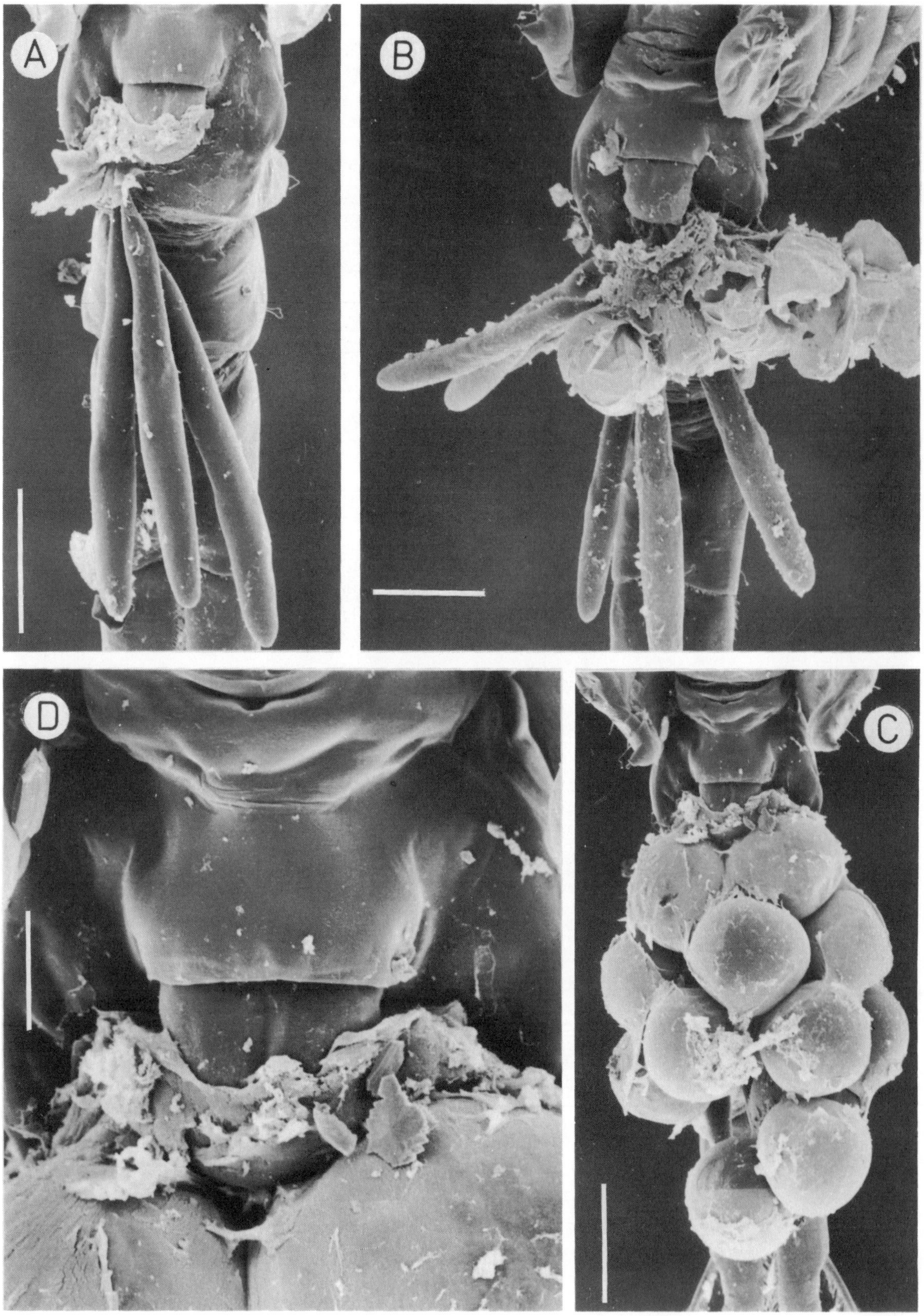

Figure 2.2.31. *Eurytemora velox*, female. **A.** Ventral view of urosome showing 3 attached spermatophores. **B.** Ventral view of urosome showing remains of egg mass and 5 attached spermatophores. **C.** Ventral view of urosome with attached egg mass. **D.** Detail of origin of egg mass at genital opening. Scale bars A-C = 100μm, D = 30μm.

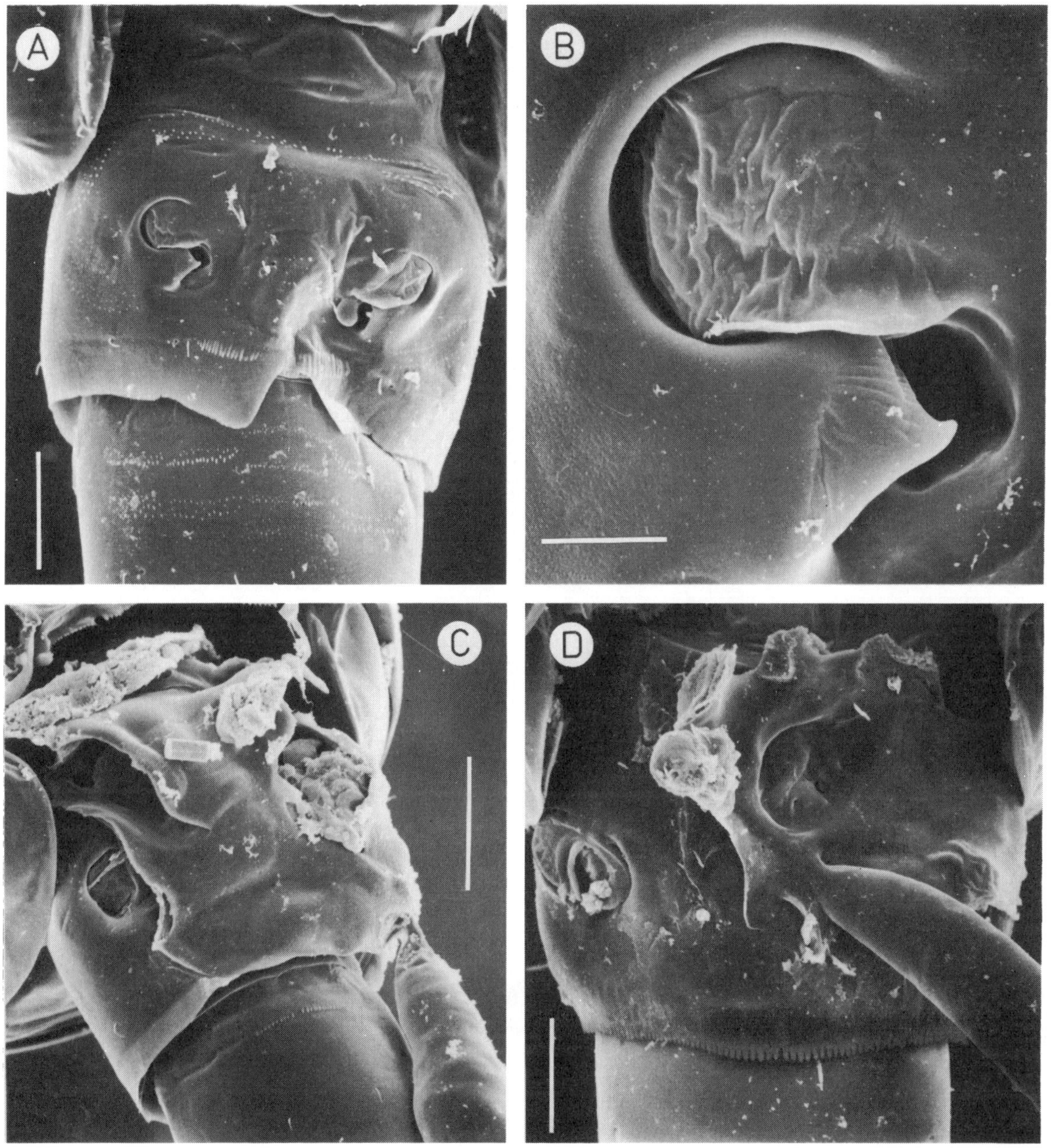

Figure 2.2.32. *Pseudocyclops* species. **A.** Species 1, female genital double somite showing paired genital apertures. **B.** Detail of right genital aperture. **C.** Species 2, female genital double somite with spermatophore attached over left genital aperture. **D.** Species 3, same. Scale bars A,C = 30μm, B = 5μm, D = 20μm.

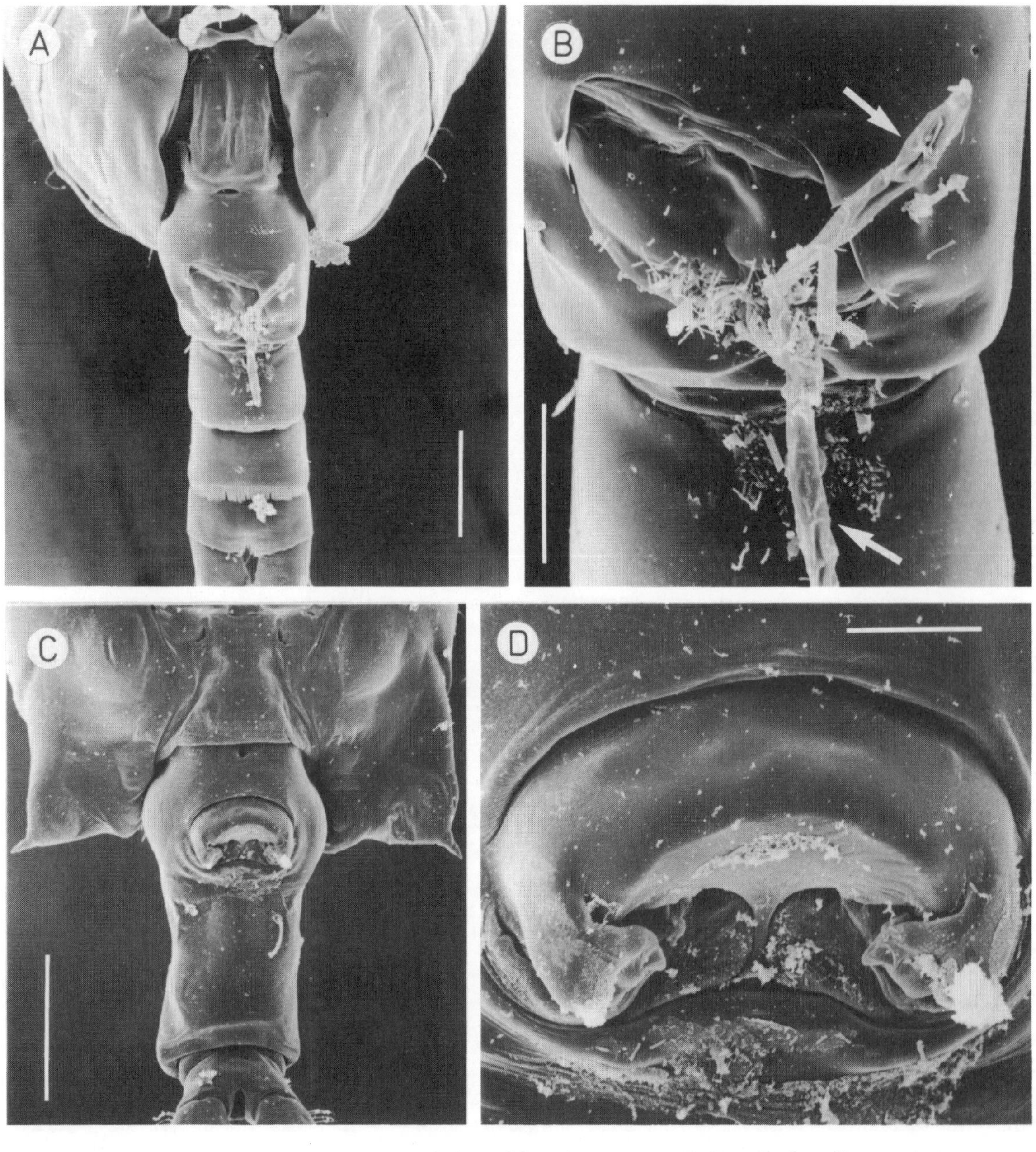

Figure 2.2.33. **A.** *Stephos canariensis*, ventral view of female urosome. **B.** Detail of median genital aperture, showing discharged spermatophores (arrowed). **C.** *Tropodiaptomus* sp., ventral view of female genital double somite. **D.** Detail of median genital aperture. Scale bars A =50μm, B,D = 20μm, C = 100μm.

2.3 MISOPHRIOIDA Gurney 1933

Misophrioids occur in shallow coastal waters, in the hyperbenthic community in the deep sea, in the deep-water plankton below about 2000 metres and in anchialine caves on volcanic islands around the world (Boxshall, 1989). They are opportunistic gorgers, feeding on a variety of other animals, including copepods and coelenterates (Boxshall & Roe, 1980). They exhibit a suite of highly specialised characters associated with the adoption of gorging as a feeding strategy including, a distensible gut, exoskeletal modifications to allow prosomal swelling, loss of the heart and retention of the antennary glands as the excretory organs of the adult (Boxshall, 1984). The biogeography of the Misophrioida was reviewed by Boxshall (1989) who postulated that the order originated in the deep-sea hyperbenthic community and secondarily emerged to colonise shallow water. Anchialine caves were colonised by two different routes: one via shallow water (*Misophria* Boeck), the other by a complex sequence of vicariance events in three dimensions.

Character set of ancestral misophrioid

Copepoda. Prosome comprising cephalosome and 4 free pedigerous somites; urosome 6-segmented in male, indistinctly 6-segmented in female due to partial fusion of genital and first abdominal somites (figure 2.3.11A). First pedigerous somite free but enclosed dorsally and laterally by carapace-like extension of posterior margin of dorsal cephalic shield. Prosome-urosome articulation between fourth and fifth pedigerous somites (podoplean position). Genital apertures paired in both sexes, located ventrally at posterior border of genital somite in male, in anterior third of genital double somite in female. Seminal receptacles fused. Copulatory pores paired (figures 2.3.15A and 2.3.16). Rostrum defined at base (figure 2.3.10C). Caudal rami with 7 setae (figure 2.3.12C). Nauplius eye absent. Antennules 27-segmented in female (figures 2.3.1A and 2.3.2A); apical segment double in both sexes, comprising fused ancestral segments XXVII and XXVIII. Antennules 25-segmented in male, bilaterally symmetrical, geniculate (figure 2.3.1B) with geniculation located between segments homologous with XX and XXI of the female; segments XIX and XX fused proximal to geniculation and XXI and XXII fused distal to geniculation. Male antennule with sheath on segment XV partly enclosing segment XVI (figures 2.3.2C and 2.3.3C-E). Antenna biramous with 8-segmented exopod and 3-segmented endopod; coxa unarmed, basis with 2 inner setae, first to third endopodal segments with 2, 6 and 7+2 setae respectively (figures 2.3.5 and 2.3.6A-B): exopodal segments 1 to 7 representing ancestral segments II-VIII, segment 8 representing fused ancestral segments IX-X (figures 2.3.5A and 2.3.6A); setal formula 1,1,1,1,1,1,1,4. Labrum an undivided muscular lobe (figure 2.3.7B). Mandible with large coxal gnathobase (figure 2.3.5B) and biramous palp (figure 2.3.5B-D); exopod 5-segmented, setal formula 1,1,1,1,2; endopod 2-segmented, setal formula 4,8; basis bearing 3 setae on inner margin. Paragnaths separate (figure 2.3.7A). Maxillule (figures 2.3.8A, 2.3.9A and 2.3.10A-B) with large praecoxal endite bearing 15 elements; coxa with single endite bearing 6 setae, and vestigial epipodite incorporated into segment, represented by 8 setae; basis with 1 seta on outer margin representing exite (figure 2.3.8A); 2 widely separated endites present, proximal endite well developed, with 4 setae; distal endite largely incorporated into segment, represented by 4 setae; exopod 1-segmented with 11 setae (figure 2.3.10A), endopod with 2 free segments, proximal segment representing double segment; setal formula (3,3)6. Maxilla 6-segmented (figure 2.3.6C-D); praecoxa and coxa each with 2 endites, endite formula 7,3,3,3 (figure 2.3.6C); allobasis with well developed proximal (basal) endite forming a claw bearing 4 setae, distal (endopodal) endite vestigial, represented by 3 setae; outer coxal seta absent; free endopod 3-segmented (figure 2.3.9B-D), setal formula 2,2,4. Maxilliped 9-segmented (figures 2.3.7C, 2.3.8B and 2.3.10D), comprising praecoxa with 1 endite, coxa with 3 endites, basis and 6-segmented endopod, with proximal endopodal segment incompletely fused to basis; praecoxal and coxal endite formula 1,2,4,3; basis with 3 setae; endopod setal formula 2,2,2,2,2+1,5. Swimming legs 1-4 biramous with 3-segmented rami, members of each leg pair joined by intercoxal sclerite; inner coxal seta and outer seta on basis present, inner seta on basis of first leg only; first exopodal segment with 1 outer spine. Spine and seta formula for legs 1 to 5:

	coxa	basis	exopod segment 1 2 3	endopod segment 1 2 3
leg 1	0 – 1	1 – I	I – 1; I – 1; III,I,4	0 – 1; 0 – 2; 1,2,3
leg 2	0 – 1	1 – 0	I – 1; I – 1; III,I,5	0 – 1; 0 – 2; 1,2,3
leg 3	0 – 1	1 – 0	I – 1; I – 1; III,I,5	0 – 1; 0 – 2; 1,2,3
leg 4	0 – 1	1 – 0	I – 1; I – 1; III,I,5	0 – 1; 0 – 2; 1,2,2
leg 5 female	0 – 0	1 – 0	I – 0; I – 1; 1,I,1	2
leg 5 male	0 – 0	1 – 0	I – 0; 0 – 1; 2,I,2	2

Fifth legs biramous; members of leg pair joined by intercoxal sclerite; praecoxa absent; separate coxa and basis present; basis with outer seta; inner coxal seta absent; exopod 3-segmented in both sexes and bearing 6 setae in female and 7 setae in male; endopod 1-segmented (figures 2.3.11D and 2.3.12D-E) and bearing 2 setae in both sexes. Sixth legs confluent in female, separate in male, represented by opercular plate closing off genital openings (figures 2.3.11B, 2.3.12A-B and 2.3.15-16). Eggs loosely attached to female urosome, not contained in sacs.

Remarks

The Misophrioida is a small order, comprising only 20 described species all placed in a single family, the Misophriidae, at present. The ordinal diagnosis is based on consideration of all genera, the neritic *Misophria*, the deep-sea genera *Archimisophria* Boxshall, *Benthomisophria* Sars, *Misophriella* Boxshall and *Misophriopsis* Boxshall, the cavernicolous genera *Speleophria, Expansophria, Palpophria* and *Dimisophria* described by Boxshall & Iliffe (1986, 1987), and *Boxshallia* described by Huys (1988b).

Female Genital System: Several genera including *Misophria, Archimisophria* and *Expansophria* have a dorsal suture partially separating genital and first abdominal somites in the female but a full genital double somite is present in *Speleophria, Boxshallia* and *Palpophria.* Three different arrangements of the female genital apparatus are found within this small order (figure 2.3.16). In *Misophria* paired copulatory pores are present, located close together on the ventral surface of the first abdominal somite and posterior to the gonopores and sixth legs (figure 2.3.15A-B). Ducts from the pores lead to a common copulatory duct which enters a median seminal receptacle. Paired spermatophores are deposited by the male and these discharge via the copulatory pores (figures 2.3.15C-D). In an as yet undescribed new species of *Misophriopsis* the arrangement is similar to *Misophria* except that the paired pores have fused to form a single copulatory pore and a common copulatory duct is present. In *Boxshallia* and *Speleophria* (figure 2.3.15E) the single copulatory pore is located more anteriorly than in the new species of *Misophriopsis* and is partly concealed beneath the confluent sixth legs that form the plate closing off the gonopores. The sixth legs are confluent (figure 2.3.20B) but still defined basally in all female misophrioids, an arrangement ensuring that eggs are released in pairs in those genera with symmetrical reproductive systems.

Caudal Rami: The caudal rami retain 7 setae in *Speleophria* species. The anterolateral accessory seta (seta I) on the lateral margin is particularly well developed in *S.bivexilla* Boxshall & Iliffe (figure 2.3.12C). In other genera, such as *Boxshallia*, only 6 setae remain, with seta I lacking (figure 2.3.17C).

Female Antennule: There are 27 segments in the antennules of female *Archimisophria, Boxshallia, Dimisophria* and some species of *Speleophria*. In *Expansophria* the antennules are 26-segmented due to fusion of ancestral segment XXVI with the apical double segment. In the antennules of the *Misophria* lineage (see Boxshall, 1989) there is considerable fusion among the proximal segments. In *Misophriella* ancestral segments II to VI and IX to XII are fused, and in *Misophriopsis* and *Misophria* (figure 2.3.3A-B) further segments are incorporated into the more proximal of these 2 compound segments (figure 2.3.4).

Male Antennule: Male antennules are at most 25-segmented. In *Archimisophria* this condition is derived from a 27-segmented state by fusion of ancestral segments XIX and XX proximal to the geniculation, and segments XXI and XXII distal to the geniculation (figure 2.3.1B). The antennules of male misophrioids are also characterised by the presence of a sheath on ancestral segment XV, which largely encloses segment XVI. This sheath is best developed in the new species of *Misophriopsis* (figures 2.3.3D-E). It is most expanded dorsally so that it conceals most of the dorsal surface of segment XVI but it is incised ventrally forming a short rim around the base of segment XVI. A distinct sheath is also present in *Boxshallia* (arrowed in figure 2.3.2C) and in *Expansophria dimorpha* Boxshall & Iliffe. The sheath is secondarily lost in *Archimisophria discoveryi* Boxshall (figure 2.3.1B). Many additional segmental fusions are found in misophrioid males (see figure 2.3.4). In *Boxshallia* and *Misophriopsis* there are fusions proximally of segments IX to XII and distally of segment XXIII to the double segment XXI-XXII. In the latter genus segments XXIV-XXVIII and II to VI are also fused.

Antenna: The misophrioid antenna has both rami well developed. A maximum of 8 segments in the exopod is retained in *Archimisophria* (figure 2.3.6A) and in *Expansophria galapagensis* Boxshall & Iliffe (figure 2.3.21D). In the former the setal formula is 1,0,1,1,1,1,0,4 and in the latter 1,1,1,1,1,1,1,4. The distal segment represents the fused ninth and tenth ancestral segments, as indicated by the presence of 4 setae. The exopod is 7-segmented in *Boxshallia* and 6-segmented in several other genera. The antennary endopod is basically 3-segmented although the second and third segments are often partially fused. The first segment bears a maximum of 2 setae (figure 2.3.5A). The second segment bears a maximum of 6 setae, as in *Speleophria campaneri* Boxshall & Iliffe, although 5 setae, as in *Boxshallia* (figure 2.3.5A) or 4 setae, as in *Archimisophria* (figure 2.3.6A) are commonly found. The third segment carries a maximum of 9 setae, as in *Archimisophria*, arranged in a 7 + 2 configuration. We interpret the 7 setae (numbered 1 to 7 in figure 2.3.6B) as the original armature of the compound third segment (III-IV) of the podoplean antennary endopod and the 2 additional setae (arrowed in figure 2.3.6B) as belonging to the second segment but which have secondarily shifted their site of origin to near the apex of the ramus. In *Boxshallia* (figure 2.3.5A) 7 setae are present on the apex of the endopod as in all misophrioids other than *Archimisophria* and *Expansophria*.

Labrum: The labrum of misophrioids is a muscular lobe (Boxshall, 1982) which can be relatively large and may be ornamented with rows of spinules or setules (figure 2.3.7B).

Paragnaths: The paragnaths are typically simple lobes bearing patches or rows of fine setules, but in *Archimisophria squamosa* Alvarez the paragnaths are each armed with 3 well developed setae (figure 2.3.7A). These are novel elements.

Mandible: The majority of misophrioids retain a mandible with a well devloped, biramous palp (figure 2.3.5B-D). Only *Palpophria* exhibits a major modification in mandibular morphology, with its extremely elongate, uniramous palp (Boxshall & Iliffe, 1987). The basis is armed with 3 setae only in *Boxshallia* (figure 2.3.5B), all other misophrioid genera having 1 seta at most. A 5-segmented exopod on the mandibular palp with a setal formula of 1,1,1,1,2 is found in *Speleophria bivexilla* (figure 2.3.5D). *Misophria* and *Boxshallia* display partial fusion of exopodal segments (figure 2.3.5B-C) although both retain all the ancestral setation elements on this ramus. The 2-segmented endopod is typical of most genera, but the ancestral setal formula of 4,8 is not found in any extant species. *Boxshallia* has 4 setae on the first endopodal segment and *Misophria* has 8 setae on the second (figure 2.3.5C).

Maxillule: The outer seta on the basis of the maxillule is present in two new species of *Speleophria* (figure 2.3.8A) described by Boxshall & Iliffe (1990) and was overlooked in *Speleophria bivexilla* by Boxshall & Iliffe (1986). *Misophriopsis* is the only podoplean with 8 setae representing the epipodite on the coxa of the maxillule. Several other misophrioids, such as *Expansophria*, *Archimisophria* (figure 2.3.10A), *Speleophria* (figure 2.3.8A) and *Boxshallia* (figure 2.3.9A) have 7 setae. The greatest reduction within the order occurs in *Palpophria* and *Dimisophria* which have only 2 and 1 setae respectively. A maximum of 6 setae on the coxal endite and 4 on each of the basal endites is found in *Boxshallia* and *Misophriopsis*. The exopod carries a variable number of setae. The maximum is 11 setae, as in *Archimisophria* (figure 2.3.10A), and the minimum occurs in *Expansophria* species which have 2 or 3 setae only. The segmentation of the endopod is indistinct, with the first and second segments nearly completely fused. In *Speleophria scottodicarloi* Boxshall & Iliffe the setation pattern is 3,2,6 (figure 2.3.8A) but the maximum is found in *Misophriopsis*, which has a 3,3,6 formula. In *Archimisophria squamosa* the endopodal formula is reduced to 2,2,6 (figure 2.3.10B).

Maxilla: The basic segmentation of the maxilla (figure 2.3.6C) is common to most misophrioids. In all genera the basis and first endopodal segment are completely fused to form an allobasis (figure 2.3.9B-D). The maximum setation of 7,3 is exhibited by the praecoxal endites of *Archimisophria* (figure 2.3.6D). The coxal endites each have 3 setae in most species. The basal endite comprises a claw plus 3 setae and the endopodal endite is represented by 3 setae, 1 located on the anterior surface, 1 on the posterior surface and 1 migrated onto the basal endite. This ancestral setation is retained in *Archimisophria* (figure 2.3.9B-C) and *Speleophria* (2.3.9D). These two genera also retain the maximum setation pattern of the free endopod (2,2,4).

Maxilliped: The 9-segmented condition of the maxilliped is not retained in any extant misophrioid. Three separate protopodal segments are found in *Archimisophria* (figure 2.3.7C) but the endopod is only 5-segmented whereas *Speleophria* (figure 2.3.8B) and *Boxshallia* (figure 2.3.10D) exhibit a 6-segmented endopod but the praecoxa and coxa are fused to form a syncoxa. Typically the 5-segmented endopodal condition arises by incorporation of the first endopodal segment into the basis, with subsequent loss of its armature. It is, however, likely that reduction to 5 segments has occurred independently by fusion of endopodal segments. In *Expansophria galapagensis*, for example, the large fourth segment bearing 2 setae on its inner margin (figure 2.3.20C), may represent a double segment (IV-V). The praecoxal endite is represented by a single seta in *Archimisophria* (figure 2.3.7C), *Expansophria* (figure 2.3.20D) and *Boxshallia* (figure 2.3.10D). The setal formula of the coxal endites was primitively 2,4,3, as found in *Speleophria* (figure 2.3.8A) but various reductions are found, such as 2,3,3 (in *Boxshallia*) and 2,4,2 (in *Archimisophria*). The ancestral setation for the endopod is retained in *Speleophria* (figure 2.3.8A) which shows the full 2,2,2,2,2+1,5 formula.

Fifth Leg: The fifth legs of misophrioids are particularly variable. In *Misophriopsis dichotoma* Boxshall (figure 2.3.11D) and an as yet undescribed new species of *Misophriopsis* (figure 2.3.12E) the endopod of the fifth leg is 1-segmented, bearing 1 or 2 long setae. In *Misophria* (figure 2.3.12D) the endopod is separated from the basis by a partial suture. In *Benthomisophria* and *Boxshallia* the endopod is represented by a seta only (figure 2.3.11E) and it is absent in other genera. An intercoxal sclerite is present in *Boxshallia* (figure 2.3.11E) and *Speleophria*. The coxa and basis are retained as separate segments in these two genera, and in *Misophriella*, *Misophria*, *Archimisophria* (figure 2.3.11C) and in *Expansophria* (figure 2.3.21C) but are fused in other genera, or the entire limb is reduced. In *Expansophria apoda* Boxshall & Iliffe the entire fifth leg is lost. The 3-segmented exopod is retained in *Archimisophria* (figure 2.3.11C), *Expansophria* and the new *Misophriopsis* species. There is often sexual dimorphism in the fifth legs but the maximum segmentation is the same for both sexes: 3 exopodal segments and 1 endopodal segment. The maximum setation of the exopod is retained in the female of *Speleophria campaneri* (6 setae) and in the male of *Misophriopsis* (7 setae).

The variation in segmentation and setation of the fifth legs is summarised for females and males in schematic figures 2.3.13 and 2.3.14 respectively. The arrows indicate how the different states of the legs can be derived and do not indicate any ancestor-descendant relationship between the taxa named. These diagrams allow the homologies of the individual armature elements of the fifth legs to be traced through the different genera.

Differential Diagnosis: Misophrioids are most readily distinguished from other copepods with podoplean-type tagmosis by the numerous plesiomorphies they exhibit. Misophrioids are the only podopleans that possess at least 16 antennulary segments in combination with more than 4 segments in the antennary exopod. The possession of 6 segments in the endopod of the maxilliped is also a unique plesiomorphy for the podopleans.

Misophrioids also possess unique apomorphies such as the carapace-like extension of the cephalosome. The carapace extends posteriorly from the rear margin of the dorsal cephalic shield (figure 2.3.18B) and completely encloses, both dorsally and laterally, the first pedigerous somite beneath. In figure 2.3.18A the carapace of *Misophria pallida* Boeck is visible as a slightly raised, lighter coloured area. In *Benthomisophria* species (figures 2.3.19A and 2.3.20A) the carapace is highly ornamented with a system of strengthening ridges and lamellae, although the thin and flexible integument of the first pedigerous somite beneath is smooth. The presence of the well developed carapace is linked to the adoption of an opportunistic gorging feeding strategy (Boxshall, 1984) and is associated with other structures such as the notched lateral margins of the cephalosome (figure 2.3.19A) and the presence of lateral areas of cone organs on the dorsal cephalic shield (figure 2.3.19A-C). Some cavernicolous taxa have secondarily lost the carapace. *Expansophria galapagensis* for example, lacks a carapace but the first pedigerous somite is modified to allow considerable distension (figure 2.3.21A-B) and it is probable that this form retains a similar opportunistic feeding strategy. In *Archimisophria squamosa* the posterior margin of the dorsal cephalic shield is only slightly produced posteriorly, not forming a large carapace. The posterior extension largely covers the first pedigerous somite when the animal has an empty midgut (figure 2.3.17B) but leaves it exposed when the midgut is full (figure 2.3.17A).

Misophrioids are the only copepods that are known to primitively lack a nauplius eye at all stages of their life cycle. However, it is possible that the Gelyelloida and Platycopioida may also lack the nauplius eye. Other anatomical characters appear to be unique to the Misophrioida, such as the neotenic retention of antennary glands as the functional excretory organs of the adult (Boxshall, 1982). Comparative data are lacking from several other orders but in the Calanoida, Cyclopoida and Harpacticoida at least, the adult excretory organs are the maxillary glands.

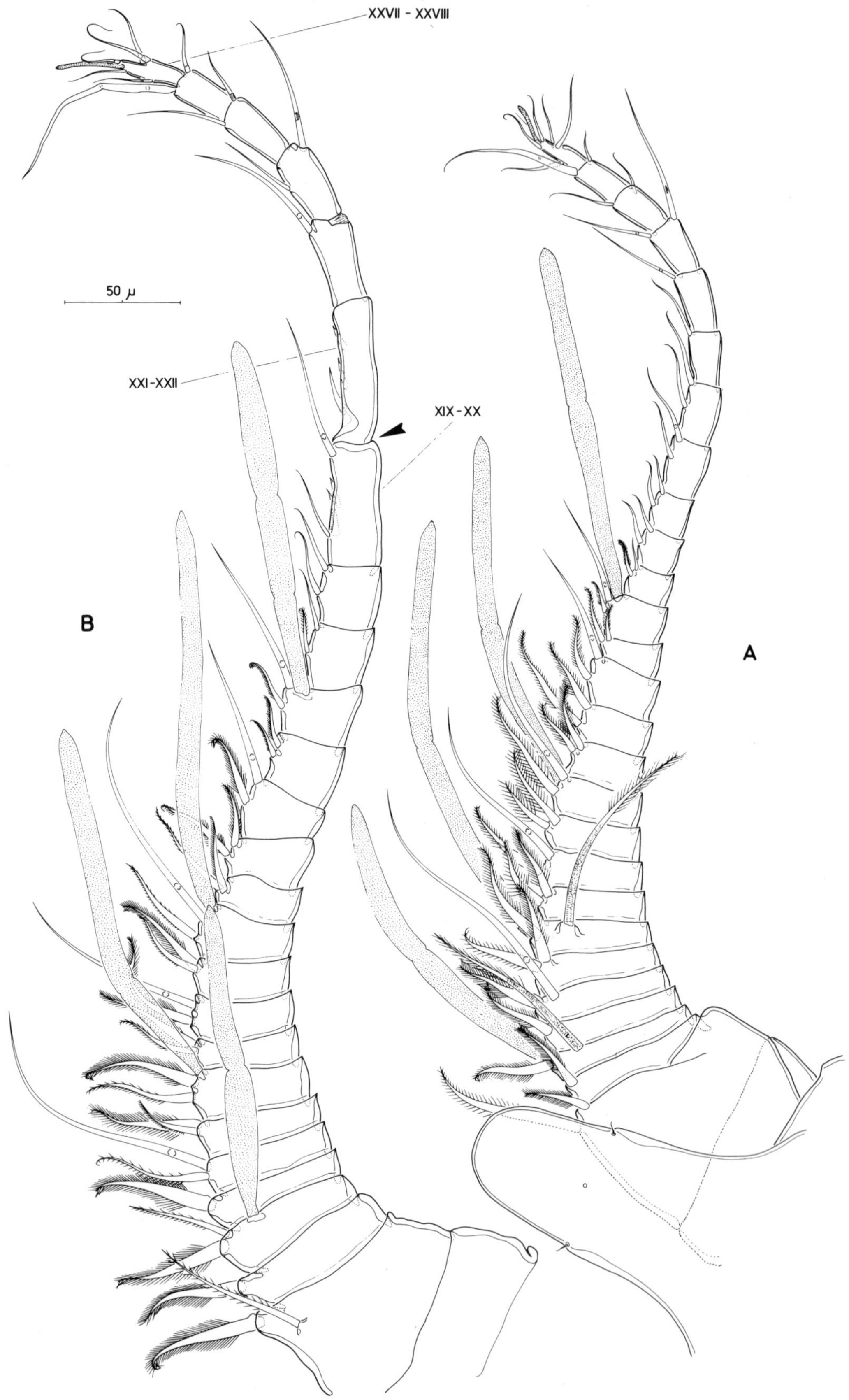

Figure 2.3.1. *Archimisophria discoveryi.* **A.** Female antennule and rostrum. **B.** Male antennule, with arrow marking geniculation.

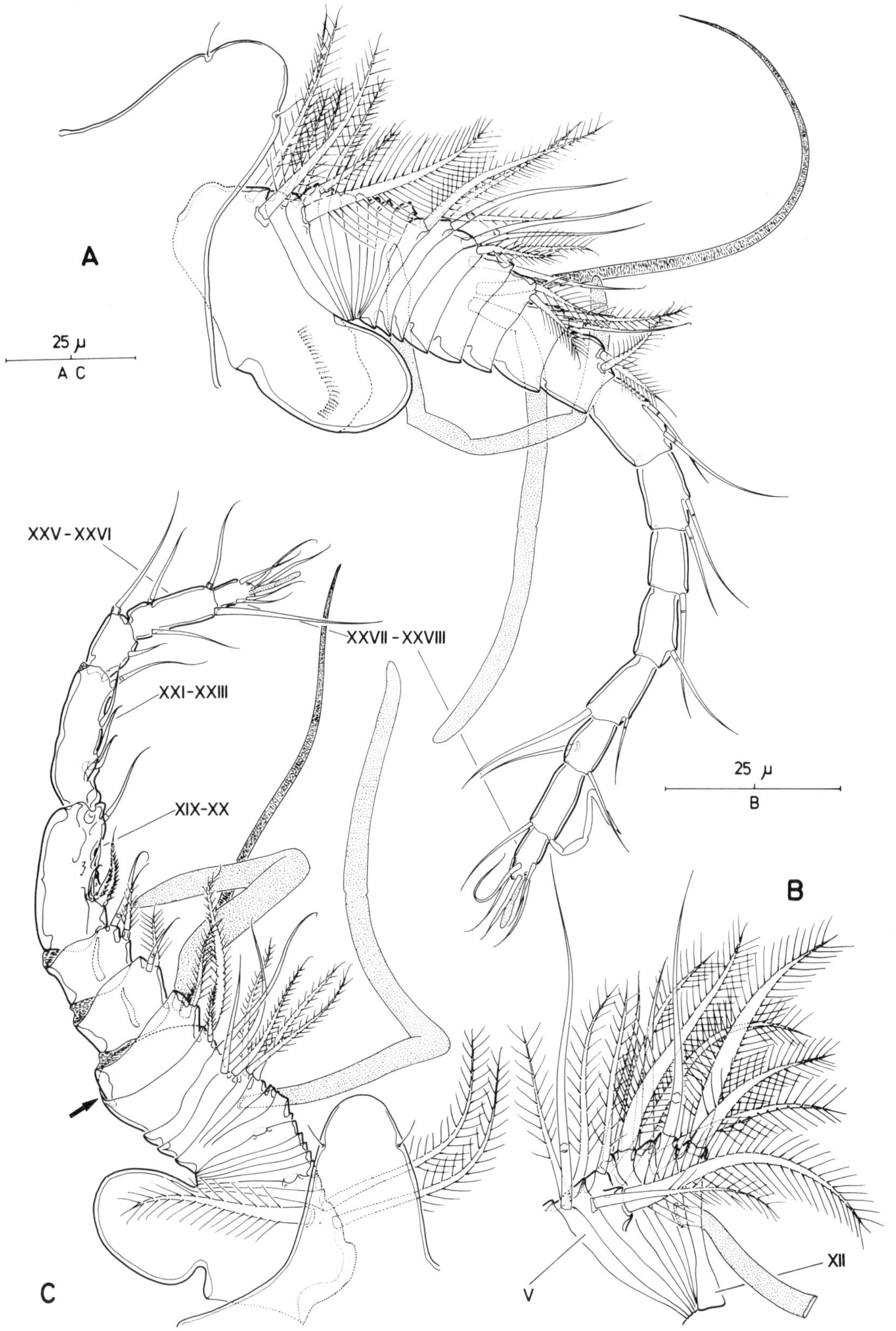

Figure 2.3.2. *Boxshallia bulbantennulata*. **A.** Female antennule and rostrum, with setation of segments V to XII omitted. **B.** Segments V to XII showing setation. **C.** Male antennule and rostrum, with arrow marking sheath on segment XV.

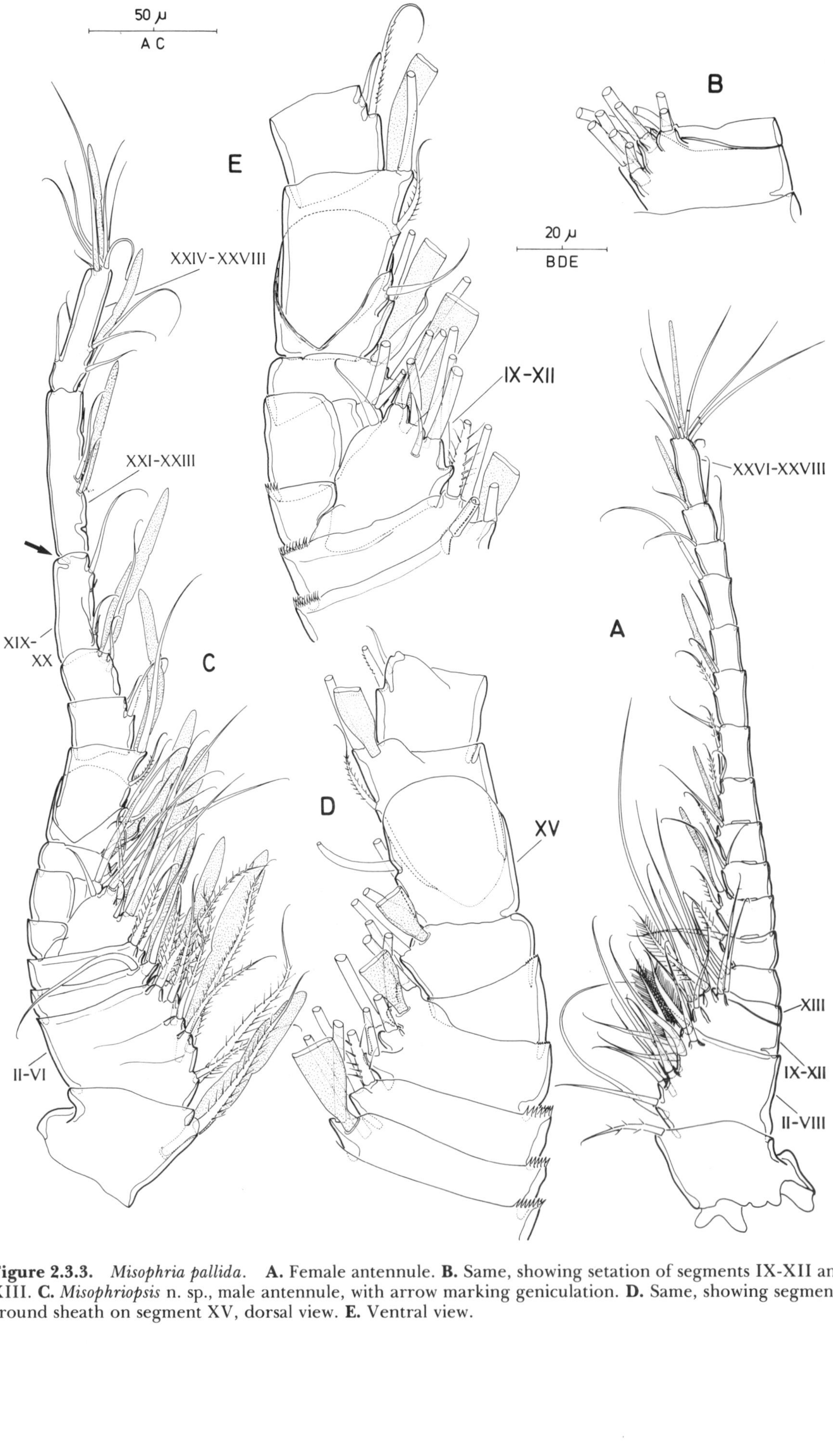

Figure 2.3.3. *Misophria pallida*. **A.** Female antennule. **B.** Same, showing setation of segments IX-XII and XIII. **C.** *Misophriopsis* n. sp., male antennule, with arrow marking geniculation. **D.** Same, showing segments around sheath on segment XV, dorsal view. **E.** Ventral view.

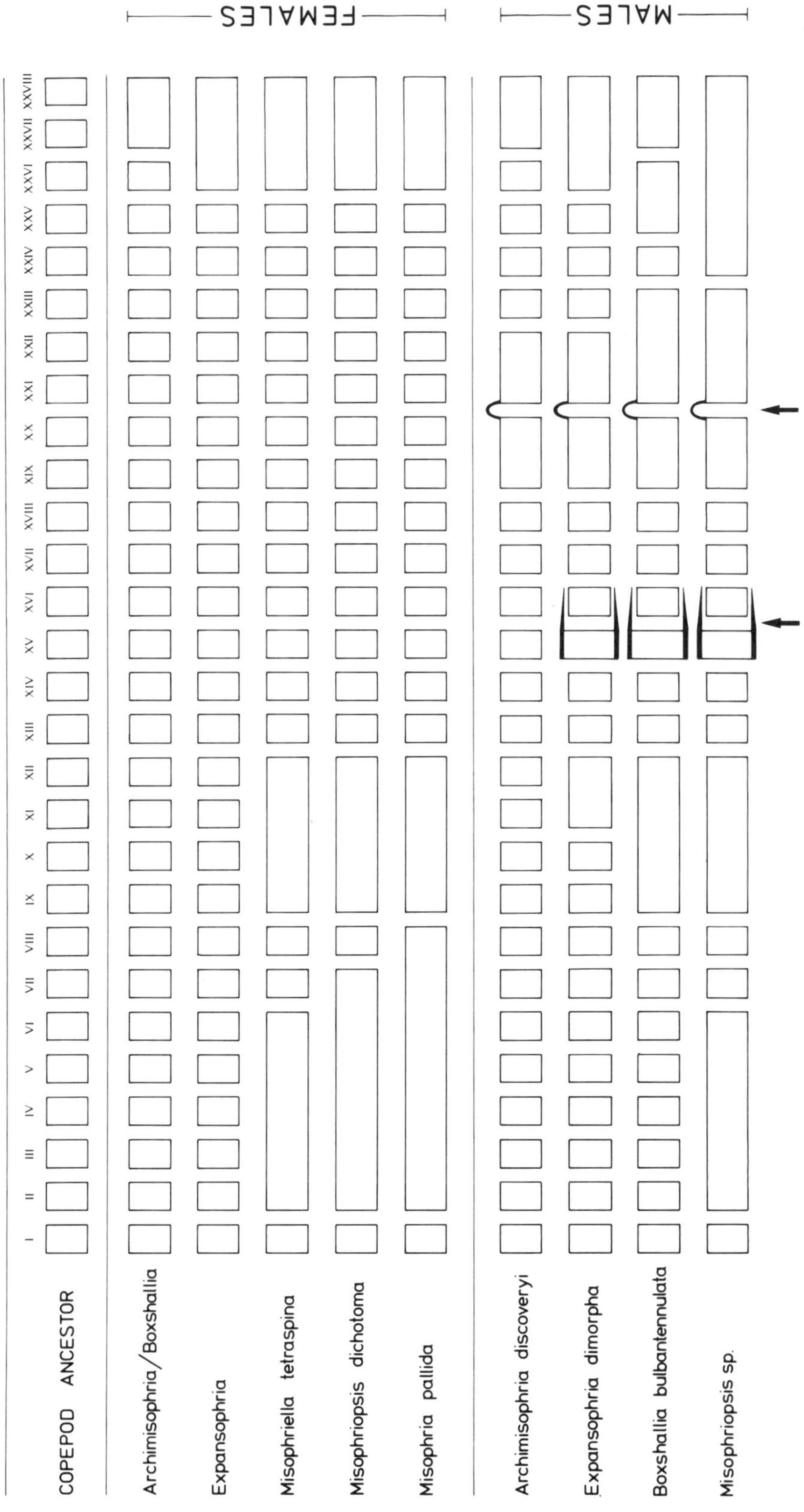

Figure 2.3.4. Schematic comparison of segmental homologies in male and female antennules in the Misophrioida; showing location of geniculation and sheath in males.

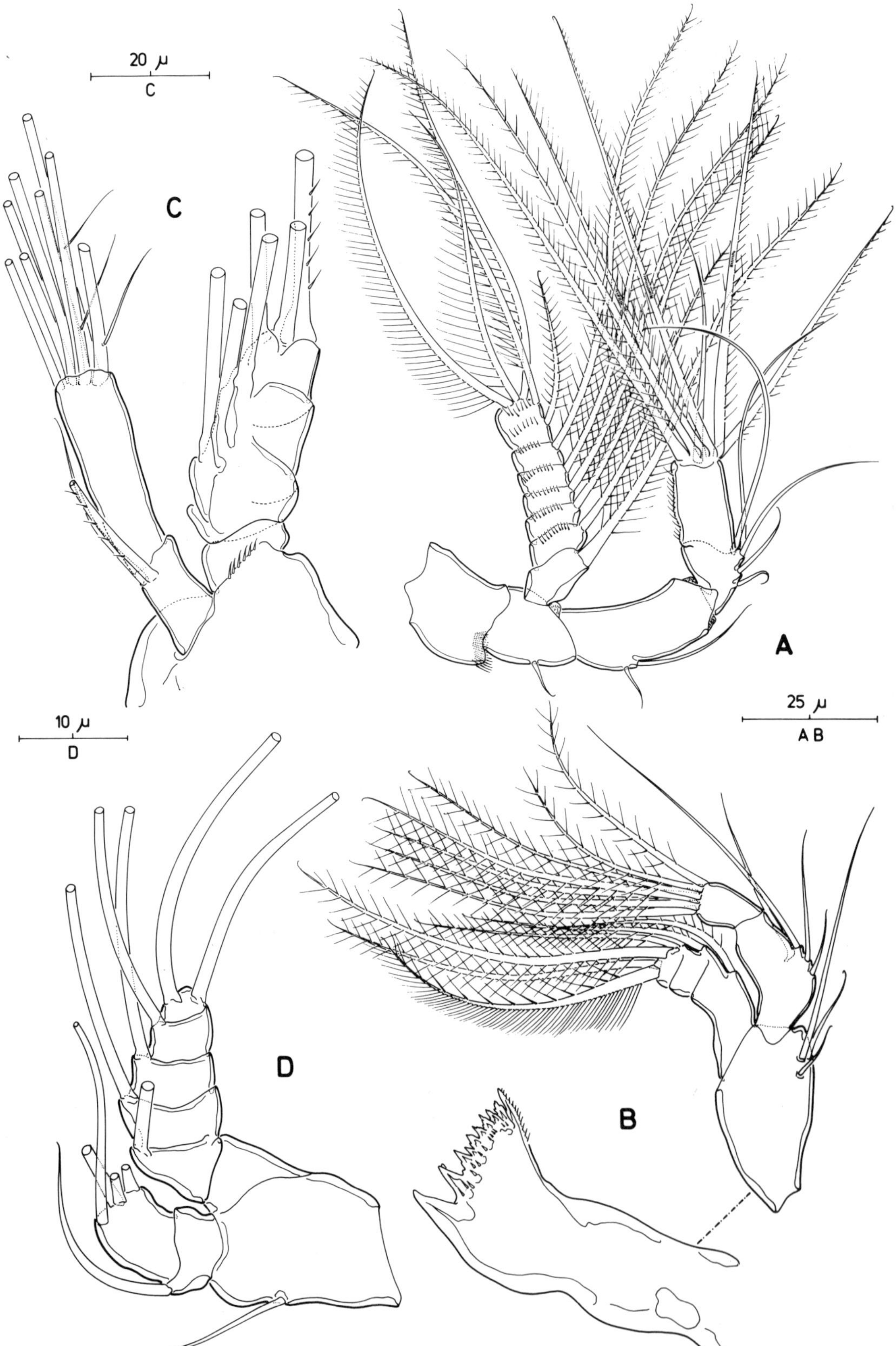

Figure 2.3.5. **A.** *Boxshallia bulbantennulata*, antenna. **B.** Mandible. **C.** *Misophria pallida*, rami of mandibular palp. **D.** *Speleophria bivexilla*, mandibular palp.

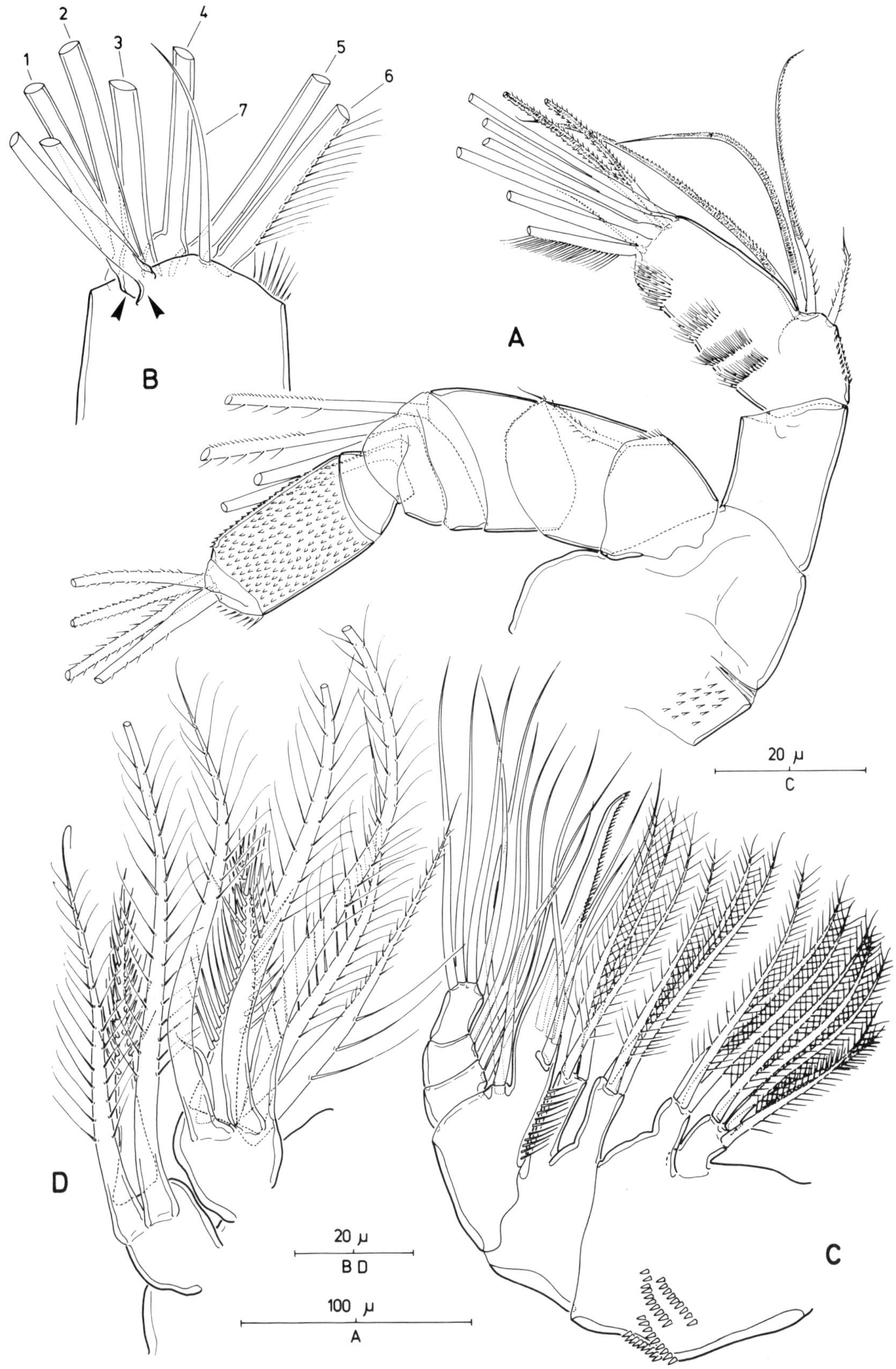

Figure 2.3.6. **A.** *Archimisophria discoveryi*, antenna. **B.** Same, tip of endopod with arrows indicating pair of setae that migrated distally from second endopodal segment. **C.** *Boxshallia bulbantennulata*, maxilla. **D.** *A. discoveryi*, praecoxal endites of maxilla.

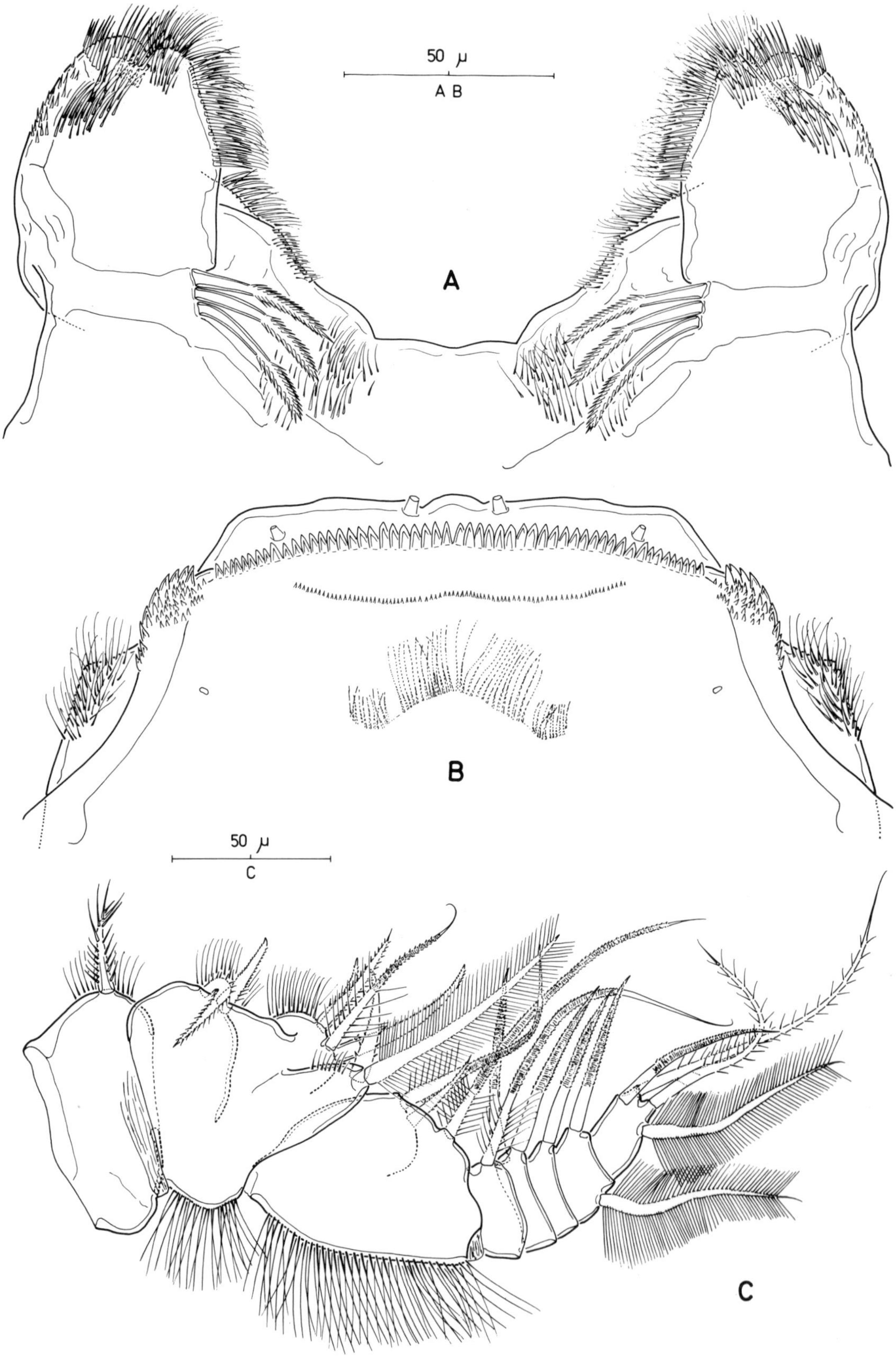

Figure 2.3.7. **A.** *Archimisophria squamosa*, paragnaths. **B.** *A.squamosa*, labrum. **C.** *A.discoveryi*, maxilliped.

Figure 2.3.8. **A.** *Speleophria scottodicarloi*, maxillule. **B.** *S.bivexilla*, maxilliped.

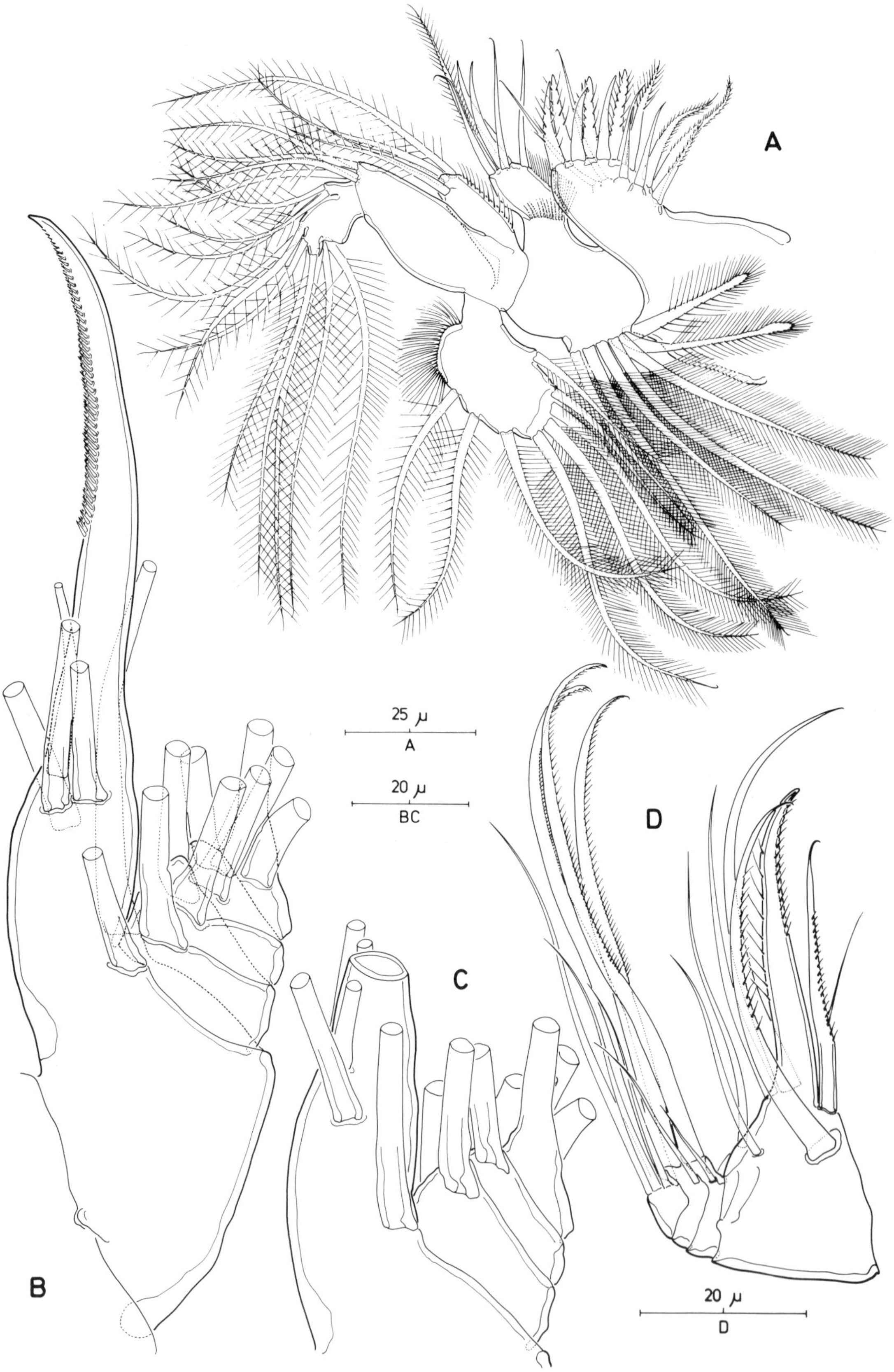

Figure 2.3.9. **A.** *Boxshallia bulbantennulata*, maxillule. **B.** *Archimisophria squamosa*, maxillary allobasis and free endopod. **C.** Same, other side. **D.** *Speleophria bivexilla*, maxillary allobasis and free endopod.

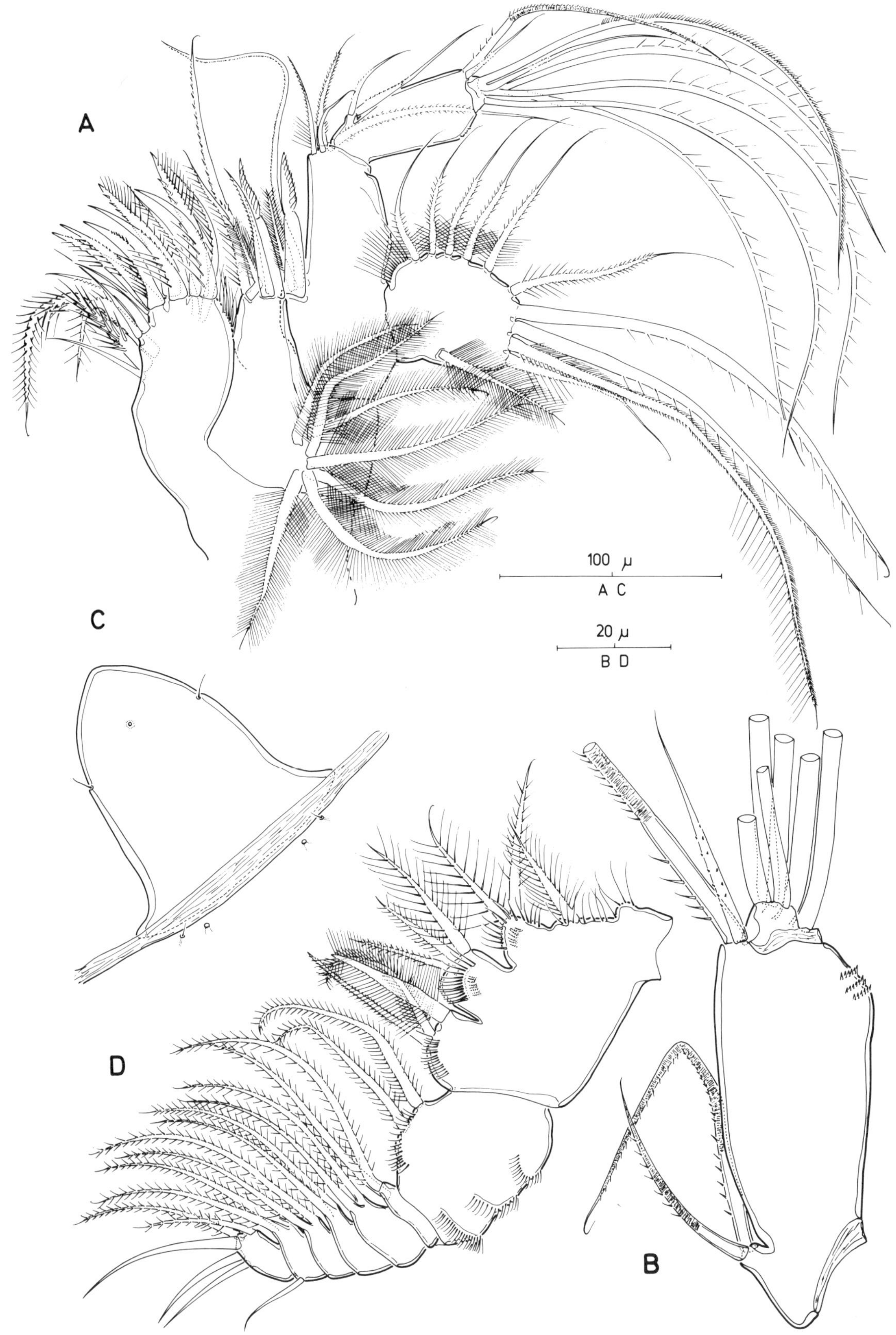

Figure 2.3.10. **A.** *Archimisophria squamosa*, maxillule. **B.** Same, endopod. **C.** *A.discoveryi*, rostrum. **D.** *Boxshallia bulbantennulata*, maxilliped.

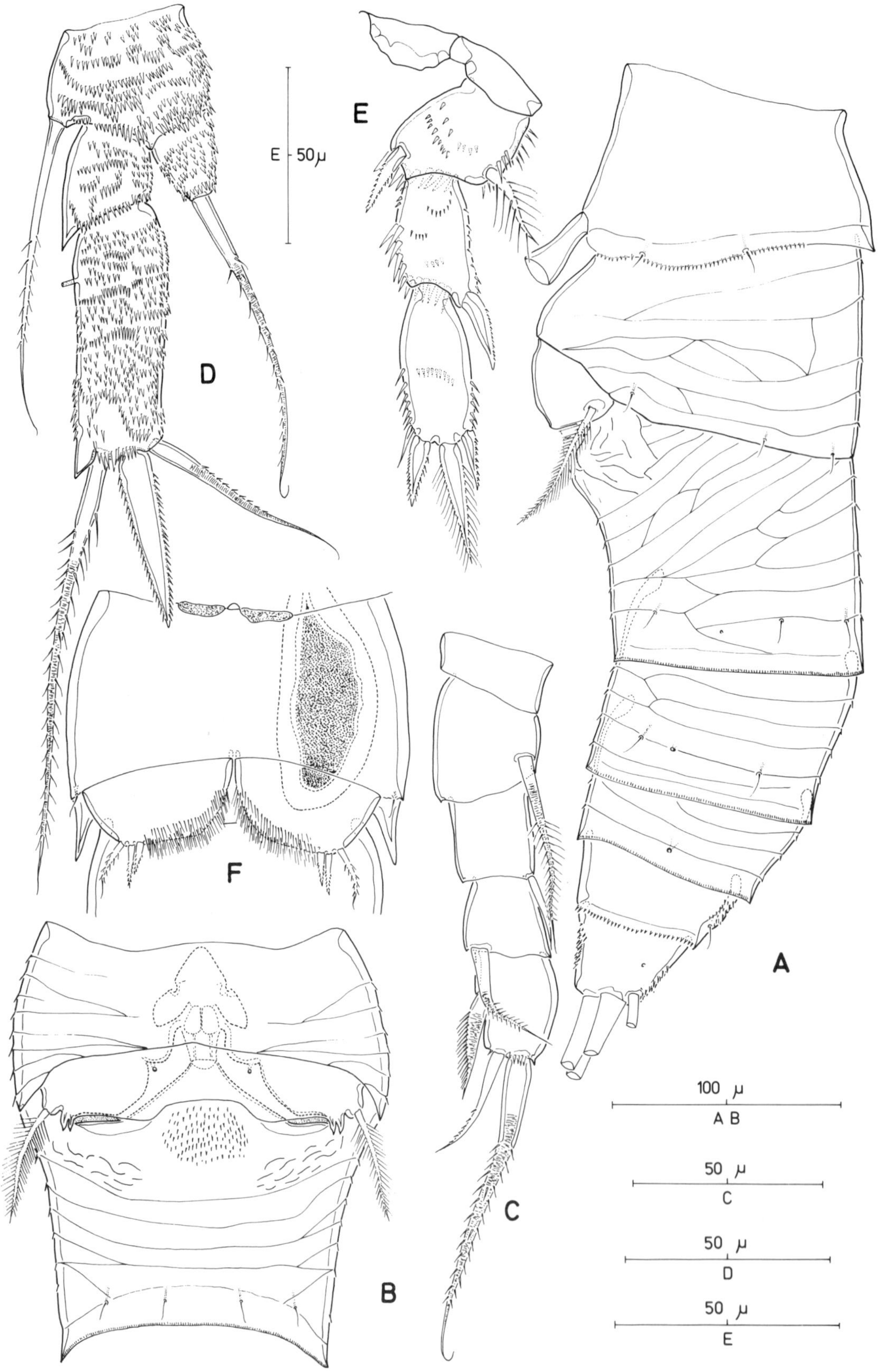

Figure 2.3.11. **A.** *Archimisophria discoveryi*, female urosome, lateral view. **B.** Genital double somite, ventral view. **C.** *A.squamosa*, female fifth leg. **D.** *Misophriopsis dichotoma*, female fifth leg. **E.** *Boxshallia bulbantennulata*, female fifth leg and intercoxal sclerite. **F.** *B.bulbantennulata*, male genital somite and sixth legs.

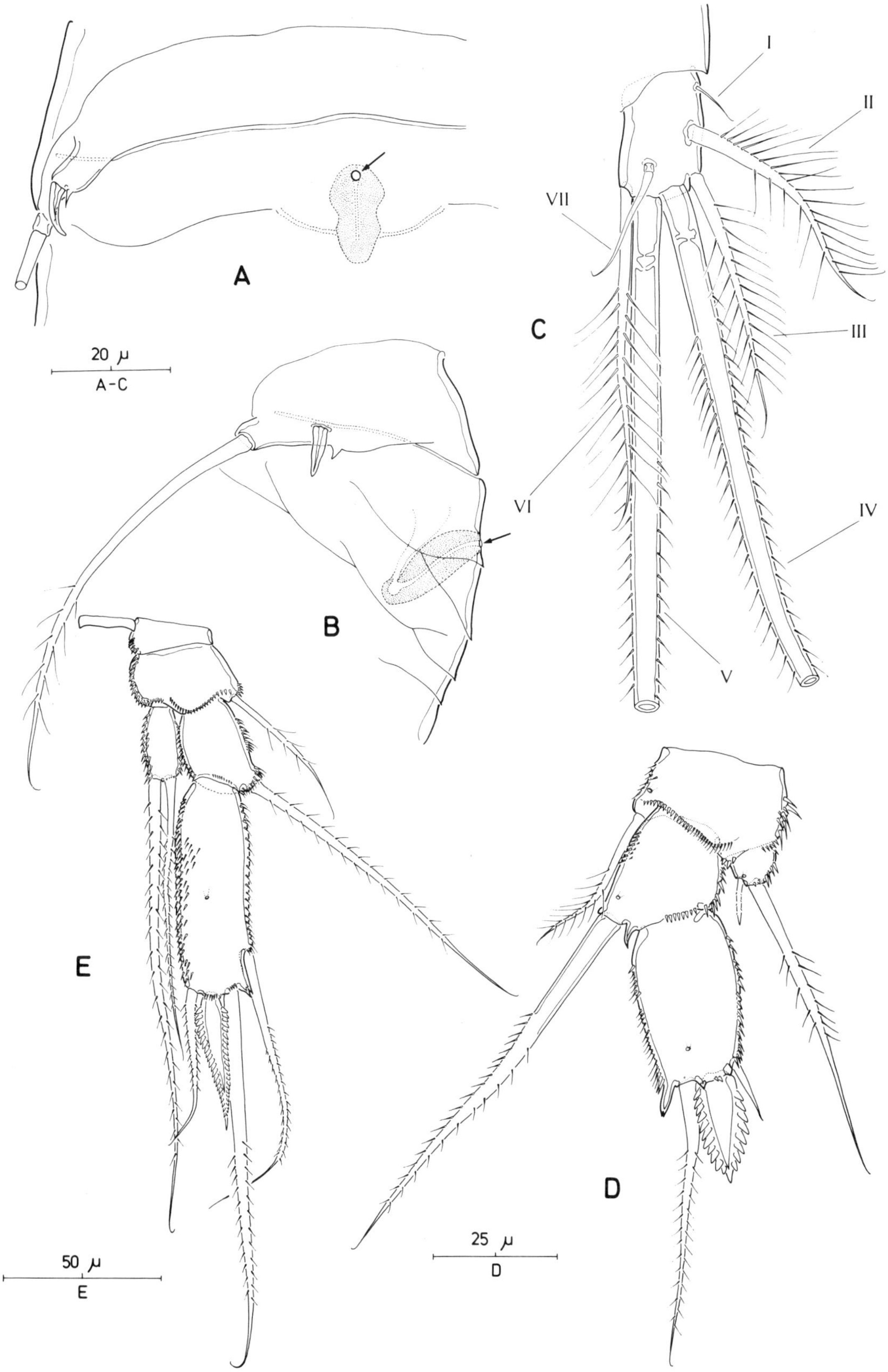

Figure 2.3.12. **A.** *Misophriopsis* n. sp., female genital area, with copulatory pore marked by arrow, ventral view. **B.** Lateral view. **C.** *Speleophria bivexilla*, caudal ramus, dorsal view. **D.** *Misophria pallida*, female fifth leg. **E.** *Misophriopsis* n. sp., female fifth leg.

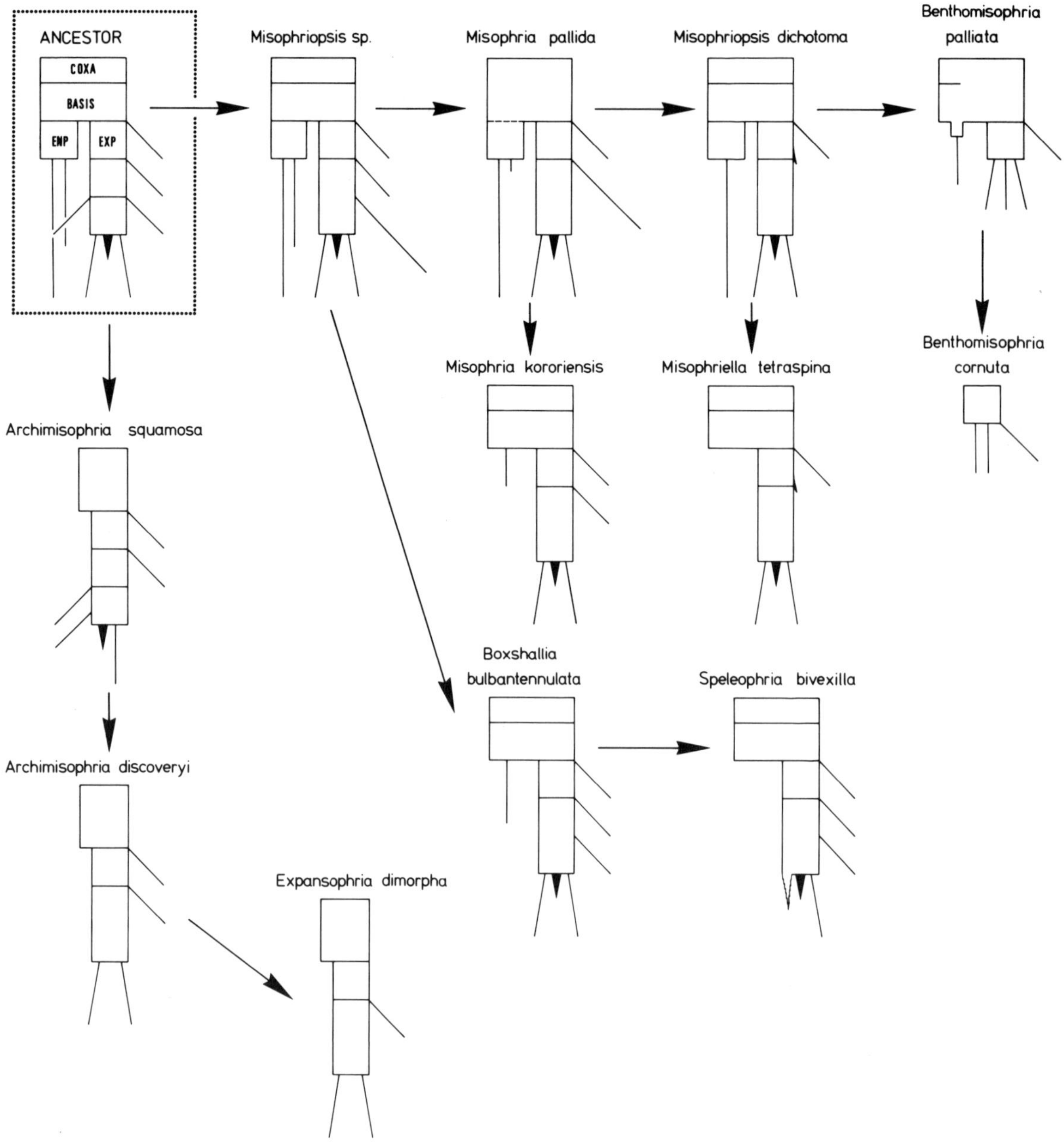

Figure 2.3.13. Schematic comparison of patterns of setation and segmentation of the female fifth leg in the Misophrioida. The arrows indicate possible derivations of setation and segmentation patterns and are not indicative of ancestor-descendant relationships between taxa.

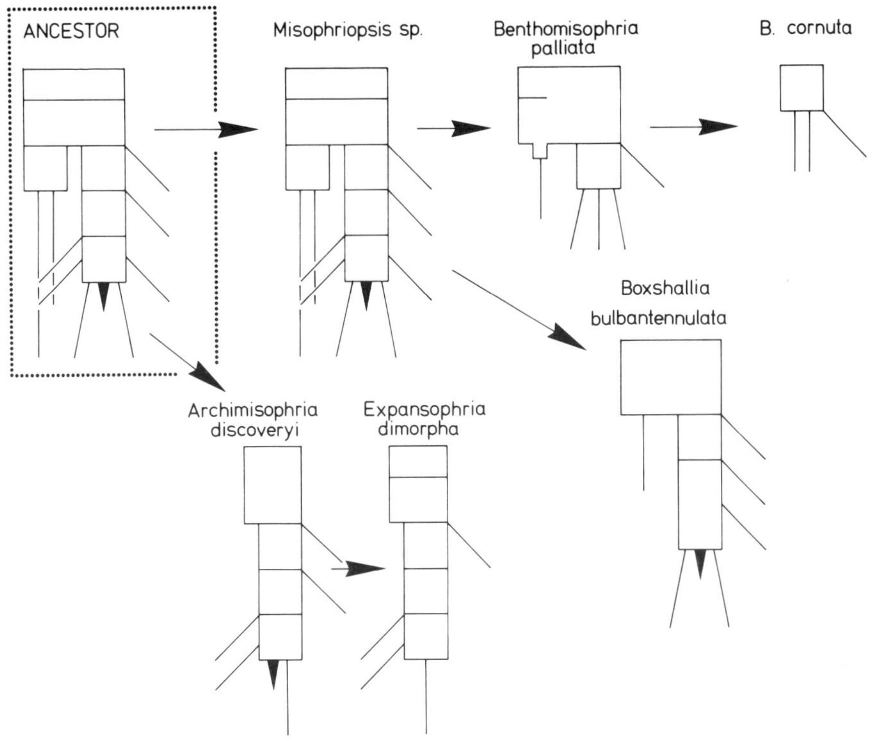

Figure 2.3.14. Schematic comparison of patterns of setation and segmentation of the male fifth leg in the Misophrioida. The arrows indicate possible derivations of setation and segmentation patterns and are not indicative of ancestor-descendant relationships between taxa.

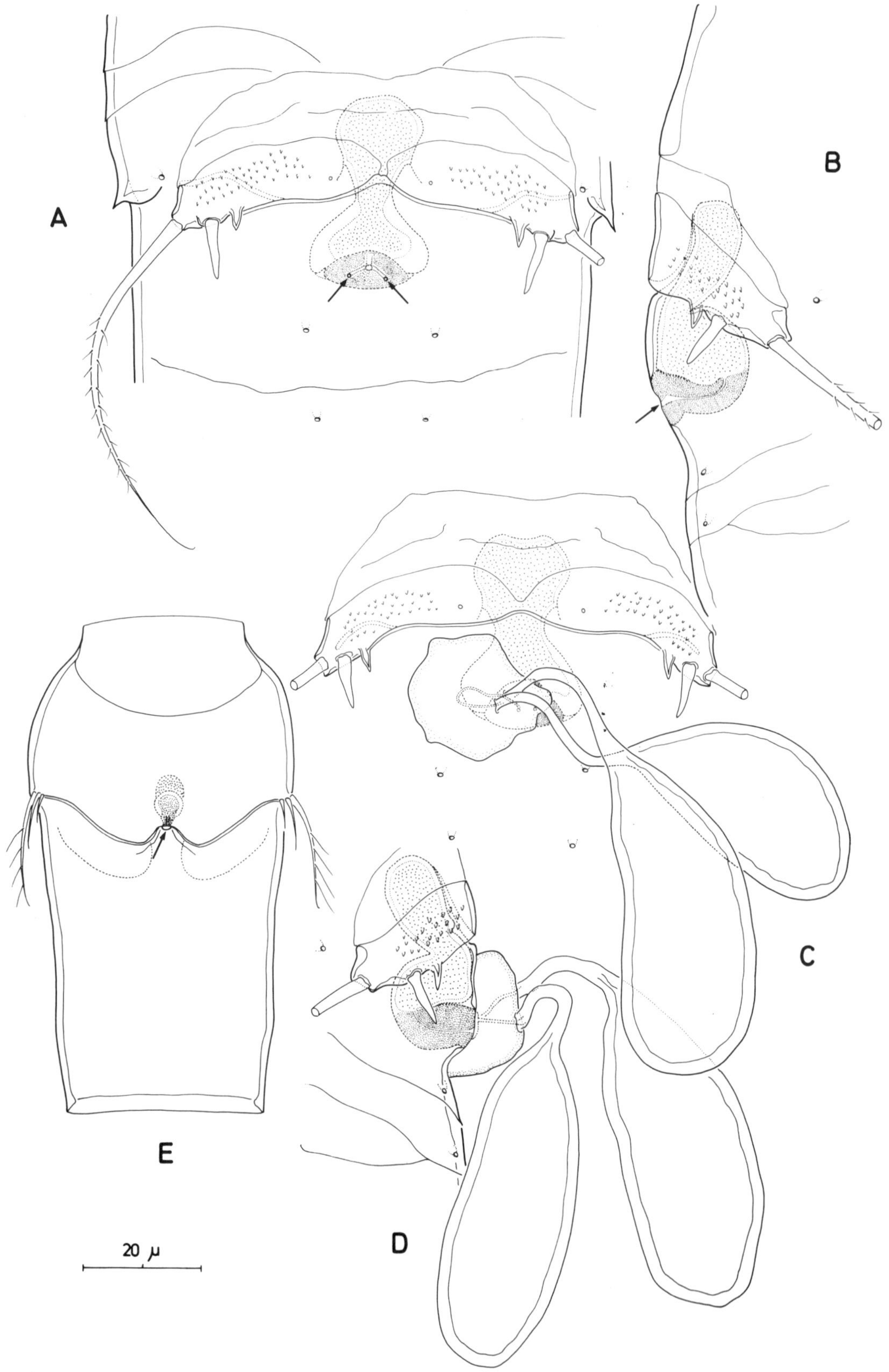

Figure 2.3.15. **A.** *Misophria pallida*, female genital area (with paired copulatory pores arrowed), ventral view. **B.** Lateral view. **C.** Attached spermatophores with their spermatophore tubules leading to copulatory pores, ventral view. **D.** Lateral view. **E.** *Speleophria bivexilla*, female genital double somite (with copulatory pore arrowed).

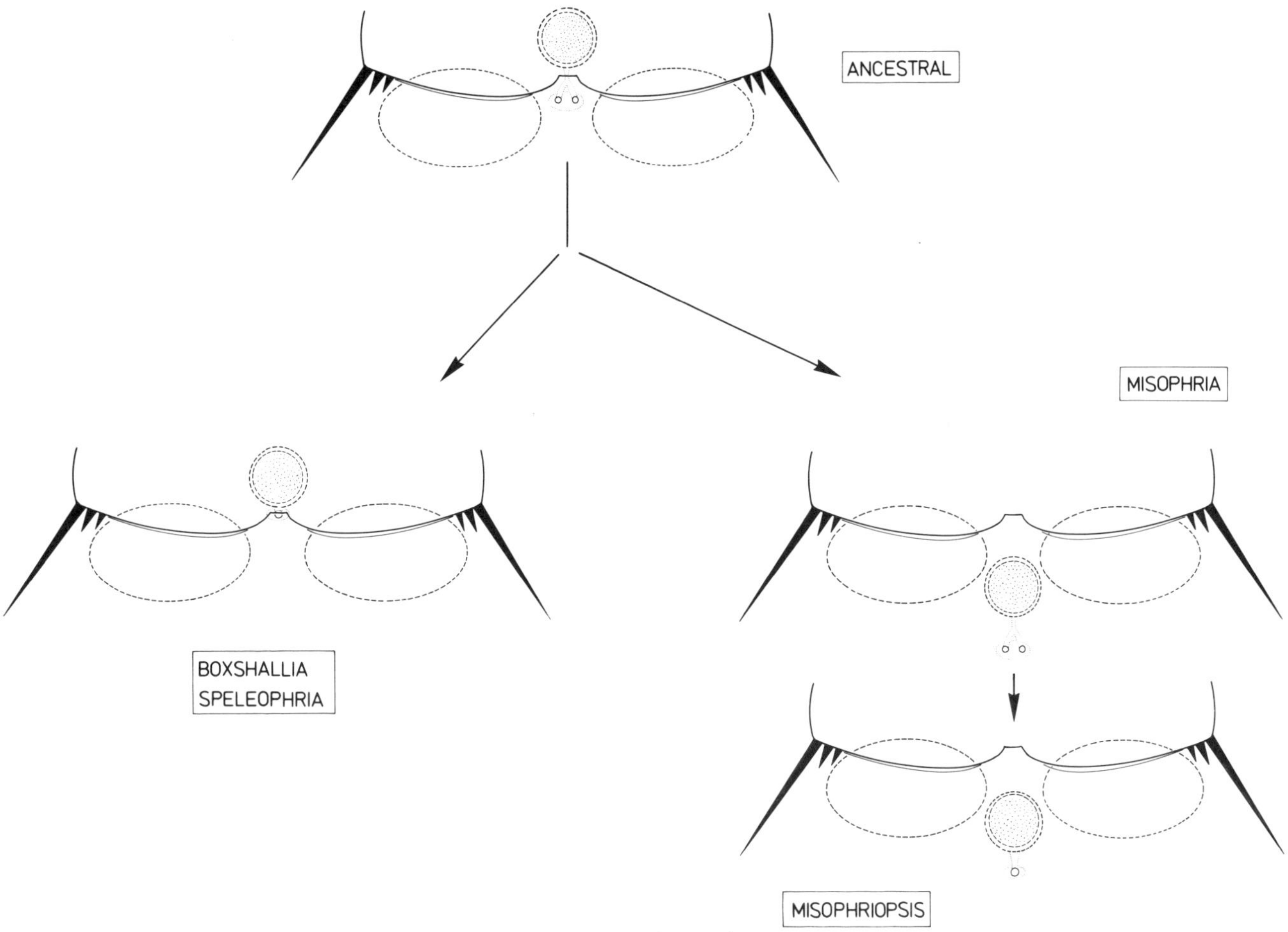

Figure 2.3.16. Schematic diagrams of female genital apertures in Misophrioida, showing fusion of the copulatory pores in *Boxshallia* and *Speleophria*, posterior shift of the copulatory pores in *Misophria*, and fusion plus posterior shift in *Misophriopsis*. The median seminal receptacle is stippled.

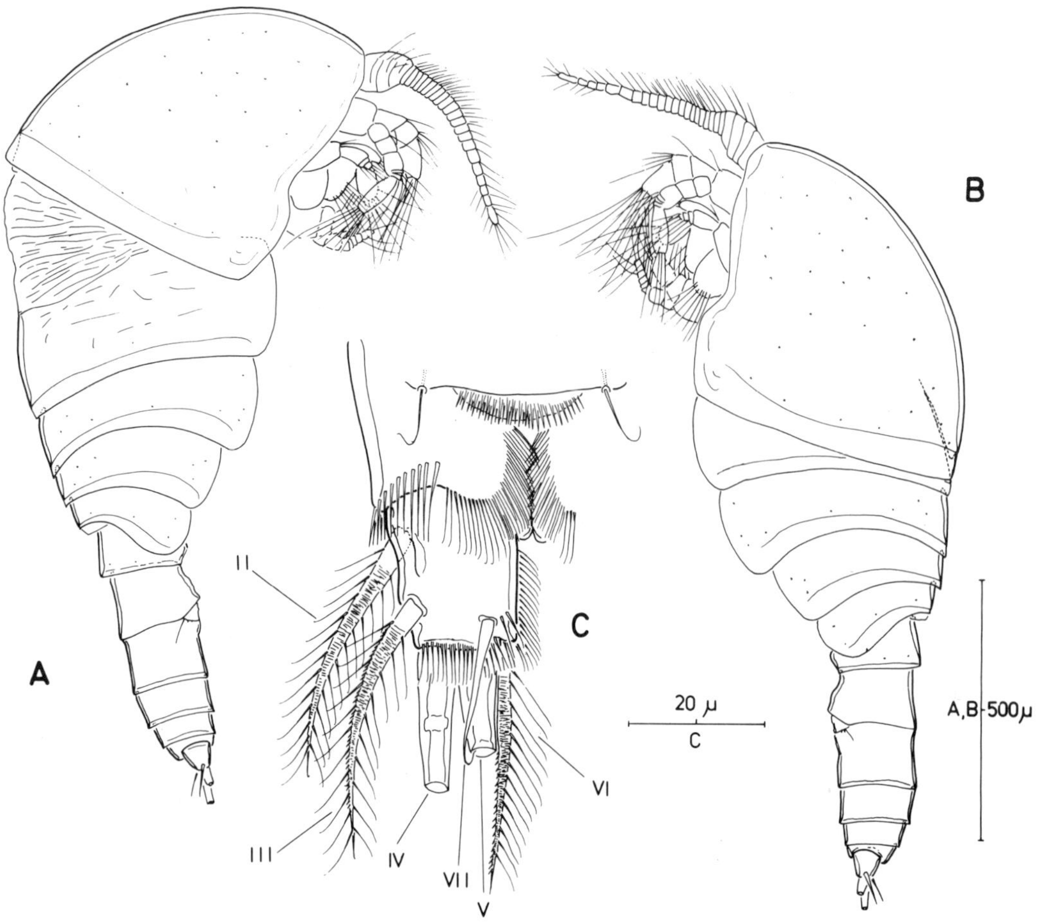

Figure 2.3.17. **A.** *Archimisophria squamosa*, female, lateral view with first pedigerous somite fully exposed. **B.** With first pedigerous somite almost completely concealed beneath posterior margin of cephalic shield. **C.** *Boxshallia bulbantennulata*, caudal ramus and part of anal somite, dorsal view.

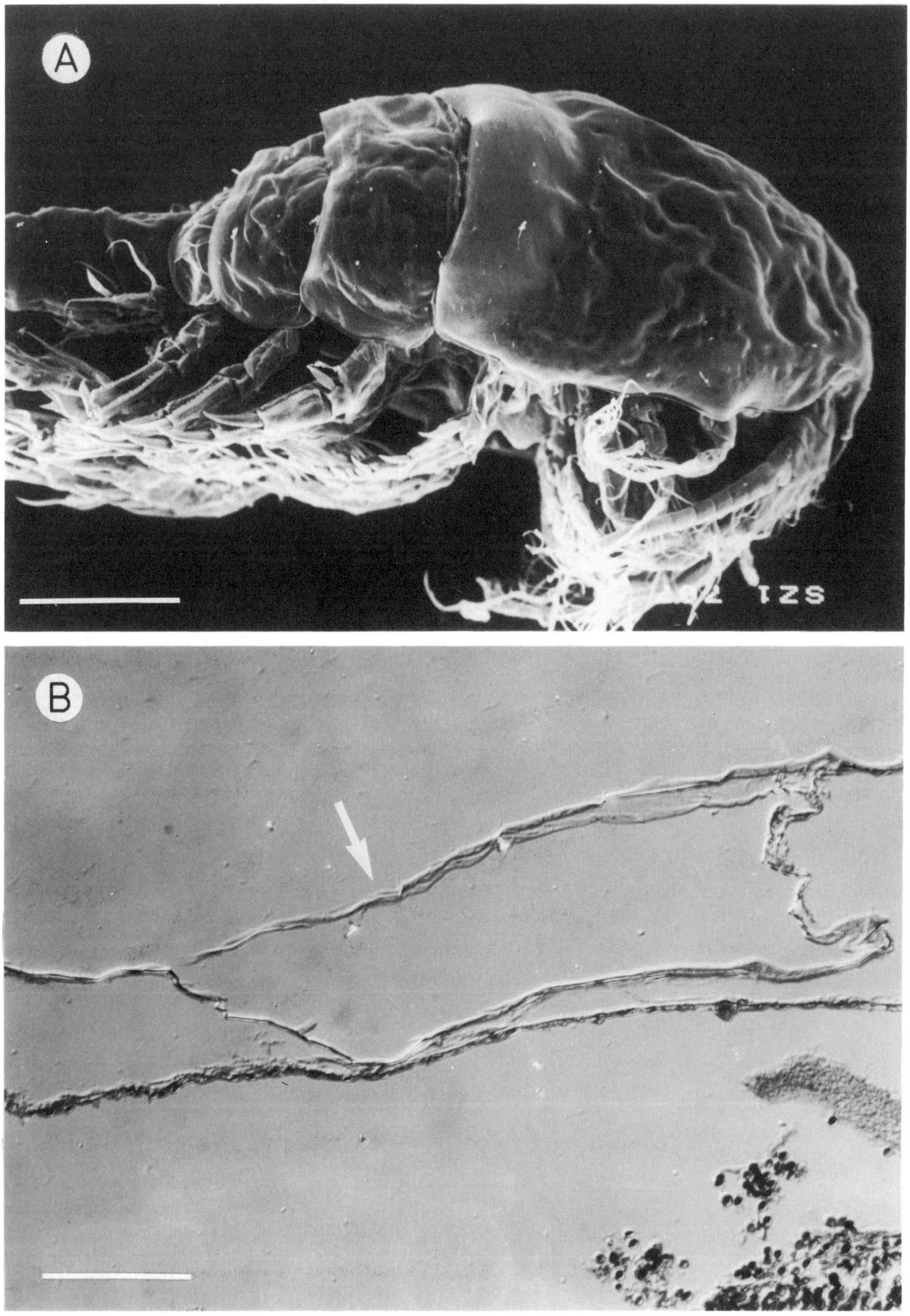

Figure 2.3.18. *Misophria pallida*, female. **A.** Lateral view, showing raised carapace-like extension of rear margin of dorsal cephalic shield. **B.** Median longitudinal section through carapace-like extension (arrowed) and dorsal part of first pedigerous somite. Scale bars A = 300μm, B = 50μm.

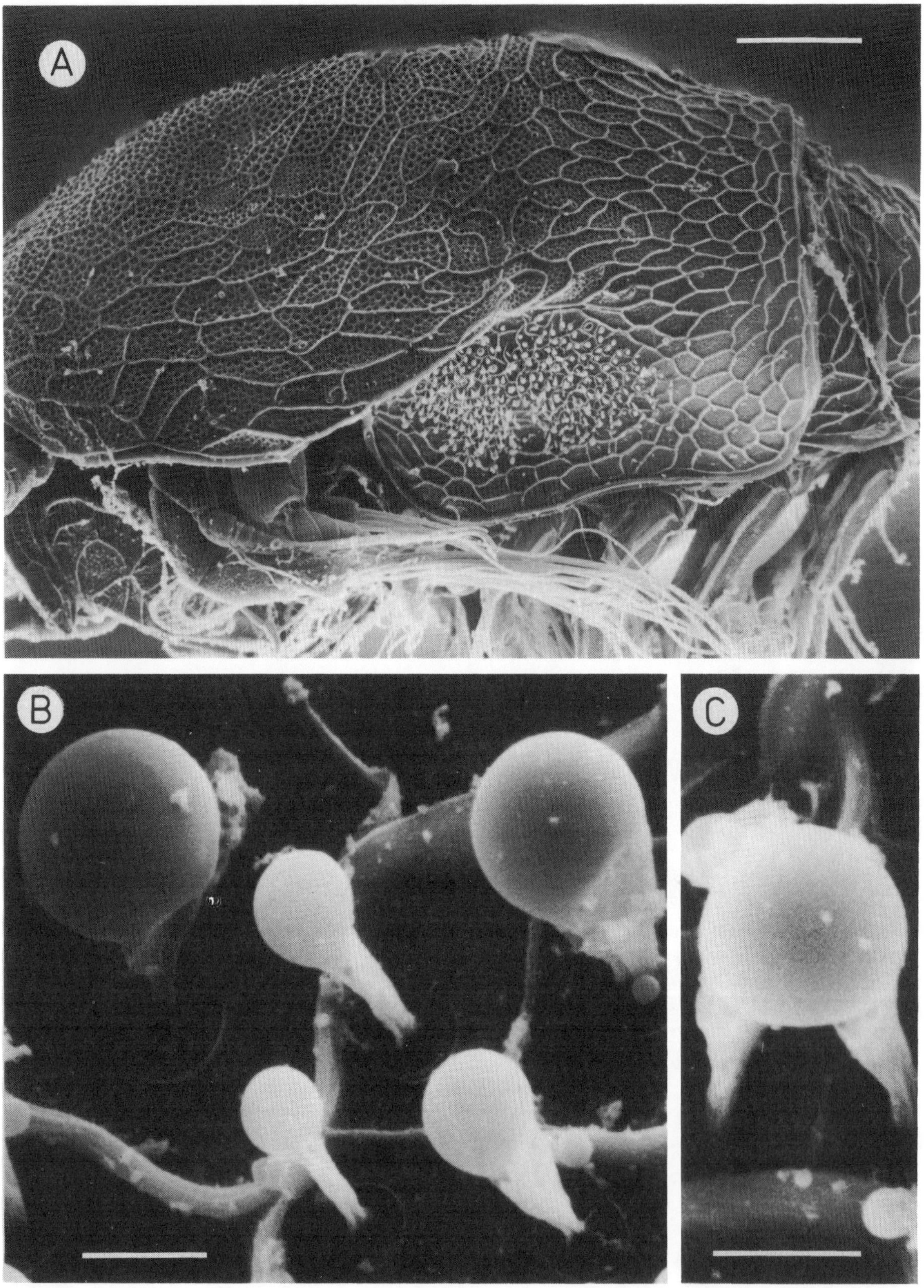

Figure 2.3.19. *Benthomisophria cornuta*. **A.** Lateral view of cephalosome, showing posterior carapace-like extension of dorsal cephalic shield, notched margin of shield, and lateral area of cone organs. **B.** Detail of cone organs. **C.** Large globule of secretion formed by coalescence of apical globules from adjacent cone organs. Scale bars A = 100μm, B-C = 4μm.

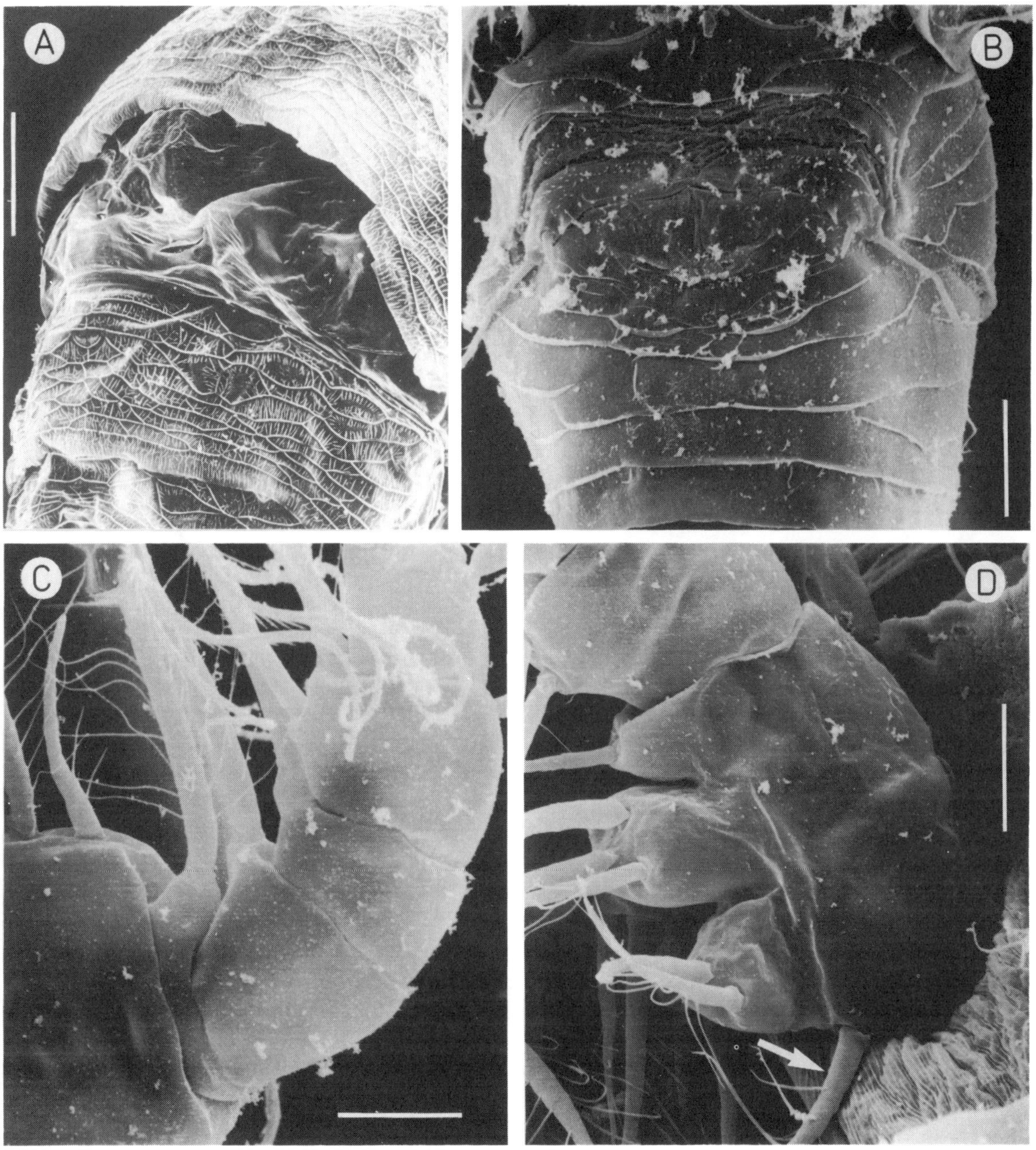

Figure 2.3.20. **A.** *Benthomisophria palliata*, dorsal view of middle of prosome, showing slightly damaged, ornamented, carapace-like extension and the smooth integument of first pedigerous somite beneath. **B.** *Misophria pallida*, ventral view of female genital region. **C.** *Expansophria galapagensis*, maxillipedal endopod. **D.** Maxillipedal syncoxa, with praecoxal seta arrowed. Scale bars A = 100μm, B = 25μm, C = 8μm, D = 10μm.

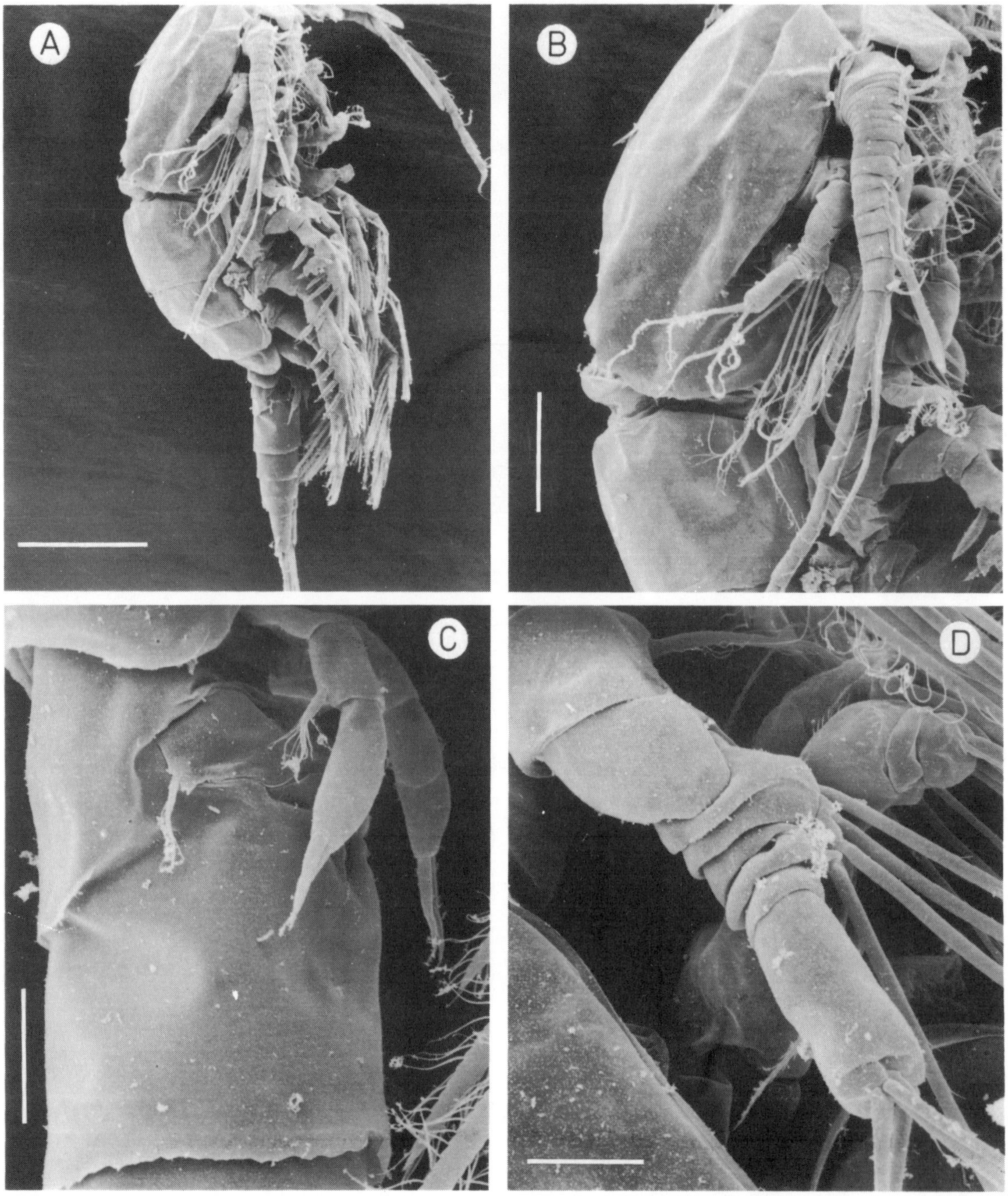

Figure 2.3.21. *Expansophria galapagensis*, female. **A.** Lateral view. **B.** Detail of cephalosome - first pedigerous somite boundary, showing folds of integument that allow distension of prosome. **C.** Fifth legs and genital somite, ventro-lateral view. **D.** Antennary exopod, lateral view. Scale bars A = 150μm, B = 60μm, C = 20μm, D = 15μm.

2.4 HARPACTICOIDA Sars 1903

Harpacticoids are primarily benthic organisms. Those inhabiting the sediment can be categorised as interstitial, burrowing or epibenthic forms (Hicks & Coull, 1983). Interstitial species are small animals with elongate worm-like bodies (figure 2.4.2A) that occupy in the spaces between the sediment particles. Burrowing forms are generally broader forms with a wide anterior end and a tapering, fusiform body. The epibenthic or surface-living forms are typically larger and exhibit a variety of body shapes from worm-like and fusiform to dorsoventrally flattened and compressed. A few harpacticoids have become planktonic (Boxshall, 1979) and often have structural features, such as the elongate caudal rami of *Aegisthus* Giesbrecht, the elongate caudal setae of *Miracia* Dana, or the internal oil droplets of *Microsetella* Brady & Robertson, that slow the rate of sinking. Finally, some harpacticoids are associates of other animals. *Balaenophilus unisetus* Aurivillius occurs only on the baleen plates of baleen whales (Vervoort & Tranter, 1961). Hicks (1988) described a group of new taxa in the subfamily Donsiellinae that are found in the burrows made in submerged wood by the wood-boring isopods of the genus *Limnoria* Leach and by teredinid shipworms. Several canuellid genera, including *Sunaristes* Hesse, *Parasunaristes* Fiers and *Brianola* Monard, and a range of species from other families live in association with hermit crabs, inside their shells (Ho, 1988). Another favoured microhabitat exploited by harpacticoids is the protected gill chamber of decapod crustaceans. Members of the Cancrincolidae inhabit the gill chambers of their hosts which include not only aquatic decapods but also land crabs. Other genera, such as *Myctiricola* Nicholls and *Harrietella* Scott live as external associates on the bodies of crustacean hosts. The group of genera comprising the tisbid subfamily Cholidyinae are all associates of cephalopod molluscs (Avdeev, 1982, 1983, 1986).

Character set of ancestral harpacticoid

Copepoda. Prosome comprising cephalosome and 4 free pedigerous somites; urosome 6-segmented in male, indistinctly 6-segmented in female due to partial fusion of genital and first abdominal somites. Prosome-urosome articulation between fourth and fifth pedigerous somites (podoplean position). Genital apertures paired in both sexes (figures 2.4.25B-D and 2.4.27A-C), located ventrally near anterior border of genital somite in female, at posterior border of genital somite in male. Copulatory pores paired, located at medial edge of ventral genital apertures on female genital somite. Seminal receptacles paired. Rostrum defined at base (figures 2.4.2A-B and 2.4.3). Caudal ramus with 7 setae (figure 2.4.24C-D). Nauplius eye present. Antennules 9-segmented in female (figure 2.4.5A); probable segmental fusion patterns I, II-VIII, IX-XIV, XV-XVII, XVIII-XX, XXI-XXIII, XXIV, XXV, XXVI-XXVIII. Male antennules 14-segmented and bilaterally symmetrical in male (figure 2.4.4), geniculate with geniculation located between ancestral segments XX and XXI. Male segmental fusions III-VIII, IX-XII, XIV-XVI, XIX-XX, XXI-XXII and XXVI-XXVIII. Antenna biramous with 8-segmented exopod and 3-segmented endopod (figure 2.4.7A-B); coxa without seta; basis with 1 inner seta; first to third endopodal segments with 2, 5 and 7 setae respectively; exopodal segments 1 to 7 representing ancestral segments II to VIII, segment 8 representing ancestral segments IX-X; setal formula 1,1,1,1,1,1,1,4. Labrum an undivided muscular lobe (figure 2.4.9A-B). Mandible with large coxal gnathobase and biramous palp (figure 2.4.10); exopod 5-segmented, setal formula 1,1,1,1,2; endopod 2-segmented, setal formula 3,9; basis bearing 4 setae on inner margin. Paragnaths separate, small hirsute lobes (figure 2.4.9C). Maxillule with large praecoxal endite bearing armature of 14 elements; coxa with single endite bearing 6 setae, and vestigial epipodite incorporated into segment, bearing 5 setae; basis with seta on outer margin representing exite (figure 2.4.12A), 2 endites closely set, proximal endite well developed, with 4 setae; distal endite largely incorporated into segment, represented by 4 setae; exopod 1-segmented, with 11 setae; endopod 2-segmented, setal formula (3,2)6. Maxilla 7-segmented (figures 2.4.13-14); praecoxa and coxa each with 2 endites; endite formula 6,3,3,3; basis with well developed endite bearing a claw and 3 setae, outer coxal seta absent; free endopod 4-segmented, setal formula 3,2,2,4. Maxilliped indistinctly 5-segmented (figures 2.4.15-16), comprising praecoxa with 1 endite, coxa with 3 endites, basis and 2-segmented endopod; syncoxal formula 1,2,4,3; basis with 2 setae; endopod setal formula 5+1,5. Swimming legs 1-4 biramous with 3-segmented rami; members of leg pairs joined by intercoxal sclerite; inner coxal seta (figure

2.4.17A-B) and outer seta on basis present, inner seta on basis of first leg only; first exopodal segment with 1 outer spine. Spine and seta formula for legs 1 to 4:

	coxa	basis	exopod segment	endopod segment
			1 2 3	1 2 3
leg 1	0 – 1	1 – I	I – 1; I – 1; III,I,3	0 – 1; 0 – 1; 1,2,2
leg 2	0 – 1	1 – 0	I – 1; I – 1; III,I,3	0 – 1; 0 – 2; 1,2,3
leg 3	0 – 1	1 – 0	I – 1; I – 1; III,I,4	0 – 1; 0 – 2; 1,2,3
leg 4	0 – 1	1 – 0	I – 1; I – 1; III,I,4	0 – 1; 0 – 2; 1,2,2

Fifth legs biramous (figures 2.4.20-21); praecoxa absent; coxae joined by intercoxal sclerite; inner coxal seta absent; primitively sexually dimorphic with exopod 3-segmented and bearing up to 8 setae in male, 1-segmented with up to 8 setae in female; endopod 1-segmented with a maximum of 6 setae in the female and 4 in the male. Sixth legs represented by opercular plates closing off genital openings. Eggs contained within paired egg sacs (figure 2.4.2A,C).

Remarks

The diagnosis is based on the study of a wide range of generalised and specialised families including the Canuellidae, Longipediidae, Neobradyidae, Cerviniidae, and Aegisthidae. The most plesiomorphic states for most mouthparts are exhibited by members of the Canuellidae and Longipediidae.

First Pedigerous Somite: The only harpacticoids that retain a free first pedigerous somite are the Canuellidae, Chappuisiidae, Phyllognathopodidae, Cerviniidae, Rotundiclipeidae, Aegisthidae and probably some members of the Latiremidae (Huys & Kunz, 1988). Petkovski's (1977) report of the free first pedigerous somite in *Cubanocleta noodti* Petkovski is erroneous (Huys, 1990b). In other harpacticoids the first pedigerous somite is incorporated into the cephalothorax (figures 2.4.31A and 2.4.32A).

Caudal Rami: The new nomenclatural system for the setation elements of caudal rami was established by Huys (1988c) using the harpacticoid *Caligopsyllus* Kunz. The 7 elements on the caudal rami of *Ambunguipes rufocincta* (Brady) are all identified by their Roman numerals in figure 2.4.24C-D. Boxshall (1979) reported 9 elements on the caudal rami of *Bathyidia remota* Farran and two closely related genera. Reexamination of *B.remota* (figure 3.12.1B-C) revealed the basic 7 elements plus several conspicuous tube pores located along the distal margin. These tube pores are unusually large and are branched. Lang (1948a) reported additional armature on the caudal rami of *Canuella perplexa* Scott & Scott but only the basic 7 elements are present (figure 3.12.1D).

Female Genital System: The great majority of harpacticoids, including the plesiomorphic families Canuellidae and Longipediidae are characterised by the presence of a genital double somite in the female, formed by fusion of the genital and first abdominal somites. Only some Latiremidae, an as yet undescribed member of the Tetragonicipitidae, and the cancrincolid *Abscondicola* Fiers possess unfused genital and first abdominal somites. Fiers (1990) analysed the ontogeny of the latter genus and suggested that lack of a double somite was secondary in this case, due to heterochrony. Fusion of the genital and first abdominal somites typically takes place at the moult from fifth copepodid to adult and Fiers found evidence in the form of the sixth legs that a delay in fusion of these somites had occurred. It is possible that a similar explanation might apply to the latiremids and tetragonicipitid, in which case the presence of a genital double somite in the female is the ancestral state of the Harpacticoida.

The arrangement of the female genital apertures is variable within the Harpacticoida. The most primitive state is found in the canuellid genera related to *Canuellina* Gurney. On each side the genital aperture comprises a gonopore (the oviduct opening) and a copulatory pore covered by an operculum derived from the sixth legs. Each copulatory pore (arrowed in figures 2.4.24B,D-E and 2.4.25A-D) leads via a copulatory duct into a seminal receptacle (stippled in figures 2.4.24B-E and 2.4.25A-D). This state is shown in *Canuellina insignis* Gurney, except that the paired seminal receptacles are fused in the midline to form a median bilobed receptacle (figure 2.4.25B). In

Sunaristes dardani Humes & Ho the copulatory pores have migrated medially, each being covered by a spinous process that might possibly represent one of the 3 armature elements of the sixth legs (figure 2.4.25C). In *Canuella* Scott & Scott the copulatory pores have undergone posterior migration. A subsurface, sigmoid copulatory duct connects each pore (arrowed in figure 2.4.25D) with its seminal receptacle. Each pore is covered by a small flap (figure 2.4.29E). The lateral margins of these flaps are free (figure 2.4.30B) but they do not represent a direct connection with the slit-like genital aperture which does not extend medial to the level at which the copulatory duct enters the seminal receptacle. Paired spermatophores are placed over the copulatory pores during copulation (figure 2.4.29A-D) and discharge into the seminal receptacle via the copulatory pores. The cerviniid and aegisthid condition, in which a single copulatory pore is present just posterior to the slit formed by fusion of the genital apertures can be derived from the *Canuellina* condition by medial migration and fusion.

Most harpacticoid families have a single, copulatory pore positioned in the ventral midline posterior to the level of the genital apertures (figure 2.4.31B). This may well have arisen independently a number of times within the Harpacticoida. In *Thompsonula curticauda* Wilson there is no surface connection between the copulatory pore (arrowed) and the genital apertures (figure 2.4.24B). In *Ambunguipes* Huys there are surface folds in the integument but no direct connection between the pore and the genital apertures. The pore is covered by novel structures, the epicopulatory plate and bulb (figure 2.4.24C-D), but is clearly visible if the epicopulatory bulb is removed (figure 2.4.30C-E). In *Laophontopsis* Sars (figure 2.4.24E) the genital apertures have fused medially to form a transverse genital slit anterior to the copulatory pore (arrowed). Finally, in *Longipedia* Claus the genital apparatus is condensed into a compact median genital field (figures 2.4.25A and 2.4.28A-C). A single copulatory pore is present (small arrow) immediately posterior to a common genital aperture (large arrow).

Male Antennule: The largest numbers of antennulary segments are found in *Hamondia* Huys and *Ambunguipes rufocincta* for males (Huys, 1990a). Prior to the discovery of the 14 segments in the antennules of *Hamondia* and *Ambunguipes* the highest number recorded for males was 10 (Lang, 1948a). It is now possible to identify the homology of the antennulary segments in harpacticoids by reference to the antennules of male *Hamondia* (figure 2.4.4A) and *Ambunguipes* (figure 2.4.4B-C). The armature of these two antennules is used to construct figure 3.4.2 and allows comparison with the ancestral copepod antennule. *Hamondia* is the Rosetta stone of harpacticoid antennules, retaining sufficient armature elements to enable to precise recognition of the segments: the first (I) and second (II) segments are single segments, the third with its 12 setae represents 6 fused segments (III-VIII), the fourth with 8 setae and 1 aesthetasc represents 4 segments (IX-XII), the fifth (XIII) is a single segment, the sixth with 6 setae and 1 aesthetasc is a triple segment (XIV-XVI), the seventh (XVII) and eighth (XVIII) are single, the ninth with its 3 setae is a double (XIX-XX), the tenth is also a double with 3 setae (XXI-XXII), the eleventh (XXIII) is a single, the twelfth and thirteenth both have an anterior and a posterior margin seta and are single (XXIV and XXV respectively), and the fourteenth (apical) segment has 8 setae (XXVI-XXVIII). Confidence in the accuracy of these homologies is provided by the positioning of the geniculation at the articulation between segments XX and XXI, as in other podoplean and calanoid copepods. This is further reinforced by the presence of posterior margin setae on segments XXIV and XXV, as in the ancestral condition.

Ambunguipes (figure 2.4.4B) shows the same segmentation as *Hamondia* but the correspondence of the setal counts is not quite so precise due to further loss of elements (Huys, 1990a). The sixth segment, for example, carries only 5 true setae and 1 aesthetasc, rather than the 6 setae of *Hamondia*. However, the situation is complicated by the presence on this segment of 14 hair-like, setoid ornamentation elements (figure 2.4.4C). Further fusions between segments have taken place in *Geeopsis* Huys but the segmental homologies are still identifiable in the male (figure 2.4.5B-C).

Lang (1948a) defined 3 different types of male antennules in the Harpacticoida. These are compared in figure 2.4.6A-C. The least modified type is haplocer, as found in *Neobradya pectinifera* Scott (figure 2.4.6A), in which the middle segments of the antennule are only slightly modified and there are at least 2 segments distal to the geniculation. The intermediate type is subchirocer, as found in *Paramesochra mielkei* Huys (figure 2.4.6B), in which the middle segments are markedly swollen and there are 2 segments distal to the geniculation. The most derived type is chirocer, as found in *Caligopsyllus primus* Kunz (figure 2.4.6C) in which the segment proximal to the geniculation is very thick-walled and swollen, and there is only a single segment distal to the geniculation. Dahms (1988) found no correlation between type of antennule and taxonomic affinities. Within a single genus closely related species exhibiting either chirocer or subchirocer antennules can be found. By tracing development through the copepodid stages, Dahms also showed that chirocer antennules have originated several times independently within the Harpacticoida.

Female Antennule: The largest number of antennule segments in a female harpacticoid is 9. This number occurs widely in the oligoarthran families and the case of *Neobradya pectinifera* is typical (Huys, 1987a). The homology of the antennulary segments of female *Geeopsis* (figure 2.4.5A) can only be identified precisely for the distalmost segments. The sixth segment with its 4 setae representing fused segments XXI-XXIII, the seventh and eighth with 1 anterior and 1 posterior seta each represent ancestral segments XXIV and XXV respectively, and the apical segment represents XXVI-XXVIII. The homologies of the proximal segments are not obvious because of loss of armature elements. However, comparison of the 9-segmented condition of the antennules of female oligoarthrans with the 4-segmented antennules of female polyarthrans, such as *Sunaristes dardani*, allows the homologies of these proximal segments to be established with reasonable certainty. The maximum armature of the antennules of female harpacticoids are given in table 2. All the setation counts for the Oligoarthra are derived from female *Hamondia* except segment 2 (*Tisbe trisetosa* Volkmann) and segment 3 (*Alteutha interrupta* (Goodsir)).

Table 2. Antennulary segments, armature and segmental homologies in female harpacticoids

	Oligoarthra			Polyarthra	
Seg. No.	Armature	Homology	Seg. No.	Armature	Homology
1	1	I	1	3	I
2	13	II–VIII			
3	11	IX–XIV	2	27 + 2ae	II–XVII
4	6 + ae	XV–XVII			
5	3	XVIII–XX	3	5	XVIII–XX
6	4	XXI–XXIII			
7	2	XXIV			
8	2	XXV	4	15 + ae	XXI–XXVIII
9	7 + ae	XXVI–XXVIII			

The aesthetasc on compound segment 4 in oligoarthrans is probably derived from ancestral segment XVI, as it is located just subterminally. The uncertain homology for the oligoarthrans in Table 2 is segment 5 which we believe represents 3 fused ancestral segments but which retains only 3 setae providing evidence of a double origin. The evidence for the triple nature of segment 5 in oligoarthrans comes from comparison with polyarthran antennules, even though they are 4-segmented at most. The fourth segment of polyarthrans carries 15 setae, the same number as the sixth to ninth segments inclusive of oligoarthrans. It presumably represents fused segments XXI to XXVIII. Polyarthran segment 2 bears 1 subterminal aesthetasc which is homologous with that of male harpacticoids and is derived from segment XVI. The other aesthetasc is located midway along the compound segment and is probably derived from ancestral segment XI since there are 12 setae distal to it on the segment (representing 6 segments, i.e. XII-XVII). We therefore postulate that segment 2 of polyarthrans is homologous with fused segments 2 to 4 of oligoarthrans. Polyarthran segment 3 is thus homologous with oligoarthran segment 5 and, since it bears 5 setae, provides the missing evidence of this segment's triple origin (XVIII-XX). The only remaining anomaly is the presence of 3 setae on the first antennulary segment of polyarthrans. It is probable that this represents the plesiomorphic neocopepodan condition, also retained in some representatives of the Calanoida (figure 2.2.7B). Supporting evidence for this assumption can be found in the ontogenetic studies of Dahms (1989a) who found that 3 setae were present on the first antennulary segment of the first copepodids of *Tisbe gracilis* (Scott) and *Ectinosoma melaniceps* Boeck which, in the adult, possess a single seta only on this segment.

Antenna: The two polyarthran families, Canuellidae and Longipediidae, are the only harpacticoids in which a 3-segmented antennary endopod and an 8-segmented exopod are retained. The coxa is unarmed in all harpacticoids and the basis bears at most 1 seta (figure 2.4.8A). In both *Canuella* (figures 2.4.7B and 2.4.32B) and *Longipedia* (figure 2.4.7A) the setal formula of the exopod is 1,1,1,1,1,1,1,4 indicating that the apical segment is derived by fusion of the ninth and tenth ancestral segments. The maximum number of segments found in other harpacticoids is 4, as in *Neobradya pectinifera* (figure 2.4.8A). Further reductions occur within the order to a 3-segmented (figure 2.4.8B-C), 2-segmented and 1-segmented state (figure 2.4.9A). The exopod is absent in most Ancorabolidae and the entire antenna is absent in the deep-sea cerviniid *Tonpostratiotes* Itô.

The 3-segmented antennary endopod of *Longipedia* (figure 2.4.7A) bears the maximum setation, with a 2,5,7 setal formula. In *Canuella* (figure 2.4.7B) there is a 1,5,7 formula. In the majority of harpacticoids the second and third endopodal segments are fused to form a double segment (figure 2.4.8A-B) and setation is further reduced. However, the 7 apical setae are commonly retained and 2 of these are fused basally. These 2 fused setae (arrowed in figure 2.4.8A) represent the original armature elements of the fourth endopodal segment, which is fully incorporated into the third in all podopleans. The 2 serrated hyaline frills on the outer margin of the endopod near its tip are derived from the third and fourth segments (figure 2.4.8B-C). Other modifications to the antenna within the Harpacticoida include the fusion of the first endopodal segment to the basis, to form an allobasis, as in *Hamondia* (figure 2.4.8C) and *Leptastacus* Scott (figure 2.4.9A).

Mandible: The 2-segmented mandibular endopod found in the Canuellidae (figure 2.4.10A) and Longipediidae is treated as the plesiomorphic state despite the reports of a 3-segmented endopod in the Paramesochridae (Lang, 1948a). In *Paramesochra* Scott and *Caligopsyllus* (figure 2.4.11C) the second segment is unarmed and the apparent third segment has apical armature elements that all lack a proximal articulation (Huys, 1988c). The third segment is here interpreted as the confluent bases (arrowed in figure 2.4.11C) of the apical armature elements rather than a true segment. The maximum setation of the endopod is 3,9. *Sunaristes dardani* retains 3 setae on the first segment but has only 8 on the second. *Scottolana antillensis* Fiers and *S.dissimilis* Fiers have 9 setae on the distal segment (Fiers, 1982, 1984). The mandibular exopod of the ancestral harpacticoid was 5-segmented although in extant harpacticoids a maximum of 4 segments is found. In cerviniids and, for example, *Neobradya* Scott (figure 2.4.10D), the armature formula is 2,1,1,2 indicating that it is derived from the ancestral 5-segmented condition by fusion of the two proximal segments, each of which primitively bears a single seta. However, in the canuellid *Sunaristes dardani* (figure 2.4.10A) the 4-segmented exopod has a 1,1,1,3 formula indicating that the ramus is derived by fusion of the 2 distal segments. The exopod is unsegmented in genera such as *Thompsonula* Scott (figure 2.4.10B) and *Caligopsyllus* (figure 2.4.11C) although the ancestral total of 6 setae is retained in the former. *Thompsonula hyaenae* Thompson possesses 4 setae on the medial margin of the basis (figure 2.4.10B). In some forms the mandible is highly specialised. *Rotundiclipeus canariensis* Huys, for example, has an elongate, stylet-like gnathobase and a 2-segmented palp (figure 2.4.10C), the proximal segment of which represents the basis.

Maxillule: No podopleans retain a discrete coxal epipodite on the maxillule. In harpacticoids it is represented by a maximum of 5 setae on the outer surface of the coxa, as found in *Longipedia* (figure 2.4.12A). The articulating segment bearing 2 setae in *Sacodiscus* Wilson (figure 2.4.11B) and *Scutellidium* Claus referred to by Lang (1948a, 1965) as the epipodite, is here reinterpreted as the exopod. *Longipedia* is the only harpacticoid in which a seta is present on the outer margin of the maxillulary basis (figure 2.4.12A) (Itô, 1980; Fig. 7). The maximum armature found on the praecoxal arthrite is 14 elements, as in *Longipedia* (figure 2.4.12B). The coxal endite bears a maximum of 6 setae, as in *Sunaristes dardani* (figure 2.4.11A). Both of the basal endites have a maximum of 4 setae, as found in the canuellids *Sunaristes dardani* and *Ellucana longicauda* (Sewell) (figure 2.4.12C). The endopod is at most 2-segmented, with the proximal segment representing the fused first and second segments. The third ancestral segment is distinct in the canuellids and longipediids but only the former retain the maximum setation of (3,2)6 (figures 2.4.11A and 2.4.12C). The maximum setation of the maxillulary exopod is 11 setae, as found in *Ellucana longicauda* (figure 2.4.12C).

Maxilla: A separate praecoxa and coxa in the maxilla are retained in *Longipedia minor* Scott & Scott (figure 2.4.13A-B) and *Canuella perplexa* (figure 2.4.13C-D), but in both of these genera the number of free endopodal segments is reduced by fusion. In *Tachidiopsis cyclopoides* Sars (figure 2.4.14B-C) the basis is free and not fused to the endopod but the endopod is only 3-segmented due to fusion of the first and second segments to form a double segment bearing 5 setae (3 setae originating on the first endopodal segment and 2 from the second). The 2 distal segments bear 2 and 4 setae. The ancestral setal formula of the maxillary endopod is 3,2,2,4. The basis of *T.cyclopoides* bears 4 elements, 1 of which forms the claw. In *Neobradya pectinifera* all 4 basal elements are still discrete from the segment but the precursor of the claw (arrowed in figure 2.4.14A) is partly fused. In *N.pectinifera* the free endopod is 3-segmented as the first endopodal segment is fully incorporated into the basis, forming the maxillary allobasis. In the great majority of all harpacticoids the first endopodal segment is fused with the basis and there are often further fusions between other endopodal segments, as in *Longipedia* and *Canuella*. Despite the segmental fusions both *Longipedia* and *Canuella* retain the original total of 15 armature elements on the basis and endopod.

Maxilliped: The maxilliped in some Canuellidae and in *Longipedia* retains a single proximal seta representing the praecoxal endite (arrowed in figure 2.4.16A). The praecoxal segment itself is partly defined in genera such as *Neobradya* (figure 2.4.15C) and *Tachidiopsis* Sars (figure 2.4.15D) but in both of these genera the praecoxal enditic seta is absent. The endites of the coxa are best defined in the syncoxa of *Canuella* (figure 2.4.15A) and *Longipedia* (figure 2.4.16A) which have a formula of 1,2,4,3. The syncoxal setation is reduced in the majority of harpacticoids. The basis bears a maximum of 2 setae in all harpacticoids (figures 2.4.15A-E and 2.4.16A-B). The endopod is at most 2-segmented and bears a total of 11 setae in the Canuellidae and Longipediidae. The presence of a weak suture in some species of *Sunaristes* (figure 2.4.15E) indicates that the ancestral endopod setal formula is 5+1,5. The outer seta on the first segment is an important reference point as this is presumably homologous with the outer seta on the fifth endopodal segment of misophrioids. The second segment is therefore homologous with the sixth segment of misophrioids. The proximal endopodal segment of harpacticoids therefore represents at least the fused second to fifth segments of the ancestral endopod. The first segment is probably incorporated either into the basis, since this is the trend within the misophrioids and calanoids, or possibly into the compound proximal endopodal segment. The maxilliped often functions as a raptorial limb and is frequently subchelate, as in *Alteutha oblonga* (Goodsir) (figure 2.4.16B) and *Namakosiramia californiensis* Ho & Perkins (figure 2.4.16D). In *Alteutha* Baird the maxillipeds are both inserted on a raised area of the ventral body surface, the pedestal. The maxilliped is very reduced in forms such as *Chappuisius inopinus* Kiefer (figure 2.4.16C) and is vestigial in some, such as *Cylindropsyllus* Brady.

Swimming Legs: The Canuellidae and Longipediidae are the only harpacticoid families with an inner coxal seta on legs 1 to 4 (arrowed in figure 2.4.17A-B). Sewell's (1940) report of this seta in *Neodactylopus cyclopoides* Nicholls (as *Eudactylopus ?anomala* Sewell) is erroneous. The maximum setation of the rami given in the spine and seta formula in the diagnosis is exhibited by *Canuella*, except for the absence of the inner seta on the first exopodal segment. This inner seta can be found in several other harpacticoids, including many cerviniids. In *Scottopsyllus langi* Mielke, *S.robertsoni* (Scott & Scott) and *S.pararobertsoni* Lang there has been a secondary increase in the number of inner basal setae on the first leg (figure 2.4.18A).

The first leg is variously modified in harpacticoids (figures 2.4.18A-D) and can function as a feeding appendage and raptorial limb rather than only as a swimming leg. It provides an extremely useful set of characters used by Lang for distinguishing between families (Lang, 1948a). A most unusual first leg is found in the new family of anchialine cave forms, the Superornatiremidae. The two genera that comprise this family have numerous additional setation elements on both rami of the first legs (figures 2.4.19A-B). Their spine and seta formulae are:

	coxa	basis	exopod segment 1 2 3	endopod segment 1 2 3
Superornatiremis Huys	0 – 0	1 – 1	III – 0; II – 1; IV,I,2	0 – 1; 2 – 1; 2,2,2
Neoechinophora Huys	0 – 0	I – 1	III – 0; II – 1; III,I,2	0 – 1; 1 – 1; 2,3,2

The presence of 3 and 2 spines on the outer margins of the first and second exopodal segments respectively are unique features, as are the presence of 1 or 2 setae on the outer margin of the second endopodal segment. It is interesting to note that despite the secondary multiplication of these outer margin elements on both rami the inner margins of the first leg rami exhibit many derived setation features shared with many other harpacticoids, such as the loss of the inner seta on exopodal segment 1 and the presence of only 1 inner seta on the second endopodal segment. The terminal endopodal segments bear 6 and 7 setae in these two genera and in both there are 2 setae on the outer margin. No other copepods have 2 outer setae on this segment in the first leg and we interpret the presence of more than 5 setae as a secondary state originating within the Harpacticoida.

The presence of only 3 setae on the inner margin of the third exopodal segment of the second swimming leg is an apomorphy for the Harpacticoida. Sars (1903-1911) figured 4 setae on this margin in *Phyllothalestris mysis* (Claus) but Lang (1948a) stated that this was an error. Reexamination of material of *P.mysis* confirms Lang's observation that only 3 setae are present.

Fifth Legs: The fifth legs of most harpacticoids are characterised by the fusion of endopod and basis to form a baseoendopod (figure 2.4.21A-E). However, in some primitive families the endopod is retained as a separate ramus. In both sexes of *Longipedia minor* (figure 2.4.20A-B), in male *Neobradya pectinifera* (figure 2.4.20C) and *Tachidiopsis bozici* Bodin (figure 2.4.20D) the endopod is represented by a single segment separated by a partial or complete proximal suture. In *Eucanuella* Scott (family Cerviniidae) and *Parastenhelia spinosa* (Fischer) (family Parastenheliidae) the exopod is 3-segmented in the male (figure 2.4.21B). It is at most 1-segmented in the females of the same genera (figure 2.4.21A). In representatives of some other families, such as the Tetragonicipitidae, Cerviniidae, Superornatiremidae and Tisbidae, a 2-segmented exopod is found in the male (figure 2.4.21D). The great majority of harpacticoids have a 1-segmented exopod (figures 2.4.21E and 2.4.22A-B). The male of *T.bozici* and both species of the Chappuisiidae are the only harpacticoids with a separate coxa and basis in the fifth leg (figure 2.4.20D). An intercoxal sclerite is retained in some members of the Thalestridae and Diosaccidae. In some families the exopod fuses to the baseoendopod to produce an undivided, plate-like limb (figures 2.4.22D-E).

The maximum setation of 4 setae on the endopod of the male fifth leg is found in a representative of a newly discovered and as yet undescribed new family of harpacticoids from the Great Barrier Reef in Australia (figure 2.4.21C). Three endopodal setae are common in the Thalestridae, Tetragonicipitidae (figure 2.4. 21D) and Canthocamptidae. The latter family also exhibits the maximum number (6 setae) on the female endopod, as in *Mesochra lilljeborgi* Boeck (figure 2.4.21E). Six endopodal setae are also found in members of the genus *Cletocamptus*. In some forms, *Chappuisius inopinus* for example, no endopodal armature elements are retained (figure 2.4.22C). The maximum setation on the exopod of the fifth leg is 8 setae in both sexes. Eight setae are present in female *Parastenhelia spinosa* (figure 2.4.21A) and in *Antiboreodiosaccus crassus* (Giesbrecht). In the male 8 setae are found in *Longipedia coronata* Claus (figure 2.4.22A). *Ambunguipes rufocincta* has 7 endopodal setae in the male and further reductions in setation are common within the order. In male *Parastenhelia spinosa* the exopod is 3-segmented but carries only 7 setae (figure 2.4.21B). The hypothetical ancestral setation and segmentation patterns are given schematically in figure 2.4.23. This shows the derivation of the setation and segmentation patterns in the various taxa discussed above.

The fifth legs are nearly always sexually dimorphic in harpacticoids, either in the number of segments or in the number of armature elements. The only exceptions are the Rotundiclipeidae (figures 2.4.22F-G) in which the fifth leg is so reduced that only 2 setae remain, and the Cristacoxidae.

Sixth Legs: The sixth legs and genital field of the males are particularly complex in the Canuellidae (figure 2.4.32C). Por (1983) first introduced the term 'petasma' to described the male gonopodial apparatus of the canuellid *Scottolana uxoris* Por. Later Por (1984b) homologised the canuellid male sixth leg with the petasma of the Euphausiiacea, Decapoda, Peracarida and Syncarida. Glatzel (1988) proposed to abandon the term petasma in canuellids since these structures are not homologous. The sixth leg of male *Canuella perplexa* retains the original complement of 3 armature elements, implanted along the inner margin of the leg (figure 2.4.26A). The inner part of the leg forms a secondary process that is bifid distally. In *Sunaristes* only 2 armature elements remain (figure 2.4.26C) and in *Canuellina* all elements are lost. In harpacticoid development (figure 3.16.4) the sixth legs are typically not sexually dimorphic at the fourth copepodid stage. Differences can appear at the fifth copepodid. In *Orthopsyllus* Brady & Robertson for example, the male fifth copepodids have only 2 setae on each leg compared to 3 in the female. By the adult stage the male sixth legs are asymmetrical, with the left leg forming the functional genital operculum closing the gonopore on that side. The female sixth legs are symmetrical, each closing off its respective gonopore. The single copulatory pore lies some distance posterior to the level of the gonopores.

In the majority of harpacticoids a much simpler sixth leg is found in the male. In the Cerviniidae and a few other families both members are symmetrical, not fused medially and are free at the base. In *Rhynchothalestris helgolandica* (Claus) (figure 2.4.26B) and the Neobradyidae the members are fused but retain their basic symmetrical arrangement. Most families exhibit asymmetrical sixth legs in the male (figure 2.4.26D), with only one functional sixth leg present. Both sinstral and dextral configurations are found, according to whether the testis and vas deferens on the left or right side are developed. Examples of this arrangement are the Thompsonulidae, Hamondiidae and families of the Laophontoidea (Huys, 1990a,b; Huys & Gee, 1990). The cancrincolid genera also have asymmetrical male sixth legs with a functional aperture on one side only, but this condition is difficult to detect since both sixth legs have lost all armature.

Differential Diagnosis: The Harpacticoida is a distinctive order within the Podoplea. Harpacticoids possess short antennules with few segments, 9 at most in females, 14 at most in males. The great majority of harpacticoids have a baseoendopod on the fifth leg in both sexes. Those that possess a discrete endopod typically have a maximum of 2 setae on it.

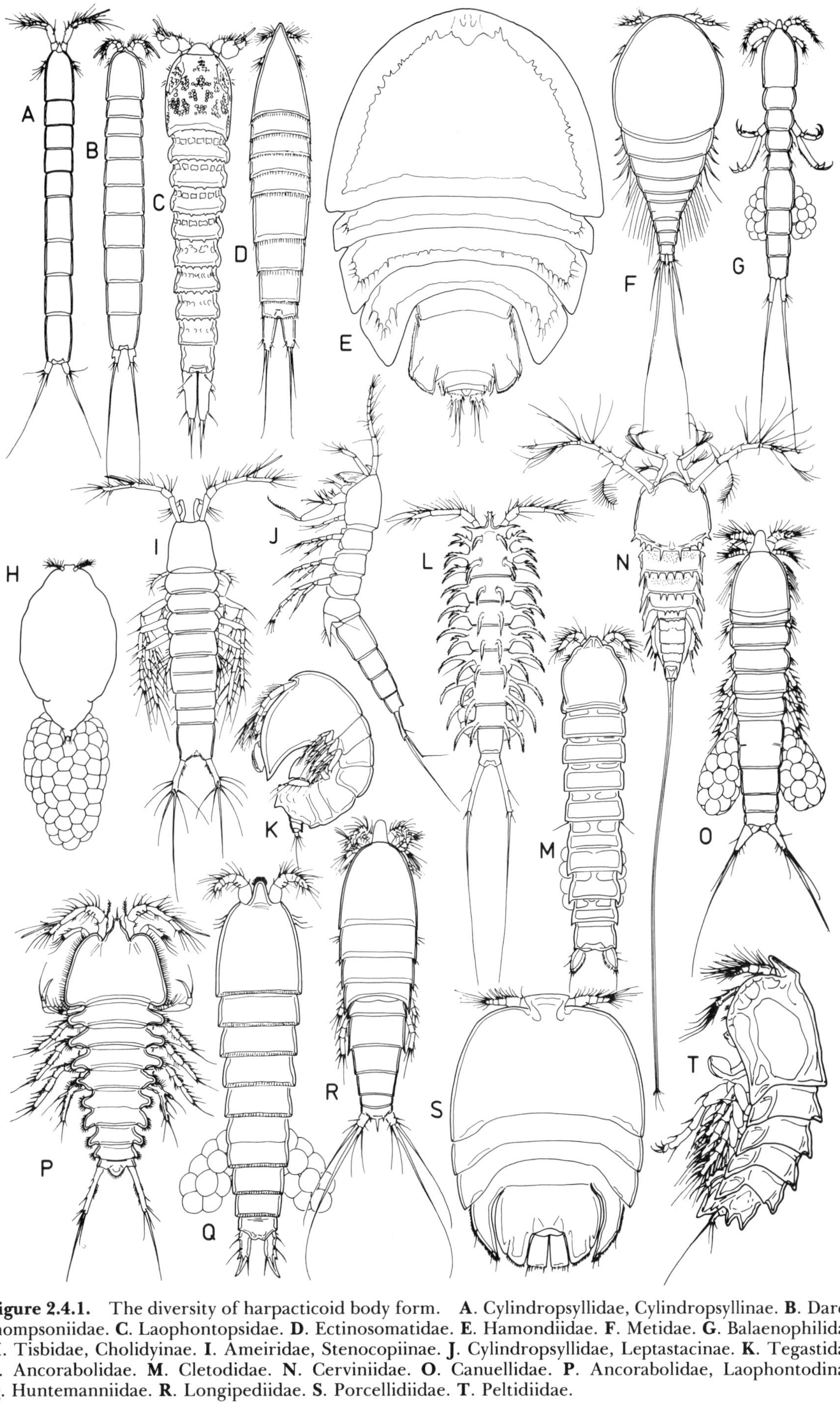

Figure 2.4.1. The diversity of harpacticoid body form. **A**. Cylindropsyllidae, Cylindropsyllinae. **B**. Darcythompsoniidae. **C**. Laophontopsidae. **D**. Ectinosomatidae. **E**. Hamondiidae. **F**. Metidae. **G**. Balaenophilidae. **H**. Tisbidae, Cholidyinae. **I**. Ameiridae, Stenocopiinae. **J**. Cylindropsyllidae, Leptastacinae. **K**. Tegastidae. **L**. Ancorabolidae. **M**. Cletodidae. **N**. Cerviniidae. **O**. Canuellidae. **P**. Ancorabolidae, Laophontodinae. **Q**. Huntemanniidae. **R**. Longipediidae. **S**. Porcellidiidae. **T**. Peltidiidae.

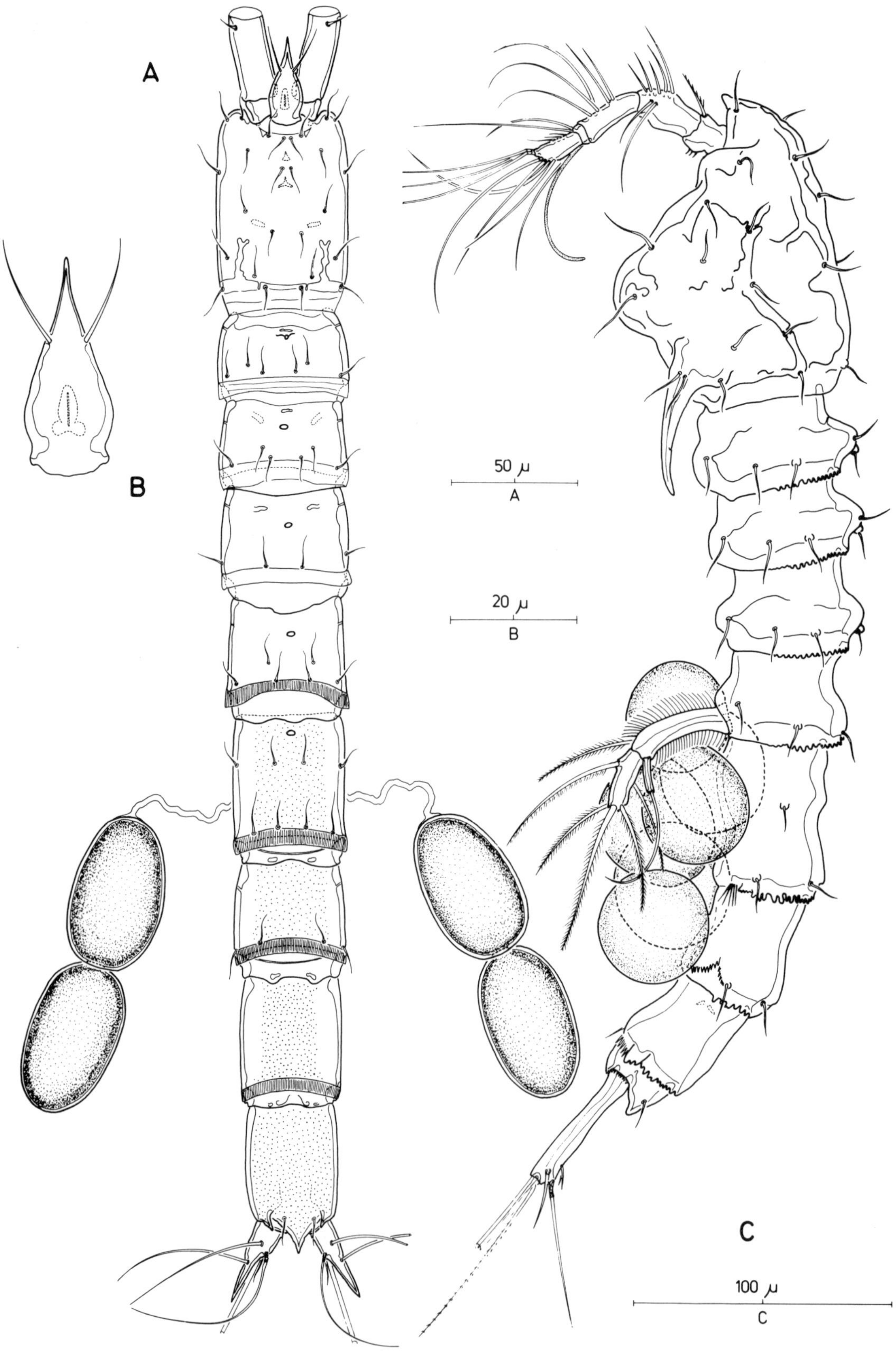

Figure 2.4.2. **A.** *Leptopontia* sp., female, dorsal view (distal segments of antennules omitted). **B.** Rostrum. **C.** *Laophontodes bicornis*, lateral view.

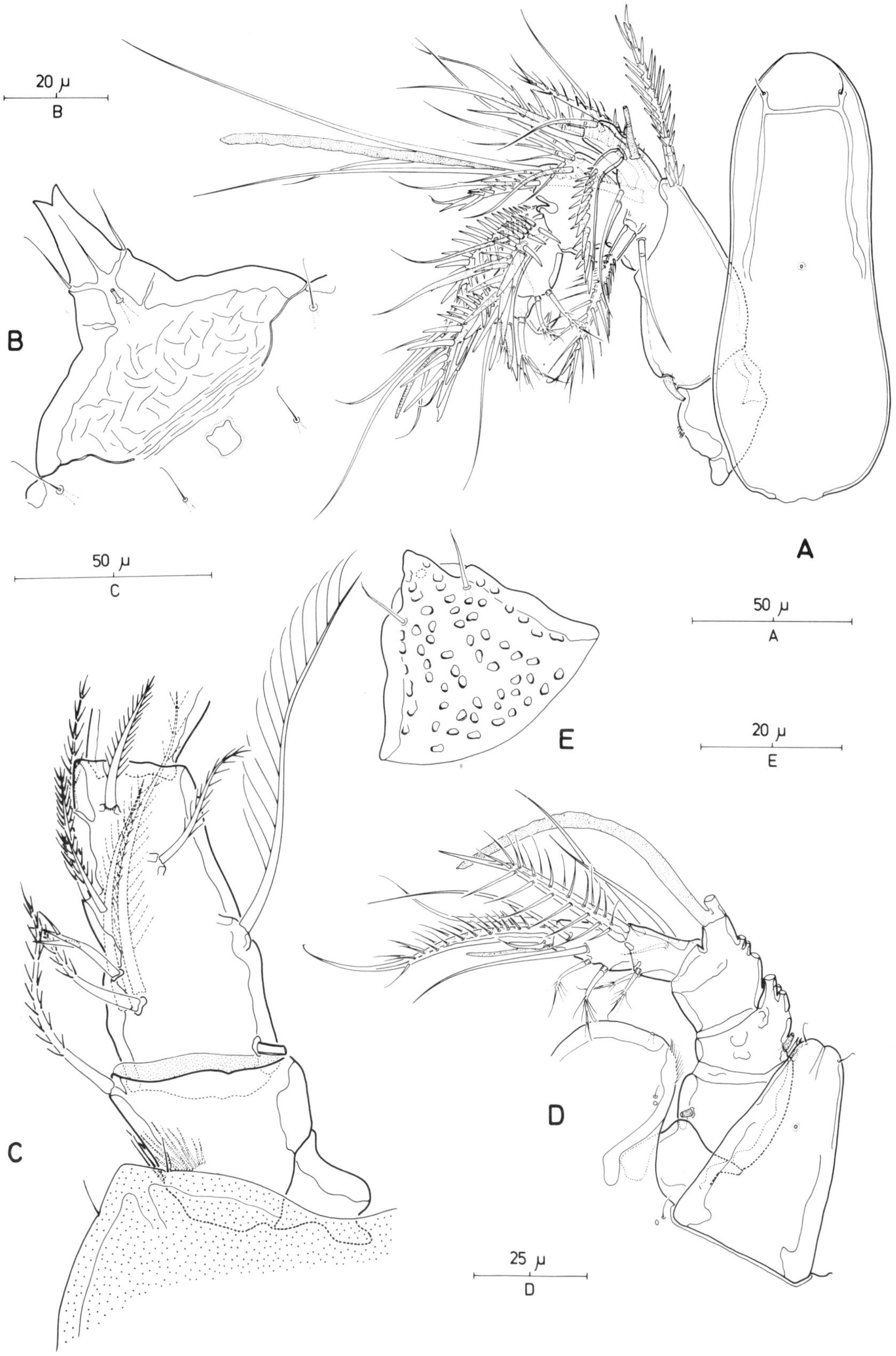

Figure 2.4.3. **A.** *Thompsonula hyaenae*, female, rostrum and antennule. **B.** *Sarsocletodes typicus*, rostrum. **C.** *Neobradya pectinifera*, female, rostrum and proximal segments of antennule. **D.** *Caribbula elongata*, female, rostrum and antennule, with setae of proximal segments omitted. **E.** *Cristacoxa petkovskii*, rostrum.

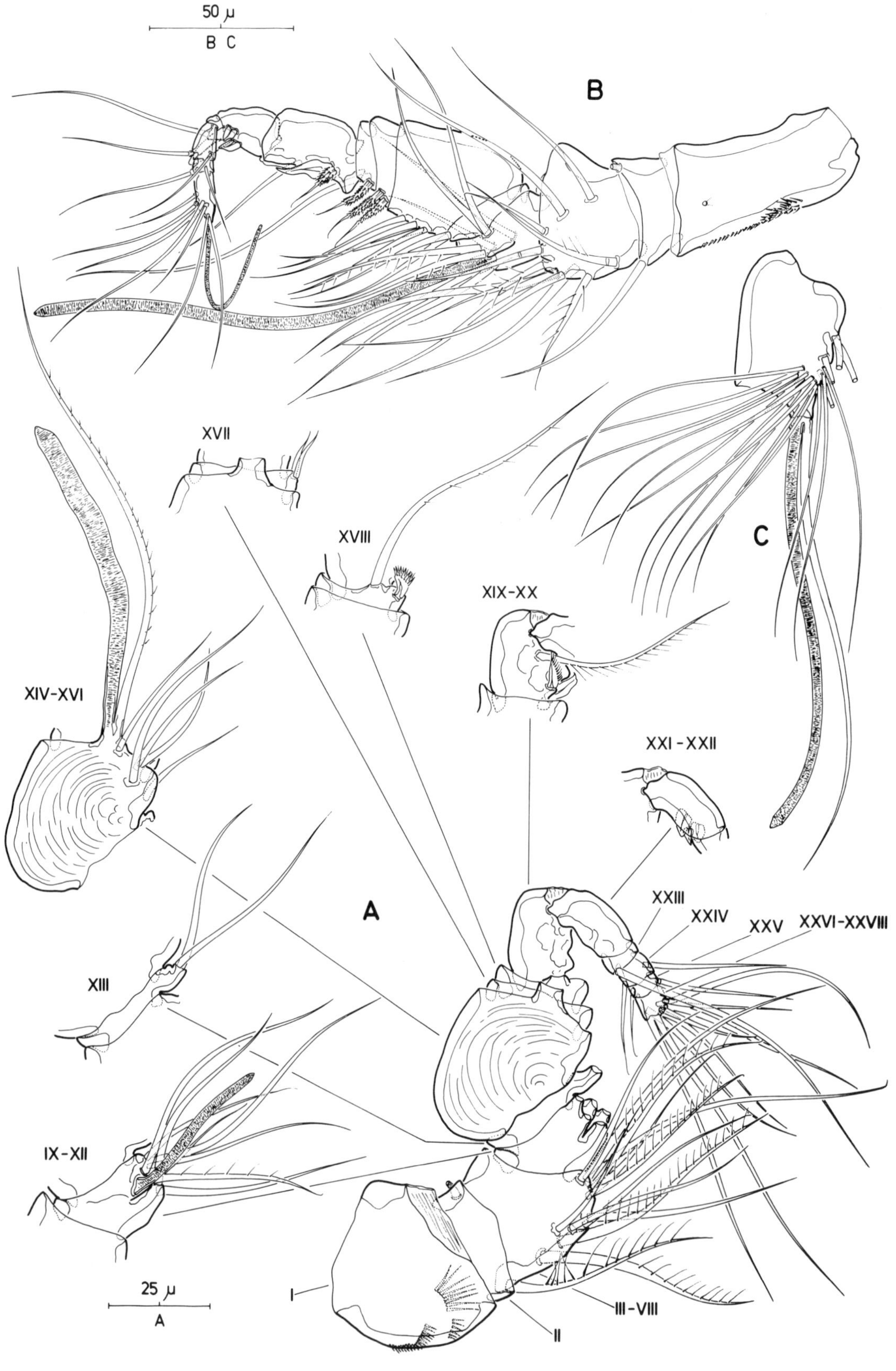

Figure 2.4.4. **A.** *Hamondia superba*, male antennule. **B.** *Ambunguipes rufocincta*, male antennule, ventral view (dorsal setae, aesthetasc and setoid elements of segment 6 omitted). **C.** Segment 6, dorsal view showing setoid elements and setae not drawn in B.

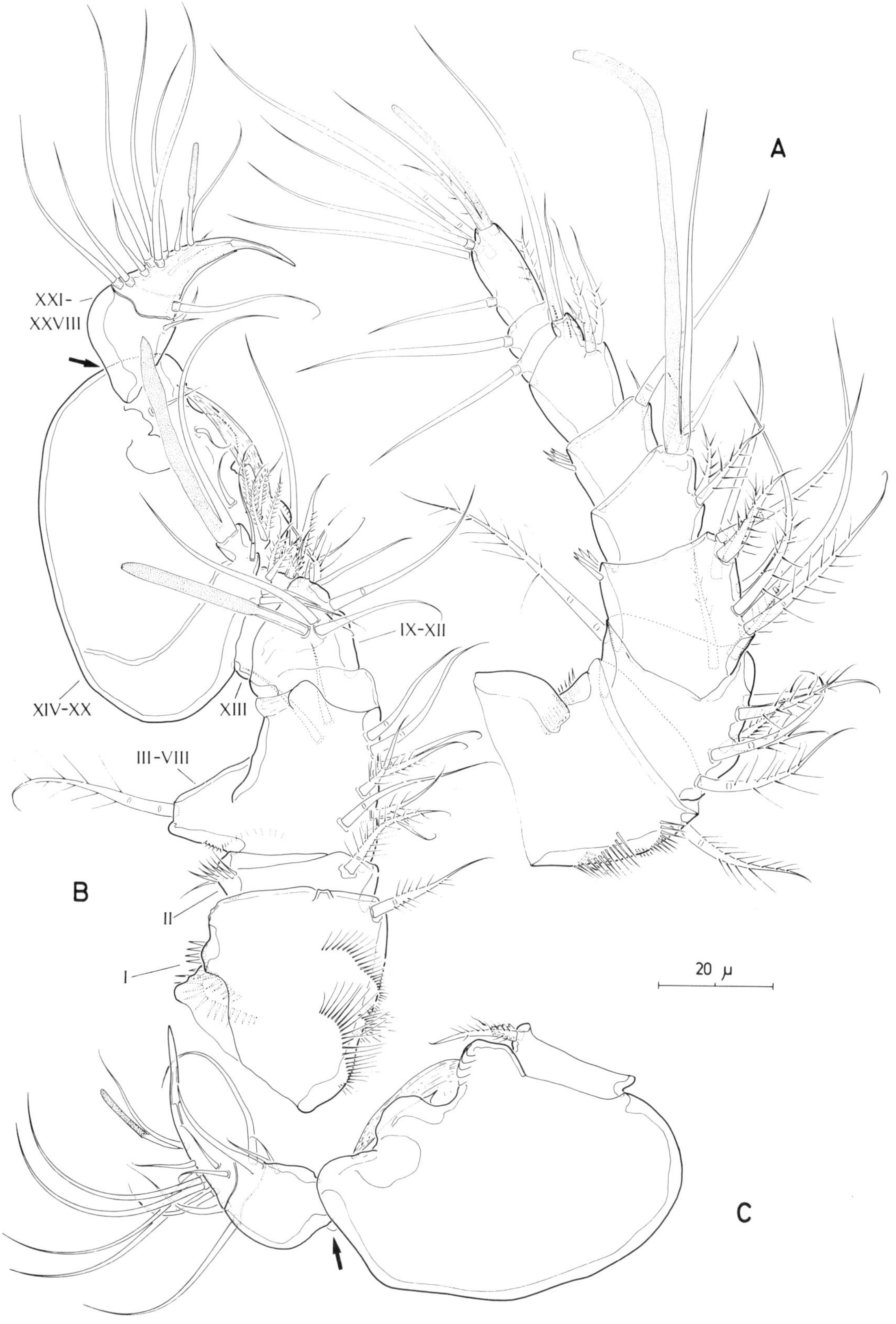

Figure 2.4.5. *Geeopsis incisipes.* **A.** Female antennule. **B.** Male antennule, ventral view. **C.** Segments 5-8, dorsal view. [Arrows indicate neocopepodan geniculation.]

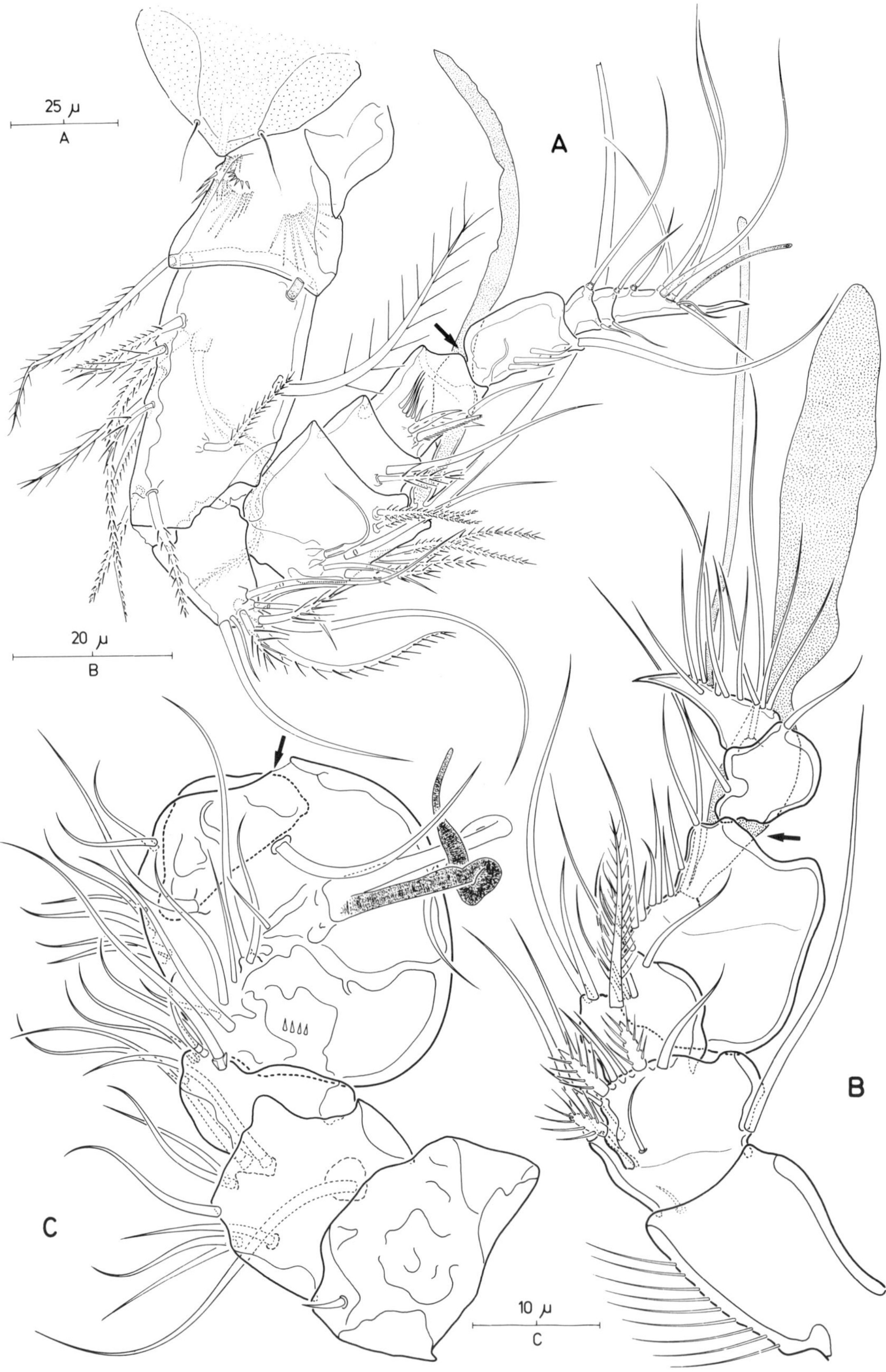

Figure 2.4.6. Composition of male antennules showing the three types defined by Lang (1948a). **A.** *Neobradya pectinifera*, haplocer type. **B.** *Paramesochra mielkei*, subchirocer type. **C.** *Caligopsyllus primus*, chirocer type. [Arrows indicate neocopepodan geniculation.]

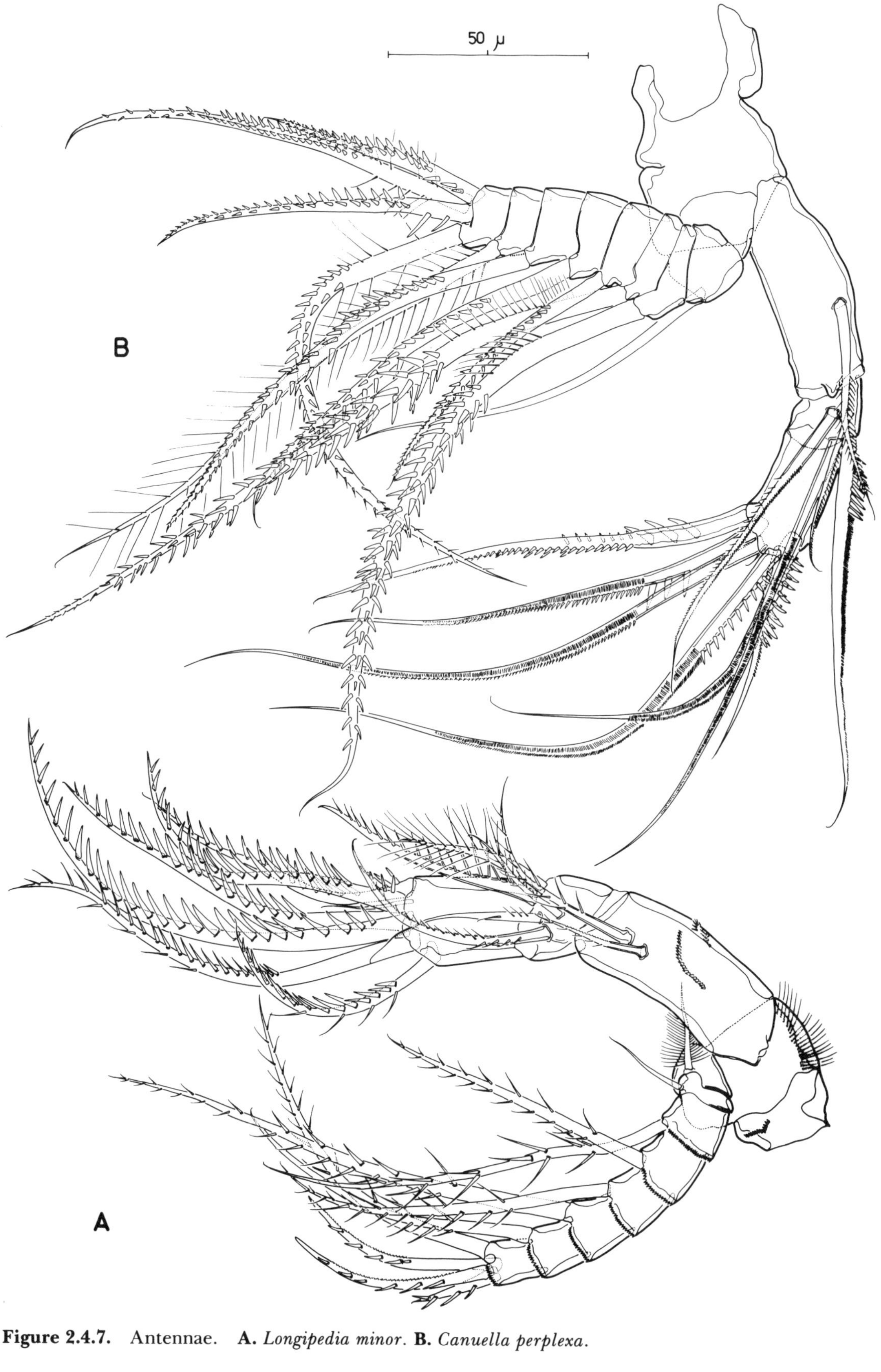

Figure 2.4.7. Antennae. **A.** *Longipedia minor*. **B.** *Canuella perplexa*.

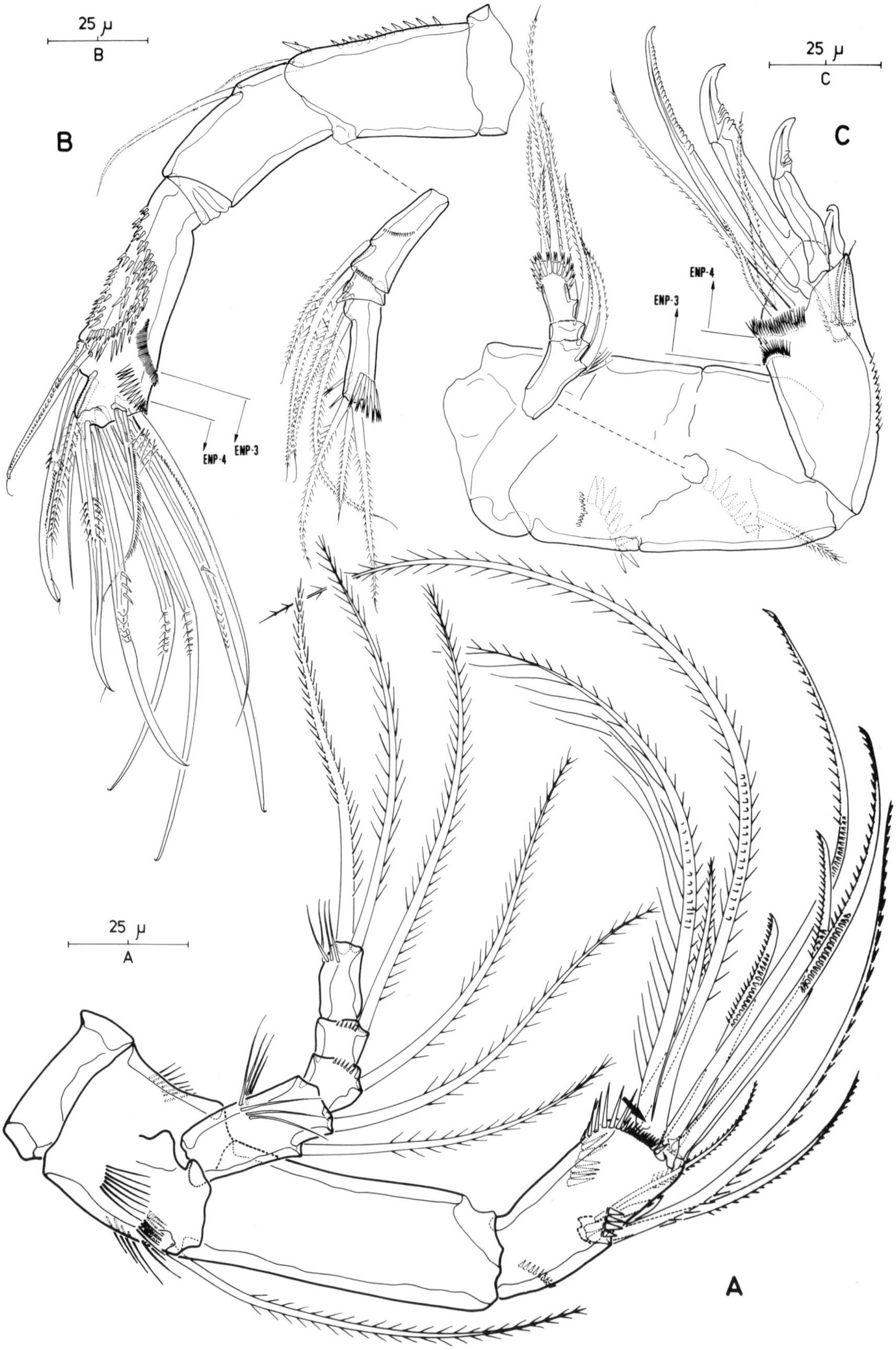

Figure 2.4.8. Antennae. **A.** *Neobradya pectinifera*, arrow indicates two fused setae derived from fourth endopod segment. **B.** *Ambunguipes rufocincta*, with serrate hyaline frills derived from endopodal segments 3 and 4 arrowed. **C.** *Hamondia superba*, with serrate hyaline frills derived from endopodal segments 3 and 4 arrowed.

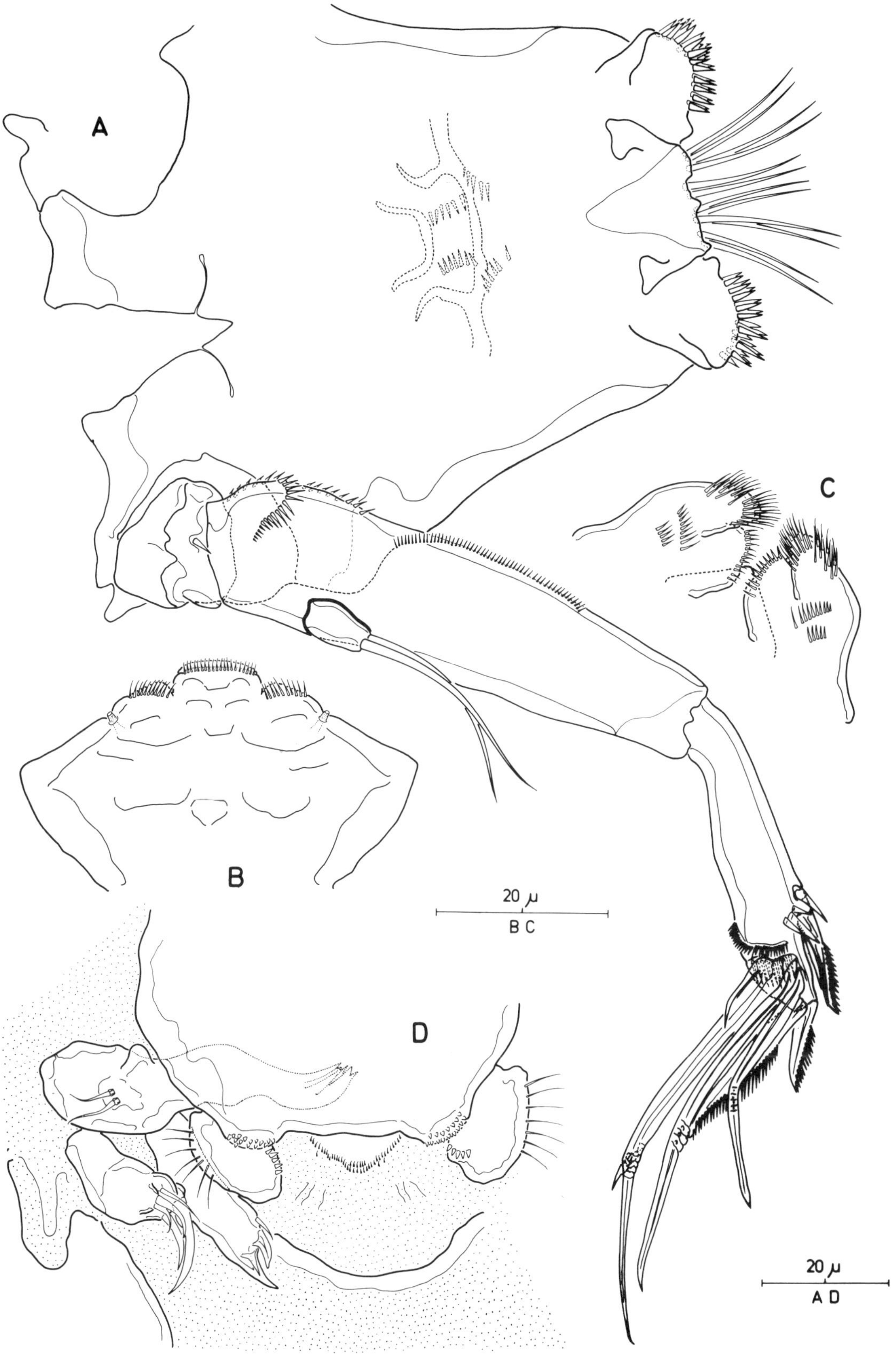

Figure 2.4.9. **A.** *Leptastacus* sp., labrum and right antenna, anterior view. **B.** *Cristacoxa petkovskii*, labrum. **C.** Paragnaths. **D.** *Namakosiramia californiensis*, oral area showing paragnaths, labrum and mouthparts.

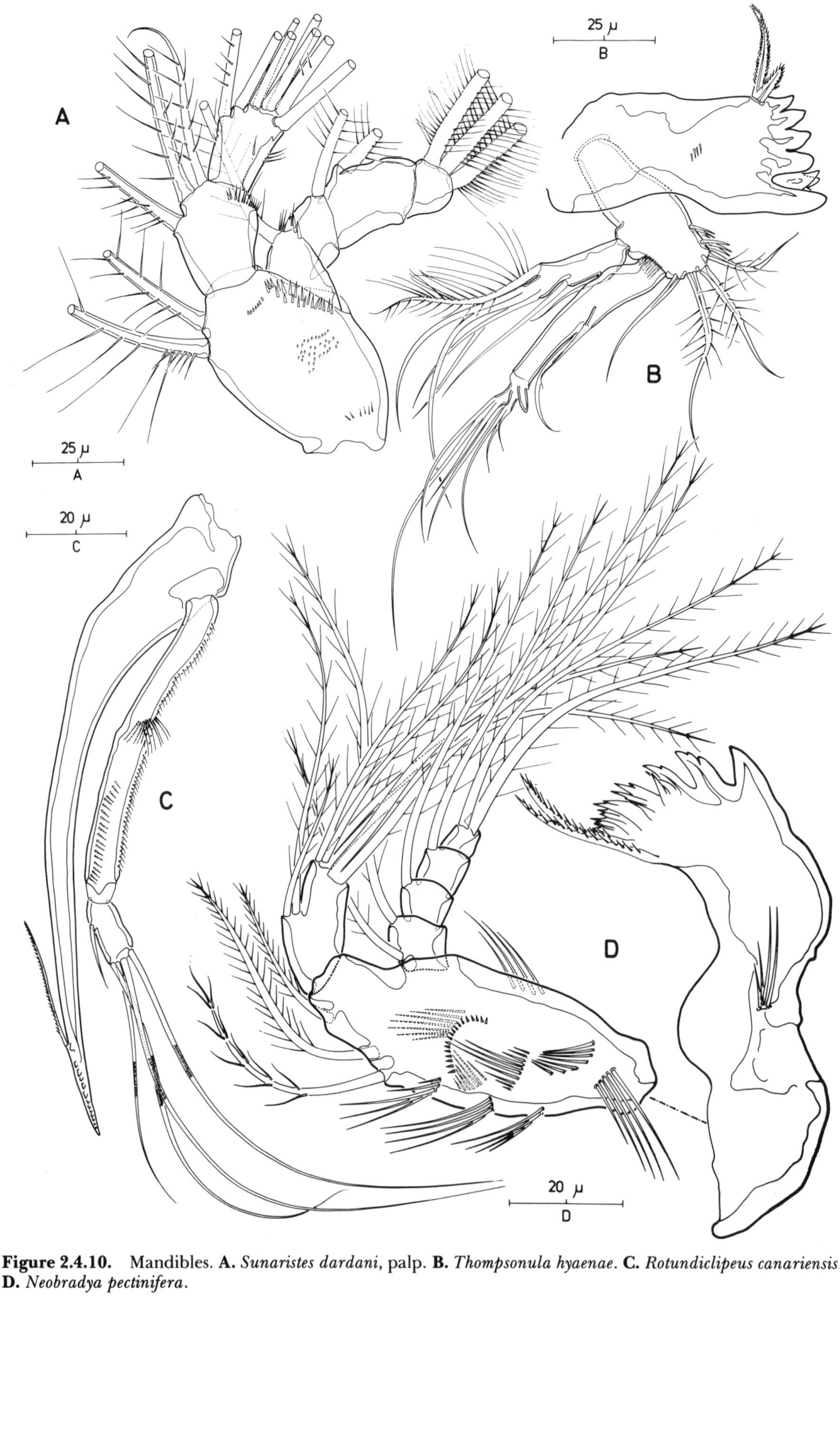

Figure 2.4.10. Mandibles. **A.** *Sunaristes dardani*, palp. **B.** *Thompsonula hyaenae*. **C.** *Rotundiclipeus canariensis*. **D.** *Neobradya pectinifera*.

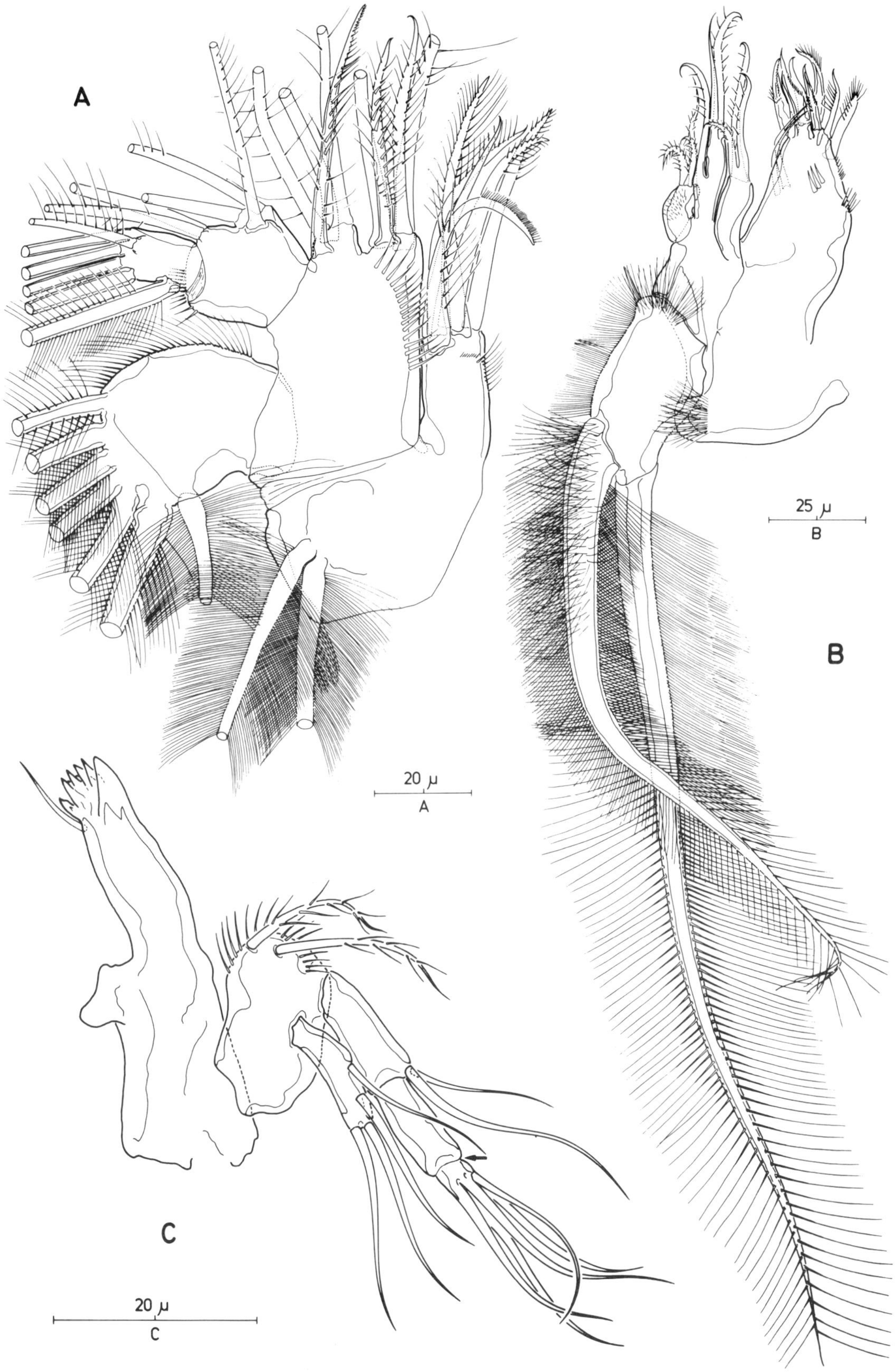

Figure 2.4.11. **A.** *Sunaristes dardani*, maxillule (praecoxa omitted). **B.** *Sacodiscus littoralis*, maxillule. **C.** *Caligopsyllus primus*, mandible (arrow indicates confluent bases of apical setae).

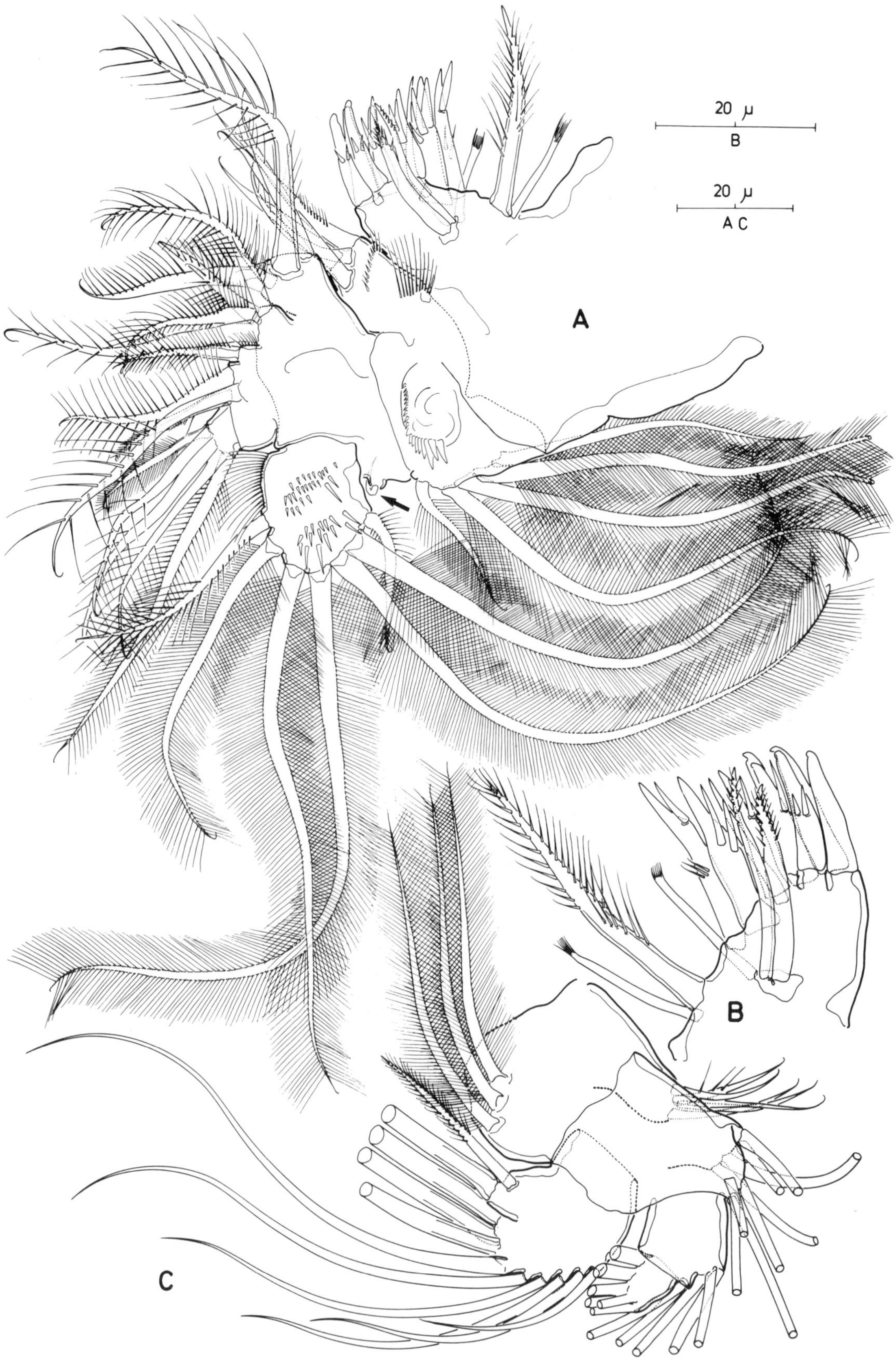

Figure 2.4.12. **A.** *Longipedia minor*, maxillule. [Arrow indicates exite on basis]. **B.** Detail of praecoxal arthrite. **C.** *Ellucana longicauda*, maxillule (praecoxa omitted).

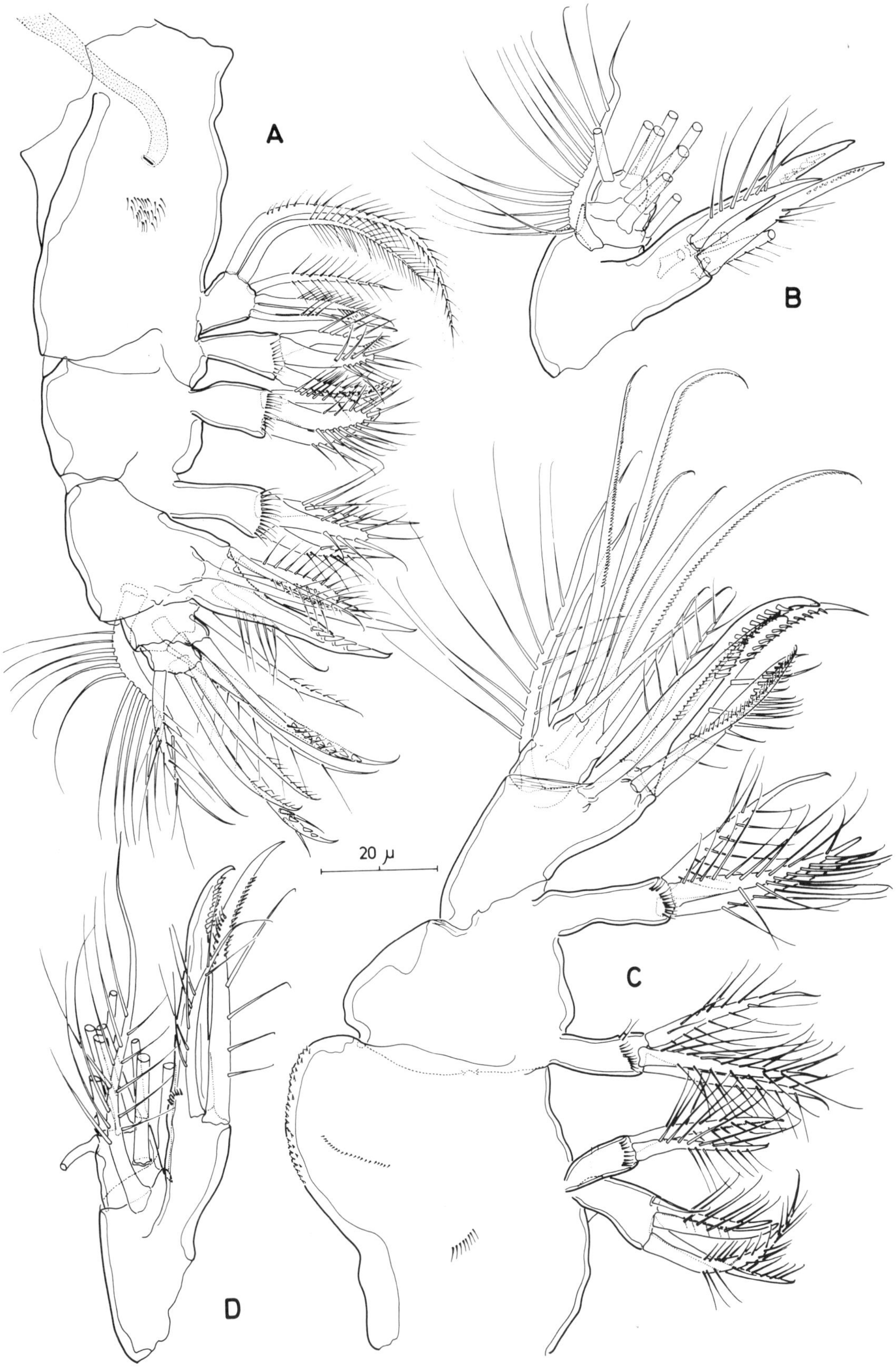

Figure 2.4.13. **A.** *Longipedia minor*, maxilla, showing pore of maxillary gland. **B.** Maxillary basis and endopod, other view. **C.** *Canuella perplexa*, maxilla. **D.** Maxillary basis and endopod, with two posterior elements on baseoendopod omitted.

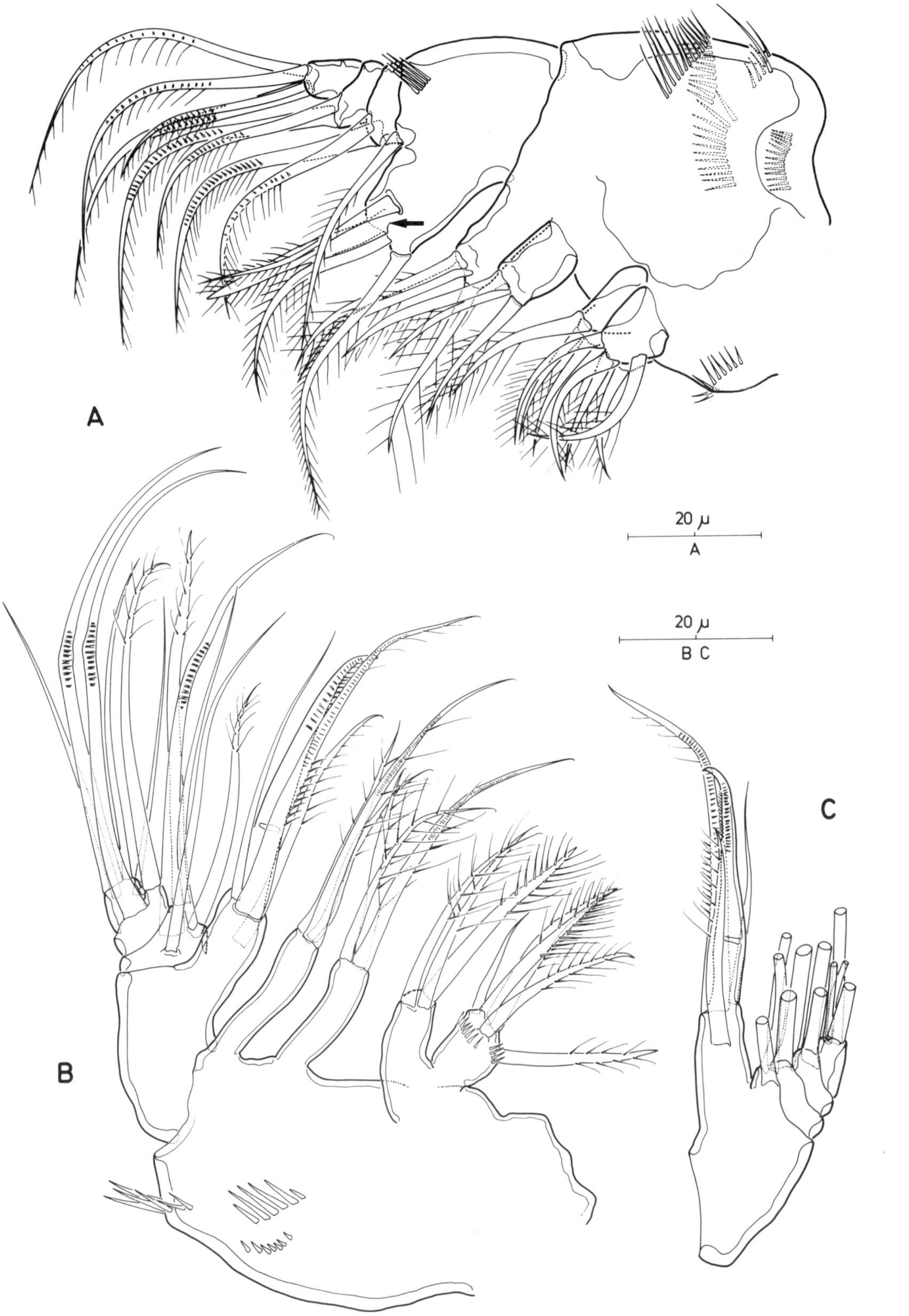

Figure 2.4.14. **A.** *Neobradya pectinifera*, maxilla, arrow indicating 'precursor' of claw. **B.** *Tachidiopsis cyclopoides*, maxilla. **C.** Detail of maxillary basis and endopod.

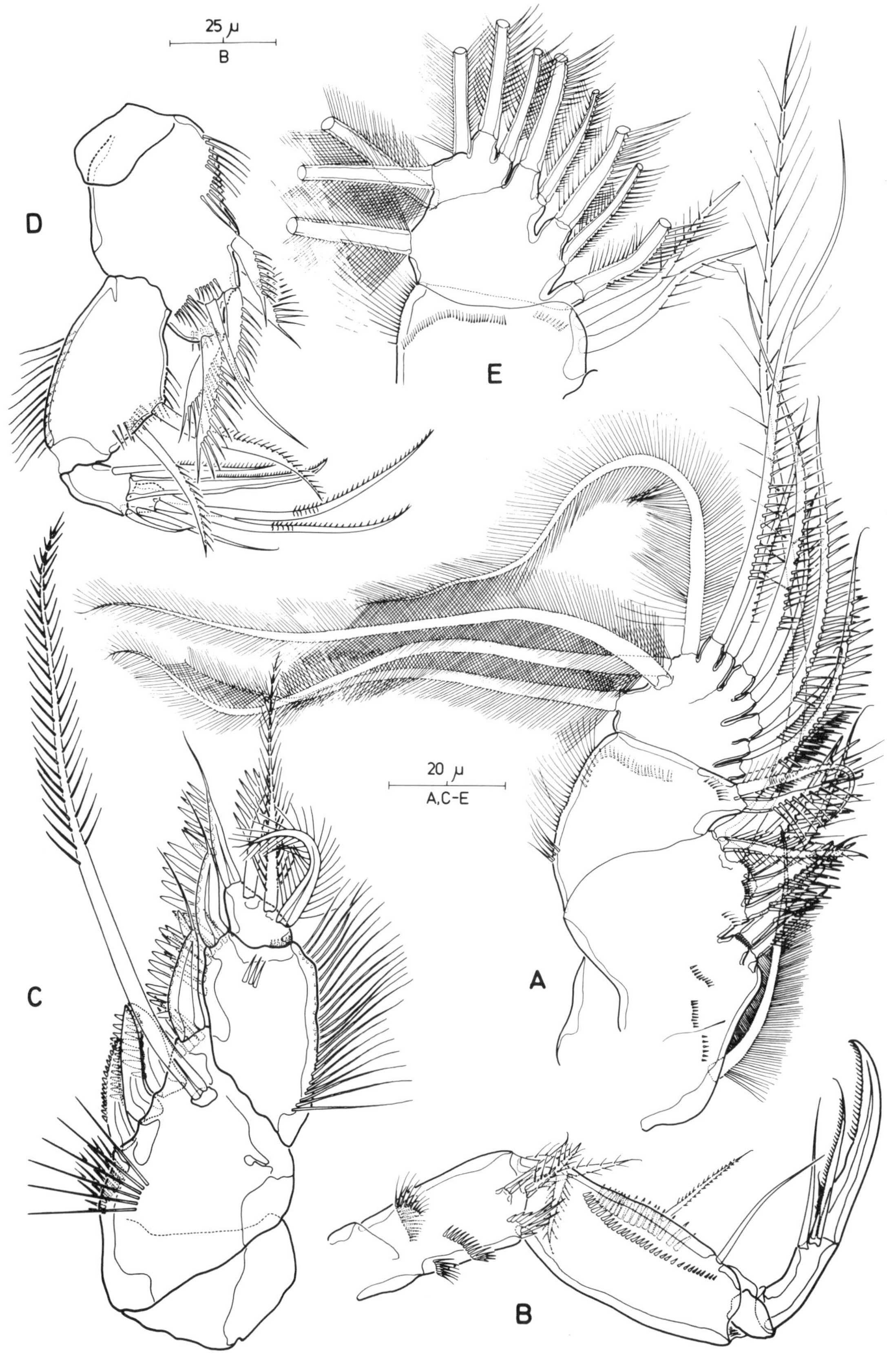

Figure 2.4.15. Maxillipeds. **A.** *Canuella perplexa*. **B.** *Pholenota spatulifera*. **C.** *Neobradya pectinifera*. **D.** *Tachidiopsis cyclopoides*. **E.** *Sunaristes dardani*, basis and endopod.

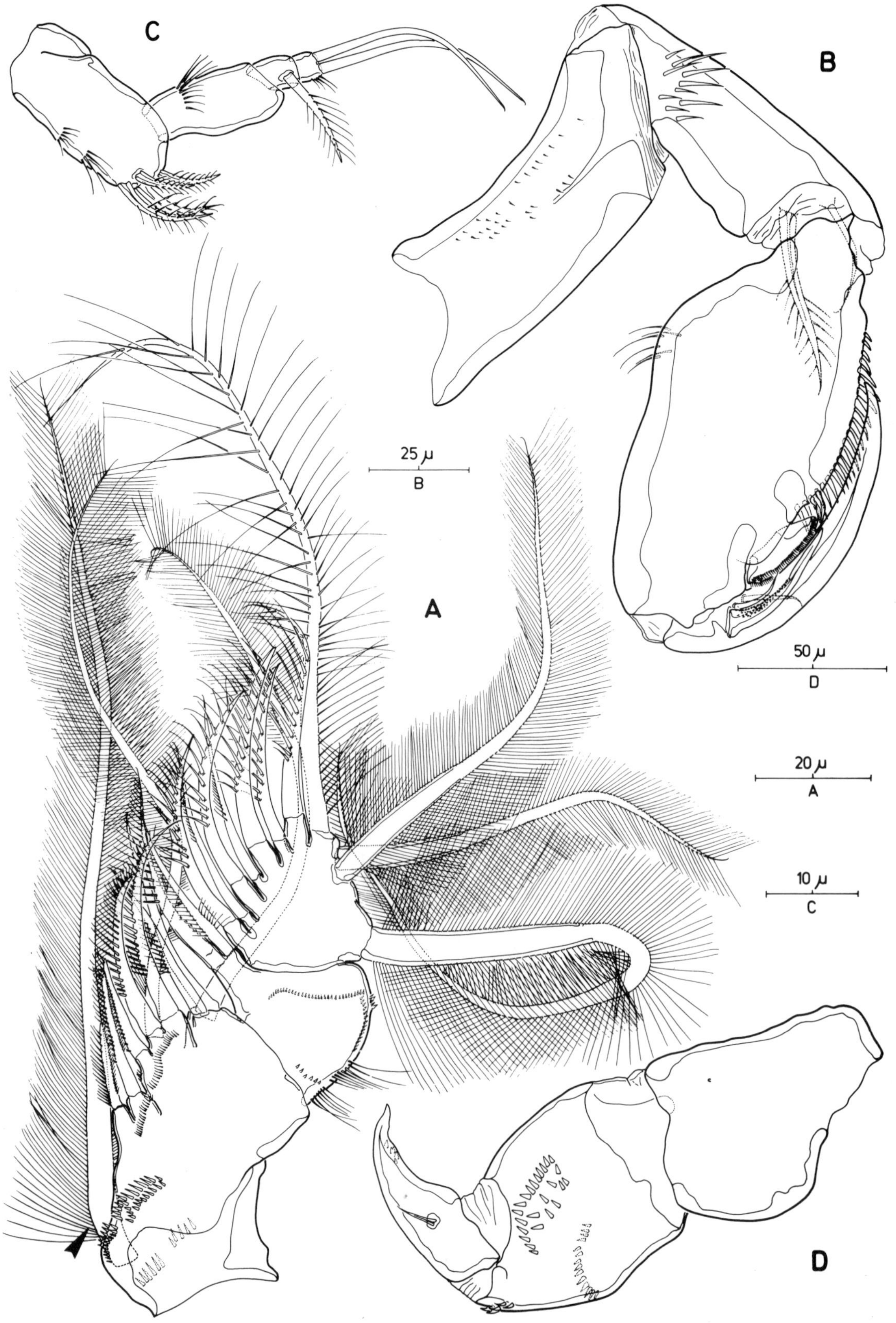

Figure 2.4.16. Maxillipeds. **A.** *Longipedia minor*, (praecoxal endite arrowed). **B.** *Alteutha oblonga*, showing pedestal. **C.** *Chappuisius inopinus*. **D.** *Namakosiramia californiensis*.

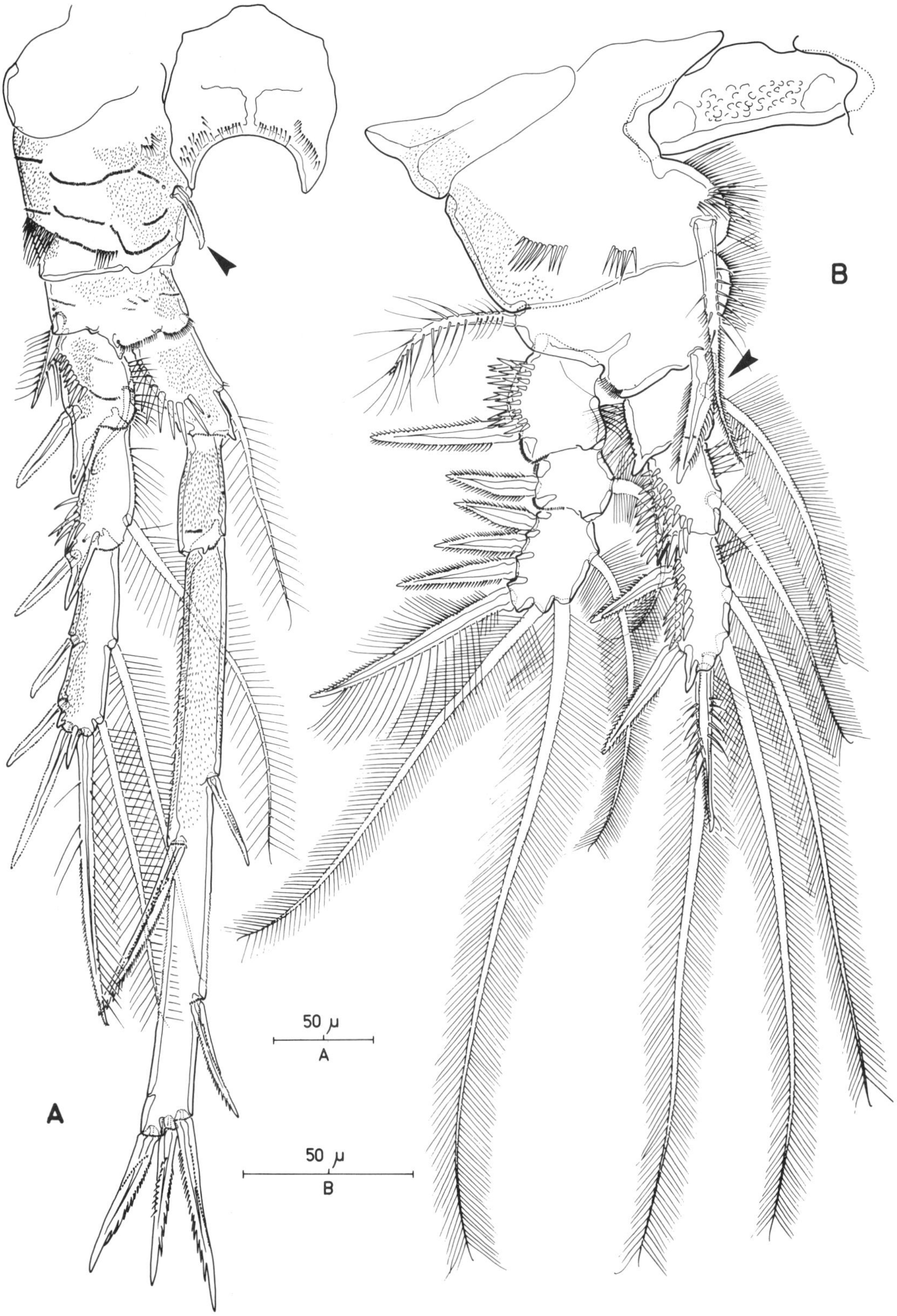

Figure 2.4.17. **A.** *Longipedia minor*, second leg, anterior view. **B.** *Canuella perplexa*, first leg, anterior view. Inner coxal seta arrowed.

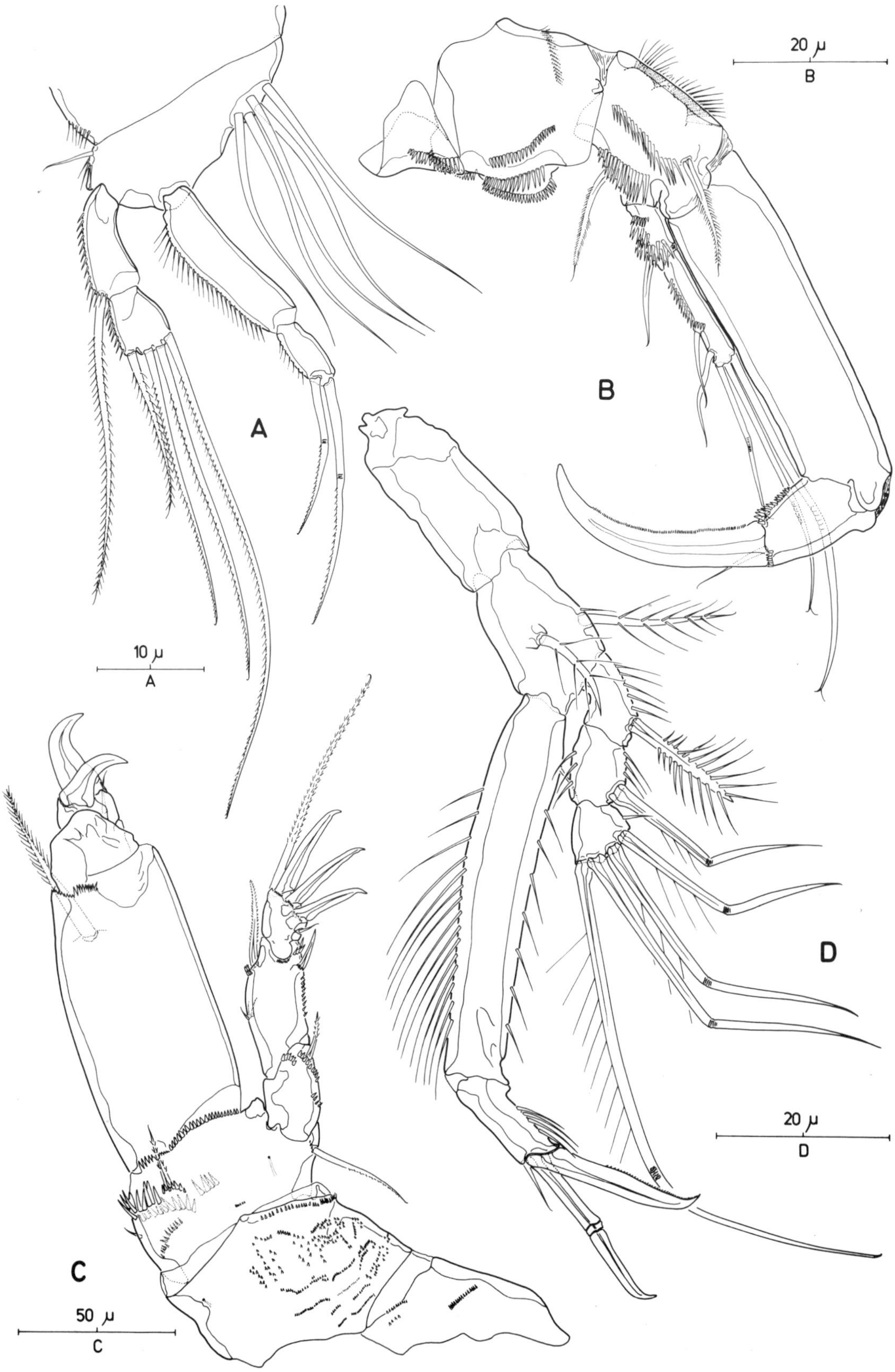

Figure 2.4.18. First legs. **A.** *Scottopsyllus langi*, showing duplicated elements on inner margin of basis. **B.** *Laophonte cornuta*. **C.** *Hamondia superba*. **D.** *Laophontodes bicornis*.

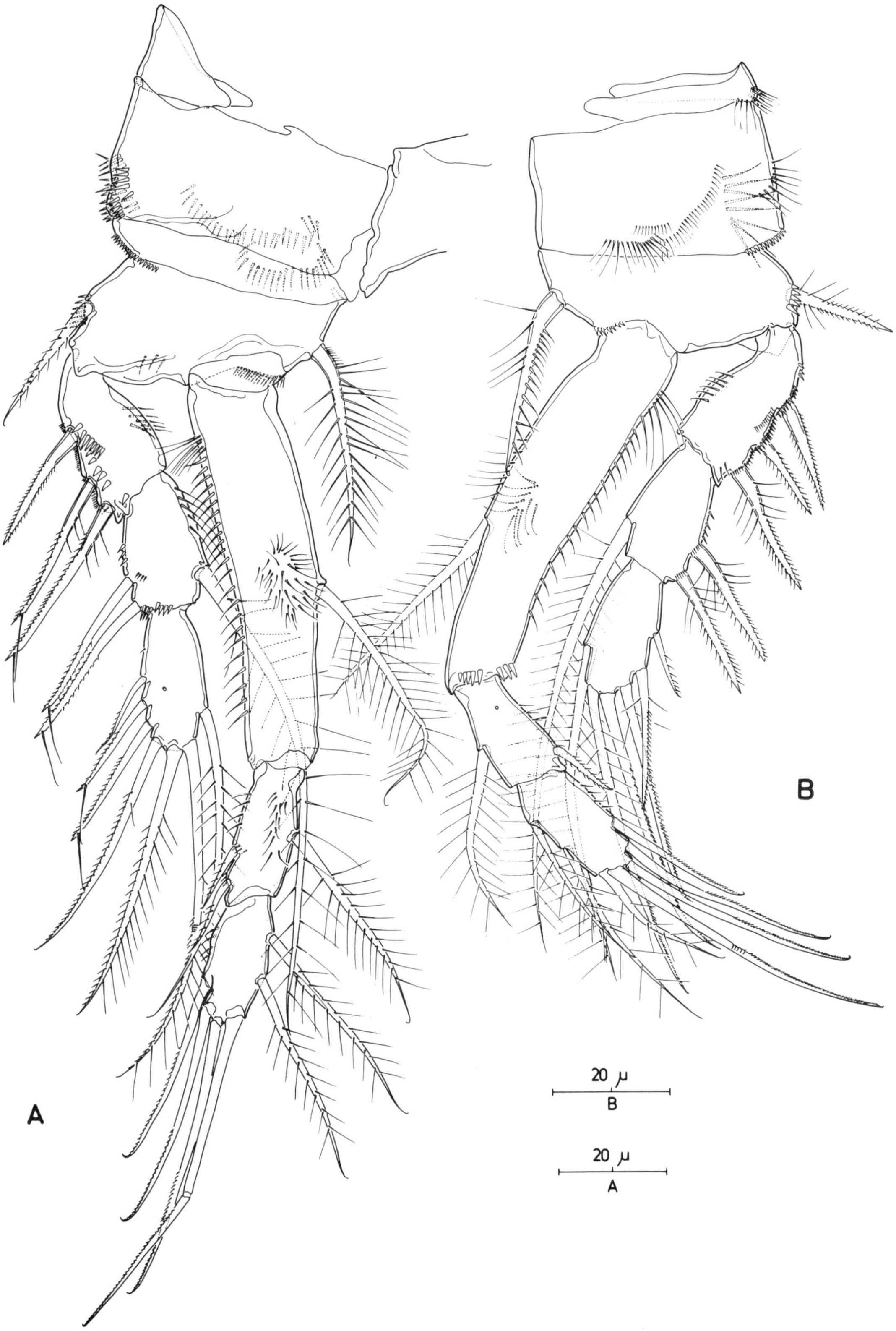

Figure 2.4.19. First legs. **A.** *Superornatiremis mysticus*. **B.** *Neoechinophora fosshageni*.

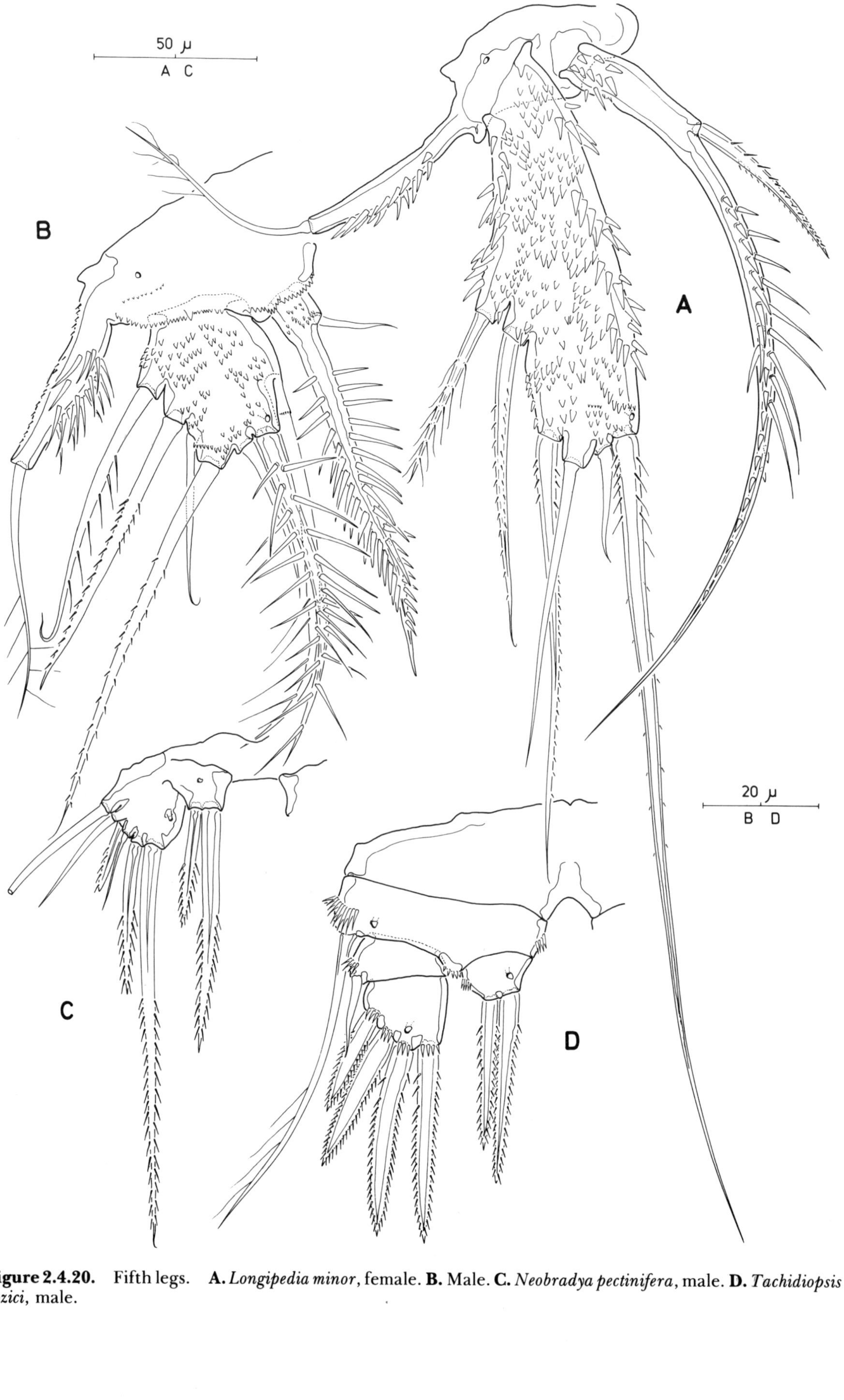

Figure 2.4.20. Fifth legs. **A.** *Longipedia minor*, female. **B.** Male. **C.** *Neobradya pectinifera*, male. **D.** *Tachidiopsis bozici*, male.

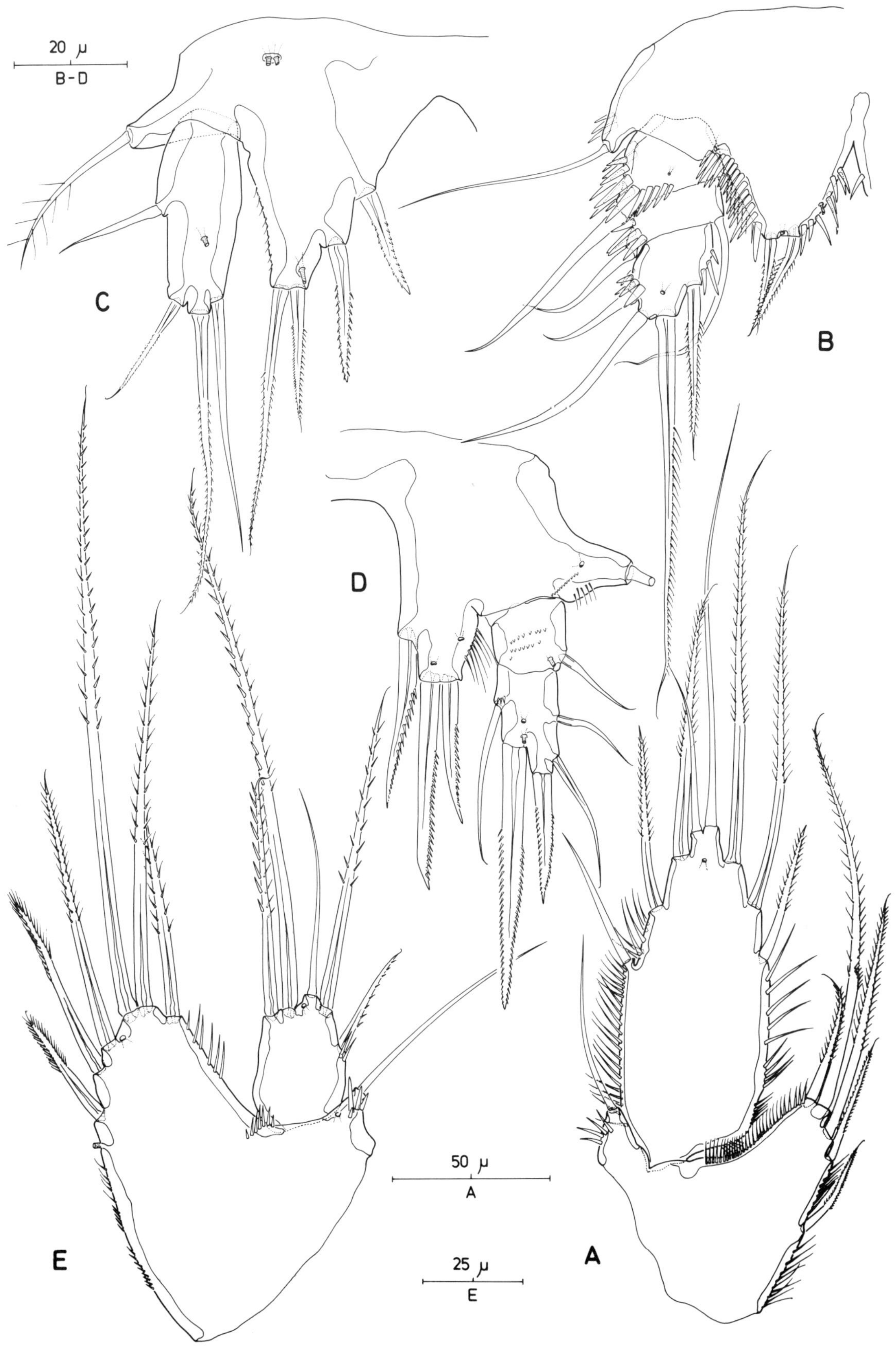

Figure 2.4.21. Fifth legs. **A.** *Parastenhelia spinosa*, female. **B.** Male. **C.** New family from Great Barrier Reef, male. **D.** *Tetragoniceps bergensis*, male. **E.** *Mesochra lilljeborgi*, female.

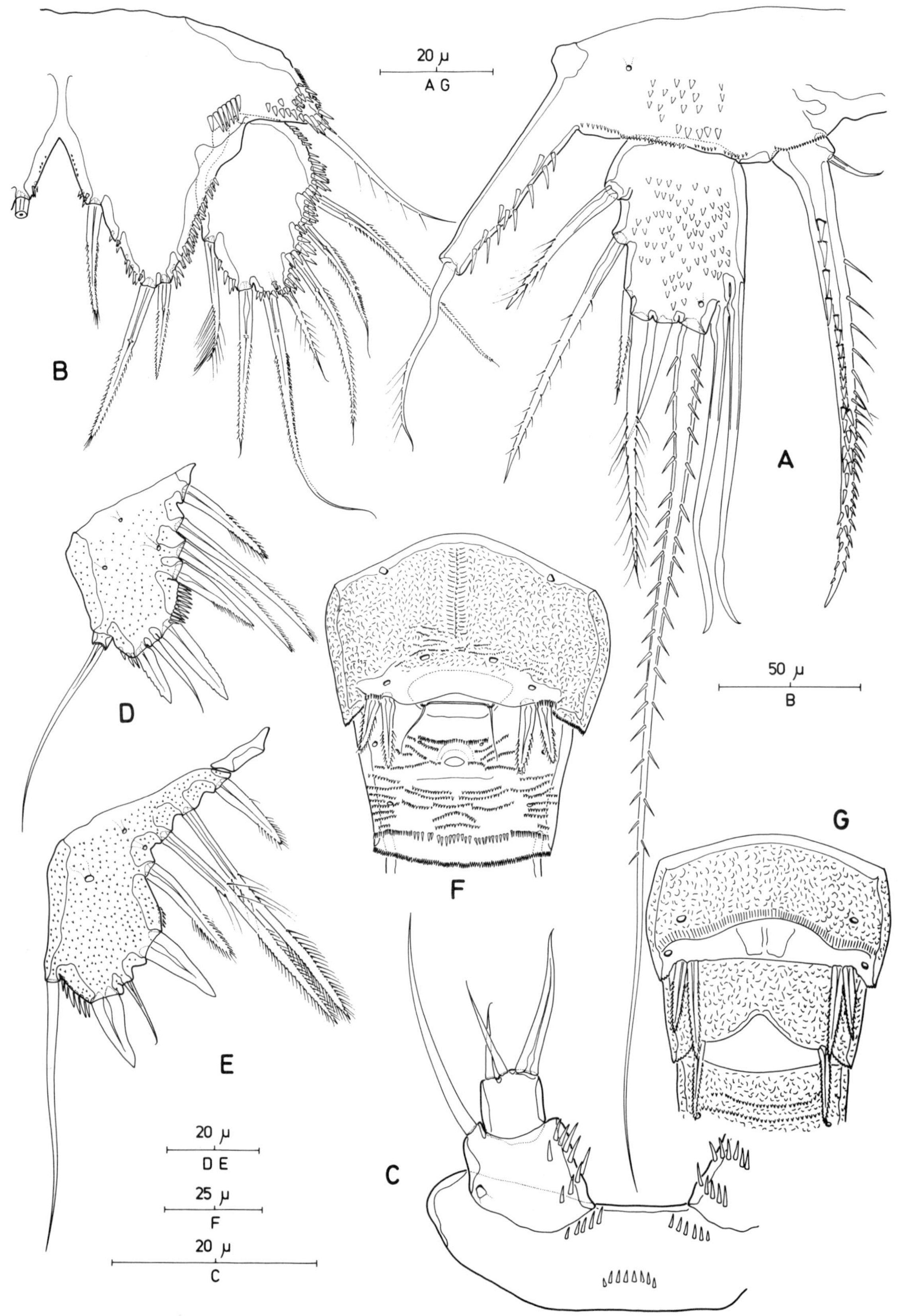

Figure 2.4.22. Fifth legs. **A.** *Longipedia coronata*, male. **B.** *Ambunguipes rufocincta*, male. **C.** *Chappuisius inopinus*, male. **D.** *Noodtorthopsyllus psammophilus*, male. **E.** Female. **F.** *Rotundiclipeus canariensis*, female. **G.** Male.

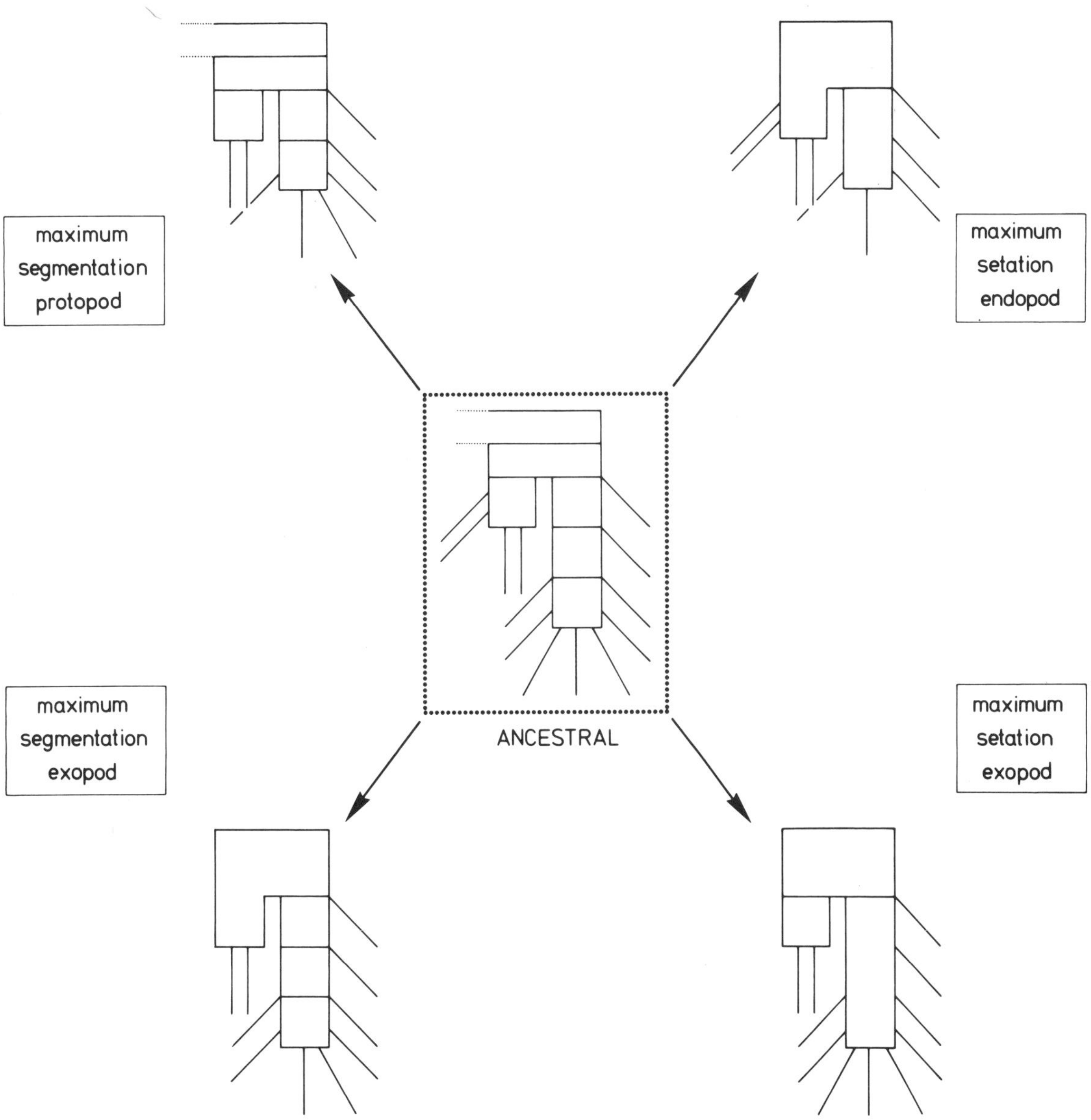

Figure 2.4.23. Schematic diagram showing derivation of ancestral condition of male fifth legs from maximum numbers of segments and setation elements in extant harpacticoids. Maximum segmentation of the protopod is retained in *Tachidiopsis bozici*, maximum segmentation of the exopod is retained in *Eucanuella* and *Parastenhelia spinosa*, maximum setation of the endopod is retained in the as yet undescribed new family of Harpacticoida from the Great Barrier Reef, and maximum setation of the exopod is retained in *Longipedia coronata*.

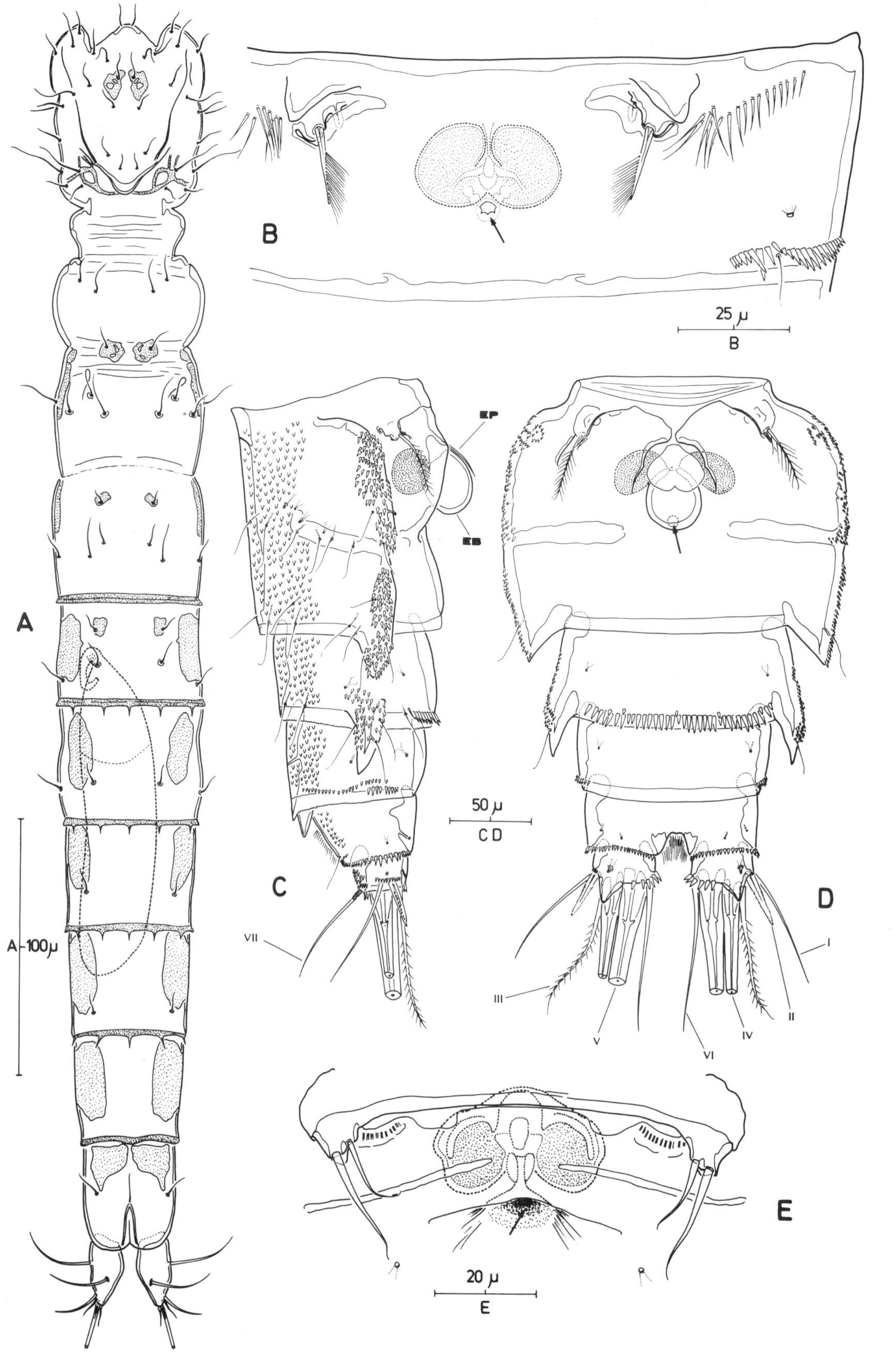

Figure 2.4.24. **A.** *Apodopsyllus* sp., male, dorsal view. **B.** *Thompsonula curticauda*, female genital complex. **C.** *Ambunguipes rufocincta*, urosome (excluding somite bearing fifth legs), lateral view. [EP = epicopulatory plate; EB = epicopulatory bulb]. **D.** Ventral view. **E.** *Laophontopsis borealis*, female genital complex. [Arrows indicate copulatory pores.]

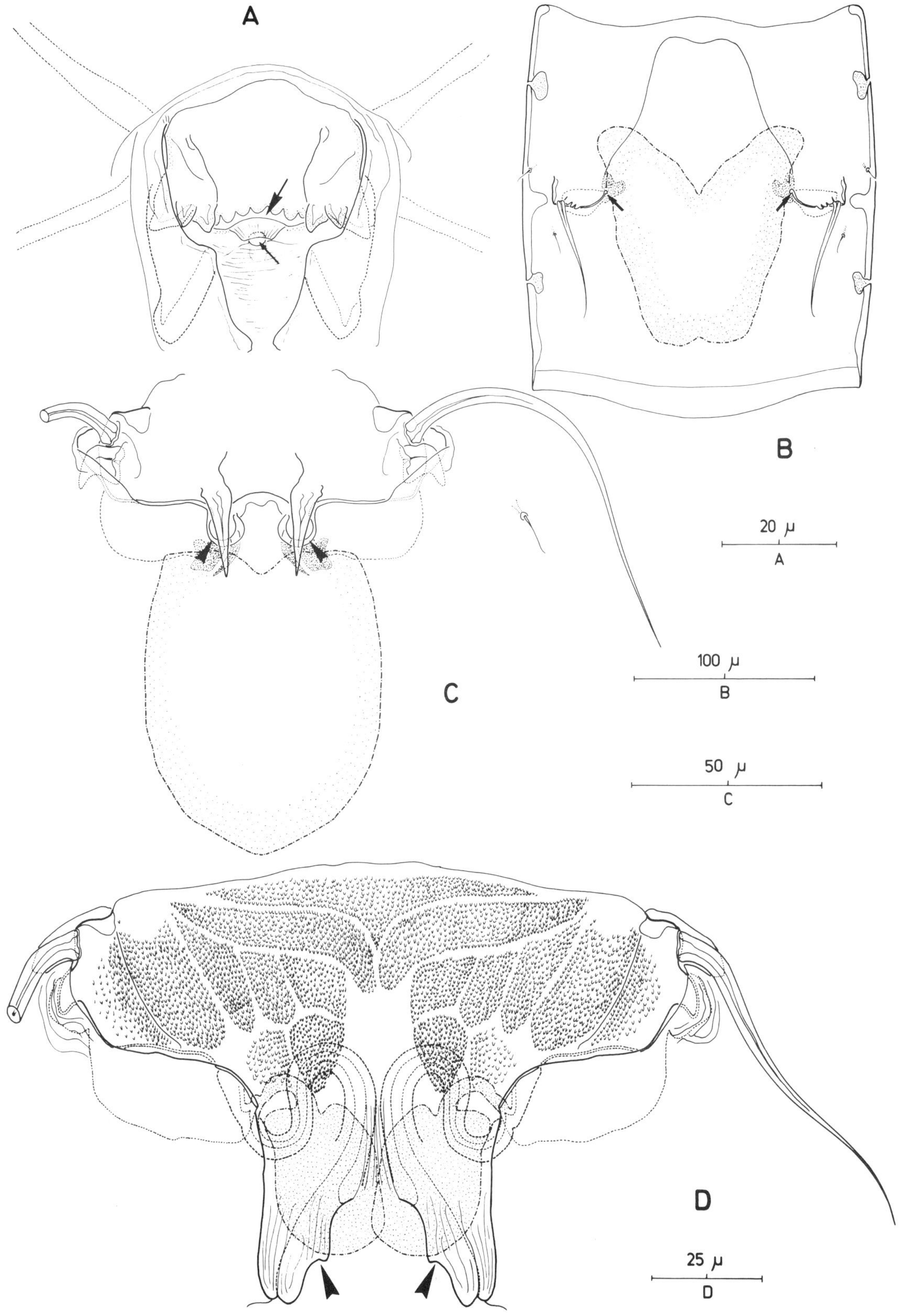

Figure 2.4.25. **A.** *Longipedia scotti*, female genital complex. [Large arrow indicates fused gonopores, small arrow indicates copulatory pore.] **B.** *Canuellina insignis*, genital double somite. **C.** *Sunaristes dardani*, female genital complex. **D.** *Canuella perplexa*, female genital complex. [Arrows in B-D indicate paired copulatory pores.]

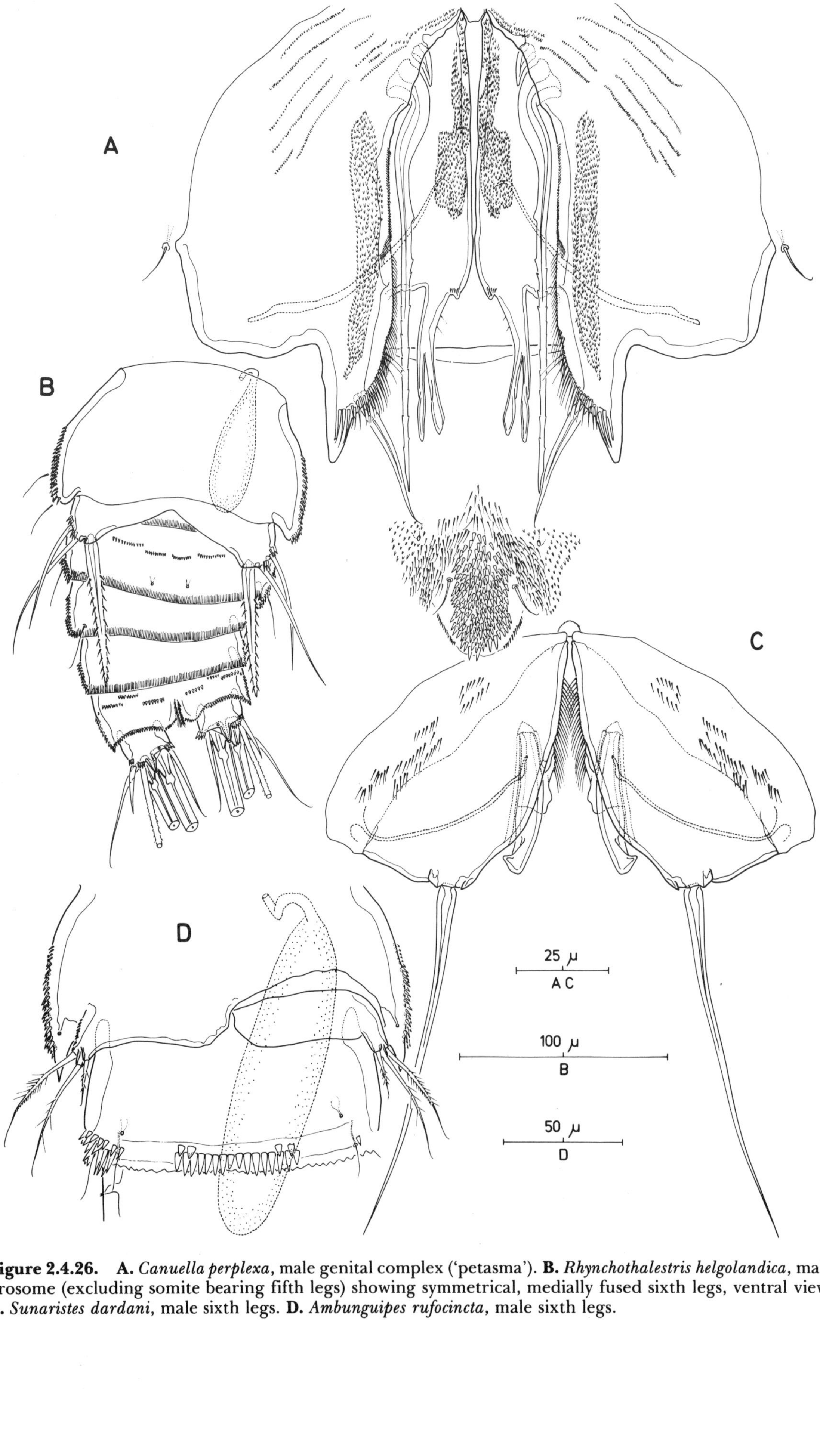

Figure 2.4.26. **A.** *Canuella perplexa*, male genital complex ('petasma'). **B.** *Rhynchothalestris helgolandica*, male urosome (excluding somite bearing fifth legs) showing symmetrical, medially fused sixth legs, ventral view. **C.** *Sunaristes dardani*, male sixth legs. **D.** *Ambunguipes rufocincta*, male sixth legs.

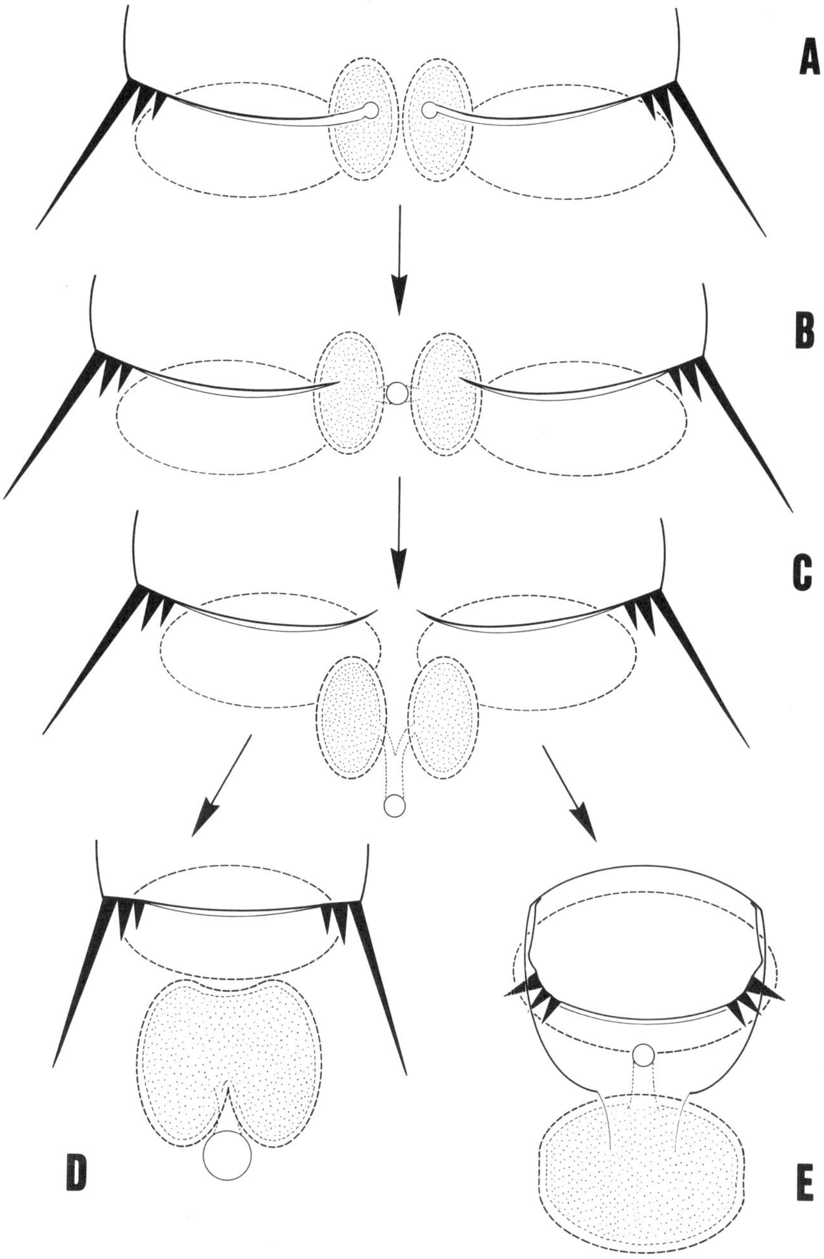

Figure 2.4.27. Schematic diagrams of female genital apertures in Harpacticoida. **A.** Ancestral condition with paired copulatory pores. **B.** Copulatory pores fused to form isolated median pore. **C.** Posterior migration of median copulatory pore. **D.** Fusion of seminal receptacles and of genital apertures. **E.** Relocation of copulatory pore within median genital aperture (Longipediidae.)

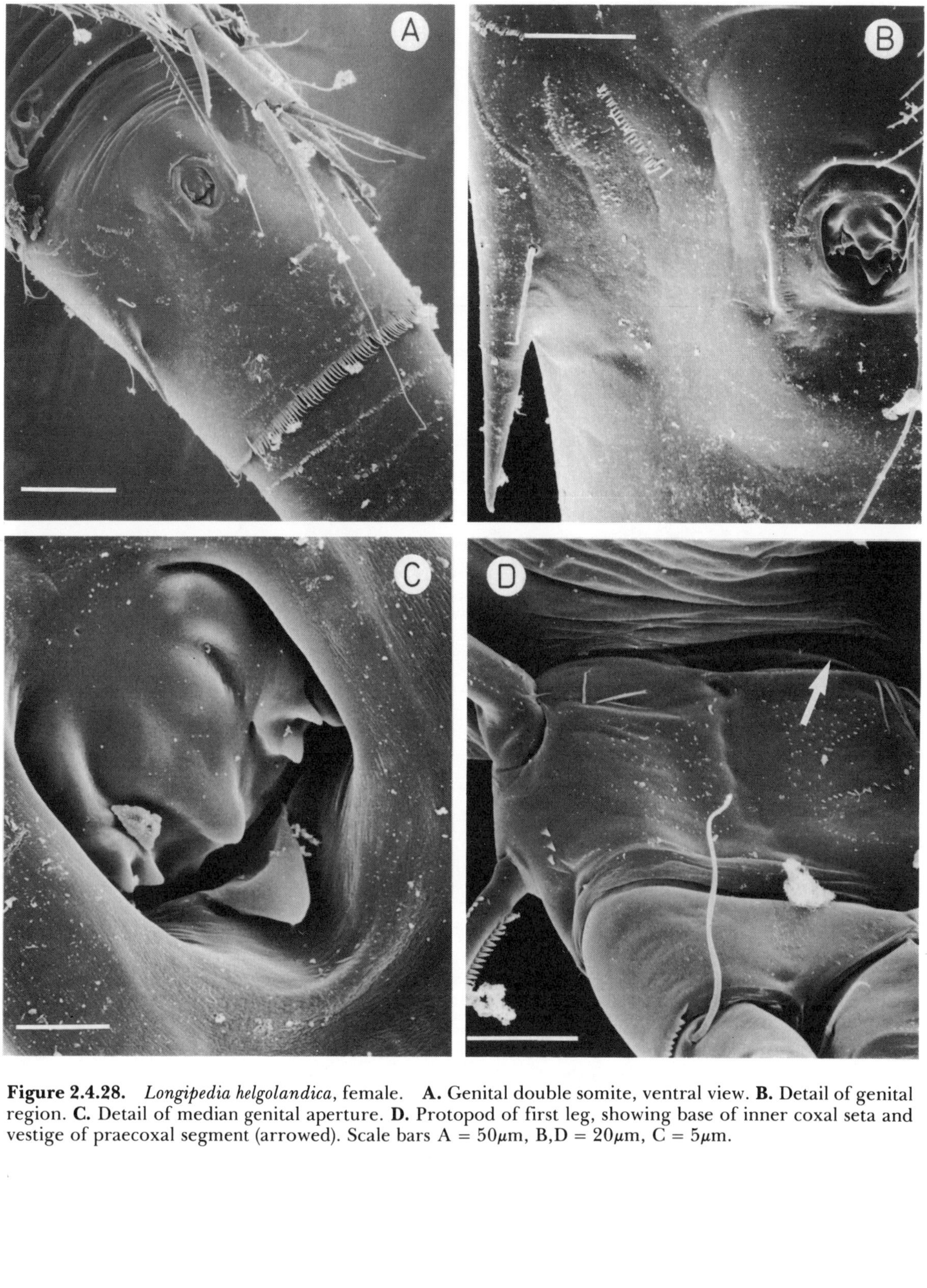

Figure 2.4.28. *Longipedia helgolandica*, female. **A.** Genital double somite, ventral view. **B.** Detail of genital region. **C.** Detail of median genital aperture. **D.** Protopod of first leg, showing base of inner coxal seta and vestige of praecoxal segment (arrowed). Scale bars A = 50μm, B,D = 20μm, C = 5μm.

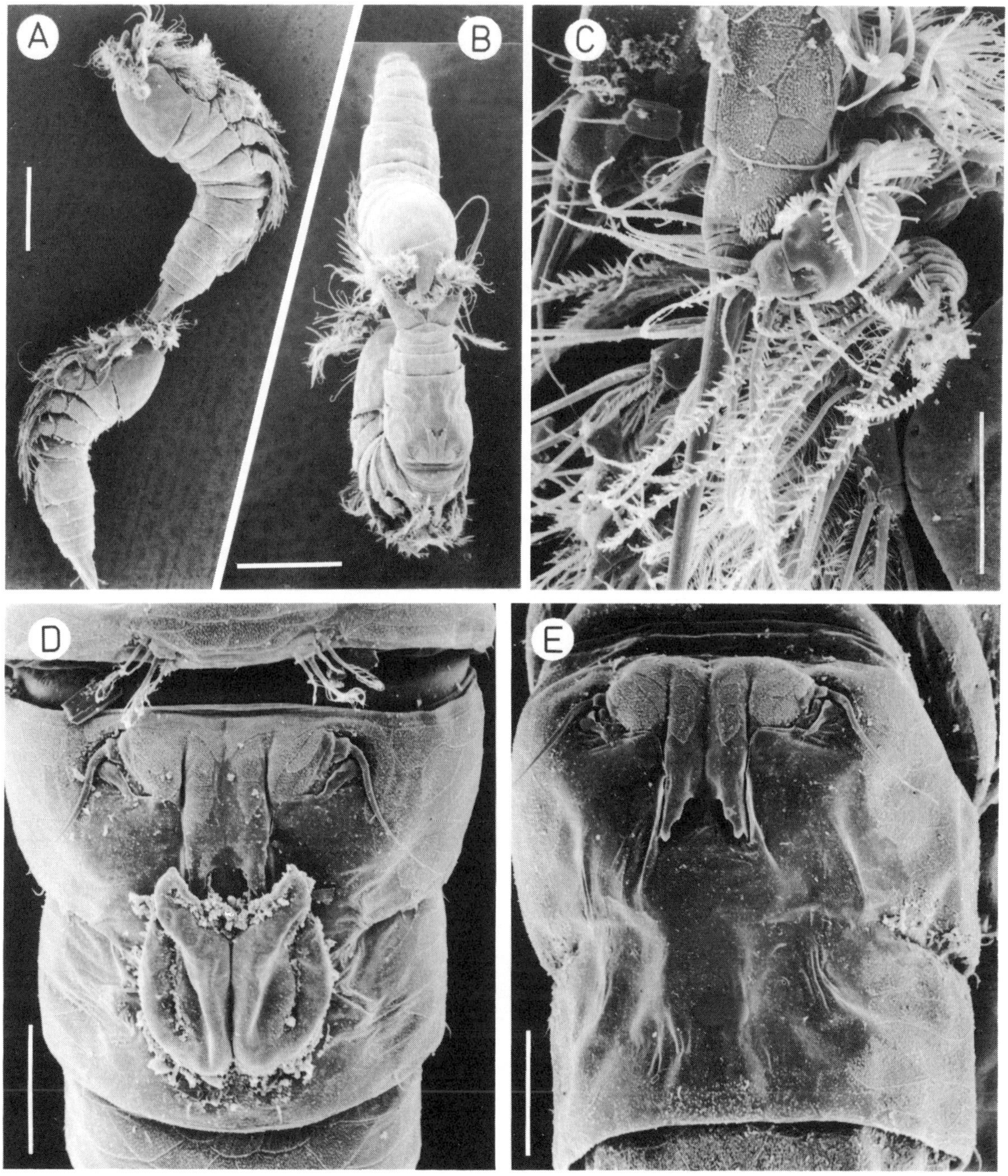

Figure 2.4.29. *Canuella perplexa.* **A.** Adult male holding adult female by the caudal rami. **B.** Same. **C.** Detail of male antennules grasping female caudal rami. **D.** Female genital double somite with pair of spermatophores attached. **E.** Same, without spermatophores. Scale bars A,B = 250μm, C-E = 50μm.

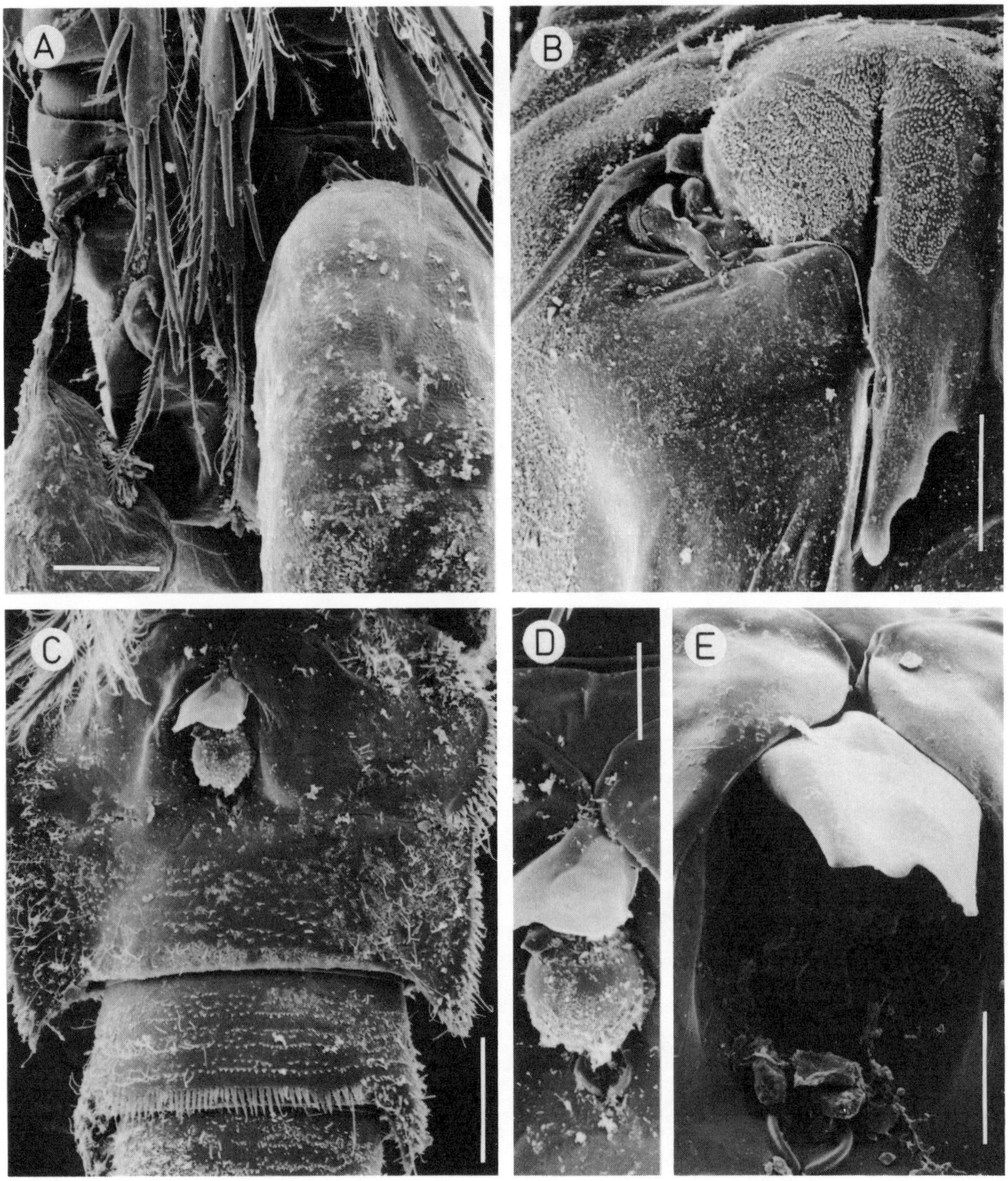

Figure 2.4.30. **A.** *Canuella perplexa*, female, ventral view of egg sacs (egg sac on right side deformed). **B.** Detail of genital aperture on right side. **C.** *Ambunguipes rufocincta*, female genital double somite. **D.** Detail showing epicopulatory plate and bulb. **E.** Same, with bulb removed showing position of copulatory pore. Scale bars A,C = 50μm, B,D = 20μm, E = 10μm.

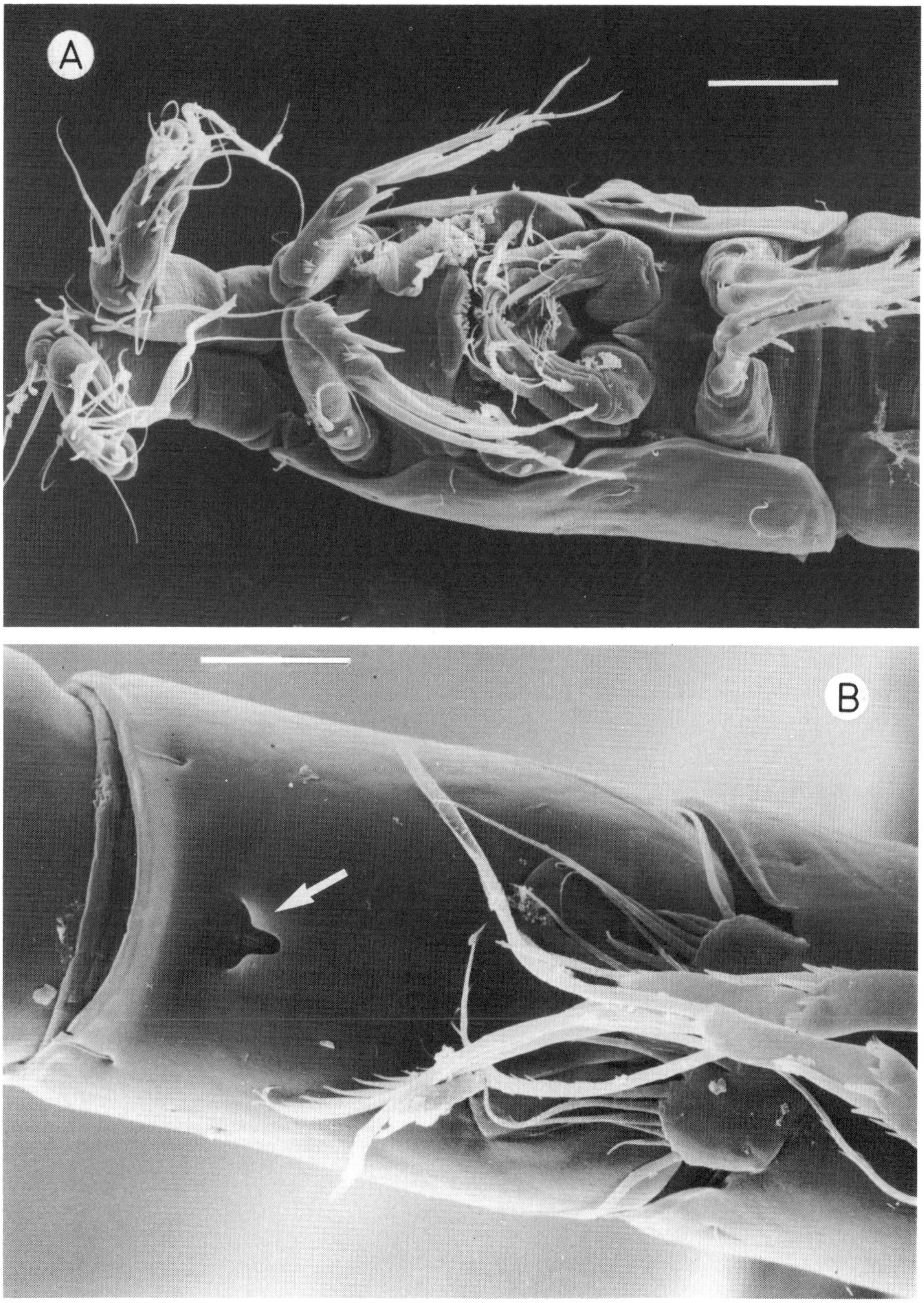

Figure 2.4.31. *Cylindropsyllus laevis*. **A.** Cephalothorax of male, ventral view showing vestigial maxillipeds. **B.** Genital double somite of female, ventral view showing median copulatory pore (arrowed). Scale bars A = 50μm, B = 20μm.

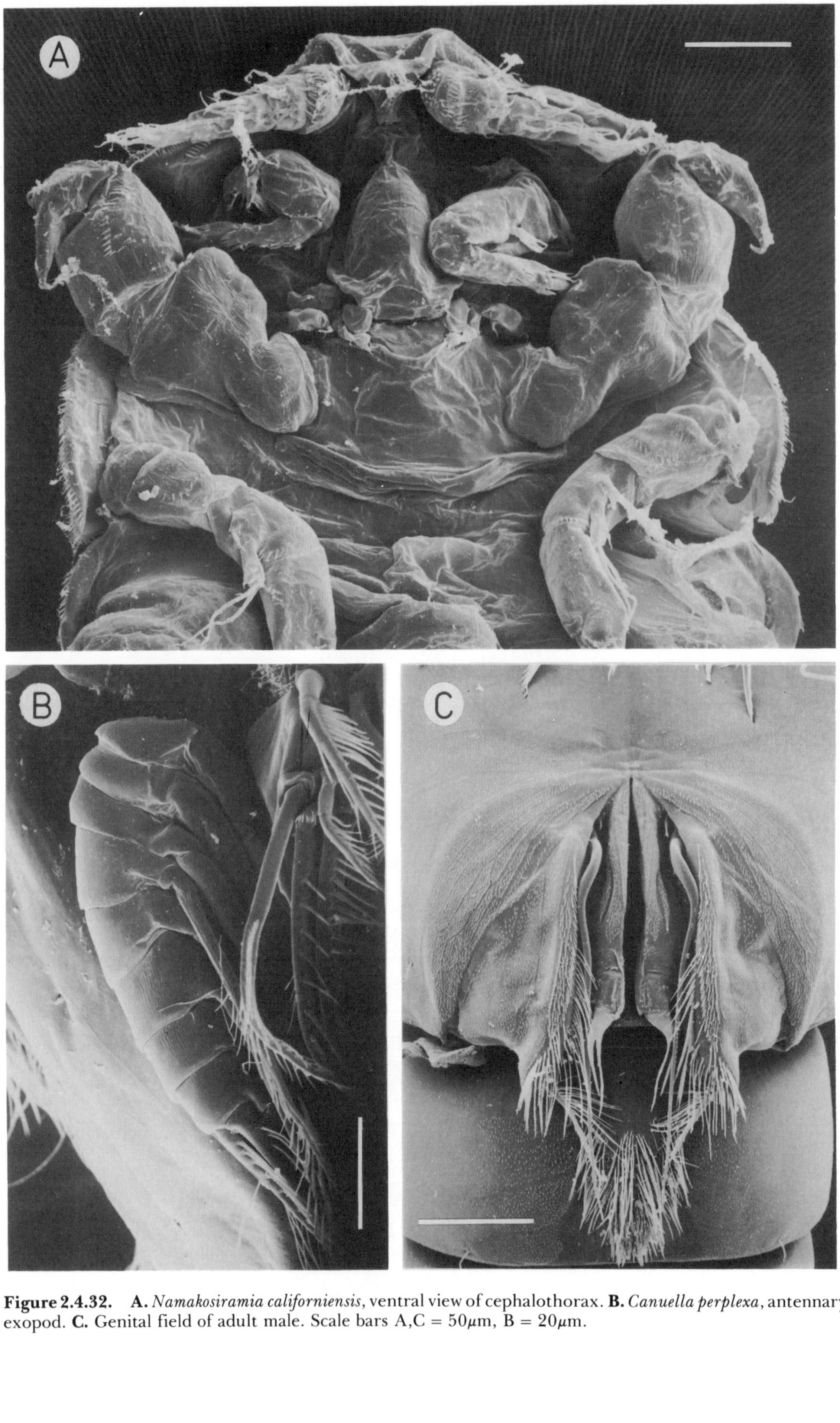

Figure 2.4.32. **A.** *Namakosiramia californiensis*, ventral view of cephalothorax. **B.** *Canuella perplexa*, antennary exopod. **C.** Genital field of adult male. Scale bars A,C = 50μm, B = 20μm.

2.5 MONSTRILLOIDA Sars 1903

All monstrilloids have endoparasitic naupliar and early postnaupliar stages and free-swimming, non-feeding adults. Monstrilloid females carry their eggs on long ovigerous spines. These eggs hatch into nauplii that locate a host and burrow into its tissues. The known hosts are polychaete worms (Malaquin, 1901; Caullery & Mesnil, 1914; Hartman, 1961) and prosobranch molluscs (Pelseneer, 1914). Once they have entered the host's blood system the nauplii transform into a sac-like body bearing root-like anterior processes. After development is complete the monstrilloid leaves the host as a last copepodid stage and undertakes a single moult into the adult.

Character set of ancestral monstrilloid

Copepoda. Prosome comprising cephalothorax incorporating first pedigerous somite (=second thoracic somite) and 3 free pedigerous somites; urosome 4-segmented in female (figure 2.5.1A), 5-segmented in male (figure 2.5.8A-B). Prosome-urosome articulation between fourth and fifth pedigerous somites (podoplean position). Genital double somite in female formed by ventral fusion of genital and first abdominal somites; dorsal suture present marking plane of fusion (figure 2.5.2D). Genital apertures paired in male and ventrally located, often on bifid genital prominence (figure 2.5.8A-D). Female with median genital aperture located anterior to ovigerous spines on ventral surface of genital double somite (figure 2.5.4C-E). Large median copulatory pore present on ventral surface of genital double somite (figure 2.5.12B). Seminal receptacles fused. Rostrum absent in adult (figure 2.5.7A-B). Caudal ramus with 6 setae, seta I lacking (figure 2.5.2C). Nauplius eye present. Antennules anteriorly directed; indistinctly 4-segmented in female (figure 2.5.3D); 5-segmented, bilaterally symmetrical and geniculate in male, geniculation between segments 4 and 5 (figures 2.5.5 and 2.5.6). Segment distal to geniculation in male representing fused segments XXI to XXVIII. Antenna to maxilliped absent in adult (figure 2.5.10A). Small median process with apical opening present in centre of ventral surface of cephalosome (figures 2.5.9A-C and 2.5.10A-C). Swimming legs 1-4 biramous, with 3-segmented rami (figure 2.5.2A); members of leg pair joined by intercoxal sclerite; coxa and basis incompletely fused in all legs; inner coxal seta absent; outer seta on basis present, inner seta on basis of first leg absent; first segment of exopod of leg 1 with 1 spine on outer margin. Spine and seta formula for legs 1 to 4:

	coxa	basis	exopod segment 1 2 3	endopod segment 1 2 3
leg 1	0 – 0	1 – 0	I – 1; 0 – 1; I,I,3	0 – 1; 0 – 1; 1,2,2
leg 2	0 – 0	1 – 0	I – 1; 0 – 1; I,I,4	0 – 1; 0 – 1; 1,2,2
leg 3	0 – 0	1 – 0	I – 1; 0 – 1; I,I,4	0 – 1; 0 – 1; 1,2,2
leg 4	0 – 0	1 – 0	I – 1; 0 – 1; I,I,4	0 – 1; 0 – 1; 1,2,2

Female fifth leg bilobed; inner and outer lobes bearing 2 and 3 setae and representing endopod and exopod respectively (figure 2.5.1C). Male fifth leg comprising a tiny lobe bearing a single seta (figure 2.5.7D-E). Intercoxal sclerite absent between fifth legs of both sexes; inner coxal seta absent. Sixth legs represented by single opercular plate closing off median genital aperture in female, and by paired plates closing genital apertures in male. Eggs borne in masses on ovigerous spines (figures 2.5.1A and 2.5.4A), not enclosed in sacs. Nauplius stages endoparasitic, with paired root-like processes. Copepodid stages endoparasitic, developing within membranous sac inside host (figure 2.5.3A).

Remarks

The phylogenetic relationships of the Monstrilloida have always been problematical, due largely to the lack of mouthparts in the adults but also to the presence of two very different families, the Monstrillidae and the Thespesiopsyllidae. These two families are classified together solely on the basis of the absence of mouthparts from the antennae through to the maxillipeds. It is, however, very difficult to assess the homology of a state of complete absence as found in these families. The relationship between the Thespesiopsyllidae to the Monstrilloida Genuina was questioned by

Fosshagen (1970) who suggested that the true affinities of this family might lie with the Cyclopoida siphonostoma (now treated as a separate order, the Siphonostomatoida). We have re-examined representatives of both families in detail. The diagnosis given above is based solely on the Monstrillidae because, as a result of this study, the Thespesiopsyllidae is herein transferred to the Cyclopoida. *Thespesiopsyllus paradoxus* (Sars) has a median copulatory pore located on the ventral surface of the genital double somite at the same level as the dorsolateral oviduct openings (figure 2.8.35E). This is an apomorphy of most Cyclopoida except for the family Oithonidae and a few representatives of other families. *T.paradoxus* also bears paired egg sacs, as is typical for the Cyclopoida, rather than the ovigerous spines of the Monstrillidae. A detailed comparison of characters of the Monstrillidae and Thespesiopsyllidae is given in Table 3.

Table 3. Comparison of the Monstrillidae and Thespesiopsyllidae

Character	Monstrillidae	Thespesiopsyllidae
Female genital apertures	median, fused	paired, lateral
Caudal ramus	6 setae	7 setae
Antennules (female)	4 segments	15 segments
(male)	5 segments	13 segments
Segments distal to geniculation	1	2
Rostrum of adult	absent or rudimentary	present
Oral structures	conical opening	labrum
Legs 1 to 3	coxa/basis partly fused	free
Inner coxal seta	absent legs 1 to 4	present
Leg 4 exopod	3-segmented	2-segmented
endopod	3-segmented	1-segmented
intercoxal sclerite	present	absent
Leg 5 (female)	biramous	uniramous
Leg 5 exopod (female)	fused to protopod, 1-segmented	free
Leg 6	ovigerous spines or median operculum	paired opercula
Eggs	carried on ovigerous spines	paired egg sacs

The Monstrillidae is in urgent need of revision. The genera are poorly defined and most species are inadequately described. The diagnosis is based on the genera *Monstrilla* Dana, *Thaumaleus* Krøyer and *Monstrillopsis* Sars which we accept as valid. The genus *Strilloma* Isaac is too poorly characterised (Isaac, 1974b) to be a usable taxon. *Thaumatohessia* Giard was inadequately described and should be treated as a *genus inquirendum* but the reported presence of rudimentary mouthparts raises severe doubts as to its validity.

Body Segmentation: All monstrilloids have a cephalothorax fully incorporating the first pedigerous somite (figure 2.5.1A-B). The genus *Monstrilla* retains the highest number of urosome somites, 4 in female (figure 2.5.1A) and 5 in male (figure 2.5.8A-B). The posterior, rather than dorsal, position of the anus on the anal somite is shown in figure 2.5.12D.

Caudal Rami: *Monstrilla* possesses the largest number of setae on the caudal rami. Six seta are retained, with seta I being lost (figure 2.5.2C). Other genera are characterised by further reduction in the number of caudal setae. At least some species of *Monstrillopsis*, for example, have only 4 setae on the caudal ramus in the male (figure 2.5.8C).

Female Genital System: The female of *Monstrilla helgolandica* Claus has a 4-segmented urosome. The large genital double somite bears a suture dorsally marking the plane of fusion of the genital and first abdominal somites. No female monstrilloids retain a fully separate genital somite. The genital double somite bears the paired ovigerous spines ventrally about at the midlevel. Anterior to the origin of the ovigerous spines is a single, median genital aperture closed off by a large subrectangular flap (figures 2.5.4C-E and 2.5.12B). This flap is a rather fleshy, muscular area that is unarmed. It closes off the common genital antrum, opening to release the eggs. Paired oviducts open laterally into the genital antrum (figure 2.5.4C-E). A single median copulatory pore is present (arrowed in figures 2.5.2B,D, 2.5.4C-E and 2.5.12B). It is unusually large and opens directly into the median seminal receptacle (stippled in figure 2.5.4D-E). There is a single median receptacle duct leading from the seminal receptacle to the genital antrum.

Ovigerous Spines and Eggs: The ovigerous spines are often considerably longer than the urosome and are closely adpressed (figure 2.5.1C). These spines may be more than twice the length of the entire body in some species (figure 2.5.4A). Egg masses are carried on the ovigerous spines (figure 2.5.4B). The eggs are attached by means of a mucous substance secreted by the terminal part of the oviduct (Malaquin, 1901) and are not enclosed in any type of egg sac (figure 2.5.11B). The presence of two egg masses on the extremely long ovigerous spines of the female illustrated in figure 2.5.4A indicates that these ovigerous spines are capable of growth and confirms that monstrilloids produce batches of eggs iteratively, as do most other copepod groups.

The homology of the ovigerous spines is difficult to determine. There are alternative interpretations; either the ovigerous spines represent the sixth legs or they are novel structures. At the fifth copepodid stage the ovigerous spines are already well developed (figure 2.5.3B-C). They are filled with soft tissue but have no intrinsic musculature. The distal tip is pinnate and separated from the bulk of the ovigerous spine by a weak suture, suggesting a possible derivation from an articulating spinous element. At this stage the copulatory pore is absent and there is no evidence to suggest the gonopore is present. On the basis of this evidence one of us (Huys) interprets the ovigerous spines as representing part of the sixth legs. The presence of similar, paired articulating spines on the male genital prominence of *Monstrilla helgolandica* is interpreted as further evidence in support of this interpretation. The alternative interpretation (preferred by Boxshall) is that the muscular flap closing off the median genital aperture in the female is homologous with the genital operculum of other copepods and is derived from the fused sixth legs. The paired flaps closing the paired genital apertures of the males (figure 2.5.11D-E) are also derived from the sixth legs. This interpretation suggests that the ovigerous spines are novel structures.

Male Genital System: In male *Monstrillopsis dubia* (Scott) the urosome is 5-segmented and the genital somite possesses a massive, posteroventrally directed genital prominence which is bifid distally (figure 2.5.11C). In *M.dubia* the two distal lobes are unarmed. The genital openings are positioned at the tip of the genital prominence between the distal lobes. The paired openings are adjacent at the ventral midline, but each is closed off by a separate opercular flap, possibly representing the sixth leg (figure 2.5.11D-E). The paired vasa deferentia open close together on the genital prominence and elongate spermatophores are extruded (figure 2.5.8C-D). In *Monstrilla* the genital prominence is smaller (figures 2.5.7D-E and 2.5.8A-B) than in *Monstrillopsis* species. The paired genital apertures are in a similar position, either side of the midline, and spermatophores are extruded in pairs. Male *Monstrilla longicornis* Sars have posterolateral lobes on the genital prominence and each bears a weakly articulated spinous element distally (figure 2.5.7D-E). No such spinous processes are present in *M.helgolandica* (figure 2.5.8A-B).

Rostrum: Davis & Green (1974) figured a large rostrum for *M.nasuta* Davis & Green but this is the only monstrilloid with an anteriorly directed structure of this kind in the adult (figure 2.5.7A-B). In other monstrilloids the rostrum is either absent or represented by a slight extension of the anterior margin of the dorsal cephalic shield wrapped around the frontal surface of the cephalothorax. We interpret the presence of a rostrum of *M.nasuta* as a secondary condition, probably resulting from heterochrony since a similar structure is present in late copepodid stages of other monstrilloids but is gradually absorbed prior to emergence of the free adult.

Female Antennule: The antennules of female monstrilloids are indistinctly 4-segmented, although in *Monstrilla longiremis* Giesbrecht, for example, only the proximal segment is clearly defined (figure 2.5.3D). In *M.grandis* Giesbrecht (figure 2.5.1A) and in the *Monstrilla* species illustrated in figure 2.5.9D the first and second segments are both clearly defined. Establishing segmental homologies with the ancestral copepod state is impossible because of the great reductions in numbers of setation elements. It is possible to state, from the setation pattern, that at least segments XXVI to XXVIII are fused. Comparison with the male, and assuming that the aesthetasc present in both sexes is homologous, suggests that probably segments XXI to XXVIII are fused. Branched setae are found only in the distal part of the limb, corresponding to fused segments XXI-XXVIII of the male.

Male Antennule: The maximum number of segments in the male antennule is 5, as found in *Thaumaleus longispinosus* (Bourne) (figure 2.5.7C) and *Monstrillopsis* species (figure 2.5.5B). Reductions in segment numbers occur widely with segmental boundaries partly or completely disappearing (figures 2.5.5A and 2.5.6A). A single segment exists distal to the geniculation. This distal segment represents ancestral segments XXI to XXVIII. Proximal to the geniculation lies a clearly compound segment which, although its ancestral segmental composition cannot be determined indicates that segments XIX and XX at least must be fused. This compound segment bears the single conspicuous aesthetasc found on male monstrilloid antennules and we speculate that this aesthetasc probably is homologous with that of ancestral segment XVI. Too few setation elements remain to allow identification of segmental homologies in the proximal part of the limb.

The structure of the male antennule provides the most useful characters to distinguish between the monstrilloid genera. There are 4 types. The first is characterised by the lack of modification of the distal (XXI-XXVIII) segment. It is slender and elongate, and typically bears 2 spinous elements apically (figures 2.5.5A and 2.5.6E). It is found in most *Monstrilla* species. The second type is characterised by the presence of a hyaline bump proximally on the medial margin of segment XXI-XXVIII and by this segment tapering distally to a curved tip (figure 2.5.5B) homologous with one of the spinous elements of the first type. This is the *Monstrillopsis* type. The third type is characterised by the presence of 5 serrate ridges located on the anterior margin of the segment in its distal third (figure 2.5.6A-D). This type is found in some *Monstrilla* species such as *M.helgolandica*. The fourth type is found in *Thaumaleus* species and is clearly derived from the third type. The ridges are reduced but are still discernible as 5 marginal structures (see inset in figure 2.5.7C) on the swollen distal segment. The branched setae are typically found on the distal segment only, except in the *M.helgolandica* type which lacks such setae.

Swimming Legs: The swimming legs of monstrilloids are extremely uniform, with many species exhibiting the ancestral spine and seta formula. The hoop-like lateral sclerite representing the praecoxa is present in all legs (figure 2.5.2A), as is the intercoxal sclerite. The coxa and basis are partly fused in all species.

Fifth Leg: The fifth leg of female *M.grandis* is biramous but both rami are fused to the protopodal part of the limb. The 3 setae on the exopod and the 2 setae on the endopod represent the maximum setation found in the Monstrilloida. The same setation pattern of 3 exopodal and 2 endopodal setae is found in *Monstrilla orcula* Scott and *M.cymbula* Scott (Scott, 1909). Other genera possess a single endopodal seta, or the endopodal lobe is unarmed (figure 2.5.3C). The male fifth leg is missing in *Monstrillopsis* (figures 2.5.8A-D and 2.5.11C), *Thaumaleus* and in some species of *Monstrilla*. The small lobe bearing a single seta is present in *M.grandis* although Isaac (1974a) reported a male of this species with 3 setae on each leg. Sars (1921) figured the male of *M.longicornis* with 2 setae on each fifth leg. We have examined numerous males of this species and found only 1 seta (figure 2.5.7D-E). The presence of more than 1 seta on male fifth legs in the Monstrilloida remains to be confirmed but it is possible that this is a variable character since Sars (1921) mentioned some specimens of *M.longicornis* with only 1 seta as well as those he figured with 2 setae.

Differential Diagnosis: The monstrilloids exhibit many unique apomorphies, most of which are linked to their unusual biology. The nauplii of monstrillids live as endoparasites of polychaete worms and gastropod molluscs. The nauplii obtain nourishment via absorptive processes. These vary in number and form with genus. Three pairs of long processes are found in *Monstrilla*, 2 or less in other genera. There are sometimes vestiges of these processes visible on the ventral surface of the cephalothorax of the free-swimming adult. The larvae emerge from their host at the fifth copepodid stage and moult once into the adult at the beginning of the planktonic phase.

Monstrilloids are readily recognised by the absence of mouthparts, the form of the anteriorly directed antennules in both sexes, and the presence of ovigerous spines in the females. Monstrilloids lack egg sacs, instead the eggs are attached to the paired ovigerous spines. These spines are located posterior to the median genital aperture of the female. The origin of the ovigerous spines is unclear. Either they represent an isolated part of the sixth legs that carries the setation element, or they are a novel structure. Identifying the homology of the ovigerous spines requires a detailed examination of the ontogeny of the reproductive apparatus of the female.

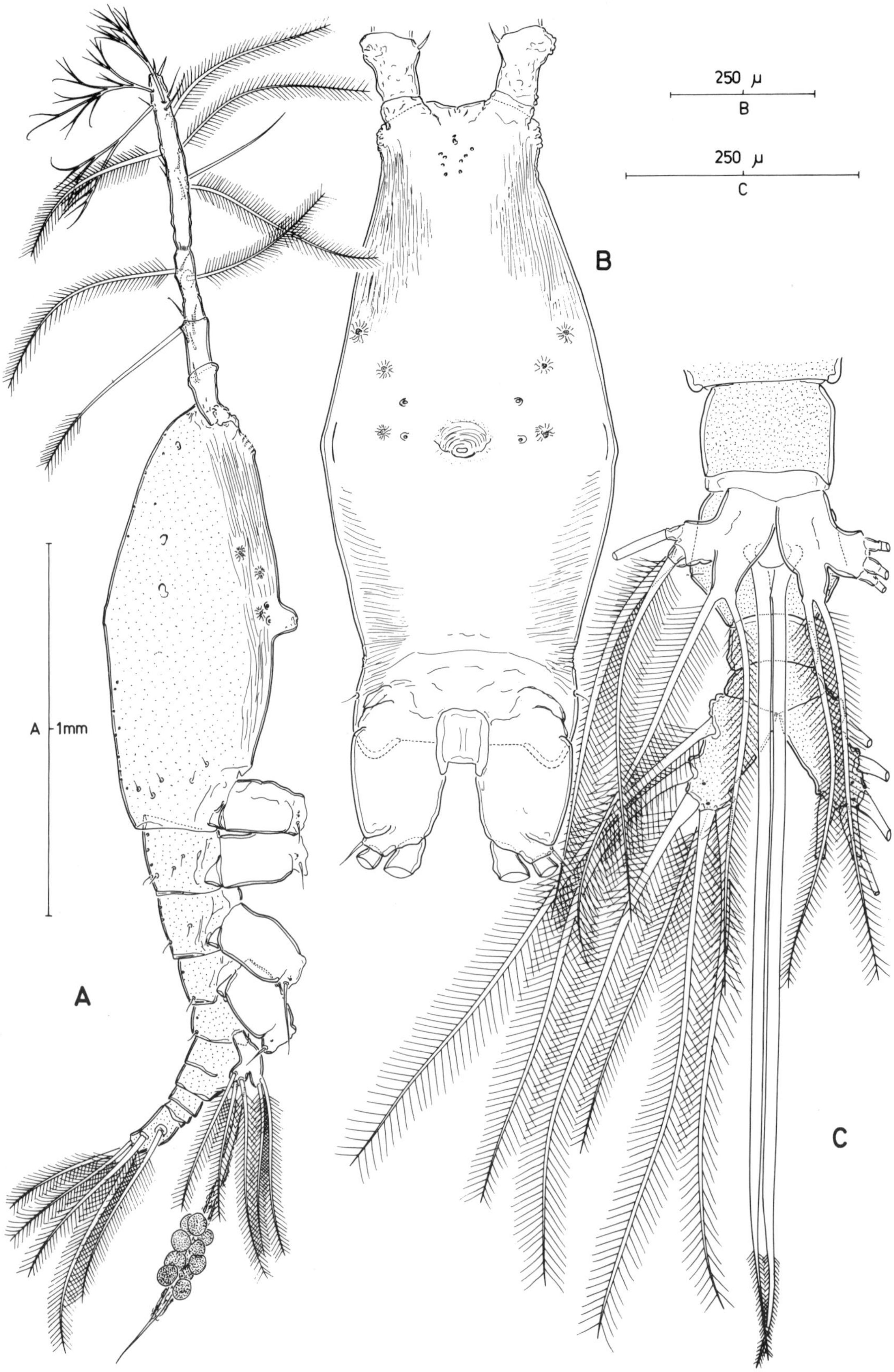

Figure 2.5.1. *Monstrilla grandis.* **A.** Female, lateral view. **B.** Cephalothorax, ventral view. **C.** Urosome, ventral view.

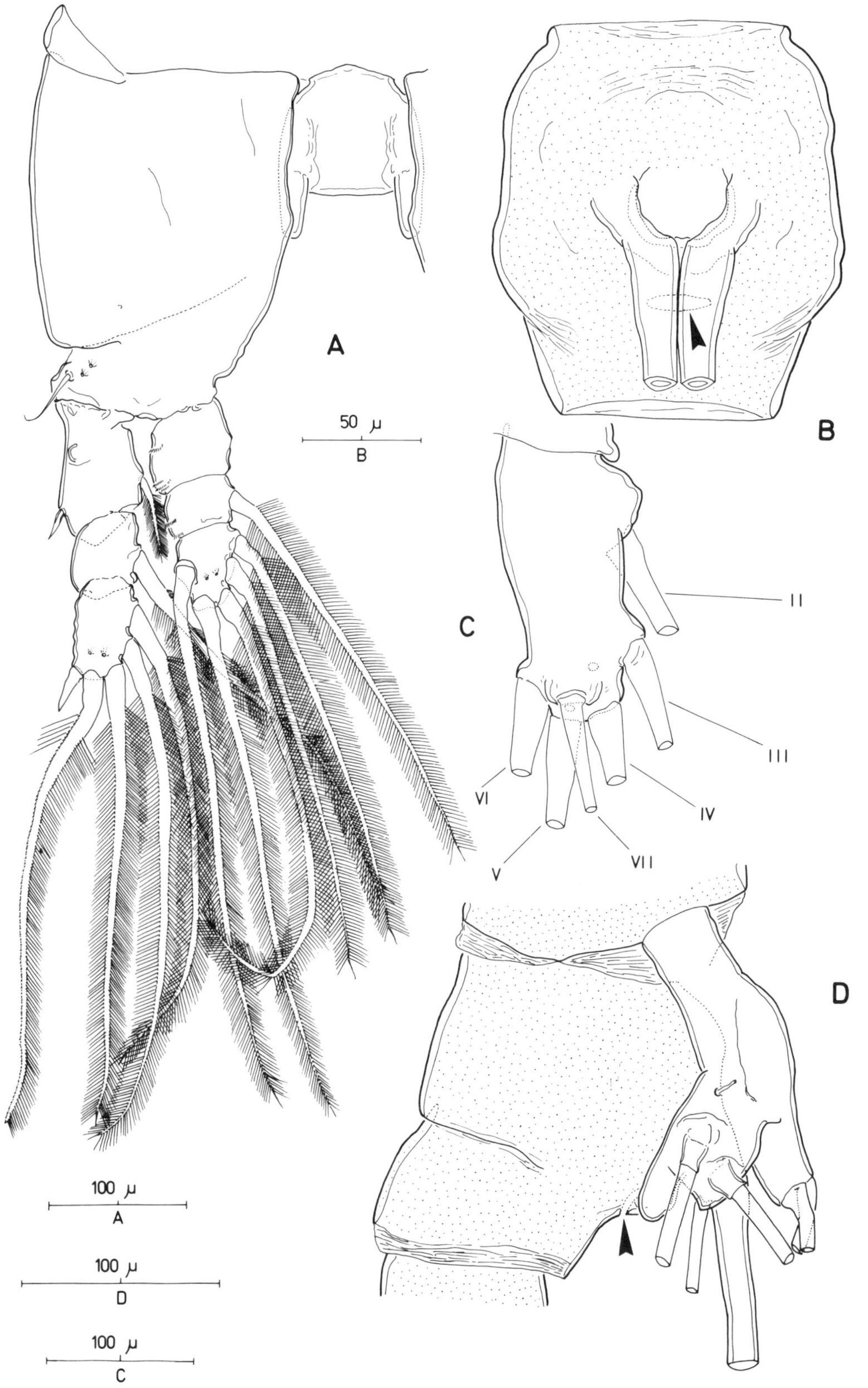

Figure 2.5.2. *Monstrilla grandis*. **A.** Second swimming leg, anterior view. **B.** Female genital double somite, ventral view. **C.** Caudal ramus, dorsal view. **D.** Fifth leg and female genital double somite, lateral view. [Copulatory pores arrowed in B and D.]

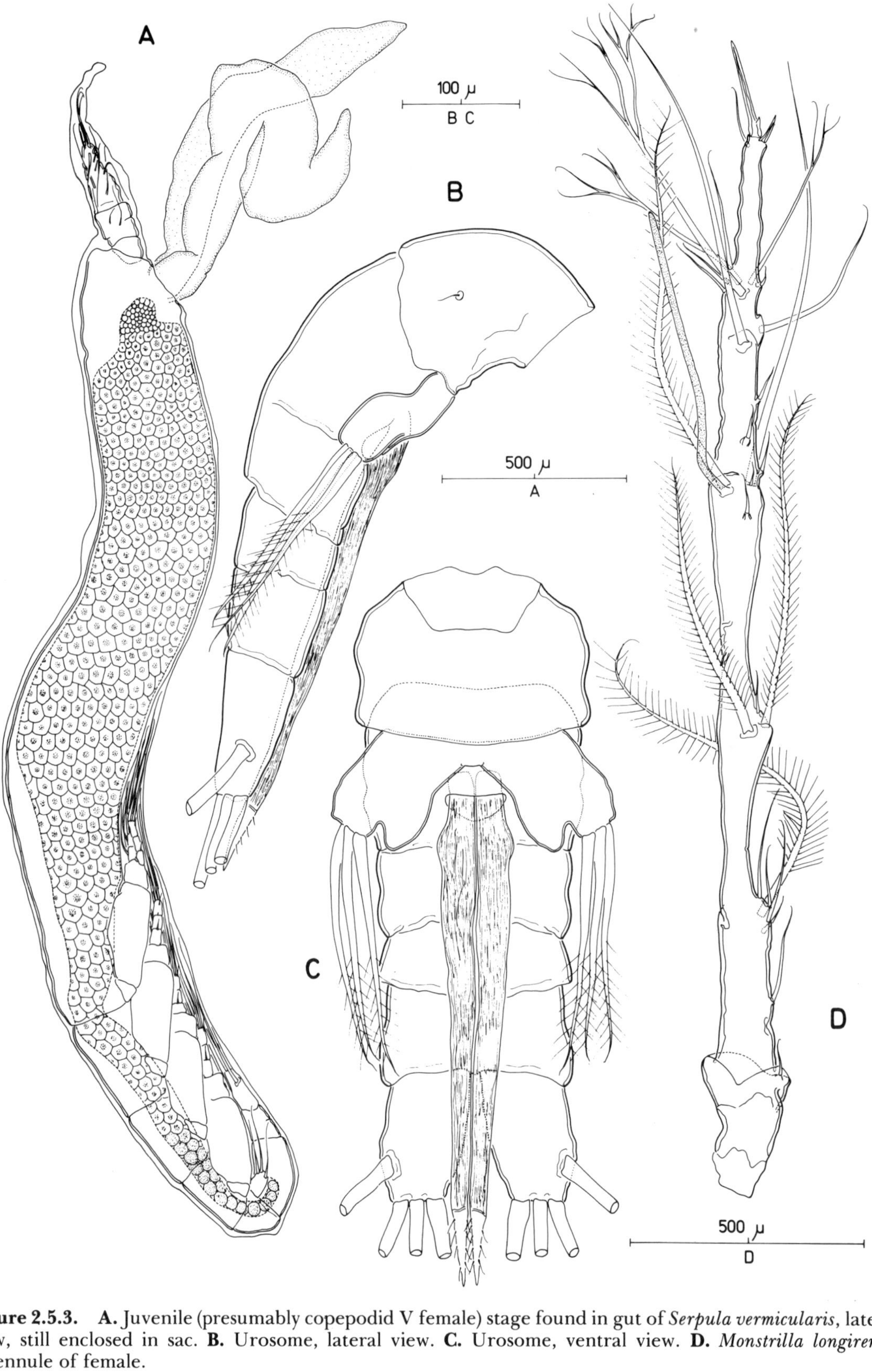

Figure 2.5.3. **A.** Juvenile (presumably copepodid V female) stage found in gut of *Serpula vermicularis*, lateral view, still enclosed in sac. **B.** Urosome, lateral view. **C.** Urosome, ventral view. **D.** *Monstrilla longiremis*, antennule of female.

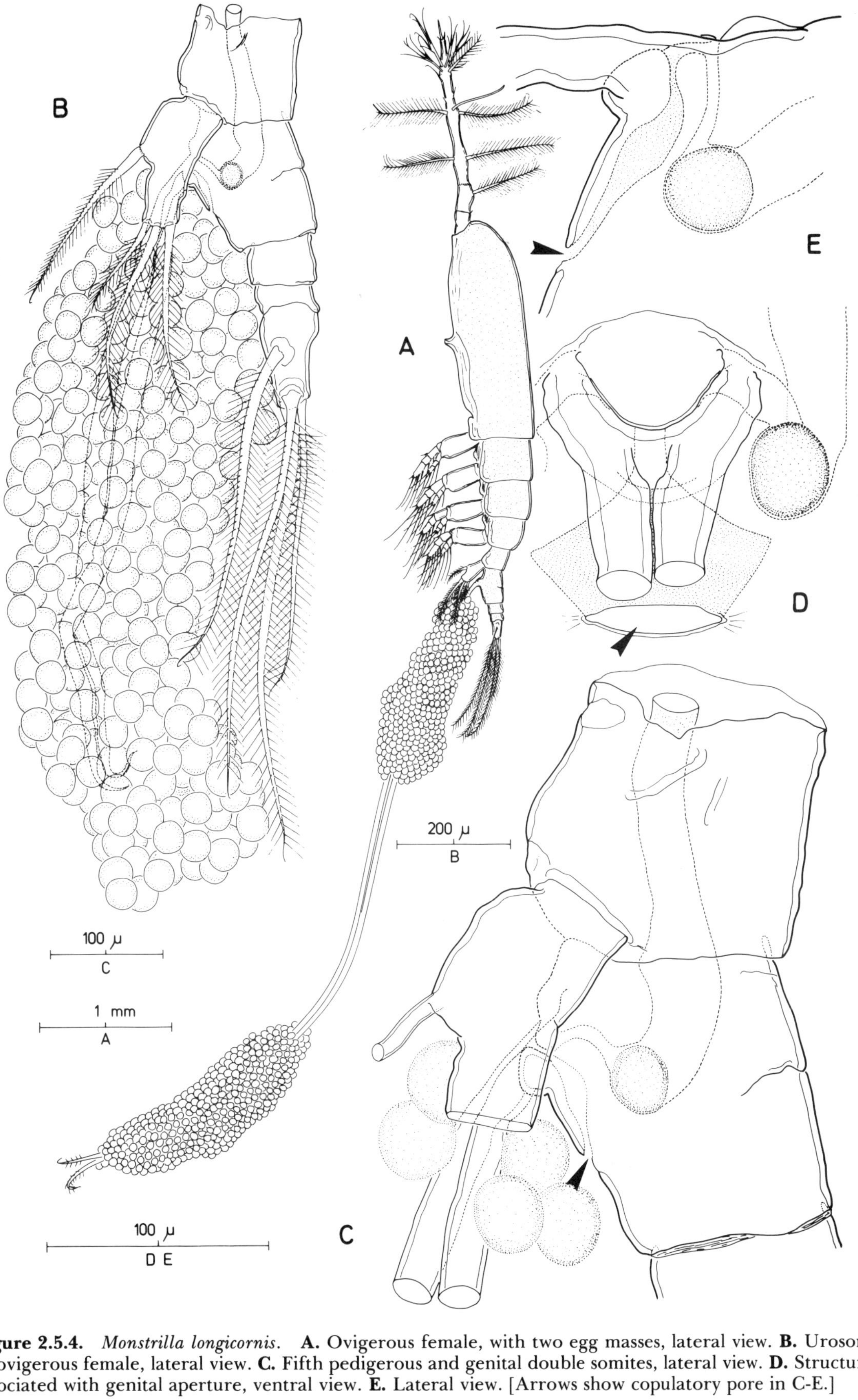

Figure 2.5.4. *Monstrilla longicornis.* **A.** Ovigerous female, with two egg masses, lateral view. **B.** Urosome of ovigerous female, lateral view. **C.** Fifth pedigerous and genital double somites, lateral view. **D.** Structures associated with genital aperture, ventral view. **E.** Lateral view. [Arrows show copulatory pore in C-E.]

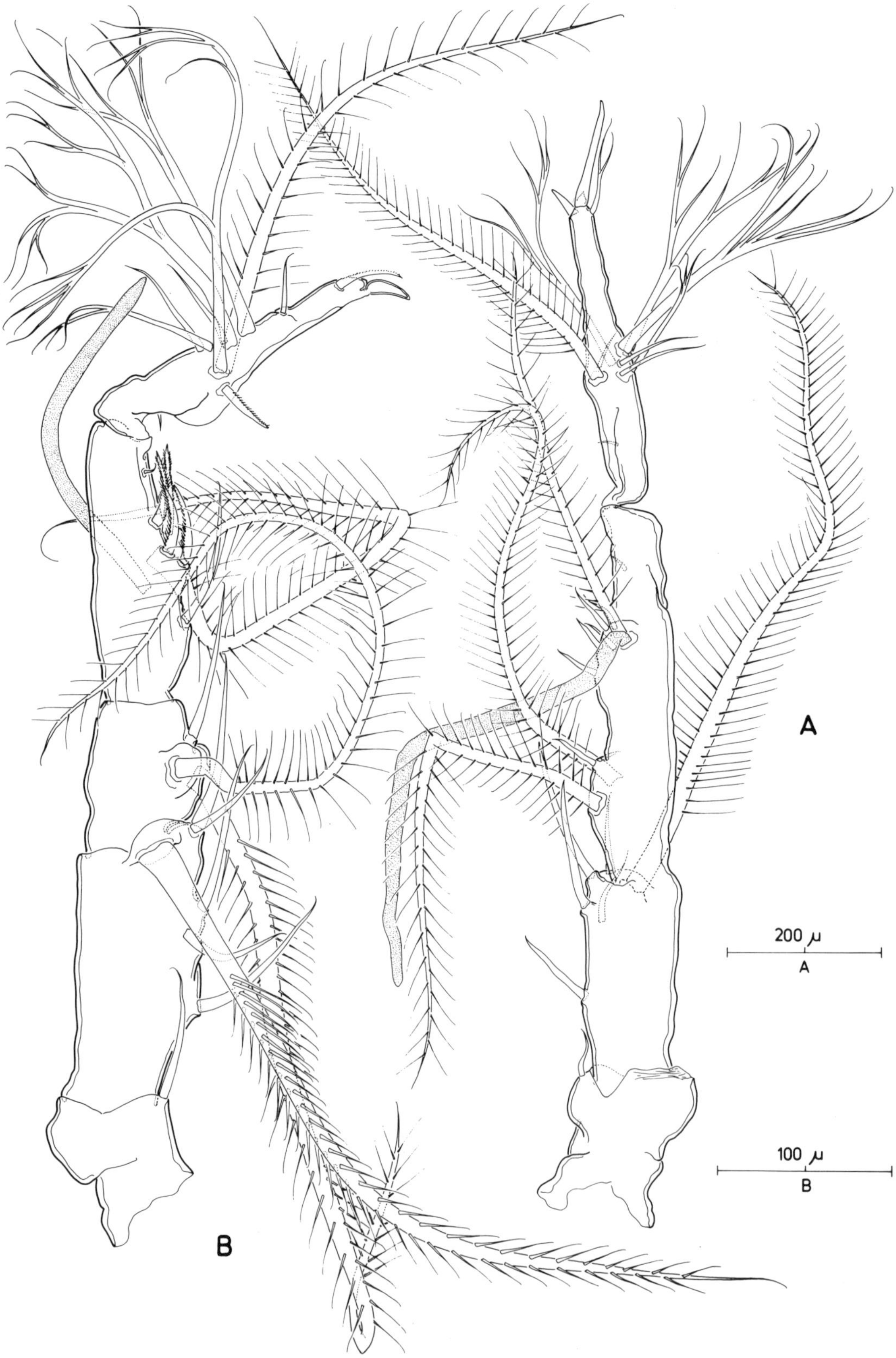

Figure 2.5.5. **A.** *Monstrilla longicornis*, antennule of male. **B.** *Monstrillopsis* sp., antennule of male.

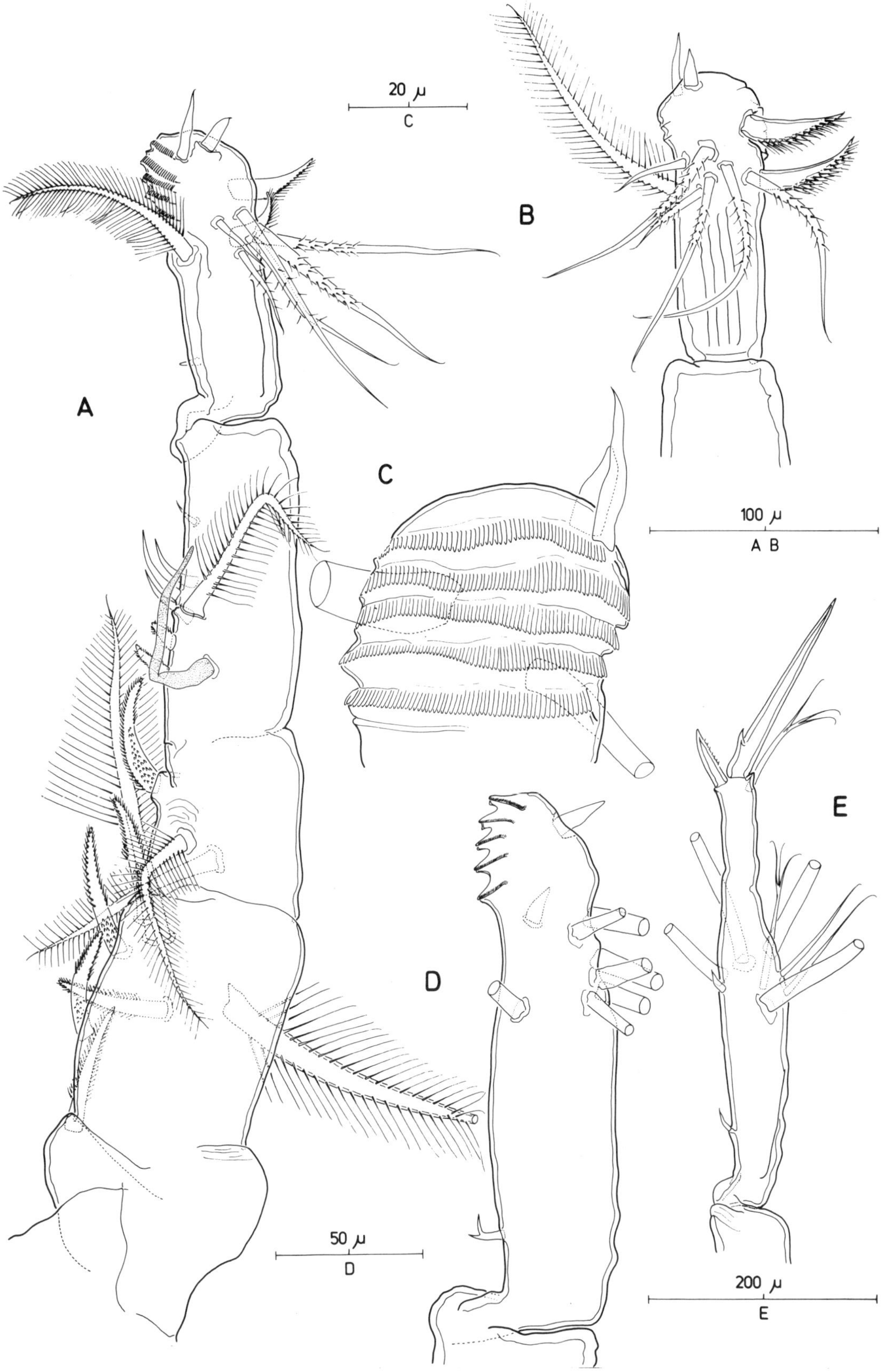

Figure 2.5.6. **A.** *Monstrilla* sp., antennule of male. **B.** Distal segment, posterior view. **C.** Tip of distal segment, anterior view. **D.** *Monstrilla helgolandica*, distal segment of male antennule. **E.** *Monstrilla longiremis*, distal segment of male antennule.

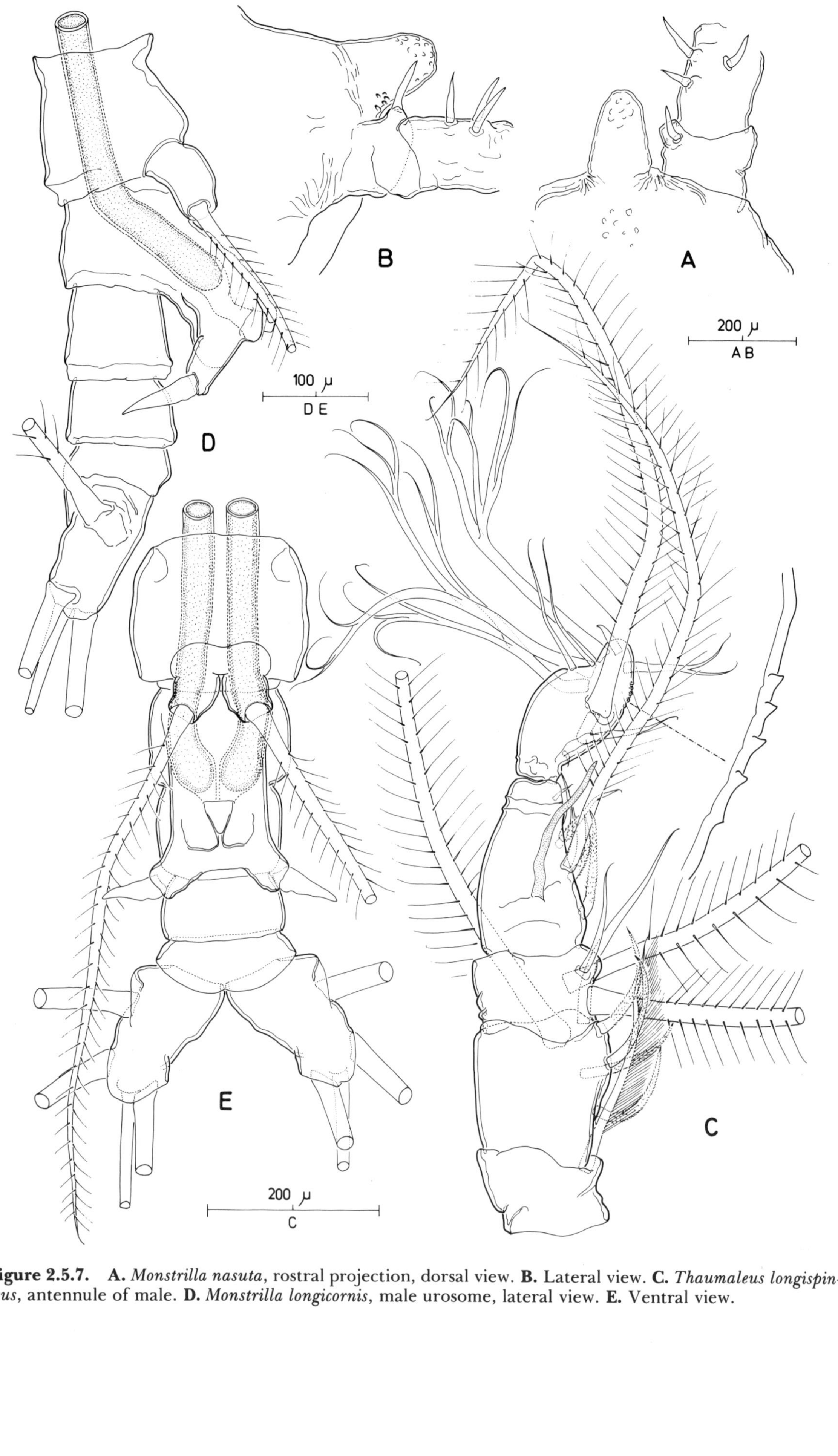

Figure 2.5.7. **A.** *Monstrilla nasuta*, rostral projection, dorsal view. **B.** Lateral view. **C.** *Thaumaleus longispinosus*, antennule of male. **D.** *Monstrilla longicornis*, male urosome, lateral view. **E.** Ventral view.

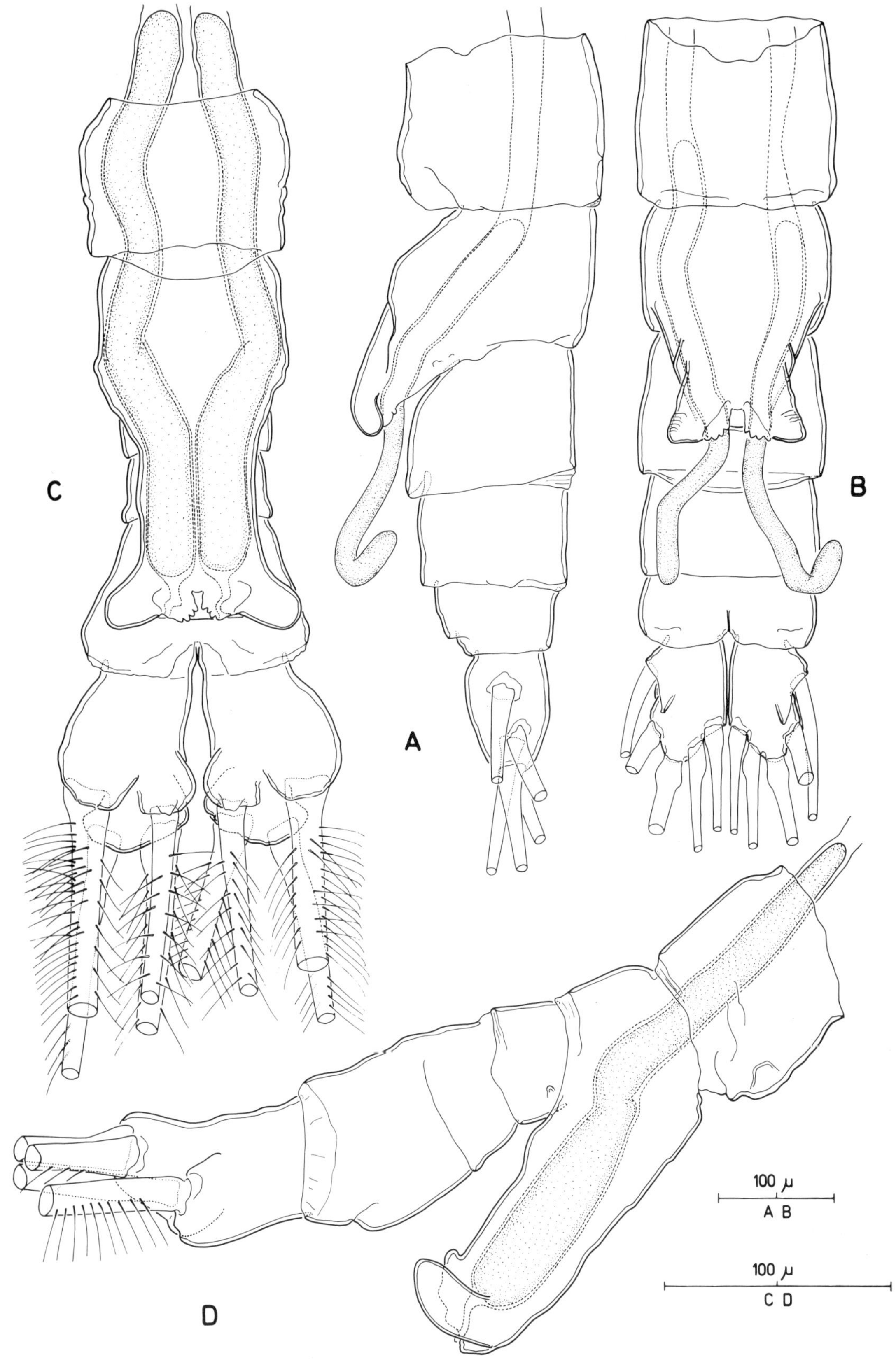

Figure 2.5.8. **A.** *Monstrilla helgolandica*, male urosome with spermatophores partly discharged, lateral view. **B.** Ventral view. **C.** *Monstrillopsis* sp., male urosome, ventral view. **D.** Lateral view.

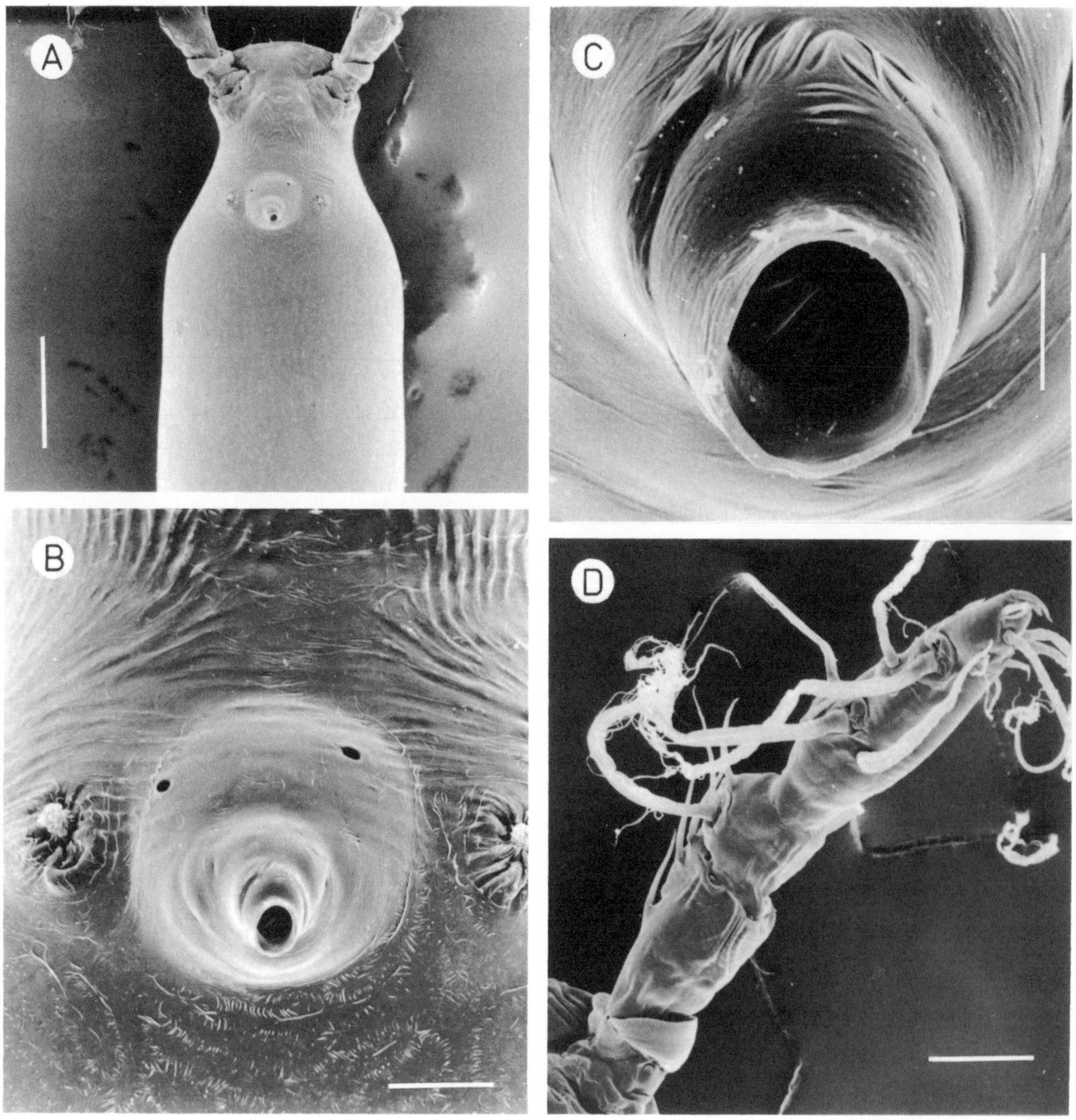

Figure 2.5.9. *Monstrilla* sp., female. **A.** Anterior part of cephalothorax, ventral view. **B.** Detail of oral region showing mouth cone and adjacent pores and scars. **C.** Detail of mouth cone. **D.** Antennule, ventral view. Scale bars A = 100μm, B = 20μm, C = 5μm, D = 40μm.

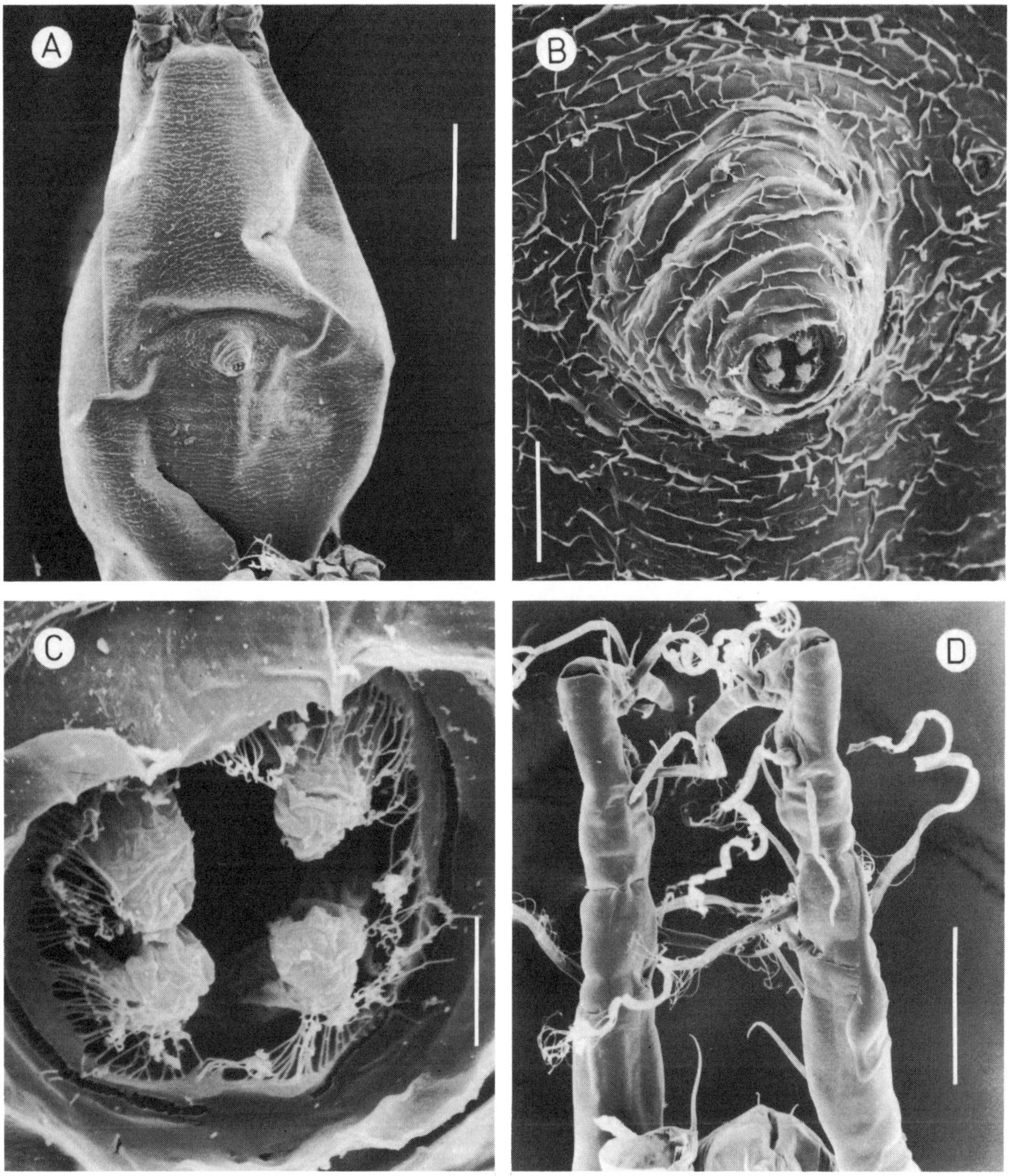

Figure 2.5.10. **A.** *Monstrilla helgolandica* female, cephalothorax, ventral view. **B.** Detail of oral region. **C.** Detail of mouth cone. **D.** *Monstrilla* sp., male antennule, ventral view. Scale bars A = 200μm, B = 30μm, C = 5μm, D = 100μm.

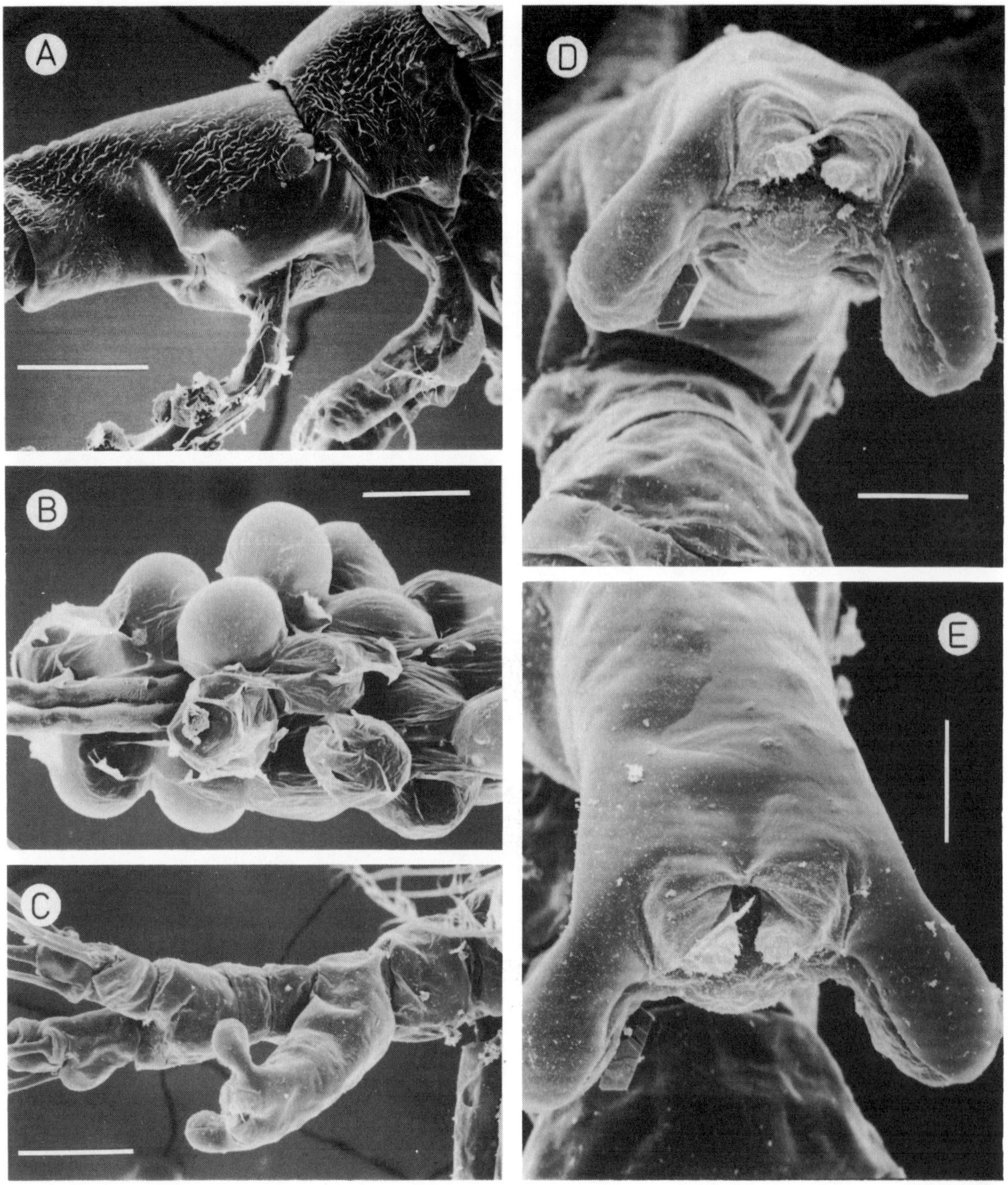

Figure 2.5.11. **A.** *Monstrilla helgolandica* female, lateral view of fifth pedigerous and genital double somites. **B.** Detail of egg mass attached to ovigerous spines. **C.** *Monstrillopsis dubia* male, lateral view of urosome. **D.** Detail of genital prominence showing gonopores, posterior view. **E.** Detail of genital prominence showing gonopores, ventral view. Scale bars A = 75μm, B = 20μm, C = 100μm, D,E = 30μm.

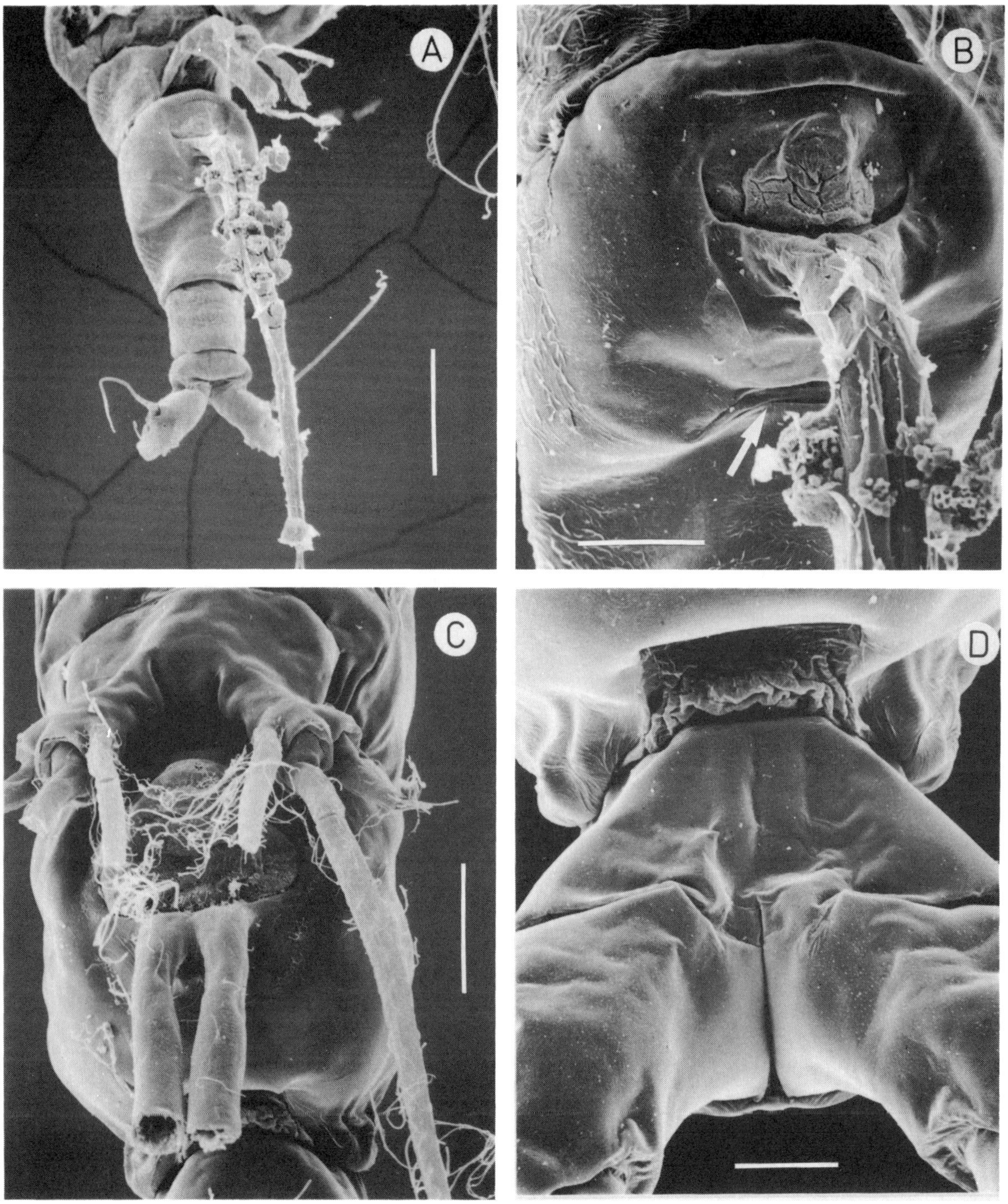

Figure 2.5.12. **A.** *Monstrilla helgolandica* female, urosome, ventral view. **B.** Detail of genital aperture, showing bases of ovigerous spines and position of copulatory pore (arrowed). **C.** *Monstrilla* sp. female, anterior part of urosome showing fused fifth legs and broken ovigerous spines. **D.** Posterior part of urosome showing slit-like anus. Scale bars A = 100μm, B = 20μm, C = 100μm, D = 10μm.

2.6 MORMONILLOIDA Boxshall 1979

The two species of the Mormonilloida, *M.phasma* and *M.minor*, are widely distributed in the world's oceans at depths of 400 to 1500 metres (Boxshall, 1979). The females of both species have a large filter basket of setae and are particle-feeders. Ruth Böttger-Schnack recently found several females carrying paired egg sacs, females with spermatophores attached and males of both species of *Mormonilla* in the Red Sea (Huys et al., in press).

Character set of ancestral mormonilloid

Copepoda. Prosome comprising cephalosome and 4 free pedigerous somites (figure 2.6.1); urosome 4-segmented in female (figure 2.6.2C), 5-segmented in male (figure 2.6.1A-B). Prosome-urosome articulation between fourth and fifth pedigerous somites (podoplean position). Female with genital double somite comprising fused genital and first abdominal somites (figure 2.6.2A-D); with single median genital aperture located ventrally on surface of double somite. Single copulatory pore located within median genital aperture. Seminal receptacles fused medially. Male with paired genital apertures located ventrally on genital somite (figure 2.6.10A). Rostrum a flat sclerite on ventral surface between bases of antennules. Caudal ramus with 6 setae; seta I lacking (figures 2.6.5E-F and 2.6.10D). Nauplius eye present. Antennules 4-segmented and symmetrical (figure 2.6.3B). Setation pattern difficult to assess due to extreme reduction and migration of sites of origin. Male antennules geniculate, with reduced setation and indistinct segmentation; single segment present distal to geniculation representing fused XXI-XXVIII; segment proximal to geniculation probably representing fused XIV to XX (figure 2.6.4A-B). Antenna biramous with 8-segmented exopod in female and indistinctly 3-segmented endopod (figure 2.6.5A); coxa without seta; basis with 1 inner seta; first endopodal segment with 2 setae; setae of elongate second segment divided by migration along margin into proximal group of 5 setae remaining in position proximally on inner margin and distal group of 4 adjacent to 7 setae of third segment at apex of ramus (figure 2.6.5B). Exopodal segment 1 representing fused ancestral segments II-III, segments 2 to 8 representing segments IV to X; setal formula 2,1,1,1,1,1,1,3. Exopod 9-segmented in male (figure 2.6.4C) with ancestral segments II to X all separate; setation reduced to formula 1,0,0,0,0,1,1,1,3; endopod retaining only 11 apical elements. Labrum a massive muscular lobe in female (figure 2.6.3D-E), reduced in male (figure 2.6.8A). Mandible in female with large coxal gnathobase and biramous palp (figure 2.6.6E); basis bearing 3 setae on inner margin, distal 2 of which derived from incorporated first endopodal segment; second endopodal segment partly fused to basis, bearing 6 setae; exopod indistinctly 4-segmented, setal formula 2,1,1,2. Male mandible (figure 2.6.9A) reduced; with weak coxal gnathobase (figure 2.6.9B); basis unarmed; endopod 2-segmented, setal formula 0,5 setae; exopod indistinctly 4-segmented, setal formula 2,1,1,2 (figure 2.6.9C). Paragnaths separate (figure 2.6.3F). Maxillule (figure 2.6.7A) with small praecoxal endite (figure 2.6.7C) bearing armature of 7 elements; coxa and basis fused; coxal and proximal basal endites poorly developed, represented by 4 setae and 2 setae on inner margin, respectively (figure 2.6.7C); distal endite of basis probably lacking; epipodite incorporated into segment, represented by 2 setae on surface; outer seta of basis lacking; exopod 1-segmented with 7 setae; endopod with traces of subdivision (figure 2.6.7B), setal formula (2,1)5. Male maxillule (figure 2.6.8B-C) reduced; praecoxal arthrite vestigial; only 2 setae remaining on inner margin of fused coxa and basis; endopod 1-segmented with 4 apical setae; exopod 1-segmented with 5 apical setae. Maxilla 5-segmented in female (figure 2.6.5C); syncoxa with 4 endites, praecoxal endites sharing common origin (figure 2.6.5D); endite formula 2,3,3,3; allobasis with a large proximal (basal) endite bearing 2 setae, distal (endopodal) endite probably represented by single seta; outer coxal seta absent; free endopod 3-segmented, setal formula 1,1,4. Male maxilla (figure 2.6.8D-E) reduced to indistinctly segmented limb with 3 elements. Maxilliped in female (figure 2.0.2) 5-segmented comprising undivided protopod and 4 free endopodal segments, setal formula 1,1,1,4; syncoxal formula 0,0,2,1; basis with 3 setae. Male maxilliped reduced to unsegmented lobe bearing 2 setae (figure 2.6.9D). Swimming legs 1-4 in female biramous with 3-segmented rami except 2-segmented endopod of leg 2 and exopod of leg 4, and 1-segmented endopod of legs 3 and 4; members of leg pairs joined by intercoxal sclerite; inner coxal seta present in leg 1 (figure 2.6.7D), absent from legs 2 to 4; outer seta on basis absent; inner seta on basis of first leg present; first exopodal segment with 1 outer spine. Legs 1 to 4 in male with 3-segmented rami (figures 2.6.9E and 2.6.10C); spine and seta formula based on both sexes of *M.phasma* legs 1 to 4:

	coxa	basis	exopod segment 1 2 3	endopod segment 1 2 3
leg 1	0 – 1*	0 – I*	I – 0 ; I – 1 ; II,I,3	0 – 0; 0 – 0; 0,2,2
leg 2	0 – 0	0 – 0	*I – 0 ; 0 – 1; I,I,4	0 – 0; 0 – 0; 0,2,1
leg 3	0 – 0	0 – 0	0 – 0; 0 – 1; 0,I,3	0 – 0; 0 – 0; 0,2,1
leg 4	0 – 0	0 – 0	*I – 1 ; 0 – 1; 0,I,2	0 – 0; (0 – 1; 2)

[elements marked with * occur in female only]

Fifth legs absent in adult female; represented by 2 setae inserted either side of midline on ventral surface of fifth pedigerous somite in male (figure 2.6.10A-B)). Sixth legs of female either represented by single opercular plate closing off median genital opening (figure 2.6.2A) or by unarmed, paired flaps covering median genital aperture (figure 2.6.2E). Male sixth legs represented by unarmed genital opercula (figure 2.6.10A). Eggs contained in paired median sacs (figure 2.6.11C).

Remarks

The order Mormonilloida was established by Boxshall (1979) to accommodate the two species of the genus *Mormonilla* which had previously been regarded as an anomalous kind of gnathostomatous cyclopoid (Sars, 1913-1918). They were known from females only and neither females carrying egg sacs or spermatophores, nor males had ever been recorded. Boxshall (1979) noted that both species co-occurred in the North Atlantic and exhibited virtually identical depth distributions. Huys et al. (in press) described the male of *Mormonilla* using material collected by fine mesh plankton nets in the Red Sea and Arabian Sea. Mormonilloids show extreme sexual dimorphism, with differences in body segmentation, and in either the segmentation or setation of all appendages from the antennules to the sixth legs.

Female Genital System: Adult female mormonilloids have a genital double somite showing no traces of any subdivision. In *M.phasma* the genital double somite is swollen anteroventrally and the single median gonopore is located anteriorly on this protruberance (figure 2.6.2A-B). The female of *M.minor* possesses a genital double somite which is swollen midventrally and the single median gonopore is located ventrally just posterior to the midlevel of the double somite (figure 2.6.2C-D). The median gonopore is closed off by a pair of large flaps (figures 2.6.2E and 2.6.12C) representing the sixth legs. These flaps are unarmed and can be retracted into the gonopore itself by muscles that insert proximally. The intermediate stage in the retraction of the sixth leg is illustrated in figure 2.6.12D. Female *Mormonilla* have paired oviducts, each releasing two eggs per oviposition. They produce paired median egg sacs that each contain 2 eggs, one anterior and the other posterior (figure 2.6.11C-D).

Male Genital System: Male *Mormonilla* have a median testis and vas deferens (figure 2.6.1A) producing one large spermatophore at a time. The spermatophore is so large that it distorts the genital somite as it is extruded (figure 2.6.10A). The spermatophore is placed on the genital double somite of the female and discharges into the median copulatory pore within the female's genital aperture (figure 2.6.12A-B).

Antennules: The sexual dimorphism of the appendages is striking. The atrophied mouthparts in the male strongly suggest that it does not feed as an adult. The antennules of the male are well developed as geniculate appendages for grasping the female during copulation. They are better supplied with aesthetascs than those of the female. The location of the 3 large aesthetascs suggests that they were originally derived from ancestral segments VII, XI and XVI. That from segment XVI is incorporated into a large compound segment including all segments from ?XIV to XX. In the area of the antennule between the long proximal compound segment (I-VIII?) and the distal compound segment (?XIV to XX) about 5 segments are partially expressed and the appendage is flexed so that the distal part is more laterally directed. If this tentative system of segmental homologies is correct the flexure zone of 5 segments is not homologous with the proximal geniculation of the digeniculate antennule, as found in cyclopoid males, for example. The antennules of female *Mormonilla* are so reduced in their segmentation and setation that it is not possible to identify with certainty the homology of any of the remaining segments.

Antenna: The antenna is reasonably well formed in males but a significant difference is apparent in the segmentation of the exopod. In the female ancestral segments II and III are fused but IX and X are separate whereas in males II and III are free as well as IX and X. In the male endopodal segments 2 and 3 are fully fused whereas in the female there is a trace of the suture line dividing them. Male *Mormonilla* is the only podoplean with 9 exopodal segments expressed.

Mouthparts: All mouthparts are highly reduced in the male, except the mandibular endopod which retains 2 free segments whereas in the female the first endopodal segment is incorporated into the basis.

Maxilliped: There are differences in segmentation of the maxilliped between the females of the only two species in this order (figure 2.0.2). The maximum segmentation is expressed in *M.minor* (figure 2.6.6C-D) which has a compound proximal segment and a 3-segmented endopod with a setal formula of 1,1,4. *M.phasma* also has a compound proximal segment but has only 2 endopodal segments (figure 2.6.6A-B). The endopodal formula is 3,4 but the elements on the first segment are divided into a proximal group of 2 setae and a single distal seta. Study of the maxillipedal musculature pattern in *M.phasma* shows that the coxal-basal hiatus is located proximally in the compound proximal segment (along the oblique plane arrowed in figure 2.6.7E). The part of the segment distal to this plane represents the basis and it bears 3 setae in *M.phasma*. In *M.minor*, however, the part of the segment distal to the coxal-basal plane bears the cluster of 3 basal setae plus an isolated distal seta, which we interpret as representing the armature of an incorporated first endopodal segment. If, as the setation suggests, the first endopodal segment is fused with the second in *M.phasma* to produce a triple segment, the ancestral mormonilloid condition would therefore be a single protopodal segment (representing syncoxa plus basis) and an endopod of 4 free segments with a 1,1,1,4 formula.

Swimming Legs: The swimming legs exhibit a greater number of endopodal segments in males than in females. All rami of the male legs are 3-segmented, although the second and third endopodal segments of leg 4 are almost completely fused. Some setation differences between the sexes are related to the role of the first leg in forming the posterior wall of the feeding basket in the female. The primary function of the legs in the non-feeding males is locomotion, as they search for females for mating. The spine and setal formula given in the ancestral character set combines elements from the male and female.

Differential Diagnosis: Mormonilloids differ from all other podopleans in the retention of a 9-segmented antennary exopod in males and an 8-segmented exopod in females bearing 2 setae on the first segment and only 3 setae on the distal segment. Within the Podoplea only the Mormonilloida and Monstrilloida primitively have a fused, median genital aperture in the female. Mormonilloids can be distinguished from female monstrilloids by their possession of mouthparts and their lack of fifth legs.

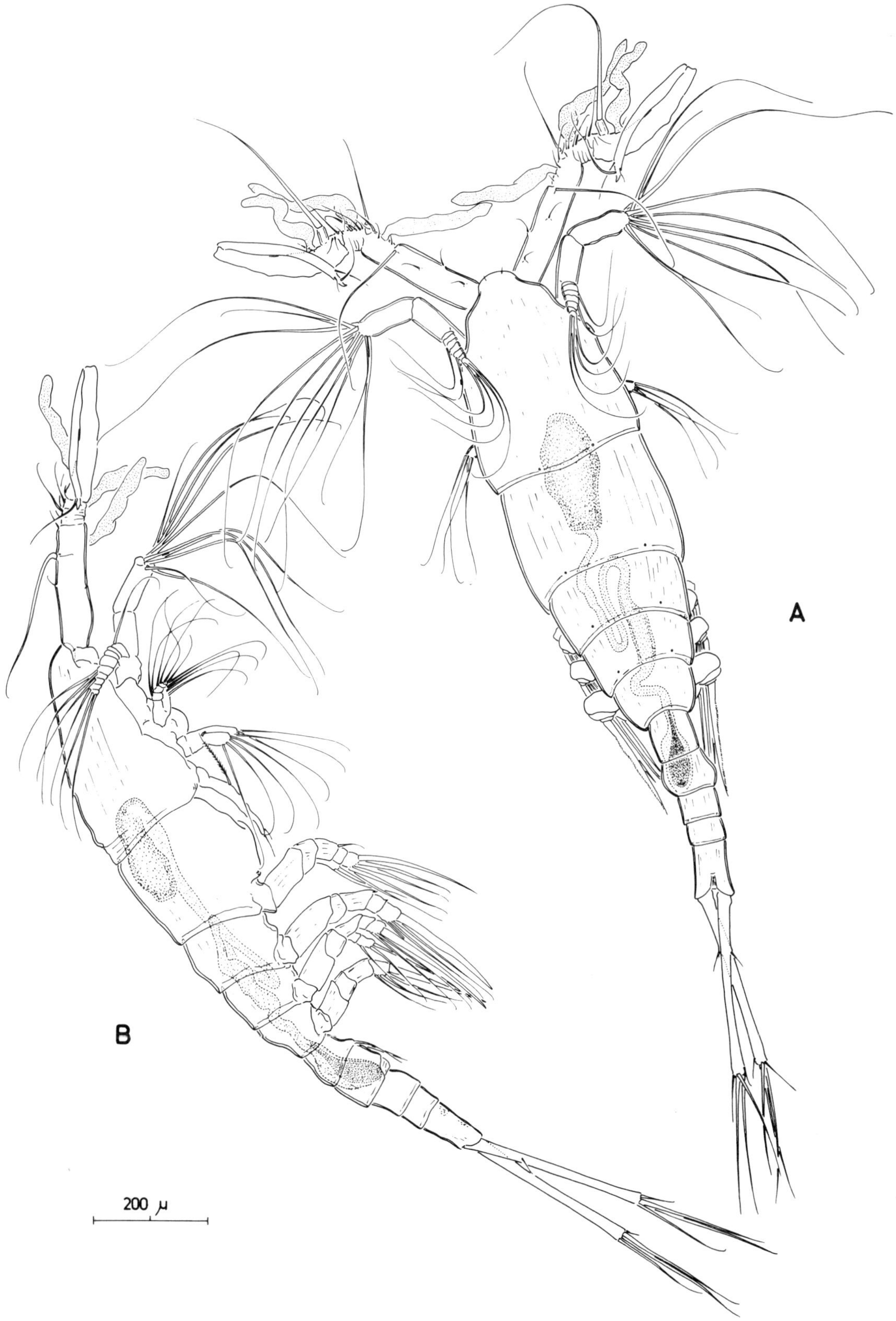

Figure 2.6.1. *Mormonilla phasma.* **A.** Male, dorsal view. **B.** Male, lateral view.

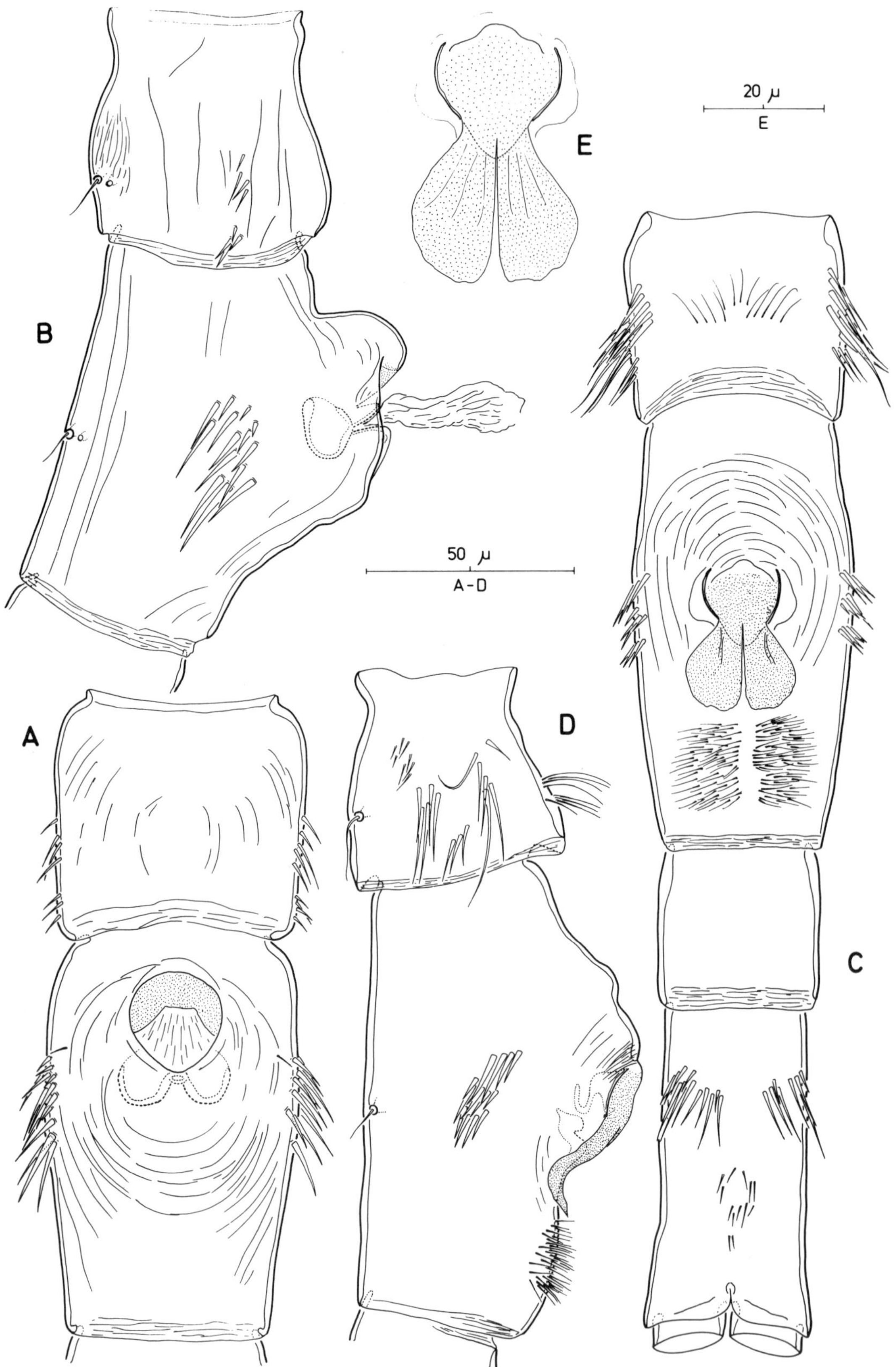

Figure 2.6.2. **A.** *Mormonilla phasma*, female genital double somite and first urosome somite, ventral view. **B.** Lateral view. **C.** *M.minor*, female urosome (caudal rami omitted), ventral view. **D.** Genital double somite and first urosome somite, lateral view. **E.** Sixth legs closing off genital apertures.

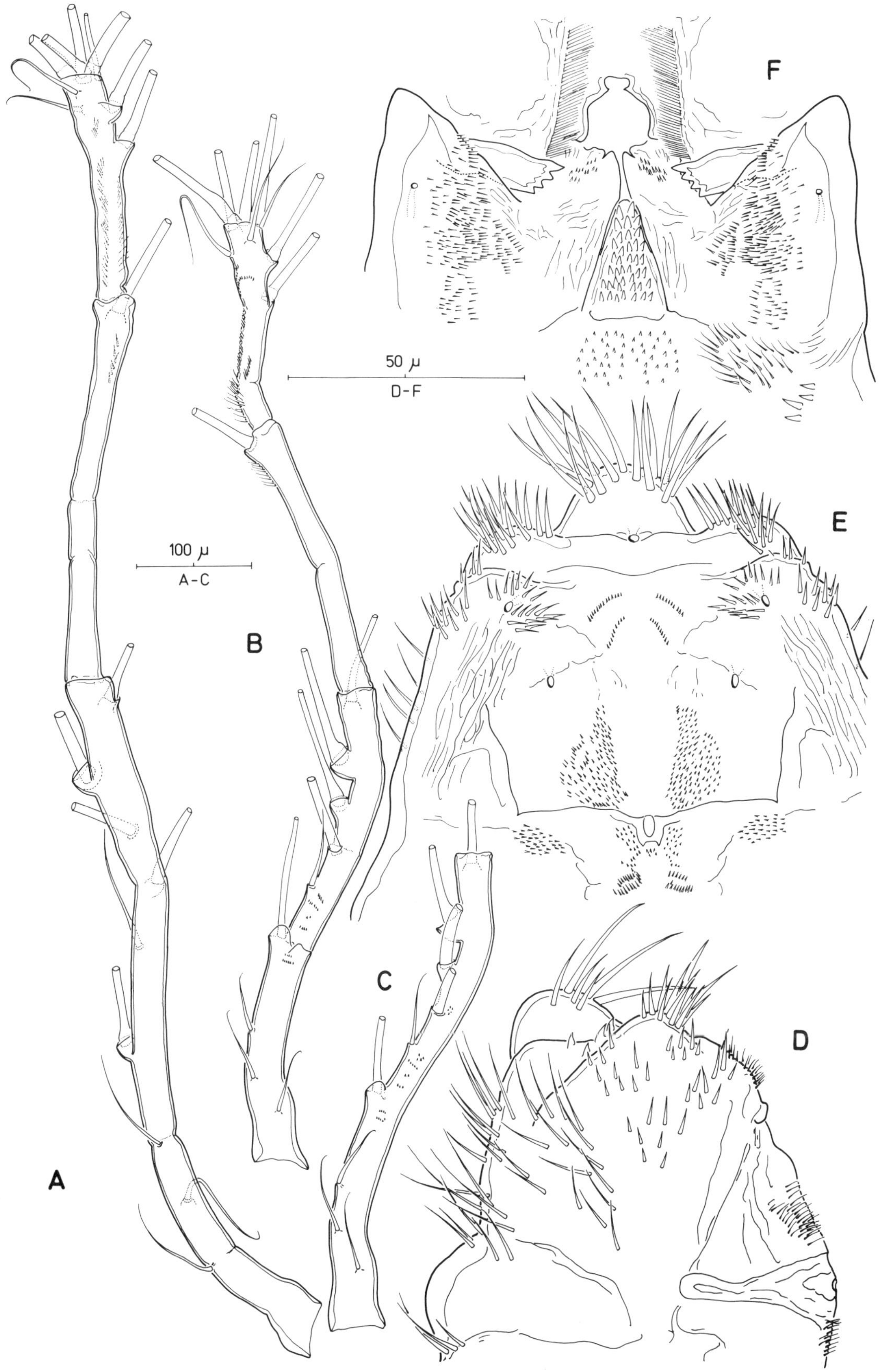

Figure 2.6.3. **A.** *Mormonilla phasma*, female antennule. **B.** *M.minor*, female antennule. **C.** Proximal part of antennule of another specimen. **D.** *M.phasma*, labrum of female, lateral view. **E.** Labrum, posterior view. **F**. Paragnaths, posterior view.

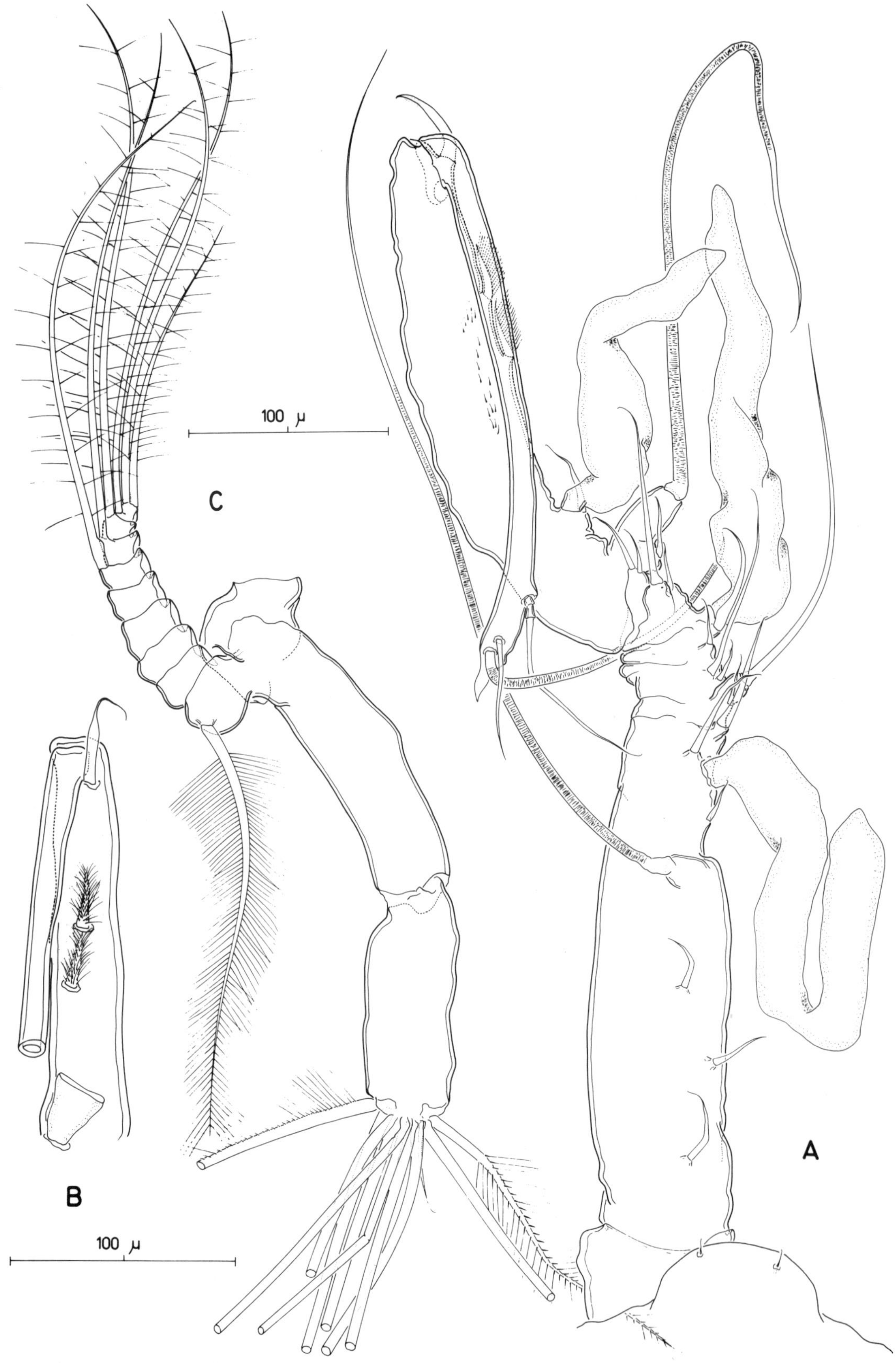

Figure 2.6.4. *Mormonilla phasma*, male. **A.** Antennule. **B.** Antennulary segments around geniculation, anterior view. **C.** Antenna.

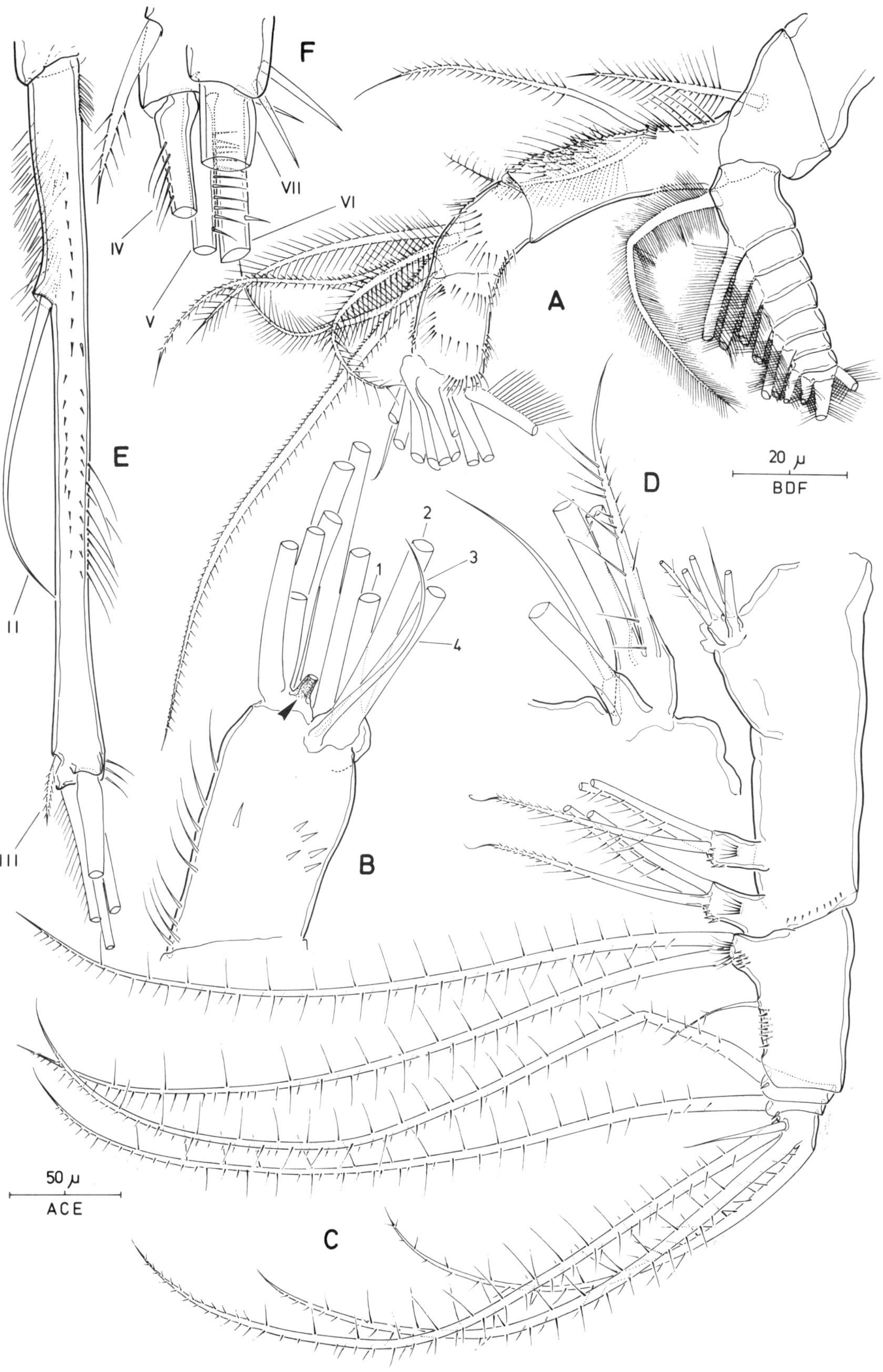

Figure 2.6.5. *Mormonilla phasma*, female. **A.** Antenna. **B.** Distal part of antennary endopod. **C.** Maxilla. **D.** Praecoxal endites of maxilla. **E.** Caudal ramus, dorsal view. **F.** Caudal ramus, detail of posterior part. [Arrow in **B** indicates tube pore, numbers 1-4 indicate setae derived from second endopodal segment.]

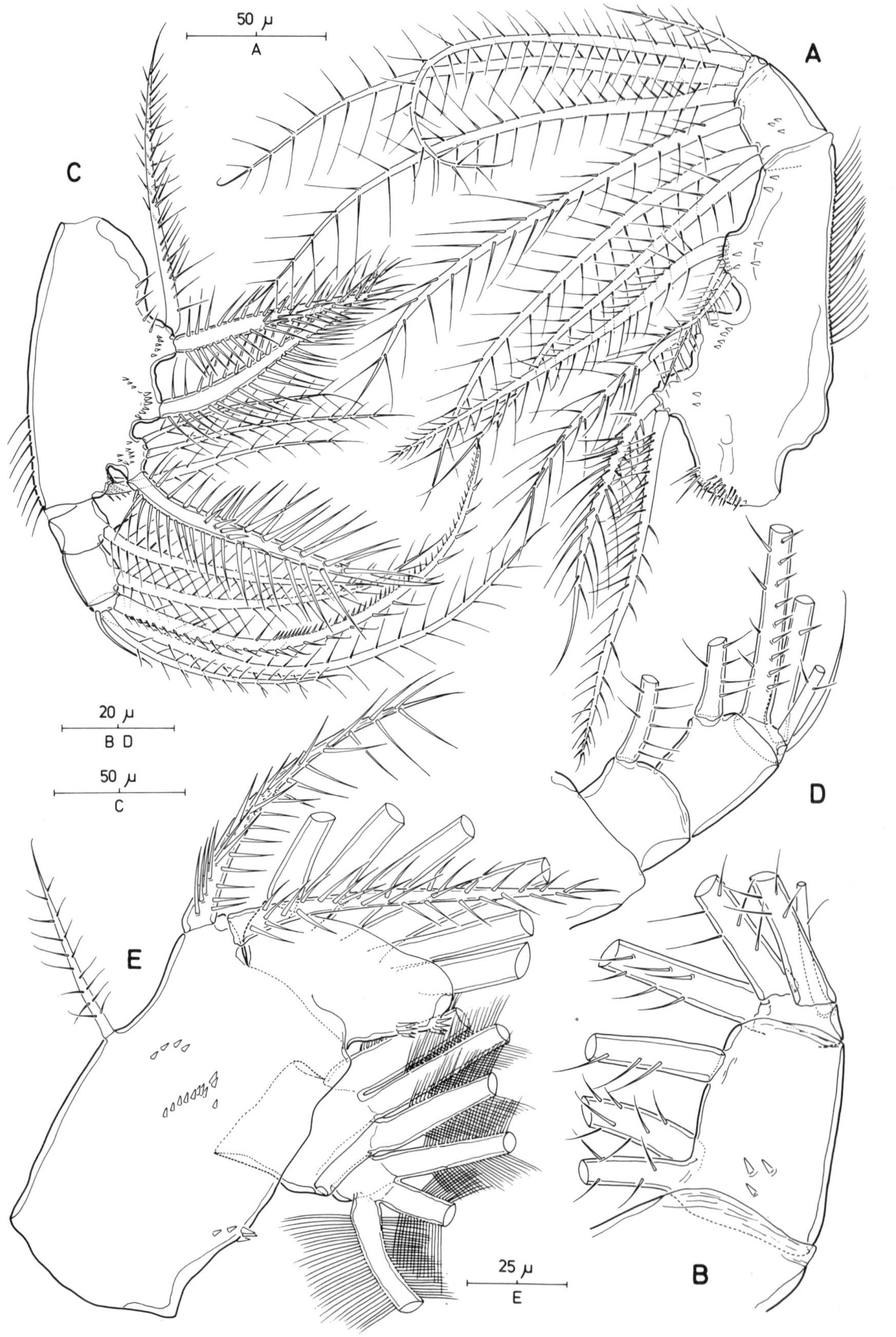

Figure 2.6.6. **A.** *Mormonilla phasma*, female maxilliped. **B.** Maxillipedal endopod. **C.** *M.minor*, female maxilliped. **D.** Maxillipedal endopod. **E.** *M.phasma*, female mandibular palp.

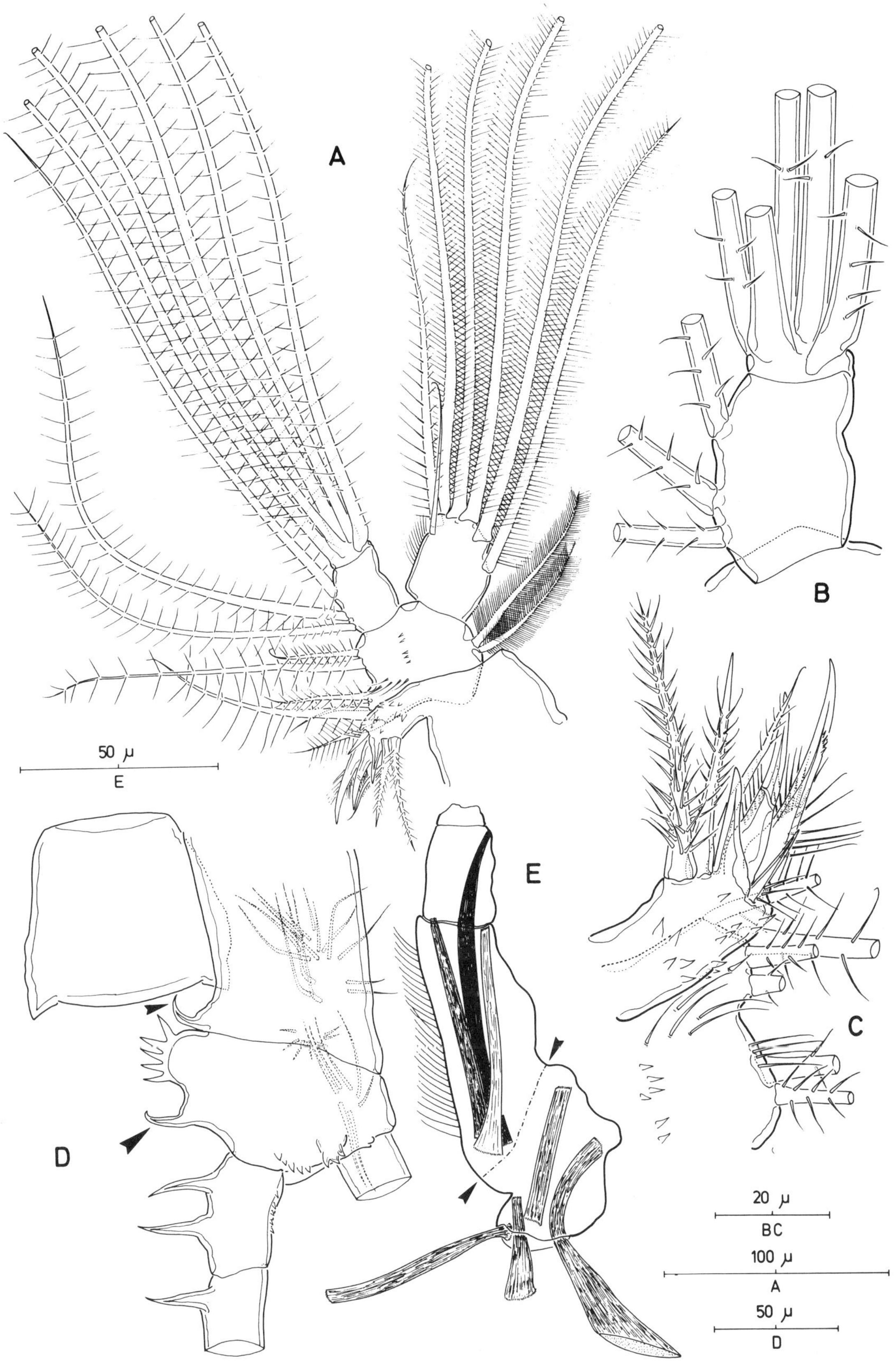

Figure 2.6.7. *Mormonilla phasma*, female. **A.** Maxillule. **B.** Maxillulary endopod. **C.** Endites of maxillulary praecoxa, coxa and basis. **D.** Intercoxal sclerite, protopod and proximal endopod segments of first swimming leg, with modified inner coxal and inner basal setae arrowed. **E.** Musculature of maxilliped, with coxal-basal plane of fusion arrowed.

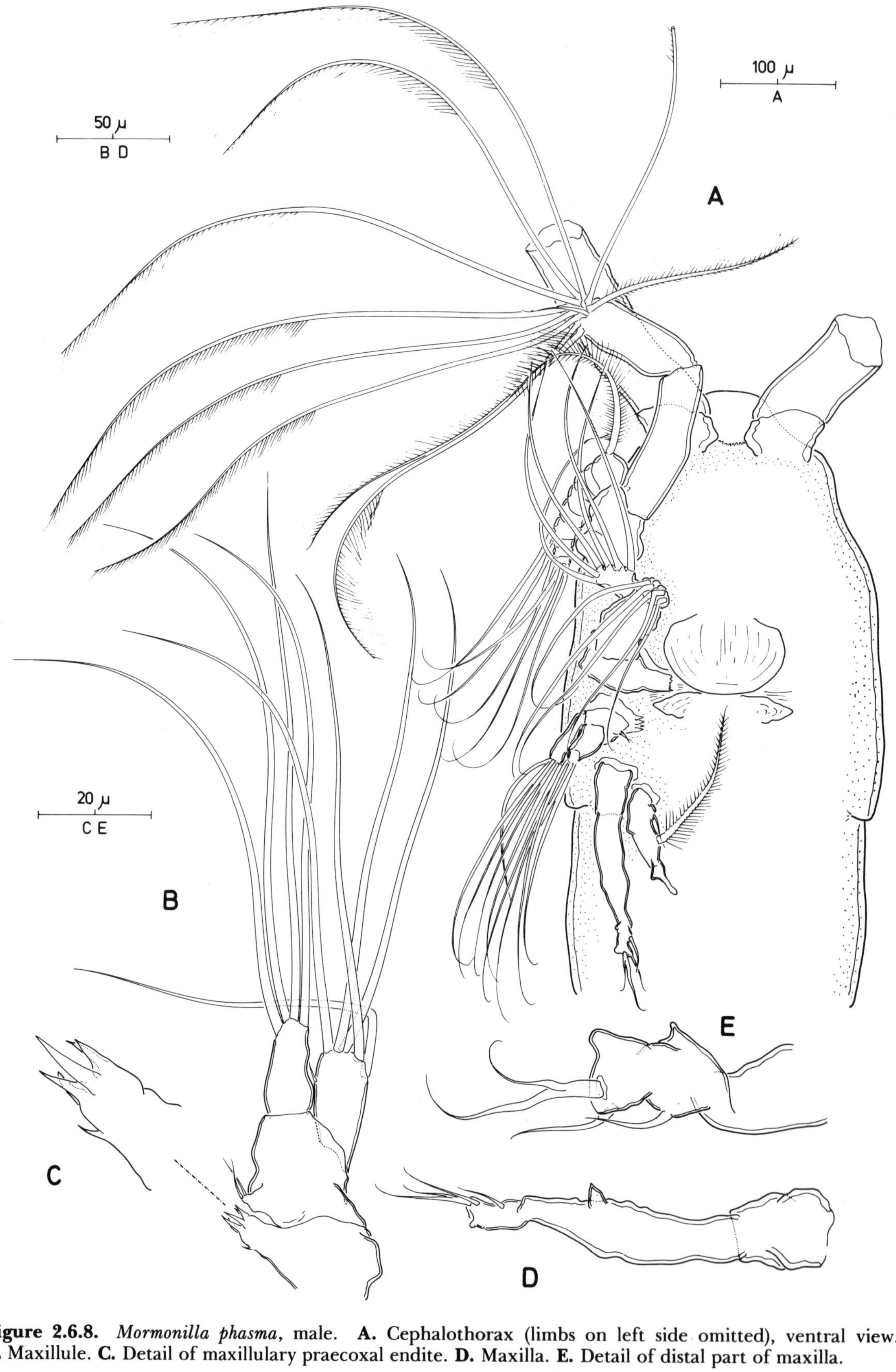

Figure 2.6.8. *Mormonilla phasma*, male. **A.** Cephalothorax (limbs on left side omitted), ventral view. **B.** Maxillule. **C.** Detail of maxillulary praecoxal endite. **D.** Maxilla. **E.** Detail of distal part of maxilla.

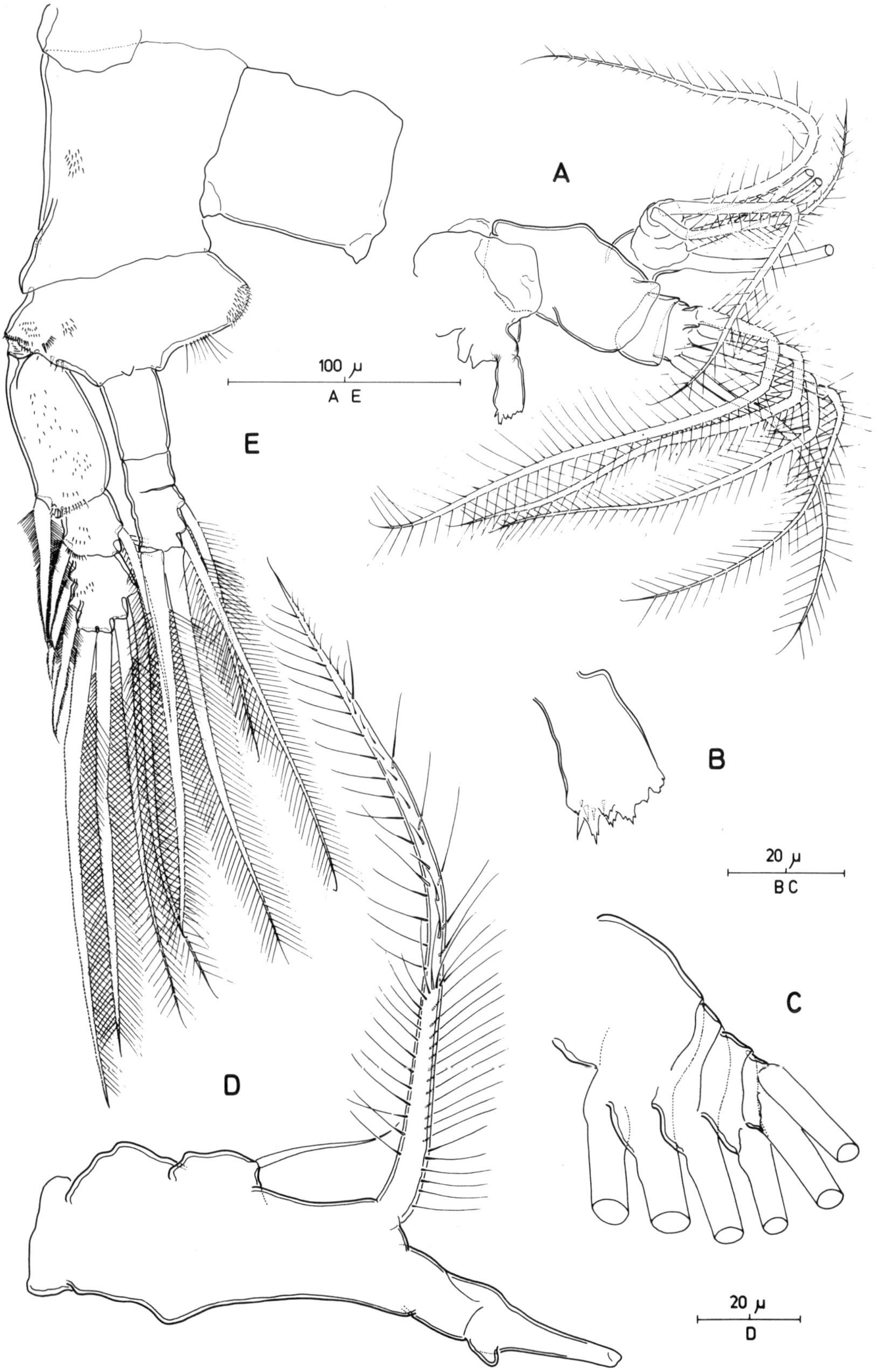

Figure 2.6.9. *Mormonilla phasma*, male. **A.** Mandible. **B.** Mandibular gnathobase. **C.** Mandibular exopod. **D.** Maxilliped. **E.** First swimming leg.

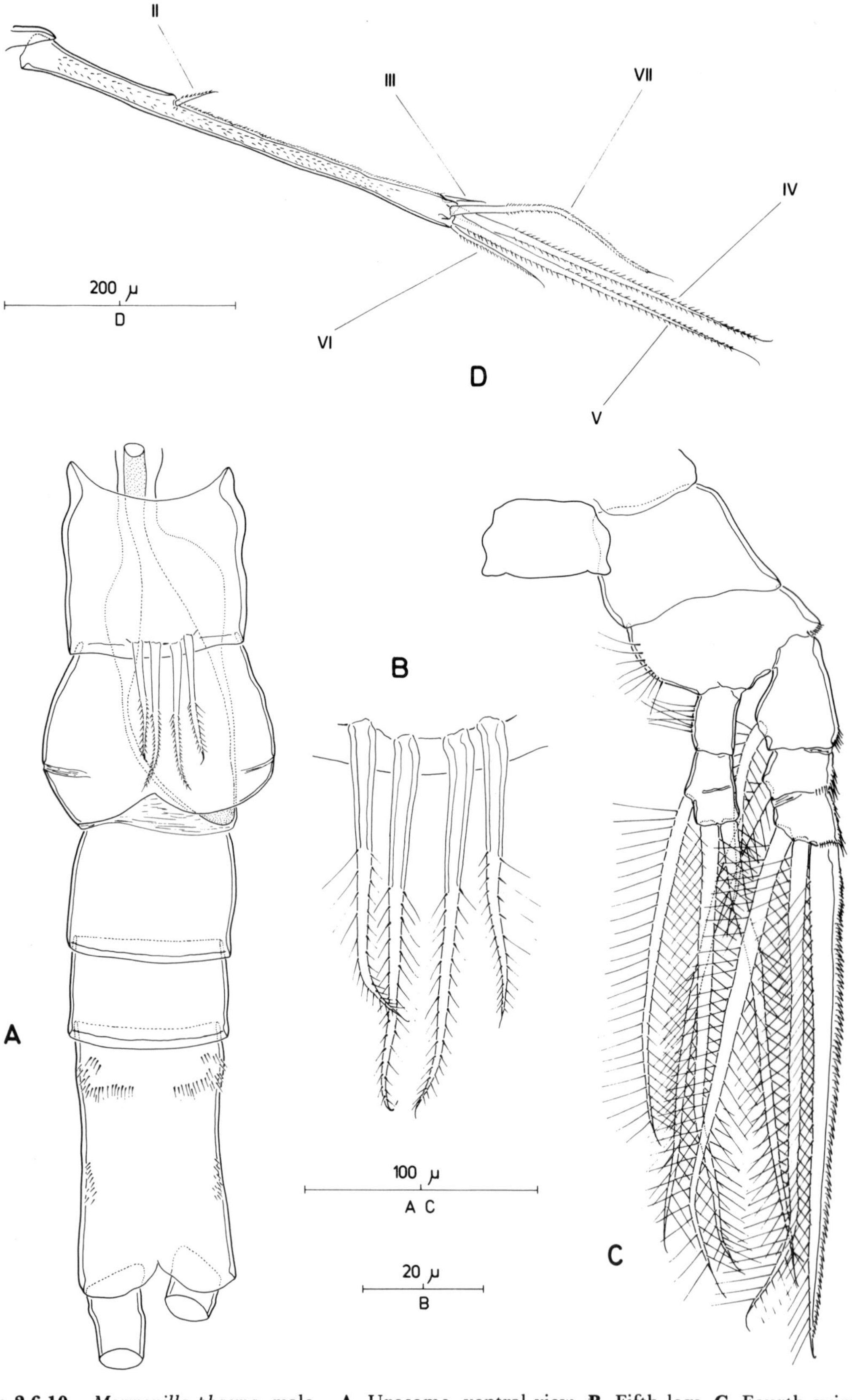

Figure 2.6.10. *Mormonilla phasma*, male. **A.** Urosome, ventral view. **B.** Fifth legs. **C.** Fourth swimming leg. **D.** Caudal ramus, dorsal view.

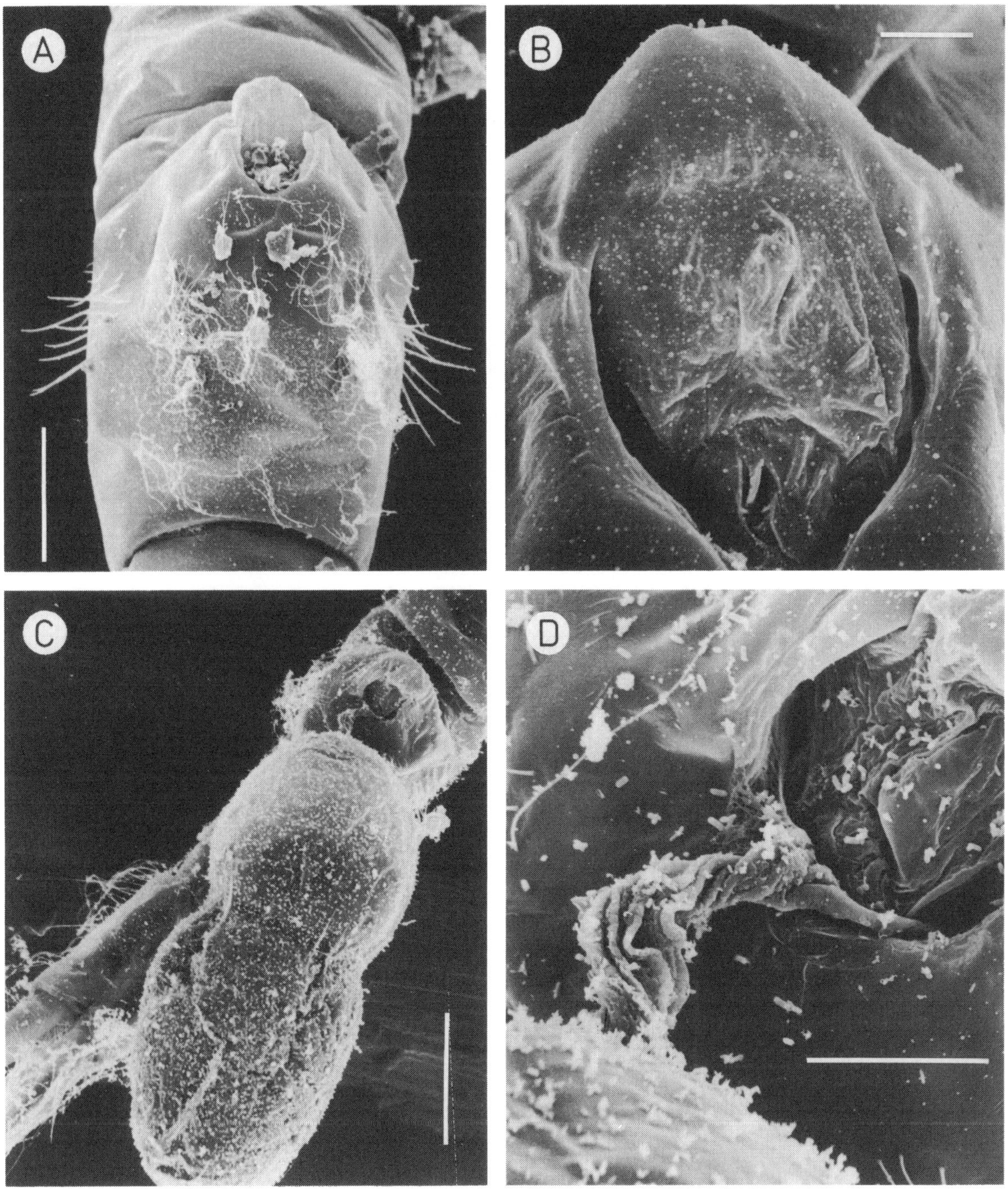

Figure 2.6.11. *Mormonilla phasma*, female. **A.** Genital double somite, ventral view. **B.** Genital aperture, ventral view. **C.** Urosome with attached egg sac, ventral view. **D.** Origin of egg sac, ventral view. Scale bars A = 30μm, B = 5μm, C = 50μm, D = 10μm.

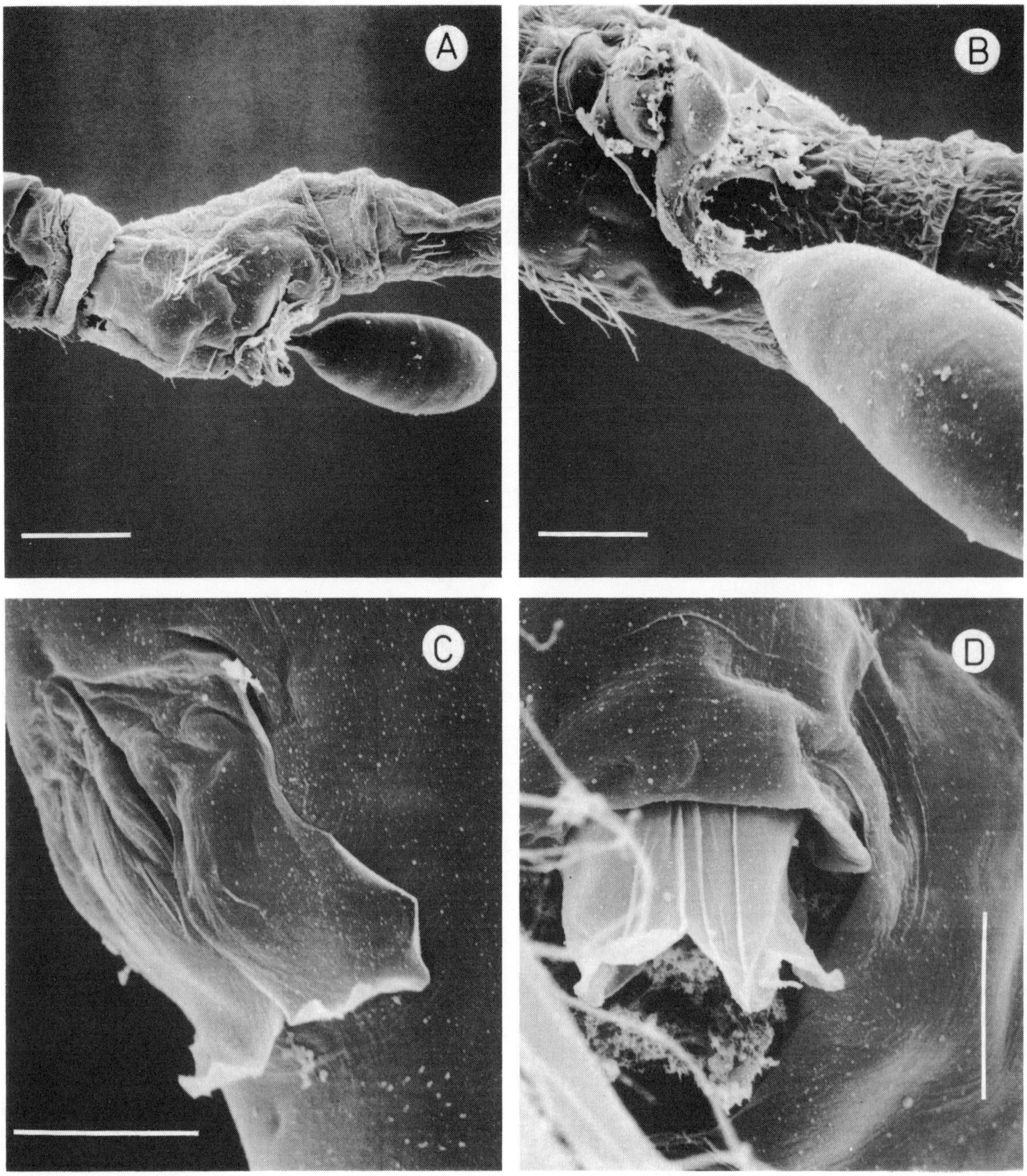

Figure 2.6.12. *Mormonilla minor*, female. **A.** Urosome with attached spermatophore, lateral view. **B.** Genital double somite, showing neck of attached spermatophore, ventral view. **C.** Closed genital aperture, ventrolateral view. **D.** Partly open genital aperture, showing withdrawn opercula formed from sixth legs. Scale bars A = 40μm, B = 20μm, C-D = 10μm.

2.7 GELYELLOIDA Huys 1988

The two known species of *Gelyella* are found only in the subterranean water of karstic systems in France (Rouch & Lescher-Moutoué, 1977) and in Switzerland (Moeschler & Rouch, 1988).

Character set of ancestral gelyelloid

Copepoda. Prosome comprising cephalosome and 4 free somites, the first 3 only being pedigerous; urosome 5-segmented in female (figure 2.7.1B), 6-segmented in male (figures 2.7.3A and 2.7.5A). Prosome-urosome articulation not distinct. Genital double somite in female (figure 2.7.4A) comprising fused genital and first abdominal somites. Female with transverse, median genital slit containing a single copulatory pore and paired gonopores (figure 2.7.4B). Seminal receptacles fused. Genital apertures paired and located ventrally at posterior border of genital somite in male. Rostrum delimited at base (figure 2.7.1B). Caudal ramus with 7 setae (figure 2.7.2D). Nauplius eye unconfirmed. Antennules indistinctly 14-segmented in female (figure 2.7.1A); 13-segmented in male (figure 2.7.3B), bilaterally symmetrical, geniculate between 11th and 12th segments, with 2 segments distal to geniculation. Antenna biramous with 7-segmented exopod (figure 2.7.5B) and 3-segmented endopod (figure 2.7.2C), coxa and basis without setae; first to third endopodal segments with 1, 5 and 7 setae respectively; exopodal segments 1 to 6 representing ancestral segments III to VIII, segment 7 representing fused ancestral segments IX-X; setal formula 1,1,1,1,1,1,4. Labrum an undivided muscular lobe. Mandible with large coxal gnathobase and biramous palp (figure 2.7.3C); basis with 1 seta on inner margin; exopod indistinctly 4-segmented, setal formula 1,1,1,3; endopod 2-segmented, setal formula 3,7. Paragnaths separate. Maxillule biramous (figure 2.7.1C), praecoxa and coxa partly fused, each with well developed endite; praecoxal endite with armature of 9 elements; coxal endite with 4 setae; no vestige of coxal epipodite retained; basis without seta on outer margin; endites widely separated, proximal endite well developed, with 3 setae; distal endite incorporated into segment, represented by 3 setae; endopod 1-segmented, with setal formula (2,2)5; exopod 1-segmented with 3 setae. Maxilla 5-segmented; syncoxa with 3 endites, endite formula 0,3,2,2; allobasis with large proximal (basal) endite bearing 3 setae, distal (endopodal) endite represented by 2 setae; outer coxal seta absent; free endopod 3-segmented, setal formula 2,2,4 (figure 2.7.4E). Maxilliped 4-segmented, comprising large syncoxa, basis and 2-segmented endopod (figure 2.7.3D); syncoxal formula 0,2,2,1; basis with 2 setae; endopod formula 1,5+1. Swimming legs 1-3 reduced, biramous with endopod 1-segmented or vestigial, exopod 1-segmented in female, 3-segmented in legs 2 and 3 of male. Coxae of legs 1-3 fused medially into broad plate (figure 2.7.2A-B); intercoxal sclerite absent; inner coxal seta absent; outer spine present on basis of legs 1 and 2, inner seta on basis of first leg absent; first exopodal segment with 1 outer spine. Spine and seta formula of legs 1 to 3:

	coxa	basis	exopod segment 1 2 3	endopod
leg 1	0 – 0	1 – 0	I – 0; III,I,2	0,1,0
leg 2	0 – 0	1 – 0	I – 0; I – 0; II,I,2	0,1,0
leg 3	0 – 0	0 – 0	I – 0; I – 0; II,I,1	1,1,0

Fourth and fifth legs absent in adults of both sexes. Sixth legs represented by unarmed flaps closing off paired, ventral genital apertures of male (figure 2.6.5A). No trace of sixth legs observable in female. Egg release mechanism unknown.

Remarks

Huys (1988a) redescribed *Gelyella droguei* Rouch & Lescher-Moutoué from the type material and removed the family from the Harpacticoida. He established a new order, the Gelyelloida, for this copepod. The diagnosis is adapted from that given by Huys (1988a). A second species, *Gelyella monardi*, has recently been described from a karstic spring in Switzerland by Moeschler & Rouch (1988). It is closely related to the type species.

Antennule: The segmentation of the antennule is hard to discern in *Gelyella*. In *G.droguei* it was originally described as 5-segmented in the female and 9-segmented in the male (Rouch & Lescher-Moutoué, 1977). The same condition was found in *G.monardi* although differences in the apparent homology of the segments led Moeschler & Rouch (1988) to suggest that the number of segments in the male might be about 12. Reexamination of *G.droguei* indicates that the male has 13 segments expressed and the female 14 (figures 2.7.3B and 2.7.1A). The small seventh segment of the male is deeply incised along its dorsal margin virtually forming an incomplete hoop. This closely resembles the condition of segment XV in male cyclopoids and misophrioids and may be interpreted as a vestige of a proximal geniculation mechanism that involves segment XV and XVI in these two orders. There is no trace of a sheath around the eighth (XVI) segment. The large aesthetasc retained in the male (and in the female) is therefore derived from segment XVI. Two segments are found distal to the geniculation in the male, probably representing segments XXI-XXIII and XXIV-XXVIII.

Mandible: The mandibular exopod is indistinctly segmented but it retains the full ancestral complement of 6 setae, the maximum found in any podoplean. Huys (1988a) interpreted the exopod as 5-segmented with a setal formula of 0,1,1,1,3. After reexamination we now interpret this as a 4-segmented condition, with a formula of 1,1,1,3 (figure 2.7.5C). The 4-segmented condition being derived by fusion of the 2 distal segments of an ancestral 5-segmented condition.

Differential Diagnosis: The Gelyelloida are readily distinguishable from all other copepods by their fused coxae and the loss of the intercoxal sclerites connecting the swimming legs. The fourth and fifth legs are lost in both sexes. The antennary exopod is 7-segmented. The presence of 4 setae on the apical segment of the antennary exopod indicates that this is a double segment, derived by fusion of the ninth and tenth ancestral segments. Each of the other antennary exopod segments in *Gelyella* is single and the first and second ancestral segments are lost.

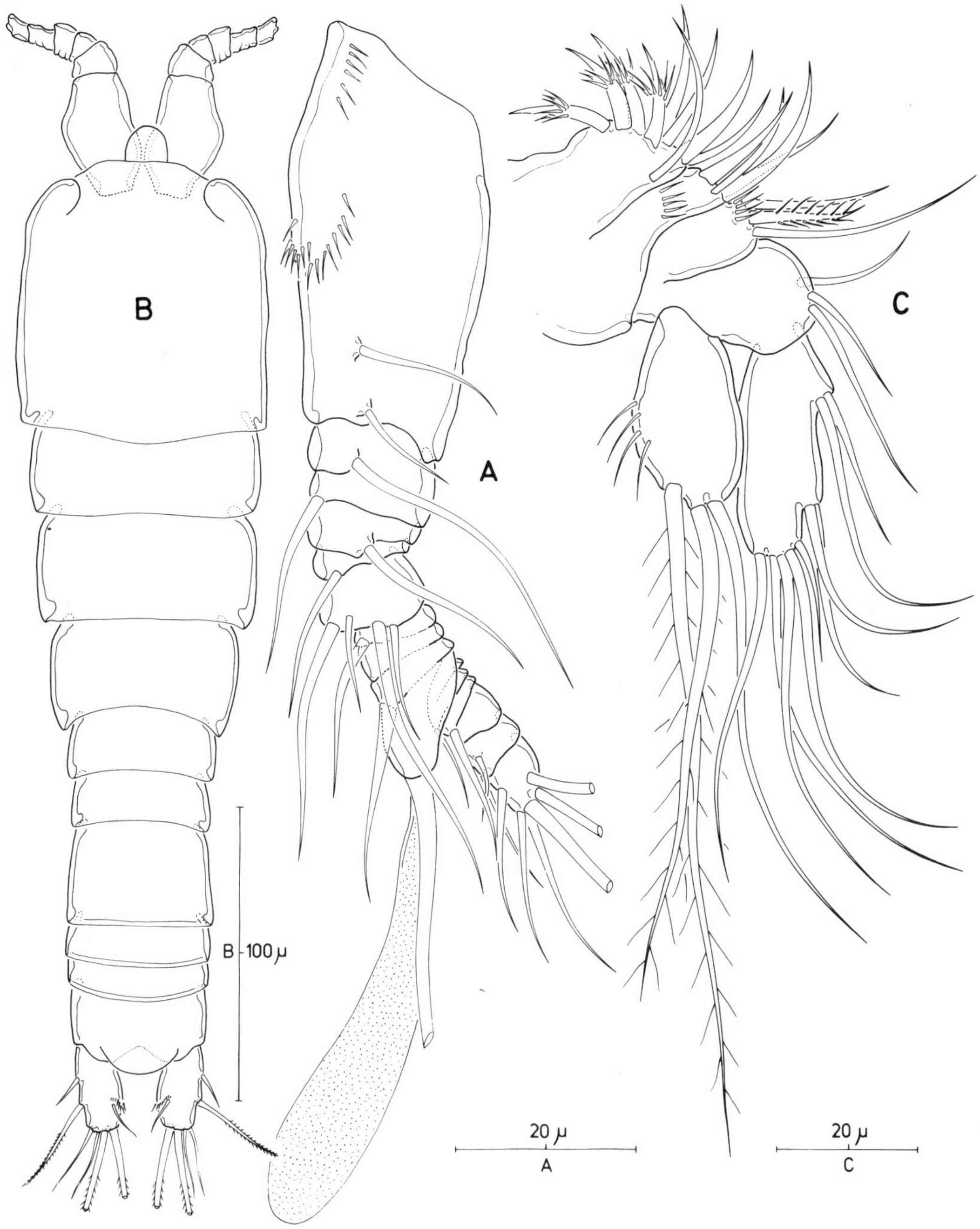

Figure 2.7.1. *Gelyella droguei.* **A.** Female antennule. **B.** Female, dorsal view. **C.** Maxillule.

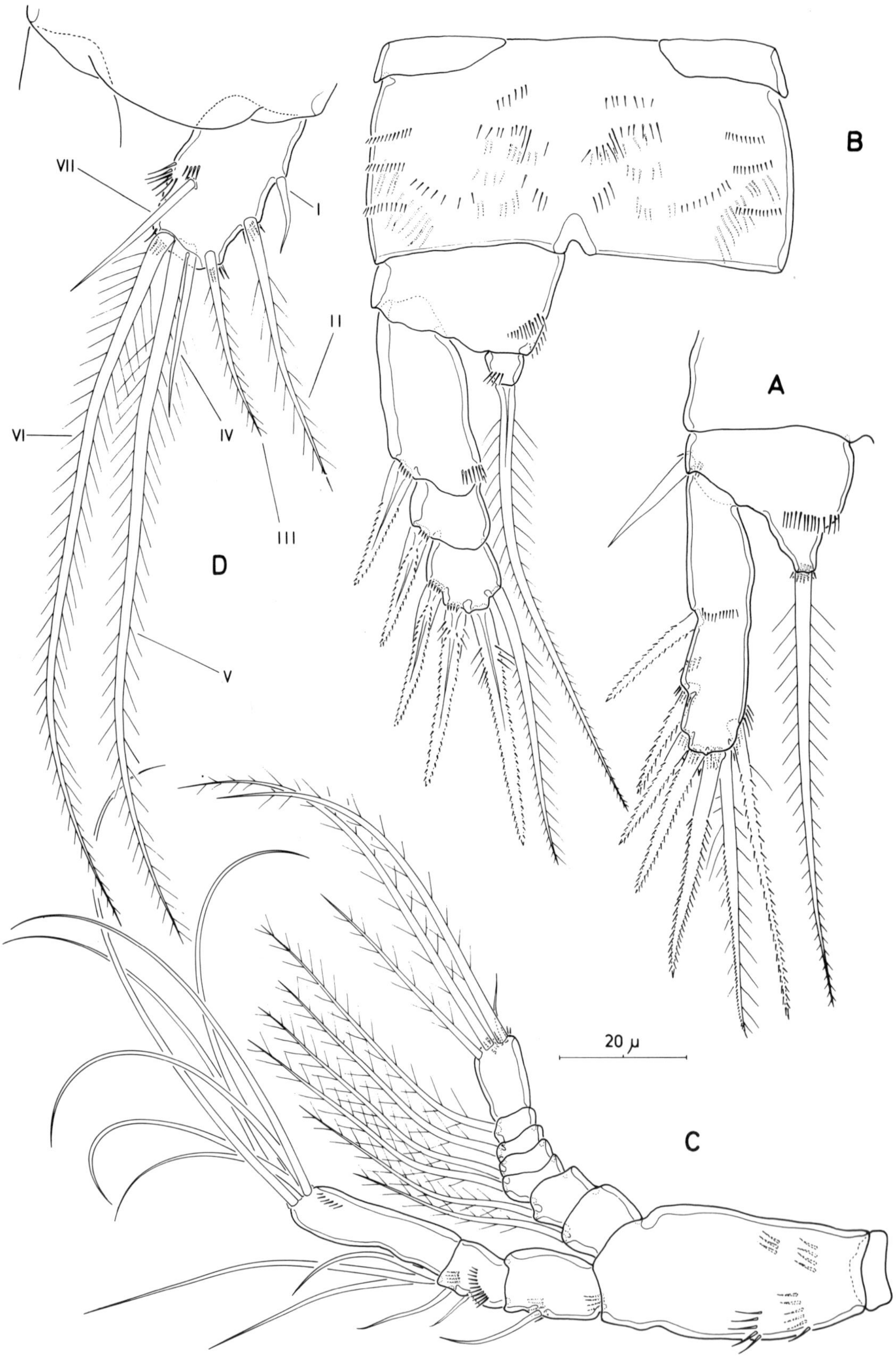

Figure 2.7.2. *Gelyella droguei.* **A.** Second swimming leg, female. **B.** Third swimming leg of male, showing fused coxae and lack of intercoxal sclerite. **C.** Antenna. **D.** Right caudal ramus, dorsal view.

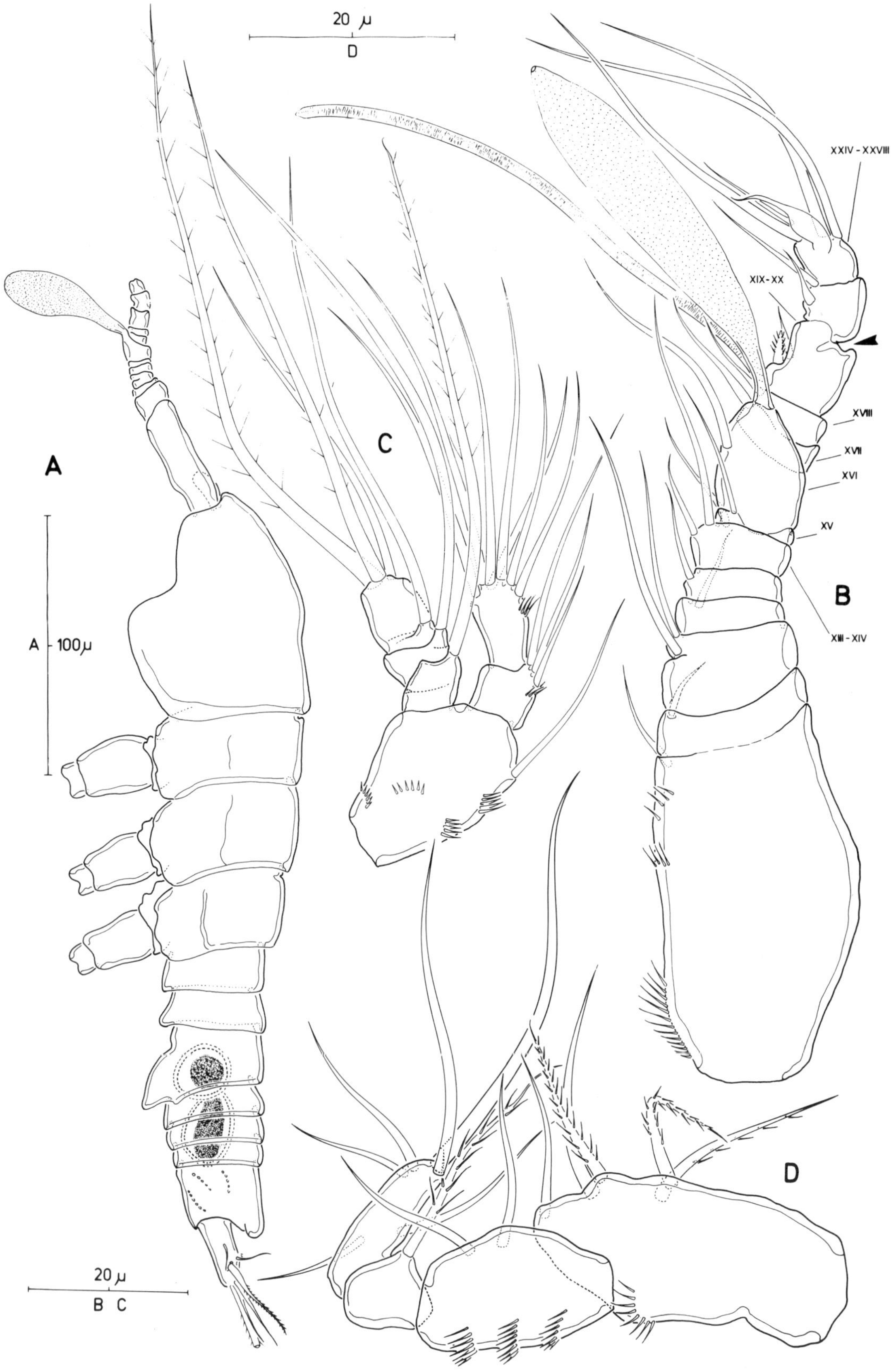

Figure 2.7.3. *Gelyella droguei.* **A.** Male, lateral view. **B.** Male antennule, with geniculation arrowed. **C.** Mandibular palp. **D.** Maxilliped.

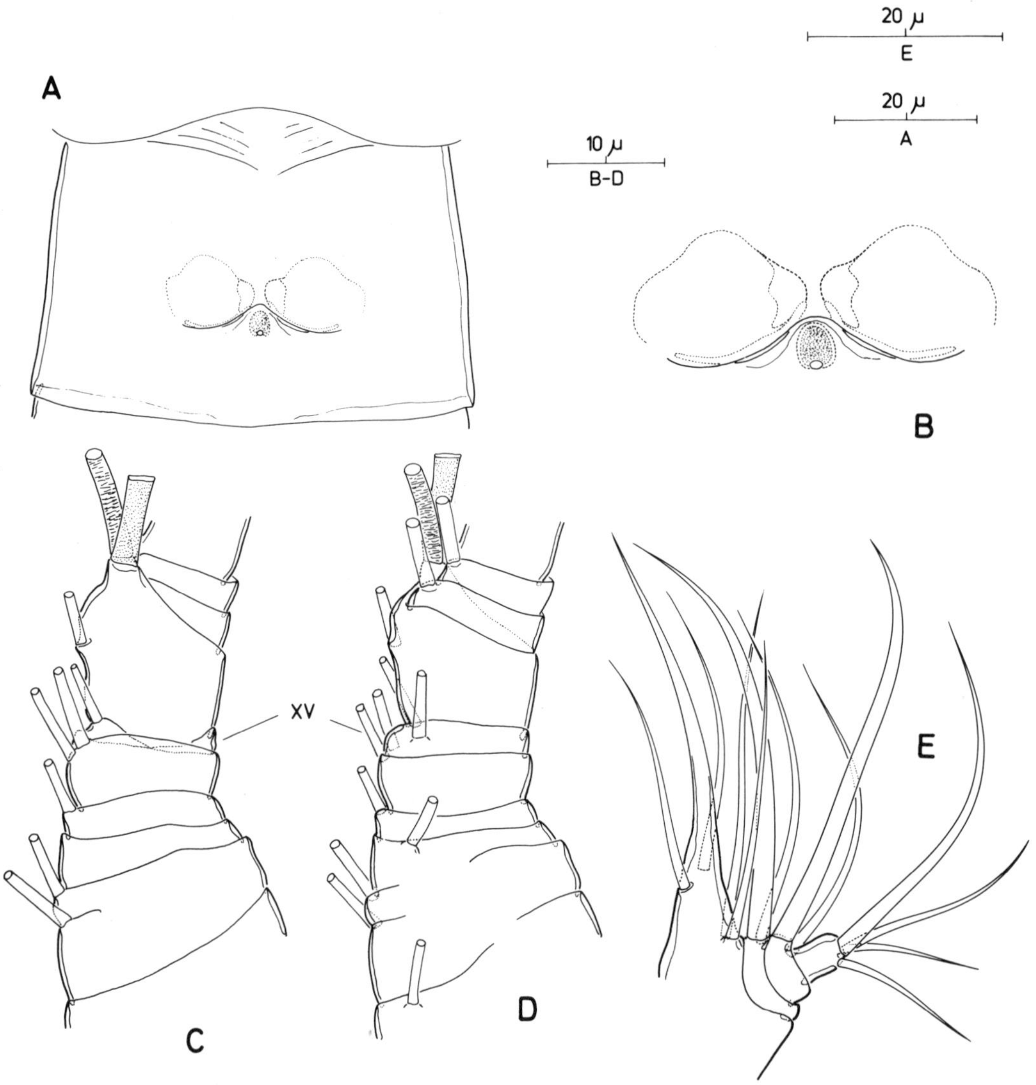

Figure 2.7.4. *Gelyella droguei.* **A.** Female genital double somite, ventral view. **B.** Female genital apertures, ventral view. **C.** Middle part of male antennule, showing modification of segment XV, ventral. **D.** Same, dorsal view. **E.** Allobasis and endopod of maxilla.

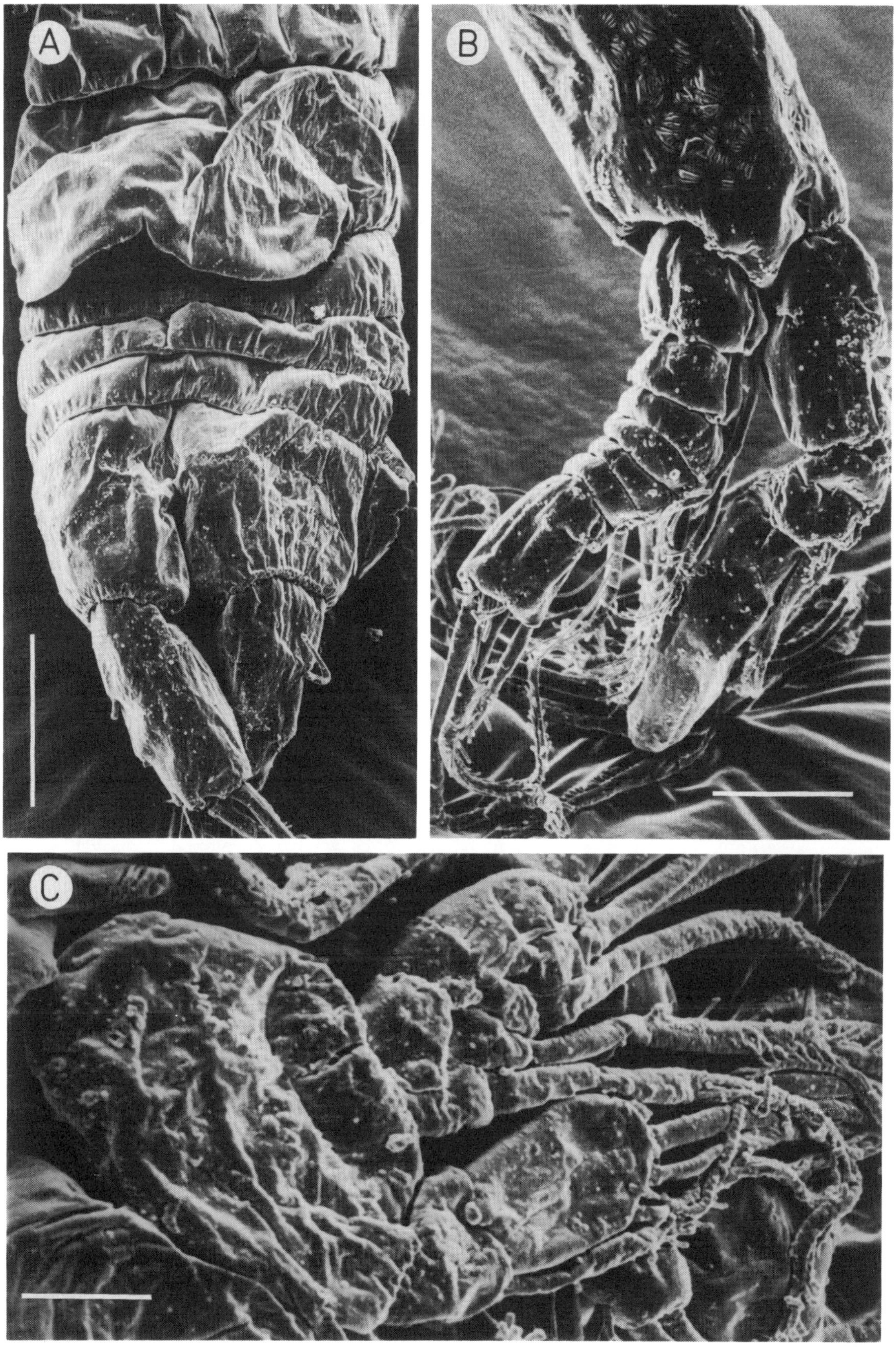

Figure 2.7.5. *Gelyella droguei.* **A.** Male urosome, ventral view. **B.** Antenna. **C.** Mandibular palp. Scale bars A = 20μm, B = 10μm, C = 5μm.

2.8 CYCLOPOIDA Burmeister 1835

The cyclopoids are by far the most abundant and successful group of copepods in fresh water. The family Cyclopidae contains an enormous number of genera and species (cf. Dussart & Defaye, 1985) from all kinds of freshwater habitats including standing water bodies such as lakes, ponds, ditches, temporary pools and wells, and running water such as streams and rivers. They are also widely distributed in groundwater (Lescher-Moutoué, 1974a, b). Many of these cyclopids are predatory (Fryer, 1957). The other free-living cyclopoids are primarily marine in distribution; the family Cyclopinidae being predominantly benthic and the Oithonidae planktonic. Many cyclopoids are parasitic including the marine families Notodelphyidae, Mantridae, Archinotodelphyidae and Ascidicolidae (found mainly in association with tunicate hosts), and the freshwater families Lernaeidae (found on fishes) and Ozmanidae (found in gastropod molluscs).

Character set of ancestral cyclopoid

Copepoda. Prosome comprising cephalosome and 4 free pedigerous somites; urosome 6-segmented in both sexes. Prosome-urosome articulation between fourth and fifth pedigerous somites (podoplean position). Genital apertures paired and located ventrally in both sexes; sited at posterior border of genital somite in male, anteriorly on the genital somite in female. Seminal receptacles paired. Rostrum fused at base. Caudal ramus with 7 setae (figure 2.8.25D). Nauplius eye present. Antennules 26-segmented in female (figure 2.8.2A), apical segment (figure 2.8.2B) comprising fused ancestral segments XXVI to XXVIII; modified by fusion and bilaterally digeniculate in male, with geniculations between segments homologous with segments XV and XVI, and between XX and XXI of the female. Male antennule with sheath on segment XV partly enclosing segment XVI (figures 2.8.4B, 2.8.5 and 2.8.6B-C), and with segments XI to XIV modified. Antenna biramous (figure 2.8.2C); exopod represented by small process on basis bearing 3 setae (figure 2.8.2D), endopod 3-segmented; coxa with a single seta; basis with 2 inner setae; first to third endopodal segments with 1, 9 and 7 setae respectively (figure 2.8.12C). Labrum an undivided muscular lobe. Mandible with large coxal gnathobase (figure 2.8.15A) and biramous palp (figure 2.8.16); exopod 4-segmented, setal formula 1,1,1,2; endopod 2-segmented, setal formula 6,10 (figure 2.8.16A); basis bearing 2 setae on inner margin. Paragnaths separate (figure 2.8.11C). Maxillule (figure 2.8.18) with large praecoxal endite bearing armature of 12 elements; coxa with endite represented by single seta only; vestigial epipodite incorporated into segment, bearing 3 setae; basis without seta on outer margin; basal endites weakly developed, proximal endite represented by 3 setae, distal endite by 5 setae on inner margin; endopod indistinctly 2-segmented, setal formula 5,5; exopod 1-segmented with 4 setae. Maxilla 6-segmented (figure 2.8.20A); praecoxa and coxa each with 2 endites, endite formula 4,1,3,3; basis with a large endite bearing 3 elements, outer coxal seta absent; free endopod 3-segmented, proximal segment double representing fused first and second endopodal segments, setal formula (2+2),2,4. Maxilliped 7-segmented (figure 2.8.20B) comprising syncoxa, basis and 5-segmented endopod; syncoxal formula 0,1,3,2; basis with 2 setae; endopod setal formula 1,2,2,1+1,4. Swimming legs 1-4 biramous with 3-segmented rami; members of leg pairs joined by intercoxal sclerite; inner coxal seta and outer seta on basis present; inner seta on basis of first leg present; first exopodal segment with 1 outer spine. Spine and seta formula of legs 1 to 4:

	coxa	basis	exopod segment 1 2 3	endopod segment 1 2 3
leg 1	0 – 1	1 – I	I – 1; I – 1; III,I,4	0 – 1; 0 – 2; 1,2,3
leg 2	0 – 1	1 – 0	I – 1; I – 1; III,I,5	0 – 1; 0 – 2; 1,2,3
leg 3	0 – 1	1 – 0	I – 1; I – 1; III,I,5	0 – 1; 0 – 2; 1,2,3
leg 4	0 – 1	1 – 0	I – 1; I – 1; II,I,5	0 – 1; 0 – 2; 1,2,2

Fifth legs uniramous, with separate coxa and basis; praecoxa absent; coxae joined by intercoxal sclerite (figure 2.8.25C); inner coxal seta and outer seta on basis present (figure 2.8.33B,D); endopod absent; exopod 2-segmented (figure 2.8.33A-D and 2.8.36B) and bearing up to 7 elements in female and 6 in male. Sixth legs represented by opercular plates closing off genital openings of female, and by paired flaps closing off genital apertures of male. Eggs contained within paired egg sacs.

Remarks

This diagnosis is based on members of all families, especially the Cyclopinidae, Oithonidae, Archinotodelphyidae, Mantridae, and Notodelphyidae. The family Thespesiopsyllidae is here transferred to the Cyclopoida from the Monstrilloida on the basis of its female genital apparatus and the structure of the male antennule.

Thespesiopsyllidae: The Thespesiopsyllidae was studied in detail in order to establish its ordinal affinities. The prosome is 4-segmented (figure 2.8.34A), with the first pedigerous somite fully incorporated into the cephalothorax. The urosome is 5-segmented in both sexes (figure 2.8.36A,D) although the fusion of genital and first abdominal somites into a double somite is incomplete ventrally in *Thespesiopsyllus* Wilson and there are dorsal and ventral sutures in *Orientopsyllus* Sewell. A broad, rounded rostrum is present, fused with the cephalothoracic shield (figure 2.8.34B). The caudal rami have 7 setae (figure 2.8.35C). The female antennule is 15-segmented (figure 2.8.35A) and that of the male 14-segmented, with the geniculation between segments 12 and 13 (homologous with ancestral segments XIX-XX and XXI-XXIII respectively) (figure 2.8.35B). The antennae to maxillipeds are all missing in the adult although a vestige of the labrum is present on the ventral cephalothoracic surface (figure 2.8.34D) and paired scars marking the position of other limbs can be observed (figure 2.8.34C). The fourth and fifth legs are sexually dimorphic. The female fourth leg (figure 2.8.36C) is biramous, with a 2-segmented exopod and 1-segmented endopod, whereas that of the male is uniramous, lacking an endopod (figure 2.8.36E). The female fifth leg comprises an unarmed protopodal segment plus a 2-segmented exopod (figure 2.8.36B) bearing 1 large seta whereas that of the male has a 1-segmented exopod bearing 4 setae or spines (figure 2.8.36F). The sixth legs of both species are armed with 2 spinous processes. In the male the sixth legs are ventral (figure 2.8.35F), in the female they are lateral (figure 2.8.35D).

Urosome Segmentation: A 6-segmented urosome in the female is retained in some members of the family Notodelphyidae, such as *Notodelphys* Allman (figures 2.8.32E and 2.8.40C). In the great majority of cyclopoids the genital and first abdominal somites are fused to form a genital double somite, as in the Cyclopinidae (figure 2.8.28), the Oithonidae (figure 2.8.30) and the Archinotodelphyidae (figures 2.8.31A-F). In the Thespesiopsyllidae (figure 2.8.35E) the fusion in incomplete.

Female Genital System: The arrangement of the female genital apertures within the Cyclopoida is remarkably variable, with 4 major evolutionary trends discernible. These four trends are shown schematically in figure 2.8.37). The first (figure 2.8.37A) involves the fusion of the copulatory pores and seminal receptacles, and the lateral migration of the gonopores. In the Ozmanidae (figure 2.8.27A-B) the common median seminal receptacle is small and is connected to the laterally located genital antra via long receptacle ducts. The copulatory pore is located just posterior to the level of the seminal receptacle. In *Euryte* Philippi the median seminal receptacle is relatively larger. Small, but distinct, receptacle ducts which open into the genital antra, are present (figure 2.8.29). The single copulatory pore leads to the seminal receptacle via a short copulatory duct which connects, about midway along its length, with a pair of transverse ducts. These transverse ducts are novel structures found only within the Cyclopidae. In the Cyclopinae the ancestral receptacle ducts appear to be absent (figure 2.8.32A-D) and the new transverse ducts are the only functional ducts for transport of spermatozoa to the paired, lateral genital antra. The seminal receptacle can extend considerably both anteriorly and posteriorly within the Cyclopinae and its precise form is an important generic level character in the subfamily.

The second evolutionary trend in cyclopoid genital structure (figure 2.8.37B) is characterised by fusion of the sixth legs, copulatory pores and seminal receptacles, as exhibited in the Cyclopinidae. *Pterinopsyllus* Brady retains a bilobed seminal receptacle (figure 2.8.26), indicating its derivation by fusion of paired receptacles. The median copulatory pore opens into the receptacle via a short copulatory duct. The gonopores are connected to the receptacle by long receptacle ducts. The gonopores are laterally located and covered by opercula derived from the sixth legs. In the

Cyclopininae the seminal receptacles are completely fused, as in *Cyclopinoides schulzi* Herbst (figure 2.8.28B-C) and *Cyclopina gracilis* Claus (figure 2.8.28D-E). Primitively, however, the gonopores and sixth legs are ventrally located, as in *Cyclopicina longifurcata* (Scott) (figure 2.8.25AB) and an as yet undescribed new interstitial genus of cyclopinid (figure 2.8.28A). In more advanced cyclopinid genera, such as *Cyclopinoides* Lindberg and *Cyclopina* Claus, the gonopores have migrated to the lateral margins of the double somite. The heavily sclerotised copulatory ducts are typical of the Cyclopinidae. Combination of the plesiomorphic features of the Pterinopsyllinae and Cyclopininae results in a hypothetical ancestral cyclopinid condition from which both were derived (figure 2.8.37B).

The evolutionary trend leading to the condition exhibited by the Oithonidae is simple (figure 2.8.37C). In the oithonids the genital apertures are located laterally on the genital double somite and are closed off by the modified sixth legs. Each aperture contains both a copulatory pore and an oviduct opening. The apertures are slit-like, extending transversely round the side of the body. The gonopores from where the egg sacs emerge are sited in the dorsal part of each aperture near the setiferous lobe representing the sixth legs. The spermatophores discharge into the copulatory pore located in the ventral slit-like extension of the aperture (figures 2.8.30 and 2.8.40A-B), as also indicated by Ferrari & Bowman (1980; figs 1c, 10d) and Nishida (1985; fig. 51d). The seminal receptacles are paired and can be found laterally in the double somite, lying beneath each genital aperture (figure 2.8.30A).

The fourth evolutionary trend in cyclopoid genital structure (figure 2.8.37D) is exhibited by the parasitic families, excluding the Ozmanidae and Lernaeidae (figure 2.8.31G). The least modified condition found within this group of families is that of *Archinotodelphys polynesiensis* Monniot (figure 2.8.31A-C) in which the gonopores and seminal receptacles are located laterally but the copulatory pores remain on the ventral surface either side of the midline. In other archinotodelphyids, such as *A.typicus* Lang, only a single, common copulatory pore is present, connected to each receptacle via long copulatory ducts (figure 2.8.31D-F). This basic arrangement, with a median copulatory pore, is also found in the Notodelphyidae (figure 2.8.32E), Mantridae (figure 2.8.30F-G) and Thespesiopsyllidae (figure 2.8.35D-E). It is also found in some members of the Ascidicolidae, such as *Ascidicola rosea* Thorell (figure 2.8.32F) in which the copulatory pore is exposed despite the extreme dorsal and lateral development of the fifth legs to form the brood pouch. In a small number of ascidicolids, such as *Enterocola fulgens* van Beneden, the copulatory pores are still separate but there is extreme development of the seminal receptacles which fuse medially. Other species of *Enterocola* van Beneden exhibit the typical ascidicolid condition (see Illg & Dudley, 1980).

The variability of the female genital apparatus within the Cyclopoida, and the retention of paired copulatory pores in plesiomorphic species, such as *Archinotodelphys polynesiensis* (figure 2.8.31A-C), indicates that the ancestral cyclopoid must have had the basic copepod system with paired, ventral apertures.

Female Antennule: The most plesiomorphic character states for most appendages are found in the family Cyclopinidae. The maximum number of 26 antennulary segments is found in female *Cyclopicina* Lindberg (Huys & Boxshall, 1990a). This antennule differs from the 27-segmented antennule of misophrioids in the incorporation of ancestral segment XXVI into the compound apical segment representing fused segments XXVII and XXVIII. All female cyclopoids, *Notodelphys allmani* Thorell for example, possess this triple segment (figure 2.8.3C). Most female cyclopoids exhibit further segmental fusions in the proximal part of the antennule. In *Euryte robusta* Sars the first segment represents fused ancestral segments I to V and the second VI to VII (figure 2.8.3A), whereas in *Cyclopinoides longicornis* (Boeck) the fusion pattern is different, I-II, III-V, VI-IX and XII-XIV (figure 2.8.4A). The antennules of female *Oithona nana* Giesbrecht are indistinctly segmented (figure 2.8.6A) and the homology of the segments is difficult to ascertain. The pattern of segmental homologies traditionally attributed to oithonid antennules by taxonomists (cf. Nishida, 1985) is misleading because comparison is based on Giesbrecht's original 25 segment scheme. The shortened antennules of females belonging to the Mantridae (figure 2.8.8D), Archinotodelphyidae (figure 2.8.9A) and Notodelphyidae (figure 2.8.3B-C) show great similarity in segmental fusion patterns. An important fusion common to all is that between ancestral segments XV and XVI. This double segment becomes a triple in the Mantridae and Archinotodelphyidae, by the incorporation of segment XIV. In the Ozmanidae the female antennules are greatly reduced, virtually lacking in any functional articulations (figure 2.8.8A).

Male Antennule: Male antennules are structurally complex in the Cyclopoida. They exhibit considerable fusion between segments and the ancestral condition is the possession of a digeniculate antennule on both sides. The maximum number of segments known is 17, as found in many members of the family Cyclopidae, such as *Macrocyclops albidus* (Jurine) (figure 2.8.5A), and in the cyclopinid *Cyclopinoides longicornis* (Figure 2.8.4B-D). Comparison between the fusion patterns of antennulary segments in *Macrocyclops* Claus and *Cyclopinoides* reveals that the 17 segments are not entirely homologous (figure 2.8.10). *Macrocyclops* and other genera of the subfamily Cyclopinae are the only cyclopoids with 3 segments distal to the distal geniculation located between ancestral segments XX and XXI. These 3 segments represent a triple segment (XXI-XXIII), a double (XXIV-XXV) and the compound apical segment (XXVI-XXVIII). In all other cyclopoids the double segment is incorporated into the compound apical segment (XXIV-XXVIII), leaving only 2 segments distal to the geniculation. The first segment of *Macrocyclops* represents fused I-VI and VII is free whereas in *Cyclopinoides* I and II are free but III-V and VI-VII are fused. It is possible to infer from this analysis that the ancestral cyclopoid male had at least 20 antennulary segments. This analysis identifies five fusions common to all known male cyclopoids: ancestral segments III-V, XIX-XX, XXI-XXIII, XXIV-XXV and XXVI-XXVIII. The male of *Cyclopicina longifurcata*, the female of which has 26 segments, is unknown but it is possible that the male of this species has up to 22 segments, with segments III to V being free, as in the female.

The distal geniculation of male cyclopoids is located at the articulation between ancestral segments XX and XXI. This geniculation is retained in the Cyclopinidae, Cyclopidae, Oithonidae, Ozmanidae, Thespesiopsyllidae, Archinotodelphyidae, Notodelphyidae and Mantridae. The male antennules of the Ascidicolidae and Lernaeidae have reduced segmentation and are secondarily non-geniculate.

The proximal geniculation is found in four families, the Cyclopinidae, Cyclopidae, Oithonidae and Ozmanidae, located between ancestral segments XV and XVI. In the first three of these families it is an elaborate structure involving other segments. The segment homologous with XV is deeply incised along its dorsal margin (figure 2.8.5A-C). Segment XVI extends into the gap created by this incision but extensive arthrodial membrane is present around the entire joint and is largely enclosed by the sheath-like distal extension of segment XV. This geniculation allows pronounced dorsoventral flexion. The articulations between segments XI to XIV are provided with extensive areas of arthrodial membrane posteriorly that would allow some posterior telescoping of these segments (figures 2.8.5 and 2.8.7). Despite its complexity, the overall structure of this region of the male antennule is remarkably consistent in the Cyclopinidae (figure 2.8.4B-D), Cyclopidae (figures 2.8.5A-C and 2.8.7A-F) and Oithonidae (figure 2.8.6B-D). The sheath on segment XV is much reduced in the Ozmanidae, but is recognisable (figure 2.8.8B-C).

The absence of the proximal geniculation in the other cyclopoid families is probably secondary since ancestral segments XV and XVI are fused in both sexes. In *Archinotodelphys profundus* Monniot (figure 2.8.9) a trace of the segmental boundary remains but it is no longer a functional articulation. In *Thespesiopsyllus* these 2 segments are also fused (figure 2.8.35B). In *Archinotodelphys profundus* (figure 2.8.9B-D), the only archinotodelphyid for which the male is known, a modified segment homologous with segment XIV is present proximal to the double XV-XVI segment. This segment does not consist of a complete ring of thickened integument but has a membranous insert. A similar modification is found in the notodelphyid *Notodelphys elegans* Thorell (figure 2.8.11A-B) and, as noted by Fosshagen (1970), *Thespesiopsyllus paradoxus* has a conspicuous groove on the seventh segment from the end (= segment XIV). Two families, the Ascidicolidae and Lernaeidae, have lost both geniculations because of the extreme fusion and reduction of the antennules in both sexes.

Antenna: *Cyclopicina* is the only podoplean to possess a seta on the coxa of the antenna in the adult (figure 2.8.2C). The Cyclopidae (figure 2.8.12C) and Cyclopinidae (figure 2.8.2C) are the only families containing members that retain 2 inner setae on the antennary basis. The presence of only 1 basal seta is shared by all other cyclopoid families. The maximum setation of the antennary endopod, 1, 9 and 7 setae on the first to third segments respectively (figure 2.8.12C), is found only in the subfamily Cyclopinae of the Cyclopidae. Reports of more than 7 terminal setae in the Cyclopidae (Fiers & van de Velde, 1984; Fiers, 1986) require confirmation. Only certain genera of Cyclopidae, such as *Cyclops* Müller, have retained 9 setae on the second endopodal segment. The number of setae on the second endopodal segment has undergone repeated reductions in the cyclopoids. Eight setae are found in *Acanthocyclops sensitivus* (Graeter & Chappuis), 7 in *Cryptocyclops bicolor* (Sars) (figure 2.8.12D) and 6 in *Microcyclops demetiensis* (Scourfield). Five setae are found in some members of the subfamily Cyclopinae and is the maximum found in all other cyclopoid families (figures 2.8.12A and 2.8.13E) and the remaining two subfamilies of the Cyclopidae, the Euryteinae (figure 2.8.12B) and Halicyclopinae.

The modification of the inner terminal element on endopodal segment 3 to form a well developed claw is a synapomorphy linking the Mantridae (claw arrowed in figure 2.8.13E), Notodelphyidae (figure 2.8.13C-D), Archinotodelphyidae (figure 2.8.13A-B), Ascidicolidae (figure 2.8.14A) and Lernaeidae (figure 2.8.14C). In some representatives of the last two families the claw is secondarily lost. The homologue of this claw on the antenna of *Ozmana* Ho & Thatcher is the smallest of the series of distal margin elements and does not appear to be modified other than to form part of the distal series of hook-like elements (figure 2.8.14D). The exopod of the antenna is represented by a minute lobe bearing 3 setae in *Cyclopicina* (figure 2.8.2C-D). A maximum of 2 exopodal setae is known for other cyclopoids, including *Oithona* Baird (figure 2.8.14B), *Notodelphys allmani* (figure 2.8.13C), and *Archinotodelphys typicus* (figure 2.8.13A).

An allobasis formed by the incorporation of the first endopodal segment into the basis is found in some species of *Pterinopsyllus* (figure 2.8.12A) and in *Mantra* Leigh-Sharpe (figure 2.8.13E). In virtually all members of the Notodelphyidae and Ascidicolidae endopodal segments 2 and 3 are fused to form a double segment (figures 2.8.13C and 2.8.14A). The only exception in the Notodelphyidae is *Doropygopsis longicauda* (Aurivillius) which retains both as separate segments.

Mandible: There are 2 setae on the mandibular basis in *Cyclopicina* (figure 2.8.15B) compared to 1 or none in other cyclopoids. The characteristic mandible of *Oithona* appears to possess 3 setae on an unusually large basis but the broad basis is almost completely fused to the first endopodal segment. The armature of the incorporated endopodal segment comprises 2 setae, 1 of which is conspicuously spinulate. The configuration of the oithonid mandibular palp greatly facilitates interpretation of the mandible of *Cyclopetta difficilis* Sars. In *C.difficilis* 2 setae are present on the basis but one of them is derived from the incorporated first endopodal segment. The maximum setation of the mandibular exopod found in cyclopoids is 1,1,1,2, as found in *Cyclopicina* (figure 2.8.15B). The 1,1,1,3 formula shown in *Cyclopina gracilis* by Sars (1913-1918) is incorrect. Reexamination of *C.gracilis* revealed a 1,1,1,2 formula (figure 2.8.17A). The highest setal numbers on the proximal endopodal segment are found in the Archinotodelphyidae and Mantridae. Six setae are present in *Archinotodelphys polynesiensis* (figure 2.8.16A) and 5 in *Mantra speciosa* Leigh-Sharpe (figure 2.8.16B). The distal endopodal segment carries a maximum of 10 setae, as found in *A.polynesiensis* and a range of notodelphyid species, such as *Notodelphys echinata* Monniot (Monniot, 1961) and *Doropygus spinosus* Jones (Jones, 1980). In the Cyclopidae the entire mandibular palp is reduced to a vestigial segment bearing up to 3 setae (figure 2.8.16C), or is lost completely. The mandibular palp is also absent in the Ozmanidae.

Maxillule: The epipodite of the maxillule is represented by 3 surface setae in *Cyclopicina* (figure 2.8.15C). The record of 3 setae on the epipodite of *Cyclopinodes elegans* (Scott) (Scott, 1894) is erroneous as only 2 setae are present (figure 2.8.19A). Two setae are common in other cyclopinid genera and in other families. The coxal endite is present in members of the families Archinotodelphyidae, Notodelphyidae and Oithonidae as a small lobe bearing a strong apical seta (arrowed in figure 2.8.18B). Huys & Boxshall (1990a) stated that the maxillulary coxal endite is absent in all cyclopinids including *Cyclopicina* and suggested that the loss of the endite might represent a synapomorphy between the Cyclopinidae and Cyclopidae. However, reexamination of *Cyclopinodes elegans* revealed the presence of a coxal endite (figure 2.8.19B). The maximum number of elements on the praecoxal arthrite is 12, as in *C.elegans*. The arthrite is especially well developed in the Cyclopidae and has sometimes been drawn as an articulating segment with 3 armature elements located proximally (cf. Gurney's figure (1933, fig. 1302) of *Macrocyclops fuscus* (Jurine)). The position of the posterior surface fold at the base of the arthrite is shown by the dotted line in figure 2.8.18A and the 3 proximal elements form part of the marginal armature of the arthrite.

In the Euryteinae the maxillulary palp itself forms a gnathobase-like structure along the ventral surface of the arthrite (figure 2.8.19C-D).

The greatest numbers of setae representing the basal maxillulary endites (3 + 5) are found in *Archinotodelphys polynesiensis* (figure 2.8.18A). The distal endite is represented by 4 setae in *A.typicus*, *Pararchinotodelphys gurneyi* Illg and the Mantridae (figure 2.8.18C) and by a maximum of 3 setae in all other cyclopoids. In the specialised maxillule of the Oithonidae the distal endite is located at the outer margin of the basis (figure 2.8.17D). This unusual configuration is also found in the cyclopinids *Psammocyclopina hindleyi* Wells and *Procyclopina polyarthra* Herbst. Oithonids retain the ancestral condition of 3 setae representing the proximal endite on the basis (figure 2.8.17D). The setation of these endites in the Cyclopinidae is typically 3 + 2, as in *Cyclopinodes elegans* (figure 2.8.19A-B). In members of the Notodelphyidae the endites are confluent on the inner margin of the basis and are represented by a maximum of 4 setae.

The maximum of 4 setae on the maxillulary exopod is widespread amongst the Cyclopinidae and other less transformed families. The setation of the maxillulary endopod in *Cyclopicina* is 1 + 1, 5 with the proximal setae representing the combined armature of the fused first and second ancestral segments. In *Mantra* the endopod setal formula is 5, 4, with the 5 proximal elements representing the maximum number found on this double segment within the Cyclopoida. The ancestral endopodal setation of 5, 5 is retained in *Archinotodelphys polynesiensis* (figure 2.8.18A).

Maxilla: The basic segmentation of the maxilla in cyclopoids provides a unique apomorphy of the order. In all families in which the maxillary endopod is sufficiently well developed for the setal patterns to be determined, the proximal endopodal segment is double, representing the fused first and second ancestral segments. This double segment primitively bears 4 setae but the number is often secondarily reduced. The first ancestral endopodal segment is never fused to the basis in cyclopoids. The middle endopodal segment represents the third ancestral segment and carries 2 setae. The distal segment is the fourth ancestral segment and retains its full complement of 4 setae. The basic setal formula for the cyclopoid endopod is (2 + 2), 2, 4 and is found in the Cyclopinidae, some Archinotodelphyidae, and the Oithonidae. In the Mantridae, Notodelphyidae and *Archinotodelphys typicus* the formula (1 or 2), 1, 4 is typical.

Maxilliped: The basic segmentation of the maxilliped (syncoxa, basis and 5-segmented endopod) is found in *Cyclopicina* (figure 2.8.20B). Many authors have illustrated cyclopoid maxillipeds with a subdivision of the syncoxa, usually shown by an oblique line drawn between the middle and distal endites (cf. Nishida, 1985: fig. 51e, for example). Detailed examination of the maxillipeds of primitive representatives of several cyclopoid families (figures 2.8.23 and 2.8.24B-E) revealed no true articulation at this position. Surface folds of integument are often present but these are derived as extensions of the origin of the endite and not from a true articulation. This integumental fold permits some limited retraction of the distal endite into the proximal part of the syncoxa.

The syncoxa bears 3 clusters of setae representing 3 coxal endites. The praecoxal endite is lost in cyclopoids, producing an enditic setation formula of 0,1,3,2, as found in many cyclopinids, such as *Cyclopicina* (figure 2.8.20B) and *Cyclopinoides schulzi* Herbst (figure 2.8.24B), *Mantra* (figure 2.8.24E) and *Archinotodelphys polynesiensis* (figure 2.8.24D). In *Oithona* the syncoxal setation is reduced to 1,2,2 (figure 2.8.23D), and it is further reduced in *Euryte* which retains only 2 setae (figure 2.8.24C). In the Notodelphyidae (figure 2.8.23B) and in a single archinotodelphyid, *Archinotodelphys typicus* (figure 2.8.23A), supernumerary setae are present on the middle and distal endites. In notodelphyid genera a setal formula of 0,0,5,5 is typical and in *A.typicus* the formula is 0,1,5,5. These are considered in the section on additions in chapter 4.

The basis in cyclopoids bears 2 inner setae, as in *Cyclopicina* (figure 2.8.20B). Reports of 3 setae on the basis of *Cyclopina ensifera* Grandori (see Petkovski, 1955) and *Cyclopinoides schulzi* (Herbst, 1964) are wrong. Only 2 setae are present in these species (figure 2.8.24B). The maximum setation of the endopod is 1,2,2,1+1,4 and is found only in *Cyclopicina* (figure 2.8.20B). The outer seta on the subapical segment is found only in *Cyclopicina* and provides an important reference point, indicating that the 5-segmented endopod of cyclopoids is derived from the ancestral 6-segmented condition by the loss of the first segment. Outside of the Cyclopinidae a maximum of only 2 endopodal segments is found, except in some species of the Euryteinae which can have 3 segments (figure 2.8.24C). The maxilliped is missing in the ascidicolid subfamily Enterocolinae and in the Ozmanidae.

Male Fifth Leg: The ancestral state of the fifth leg of cyclopoid males is retained in species of the cyclopinid genera *Metacyclopina* Lindberg (figure 2.8.33D) and *Cyclopinodes* Wilson (figure 2.8.33B). It comprises a separate coxa, basis and 2-segmented exopod. An intercoxal sclerite is present connecting the fifth legs in these genera and in *Herbstina* Huys & Boxshall (figure 2.8.33C). The same two genera also have retained an inner coxal seta and display the maximum exopodal setation of 1-1;4. A separate coxa and basis is also found in *Pterinopsyllus, Cyclopinoides* and *Psammocyclopina* Wells but in these genera either the exopod is 1-segmented or the inner coxal seta is lost (figure 2.8.33A). A few members of the Cyclopidae also retain separate coxa and basis, for example *Neocyclops* Gurney and *Euryte.* A 2-segmented exopod also occurs in *Pseudocyclopinodes* Lang and *Neocyclopina* Herbst within the Cyclopinidae, and in *Neocyclops* which is the only cyclopid to exhibit this state. A few cyclopids, such as members of the subfamily Halicyclopinae, have 5 exopodal setae, but otherwise 4 is the maximum number for the non-cyclopinid families.

Female Fifth Leg: The ancestral state of the female fifth leg is not found in any extant cyclopoid. A separate coxa and basis is found in several genera of the Cyclopinidae, such as *Cyclopinoides* (figure 2.8.28B) and *Pterinopsyllus* (figure 2.8.26A-B), and in two cyclopid genera, *Euryte* (figure 2.8.29A) and *Neocyclops.* In the Cyclopinidae the intercoxal sclerite is commonly retained connecting the ventrally located fifth legs. In *Pterinopsyllus* the coxae fuse with the sclerite to form a common transverse plate (figure 2.8.26A). In the Cyclopidae an intercoxal sclerite is found only in *Euryte, Ancheuryte* Herbst and *Neocyclops.* The intercoxal sclerite is absent in all other families, even the Thespesiopsyllidae in which the fifth legs are located close together on the ventral surface of the somite (figure 2.8.36A). A 2-segmented exopod on the female fifth leg is found only in *Thespesiopsyllus* (figure 2.8.36B).

The inner coxal seta of the female fifth leg is retained only in some cyclopinid genera, including *Pseudocyclopinodes, Cyclopinodes, Cyclopinopsis* Smirnov, *Psammocyclopina* and *Metacyclopina* in the Cyclopininae and both genera of the Pterinopsyllinae. The outer basal seta is present in the great majority of all cyclopoids. *Cyclopicina longifurcata* is the only cyclopoid possessing 2 elements on the outer margin of the fifth leg exopod (figure 2.8.25C). *Archinotodelphys polynesiensis* possesses a total of 6 setae (figure 2.8.31B) consisting of 3 on the inner margin, 2 distally and 1 on the outer margin. The total number of ancestral elements in the Cyclopoida was presumably 7, with 2 on the outer margin, 2 distally and 3 on the inner margin. Species of the ascidicolid genus *Styelicola* Lützen have a 1-segmented exopod bearing 6 setae on the distal and inner margins. All other cyclopoids have a maximum of 4 setae, having lost the proximal outer seta and retained only the distalmost inner seta.

The female fifth legs are highly modified within the family Ascidicolidae (Illg & Dudley, 1980). In *Ascidicola* Thorell species the fifth legs are expanded to form hollow plates each of which functions as a brood pouch protecting the egg sac. In *Styelicola* the fifth leg is less expanded and retains an articulated and setose exopod (referred to as the endopod by Illg & Dudley (1980)). In other ascidicolids the fifth legs form pediform projections that probably incorporate protrusions of the actual somite. In some subfamilies, such as the Botryllophilinae, these projections support the dorsal ovisacs, which are usually fused into a common dorsal mass.

Mating: The possession of digeniculate antennules in male cyclopoids is correlated with a primitive mating position in which the male grasps the fourth legs of the female in a ventral to ventral orientation (figure 2.8.38B). In this position the paired spermatophores are transferred from the apertures of the male to the ventral surface of the female genital double somite on the tips of the male fourth legs (Hill & Coker, 1930). It can be inferred from the configuration of the female genital openings and the typical mating posture that in the ancestral cyclopoid stock the male placed a pair of spermatophores ventrally on the female's genital somite. These discharged directly into the copulatory pores contained within the paired, ventral genital apertures of the female. This basic copulatory mechanism is still found in those cyclopoids (the majority) with a single ventral copulatory pore. It is interesting to note that spermatophore placement is still the same in most oithonids, despite the lateral migration of the genital apertures containing the copulatory pores. In these oithonids (eg. *Oithona nana*, figures 2.8.30C-E and 2.8.40A-B) the spermatophores discharge via long spermatophore tubules that extend round the ventrolateral surface and into the copulatory pores located within the slit-like apertures. In a few oithonids, such as *O.setigera*

Dana, copulation must be modified since the spermatophores appear to be placed singly on each genital aperture (figure 2.8.30A-B).

Differential Diagnosis: Cyclopoids can be distinguished from other podopleans by the possession of a combination of digeniculate antennules bearing a sheath on segment XV in the males with the lack of a defined antennary exopod. The antennary exopod is represented by up to 3 setae but no exopodal segment remains. Those other podopleans with digeniculate antennules, the Misophrioida and Gelyelloida, both possess a multisegmented antennary exopod. Cyclopoids are also characterised by the fusion of the first and second endopodal segments of the maxilla, and by a 4-segmented mandibular exopod derived by loss of the ancestral first exopodal segment.

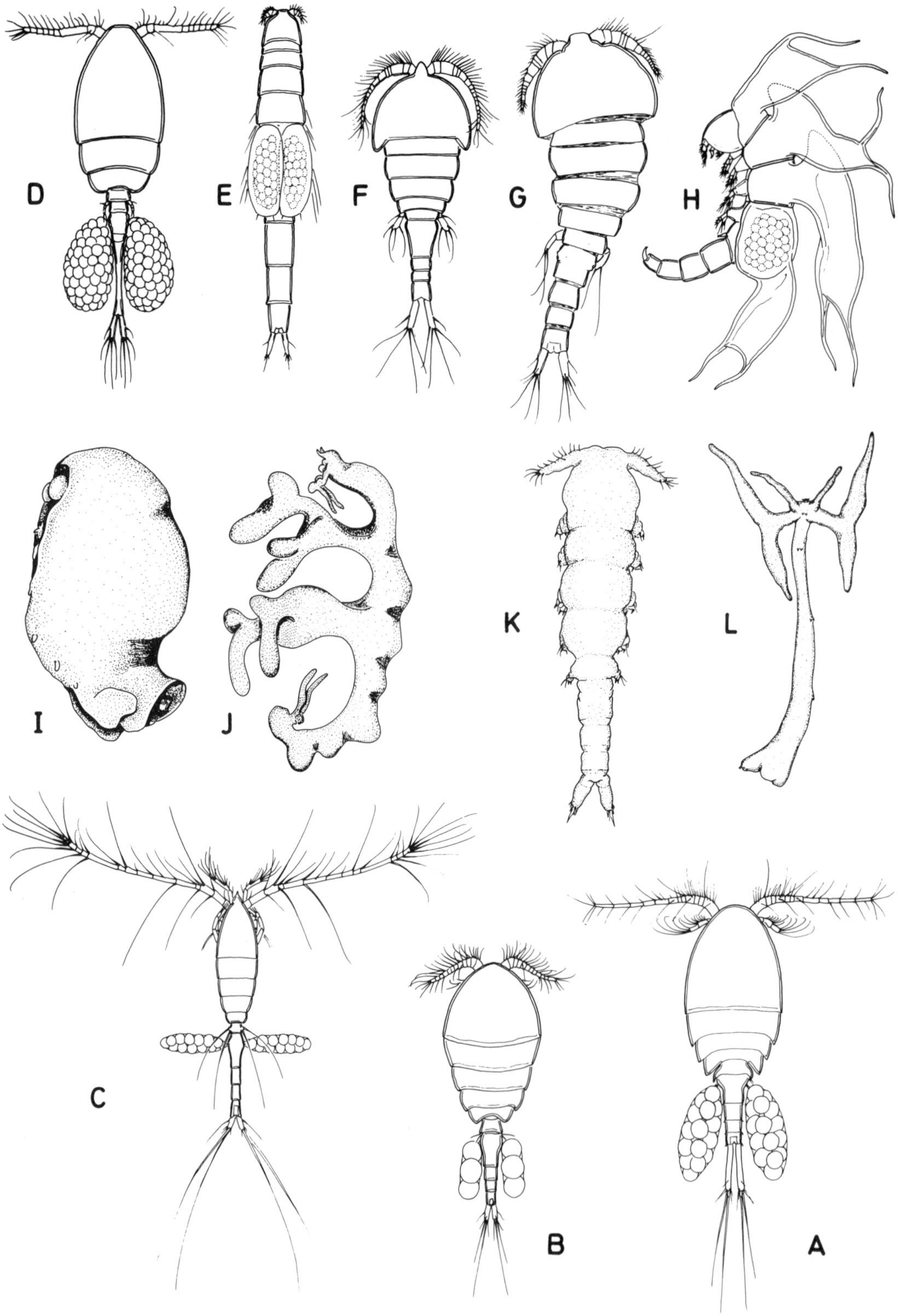

Figure 2.8.1. The diversity of cyclopoid body form. **A**. Cyclopidae. **B**. Cyclopinidae. **C**. Oithonidae. **D**. Thespesiopsyllidae. **E**. Ascidicolidae. **F**. Archinotodelphyidae. **G**. Mantridae. **H**. Notodelphyidae. **I**. Chordeumiidae. **J**. Cucumaricolidae. **K**. Ozmanidae. **L**. Lernaeidae.

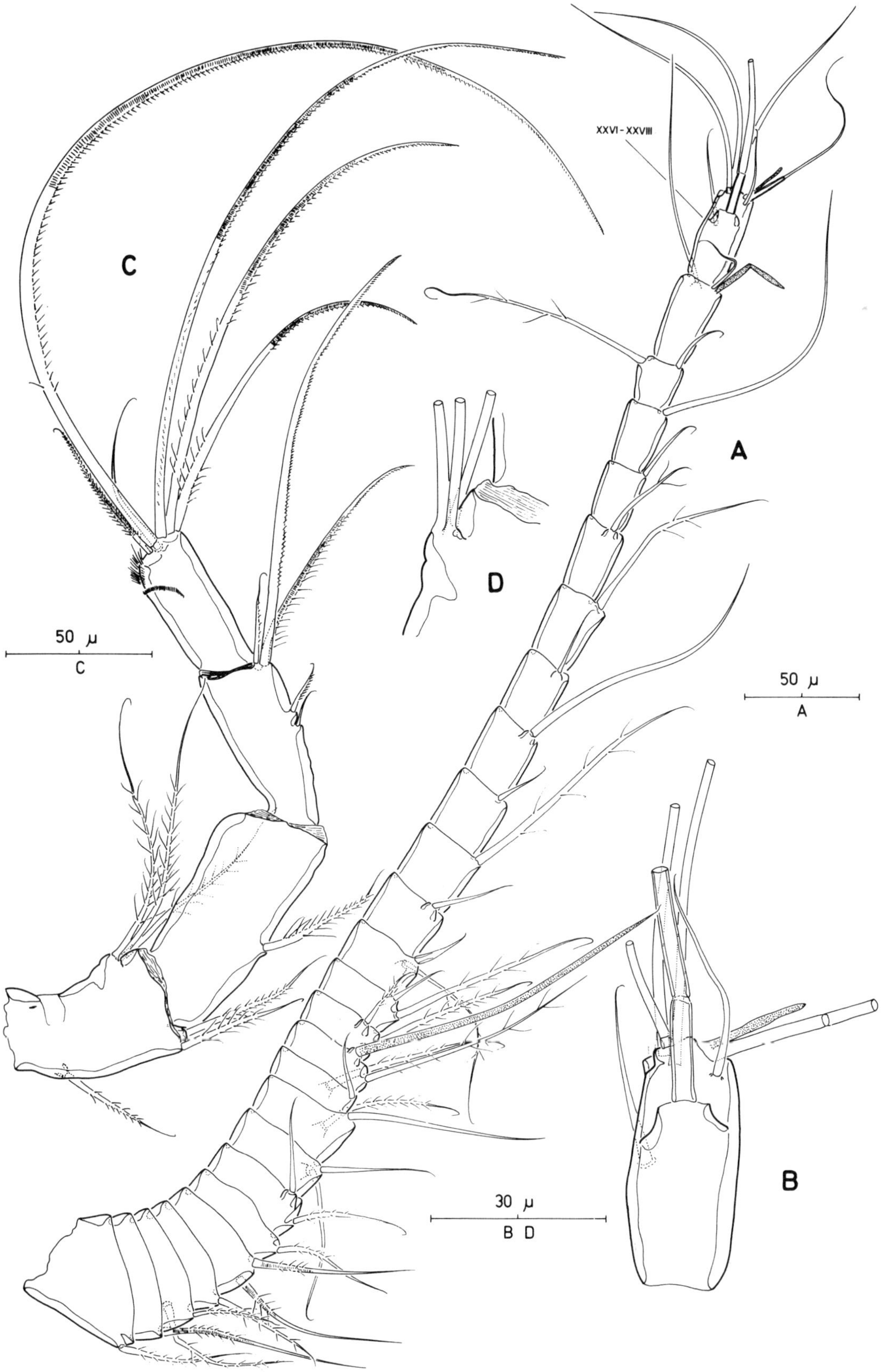

Figure 2.8.2. *Cyclopicina longifurcata*. **A.** Female antennule. **B.** Distal antennulary segment XXVI-XXVIII. **C.** Antenna. **D.** Antennary exopod, detail.

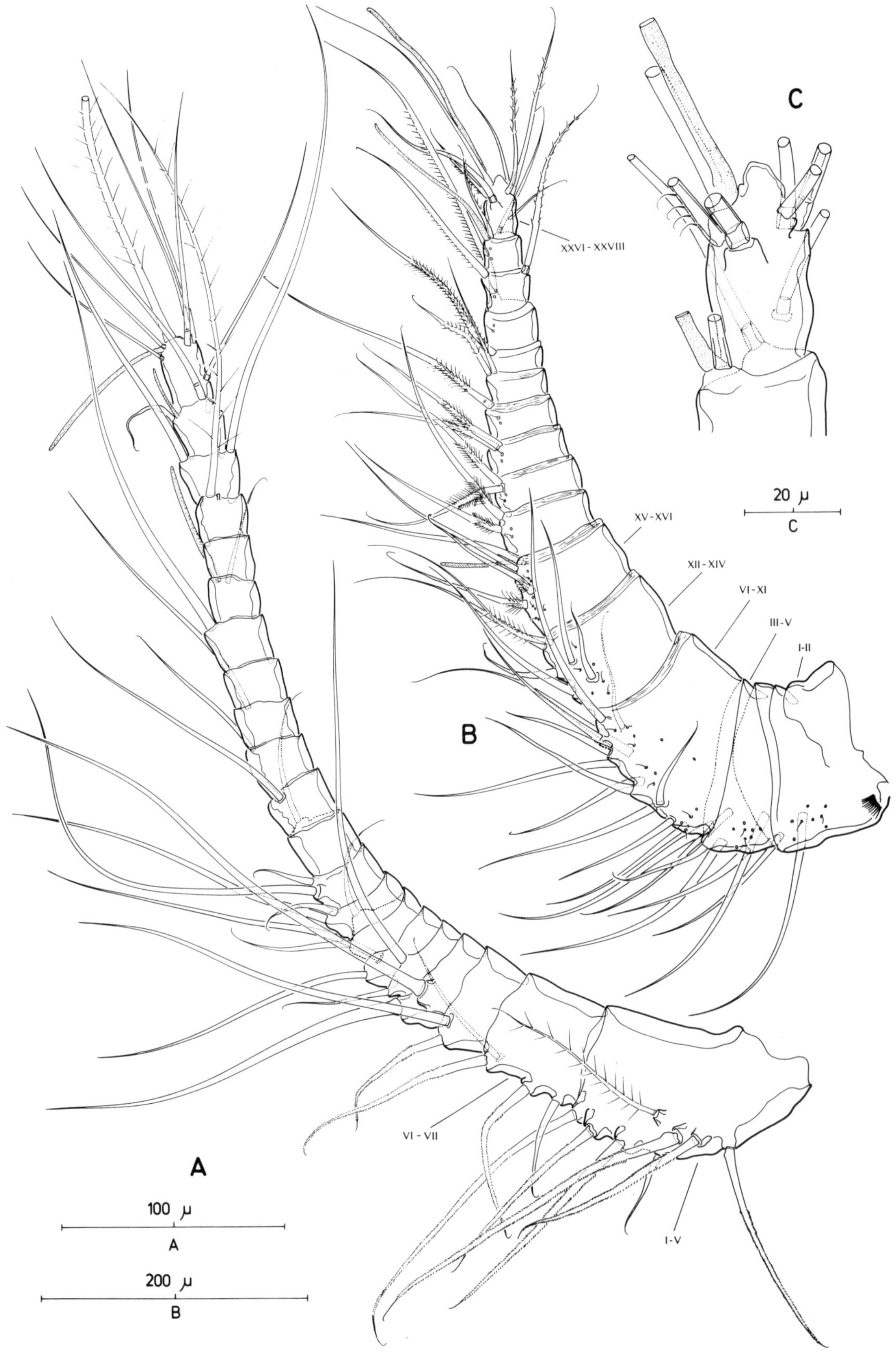

Figure 2.8.3. **A.** *Euryte robusta*, female antennule. **B.** *Notodelphys allmani*, female antennule. **C.** Same, distal segment.

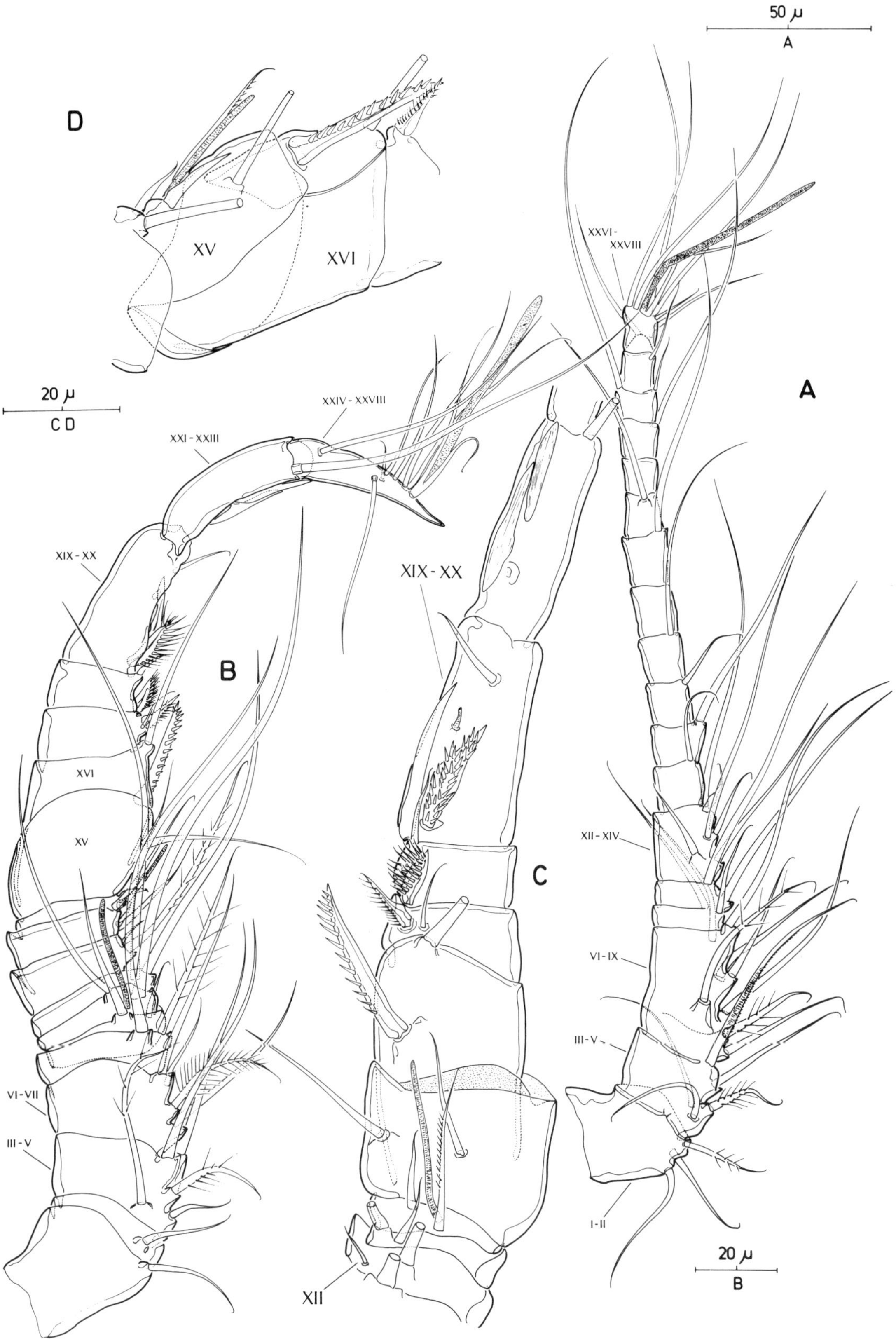

Figure 2.8.4. *Cyclopinoides longicornis*. **A.** Female antennule. **B.** Male antennule, ventral view. **C.** Male, antennule, anterior view of segments XII to XXIII. **D.** Male antennule, dorsal view of segments XV and XVI.

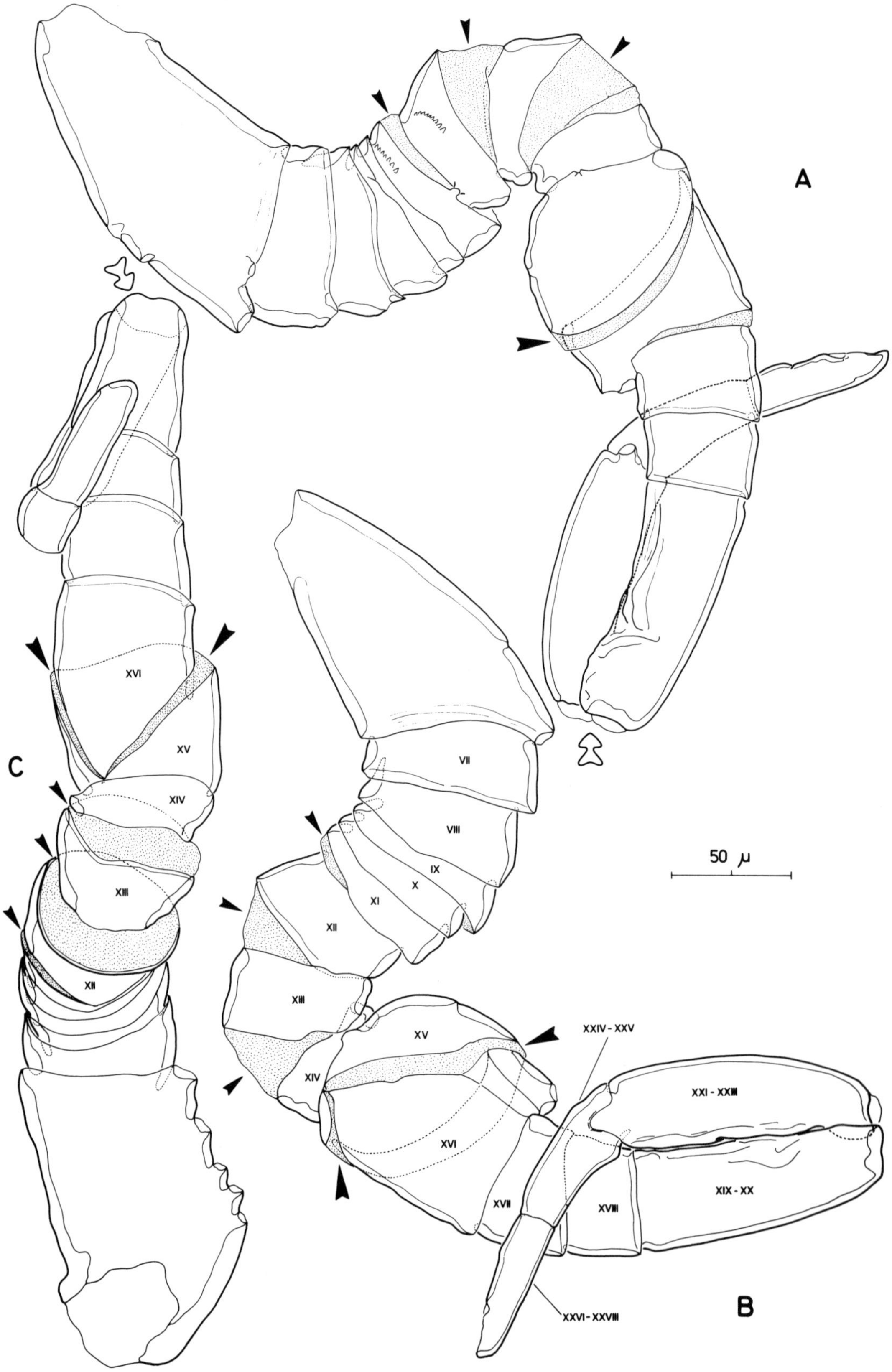

Figure 2.8.5. *Macrocyclops albidus*, male antennule. **A.** Ventral view. **B.** Dorsal view. **C.** Posterior view. [White arrow indicates neocopepodan geniculation; large black arrows indicate sheath between XV and XVI; small black arrows show arthrodial membranes.]

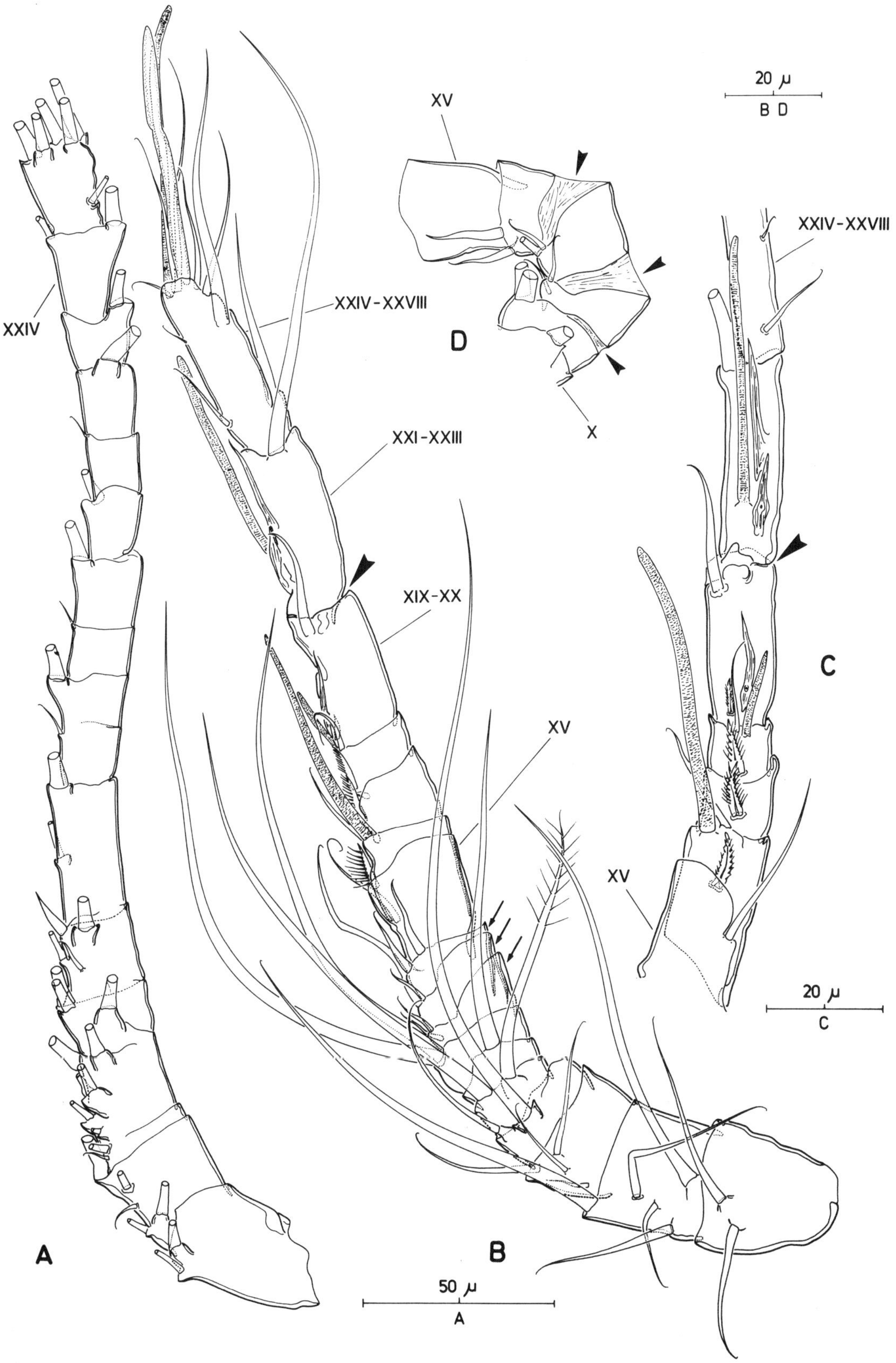

Figure 2.8.6. *Oithona nana*. **A.** Female antennule. **B.** Male antennule, ventral view. [Large arrow indicates neocopepodan geniculation; small arrows indicate telescoping segments.] **C.** Male antennule, anterior view of segments XV to XXIII. [Geniculation arrowed.] **D.** Male antennule, ventral view of segments X to XV (in clasping mode with arthrodial membranes fully exposed).

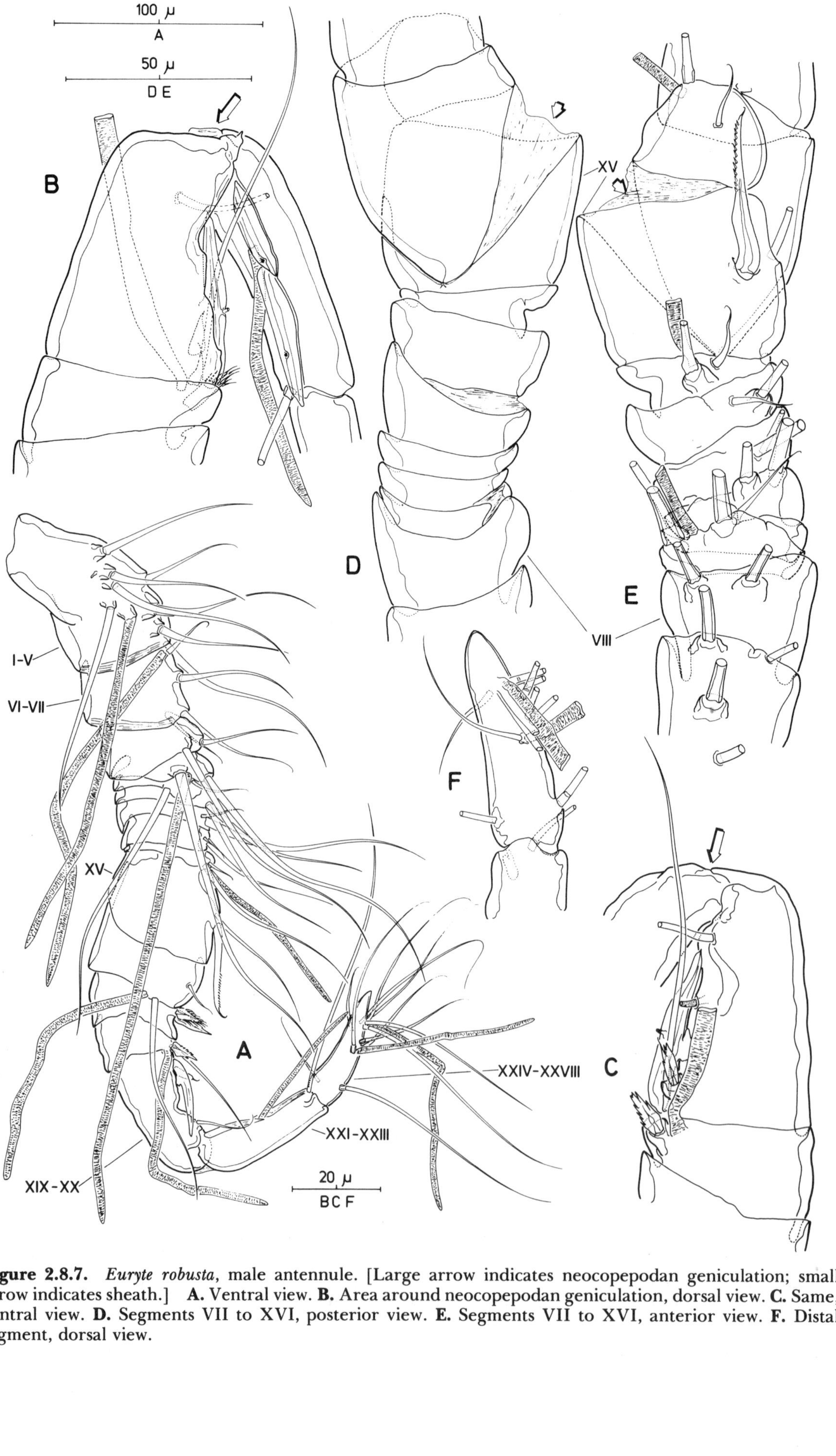

Figure 2.8.7. *Euryte robusta*, male antennule. [Large arrow indicates neocopepodan geniculation; small arrow indicates sheath.] **A.** Ventral view. **B.** Area around neocopepodan geniculation, dorsal view. **C.** Same, ventral view. **D.** Segments VII to XVI, posterior view. **E.** Segments VII to XVI, anterior view. **F.** Distal segment, dorsal view.

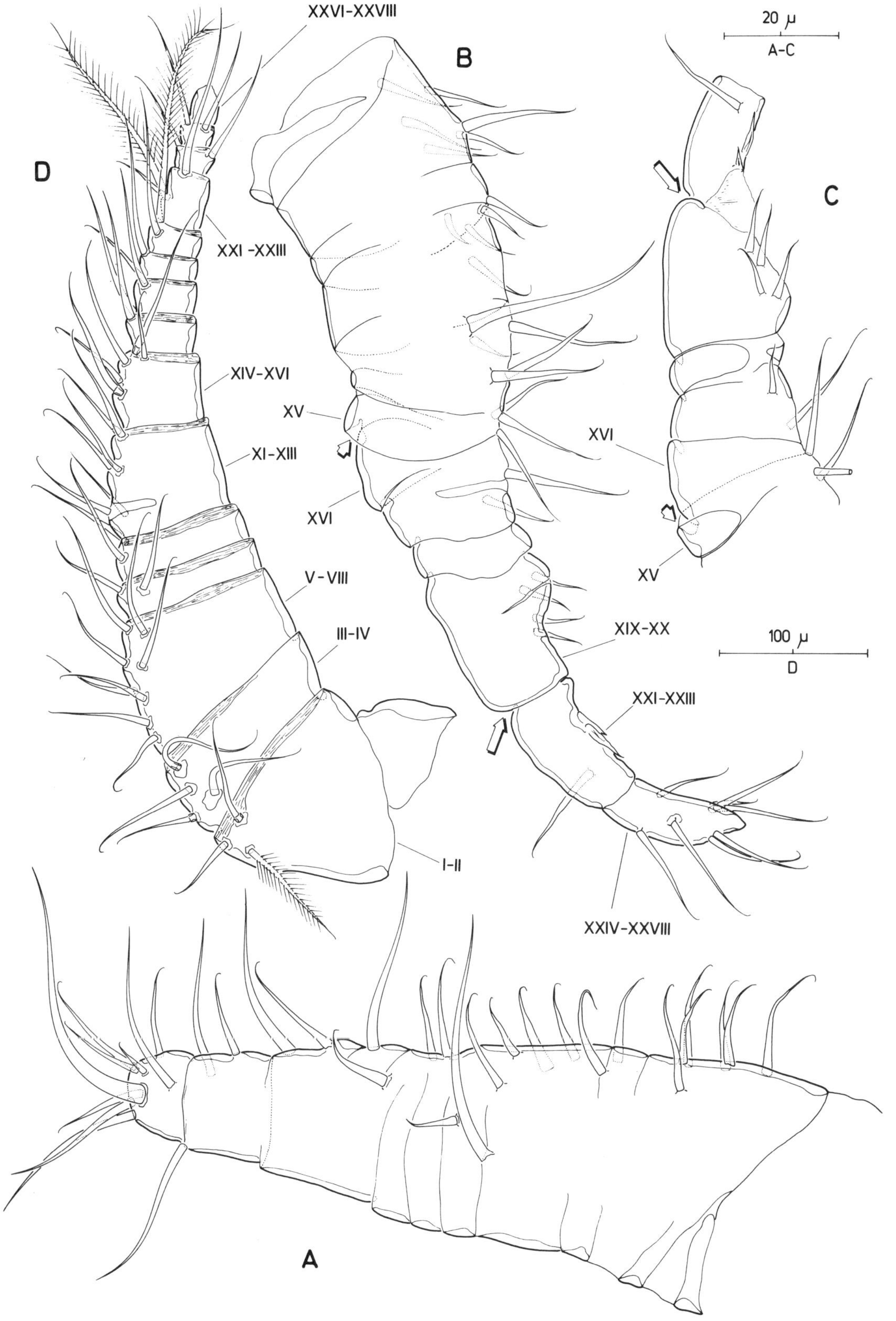

Figure 2.8.8. **A.** *Ozmana haemophila*, female antennule. **B.** Male antennule, dorsal view. **C.** Male antennule, ventral view of segments XV to XXIII. [In B-C: large arrow indicates neocopepodan geniculation; small arrow indicates sheath.] **D.** *Mantra speciosa*, female antennule with distal armature missing, ventral view.

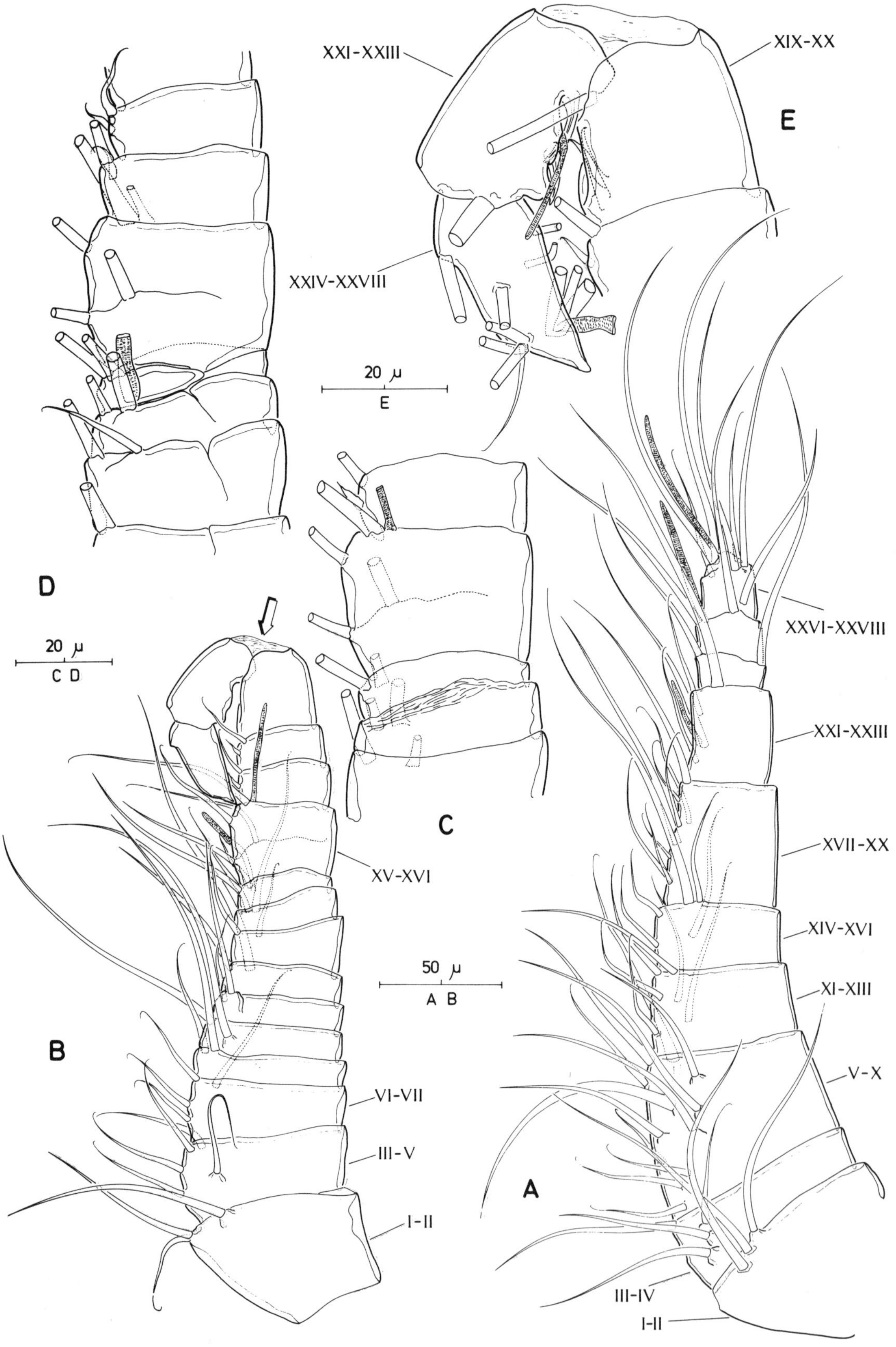

Figure 2.8.9. *Archinotodelphys profundus.* **A.** Female antennule, ventral view. **B.** Male antennule, ventral view (setation of distal segments omitted). [Geniculation arrowed.] **C.** Male antennule, segments XII to XVII, ventral view. **D.** Male antennule, segments XII to XVII, dorsal view. **E.** Male antennule, distal segments, ventral view.

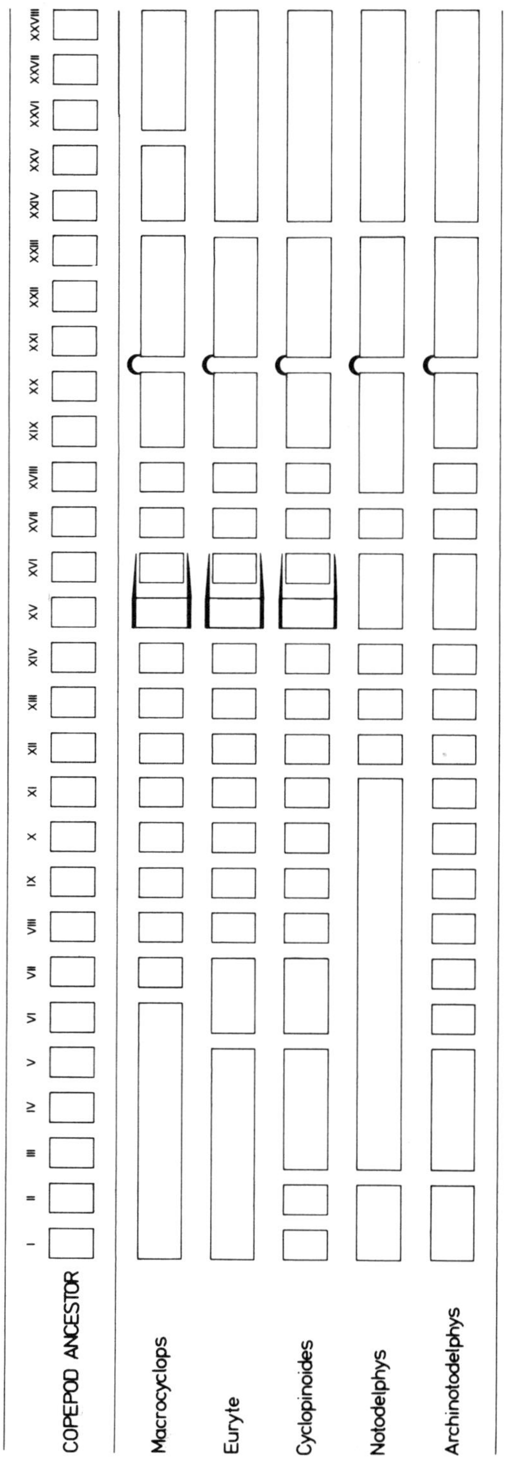

Figure 2.8.10. Schematic comparison of segmental homologies in the antennules of male cyclopoids.

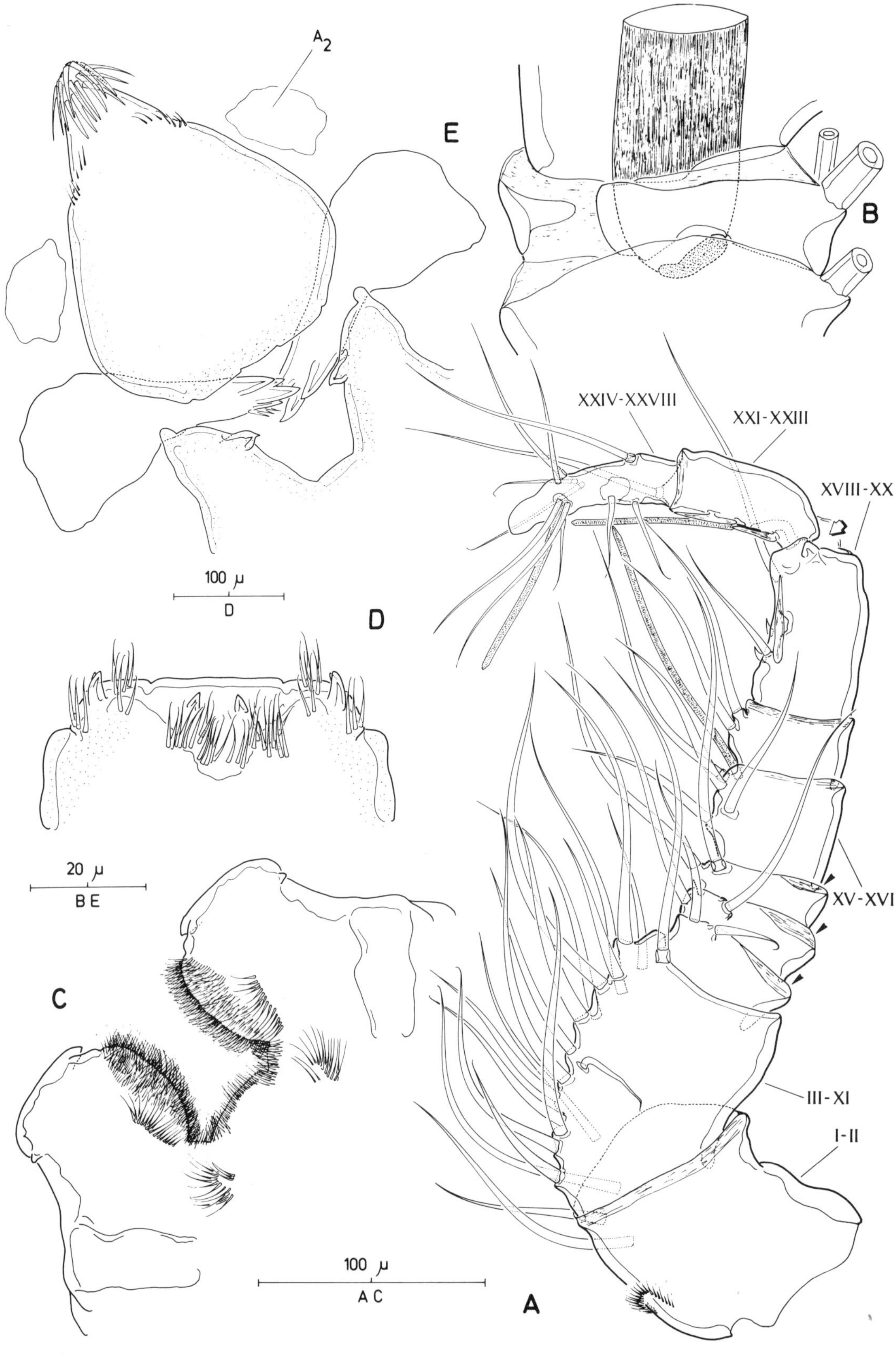

Figure 2.8.11. **A.** *Notodelphys elegans*, male antennule, ventral view (ornamentation of setae omitted). [White arrow indicates geniculation; small arrows indicating arthrodial membranes.] **B.** Male antennula, dorsal view of segments XIII and XIV showing insertion site of muscle. **C.** Paragnaths. **D.** *Mantra speciosa*, labrum. **E.** *Oithona nana*, oral area showing labrum, mandibular gnathobases and paragnaths (A_2 indicates position of antenna).

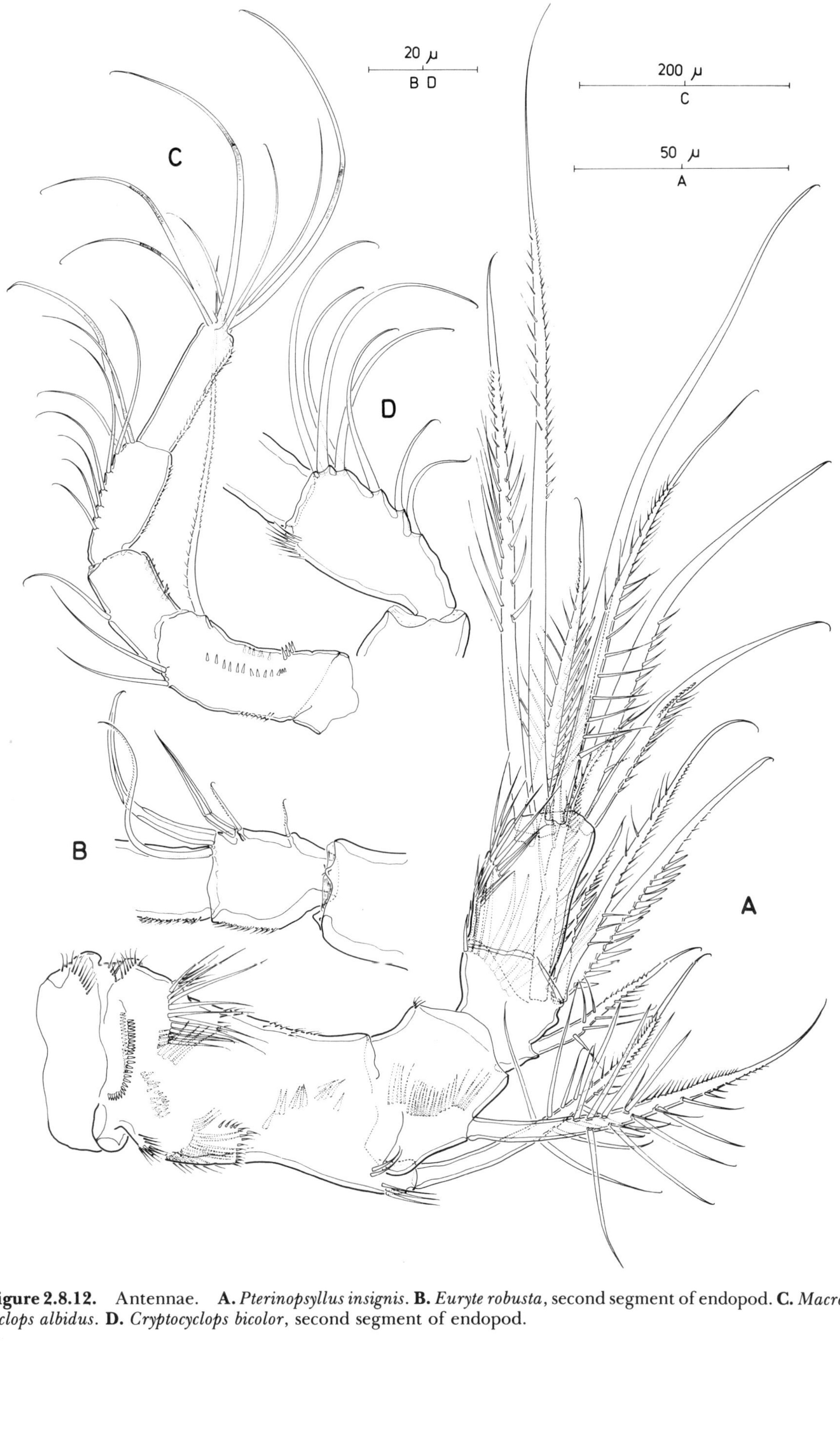

Figure 2.8.12. Antennae. **A.** *Pterinopsyllus insignis*. **B.** *Euryte robusta*, second segment of endopod. **C.** *Macrocyclops albidus*. **D.** *Cryptocyclops bicolor*, second segment of endopod.

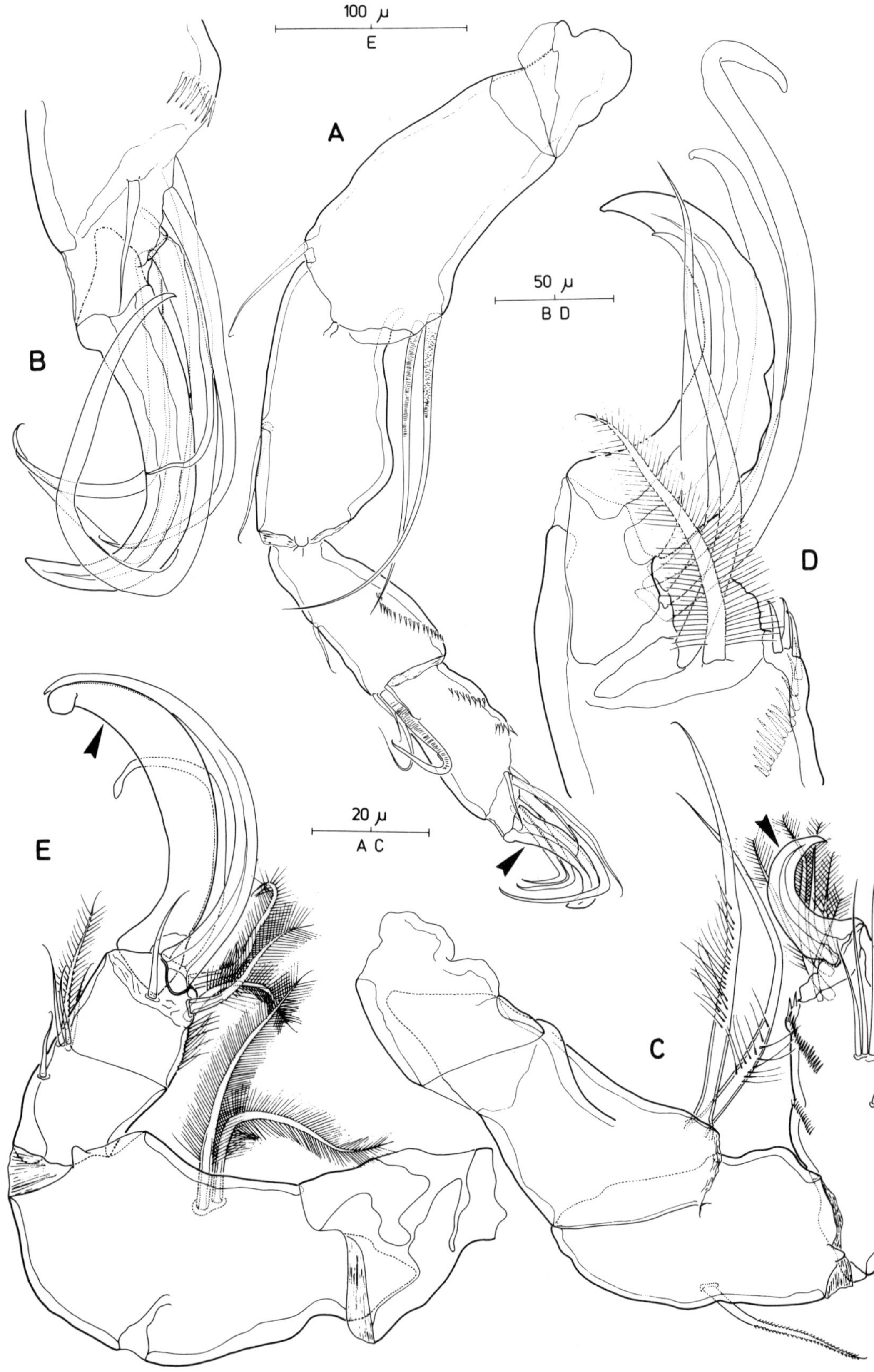

Figure 2.8.13. Antennae. **A.** *Archinotodelphys typicus*. **B**. Detail of endopodal apex. **C.** *Notodelphys allmani*. **D.** Detail of endopodal apex. **E.** *Mantra speciosa*. [Arrow indicates modified claw.]

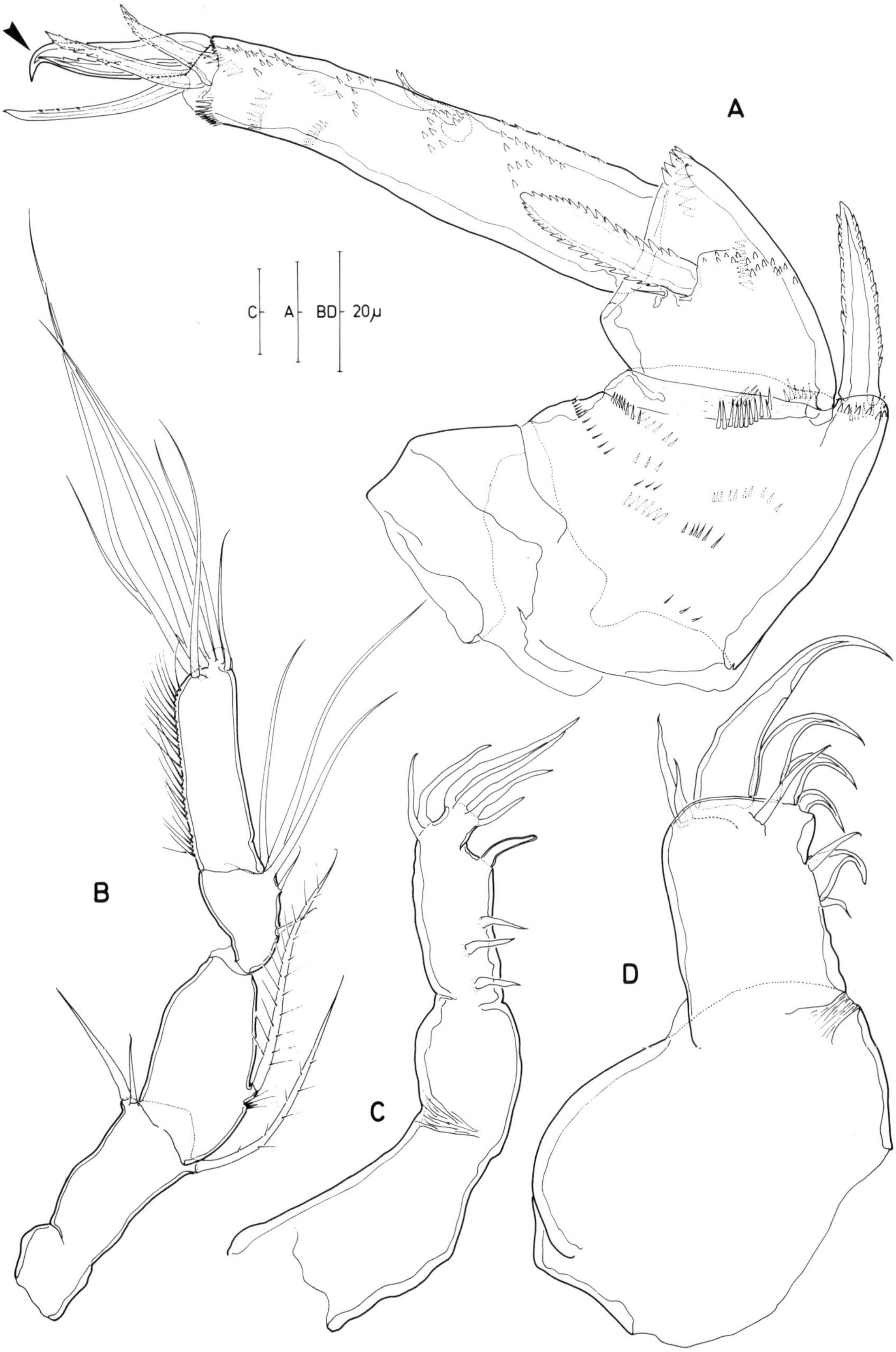

Figure 2.8.14. Antennae. **A.** *Ascidicola rosea*, with modified claw homologous with that of archinotodelphyids, mantrids and notodelphyids arrowed. **B.** *Oithona nana*. **C.** *Lamproglena pulchella*. **D.** *Ozmana haemophila*.

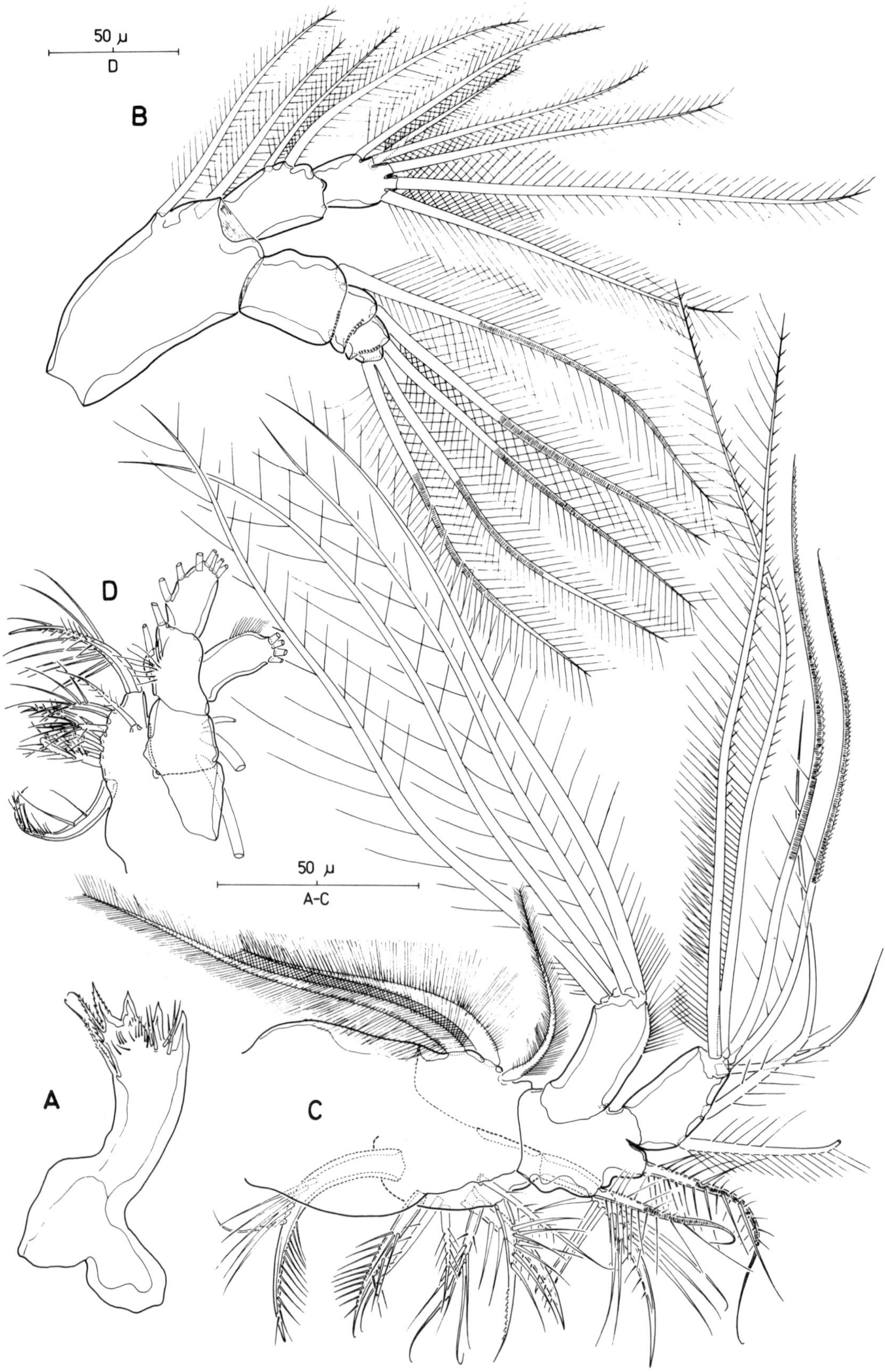

Figure 2.8.15. *Cyclopicina longifurcata*. **A.** Mandibular gnathobase. **B.** Mandibular palp. **C.** Maxillule, posterior view. **D.** Maxillule, anterior view.

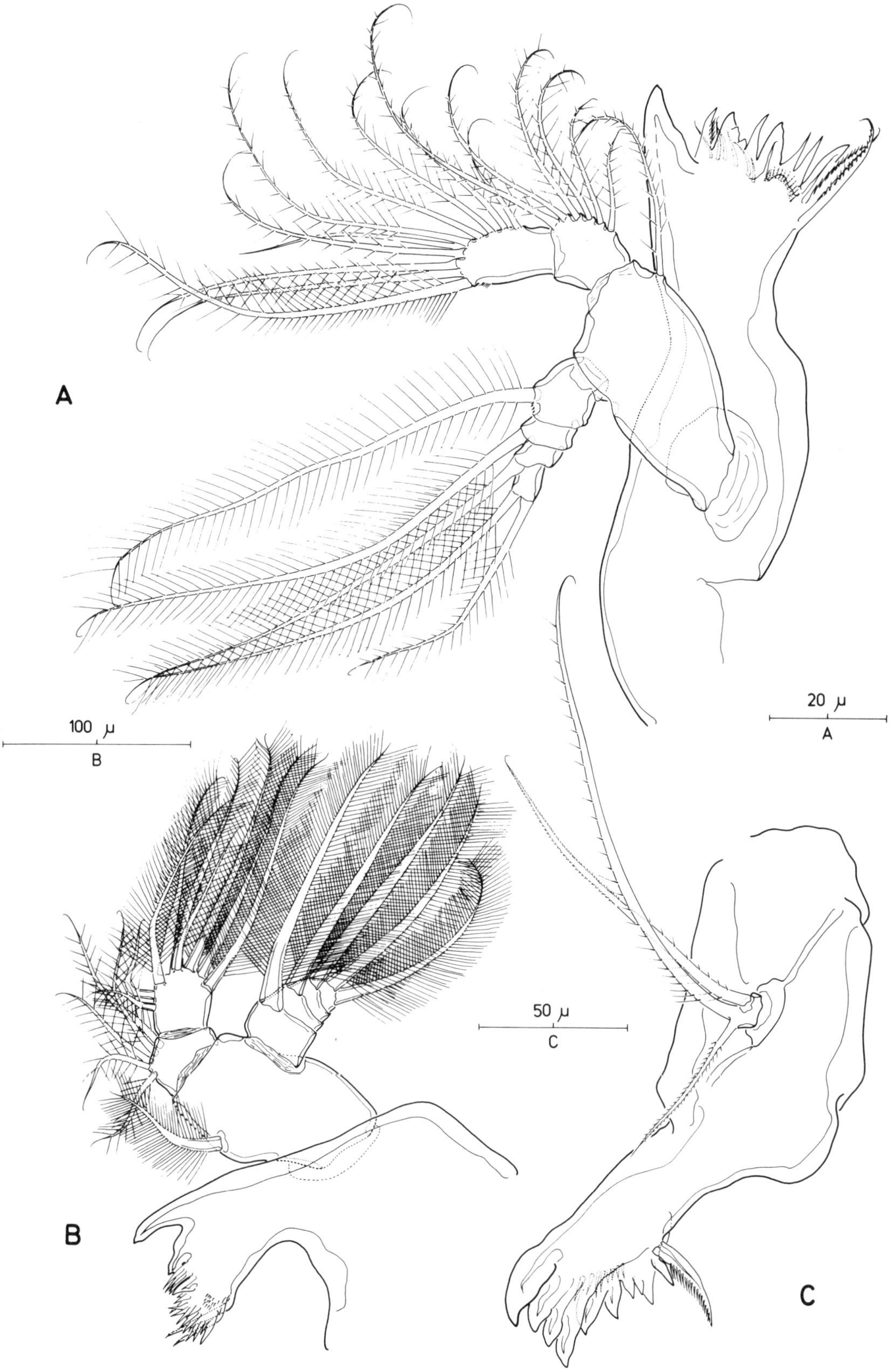

Figure 2.8.16. Mandibles. **A.** *Archinotodelphys polynesiensis*. **B.** *Mantra speciosa*. **C.** *Euryte robusta*.

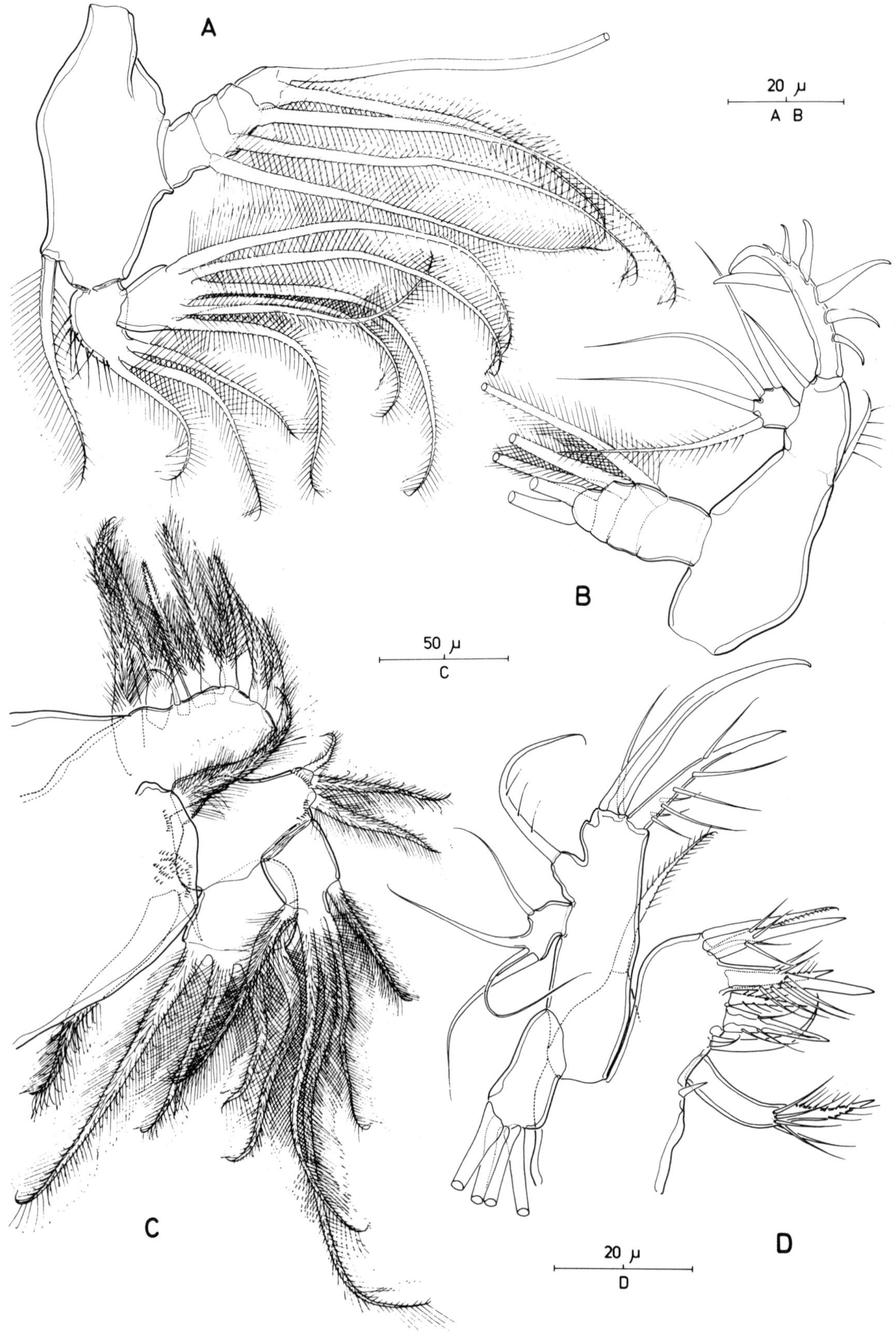

Figure 2.8.17. **A.** *Cyclopina gracilis*, mandibular palp. **B.** *Oithona nana*, mandibular palp. **C.** *Notodelphys allmani*, maxillule. **D.** *O.nana*, maxillule.

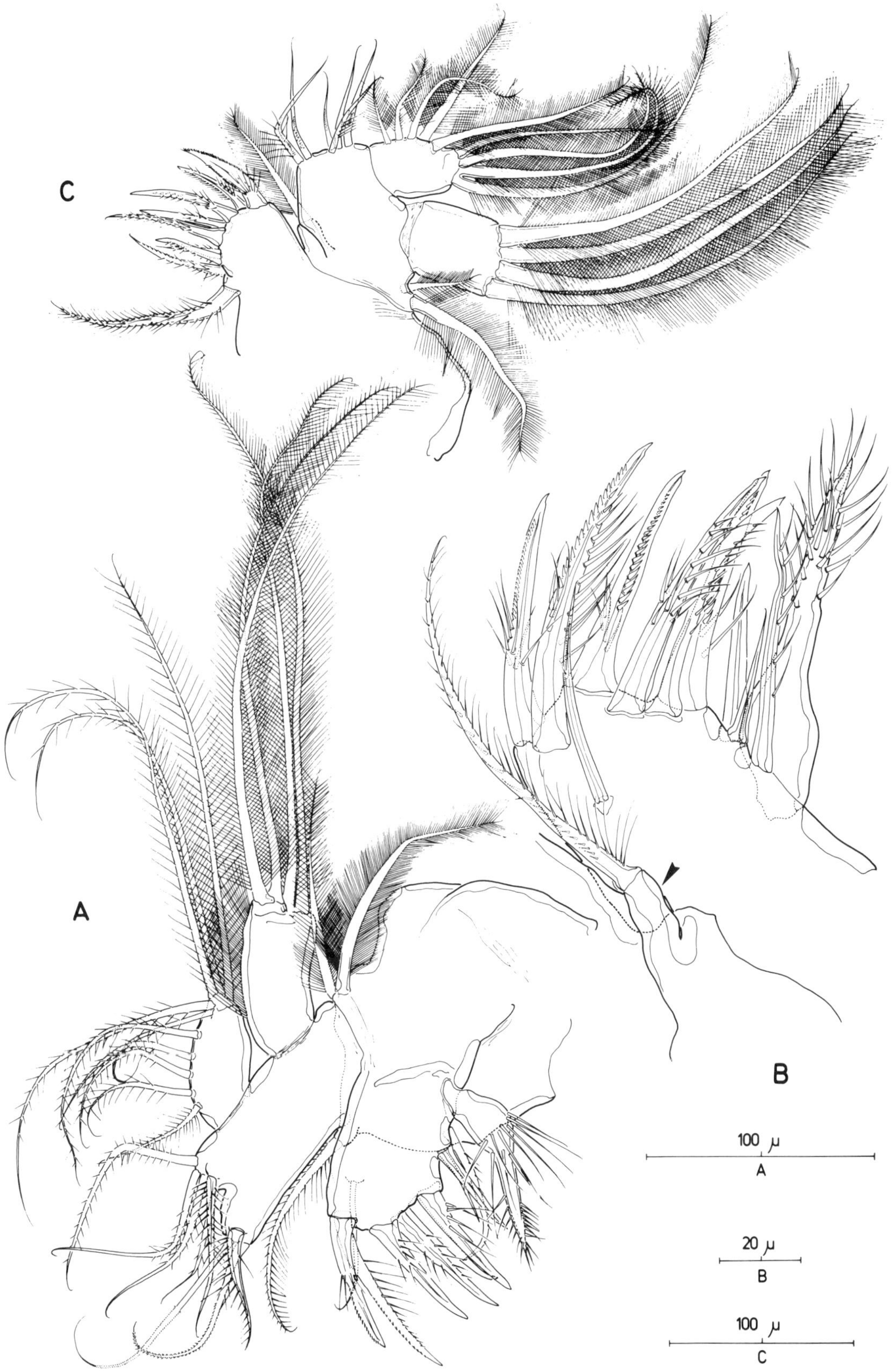

Figure 2.8.18. **A.** *Archinotodelphys polynesiensis*, maxillule. **B.** Praecoxal arthrite and coxal endite (arrowed). **C.** *Mantra speciosa*, maxillule.

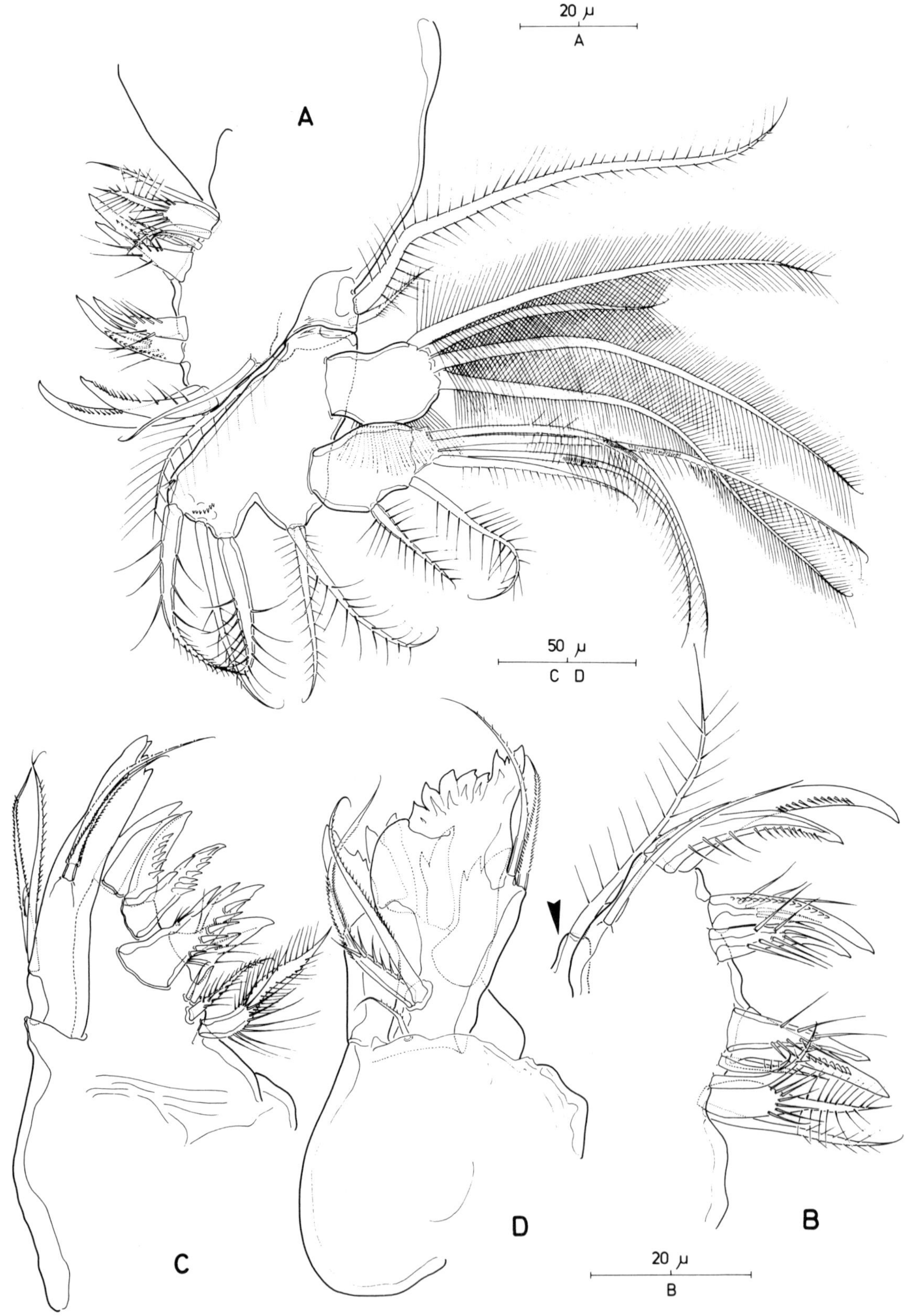

Figure 2.8.19. **A.** *Cyclopinodes elegans*, maxillule. **B.** Arthrite and coxal endite (arrowed). **C.** *Euryte robusta*, detail of maxillulary arthrite, medio-dorsal view. **D.** Maxillule, anterior view.

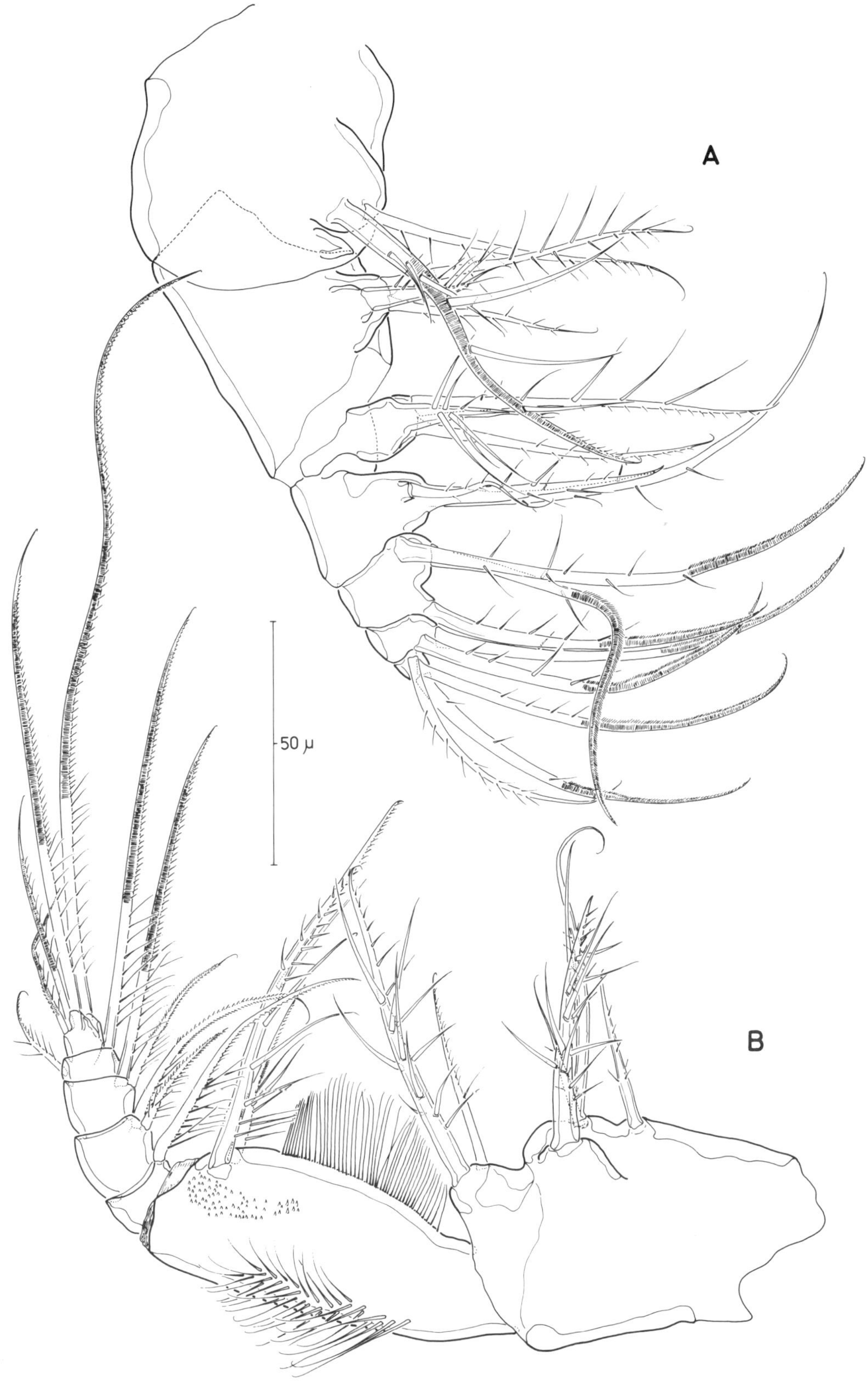

Figure 2.8.20. *Cyclopicina longifurcata*. **A.** Maxilla. **B.** Maxilliped.

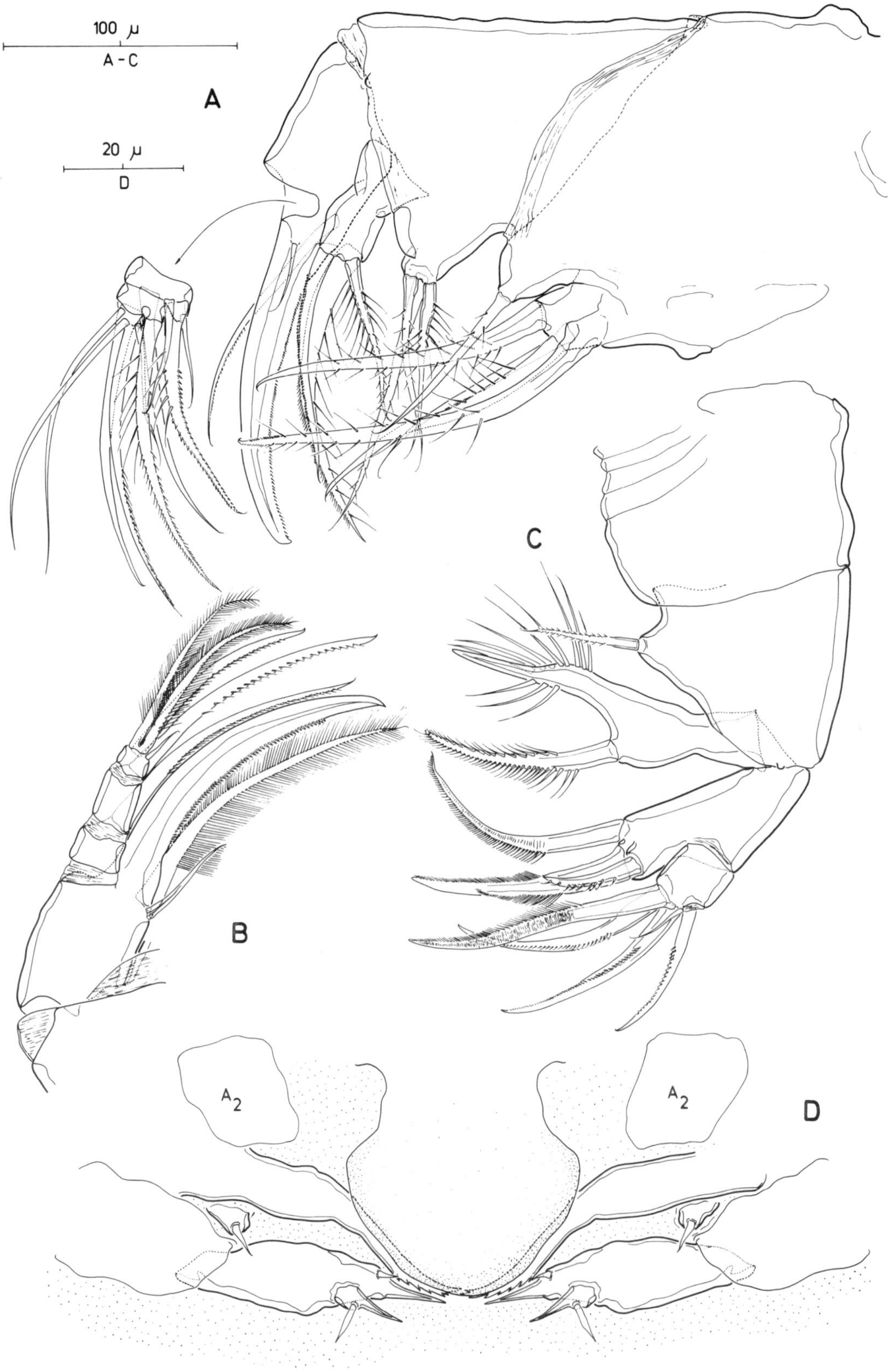

Figure 2.8.21. **A.** *Archinotodelphys polynesiensis*, maxilla. **B.** *Notodelphys allmani*, maxillary basis and endopod. **C.** *Euryte robusta*, maxilla. **D.** *Ozmana haemophila*, oral area showing labrum, mandibles, maxillules and maxillae (A_2 indicates base of antenna).

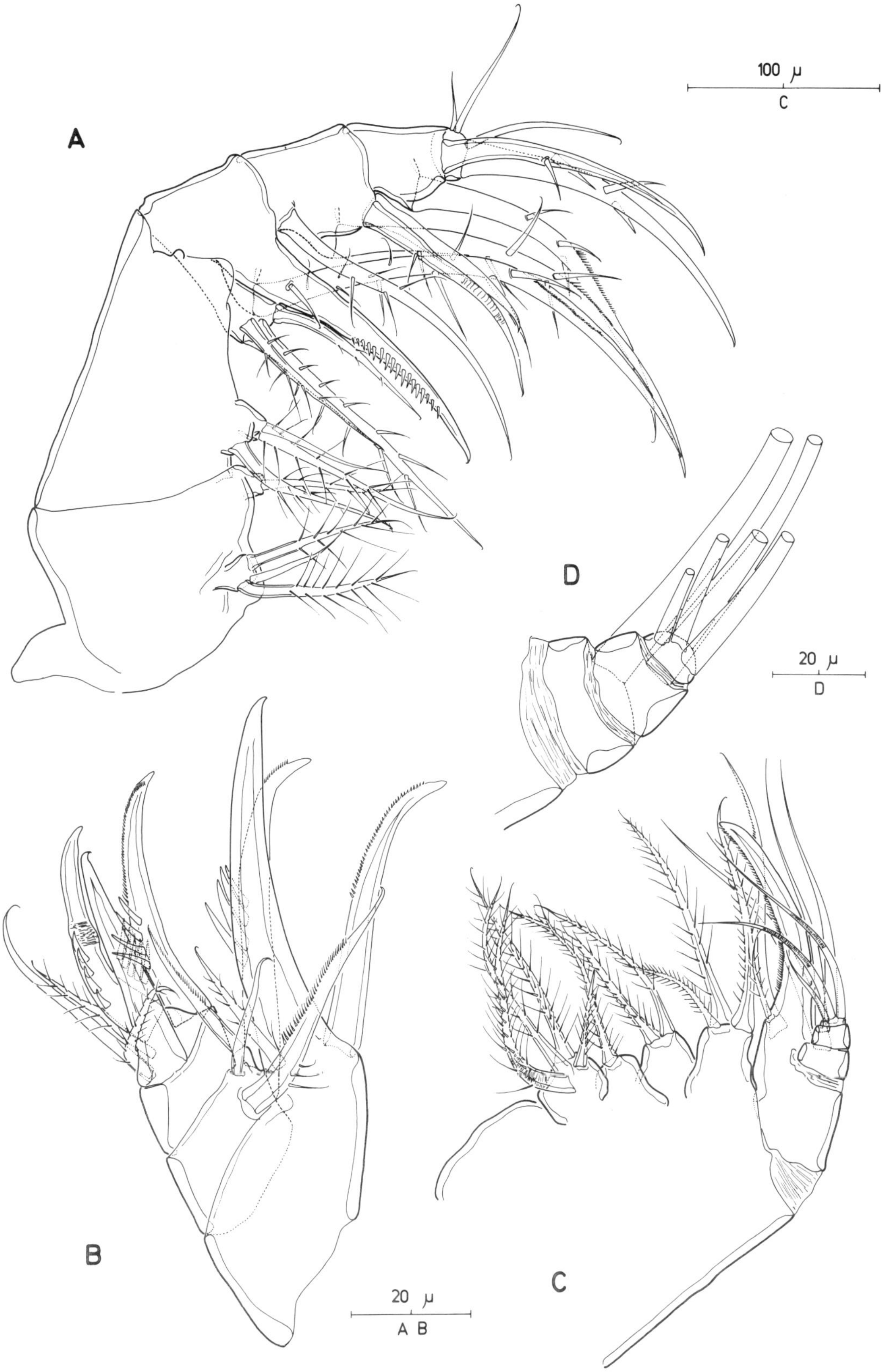

Figure 2.8.22. **A.** *Oithona nana*, maxilla. **B** *Pterinopsyllus insignis*, basis and endopod. **C.** *Mantra speciosa*, maxilla. **D.** Maxilla, endopod.

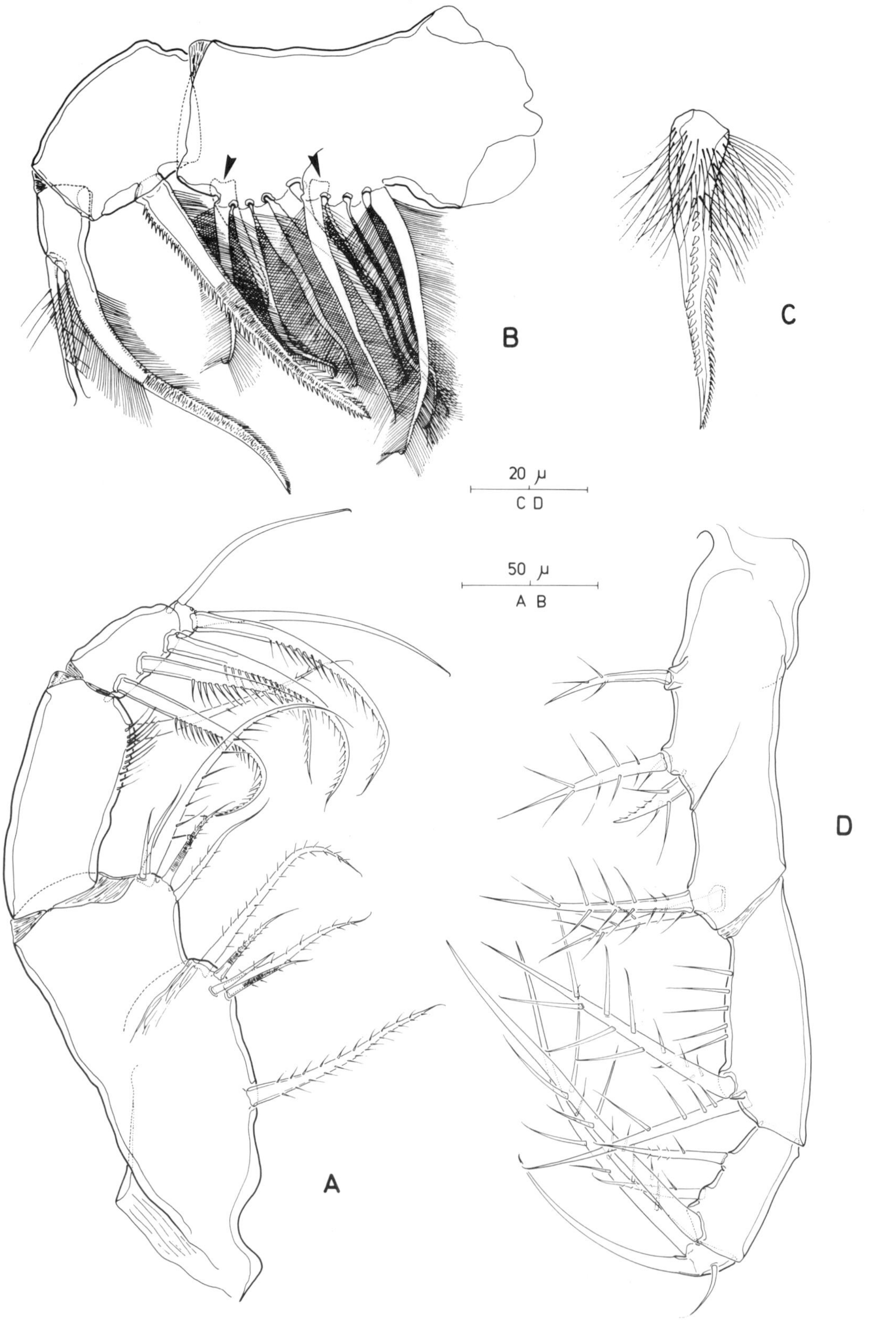

Figure 2.8.23. **A.** *Archinotodelphys typicus*, maxilliped. **B.** *Notodelphys allmani*, maxilliped (posterior spines arrowed). **C.** Detail of posterior spine. **D.** *Oithona nana*, maxilliped.

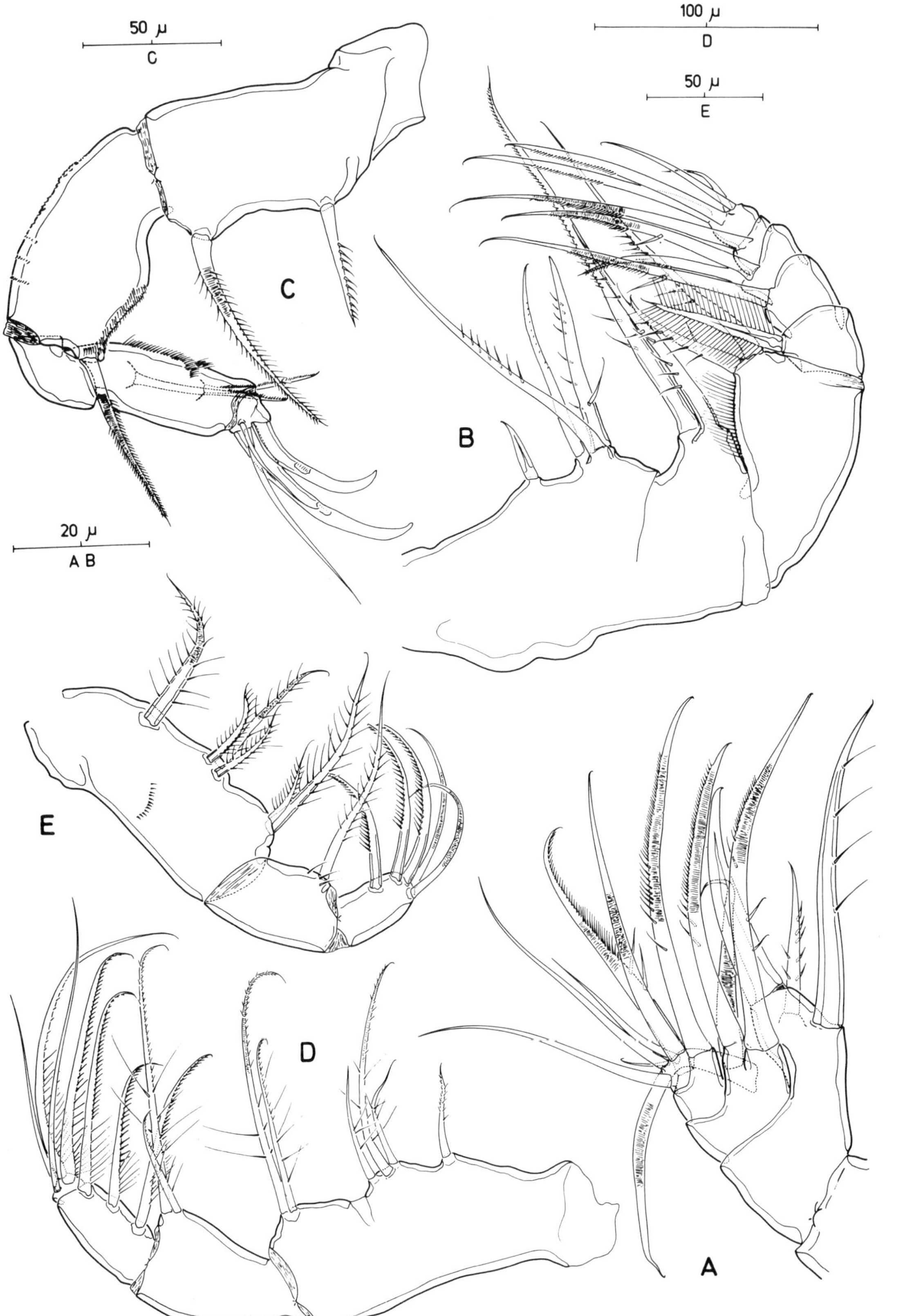

Figure 2.8.24. **A.** *Cyclopinoides schulzi,* maxillary basis and endopod. **B.** Maxilliped. **C.** *Euryte robusta,* maxilliped. **D.** *Archinotodelphys polynesiensis,* maxilliped. **E.** *Mantra speciosa,* maxilliped.

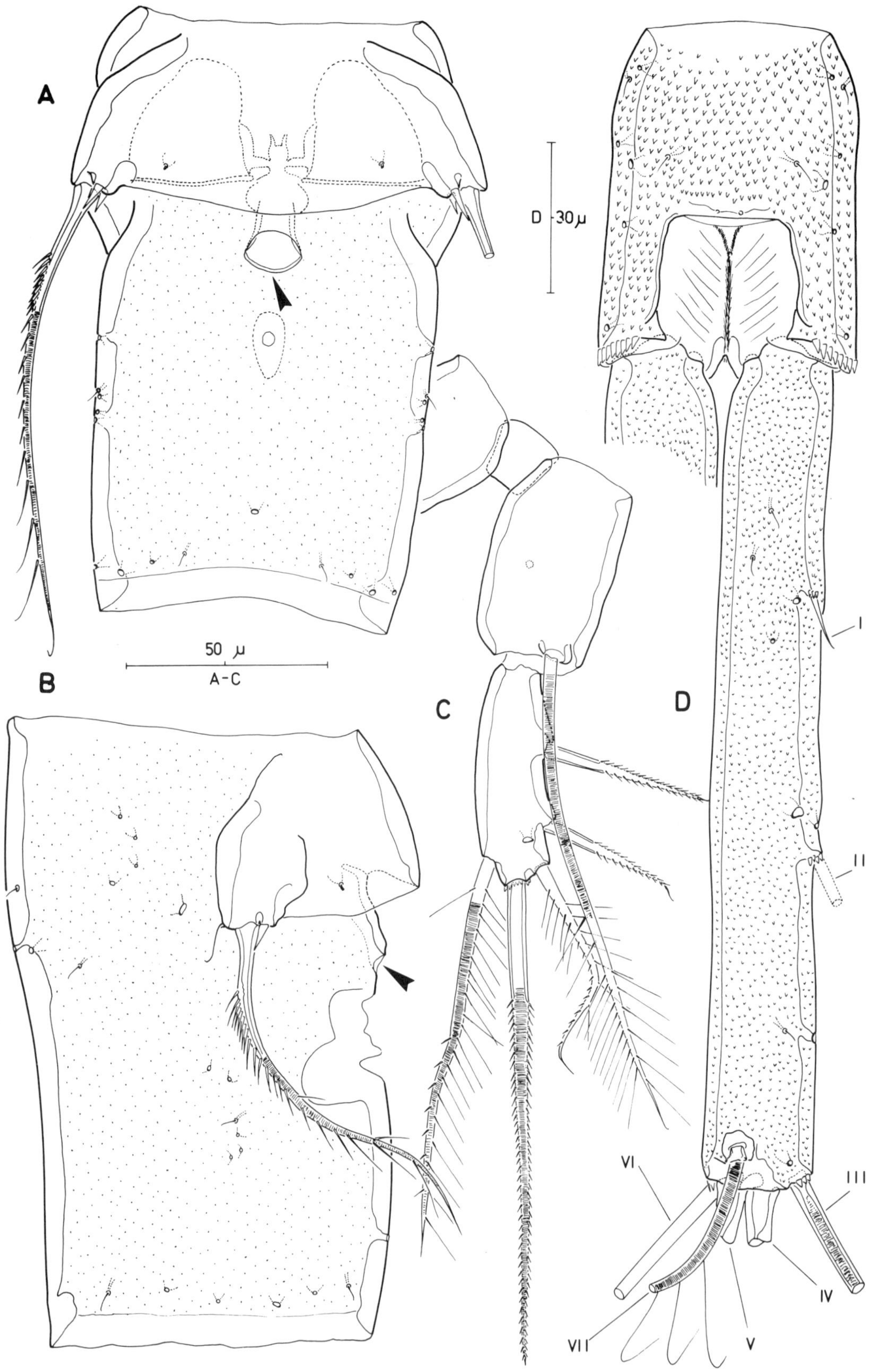

Figure 2.8.25. *Cyclopicina longifurcata*. **A.** Female genital double somite, ventral view. **B.** Lateral view. **C.** Female fifth leg. **D.** Anal somite and caudal ramus, dorsal view. [Copulatory pore arrowed in A and B.]

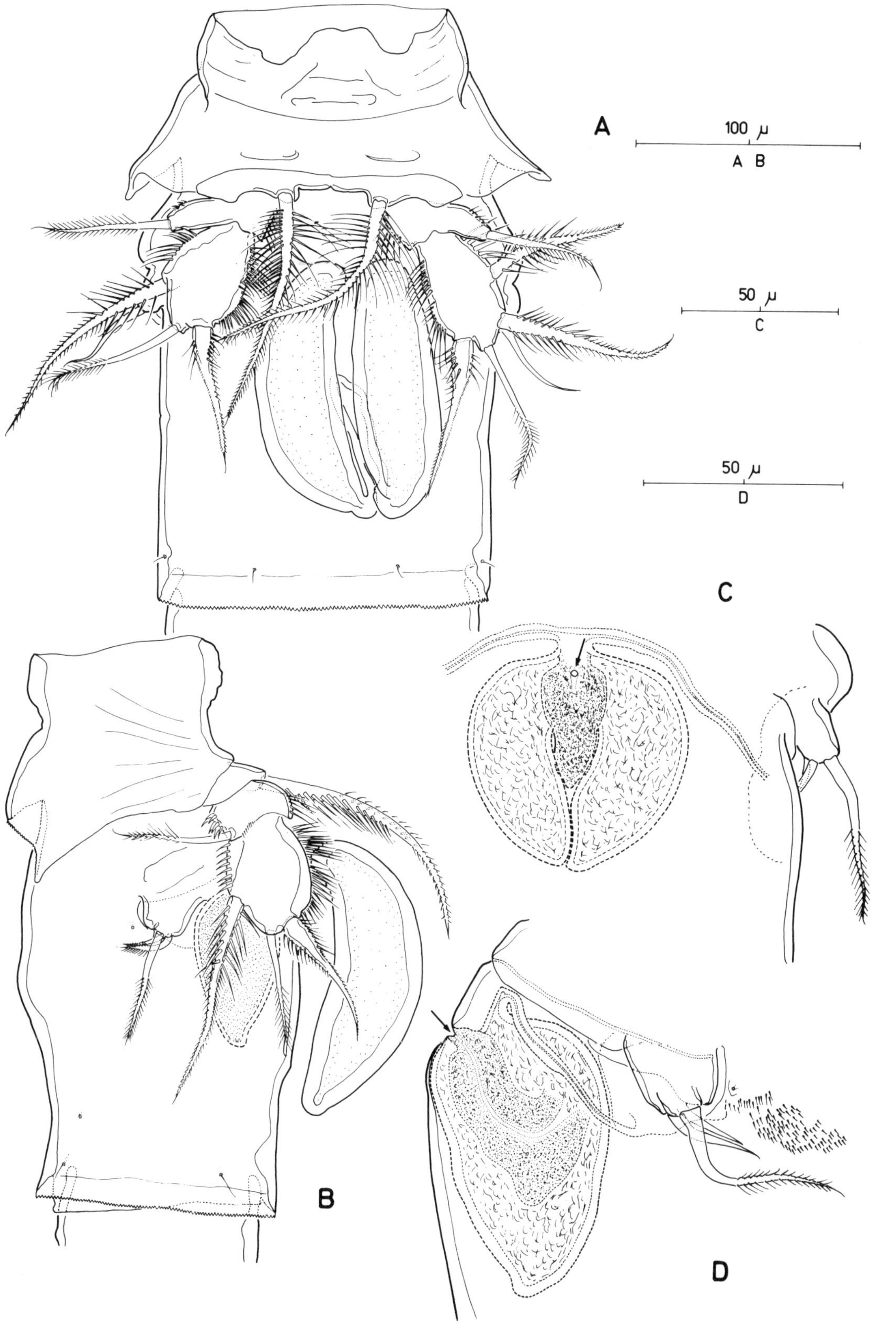

Figure 2.8.26. *Pterinopsyllus insignis.* **A.** Female genital double somite (with attached spermatophores) and fifth pedigerous somite (right fifth leg aberrant), ventral view. **B.** Lateral view. **C.** Genital field after removal of spermatophores, ventral view. **D.** Lateral view. [Copulatory pore arrowed in C and D.]

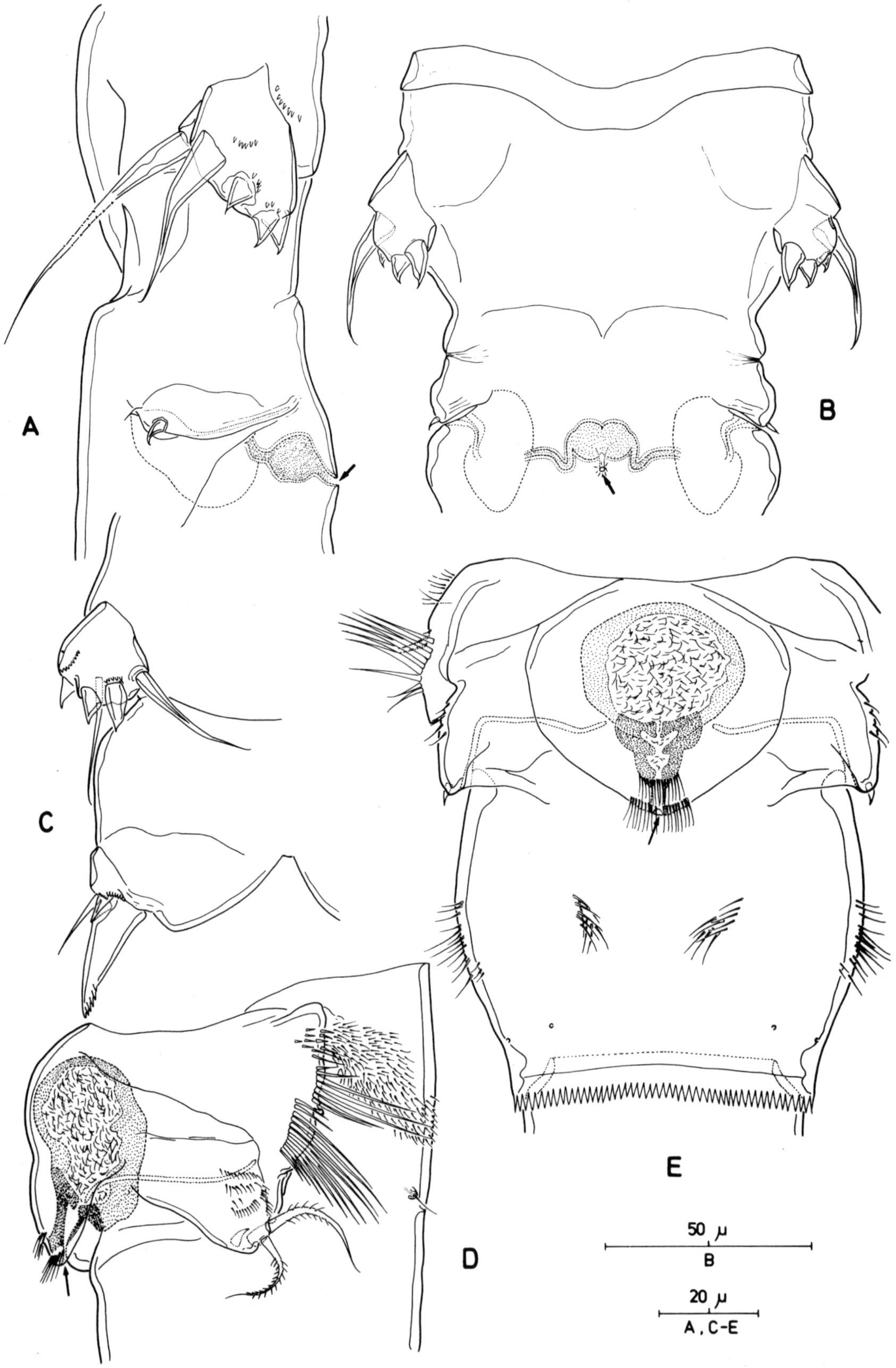

Figure 2.8.27. **A.** *Ozmana haemophila*, female genital double somite and fifth pedigerous somite, lateral view. **B.** Ventral view. **C.** Male fifth and sixth legs, ventral view. **D.** *Cyclopinodes elegans*, anterior half of female genital double somite, lateral view. **E.** Genital double somite, ventral view. [Copulatory pore arrowed in A, B, D and E.]

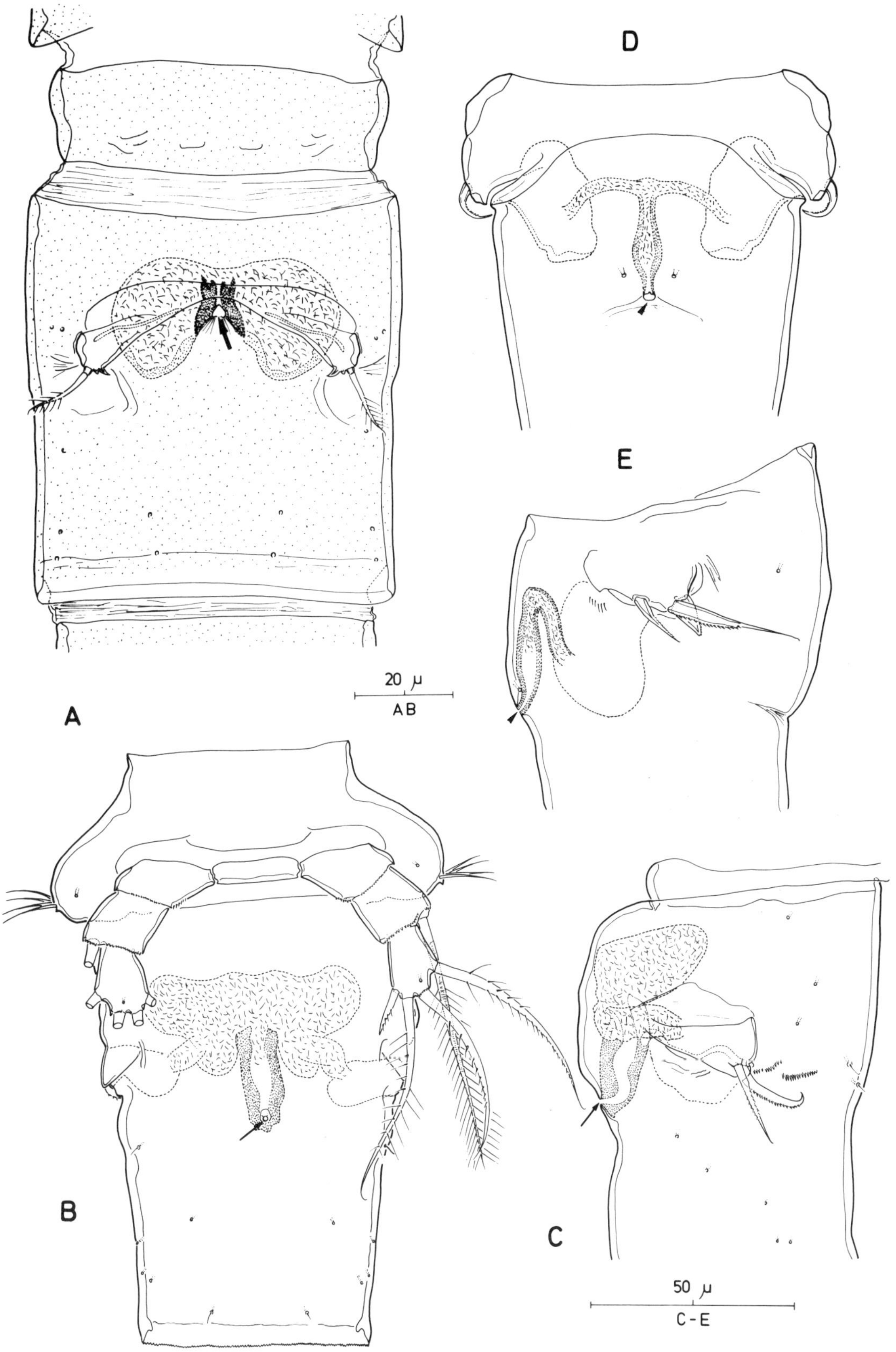

Figure 2.8.28. **A.** Undescribed new genus of interstitial cyclopinid, female genital double somite, ventral view. **B.** *Cyclopinoides schulzi*, female genital double somite and fifth pedigerous somite, ventral view. **C.** Anterior half of female genital double somite, lateral view. **D.** *Cyclopina gracilis*, anterior part of female genital double somite, ventral view. **E.** Lateral view. [Copulatory pore arrowed in A-E.]

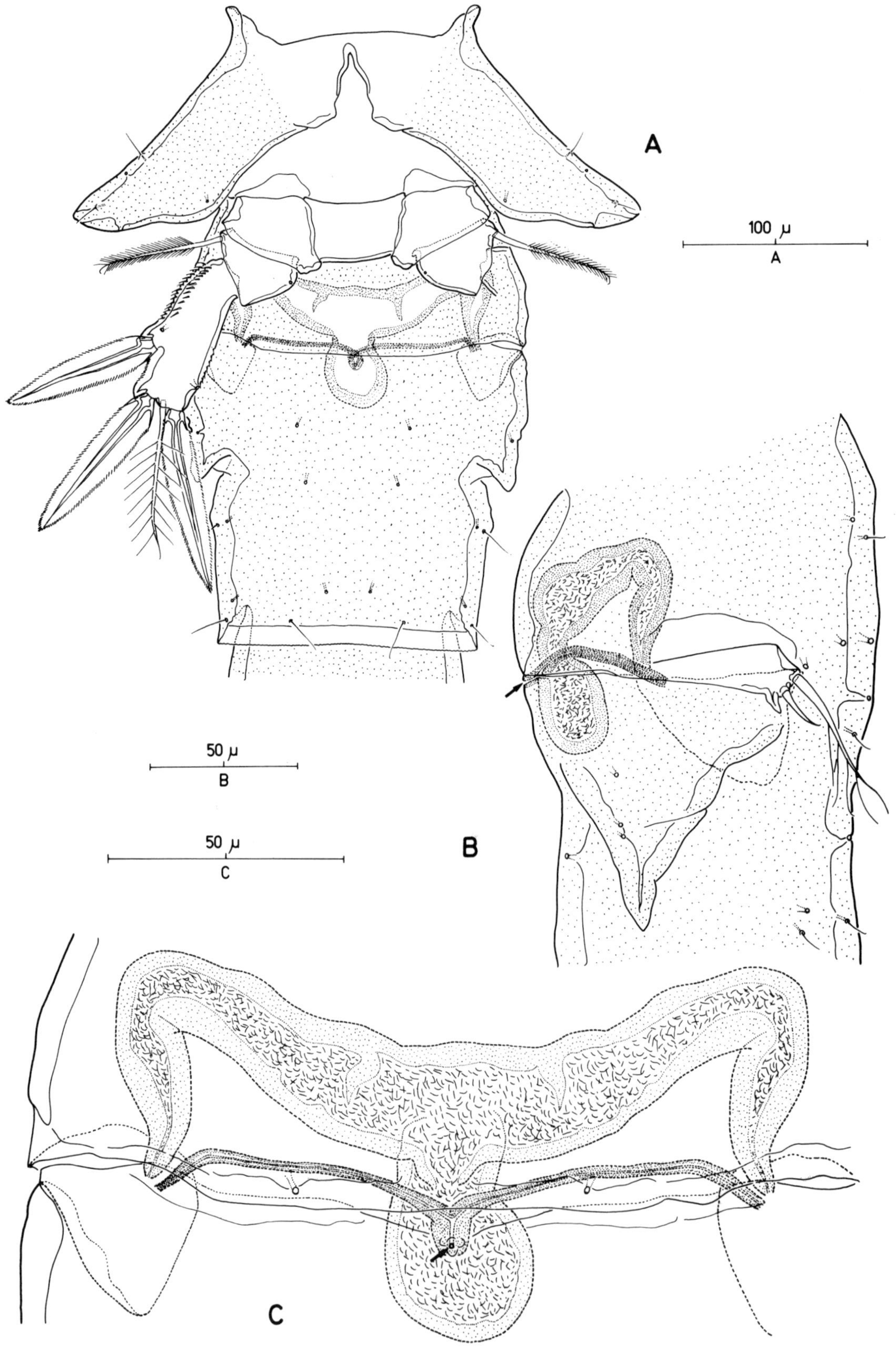

Figure 2.8.29. *Euryte robusta.* **A.** Female genital double somite and somite bearing fifth legs (exopod of left fifth leg omitted), ventral view. **B.** Genital complex, lateral view. **C.** Genital complex, ventral view. [Copulatory pore arrowed in B and C.]

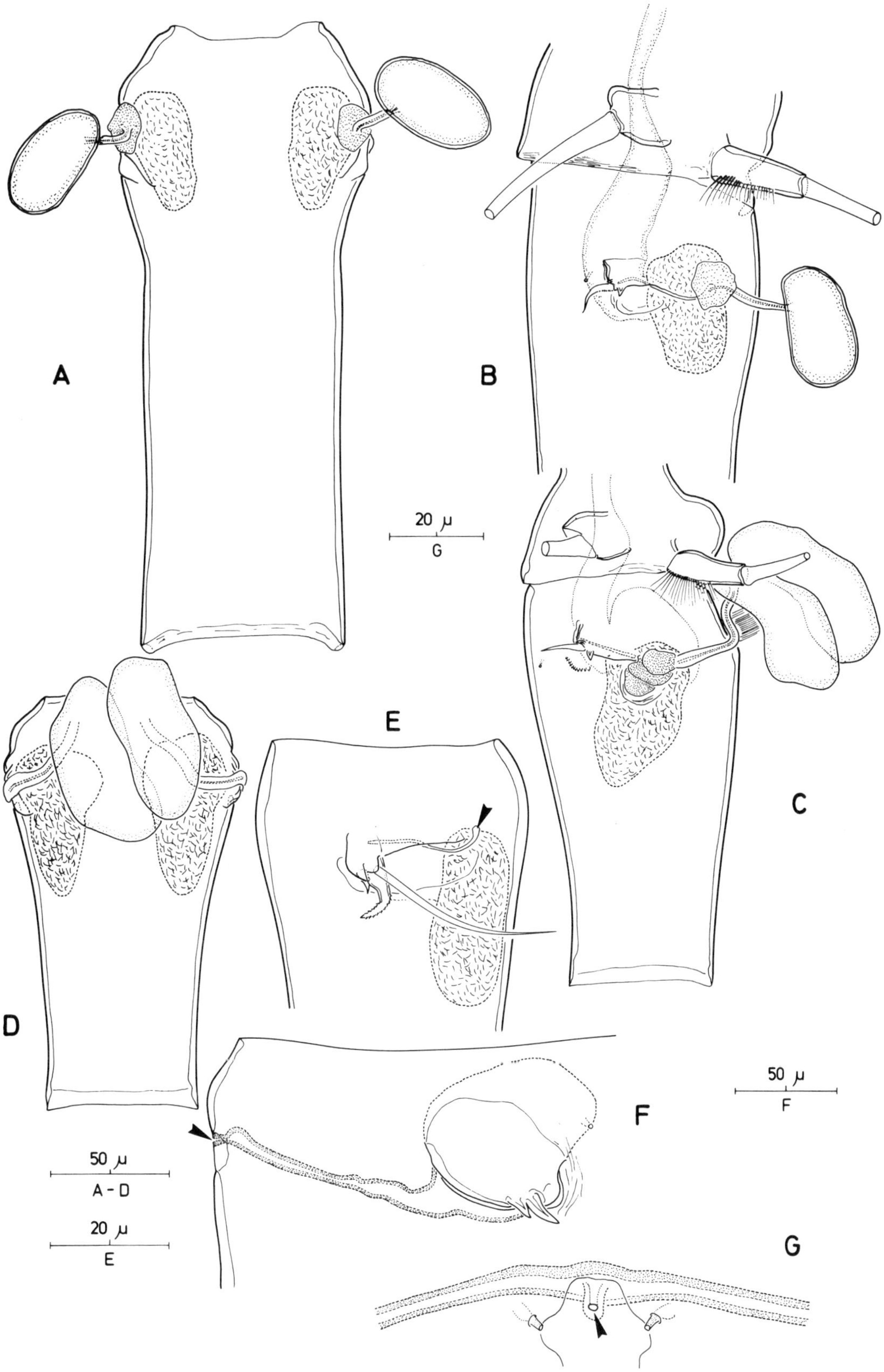

Figure 2.8.30. **A.** *Oithona setigera*, female genital double somite (spermatophores attached), ventral view. **B.** Fifth leg and anterior part of genital double somite, lateral view. **C.** *Oithona* sp., female genital double somite (spermatophores attached midventrally), ventral view. **D.** Same, lateral view. **E.** *Oithona nana*, genital complex, lateral view. [Copulatory pore arrowed.] **F.** *Mantra speciosa*, female genital complex, lateral view. **G.** Copulatory pore (arrowed) and ducts, ventral view.

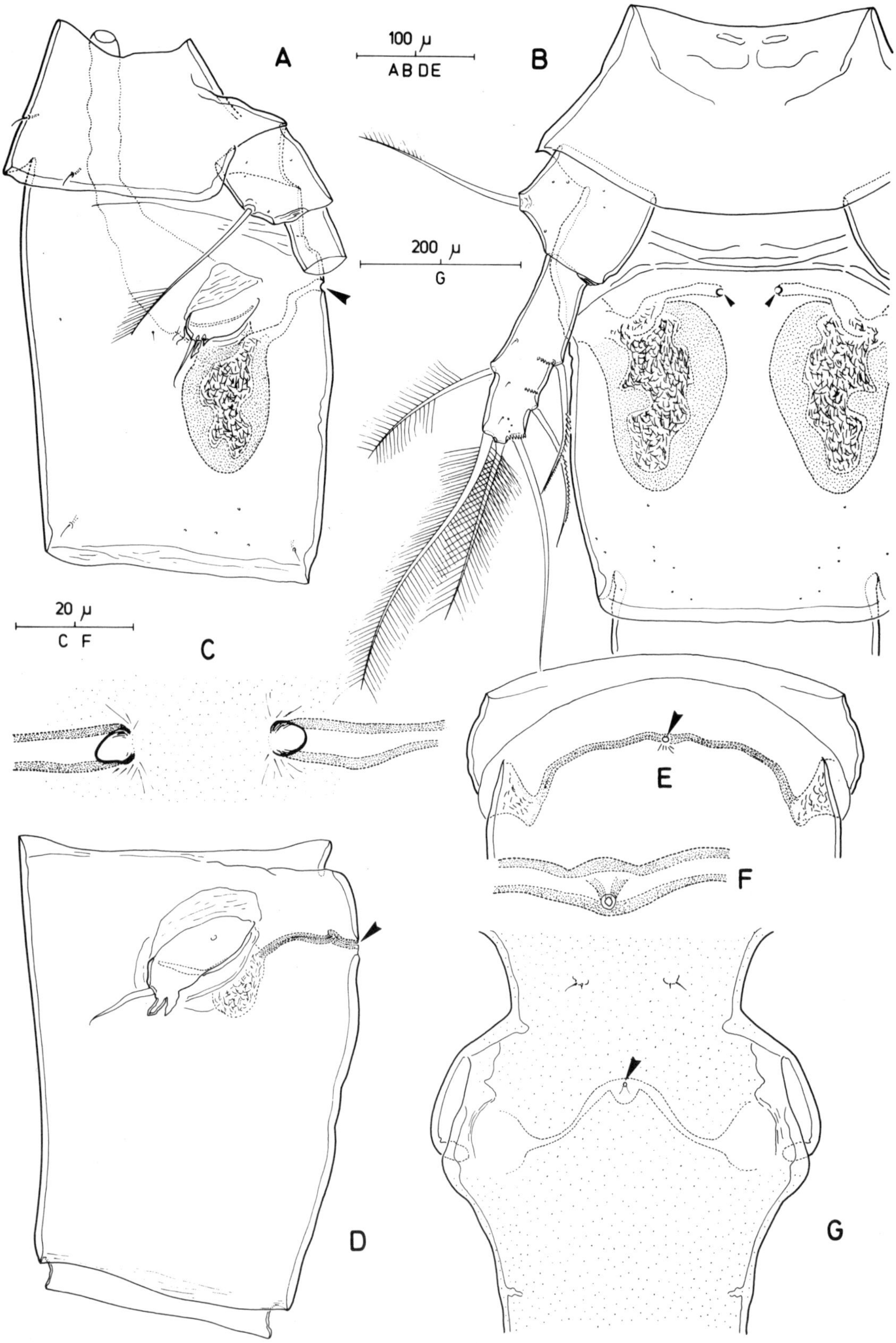

Figure 2.8.31. **A.** *Archinotodelphys polynesiensis*, female genital double somite and somite bearing fifth legs, lateral view. **B.** Ventral view (left fifth leg omitted). **C.** Detail of copulatory pores. **D.** *A.typicus*, female genital double somite, lateral view. **E.** Ventral view. **F.** Detail of copulatory pore and ducts. **G.** *Lamproglena monodi*, female genital double somite, ventral view. [Copulatory pores arrowed in A-B, D-E, G.]

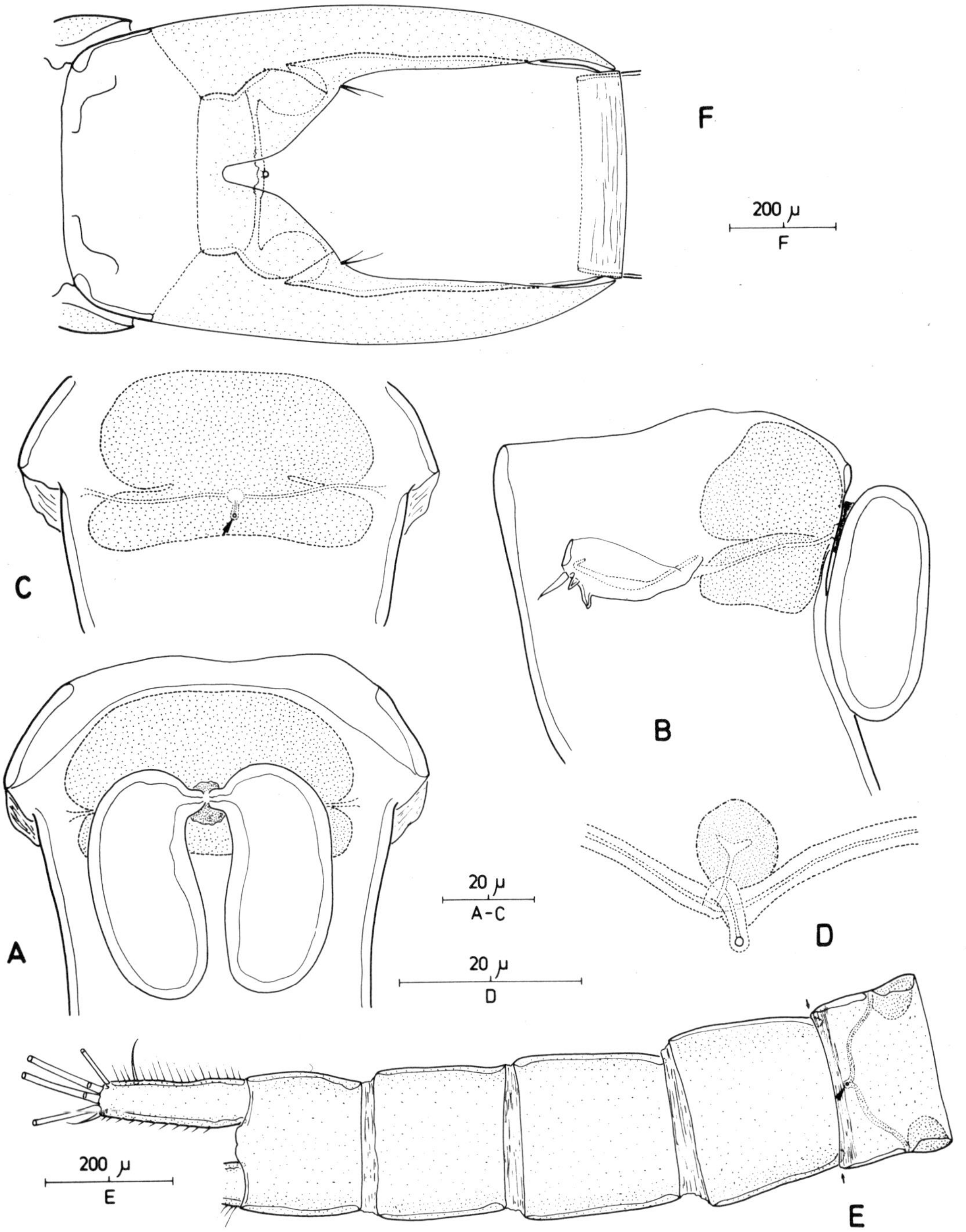

Figure 2.8.32. **A.** *Cryptocyclops bicolor*, anterior half of genital double somite (with attached spermatophores), ventral view. **B.** Same, lateral view. **C.** Anterior half of genital double somite (spermatophores removed). **D.** *Macrocyclops albidus*, area around copulatory pore. **E.** *Notodelphys allmani*, female urosome (excluding somite bearing fifth legs), ventral view. **F.** *Ascidicola rosea*, genital double somite and somite bearing fifth legs, ventral view. [Copulatory pore arrowed in C and E.]

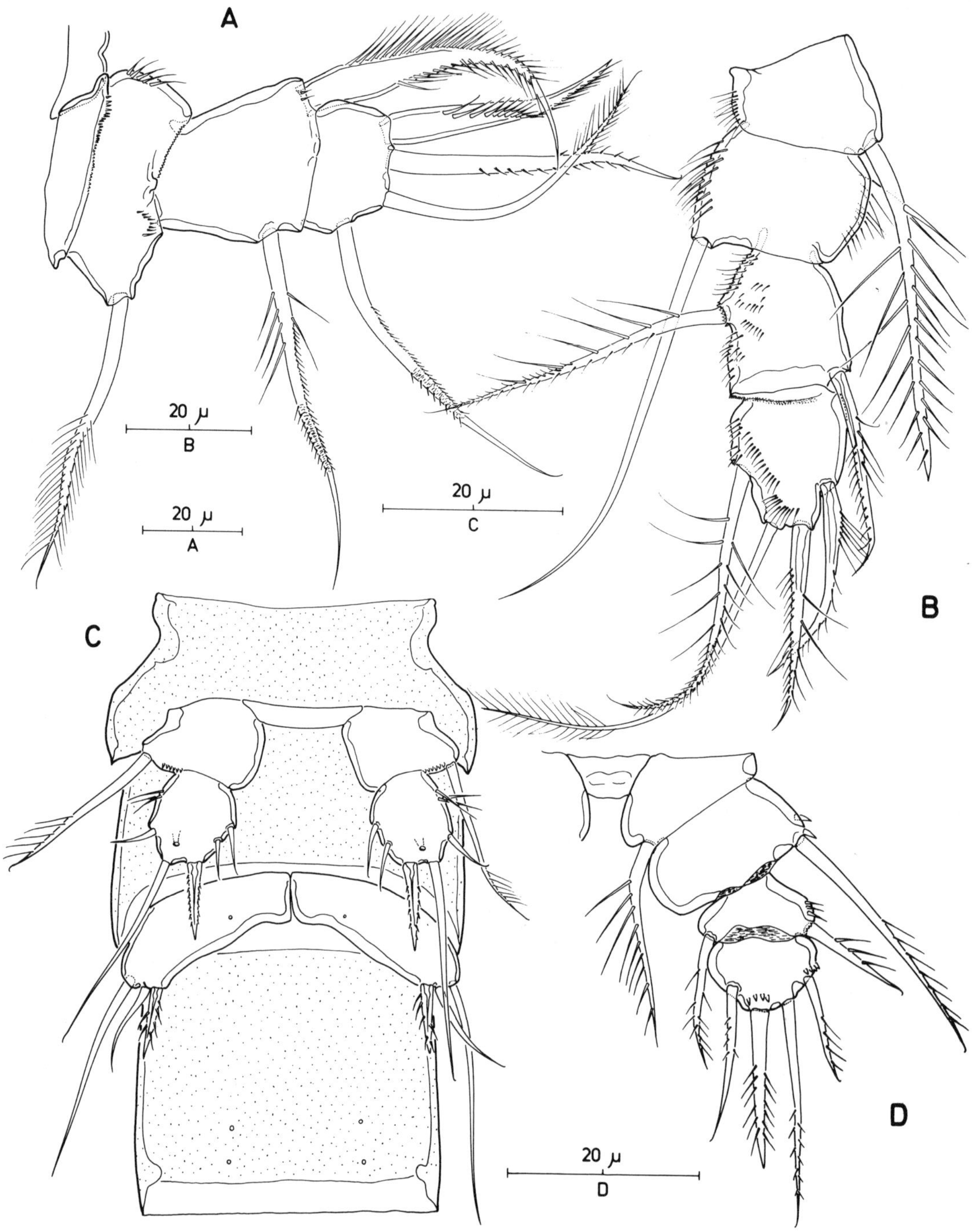

Figure 2.8.33. **A.** *Pterinopsyllus insignis*, male fifth leg. **B.** *Cyclopinodes elegans*, male fifth leg. **C.** *Herbstina exigua*, male fifth and sixth legs. **D.** *Metacyclopina* aff. *harpacticoidea*, male fifth leg.

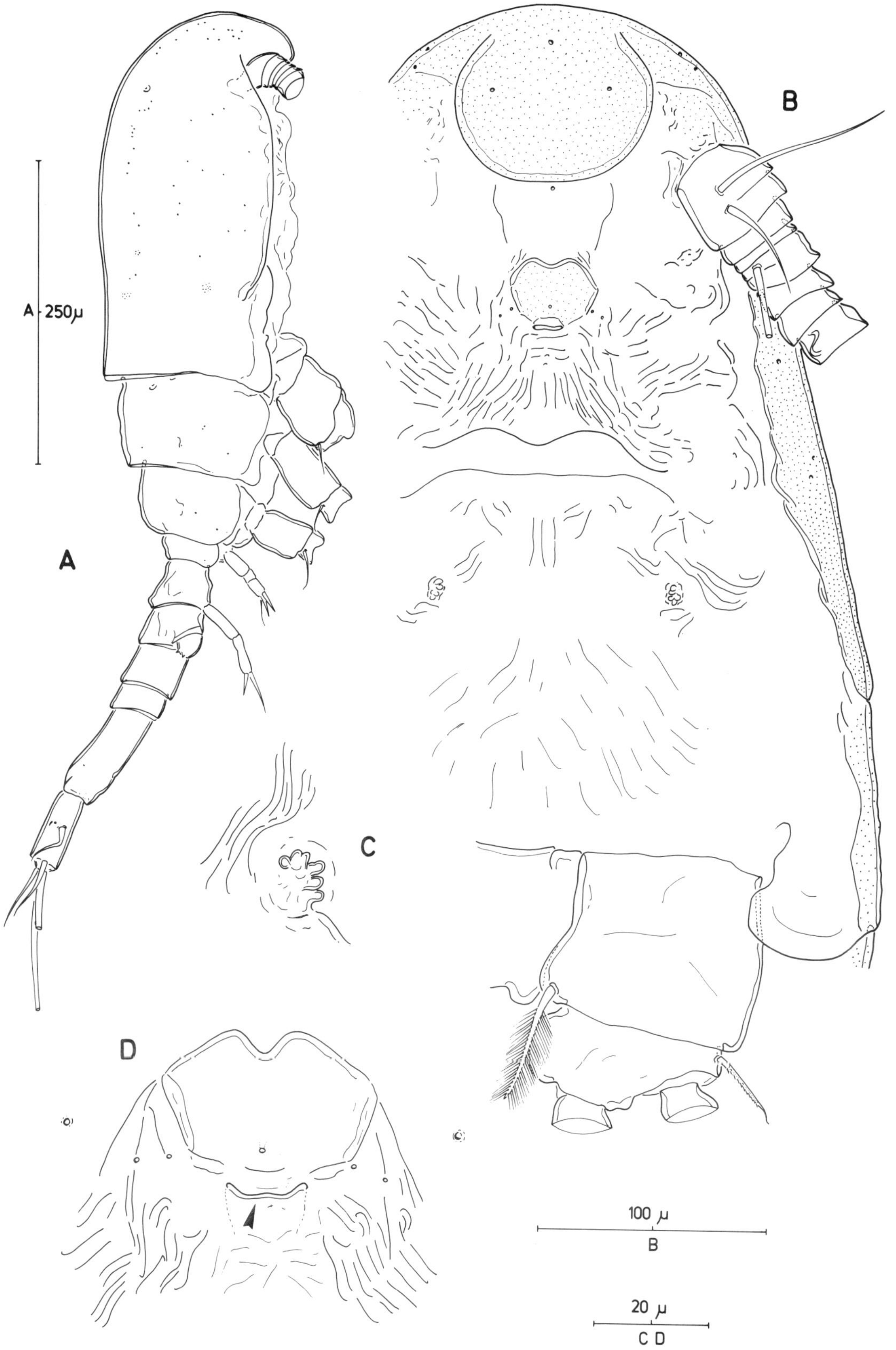

Figure 2.8.34. *Thespesiopsyllus paradoxus*. **A.** Male, lateral view. **B.** Cephalothorax, ventral view. **C.** Surface scar, possibly representing vestige of appendage. **D.** Oral aperture (arrowed) and labrum.

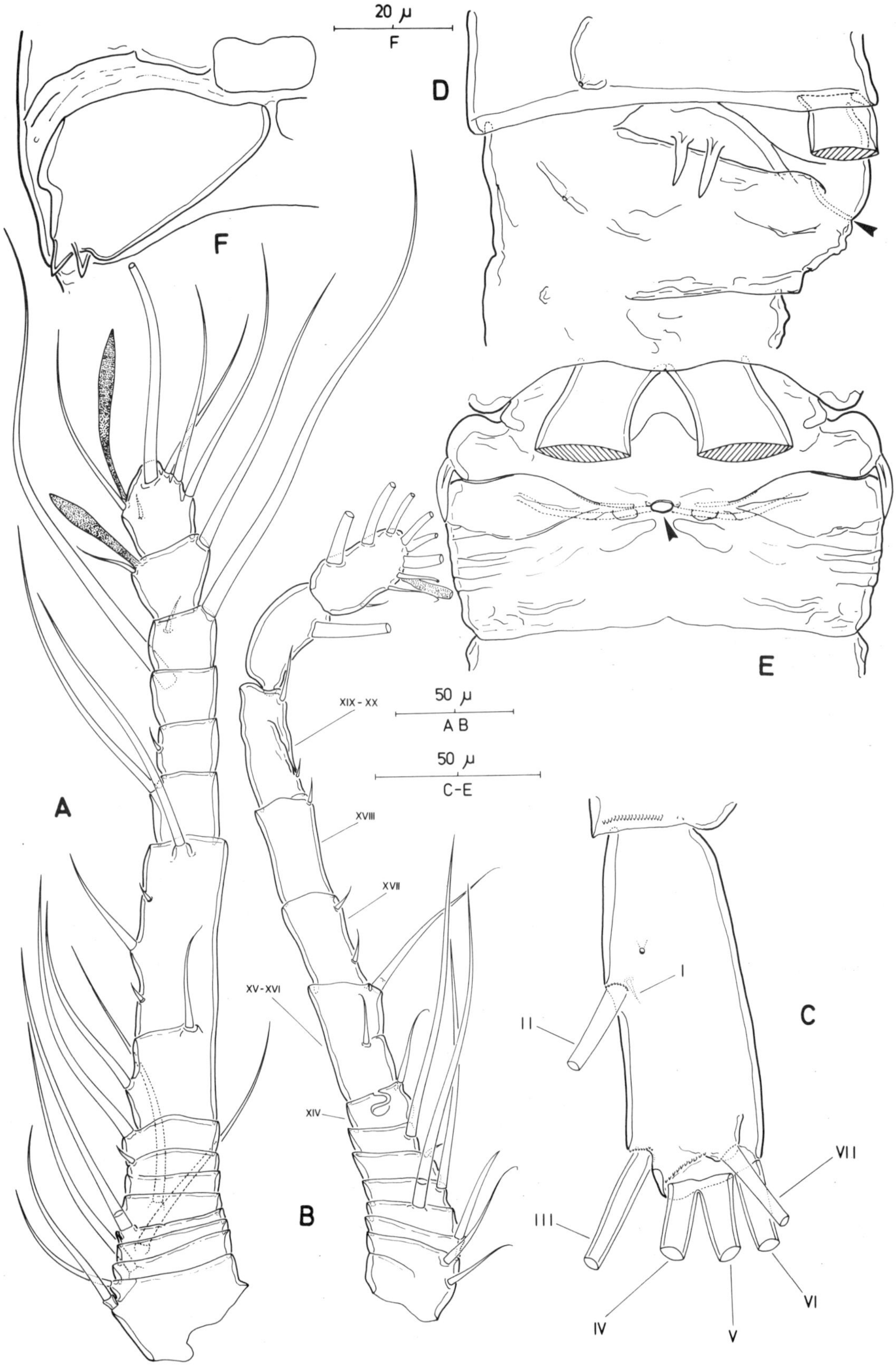

Figure 2.8.35. *Thespesiopsyllus paradoxus.* **A.** Female antennule. **B.** Male antennule. **C.** Caudal ramus, dorsal view. **D.** Female genital complex, lateral view. **E.** Female genital complex, ventral view. **F.** Male sixth leg. [Copulatory pore arrowed in D-E.]

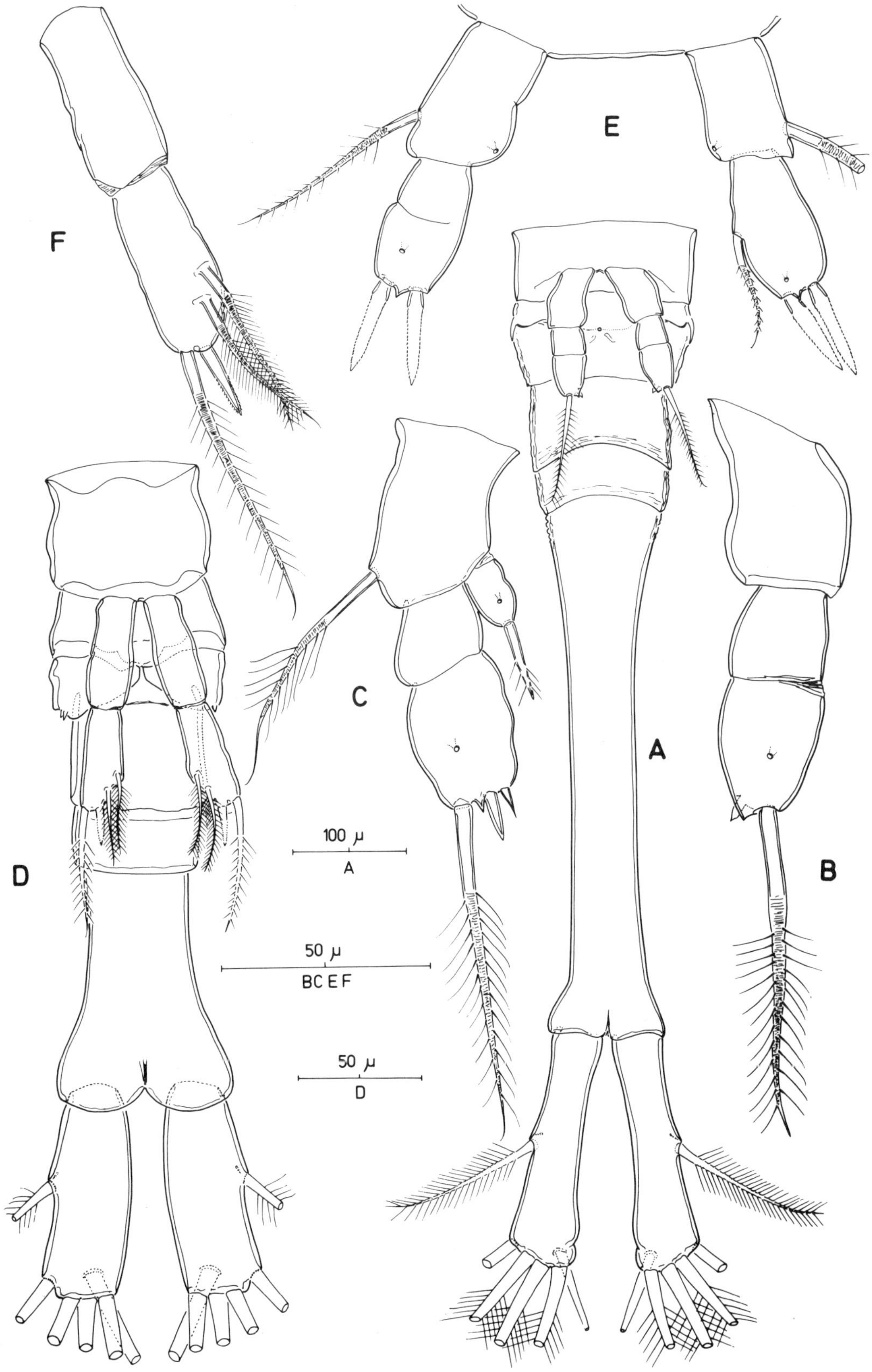

Figure 2.8.36. *Thespesiopsyllus paradoxus.* **A.** Urosome of female, ventral view. **B.** Female fifth leg. **C.** Female fourth leg. **D.** Urosome of male, ventral view. **E.** Male fourth leg. **F.** Male fifth leg.

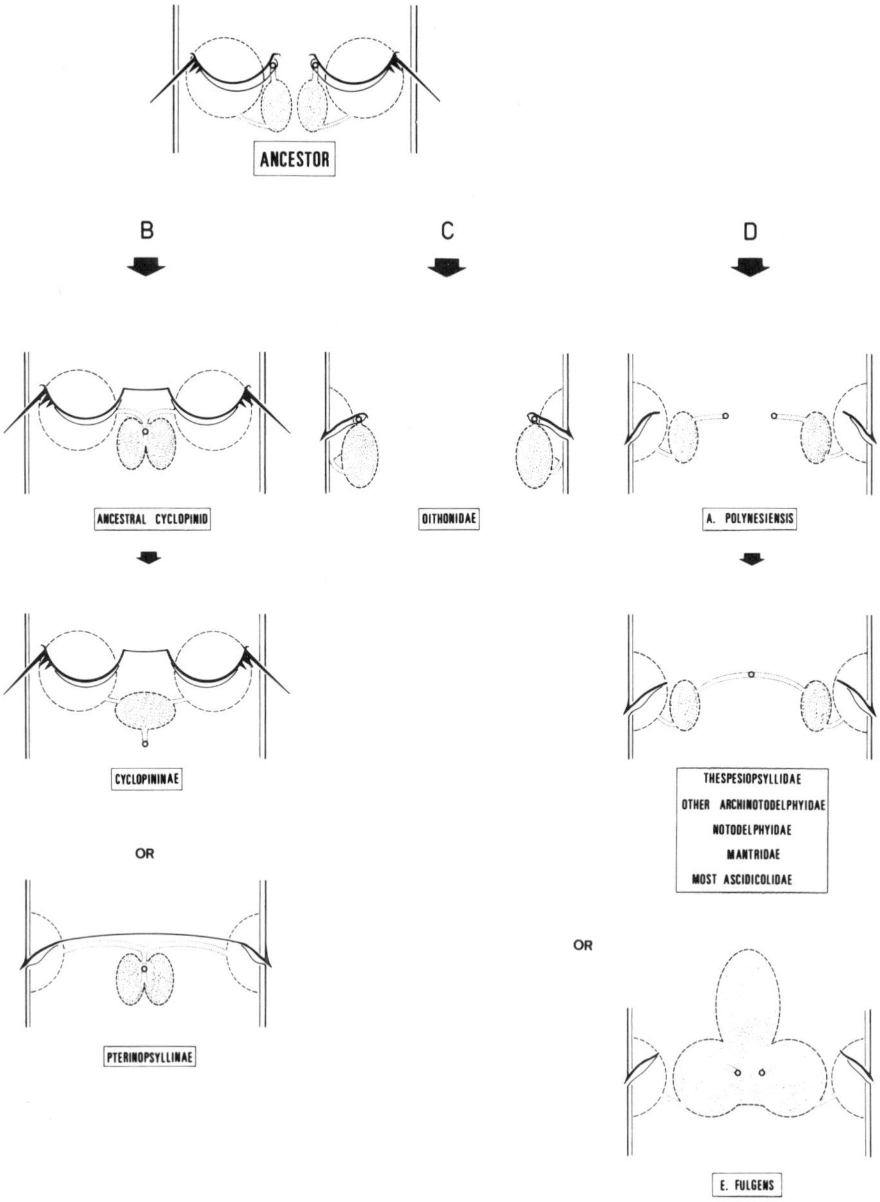

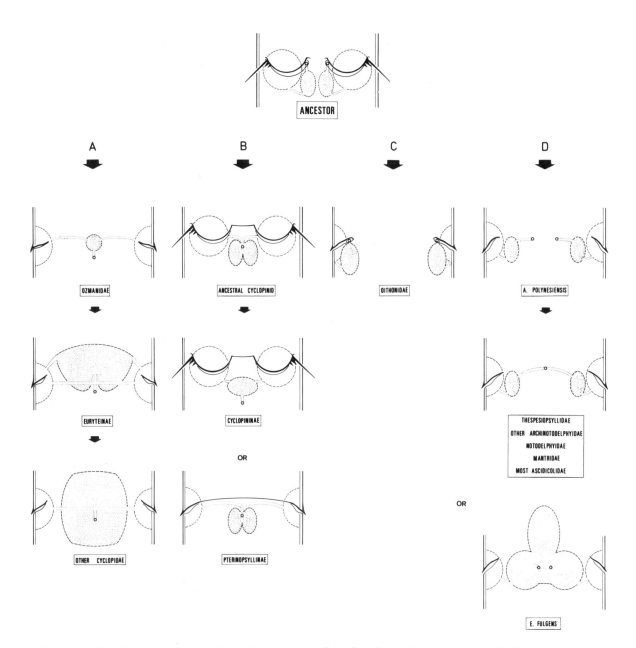

Figure 2.8.37. Evolutionary trends in the structure of the female genital system. **A.** Fusion of copulatory pores and seminal receptacles, lateral migration of gonopores. **B.** Fusion of sixth legs, copulatory pores and seminal receptacles. **C.** Lateral migration of copulatory pores, gonopores and seminal receptacles. **D.** Lateral migration of gonopores and seminal receptacles only, development of transverse copulatory ducts.

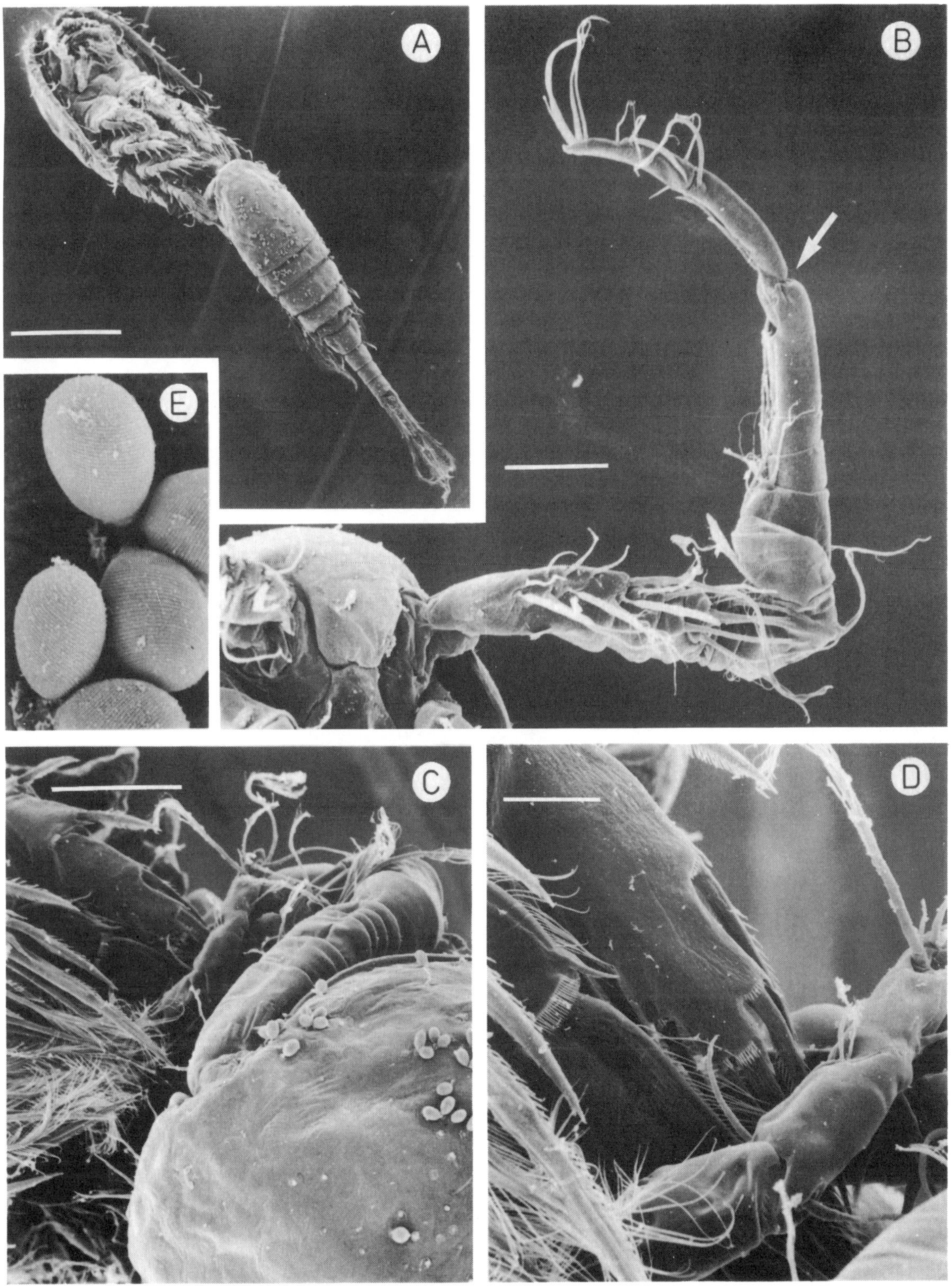

Figure 2.8.38. **A.** Mating pair of *Cyclops vicinus* in position for spermatophore transfer. **B.** *Mesocyclops rarus*, male antennule with proximal geniculation flexed, distal geniculation arrowed. **C.** Detail showing right male antennule grasping fourth leg of female. **D.** Detail showing part of antennule distal to neocopepodan geniculation passing across anterior face of both rami of female fourth leg. **E.** Protistans attached to integument of male *Cyclops*. Scale bars A = 500μm, B = 50μm, C = 100μm, D = 30μm.

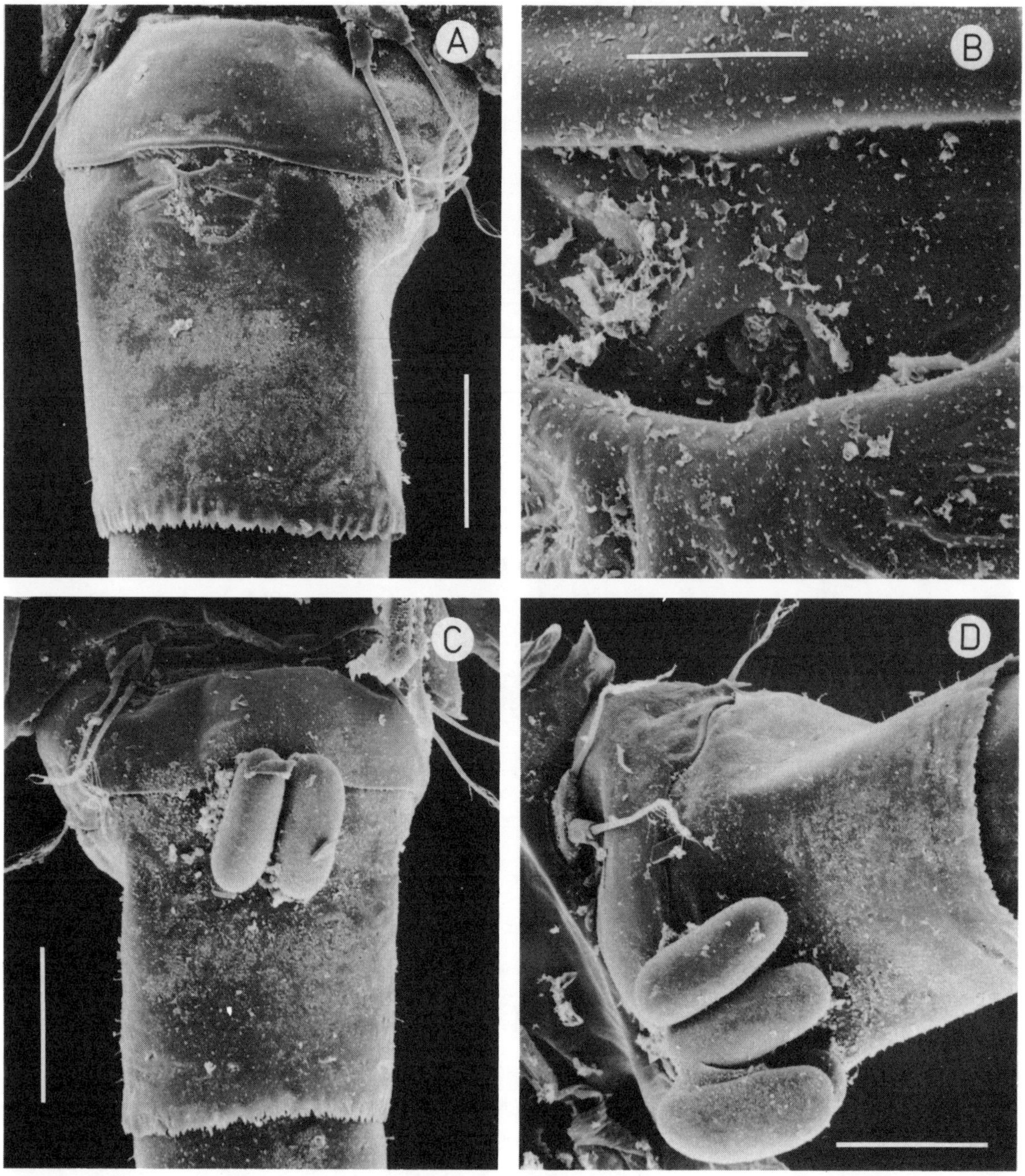

Figure 2.8.39. **A.** *Cyclops vicinus*, female genital double somite, ventral view. **B.** Detail of copulatory pore, ventral view. **C.** *Cyclops vicinus*, female genital double somite with pair of spermatophores attached, ventral view. **D.** Female genital double somite with 2 pairs of spermatophores attached, ventro-lateral view. Scale bars A,C-D = 50μm, B = 5μm.

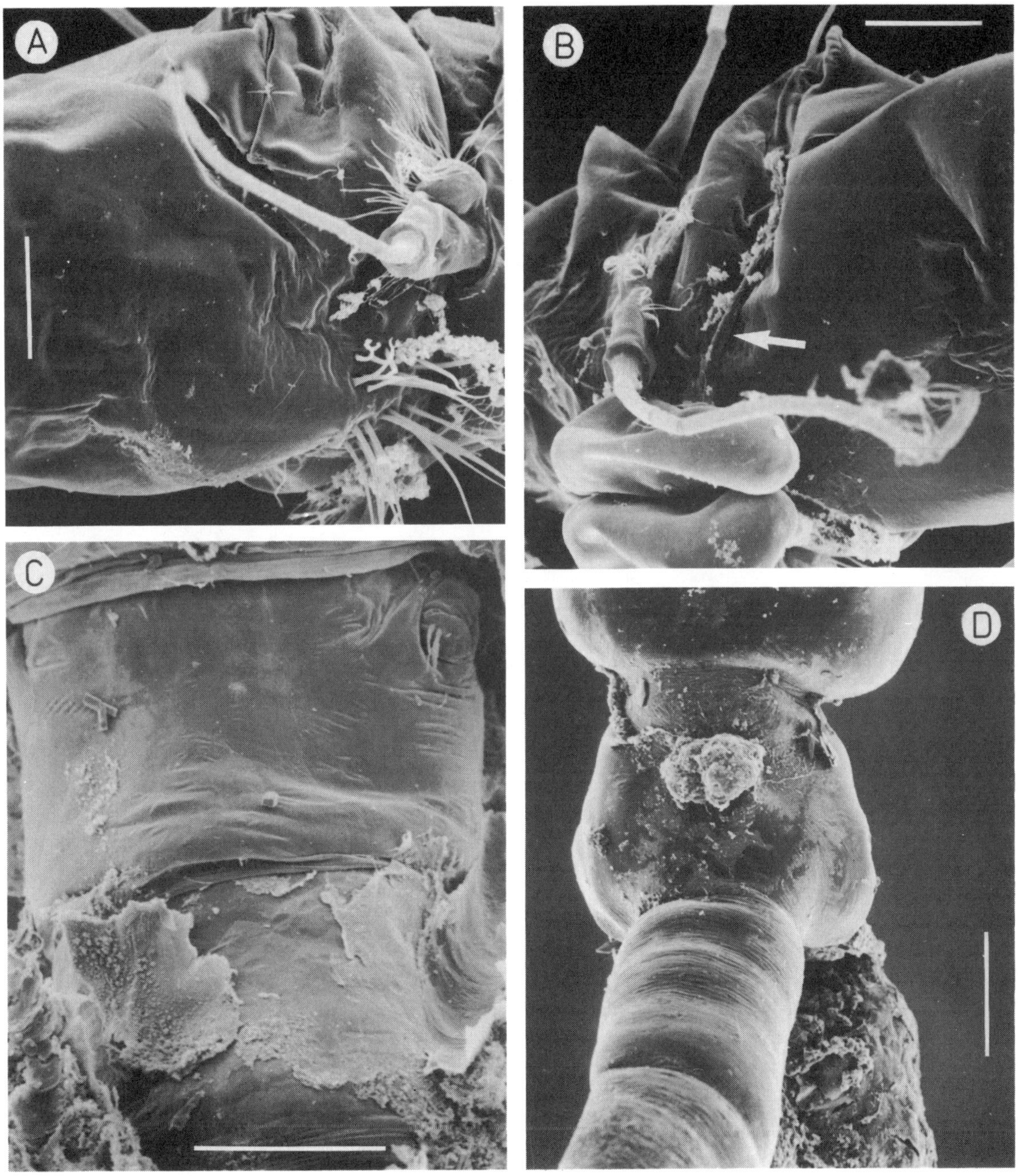

Figure 2.8.40. **A.** *Oithona nana*, female genital double somite, lateral view. **B.** Female genital double somite with spermatophores attached, lateral view (arrow indicates spermatophore tubule). **C.** *Notodelphys allmani*, female genital region with brood sac removed, showing genital somite clearly separate from fifth pedigerous and first abdominal somites, and antero-lateral location of gonopores, dorsal view. **D.** *Lamproglena monodi*, female genital double somite with spermatophores attached midventrally and egg sac attached dorsally, ventral view. Scale bars A-B = 20μm, C-D = 100μm.

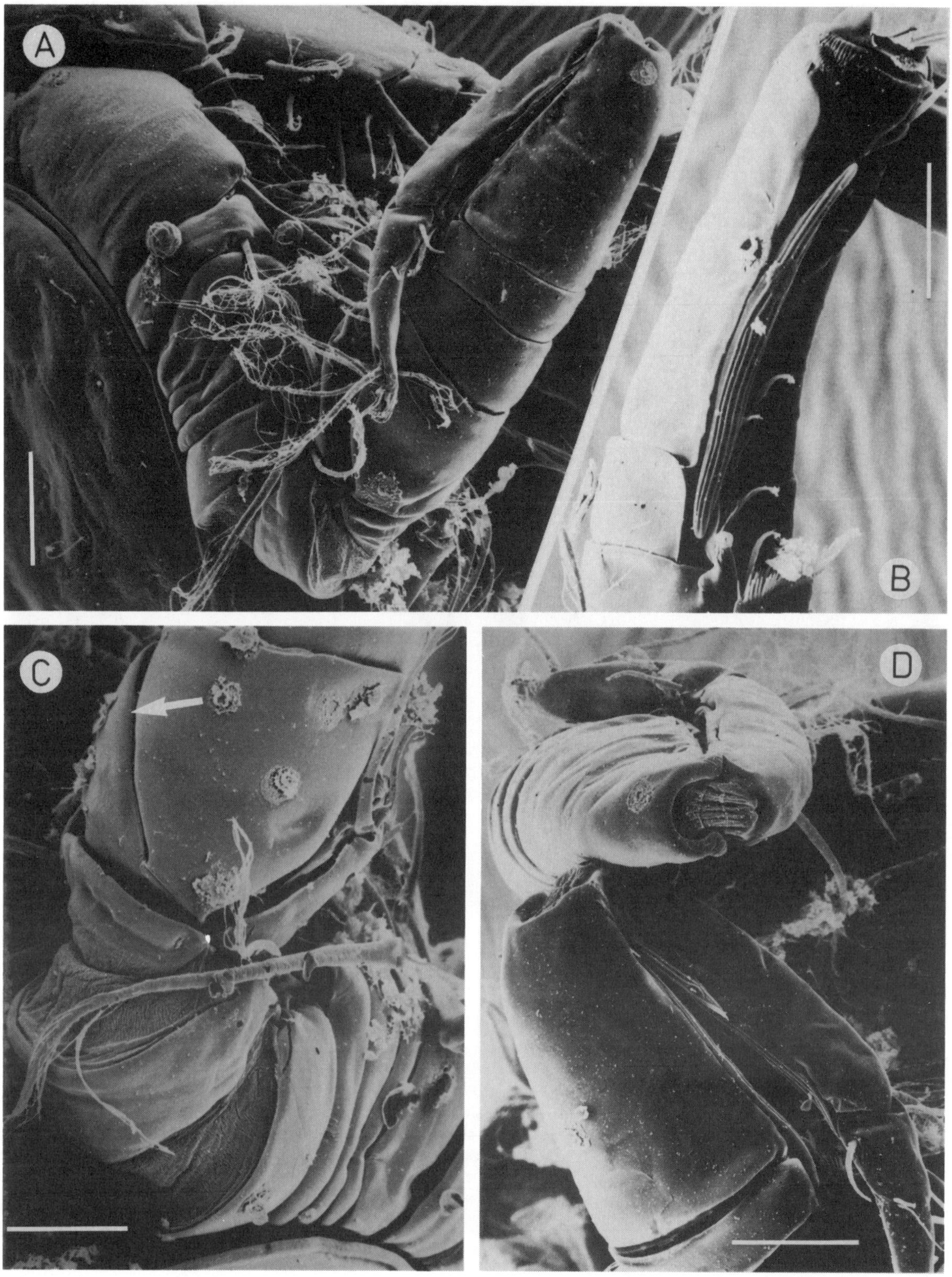

Figure 2.8.41. *Cyclops strenuus*, male antennule. **A.** Lateral view, with both geniculations flexed. **B.** Detail of segments XVIII to XIX-XX, showing modified setae. **C.** Proximal geniculation showing sheath (arrowed) around segment XVI. **D.** Distal geniculations of both antennules, showing arthrodial membrane (above) and specialised setae on segment XXI-XXIII. Scale bars A = 30μm, B-D = 20μm.

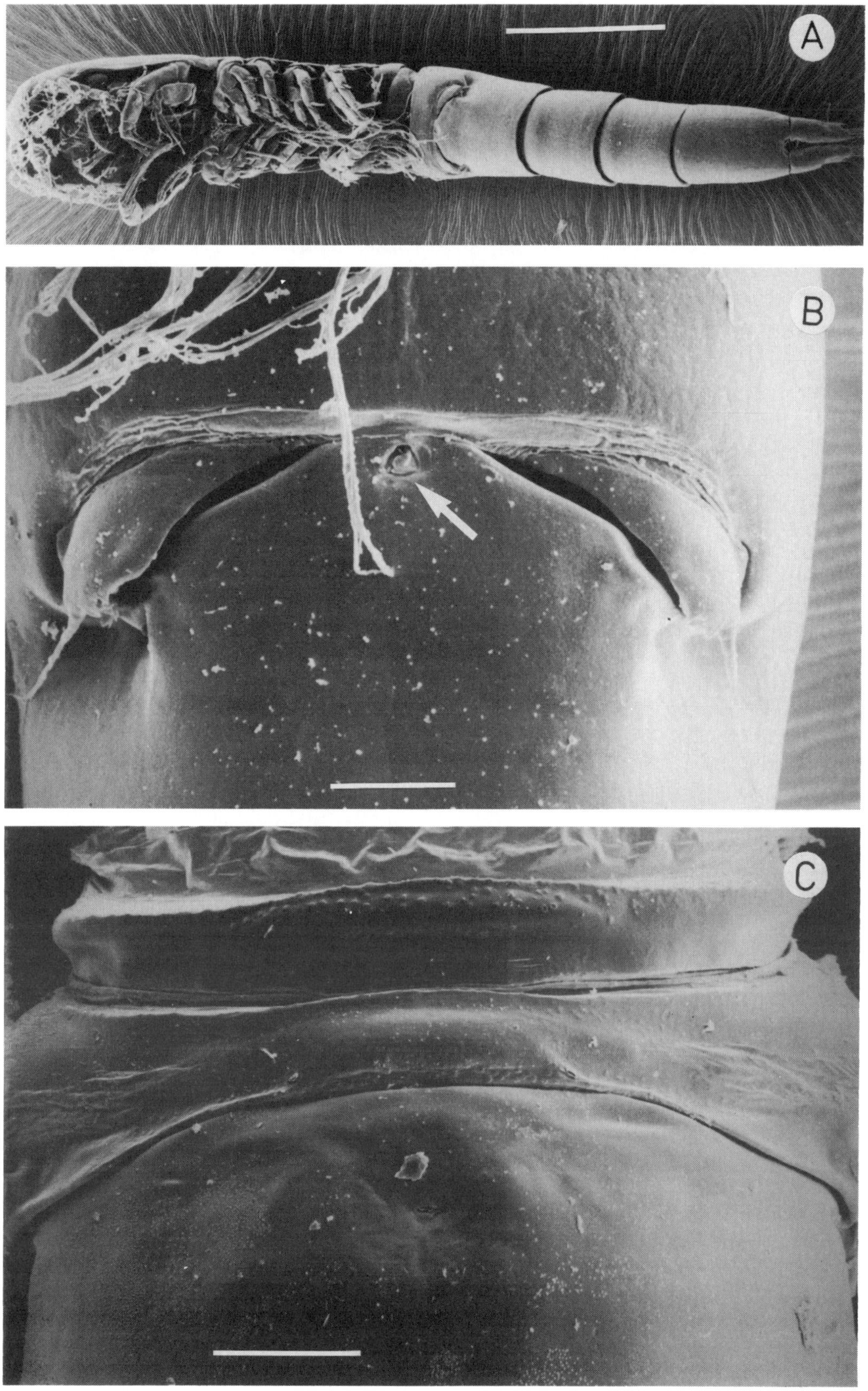

Figure 2.8.42. Undescribed new genus of interstitial cyclopinid. **A.** Ventral view of female. **B.** Genital apertures and median copulatory pore (arrowed). **C.** *Pterinopsyllus insignis*, anterior part of female genital double somite showing 'pseudosomite' and copulatory pore. Scale bars A = 100μm, B = 10μm, C = 20μm.

2.9 SIPHONOSTOMATOIDA Thorell 1859

All siphonostomatoids are parasites or associates of other animals. In excess of 1550 species are known and, of these, about 1050 are parasites of fishes (and mammals) and about 500 are parasites or associates of invertebrate hosts. The order is largely marine although a small number of fish parasites is found in freshwater. This is a relatively diverse group containing many highly transformed types. Some members of the family Nicothoidae have lost all of their appendages and are reduced to a spherical body attached to their crustacean host by means of absorptive rootlets derived from the oral cone (Lincoln & Boxshall, 1983).

Character set of ancestral siphonostomatoid

Copepoda. Prosome comprising cephalothorax incorporating first pedigerous (=second thoracic somite), and 3 free pedigerous somites (figure 2.9.2B); urosome 6-segmented in both sexes (figure 2.9.2A). Prosome-urosome articulation between fourth and fifth pedigerous somites (podoplean position). Genital apertures paired and ventrally located in both sexes, sited at posterior border of genital somite in male. Copulatory pores paired; present within each genital aperture, beneath genital operculum. Seminal receptacles paired. Rostrum fused to cephalosome. Caudal ramus with 7 setae (figure 2.9.2C-D). Nauplius eye present. Antennules 21-segmented in female; ninth segment compound representing fused segments IX to XII of the ancestral antennule; segments representing XXII-XXIII, XXIV-XXV and XXVI-XXVIII fused (figure 2.9.13). Male antennules 19-segmented; bilaterally geniculate, modified by fusion of ancestral segments XIX and XX, with only 2 compound segments distal to geniculation representing fusions of XXI to XXIII and XXIV to XXVIII; segments IX to XI incompletely fused (figure 2.9.14). Antenna biramous (figure 2.9.15A-B); with 1-segmented exopod and 3-segmented endopod; coxa and basis both unarmed; first to third endopodal segments with 0, 1 and 4 setae respectively; exopod bearing 3 setae. Labrum a well developed muscular lobe forming anterior part of oral cone (figure 2.9.19). Mandible (figure 2.9.20A) reduced to a stylet-like gnathobase and 2-segmented palp bearing 2 setae on apical segment, first segment (basis) unarmed. Paragnaths fused medially into a labium forming the posterior part of the oral cone. Maxillule reduced; bilobed, inner lobe representing praecoxal endite, armed with 5 setae; outer lobe representing palp, armed with 4 setae (figure 2.9.21A). Maxilla 3-segmented; proximal part representing praecoxa and coxa, distal part claw-like, representing basis and endite; praecoxa and coxa lacking defined endites; basal endite with 3 elements (figure 2.9.21E); outer coxal seta absent; endopod absent. Maxilliped 6-segmented comprising syncoxa, basis and an indistinctly 4-segmented, subchelate endopod bearing a terminal claw (figure 2.9.23); syncoxa and basis each with 1 seta; endopod setal formula 2,(1,1),1+claw. Swimming legs 1-4 biramous with 3-segmented rami; members of leg pairs joined by intercoxal sclerite; inner coxal seta and outer seta on basis present; inner seta on basis of first leg present; first exopodal segment with 1 outer spine and 1 inner seta. Spine and seta formula of legs 1 to 4:

	coxa	basis	exopod segment	endopod segment
			1 2 3	1 2 3
leg 1	0 – 1	1 – I	I – 1; I – 1; III,I,4	0 – 1; 0 – 2; 1,2,3
leg 2	0 – 1	1 – 0	I – 1; I – 1; III,I,5	0 – 1; 0 – 2; 1,2,3
leg 3	0 – 1	1 – 0	I – 1; I – 1; III,I,5	0 – 1; 0 – 2; 1,2,3
leg 4	0 – 1	1 – 0	I – 1; I – 1; III,I,5	0 – 1; 0 – 2; 1,2,2

Fifth legs biramous, with single segmented protopod not joined by intercoxal sclerite; inner coxal seta absent; outer seta on basis present; exopod 1-segmented bearing 6 setae (figure 2.9.24B); endopod represented by single seta on apex of inner margin of protopod (figure 2.9.24A, C-D). Sixth legs represented by opercular plates closing off genital openings of female (figure 2.9.26C), and by paired flaps closing off genital apertures of male (figure 2.9.30A). Eggs carried in paired sacs.

Remarks

The diagnosis is based primarily on the plesiomorphic families Asterocheridae, Dirivultidae and Megapontiidae, on the Cretaceous fossil *Kabatarina pattersoni* described from the gills of a Lower Cretaceous fossil fish (Cressey & Boxshall, 1989), and on the eudactylinids *Bariaka* Cressey and *Jusheyus* Deets & Benz. The last 2 genera are the only siphonostomatoids in which the genital somite is retained separate from the first abdominal somite in the female. In all others the genital and first abdominal somites are fused to form a genital double somite in the female, as seen in the plesiomorphic families Asterocheridae and Dirivultidae. Virtually all the families parasitic on fishes, except the Eudactylinidae, share a further segmental fusion, with the fifth pedigerous somite being incorporated into the genital double somite to form a genital complex in the female (Boxshall, 1990a).

Cephalothorax: All siphonostomatoids have the first pedigerous somite fully fused with the cephalosome to form a cephalothorax (figure 2.9.2B). No trace of a suture separating the first pedigerous somite is retained in any siphonostomatoid. Humes (1987) reported a slight separation of this somite from the cephalosome in the dirivultid *Scotoecetes introrsus* Humes but on reexamination this proved to be an artefact. Further incorporations of posterior pedigerous somites into the cephalothorax are common within the order, especially amongst the more transformed parasitic families, in which all traces of external segmentation are sometimes lost.

Female Genital System: In the primitive eudactylinid *Bariaka alopiae* Cressey the genital apertures are located at the extreme ventrolateral angles of the genital somite, close to the posterior margin (figure 2.9.29A). The copulatory pores are contained within the genital aperture and are not isolated as in virtually all other siphonostomatoids. The seminal receptacles are paired in *Bariaka*, as in the majority of siphonostomatoids. Since *Bariaka* is also one of the only 2 siphonostomatoid genera that retain separate genital and first abdominal somites, this leads to the inference that the ancestral siphonostomatoid probably had paired ventral genital apertures in the female, each aperture containing a copulatory pore and a gonopore. Lateral migration of this ancestral type of aperture took place in other eudactylinid genera, such as *Carnifossorius* Deets & Ho and *Heterocladius* Deets & Ho.

A common arrangement of the genital apparatus in female siphonostomatoids is illustrated by *Asterocheres reginae* Boxshall & Huys (figures 2.9.26A-B and 2.9.34A-B) and *Pontoeciella abyssicola* (Scott) (figure 2.9.34C-D). The oviduct openings (gonopores) are paired and laterally located. There are paired copulatory pores located on the ventral surface on each side of the genital double somite. Each copulatory pore discharges via a short copulatory duct, into a seminal receptacle. This is the typical arrangement of the female apparatus found in other cyclopiform families, such as the Brychiopontiidae (figure 2.9.26D-E), Dirivultidae (figures 2.9.27 and 2.9.28A-D) and Ecbathyriontidae (figure 2.9.29C-D). The gonopores are located laterally or dorsolaterally on the genital double somite and the paired copulatory pores remain on the ventral surface. This basic system is also found in more transformed families that are associated with invertebrate hosts, such as the Stellicomitidae. In *Stellicomes supplicans* Humes the position of the egg sacs, each containing a single egg (figure 2.9.30C), shows the dorsal position of the tiny gonopore (figure 2.9.30F). The ventral location of the copulatory pores is shown in figure 2.9.30D-E with the unusually shaped spermatophores fixed in position. The typical condition found in cyclopiform siphonostomatoids, as described above for *Asterocheres reginae*, could be derived from this ancestral pattern by migration of the gonopore onto the lateral or dorsolateral surface, whilst leaving the copulatory pore isolated in its original position on the ventral surface.

There are several other arrangements of the female genital system exhibited within the order. Some modifications simply involve the migration of the copulatory pores. In the dirivultid *Chasmatopontius thescalus* Humes, for example, the copulatory pores have migrated posterodorsally and can be found on the dorsal surface of the double somite near the posterolateral angles (arrowed in figure 2.9.28B). Spermatophore tubules do not cross over in this genus (figure 2.9.28A). The copulatory ducts connecting the pores with the seminal receptacles lying beneath the gonopores are heavily sclerotised in *C.thescalus*. The genital apparatus of female members of the family Lernanthropidae is similar to that of *Chasmatopontius* Humes, with a sclerotised copulatory duct passing forwards from the posterolaterally located copulatory pores (figure

2.9.29B). The pattern may vary even between species of a single genus. In the dirivultid *Stygiopontius stabilitus* Humes the copulatory pores are located just ventral to the lateral margin of the double somite, very close to the gonopores which lie just dorsal to the same margin (figure 2.9.27A-B). In *Stygiopontius cinctiger* Humes the copulatory pores can be found at the extreme posterior border of the double somite in the lateral position (figure 2.9.27C-D). The system found in *Fissuricola caritus* Humes (figure 2.9.28C-D) is very similar to that of *Stygiopontius stabilitus*.

In *Lepeophtheirus pectoralis* Müller the genital apertures are ventrally located. The paired copulatory pores lie either side of the midline on the ventral surface of the genital complex (figure 2.9.25A-B) and the gonopores are positioned ventrolaterally. The seminal receptacles are fused but this is secondary and is not the ancestral condition. The gonopores are overlain by the fifth legs and each is closed off by an unarmed opercular plate representing the sixth leg. In *L.pectoralis* the spermatophores are transferred in pairs and each spermatophore typically discharges into the copulatory pore on the other side of the body (figure 2.9.25B). This crossing of the spermatophore tubules is very characteristic and has been observed in a wide range of families, including the Caligidae and Asterocheridae. The caligid condition, as exemplified by *Lepeophtheirus pectoralis*, can be derived from the ancestral *Bariaka*-like state by medial migration of the copulatory pores. A similar process of medial migration must be postulated for the highly transformed family of sponge parasites, the Spongiocnizontidae, because in *Spongiocnizon vermiformis* Stock the paired copulatory pores are sited close together, either side of the ventral midline, and the gonopores are also ventrally located (figure 2.9.28E-F).

Female Antennule: The antennule of female siphonostomatoids has a maximum of 21 segments. This is found in several asterocherid genera, such as *Asterocheres* Boeck and *Mesocheres* Norman & Scott, and in the fossil *Kabatarina*. In *Asterocheres reginae* the antennules are 21-segmented in the female: ancestral segments I to VIII are free, IX to XII are fused, XIII to XXI are free, XXII and XXIII are fused, as are XXIV to XXV and XXVI to XXVIII (figure 2.9.4A-E). The large aesthetasc present on ancestral segment XXI is remarkably conservative within the order and serves as a valuable reference point in the identification of segmental homologies. *Tuphacheres micropus* Stock was reported as possessing a 21-segmented antennule (Stock, 1965) but reexamination revealed this to be 17-segmented. Basically similar segmentation is expressed in female *Ecbathyrion prolixicauda* Humes (figure 2.9.6A-C) although the fusion of segments I to III and XV to XVI reduces the total number of segments to 18. *Brychiopontius falcatus* Humes has an indistinctly 18-segmented condition, derived by fusion of the proximal segments I to IV (figure 2.9.7A). The compound segment IX-XII is characteristic of all female siphonostomatoids and retains all 8 of its original setae in *Ecbathyrion* Humes (figure 2.9.6B) and *Brychiopontius* Humes (figure 2.9.7B). The antennule of female *Scotoecetes introrsus* is only 11-segmented, due to further segmental fusions; the segments expressed being I-VIII, IX-XII, XIII, XIV, XV-XVI, XVII, XVIII, XIX, XX, XXI and XXII-XXVIII (figure 2.9.9A). The similar total number of segments in *Acontiophorus* Brady represents a different fusion pattern as segment I is free, as are segments XXII-XXIII and XXIV-XXV (figure 2.9.11A).

The antennules of siphonostomatoids found on fish hosts are typically more reduced. The largest numbers found are in the plesiomorphic eudactylinid genera *Bariaka* and *Protodactylina* Laubier. In *B.alopiae* the female antennule has 18 segments fully separated but is indistinctly 20-segmented (figure 2.9.10D) whereas in *P.pamelae* Laubier it is indistinctly 18-segmented but with only 12 fully separated (figure 2.9.10B-C). The compound segment IX-XII is clearly defined in both of these genera and provides a powerful apomorphy uniting the families associated with invertebrate hosts and those parasitic on vertebrate hosts (see figure 2.9.13).

Male Antennule: Male antennules are primitively geniculate with the geniculation located between compound segments XIX-XX and XXI-XXIII. In all siphonostomatoids a maximum of 2 compound segments (representing XXI-XXIII and XXIV-XXVIII) is found distal to the geniculation (figure 2.9.14). In *Ecbathyrion*, a total of 3 segments was shown in this distal part (Humes, 1987) but only 2 were found on reexamination (figure 2.9.6D). *Hermacheres montastreae* Stock was also originally shown as possessing 3 segments distal to the geniculation (Stock, 1989) but our studies revealed only 2 segments (figure 2.9.8C).

A maximum of 19 segments is expressed in male siphonostomatoids, as found in *Collocheres comanthiphilus* Humes. The segmental fusions are IX-XI, XIX-XX, XXI-XXIII and XXIV-XXVIII (figure 2.9.3A). In this species segment XII is free (figure 2.9.3B-C) and is not incorporated into compound segment IX-XI as it is in all siphonostomatoid females. Segment XII is also free from compound segment IX-XI in male *Ecbathyrion* (figures 2.9.6D-F). In all other males available for study, *Asterocheres reginae* for example, segment XII was incorporated into the quadruple segment IX-XII (figure 2.9.5A-E), as in females. Several members of the Dirivultidae show partial separation of segments IX to XII, such as *Scotoecetes introrsus* (figure 2.9.9B-F), *Stygiopontius* Humes (figure 2.9.8A-B) and some species of *Aphotopontius* Humes. These 4 segments are fused along their anterior edges but their free posterior margins allow some flexure. They form part of a proximal geniculation mechanism which also involves segment XIII. This latter segment forms an important part of the proximal geniculation and represents a major flexing point in the limb even when segments IX to XII are completely fused, as they are in most siphonostomatoids. In some genera, *Asterocheres* for example, segment XIII possesses a membranous insert facilitating flexure (figure 2.9.5D). In most dirivultids a large spinous process arises from segment XIII (figure 2.9.9C-F). Also in this family segment II is frequently modified, as in *Stygiopontius quadrispinosus* in which this segment is horseshoe-shaped and permits posterior flexure of the whole limb (figure 2.9.8A-B).

The antennule of male *Eudactylinella alba* Wilson (figure 2.9.11B-C) retains a high number of segments (Deets & Ho, 1988) and provides an important link between the families parasitic on fishes and those associated with invertebrates. Two segments (XXI-XXIII and XXIV-XXVIII) are present distal to the geniculation, with segment XXI bearing the prominent aesthetasc as is typical for the order. The proximal part of the limb retains sufficient setation elements for the fusion pattern to be elucidated: the pattern is I, II-III, IV-VI, VII, VIII, IX-XII, XIII, XIV, XV-XVII, XVIII, XIX-XX, XXI-XXIII, XXIV-XXVIII. This can be readily derived from the ancestral siphonostomatoid pattern (figure 2.9.14) and provides further evidence uniting the order.

Antennules with reduced numbers of segments are common within the Siphonostomatoida. Species of the Nanaspididae have short bilaterally geniculate antennules with up to 6 segments. In males of *Nanaspis moluccana* Humes, for example, the subapical segment is massive and there is a single segment distal to the geniculation (Humes, 1980a). This antennule closely resembles the chirocer antennules found in many harpacticoids. Males of the closely related family Stellicomitidae differ from the nanaspidids primarily in their non-geniculate antennules.

Biramous antennules have been reported twice in the Siphonostomatoida but both reports are based on misinterpretations. Stock (1967) reported a biramous antennule in *Spongiocnizon vermiformis*, identifying the offset lobe arising at the base of the terminal segment as the exopod. Boxshall (1985), without examining the material, suggested that the offset lobe might represent the terminal segment of a uniramous appendage, displaced by the asymmetrical growth of the penultimate segment. Reexamination of the original material of *S.vermiformis* reveals both interpretations to be wrong. The offset lobe does not bear an apical seta as reported by Stock (1967) and is an aesthetasc, almost certainly that originally from ancestral segment XXI. In both sexes the antennule is only 2-segmented (figure 2.9.12A-E) with the basal segment probably representing segments I-XX and the terminal segment representing XXI-XXVIII. The male antennule is geniculate and has a subchelate structure provided by the claw-like terminal segment which opposes the strong process on the basal segment. Biramous antennules were also reported in the male of the parasitic nicothoid *Paranicothoe cladocera* Carton, by Carton (1970). Boxshall (1985) suggested that the small articulated lobe at the base of the distal seta on the second compound antennulary segment, interpreted by Carton as the exopod, could equally well be interpreted as the swollen base of an articulated seta. Reexamination of *P.cladocera* reveals that Boxshall's interpretation was correct. The articulated seta is arrowed in figure 2.9.12F.

Antenna: A separate coxa and basis are retained in the antenna of most of the cyclopiform families of siphonostomatoids, including the Asterocheridae (figure 2.9.15A), Dirivultidae (figure 2.9.15D), Brychiopontiidae (figure 2.9.15E), and Ecbathyriontidae (figure 2.9.17C). These 2 segments are separate even in the highly condensed antenna of *Spongiocnizon* Stock & Kleeton in which the limb is a tapering, 4-segmented structure consisting of coxa, basis and 2-segmented endopod (figure 2.9.17B). In most of the families parasitic on fish the coxa and basis are free, as in the Caligidae (figure 2.9.17E). In the primitive eudactylinid *Eudactylinella alba* the coxa and basis are both large, well developed segments and the articulation between them forms the main flexing point of the limb (figure 2.9.17D). The typical configuration shows a small coxa and comparatively large basis, but in the plesiomorphic families Dirivultidae and Eudactylinidae these segments are more equal in size, and it is possible that this represents the ancestral condition. In *Hyalopontius* Sars the basis and first endopodal segment are fused to form an allobasis bearing the exopod about at midlength (figure 2.9.17A). The coxa and basis are unarmed in all siphonostomatoids.

The antennary exopod is given as 1-segmented in the diagnosis. The exopod of *Dermatomyzon nigripes* Brady & Robertson is shown by Giesbrecht (1899) as indistinctly 2-segmented but re-examination of this species revealed a 1-segmented condition (figure 2.9.16B and see Boxshall, 1990b). *Rhynchomyzon compactum* Alvarez was described as possessing a clearly 2-segmented exopod (Alvarez, 1988). Re-examination of the type material of *R.compactum* revealed that the exopod is only 1-segmented (figure 2.9.16E). Nicholls (1944) illustrated a 2-segmented exopod on the antenna of *Australomyzon* Nicholls but re-examination of the types of *A.typicus* Nicholls showed that this was also erroneous and the exopod is only 1-segmented (figure 2.9.15C). Heegaard (1940) reported a 2-segmented exopod in the lernaeopodid genus *Euclavellisa* Heegaard but this requires confirmation as it is the only siphonostomatoid reported with this character that we have been unable to examine.

The antenna becomes uniramous in many families, by loss of the exopod. This is typical of the families parasitic on fish, although members of the families Lernaeopodidae and Sphyriidae have a distinct, 1-segmented exopod. The loss of the exopod in most families of fish parasites appears to be correlated with the modification of the limb as a subchelate or claw-like structure used for attachment to the host (figure 2.9.17E). At least some members of the plesiomorphic family Eudactylinidae, such as *Eudactylinella alba*, have not completely lost the exopod as it is represented by a single seta on the outer margin of the basis (figure 2.9.17D).

The maximum armature on the exopod is 3 setae and is retained in a wide variety of the cyclopiform families and in the Lernaeopodidae, at least in the copepodid stage (Kabata, 1979). The numbers of exopodal setae are often reduced, as in *Hammatimyzon* Stock (figure 2.9.18A-B) which has only 2 setae.

The first segment of the antennary endopod is typically much longer than the second, although in some genera, such as *Acontiophorus*, these segments are of similar length (figure 2.9.16A). The second and third endopodal segments are separated by a complete suture in *Asterocheres reginae* (figure 2.9.15A-B) and this represents the ancestral siphonostomatoid condition. In the dirivultid *Scotoecetes introrsus* the second and third segments are partly fused (figure 2.9.15D) but in the great majority of siphonostomatoids these 2 segments are completely fused (cf. figures 2.9.15 to 2.9.18). The double terminal segment is often claw-like forming a prehensile part which is typically used for attachment to the host. In the caligiform families the entire endopod forms a unitary claw, derived by fusion of all 3 segments (Boxshall, 1990a).

The antennary armature is sparse. The first endopodal segment is always unarmed. The second carries a single seta on the medial margin (figure 2.9.15B,D) which is usually visible proximally on the margin of the double terminal segment found in most siphonostomatoids. The third segment carries 4 setae around its distal margin, one of which is commonly larger than the others and somewhat claw-like (figure 2.9.16A-B). In *Brychiopontius falcatus* one of the distal elements is modified as a spatulate blade rather than a claw (figure 2.9.15E).

Mandible: The ancestral state of the mandible is found in some asterocherids, such as *Asterocheres reginae*, and some Entomolepidae. The coxa is drawn out to form a slender, stylet-like gnathobase and a 2-segmented palp is present (figure 2.9.20A). The 2 segments of the palp presumably represent the basis plus a 1-segmented ramus. The basis is unarmed and the ramus bears a maximum of 2 setae on its apex. There is no evidence to indicate which ramus is present. The palp is commonly reduced to a single segment and is lacking altogether in many families, including cyclopiform families such as the Brychiopontiidae (figure 2.9.20D), Ecbathyriontidae (figure 2.9.20C) and Megapontiidae (figure 2.9.20E-F), as well as in all those families that parasitise fishes. The mandible of the caligiform and dichelesthiiform families is a rod-shaped stylet bearing teeth on one side near the apex (figure 2.9.20G-H). This type of mandibular stylet is often figured as comprising 3 or 4 segments but these represent annulations and are not true segments. No muscles pass into the mandibular stylet (Boxshall, 1990a).

Maxillule: The basic bilobed structure of the maxillule is retained in many families. The homology of the lobes of the maxillule was reviewed by Boxshall (1990a). These lobes are commonly referred to as inner and outer lobes, or as endopod and exopod (Deets & Ho, 1988). The maxillulary musculature supports the suggestion made by Giesbrecht (1899) that the inner and outer lobes represent the praecoxal gnathobase and the palp respectively (Boxshall, 1990a). The palp is often delimited basally by a well defined articulation (figure 2.9.21A-B). The maximum setation of the lobes of the maxillule is found in several asterocherid genera, such as *Sinopontius* Boxshall (Boxshall, 1990b), and in the Brychiopontiidae (figure 2.9.21A). Five setae are found on the praecoxal gnathobase and 4 on the palp. Reductions in setal numbers are widespread, with both 4+4 and 4+3 formulae being common (figures 2.9.18D and 2.9.21B). In *Pontoeciella abyssicola* the maxillule is unilobate with 2 apical setae (figure 2.9.33D) but it is not known which lobe has been retained.

The caligiform families of fish parasites have a particular type of modified maxillule. The palp is reduced to a small papilla bearing 3 apical setae and the gnathobase forms a large, spinous process that may be simple, bifid (figure 2.9.21C) or trifid. The 2 parts of the maxillule are separate because much of the praecoxal segment has been incorporated into the ventral cephalic surface.

Maxilla: The basic siphonostomatoid maxilla is 3-segmented, comprising praecoxa, coxa and claw-like basis (Boxshall, 1990a) and is found in the Cretaceous fossil *Kabatarina pattersoni* (Cressey & Boxshall, 1989). In the great majority of recent forms praecoxa and coxa are fused to produce a syncoxa, although in some species, such as *Asterocheres reginae*, a partial suture near the base of the syncoxa may represent a vestige of the praecoxal-coxal articulation (figure 2.9.21D). The distal, claw-like segment is formed from the basis and basal endite (Boxshall, 1990a). There is no trace of the endopod in any siphonostomatoid.

The syncoxa is typically unarmed (figures 2.9.21E-F and 2.9.22) although the medial surface is sometimes produced into myxal processes, as in *Brychiopontius* (figure 2.9.22E). However, in a few asterocherids an aesthetasc-like element has been observed on the praecoxal part of the syncoxa. Ho (1984) found this element in *Asterocheres aesthetes* Ho, and Boxshall (1990b) found it in *Sinopontius aesthetascus* Boxshall and *Inermocheres quadratus* Boxshall. It is also present in *Asterocheres reginae* (figures 2.9.21D and 2.9.31A,C). The presence of an aesthetasc or aesthetasc-like element on any copepod appendage other than the antennules is very unusual, with only a few cases recorded in harpacticoid families such as the Paranannopidae (Huys & Gee, in press). This element on the maxilla resembles an aesthetasc as it is thin-walled and somewhat flaccid in preserved material. However, an alternative interpretation is that it might represent a tubular extension around the external opening of the maxillary gland. A short tube pore at the opening of the maxillary gland is present in a similar position on the syncoxa of *Nicothoe astaci* Audouin & Milne-Edwards (figure 2.9.21E), and in *Scotoecetes introrsus* the pore of the maxillary gland is carried on a raised process (figure 2.9.22B).

In some Asterocheridae there is a small hyaline process in the axil of the maxillary claw, as in *Asterocheres reginae* (figure 2.9.21D). This process does not appear to be a true armature element.

The maxillary basis is typically drawn out to form a claw-like enditic process armed with a maximum of 2 additional elements. In some asterocherids, such as *Asterocheres reginae*, a pair of tiny setae are positioned along the basal claw (arrowed in figure 2.9.21D). In *Nicothoe astaci* the claw has serrated margins and bears a large, articulated, claw-like spine also with serrated margins plus a small seta (arrowed in figure 2.9.21E). In the Ecbathyriontidae and some genera of the family Dirivultidae (Humes, 1987) a very large and conspicuous seta is present right at the base of the basal claw. The precise site of origin of this seta is difficult to ascertain as it arises in an area of folded flexible integument. Humes (1987) interpreted it as originating on the syncoxa. Boxshall (1990a) found that in *Stygiopontius hispidulus* Humes this seta lies on a small process delineated by integumental folds on each side but that it appears to be more firmly attached to the basal claw. In this case it represents an element of the armature of the basal endite. Examination of other dirivultids, such as *Stygiopontius cinctiger* (figure 2.9.22A) and *Scotoecetes introrsus* (figure 2.9.22B), and the Ecbathyriontidae (figure 2.9.22C) reveals that this seta is an unusually well developed basal endite element. In the majority of siphonostomatoids only a single additional element remains on the enditic claw (figure 2.9.22D-E). This may be located at the base, in the middle, or near the apex of the claw. The 2 elements at the tip of the bifurcate enditic claw in the caligiform families, such as in *Lepeophtheirus salmonis* (figure 2.9.21F-G), were referred to by Kabata (1979) as the calamus and canna. These elements are interpreted here as the fused enditic claw plus a second fused element; both are derived from original armature elements of the basal endite.

Maxilliped: The fossil *Kabatarina* is the only siphonostomatoid that has been reported as retaining a separate praecoxa and coxa on the maxilliped (Cressey & Boxshall, 1989). In all recent forms these ancestral segments are fused to form a syncoxa. In many siphonostomatoids the maxillipeds are located on a prominent pedestal (see figure 2.9.23A) and this is often interpreted and figured erroneously as a discrete proximal segment. We consider it possible that the proximal part of the maxilliped of the fossil *Kabatarina* could equally well represent a pedestal rather than a separate praecoxal segment. The bases of all the appendages were more or less covered with an overgrowth of the mineral apatite which made observations difficult. We therefore prefer to reinterpret the maxilliped of the fossil as comprising syncoxa, basis and endopod, with the whole limb sitting on a raised pedestal. The maximum armature of syncoxa and basis (1,1) is widespread throughout the order (figure 2.9.23).

The endopod of the maxilliped displays a maximum of 3 free segments, as in *Ecbathyrion* (figure 2.9.23A), *Nicothoe* Audouin & Milne Edwards (figure 2.9.16C-D), and *Brychiopontius* (figure 2.9.23B). However, in *Asterocheres reginae* the endopod has only 2 clearly separated segments although the presence of incomplete sutures, with associated armature elements (figure 2.9.23C-E), subdividing the proximal segment, indicates that this is probably derived from a 4-segmented condition. We conclude that the typical 3-segmented endopod with a setal formula of 2,2,1+claw is derived from an original indistinctly 4-segmented ramus with 2,(1,1),1+claw armature.

There is a marked tendency towards fusion of the endopodal segments and the terminal claw to form a powerful compound subchela, as is found in the caligiform families (figure 2.9.23F). In representatives of these families, such as *Lepeophtheirus* Nordmann, the protopodal segments are also fused into a single massive segment containing powerful, pinnate adductor muscles (Boxshall, 1990a).

Swimming Legs: The full setation of the swimming legs is retained in a wide range of taxa, including *Asterocheres reginae*.

Fifth Legs: The fifth leg has a maximum of 2 segments, a proximal segment representing the fused coxa and basis and a distal 1-segmented exopod. In some species, such as *Scottocheres elongatus* (Scott & Scott) (figure 2.9.24A), *Dermatomyzon nigripes* (figure 2.9.24D), *Acontiophorus scutatus* (Brady & Robertson) (figure 2.9.24C) and *Paracontiophorus* Eiselt, the protopod bears a small inner seta representing a vestige of the endopod. This is lost in the great majority of siphonostomatoids. The protopod is armed with an outer margin seta. This seta often remains, inserted on the surface of the somite, even when the protopod has been totally incorporated into the somite.

No siphonostomatoids retain an intercoxal sclerite between the fifth legs. The configuration of the fifth legs in plesiomorphic genera such as *Dermatomyzon* Claus and *Scottocheres* Giesbrecht indicates that the evolutionary trend within the order is for the fused protopodal segments to expand transversely. This has a dual effect of causing the protopods to meet in the midline and of carrying the exopod into a more laterally located position. The subsequent incorporation of the protopod into the somite leaves the free exopod isolated on the lateral surface of the somite. Only a single free exopodal segment is ever found and the maximum number of setae on this segment is 6, as found in *Nicothoe astaci* (figure 2.9.24B). Sexual dimorphism commonly occurs in the armature of the fifth legs. Males of many genera, such as *Dermatomyzon*, carry 5 elements on the exopod, 2 of which are located on the medial margin. In the corresponding females the 2 medial setae are absent. This dimorphism occurs in members of the Asterocheridae, Dirivultidae and other families.

In the Dirivultidae the fifth legs including the protopods have migrated and are typically located ventrolaterally or laterally (figure 2.9.27C). In some dirivultids the protopod and exopod are fused, forming a single compound segment, as in *Stygiopontius stabilitus* (figure 2.9.27A-B).

Differential Diagnosis: The Siphonostomatoida is a well defined order diagnosed by the form of the mandible and by the formation of an oral cone from the labrum and the medially fused paragnaths (the labium). Boxshall (1990a) reviewed adaptive radiation in structure of the oral cone within the Siphonostomatoida. The oral cone comprises an anterior lip, the labrum, and a posterior lip, the labium, which are produced together into a tapering tubular structure that opens distally. Primitively, labrum and labium are loosely associated and part readily to allow movement of the mandibular stylet between them, as in the dirivultids. In more advanced forms labrum and labium are held together along their lengths by a complex arrangement of interlocking ridges and grooves, and the mandibular stylets lie within the central lumen of the cone (figures 2.9.31-33).

The labrum is typically robust and contains powerful muscles (figure 2.9.19) that produce the suction necessary to draw food up into the oesophagus. The labium is derived from the fused paragnaths (Boxshall, 1986a) and is provided with one median and a pair of lateral muscles. These muscles originate on the ventral surface of the anterior ventral cephalic tendon in *Hyalopontius typicus* Sars (Boxshall, 1990a), and pass through channels in the suboesophageal ganglion before inserting in the labium. The median muscle inserts on a tendinous sheet, probably representing the plane of fusion of the paired paragnaths. The paired muscles pass to the tip of the labium where they probably are responsible for moving the flared oral disc (figure 2.9.19).

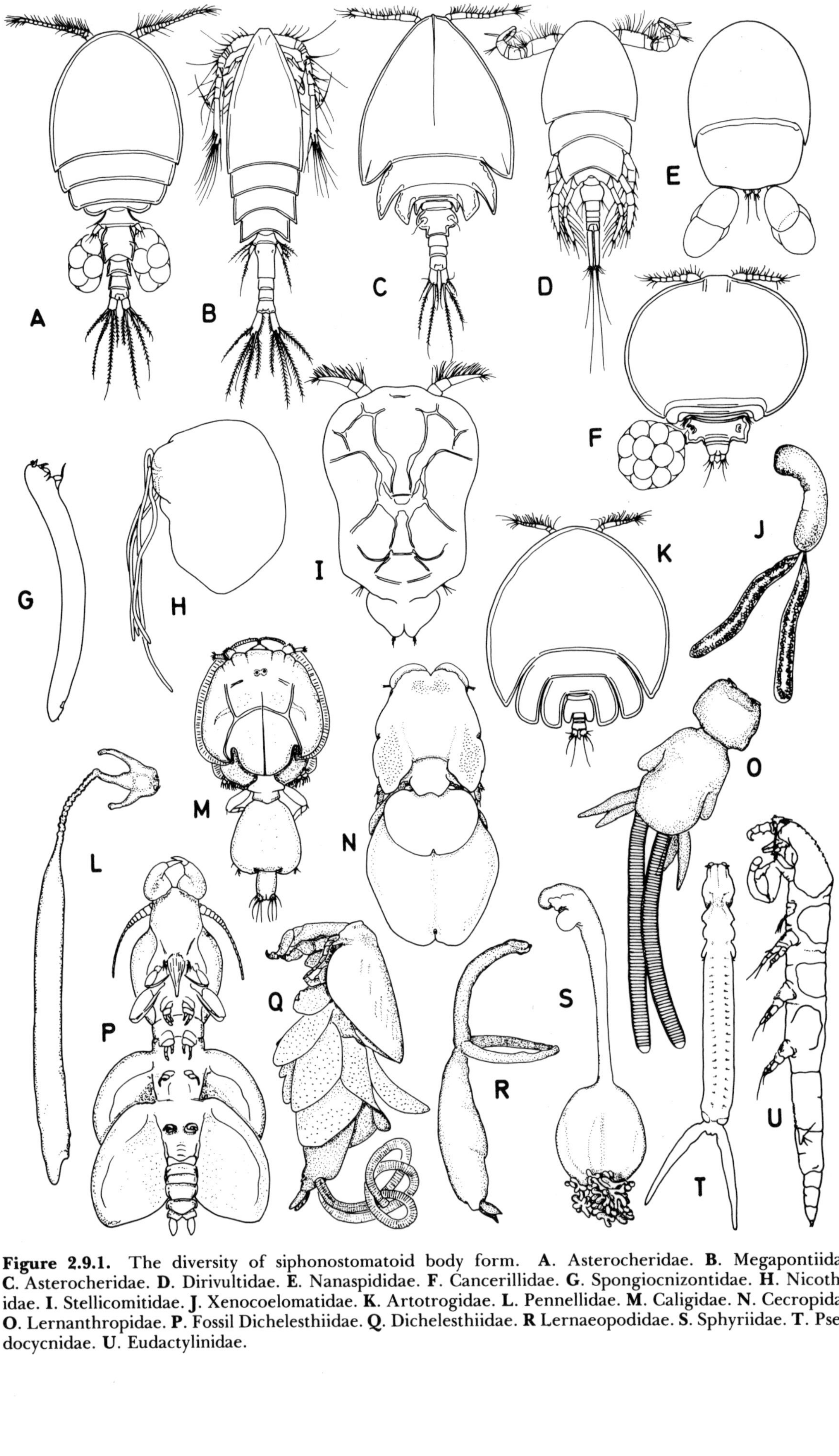

Figure 2.9.1. The diversity of siphonostomatoid body form. **A.** Asterocheridae. **B.** Megapontiidae. **C.** Asterocheridae. **D.** Dirivultidae. **E.** Nanaspididae. **F.** Cancerillidae. **G.** Spongiocnizontidae. **H.** Nicothoidae. **I.** Stellicomitidae. **J.** Xenocoelomatidae. **K.** Artotrogidae. **L.** Pennellidae. **M.** Caligidae. **N.** Cecropidae. **O.** Lernanthropidae. **P.** Fossil Dichelesthiidae. **Q.** Dichelesthiidae. **R** Lernaeopodidae. **S.** Sphyriidae. **T.** Pseudocycnidae. **U.** Eudactylinidae.

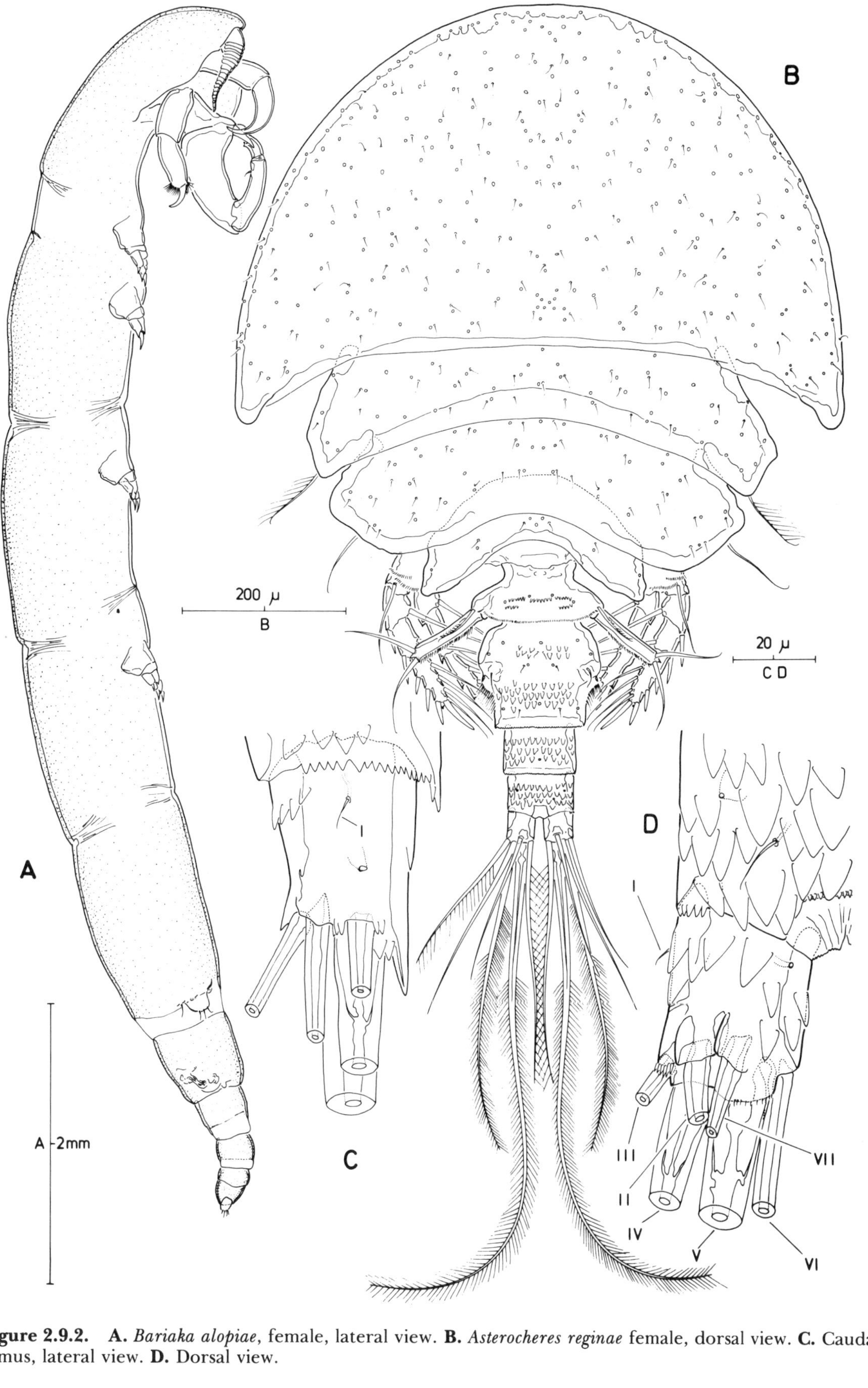

Figure 2.9.2. **A.** *Bariaka alopiae*, female, lateral view. **B.** *Asterocheres reginae* female, dorsal view. **C.** Caudal ramus, lateral view. **D.** Dorsal view.

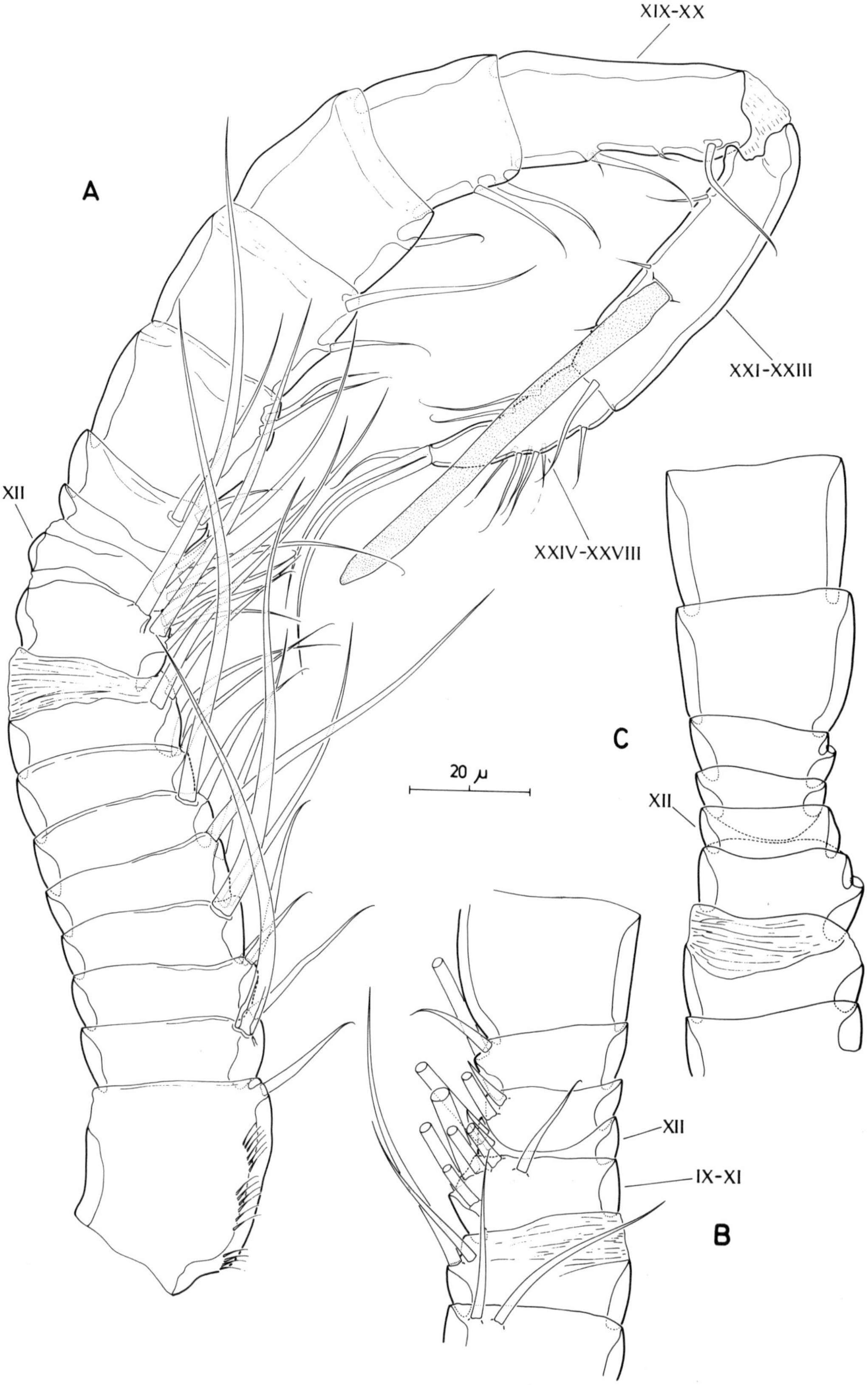

Figure 2.9.3. *Collocheres comanthiphilus.* **A.** Male antennule. **B.** Detail of compound segment IX-XI, showing free segment XII. **C.** Detail of specialised segments forming proximal geniculation, with setae removed.

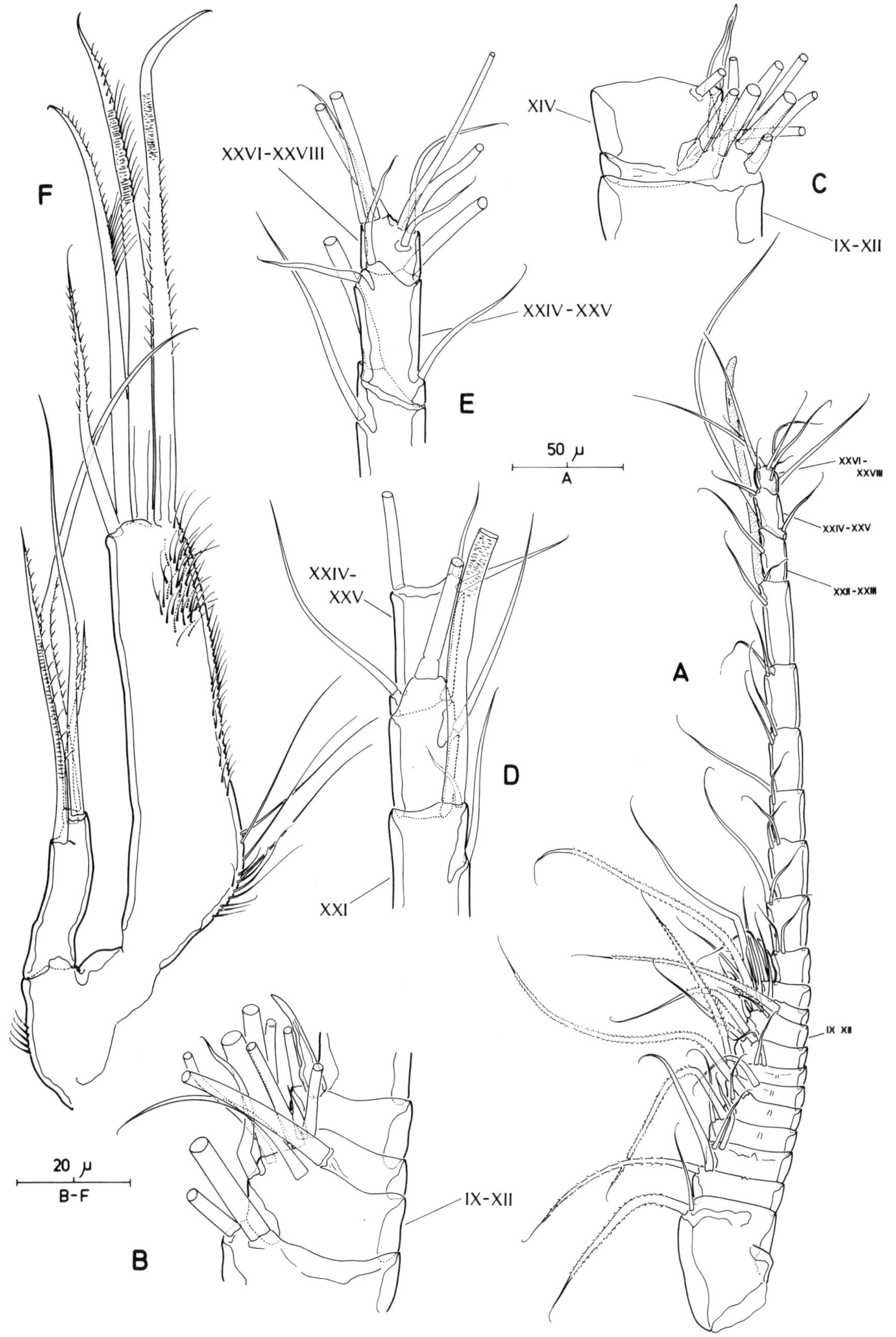

Figure 2.9.4. *Asterocheres reginae*. **A**. Female antennule. **B**. Detail of segments IX-XII, ventral view. **C**. Same, dorsal view. **D**. Detail of segments XXI to XXIV-XXV. **E**. Detail of apex. **F**. Maxillule.

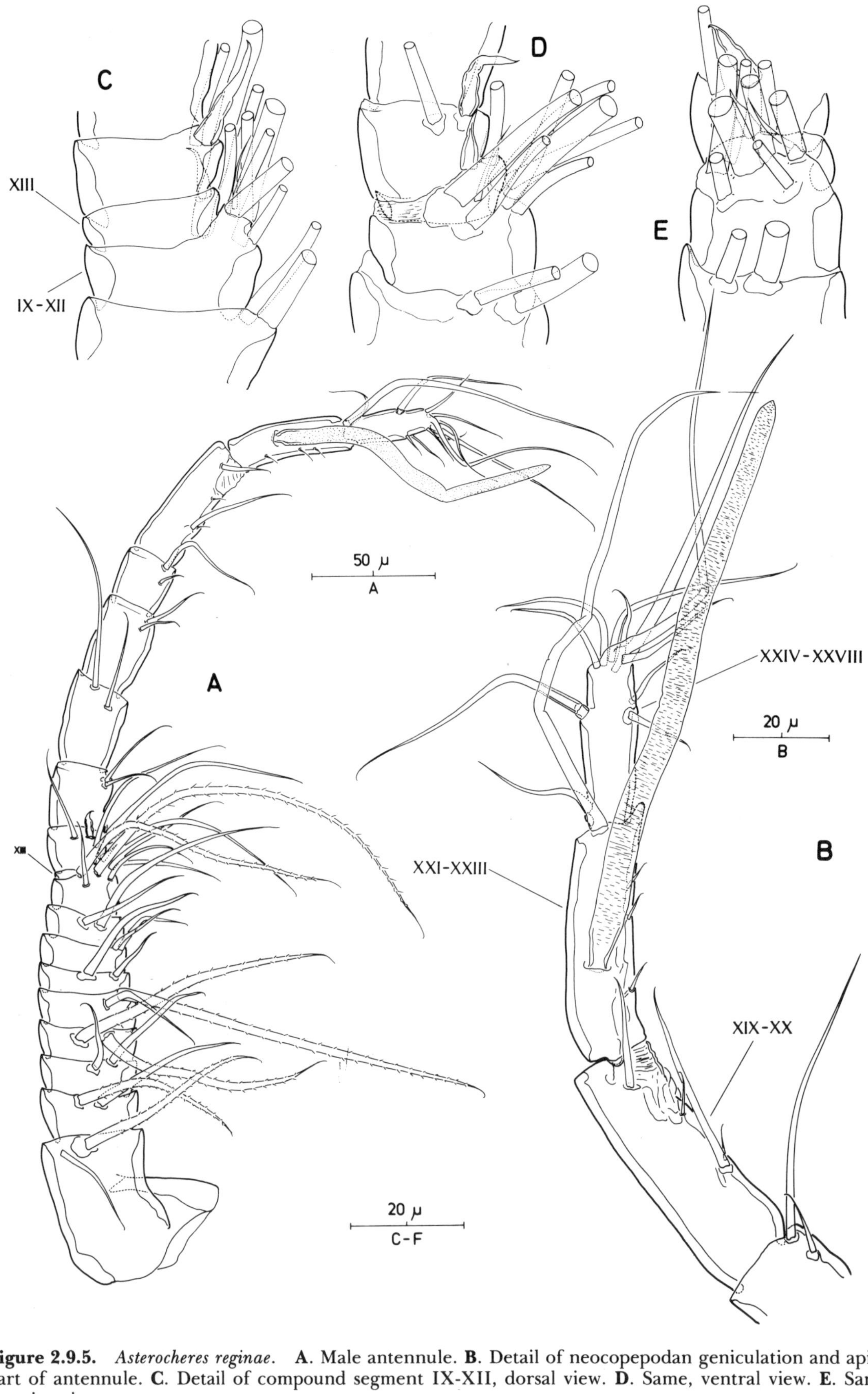

Figure 2.9.5. *Asterocheres reginae*. **A**. Male antennule. **B**. Detail of neocopepodan geniculation and apical part of antennule. **C**. Detail of compound segment IX-XII, dorsal view. **D**. Same, ventral view. **E**. Same, anterior view.

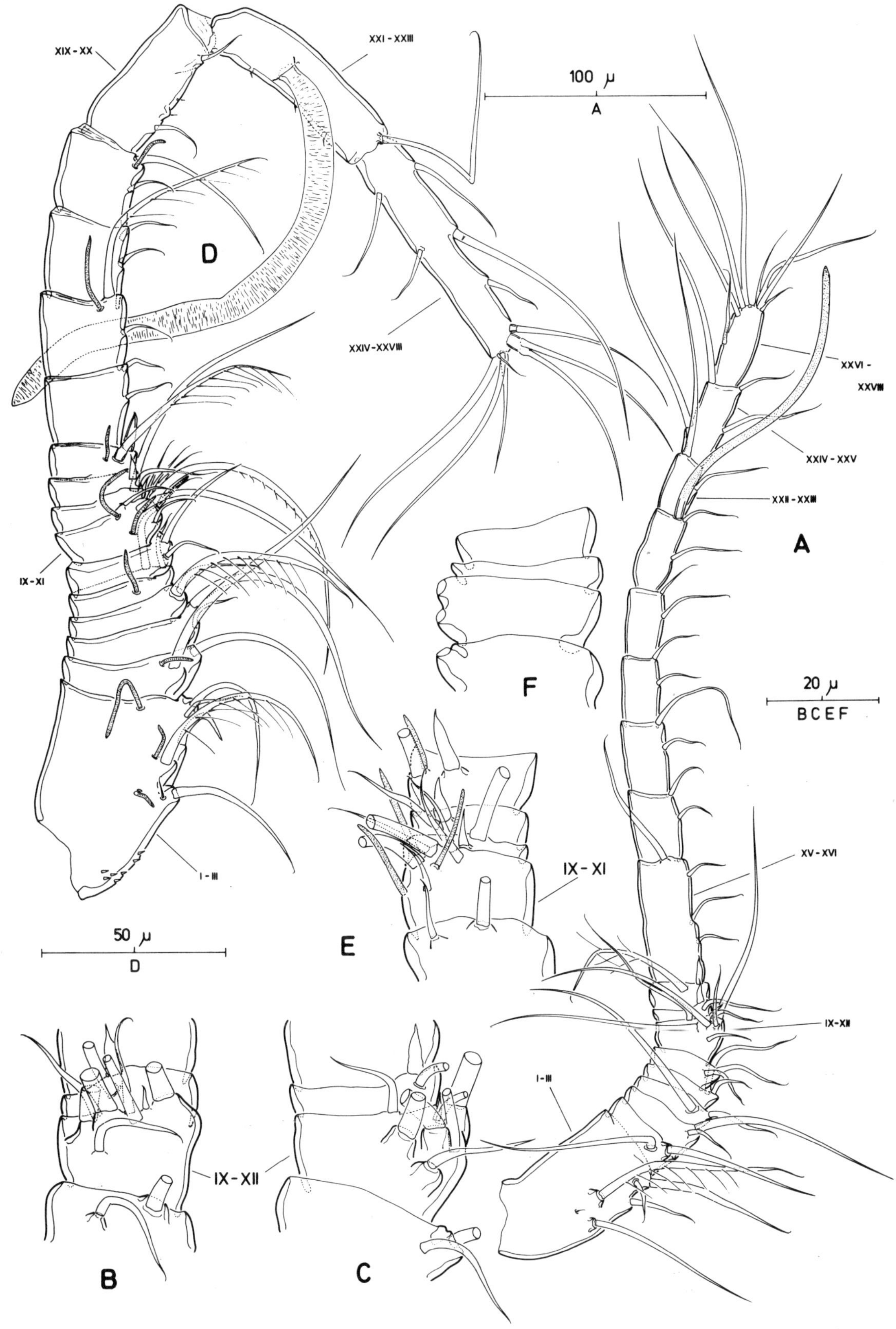

Figure 2.9.6. *Ecbathyrion prolixicauda.* **A**. Female antennule. **B**. Detail of compound segment IX-XII, anterior view. **C**. Same, ventral view. **D**. Male antennule. **E**. Detail of compound segment IX-XI. **F**. Same, with setae removed to show segmentation.

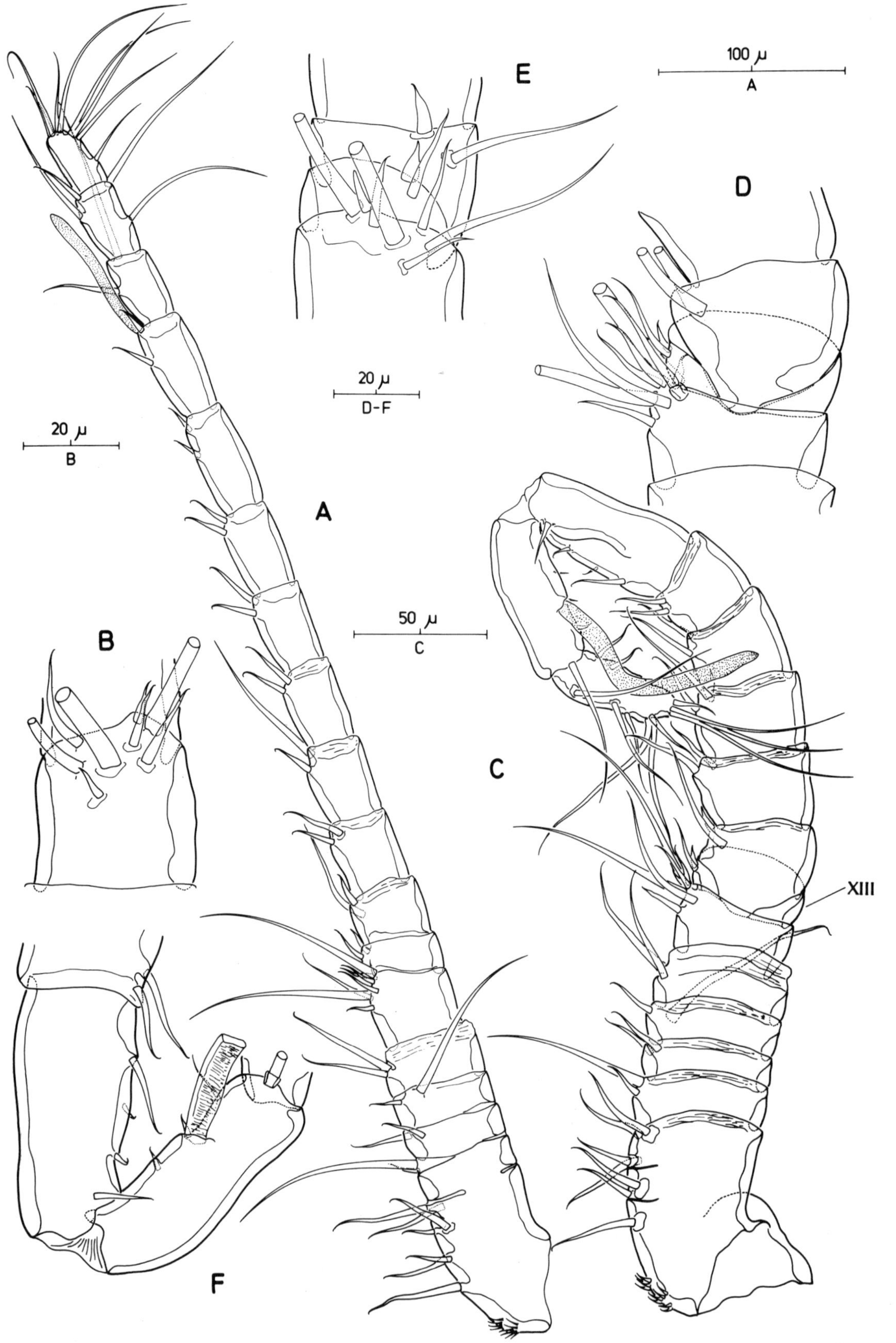

Figure 2.9.7. *Brychiopontius falcatus.* **A.** Female antennule. **B.** Female antennulary segments IX-XII, anterior view. **C.** Male antennule. **D.** Male antennulary segments IX-XIV. **E.** Anterior view of segments IX-XIV. **F.** Segments around geniculation.

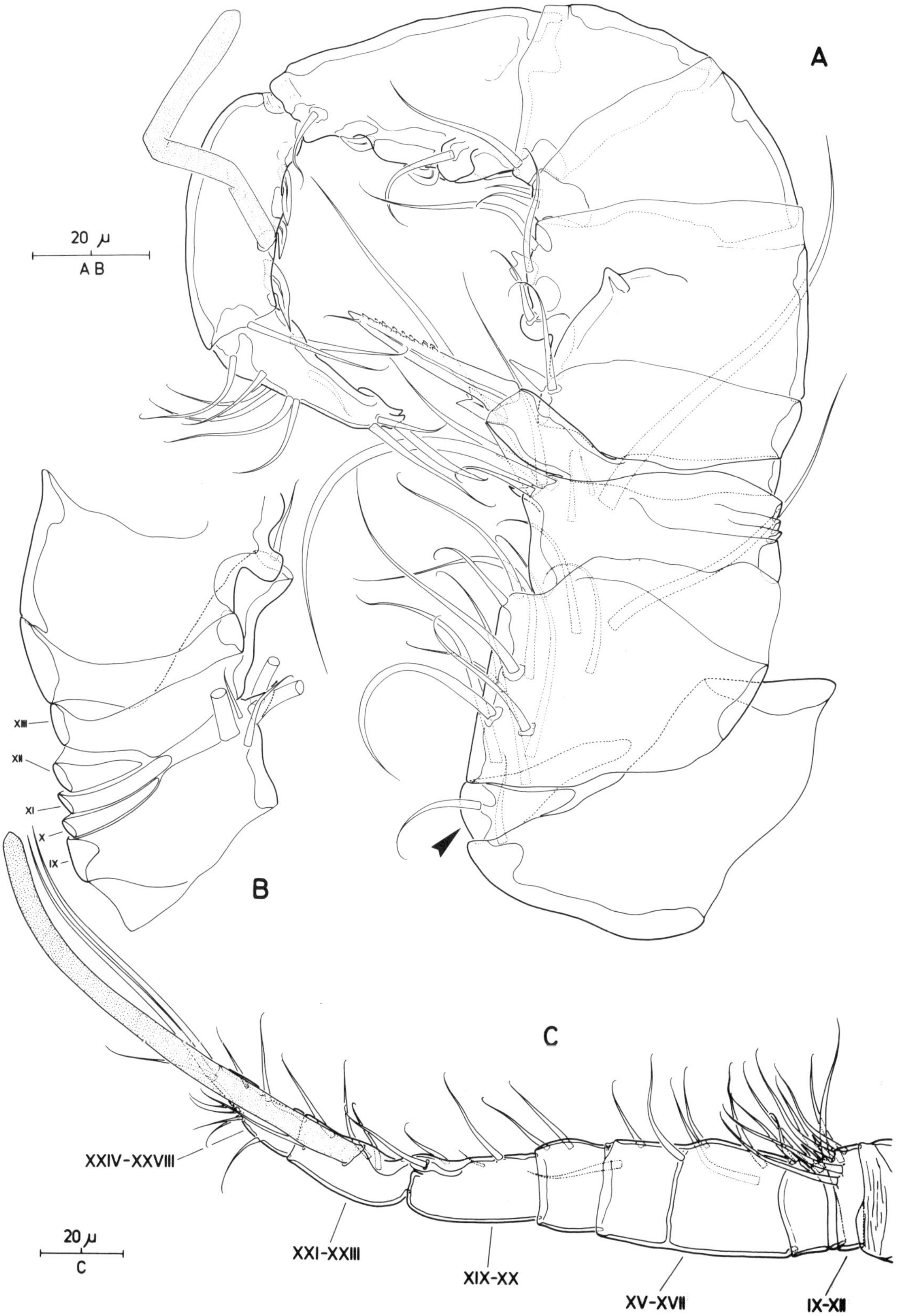

Figure 2.9.8. **A.** *Stygiopontius quadrispinosus*, male antennule (modified, horseshoe-shaped segment II arrowed). **B.** Detail of segments IX-XV. **C.** *Hermacheres montastreae*, distal part of male antennule.

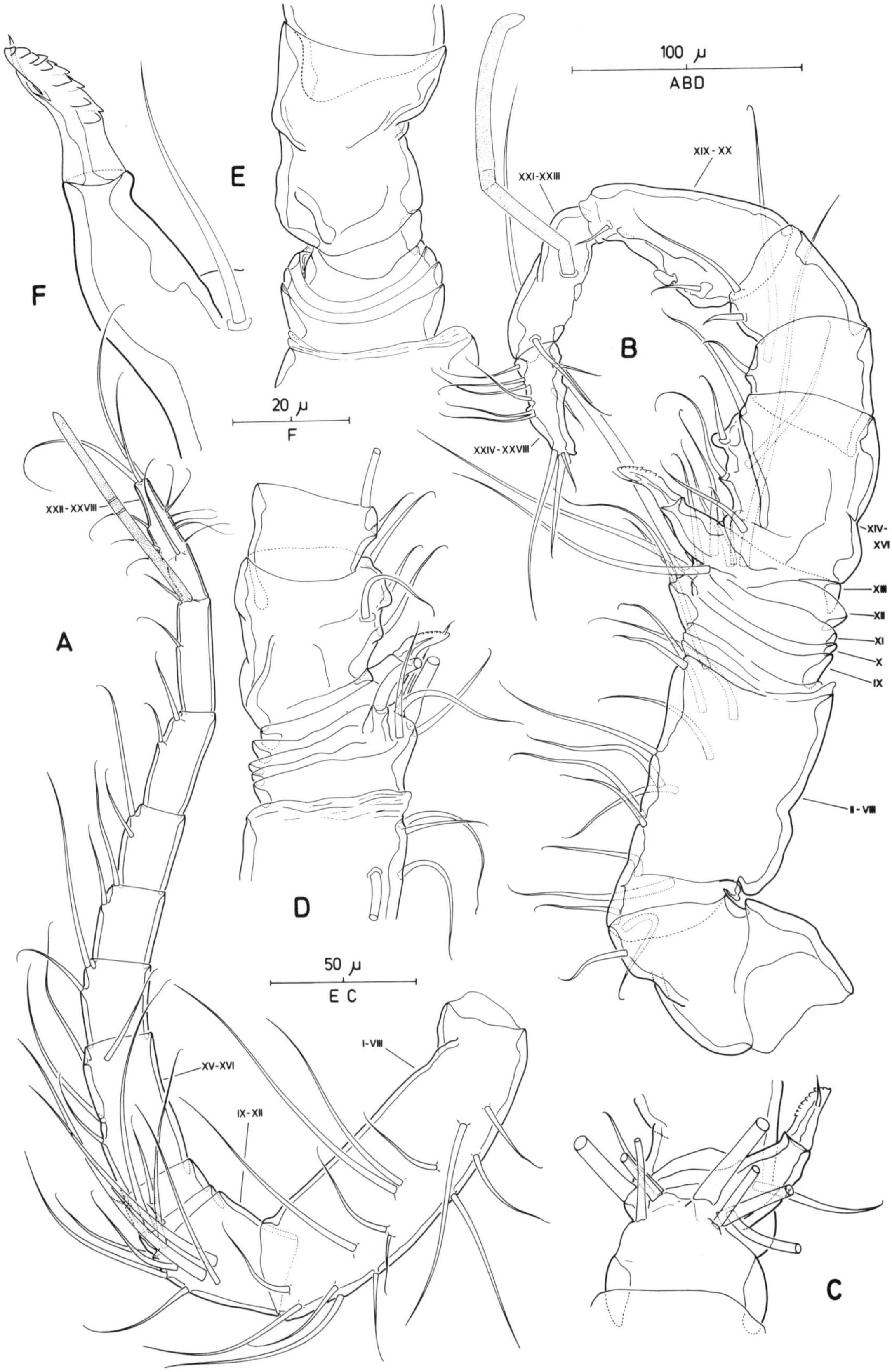

Figure 2.9.9. *Scotoecetes introrsus.* **A.** Female antennule. **B.** Male antennule, with partially fused segments IX to XIII numbered, dorsal view. **C.** Detail showing fused anterior margins of segments IX to XII, anterior view. **D.** Detail of segments IX to XIV-XVI, ventral view. **E.** Same, with setae removed to show segmentation. **F.** Detail of process on segment XIII.

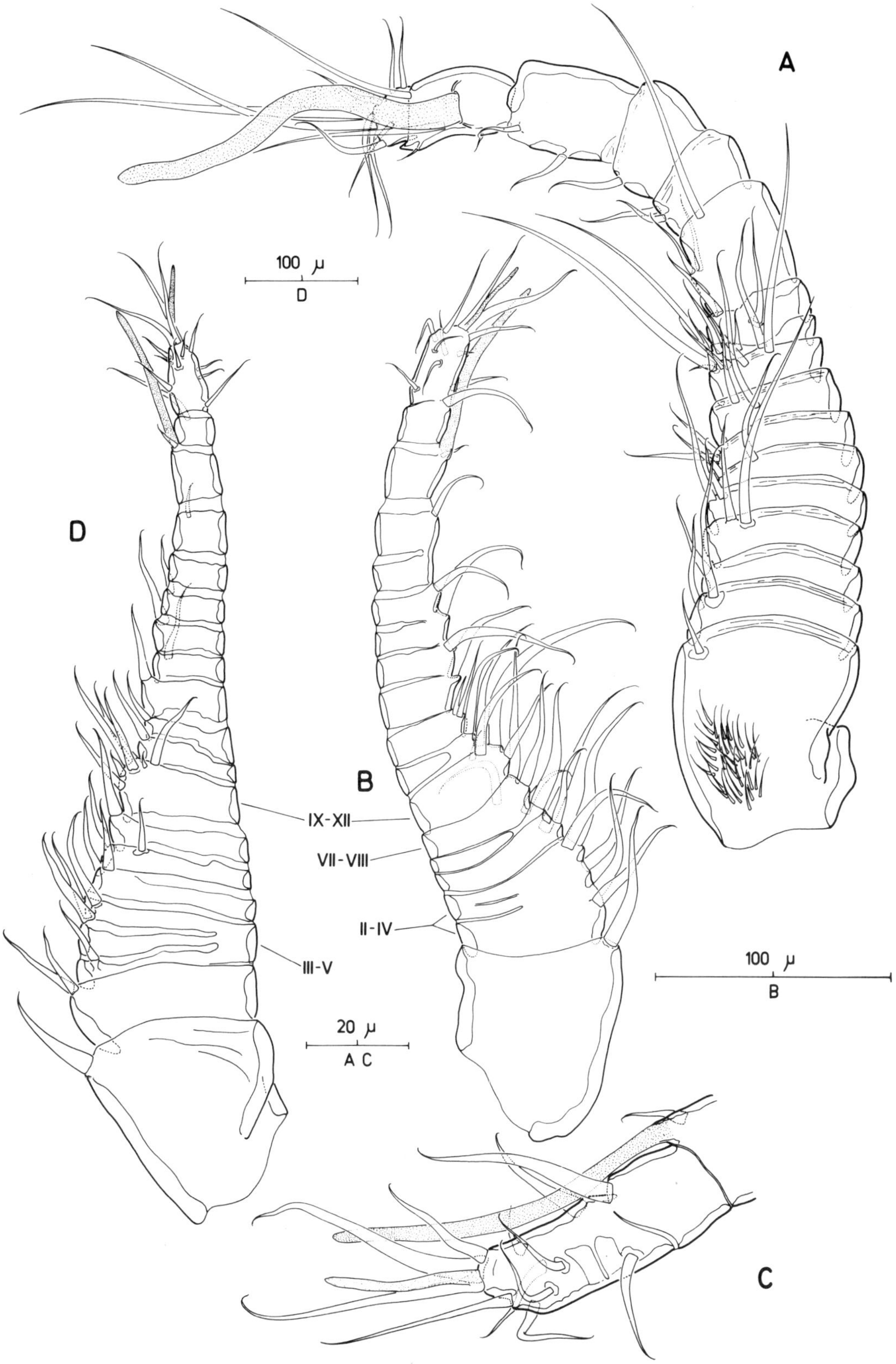

Figure 2.9.10. **A.** *Tuphacheres micropus*, male antennule. **B.** *Protodactylina pamelae*, female antennule. **C.** Female antennulary segment XXII-XXVIII. **D.** *Bariaka alopiae*, female antennule.

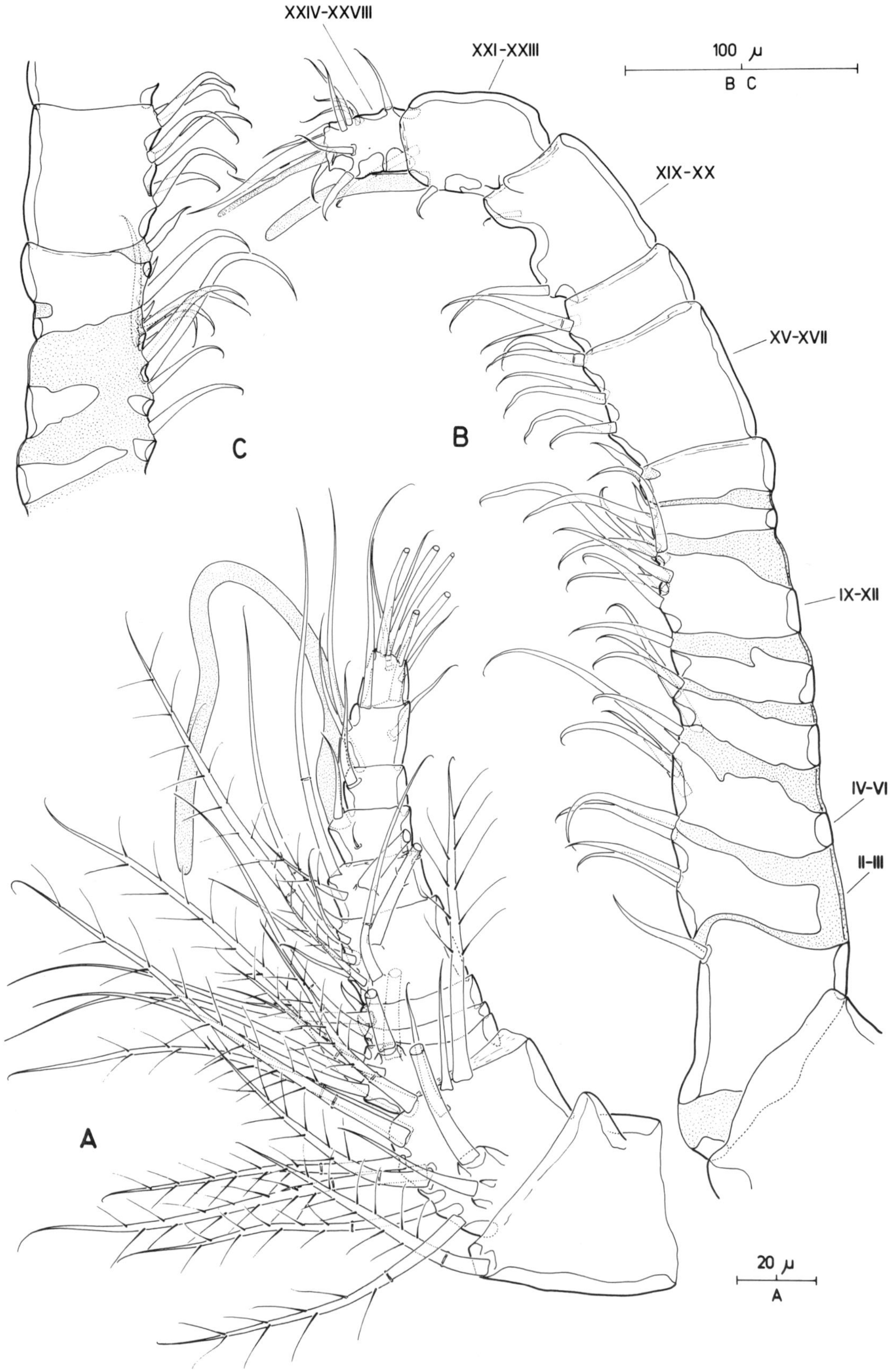

Figure 2.9.11. **A.** *Acontiophorus scutatus*, female antennule. **B.** *Eudactylinella alba*, male antennule. **C.** Male antennulary segments VIII to XVII.

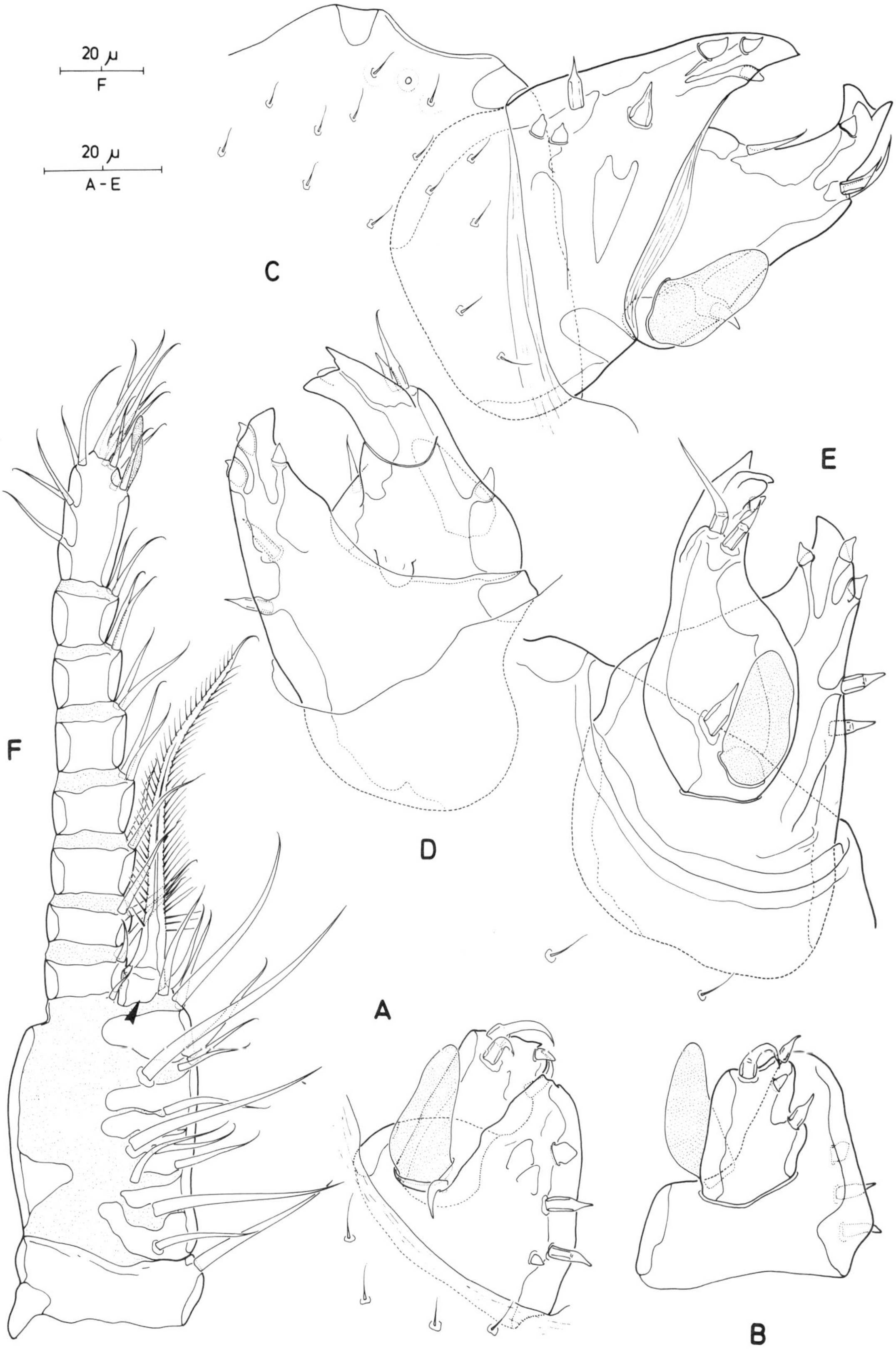

Figure 2.9.12. **A.** *Spongiocnizon vermiformis*, female antennule, dorsal view. **B.** Ventral view. **C.** Male antennule, dorsal view. **D.** Ventral view. **E.** Postero-lateral view. **F.** *Paranicothoe cladocera*, male antennule, with arrow showing seta with swollen base that was misinterpreted as the exopod.

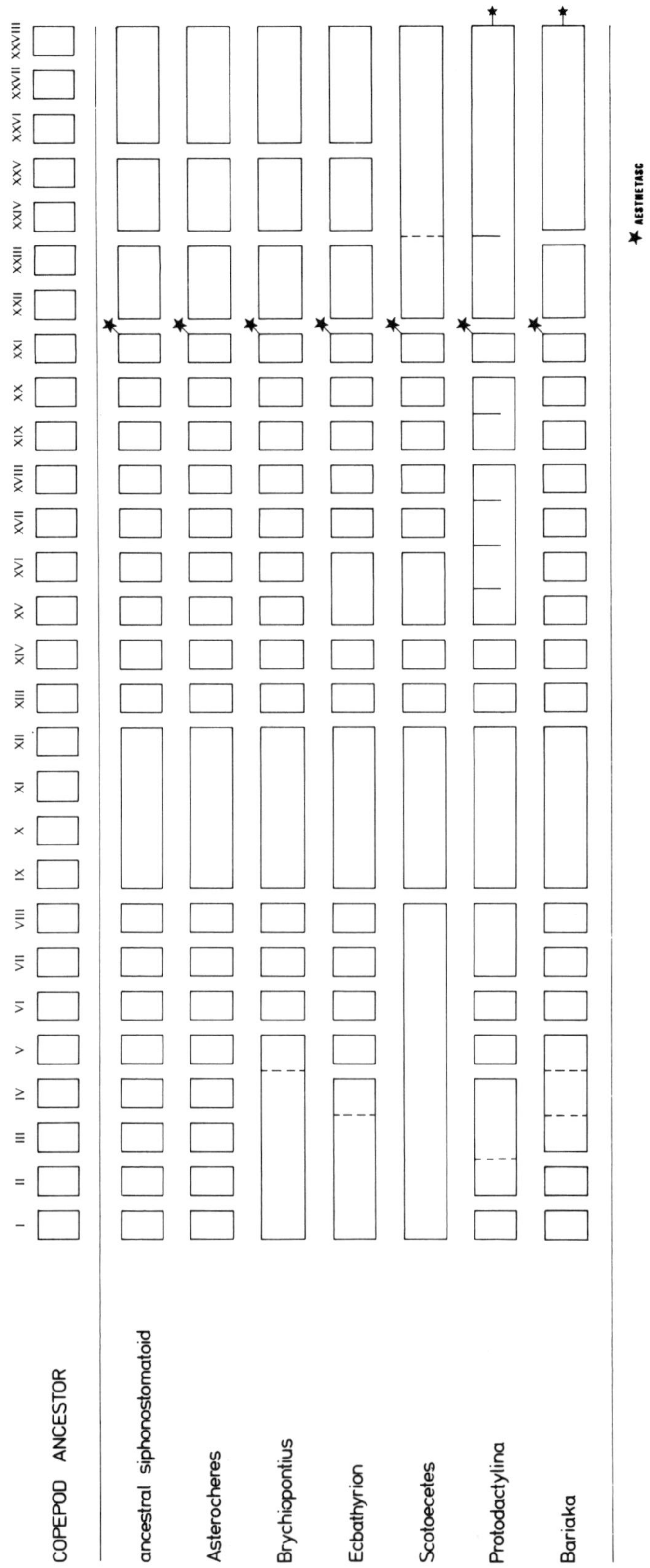

Figure 2.9.13. Schematic comparison of segmental homologies in the antennules of female siphonostomatoids.

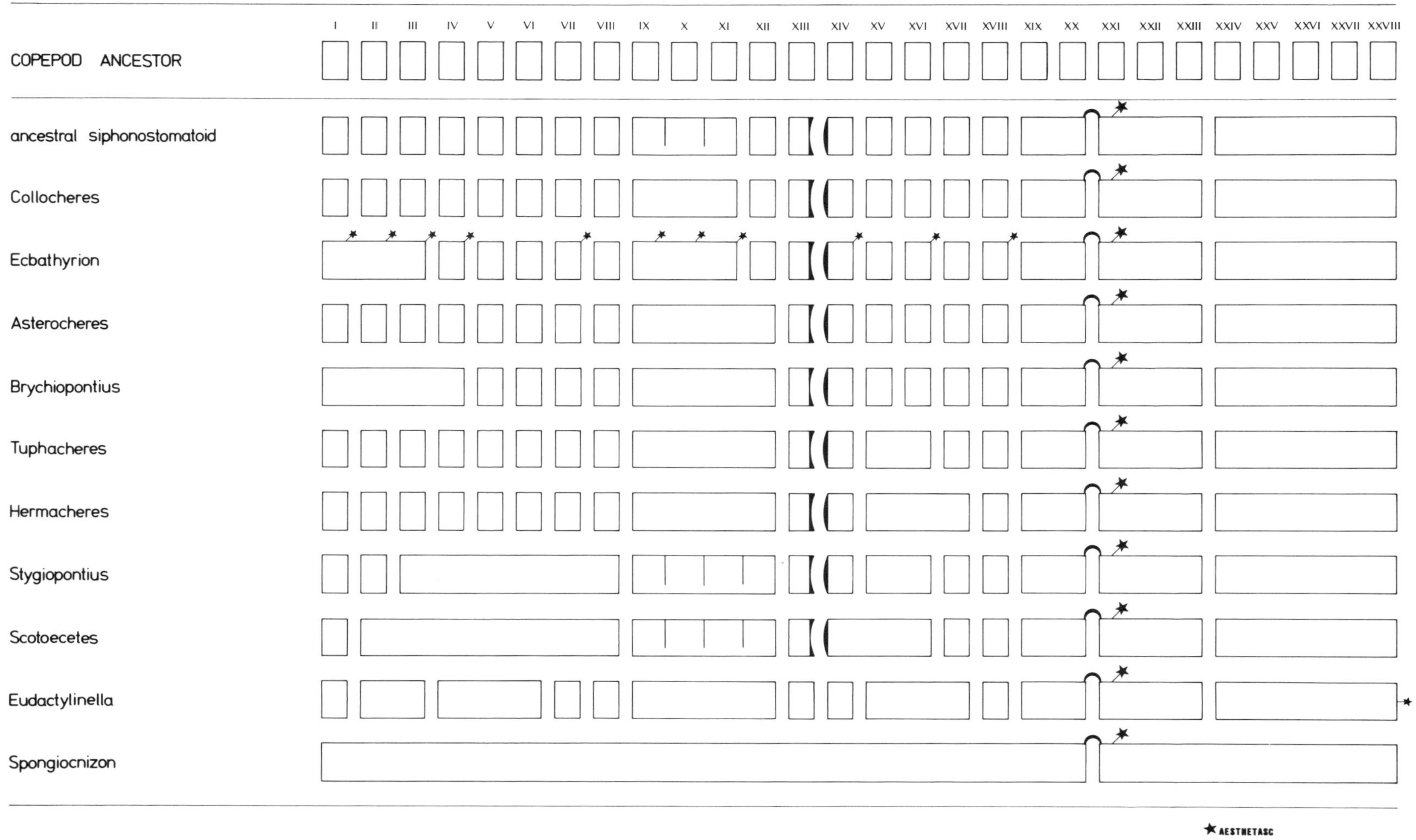

Figure 2.9.14. Schematic comparison of segmental homologies in the antennules of male siphonostomatoids, showing positions of aesthetascs, the neocopepodan geniculation and the modified joint between XIII and XIV.

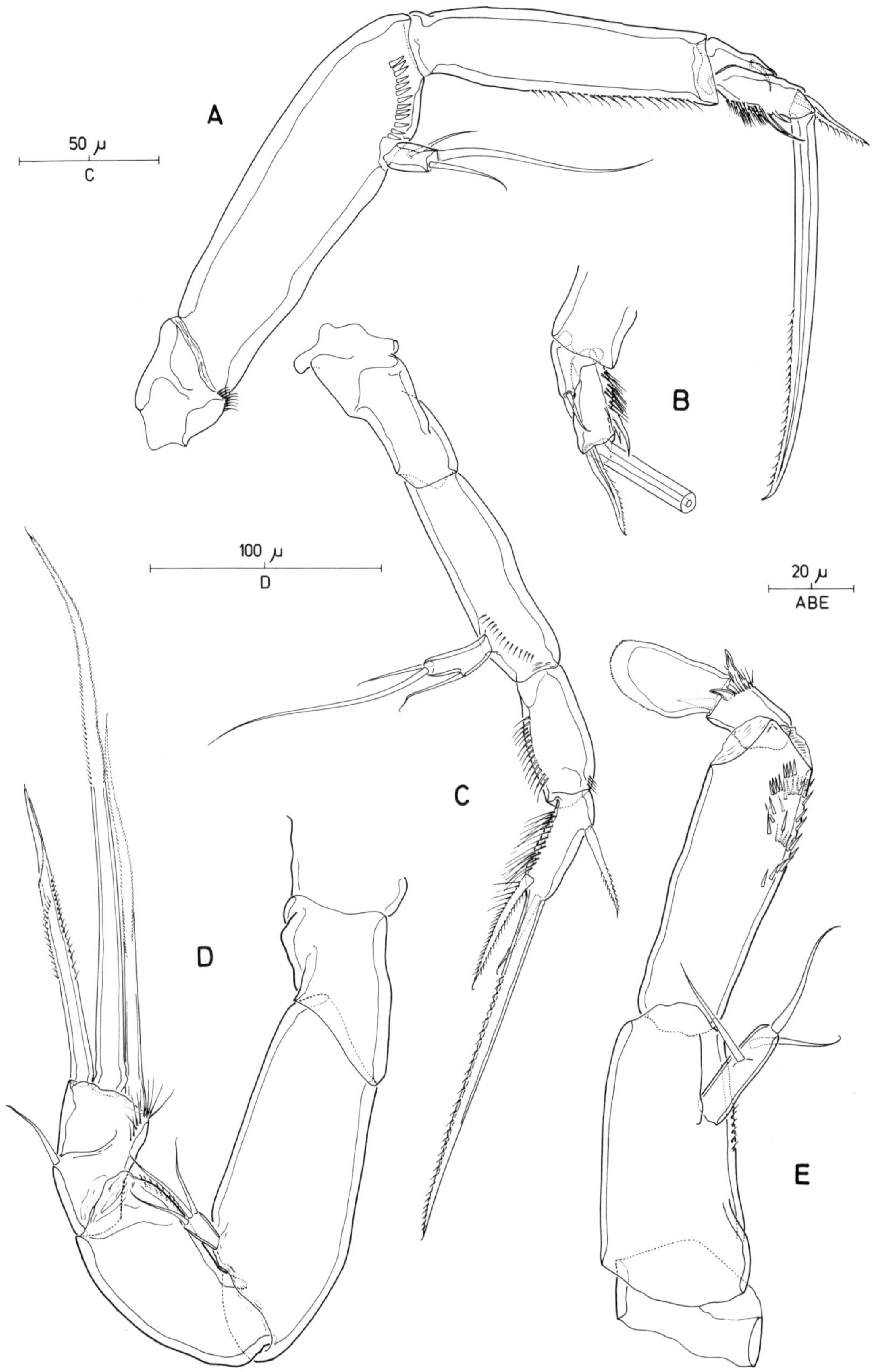

Figure 2.9.15. Antennae. **A**. *Asterocheres reginae*. **B**. Detail of apex of endopod. **C.** *Australomyzon typicus*. **D.** *Scotoecetes introrsus*. **E.** *Brychiopontius falcatus*.

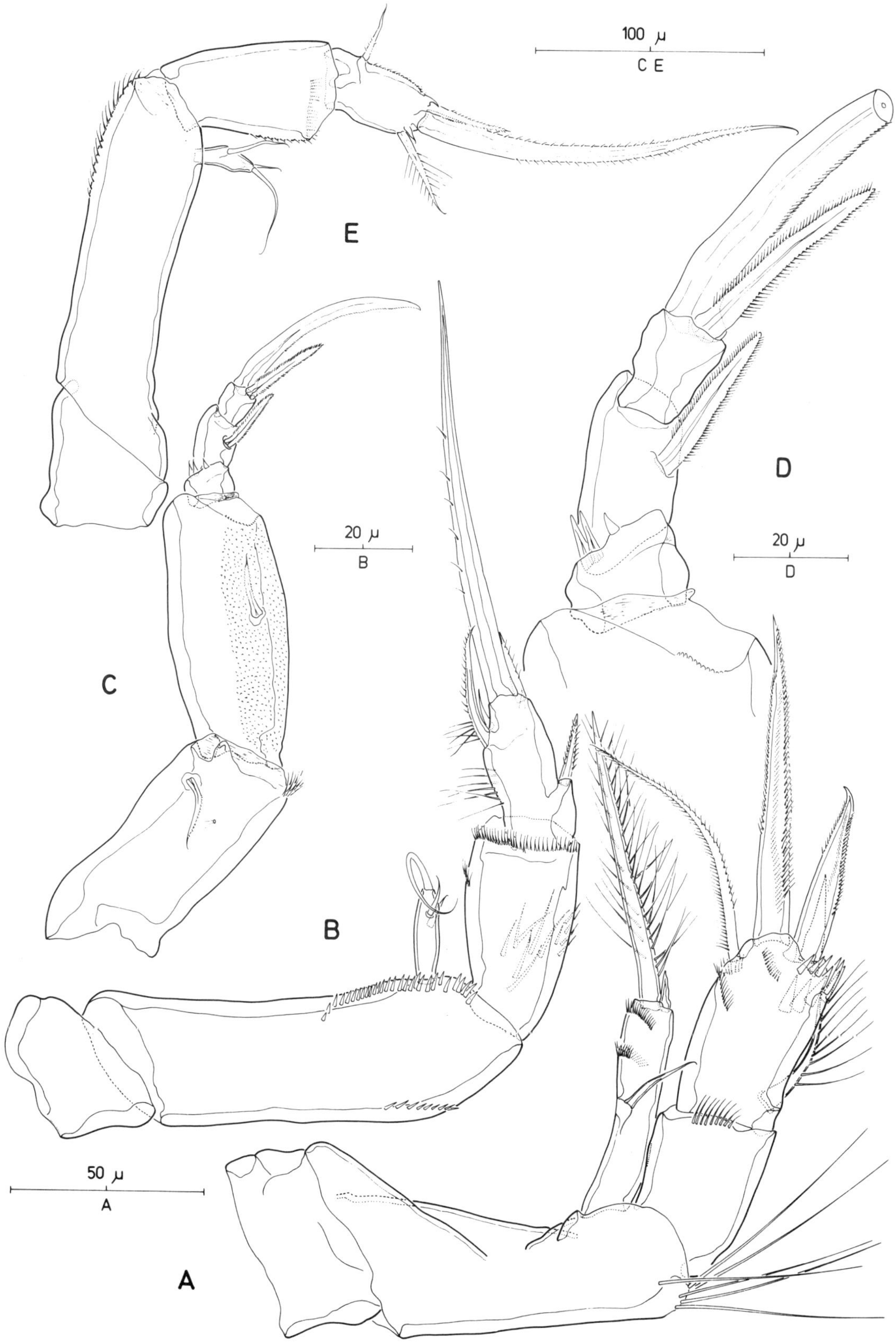

Figure 2.9.16. Antennae. **A.** *Acontiophorus scutatus*. **B.** *Dermatomyzon nigripes*. **C.** *Nicothoe astaci*, maxilliped. **D.** Detail of endopod of maxilliped. **E.** *Rhynchomyzon compactum*, antenna.

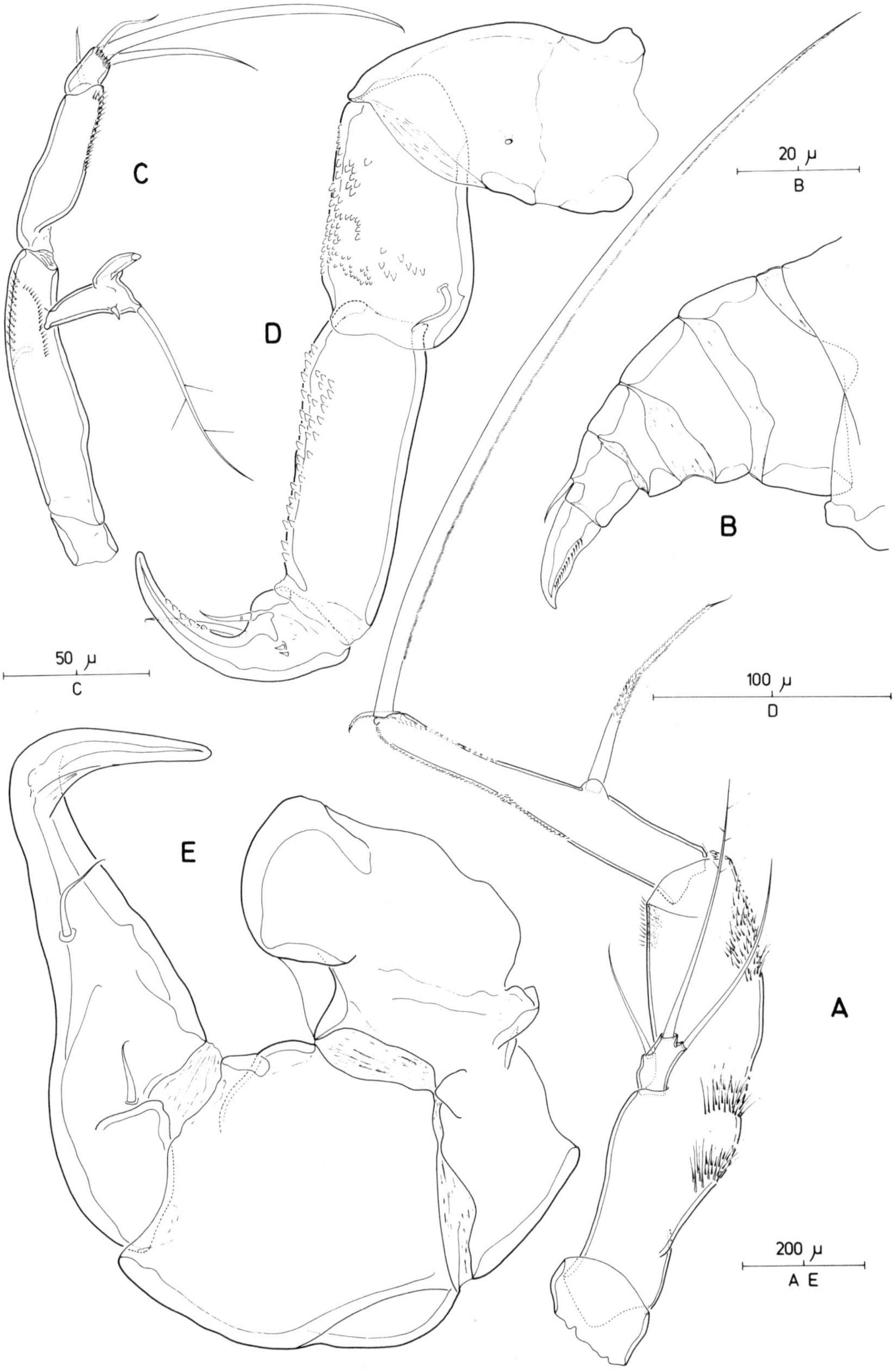

Figure 2.9.17. Antennae. **A.** *Hyalopontius typicus*. **B.** *Spongiocnizon vermiformis*. **C.** *Ecbathyrion prolixicauda*. **D.** *Eudactylinella alba*, male. **E.** *Lepeophtheirus salmonis*.

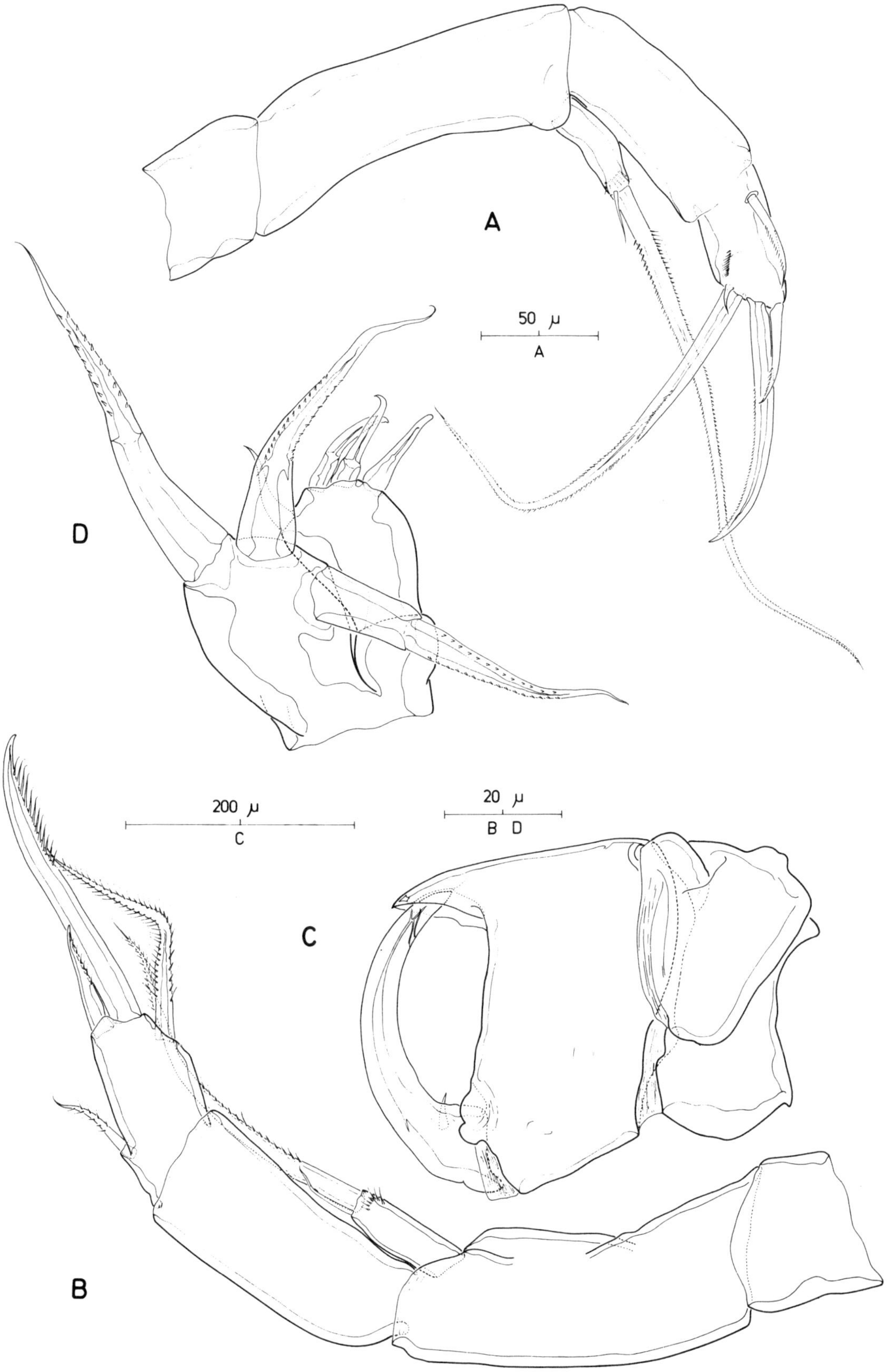

Figure 2.9.18. Antennae. **A.** *Hammatimyzon dimorphum*, female. **B.** *H.dimorphum* male. **C.** *Lernaeocera* sp. **D.** *Nicothoe astaci*, maxillule.

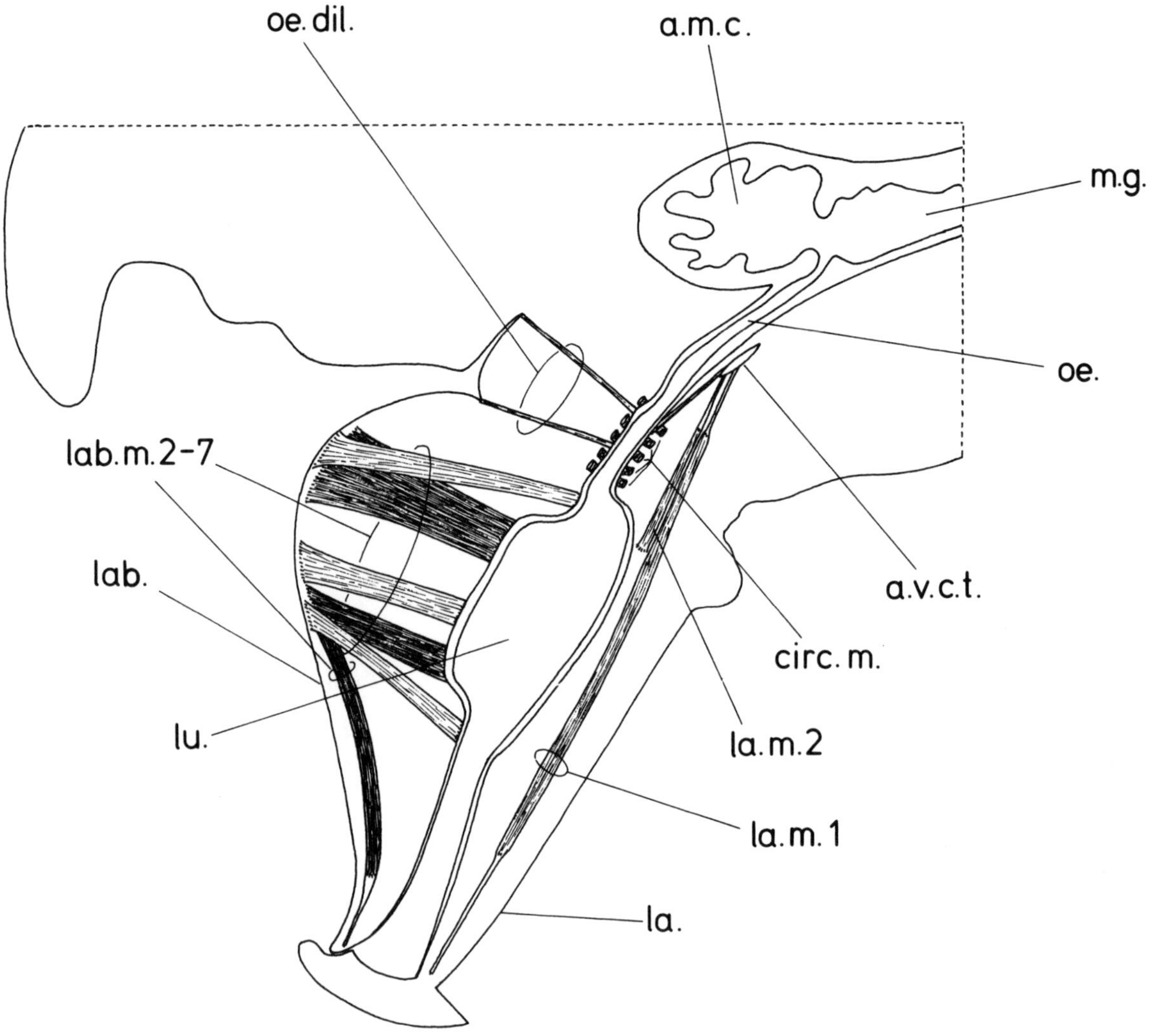

Figure 2.9.19. Median longitudinal section through oral cone of *Hyalopontius typicus* showing labral and labial musculature. [Abbreviations: **a.m.c.** = anterior midgut caecum, **a.v.c.t.** = anterior ventral cephalic tendon, **circ.m.** = circular muscles, **la.** = labium, **lab** = labrum, **lab.m.2-7** = labral muscles 2-7, **la.m.1-2** = labial muscles 1-2, **lu.** = lumen, **mg.** = midgut, **oe.** = oesophagus, **oe.dil.** = oesophageal dilator muscles.]

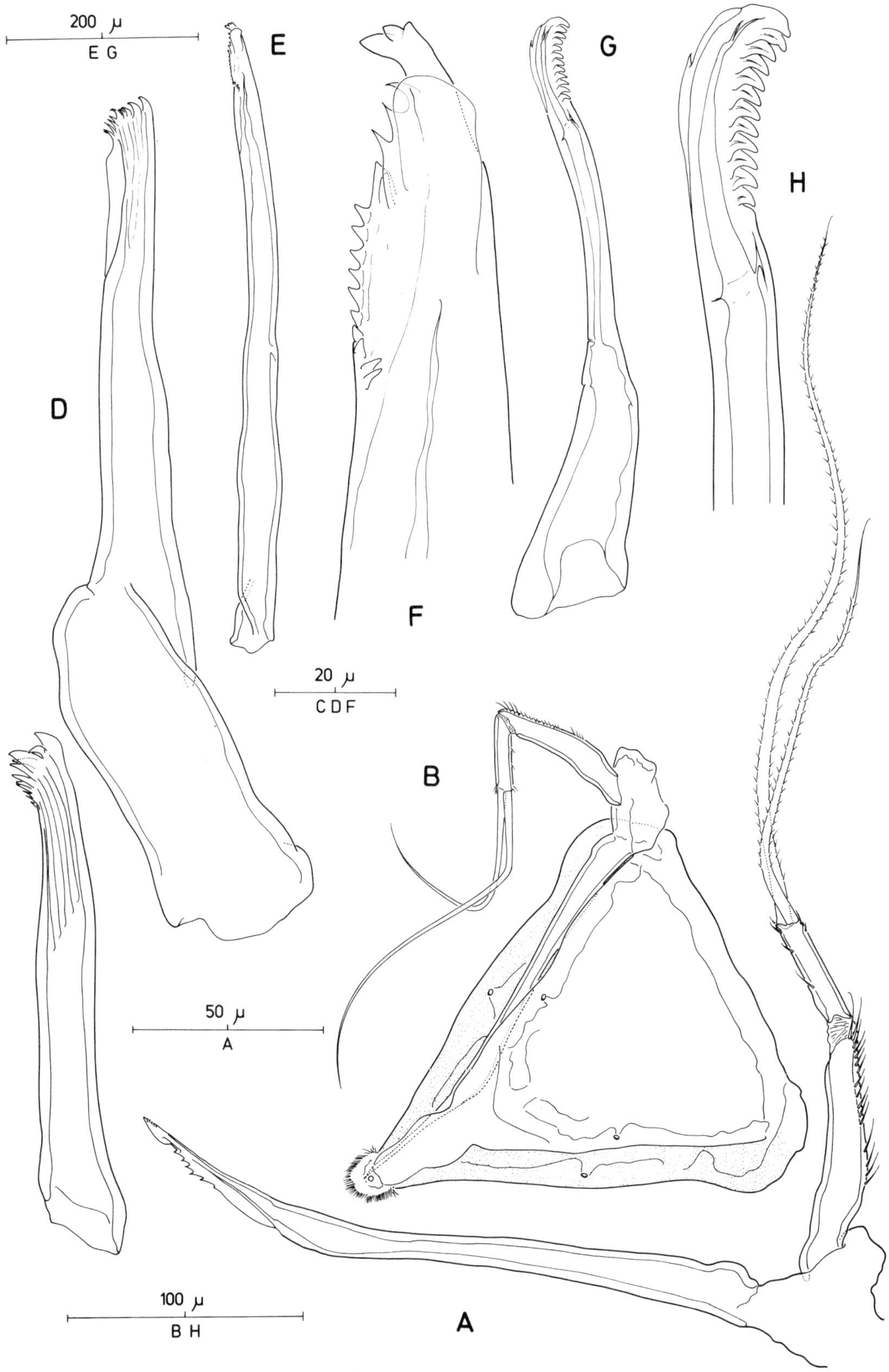

Figure 2.9.20. **A.** *Asterocheres reginae*, mandible. **B.** Oral cone and mandible. **C.** *Ecbathyrion prolixicauda*, mandible. **D.** *Brychiopontius falcatus*, mandible. **E.** *Hyalopontius typicus*, mandible. **F.** Distal end of gnathobase. **G.** *Lepeophtheirus salmonis*, mandible. **H.** Distal end of gnathobase.

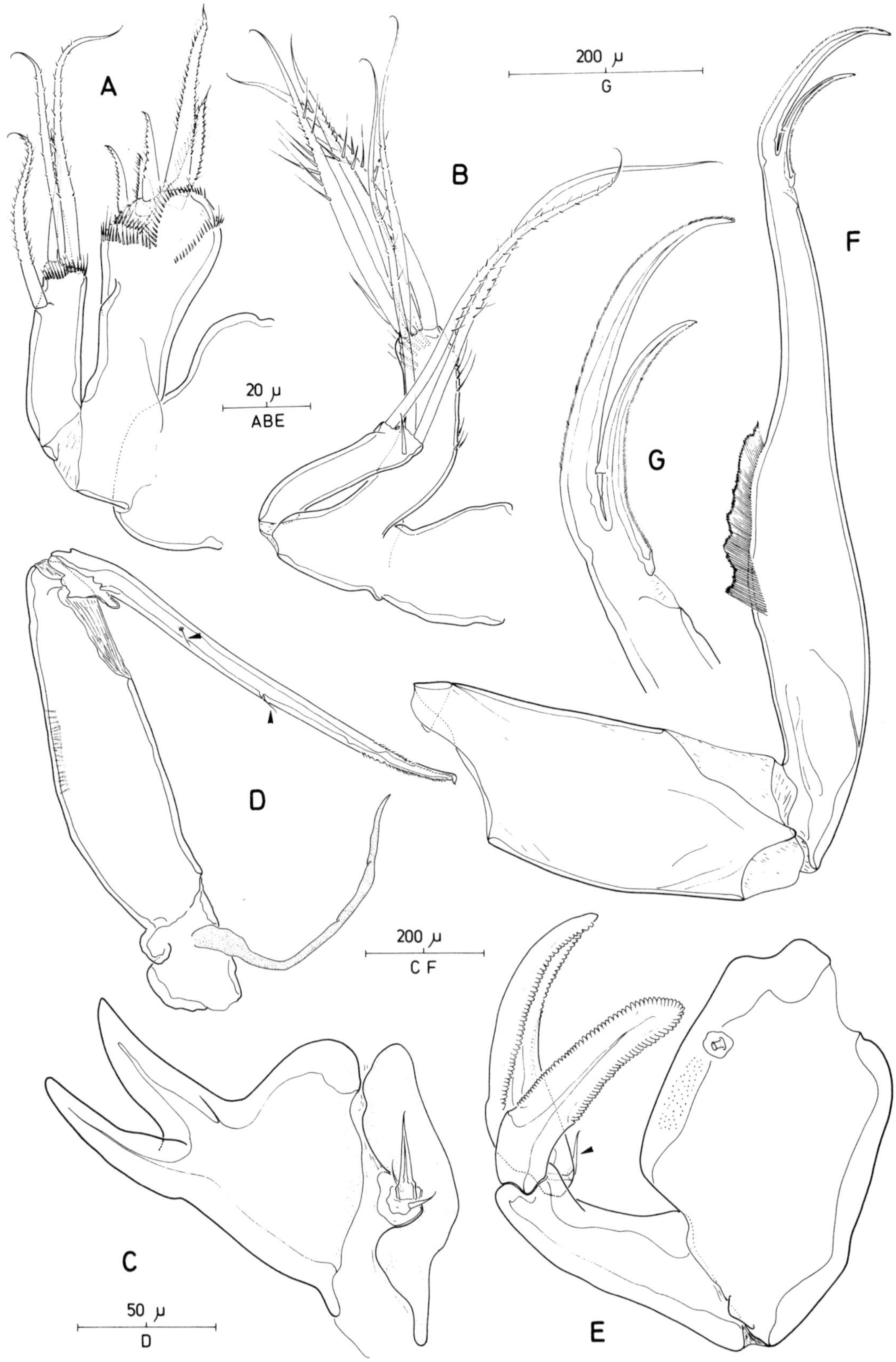

Figure 2.9.21. **A.** *Brychiopontius falcatus*, maxillule. **B.** *Ecbathyrion prolixicauda*, maxillule. **C.** *Lepeophtheirus salmonis*, maxillule. **D.** *Asterocheres reginae*, maxilla (minute setae arrowed). **E.** *Nicothoe astaci*, maxilla (minute seta arrowed). **F.** *L.salmonis*, maxilla. **G.** Distal end of maxillary allobasis.

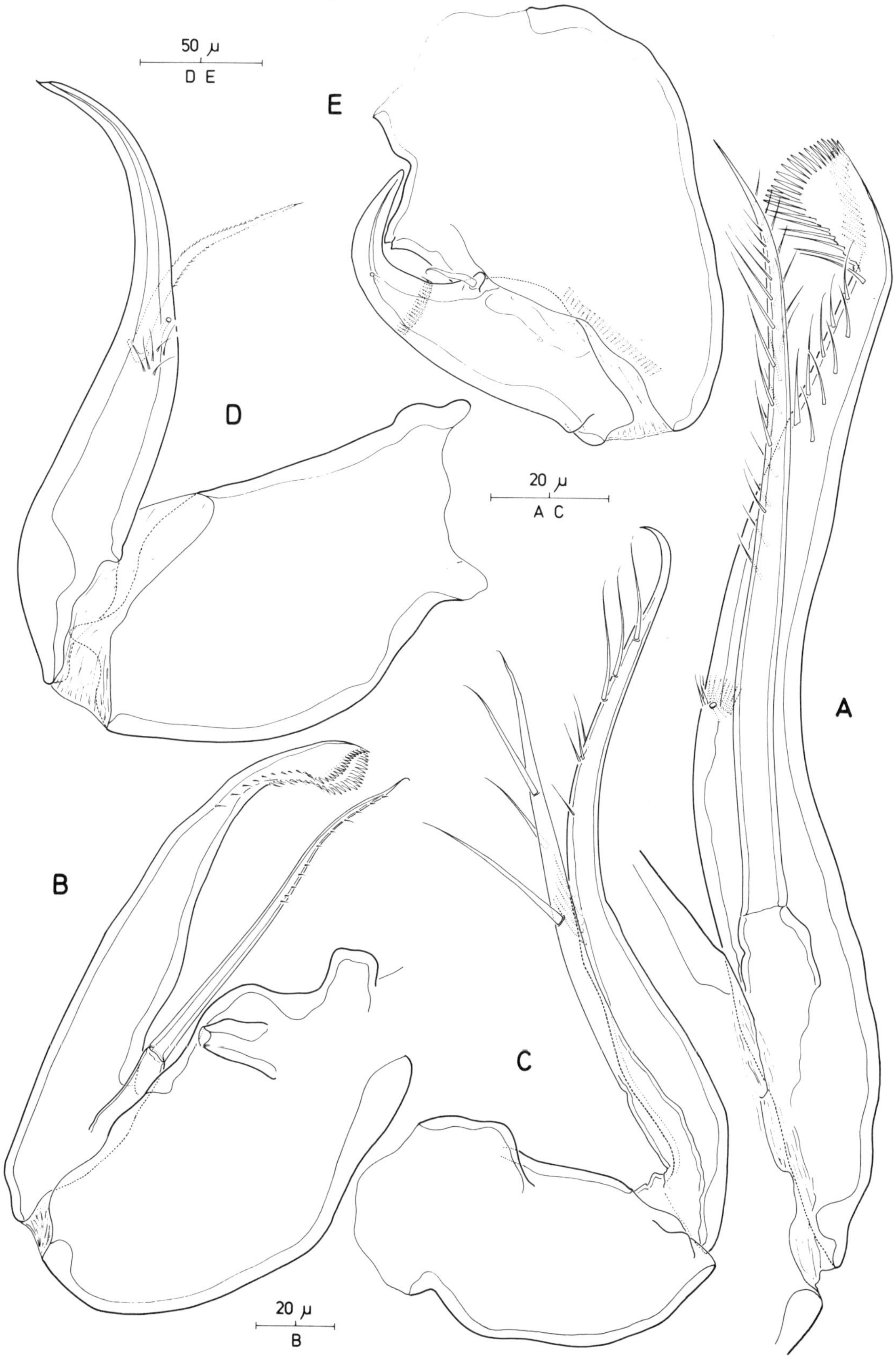

Figure 2.9.22. Maxillae. **A.** *Stygiopontius cinctiger* (basis only). **B.** *Scotoecetes introrsus.* **C.** *Ecbathyrion prolixicauda.* **D.** *Hammatimyzon dimorphum.* **E.** *Brychiopontius falcatus.*

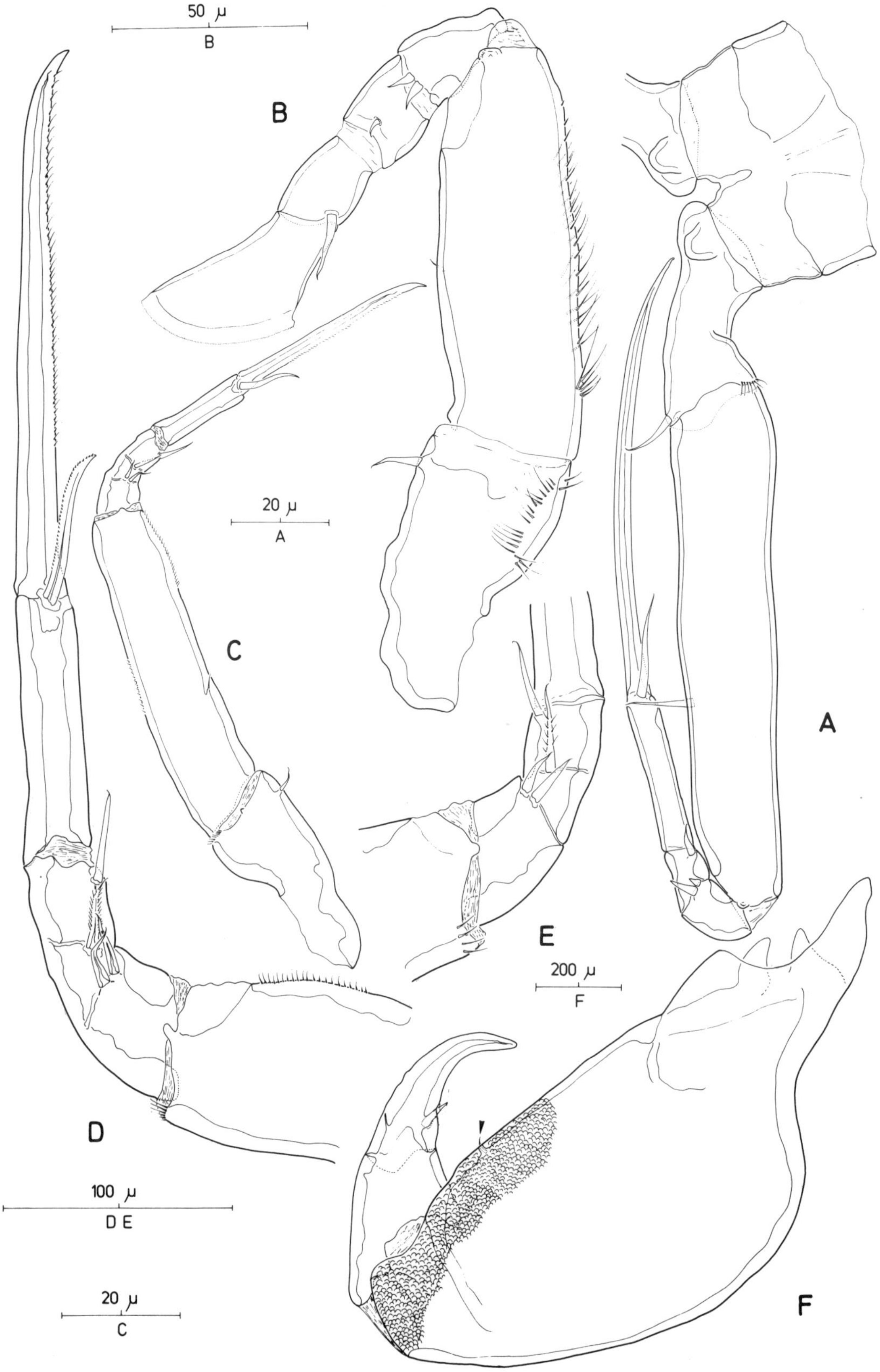

Figure 2.9.23. Maxillipeds. **A.** *Ecbathyrion prolixicauda* (including pedestal). **B.** *Brychiopontius falcatus*. **C.** *Asterocheres reginae*, female maxilliped. **D.** Female endopod. **E.** Male endopod, proximal segments. **F.** *Lepeophtheirus salmonis* (minute seta derived from basis arrowed on protopod).

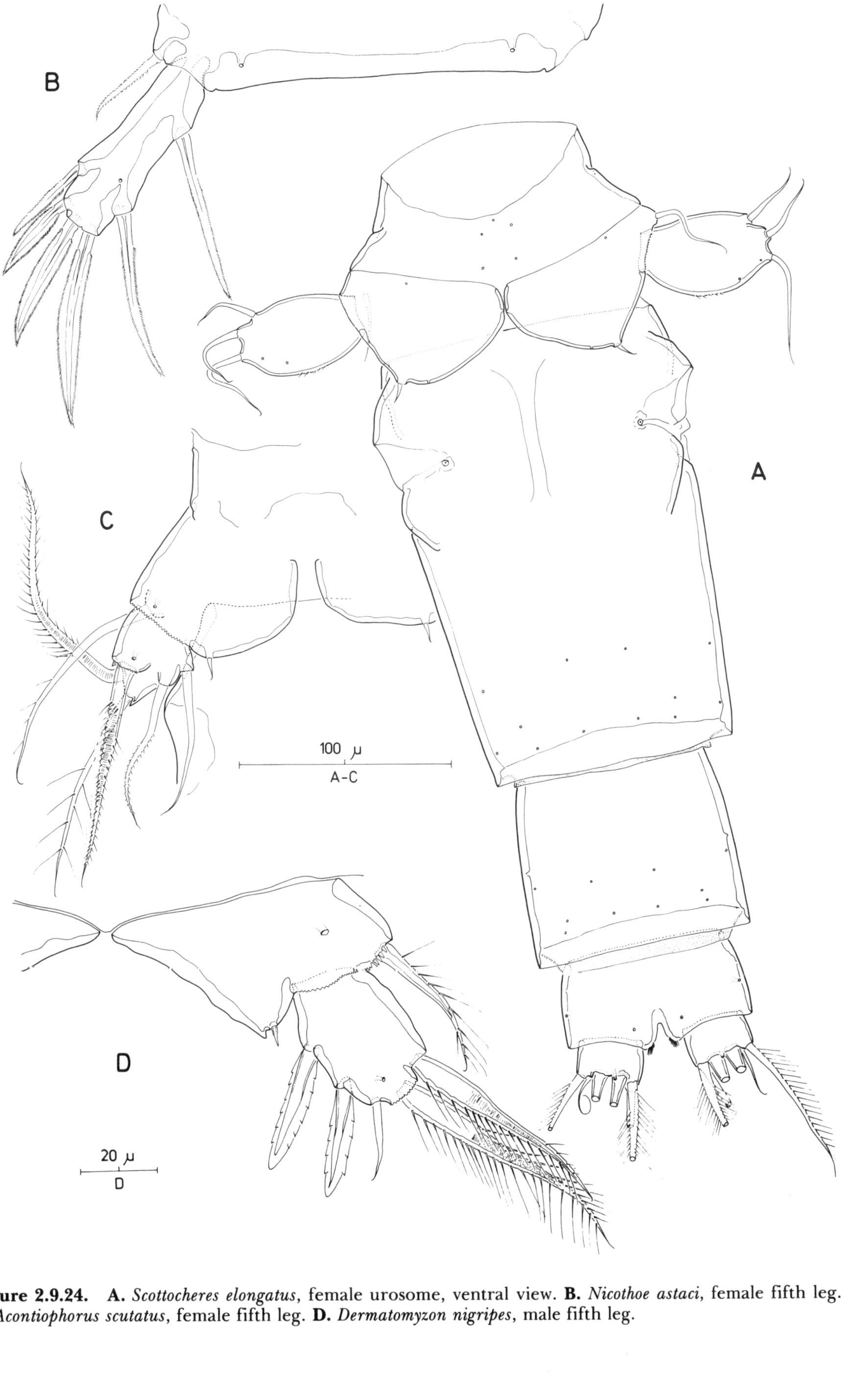

Figure 2.9.24. **A.** *Scottocheres elongatus*, female urosome, ventral view. **B.** *Nicothoe astaci*, female fifth leg. **C.** *Acontiophorus scutatus*, female fifth leg. **D.** *Dermatomyzon nigripes*, male fifth leg.

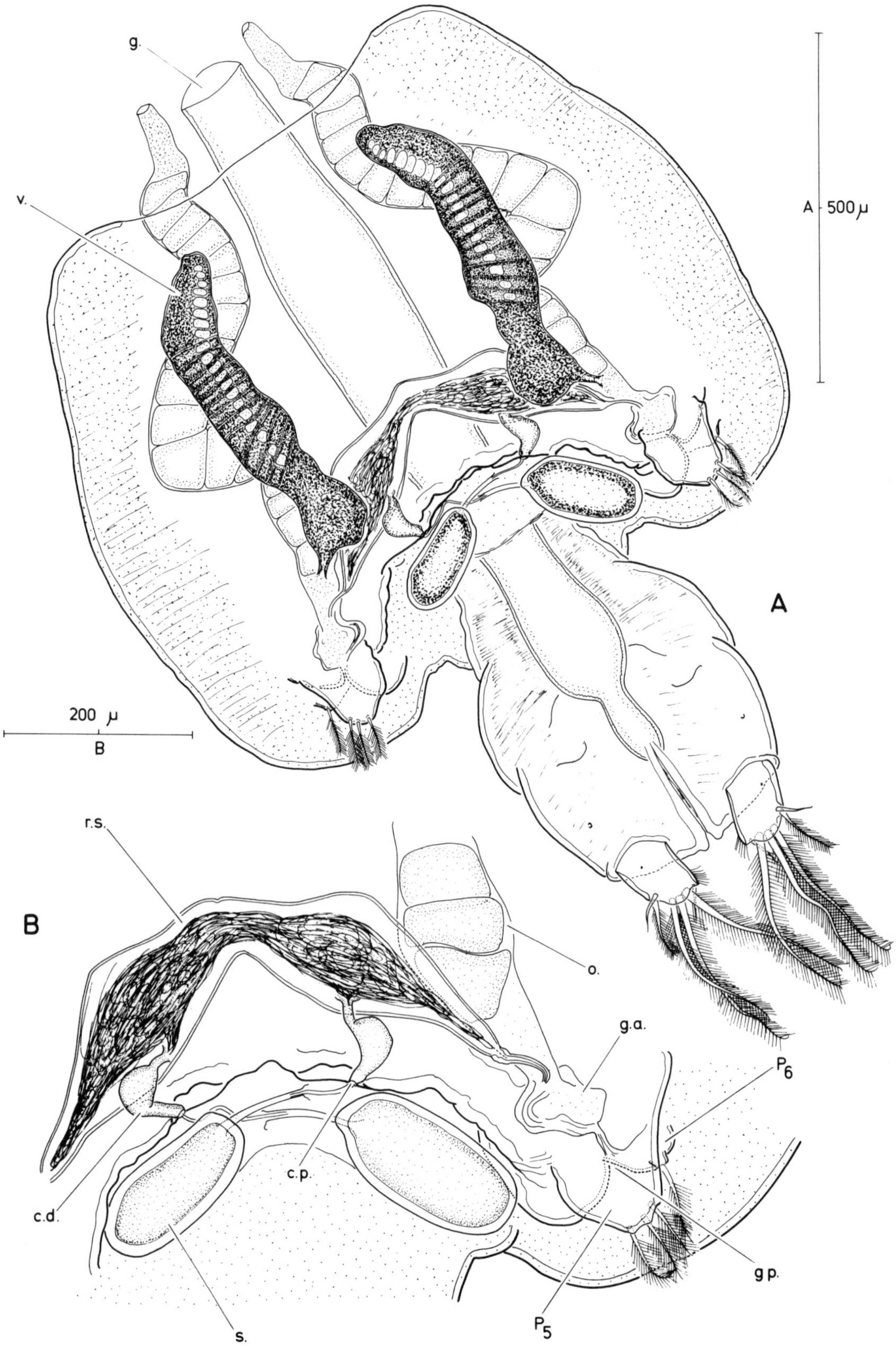

Figure 2.9.25. *Lepeophtheirus pectoralis* female. **A.**. Genital complex and abdomen, showing internal anatomy. **B.** Detail of genital apertures. [Abbreviations: **g.** = gut; **v.** = vitellarium; **o.** = oviduct; **r.s.** = seminal receptacle; **c.d.** = copulatory duct; **s.** = spermatophore; **g.a.** = genital antrum; **c.p.** = copulatory pore; **gp.** = gonopore.]

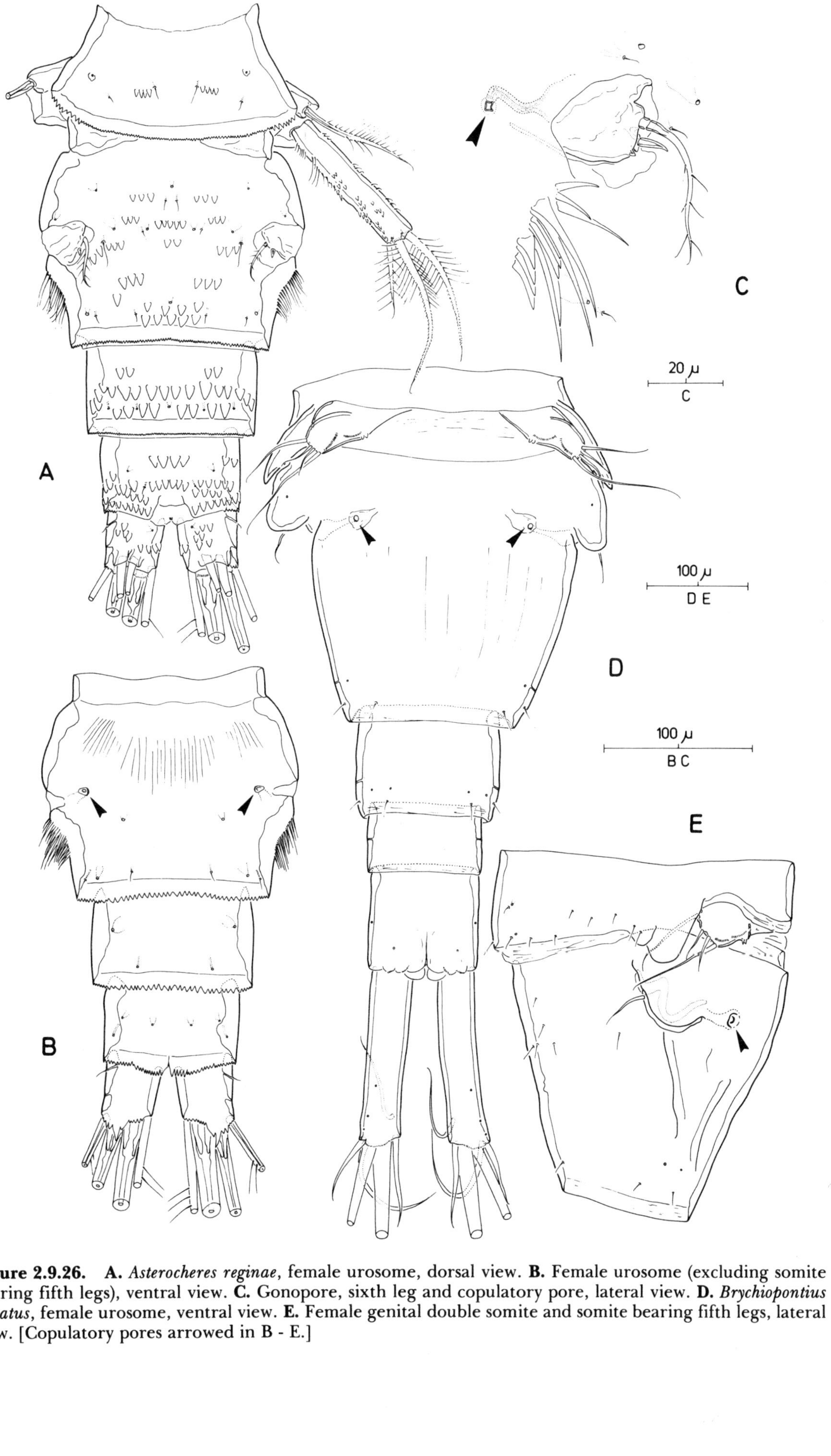

Figure 2.9.26. **A.** *Asterocheres reginae*, female urosome, dorsal view. **B.** Female urosome (excluding somite bearing fifth legs), ventral view. **C.** Gonopore, sixth leg and copulatory pore, lateral view. **D.** *Brychiopontius falcatus*, female urosome, ventral view. **E.** Female genital double somite and somite bearing fifth legs, lateral view. [Copulatory pores arrowed in B - E.]

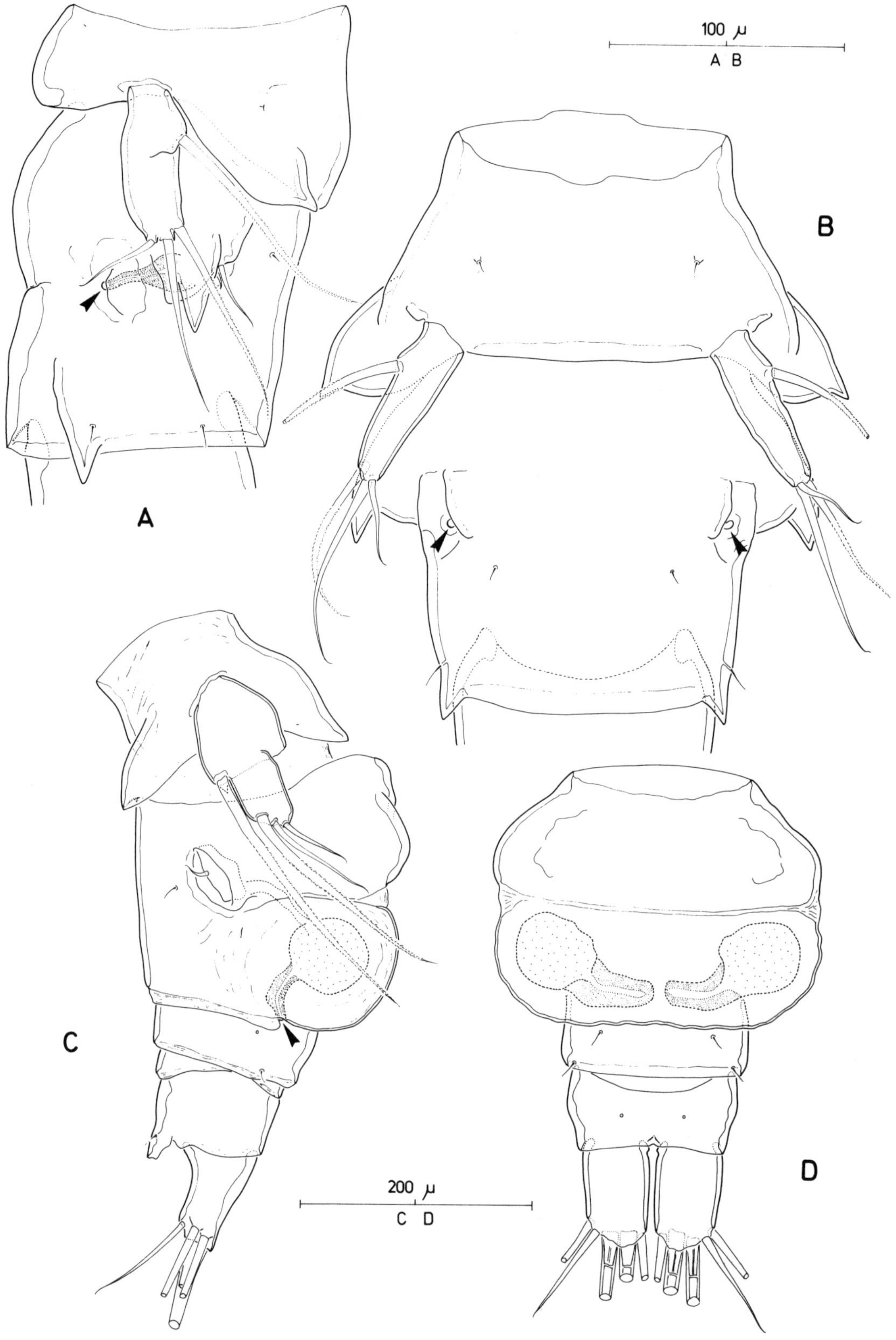

Figure 2.9.27. **A.** *Stygiopontius stabilitus*, female genital double somite and somite bearing fifth legs, lateral view. **B.** Ventral view. **C.** *S.cinctiger*, female urosome, lateral view. **D.** Female urosome (excluding somite bearing fifth legs), ventral view. [Copulatory pores arrowed in A - C.]

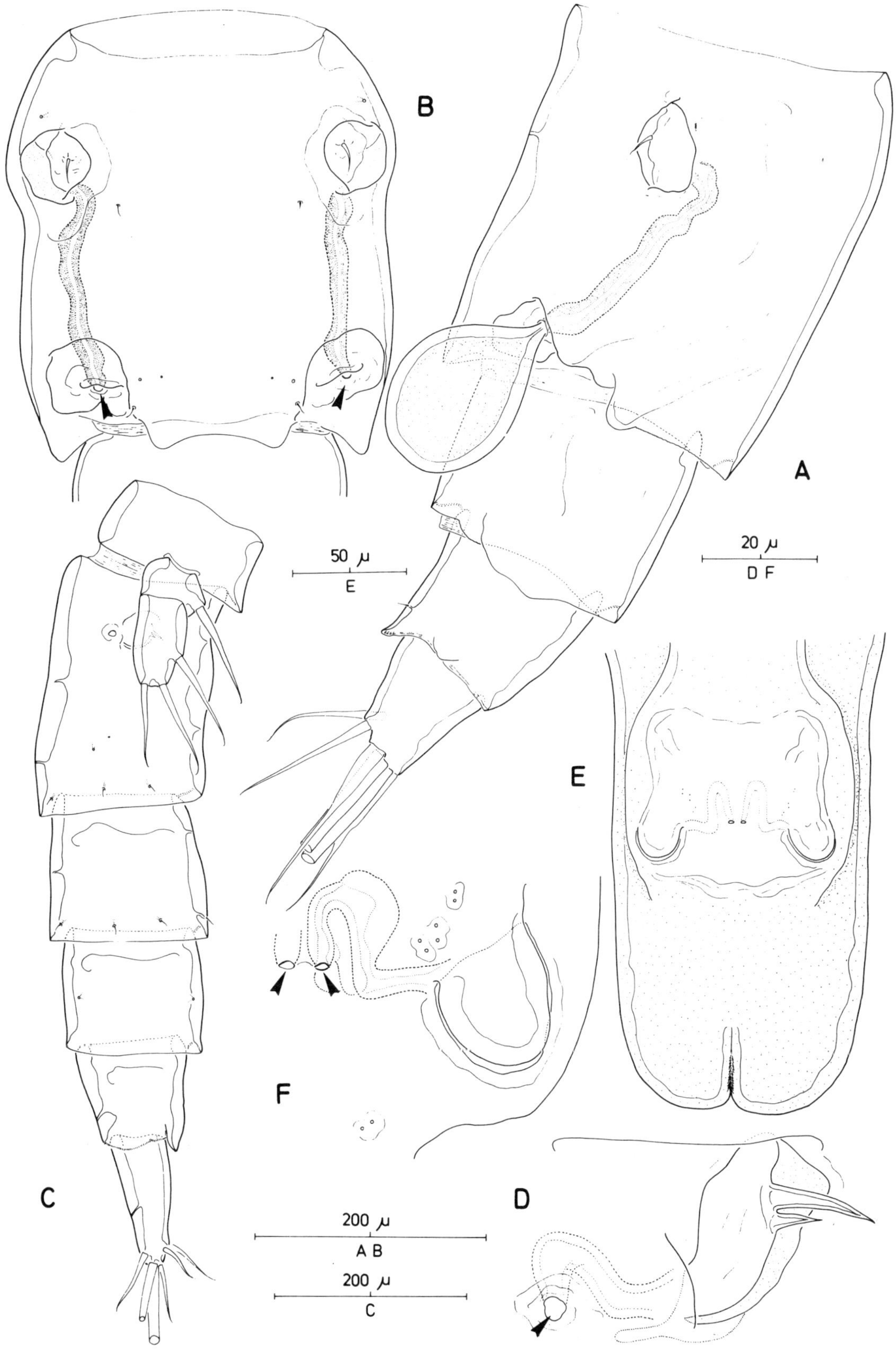

Figure 2.9.28. **A.** *Chasmatopontius thescalus*, female urosome (excluding fifth pedigerous somite), with spermatophore attached, lateral view. **B.** Female genital double somite, dorsal view. **C.** *Fissuricola caritus*, female urosome, lateral view. **D.** Female gonopore and copulatory pore, lateral view. **E.** *Spongiocnizon vermiformis*, genitoabdominal region of female, ventral view. **F.** Left gonopore and copulatory pores, ventral view. [Copulatory pores arrowed in B, D and F.]

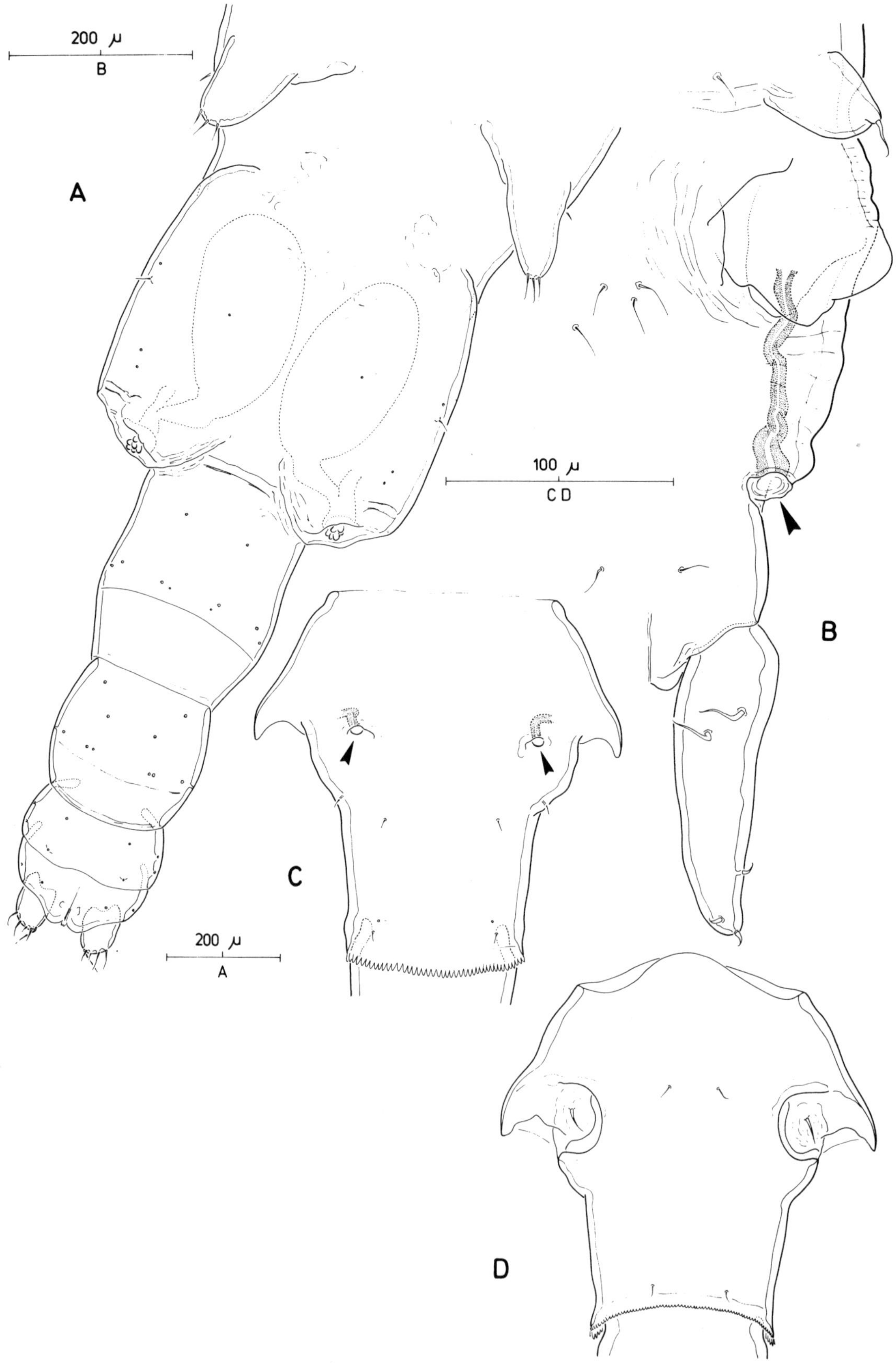

Figure 2.9.29. **A.** *Bariaka alopiae*, female urosome, ventral view. **B.** *Lernanthropus kroyeri*, left half of female urosome, ventral view. **C.** *Ecbathyrion prolixicauda*, female genital double somite, ventral view. **D.** Dorsal view. [Copulatory pores arrowed in B and C.]

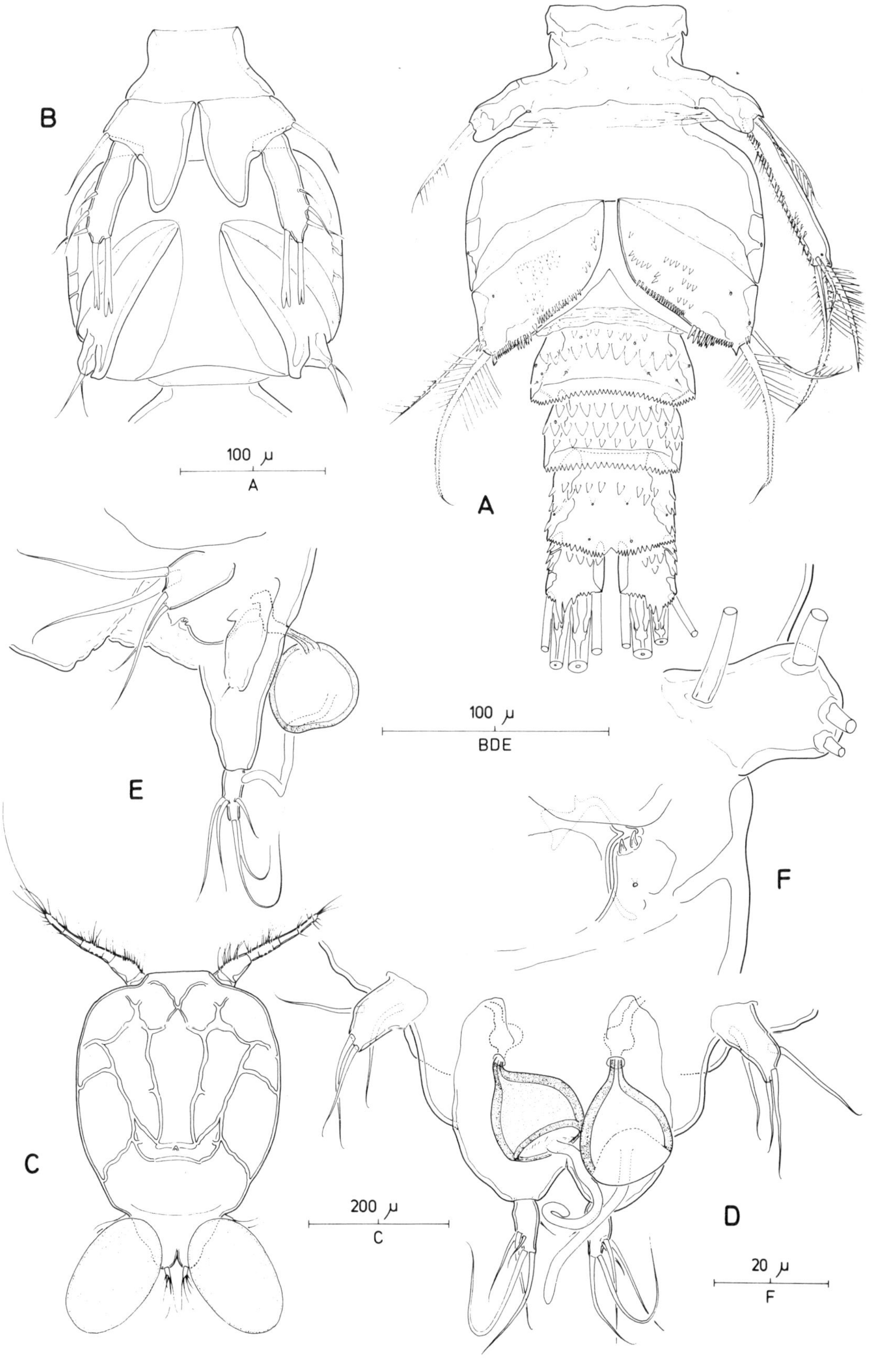

Figure 2.9.30. **A.** *Asterocheres reginae*, male urosome (right fifth leg removed), ventral view. **B.** *Collocheres comanthiphilus*, male genital somite and somite bearing fifth legs, ventral view. **C.** *Stellicomes supplicans*, ovigerous female, dorsal view. **D.** Female urosome (spermatophores attached), ventral view. **E.** Lateral view. **F.** Female gonopore, dorsal view.

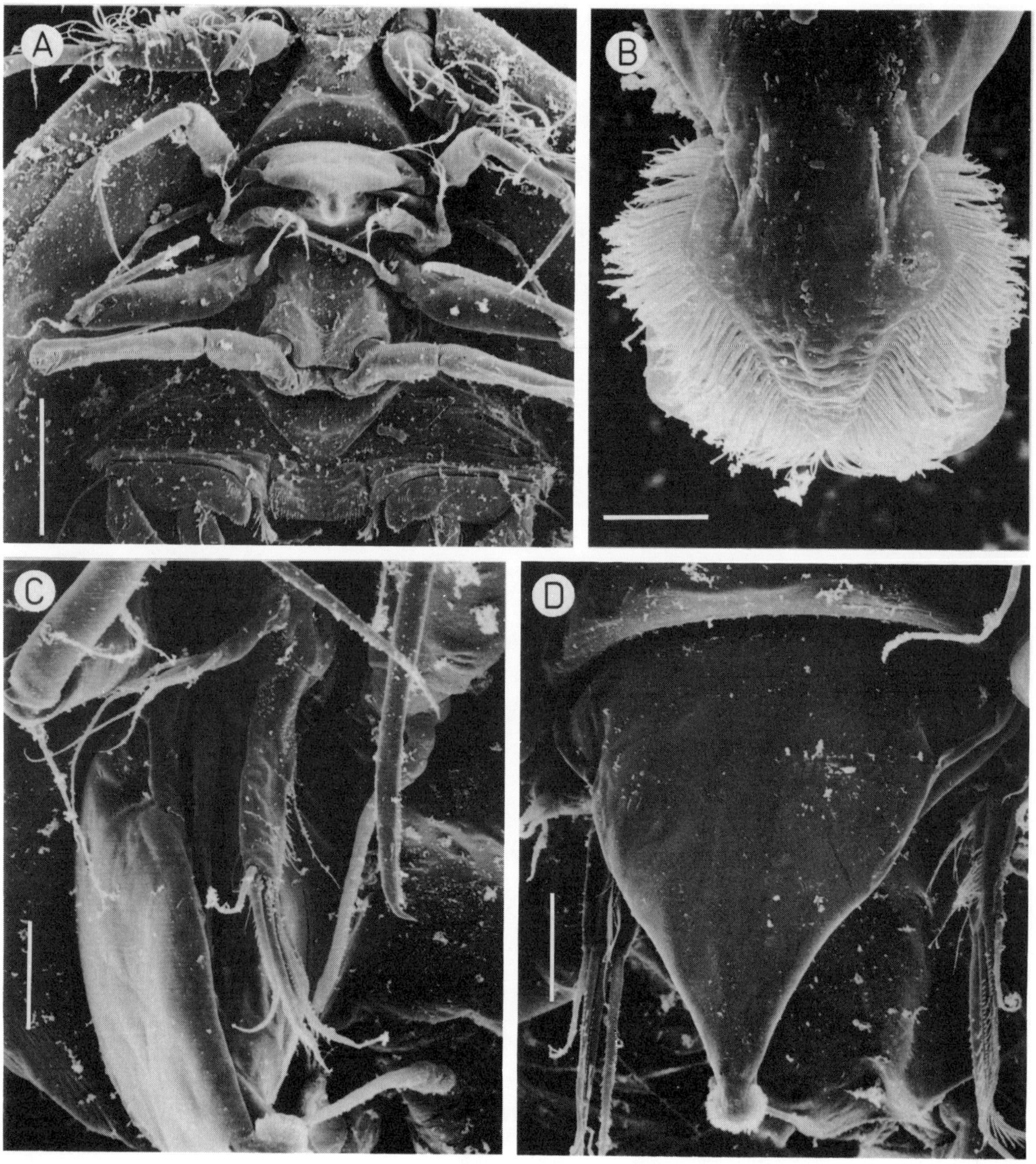

Figure 2.9.31. *Asterocheres reginae*. **A.** Cephalothorax, ventral view. **B.** Tip of labrum, ventral view. **C.** Lateral view of oral cone showing slit between labrum and labium, maxillule and aesthetasc-like element on syncoxa of maxilla. **D.** Oral cone, anterior view. Scale bars A = 100μm, B = 5μm, C-D = 30μm.

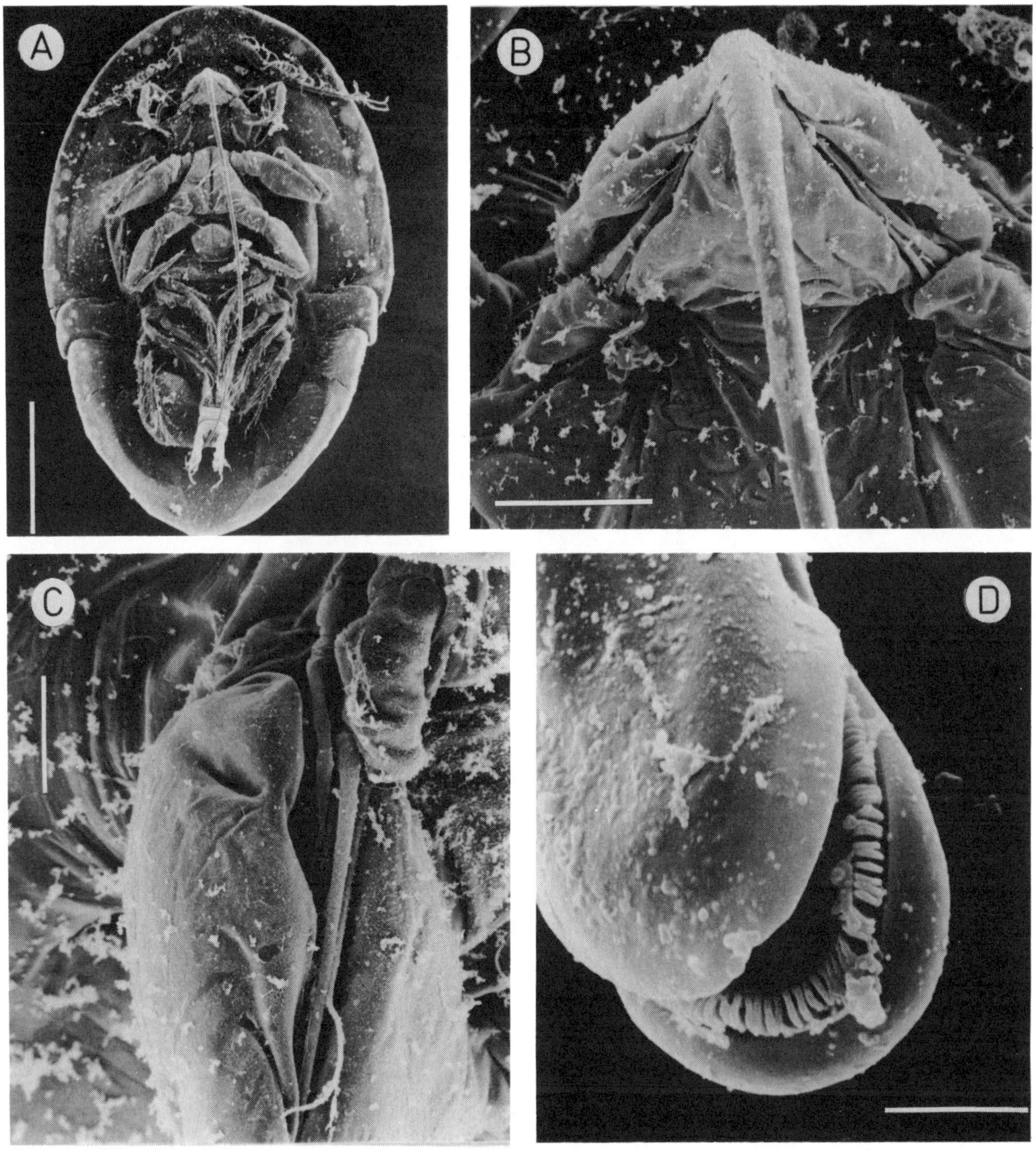

Figure 2.9.32. *Entomopsyllus adriae* female. **A.** Ventral view showing elongate oral cone divided into proximal bulb and distal siphon. **B.** Proximal bulb of oral cone and base of siphon, ventral view. **C.** Lateral view of bulb of oral cone showing mandible and maxillule entering slit between labrum and labium. **D.** Tip of oral cone. Scale bars A = 250μm, B = 40μm, C = 20μm, D = 2μm.

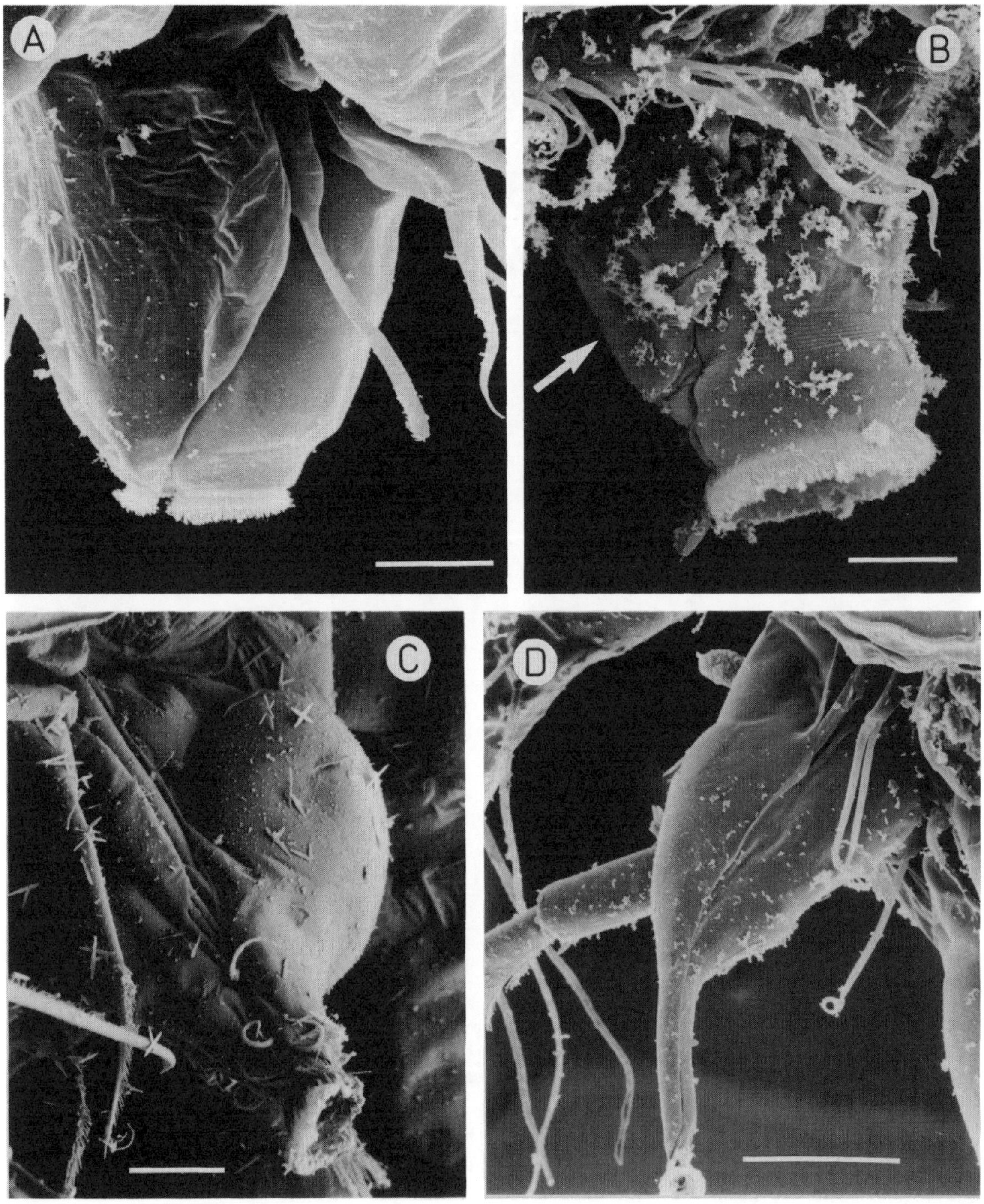

Figure 2.9.33. **A.** *Lernaeocera branchialis* copepodid stage, lateral view of oral cone with mandible displaced, showing distal opening comprising both labrum and labium. **B.** Adult showing reduced labrum (arrowed) and distal opening comprising only labium. **C.** *Hyalopontius typicus* female, lateral view of oral cone showing mandible and maxillule entering slit between labrum and labium. **D.** *Pontoeciella abyssicola* female, lateral view of oral cone showing boundary between labrum and labium. Scale bars A = 30μm, B,D = 40μm, C = 100μm.

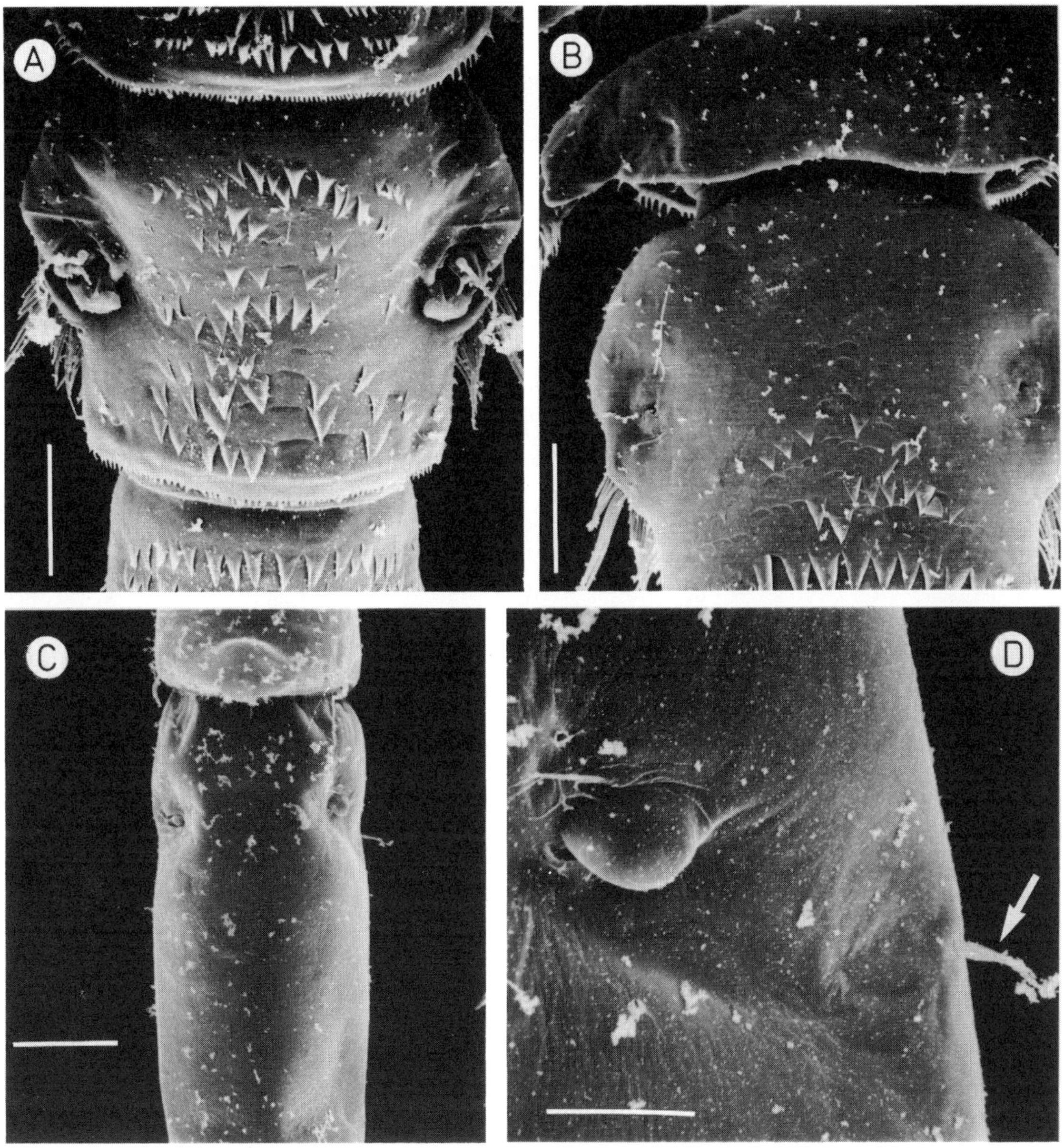

Figure 2.9.34. **A.** *Asterocheres reginae*, female genital double somite, dorsal view. **B.** Ventral view. **C.** *Pontoeciella abyssicola*, female genital double somite, ventral view showing copulatory pores. **D.** Detail of copulatory pore and dorso-lateral seta (arrowed) marking position of gonopore. Scale bars A-C = 30μm, D = 10μm.

2.10 POECILOSTOMATOIDA Thorell 1859

Virtually all poecilostomatoids are parasites or associates of other animals and the great majority is marine. This is perhaps the most diverse order of copepods in terms of gross body morphology (figure 2.10.1). It contains primitive representatives, such as *Hemicyclops* Boeck, that have a typical cyclopiform body and live in loose associations, sharing the burrows built by decapod crustaceans for example. It also contains a large number of highly derived families exhibiting a range of bizarre morphologies, including the Corallovexiidae (which parasitise coelenterates), the Chondracanthidae and Philichthyidae (which parasitise fishes), the Splanchnotrophidae and Mytilicolidae (which parasitise molluscs), and the Nereicolidae (which parasitise polychaetes). Four families are planktonic and can be abundant in oceanic communities. Of these the Corycaeidae and Sapphirinidae are visual predators, utilising a variety of prey organisms. The Oncaeidae are surface feeders and tend to be associated with mucoid aggregates and abandoned larvacean houses.

Character set of the ancestral poecilostomatoid

Copepoda. Prosome comprising cephalosome and 4 free pedigerous somites (figure 2.10.21A); urosome 6-segmented in both sexes (figures 2.10.19B and 18B). Prosome-urosome articulation between fourth and fifth pedigerous somites (podoplean position). Genital apertures paired in both sexes, located ventrally in anterior part of genital somite in female, ventrally at posterior border of genital somite in male (figure 2.10.23C). Seminal receptacles paired. Rostrum fused to cephalosome (figure 2.10.2F). Caudal ramus with 7 setae (figure 2.10.19C). Nauplius eye present (figure 2.10.23A-B). Antennules 8-segmented (figures 2.10.2-7), not geniculate in male but with vestige of geniculation (figure 2.10.2C-E). Antenna uniramous (figure 2.10.8A-D); with 3-segmented endopod, exopod entirely lacking; coxa and basis fused, with 1 seta on inner distal margin; first to third endopodal segments with 1, 4 and 7 setae respectively. Labrum a well developed muscular lobe (figure 2.10.11D). Mandible reduced; gnathobase small bearing 1 articulated seta and a distal array of single and multicusped non-articulating blades; palp 1-segmented bearing 1 medial and 3 terminal setae (figure 2.10.11F). Paragnaths separate (figure 2.10.16A). Maxillule reduced (figure 2.10.19E); bilobed, inner lobe representing praecoxal endite bearing 3 setae; outer lobe, defined at base, representing reduced palp, armed with 5 setae. Maxilla 2-segmented (figure 2.10.13D); proximal segment representing syncoxa, distal segment representing basis; syncoxa with 2 + 1 setae representing both coxal endites; basis drawn out into spinous process armed with 3 elements. Maxilliped sexually dimorphic (figure 2.10.14A-B); 4-segmented in female (figure 2.10.13E); 4-segmented with fourth segment fused with claw in male; first and second segment (syncoxa and basis respectively) each bearing 2 setae in both sexes; basis more robust and muscular in male than female (figure 2.10.14A-B): endopod setal formula 2, 4 for female and 0,1+claw for male. Swimming legs 1-4 biramous with 3-segmented rami; members of leg pairs joined by intercoxal sclerite; inner coxal seta and outer seta on basis present; inner seta on basis of first leg present (figure 2.10.22A); first exopodal segment with 1 outer spine, without inner seta. Spine and seta formula of legs 1 to 4:

	coxa	basis	exopod segment 1 2 3	endopod segment 1 2 3
leg 1	0 – 1	1 – I	I – 0; I – 1; III,I,4	0 – 1; 0 – 1; I,2,3
leg 2	0 – 1	1 – 0	I – 0; I – 1; III,I,5	0 – 1; 0 – 2; I,II,3
leg 3	0 – 1	1 – 0	I – 0; I – 1; III,I,5	0 – 1; 0 – 2; I,II,3
leg 4	0 – 1	1 – 0	I – 0; I – 1; II,I,5	0 – 1; 0 – 2; I,II,2

Fifth legs uniramous (figure 2.10.18C-E), with single segmented protopod joined by intercoxal sclerite; inner coxal seta absent; outer seta on basis present; exopod 1-segmented bearing 4 setae; endopod absent. Sixth legs represented by opercular plates bearing 3 setae closing off genital openings of female (figure 2.10.20C-D), and by paired flaps closing off genital apertures of male. Eggs carried in paired sacs (figure 2.10.24B).

Remarks

The diagnosis is based on representatives of the most primitive families, Clausidiidae, Paralubbockiidae, Oncaeidae and Erebonasteridae, and derived families such as the Corycaeidae and Lichomolgidae. A 6-segmented urosome in the female is retained in some species of *Hemicyclops* (figure 2.10.19B), in the xarifiid *Zazaranus* Humes, in some members of the Clausiidae, the Philichthyidae (Kabata, 1979) and the Philoblennidae (Avdeev et al., 1986). In the great majority of poecilostomatoids the genital and first abdominal somites are fused to form a genital double somite, as in the Erebonasteridae (figure 2.10.16C), Paralubbockiidae (figure 2.10.18A) and the Oncaeidae (figure 2.10.21B). Some members of the Taeniacanthidae are shown with separate genital and first abdominal somites (Dojiri & Cressey, 1988) but detailed study of female *Taeniacanthus wilsoni* Scott revealed an intermediate condition in which these somites are partly fused, being separated by a furrow rather than a functional articulation (figure 2.10.17F-G).

Female Genital System: Two different arrangements of the female genital system are found in poecilostomatoids. One occurs only in the Erebonasteridae, the other in all remaining families. In erebonasterids the genital and first abdominal somites are fused to form a genital double somite which carries the gonopores laterally and the paired copulatory pores midventrally (figures 2.10.17A-B and 2.10.16F). The copulatory pores lie close together in a slight depression on the midventral surface (figures 2.10.16F and 2.10.17C-E). In all erebonasterids the large copulatory ducts leading from the copulatory pores to the seminal receptacles are highly sclerotised and readily visible through the integument of the body wall. The voluminous seminal receptacles are located laterally in the double somite (figure 2.10.16E). The oviducts transport the large eggs to the genital antra which lie beneath the laterally located gonopores. In all other poecilostomatoids the copulatory pores are located within the lateral or dorsolateral genital apertures. Each is concealed beneath the genital operculum formed by the sixth legs. Spermatophores are placed on the genital somite or double somite by the male and discharge into the paired receptacles (hatched line in figure 2.10.20A) via the genital aperture (figure 2.10.21B).

These two systems differ substantially but, when combined, they provide useful information on the ancestral condition of the Poecilostomatoida. The typical poecilostomatoid condition in which both copulatory pores and gonopores lie together within the genital apertures is the ancestral copepod condition but it differs in that the apertures have migrated onto the lateral surface of the genital somite. The erebonasterids, with their ventrally located copulatory pores, indicate that the copulatory pores must have originally been ventral. These two states can be derived from an ancestral poecilostomatoid condition resembling that of the ancestral copepod stock in which the genital apertures, containing the copulatory pores, are located ventrally on the genital somite. Such a system is found in the lamippid *Lamippe concinna* Humes (figure 2.10.5D), although the apparent ventral position of the paired genital apertures may result partly from allometric growth in this highly transformed parasite.

Antennules: In the lineage comprising the Oncaeidae and Paralubbockiidae and in the anthessiid *Rhinomolgus anomalus* Sars the antennules are sexually dimorphic, with the distal 3 segments fused into a compound terminal segment in the male (figures 2.10.2C-E and 2.10.3A-B). The musculature operating this terminal segment in the male resembles that operating the geniculation mechanism in the male antennules of other orders (see chapter 3.4). We interpret this modification of the distal part of the male antennule as representing a vestige of the geniculation mechanism of the ancestral podoplean type. The compound distal segment of male *Oncaea* (figure 2.10.2E) represents the part of the antennule that lies distal to the geniculation, i.e. from ancestral segment XXI to the apex (segment XXVIII). This vestige of the ancestral geniculation mechanism is lost in other poecilostomatoids. However, it is possible to establish the segmental homologies of the more distal part of the antennule in both sexes by using the position of the vestigial geniculation in males as a reference point. In the proximal part the homologies remain uncertain (figures 2.10.6-7). The first two segments of a 7-segmented antennule represent ancestral segments I to XIV but the loss of setation elements renders the identification of precise homologies impossible at present.

The antennules of poecilostomatoids are short, with a maximum of 8 segments as found in the female of *Boylea longispica* Cressey and *Metataeniacanthus vulgaris* Cressey & Cressey. In *Boylea longispica* the distal fusions are XIV-XVII, XVIII-XX, XXI-XXIII, XXIV and XXV are free, and

XXVI-XXVIII (figure 2.10.5A). The articulations expressed in *Boylea* Cressey and *M.vulgaris* represent the ancestral condition of the Poecilostomatoida. Including the two proximal segments of indeterminate homology produces an ancestral segment number of 8 for the order. It is possible that this may have been even higher because *Stellicola flexilis* Humes exhibits a partial subdivision of its third segment (arrowed in figure 2.10.4C-F). This might indicate that the XIV-XVII compound segment was represented by 2 separate segments in the ancestral poecilostomatoid. In all other poecilostomatoids 7 is the maximum number of segments. Comparison of the antennules in representatives of the Erebonasteridae and Clausidiidae (figure 2.10.6) reveals that the segments are not all homologous. In *Clausidium vancouverense* (Haddon) (figure 2.10.4A) and *Hemicyclops carinifer* Humes (figure 2.10.2A) the fusions in the distal part of the 7-segmented female antennule are XIV-XVII, XVIII-XX, XXI-XXIV, XXV is free, and XXVI-XXVIII. In *Centobnaster humesi* Huys & Boxshall (figure 2.10.3C) the fusions in the distal part are XIV-XX, XXI-XXIII, XXIV and XXV are free, and XXVI-XXVIII. Combining the segments exhibited by these clausidiids and erebonasterids produces a total of 8 expressed segments, conforming to the scheme of segmental homologies noted for *Boylea* and *Metataeniacanthus vulgaris* (figure 2.10.6).

The setation of the antennules is reduced in all poecilostomatoids but there are certain features that are relatively uniform throughout the more plesiomorphic families. Aesthetascs, for example, are typically retained on the compound segment incorporating segment XXI, on segment XXV and on the tip of the triple apical segment XXVI-XXVIII (figure 2.10.6). Sexually dimorphic aesthetasc patterns are found in several lichomolgids. Male *Xenomolgus varius* Humes & Stock, for example, possesses 2 aesthetascs on the second antennulary segment and 1 on the fourth segment (figure 2.10.5B). These are absent in the female. The proximal position of the aesthetasc on the fourth segment in *X.varius* strongly suggests that it represents the element derived from ancestral segment XVIII. The distal aesthetasc on the second segment has 4 setae distal to it on the anteroventral surface of the segment. These setae probably represent the armature of ancestral segments XII and XIII, from which we infer that the aesthetasc is derived from ancestral segment XI. Aesthetasc-like elements are present on the proximal part of the antennule in male *Paralubbockia* Boxshall (figure 2.10.3B) but these may be derived secondarily by modification of other original setation elements. The male of *Mecomerinx notabilis* (Humes & Cressey) has a total of 7 aesthetascs (Humes, 1977). Two are situated on the second segment (probably derived from segments VII and XI) and 2 on the fourth (derived from segments XVIII and XIX), and one each on the fifth to seventh segments (derived from segments XXI, XXV and XXVIII respectively). A total of 9 aesthetascs was found in the male of *Mecra ellipsaria* Humes and this is the largest number known for any poecilostomatoid. Five of the aesthetascs are carried on the long second segment and one each on the fourth to seventh segments (Humes, 1980b).

Antenna: The antenna of poecilostomatoids is characterised by the complete absence of the exopod in the later copepodid and adult stages. With one exception, all poecilostomatoids have the antennary coxa and basis fully fused into a coxobasis, typically bearing a single distal (= basal) seta. The exception is *Rhinomolgus anomalus* which Sars figures with a small discrete coxa (Sars, 1913-1918; pl. CV, fig.a2,). This proximal structure may represent a pedestal upon which the limb has its origin, and it requires reexamination. In *Paraergasilus remulus* Cressey the coxa and basis appear to be separated (Cressey & Collette, 1970; fig. 64) but examination of the closely related *P.minutus* (Fryer) (figure 2.10.9F) revealed no trace of a suture subdividing the coxobasis. The basic poecilostomatoid antenna can be found in *Hemicyclops carinifer* (figure 2.10.8A). The coxobasis has 1 seta and the 3 endopodal segments are separate, with an armature formula of 1,4,6. The maximum number of 7 elements on the third endopodal segment is found in various groups, including the Oncaeidae. In *Oncaea venusta* Philippi (figure 2.10.8B) the raptorial antenna has the second and third endopodal segments fused to form a double apical segment but this bears proximal and distal groups of 4 and 7 elements respectively representing the armature of the original segments. In *Lamippe concinna* the antenna is 3-segmented, comprising unarmed coxobasis, unarmed first endopodal segment and the double apical segment representing the fused second and third endopodal segments (figure 2.10.5C). In *Paralubbockia* the first endopodal segment is fused to the coxobasis (figure 2.10.8C) and the second and third endopodal segments are also fused, resulting in a 2-segmented appendage. In *Cotylemyzon* Stock (figure 2.10.8D) one of the 3 elements on the second endopodal segment is modified as a sucker.

A segmented exopod is present on the antenna of naupliar poecilostomatoids (Izawa, 1987). A vestige of the exopod remains on the antenna of the first copepodid stage but is lost in subsequent copepodid stages (Izawa, 1987). The structure referred to as the antennary exopod in the third copepodid of the chondracanthid *Acanthochondria cornuta* Müller by Heegaard (1947: figure 124) is the atrophied and displaced terminal segment of the endopod (see Ho, 1984b).

The antenna of corycaeids is sexually dimorphic, as in *Farranula* Wilson. The female has a 4-segmented limb comprising coxobasis, with 1 powerful spinulate seta, and a 3-segmented endopod consisting of a long first segment bearing a similar spinulate seta proximally, a short second segment armed with 2 elements and an apical segment drawn out into a spiniform process and armed with 2 claws and 5 setae (figure 2.10.9D-E). The male also has a coxobasis bearing a powerful spinulate seta, an elongate first endopodal segment with a proximal spinulate seta, and a short second endopodal segment armed with 2 setae. However, the apical segment is fused to the single terminal claw and it carries 6 small elements around its base (figure 2.10.9B-C).

Accessory Antennule: The family Chondracanthidae comprises about 160 species all of which are parasites of marine fishes. They attach to their host by means of modified, hook-like antennae. Approximately one quarter of known chondracanthids possess an 'accessory antennule' at the base of the antennae. Ho (1984b) studied the homology of this 'accessory antennule' and showed that it represents the reduced and offset terminal endopodal segment of the antenna.

Postantennal Process: Some genera of the family Taeniacanthidae possess a large postantennal process, originating on the ventral surface of the cephalosome, just lateral to the base of the antennule (figure 2.10.9A). This process has been interpreted as the first maxilla (maxillule) by some authors (e.g. Heegaard, 1947, in which the taeniacanthids and bomolochids were treated as part of the Ergasilidae) but is not a true appendage. It represents an elaboration of a sclerite forming part of the ventral cephalosomic wall.

Mandible: The presence of a falcate mandible was treated as diagnostic of the Poecilostomatoida by Kabata (1979) but the families Oncaeidae (figure 2.10.10A-B), Corycaeidae, Clausidiidae (figure 2.10.10C) and Erebonasteridae (figure 2.10.11B-C, E-F) all contain representatives with separate blades on the distal margin of the mandibular gnathobase, rather than the falcate lash. The discovery of *Centobnaster* Huys & Boxshall revealed a different type of mandibular gnathobase for the Poecilostomatoida. *Centobnaster* has a gnathobase armed with complex, multicusped teeth that are not articulated basally like the distal blades on the mandibles of oncaeids (figure 2.10.10C, for example) or clausidiids. There is a single articulated element, modified as a broad, brush-like structure, located midway along the dorsal surface of the gnathobase (figure 2.10.11B-C). This articulated element is present on virtually all copepod mandibular gnathobases. The distal margin forms an array of single and multicusped, non-articulated blades that resemble those of the typical copepod gnathobase. Two other erebonasterid genera, *Amphicrossus* Huys (figure 2.10.11F) and *Tychidion* Humes (figure 2.10.11E), have similar gnathobases although the distal margin array is organised into 3 distinct blades. In *Erebonaster* Humes (figure 2.10.16B) the same 3 blades can be recognised but they are slender and more setiform in appearance. Comparison of all 4 erebonasterid genera suggests that the distal elements of *Centobnaster* are also interpretable as 3 blades. The 7 teeth along the dorsal margin comprise 1 blade comparable with the single blade (bearing teeth along its dorsal margin) in the same position on the mandible of *Amphicrossus*. The simple blade at the dorsodistal angle is comparable with the simple blade in the same position in *Tychidion*. The 4 remaining teeth represent the third blade which is dentate along its ventral margin in *Amphicrossus*.

It is difficult to interpret the evolutionary sequence of changes in gnathobase armature within the Poecilostomatoida (figure 2.10.12). The basic copepod mandible has an articulated dorsal seta (marked with a star in figure 2.10.12) on the gnathobase which is clearly retained in primitive poecilostomatoids and the distal margin bears a complex array of single and multicusped blades. This most closely resembles the erebonasterid condition, which is therefore presumed to be closest to the ancestral poecilostomatoid condition. There is a clear trend within the Erebonasteridae for the blades to become more clearly demarcated from the segment basally, but they are not articulated. In other primitive families, such as Oncaeidae and Clausidiidae, there is a maximum of 5 elements, all articulated at their bases. The most dorsal of these is the ancestral articulated element but there are 4 elements derived from blades, rather than the 3 present in erebonasterids.

The falcate blade or lash has obviously evolved within the order. It appears to be derived by enlargement and specialisation of the middle element of the 5 ancestral gnathobase elements (figure 2.10.10B) and some species of *Hemicyclops* show an early stage in the modification of this element. A similar process has occurred, presumably in parallel, within the Oncaeidae. *Oncaea* typically has 5 articulated distal blades but in *Lubbockia* Claus the middle element has become lash-like, i.e. elongate and dentate along its convex margin. In the assemblage of families that parasitise fish the mandible also becomes lash-like. In the Chondracanthidae, in particular, the mandible is drawn out into a lash-like structure armed along both margins with relatively large teeth. A similar mandible, but with 2 lash-like elements, is present in the Philichthyidae. In the Ergasilidae 3 blades remain and all are more or less dentate, however, the teeth extend over the anterior surface of the central element and are not just located marginally. The closely related families Taeniacanthidae and Bomolochidae have 2 or 3 discrete blades apically but the homologies of these blades with the elements retained in other fish parasites cannot be confirmed.

The typical condition of the poecilostomatoid mandible is found in the Lichomolgidae, in which only the middle element remains on the mandible and it is produced into a long, bilaterally toothed lash (figure 2.10.10D). This true lash is characterised by the gradual incorporation of the more proximal elements into the lash (figure 2.10.12, V-VI). The ornamentation of fine spinules or denticles along their outer margins eventually becomes continuous with the marginal ornamentation of the central lash. The mandible of the Anthessiidae and Myicolidae may represent an intermediate stage in this process of gradual incorporation. It has the dominant lash with its spinulose margins and the 2 proximal elements on the ventral margin are reduced but the dorsal seta (marked with a star in figure 2.10.12) is well developed and still separate.

The report of a palp on the mandible of *Cotylemyzon vervoorti* Stock (Stock, 1982) is erroneous. Ho (1984a) suggested that the 'palp' in *C.vervoorti* represents a cluster of terminal elements on a slightly protruded sclerite. Reexamination of this material (figure 2.10.10E) confirms Ho's interpretation. The maxillule was erroneously interpreted as the mandibular palp of poecilostomatoids by Sars (1913-1918). The only poecilostomatoids retaining a mandibular palp are the 4 genera of the Erebonasteridae (Humes, 1988; Huys, in press; Huys & Boxshall, 1990b) (figure 2.10.11B, E-F and 2.10.16B). *Tychidion* is here recognised as an erebonasterid, as indicated by the possession of paired ventral copulatory pores on the genital double somite of the female. Leigh-Sharpe (1934) illustrated a palp on the mandible of *Mantra*, which was subsequently placed in the Poecilostomatoida. Study of the type material has revealed that *Mantra* is a valid genus (and family) of Cyclopoida (Huys, 1990c).

In *Paralubbockia* there is pronounced sexual dimorphism in the structure of the mandible. In the female (figure 2.10.15A) the well developed gnathobase is armed with 3 elements and a row of strong spinules whereas in the male (figure 2.10.15B) the entire gnathobase is small and weakly sclerotised. The same number of gnathobasic elements as in the female is present but they too are weakly developed. It is probable that the adult male of *Paralubbockia* is non-feeding. In some poecilostomatoid families the mandible is highly reduced and in a few, such as the Mytilicolidae, the mandible is completely absent.

Maxillule: The maxillule is reduced in all poecilostomatoids and is typically described as bilobed. The structure of the maxillule in the clausidiid *Hemicyclops carinifer* (figure 2.10.19E) indicates that the inner lobe represents the praecoxal arthrite and the outer lobe represents the rest of the palp. In both sexes of *Paralubbockia* the maxillule (figure 2.10.13B-C) has a produced praecoxal endite bearing 3 elements and a distinct palp bearing 4 setae. The palp is clearly articulated at its base. The outermost seta of the outer lobe in *H.carinifer* is positioned on the trace of a suture line, possibly representing the coxal-basal boundary. On this basis we interpret this outer seta as the vestige of the coxal epipodite. Further evidence supporting our interpretation is provided by the location of this seta midway along the outer maxillulary margin in another clausidiid *Clausidium vancouverense* (figure 2.10.13A). The seta representing the epipodite is absent in *Paralubbockia*. In many other poecilostomatoids the maxillule is further reduced, to a single lobe, and it can be lost altogether.

The maximum setation of the maxillule is found in species of *Hemicyclops*. In *H.carinifer* (figure

2.10.19E) the inner lobe (praecoxal endite) bears 3 setae and the outer lobe (palp) bears 5 setae one of which is the vestigial coxal epipodite. The other 4 setae would therefore represent the basal, endopodal and exopodal elements. Sars (1913-18) figured a total of 9 setae on the maxillule of *H.purpureus* Boeck, and 4 of these appear to be located on the praecoxal endite. Reexamination of this poecilostomatoid, the only species reported with more than 3 praecoxal elements, revealed the typical armature of 3 praecoxal and 5 palp setae (figure 2.10.5E). The extra seta was the result of superimposing 1 of the mandibular setae on the maxillule.

Maxilla: *Hemicyclops carinifer* illustrates the basic segmentation of the poecilostomatoid maxilla (figure 2.10.21C) with a large proximal segment, the syncoxa, and a small distal segment, the basis. The large proximal syncoxa bears the vestiges of 2 endites distally; both endites have a swollen base. The proximal endite bears 2 setae, the distal is drawn out into a spinous process. In the majority of species the syncoxal endites are lacking, as in *Oncaea venusta* (figure 2.10.21D). In *Clausidium vancouverense* the syncoxa bears the trace of an oblique suture line subdividing the double segment (figure 2.10.13D). It is possible that this line represents a vestige of the praecoxal-coxal boundary, but there is little supporting evidence for this interpretation.

Maxilliped: Poecilostomatoids can be readily distinguished by their sexually dimorphic maxillipeds (cf. figures 2.10.14A and B). The female maxilliped is basically 4-segmented (figure 2.10.13E) whereas that of the male is 4-segmented with the distal segment fully fused to the claw. The male maxilliped of *Pseudolubbockia dilatata* Sars, as described by Heron & Damkaer (1969: figures 5 and 10a) is 5-segmented with an endopodal formula of 0,2,0+claw but we have been unable to verify this structure and regard it as doubtful. This species needs to be reexamined. The ancestral segmentation and setation of the maxilliped of both sexes are clearly illustrated by *Hemicyclops*. The basis is much more robust in the male than in the female, and the claw is typically longer in the male. The syncoxa and basis each have 2 setae in both sexes but the robust basis of the male (figure 2.10.14B) is more muscular and has additional rows of spinules on its medial surface. In the male the endopod comprises a small, unarmed free segment plus the large terminal claw incorporating the distal endopodal segment. The claw bears a single seta proximally, confirming that it incorporates at least one other endopodal segment. In female *Hemicyclops* (figure 2.10.14A) the small first endopodal segment is also unarmed. The apical segment is claw-like and carries 3 other armature elements. The maximum setation of the female maxilliped is found in *Clausidium vancouverense* which has 2 setae on the syncoxa, 2 on the basis, 2 on the first endopodal segment and 4 on the second. All 4 elements on the second endopodal segment are articulated basally (figure 2.10.13E) and this indicates that the claw on the last endopodal segment in female *Hemicyclops* is probably derived from a modified armature element and is not homologous with that of the male. This dimorphism in maxilliped structure is clearly related to the mating behaviour of poecilostomatoids, in which the males typically grasp the females around the prosome-urosome junction with their maxillipeds. Many poecilostomatoid families, such as the Ergasilidae, show the most extreme sexual dimorphism possible, in which the maxilliped is a well developed raptorial limb in the male and completely absent in the female.

The maxillipeds vary within the order. Most poecilostomatoids, other than clausidiids such as *Hemicyclops* and *Clausidium* Kossmann, erebonasterids such as *Tychidion*, and some members of the Taeniacanthidae, lack the setae on the syncoxa. The maxilliped of male *Oncaea* lacks free endopodal segments (figure 2.10.14E-F). The segments are presumably incorporated into the base of the claw. Female *Oncaea* retains a free endopodal segment but the claw only has 2 setae at its base (figure 2.10.14D) rather than the 3 found in *Hemicyclops* and *Tychidion*.

Swimming Legs: The maximum setation of swimming legs 1 to 4 is found in the clausidiid genus *Hyphalion* Humes. A useful diagnostic character of the Poecilostomatoida is the absence of the seta on the inner margin of the first exopodal segment in legs 1 to 4 (figure 2.10.22A-C). This seta typically appears at the copepodid III stage (for legs 1 to 3) and at the copepodid IV stage (for leg 4) but it is absent throughout development in poecilostomatoids. Only a single inner seta is present on the second endopodal segment of the first leg (figure 2.10.22A). In *Chauliolobion bulbosum* Humes the first leg bears a large spiniform process on the outer margin of the coxa (figure 2.10.22C-D). This resembles a modified armature element but it is not articulated basally and can be regarded as a prolongation of the segmental margin. The small outer sclerite at the base of legs 1 to 4 in *Amphicrossus* (figure 2.10.22A) is a vestige of the praecoxa.

Fifth Legs: The fifth legs of *Centobnaster* (figure 2.10.18C) and *Tychidion* (figure 2.10.18D) are the most plesiomorphic within the order. They are ventral in position and are connected by a small intercoxal sclerite (Huys & Boxshall, 1990b). The males of serpulidicolids such as *Serpulidicola placostegi* Southward, also retain ventrally located fifth legs and have a minute remnant of the intercoxal sclerite joining the protopodal segments (figure 2.10.18E). In virtually all other poecilostomatoids, except *Paralubbockia*, the fifth legs are lateral or dorsolateral in position, as in *Hemicyclops carinifer* (figure 2.10.19A-B). In both sexes of *Paralubbockia* the legs are located midventrally but there is no intercoxal sclerite and the base of the limb is fused to the somite (figure 2.10.18A-B).

The primitive fifth leg in poecilostomatoids has 4 elements on the free exopodal segment in both sexes, although this number is often reduced. Three of these elements (the two outermost, and the innermost) are primitively spiniform with serrate margins and the fourth is setiform. The single protopodal segment, formed by fusion of coxa and basis, bears the outer basal seta.

Differential Diagnosis: The Poecilostomatoida is best characterised by its strongly sexually dimorphic maxillipeds and by the structure of the bilobate maxillule.

Note Added in Proof: While this volume was in press Mark Holmes (National Museum of Ireland) sent us a male of *Pseudolubbockia dilatata*. The maxilliped has a 3-segmented endopod as reported by Heron & Damkaer (1969) but the endopodal armature formula is 0,2,1+claw. This represents the ancestral state of the male poecilostomatoid maxilliped. The ancestral character set and the discussions on pages 289 and 350 should be amended accordingly.

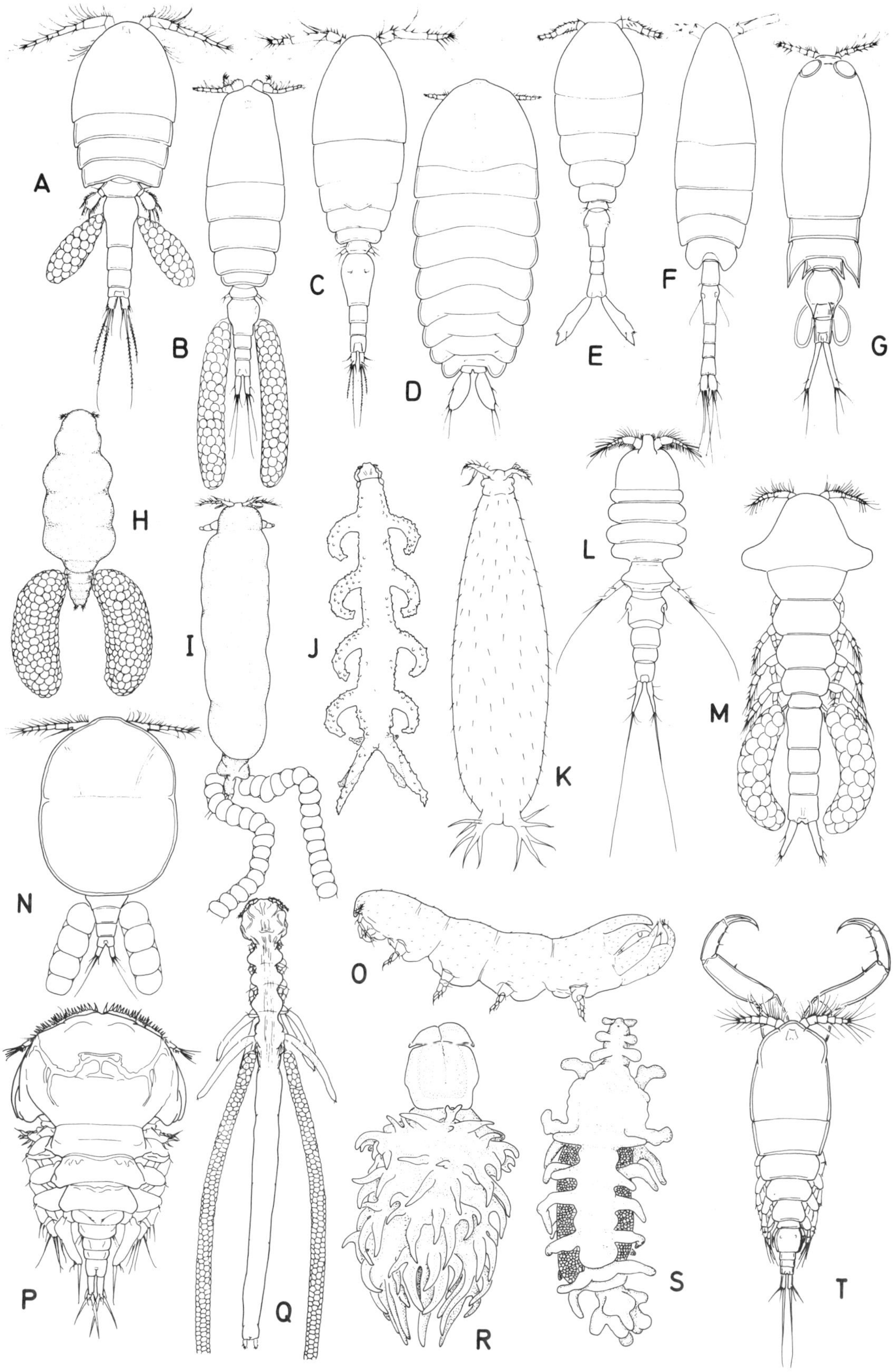

Figure 2.10.1. The diversity of poecilostomatoid body form. **A**. Clausidiidae. **B**. Sabelliphilidae. **C**. Oncaeidae. **D**. Sapphirinidae. **E**. Urocopiidae. **F**. Paralubbockiidae. **G**. Corycaeidae. **H**. Philoblennidae. **I**. Spiophanicolidae. **J**. Corallovexiidae. **K**. Lamippidae. **L**. Erebonasteridae. **M**. Clausiidae. **N**. Eunicicolidae. **O**. Xarifiidae. **P**. Taeniacanthidae. **Q**. Telsidae. **R**. Chondracanthidae. **S**. Philichthyidae. **T**. Ergasilidae.

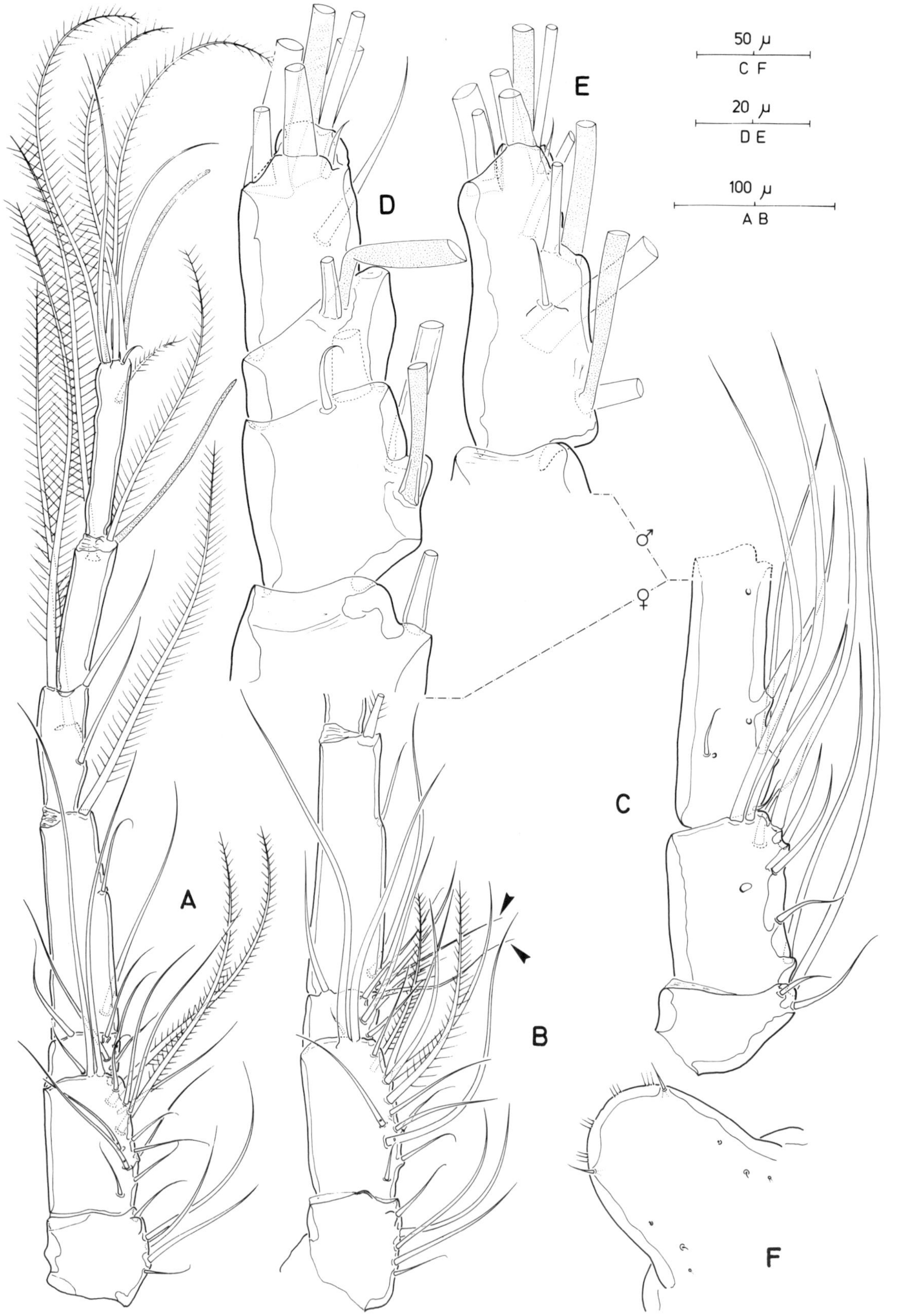

Figure 2.10.2. **A.** *Hemicyclops carinifer*, female antennule. **B.** First four segments of male antennule (extra setae arrowed). **C.** *Oncaea media* f. *minor*, proximal part of antennule (for both sexes). **D.** Distal part of female antennule. **E.** Distal part of male antennule. **F.** *Erebonaster protentipes*, rostrum.

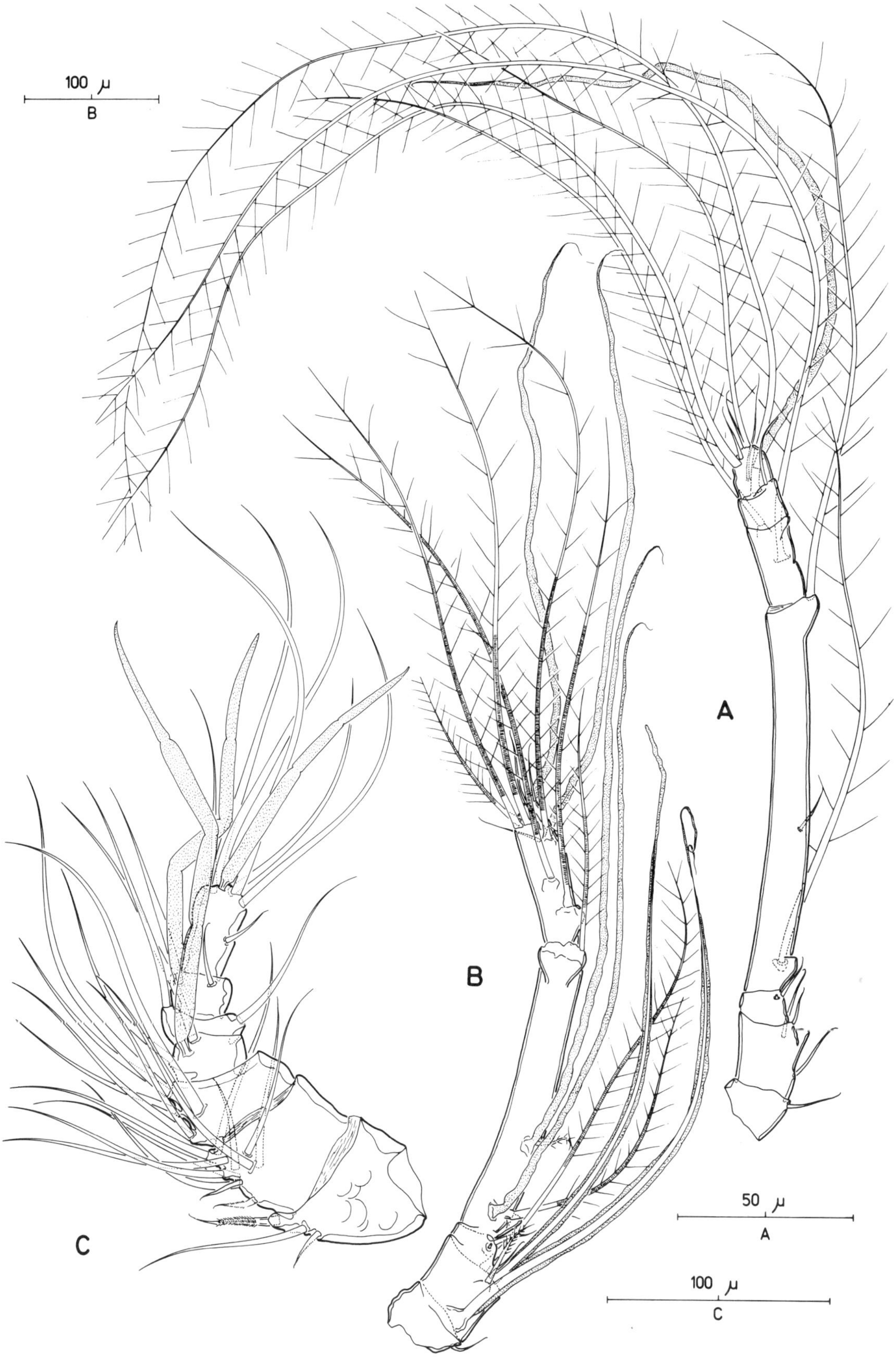

Figure 2.10.3. Antennules. **A.** *Paralubbockia longipedia*, female. **B.** Male. **C.** *Centobnaster humesi*, female.

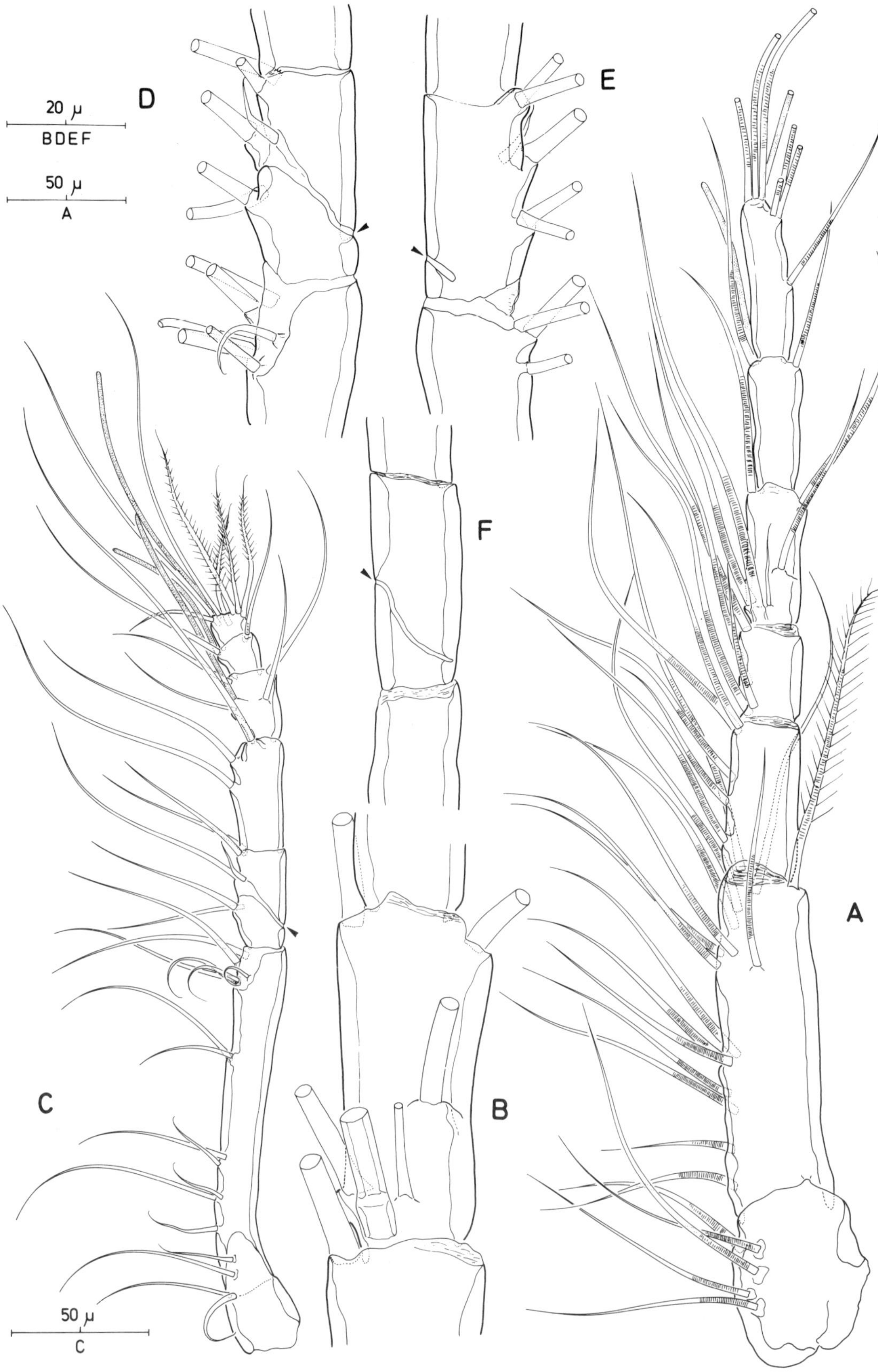

Figure 2.10.4. Antennules. **A.** *Clausidium vancouverense*, female. **B.** Fifth segment. **C.** *Stellicola flexilis*, male. **D.** Ventral view of third segment. **E.** Dorsal view of third segment. **F.** Posterior view of third segment. [Arrows in C-F indicate partial suture dividing segment 3.]

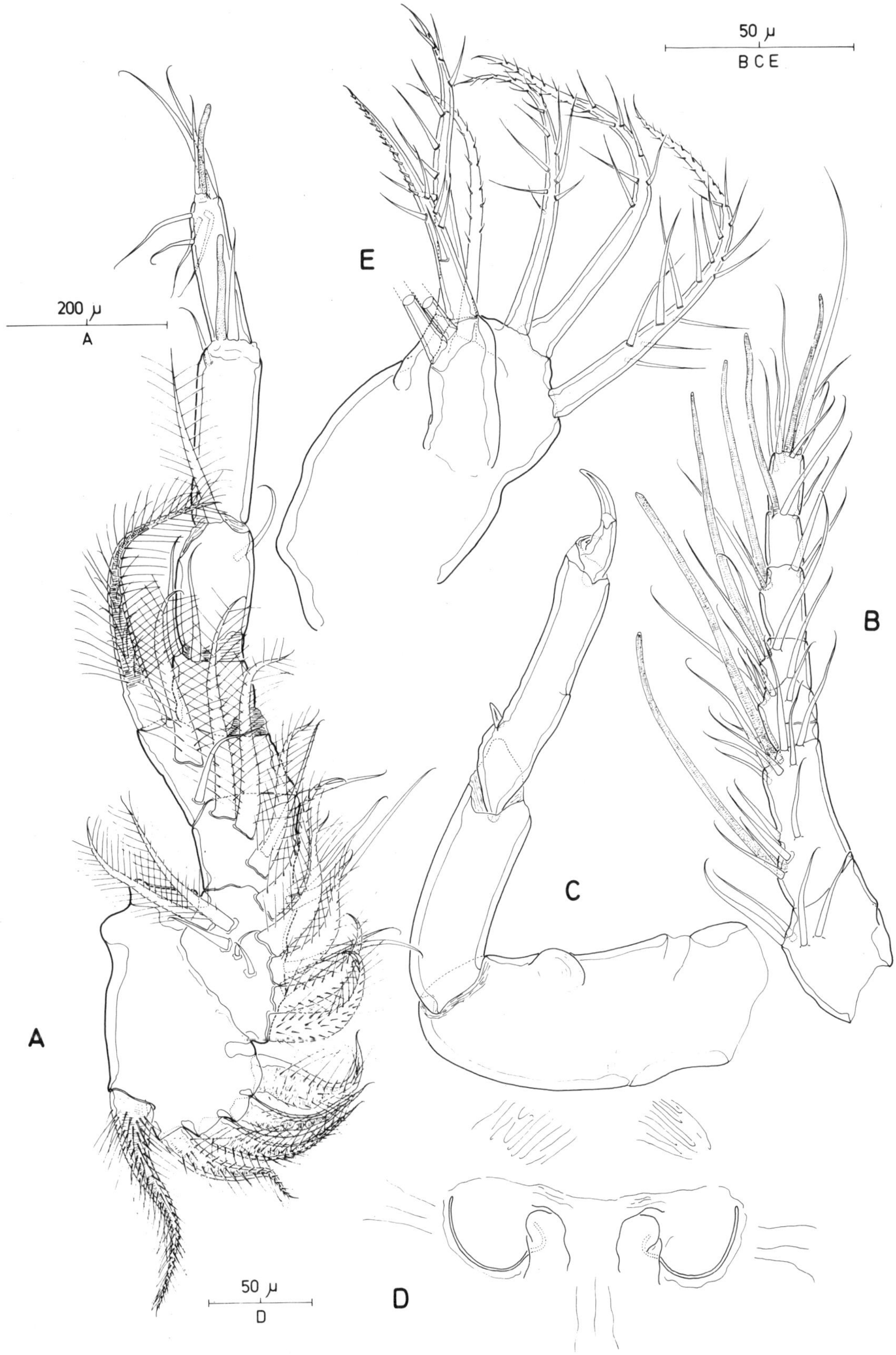

Figure 2.10.5. **A**. *Boylea longispica*, female antennule. **B**. *Xenomolgus varius*, male antennule. **C**. *Lamippe concinna*, antenna. **D**. Gonopores, ventral. **E**. *Hemicyclops purpureus*, maxillule.

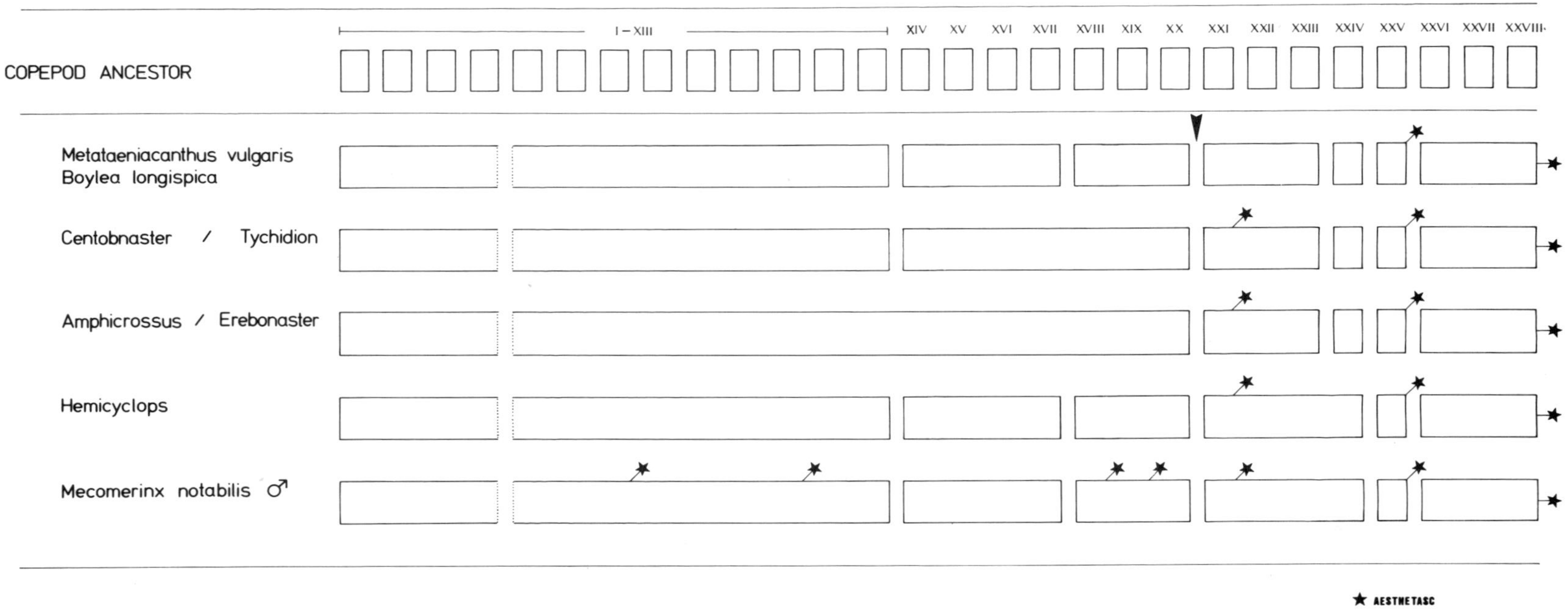

Figure 2.10.6. Schematic comparison of segmental homologies in the antennules of some poecilostomatoids not showing sexual dimorphism in segmentation pattern. Positions of aesthetascs are indicated and the arrow shows the position of the lost neocopepodan geniculation.

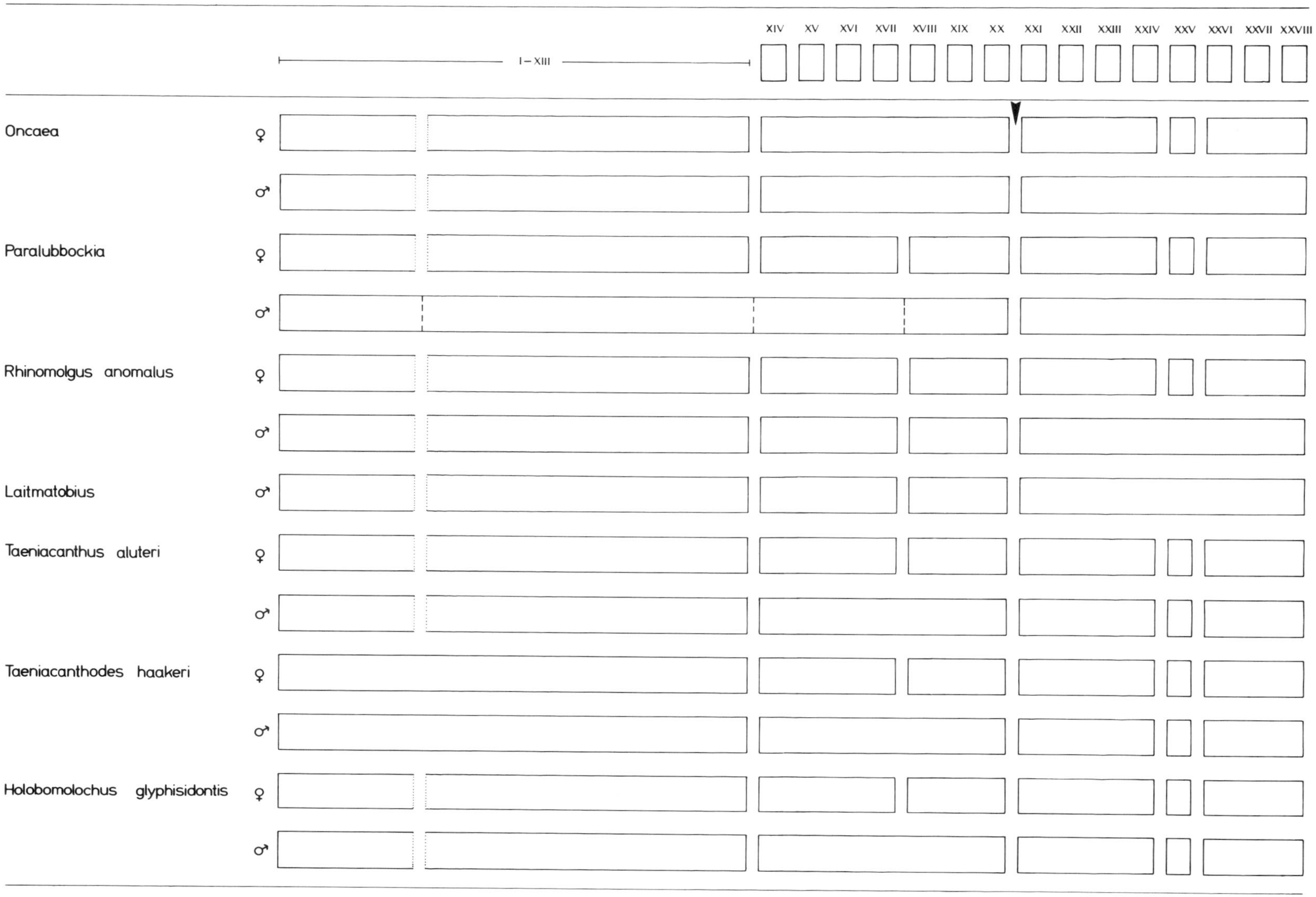

Figure 2.10.7. Schematic comparison of segmental homologies in the antennules of some poecilostomatoids showing sexual dimorphism either proximal or distal to presumed geniculation. The arrow indicates the position of the lost neocopepodan geniculation.

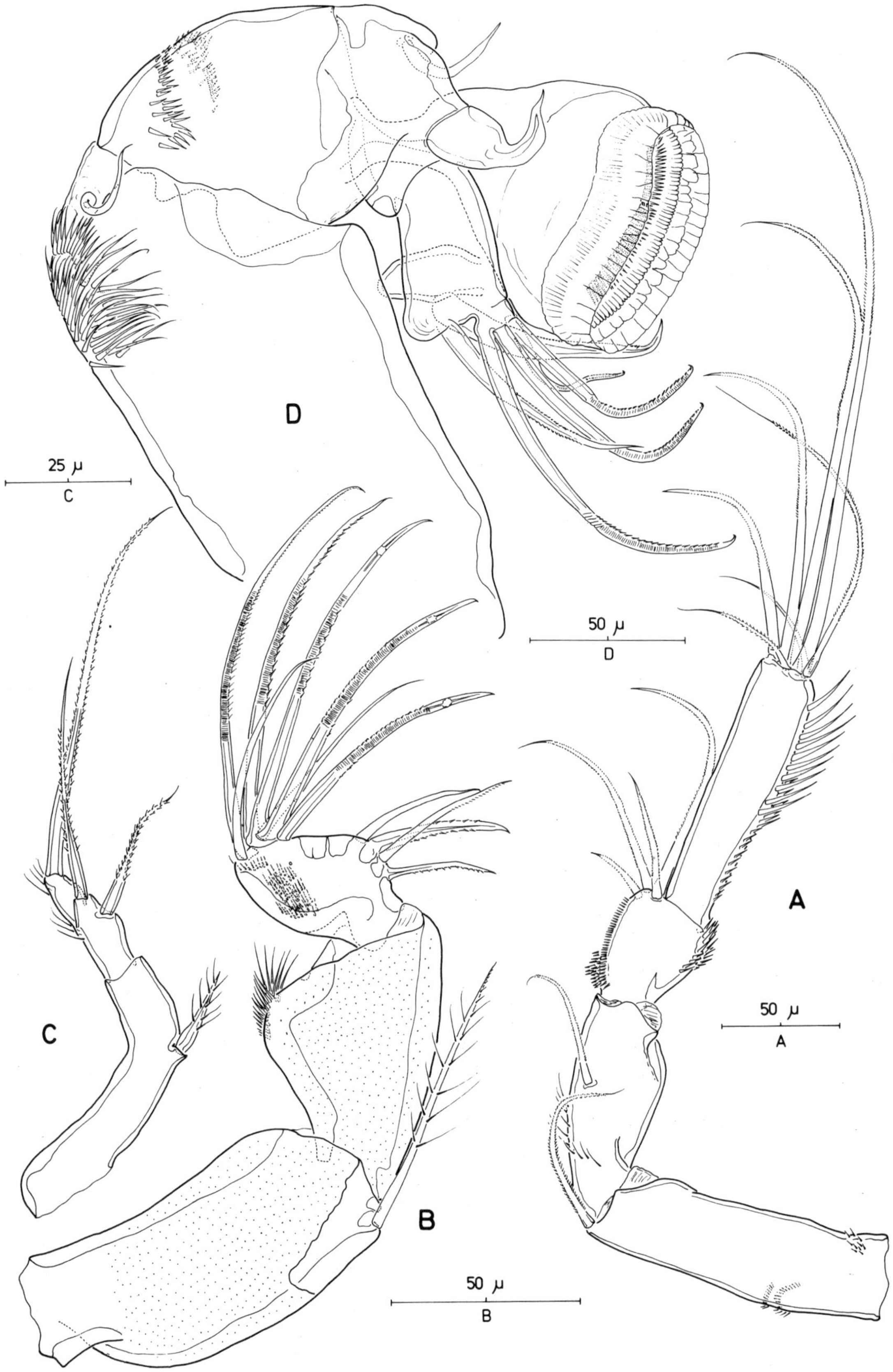

Figure 2.10.8. Antennae. **A.** *Hemicyclops carinifer*. **B.** *Oncaea venusta*. **C.** *Paralubbockia longipedia*. **D.** *Cotylemyzon vervoorti*.

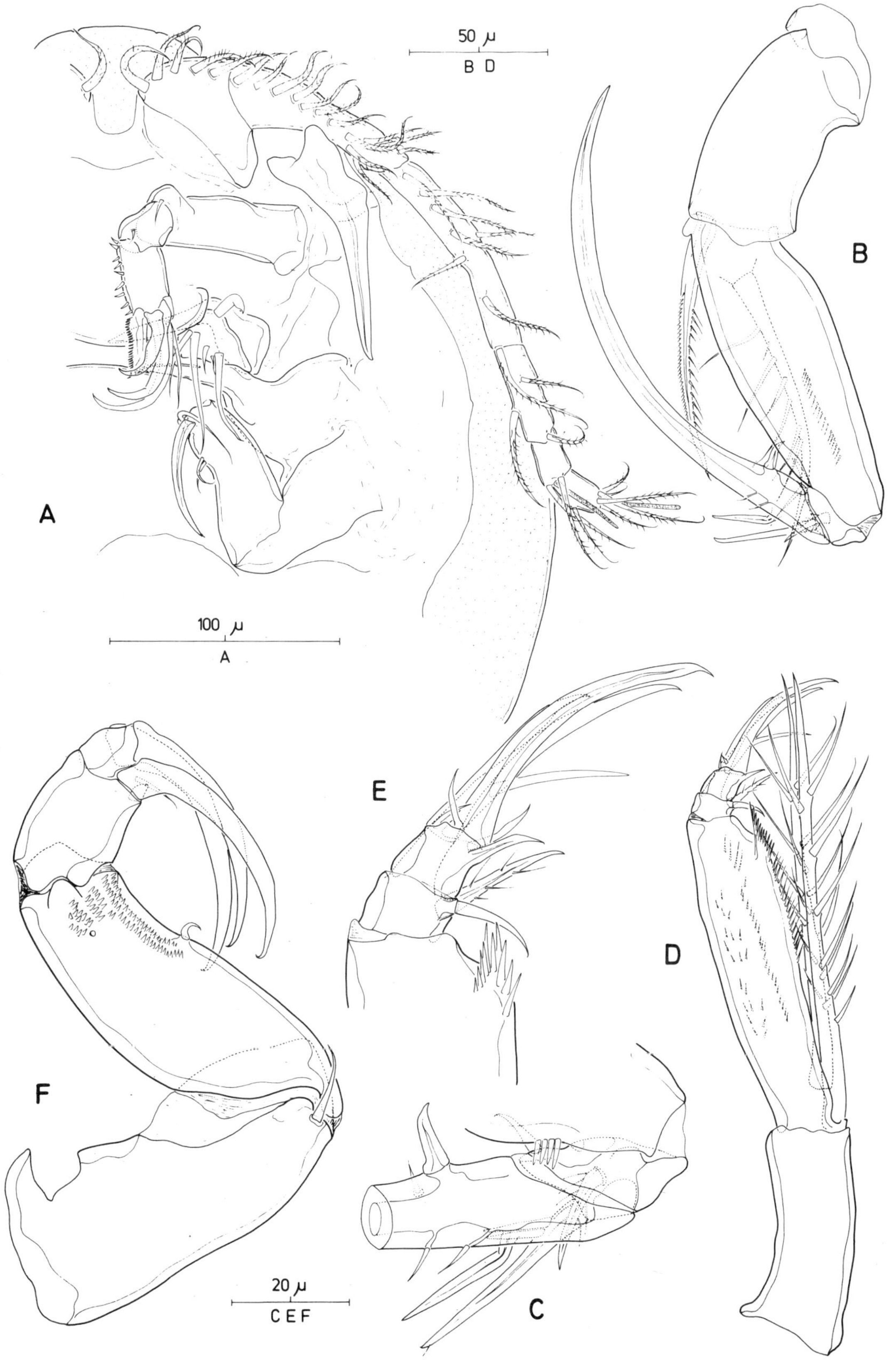

Figure 2.10.9. **A.** *Taeniacanthus wilsoni*, anterior part of cephalosome, ventral view showing postantennal process. **B.** *Farranula gibbula*, male antennule. **C.** Detail of second and third endopodal segments. **D.** *Farranula gibbula*, female antenna. **E.** Detail of distal segments. **F.** *Paraergasilus minutus*, female antenna.

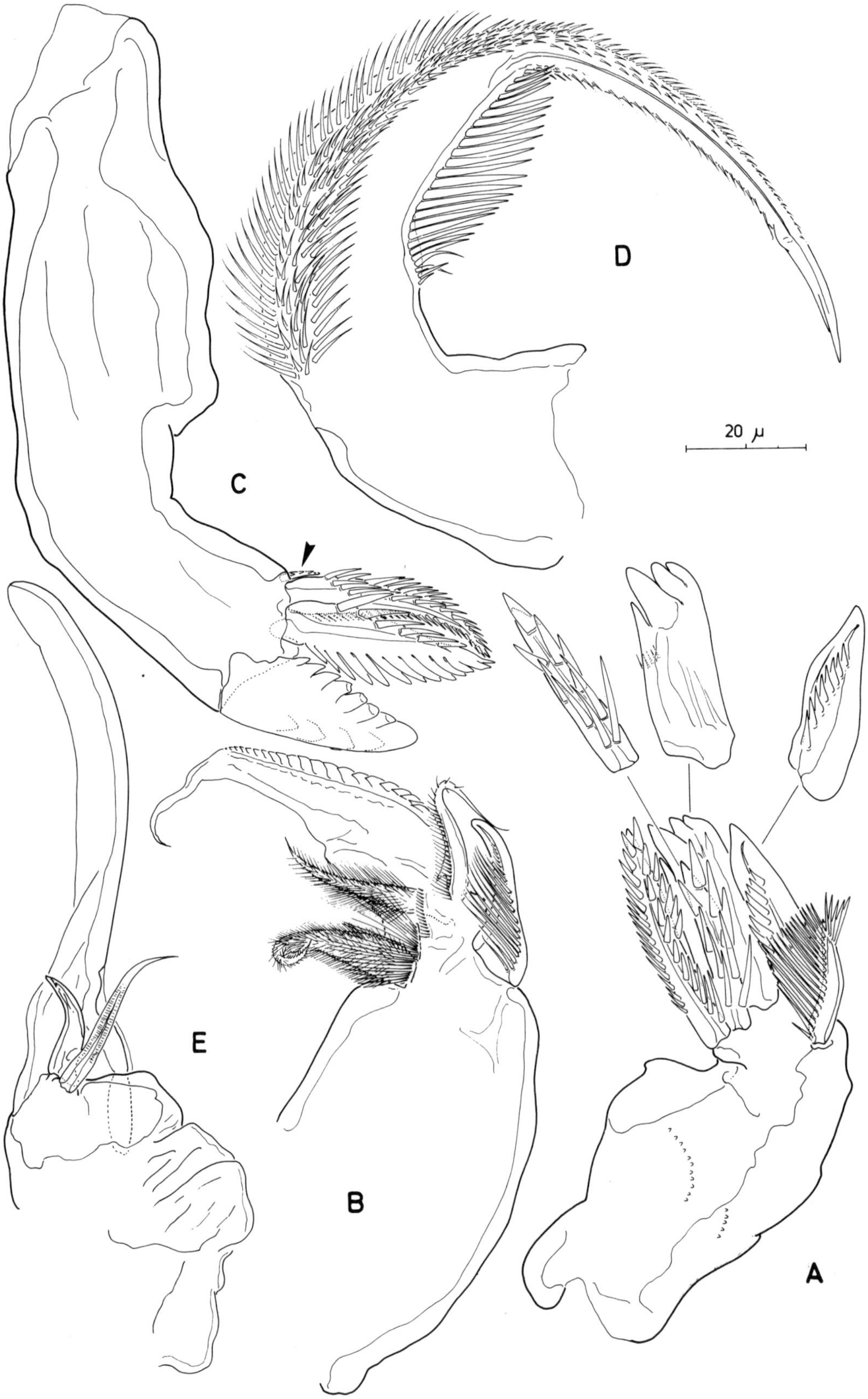

Figure 2.10.10. Mandibles. **A.** *Oncaea venusta*. **B.** *Lubbockia extenuata*. **C.** *Hemicyclops carinifer* with dorsal blade arrowed. **D.** *Lichomolgus forficula*. **E.** *Cotylemyzon vervoorti*.

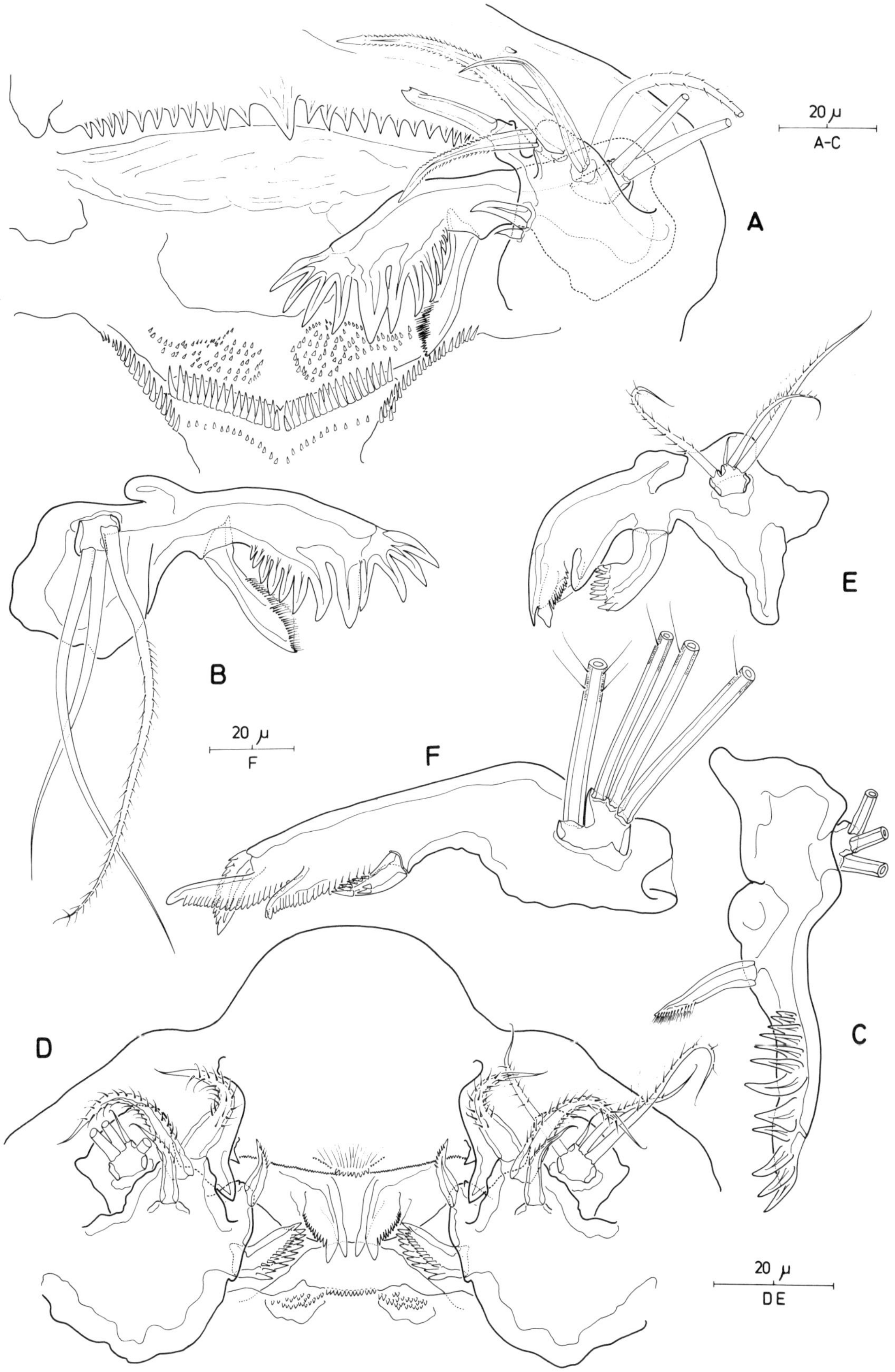

Figure 2.10.11. **A.** *Centobnaster humesi*, oral area. **B - C.** Mandible. **D.** *Tychidion guyanense*, oral area. **E.** Mandible. **F.** *Amphicrossus pacificus*, mandible.

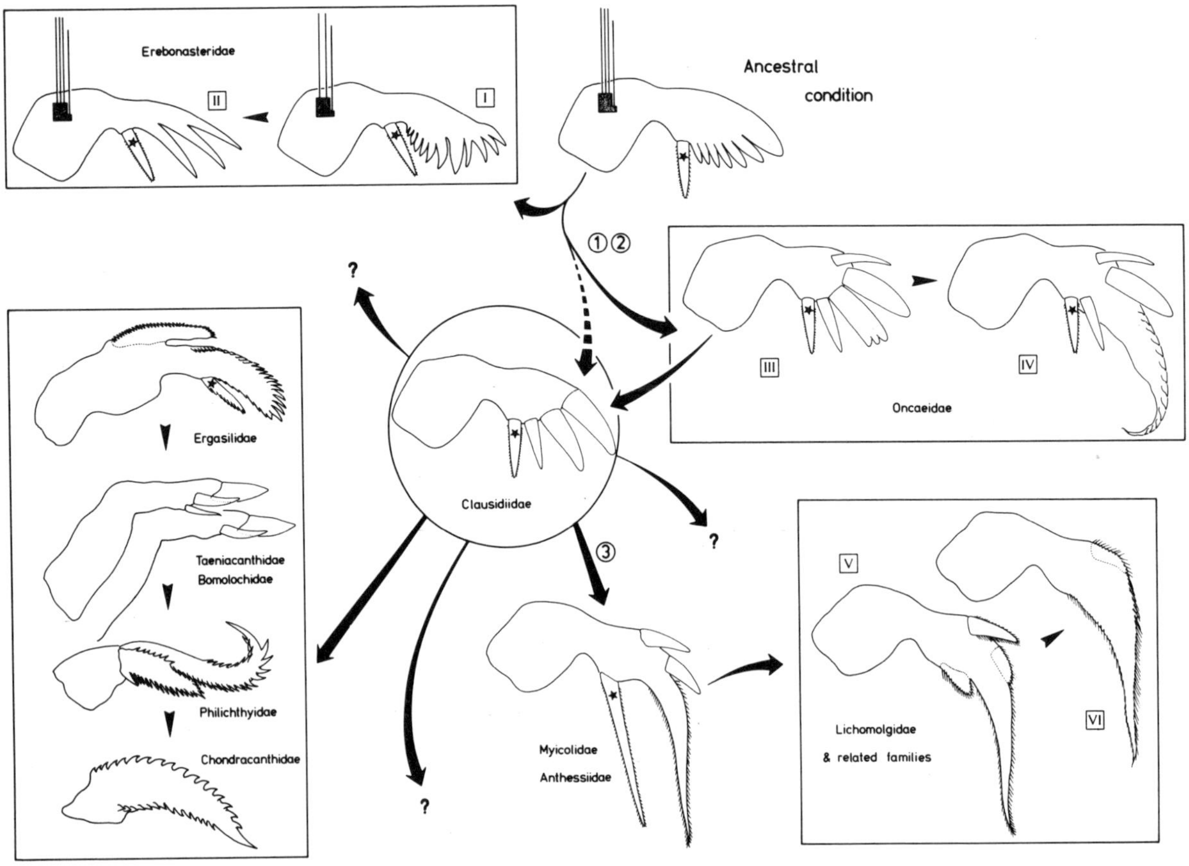

Figure 2.10.12. Schematic representation of changes in mandibular structure in poecilostomatoids. The arrows indicate possible derivations of structure and are not necessarily indicative of an ancestor-descendant relationship between taxa. [Key: I = Erebonasterids with an array of multicusped blades along distal margin of gnathobase, such as *Centobnaster*, II = Erebonasterids with a discrete number of simple blades not separated from margin of gnathobase, such as *Erebonaster* and *Amphicrossus*, III = Oncaeids with 5 articulated blades on the distal margin of the gnathobase, such as *Oncaea*, IV = Oncaeids with the central element fused to the gnathobase and modified as a lash-like process, as found in some species of *Lubbockia*, V = Lichomolgids showing transitional types of mandibles with the proximal elements not yet incorporated into the lash, such as *Lichothuria* Stock, *Chauliolobion* and *Lecanurius* Kossmann, and VI = Lichomolgids in which the proximal elements are fully incorporated into the margins of the lash, such as *Lichomolgus*. Numerals 1-3 indicate important evolutionary events, 1 = loss of palp, 2 = evolution of 5 distal articulating elements, 3 = formation of a true lash. The element marked with a star is the articulated dorsal seta that is found in most other orders of copepods.]

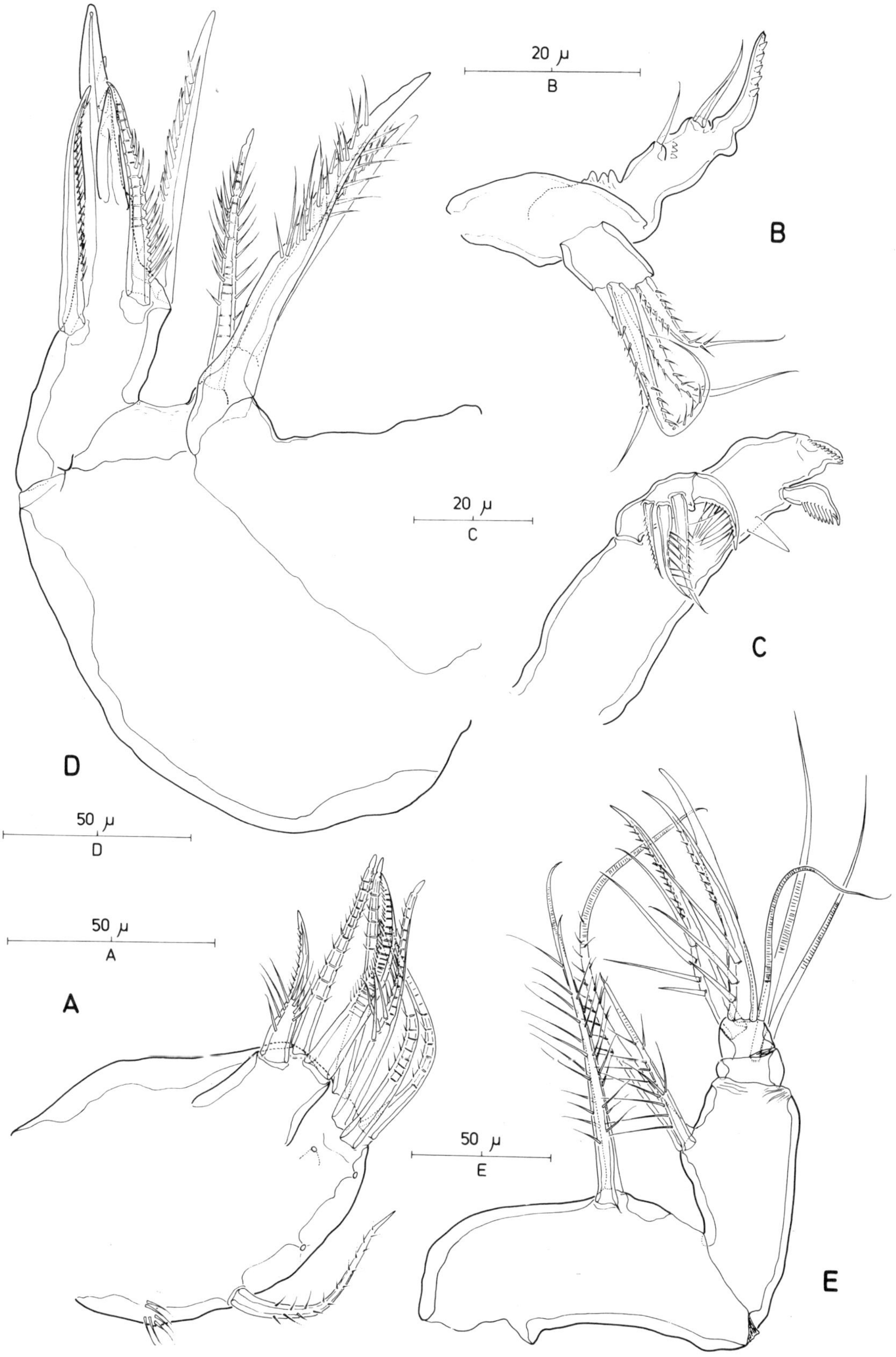

Figure 2.10.13. **A.** *Clausidium vancouverense*, maxillule. **B.** *Paralubbockia longipedia*, female maxillule. **C.** Male maxillule. **D.** *C.vancouverense*, maxilla. **E.** Maxilliped.

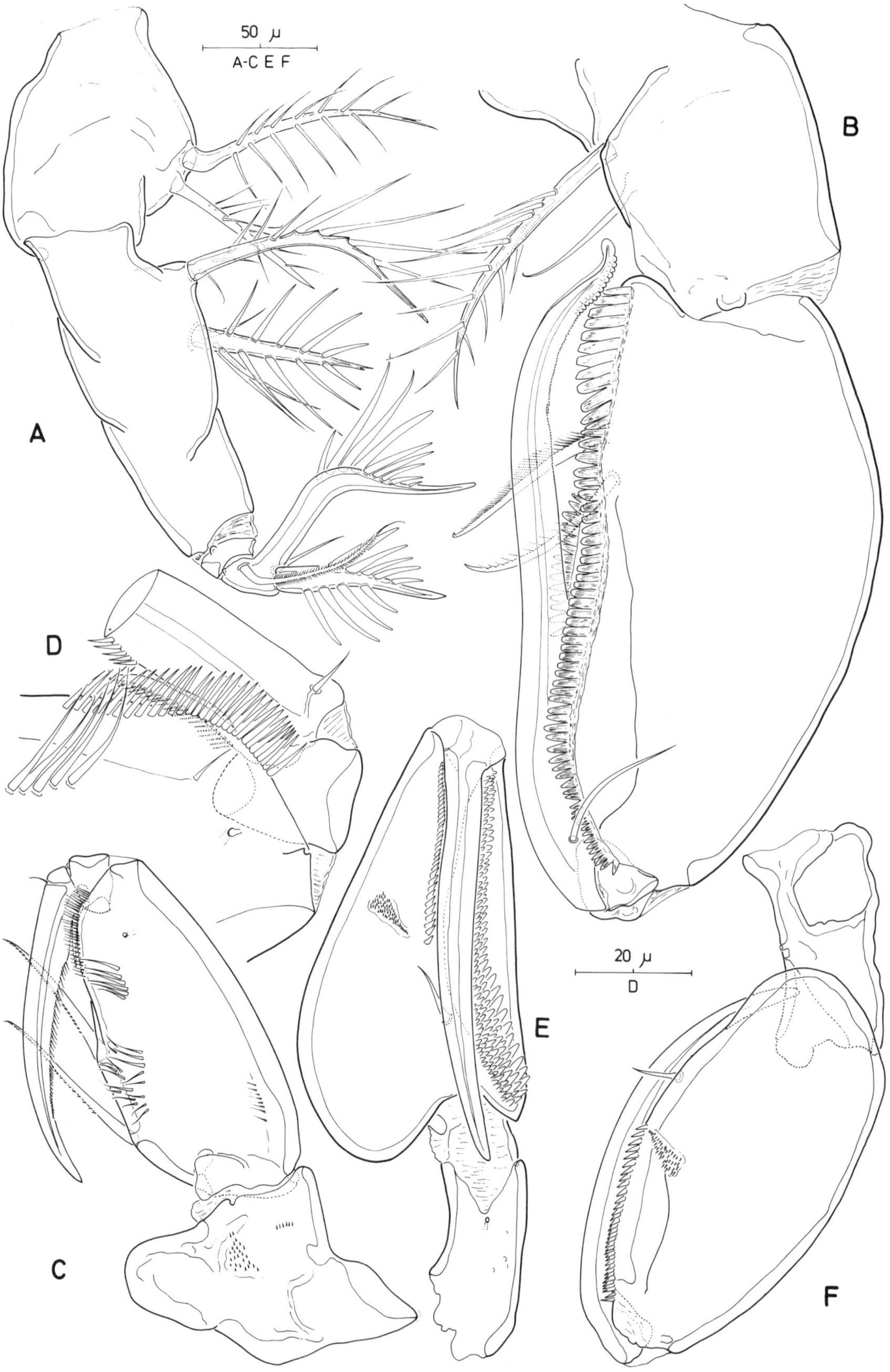

Figure 2.10.14. **A.** *Hemicyclops carinifer*, female maxilliped. **B.** Male maxilliped. **C.** *Oncaea media* f. *minor*, female maxilliped. **D.** Endopod of female maxilliped. **E.** Male maxilliped, anterior view. **F.** Male maxilliped, lateral view.

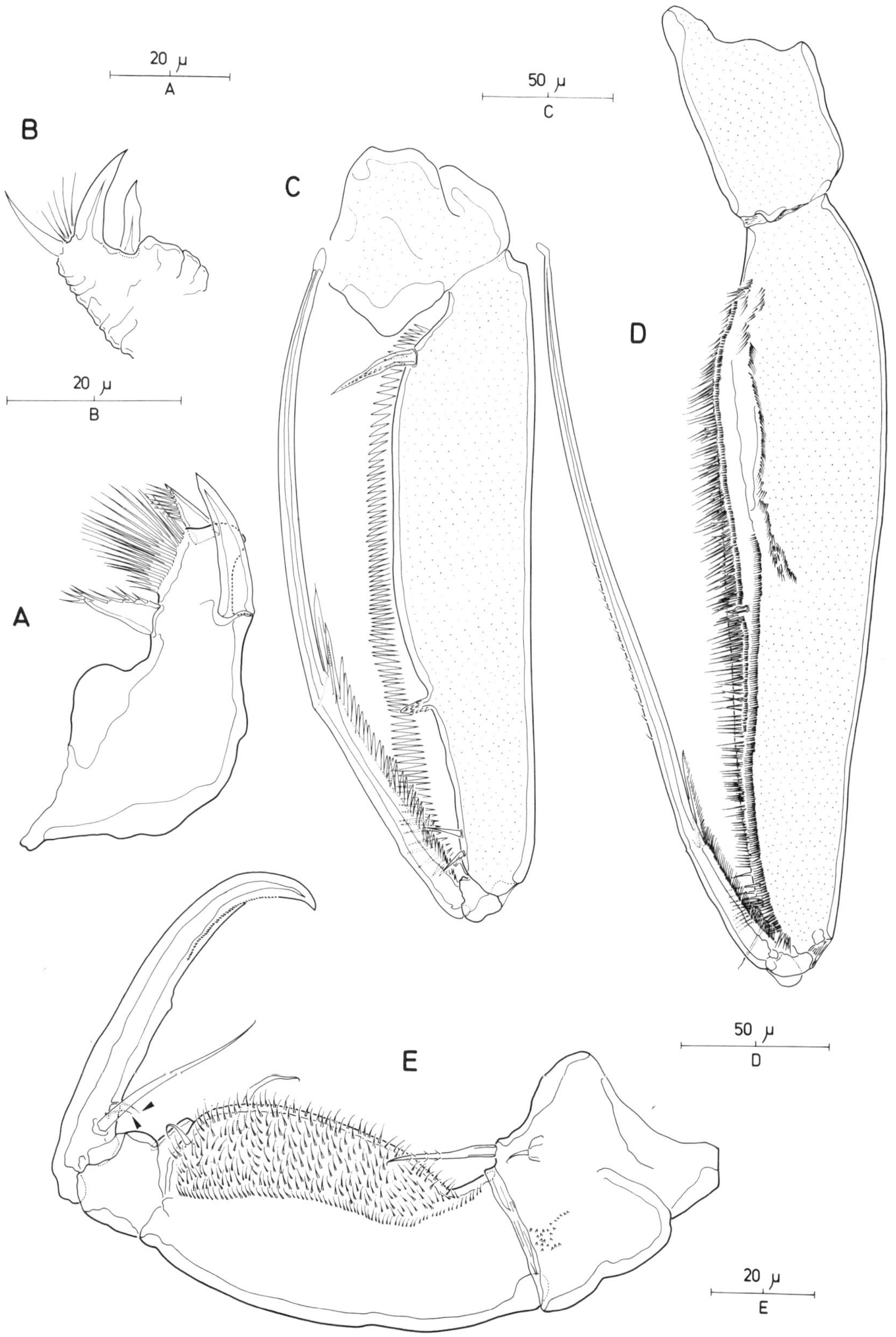

Figure 2.10.15. **A.** *Paralubbockia longipedia*, female mandible. **B.** Male mandible. **C.** Female maxilliped. **D.** Male maxilliped. **E.** *Tychidion guyanense*, female maxilliped (minute endopodal setae arrowed).

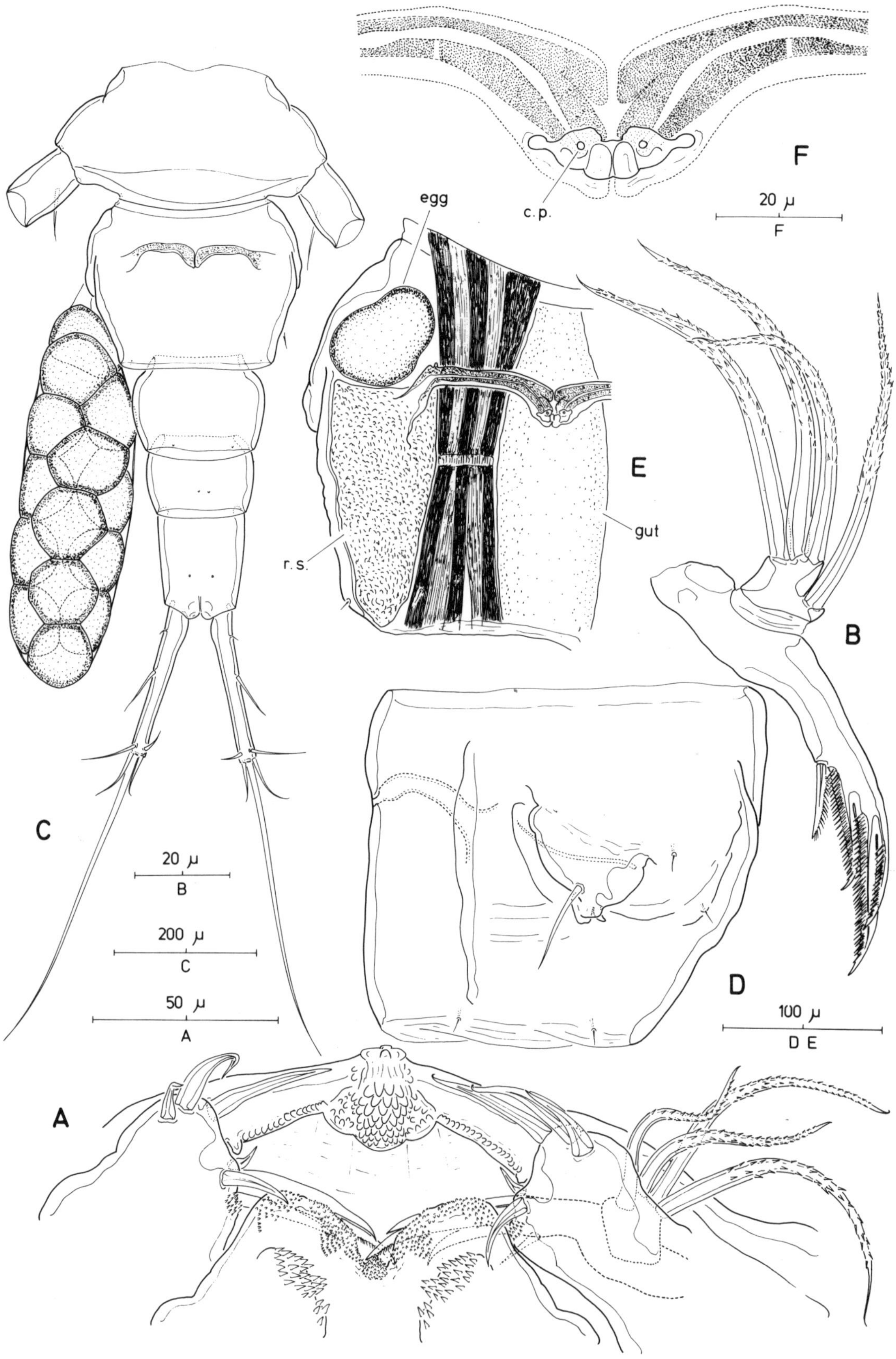

Figure 2.10.16. *Erebonaster protentipes.* **A.** Oral area showing labrum, paragnaths, maxillules and mandibles (right mandibular palp omitted). **B.** Mandible. **C.** Female urosome, ventral view. **D.** Female genital double somite, lateral view. **E.** Female genital double somite, lateral internal view (**r.s.** = seminal receptacle). **F.** Detail of copulatory pores (**c.p.**) and copulatory ducts.

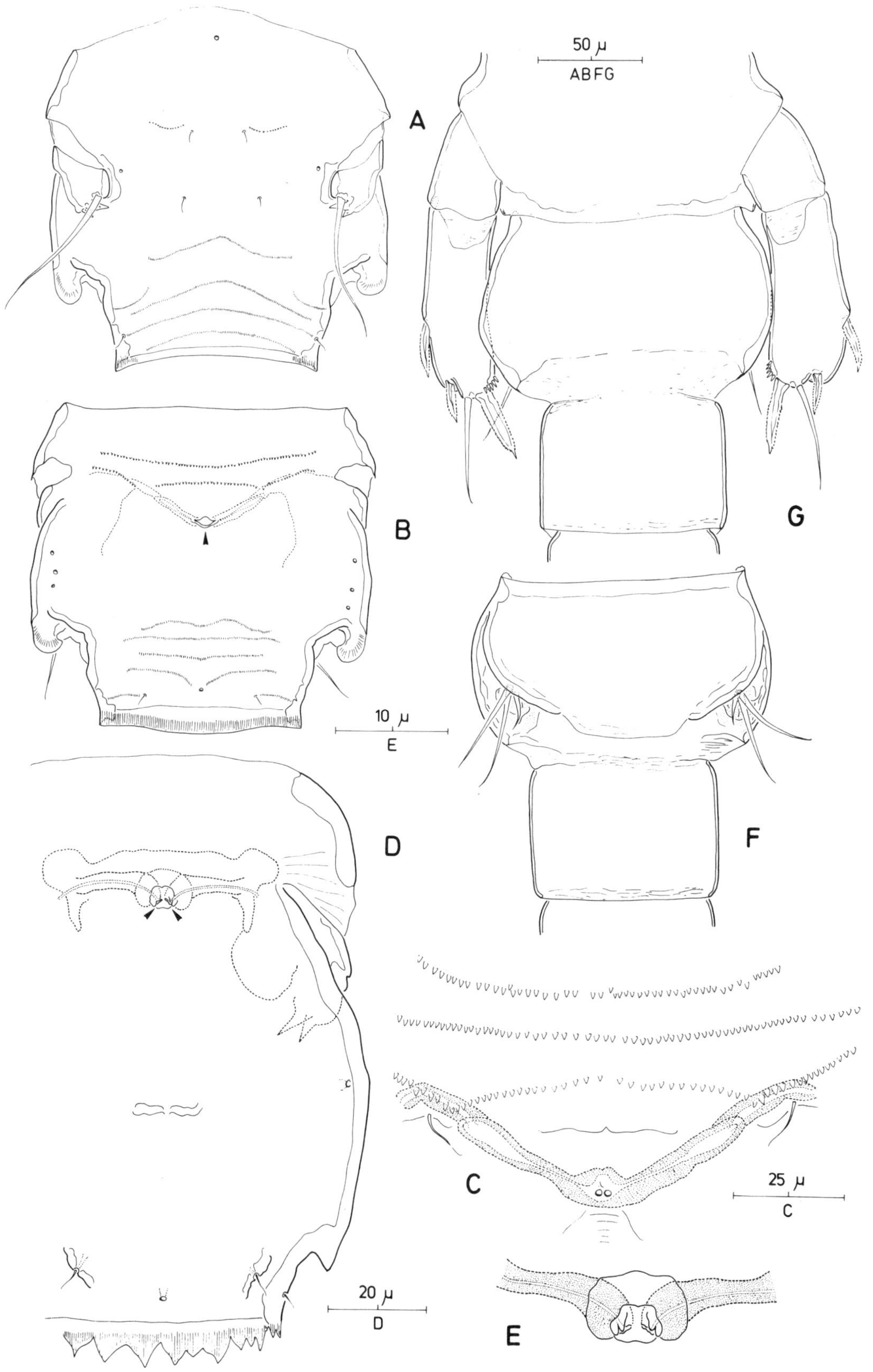

Figure 2.10.17. **A.** *Centobnaster humesi*, genital double somite, dorsal view. **B.** Ventral view. **C.** Copulatory pores. **D.** *Tychidion guyanense*, genital double somite, ventral view. **E.** Copulatory pores. **F.** Genital double somite, dorsal view. **G.** *Taeniacanthus wilsoni*, genital double somite and somite bearing fifth legs, ventral view. (Copulatory pores arrowed in B and D)

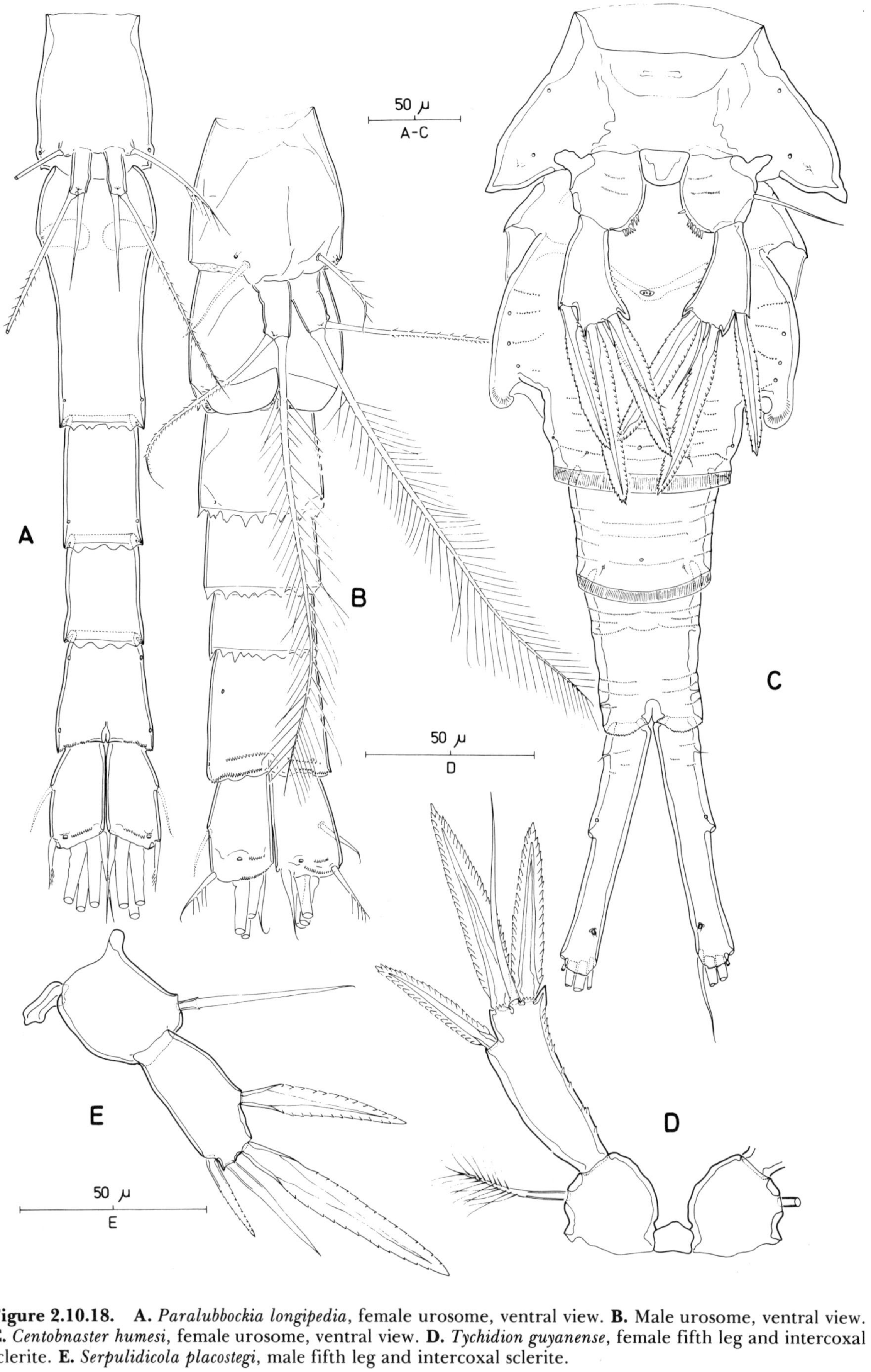

Figure 2.10.18. **A.** *Paralubbockia longipedia*, female urosome, ventral view. **B.** Male urosome, ventral view. **C.** *Centobnaster humesi*, female urosome, ventral view. **D.** *Tychidion guyanense*, female fifth leg and intercoxal sclerite. **E.** *Serpulidicola placostegi*, male fifth leg and intercoxal sclerite.

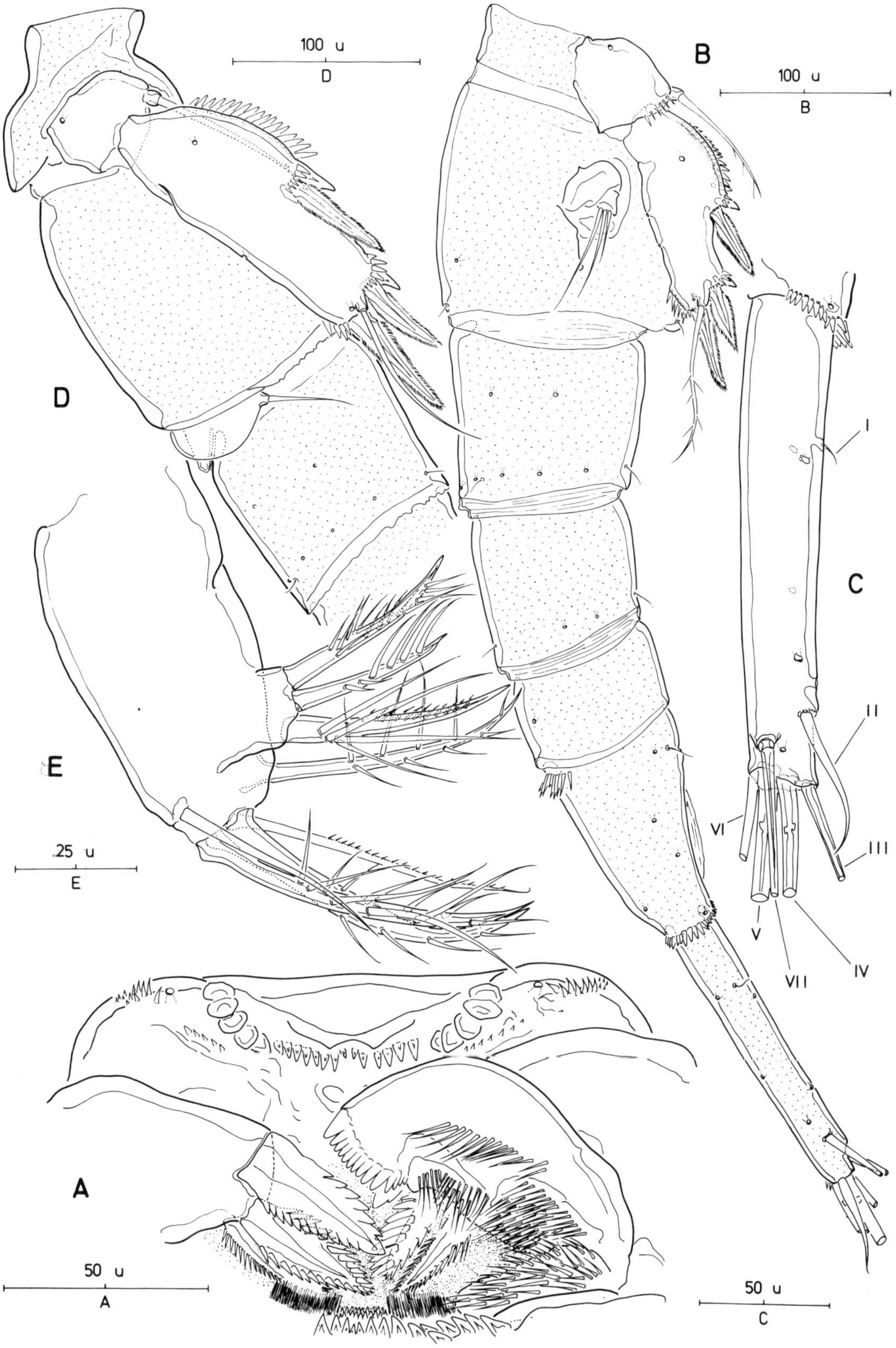

Figure 2.10.19. *Hemicyclops carinifer*. **A.** Oral area showing labrum, mandible and paragnath (right paragnath omitted). **B.** Female urosome, lateral view. **C.** Caudal ramus, dorsal view. **D.** First three urosome somites of male, lateral view. **E.** Maxillule.

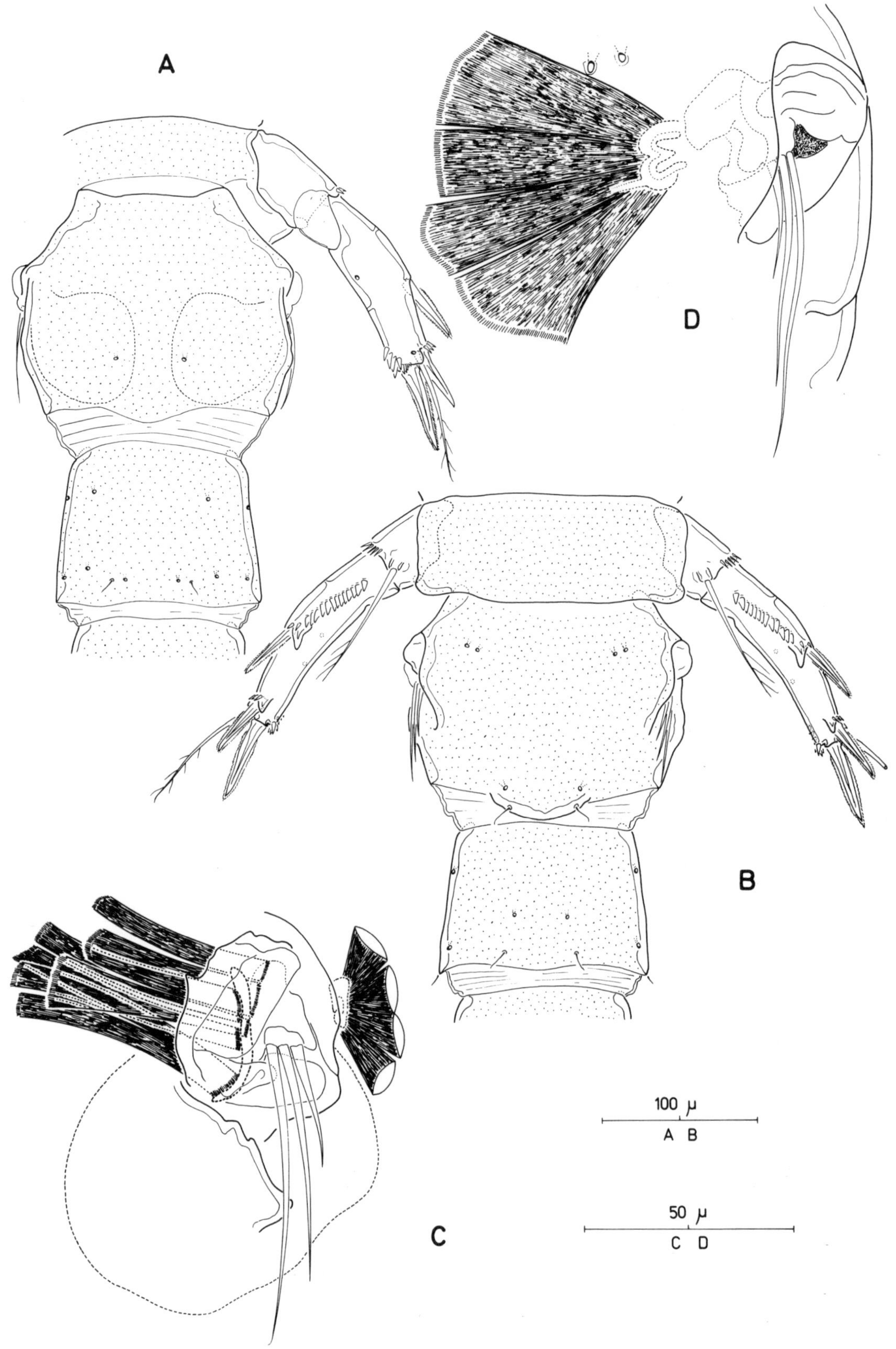

Figure 2.10.20. *Hemicyclops carinifer*. **A.** First three urosome somites of female (dotted lines showing seminal receptacles), ventral view. **B.** Dorsal view. **C.** Genital aperture and associated muscles, latero-dorsal view. **D.** Lateral view.

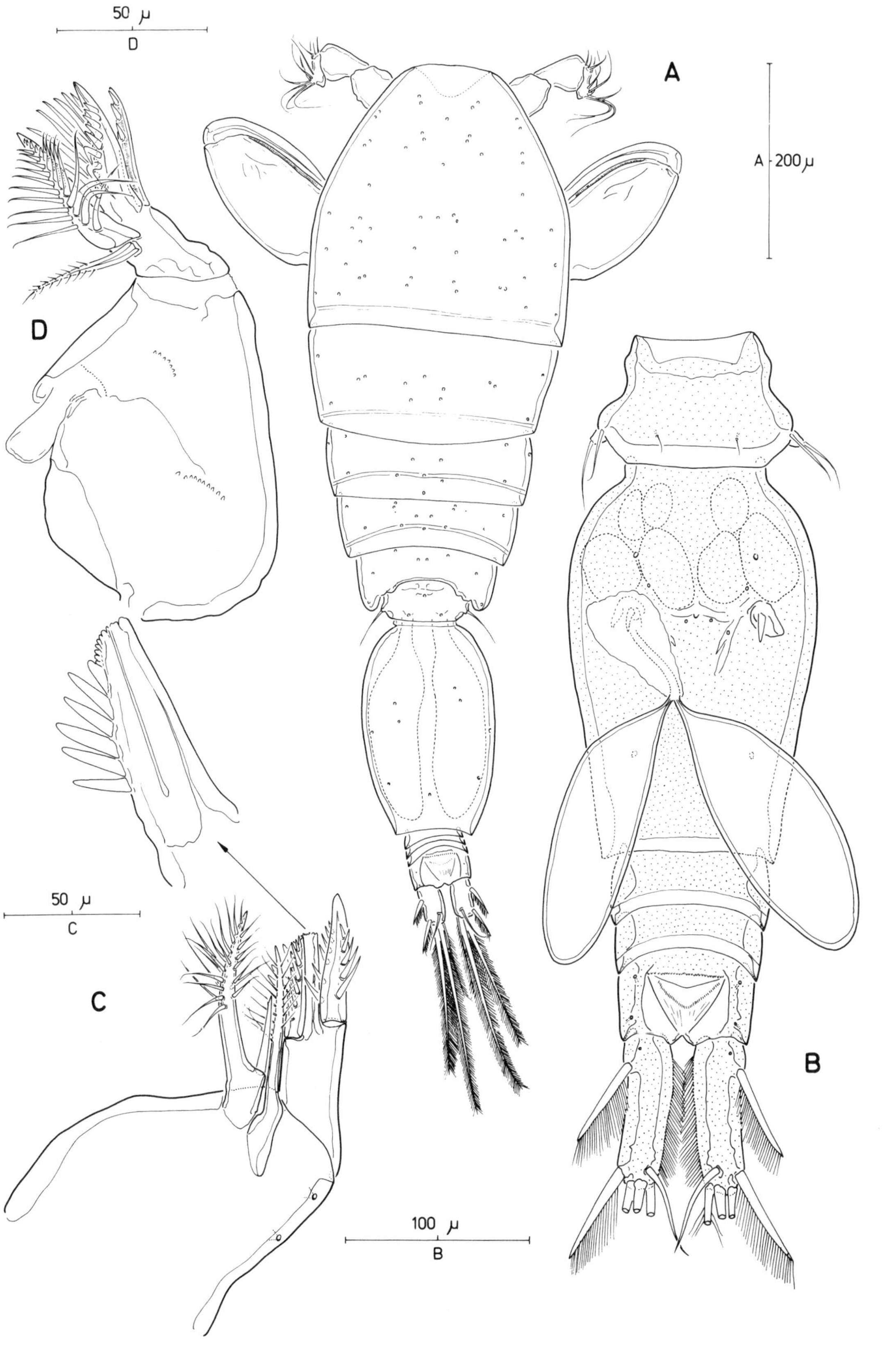

Figure 2.10.21. **A.** *Oncaea media* f. *minor*, male, dorsal view. **B.** *Oncaea venusta*, female urosome (with attached spermatophores), dorsal view. **C.** *Hemicyclops carinifer*, maxilla. **D.** *O.venusta*, maxilla.

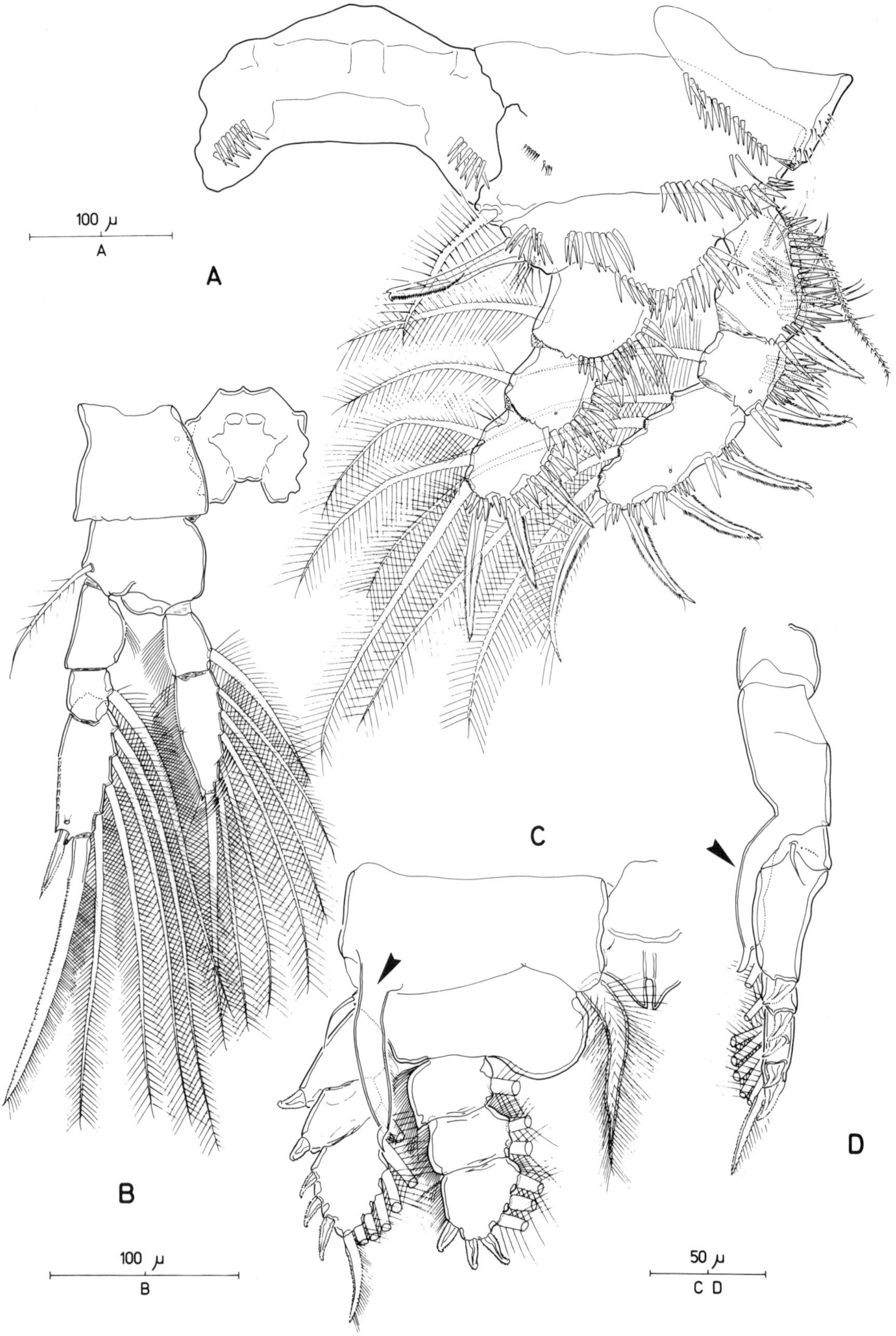

Figure 2.10.22. **A.** *Amphicrossus pacificus*, first leg. **B.** *Paralubbockia longipedia*, first leg. **C - D.** *Chauliolobion bulbosum*, second leg with arrows indicating lateral process on coxa.

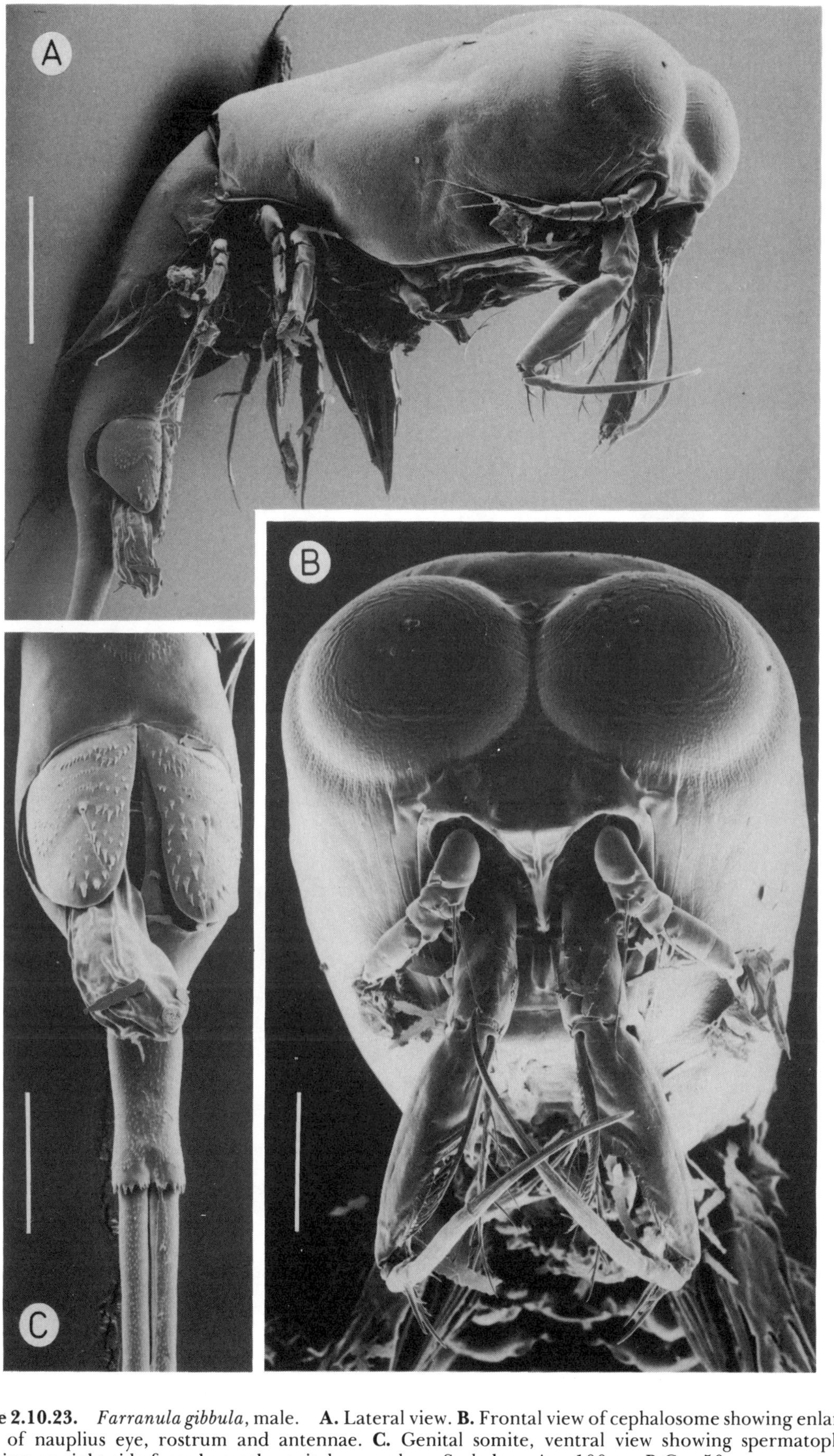

Figure 2.10.23. *Farranula gibbula*, male. **A.** Lateral view. **B.** Frontal view of cephalosome showing enlarged lenses of nauplius eye, rostrum and antennae. **C.** Genital somite, ventral view showing spermatophore emerging on right side from beneath genital operculum. Scale bars A = 100μm, B-C = 50μm.

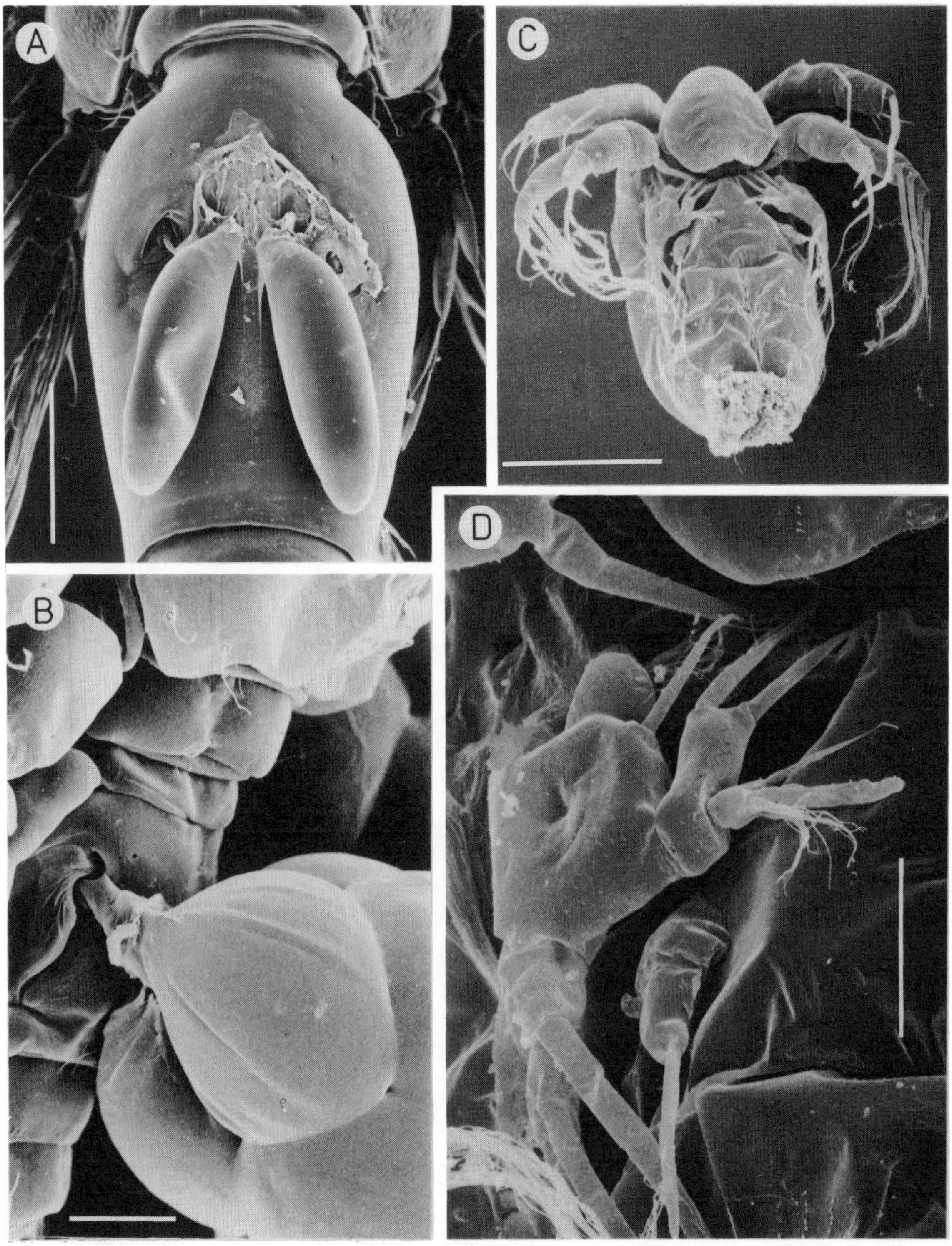

Figure 2.10.24. **A.** *Oncaea venusta*, female genital double somite with spermatophores attached, dorsal view. **B.** *Ergasilus sieboldi*, lateral view of female genital double somite showing egg sac originating anteriorly in slit-like genital aperture. **C.** Fifth nauplius, ventral view. **D.** Detail showing naupliar mandible. Scale bars A = 75μm, B = 20μm, C = 100μm, D = 20μm.

Chapter 3

EVOLUTIONARY TRENDS WITHIN THE COPEPODA

3.1 BODY SEGMENTATION

a. Ancestral state

The body of a copepod primitively comprises an anterior cephalosome of 6 somites and a posterior trunk of 9 somites plus the anal 'somite' which represents the telson. The cephalosome consists of 5 cephalic somites and the first thoracic somite which bears the maxillipeds. The trunk comprises the second to sixth thoracic somites each of which bears a pair of biramous swimming legs, the genital (seventh thoracic) somite bearing the paired, ventral genital openings in both sexes, and 4 postgenital abdominal somites which are limbless although the anal somite (=telson) bears a pair of setiferous caudal rami.

Cephalosome: The cephalosome incorporates the first thoracic somite in all copepods. This represents an apomorphy relative to the mystacocarid condition, in which the maxilliped bearing somite is not fused with the cephalon even though the sixth appendage is modified as a feeding appendage. The cephalosome should strictly be referred to as a cephalothorax but we retain cephalosome as a useful term for the anterior division of the ancestral copepod. Cephalothorax can then be used for those copepods in which one or more of the pedigerous somites is also incorporated into the anterior division of the body.

Telson and Caudal Rami: The homology of the structures present at the rear end of crustaceans has been the subject of much debate. Bowman (1971) fueled the controversy by attempting to distinguish between a true telson and an anal somite, and between caudal rami and uropods. Bowman interpreted the last segment of the copepod abdomen as an anal somite which bears paired uropods (=caudal rami) and a dorsal anal operculum representing a rudimentary, non-articulated telson. Schminke (1976) refuted many of Bowman's arguments but confined his analysis to the malacostracan groups.

Some authors (e.g. Kabata (1979) and Vaupel Klein (1982)) have continued to use Bowman's system of homologies for the posterior structures of copepods but we reject this system. Ontogenetic evidence indicates that the anal 'somite' is a telson (defined as a terminal unit having its mesoderm derived directly from the teloblasts after budding of the metameres has ceased) and is not a true somite (Boxshall, 1985). However, according to Dudley (1966) the anal somite of copepods is a somitic complex in which division is suppressed, and is not completely homologous with the telson. Further evidence contradicting Bowman's interpretation is the absence of an operculum in the most primitive groups of copepods, including the Platycopioida and the most plesiomorphic calanoid family, the Pseudocyclopidae. Whilst accepting that the terminal division of the copepod body represents the telson we propose to continue the established practice of referring to it as the anal somite. As a consequence of recognising the anal somite as the telson, we refer to its 'appendages' as the caudal rami. Copepods do not possess uropods.

Abdominal Annulations: There are a few copepods that appear to have more than 4 abdominal somites. For example, the siphonostomatoid *Caligus quinqueabdominalis* Heegaard and several species in the cyclopoid family Ascidicolidae (see Illg & Dudley, 1980; Ooishi & Illg, 1988) have between 5 and 8 apparent somites. However, these represent secondary annulations of the basic abdominal somites.

b. Transformations

Cephalothorax: The second thoracic somite (=first pedigerous somite) is commonly fused with the cephalosome to form a cephalothorax derived from 7 original somites. Representatives with a cephalothorax are known from most copepod orders and in the Cyclopoida (Gurney 1933), Harpacticoida (Lang, 1948a) and Calanoida (Giesbrecht, 1892) the great majority displays this condition. All siphonostomatoids and monstrilloids have a cephalothorax but the other eight orders contain at least one representative that retains the second thoracic somite as a free somite. All members of the Platycopioida, Mormonilloida and Gelyelloida retain a defined first pedigerous somite but in the first two of these three orders the joint is marked only by a suture line without arthrodial membrane and is non-functional.

Genital Double Somite: The most common fusion between body somites is the formation of a genital double somite from the genital and first abdominal somites in the female. All Calanoida, Mormonilloida, Gelyelloida, and Monstrilloida, the majority of the Harpacticoida, Siphonostomatoida, Poecilostomatoida and Cyclopoida, and some representatives of the Misophrioida (for example, *Speleophria* and *Boxshallia*) possess a genital double somite. Only the Platycopioida does not show this condition.

Other Fusions: A great variety of fusions between other somites is also found in the copepods. Fusions of pedigerous somites are common in the Calanoida, *Euaugaptilus* for example (see Boxshall, 1985), has the fourth and fifth pedigerous somites fused into a single unit at the rear end of the prosome. Many of the more highly transformed parasites exhibit fusions between some pedigerous somites and the genital somite. The majority of siphonostomatoids parasitic on fishes (for example, the caligiform families) have the fifth pedigerous somite incorporated into a genital complex with the genital double somite. However, such fusions are important in analysing phylogenetic relationships only within these particular orders and have no significance at the ordinal level.

Modifications in Interstitial forms: In some interstitial harpacticoids, such as the paramesochrid *Apodopsyllus* Kunz, the somite boundaries within the urosome are very poorly defined (figure 2.4.24A). This may enhance their ability to perform more worm-like movements within the sediment. Other small interstitial forms, including the harpacticoids *Paramesochra mielkei* and *Intermedopsyllus intermedius* (Scott & Scott) and the cyclopoids *Psammocyclopina hindleyi* and *Metacyclopina* aff. *harpacticoidea* Klie (Klie, 1949) possess a secondary 'pseudosomite' separated off from the anterior end of the genital double somite (arrowed in figure 3.1.1A-C). These secondary subdivisions may provide another mechanism allowing a greater versatility of urosomal movements.

3.2 TAGMOSIS

a. Ancestral state

The main tagmata are the anterior prosome and posterior urosome, separated by the hinge joint between the sixth thoracic somite and the genital somite (the gymnoplean position).

Kabata (1979), Boxshall (1986c) and Ho (1990) considered the Gymnoplea and Podoplea to be monophyletic, presumably on the assumption that the two types of prosome-urosome articulation are apomorphies that evolved independently from a common ancestor that lacked prosome-urosome differentiation. Marcotte (1982) however, considered that the podoplean-type joint could be the ancestral one and the gymnoplean-type derived. This would indicate a polyphyletic or paraphyletic status for the Podoplea. We regard the gymnoplean type of tagmosis as the ancestral condition on the basis of out-group comparison. A homologous boundary (arrowed in figure 3.2.1A-B,D) is present in related maxillopodan taxa such as the Thecostraca (Grygier, 1987) and the Tantulocarida (Boxshall & Lincoln, 1987), dividing the trunk into an anterior locomotory tagma of 6 thoracic somites and a posterior tagma, the first somite of which is the genital somite, at least in the male (figure 3.2.1A-D). The posterior tagma includes the genital somite bearing the seventh thoracopods which are associated with the genital apertures in both sexes of copepods. In the Thecostraca (both Facetotecta and Ascothoracida) and the Tantulocarida the male genital

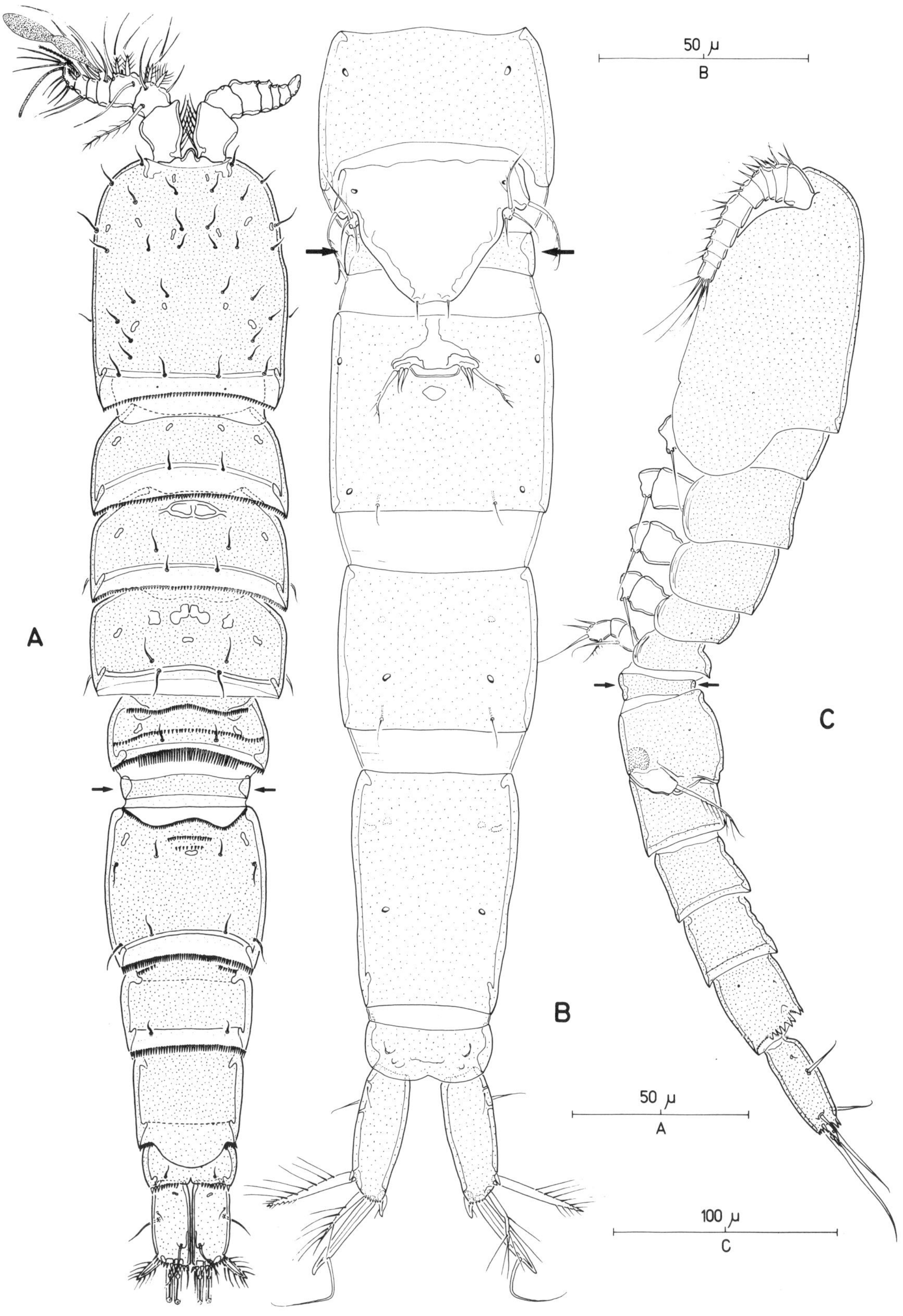

Figure 3.1.1. **A.** *Paramesochra mielkei*, female, dorsal view. **B.** *Intermedopsyllus intermedius*, urosome of female, ventral view. **C.** *Metacyclopina* aff. *harpacticoidea*, female, lateral view. [Arrows indicate 'pseudosomite'.]

apertures are associated with the seventh thoracopod (fine arrows in figure 3.2.1). The fossil Orstenocarida show a similar tagmosis (Müller & Walossek, 1988). Orstenocarids are the only maxillopodans with a well developed seventh thoracopod (figure 3.2.1C) and this limb is not modified as a copulatory device or intromittent organ.

On the basis of out-group analysis the Gymnoplea, comprising the Platycopioida and Calanoida, proves to be a paraphyletic taxon, diagnosed only by plesiomorphies.

There have been isolated reports of vestiges of paired limbs on the postgenital abdominal somites. *Limnocletodes behningi* Borutzky has paired setiferous lobes on the first and second postgenital somites that Smirnov (1933) interpreted as vestigial appendages. He further surmised that the ancestral copepod originally had paired appendages on all somites. Grygier (1983) suggested that these structures were probably not limbs but fused papillae similar to those widely found in the Cletodidae. Examination of *Limnocletodes secundus* Sewell revealed serially homologous ornamentation elements (figure 3.2.2A) around the lateral and ventrolateral margins of the postgenital somites. There is no evidence to suggest that these are anything other than papillate somitic sensilla. Similar ornamentation elements are positioned laterally around the margin of the genital double and succeeding abdominal somites in numerous members of the Cletodidae (figure 3.2.2B).

b. Transformations

The gymnoplean-type of tagmosis in which the articulation between prosome and urosome lies between the fifth pedigerous and genital somites is found in the Platycopioida and Calanoida. In all other orders the prosome-urosome articulation primitively lies between the fourth and fifth pedigerous somites. This is the podoplean type of tagmosis. The podoplean type of tagmosis therefore is derived and constitutes a unique apomorphy uniting the eight orders grouped in the superorder Podoplea. In both the gymnoplean and podoplean tagmosis patterns the urosomal somites are hoop-like and are not differentiated into tergum, pleura and sternum. The podoplean condition is, therefore, characterised by the failure of the pleural folds, in particular, of the fifth pedigerous somite to differentiate. In vermiform and fusiform harpacticoids the distinction between prosome and urosome is poorly defined externally. Por (1984b) introduced the term dolichoplean for those vermiform types in which the prosome-urosome boundary is secondarily reduced. The Dolichoplea is not, however, a valid taxon.

Reductions of Fourth Pedigerous Somite: In some podopleans, such as the cyclopoid *Thespesiopsyllus* (figure 2.8.34A) and the siphonostomatoid *Cancerilla* Dalyell, the fourth pedigerous somite has become so reduced that it has been suggested that the prosome-urosome boundary lies between the third and fourth pedigerous somites. Close examination of these forms reveals that the tagma boundary remains in the podoplean position. Somites anterior to this boundary have tergites with well defined epimeral areas whereas true urosomal somites lack defined epimeral areas and do not have terga and pleura differentiated from the original hoops of integument that appear during ontogeny.

Trunk Musculature: The basic longitudinal trunk muscles of copepods comprise a pair of large dorsal muscles and a pair of smaller ventral muscles. The dorsal muscles originate dorsolaterally on the dorsal cephalic shield about at the level of the maxillary somite. The ventral muscles originate on the postmaxillulary and postmaxillary apodemes. In some podopleans and gymnopleans an oblique muscle passes from its ventral origin on the postmaxillary apodeme to join the dorsal muscle bundle about at the level of the second pedigerous somite. In gymnopleans, such as *Euaugaptilus* (figure 3.2.3A) and podopleans, such as *Benthomisophria* (figure 3.2.3B), bundles of the dorsal muscles insert at each prosomal somite boundary and just inside the urosome. The dorsal muscles continue down the urosome, finally inserting in the anal somite. The ventral muscles pass posteriorly through the prosome with, at most, indirect tendinous attachments at the intersomitic boundaries, to insert just inside the urosome. They continue along the urosome to finally insert on the anal somite. The longitudinal trunk muscles are responsible for the gross movements of the urosome.

Ontogeny: First copepodid stages of both gymnoplean and podoplean copepods have 5 postcephalosomic trunk somites. There seems to be a functional tagma boundary between the third and

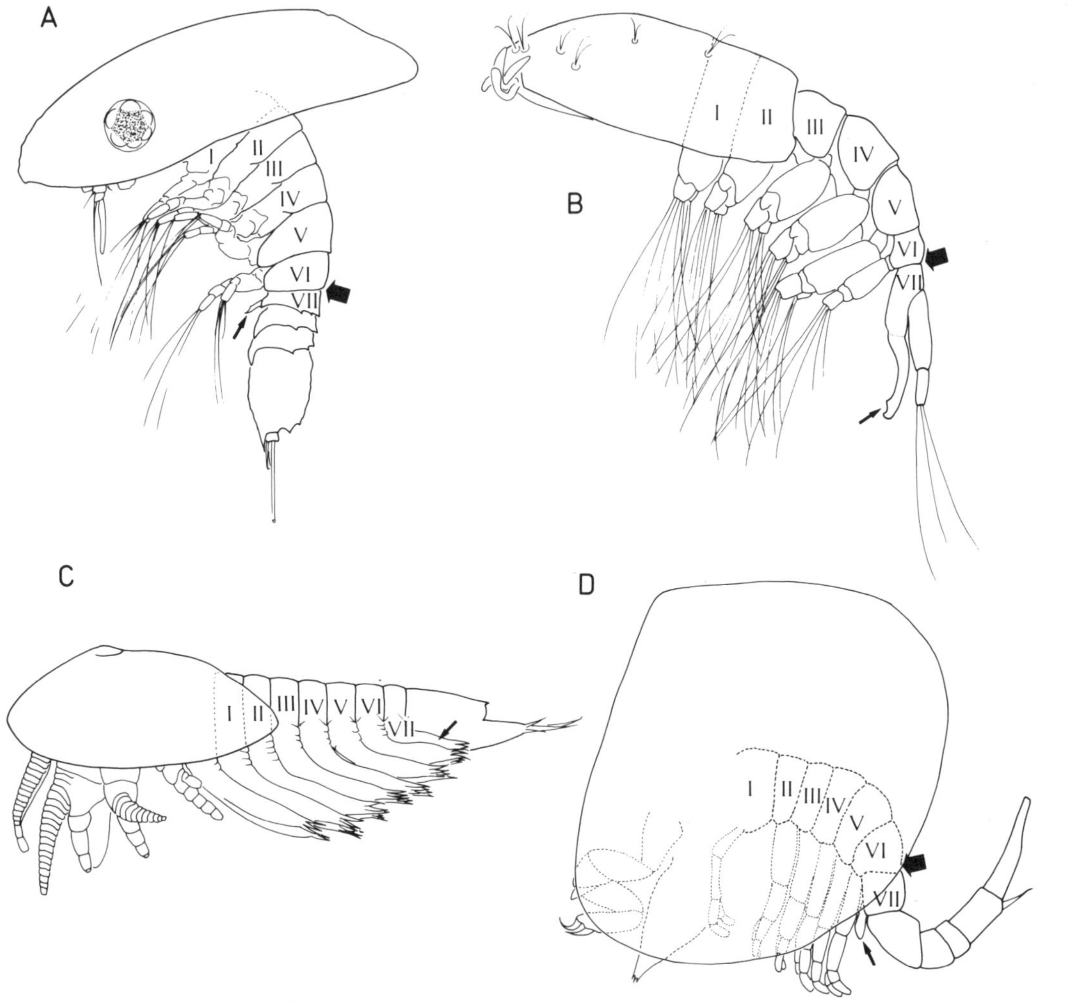

Figure 3.2.1. Major tagma boundaries in maxillopodan taxa. **A.** Facetotectan. **B.** Adult male tantulocaridan. **C.** Orstenocaridan. **D.** Ascothoracid. [Large arrows indicate boundary between locomotory thoracic tagma and posterior tagma; small arrows indicate seventh trunk limb.]

fourth of these trunk somites in gymnopleans but not in podopleans (figure 3.2.4) (see references in Boxshall (1985)). This tagma boundary is not morphologically specialised but is a flexure point defined by the behaviour of the animal. At the second copepodid stage the functional flexure point is located between the fourth and fifth postcephalosomic somites in both podopleans and gymnopleans. This is the definitive position of the prosome-urosome boundary in adult podopleans. The definitive prosome-urosome boundary in gymnopleans, between the fifth and sixth postcephalosomic somites, is attained at the third copepodid stage. The fixation of the tagma boundary one moult earlier in development may indicate a heterochronic origin for the podoplean tagmosis. After fixation of the boundary the joint is able to become more highly modified by the development of condyles.

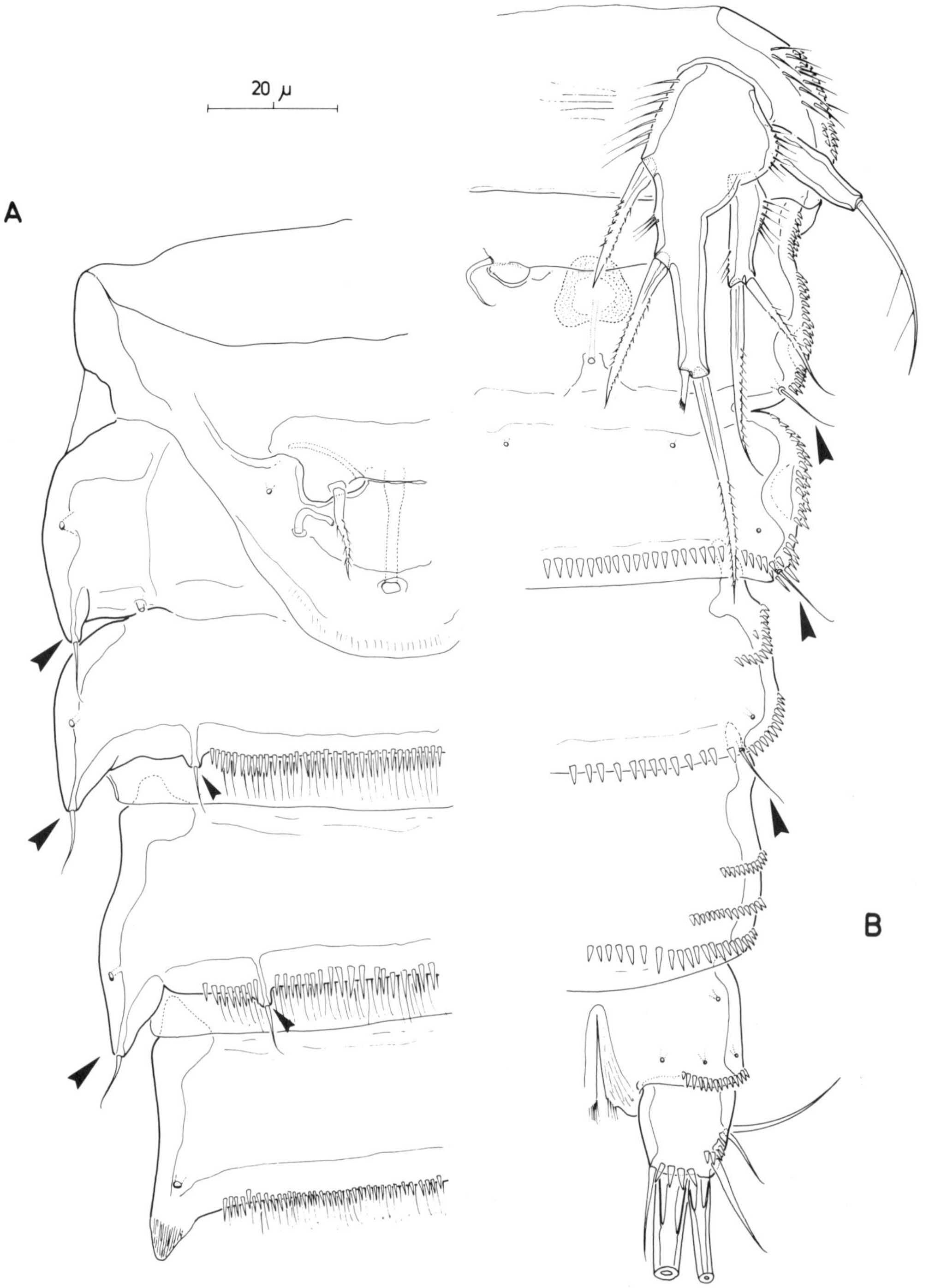

Figure 3.2.2. Abdominal ornamentation. **A**. *Limnocletodes secundus*. **B**. *Cletodes* sp. [Arrows indicate ornamentation elements, often on raised processes, that could be misinterpreted as vestigial swimming legs.]

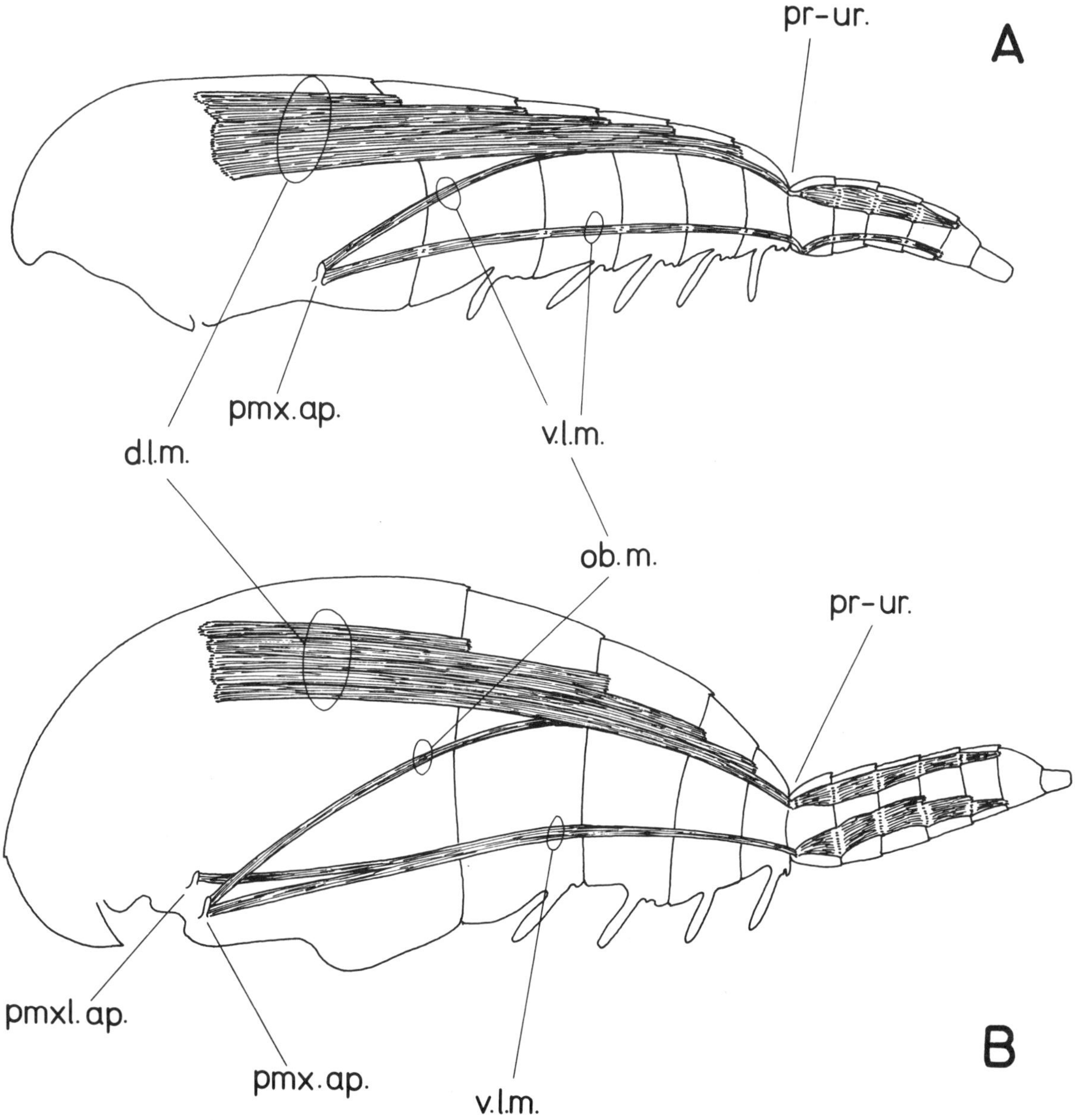

Figure 3.2.3. Comparison of the longitudinal trunk musculature between gymnoplean (A) and podoplean (B) tagmosis. [Abbreviations: **d.l.m.** = dorsal longitudinal trunk muscles, **ob.m.** = oblique muscles, **pmx.ap.** = postmaxillary apodeme, **pmxl.ap.** = postmaxillulary apodeme, **pr-ur.** = prosome-urosome boundary, **v.l.m.** = ventral longitudinal trunk muscles.]

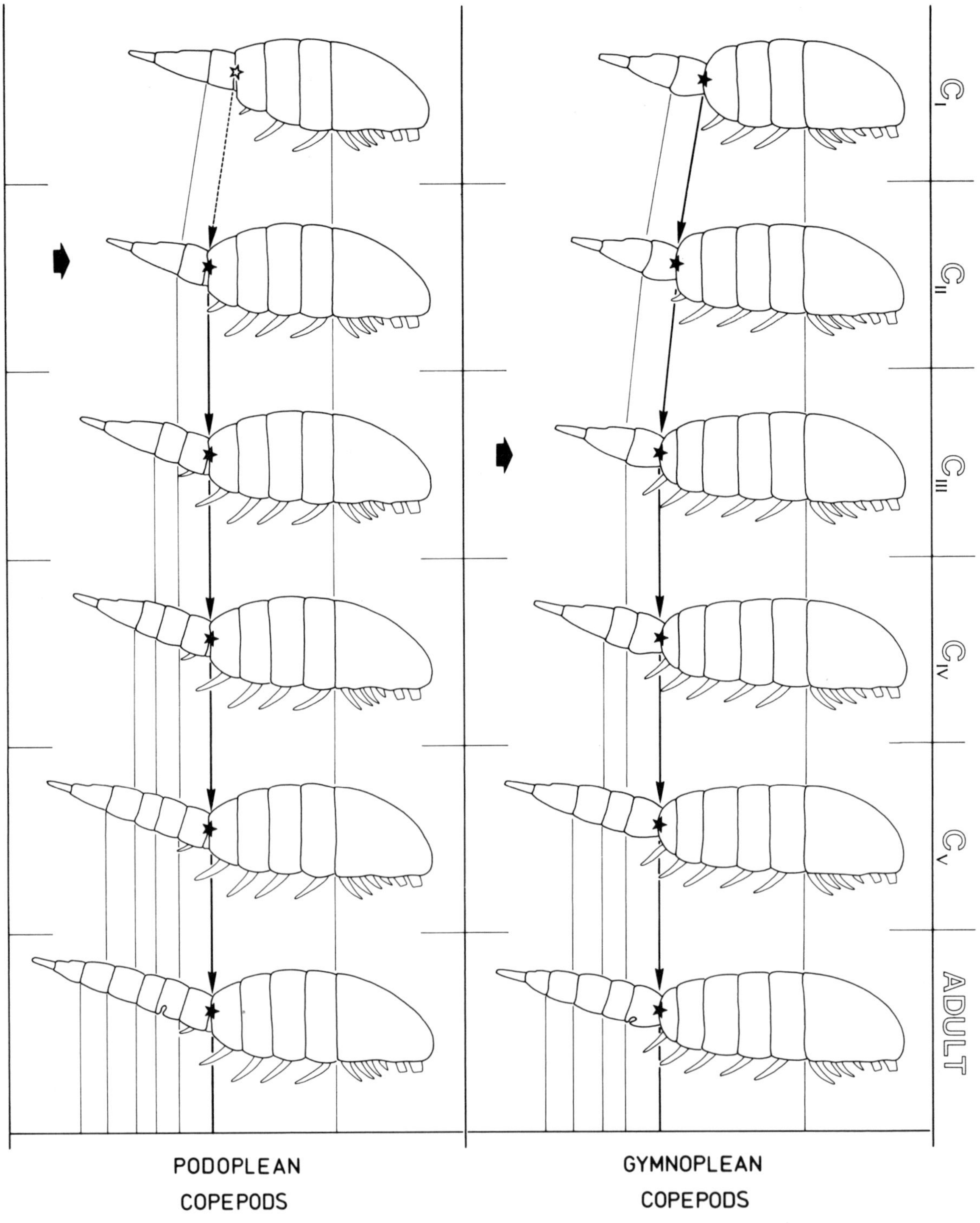

Figure 3.2.4. Comparison of the development pattern in podoplean and gymnoplean copepods. [CI-CV = first copepodid to fifth copepodid: solid stars indicate flexure planes, hollow stars indicate poorly defined flexure planes, arrows indicate the stage at which the definitive tagmosis is attained and specialisation of the joint commences.]

3.3 GENITAL APPARATUS AND SIXTH LEG

a. Ancestral State

The primitive condition of the Copepoda is a bilaterally symmetrical, paired reproductive system in both sexes. Gonads, gonoducts and genital openings are all paired, and the genital openings are located on the ventral body surface at the posterior margin of the genital somite. Spermatozoa transfer is by means of paired spermatophores. The spermatophores discharge via spermatophore tubules into a pair of copulatory pores, each of which primitively lies within the genital aperture of the female, concealed beneath the lobe of the genital operculum. Spermatozoa pass into the copulatory pores and along the paired copulatory ducts into the paired seminal receptacles where they are stored. Spermatozoa are released via the paired receptacle ducts into the genital antrum where fertilisation takes place. Fertilised eggs are released through the gonopores that represent the oviduct openings. The sixth legs are associated with the genital openings in both sexes. Each leg is reduced to a plate-like operculum that closes off the opening. The plates are symmetrical and bear up to 3 setae or spines in both sexes.

The plesiomorphic arrangement is retained in the males of all orders. It is also retained in females of the Platycopioida. In females of the calanoid genera *Pseudocyclops* (figure 2.2.32A) and *Boholina*, and the harpacticoid genus *Canuellina* (figure 2.4.25B) the basic system of paired, ventral apertures is retained but the genital and first abdominal somites are fused to form a genital double somite and the apertures have migrated anteriorly.

b. Transformations of the Female System

Analysis of the variation expressed in the arrangement of the female genital system in the Copepoda reveals that a number of independent processes have taken place. The first of these is the migration of the genital apertures, the second is the fusion of the genital apertures, and the third is the isolation of the copulatory pores remote from the gonopores.

i) Migration of the genital apertures

In all female Poecilostomatoida (except members of the family Erebonasteridae) the paired genital apertures have migrated to the lateral or dorsolateral surface of the genital somite. No other changes have taken place, i.e. the copulatory pore and gonopore lie beneath the operculum on each side. This migration has both anterior and dorsal components, as shown by the poecilostomatoid *Hemicyclops carinifer*, a species in which the genital and first abdominal somites are not fused to form a double somite. Here the female genital apertures are positioned on the lateral surface close to the anterior margin of the genital somite (figures 2.10.19B and 2.10.20A-D). The dorsal migration takes place gradually during ontogeny. Malt (1986) found that the sixth legs of *Oncaea media* Giesbrecht first appeared at the fifth copepodid stage as a small triangular flap located laterally on the genital double somite. In the adult they close off the genital apertures and are located dorsally on the double somite.

A similar anterior and dorsal migration has taken place in female cyclopoids of the family Notodelphyidae. *Notodelphys* itself has a separate genital somite, totally enclosed by the brood pouch in the adult female, and the genital apertures are located on the dorsolateral surface very close to the anterior margin of the genital somite (figure 2.8.40C).

In females of the cyclopoid family Oithonidae the genital apertures have migrated to the lateral surface of the genital double somite. Each has become elongated transversely around the side of the somite. The dorsal part of the aperture is closed off by setose flaps derived from the sixth legs and the egg sacs are extruded from this part. Each spermatophore discharges via a spermatophore tubule which extends into the slit-like ventral part of the aperture (figures 2.8.30A-E and 2.8.40A-B) where the copulatory pore leading to the copulatory duct and seminal receptacle is located.

ii) Fusion of the gonopores

The medial migration and fusion of the gonopores resulting in the formation of a single median genital aperture on the genital somite is found in females of the Mormonilloida (figure 2.6.2A-E), the Monstrilloida (figure 2.5.4C-E), the harpacticoid family Longipediidae, and in most female calanoids (Vaupel Klein, 1982; Blades, 1977; Blades & Youngbluth, 1979).

In the majority of female calanoids, excluding the families Pseudocyclopidae and Boholinidae, and at least some members of the Arietellidae, the sixth legs are fused to form a common operculum. In *Mesaiokeras* paired gonopores and seminal receptacles are retained beneath this common operculum. In *Paracyclopia* Fosshagen the gonopores are fused so that the common operculum closes off a common gonopore but paired seminal receptacles are retained. Finally, in *Stephos* Scott a functional receptacle is retained on one side of the body only.

In female *Longipedia* there is a compact, median genital field closed off by a complex operculum armed with a median and 3 pairs of lateral spinous processes (figure 2.4.28C). Within this genital field lies a common genital aperture (large arrow in figure 2.4.25A) through which the eggs are laid and a single median copulatory pore (small arrow in figure 2.4.25A) into which the spermatophore discharges.

iii) Isolation of the copulatory pores

In the females of many copepods the copulatory pores are more or less widely separated from the gonopores and are no longer covered by opercula derived from the sixth legs. The simplest examples of this type are in the Siphonostomatoida. In the caligid *Lepeophtheirus pectoralis* the paired copulatory pores are located just medial to the opercular plates that close off the paired gonopores (figure 2.9.25A-B). This arrangement is probably derived by the medial migration of the copulatory pores away from their opercula, which remained in the original ventrolateral position. A similar arrangement is found in the canuellid harpacticoid *Sunaristes dardani* (figure 2.4.25C) although the paired copulatory pores are covered by an isolated spinous process which might be derived from a modified armature element of the sixth leg. In the cyclopoid *Archinotodelphys polynesiensis* (figure 2.8.31B) separate, paired copulatory pores are retained either side of the ventral midline but the gonopores have migrated further, onto the lateral surface of the somite. In the siphonostomatoid *Asterocheres* the gonopores have migrated further still, onto the dorsal surface of the somewhat flattened genital double somite (figure 2.9.34A-B). The paired copulatory pores remain on the ventral surface but have moved laterally and no longer lie close to the midline. In *Chasmatopontius* the copulatory pores have been displaced posteriorly and laterally, lying on the lateral surface of the genital double somite close to its posterior margin (figure 2.9.28A). The arrangement of the pores in *Lernanthropus kroyeri* van Beneden (figure 2.9.29B) is similar to that of *Chasmatopontius*. In the misophrioid genus *Misophria* (figure 2.3.15A-D) and the harpacticoid genus *Canuella* (figure 2.4.29D-E) paired copulatory pores are retained but they have migrated back along the ventral surface and lie some distance posterior to the level of the gonopores.

Paired Midventral Copulatory Pores: The aberrant poecilostomatoid family Erebonasteridae also has paired copulatory pores but they are located very close together within a common depression in the ventral surface of the genital double somite (figures 2.10.16C-F and 2.10.17B-E). In erebonasterids the gonopores are situated dorsolaterally on the double somite.

Median Copulatory Pore: The presence of a single, median, ventral copulatory pore is characteristic of all monstrilloids and gelyelloids, the majority of harpacticoids, the majority of cyclopoids and some representatives of the Misophrioida and Calanoida. Although in monstrilloids the copulatory pore is large it has hitherto been overlooked, probably because it is located in a depression on the ventral surface of the genital double somite and is concealed by the overlying ovigerous spines (figure 2.5.12B). In *Gelyella* the copulatory pore lies on the ventral midline just between the close-set gonopores (figure 2.7.4A-B). In most harpacticoids the single copulatory pore is isolated on the mid-ventral surface of the double somite, a considerable distance posterior to the level of the gonopores (figure 2.4.31B). In the Cyclopoida the female genital system is highly variable (cf. figure 2.8.37) but there is typically a single copulatory pore situated on the midventral surface whilst the gonopores are located either ventrally, as in *Cyclopicina*, laterally or dorsolaterally, as in the Cyclopidae. In the misophrioid *Misophriopsis* the single copulatory pore is located a small distance behind the gonopores but in two other genera, *Boxshallia* and *Speleophria*, the pore (and median seminal receptacle) is positioned more anteriorly (figure 2.3.16). Only two described calanoid species are known to possess an isolated copulatory pore, both of them arietellids. In *Paramisophria platysoma* and in *P.cluthae* (figure 2.2.29A-B,E) a single copulatory pore is located on the left side of genital double somite and asymmetrical copulatory ducts connect it with the paired seminal receptacles that lie beneath the genital apertures (Ohtsuka & Mitsuzumi, 1990). In an as yet undescribed new species of *Paramisophria* the single copulatory pore is medially positioned on the genital double somite (figure 2.2.29C-D).

Independent Evolution: It is apparent that isolation of the copulatory pores from the gonopores has occurred independently several times in the Copepoda. Isolated pores are found in the Calanoida, Misophrioida, Harpacticoida, Cyclopoida, Gelyelloida, Monstrilloida, Siphonostomatoida and Poecilostomatoida. Each arrangement is unique in some way, indicating that the isolation is the product of convergence.

iv) Loss of the sixth legs

The sixth legs form the opercula that close off the paired female genital apertures. They are fused medially in misophrioids such as *Misophria* (figure 2.3.15A) but are still clearly defined from the somite basally. Fusion ensures that both genital apertures open simultaneously and, in forms such as *Misophria pallida* with large lecithotrophic eggs, that eggs are laid in pairs. Formation of a single, median genital aperture results in total fusion of the sixth legs to form a common genital operculum. In the harpacticoid *Longipedia* the common operculum bears 3 pairs of spinous processes, probably representing the ancestral armature of the sixth legs. In *Mormonilla* and in most calanoids the common operculum is unarmed. In the Calanoida ontogenetic studies have shown no trace of any armature on the sixth legs at any stage during female development but the opercular musculature that opens the genital antrum appears to be homologous with the muscles operating the sixth legs in female misophrioids (Boxshall, 1982), suggesting that the common operculum is derived from the fused sixth legs. For comparison, the sixth leg typically appears at the fourth copepodid stage in podoplean orders such as the Harpacticoida, Misophrioida and Cyclopoida. The total loss of the armature of the female sixth legs throughout ontogeny in the Calanoida can be interpreted as evidence of the involvement of a heterochronic mechanism that ontogenetically delayed the appearance of armature elements, rather than as the end point of a gradual reduction series, in which case intermediate conditions might be expected.

c. Transformations of the Male System

In comparison to the female system relatively little variation occurs in fundamental arrangement of the reproductive system of male copepods. In males of the Monstrilloida the genital apertures have migrated medially but have remained separate. The genital flaps (sixth legs) are distinct but adjacent basally. This migration is partly a passive process caused by the differential growth of the genital prominence on the ventral surface of the male genital somite (figures 2.5.8A-D and 2.5.11C-E).

Sixth Legs: The sixth legs are an important part of the genital apparatus. In the great majority of copepods they remain relatively simple flaps, with or without any armature elements. There is great variation in their degree of development. In both sexes of the Platycopioida they are extremely reduced (figure 2.1.11A-B,E) whereas in the male of various harpacticoids, *Canuella perplexa* for example, they can form an elaborate petasma-like structure (figure 2.4.32C). Por (1984b) suggested that the male petasma of canuellids was homologous with first pleopods of male malacostracans. Since these structures occur on different body somites, seventh and ninth trunk somites respectively, they are clearly not homologous. The structures in the male genital field of *Canuella* have been described and named by Glatzel (1988) but their role during mating is not well understood. They may be involved in species recognition or they may assist in spermatophore placement. In calanoids no trace can be found either of a defined sixth leg or of any armature elements at any stage during their ontogeny whereas in male podopleans the sixth legs first appear at the fourth copepodid stage (figure 3.16.4). It seems likely that the total loss of the armature of the sixth legs in male calanoids is the result of a heterochronic process (as in the female), rather than representing the end point of a process of gradual reduction and loss.

Asymmetry: Asymmetry of the male reproductive system is apparent within several orders. The Calanoida is characterised by asymmetry. In mature calanoid males there is typically a single median testis and only one functional vas deferens and gonopore, usually on the left side. Similarly in harpacticoids the testis is median and there is typically a single functional vas deferens and gonopore, most frequently on the left side (in 70 per cent of taxa) but sometimes on the right (Lang, 1948a; Fahrenbach, 1962). Typically in harpacticoids only the functional sixth leg is capable of movement relative to the somite, that on the non-functional side is fused to the somite. This condition can even be observed in male cancrincolids (figure 3.16.3B) although in this family the male sixth legs have lost all armature elements. In some cerviniid harpacticoids, however, the reproductive system is symmetrical, with paired vasa deferentia, each producing a spermatophore. The newly discovered male of *Mormonilla* has a median testis and single median vas deferens. In most other orders there are paired, functional vasa deferentia and gonopores in the male and spermatophores are typically deposited in pairs. However, in particular genera and families within these orders a secondary asymmetry may have evolved. In the siphonostomatoid *Hyalopontius* for example, only a single testis and vas deferens develop in the adult male and the genital aperture is functional on the right side of the body only (Boxshall, 1990a).

3.4 ANTENNULE

a. Ancestral State

Female Antennule: The female antennule is 28-segmented. Each segment from II to XXI primitively possessed a trithek consisting of 2 setae and an aesthetasc located on the anteroventral margin of the segment (Giesbrecht, 1892). These elements are typically arranged with one seta midway along the segment and the other seta plus the aesthetasc located distally. The first segment can possess up to 4 elements, representing a trithek plus an additional proximal seta. Segments XXII and XXIII originally possessed only one seta and an aesthetasc, both located distally on the anteroventral margin. The next four segments (XXIV to XXVII inclusive) each bear a trithek. One seta and the aesthetasc are positioned distally on the anteroventral margin but the other seta is located distally on the posterior margin. The apical segment (XXVIII) possesses a maximum of 4 setae and an aesthetasc.

Male Antennule: The male antennule is similar to that of the female but may have been geniculate at a position corresponding to the articulation between segments XX and XXI of the female antennule. We are uncertain whether to regard this geniculation as the ancestral condition of the Copepoda because it is absent in the Platycopioida. The antennules of the male of the platycopioid *Antrisocopia* (see section 2.1) are bilaterally geniculate but the geniculation lies between segments homologous with ancestral segments XXIV and XXV. This is a unique condition and is not homologous with the geniculation located between segments XX and XXI of the Calanoida and Podoplea. The ancestral condition of the lineage comprising the Calanoida and the Podoplea is for both left and right antennules to be geniculate between segments XX and XXI. It is possible to interpret the absence of this geniculation from the Platycopioida as a plesiomorphy or as an apomorphy. In the former case, the ancestral copepod state is the lack of a geniculation and, therefore, the two different geniculations are both apomorphies. In the latter case, the absence of the geniculation in the Platycopioida is regarded as a secondary state and, therefore, the ancestral copepod possessed antennules geniculate between segments XX and XXI. Without a relevant out-group both alternatives are equally parsimonious, but the evolution of a different geniculation mechanism in *Antrisocopia* tends to suggest that the Platycopioida primitively lacked the geniculation between segments XX and XXI.

Giesbrecht (1892) recognised the pattern of antennulary setation as an important taxonomic character. The setation patterns exhibited by female calanoids and female misophrioids, such as *Archimisophria*, are easily derived from a common ancestral pattern (Boxshall, 1983). Although both forms have 27-segmented antennules there is good evidence that the ancestral copepod had 28-segmented antennules. In misophrioids and calanoids with 27-segmented antennules the apical segment bears up to 7 elements 1 of which is located midway along the posterior margin of the segment. This seta marks the plane of fusion of ancestral segments XXVII and XXVIII. Vaupel Klein (1982) noted that many calanoids showed, on the apical segment, traces of the suture line that formerly separated these two segments. In the Platycopioida the setation pattern indicates that original segments XXVII and XXVIII are still unfused. In all platycopioids there is some fusion proximally but by using the apex as a reference point it is apparent that in *Platycopia* the

Figure 3.4.1. Schematic comparison of segmental homologies in the female antennules of a range of copepod orders.

fourth segment proximal to the apex bears a seta on the posterior margin. This is equivalent to ancestral segment XXIV (the most proximal segment of calanoid and misophrioid antennules to carry a posterior seta) indicating that ancestral segments XXV, XXVI, XXVII and XXVIII are all unfused. The posterior seta on segment XXIV is usually very well developed and is retained in all platycopioids even when the posterior setae of more distal segments are lost or have migrated. In all platycopioids both setae and the aesthetasc of segment XXVI are located distally on the anterior margin. Segment XXII is unarmed in all platycopioids but XXIII has a distal seta only on the anterior margin in platycopioids, the proximal seta being lost as in other copepods (cf. figure 2.1.4). This segment also serves as a reference point in identifying the homologies of the distal segments.

There is controversy over the nature of the antennule of the ancestral copepod (see discussion in Boxshall et al., 1984) and various ancestral segment numbers have been proposed, the largest being 31 by Gurney (1931). This has been added to recently by Grygier (1987) who proposed that an 8-segmented antennule was a synapomorphy of the class Maxillopoda (including the subclass Copepoda), based on the presence of 8-segmented antennules in the Mystacocarida and the Ostracoda, and on the appearance of 8 segments during the ontogeny of the Thecostraca. Grygier (1987) made this proposal after careful analysis of segmental armature to determine homology. A similar analysis of the different copepod orders (cf. figure 3.4.1) reveals powerful homologies between the multisegmented antennules of the Platycopioida, Calanoida, Siphonostomatoida, Misophrioida and Cyclopoida. Consideration of the geniculation in male antennules allows this system of homologies to be extended to other orders, such as the Harpacticoida, with their low numbers of antennulary segments (figure 3.4.2). On the basis of careful comparison, the segmental homologies can be elucidated and now there can be little doubt that a multisegmented antennule is ancestral to the Copepoda.

b. Transformations

i) Segmental fusion in females

There are innumerable modifications to female antennules within the Copepoda (cf. figures 2.1.4, 2.2.9, 2.3.4, 2.9.13 and 2.10.6-7). The simplest involve fusions between ancestral segments and all copepods exhibit at least one fusion since the maximum number of segments known in any extant copepod is 27 and the ancestral number is 28 (figure 3.4.1). The fusion of original segments XXVII and XXVIII to form a double apical segment is an apomorphy of all copepods other than the platycopioids which retain a separate 28th segment but exhibit a maximum of 23 antennulary segments because of fusion amongst the proximal segments. The 27-segmented condition is found in some calanoids, such as *Exumella polyarthra*, and some misophrioids, such as *Archimisophria*.

In all orders other than the Platycopioida, Calanoida, and Misophrioida the maximum number of segments reported is 26, in the cyclopoid *Cyclopicina longifurcata*, and the apical segment represents a triple segment incorporating ancestral segment XXVI as well as XXVII and XXVIII (figure 2.8.2A-B). The maximum segment number found in the remaining orders is 21 in the Siphonostomatoida (in the genera *Mesocheres, Asterocheres* and the fossil *Kabatarina*). The ancestral siphonostomatoid antennule was 21-segmented (figure 2.9.13) and was characterised by fusion proximally between segment IX and XII to form a quadruple segment. There is also fusion distally of segments XXII to XXIII and XXIV to XXV.

The maximum segment numbers in the remaining orders are 14 in the Gelyelloida, 9 in the Harpacticoida, 8 in the Poecilostomatoida, 4 in the Monstrilloida and Mormonilloida. Except for the Harpacticoida, it is not possible to fully establish the segmental homologies of the reduced antennules in the females of these orders but this is possible for the males, at least in part. Detailed comparison between the oligoarthran and polyarthran limbs (see table 2 in chapter 2.4) resulted in a system of homologies for the 9-segmented antennules of female harpacticoids. The segmental fusion patterns are I, II-VIII, IX-XIV, XV-XVII, XVIII-XX, XXI-XXIII, XXIV, XXV, XXVI-XXVIII. In female poecilostomatoids it is possible to determine the homologies for the more distal segments only.

ii) Segmental fusion in males

Male antennules are basically similar to those of the female except they are typically geniculate to enable them to function as grasping organs. Comparison of the male and female antennules of calanoids and misophrioids reveals that the geniculation present in these two orders lies between ancestral segments XX and XXI. Such a geniculation is also present in male cyclopoids, siphonostomatoids, harpacticoids, gelyelloids, monstrilloids and mormonilloids. The antennules of male poecilostomatoids are too reduced to permit the identification of this segmental boundary with certainty, although in the plesiomorphic families Oncaeidae and Paralubbockiidae some vestige of a geniculation may be present (Boxshall & Huys, 1988-89). The platycopioids, however, lack such a geniculation. The antennules of male *Platycopia* species are non-geniculate. The male of *Nanocopia* is unknown. The extremely primitive platycopioid *Antrisocopia* has bilaterally symmetrical, geniculate antennules in the male but the geniculation lies between ancestral segments XXIV and XXV, and is, therefore, not homologous with the geniculation located between segments XX and XXI of calanoids and podopleans. The detailed comparisons below are made using the geniculate antennule of male calanoids, which in extant calanoids is present on one side only (either the right or the left side), or is secondarily lost altogether.

Males of all orders exhibit some fusions of antennulary segments (figure 3.4.2), either around the geniculation at the boundary between segments XX and XXI, or in the part distal to the geniculation. The setation pattern provides the reference points that enable the fusions to be identified. As in the females, males of all orders other than the Platycopioida have ancestral segments XXVII and XXVIII fused to form a double segment and all the podoplean orders, with the exception of the Misophrioida, have a triple apical segment incorporating segment XXVI as well. In many cases this triple segment undergoes additional fusions incorporating yet more segments into a compound apical unit. Proximal to the geniculation segments XIX and XX are free in calanoids but are fused in all podoplean orders. In the Platycopioida segments XVIII to XX are fused but this compound segment is not associated with a geniculation and is here interpreted as an independent fusion.

Distal to the geniculation segments XXI and XXII are fused in harpacticoids and misophrioids. In the geniculate antennules of calanoid males segments XXI to XXIII form a triple unit although XXI is only incompletely fused to the other two. In cyclopoids, gelyelloids and siphonostomatoids segments XXI to XXIII are fused to form a triple segment but this is treated as a distinct character state from that found in calanoid males because of the incomplete incorporation of segment XXI in the Calanoida. Ancestral segments XXIV and XXV fuse to form a double segment in the Calanoida and Cyclopoida. In gelyelloids and siphonostomatoids both are incorporated into a compound apical segment comprising segments XXIV to XXVIII. In monstrilloids and mormonilloids only a single segment is present distal to the geniculation, presumably comprising fused ancestral segments XXI to XXVIII.

In siphonostomatoids a total of 19 segments is expressed, with segments IX to XI fused to form a triple segment. Segments IX to XI are incompletely fused in some dirivultids (figure 2.9.9B), but in the majority of families this fusion is complete and segment XII is also incorporated to form a quadruple segment (figure 2.9.14). Segment XIII is often modified by the inclusion of a membranous insert. The boundary between segments XIII and XIV is typically well defined and forms a proximal geniculation.

The Harpacticoida is characterised by very short antennules. Male harpacticoids have at most 14 segments in their antennules, which are bilaterally geniculate. The reduction in segment numbers has taken place mostly in the proximal part of the limb. By careful reference to the setation pattern the homologies of the harpacticoid antennulary segments can be established. The key species in this process are *Ambunguipes rufocincta* (figure 2.4.4B-C) and the recently described *Hamondia superba* Huys (figure 2.4.4A), both of which have 14 segments in the male. These are the Rosetta stone copepods that enabled the information contained in the harpacticoid antennule to be decoded and assimilated into the overall copepod system. The setation of 0, 1, 12, 8+1 aesthetasc, 2, 6+1 aesthetasc, 2, 2, 3, 3, 1, 1+1, 1+1, and 8 corresponds only with the following pattern of segmentation I, II, III-VIII, IX-XII, XIII, XIV-XVI, XVII, XVIII, XIX-XX, XXI-XXII, XXIII, XXIV, XXV, XXVI-XXVIII. The accuracy of this fusion pattern is supported by the location of the geniculation between segments XX and XXI. This newly recognised series of homologies indicates that the antennules of harpacticoids are secondarily shortened by fusion.

Digeniculate Antennule: The antennules of male cyclopoids are referred to as digeniculate. The distal geniculation lies between ancestral segments XX and XXI and is found in the great majority

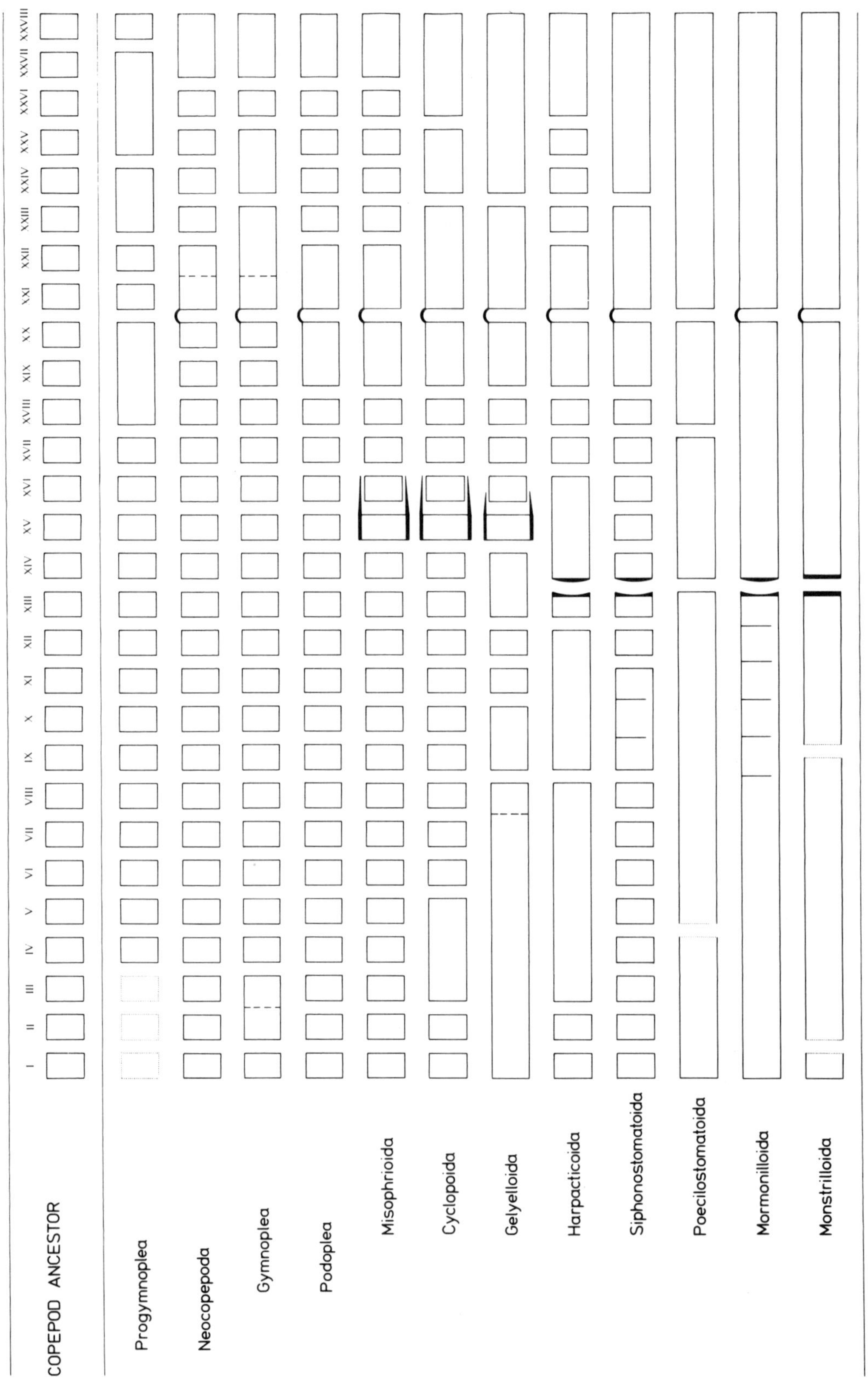

Figure 3.4.2. Schematic comparison of segmental homologies in the male antennules of a range of copepod orders, showing the positions of the neocopepodan geniculation, the sheath and the proximal modified joint (XIII-XIV).

of all copepods. The proximal geniculation lies between ancestral segments XV and XVI but it typically involves some modification to the articulations between the more proximal segments XII, XIII and XIV. A conspicuous feature of the proximal geniculation is the large sheath-like distal extension of segment XV that partly encloses segment XVI (figures 2.8.5A-C and 2.8.41C). This structure is retained in most families of cyclopoids. It can also be detected, in a much reduced form, in the Gelyelloida (figure 2.7.4C-D). A sheath on segment XV is also present in misophrioids, such as *Misophriopsis* (figure 2.3.3D-E) and *Boxshallia*, although it is absent in *Archimisophria discoveryi*. Its absence in *Archimisophria* is surprising, since there is no trace of a sheath on segment XV. If the sheath was primitively present in the Misophrioida then it must have been secondarily lost in *Archimisophria*. The lack of any vestige of the sheath in *Archimisophria* can be interpreted as indicating that the loss was brought about by a heterochronic process that delayed the appearance of the adult male condition and retained the copepodid V condition in the adult.

Partial Homologies: The fusions between the segments in male monstrilloids (figures 2.5.5 and 2.5.6) and mormonilloids (figure 2.6.4A) cannot be identified with certainty for the part proximal to the geniculation. There is only a single segment distal to the geniculation and this presumably represents ancestral segments XXI to XXVIII fused. In the poecilostomatoids the lack of a functional geniculation in adult males removes a possible reference point useful in the identification of homologies in taxa with such reduced antennules. In *Paralubbockia*, the Oncaeidae and *Rhinomolgus* the antennules are sexually dimorphic, with the three distalmost segments of the female being fused into a single segment in the male. Using evidence from the musculature Boxshall & Huys (1988-89) interpreted this as representing a vestige of the geniculation, suggesting that the compound distal segment represented the part of the limb distal to the geniculation (i.e. segments XXI to XXVIII). Several poecilostomatoids, representing the plesiomorphic families Bomolochidae and Taeniacanthidae, exhibit a sexually dimorphic, segmental fusion pattern with the compound segments XIV-XVIII and XIX-XX of the female combining to form a single long segment, representing XIV-XX, in the male (figure 2.10.7).

iii) Antennules and mating

In the great majority of copepods the antennules of the male are modified for grasping the adult female during mating and precopulatory mate guarding, in which an adult male clasps a juvenile, copepodid I to V stage female (Boxshall, 1990c). Antennulary grasping is a primitive characteristic of all calanoids and podopleans, although it is secondarily lost in some forms. Even the platycopioid *Antrisocopia* has evolved an antennulary clasping mechanism, but this is not homologous with that of calanoids and podopleans. Only *Platycopia* and *Nanocopia* primitively lack a specialised antennulary geniculation. Boxshall (1990c) failed to find any evidence of precopulatory mate guarding in calanoids but he suggested that this behaviour was primitive to podopleans. Our analysis of antennulary structure suggests that mate guarding and mate grasping during copulation are the major determinants of the form of male antennules in the Podoplea. Two basic types of antennule are found (figure 3.4.3): the digeniculate misophrioid-cyclopoid type, also found in the Gelyelloida to a lesser extent (as described above), and the siphonostomatoid type which is also found in the Harpacticoida and Mormonilloida.

The misophrioid-cyclopoid type of digeniculate male antennule is divided into 3 sections, proximal, middle and distal, by a proximal geniculation at segmental boundary XV-XVI and a distal geniculation at segmental boundary XX-XXI. This arrangement allows the antennules to firmly clasp the female fourth swimming legs across their posterior (middle section) and anterior surfaces (distal section) during copulation (figures 2.8.38 and 3.4.3). The male may initially grasp a different part of the female, for example, Gophen (1979) noted that *Mesocyclops leuckarti* (Claus) males initially held onto the female in the vicinity of the caudal rami, using its geniculate antennules. The male then changed position to attach to the female's fourth legs. Mating behaviour in misophrioids is unknown but the similarity of the antennule of male misophrioids suggests that they employ the same orientation and grasping position as cyclopoids during copulation. The extreme reduction of the proximal geniculation in gelyelloids is presumably correlated with the loss of the fourth swimming legs in this order.

A second type of geniculate antennule, the siphonostomatoid type, is found in the Podoplea. It is divided into proximal, middle and distal sections by a proximal geniculation located at the XIII-XIV segmental boundary and a distal geniculation at the XX-XXI boundary. The proximal section

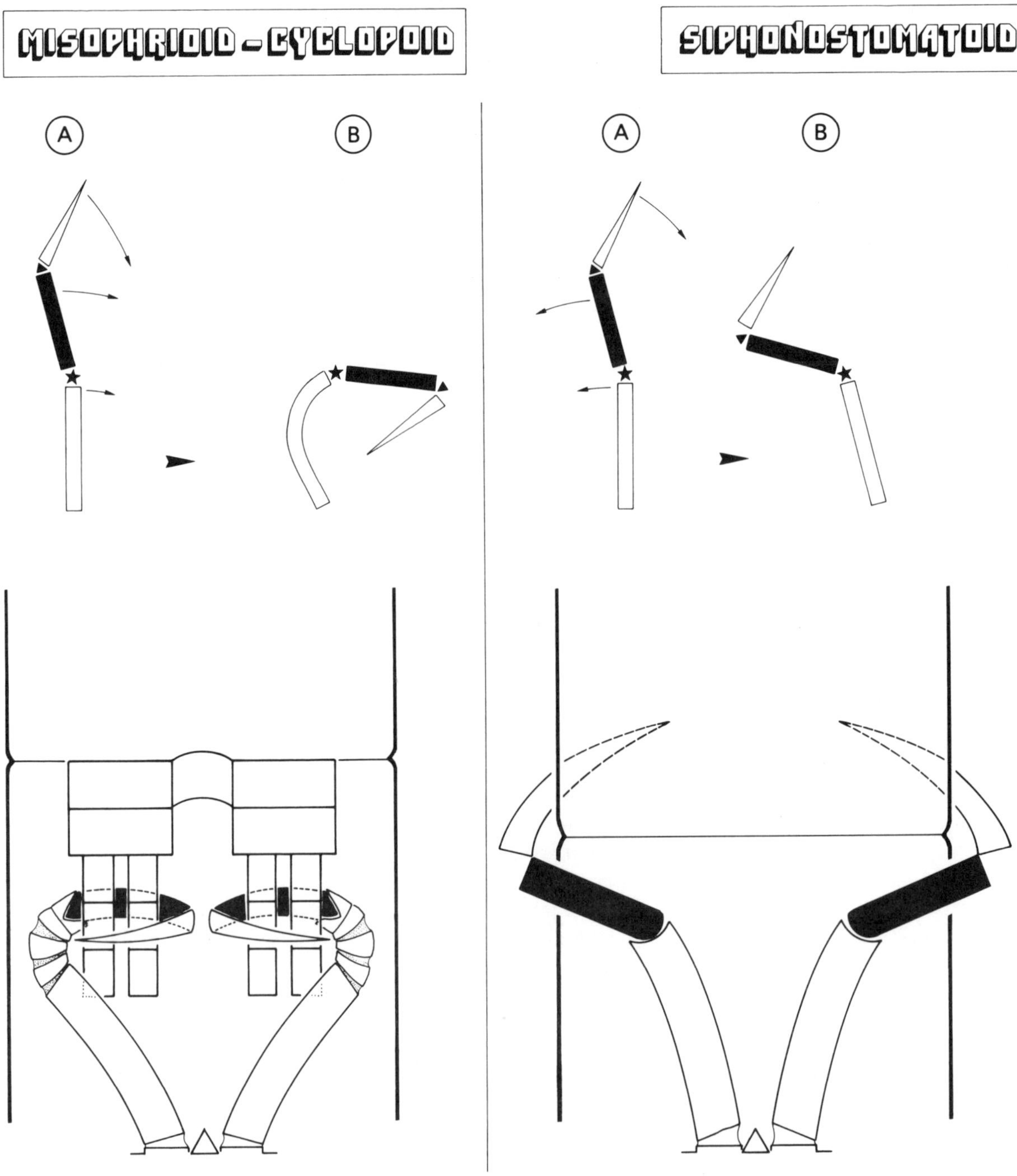

Figure 3.4.3. Schematic comparisons of functional morphology of the two main types of digeniculate antennules of male podopleans. From its resting position the misophrioid-cyclopoid type flexes medially (as indicated by arrows) at both the proximal and distal geniculations, whereas from its resting position the siphonostomatoid type flexes laterally at the proximal geniculation and medially at the distal geniculation. The misophrioid-cyclopoid type has a relatively narrow gape and is primitively used to grasp the fourth legs of the female. The siphonostomatoid type has a wider gape and is used to hold round the body. [A = resting position, B = flexed position, after movement indicated by arrows; the neocopepodan geniculation (between XX and XXI) is marked by a triangle, the proximal geniculation is marked by a star]

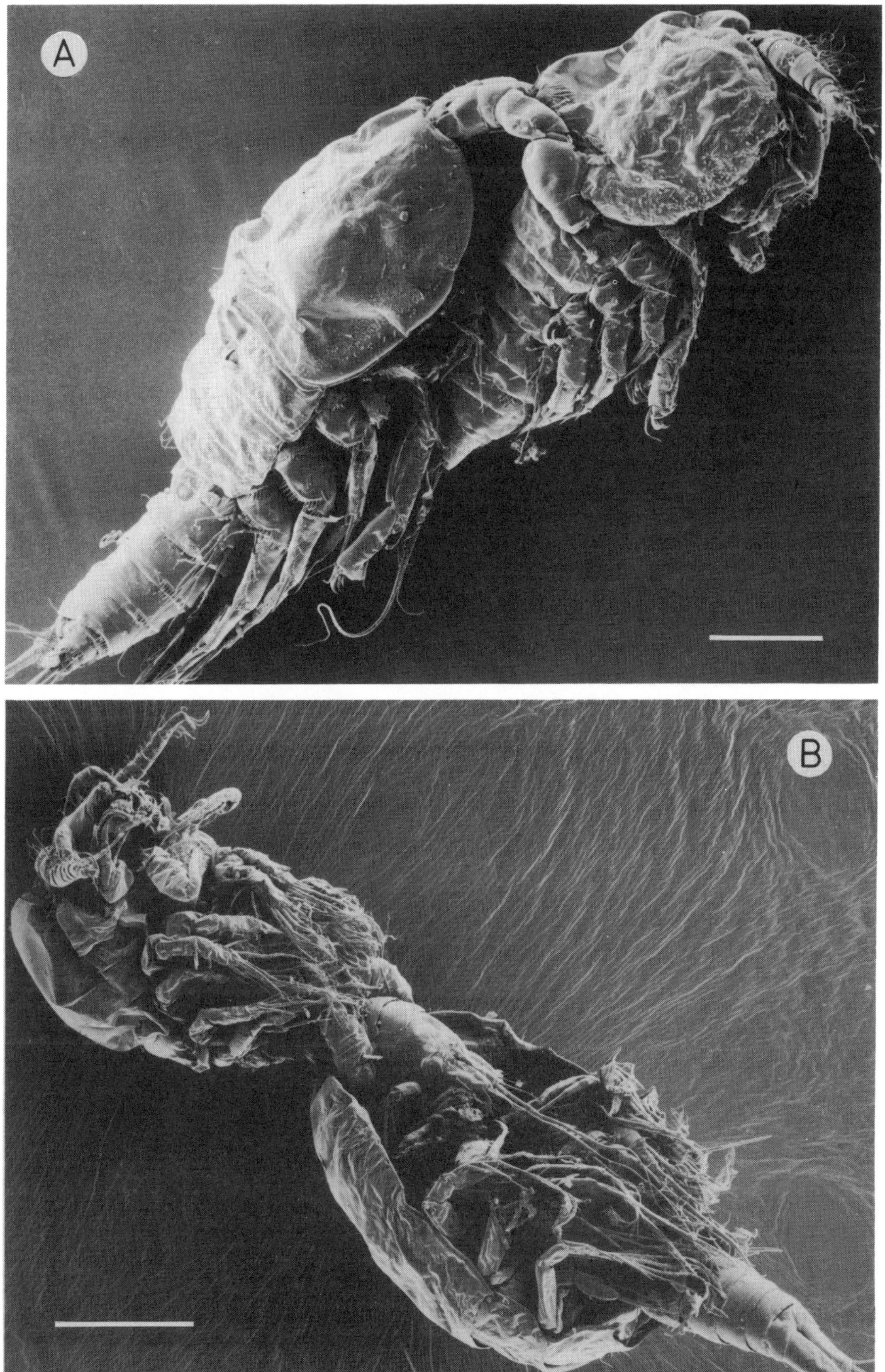

Figure 3.4.4. Precopulatory mate guarding. **A.** Adult male of *Tigriopus japonicus* grasping female copepodid stage. **B.** Adult male of *Stygiopontius quadrispinosus* grasping female copepodid V with its geniculate antennules. Scale bars = 100μm.

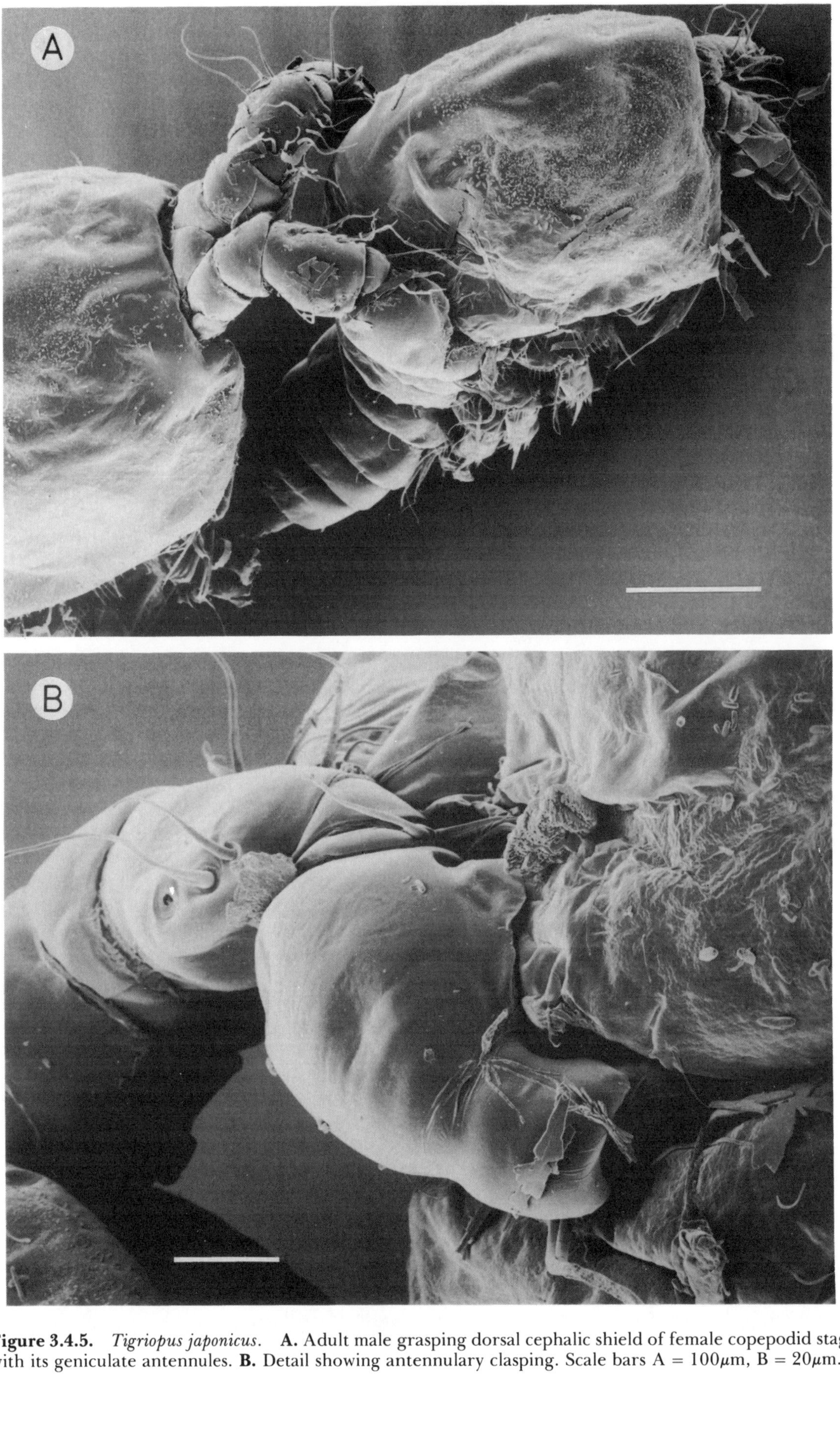

Figure 3.4.5. *Tigriopus japonicus.* **A.** Adult male grasping dorsal cephalic shield of female copepodid stage with its geniculate antennules. **B.** Detail showing antennulary clasping. Scale bars A = 100μm, B = 20μm.

of this type of antennule is directed anteriorly or anterolaterally and outward flexure at the proximal geniculation directs the middle section more laterally. Flexure at the distal geniculation directs the distal section anteromedially. This arrangement permits a wider grasp of the female by the adult male during copulation or precopulatory mate guarding (figure 3.4.3). In the Siphonostomatoida and Harpacticoida the male typically holds the female dorsally around the margins of the dorsal cephalothoracic shield or around the urosome, during any precopulatory mate guarding phase (figures 3.4.4 to 3.4.6) and a wide grasp is clearly advantageous. Some harpacticoids are known to hold females by the fourth legs or caudal rami during mating but we regard this as a derived behaviour pattern. The modified antennule of male *Mormonilla* also flexes outwards proximally and the setation pattern indicates that this flexure plane may well be homologous with the XIII-XIV segmental boundary.

The role of grasping the female during copulation and precopulatory mate guarding has been taken over by the antennae and, especially, by the sexually dimorphic maxillipeds in male poecilostomatoids. There has been a consequent reduction both in size and in the numbers of antennulary segments in male poecilostomatoids, and the secondary loss of the geniculation at the XX-XXI boundary. The geniculate antennules of male monstrilloids insert frontally and are anteriorly directed. They are used to grasp the female during copulation but they have only a single geniculation homologous with that at the XX-XXI boundary.

iv) Setation

In the great majority of copepods some ancestral setation elements are lost. The setation is, however, surprisingly conservative so that forms with short antennules, such as the harpacticoids, still retain sufficient setae to permit the identification of segmental homologies. The aesthetascs are less highly conserved and, in the podopleans particularly, only small numbers of aesthetascs are retained. We will not attempt to document all the losses of setation elements but there are some major features that should be mentioned.

In the podoplean orders aesthetascs are retained on certain segments only. Some of these segments can be categorised as key segments because of the stability of their armature throughout the podoplean orders. The segment homologous with ancestral segment VII retains its aesthetasc in at least some Misophrioida (e.g. *Archimisophria*), Harpacticoida (e.g. the Cerviniidae), Siphonostomatoida (e.g. *Ecbathyrion*) and probably also in male Mormonilloida and Poecilostomatoida (e.g. *Mecomerinx* Humes). The segment homologous with ancestral segment XI retains its aesthetasc in at least some members of the Misophrioida (e.g. *Archimisophria*), Harpacticoida (e.g. *Hamondia*), Cyclopoida (e.g. *Cyclopicina*) and Siphonostomatoida (e.g. *Ecbathyrion*). The homologous aesthetasc is probably also present in male Mormonilloida (see chapter 2.6) and male Poecilostomatoida (e.g. *Mecomerinx*). Similarly, segment XVI retains its aesthetasc in the same four orders, although within the Cyclopoida it is absent in *Cyclopicina* but present in other genera, such as *Oithona*. In addition it is present in the Gelyelloida and probably also the Monstrilloida and males of the Mormonilloida. This is the aesthetasc that is so prominent on the geniculate antennules of male harpacticoids. More distally, the aesthetascs on segments XXI and XXV are also present in misophrioids (e.g. *Misophriopsis*), cyclopoids (e.g. *Euryte*), and poecilostomatoids (e.g. *Hemicyclops*, see figure 2.10.6). The aesthetasc of segment XXI is particularly stable within the Siphonostomatoida (figure 2.9.13) and its apparent position on the limb is used as a generic level character in families such as the Asterocheridae. It is retained even in highly transformed siphonostomatoids such as *Spongiocnizon* which is vermiform and has only 2 antennulary segments (figure 2.9.12A-E). The aesthetasc of segment XXV is lost in siphonostomatoids. Most copepods of all orders retain the apical aesthetasc derived from ancestral segment XXVIII. The highly conserved armature of the key segments VII, XI, XVI and XXI suggests that they may be associated with important segmental boundaries that are expressed early in the copepodid or even naupliar phase of development.

3.5 ANTENNA

a. Ancestral State

The antenna is originally a biramous limb comprising a 2-segmented protopod consisting of a separate coxa and basis, a 10-segmented exopod and a 4-segmented endopod. In the ancestral

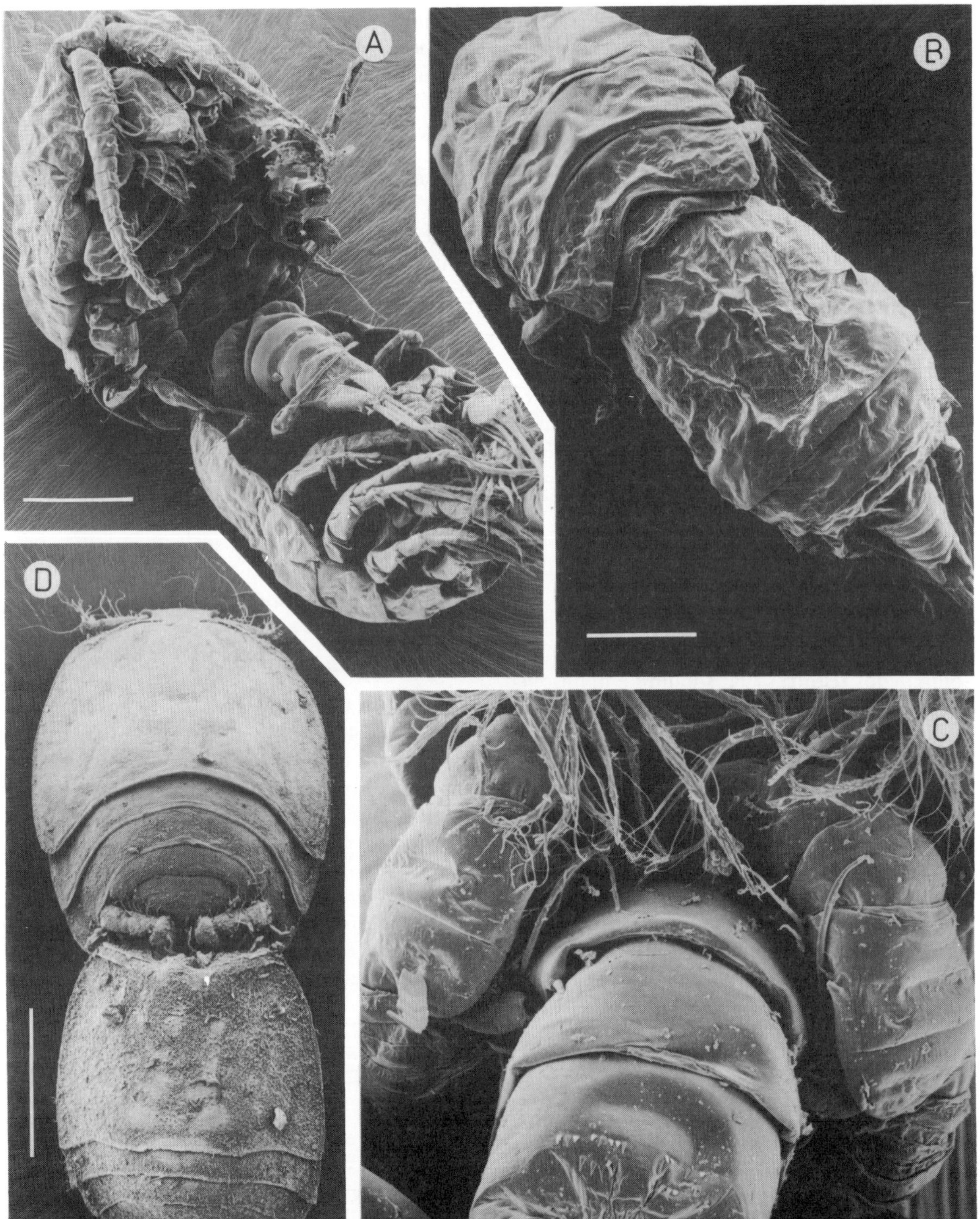

Figure 3.4.6. **A.** *Stygiopontius quadrispinosus*, mating pair of adults, showing male grasping female urosome with its antennules and maxillipeds, ventral view. **B.** Dorsal view. **C.** Detail of male antennules clasping female copepodid V stage urosome, ventral view. **D.** *Porcellidium* sp., male grasping female using antennules, dorsal view. Scale bars A-B = 100μm, C = 20μm, D = 200μm.

state the coxa bears a single seta medially, and the basis has 2 setae. Each exopodal segment of the adult bears an inner seta except the apical segment which carries 3 setae. The endopod is armed with 2 setae on the inner margin of the first segment, 9 on the inner margin of the second segment, 5 on the third and 2 on the minute fourth segment.

b. Transformations

i) Protopod

The original coxa and basis are often fused to form a coxobasis. This is a diagnostic character of the Poecilostomatoida and can be found in derived representatives of many other orders. In some poecilostomatoids, such as the Paralubbockiidae, subsequent fusion of the first endopodal segment occurs, resulting in the formation of a triple segment (a coxo-allobasis). The formation of an allobasis, comprising fused basis and first endopodal segment, is also widespread in many copepod orders including the Harpacticoida and Siphonostomatoida, and is even found in some calanoids, such as *Acartia* Dana (figure 2.2.12A) and the Pseudocyclopiidae. In the Monstrilloida and the cyclopoid family Thespesiopsyllidae the entire antenna is absent. This is also the case in the cerviniid genus *Tonpostratiotes* (Itô, 1982b) and in a number of highly transformed parasitic forms.

Coxal Seta: The coxal seta is retained only in calanoids and the monotypic cyclopoid genus *Cyclopicina*. All other adult copepods have lost this seta. Representatives of the Calanoida, Misophrioida and Cyclopoida retain 2 basal setae. A single basal seta is found in the Harpacticoida, Mormonilloida and Poecilostomatoida whilst none is present in the Platycopioida, Gelyelloida and Siphonostomatoida. Up to 3 coxal setae are present in all planktotrophic copepod nauplii, acting as the primary gnathobasic element for the naupliar feeding mechanism.

ii) Exopod

The antenna displays many modifications within the Copepoda. In particular there is a pronounced trend towards the reduction of the exopod, its replacement by one or more setae, and, ultimately, its complete loss. The maximum numbers of exopodal segments in the adult for each order are: Calanoida 10 segments, Platycopioida and male Mormonilloida 9 segments, Misophrioida, Harpacticoida and female Mormonilloida 8 segments, Gelyelloida 7 segments, and Siphonostomatoida 1 segment. No free exopodal segments are present in the remaining orders.

Park (1986) suggested that the ancestral calanoid possessed a 10-segmented antennary exopod and that the first to ninth segments each carried 1 seta, with the tenth carrying 3 setae. Comparison between the antennary exopods of a range of calanoid genera (figure 2.2.15) confirmed the validity of this basic pattern. Based on this ancestral calanoid pattern, which we also attribute to the ancestral copepod, it is possible to interpret the patterns of fusion of the exopodal segments in those orders that retain a multisegmented ramus. These multisegmented exopods and their setation elements are shown diagrammatically in figure 3.5.1. In the exopod of platycopioids segment I is free, ancestral segments IV and V are fused, and segments VI and VII are incompletely fused. In all adult podopleans ancestral segment I is missing, neither the seta nor any trace of the segment can be detected. In males of the Mormonilloida all the remaining 9 (II to X) segments are free whereas in females ancestral segments II and III are fused into a double basal segment armed with 2 setae, but segments IX and X are free. In the Misophrioida and Harpacticoida ancestral segments II and III are free but IX and X are fused into a double apical segment bearing 4 setae. The 8-segmented condition found in female Mormonilloida is, therefore, not homologous with that of the Misophrioida and Harpacticoida. In the Gelyelloida ancestral segment II and its seta are absent and segments IX and X are fused into a double apical segment bearing 4 setae.

Reduced Exopod: In the Siphonostomatoida the exopod is frequently lost. Amongst the numerous families of siphonostomatoids that parasitise fishes, for example, a free exopod is retained only in the Lernaeopodidae and Sphyriidae. In these families and in the other cyclopiform families in which it is retained, such as the Asterocheridae, Entomolepidae, and Ecbathyriontidae, it consists of 1 free segment bearing up to 3 setae. A few species, such as *Rhynchomyzon compactum* and *Australomyzon typicus*, have been described as possessing a clearly 2-segmented antennary exopod (Alvarez, 1988; Nicholls, 1944). Subsequent re-examination of these species revealed that the exopod is 1-segmented in both. There remain a few reports of 2-segmented exopods in the

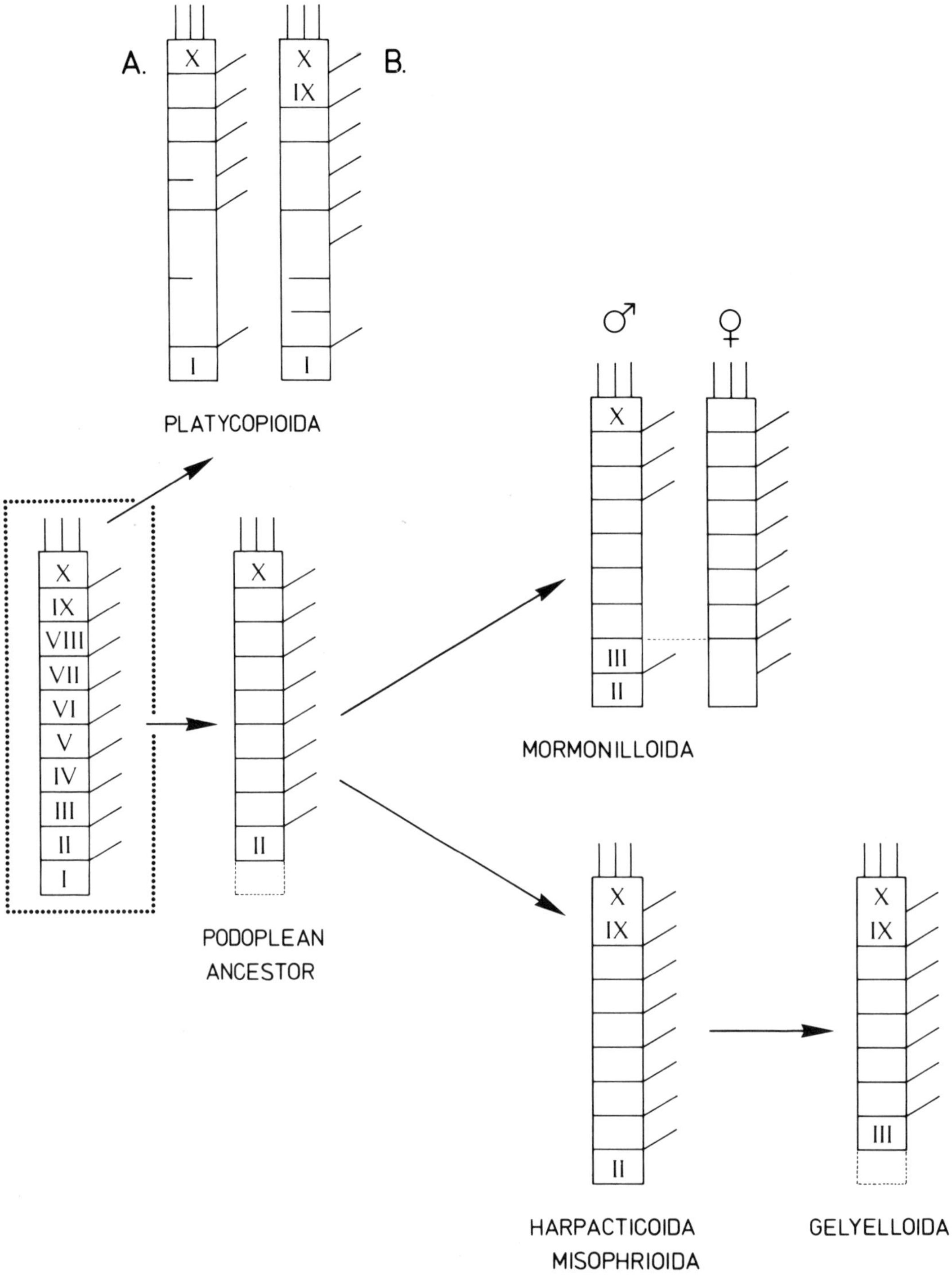

Figure 3.5.1. Evolution of setation patterns and segmentation of antennary exopod in various copepod orders. The arrows indicate possible derivations of segmentation patterns and are not necessarily indicative of an ancestor-descendant relationship between taxa. The 10-segmented ancestral form is taken from the analysis of exopodal segmentation in calanoid antennae (figure 2.2.15). Platycopioid A is *Antrisocopia*, B is *Platycopia*.

literature, for example *Euclavellisa* (cf. Heegaard, 1940), and it is possible that the ancestral state for the siphonostomatoids is 2-segmented, but this requires confirmation.

There is no free exopod in Cyclopoida and Poecilostomatoida. In adult Cyclopoida the exopod is represented by a small lobe fused to the basis bearing a maximum of 3 setae. This is found only in *Cyclopicina* (figure 2.8.2C-D). In other members of the Cyclopinidae there are either 1 (as in *Cyclopina*, *Cyclopuella* Por, and *Afrocyclopina* Wells) or 2 setae (as in *Arctocyclopina* Mohammed & Neuhof, *Cycloporella* Monchenko and *Cyclopidina* Steuer). Two setae are commonly also found in the Oithonidae, the Mantridae and the Notodelphyidae. In the Poecilostomatoida the exopod is completely absent, not even a seta remains. However in both of these orders a well developed and multisegmented exopod is present in the nauplii but degenerates during the copepodid phase (Dudley, 1966; Do et al., 1984). A setiferous vestige is present in the first copepodid that is lost by the second copepodid in poecilostomatoids and reduced to its adult form of up to 3 setae in cyclopoids. The ontogeny of the antennary exopod is different in the siphonostomatoids. Kabata & Cousens (1973) showed, in the lernaeopodid *Salmincola*, that the multisegmented antennary exopod of the nauplius is transformed into its adult condition (1-segmented with 3 setae) at the moult into the first copepodid.

ii) Endopod

A number of modifications of the endopod are also found. The original 4-segmented condition is retained in only a few calanoids (figure 2.2.11A,C). This endopod, with its full setation, is shown diagrammatically in figure 3.5.2A. In the great majority of copepods, including all podopleans, the fourth endopodal segment is completely fused to the third. The number of endopodal segments is often further reduced from 3 to 2. In all calanoids, except the family Pseudocyclopidae (figures 2.2.14A and 3.5.2Ba), the third segment (representing ancestral segments III-IV) is reduced to a small lobe fused to the apex of the second segment and bearing 7 setae (figure 3.5.2Bb). The second segment has a distal expansion on the inner margin bearing the ancestral complement of 9 setae (figure 2.2.12D).

Setation: The basic antennary endopod of podopleans comprises 3 segments, with the third derived by fusion of ancestral segments III and IV. Close examination of the setation of these segments is necessary before it is possible to interpret the endopodal structure of mormonilloids and misophrioids. The basic podoplean setation is 2,9,7 (as in figure 3.5.2Ba). In female *Mormonilla* the second segment bears only 5 setae and the tip of the endopod carries 11 setae, 4 of which are inserted on a small lobe. A total of 16 setae are present on the second and third segments, as in the ancestral podoplean, but their distribution is atypical (figure 3.5.2C). In *Mormonilla* the second and third segments are partly fused, being separated only by a partial suture on one side (figure 2.6.5A). We consider that this condition was probably derived by the distal migration of the 4 elements inserted on the lobe offset from the tip of the ramus (numbered 1 to 4 in figure 2.6.5B), from their original position on the second segment. This migration is possible because of the partial fusion of the 2 segments involved. In some members of the Misophrioida a similar migration has occurred. In *Archimisophria* endopodal segments 2 and 3 are incompletely fused (figure 2.3.6A). At the tip of the ramus are 9 setae, 7 of which (numbered 1 to 7 in figure 2.3.6B) represent the armature elements of the ancestral podoplean compound third segment (figure 3.5.2Ba). The other 2 setae (arrowed in figure 2.3.6B) are offset from the apex and are probably derived from the second segment. Again, we postulate that migration of these elements has occurred (figure 3.5.2Db), and that it was possible because of the partial fusion between second and third segments. However, the presence, in some species of *Speleophria*, of 6 setae on the second endopodal segment, suggests that the distal migration must have occurred independently in mormonilloids (in which 4 setae migrated leaving 5 on the second segment) and misophrioids (in which 2 setae migrated leaving 6 on the second segment and 1 unaccounted for, presumed lost).

The Harpacticoida contains many examples of modified antennary endopods. The basic harpacticoid condition (figure 3.5.2E) is found in *Longipedia*. All families other than the Canuellidae and Longipediidae have a maximum of 2 endopodal segments due to the fusion of the second and third (= III-IV) segments. The presence of 5 setae on the second endopodal segment is shared with the Gelyelloida and Mormonilloida.

The modifications of the setation pattern are characteristic of certain orders. Poecilostomatoids typically exhibit a 1,4,7 setation pattern on the first to third endopodal segments respectively (figure 3.5.2F). This pattern is found both in planktonic families, such as the Oncaeidae, and associated families such as the Clausidiidae. The pattern is strongly reduced in the plesiomorphic family Paralubbockiidae (Boxshall & Huys, 1990). Individual setation elements are sometimes transformed. For example, one element on the second endopodal segment of *Cotylemyzon* forms an enormous sucker (figure 2.10.8D). Ho (1986) grouped the parasitic cyclopoid families Archinotodelphyidae, Notodelphyidae, Lernaeidae and Ascidicolidae together on the possession of a distal claw on the antennary endopod. Ho & Thatcher (1989) later added the Ozmanidae to this group of parasitic families sharing an antennary endopodal claw. The close resemblance of the antenna of the primitive lernaeid *Lamproglena* (figure 2.8.14C) and that of *Ozmana* (figure 2.8.14D) is remarkable. Both retain the ancestral 7 distal elements and both have 3 elements derived from the second endopodal segment on the medial margin of the compound apical segment. Several of the distal elements are somewhat claw-like in these two genera but the evidence for homologising any one element with the strongly curved, heavily chitinised claw of archinotodelphyids (figure 2.8.13A), mantrids (figure 2.8.13E), notodelphyids (figure 2.8.13C) and ascidicolids (figured by Illg & Dudley (1980) for *Styelicola lighti* Illg & Dudley) is weak.

Raptorial Antennae: In many associated copepods the antennae are important raptorial limbs and the endopod forms a grasping claw. Within the Poecilostomatoida the third endopodal segment bears 1 to 3 powerful claw-like elements in members of the Ergasilidae. These claws are typically used by the adult female to grasp around the gill filaments of the host. In members of the Corycaeidae one or more elements of the third endopodal segment are claw-like in both sexes (figure 2.10.9B-E). Similar modifications are seen in parasitic members of the Siphonostomatoida; an armature element on the third segment commonly forming a terminal claw used for attachment to the host in parasitic forms. In the large caligiform fish parasites the endopodal segments become highly sclerotized and fused into a powerful unitary claw. In the Pennellidae the broad middle segment (basis) is produced into a spinous process opposing the movable distal segment (figure 2.9.18C). In several poecilostomatoid families it is an element of the second endopodal segment that develops to form the dominant claw. Ho (1984b) identified the tendency for the third endopodal segment to atrophy in some of these cases. The offset, atrophied distal endopodal segment in some genera of the Chondracanthidae was formerly referred to as the accessory antennule.

Antenna of *Acartia*: In the calanoid family Acartiidae the endopod is modified by fusion of basis and first endopodal segment. The resulting allobasis bears 9 setae (figure 2.2.12A) arranged in a proximal group of 8 and an isolated distal seta. The 8 proximal setae are interconnected by means of tiny tendinous strands extending from a single muscle inserting adjacent to the last seta (figure 2.2.12B). This mechanism enables the 8 setae to be moved as a single unit and we interpret this as evidence that there has been a secondary increase in the number of setae on that part of the allobasis derived from the basis. The isolated distal seta probably represents a single seta derived from the incorporated first endopodal segment.

3.6 LABRUM

a. Ancestral State

The labrum is typically an undivided muscular lobe, posteroventrally directed and overlying the mouth opening. In most orders this original state is retained.

b. Transformations

In the Platycopioida the labrum is tripartite, with a long median lobe flanked by bulbous lateral lobes. This is treated as a derived condition here as the simple labrum is typical of most other crustacean groups. A tripartite labrum is known in some harpacticoids, such as *Leptastacus* (see Huys, 1987b), but this is clearly a convergence as the labrum is very swollen with a short median lobe. In the majority of Poecilostomatoida the labrum is bilobed, with a marked median incision, however, there are primitive representatives of this order with an undivided labrum such as *Hemicyclops* species.

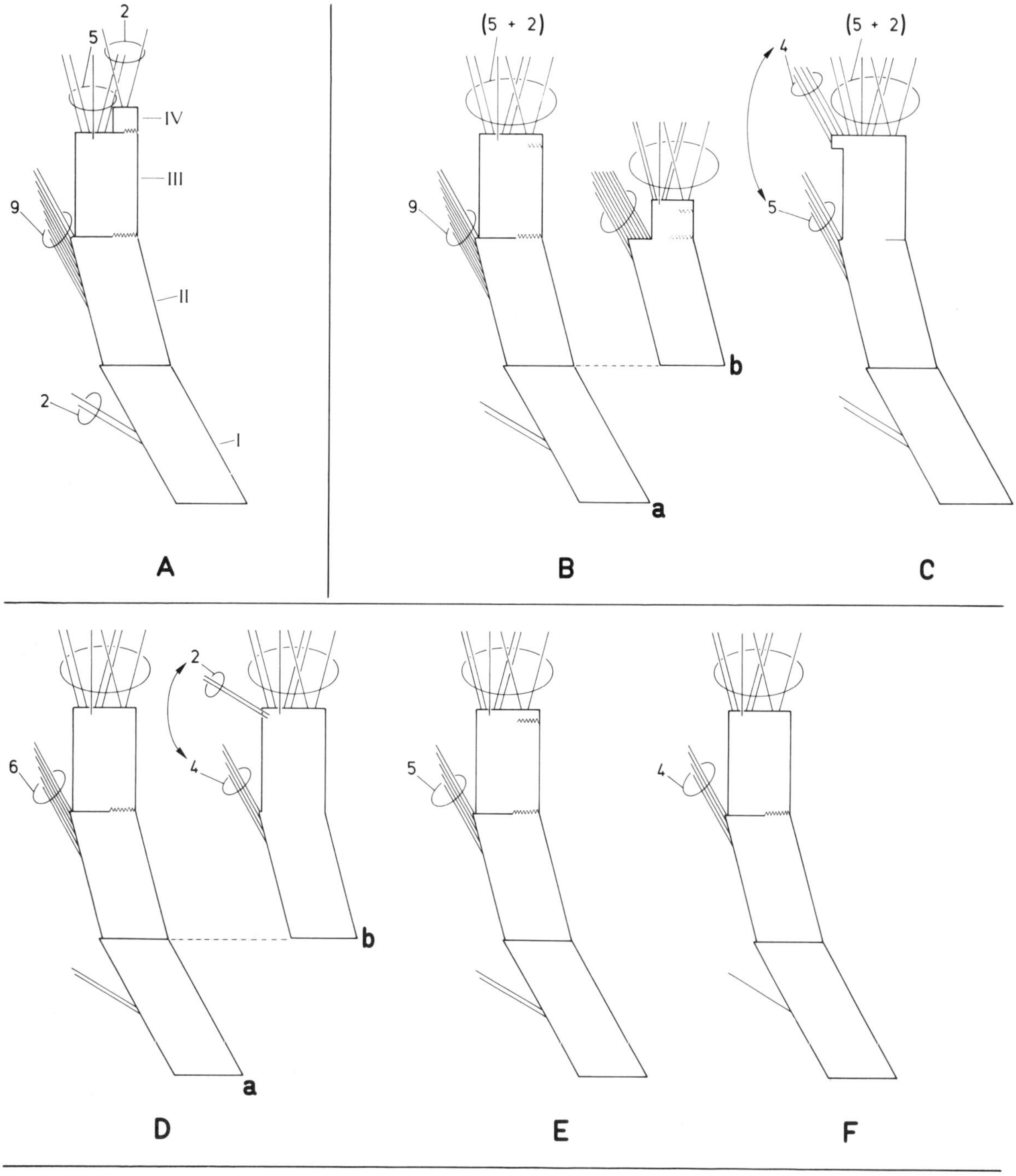

Figure 3.5.2. Evolution of setation patterns of antennary endopod in various copepod orders. A. Ancestral copepod, showing full endopodal setation. B. Calanoida, showing the *Pseudocyclops* (a) form and typical (b) form. C. Mormonilloida, showing distal migration of 4 setae from second segment. D. Misophrioida, showing the *Speleophria* (a) type and *Archimisophria* (b) type. E. Harpacticoida. F. Poecilostomatoida.

Oral Cone: In the Siphonostomatoida the labrum forms the upper lip of the oral cone. Both labrum and labium are often produced together into a tapering tubular structure, the oral cone, that opens distally. The musculature of the oral cone is mainly in the labrum and is typically concentrated in the proximal part (figure 2.9.19). In species with an elongate oral cone, such as *Entomopsyllus adriae* (Eiselt) (figure 2.9.32A-D), the labral muscles form a proximal sucking bulb at the base of the cone and the distal part is produced into a siphon which may be as long as the entire body (Boxshall, 1990a). This kind of oral cone is used for feeding on fluids. The fish parasitic siphonostomatoids tend to have their musculature distributed along the full length of the oral cone. This kind of oral cone can be used for transporting fine particulate matter in addition to fluids.

3.7 MANDIBLE

a. Ancestral State

The plesiomorphic mandible is a biramous limb comprising a 2-segmented protopod consisting of a separate coxa and basis, a 5-segmented exopod and a 2-segmented endopod. The coxa has a well developed gnathobase armed with several blades distally and 2 setae near the dorsodistal angle. The basis bears 4 setae on the inner margin. Each exopodal segment is armed with a single seta on the inner margin, except for the apical segment which carries 2 setae. The first endopodal segment bears 6 setae on its inner margin. The second bears 11 setae around the apex.

b. Transformations

i) Gnathobase

Profound changes have occurred in the mandibular gnathobase of siphonostomatoids. The gnathobase, which is coxal in origin, is drawn out into a long stylet, typically bearing 1 or more minute teeth at its tip. The stylet passes medially into the oral cone via the slit between the labrum and labium (Boxshall, 1986a). There is convergent formation of a stylet-like gnathobase in members of the Tisbidae (Marcotte, 1977) and in the Rotundiclipeidae (Huys, 1988b).

Until the discovery of the Erebonasteridae, particularly *Centobnaster*, it appeared that the Poecilostomatoida primitively lacked the coxal gnathobase consisting of an array of single and multicusped blades along the distal margin. *Centobnaster* possesses a coxal gnathobase with 3 clusters of distal margin blades and a dorsodistal articulated element (figure 2.10.11A-C). The articulated element on the dorsal margin, is probably homologous with the seta located in the same position in representatives of other orders, such as the Cyclopoida (figure 2.8.16C). Within the Erebonasteridae there is a trend towards the clusters of blades becoming more clearly demarcated from the segment basally, but they are not articulated (figure 2.10.16B). Subsequent evolution within the Poecilostomatoida appears to have involved these elements becoming articulated basally. The evolution of a mandibular gnathobase comprising a total of 5 articulated elements provided the basic condition from which all other poecilostomatoid families were derived. This condition is retained in several primitive families, including the Oncaeidae and Corycaeidae. The falcate mandible with its long gnathobasic lash armed with rows of teeth bilaterally has obviously evolved within the order. It appears to be derived by enlargement and specialisation of the middle element of the 5 ancestral gnathobase elements (figure 2.10.10B) but there is evidence that a lash-like mandible has evolved at least 3 times within the Poecilostomatoida (see chapter 2.10 and figure 2.10.12).

ii) Palp

There is a trend towards the reduction in numbers of segments in the rami and in the entire palp. The ancestral number of 5 exopodal segments is retained in the Platycopioida, Calanoida, Misophrioida and Harpacticoida. A maximum of 4 segments is found in the exopod of the Gelyelloida, Mormonilloida and Cyclopoida. In female Mormonilloida the 4-segmented condition arises as a result of fusion of the 2 proximal segments of the ancestral 5-segmented ramus, as indicated by the 2,1,1,2 setal formula. In the Gelyelloida the 4-segmented condition arises as a result of fusion of the 2 distal segments, as indicated by the 1,1,1,3 setal formula. In the Cyclopoida the 4-segmented condition with its 1,1,1,2 setal formula arises as a result of the loss, or total incorporation, of the first ancestral exopodal segment and the loss of its seta.

A 2-segmented endopod is retained in the Calanoida, Misophrioida, Gelyelloida, Cyclopoida, and Harpacticoida. The maximum setation in these orders is Calanoida 4,11 (proximal, distal segment), Misophrioida 4,8, Gelyelloida 3,7, Cyclopoida 6,10 and Harpacticoida 3,9. The endopod is 1-segmented in the Platycopioida and bears 6 setae. The endopod is reduced to a single free segment in female Mormonilloida, as the first endopodal segment with its armature of 2 setae is incorporated into the basis. The free segment bears 6 setae. In male Mormonilloida the first endopodal segment is free but unarmed. In the Siphonostomatoida and Poecilostomatoida the entire palp is very reduced. In the former the palp forms a simple process, comprising a maximum of 2 segments, armed with 2 apical setae. In the great majority of poecilostomatoids the palp is lacking altogether but in the family Erebonasteridae only, it is represented by a single segment armed with up to 4 setae (Humes, 1987). In the Monstrilloida the mandible is absent in the adult.

Table 4. Comparison of mandibular palp setation in copepod orders

	basis	end1	end2	exp1	exp2	exp3	exp4	exp5
Platycopioida	(0	--- 0)	6	1	1	1	1	2
Calanoida	4	4	11	1	1	1	1	2
Misophrioida	3	4	8	1	1	1	1	2
Harpacticoida	4	3	9	1	1	1	1	2
Mormonilloida*	(1	--- 2)	6	(–2–	)	1	1	2
Gelyelloida	1	3	7	1	1	1	(–3–	)
Cyclopoida	2	6	10	(0)	1	1	1	2

*female only

The setation of the basis and rami shows a clear reduction in many orders (Table 4). In those orders in which a separate basis is retained there is a maximum of 4 setae on the inner margin of the basis, as found in the Calanoida and Harpacticoida. There are 3 setae in the Misophrioida, 2 in the Cyclopoida, only 1 in the Gelyelloida, and none in the Platycopioida. In female Mormonilloida there are 3 setae on the basis but only the proximal seta is basal in origin, the 2 distal setae being derived from the first endopodal segment which is fully incorporated into the basis. The first segment of the 2-segmented palp of the Siphonostomatoida presumably represents the basis, but is unarmed.

3.8 PARAGNATHS

a. Ancestral State

The plesiomorphic paragnaths are paired setulose lobes located between the bases of the mandibles and maxillules either side of the mouth.

Vaupel Klein (1982) identified the calanoid labium as a purely sternal structure, not related to any paired true appendage. He referred to the paragnaths as the cleft labium, presumably regarding the median lobate condition as plesiomorphic. We regard the medial fusion of the paragnaths to form a labium as the derived state. Other structures located posterior to the mouth in the ventral midline have been referred to as a labium. For example, some poecilostomatoids have been described as possessing paired paragnaths and a labium. The term labium should be restricted in usage to a median lobe formed by fusion of the paragnaths.

b. Transformations

The only major modification involving the paragnaths has occurred in the Siphonostomatoida.

Here the paragnaths are fused medially to form the labium which acts as the lower lip of the oral cone (Boxshall, 1986a; 1990a). There is little musculature within the labial part of the oral cone (figure 2.9.19). In *Hyalopontius*, for example, a pair of muscles, originating on the anterior ventral cephalic tendon, passes to the tip of the labium and appears to be responsible for movement of the oral disc at the tip of the cone (Boxshall, 1990a).

The paragnaths are separate lobes in most calanoids but are often referred to as the bifid labium. The paragnaths of the misophrioid *Archimisophria* are unique in their possession of 3 setae in addition to their normal ornamentation of spinules and setules (figure 2.3.7A).

3.9 MAXILLULE

a. Ancestral State

The plesiomorphic maxillule is biramous and has a 3-segmented protopod consisting of a separate praecoxa, coxa and basis. The praecoxa has a well developed gnathobasic endite which is movable and is often referred to as an arthrite. The praecoxal arthrite carries an armature of 16 elements. The coxa bears a single elongate endite bearing 6 setae and a well developed exite, the epipodite, which is discrete from the coxa and carries 9 setae. The basis bears 2 endites, the proximal being well developed and armed with 4 setae, the distal largely incorporated into the segment and represented by 5 setae. It also carries a distinct exite bearing 2 setae. The exopod is a single segment armed with a row of 11 marginal setae. The endopod consists of 3 segments, first to third segments armed with 6, 4 and 7 setae respectively.

The report by Alvarez (1985) of a 2-segmented maxillulary exopod in *Archimisophria squamosa* is an error of interpretation. The apparent segmental boundary probably represents a fold in the integument of the ramus. The armature elements on the margin of the exopod in some calanoids, such as *Pseudocyclops* (figure 2.2.20B), are divided into a proximal group of 5 and distal group of 6 setae by a partial suture which could represent a vestige of an intersegmental articulation.

b. Transformations

The maxillule has undergone many modifications within the Copepoda and several of these are highly informative in the analysis of phylogenetic relationships. A discrete lobate exite on the basis is retained only in the Platycopioida. In the Calanoida this exite is vestigial, represented by a single seta only located on the outer surface of the basis. Amongst the podoplean orders there is a single seta representing the exite on the basis in the harpacticoid *Longipedia* and in the misophrioid *Speleophria*, but in all other podoplean groups no vestige of the exite remains.

Coxal Endite: The coxal endite is a well developed setose lobe in the Platycopioida (3 setae), Calanoida (5 setae), Harpacticoida (6 setae), Misophrioida (6 setae) and Gelyelloida (4 setae). In female Mormonilloida it is largely incorporated into the segment, being represented by a slight swelling on the inner margin armed with 4 setae. In the Cyclopoida it is represented by a single seta on a small process but is often lost.

Epipodite: The coxal epipodite is absent in Platycopioida and Gelyelloida. It is retained as a discrete movable lobe bearing up to 9 setae in the Calanoida (Boxshall, 1985) but in the Harpacticoida, Misophrioida, Cyclopoida, and female Mormonilloida it is incorporated into the coxa and is represented only by the setae on the outer surface of the segment. The maximum number of setae found in each order is 8 (Misophrioida), 5 (Harpacticoida), 3 (Cyclopoida), and 2 (Mormonilloida). It is possible that the isolated seta on the outer margin of the maxillule of some poecilostomatoids, as found in *Clausidium vancouverense*, represents the epipodite (see chapter 2.10).

Exopod: The exopod carries a maximum of 11 setae in the Calanoida, Misophrioida and Harpacticoida, 7 in the Mormonilloida, 4 in the Cyclopoida and 3 in the Gelyelloida. In the last 2 groups the reduction in setal numbers includes the loss of all the setae from the inner margin of the ramus, with only distal margin setae remaining. In the Platycopioida the exopod is probably represented by a single outer seta on the reduced palp.

Endopod: The endopod was originally 3-segmented and this state is retained only in the Calanoida. A 2-segmented condition in which ancestral segments 1 and 2 are fused is present in the Misophrioida, Harpacticoida and Mormonilloida. In the Cyclopoida segment 3 is partly fused to the proximal double segment. An unsegmented condition in which all 3 segments are fused is found in Gelyelloida. The setal formula for the endopod comprises 3 numbers corresponding to the original 3 segments in all these orders because the setae are arranged in 3 groups irrespective of segmental fusions. The endopodal setal formulae are: 6,4,7 in calanoids, 3,3,6 in misophrioids, 3,2,6 in harpacticoids, 2,1,5 in mormonilloids, 2,2,5 in gelyelloids and (5),5 in cyclopoids. The limb is lacking in the Monstrilloida.

Bilobate Maxillules: The entire limb is profoundly reduced in the Poecilostomatoida and Siphonostomatoida. In the siphonostomatoids it forms a bilobed structure in which the inner lobe represents the praecoxal endite and the outer lobe represents the palp (Boxshall, 1990a). There is strong supporting evidence in the intrinsic musculature, for this interpretation of the 2 lobes. In the poecilostomatoids the structure of the limb in clausidiids suggests that the inner lobe represents the reduced praecoxal arthrite and that the outer lobe represents the palp. Although primitively poecilostomatoids have 3 setae on the inner lobe (praecoxal) and 5 on the outer (palp) whereas siphonostomatoids have 5 and 4 respectively the basic bilobed structure of the maxillule in these two orders appears to be homologous (see figure 4.5.1). It is possible, however, that the bilobed condition in these two orders is the result of parallel evolution because significant differences between the maxillule types are apparent. The poecilostomatoid type can be readily derived from the ancestral limb by reduction since vestiges of the basic components of the limb remain, including the epipodite which is represented by a single seta. In siphonostomatoids the form of the two lobes, with all setation elements located distally, is different and their intimate association with the oral cone makes their derivation less clear.

3.10 MAXILLA

a. Ancestral State

The maxilla is uniramous and 7-segmented, consisting of a praecoxa, coxa, basis and a short, 4-segmented endopod. The praecoxa bears 2 well defined endites; proximal endite with 10 setae, distal with 3 setae. The coxa also has 2 well developed endites each armed with 3 setae and bears, on the outer margin, a single seta which probably represents the epipodite. The basis has a single endite bearing 4 setae. Endopodal segments 1 to 4 carry 4,3,2,4 setae.

b. Transformations

One of the most common modifications of the maxilla is the fusion of the praecoxa and coxa to form a syncoxa. In many copepods the praecoxal-coxal suture is present but no arthrodial membrane is retained so it is no longer a functional articulation, as in the misophrioid *Benthomisophria* (Boxshall, 1985). In many others the suture line is lost producing a syncoxa with 4 endites. All recent siphonostomatoids possess a syncoxa but the Cretaceous fossil *Kabatarina* has retained separate praecoxa and coxa.

Outer Coxal Seta: The seta on the outer margin of the coxa of some calanoids can be interpreted as a serial homologue of the maxillulary epipodite, and therefore, as the vestigial epipodite. This is lost in all podopleans and in the Platycopioida.

Syncoxal Endites: The syncoxal endites are lost in siphonostomatoids although in several species a single armature element is present proximally on the medial surface of the syncoxa. For example, the asterocherids *Asterocheres aesthetes* and *Sinopontius aesthetascus* both possess an aesthetasc on the syncoxa in this position. This has also been noted in other asterocherids (figure 2.9.21D). No aesthetascs are present on the praecoxal or coxal endites of free-living copepods and none is postulated for the ancestral copepod. If this structure is a true aesthetasc it is necessary to infer that either it represents a novel element or it represents a transformed seta in these siphonostomatoids. An alternative explanation is that despite its superficial resemblance to an aesthetasc this structure represents a tubular extension of the external pore of the maxillary gland which typically opens in this approximate position. Weakly developed endites are present in the Poecilostomatoida, one bearing 2 setae and the other reduced to a single seta. They are located distally on the medial surface of the syncoxa and are probably derived by reduction of the coxal endites. The maximum armature of the syncoxal endites for each order is given in Table 5.

Table 5. Maximum setation of praecoxal and coxal endites

	praecoxal:proximal	distal	coxal:proximal	distal
Platycopioida	4	1	3	3
Calanoida	10	3	3	3
Misophrioida	7	3	3	3
Harpacticoida	6	3	3	3
Mormonilloida	2	3	3	3
Gelyelloida	0	3	2	2
Cyclopoida	4	1	3	3
Poecilostomatoida	0	0	2	1
Siphonostomatoida	0	0	0	0

Endopodal Reductions: Another common trend is the reduction in number of endopodal segments. This occurs within most orders. In some calanoids and harpacticoids all endopodal segments are free. In many other representatives of these two orders and in all platycopioids, misophrioids and gelyelloids the first endopodal segment is fused with the basis to form an allobasis. This allobasis bears 2 endites, the proximal being basal in origin, the distal being derived from the first endopodal segment. In these orders the 3 endopodal segments that remain free are the second to fourth ancestral segments. Three apparent segments are also present in cyclopoids but they are not homologous since the proximal segment is double, derived by fusion of the first and second ancestral endopodal segments. In every cyclopoid examined in which the maxillary endopod preserves recognisable segmentation the basis is free and this double endopodal segment is present. In no case has an allobasis been found.

Table 6. Comparison of setation of maxillary basis and endopod

	basis	endopod 1	2	3	4
Platycopioida	(4 +	1)	1	2	3
Calanoida	4	4	3	2	2
Misophrioida	(4 +	3)	2	2	4
Harpacticoida	4	3	2	2	4
Mormonilloida	(2 +	1)	1	1	4
Gelyelloida	(3 +	2)	2	2	4
Cyclopoida	3	(2 +	2)	2	4

Subchelate Maxilla: In siphonostomatoids the maxilla is modified into a subchelate appendage. The distal claw is formed by specialisation of the endite of the basis and is armed with up to 2 additional enditic setae. The loss of the entire endopod appears to be associated with the formation of the basal claw. In the Poecilostomatoida the distal maxillary segment represents the basis with its endite and no trace of the endopodal segments remains.

Endopodal Setation: The setation of the maxillary endopod is rarely figured accurately in taxonomic drawings. We have been unable to verify many of the published setal counts for this

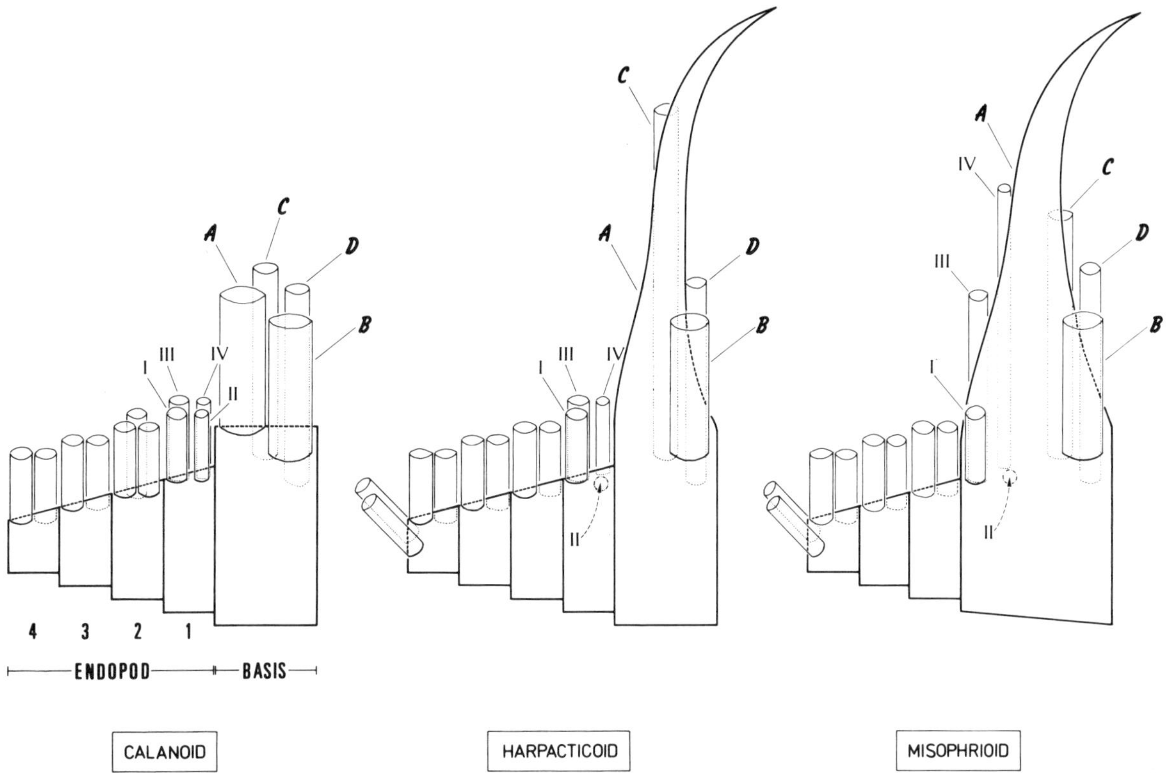

Figure 3.10.1. Comparison of homologous segments and setae on the maxillary endopod and basis in calanoids, misophrioids and harpacticoids. Homologous setation elements are indicated by letters on the basis and Roman numerals on the first endopodal segment.

ramus and therefore we have only used counts verified by examination of material (listed in Appendix 1) in our phylogenetic analysis. The simple numbers of setation elements on the maxillary basis and endopod are given in Table 6.

In order to extract the maximum information content it is necessary to identify each element on the basis and first endopodal segments individually. The four ancestral elements on the basis are termed A to D, those on the first endopodal segment I to IV. The primitive setation patterns of maxillary basis and endopod of the Calanoida, Misophrioida and Harpacticoida are compared in figure 3.10.1. In the Calanoida elements A to D are retained on the basis and I to IV on the first endopodal segment. In the Harpacticoida the first endopodal segment carries only 3 setae, seta II is lost. One seta is also lost from the second endopodal segment which carries 3 in calanoids. The losses of this seta and of seta II on the first endopodal segment are shared by all podoplean orders. The fourth endopodal segment carries 4 setae, as do other podoplean orders, and we interpret the loss of 2 setae from the apical segment as an apomorphy of the Calanoida. Only 1 seta is lost in platycopioids which retain 3 apical setae.

Despite the differences in segmental fusions of basis and endopod in the Cyclopoida and the Gelyelloida they share two changes in setation (figure 3.10.2); the loss of seta D from the basis and the loss of seta IV from the first ancestral endopodal segment. These setae may also be lost in female Mormonilloida, which possess a total of 3 setae on the allobasis, but it is not possible to accurately confirm the homology of the missing setae.

3.11 MAXILLIPED

a. Ancestral State

The maxilliped is uniramous, consisting of a 3-segmented protopod and a 6-segmented ramus, the endopod. The first and second protopodal segments, the praecoxa and coxa, carry 1 and 3

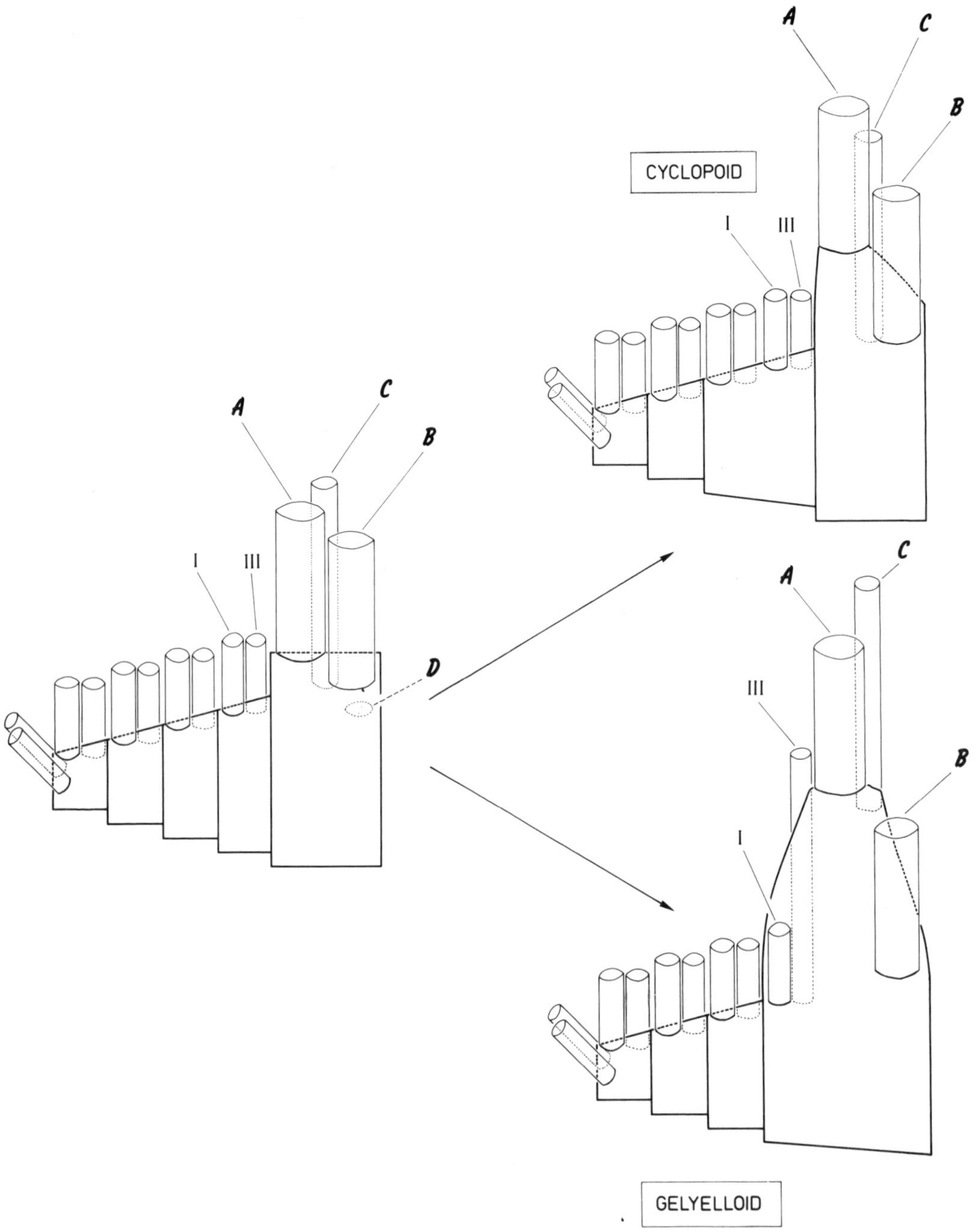

Figure 3.10.2. Comparison of homologous segments and setae on the maxillary endopod and basis of cyclopoids and gelyelloids. The same convention of identifying setation elements is used as in figure 3.10.1.

endites respectively. The praecoxal and coxal endite formula is 1, 2, 4, 4. The coxa also bears a single outer seta probably representing the epipodite. The basis bears 3 setae on its medial margin. The first to sixth endopodal segments bear 2, 4, 4, 3, 3+1 and 5 setae respectively.

Boxshall (1983, 1985) investigated the segmental structure of the maxilliped of *Archimisophria* and finally concluded (1985) that the praecoxa and coxa each have 2 endites. Further study of this appendage in a related species has revealed conflicting evidence. We now interpret the line across the appendage at the level of the second and third endites as an integumental fold whereas the true separation between praecoxa and coxa is marked by the suture line separating first and second endites. The outer coxal seta is present only in some calanoids (Ferrari, 1985). A seta in this position was shown in the harpacticoid *Brianola pori* Hamond but reexamination of the specimen (Hamond, pers.comm.) failed to confirm the presence of this seta.

b. Transformations

A common modification is the fusion of praecoxa and coxa to form a syncoxa. A syncoxa is primitively found in the Platycopioida, Calanoida, Cyclopoida, Gelyelloida, Mormonilloida and Poecilostomatoida. The monstrilloids lack a maxilliped in the adult. The Harpacticoida and Misophrioida each contain representatives that retain indistinctly separated praecoxa and coxa. The only siphonostomatoid with an apparently separate praecoxa and coxa is the fossil *Kabatarina*. Cressey & Boxshall (1989) described the maxilliped as comprising a 3-segmented proximal part and a distal subchela. We now consider that the first segment, interpreted as praecoxa by Cressey & Boxshall, probably represents the maxillipedal pedestal which is so widespread within the order. Siphonostomatoids lack endites on the syncoxa although the single seta located on the distomedial margin of the syncoxa probably represents a vestige of the distal coxal endite. The 2 setae on the syncoxa of poecilostomatoids probably represent the 2 coxal endites. In female *Mormonilla minor* the praecoxa, coxa, basis and first endopodal segment are fused into a compound proximal segment (figures 2.6.6C and 2.0.2).

Table 7. Comparative setal formula of maxillipedal protopod

	Syncoxal endites				
	1	2	3	4	Basis
Platycopioida	0	0	0	2	2
Calanoida	1	2	4	4	3
Misophrioida	1	2	4	3	3
Harpacticoida	1	2	4	3	2
Mormonilloida*	0	0	2	1	3
Gelyelloida	0	2	2	1	2
Cyclopoida	0	1	3	2	2
Siphonostomatoida	(– – – – – 1 – – – – –)				1
Poecilostomatoida	(– – – – – 2 – – – – –)				2

*females only

Setation: The setation formulae for the orders are compared in Table 7. The ancestral number of 3 setae on the basis is retained in the Calanoida, Misophrioida and Mormonilloida. All other orders have 2 except the Siphonostomatoida with 1 and the Monstrilloida in which the limb is absent. In some cyclopoids belonging to the Notodelphyidae, and in *Archinotodelphys typicus*, the syncoxal formula is 0,1,5,5 or 0,0,5,5. We interpret this as a secondary increase in setal numbers (see chapter 3.16).

Endopodal Segmentation: The number of endopodal segments is commonly reduced by fusion. In many orders there are only 5 free endopodal segments because the proximal segment has become incorporated into the basis (see Table 8). This serves to increase the apparent number of

3 setae on the basis but the distal elements are derived from the first endopodal segment. The endopod is treated as 6-segmented in the Platycopioida, Calanoida and Misophrioida because the proximal segment is incompletely fused to the basis. In the Cyclopoida the endopod is 5-segmented, presumably as a result of the complete incorporation of the ancestral first endopodal segment into the basis. In the Siphonostomatoida the endopod is indistinctly 4-segmented, and in the Harpacticoida, Gelyelloida, and Poecilostomatoida it is 2-segmented. In the Mormonilloida the maxilliped is sexually dimorphic. In the non-feeding males it is extremely reduced. In female *Mormonilla* the ancestral condition is a single protopodal segment representing syncoxa plus basis and a 4-segmented endopod (see figure 2.0.2). There is also sexual dimorphism in the maxillipedal structure in the Poecilostomatoida, with the basis of the male being much larger and more robust than that of the female. The male has a 2-segmented endopod with the second segment incorporated into the terminal claw, whereas the endopod of the female is 2-segmented with the second segment bearing a claw-like element that is usually fused to the segment basally. There is further fusion within each group, particularly the Siphonostomatoida. In the siphonostomatoid families parasitic on fish fusion within the endopod commonly results in the formation of a single rigid subchela representing the entire ramus.

Table 8. Comparison of setal formulae for maxillipedal endopod

endopodal segments	1	2	3	4	5	6
Platycopioida	1	2	2	1	1	4
Calanoida	2	4	4	3	3 + 1	4
Misophrioida	2	2	2	2	2 + 1	5
Cyclopoida	(–)	1	2	2	1 + 1	4
Harpacticoida	(– – – – – – 5 + 1 – – – – – –)					5
Gelyelloida	(– – – – 1 – – – –)				(– – 5 + 1 – –)	
Mormonilloida: female	1	1	1	4		
Siphonostomatoida	2	(1	1)	1 + claw		
Poecilostomatoida: male	0	1 + claw				
: female	2	4				

The presence of an outer margin seta on the fifth endopodal segment provides a useful reference point for the identification of segmental homologies. In the Calanoida and Misophrioida the outer margin seta occurs on segment 5. In the Cyclopoida the first endopodal segment is lacking, presumably incorporated into the basis, and the outer margin seta occurs on segment 4. The presence of an outer margin seta on the first segment of the 2-segmented endopod of harpacticoids indicates that the fifth ancestral segment must be incorporated into the compound proximal segment whereas the presence of the outer margin seta on the distal segment in the 2-segmented endopod of *Gelyella* indicates that the ancestral fifth segment is incorporated into the compound distal segment. The 2-segmented conditions found in the Harpacticoida and Gelyelloida are therefore not homologous.

3.12 SWIMMING LEGS 1-4

a. Ancestral State

The first four pairs of thoracopodal swimming legs all share the same segmentation and setation plan. The protopod consists of a well developed coxa and basis, and a remnant of the praecoxa. The latter is represented by the sclerite located laterally at the base of the leg. The coxae of each member of a leg pair are fused medially to a rigid intercoxal sclerite which ensures that they beat in unison. The coxa bears a single inner seta. The basis bears an inner seta or spine and an outer seta. The endopod is 3-segmented and is armed with 1 inner seta on the first segment, 2 on the second and a total of 8 elements on the third arranged with 2 on the outer margin, 2 on the distal margin and 4 on the inner margin. The exopod is 3-segmented. The first segment has 1 or 2 spines on the outer margin and an inner seta. The second segment has one outer spine and an inner seta. The third segment has 3 spines on the outer margin, a terminal spine and 5 setae along the inner margin.

Protopodal Segmentation: The protopod is clearly 3-segmented in most harpacticoids, as in *Neobradya pectinifera* (see Huys, 1987a, fig. 4A). The praecoxa is well developed in the first leg of *N.pectinifera* and in the legs of *Hamondia* and *Ambunguipes* (Huys, 1990a). In most harpacticoid legs it is reduced to a sclerite located round the lateral part of the coxa (figure 2.4.19A-B). Boxshall (1985) described a pouch of flexible integument lying lateral to the limb base in the calanoid *Euaugaptilus placitus* Scott. A promotor muscle (th.pr.m.3) inserts on this area. This pouch presumably represents the remnant of the praecoxa. No vestige of the praecoxa was found in *Benthomisophria* by Boxshall (1982) but Huys (1988b) shows minute lateral sclerites on some legs of *Boxshallia* which are probably praecoxal in origin. The 3-segmented condition of the protopod, found in at least the Calanoida, Misophrioida, Harpacticoida, Monstrilloida, Siphonostomatoida and Poecilostomatoida, is here regarded as the ancestral copepod state.

Armature: The spine and seta formula of copepod legs is an important systematic tool from species level to ordinal level. There is, however, uncertainty about the formula attributed to the exopod of the ancestral copepod. In the Platycopioida there are 2 spines on the outer margin of the first exopodal segment. In all other described copepods there is only one. The report of 2 outer setae on this segment of the third leg of *Pseudocyclopia caudata* Scott by T.Scott (1894) is erroneous. The general oligomerization principle that has become apparent during our analysis would suggest that the 2-spined state is ancestral and that the 1-spined state is apomorphic for other copepods. Out-group analysis is uninformative since potential out-groups either have very reduced thoracopods, such as the Mystacocarida, or have thoracopods in which the nature of the spine formula is different, such as the Thecostraca. The uncertainty has increased since the discovery in anchialine cave habitats of two new genera, *Superornatiremis* and *Neoechinophora*, belonging to a recently discovered new family of harpacticoids, the Superornatiremidae, which possess 3 spines on the outer margin of the first exopodal segment, 2 on the outer margin of the second and 1 or 2 spines on the outer margin of the second endopodal segment (figure 2.4.19A-B). The possession of outer margin elements on the second endopodal segment is unique within the Copepoda. The increase in number of elements in this relatively advanced family of harpacticoids is interpreted here as a secondary phenomenon and it raises the possibility of the increase in the Platycopioida also being secondary. However, at present we have tentatively interpreted the platycopioid condition as plesiomorphic, and this interpretation is supported by these spines being in a state of reduction within the order, or having been lost.

Segmentation of Rami: The rami of the legs are primitively 3-segmented in copepods. Rarely aberrant individuals have been found which appear to have more segments but these are almost certainly teratological in origin. Vaupel Klein (1984) found a *Euchirella messinensis* with a partly subdivided third exopodal segment on one side of one leg. In view of the probable derivation of the copepod swimming leg rami from an ancestral crustacean with 6 or 7 segments (cf. Itô, 1982a) Vaupel Klein interpreted this leg as an atavism. We regard this as highly improbable. Humes & Stock (1973) also reported an aberrant specimen of *Serpuliphilus tenax* Humes & Stock which had a 4-segmented exopod.

b. Transformations

Fusion or loss of intercoxal sclerite: A unique modification of the swimming legs is found in the Gelyelloida (Huys, 1988a). The coxae of the members of each leg pair are fused medially and the characteristic intercoxal sclerites appear to be absent, or are so reduced that they are represented only by the tiny sclerotised crescents on the mid-distal margin of the fused coxae. Also in the Gelyelloida the fourth legs are entirely lacking. In the harpacticoid *Orthopsyllus* (figure 3.12.1A) the intercoxal sclerites are secondarily lost, as they are in many parasitic forms within other orders.

Segmental Fusion: Fusion and loss of the ramal segments occur frequently in most copepod orders, and one or both rami can also be lost. In many harpacticoids the first pair of legs functions

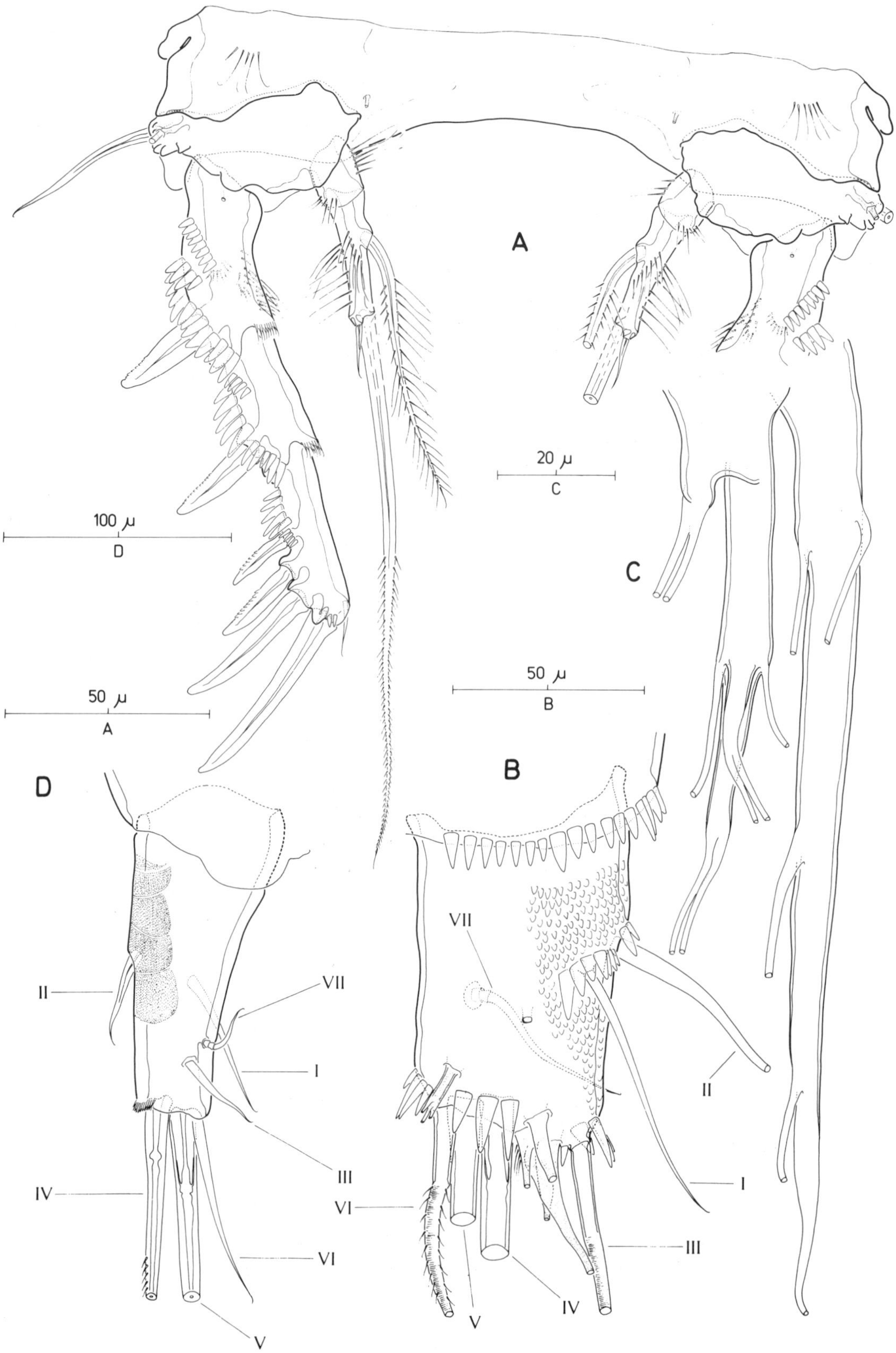

Figure 3.12.1. **A**. Second swimming leg of *Orthopsyllus* sp., showing fusion of members of leg pair and loss of intercoxal sclerite. **B**. *Bathyidia remota*, caudal ramus. **C**. Detail of distal tube pores on caudal ramus. **D**. *Canuella perplexa*, caudal ramus.

as a raptorial limb and has a role in feeding. This adaptation often involves changes in proportional lengths of limb segments and the formation of a subchela from one of the armature elements.

Setation: Modifications of the setation formula are very common and provide useful systematic characters. The Platycopioida, for example, are the only order in which an inner seta is present on the basis of legs 2 to 5. The Platycopioida, however, have lost the inner seta from the coxa of all of the swimming legs. There is never an outer seta on the coxa (Gurney, 1931; Lang, 1948a). Reports of such a seta, for example in *Scottopsyllus minor* Scott & Scott by Nicholls (1935), *Enhydrosoma vervoorti* Fiers by Fiers (1987), and in *Neopeltopsis hicksi* Pallares by Pallares (1979) are erroneous. The outer digitiform process on the coxa of the second and third legs of the poecilostomatoid genus *Chauliolobion* Humes (Humes, 1975; 1980a) is a novel structure and is not derived from a spine or seta (figure 2.10.22C-D). In some members of the Paramesochridae there is a secondary increase in the number of inner basal setae. Both Lang (1948a; 1965) and Mielke (1984) show 5 setae on the inner margin of the basis of the first leg (figure 2.4.18A) of such paramesochrids. Itô & Burton (1980) showed an aberrant third leg in *Thermomesochra reducta* Itô & Burton with 2 outer setae on the basis.

The spine and seta formula for the rami of the swimming legs is regularly used to separate families, genera and species. The formula is basically stable within a species, although individual variation has been reported. At the ordinal level a great deal of information is present in this formula. The podoplean orders differ from the Platycopioida and Calanoida in the total number of elements on the third segment of the endopod: the podopleans having a basic 6,6,6,5 pattern for legs 1 to 4 whereas the Platycopioida and Calanoida have 7,7,7,6 and 6,8,8,7 respectively. Using legs 2 and 3 as a comparison it is clear that this increase is due to the presence of 2 setae on the lateral margin and 4 on the inner margin of this segment as compared to maxima of 1 and 3 respectively in podopleans.

The use of total number of elements, however, is misleading because it can conceal the true homology of elements. For example the Platycopioida, the Harpacticoida, the Cyclopoida and the Poecilostomatoida each have a total of 8 elements on the third exopodal segment of leg 4 but in the Platycopioida and the Harpacticoida this is derived from a spine and seta formula of III,I,4 whereas in the Cyclopoida and Poecilostomatoida the original formula is II,I,5. These two states are not homologous. Spine and seta formulae are given in each ordinal diagnosis in chapter 2 and provide sufficient detail for accurate comparison.

Other minor setation characters have proved to be distinctive at high taxonomic levels. For example, no poecilostomatoids retain an inner seta on the first exopodal segment in legs 1 to 4. Similarly no harpacticoids or poecilostomatoids possess more than 1 seta on the inner margin of endopodal segment 2 of leg 1 but they retain the original complement of 2 setae on this segment in legs 2 to 4. Platycopioids and monstrilloids have only 1 seta on this segment in legs 1 to 4. All other orders, excluding the Mormonilloida and Gelyelloida with their extremely reduced legs, have 2 setae on this segment in legs 1 to 4 in at least some representatives.

3.13 FIFTH LEG

a. Ancestral State

The fifth leg is similar to the other swimming legs in segmentation and in the presence of a distinct intercoxal sclerite. It has fewer armature elements on the third endopodal segment, carrying only 6 setae, and on the third exopodal segment which has a total of 8 elements. There is an inner seta on the basis. There is no sexual dimorphism. The spine and seta formula is as follows:

	coxa	basis	exopod segment	endopod segment
			1 2 3	1 2 3
leg 5	0 – 1	1 – 1	II – 1; I – 1; III,I,4	0 – 1; 0 – 1; 2,2,2

b. Transformations

The fifth legs are highly modified in many copepods. In the Gelyelloida the fifth legs are lacking in the adults of both sexes. The fifth legs are commonly sexually dimorphic, especially when those of the male are involved in grasping the female and transferring the spermatophore during copulation, as in calanoids. Sexual dimorphism occurs in the basic segmentation pattern of the Misophrioida, Harpacticoida and Cyclopoida. Sexual dimorphism is also expressed in the Mormonilloida, in which females lack a fifth leg completely but males have 4 setae on the ventral body surface, 2 on each side of the midline.

Praecoxal vestige: The small lateral hoop-like sclerite representing the praecoxa is present in the fifth legs of platycopioids and calanoids. All the podoplean orders have lost this praecoxal vestige so the protopod is 2-segmented at most.

Endopodal Reduction and Loss: Another common trend is towards the reduction and loss of the endopod within the podoplean lineage. The endopod is reduced in all podoplean orders. It is retained as a single free segment in some Misophrioida (figures 2.3.11D and 2.3.12D-E), in both sexes of the harpacticoids *Longipedia* (figure 2.4.20A-B) and in the males of *Tachidiopsis bozici* (figure 2.4.20D) and *Antarcticobradya tenuis* Brady (figure 2.4.20C). In the Misophrioida the endopod bears 1 or 2 apical setae, in *Misophriopsis* species, or is represented by a single seta on the distal margin of the basis. In the harpacticoids listed above which have a discrete endopod a maximum of 2 setae is present on the endopod, but in the other harpacticoids, in which the endopod and basis are fused to form a baseoendopod, up to 4 setae are found in the male and 6 in the female. This indicates that the ancestral harpacticoid presumably had a free endopodal segment bearing a maximum of 6 and 4 setae in the female and male respectively. In the Monstrilloida the fifth legs are bilobed. The 2 distal lobes represent endopod and exopod and both are fused to the protopod. The endopodal lobe bears a maximum of 2 setae in *Monstrilla grandis* (figure 2.5.1C). In the Siphonostomatoida the endopod is represented by a small seta on the inner margin of the protopod of a few species, *Dermatomyzon nigripes* for example. The endopod is absent in most other siphonostomatoids and in the Cyclopoida and Poecilostomatoida.

The Monstrilloida and Siphonostomatoida primitively share a baseoendopod in which the endopod is incorporated into the basis and bears a maximum of 2 endopodal setae. The great majority of harpacticoids also possess a baseoendopod but the retention of a free endopodal segment in some plesiomorphic forms, such as *Longipedia*, indicates that it must have evolved in parallel to that of the Monstrilloida-Siphonostomatoida group. There is no indication of the endopod of the fifth legs at any stage in the ontogeny of poecilostomatoids, Typically in podopleans the rudiment of the fifth leg appears at the third copepodid stage. In the third copepodid of *Benthomisophria palliata* Sars this rudiment carries 4 setae (Boxshall & Roe, 1980), the innermost of which can be identified as the endopodal seta of the adult. No such endopodal lobe or endopodal seta appears during the copepodid phase of poecilostomatoids or cyclopoids. The fifth leg is often bilobed at the fourth copepodid stage in cyclopoids (see Dudley, 1966) but the outer lobe is the vestige of the protopod bearing the single outer basal seta and the inner lobe represents the exopod.

Exopodal reduction: The exopod is also reduced within the podoplean line. A 3-segmented exopod is retained in some male harpacticoids, such as the cerviniid *Eucanuella* and some species of *Parastenhelia* Thompson & Scott, and in some male misophrioids. A maximum of 2 exopodal segments is found in female misophrioids and male and female cyclopoids. A single free exopodal segment is found in female harpacticoids, in both sexes of Siphonostomatoida, and in Poecilostomatoida. In the majority of the members of these last 2 orders the fifth leg is a single free segment (the exopod) located laterally on the somite.

Lateral Migration: The lateral migration of the fifth legs occurs in several podoplean groups. The typical siphonostomatoid fifth leg is a single free segment (the exopod) located laterally on the somite. The plesiomorphic condition present in *Dermatomyzon* indicates that this configuration is derived in stages. Initially the single protopodal segment broadens considerably, carrying the exopod to a more ventrolateral position (figure 2.9.24A). The fusion of the protopod to the somite (figure 2.9.24B) and its eventual incorporation into it leaves the free exopodal segment located laterally and the outer basal seta situated dorsal to it, on the surface of the somite. A similar process has taken place independently in the Poecilostomatoida, with the primitive ventral position of the fifth legs being retained only in the families Erebonasteridae and Paralubbockiidae, and in males of *Serpulidicola* Southward, and in the Cyclopoida, with ventral fifth legs retained in some genera of the families Cyclopinidae and Cyclopidae. A second mode of lateral migration involving the entire fifth legs (including the protopodal segment) has also occurred in some siphonostomatoids. In dirivultids, for example, the fifth legs are laterally located (figure 2.9.27C) but the protopodal segment does not form a broad transverse plate. The only prerequisite for this migration is the loss of the intercoxal sclerite.

Intercoxal Sclerites: Intercoxal sclerites joining the members of the fifth leg pair are present in all orders except the Siphonostomatoida, Monstrilloida, Gelyelloida and Mormonilloida. In the last 2 orders the fifth legs are either absent or so reduced that no free segments remain.

Setation: An inner seta on the coxa of the fifth legs is found only in a few species of two orders. In the Cyclopoida it is retained in some members of the family Cyclopinidae, such as female *Cyclopinodes elegans* (figure 2.8.33B). In the Calanoida it is retained in some members of the Augaptilidae, such as female *Haloptilus oxycephalus* (figure 2.2.25A), and in the family Boholinidae. All other copepods have lost this seta. An inner seta on exopodal segment 1 is retained only in the Platycopioida, all other orders have no inner margin element on this segment. The Calanoida have 6 setae on the third endopodal segment arranged in a 2,2,2 pattern. All other orders have only 5 setae arranged in a 1,2,2 configuration.

Some armature elements are highly conservative. The outer basal seta is retained in the majority of copepods. Even in orders such as the Poecilostomatoida and Siphonostomatoida that typically have reduced fifth legs the basal seta is present and in those forms that have just a single free segment, or no free segment at all, the basal seta is inserted on the surface of the somite just dorsal to the segment, lobe or seta that represents the exopod. The inner seta on the first exopodal segment (seta '*l*' in figure 1.5.8) is present only in the Platycopioida, so its loss represents a synapomorphy of all calanoids and podoplean orders.

3.14 CAUDAL RAMI

a. Ancestral State

The caudal rami are unsegmented, articulating lobes situated posteriorly on the anal somite. In their most generalised form they are cylindrical in shape, and rectangular in dorsal view. Each ramus carries 7 setae; the anterolateral accessory seta (I), anterolateral seta (II), posterolateral seta (III), outer terminal seta (IV), inner terminal or principal seta (V), terminal accessory seta (VI) and dorsal seta (VII).

The terminology used for the caudal setae follows that proposed by Huys (1988c) for the generalised paramesochrid caudal ramus. The presence of six setae has previously been regarded as typical for copepods but the 7 setae named by Huys can be found in the Platycopioida, Calanoida, Gelyelloida, Cyclopoida, Poecilostomatoida, Siphonostomatoida and Misophrioida, as well as in the Harpacticoida. The anterolateral accessory seta (seta I) is relatively large in *Gelyella* (figure 2.7.2D), in the misophrioid genus *Speleophria* (figure 2.3.12C), and in many harpacticoids (figure 2.4.24D). In other orders we have often found it to be minute. It has rarely been figured and may be secondarily absent from many taxa.

More than 7 elements on the caudal rami have been reported from various copepods. Lang (1948a) reported an additional element in *Canuella perplexa* (figure 3.12.1D) but this was an error. Boxshall (1979) reported 9 elements on the caudal rami of the tisbid genera *Volkmannia* Boxshall, *Neotisbella* Boxshall and *Bathyidia* Farran. Reexamination of *B.remota* (figure 3.12.1B-C) revealed that the extra setae were extremely elongate and branching tube pores rather than setation elements.

b. Transformations

The caudal rami are found in a great variety of shapes and sizes in the Copepoda. They may exceed the entire length of the body, as in the Aegisthidae (Boxshall, 1979; Huys, 1988e), or they may be incorporated into the anal somite as in the cyclopoid family Chordeumiidae (Boxshall, 1988), or lost as in the Spongiocnizontidae (figure 2.9.28E). There are also many modifications to the armature; with setae being lost or transformed. Two orders, the Monstrilloida and the Mormonilloida, are characterised by the loss of seta I and have a maximum of 6 setae.

3.15 OTHER CHARACTERS

a. Carapace

A carapace-like extension of the dorsal cephalic shield is found in several misophrioid genera (Boxshall, 1982). This structure encloses the first free pedigerous somite both laterally and dorsally (figure 2.3.20A). It has been treated herein as an autapomorphy of the Misophrioida although it has been secondarily reduced or lost in a number of cavernicolous genera, such as *Expansophria* (figure 2.3.21A-B). It was interpreted by Boxshall (1984) as a functional adaptation to gorging as an opportunistic feeding strategy. It is apparently derived as an outgrowth from the posterior margin of the maxilliped-bearing somite (figure 2.3.18B) and is not homologous with the carapace of thecostracans which is maxillary in origin (Newman, in Hessler & Newman, 1975).

Examination of some plesiomorphic cyclopoids belonging to the family Cyclopinidae revealed the presence of a similar structure in several genera. In *Pterinopsyllus* a complete carapace is present, enclosing the first pedigerous somite both dorsally and laterally (figure 3.15.1A). In *Cyclopinodes elegans* the carapace is reduced to posterolateral lobe-like expansions that cover the lateral margins of the first pedigerous somite and partly overlap onto the second (figure 3.15.1B-C).

b. Intermaxillipedal Process

A variety of structures can be found along the midventral surface of the cephalosome in copepods, including the intermaxillipedal process of the Platycopioida and the intermaxillary swellings of misophrioids (Boxshall, 1982). The former is well developed and bears strong teeth in species of *Platycopia* (figure 2.1.12C), but is poorly developed in *Nanocopia* and *Antrisocopia*. This process is treated as an autapomorphy of the Platycopioida. It is not regarded as homologous with the small, ornamented swellings found between the maxillipeds in other orders. The sternal furca of caligiform siphonostomatoids lies in the ventral midline between the maxillipeds and first swimming legs. In his study of caligid musculature Boxshall (1990a) showed that the sternal furca is derived by elaboration of the median intersomitic sclerite. There is also a prominent process between the maxillipeds in *Aphotopontius probolus* Humes (Humes, 1990).

c. Nauplius Eye

The nauplius eye is a crustacean character and is primitively present in copepods. It has been secondarily lost in the Misophrioida (Boxshall, 1984) and it has not been recorded in either the Platycopioida or the Gelyelloida. Both of these orders have strong links with subterranean habitats, as does the Misophrioida, and it is possible that they also lack the nauplius eye.

The basic nauplius eye is tripartite, comprising a pair of dorsal ocelli and a median ventral ocellus. The nauplius eye has become very elaborate in some copepods and an amazing array of optical systems involving mirrors, lenses and combinations of mirrors and lenses is found (Land, 1984). Elaborate nauplius eyes are found in some Calanoida (families Pontellidae, Phaennidae and Centropagidae), some Poecilostomatoida (families Corycaeidae and Sapphirinidae), some Monstrilloida, some Harpacticoida (Miraciidae) and some Siphonostomatoida (Caligidae and Pennellidae). These modifications all appear to have evolved independently within the orders and provide little information relevant to ordinal relationships.

d. Rostrum

The rostrum is extremely variable in copepods, both between and within orders. In order to analyse this variation it is necessary to unambiguously define the nature of a rostrum. In copepods

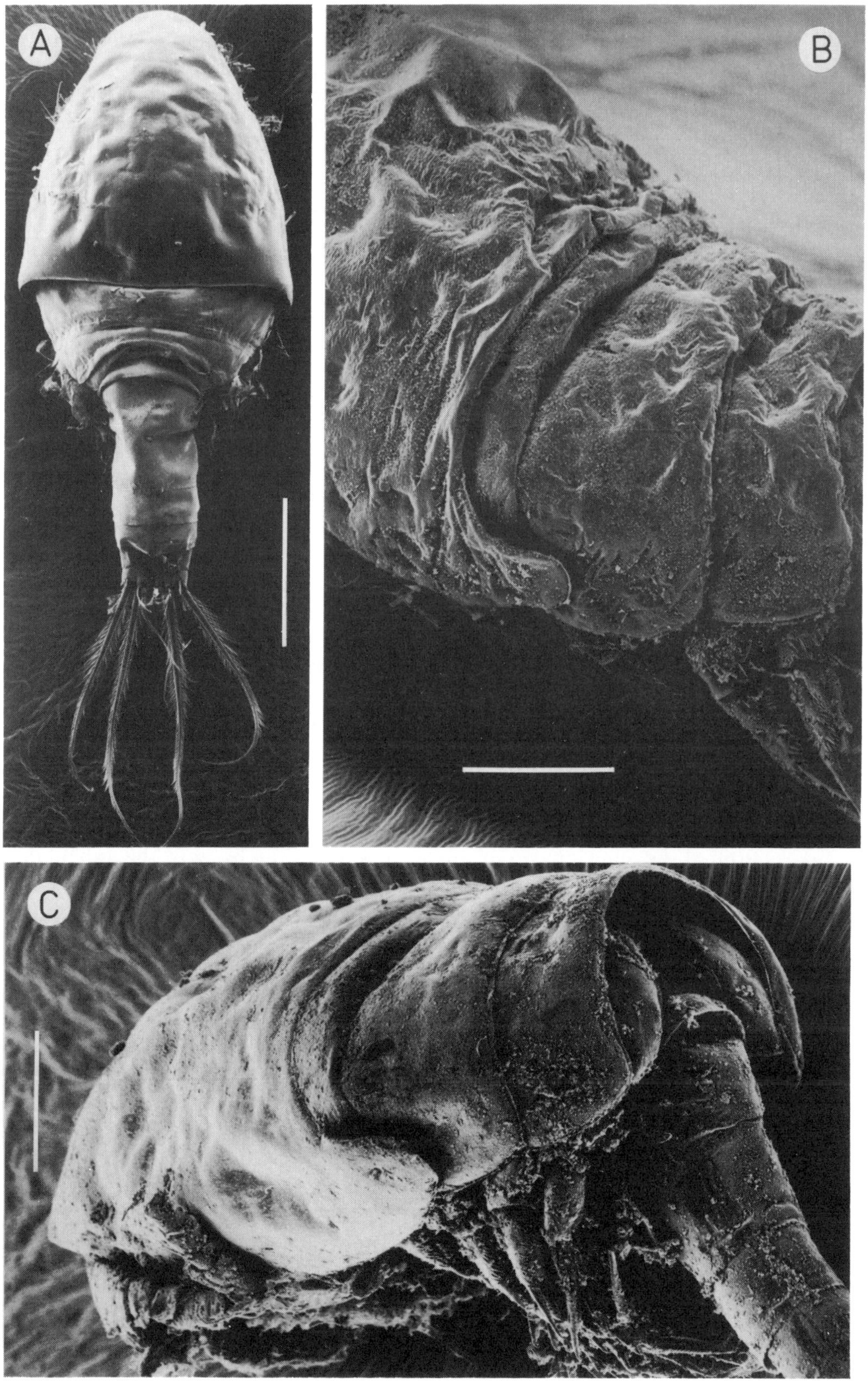

Figure 3.15.1. **A.** *Pterinopsyllus* sp., dorsal view showing carapace-like extension from rear margin of dorsal cephalic shield enclosing first pedigerous somite. **B.** *Cyclopinodes elegans*, lateral view of middle part of prosome showing postero-lateral extensions of dorsal cephalic shield over epimeral regions of first pedigerous somite. **C.** *Cyclopinoides longicornis*, postero-lateral view of prosome showing postero-lateral extensions of dorsal cephalic shield. Scale bars A = 200μm, B = 75μm, C = 50μm.

the term rostrum has been applied uncritically to virtually any structure located at the anterior end of the dorsal cephalosomic shield, between the bases of the antennules. The glossary of crustacean terms in Moore & McCormick (1969) defines a rostrum as 'an anteriorly projecting, unpaired, usually rigid median extension of carapace between eyes or eyestalks' and a rostral plate as an 'anteriorly projecting, unpaired, movably articulated, median extension of carapace'. Neither of these definitions is particularly relevant to the Copepoda. In copepods there are other structures, typically a large median pore and an associated pair of frontal sensilla (referred to here as the rostral sensory complex), located at or near the anterior margin of the dorsal cephalosomic shield, that can be used to establish reference points. We define the copepod rostrum as a median extension of the anterior margin of the dorsal cephalosomic shield that carries the rostral sensory complex. The rostrum is typically continuous with the dorsal shield but may be directed anteriorly, ventrally or posteroventrally between the bases of the antennules.

There are two basic types of copepod rostrum: the first is a projecting lobe lying between the bases of the antennules, the second wraps around the frontal surface of the prosome and scarcely projects at all. The projecting type exists in a wide variety of states. It may be very well developed, tapering either to a sharply pointed tip as in the calanoid *Pseudocyclops* (figure 3.15.2D) and Platycopioida (figure 2.1.10D), or to a less pointed or even rounded tip as in the cyclopoids *Cyclops strenuus* Fischer (figure 3.15.4A) and *Pterinopsyllus* (figure 3.15.4D) respectively. The pointed rostrum can also be strongly curved, as in *Oithona helgolandica* Claus (figure 3.15.3C). In the Calanoida the rostrum is usually of the projecting type but it is typically bifid, and the resulting paired structures are referred to as rostral filaments (figure 3.15.2A-B). The projecting type of rostrum may be secondarily separated from the dorsal shield by a proximal suture, as in the misophrioid *Archimisophria discoveryi* (figure 2.3.10C) and the harpacticoid *Canuella perplexa* (figure 3.15.3B). In the latter the rostral sensory complex is not visible in frontal view because the paired sensilla lie on the laterodistal margins and the median pore is located on the posterior surface. In some cases, such as the male of *Pseudocyclops*, a projecting lobe separated from the dorsal shield by a proximal suture, is present between the bases of the antennules but the rostral sensory complex remains on the dorsal shield (figure 2.2.24B). We refer to such an articulating structure which lacks the rostral sensory complex, as a pseudorostrum because it is clearly not homologous with the defined rostrum of *Archimisophria* which bears the rostral sensory complex.

The second type of rostrum is represented by the frontal margin of the dorsal cephalic shield that is wrapped around the anterior end of the head between the bases of the antennules. This type of rudimentary rostrum is found in, for example, the calanoid family Stephidae (figure 3.15.2C) and the poecilostomatoid family Ergasilidae (figure 3.15.4C). The frontal sensilla and median pore are clearly visible in this latter example. The wrap-around type of rostrum can also be separated from the dorsal shield by a proximal suture as in the cyclopoid family Chordeumiidae (figure 3.15.3A).

Further modifications and elaborations of the rostrum can occur. In the misophrioid *Benthomisophria* the posteroventrally directed rostrum is fused to the labrum. In the harpacticoid *Nannopus palustris* Brady the small rostrum is provided with a dense fringe of long setules (figure 3.15.4B). In the siphonostomatoid *Lernaeocera branchialis* (Linn.) the rostrum forms a broad plate extending over the bases of the antennae (figure 3.15.3D) and carries, postero-distally, the opening of the gland secreting the frontal filament which serves to attach the chalimus larval stages to the host.

e. Operculum and Pseudoperculum

In most copepods the anus opens dorsally on the anal somite, some distance anterior to the rear margin of the somite. It is more or less covered by an operculum formed as a posterior extension of the dorsal surface of the somite. This operculum may be highly ornamented with rows of spinules, especially in some harpacticoids. An operculum is present in the Harpacticoida, Misophrioida, Cyclopoida, Siphonostomatoida, Poecilostomatoida and Gelyelloida. There is no operculum in the Platycopioida, Monstrilloida and in the plesiomorphic calanoid family Pseudocyclopidae. In these forms the anus lies terminally, on the posterior surface of the anal somite, between the caudal rami.

In some harpacticoids the operculum is lost and the anus is covered by a pseudoperculum derived as a posterior outgrowth of the somitic hyaline frill of the preanal somite. The presence

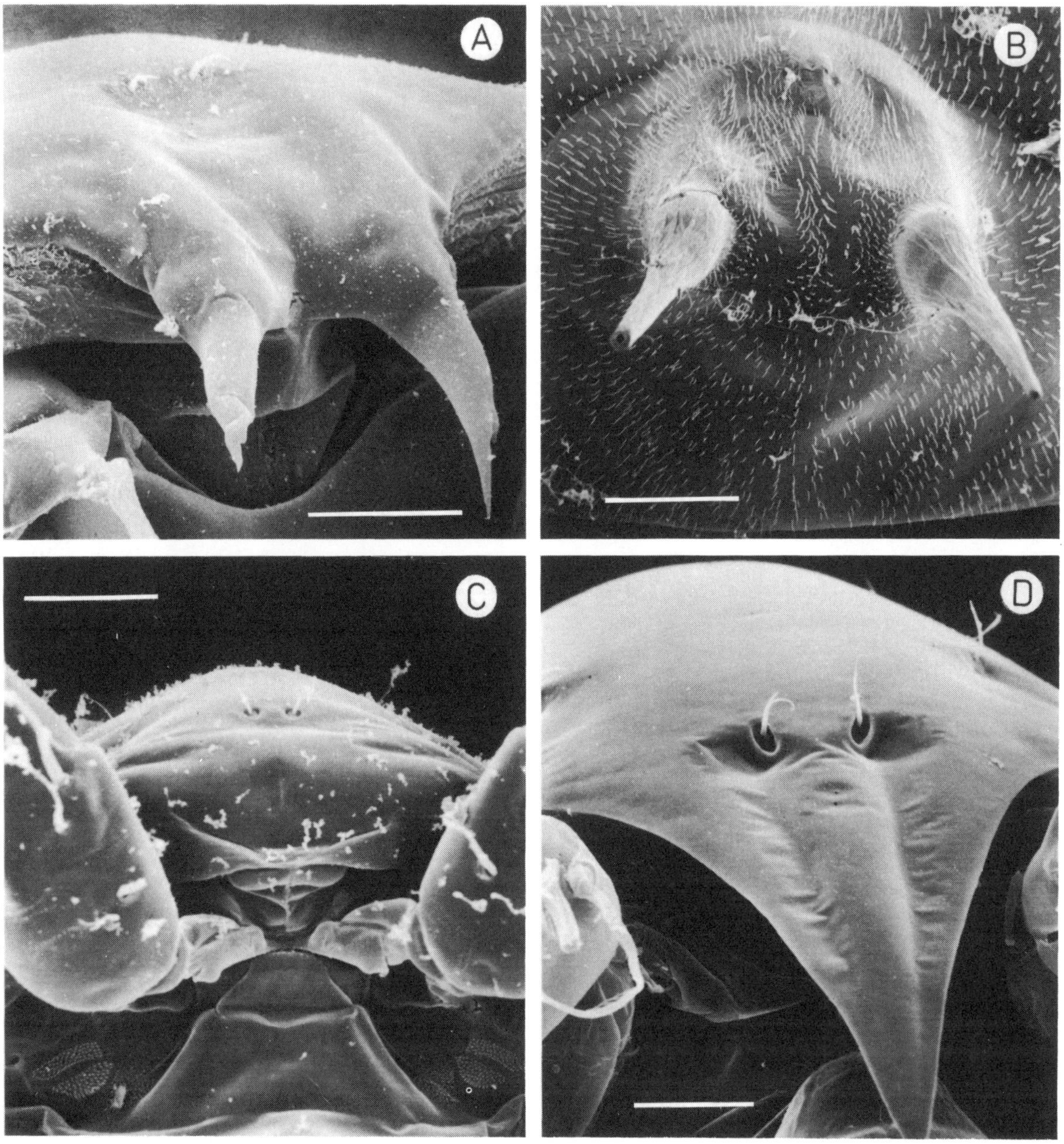

Figure 3.15.2. Rostral area. **A.** *Tropodiaptomus* sp. **B.** *Centraugaptilus horridus*. **C.** *Stephos canariensis*. **D.** *Pseudocyclops* sp. Scale bars A,C-D = 20μm, B = 100μm.

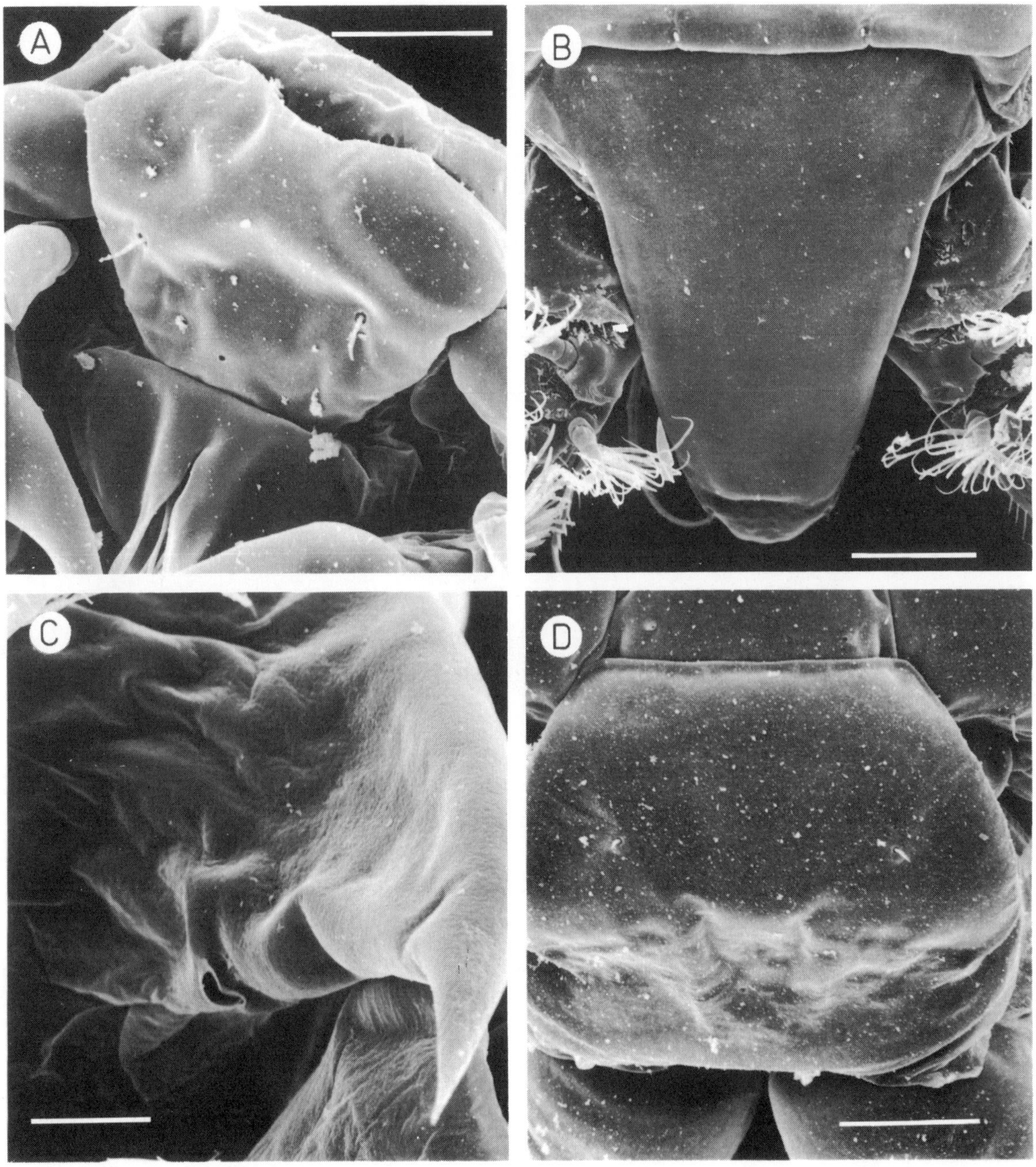

Figure 3.15.3. Rostral area. **A.** *Parachordeumium amphiurae*. **B.** *Canuella perplexa*. **C.** *Oithona helgolandica*. **D.** *Lernaeocera branchialis* copepodid stage. Scale bars A = 10μm, B = 20μm, C = 5μm, D = 30μm.

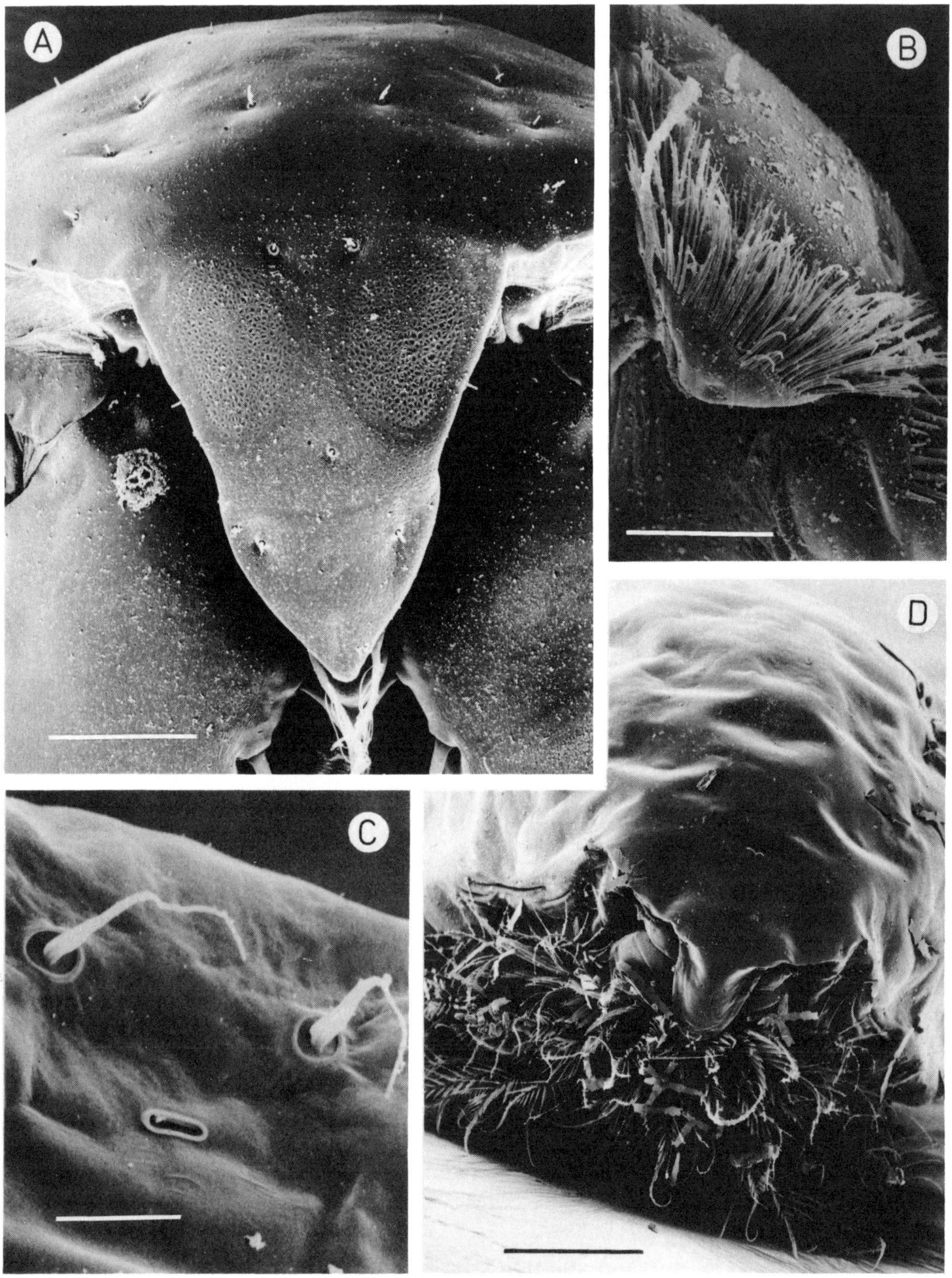

Figure 3.15.4. Rostral area. **A.** *Cyclops strenuus*. **B.** *Nannopus palustris*. **C.** *Ergasilus sieboldi*. **D.** *Pterinopsyllus* sp. Scale bars A-B = 20μm, C = 5μm, D = 75μm.

of a particularly well developed pseudoperculum in the Paranannopidae and Neobradyidae is probably correlated with the deeply incised form of the anal somite in these families. In *Mychophilus* Hesse and other members of the Enteropsinae the anus has secondarily migrated forwards and lies on the dorsal surface of the urosome above the genital apertures (Illg & Dudley, 1980). In some parasitic forms the anus is absent altogether.

f. Egg Sacs

Egg sacs have long been regarded as typical of the Copepoda but many copepod orders lack them, including the Platycopioida, Misophrioida, Monstrilloida, and probably the Gelyelloida. True egg sacs are present in the Harpacticoida, Mormonilloida, Cyclopoida, Siphonostomatoida and Poecilostomatoida. Many calanoids appear to have egg sacs but close examination of these egg masses, for example in *Eurytemora velox* (Lilljeborg), has failed to reveal an enclosing egg sac membrane (figure 2.2.31C). Members of the calanoid family Arietellidae are reported to have paired egg sacs (Sekiguchi, 1974; Ohtsuka & Mitsuzumi, 1990) but it is not known whether these are true egg sacs with enclosing sac membranes. Webb & Weaver (1988) suggested that free-spawning of eggs into the water column evolved secondarily in calanoids, as an adaptation to pelagic existence. They considered that selection pressure favoured the evolution of free spawning in areas where visual predation was intense since it had been demonstrated (Vuorinen et al., 1983) that visual predators will select for ovigerous females over non-ovigerous females of equal body size. However, if the lack of true egg sacs is primitive in calanoids it would suggest that a different hypothesis should have been tested. For example, that egg masses are retained on the body of female calanoids in habitats that are highly turbid, such as estuaries, because there is reduced visual predation.

Egg sacs can be used as taxonomic characters. The complex of caligiform and dichelesthiiform families within the Siphonostomatoida are characterised by their possession of linear egg sacs containing a single column of closely packed, disc-shaped eggs. These uniseriate egg sacs represent an apomorphic character state, the plesiomorphic state being the more ovoid, multiseriate sac. *Mormonilla* females carry two median egg sacs containing just 2 eggs each, arranged antero-posteriorly (figure 2.6.12C).

g. Heart

A muscular heart with several ostia is present in *Calanus* (Lowe, 1935) but in another calanoid, *Epilabidocera* Wilson, Park (1965) found only anterior and posterior ostia. Tiemann (in Boxshall et al., 1984) regarded the possession of a heart as the plesiomorphic state for the Copepoda because a heart is present in other crustaceans. A reduced heart is present in the misophrioid *Misophria pallida* (Giesbrecht, 1892; Boxshall, 1982) but not in either species of *Benthomisophria*. Fanta (1973) reported a pulsating dorsal vessel in the nauplius of the harpacticoid *Euterpina acutifrons* (Dana). It is assumed that in the great majority of podopleans the heart has been lost.

3.16 SECONDARY ADDITIONS AND CHARACTER REVERSALS

a. Secondary Additions

A secondary addition is defined as any segment, setation element or other structure present that did not have a homologue in the ancestral copepod. We include here setation elements that are probably derived by duplication or multiplication of one or more existing elements as well as elements that arise *de novo* and not from any precursor. Novel structures that can also be classified as secondary additions include the carapace (see chapter 3.15a) of misophrioids and cyclopinids, and the antennulary sheath (see chapter 3.4b) of male cyclopoids and misophrioids. Ornamentation elements are insufficiently well known to be considered here either as ancestral or secondary structures.

i) Antennule

Males in some calanoid families possess a quadrithek of armature elements, consisting of 2 setae and 2 aesthetascs, on some or most antennulary segments, instead of the usual trithek which has only 1 aesthetasc. This was recognised by Giesbrecht when he introduced the trithek/quadrithek scheme in his Bay of Naples monograph in 1892. Giesbrecht's figures indicate that quadritheks are found on some segments in males of at least some members of the following familes; Calanidae, Paracalanidae, Aetideidae, Candaciidae, Euchaetidae, Clausocalanidae and Eucalanidae (figure 3.16.1). This condition is best exemplified by ***Eucalanus attenuatus*** (Giesbrecht, 1892: Taf. 11, figure 1) in which every ancestral segment from II to XXIV has 2 aesthetascs. Segments I, XXV, XXVI and XXVII-XXVIII each possess only 1 aesthetasc (figure 2.2.7D). The presence of these additional aesthetascs in advanced calanoid families is here interpreted as secondary duplication because they are not present in the most plesiomorphic calanoid families, such as the Pseudocyclopidae, Ridgewayiidae, Arietellidae and Boholinidae. These primitive families are typically members of the near-bottom community and this leads to the speculation that duplication of aesthetascs in males occurred at the point in the calanoid lineage when the open pelagic environment was invaded.

Comparison of aesthetasc numbers in various families of pelagic calanoids, using the excellent figures in Giesbrecht's (1892) Gulf of Naples monograph, is given in figure 3.16.1. The Eucalanidae exhibit quadritheks on nearly all antennulary segments. No other families approach this condition. The Metridinidae and Augaptilidae show duplication on the majority of the proximal segments, from ancestral segment II to XIII, but not distally. The remaining families figured show further reductions and these tend to follow a pattern. For example, the additional aesthetasc tends to be lost from each of the even-numbered segments (ancestral segments II, IV, VI, VIII, X, and XII) with those on the odd-numbered segments remaining. If, as we have speculated these aesthetascs evolved when the calanoid lineage invaded the pelagic realm, their subsequent loss on some or most segments represents a return to the original state, as retained in the primitive near-bottom families. The loss of these additional aesthetascs appears to represent a character reversal although we have no direct evidence that it is the additional (rather than the original) aesthetasc that is secondarily lost.

In the cyclopoid family Ascidicolidae the males of some genera, including *Haplostoma* Canu and *Botryllophilus* Hesse, possess large numbers of aesthetascs on the first segment of the antennule (Illg & Dudley, 1980). Ooishi & Illg (1977) reported 191 aesthetascs on the expanded first antennulary segment of male *Haplostoma setiferum* Ooishi & Illg. Most were arranged in a closely set rosette configuration on the hemispherical expansion of the segment. This constitutes a clear example of multiplication of elements, since only 28 aesthetascs, one per segment, are presumed to have been present on the entire appendage in the ancestral copepod.

The setoid elements present on the antennules of male *Ambunguipes rufocincta* have been discussed in chapter 2.4. They are ornamentation rather than setation elements and, as such, do not represent a secondary addition.

ii) Antenna

In the calanoid family Acartiidae the endopod of the antenna is modified by fusion of basis and first endopodal segment. The resulting allobasis bears 9 setae (figure 2.2.12A) arranged in a proximal group of 8 and an isolated distal seta, which is probably derived from the incorporated first endopodal segment. The 8 proximal setae are interconnected by means of minute tendinous strands extending from a single muscle which inserts just proximal to the first seta. The mechanism connecting the 8 setae ensures that they form a functional unit and we interpret this as evidence that there has been a secondary multiplication in the number of setae on that part of the allobasis derived from the basis.

iii) Mandible

Among the Harpacticoida the Longipediidae and Canuellidae retain the plesiomorphic 2-segmented state of the mandibular endopod. In the oligoarthran families some 2-segmented endopods are found but the typical condition is a 1-segmented endopod derived by fusion of first and second ancestral segments. However, in some members of the Paramesochridae the endopod appears to be 3-segmented. In these forms the distal segment is not a true segment but is formed from the confluent bases of the apical setae, as indicated by their lack of articulations basally (figure 2.4.11C). This does not, therefore, constitute a secondary addition of a segment.

ANCESTRAL SEGMENT N°		I	II	III	IV	V	VI	VII	VIII	IX	X	XI	XII	XIII	XIV	XV	XVI	XVII	XVIII	XIX	XX	XXI	XXII	XXIII	XXIV	XXV	XXVI	XXVII–XXVIII
GIESBRECHTIAN SEGMENT N°		1	2			3	4	5	6	7	8	9	10	11	12	13	14	15	16	17	18	19	20	21	22	23	24	25
EUCALANIDAE	GIESBRECHT: Taf.11; Fig.1	1	1	3	2	2	2	2	2	2	2	2	2	2	2	2	2	2	2	2	2	2	2	2	2	1	0	1
CALANIDAE	FLEMINGER (1985)	1	1	2	1	2	1	2	1	2	1	2	1	1	1	1	1	1	1	1	1	1	1	1	1	1	0	1
AETIDEIDAE	GIESBRECHT: Taf.14; Fig.13	1	1	2	1-2	2	2	2	2	2	1	1-2	1	1	1	1	1	1	1	1	1	1	0	1	1	1	0	1
METRIDINIDAE	GIESBRECHT: Taf.32; Fig.6 Taf.33; Fig.1	1	2	2	2	2	2	2	2	2	2	2	2	2	1	1	1	1	1	1	1	1	0-1	0	1	1	0	2
AUGAPTILIDAE	GIESBRECHT: Taf.28; Fig.2	1	1	2	1	2	1	3	2	2	1	2	1	2	1	1	1	1	1	1	1	1	1	1	0	1	0	1
EUCHAETIDAE	GIESBRECHT: Taf.16; Fig.29	1	2	2	1	1	1	1	1	1	0	1	1	1	1	1	1	1	1	1	1	1	0	1	1	0	0	1
SCOLECITHRICIDAE	GIESBRECHT: Taf.13; Fig.1	1	1	2	1	2	1	2	1	2	1	1	1	1	1	1	1	1	1	1	1	1	0	0	1	1	0	1
CLAUSOCALANIDAE	GIESBRECHT: Taf.10; Fig.7	1	1	2	1	2	1	2	1	2	0	1	0	0	0	0	1	0	1	1	1	1	0	1	1	0	0	1
PARACALANIDAE	GIESBRECHT: Taf.9; Fig.5	1	1	2	1	2	1	2	1	2	1	2	1	1	1	1	1	1	1	1	1	1	1	1	1	1	0	1
CANDACIIDAE	GIESBRECHT: Taf.21; Fig.5	1	0	2	1	2	1	2	1	1	1	1	1	1	1	1	1	1	1	1	1	1	0	0	0	1	0	1
SPINOCALANIDAE	DAMKAER (1975): Table 4	1	1	2	1	2	1-2	2	1	2	1-2	2	1	1	1	1	1	1	1	1	1	1	0-1	1	1	1	0	1
STEPHIDAE	Present account: Fig.2.2.6C	1	1	2	1	1	1	1	1	1	0	1	0	0	1	0	1	0	0	0	1	1	0	1	1	0	0	1

Figure 3.16.1. Schematic comparison of segmentation and segmental aesthetasc numbers in advanced calanoid families. [Data mostly derived from figures in Giesbrecht (1892).]

iv) Paragnaths

The setae on the paragnaths of *Archimisophria* are novel and are interpreted here as an autapomorphy. The report of similar setae on the paragnaths of enterocoline ascidicolids (Ooishi, pers. comm.) requires confirmation.

v) Maxilla

Sars (1924) described the calanoid *Augaptilina scopifera* Sars on the basis of a single female collected in the Bay of Biscay. Both the maxilla and the maxilliped of this species were 'distinguent notablement par l'armure très singulière de la partie terminale; car à la place des épines usuelles, il y a ..... cinq faisceaux bien définis de nombreux filets extrêmement minces et densement serrés, arrangés en forme de balai.' The plates (Sars, 1925: Pl. CVIII, figs 8-10) show these dense brushes of fine, serrated setae on the basis and the four endopodal segments of the maxilla and on the 5 free endopodal segments of the maxilliped. It is difficult to discern the precise structure of these setae from the figures but reexamination of the type specimen confirmed Sars' observations (figure 3.16.2A-B). However, the components of the brushes are not clearly articulated basally. The presence of these brushes in a relatively advanced genus within the Augaptilidae is here interpreted as a secondary condition, probably resulting from subdivision of the original elements.

vi) Maxilliped

In all members of all podoplean orders the maximum setation formula of the syncoxa of the maxilliped is 1,2,4,3, as found in the Misophrioida and Harpacticoida. In the outgroup of the Podoplea, the Calanoida, the formula is 1,2,4,4, and this formula is here accepted as the ancestral copepod state. It is therefore remarkable that in the cyclopoid family Notodelphyidae the typical formula is 0,0,5,5, and in a single archinotodelphyid species, *Archinotodelphys typicus*, a formula of 0,1,5,5 is found (figure 2.8.23A). It is difficult to interpret this condition. The total number of setae in *A.typicus* is 11, the same as for the ancestral podoplean, but their distribution on the surface of the syncoxa (with 3 distinct groups, apparently corresponding to endites) does not readily allow an interpretation involving the rearrangement of existing setae. It is possible that rearrangement has occurred but we prefer to postulate that additional elements have been added to the 2 distal endites.

The maxilliped of *Augaptilina scopifera* (figure 3.16.2B) has been discussed above, in the section on maxillae (v).

vii) First swimming leg

The Superornatiremidae, a new family of anchialine cave inhabiting harpacticoids exhibit the most remarkable first legs in the whole of the Copepoda. Species of the 2 genera comprising this family possess numerous atypical setation elements on both rami of the first swimming legs (figure 2.4.19A-B). The first exopodal segment bears 3 spines on the outer margin and the second segment bears 2 spines. Either 1 or 2 setae are present on the outer margin of the second endopodal segment, and 2 setae are present on the outer margin of the third endopodal segment. No other copepods possess more than 2 spines on the outer margin of exopodal segment 1 or more than 1 spine on the outer margin of segment 2. No other copepods possess any armature elements at all on the outer margin of the second endopodal segment and no other copepods possess more than 1 seta on the outer margin of the third endopodal segment of the first swimming leg. All of these additional elements are here regarded as secondary.

In the paramesochrid *Scottopsyllus langi* and two of its congeners a total of 5 setae is present at the inner angle of the basis of the first swimming leg (figure 2.4.18A). A single seta only is present at this position in plesiomorphic harpacticoids, such as the Longipediidae and Canuellidae, and in the ancestral stocks of other orders. This is here interpreted as an example of secondary multiplication.

b. Character Reversals

A character reversal is one in which a plesiomorphic character state is regained by a descendant of an ancestor characterised by an apomorphic state of the same character. We distinguish between two categories of character reversal. One is the secondary loss of a novel character state, and the other is a true reversal controlled by a genetic switch mechanism that suppresses the apomorphic state in favour of the plesiomorphic state. Only in the latter category is there any certainty that

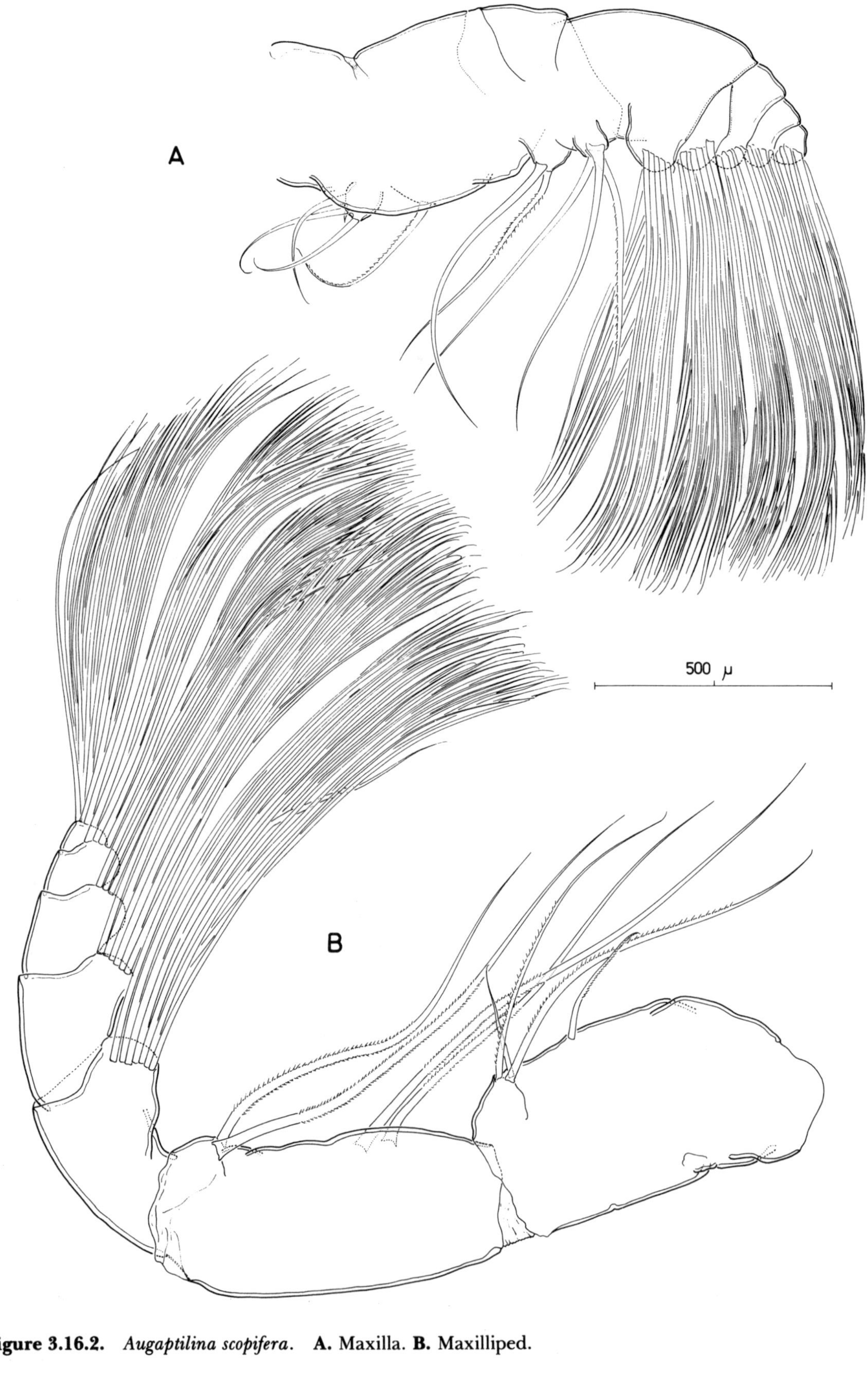

Figure 3.16.2. *Augaptilina scopifera*. **A.** Maxilla. **B.** Maxilliped.

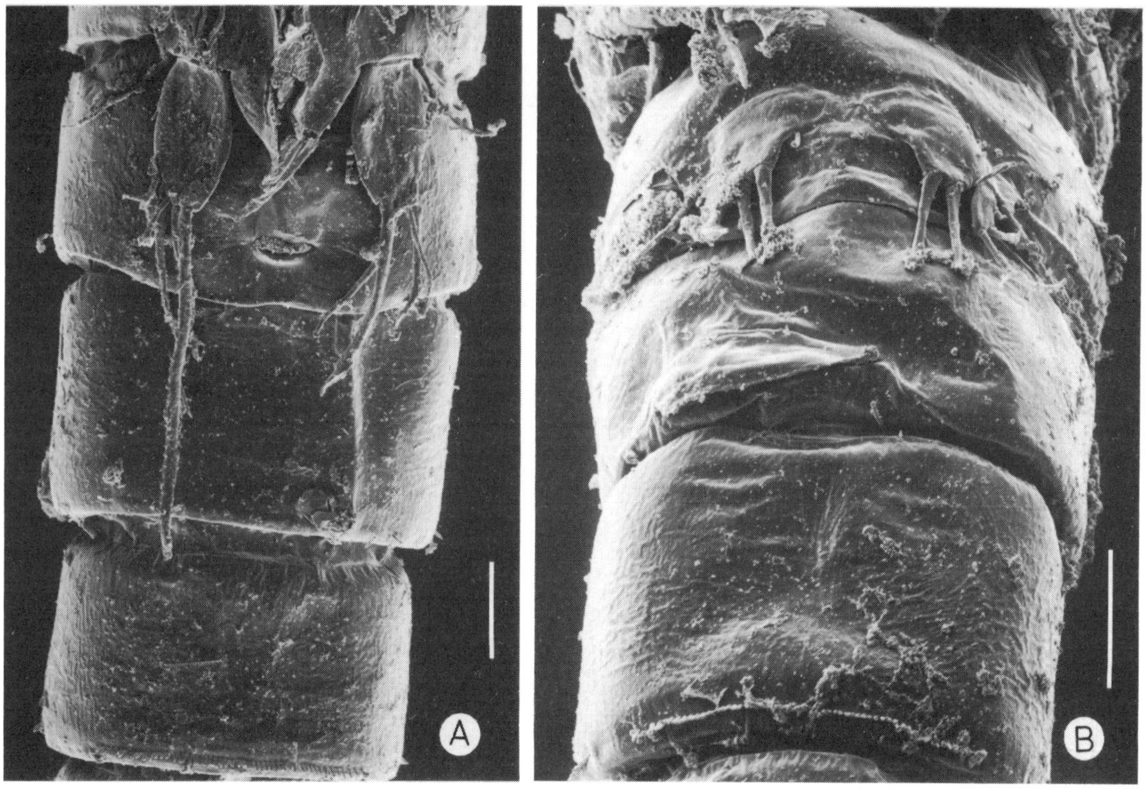

Figure 3.16.3. *Cancrincola abbreviata*. **A**. Female urosome, showing fifth legs and separate genital and first abdominal somites, ventral. **B**. Male urosome, ventral. Scale bars = 20μm.

the original and the secondary plesiomorphic states are the same. In this analysis we have identified a small number of examples of the former category, the secondary loss of novel structures, but we have failed to find any convincing example of true character reversal.

i) Loss of Genital Double Somite

The adult females of the three genera that comprise the harpacticoid family Cancrincolidae have 6-segmented urosomes in which the genital and first abdominal somites are free (figure 3.16.3A) (Fiers, 1990). This is the ancestral copepod condition but the phylogenetic affinities of this family to other oligoarthran families indicates that its ancestor would have possessed a genital double somite comprising fused genital and first abdominal somites in the adult female. For example, in many of its other features the Cancrincolidae appears relatively more derived than the closely related Ameiridae but all ameirids possess a genital double somite. In simplistic terms the possession of separate genital and first abdominal somites by cancrincolids constitutes a character reversal, since the immediate ancestor of this family within the Oligoarthra almost certainly possessed a genital double somite.

Fiers (1990) described the copepodid stages of two species of *Cancrincola* Wilson and of *Abscondicola humesi* Fiers and noted that in *A.humesi* the sixth legs did not appear until the fifth copepodid stage in females and not until the adult in males. He also found that the copepodids of *Cancrincola* never exhibit a normal genital field incorporating the sixth legs in females or a typical genital plate in males. Typically the sixth legs appear at the fourth copepodid stage in harpacticoid development (figure 3.16.4) and attain the definitive state in the adult. On the basis of the evidence provided by the delayed development of the sixth legs Fiers (1990) speculated that a heterochronic event has occurred. Post-displacement of fusion of the genital and first abdominal somites, which normally occurs at the final moult from fifth copepodid to adult female, results in the loss of the genital double somite. The presence of separate genital and first abdominal somites in cancrincolids is therefore interpreted here as a secondarily derived condition, not homologous with the primary separation found in the ancestral copepod. Strictly, therefore, this does not represent a genuine character reversal.

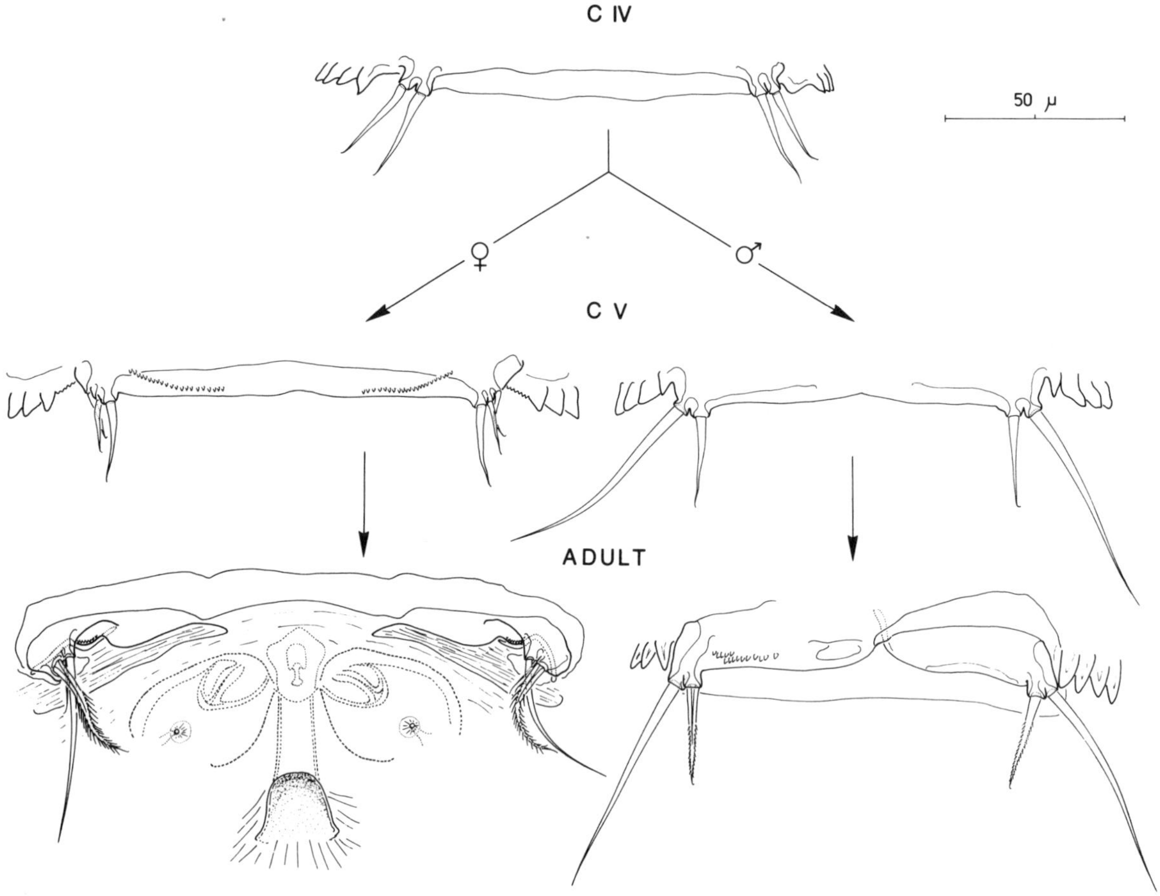

Figure 3.16.4. *Orthopsyllus* sp. Development of the sixth pair of legs from copepodid IV (CIV) stage to adult in both sexes.

ii) Loss of Carapace

A carapace-like extension from the posterior margin of the dorsal cephalic shield was present in the ancestor of the primitive podoplean order Misophrioida. Neither the Calanoida nor the Platycopioida possessed such a structure and it appears to be novel. Within the Misophrioida some genera have reduced or lost this carapace. In *Speleophria bivexilla*, for example, the carapace is reduced to posterolateral lobes and in *Expansophria* (figure 2.3.21A-B) it is absent although modifications to the prosome that allow distension of the midgut indicate that this is a secondary condition. The carapace, therefore, evolved in the ancestor of the Misophrioida and was subsequently lost by some of its descendants. This appears to be an example of character reversal but the strong evidence that the loss is secondary in genera such as *Expansophria* indicates that its absence within the Misophrioida is not an homologous character state with its primary absence in the early copepod stock, including the ancestors of the Platycopioida and Calanoida. A similar argument can be used for the distribution of the carapace within the cyclopoid family Cyclopinidae. A full carapace is present in some forms, such as *Pterinopsyllus* (figure 3.15.1A), but in others the carapace is reduced to small posterolateral lobes (figure 3.15.1B-C) or completely lost, as in *Cyclopicina*. Again, we interpret the existence of intermediate forms in which the carapace is reduced as evidence that the loss of the carapace within the Cyclopinidae is secondary - the end product of a series of progressive reductions. The end product lacks a carapace but this state is secondary and is not homologous with the primary carapace-less state of the ancestor of the Cyclopoida.

iii) Loss of Duplicated Aesthetascs

The distribution of aesthetascs on the antennules of male calanoids was analysed above (chapter 3.16a). This analysis suggests that the duplication was a single event followed by subsequent loss of the duplicated elements in certain families (figure 3.16.1). The pattern of losses indicates that certain antennulary segments are more likely to return to a 1-aesthetasc state than others. The loss of these supernumerary elements may constitute a character reversal since we have no morphological evidence whether the secondarily derived 1-aesthetasc state is homologous with the ancestral calanoid 1-aesthetasc state or not. The evidence could only be gathered by a detailed comparative ontogenetic analysis of the antennulary setation in a range of these calanoid families.

iv) Loss of Sheath on Male Antennules

The antennules of male cyclopoids and misophrioids primitively have a sheath-like expansion of segment XV that partly encloses segment XVI. In the many cyclopoids in which this sheath has been lost segments XV and XVI are fused providing evidence that the absence of the sheath is a secondary condition. Further evidence of the progressive loss of the sheath is the existence of intermediate forms, such as the Ozmanidae (figure 2.8.8B-C), in which the sheath is much reduced. The reduced condition of the sheath on the male antennule in the Gelyelloida also provides evidence of a tendency towards gradual reduction and loss within the cyclopoid-gelyelloid lineage. By comparison the complete loss of the proximal geniculation, of which the sheath on segment XV forms a part, in the misophrioid *Archimisophria* suggests the involvement of a different mechanism. We interpret the loss of the sheath without any trace, such as segmental fusions, in *Archimisophria* as the product of some heterochronic event in which the fifth copepodid type of antennule (which lacks the sheath) is retained in the adult. It is relevant to note here that the 27-segmented condition of the antennule in *Archimisophria discoveryi* is attained at the fourth copepodid stage (Boxshall, 1983).

3.17 OLIGOMERIZATION AND HETEROCHRONY

In the discussion session on the ancestral copepod held during the First International Conference on Copepoda in Amsterdam in August 1981 it was implicitly assumed that 'primary evolutionary processes in copepods proceed towards fusion of body somites, and towards reduction in the segmentation and armature of the appendages either by fusion or loss' (Boxshall et al., 1984). The detailed analysis of all orders carried out in this volume strongly supports that assumption. However, we have found a substantial body of evidence that at least two distinct mechanisms are involved in generating this trend towards oligomerization. One mechanism is progressive reduction and eventual loss of a character state in adults, the other is the heterochronic displacement of the time of appearance or transformation of characters during ontogeny, resulting in the total loss of a character state in the adult descendant. Progressive reduction in adults is by far the most common evolutionary process in the Copepoda - the whole of this book is replete with examples of segmental fusions and losses, and of reduction in setation elements. The evidence that progressive loss is involved comes in each case from the numerous intermediate forms that are found. There are fewer examples of heterochronic processes. One example, the secondary separation of the genital and first abdominal somites in females of the Cancrincolidae, has been examined in detail above (chapter 3.16) but we discuss a number of other examples below.

Sixth Legs: The sixth legs typically appear as seta-bearing rudiments at the fourth copepodid stage of development. In calanoids, however, the sixth legs never appear in this form in either sex. They are presumably represented by the unarmed genital opercula or common operculum in adult female calanoids and possibly by the very reduced operculum of male calanoids but no armature elements are apparent at any stage in ontogeny. We interpret this total loss throughout development as evidence that the appearance of sixth leg armature elements has been post-displaced, i.e. their appearance in ontogeny has been delayed beyond the definitive moult and they have been effectively lost. In contrast the sixth legs of platycopioids are extremely reduced but a vestige remains, including at least 1 setation element, and this is interpreted as evidence that the state of the platycopioid sixth leg represents the end point of a series of reductions that have taken place in adult ancestors.

Geniculate Antennules: Post-displacement of characters that usually appear late in development provides a relatively simple heterochronic mechanism that can produce instant loss of a character or character state. In particular, secondary sexual characters involved in mating behaviour could be prone to such a mechanism since many only appear at the definitive moult into the adult and a delay of a single moult would therefore result in their total loss. For example, the geniculations of male antennules typically appear only at the final moult from fifth copepodid to adult. In male calanoids a geniculate antennule is primitively retained on the right side only. The left antennule resembles that of the fifth copepodid as well as that of the female and it seems probable that the loss of the geniculation on the left side is the result of the post-displacement, by just one moult, of the geniculation that typically appears at the definitive moult. The mechanism responsible for this loss must be relatively simple because in one group of calanoid families, the Augaptiloidea, it is the right side geniculation that is lost and the left side geniculation that is retained in the adult male (see chapter 2.2). It is probable that post-displacement of the appearance of the sheath primitively associated with the proximal geniculation of the antennules of male misophrioids is responsible for the total loss of this structure in *Archimisophria*. We speculate that detailed ontogenetic studies will in the future provide evidence that post-displacement, especially of secondary sexual characters, has been the evolutionary mechanism responsible for the sudden and total loss of adult characters. This quantum process stands in marked contrast to the more widespread process of gradual reduction through a series of intermediate stages, leading to eventual loss.

Chapter 4

A NEW PHYLOGENY OF THE COPEPODA

4.1 EXISTING PHYLOGENIES

There have been a large number of different classification schemes proposed for the copepods. Many of these have not stood the test of time and we do not intend to consider them in detail. However, several different schemes have contributed substantially to the modern arrangement of the orders and we will review them briefly in chronological order. In particular we will pay attention to the development of those concepts that are central to the modern copepod classification and to the origin of the names of ordinal taxa that are still in use.

The history of copepod classification can be divided into two phases. The first of these was the gradual recognition of the unity of the Copepoda. The sheer diversity of body form and mode of life within the Copepoda caused considerable confusion among the early systematists and from the time of Linnaeus to the middle of the nineteenth century free-living and parasitic forms were classified in widely separate higher taxa which contained combinations of copepod and non-copepodan taxa (cf. Milne Edwards, 1840). The recognition of the affinity between free-living and parasitic copepods by Thorell in 1859 marked the beginning of the end of this phase although traces lingered on into the twentieth century in the form of the Branchiuran fish lice which were included with the Copepoda as recently as 1932 (cf. Wilson, 1932). The second historical phase of copepod classification started in 1859 and continues to the present day. This is the search for the natural system of phylogenetic relationships between the component orders of the Copepoda. The overlap between the two phases is understandable since they are essentially separate processes.

Latreille & Lamarck: In all the eighteenth century classifications of the Crustacea and in those of the first half of the nineteenth century the relationships between parasitic and free-living copepods were not recognised. Latreille (1802) divided the Crustacea into two subclasses, Entomostraces and Malacostraces. The copepods known at that time were placed in the Entomostraces, the parasites (*Caligus* Müller) went into the section Opercules, order Pneumonures and the free-living forms (*Cyclops*) into the section Nus, order Pseudopodes. Lamarck's primary division of the Crustacea into two orders, Heterobranches and Homobranches, included the copepods in two groups within the section Branchiopodes of the order Heterobranches (Lamarck, 1818). One group, the Franges, contained *Cyclops* together with a variety of non-copepodan taxa, the other, the Parasites, comprised *Dichelestium*, *Cecrops* Leach and *Caligus* together with *Argulus* Müller. In his later works Latreille (1817, 1829) placed the copepods in two sections of his order Branchiopodes of the Crustacea. The parasitic forms belonged in the section Poecilopes and the free-living forms, in the Lophyropes. Both of these sections also contained a variety of non-copepodan taxa.

Milne Edwards: Milne Edwards (1840) used the organization of the mouth as the basis for his classification of the Crustacea. He recognised three crustacean subclasses, the Maxillés, Suceurs and Xyphosures. Copepods were included in both the first and second of these, together with a wide variety of non-copepodan taxa. The free-living copepods were considered to be an order (the Copépodes) of the legion Entomostraca of the subclass Maxillés. He established subgroups within the Copepoda, recognising two families, Pontiens and Monocles, on the basis of the separation or fusion of the eyes. The parasitic copepods belonged to the orders Siphonostomes and Lernéens of the legion Parasites nageurs of the subclass Suceurs.

Dana: In his preliminary system Dana (1846, 1848) placed the free-living copepods in five families (the Cyclopidae, Harpacticidae, Calanidae, Corycaeidae and Miracidae) within the Cyclopacea and the parasitic copepods in three tribes (the Monstrillacea, Caligacea and Lernaeacea) within the suborder Cormostomata. Dana abandoned this system in his major work published in 1852 in which he recognised the Entomostraca as an order within the subclass Crustacea Edriophthalmia. The copepods are contained within two separate suborders, the Gnathostomata and Cormostomata, but are intermixed with other non-copepodan taxa. Dana's scheme can best be summarised in tabular form (Table 9). The primary division of the copepods in this system is to separate those with a suctorial type of mouth (the Cormostomata) from those with a relatively less modified mouth (the Gnathostomata). Dana based much of this system on the structure of the mandibular palp, the maxilla, the number of eggs sacs and eye structure.

Table 9. The position of copepods (*) in the classification of Dana (1852)

- Subclass Crustacea Edriophthalmia
  - Order Entomostraca
    - Suborder Gnathostomata
      - Legion Lophyropoda
        - *Tribe Cyclopoidea
          - *Families Calanidae
            - Cyclopidae
            - Corycaeidae
        - Tribe Daphnioidea
        - Tribe Cyproidea
      - Legion Phyllopoda
    - Suborder Cormostomata
      - Legion Poecilopoda
        - *Tribe Ergasiloidea
          - *Families Monstrillidae
            - Ergasilidae
            - Nicothoidae
        - Tribe Caligoidea
          - Families Argulidae
            - *Caligidae
            - *Dichelestidae
        - *Tribe Lernaeoidea
          - *Families Chondracanthidae
            - Anchorellidae
            - Penellidae

Baird: Baird (1850) in his study of British entomostracans adopted a classification of the division Entomostraca that derived features from Latreille (1829) and Milne Edwards (1840). In Baird's scheme the copepods are found in two legions, Lophyropoda and Paecilopoda. The Lophyropoda comprises two orders, the Ostracoda and Copepoda, with the latter containing the free-living copepods arranged in three families, the Cyclopidae, Diaptomidae and Cetochilidae. The Paecilopoda consists mostly of copepods, plus the Branchiura (as the family Argulidae), arranged in two orders. The order Siphonostoma contains the copepod families Caligidae, Pandaridae, Cecropidae, Anthosomadae and Ergasilidae. The order Lernadae comprises the families Chondracanthidae, Lernaeopodadae, Anchorelladae, Penelladae and Lerneoceradae.

Zenker & Claus: In Zenker (1854) the copepods are all grouped in three families, the Cyclopiden (or Copepoden), Siphonostomen and Lernaeoden, all of which are placed in a single order, the Entomostraca. Claus (1857) divided Zenker's Entomostraca into two, Copepoda and Parasita.

Thorell: Thorell (1859) proposed a novel system in which, for the first time, the free-living and parasitic forms were considered as a single group and were not divided on the basis of mode of life. The copepods were arranged into three series according to the structure of their oral appendages and mouths. The Gnathostoma were characterised by their large, open buccal cavities and their biting mandibles bearing a well developed palp. The Poecilostoma were characterised by their similar mouths and by their apparent lack of a mandible. The Siphonostoma had a more or less elongated oral cone which contained stylet-like mandibles. This classification fell into disuse when Claus (1862) discovered that a mandible was present in the Poecilostoma. Thorell's scheme represented the start of the second phase of copepod systematics and is summarised below:

Table 10. Thorell's (1859) classification of the Copepoda

Series Gnathostoma		Series Poecilostoma	
Families	Calanidae	Families	Corycaeidae
	Cyclopidae		Miracidae
	Notodelphyidae		Sapphirinidae
	Buproridae		Ergasilidae
Series Siphonostoma			?Monstrillidae
Families	Ascomyzontidae		Chondracanthidae
	Nicothoidae		*Lamippe*
	Dichelestidae		?*Doridicola*
	Caligidae		
	Lernaeopodidae		
	Lernaeidae		

Claus: Claus (1863) retained Zenker's Entomostraca as a taxon but uses the name Copepoda for it because all the animals within that group were characterised by their oar-like swimming legs. On the basis of anatomical and morphological features Claus subdivided the copepods into two groups, the Copepoda Carcinoidea and the Copepoda Parasitica. The former comprised all the species with a cyclopiform body shape and included all free-living forms and the temporary parasites (now known as associates). The latter comprised those species with modified bodies and included the permanent parasites.

Brady: Brady (1878-80) treated the Copepoda as an order within the legion Lophyropoda. After Thorell he divided the copepods into three sections, Gnathostoma, Poecilostoma and Siphonostoma.

Gerstaecker: Gerstaecker (1866-1879) made a preliminary attempt to examine phylogenetic relationships between families within the Copepoda. He recognised that semi-parasitic and parasitic families did not represent a single group and he suggested that it was better to establish lineages leading from free-living forms, via commensals and semi-parasites, to the highly evolved parasites.

Grobben: Grobben (1892) recognised the distinctiveness of the fish lice (Branchiura) and divided the copepods into Arguloidea and Eucopepoden. He suggested that the copepods were the most primitive of all extant Crustacea.

Canu: Canu (1892) proposed a classification of the Copepoda in which the primary subdivision into Monoporodelphya (containing families representing the Cyclopoida, Harpacticoida and Calanoida) and Diporodelphya (containing families representing the Poecilostomatoida and Siphonostomatoida) depended on characters relating to the female genital apparatus. The former possessed a single and separate copulatory pore through which the spermatophore discharged, the latter possessed two genital openings into which the spermatophores discharged. This classification was oversimplified and was not adopted by the majority of copepod workers.

Giesbrecht: In 1882 Giesbrecht rejected mouthpart structure and numbers of genital apertures as criteria for the higher level division of the Copepoda. Instead he used basic tagmosis to divide the Copepoda into two major groups, the Gymnopleoden and Podopleoden, but only in his 1892 and 1899 works did he complete his new system. The Gymnoplea was characterised by the division of the body into prosome and urosome by a major articulation located between the fifth pedigerous and genital somites. The hind part of the body was limbless and the male fifth legs were involved in copulation. Whereas in the Podoplea this articulation lies between the fourth and fifth pedigerous somites. The hind part of the body carried a vestigial pair of fifth legs which was not involved in copulation. This natural division was recognised by some copepod workers (for example, Malaquin, 1901) but many (for example, Sars, 1901-1903) regarded it as inadequate as a classification for the whole range of benthic and parasitic copepods since it was based almost solely on the planktonic forms. The Gymnoplea was divided into two tribes, Amphaskandria and Heterarthrandria, primarily on the basis of the structure of the antennules in the male. The Podoplea was divided into the tribes Ampharthrandria and Isokerandria again using differences in the male antennules and arrangement of the genital apertures. Giesbrecht's classification is summarised in Table 11.

Table 11. Giesbrecht's classification of the Copepoda

Suborder Gymnoplea					
	Tribe Amphaskandria				
		Family Calanidae			
	Tribe Heterarthrandria				
		Families Centropagidae			
		Candacidae			
		Pontellidae			
Suborder Podoplea					
	Tribe Ampharthrandria			Tribe Isokerandria	
		Families Cyclopidae			Families Oncaeidae
		Mormonillidae			Corycaeidae
		Harpacticidae			Clausidiidae
		Monstrillidae			Lichomolgidae
		Misophriidae			Ergasilidae
		Ascidicolidae			Bomolochidae
		Asterocheridae			Clausiidae
		Dichelestiidae			Nereicolidae

Sars: Sars (1901-1903) rejected Giesbrecht's division of the Copepoda and established a classification based on seven genera which he regarded as representing distinct types or suborders of copepods. These genera are *Calanus, Harpacticus* Milne Edwards, *Cyclops, Notodelphys, Monstrilla, Caligus* and *Lernaea* Linn. (= *Lernaeocera*). Each one of these genera became the 'type' of a suborder to which it lent its name, i.e. Calanoida, Harpacticoida, Cyclopoida, Notodelphyoida, Monstrilloida, Caligoida, and Lernaeoida. In the Sarsian system the basic principle upon which any given copepod is classified is its similarity to one of these basic types. It places great emphasis upon a common mode of life rather than similarities in mouthpart morphology or body tagmosis as in Thorell (1859) and Giesbrecht (1882, 1892, 1899) respectively. Sars employed Thorell's Gnathostomata, Siphonostomata and Poecilostomata as subgroups of the Cyclopoida. This represents a significant change in the concepts of these taxa since Thorell introduced them as his primary subdivisions of the Copepoda.

Calman: In his 1909 monograph on the Crustacea Calman classified the Copepoda as a subclass of the Crustacea but continued to include the fish lice as an order, the Branchiura, distinct from the true copepods which he placed in the order Eucopepoda.

Wilson: C.B. Wilson (1910) briefly summarised existing classification schemes of the Copepoda and strongly supported the Sarsian system although he indicated that it might be necessary to transfer the Lernaeidae to the Caligoida.

Schellenberg: Schellenberg (1922) implicitly questioned the validity of the order Notodelphyoida when he recognised the close relationship between the Notodelphyidae and the cyclopoids, especially *Cyclopina*, based on similarities in mouthpart structure. He reasoned that the ancestors of the Notodelphyidae must therefore be close to *Cyclopina*.

Brehm: Brehm (1927) attempted to combine what he considered to be the best features of the existing systems proposed by Giesbrecht, Sars and Wilson. The classification generated by this approach is tabulated below:

Suborder Gymnoplea
    Tribe Amphascandria
        Isokerandria
        Heterarthrandria
Suborder Podoplea
    Tribe Poecilostomata
        Monstrillidea
        Ampharthrandria
            Cyclopidea
            Cyclopinidea
            Asterocheridea
            Misophriidea
            Harpacticoidea
Suborder Philichthyes
Suborder Dichelestia
Suborder Caligi
Suborder Chondracanthi
Suborder Lernaeae
Suborder Lernaeopodae
Suborder Choniostoma
Suborder Herpyllobii

Oakley: Oakley (1930) pointed to some failings in the Sarsian scheme with respect to its treatment of the Lernaeoida. He reviewed Wilson's decision to transfer the Lernaeidae from the Lernaeoida to the Caligoida and rename the remaining two families (Chondracanthidae and Lernaeopodidae) the Lernaeopodoida. Oakley suggested that the Chondracanthidae be placed in the Cyclopoida, on the basis of mouthpart structure and the morphology of the male. He also considered that the Lernaeopodidae, together with the Choniostomatidae and probably the Herpyllobiidae, belong to the Caligoida. The Lernaeoida and its derivative the Lernaeopodoida are thus completely abandoned. Oakley then proposed a new subdivision of the Copepoda into Cyclopiformes, including all free-swimming forms (probably), Ergasilidae, Juanettidae, Chondracanthidae and Monstrillidae, and Caligiformes, including Caligidae, Dichelesthiidae, Lernaeidae, Lernaeopodidae, Choniostomatidae and Herpyllobiidae.

Gurney: Gurney (1933b) established a new order for the family Misophriidae, previously placed in the Harpacticoida by Sars. He then assimilated this into a new arrangement of the copepod orders, based mainly on the Sarsian system. Gurney's scheme is as follows:

Order Calanoida
Order Monstrilloida
Order Harpacticoida
Order Cyclopoida
    Suborder Gnathostoma
        Siphonostoma
        Poecilostoma
Order Misophrioida
Order Notodelphyoida
Order Caligoida

Later Gurney (1945) defended his placement of the Lernaeopodoida of Wilson in the order Caligoida on the basis of similarities between the copepodids of these two groups, in particular, their common possession of a frontal filament for attachment of the first copepodids to their host.

Monod & Dollfus: Monod & Dollfus (1932) adopted the system proposed by Oakley (1930) in which the copepods were divided into two groups, Cyclopiformes and Caligiformes. The former comprised the orders Monstrilloida, Calanoida, Harpacticoida, Cyclopoida and Notodelphyoida, and the latter comprised the families Caligidae, Dichelesthiidae, Sphyriidae, Lernaeidae, Lernaeopodidae, Choniostomatidae and Herpyllobiidae.

Wilson: C.B. Wilson (1932) extended the Sarsian system to include the fish lice amongst the Copepoda, as the suborder Arguloidea. Wilson recognised seven suborders of true copepods: Calanoida, Harpacticoida, Cyclopoida, Notodelphyoida, Monstrilloida, Caligoida and Lernaeopodoida.

Heegaard: Heegaard (1947) reviewed the main existing classifications and concluded that whilst it was impossible to provide a natural system of the Copepoda at that time it was possible to suggest minor changes and additions. He regarded the Calanoida as a highly derived order and considered that within the Copepoda as a whole there had been an evolutionary radiation in all directions from the Cyclopoida or a cyclopoid-like ancestor. According to Heegaard '... a radiation is thus seen from the Cyclopoida toward the Calanoida and the Harpacticoida, as well as towards the Monstrilloida and the Notodelphyoida, but also towards the parasitic copepods'. The main novelty in Heegaard's system is the division of the parasitic copepods into two groups, the Pectinata and Fistulata, on the structure of the mandible and other characters. The Fistulata contains the Ergasilidae and Chondracanthidae and was derived from lichomolgid-like ancestors within the Cyclopoida. The Pectinata contained the Caligidae, Lernaeidae, Lernaeopodidae and Dichelestidae, and was derived from a sapphirinid-like ancestor within the Cyclopoida.

Lang: Lang (1948b) provided the first major challenge to the Sarsian system when he rejected the validity of the Notodelphyoida on the basis of mouthpart structure. He stated that the notodelphyoids were of a diphyletic origin, with some, such as Enterocolidae, belonging to the poecilostomatous series and others, such as the Notodelphyidae, belonging to the gnathostomatous series. Lang concluded that the copepods (then treated as an order) should be divided into 4 suborders: the Progymnoplea comprising the Platycopiidae; the Gymnoplea comprising the rest of Sars' Calanoida; the Propodoplea comprising the Misophriidae; and the Podoplea comprising the remainder of the copepods divided into two sections, the Cyclopoida and Harpacticoida. Lang also recognised three subsections within the Cyclopoida, the Cyclopoida gnathostoma, the Cyclopoida poecilostoma and the Cyclopoida siphonostoma. This system recognises as distinct taxa the majority of the modern orders, although it attributes a different rank to several of them. Lang's new system contains most of the elements of the modern copepod classification but he did not consider the parasitic copepods in detail. He hinted that the siphonostomes parasitic on fishes may belong with the Cyclopoida siphonostoma. Lang also recommended abandoning the old established principle of separating free-living and parasitic groups at a high taxonomic level.

Bocquet & Stock: Bocquet & Stock (1963) examined the interrelationships between the major groups of parasitic copepods. They recognised the artificial nature of the Copepoda Parasitica and indicated that the members of this group belong in part to the Cyclopoida poecilostoma, and in part to the Cyclopoida siphonostoma. They also restated Lang's (1948b) view that the Notodelphyoida does not represent a monophyletic group.

Yamaguti: Yamaguti (1963) classified the copepods parasitic on vertebrate hosts in six orders. Yamaguti treated five of these orders (Cyclopidea, Lernaeopodidea, Andreinidea, Philichthyidea and Sarcotacidea) as new and referred to the sixth, the Caligidea, as of emended status. His Cyclopidea comprised four families, three of which (Tuccidae, Ergasilidae and Bomolochidae) are currently included in the Poecilostomatoida and the fourth, the Grandiunguidae, is no longer regarded as valid. The Cyclopidea of Yamaguti (1963) bears no relationship to the Cyclopoida.

Kabata: It was Kabata (1979) who formally reassessed the phylogenetic relationships of the families of copepods parasitic on fishes and produced a comprehensive classification for the Copepoda. Kabata recognised two main lineages, the Gymnoplea and Podoplea. The former comprised only the Calanoida. The Podoplea comprised the Harpacticoida, Monstrilloida, Misophrioida, Cyclopoida, Poecilostomatoida and Siphonostomatoida (figure 4.1.1). Much emphasis was placed on the body tagmosis and the mouthpart structure, especially the form of the mandibles. Using his new criteria Kabata was able to place the families of fish parasites formerly classified in the orders Caligoida, Lernaeopodoida, and Lernaeoida into their appropriate orders: the Lernaeidae in the Cyclopoida, the Chondracanthidae, Bomolochidae, Taeniacanthidae, Ergasilidae and

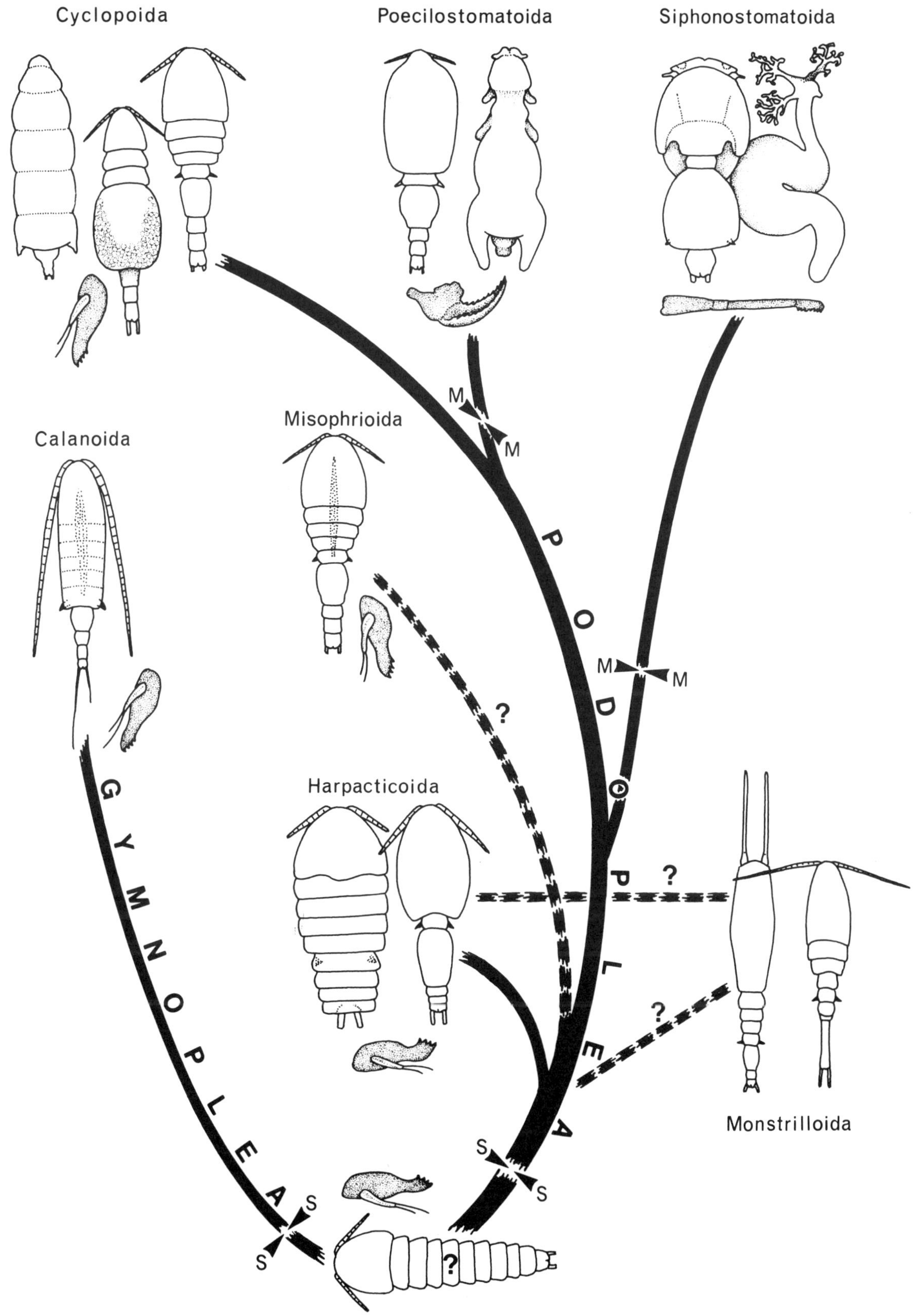

Figure 4.1.1. Scheme of phylogenetic relationships proposed by Kabata (1979).

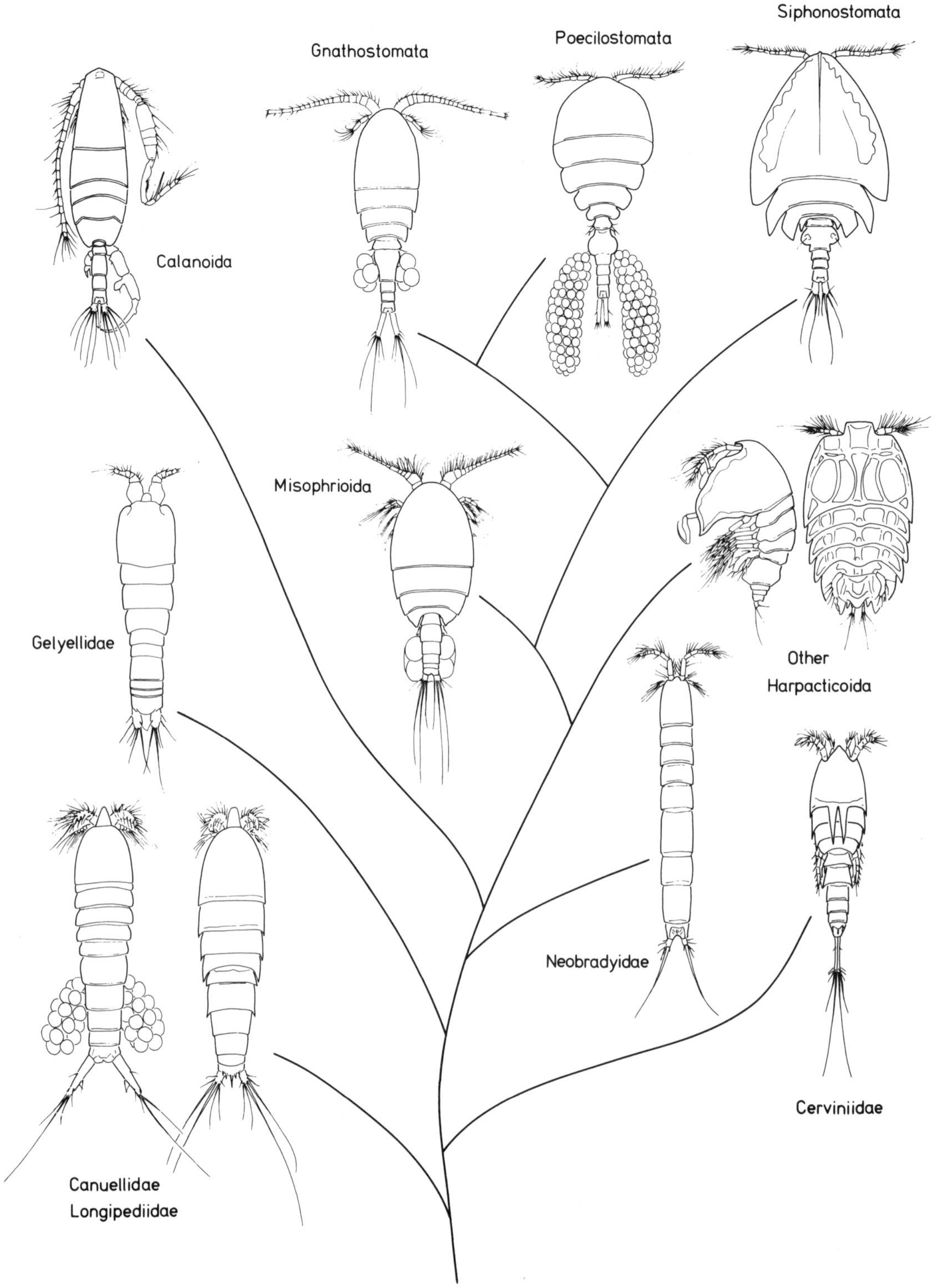

Figure 4.1.2. Scheme of phylogenetic relationships proposed by Por (1984).

Philichthyidae in the Poecilostomatoida, and the caligiform and dichelesthiiform families in the Siphonostomatoida together with the Pennellidae and Lernaeopodidae. The concept of the Copepoda Parasitica as a valid taxon was finally disposed of as having no scientific merit.

Boxshall: In 1979 Boxshall established the Mormonilloida, a new order of Podoplea, based on the genus *Mormonilla*.

Marcotte: The characteristics of the ancestral copepod were briefly considered by Marcotte (1982). He concluded that the ancestor was benthic or semibenthic and had a flexible body with clearly defined somites but lacked a rigid prosome specialised for swimming. He suggested that this ancestor might have inhabited freshwater although subsequent divergence of most orders took place in the sea. This ancestor gave rise to the Harpacticoida, and to the Calanoida. He regarded the Misophrioida as too poorly known to be considered and the Monstrilloida as problematic because of their extreme specialisation. The final great radiation, according to Marcotte, was the evolution of the Cyclopoida, Poecilostomatoida and Siphonostomatoida (which he regarded as diphyletic) into planktonic and parasitic habitats. He suggested that these 3 orders may have arisen from a common ancestor resembling the harpacticoid *Tisbe* Lilljeborg, although *Tisbe* itself was too apomorphic to be ancestral.

Stock: In his review of Kabata's (1979) monograph Stock (1981) accepted most of Kabata's phylogenetic scheme (figure 4.1.1) but suggested uniting the Cyclopoida and Poecilostomatoida within a single order, to be referred to as the Cyclopoida. This would consist of two tribes, the Gnathostomata and Poecilostomata. This proposal was based on the characteristics of forms such as *Halicyclops* Norman, *Hemicyclops* and *Anthessius* Della Valle which Stock regarded as intermediates, both in terms of morphology and mode of life, between the Cyclopoida and Poecilostomatoida. Stock restated these views in 1986.

First International Conference: At the First International Conference on Copepoda held in Amsterdam in 1981 Por, Dussart and Tiemann all made new contributions to ordinal level copepod phylogeny. These were published in 1984 together with the proceedings of an open discussion on the characters of the ancestral copepod edited by Boxshall, Ferrari and Tiemann.

Por: Por (1984b) considered that the harpacticoid family Canuellidae most closely resembled the ancestral copepod condition. His evolutionary scheme, summarised in figure 4.1.2, is based on this assumption. Por fragmented the Harpacticoida into four separate branches and derived the Gelyellidae, Calanoida and a group comprising the Misophrioida, Gnathostomata, Poecilostomata and Siphonostomata from different points within the harpacticoid lineages. This scheme did not include either the Monstrilloida or Mormonilloida, and it attributes paraphyletic status to the Harpacticoida. In this paper Por introduced the term dolichoplean for those vermiform copepods in which the prosome-urosome boundary is poorly defined.

Dussart: Dussart (1984) proposed a novel system of phylogenetic relationships between the eight recognised copepod orders. The basic arrangement of these orders was heavily influenced by Björnberg's (1972) extensive studies on copepod nauplii and naupliar musculature. Dussart's tentative scheme (figure 4.1.3) identified three main lineages, all derived independently from an ancestral cyclopoid-like form. One lineage grouped the Monstrilloida, Misophrioida, Siphonostomatoida and Cyclopoida (other than the Cyclopinidae and Oithonidae). A second lineage passed via the Cyclopinidae to the Oithonidae and then branched into two, one branch forming the Poecilostomatoida and the other the Calanoida. The third lineage comprised the Harpacticoida. This scheme results in a diphyletic origin of the Cyclopoida.

Tiemann: Tiemann (1984) examined the monophyly of the Harpacticoida, concluding that the two polyarthran families (Canuellidae and Longipediidae) should be separated from the Harpacticoida and placed as a basic taxon near the roots of the Copepoda. The Oligoarthra then becomes synonymous with the Harpacticoida.

Fosshagen: Fosshagen in Fosshagen & Iliffe (1985) established a new order, the Platycopioida, comprising the family Platycopiidae with its two genera, *Platycopia* and *Antrisocopia*, known at that time. Fosshagen placed the Platycopioida in the Gymnoplea and regarded it as the sister group of the rest of the gymnopleans (the Calanoida).

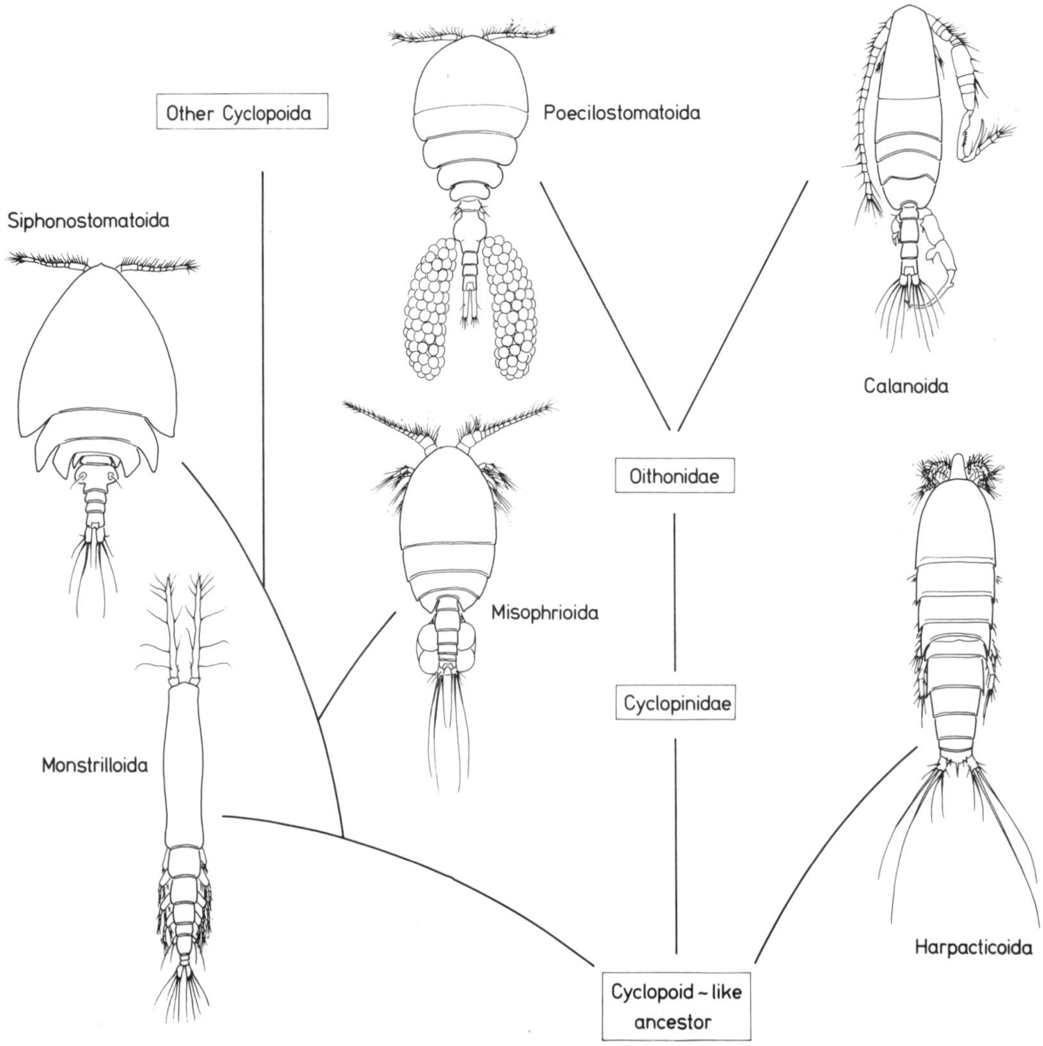

Figure 4.1.3. Simplified summary of scheme of phylogenetic relationships proposed by Dussart (1984).

Marcotte: Marcotte (1986) restated many of his earlier views (1982), namely that a benthic or epibenthic ancestor is likely for the Copepoda (figure 4.1.4) and that the harpacticoid *Tisbe* is similar to this ancestor although *Tisbe* itself is probably too derived to be the actual ancestor. Many harpacticoids remained in the epibenthic habitat. Marcotte identified a lineage of swimming taxa beginning with the natant harpacticoids such as Longipediidae and Canuellidae, leading to the Misophrioida and ultimately to the Calanoida and Mormonilloida. Another lineage comprised the inbenthic harpacticoids. Finally, he recognised a parasitic lineage leading from a *Tisbe*-like ancestor to the Cyclopoida, from which the Poecilostomatoida might have evolved. In this scheme the Siphonostomatoida are derived directly from a harpacticoid ancestor. Marcotte was mainly concerned with the ecological radiation of the copepods into a variety of habitats and did not thoroughly detail the taxonomic consequences of this scheme. It would, for example, attribute paraphyletic status to the Harpacticoida.

Starobogatov: Starobogatov's (1986) new classification of the Crustacea (translated by Grygier in Starobogatov (1988)) is radically different from all other schemes. It breaks up the Copepoda, placing the Calanoida and Platycopioida together with the Tantulocarida in the infraclass Calanioni of the subclass Cyclopiones, and all the podoplean orders known at that time in the infraclass Cyclopioni of the same subclass. The principle upon which this classification is based was strongly criticised by Boxshall & Huys (1989).

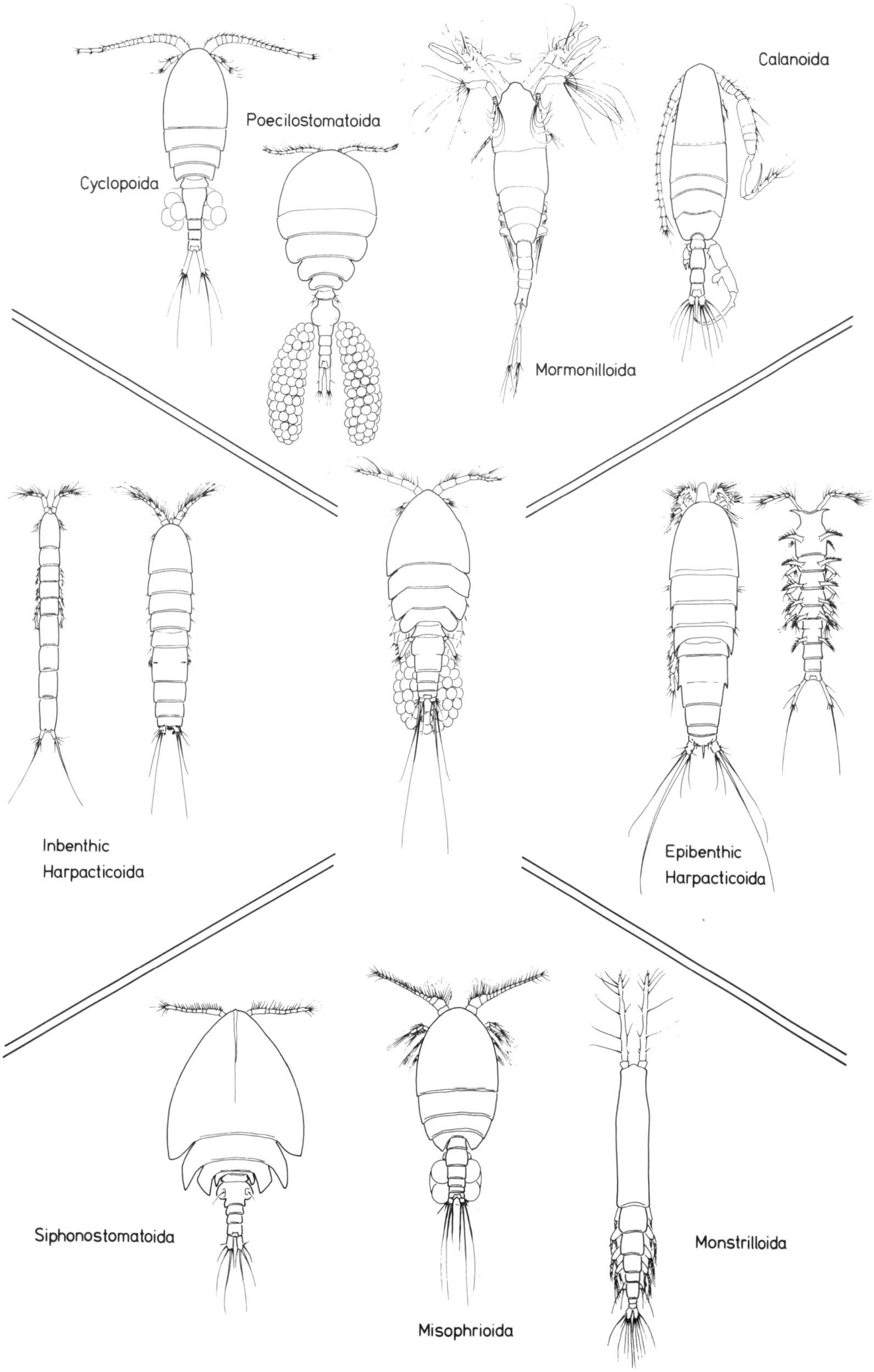

Figure 4.1.4. Scheme of phylogenetic relationships proposed by Marcotte (1986).

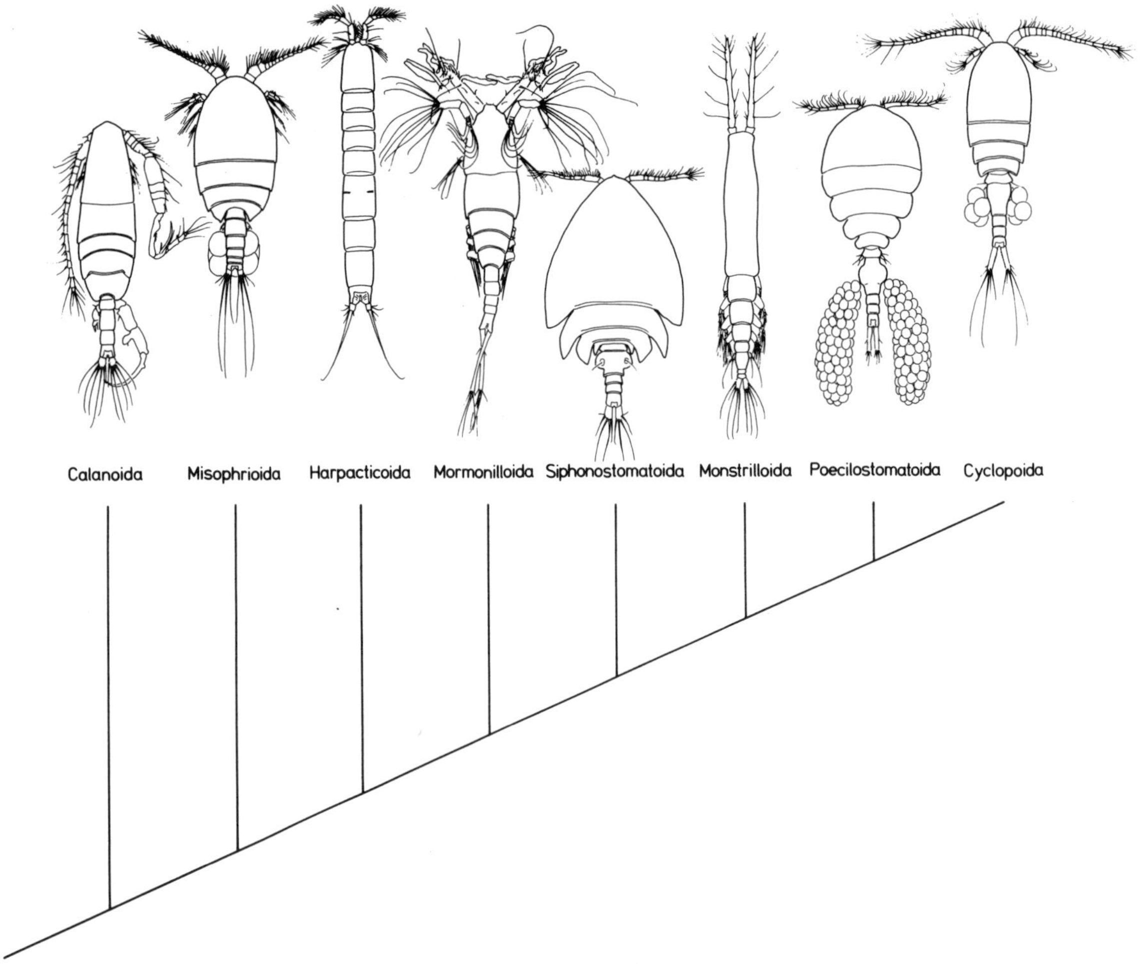

Figure 4.1.5. Scheme of phylogenetic relationships proposed by Boxshall (1986c).

Boxshall: In the panel discussion on phylogeny at the Second International Conference on Copepoda held in Ottawa in 1984 Boxshall (1986c) proposed a new phylogenetic system for the copepod orders (figure 4.1.5). This system was based on that of Kabata (1979) but utilised derived characters only in establishing relationships. The basic arrangement of the taxa placed the Gymnoplea (=Calanoida) as the sister group of the Podoplea and positioned the other orders in the sequence Misophrioida, Harpacticoida, Mormonilloida, Siphonostomatoida, Monstrilloida, Poecilostomatoida and Cyclopoida. Later Boxshall (in Schram, 1986) used a modified character set for a second analysis which resulted in the same pattern of affinities.

Izawa: In a paper discussed in more detail in the next section (chapter 4.2) Izawa (1987) noted that the Ergasilidae exhibited unusual naupliar features and suggested that there was sufficient justification for the establishment of a new order for this family.

Huys: Huys (1988a) reexamined *Gelyella* and concluded that this aberrant genus was not a harpacticoid but represented a separate order, the Gelyelloida, within the Podoplea. The Gelyelloida was considered to represent the sister group of a clade comprising the Cyclopoida, Siphonostomatoida and Poecilostomatoida. It was placed closest to the ancestral form of this assemblage because of the retention of a 7-segmented exopod on the antenna.

Ho: All ten orders were considered by Ho (1990) in his phylogenetic analysis of the Copepoda, using cladistic methods. Ho produced a matrix of 21 characters for the ten orders and, using the computer program PAUP 2.4.1 produced by David Swofford, he generated a consensus tree depicting phylogenetic relationships between the orders. There are unresolved polychotomies in this scheme but it suggests a sister group relationship between the Poecilostomatoida and

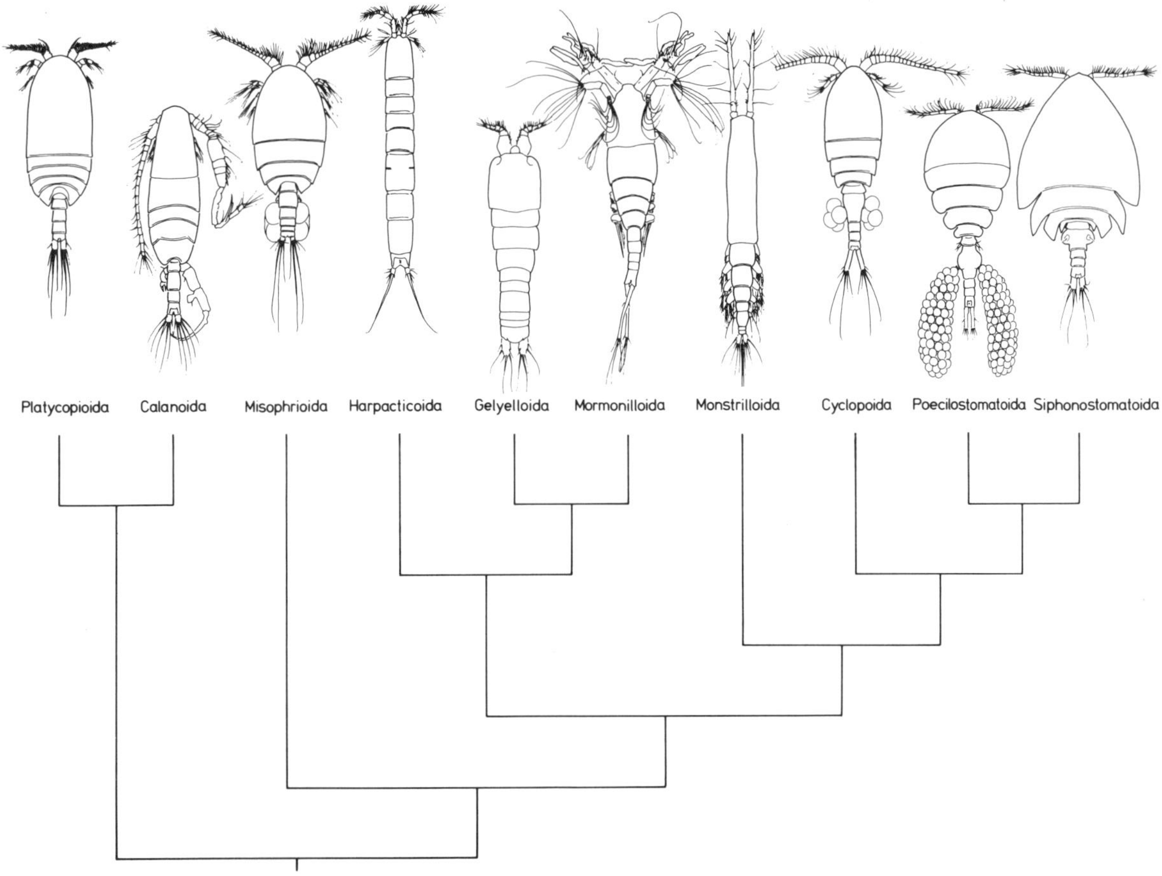

Figure 4.1.6. Scheme of phylogenetic relationships proposed by Ho (1990).

Siphonostomatoida. Ho selected a fully resolved cladogram (figure 4.1.6) as his working hypothesis on ordinal relationships.

Dahms: An in-depth study of harpacticoid nauplii by Dahms (1991) provided a detailed comparison of the naupliar characters of polyarthran and oligoarthran harpacticoids (Table 12). Dahms found several apomorphies shared by canuellids and longipediids, thus confirming the monophyly of the Polyarthra. Nauplii of the oligoarthran families also shared a number of advanced characters relative to the Polyarthra but Dahms was unable to find any naupliar synapomorphies linking the Polyarthra and Oligoarthra and, therefore, questioned the monophyletic status of the Harpacticoida. On this basis he suggested that the Polyarthra should be removed from the Harpacticoida. Dahms further discussed whether the Polyarthra should be removed either from the Podoplea or from the Copepoda on the basis of their naupliar characters alone.

Table 12. A comparison between the nauplii of Polyarthran and Oligoarthran Harpacticoids

	Polyarthra	Oligoarthra
Antennule	5 or 6-segmented	Up to 3-segmented
Antennary exopod	Up to 9-segmented	Up to 5-segmented
Mandibular endopod	Distinctly 2-segmented	1- or indistinctly 2-segmented
Labral ornamentation	On anterior surface	Marginal
Caudal process	Present	Absent
Maxilla	Absent	Present
Thoracic limb buds	Located medioventrally	Located laterally

4.2 CHARACTERS

a. Introduction

Copepod systematics at the ordinal level has been based primarily on characters relating to body plan, to the presence and segmentation of rami of particular limbs and to the major modifications of the cephalic feeding structures (Thorell, 1859; Giesbrecht, 1892; Sars 1901-21; Gurney, 1931; Lang, 1948b; Kabata, 1979; Boxshall, 1986c). Canu's (1892) attempt to base the primary division of the Copepoda on the nature of the genital systems was not adopted by subsequent reviewers. The presence of novel apomorphies, such as the carapace of misophrioids (Boxshall, 1984), or the fused coxae of the swimming legs of gelyelloids (Huys, 1988a) have been used to reinforce the distinctness of particular orders. Characters involving setation elements have occasionally been used as supplementary diagnostic characters at suprafamilial taxonomic levels. Lang (1948a) and Andronov (1974) both used the setation of the swimming legs as characters for suprafamilial divisions, of the Harpacticoida and Calanoida respectively. Fosshagen (in Fosshagen & Iliffe, 1985) used the presence of 2 spines on the outer margin of the first exopodal segment of swimming legs 2 to 5 as a supporting character when he established the order Platycopioida and Lang (1948b) used this character as diagnostic of his proposed new suborder, the Progymnoplea, accommodating the Platycopiidae. However, these are exceptions and, in general, characters involving setation have been used only at familial level and below.

The availability of modern, detailed taxonomic descriptions of representatives of all orders has revealed that patterns of setation on all the limbs are highly conservative evolutionarily and we have found that they provide a great deal of information of phylogenetic importance at higher, i.e. ordinal and superfamilial, taxonomic levels. The character set used for the cladistic analysis in this volume utilises precise details of segmentation and setation for all taxa. Adult representatives of all orders have been examined in order to verify every character employed in the analysis (Appendix 1).

Anatomy: The internal anatomy of copepods is much less useful at present in providing data upon which phylogenetic inferences may be made. The anatomy of the genital apparatus, especially the number and position of the seminal receptacles, provides several important characters but basic data are lacking for a number of orders at present. This situation is exacerbated by the widespread practice of drawing internal structures with solid lines in taxonomic illustrations thereby creating the misleading impression that they are external surface features. In his monograph on the harpacticoids Lang (1948a) emphasised the importance of the so-called genital field of the female, and used it extensively to support his scheme of phylogenetic affinities. The genital field is a misleading concept as it does not constitute a well defined character. It represents a combination of external features, such as the sixth legs, internal parts of the reproductive system, such as the seminal receptacles, and other internal features not related to the reproductive system, such as muscle insertion sites.

Studies on the skeletomusculature of the Calanoida, Misophrioida, Mormonilloida and Siphonostomatoida (Boxshall, 1982, 1985, 1990a) have provided a reference system that permits the identification of homologies between limb segments. The hiatus between the coxa and basis is particularly useful as a plane of reference, independent of setation patterns. Evidence provided by study of the musculature has been especially valuable in interpreting appendages, such as the oithonid maxilliped, which have conspicuous surface folds that resemble articulations and have caused confusion in the past. Other features of the skeletomusculature, such as the form of the ventral cephalic tendon system, are too poorly known to permit detailed comparison between orders. More information is also required before such systems are understood well enough to be used as characters in phylogenetic analysis. For example, both the Mormonilloida and Siphonostomatoida have a single functional ventral cephalic tendon, having reduced or lost the posterior tendon. In the former the posterior tendon is reduced to a strand connecting the tips of the postmaxillulary apodemes but the anterior tendon is well developed and serves as the origin of numerous muscles. In the latter the posterior tendon is lost and the anterior is reduced to a strand serving as the origin of only 4 mandibular muscles and the oral cone muscles. These differences strongly suggest that the loss of the posterior tendon in these 2 orders is the result of convergent evolution.

The presence of a heart in the Misophrioida has long been regarded as significant because it appears to be the only podoplean order in which a heart is found in the adult. Por (1984b) attributed great importance to the abdominal musculature of polyarthran harpacticoids that enables them to move the caudal rami. The phylogenetic significance of many anatomical features is difficult to assess, primarily because the anatomy is so poorly known in many orders that meaningful comparisons are not possible.

Ontogenetic Stages: The morphology of the developmental stages also provides useful characters for phylogenetic analysis. Björnberg (1986) compared the naupliar characters of the Harpacticoida, Cyclopoida and Calanoida in an attempt to determine which of the three was the most primitive. She concluded that the cyclopoid nauplius presents the greatest number of primitive features and, therefore, that the Cyclopoida is the oldest of these three groups. Björnberg also stated that the known nauplii of poecilostomatoids are like those of cyclopoids.

Boxshall (1985) compared the ontogeny of the naupliar musculature in a calanoid, a harpacticoid and a cyclopoid using the data published by Perryman (1961) on *Calanus*, and Fanta (1973 and 1976) on *Euterpina* Norman and *Oithona* respectively. He found no clear indication that any one of these genera shows more advanced features than the others. However, *Calanus* displays the most gradual increase in numbers of appendage muscles and only *Calanus* develops extrinsic maxillary muscles during the naupliar stages. It might be inferred from this that *Calanus* exhibits the most regular anamorphic pattern of development and that this represents the most plesiomorphic state.

Izawa (1987) published an extensive review of naupliar features in the Poecilostomatoida and made comparisons with the larval morphology of other copepod orders and other crustacean groups. Izawa's analysis is hard to interpret for two reasons. Firstly he adheres to the Sarsian ordinal classification, presumably because he found no characters in the naupliar feeding apparatus that could be used to discriminate between the siphonostome, poecilostome and gnathostome Cyclopoida. Secondly, he makes no attempt to differentiate between plesiomorphic and apomorphic character states. This is a more profound difficulty. Izawa uses the presence of either 1 or 2 setae on the terminal segment of the mandibular exopod as a high level discriminant. He found 2 setae in the Calanoida and the Harpacticoida. In the Siphonostomatoida he found both the 2 setae (in his 'siphonostome Cyclopoida') and 1 seta conditions (in his 'Caligoida' and 'Lernaeopodoida'). In the Cyclopoida also he found both states, with 2 setae present in the Cyclopidae and 1 seta in the Oithonidae, Ascidicolidae (as Enterocolidae) and Lernaeidae. In his 'poecilostome Cyclopoida' he found only the 1 seta state. Izawa then used the mandibular setation to place certain highly transformed parasites of problematic position. On the basis of in-group analysis of adult characters we interpret the 2 setae state as plesiomorphic. The apomorphic 1 seta state is found, therefore, in the three main parasitic orders. This character cannot be used in isolation to determine the ordinal position of such problematic taxa.

Izawa (1987) also found the nauplii of the family Ergasilidae (figure 2.10.23C-D) to be unique in many respects and suggested that this family constitutes a separate ordinal taxon related to the Cyclopoida. The naupliar mandible of *Ergasilus* is very specialised, especially in the structure and setation of the endopod (arrowed in figure 2.20.23D). We interpret these characters as providing good apomorphies defining the family Ergasilidae but the considerable number of synapomorphies between adult ergasilids and other poecilostomatoids confirm their position within this order. Izawa's work does, however, serve to illustrate the potential of larval characters at higher taxonomic levels. It provides, for example, an apomorphy between the two polyarthran harpacticoid families, Longipediidae and Canuellidae. The nauplii of both these families fail to develop a mandibular gnathobase although the possession of such a structure is probably plesiomorphic to the Harpacticoida since it is present in calanoid nauplii and in the nauplii of oligoarthran families, such as the Tachidiidae.

The excellent study of harpacticoid nauplii published by Dahms in 1991 raises a number of issues, the most important being the affinities of the Polyarthra. The antennules of nauplii of polyarthrans differ from those of all other copepod nauplii in segmentation. In *Longipedia minor* they are 6-segmented at the first nauplius stage and 5-segmented at the second. In *Canuella perplexa* they are 5-segmented throughout the naupliar phase of development. Comparison with oligoarthran antennules led Dahms to suggest that: the first segments are homologous in the

Polyarthra and Oligoarthra, segment 2 of oligoarthrans is homologous with segment 2 to 4 of polyarthrans, and segment 3 is homologous with the fifth segment of polyarthrans. This unique antennulary segmentation is only a naupliar feature, since copepodid and adult polyarthrans have short antennules, with at most 4 segments. We interpret many of the unusual features of polyarthran nauplii as derived, in particular the loss of the mandibular gnathobase and the lack of the maxillary anlagen, and it is possible that other morphological features, such as the subdivision of antennulary segments, can also be viewed as adaptations for a specialised naupliar mode of life.

b. Criteria Used in Constructing the Character Matrix.

Out-group analysis is problematic because of the specialised nature of related taxa. The phylogenetic scheme of maxillopodan taxa presented by Boxshall & Huys (1989) suggests that the Mystacocarida are the sister group of the Copepoda but the mystacocarids are highly specialised for their interstitial existence. Using mystacocarids as the out-group provides little information relevant to segmentation and setation patterns of the cephalic limbs, for example, which are so important in analysing interordinal relationships within the Copepoda. Other taxa within the maxillopodan complex are also highly specialised, for a sessile habit (Thecostraca), for parasitism (Tantulocarida and Branchiura) or for life within an enclosing bivalved shell (Ostracoda). Out-group analysis has been used where it provides an informative perspective on copepod evolution but in this account we have necessarily relied primarily upon in-group analysis.

The phylogenetic analyses presented in this chapter use the ordinal ancestral character sets generated in chapter 2 as their database. The transformations in character states and their polarity are discussed below. We accept that only homologous derived character states can be used to construct meaningful phylogenies and it is apparent that lack of critical attention to homology is at least partly responsible for the great number of phylogenies that are generated, briefly flourish, and are then lost for ever, virtually without trace. In carcinology in general and copepodology in particular it appears to us that, in practice, the rule regarding homology has been to assume that similar structures in related organisms are homologous unless there is good evidence otherwise. In order to improve the resolution of our phylogenies it is vital that we improve the quality of our character sets and this can only be achieved by adopting a new and more rigorous attitude towards homology. Everything will founder unless we make this committment. The ultimate goal must be to make a positive statement on the homology of every single character state in the character matrix.

The character matrix used to generate our new phylogeny includes only those derived character states (synapomorphies) that we can positively identify as homologous. In the course of this study we have become aware that simple counts of segment numbers in the antennule, or in the exopod of the antenna, or in the maxillary endopod, are virtually unusable. In fact, this is the case for almost all copepod appendages. For example, both the Gelyelloida and Cyclopoida have a 3-segmented endopod on the maxilla. In the former the first endopodal segment is fused to the basis so the 3 free segments are ancestral segments II, III and IV, whereas in the latter the first and second endopodal segments are fused to form a double segment so the 3 observable segments are I-II, III and IV. The two states are clearly not homologous. Similarly, simple setal counts can be very misleading. For example, the third exopodal segment of the first swimming leg has a total of 7 elements in the Calanoida and the Harpacticoida, however, in the former these are derived from a spine and setal formula of II,I,4 whereas in the latter they are derived from a III,I,3 condition. The setation elements are not all homologous.

We recognise 3 categories of characters. The first comprises characters which we can positively identify as homologous because of solid morphological evidence, such as features of the musculature, the setation pattern, or other reference point. These characters can be used in phylogenetic studies. An example of such a character is the sheath on segment XV of cyclopoids and misophrioids and its associated morphology. The second category of characters are those which cannot be used in phylogenetic studies because there is insufficient information to determine whether or not the characters are homologous. A good example of this type of character is the number of setae on the epipodite of the maxillule. It varies from 10 in the Calanoida down to 2 in the Mormonilloida (or possibly 1 in the Poecilostomatoida) but is unusable because it is not possible to precisely identify which setae of one order are homologous with which setae of another. This category of characters may be usable in the future but much more information, particularly on the vertical homology of setation elements through ontogenetic series, will be required before this happens. The third category of characters are those which are unusable because they are convergent. An example of this is the 2-segmented maxillipedal endopod which, as scored by Ho (1990) in his data matrix, would link the Harpacticoida and Gelyelloida. The two 'segments' present in these orders are compound segments representing different combinations of fused segments and, therefore, cannot be homologous.

Neither simple segmental counts nor simple setal counts were used in the character matrix unless it could be confirmed that the elements involved were homologous. Most often it was the patterns of segmental fusion, as identified by reference to the setation, the musculature, or some other reference point, that provided the usable characters. We consider that setation characters will, in future, prove to be a valuable source of characters once sufficient care is taken in the description of setation elements in the primary taxonomic literature. The ultimate extension of this process will require that every seta and spine on every segment of every appendage be named individually and criteria established for the determination of their homology. Our understanding of copepod morphology and ontogeny is as yet inadequate for this process to be taken far. However, even recognising the true nature of the problem will direct us onto the right path - the path that ultimately leads to a natural classification. We believe that this volume represents a first step along this path.

c. The Character Set.

The characters used in our analysis of phylogenetic relationships between the ten orders of copepods are listed below, together with comments on their various character states. The character states are also scored inside square brackets as for the PAUP program (see chapter 4.3). They are scored using the multistate system: 0 = the ancestral state, 1 = the derived state, 2 = a further derived state. A score of 9 = missing data, indicating either that the appendage or structure is absent in that order (e.g. the mouthparts in the Monstrilloida) or that we were unable to score the character accurately using our rigorous definition of homology.

Character 1: First pedigerous somite fused to cephalosome forming a cephalothorax.
Comments: The fusion of the first pedigerous somite to the cephalosome forming a cephalothorax is widespread within the Copepoda. The possession of a cephalothorax is the typical state of many families within orders such as the Cyclopoida, Calanoida and Poecilostomatoida which also contain members exhibiting the ancestral unfused state. However, only the Monstrilloida and Siphonostomatoida exhibit the derived state in all representatives. Out-group comparison indicates that the unfused state is ancestral since neither the first nor the second thoracic somite is incorporated into the cephalic tagma in the Mystacocarida which was identified as the sister group of the Copepoda in the analysis of Boxshall & Huys (1989).
[Score 0 = not fused, 1 = fused.]

Character 2: Tagmosis: gymnoplean tagmosis with main body articulation between fifth pedigerous and genital somites or podoplean tagmosis with articulation between fourth and fifth pedigerous somites.
Comments: The gymnoplean condition is here regarded as ancestral on the basis of out-group comparison (see chapter 3.2). It is retained in the Platycopioida and Calanoida. All other orders exhibit the podoplean condition.
[Score 0 = gymnoplean tagmosis, 1 = podoplean tagmosis.]

Character 3: Position of female genital apertures on genital somite.
Comments: The Platycopioida is the only order in which all species have the genital apertures located at the posterior margin of a discrete genital somite in the female. In most or all members of the other orders the genital and first abdominal somites are fused to form a double somite with the genital apertures located in the anterior half. However, even in those representatives of other orders in which a free genital double somite is retained, the genital apertures have migrated anteriorly, away from the posterior margin.
[Score 0 = located at posterior margin, 1 = located some distance anterior to rear margin of genital somite.]

Character 4: Female antennule with segments XXVII and XXVIII fused.
Comments: All orders except the Platycopioida have these 2 segments fused (see chapter 3.4). In most podoplean orders segment XXVI is also fused to XXVII-XXVIII making a triple segment. These orders, such as the Cyclopoida, score 1 for character 4 because XXVII and XXVIII are fused even though they are further incorporated into a compound segment.
[Score 0 = free, 1 = fused.]

Character 5: Female antennule with segment XXVI fused to double segment XXVII-XXVIII.
Comments: This character is exhibited in the simple derived state in most podoplean orders, although in some, such as the Mormonilloida, the triple segment XXVI-XXVIII may be incorporated into a larger fused unit. The ancestral unfused state is retained in the Platycopioida, Calanoida and Misophrioida (score = 0)
[Score 0 = free, 1 = fused.]

Character 6: Female antennule with segments IX to XII fused to form quadruple segment.
Comments: These 4 segments are fused in female siphonostomatoids. They are fused in harpacticoids within a larger unit IX-XIV (see table 2 in chapter 2.4) and are fused within the second compound segment of poecilostomatoid females (comprising ?IV-XIII). In all 3 of these orders the score = 1. Too few setation elements remain on the antennules of female monstrilloids to permit the identification of the segmental homologies with certainty but a score of 1 is recorded because all segments other than the proximal segment are more or less fused. Segmental homologies of the very reduced antennules of female mormonilloids and gelyelloids cannot be determined (score = 9). In all other orders these 4 segments are not fused.
[Score 0 = free, 1 = fused, 9 = indeterminate.]

Character 7: Male antennule with segments XXVII and XXVIII fused.
Comments: This is the male character equivalent to character 4. The simple derived state is exhibited only in the Calanoida and Misophrioida. It is scored as 1 for all orders other than the Platycopioida even though in some, such as the Monstrilloida and Mormonilloida, the double segment XXVII-XXVIII is subsumed within the much larger fused unit XXI-XXVIII.
[Score 0 = free, 1 = fused.]

Character 8: Male antennule with segment XXVI fused to double segment XXVII-XXVIII.
Comments: This is the male character equivalent to character 5. The simple derived state is exhibited only in the Harpacticoida and Cyclopoida, although the Gelyelloida, Mormonilloida, Monstrilloida, Siphonostomatoida and Poecilostomatoida also score 1 as the triple segment XXVI-XXVIII is subsumed within a larger fused unit (either XXIV-XXVIII or XXI-XXVIII). The ancestral unfused state is retained in the Platycopioida, Calanoida and Misophrioida (score = 0).
[Score 0 = free, 1 = fused.]

Character 9: Male antennule with geniculation present between segments XX and XXI.
Comments: The geniculation present in the platycopioid *Antrisocopia* is located between segments XXIV and XXV (see chapter 2.1) and is not homologous with that between XX and XXI. All other orders exhibit a geniculation at this point at least in some representatives. The geniculation is vestigial in the Poecilostomatoida and is detectable only by reference to the intrinsic musculature but the secondary nature of this condition indicates that the poecilostomatoids should score 2 for this character.
[Score 0 = absent, 1 = present, 2 = secondarily absent.]

Character 10: Male antennule with segments XXI and XXII fused.
Comments: These segments are free in the Platycopioida. In the Calanoida partial fusion has occurred and an incomplete suture line remains marking the boundary between segments XXI and XXII. In all podopleans these segments are completely fused although in orders other than the Harpacticoida and Misophrioida this double segment is incorporated into a larger fused unit.
[Score 0 = free, 1 = partly fused, 2 = completely fused.]

Character 11: Male antennule with segment XXIII incorporated into double segment XXI-XXII.
Comments: This character is exhibited in the simple derived state in the Cyclopoida, Gelyelloida and Siphonostomatoida. It is also scored as derived in the Mormonilloida, Poecilostomatoida and

Monstrilloida in which the triple segment is part of a larger compound unit. Segment XXIII is free in the Platycopioida, Misophrioida and Harpacticoida (score = 0). The Calanoida are scored as 0 even though segment XXIII is fused to XXII because, primitively, the fusion of XXI and XXII is not complete and XXI to XXIII cannot be regarded as constituting a triple segment.
[Score 0 = free, 1 = fused.]

Character 12: Male antennule with segments XIX and XX fused.
Comments: All podoplean orders exhibit the derived state, although in the Poecilostomatoida, Mormonilloida, and presumably the Monstrilloida the double segment forms part of a larger unit. In platycopioids segment XVIII to XX are fused to form a triple segment and must score 1 in the matrix. This fusion is typically associated with the presence of the geniculation in podopleans and the primitive lack of a geniculation in platycopioids suggests that the fusion may be convergent. The ancestral unfused state is found only in the Calanoida.
[Score 0 = free, 1 = fused.]

Character 13: Male antennule with segments XXIV and XXV fused.
Comments: These segments are free in the Harpacticoida and Misophrioida, and each is incorporated into a different compound segment in the Platycopioida. All 3 taxa score for the ancestral condition. All other orders show the derived state. In the Calanoida and Cyclopoida these 2 segments are fused to form an isolated double segment. In other podoplean orders they are incorporated into larger units, either XXIV-XXVIII (in Gelyelloida and Siphonostomatoida) or XXI-XXVIII (in Monstrilloida, Mormonilloida and Poecilostomatoida).
[Score 0 = free, 1 = fused.]

Character 14: Male antennule with segments IX to XI fused anteriorly.
Comments: These 3 segments are partly fused in the Siphonostomatoida and completely fused in the Harpacticoida and Poecilostomatoida. The simple derived state is found only in the Siphonostomatoida. In harpacticoids the triple segment IX-XI belongs to the compound unit IX-XII, whereas in poecilostomatoids it is part of a much larger compound unit incorporating about 10 original segments (from ?IV to XIII). Using the positions of the aesthetascs on the antennules of male mormonilloids as reference points the segmental homologies were tentatively identified. Segments IX to XI are fused anteriorly in the Mormonilloida (score = 1). The condition of these segments in the Monstrilloida cannot be scored because too few setation elements are retained for the segmental fusion pattern in the proximal part of the limb to be established. There is a high probability that these segments are fused in such a condensed antennule but the uncertainty is recognised in a score of 9. In all other orders these segments are not all fused anteriorly.
[Score 0 = free, 1 = fused, 9 = indeterminate.]

Character 15: Male antennule with sheath on segment XV, enclosing segment XVI.
Comments: This is a novel character expressed in the Cyclopoida, Misophrioida and, in a modified form, in the Gelyelloida. Scores of 0 are attributed to the Harpacticoida, Monstrilloida, Mormonilloida and Poecilostomatoida although in each of these cases segment XV is incorporated by fusion into a larger compound segment.
[Score 0 = absent, 1 = present.]

Character 16: Antennary exopod segment I present or absent.
Comments: The ancestral state is exhibited by the Platycopioida and Calanoida. The derived state could be detected in those podoplean orders with well developed, multisegmented exopods, the Misophrioida, Harpacticoida, Mormonilloida and Gelyelloida. The taxa that scored 9 either had no antenna (Monstrilloida), or had no exopod (Poecilostomatoida), or had the exopod so reduced that it was represented by a lobe (Cyclopoida) or a single segment (Siphonostomatoida). In neither of the last 2 cases could the segmental composition of the exopodal vestige be ascertained.
[Score 0 = present, 1 = absent, 9 = indeterminate.]

Character 17: Antennary exopodal segments IX and X fused.
Comments: The ancestral state is found in the Platycopioida, Calanoida and Mormonilloida. The simple expression of the derived state, with segments IX and X fused to form a double segment bearing 4 setae, is found in the Misophrioida, Harpacticoida and Gelyelloida. The taxa that scored

9 either had no antenna (Monstrilloida), or had no exopod (Poecilostomatoida), or had the exopod so reduced that it was represented by a lobe (Cyclopoida) or a single segment (Siphonostomatoida). In neither of the last 2 cases could the segmental composition of the exopodal rudiment be ascertained.
[Score 0 = free, 1 = fused, 9 = indeterminate.]

Character 18: Coxal seta on antenna.
Comments: The ancestral state is found only in the Calanoida and Cyclopoida. All other orders show the derived state, having lost the coxal seta, except for the Monstrilloida which lack the entire antenna and therefore score 9.
[Score 0 = present, 1 = absent, 9 = missing.]

Character 19: Antennary endopodal segments III and IV fused.
Comments: Only the calanoids show the ancestral state, retaining a 4-segmented endopod. All other orders display the derived state, except for the Monstrilloida which lack the antenna and score 9.
[Score 0 = free, 1 = fused, 9 = missing.]

Character 20: Maxillule with coxa, basis and rami fused into unsegmented palp.
Comments: The derived state is shared only by the Siphonostomatoida and Poecilostomatoida, and both score 1, despite some differences in the form of the unsegmented palp in these orders. All other orders display a more plesiomorphic state with at least one of these segments expressed, except for the monstrilloids which lack the entire maxillule.
[Score 0 = free, 1 = fused to form palp, 9 = missing.]

Character 21: Form of outer lobe on basis of maxillule.
Comments: The ancestral state, a lobate exite, is retained only in the Platycopioida. In the calanoids, misophrioids and harpacticoids the exite is represented by a seta on the outer surface of the basis and they all score 1. All other orders lack any outer seta on the basis and score 2, except for the Monstrilloida which lack the entire appendage.
[Score 0 = lobate with 2 setae, 1 = reduced to 1 seta, 2 = absent, 9 = missing.]

Character 22: First and second endopodal segments of maxillule fused to form double segment.
Comments: A 3-segmented endopod in which segments 1 and 2 are free is retained only in the Calanoida. In most other orders segments 1 and 2 are fused to form a double segment, although in the Gelyelloida and Cyclopoida this double segment is incorporated into a triple segment representing segments 1 to 3. The exceptions are the Monstrilloida, which lack the appendage, and the Platycopioida, Siphonostomatoida and Poecilostomatoida which all lack a defined endopod and therefore score 9.
[Score 0 = free, 1 = fused, 9 = missing.]

Character 23: Third endopodal segment of maxillule fused to proximal double segment.
Comments: The derived state, an unsegmented endopod representing 3 fused segments, is exhibited by the Gelyelloida and Cyclopoida although fusion is incomplete in the latter. The Calanoida, Misophrioida, Harpacticoida, and Mormonilloida all exhibit the ancestral state in which the third segment is free. The Monstrilloida, which lack the appendage, and the Platycopioida, Siphonostomatoida and Poecilostomatoida, all of which lack a defined endopod, score 9.
[Score 0 = free, 1 = fused, 9 = missing.]

Character 24: Setae on inner margin of maxillulary exopod lost.
Comments: The formulation of this character represents an attempt to assess the homology of the exopodal setae. The numbers of setae present vary from 11 to 3 but simple counts are often misleading. In those orders with significantly reduced numbers of setae the distal margin setae are retained and the setae originally belonging to the inner margin are lost. The loss of these setae constitutes the derived condition and is exhibited in the Gelyelloida and Cyclopoida. In the Calanoida, Misophrioida, Harpacticoida and Mormonilloida some inner margin setae are present. Scores of 9 are attributed to the Monstrilloida, which lack the appendage, and the Platycopioida, Siphonostomatoida and Poecilostomatoida, all of which lack a defined exopod.
[Score 0 = setae present, 1 = setae absent, 9 = missing.]

Character 25: Endopod of maxilla.
Comments: All orders of copepods have a defined endopod on the maxilla, the ancestral state, except for the Siphonostomatoida and Poecilostomatoida, both of which exhibit the derived state. The Monstrilloida lack a maxilla and score 9.
[Score 0 = present, 1 = absent, 9 = missing.]

Character 26: Seta II on endopodal segment I of maxilla lost.
Comments: The ancestral state is found only in the Calanoida, which retain setae I to IV on the first endopodal segment. Seta II is lost in all those podopleans in which this segment is expressed and the setal homologies can be determined. Scores of 9 are attributed to the Monstrilloida because the limb is missing, and to the Siphonostomatoida and Poecilostomatoida which lack the endopod. The Platycopioida and Mormonilloida are also scored 9 because in each only 1 seta originating on this segment is present and its homology cannot be determined with certainty.
[Score 0 = present, 1 = absent, 9 = missing.]

Character 27: Seta IV on endopodal segment I of maxilla lost.
Comments: The ancestral state is found in the Calanoida, Misophrioida and Harpacticoida, which retain seta IV on the first endopodal segment. The derived state, loss of seta IV, is shared only by the Gelyelloida and Cyclopoida. Scores of 9 are attributed to the Monstrilloida because the limb is missing and to the Siphonostomatoida and Poecilostomatoida which lack the endopod. The Platycopioida and Mormonilloida are also scored 9 because in each only 1 seta originates on this segment and its homology cannot be determined with certainty.
[Score 0 = present, 1 = absent, 9 = missing.]

Character 28: Seta D on basis of maxilla lost.
Comments: This character state has a similar distribution within the copepod orders as character 27 except for the platycopioids. The same comments apply and identical scores are allocated but the Platycopioida retain the ancestral condition (score = 0).
[Score 0 = present, 1 = absent, 9 = missing.]

Character 29: Seta representing proximal (praecoxal) endite of maxilliped lost.
Comments: The ancestral state is retained only in the Calanoida, Misophrioida and Harpacticoida. The derived state in which the single proximal seta is absent, is found in all other orders except the Monstrilloida (maxilliped absent).
[Score 0 = present, 1 = absent, 9 = missing.]

Character 30: Number of setae on basis of maxilliped.
Comments: The ancestral state of 3 setae on the basis is found in the Calanoida, Misophrioida and Mormonilloida. All other orders have 2 setae (score = 1) except the Siphonostomatoida which has a single seta only (score = 2) and the Monstrilloida (maxilliped absent, score = 9). This is a simple setal count and is dependent upon the assumption that the 2 setae remaining in the Platycopioida, Harpacticoida, Gelyelloida, Cyclopoida and Poecilostomatoida are homologous. There is little evidence either for or against this assumption and it remains a weak character.
[Score 0 = 3 setae, 1 = 2 setae, 2 = 1 seta, 9 = missing.]

Character 31: Inner spine on basis of swimming leg 2.
Comments: The ancestral state is exhibited only in the Platycopioida, all other orders share the derived state.
[Score 0 = present, 1 = absent.]

Character 32: Inner spine on basis of swimming leg 3.
Comments: As for the preceding character 31.
[Score 0 = present, 1 = absent.]

Character 33: Inner spine on basis of swimming leg 4.
Comments: As for character 31, except that the Gelyelloida lack fourth legs and score a 9.
[Score 0 = present, 1 = absent, 9 = missing.]

Character 34: Inner spine on basis of swimming leg 5.

Comments: As for the preceding character 33, except that the Mormonilloida lack fifth legs in the female and lack defined fifth leg segments in the male and also score 9.
[Score 0 = present, 1 = absent, 9 = missing.]

Character 35: First exopodal segment of swimming leg 2 with 2 spines on outer margin.
Comments: Two spines are present on the outer margin in the Platycopioida only, all other orders share the derived state.
[Score 0 = 2 spines, 1 = 1 spine.]

Character 36: First exopodal segment of swimming leg 3 with 2 spines on outer margin.
Comments: As for the preceding character 35.
[Score 0 = 2 spines, 1 = 1 spine.]

Character 37: First exopodal segment of swimming leg 4 with 2 spines on outer margin.
Comments: As for character 35, except that the Gelyelloida lack fourth legs and score a 9.
[Score 0 = 2 spines, 1 = 1 spine, 9 = missing.]

Character 38: First exopodal segment of swimming leg 5 with 2 spines on outer margin.
Comments: As for character 35, except that the Gelyelloida and female Mormonilloida lack fifth legs and both score 9's.
[Score 0 = 2 spines, 1 = 1 spine, 9 = missing.]

Character 39: Number of setae on inner margin of second endopodal segment of first swimming leg.
Comments: The ancestral state is exhibited by members of the Calanoida, Misophrioida, Cyclopoida and Siphonostomatoida. The derived state, with only a single inner margin seta present, is found in the Harpacticoida, Monstrilloida and Poecilostomatoida. In the Mormonilloida this margin is unarmed (score = 2). The Platycopioida and Gelyelloida both score 9 as this segment is not expressed in either order. Many members of the Calanoida, Misophrioida, Cyclopoida and Siphonostomatoida also display the derived state and it is clear that the proximal seta may be lost with relative ease. It is probably a highly convergent character state.
[Score 0 = 2 setae, 1 = 1 seta, 2 = unarmed, 9 = missing.]

Character 40: Number of elements on outer margin of third endopodal segment of swimming leg 2.
Comments: The ancestral state, in which 2 setae are present on the outer margin, is found only in the Platycopioida and Calanoida. All other orders have only 1 seta (score = 1) except the Mormonilloida, which have an unarmed inner margin (score = 2), and Gelyelloida, which lack a defined third endopodal segment (score = 9).
[Score 0 = 2 elements, 1 = 1 element, 2 = unarmed, 9 = missing.]

Character 41: Number of elements on outer margin of third endopodal segment of swimming leg 3.
Comments: As for the preceding character 40.
[Score 0 = 2 elements, 1 = 1 element, 2 = unarmed, 9 = missing.]

Character 42: Number of elements on outer margin of third endopodal segment of swimming leg 4.
Comments: As for character 40, except that the entire limb is missing in the Gelyelloida (score = 9).
[Score 0 = 2 elements, 1 = 1 element, 2 = unarmed, 9 = missing.]

Character 43: Intercoxal sclerite between fifth legs of female lost.
Comments: The ancestral state in which an intercoxal sclerite is present in the female is found in all orders except the Gelyelloida and Mormonilloida, in which the fifth leg is lost (score = 9), and the Monstrilloida and Siphonostomatoida, which share the derived state (score = 1).
[Score 0 = present, 1 = absent, 9 = missing.]

Character 44: Praecoxa of female fifth legs lost.
Comments: The ancestral state in which the praecoxa of the fifth leg is represented by a small hoop-like lateral sclerite is found in platycopioids and calanoids. All podoplean orders, except the

Gelyelloida and Mormonilloida which lack a fifth leg, have lost any vestige of the praecoxa in the fifth legs (score = 1).
[Score 0 = praecoxa present, 1 = praecoxa absent, 9 = limb missing.]

Character 45: Coxa and basis of female fifth legs fused.
Comments: A separate coxa and basis, the ancestral state, is still found in the Platycopioida, Calanoida, Misophrioida and Cyclopoida. The derived state is exhibited by the Harpacticoida, Monstrilloida, Siphonostomatoida and Poecilostomatoida. The fifth legs are absent in the Mormonilloida and Gelyelloida (score = 9).
[Score 0 = free, 1 = fused, 9 = limb missing.]

Character 46: Inner coxal seta absent from female fifth legs.
Comments: An inner coxal seta is present only in some Calanoida and Cyclopoida (score = 0). All other orders share the derived state in which this seta is lost (score = 1), except for the Gelyelloida and female Mormonilloida which lack fifth legs (score = 9).
[Score 0 = present, 1 = absent, 9 = limb missing.]

Character 47: Endopod incorporated into basis of female fifth leg.
Comments: The ancestral state of a well defined endopod is retained in the Platycopioida, Calanoida, Misophrioida and Harpacticoida (score = 0). The Siphonostomatoida and Monstrilloida exhibit the derived condition in which the endopod is incorporated and either 1 or 2 endopodal setae respectively are inserted on the surface of the baseoendopod. In the Cyclopoida and Poecilostomatoida no trace of the endopod remains and the entire fifth leg is missing in the Gelyelloida and Mormonilloida.
[Score 0 = endopod separate, 1 = endopod incorporated into basis to form baseoendopod, 9 = endopod or entire limb missing.]

Character 48: Seta *l* on exopod of female fifth leg.
Comments: Only the Platycopioida retains the ancestral state. All other orders share the derived condition, in which the seta is lost, except for the Gelyelloida and Mormonilloida in which the fifth legs are lacking (score = 9).
[Score 0 = present, 1 = absent, 9 = limb missing.]

Character 49: All exopodal segments of female fifth leg fused.
Comments: Two or more exopodal segments are present in females belonging to the Platycopioida, Calanoida, Misophrioida and Cyclopoida. In the Gelyelloida and Mormonilloida the fifth legs are lacking (score = 9) but in the Harpacticoida, Monstrilloida, Siphonostomatoida and Poecilostomatoida a compound exopodal segment is present bearing sufficient armature elements to indicate that it is derived by fusion of at least 2 segments (the derived state, score = 1).
[Score 0 = free, 1 = fused, 9 = limb missing.]

Character 50: Intercoxal sclerite between fifth legs of male lost.
Comments: As for character 43.
[Score 0 = present, 1 = absent, 9 = limb missing or vestigial.]

Character 51: Praecoxa of male fifth legs lost.
Comments: The ancestral state in which the praecoxa of the fifth leg is represented by a small hoop-like lateral sclerite is found in platycopioids and calanoids. All podoplean orders, except the Gelyelloida which lack a fifth leg and the Mormonilloida which have a vestigial fifth leg, have lost any vestige of the praecoxa in the fifth legs (score = 1).
[Score 0 = praecoxa present, 1 = praecoxa absent, 9 = limb missing or vestigial.]

Character 52: Coxa and basis of male fifth legs fused.
Comments: The ancestral condition, with separate coxa and basis, is found in the Platycopioida, Calanoida, Misophrioida, Harpacticoida, and Cyclopoida (score = 0). The derived state in which coxa and basis are fused to form a common protopodal segment is exhibited by the Monstrilloida, Siphonostomatoida and Poecilostomatoida (score = 1). The fifth legs are absent in the Gelyelloida and so reduced in the Mormonilloida that the coxa and basis are not defined (score = 9).
[Score 0 = free, 1 = fused, 9 = limb missing or coxa and basis not defined.]

Character 53: Inner coxal seta on male fifth leg lost.
Comments: As for character 46.
[Score 0 = present, 1 = absent, 9 = limb missing or vestigial.]

Character 54: Seta *b* on exopod of male fifth leg.
Comments: The ancestral state, with seta *b* present, is found only in the Platycopioida, Calanoida and Harpacticoida. The derived state is shared by the Misophrioida, Cyclopoida, Siphonostomatoida and Poecilostomatoida. The limb is absent in the Gelyelloida, and so reduced that the homology of the remaining setation elements cannot be discerned in the Mormonilloida and Monstrilloida (score = 9).
[Score 0 = present, 1 = absent, 9 = missing.]

4.3 CLADISTIC ANALYSIS OF RELATIONSHIPS BETWEEN ORDERS

a. Phylogenetic Analysis Using Parsimony (PAUP).

i) Character Matrix

Phylogenetic analysis using parsimony has become one of the orthodoxies of modern systematics. Analyses of phylogenetic relationships that do not use parsimony as the primary determinant of the shape of the evolutionary trees are considered to be subjective and unscientific. The distributions of the various states of the characters listed in chapter 4.2 are summarised in tabular form (Table 13) using the multistate scoring system. This matrix uses a hypothetical composite ancestral copepod (HYPANC) which scores 0 for all characters. Any trees generated are rooted in this hypothetical ancestor.

Table 13. Character matrix for first analysis using PAUP 2.4

Taxon	Characters 1–54
HYPANC	000000000000000000000000000000000000000000000000000000
PLATY	000000000001000001100999099011000000009000000100000010
CALAN	0011001011001000000001000000000111111110000000001001000
MISOPH	011100101201001111101100010000111111110111010101001011
HARPACT	011111111201010111101100010001111111111111011101101010
MONSTR	111111111211190999999999999999911111111111111111111119
MORMON	011119111211110101102100099910111911192222999999999999
GELYELL	011119111211101111102111011111119911999999999999999999
CYCLO	0111101112111019901021110111111111111110111010091001001
SIPHON	111111111211110991112999199912111111110111111111111111
POECILO	01111111221111099111299919991111111111111011191101111

Ordered Characters: This character matrix was analysed using the PAUP 2.4 program prepared by David Swofford of the Illinois Natural History Survey, Champaign, Illinois. The options employed were Branch-and-Bound, which is guaranteed to find all the most parsimonious trees, and the MINF optimisation which assigns character states so that the *f*-value is minimised. The characters were ordered. The use of ordered, multistate characters implies a linear sequence between character states, so that the most derived state (=2) evolved from the ancestral state (= 0) via the intermediate state (=1). The character matrix contains only 8 characters that exist in two derived states and in 6 of these one of the derived states is autapomorphic.

Three trees were generated by this analysis (figures 4.3.1A-C) but we will only briefly discuss their topology here. They differ only in the position of the order Mormonilloida. In all three trees the first order to diverge from the main copepod lineage was the Platycopioida and there are numerous characters supporting this recognition of the Platycopioida as the sister group of all other copepods. The second offshoot is the Calanoida which retains the plesiomorphic gymnoplean body tagmosis whereas the main copepod lineage that forms the sister group of the Calanoida is characterised by its podoplean tagmosis and a range of other characters. In all trees

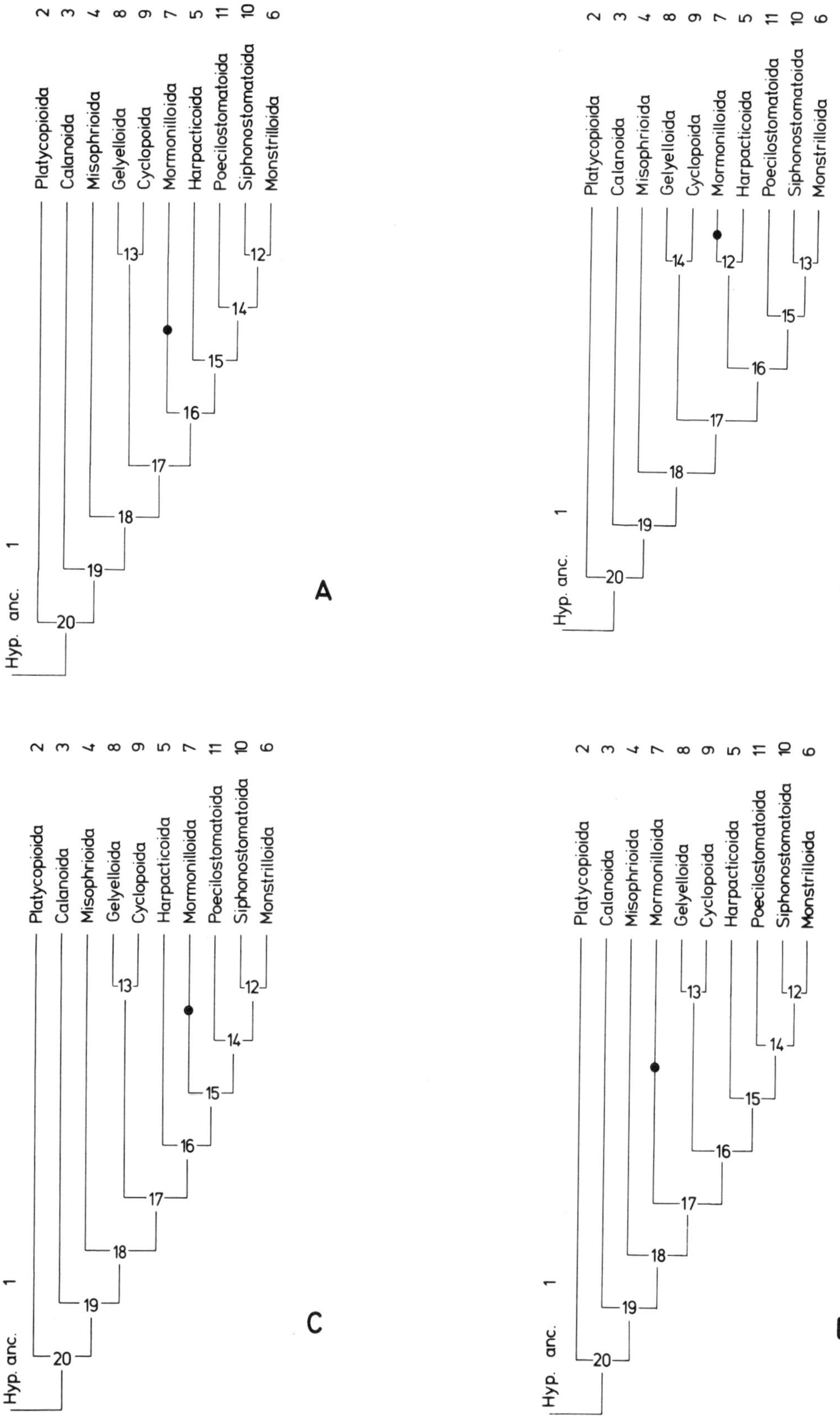

Figure 4.3.1. **A - C**. Three cladograms generated using PAUP 2.4 on an ordered character set (Table 13). **A - D**. Four cladograms generated using PAUP 2.4 on an unordered character set (Table 13). All four cladograms differ only in the relative position of the Mormonilloida (branch marked with a black spot). The numbers refer to the hypothetical ancestor (hyp. anc. = 1), the orders (2 to 11), and the branching points (12 to 20).

the first branch off the podoplean stem is the Misophrioida. The Misophrioida alone among the podoplean orders retains antennulary segment XXVI as a separate segment. The Misophrioida therefore becomes the sister group of all other podoplean orders (which have antennulary segment XXVI incorporated into a triple apical segment XXVI-XXVIII). All three trees also identify two clades within the remaining podoplean orders, a Mormonilloida-Harpacticoida-Poecilostomatoida-Siphonostomatoida-Monstrilloida clade and a Gelyelloida-Cyclopoida clade. The Mormonilloida occupies three different positions within its clade in the three trees. In the tree shown in figure 4.3.1A the Mormonilloida is the first offshoot of its clade and is the sister group of the Harpacticoida-Poecilostomatoida-Siphonostomatoida-Monstrilloida. In the tree in figure 4.3.1B the clade subdivides into two groups, one comprising the Harpacticoida and Mormonilloida, the other comprising the Poecilostomatoida, Siphonostomatoida and Monstrilloida. In the third tree (figure 4.3.1C) the Mormonilloida is the second offshoot of the clade and forms the sister group of the Poecilostomatoida-Siphonostomatoida-Monstrilloida. The branch length (= 82 steps), the consistency index (= 0.756) and the *f*-value (= 2.382) are the same for all three trees and all are fully resolved.

Unordered Characters: Many systematists prefer to use unordered character states as this does not involve any *a priori* assumptions about polarity of a transformation series from one character state to the next. An analysis using unordered character states was performed on the same matrix (Table 13), using the same options as in the previous analysis.

Four trees were generated by this analysis, three of which have the same topology as in figure 4.3.1A-C. The fourth tree also differs only in the position of the Mormonilloida. In this tree (figure 4.3.1D) the Mormonilloida is placed as the second offshoot of the podoplean lineage and it forms the sister group of the other two clades. The statistics for the trees generated by the unordered analysis are the same as for the ordered analysis: branch length = 82 steps and consistency index = 0.756.

ii) Interpretation of Trees Generated by PAUP.

The tree illustrated in figure 4.3.1A will be analysed in detail by examination of the lists of apomorphies and character state changes generated during the PAUP analysis. Forty of the 54 characters show a 100 per cent consistency, i.e. they change only once from state 0 to state 1, or twice from 0 to 1 and from 1 to 2 (if it exists in three states). Changes in the remaining 14 characters are listed in Table 14.

There are 17 individual cases of character state reversal, eight of which also constitute four cases of convergence. The following character state reversals are shown as occurring:

Character 11: male antennulary segment XXIII becomes unfused from double segment XXI-XXII in the Harpacticoida.

Character 12: male antennulary segments XIX and XX become unfused in the Calanoida.

Character 13: male antennulary segments XXIV and XXV become unfused convergently in the Misophrioida and in the Harpacticoida.

Character 17: antennary exopodal segments IX and X become unfused in the Mormonilloida.

Character 18: coxal seta on antenna regained convergently in Calanoida and Cyclopoida.

Character 19: antennary endopodal segments III and IV become unfused in the Calanoida.

Character 21: outer seta on basis of maxillule regained in Harpacticoida.

Character 29: praecoxal seta on maxilliped regained in Harpacticoida.

Character 30: third seta on basis of maxilliped regained in Mormonilloida.

Character 39: second seta on second endopodal segment of first swimming leg regained in Siphonostomatoida.

Character 46: inner coxal seta on female fifth leg regained convergently in Calanoida and Cyclopoida.

Table 14. Changes in characters with less than 100 per cent consistency in tree figured in 4.3.1A

Character No.	States	Branch	Convergence	Reversal
11	0 – 1	18 – 17		
	1 – 0	15 – Harpacticoida		+
12	0 – 1	Hypanc – 20		
	1 – 0	19 – Calanoida		+
13	0 – 1	20 – 19		
	1 – 0	15 – Harpacticoida	+	+
	1 – 0	18 – Misophrioida	+	+
15	0 – 1	17 – 13	+	
	0 – 1	18 – Misophrioida	+	
17	0 – 1	19 – 18		
	1 – 0	16 – Mormonilloida		+
18	0 – 1	Hypanc – 20		
	1 – 0	13 – Cyclopoida	+	+
	1 – 0	19 – Calanoida	+	+
19	0 – 1	Hypanc – 20		
	1 – 0	19 – Calanoida		+
21	0 – 1	20 – 19		
	1 – 2	18 – 17		
	2 – 1	15 – Harpacticoida		+
29	0 – 1	18 – 17	+	
	1 – 0	15 – Harpacticoida		+
	0 – 1	20 – Platycopioida	+	
30	0 – 1	18 – 17	+	
	1 – 2	12 – Siphonostomatoida		
	1 – 0	16 – Mormonilloida		+
	0 – 1	20 – Platycopioida	+	
39	0 – 1	17 – 16		
	1 – 0	12 – Siphonostomatoida		+
	1 – 2	16 – Mormonilloida		
46	0 – 1	Hypanc – 20		
	1 – 0	13 – Cyclopoida	+	+
	1 – 0	19 – Calanoida	+	+
53	0 – 1	Hypanc – 20		
	1 – 0	13 – Cyclopoida	+	+
	1 – 0	19 – Calanoida	+	+
54	0 – 1	19 – 18		
	1 – 0	15 – Harpacticoida		+

Character 53: inner coxal seta on male fifth leg regained convergently in Calanoida and Cyclopoida.

Character 54: seta *b* on exopod of male fifth leg regained in Harpacticoida.

This tree (and the other three trees) contains a significant number of character reversals which would necessitate the unfusing of segments in descendants of ancestors with fused segments, as well as the reappearance of setation elements which were absent in ancestors. We have examined each of these thirteen characters in the search for morphological evidence which would confirm that a reversal had taken place. The reversal of character 17, for example, involves the secondary separation of two previously fused segments in the antennary exopod. In all taxa in which these segments are fused (Misophrioida, Harpacticoida and Gelyelloida) all 4 setae are located around the apex of the double IX-X segment (see figures 2.3.6A, 2.4.7A-B and 2.7.2C) indicating that the single seta originally belonging to segment IX has migrated distally. It would therefore be reasonable to expect that if the separation of segments IX and X in the Mormonilloida resulted from the reversal of a fusion present in an ancestral form, then segment IX would be unarmed and segment X carry 4 setae. This is not the case (figure 2.6.5A), segments IX and X carry 1 and 3 setae respectively, as in the ancestral condition. We interpret this as evidence that the presence of separate segments in the Mormonilloida represents the retained ancestral condition.

Loss of Antennary Coxal Seta: Close examination of a reversal in a setation character is also instructive. The derived state of character 18 is the loss of the coxal seta on the antenna and is shared by all orders except the Calanoida and Cyclopoida. The Monstrilloida have no antenna and cannot be scored. The presence of the coxal seta in two of the 10 taxa is treated as a convergent reversal by the PAUP analysis. The tree indicates that the coxal seta was lost at a point on the lineage between the hypothetical ancestral stock of the Copepoda and the divergence of the Platycopioida. It was then regained independently in the Calanoida and Cyclopoida. For a state present in only two taxa this is the most probable outcome for any analysis that adopts the criterion that the best tree is the shortest (= most parsimonious) tree. We would place a different interpretation on the distribution of this character state, based on evidence from ontogeny. Up to 3 coxal setae are present on the antenna in the nauplii of many of the orders which lack the coxal seta in the adult. The adult coxal seta is presumably homologous with one of the coxal gnathobasic setae of the nauplius but it is not possible, at present, to determine which. In all planktotrophic copepod nauplii the antennary coxal seta (or setae) forms the primary feeding gnathobase, acting to push food particles beneath the labrum into the mouth. The coxal gnathobasic seta is present in those members of the Poecilostomatoida that possess planktotrophic nauplii, such as the Ergasilidae (figure 2.10.24C-D), even though it is absent in the adults. This seta is also present in the planktotrophic nauplii of the Calanoida, Harpacticoida, Cyclopoida and Poecilostomatoida. It is absent in the lecithotrophic nauplii of the Misophrioida (Gurney, 1933a) and in the highly specialised nauplius of the Monstrilloida (Malaquin, 1901). The nauplius stages of the Platycopioida, Mormonilloida and Gelyelloida are unknown. The appearance of this seta early in ontogeny confirms that its presence can be treated as an ancestral character state. The tree generated in the PAUP analysis treats the adult coxal seta as being regained independently in these two orders, and an explanation involving heterochrony could be advanced that makes this plausible. We prefer a different interpretation, namely that the coxal seta has been retained in adult Calanoida and Cyclopoida and lost in all other orders. This is less parsimonious since it postulates a greater number of evolutionary events (= losses of the seta) compared to losing it once then regaining it twice only, but has more supporting evidence. We know that this seta is readily lost because it disappears during the ontogeny of many harpacticoids, cyclopoids and poecilostomatoids, and has been entirely lost in the Misophrioida, with its non-feeding lecithotrophic nauplii. It may well be lost in all lecithotrophic nauplii because their feeding strategy does not require an antennary gnathobase. It is noteworthy here that the first lecithotrophic nauplius discovered in the Harpacticoida, a species of *Pseudotachidius* Scott, lacks the gnathobasic seta (Dahms, 1989b). The coxal seta in adults is not modified as a gnathobasic structure but a typical plumose seta. This suggests that its retention in adults does not result from a heterochronic (neotenic) event, since it differs in both form and function from the naupliar seta.

Relict Characters: The disjunct distribution of some plesiomorphic character states through the orders of copepods suggested to us that drawing an analogy with the biogeographical concept of relict species might provide some insight. Relict species can be defined as 'persistent remnants of formerly widespread taxa existing in restricted areas or habitats'. The coxal seta on the antenna of calanoids and cyclopoids is a good example of what we consider to be a relict character. It has a disjunct and restricted distribution through taxonomic space (according to the phylogenies illustrated in figure 4.3.1A-D) and ontogenetic criteria suggest that it was formerly more widely distributed. The antennary coxal seta is a particularly good example of a relict character because there is supporting ontogenetic evidence for our interpretation but it is possible to identify several other characters, for example, the inner coxal setae on the fifth legs of both males and females, that have a similarly disjunct distribution, occurring only in the Calanoida and Cyclopoida. Using the analogy with relict species we would interpret these as relict characters - representing previously widespread characters that are now found in a small number of phylogenetically disjunct taxa. This analogy can be extended by the implication that the disjunct distribution is generated by extinction (of intermediate ancestral forms) just as species become relict by extinction in intermediate geographical areas. The description of character distributions in taxonomic space as disjunct is applicable at finer, intraordinal, scales since these inner coxal setae on the fifth legs are retained in only a tiny minority of genera in both the Calanoida and Cyclopoida. The identical distribution of these three relict characters in taxonomic space is an analogous phenomenon to the co-occurrence of relict species in a relict fauna or flora, and requires explanation. Parsimony based techniques seem to be unable to provide this explanation since the cost (in terms of branch lengths) of losing characters repeatedly is always likely to be greater than the cost of regaining the ancestral state only twice.

Morphological Evidence: Detailed study of all these postulated character state reversals (Table 14) revealed no morphological evidence that any such reversals have taken place. In many cases our studies have exposed evidence to the contrary - evidence that indicates a different evolutionary scheme of relationships. It is perhaps, necessary to test the assumption that if a reversal had occurred there would be some morphological or anatomical evidence of this event. Let us examine the presence of a geniculation in male antennules (= character 9). The male antennules of the Platycopioida lack a geniculation between ancestral segments XX and XXI, and this character state was also attributed to the hypothetical ancestor. Poecilostomatoids also lack a geniculation, however, study of the intrinsic musculature of the sexually dimorphic antennule of *Oncaea* revealed a modified muscular pattern typical of geniculate antennules. This apparent character state reversal (returning to the ancestral non-geniculate state) is not valid since the poecilostomatoid state is secondary, rather than a return to the primary ancestral condition. The poecilostomatoid antennule was therefore scored as possessing a modified geniculation in the character matrix (Table 13). This example strongly supports the contention that there would be morphological evidence if a reversal had occurred.

Another possible example of character reversal is the change from a genital double somite back to separate genital and first abdominal somites in females of the Cancrincolidae (see Fiers, 1990 and chapter 3.16). In this case there was good morphological evidence to indicate that the so-called reversal had been brought about by a heterochronic event, post-displacement, and that the secondary separation of these two somites represented a condition that was not homologous with the primary separation of the ancestral copepod. Again, the evidence indicated that this also does not constitute a case of character reversal.

In our detailed study of the characters exhibited by the most primitive representatives of every order we have concentrated mainly on identifying homologous structures and charting their distribution patterns at higher taxonomic levels. Although loss and redevelopment of characters are documented at the specific level (cf. Ferrari, 1988a,b) our studies have failed to reveal any evidence of character reversals, except the secondary loss of novel structures, at ordinal level and above. Alternative interpretations based on genetic switch mechanisms that can make characters disappear in an ancestral form and then reappear in a descendant suffer because of lack of supporting evidence. Almost anything is theoretically possible but where is the evidence for such mechanisms? Our analysis indicates that the major evolutionary changes involve fusion and loss of body somites and of appendage segments, and loss of setation elements. In summary, evolution within the Copepoda has proceeded primarily by oligomerization (see Boxshall et al., 1984) and character reversal appears to be an extremely rare event.

b. Phylogenetic Analysis Not Using Parsimony

i) Parsimony versus Homology

In a contribution to the workshop on The Evolution of Crustacea organised by J.-O. Strømberg and E. Dahl and held at Kristineberg Marine Laboratory in Sweden during September 1990 we discussed the relative importance of homology and parsimony in the construction of evolutionary trees (Boxshall & Huys, in press). Although these criteria should be complementary we emphasised that, in any phylogenetic study, computer analysis and the construction of phylogenies are secondary processes - the primary process being the production of the character matrix. The key criterion in the production of the matrix is not parsimony but homology. Only homologous derived character states can be used to construct phylogenies and it is clear that the failure to devote sufficient attention to homology lies at the root of many of the new phylogenetic schemes that appear and then vanish with great rapidity. In order to improve the resolution and robustness of our phylogenies it is vital to improve the quality of the character sets that are used in phylogenetic studies and this can only be achieved by adopting a new attitude towards homology. We believe that the ultimate goal should be to make a positive statement on the homology of every character and character states in the data matrix.

The identification of homologous characters and character states is often difficult. Convergent evolution seems widespread amongst the arthropods in particular and exacerbates this problem. The concept of homology, as espoused by the comparative anatomists in the nineteenth century, had two central components: it described the relationship between structures that correspond in relative position and that arise from similar precursors in embryonic development. Right from its origin there has been a developmental or ontogenetic component to the concept of homology and this remains important. Boxshall & Huys (1989) argued that a simple positional-embryological definition of homology was inadequate because apparently homologous end products could arise by non-homologous developmental processes. Ferrari (1988b) also produced evidence of developmental convergence in which apparently homologous adult segmentation patterns in copepod swimming legs resulted from non-homologous developmental processes.

The advent of evolutionary theory provided the third component in the definition of homology, namely that homologous structures are derived by common ancestry. Patterns of common ancestry are best determined by cladistic analysis in which the primary criterion is parsimony. This creates the situation where homology and parsimony can come into conflict. The character matrix is constructed using homologous character states identified by comparative positional-embryological criteria and in the absence of evidence indicating the involvement of non-homologous developmental processes. This matrix is then subjected to a parsimony-based analysis which may categorise character states as convergent or resulting from reversal solely on the basis of the pattern of common ancestry (= the tree) it generates. Parsimony can therefore act as the ultimate determinant of whether two character states are homologous or not, irrespective of whether supporting morphological evidence exists.

In theory there should be no conflict between homology and parsimony but trees generated by parsimony are often described as 'counter-intuitive'. We interpret this phrase as meaning 'there is no morphological evidence to support the categorisation of certain characters as either convergent or the result of character reversal but if that is what the computer says I guess it must be right'. We believe such conflict results from the lack of attention to the development of ideas on homology and to criteria for determining homology. In this study we have concentrated on homology but the failure of the parsimony-based analysis to provide a system of phylogenetic relationships that does not require the acceptance of hypotheses of convergence and evolutionary reversal for which there is absolutely no tangible evidence leads us to conclude that the way in which the concept of homology is used in the construction of the character matrix for a PAUP analysis still lacks the sophistication necessary to accommodate the subtleties of evolutionary history, at least as far as copepods and other crustaceans are concerned.

ii) A New Phylogeny for the Copepoda.

We propose a new scheme of phylogenetic relationships for the copepod orders based on the morphological data and interpretations presented in chapter 2. This scheme is summarised in figure 4.3.2. What we have done in essence is to weight certain characters. In fact, we can generate this cladogram using PAUP merely by differential weighting of two characters, the segmentation of the antennary exopod and the presence of the sheath and proximal geniculation on the male antennule. It is possible to weight these characters by subdividing them into their minutest component parts and scoring each part as an independent character. Too little is known about the genetic control of morphology in copepods to say whether this approach could be valid so we have not done so. We have generated this cladogram by hand, since to present it as generated by PAUP (but using arbitrary weights) would give it an apparent but undeserved objectivity. Differential weighting of characters is controversial since it is based on the assumption that certain characters are more significant than others. We would seek to defend this assumption. Any change in the state of a character represents an evolutionary event. Equal weighting of characters is based

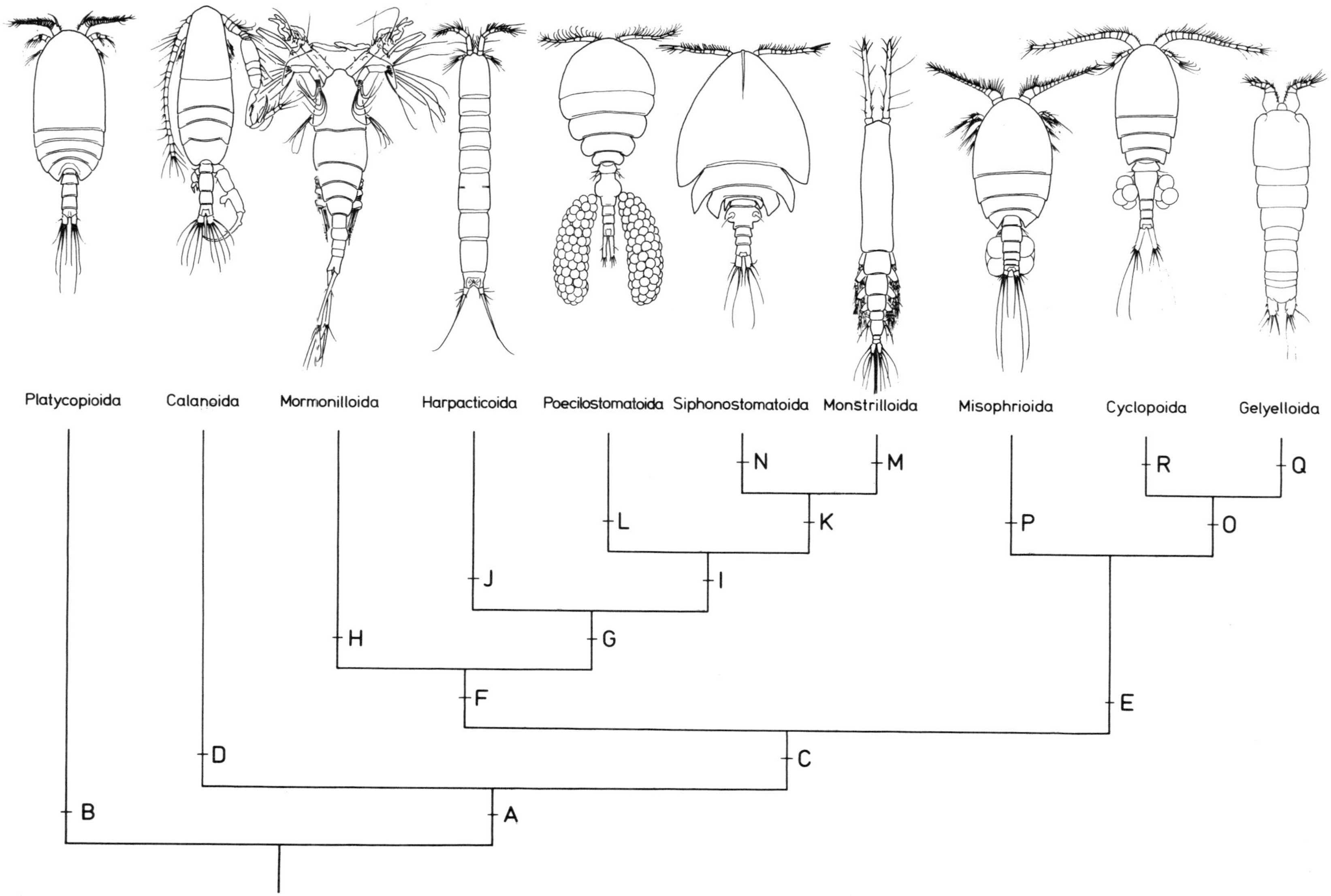

Figure 4.3.2. The proposed new phylogeny of the copepod orders. Each of the branches (clades) is identified by a capital letter. The character states defining these clades are discussed in the text.

on the assumption that each and every change in the state of any character represents a standard evolutionary event irrespective of the relative complexity or simplicity of the change. This assumption might be valid for comparing point mutations in DNA sequence data but it appears unrealistic and difficult to accept for some morphological characters. For example, it seems improbable that the evolution of a novel and complex character, such as the proximal geniculation mechanism involving the sheath on segment XV of the antennules and adjacent segments in male cyclopoids and misophrioids as well as any associated internal features such as musculature, is equivalent to the loss of a single seta, such as the coxal seta on the antenna. Loss of the coxal seta may be brought about by a point mutation in a single gene but we regard it as unlikely that the evolution of a geniculation mechanism involving several segments is controlled by a single gene. In the absence of information on the genetic control of these two characters this is also an assumption, but one that appears more reasonable as a working hypothesis. In summary we regard the gain of a novel, complex character linked to obvious anatomical features and behaviour patterns as more significant in general than the loss of a single seta, and therefore a more reliable indicator of phylogenetic affinities.

In the new phylogenetic scheme (figure 4.3.2) the Platycopioida is the first group to diverge from the main copepod lineage and the other gymnoplean order, the Calanoida, is the second. The remaining eight orders are grouped together as the Podoplea and form two clades, one comprising the Misophrioida, Cyclopoida and Gelyelloida, the other comprising the other five orders. In the first podoplean clade the Misophrioida is the first group to diverge and the Cyclopoida and Gelyelloida are terminal sister groups. In the second clade the Mormonilloida is the plesiomorphic sister group of the other four orders. Then the Harpacticoida separates, followed by the Poecilostomatoida. The Siphonostomatoida and Monstrilloida are the terminal sister groups of this clade.

Neocopepoda: The Platycopioida are an extremely primitive taxon, differing from all other copepods in an enormous number of characters. We recognise the early divergence of the Platycopioida by establishing two infraclasses of the subclass Copepoda. The infraclass Progymnoplea contains the order Platycopioida while the infraclass Neocopepoda comprises the Calanoida and all the podoplean orders. The taxon Progymnoplea was introduced by Lang (1948b) to accommodate the family Platycopiidae and is synonymous with the order Platycopioida proposed subsequently by Fosshagen in Fosshagen & Iliffe (1985). We consider this to be the appropriate name for this new infraclass. The name Neocopepoda is proposed here for the other new infraclass. The Neocopepoda (figure 4.3.2, branch A) is characterised by the following shared derived character states (synapomorphies): anterior migration of the female genital apertures (3); fusion of female antennulary segments XXVII and XXVIII (4); fusion of male antennulary segments XXVII and XXVIII (7); presence of geniculation between segments XX and XXI of male antennule (9); partial fusion of male antennulary segments XXI and XXII (10); the loss of a lobate exite on the basis of the maxillule (21); the loss of the inner spine on the basis of legs 2 to 5 (31-34); the loss of the proximal spine on the outer margin of exopodal segment 1 of legs 2 to 5 (35-38); and the loss of the inner seta (seta '*l*') on the first exopodal segment of the female fifth leg (48). The number after each character is its number in the character set given in chapter 4.2c and in the character matrix (Table 13).

Progymnoplea: The Progymnoplea (figure 4.3.2, branch B) is characterised by the retention of the plesiomorphic state of each of those characters listed as synapomorphies of the Neocopepoda and by the following shared derived character states: fusion of male antennulary segments XIX and XX (12); loss of antennary coxal seta (18); fusion of antennary endopodal segments 3 and 4 (19); loss of praecoxal seta of maxilliped (29) and presence of 2 setae on basis of maxilliped (30). The Progymnoplea is also characterised by numerous unique derived character states (autapomorphies) including: loss of armature elements on antennulary segments XVII, XIX and XXII in both sexes; fusion of antennulary segments XXIII and XXIV, and of XXV to XXVII in male; fusion of antennulary segment XVIII to double segment XIX-XX; presence of only 3 setae on antennary endopodal segment 2; fusion of antennary exopodal segments IV and V; the tripartite labrum; loss of the free first endopodal segment of the mandibular palp; the trilobate maxillulary palp; the setal formula of 4,1 for the maxillary praecoxal endites; the setal formula of 1,2,3 for the free maxillary endopod; the setal formula of 0,0,0,2 for the maxillipedal syncoxa;

the formula of 1,2,2,1,1,4 for the maxillipedal endopod; the intermaxillipedal process; the 2-segmented endopod of the first swimming leg; loss of armature of exopodal segments 1 and 2 of first swimming leg and the reduction to a tiny seta of the sixth legs in both sexes.

Podoplea: The Neocopepoda is divided into two superorders for which we use the names Gymnoplea, comprising the Calanoida alone, and the Podoplea, comprising the remaining eight orders. The superorder Podoplea (figure 4.3.2, branch C) is characterised by the following shared derived character states: tagmosis (2); complete fusion of male antennulary segments XXI and XXII (10); fusion of male antennulary segments XIX and XX (12); loss of antennary exopodal segment I (16); fusion of antennary endopodal segments 3 and 4 (19); fusion of maxillulary endopodal segments 1 and 2 (22); loss of seta 'II' on first endopodal segment of maxilla (26); presence of only 1 seta on outer margin of endopodal segment 3 of swimming legs 2-4 (40-42); loss of praecoxa of female fifth leg (44); loss of praecoxa of male fifth leg (51). The most characteristic and readily recognisable amongst these characters is the podoplean tagmosis.

Gymnoplea: The old concept of the Gymnoplea as comprising the Calanoida and Platycopioida is paraphyletic according to our new phylogenetic scheme. We, therefore, propose to restrict the concept of the Gymnoplea to accommodate only the Calanoida, which is the sole neocopepodan order retaining the ancestral gymnoplean tagmosis. The superorder Gymnoplea (figure 4.3.2, branch D) is characterised by retention of relatively plesiomorphic states of the characters listed above for the Podoplea but by few derived characters. The only shared derived character is the fusion of male antennulary segments XXIV and XXV (13). Unique derived characters include: loss of neocopepodan geniculation on left antennule only of male; loss of 2 setae (from ancestral 4 setae) on maxillary endopodal segment 4; male fifth legs asymmetrical, and armature of sixth legs lost in both sexes. All calanoids have a genital double somite in the female but this state has evolved independently in virtually every copepod order and is unreliable as an indicator of phylogenetic affinity.

MCG-Clade: The two clades within the Podoplea are not named. The Misophrioida-Cyclopoida-Gelyelloida (MCG-Clade) clade (figure 4.3.2, branch E) is characterised by the following shared derived character states (synapomorphies): the presence of a sheath on male antennulary segment XV (15); the fusion of antennary exopodal segments IX and X (17), and the loss of seta '*b*' from the exopod of the male fifth leg (54). The discovery of a carapace in some primitive cyclopoids as well as in the Misophrioida raises the possibility that its presence is an ancestral attribute of this clade. However, until the distribution of the carapace in the Cyclopinidae has been studied we will continue to treat the carapace as having evolved independently in these two orders.

MHPSM-Clade: The Mormonilloida-Harpacticoida-Poecilostomatoida-Siphonostomatoida-Monstrilloida clade (figure 4.3.2, branch F) needs a shorter name and we will use the acronym MHPSM-Clade. It is characterised by the following shared derived character states: fusion of female antennulary segment XXVI with double segment XXVII-XXVIII (5); fusion of male antennulary segment XXVI with double segment XXVII-XXVIII (8); anterior fusion of male antennulary segments IX to XI (14), and the loss of the antennary coxal seta (18). An important plesiomorphic state that is retained in this MHPSM-Clade is the full expression of the segmental boundary between segments XIII and XIV in the male antennule. This articulation forms an important part of the proximal geniculation at which the more distal part of the antennule is flexed anterolaterally.

HPSM-Clade: Within the MHPSM-Clade the first offshoot from the main lineage (figure 4.3.2, branch G) is the Mormonilloida (figure 4.3.2, branch H). The main lineage, Harpacticoida-Poecilostomatoida-Siphonostomatoida-Monstrilloida (HPSM-Clade), is characterised by the following shared derived character states: fusion of female antennulary segments IX to XII (6); fusion of antennary exopodal segments IX and X (17); presence of only 2 setae on maxillipedal basis (30); fusion of coxa and basis of female fifth legs (45), and fusion of all exopodal segments of female fifth legs (49). The first of these, fusion of female antennulary segments IX to XII, may well be a characteristic of the MHPSM-Clade because there is extensive fusion of antennulary segments in female Mormonilloida. However, because we were unable to identify the segmental homologies of the few remaining segments, this character was treated as indeterminate for the Mormonilloida.

Mormonilloida: There are numerous apomorphies for the Mormonilloida, most of them unique to this order, including: fusion of female genital apertures; sexual dimorphism in every appendage from the antennules to the caudal rami; fusion of antennary exopodal segments II and III in the female; distal migration of some antennary endopodal setae; reduced setation of swimming legs; loss of female fifth legs, and reduction of male fifth legs to 2 setae. This order is also characterised by retention of a relatively plesiomorphic state of each of the characters listed above as apomorphies for its derived sister group (characters 17, 30, 45 and 49).

PSM-Clade: The next divergence within the clade is the separation of the Harpacticoida (figure 4.3.2, branch J) from the parasitic and associated clade (figure 4.3.2, branch I) comprising the Poecilostomatoida, Siphonostomatoida and Monstrilloida (PSM-Clade). The latter is characterised by the following shared derived character states; fusion of male antennulary segments XXIV and XXV (13), fusion of maxillulary coxa, basis and rami to form an unsegmented palp (20); loss of the exite from maxillulary basis (21); loss of endopod of maxilla (25); loss of praecoxal seta on maxilliped (29); fusion of coxa and basis of male fifth legs (52), and loss of seta '*b*' on male fifth leg.

Harpacticoida: The Harpacticoida are characterised by the following derived character states: fusion of female antennulary segments II to VII, IX to XIV, XV to XVII, and XVIII to XX; fusion of male antennulary segments III to VIII, IX to XII, and XIV to XVI; presence of only 3 setae on inner margin of exopodal segment 3 of second swimming leg; presence of only 1 seta on inner margin of endopodal segment 2 of first swimming leg, and the 2-segmented maxillipedal endopod in which ancestral segment 5 is incorporated into the compound proximal segment. It is also characterised by the retention of relatively plesiomorphic states of the derived characters listed above for the PSM-Clade.

SM-Clade: The PSM-Clade divides into the Poecilostomatoida (figure 4.3.2, branch L) and the Siphonostomatoida-Monstrilloida (SM-Clade) (figure 4.3.2, branch K). The latter clade is characterised by the following shared derived character states: fusion of cephalosome and first pedigerous somite to form cephalothorax (1); loss of intercoxal sclerite between female fifth legs (43); fusion of endopod to basis forming a baseoendopod in female fifth legs (47), and loss of intercoxal sclerite between male fifth legs (50). It is possible that a baseoendopod was present in the larger PSM-Clade but without the retention of any endopodal seta on the protopod of the female fifth legs there is no evidence that the endopod is incorporated into the basis in poecilostomatoids.

Poecilostomatoida: The Poecilostomatoida is characterised by the retention of relatively plesiomorphic states of the characters listed above as derived for the SM-Clade. It is also characterised by numerous uniquely derived character states including: fusion of antennulary segments I to ?III and ?IV to XIII in both sexes; secondary loss of geniculation between segments XX and XXI of male antennule; fusion of antennary coxa and basis to form coxobasis; complete loss of antennary exopod, reduction of mandibular palp to single segment; the form of the bilobed maxillule with 3 setae on inner and 5 on outer lobes; the segmentation and structure of the sexually dimorphic maxillipeds; the presence of 1 seta on inner margin of endopodal segment 2 of first swimming leg (39); the absence of the inner seta of exopodal segment 1 of legs 1 to 4, and the armature (3 spines and 1 seta) of the fifth legs.

Siphonostomatoida: Compared to the Monstrilloida (figure 4.3.2, branch M) the Siphonostomatoida (figure 4.3.2, branch N) retains many relatively plesiomorphic character states. The Siphonostomatoida is best characterised by the form of the mandible and the presence of an oral cone. The coxal gnathobase of the mandible is drawn out to form a stylet that passes into the oral cone via lateral slits, and the mandibular palp is reduced to 2 segments with a 0,2 setal formula. The oral cone, after which the order takes its name, consists of the labrum and labium which are produced together to form a tapering tubular structure surrounding the mouth opening. Numerous other derived character states can be listed for the Siphonostomatoida including: 1-segmented antennary exopod with 3 setae; bilobed maxillule with 5 setae on inner and 3 setae on outer lobes; syncoxa of maxilliped with only 1 seta representing endites; endopod of maxilliped 4-segmented with setal formula of 2,(1,1),1 + claw.

Monstrilloida: The monstrilloids have always been easy to recognise but their phylogenetic affinities have remained obscure. The reason for this being the absence, in the adults of both sexes, of antennae, mandibles, maxillules, maxillae and maxillipeds. This order is characterised by other derived character states including: presence of only 1 seta on inner margin of endopodal segment 2 of first leg (39); fusion of female genital apertures; fusion of all segments distal to segment I of female antennule; loss of outer spine of exopodal segment 2 of swimming legs 1 to 4; fusion of exopod to baseoendopod of female fifth leg; presence of ovigerous spines on genital double somite of female, and the highly atypical naupliar and copepodid development.

CG-Clade: The first dichotomy within the MCG-Clade is the divergence of the Misophrioida (figure 4.3.2, branch P) from the Cyclopoida-Gelyelloida (CG-Clade) (figure 4.3.2, branch O). The CG-Clade is characterised by the following shared derived character states: fusion of female antennulary segment XXVI to double segment XXVII-XXVIII (5); fusion of male antennulary segment XXVI to double segment XXVII-XXVIII (8); fusion of male antennulary segment XXIII to double segment XXI-XXII (11); fusion of male antennulary segments XXIV and XXV (13); loss of outer basal seta on maxillule (21); third endopodal segment of maxillule fused to double proximal segment (23); loss of setae on inner margin of maxillulary exopod (24); loss of seta 'IV' on first endopodal segment of maxilla (27); loss of seta 'D' on basis of maxilla (28); loss of praecoxal seta on maxilliped (29), and presence of only 2 setae on basis of maxilliped (30).

Misophrioida: The Misophrioida is characterised by the loss of the antennary coxal seta (18); loss of coxal seta on fifth legs of female (46) and male (53); presence of carapace; fusion of seminal receptacles, and isolation of paired copulatory pores. It is also characterised by retention of relatively plesiomorphic states of the derived characters listed above for the CG-Clade.

Cyclopoida: Compared to its sister group, the Gelyelloida, the Cyclopoida (figure 4.3.2, branch R) retains many relatively plesiomorphic character states. It is characterised by the following uniquely derived character states: reduction of antennary exopod to small process bearing 3 setae; loss of first exopodal segment of mandible; reduction of coxal endite of maxillule to small lobe bearing 1 seta, and fusion of endopodal segments 1 and 2 to form double segment in maxilla.

Gelyelloida: The Gelyelloida (figure 4.3.2, branch Q) is characterised by the numerous derived character states including: loss of antennary coxal seta (18); reduction of sheath on segment XV of male antennule; loss of antennary exopodal segment II; fusion of exopodal segments 4 and 5 of mandible; fusion of basis and first endopodal segment of maxilla to form allobasis; gross reduction of swimming legs 1 to 3; loss of fourth swimming leg; loss of fifth swimming legs in both sexes; fusion of copulatory pores; loss of armature elements of sixth legs in male.

4.4 ECOLOGICAL RADIATION

One, admittedly subjective, test of a phylogeny for a biologist is that it should make sense according to various ecological, biogeographic and behavioural criteria. In this section we attempt to combine our new phylogenetic scheme with available data on the ecology, biogeography and behaviour of the copepod orders in order to test its explanatory power. We begin with some speculations about the ancestral copepod. Most of the phylogenetic schemes proposed in recent years for the copepods assume that the ancestor was marine and epibenthic (Kabata, 1979; Marcotte, 1982; Boxshall et al., 1984). We too envisage the ancestral copepod as a shallow-water marine form, inhabiting the sediment-water interface. It exhibited gymnoplean tagmosis, with five well developed pairs of swimming legs on the prosome, but the prosome-urosome tagma boundary lacked well defined condyles and allowed considerable flexure in all directions. This animal probably searched for particulate food along the surface of the sediment and in the base of the water column immediately above the sediment (the hyperbenthic zone). We presume that it must have been sexually dimorphic, with the male using one of its appendages for grasping the female during spermatophore transfer. We consider it most likely that the antennule was the appendage involved although it was not highly modified to perform this role.

Platycopioida: The few known species of *Platycopia* have remained in the ancestral habitat and are found in the hyperbenthic environment in shallow, neritic waters. The other two genera are monotypic and are restricted to anchialine caves. In fact, the type and only species of *Antrisocopia* and of *Nanocopia* inhabit the same cave on the Atlantic island of Bermuda (Fosshagen & Iliffe, 1988). In the course of its long evolutionary history the Platycopioida appears to have successfully invaded only one other habitat - anchialine caves.

Calanoida: The Calanoida is a large order of planktonic copepods and shows great diversity at low taxonomic levels. Members of some of the most primitive families, such as the Pseudocyclopidae and Arietellidae, typically inhabit the near-bottom hyperbenthic environment. From here the calanoids have invaded anchialine habitats, with representatives of the families Ridgewayiidae, Epacteriscidae and Boholinidae being amongst the most common members of particular anchialine cave communities. The greatest habitat shift performed by calanoids was the colonisation of the open pelagic environment. This is the largest environment on Earth and the calanoids as a group are one of the most successful, if not the most successful, of its animal inhabitants. They occur in great abundance in the epipelagic (surface to 200 metres) and mesopelagic zones (200 to 1000 metres). Here the dominant taxa are the superfamilies Megacalanoidea, Eucalanoidea and some members of the Clausocalanoidea. In the deeper bathypelagic zone (below 1,000 metres) the superfamilies Augaptiloidea and Bathypontioidea, and some families of the Clausocalanoidea, such as the Spinocalanidae, dominate. We speculate that the evolutionary doubling in number of aesthetascs on the segments of the male antennules is correlated with the colonisation of the open pelagic environment where chemical cues are of paramount importance. The superfamily Centropagoidea may have originated direct from the hyperbenthic ancestors or, more likely, from pelagic ancestors. Its members, such as the Acartiidae and Sulcanidae, are typically the dominant calanoids in neritic waters and estuaries. Some, such as the pontellids, have invaded the specialised neustonic habitat associated with the sea surface-air interface. Members of this superfamily have also successfully, and repeatedly, colonised brackish, freshwater and inland saline habitats so that several families, for example the Temoridae and the Centropagidae, have numerous neritic and freshwater representatives. By far the most successful and widespread freshwater family is the Diaptomidae, containing about 50 genera and well over 400 species (Dussart & Defaye, 1983).

Calanoids exhibit two kinds of swimming movements: slow, almost continuous swimming achieved by the anterior cephalic appendages and rapid jumping movements performed by the swimming legs. Rapid jumping is used only as part of the escape reaction and can be triggered by physical stimuli, such as vibration or changes in light intensity (Buskey et al., 1986). In the open pelagic environment the normal slow swimming movements of calanoids are adequate for feeding and generate a relatively small signal that a predator might detect. Rapid jumping movements, which generate a much larger signal, are restricted to times when an escape response has already been elicited.

Podoplea: The ancestral podoplean was epibenthic, remaining in the ancestral habitat. It exhibited the derived tagmosis, with only four pairs of well developed swimming legs on the prosome, but the prosome-urosome boundary was still relatively weakly defined permitting flexure in all directions. The typical mode of locomotion of podopleans is rapid jumping, using the four pairs of swimming legs, as described for cyclopoids by Strickler (1974). This was assumed to be the basic podoplean swimming mechanism by Boxshall (1982), however, Fosshagen & Iliffe (1988) observed that the misophrioid *Speleophria bivexilla* swam in a smooth gliding fashion when free in the water column. It is, therefore, possible that the ancestral podoplean exhibited both slow swimming, by motions of the anterior cephalic appendages, as well as rapid jumping.

The two clades within the Podoplea, the MCG-Clade and MHPSM-Clade, differ in the manner in which the male grasps the female during copulation or precopulatory mate guarding (figure 3.4.3). In the MCG-Clade the males primitively had digeniculate antennules, with a proximal geniculation mechanism that involved a sheath on segment XV, and the distal neocopepodan geniculation between segments XX and XXI. This type of antennule is adapted for clasping around the anterior and posterior surfaces of the fourth swimming legs of the female during spermatophore transfer, as observed in the Cyclopoida (Hill & Coker, 1930; Gophen, 1979; Boxshall, 1990c). The MHPSM-Clade, by comparison, is primitively characterised by a proximal geniculation on the male antennules formed by the retention of a well developed articulation between segments XIII and XIV. The distal neocopepodan geniculation is primitively present. The proximal articulation directs the distal part of the antennule more anterolaterally, producing a wider grasp and may be an adaptation to the protracted precopulatory mate guarding found in this clade, in which the male typically grasps onto the dorsal surface of the female.

Misophrioida: The most plesiomorphic order within the MCG-Clade retains the close ancestral association with the sea bed. Boxshall (1989) briefly analysed the biogeography of the known misophrioids and concluded that the group originated in the hyperbenthic habitat in the deep sea. Deep-sea hyperbenthic misophrioids exhibit a suite of highly specialised characters associated with the adoption of gorging as a feeding strategy, including a distensible midgut, exoskeletal modifications allowing prosomal swelling, loss of heart and retention of the antennary glands as the adult excretory organs (Boxshall, 1984). The loss of the nauplius eye, even in the shallow-water genus *Misophria*, was interpreted as evidence that the group originated in the deep-sea and secondarily emerged to invade shallow water. Boxshall (1989) identified two lineages within the Misophrioida, both of which have their most plesiomorphic representatives in the deep-sea hyperbenthic habitat. The *Misophria* lineage radiated to colonise shallow neritic waters and the bathypelagic zone of the oceanic water column. Secondarily a shallow-water representative colonised an anchialine cave on an island in the Palau group. All the more derived genera within the other lineage, the *Archimisophria* lineage, are found in anchialine caves, flooded lava tubes and other crevicular habitats, all on oceanic islands.

Cyclopoida: The Cyclopoida is commonly regarded as a freshwater group and it certainly has been the most successful order of copepods in freshwater. However, the primarily marine distribution of the plesiomorphic families Cyclopinidae and Oithonidae indicates that it was primitively a marine group (figure 4.4.1). The cyclopinids are closest to the ancestral cyclopoid both in the characters they exhibit and in their primarily epibenthic habit. Cyclopinids have secondarily invaded the sediment, becoming endobenthic and inhabiting the interstitial spaces between sediment particles. These interstitial cyclopinids have become vermiform and show remarkable convergence with some of the interstitial harpacticoids, such as the Paramesochridae. For example, representatives of both families have evolved the additional 'pseudosomite' just anterior to the female genital double somite (figure 3.1.1). The Oithonidae have successfully invaded the plankton. Oithonids are often numerically the most abundant family of copepods in both neritic waters and in the epipelagic of oceanic waters, but their small size greatly reduces their overall contribution to copepod biomass. They have also invaded freshwater via the estuarine route, but the number of freshwater forms is small. The main freshwater invasion was by the ancestors of the lineage comprising the Cyclopidae, Ozmanidae and Lernaeidae. We regard these three families as a monophyletic group. This clade has radiated extensively in freshwater and its members now occupy a wide range of habitats and exhibit a variety of modes of life. The Cyclopidae have colonised the open freshwater water column of lakes and other large water bodies. They are also abundant in epibenthic situations, and have colonised damp semi-terrestrial situations and subterranean habitats. One species, *Acanthocyclops spongicola* Mazepova, is a specialised associate of freshwater sponges in Lake Baikal. Some members of the Cyclopidae, in particular representatives of the subfamilies Euryteinae and Halicyclopinae, have secondarily reinvaded marine and brackish water habitats. Some of these secondarily marine cyclopids have become associates of marine invertebrate hosts, for example *Halicyclops caridophilus* Humes is found on the gills of a thallasinid decapod. This clade also contains two parasitic families, the Ozmanidae and the Lernaeidae. The close relationship between these two families can be seen in the precise configuration of the setation elements of the modified antennary endopod (figure 2.8.14C-D). The Ozmanidae is the more primitive of them since it retains digeniculate male antennules. The Ozmanidae comprises a single species that inhabits the haemocoel of a freshwater gastropod in South America. The Lernaeidae is a successful and widespread family of freshwater fish parasites.

The marine epibenthic ancestral stock of the Cyclopoida also gave rise to a lineage of associated and parasitic forms that now encompasses the families Archinotodelphyidae, Notodelphyidae,

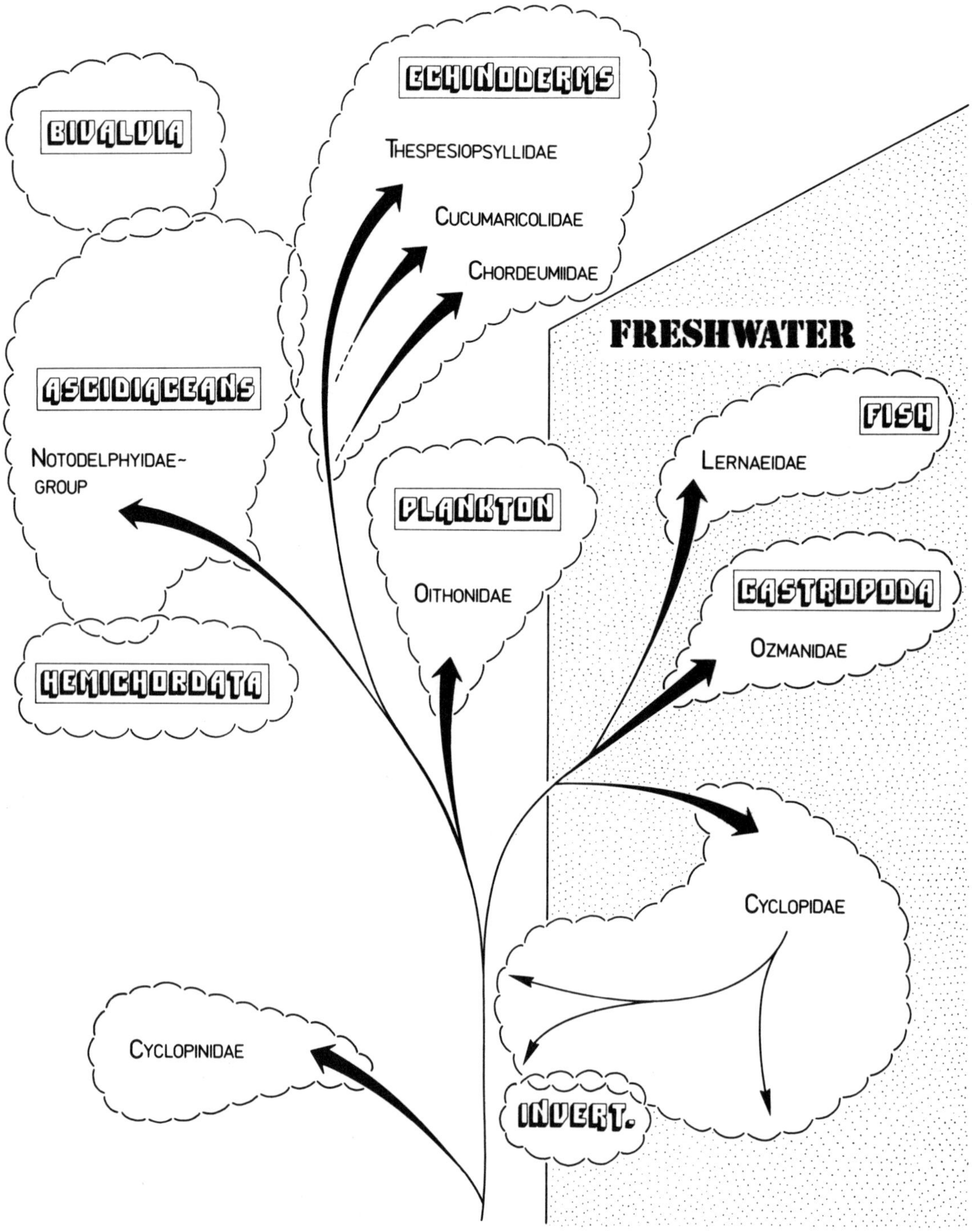

Figure 4.4.1. The ecological radiation of the Cyclopoida, showing the main habitats utilised and the dominant cyclopoid families in each. The arrows summarise the evolutionary history envisaged for the Cyclopoida from its marine epibenthic origin.

Mantridae, Thespesiopsyllidae, Ascidicolidae, Chordeumiidae and the Cucumaricolidae. This lineage is characterised by the loss of the proximal geniculation of the male antennule and by the presence of a modified distal claw on the antennary endopod. The antenna is, of course, lacking in the Thespesiopsyllidae. Members of these families utilise a variety of marine invertebrates as hosts including colonial and solitary ascidiaceans, bivalve molluscs, echinoderms and hemichordates.

Gelyelloida: Gelyelloids are a small and specialised order comprising just two species found in subterranean waters in Europe. The gelyelloids invaded freshwater independently of their sister group, the Cyclopoida, which had marine ancestors. Presumably as an adaptation to their groundwater habitat, these small copepods appear to have lost their nauplius eye and have very reduced swimming legs. The secondary reduction of the sheath on the male antennule in gelyelloids is probably correlated with the loss of the fourth legs in the female since the primary function of the sheath was to form part of a mechanism for grasping the female fourth legs during copulation.

Mormonilloida: The Mormonilloida is the first order of the large MHPSM-Clade to diverge. From its epibenthic ancestry this order has colonised the open pelagic environment in the deep mesopelagic and bathypelagic zones. Little is known about the biology of *Mormonilla* but we speculate that it also exhibits the two basic swimming modes - slow swimming using the anterior cephalic appendages, and the rapid jumping escape response. The well developed state of the antennae and the mandibular and maxillulary palps of the non-feeding adult male suggests that they might function as locomotory appendages at this stage.

Harpacticoida: The Harpacticoida is the next group to diverge within the HPSM-Clade. Harpacticoids are the dominant group of benthic copepods and have also successfully exploited an enormous variety of other habitats. They are primitively a marine epibenthic order. The most plesiomorphic clade within the Harpacticoida is the Polyarthra, a monophyletic group comprising the Longipediidae and Canuellidae. Both these families remained associated with the bottom but have planktonic nauplii. *Longipedia* is a conservative epibenthic form that also occurs off the bottom in the lower parts of the water column. The Canuellidae is a large and diverse family containing marine epibenthic species as well as forms inhabiting the deep sea down to 2,000 metres (*Intercanuella* Becker species), anchialine caves, and even associates of marine invertebrates, such as species of the genera *Sunaristes*, *Parasunaristes* and *Brianola* which are all associates of hermit crabs. The great majority of oligoarthran harpacticoids have remained in association with the sea bottom, but from their epibenthic origins they have invaded adjacent habitats including the interstitial spaces within the sediment and phytal habitats. Exploitation of phytal microhabitats has led to some obvious changes in gross morphology of the phytal specialists, for example, the dorsoventral flattening shown by the Porcellidiidae and Peltidiidae and the lateral compression shown by the Tegastidae.

Specialisation for a benthic existence has resulted in the evolution of a body form that is clearly related to sediment type. Harpacticoids inhabiting coarse sediments have exploited the interstitial spaces either by becoming progressively more vermiform in gross morphology (via a cylindrical body shape as in the Cylindropsyllidae), or by becoming smaller (as in the Paramesochridae), or both. Those inhabiting fine muddy sediments, such as the Ancorabolidae and Cerviniidae, have a spider-like habitus with long legs that project laterally and enable the animal to move over the surface of the sediment. Some larger harpacticoids, such as the Ectinosomatidae, have become endobenthic burrowers, characterised by their torpedo-shaped bodies.

There are several specialised planktonic forms within the Harpacticoida. Three families have independently colonised the marine pelagic environment, the Aegisthidae, Miraciidae and Clytemnestridae. The aegisthids are true holoplanktonic forms found in the mesopelagic and bathypelagic zones, and are characterised by adaptations, such as their extremely elongated caudal rami, that slow their rate of sinking through the water column. The miraciids are more epipelagic and some, such as *Macrosetella gracilis* (Dana), essentially exhibit a phytal surface-living biology in the epipelagic by their association with blue-green algae. The clytemnestrids are also found mainly in the epipelagic zone. Isolated members of other families have secondarily invaded the pelagic zone. The tachidiid *Euterpina acutifrons*, for example, is often abundant in shallow neritic waters

(Pugh & Boxshall, 1984). Other independent colonists of the inshore plankton include the ectinosomatid genus *Microsetella* and the thalestrid *Parathalestris croni* (Krøyer).

Harpacticoids have also radiated into freshwater. At least four separate lineages have independently invaded freshwater habitats. These four families are more or less exclusively freshwater in distribution. The plesiomorphic family Phyllognathopodidae comprises three genera, one of which (*Phyllognathopus* Mrazek) occurs in a variety of unusual microhabitats such as the leaf pools of bromeliads and the pitchers of pitcher plants. The Chappuisiidae comprises only 2 species restricted to groundwater habitats in central Europe. The Phyllognathopodidae and Chappuisiidae are primitive families and represent early but relatively unsuccessful, attempts to colonise freshwater. The Parastenocarididae contains true interstitial freshwater forms but appears to have evolved direct from a marine interstitial ancestor. It is a large and successful family, found worldwide except for New Zealand and the Caribbean Islands. The Canthocamptidae is by far the largest family of freshwater Harpacticoida. In the past this family has served as a repository for a variety of unrelated forms but the core of the family is found predominantly in freshwater. Many of the marine forms, formerly placed in the Canthocamptidae, should be transferred to other families such as the Orthopsyllidae. The ancestors of the Canthocamptidae appear to have been marine epibenthic and probably invaded freshwater via estuarine habitats. The affinities of primitive canthocamptids, such as *Mesochra* Lilljeborg, for brackish waters is in accordance with this scenario. The Canthocamptidae share a sister group relationship with the interstitial cylindropsyllids which are exclusively marine. There are numerous isolated examples of representatives of other, primarily marine, families secondarily invading freshwater, including the Ameiridae, Cletodidae, Diosaccidae, Ectinosomatidae, Harpacticidae, Laophontidae and Thalestridae.

Significant numbers of harpacticoids have entered into loose associations with an extensive range of host organisms and several have become true parasites. Most are not highly transformed in gross morphology. As was the case for the freshwater inhabiting harpacticoids there is no single lineage containing the associated forms. Harpacticoids are well adapted to benthic surface living and they appear to have spread onto the surface of available hosts almost as a horizontal extension of their ancestral mode of life. In particular several groups of phytal-living species also contain associates of sessile host groups such as the cnidarians and sponges. Members of the Donsiellinae are associated with the burrows of crustaceans and teredinid molluscs in submerged wood (Hicks, 1988). Other harpacticoids are found in association with echinoderms (e.g. *Namakosiramia* Ho & Perkins). Several other families have independently become associated with crustaceans, including the Cancrincolidae (which inhabit the gill chambers of land crabs), some members of the Canuellidae (which occupy hermit crab shells), and some species of the canthocamptid *Attheyella* Brady (which are associated with freshwater crayfish). Harpacticoids are also found in association with vertebrate hosts. The monotypic family Balaenophilidae inhabits the baleen plates of baleen whales and the tisbid genus *Neoscutellidium* Zwerner occurs on the gills of a teleost fish. Other tisbids, members of the subfamily Cholidyinae, have a more highly modified morphology adapted for life on their cephalopod mollusc hosts.

PSM-Clade: Poecilostomatoids, siphonostomatoids and monstrilloids can all be regarded as displaying an 'epibenthic' mode of life but in association with a variety of animal surfaces rather than the sediment surface. The origin of this clade and its association with metazoan hosts must date back at least to the Lower Cretaceous, since *Kabatarina* is known from that period, but may belong back in the Palaeozoic. Their cephalosomic appendages are adapted for holding onto, and for feeding on, surfaces. Their mouthparts typically have reduced palps since they no longer generate water currents for feeding, but retain functional arthrites or endites adapted for scraping or piercing the surface of the host.

Poecilostomatoida: The origin of the Poecilostomatoida is closely linked with a change in mate grasping behaviour. The ancestral behaviour pattern of the male using its geniculate antennules to hold the female during copulation is lost. Instead the male uses its maxillipeds for this purpose. This behavioural shift has resulted in the marked sexual dimorphism in the maxillipeds expressed in all known members of the order. The first offshoot of the main poecilostomatoid lineage was the Erebonasteridae. This plesiomorphic family is characterised by the retention of a 1-segmented mandibular palp and of the ancestral setation of appendages such as the maxillae and maxillipeds,

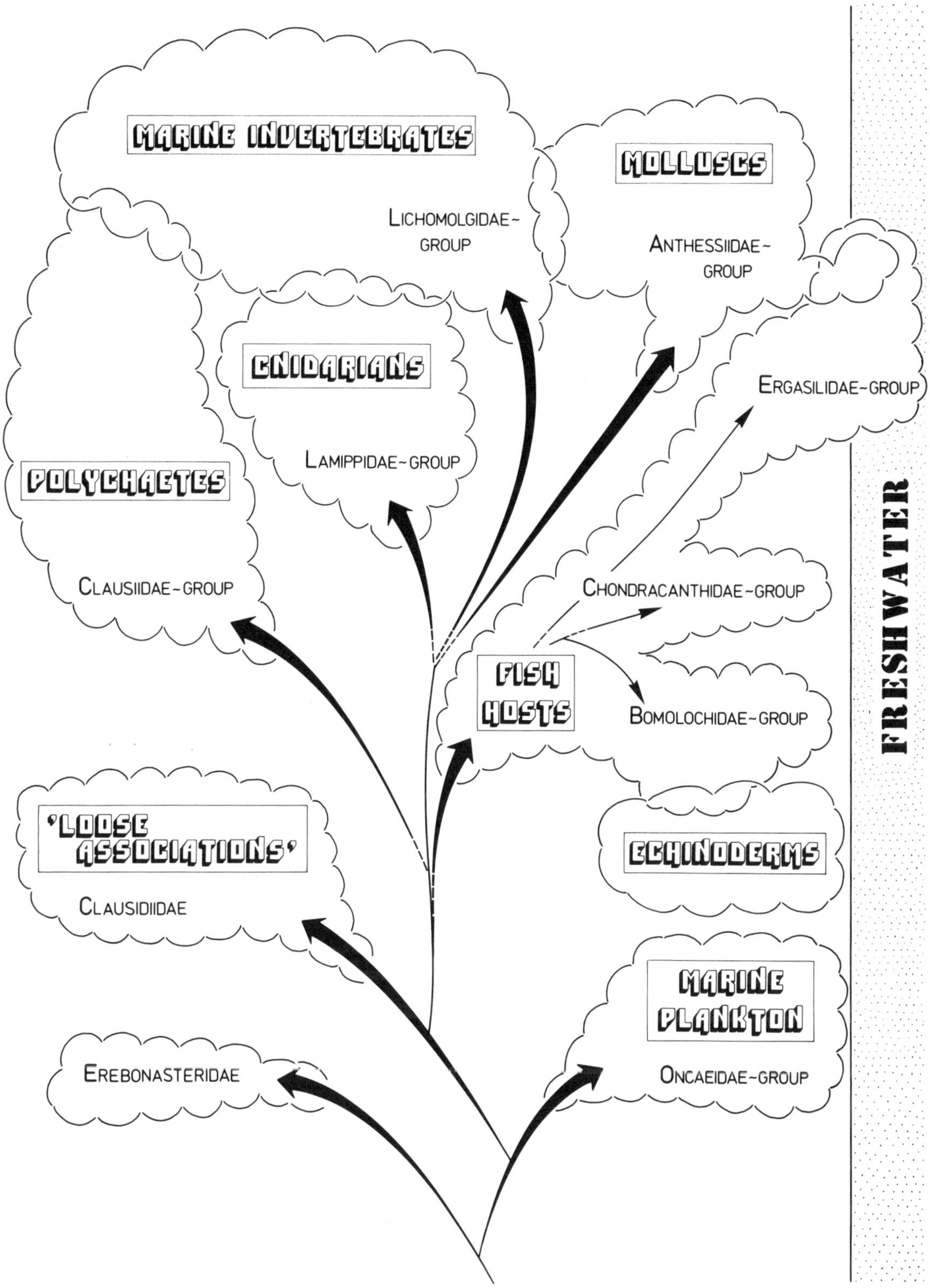

Figure 4.4.2. The ecological radiation of the Poecilostomatoida, showing the main habitats utilised and an indication of the main family groups found in each.

and by the unique arrangement of the female genital apparatus with its paired ventral copulatory pores. The erebonasterids are associates of deep-sea invertebrates.

An early habitat shift was the colonisation of the open water pelagic environment by families such as the Corycaeidae, Oncaeidae, Paralubbockiidae, Sapphirinidae and Urocopiidae. These families probably represent two different lineages, the Oncaeidae-Paralubbockiidae and Corycaeidae-Sapphirinidae-Urocopiidae, which entered the plankton independently. The Oncaeidae is a widespread family of typically small species which are abundant at all depths in the water column, especially in subtropical and tropical waters. The Sapphirinidae is a specialist epipelagic family which has adopted transparency as its primary strategy for predator avoidance. The Sapphirinidae and Corycaeidae both have elaborate nauplius eyes with well developed cuticular lenses, confirming their link with the well lit surface waters. These poecilostomatoids are caught in plankton nets and have been regarded as free-living but the little we know of their biology suggests that they are all associates of gelatinous zooplankton, such as appendicularians and salps.

The great majority of poecilostomatoids live in association with invertebrate hosts (figure 4.4.2) but about ten families occur on fish hosts. The least modified of these families, such as the Bomolochidae, tend to occupy sheltered microhabitats on the fish, including the nasal cavities, mouth, gills, and orbits. A few occur on the outer body surface. More modified forms, such as the chondracanthids, occupy the same kinds of microhabitats. Members of the Philichthyidae have become internal parasites and can be found in subcutaneous spaces in the canals of the lateral line system and in the skull bones of teleost fish. Amongst the fish parasites is the Ergasilidae which, together with the closely related Vaigamidae, represents the only major invasion of fresh water by the Poecilostomatoida. Only the adult females of these forms are parasites, typically of fish but also on fresh and brackish-water bivalve molluscs. The developmental stages and adult males are free-living. About three quarters of the known ergasilids are found in freshwater habitats, with the other quarter in brackish or coastal marine habitats. The family Taeniacanthidae is remarkable in utilising both vertebrate and invertebrate hosts. It comprises two groups of genera, one occurring on echinoderms and the other on fish.

The plesiomorphic family Clausidiidae occupies a pivotal position near the base of the phylogenetic tree of the order. This family retains a large number of plesiomorphic character states and its species are typically loosely associated with a wide range of host groups. Adaptive radiation from a clausidiid-like ancestor has generated numerous host-related lineages which have yet to be resolved. Most of the families are external associates, moving and feeding over the surface of their hosts, but some are internal parasites. The Mytilicolidae, for example, comprises species that inhabit the alimentary canal of their bivalve mollusc hosts, and members of the Lamippidae are often found inside the canals of colonial cnidarians.

Siphonostomatoida: Siphonostomatoids are all associates or parasites. They utilise a wide range of invertebrate and vertebrate hosts (figure 4.4.3). The families parasitic on vertebrates appear to form a monophyletic group characterised by the loss of the mandibular palp. Another widely distributed character shared by many of these families is the possession, by the second to fourth or fifth copepodid (= chalimus) stages, of a frontal filament that serves to temporarily attach the larva to its host. Excluding the Lernaeopodidae and the closely related Sphyriidae, the families parasitic on vertebrates also share the loss of the antennary exopod and the apomorphic uniseriate type of egg sac in which discoid eggs are tightly packed to form a cylindrical egg string. The fish parasites utilise a variety of microhabitats on their hosts. Many occur on the external body surface and fins, or on the gills. Others are found in the mouth, nostrils, cloaca and eyes. Some, typically large forms, have become mesoparasitic and live with their head end embedded in the host, acting as an anchor. A few, such as the pennellid *Peroderma* Heller, are internal parasites living deep within the body musculature of the host.

The lineage of vertebrate parasites contains the only successful colonists of freshwater within the order (figure 4.4.3). A group of lernaeopodid genera related to *Salmincola* Wilson, as identified in the phylogenetic scheme of Kabata (1979), is widely distributed on freshwater fish, particularly in the northern hemisphere. Virtually all other siphonostomatoids are marine, with rare exceptions such as *Caligus lacustris* Steenstrup & Lütken which is a common parasite of freshwater fish in Europe and the U.S.S.R.

The radiation of siphonostomatoids that utilise invertebrate hosts is poorly resolved. Several of

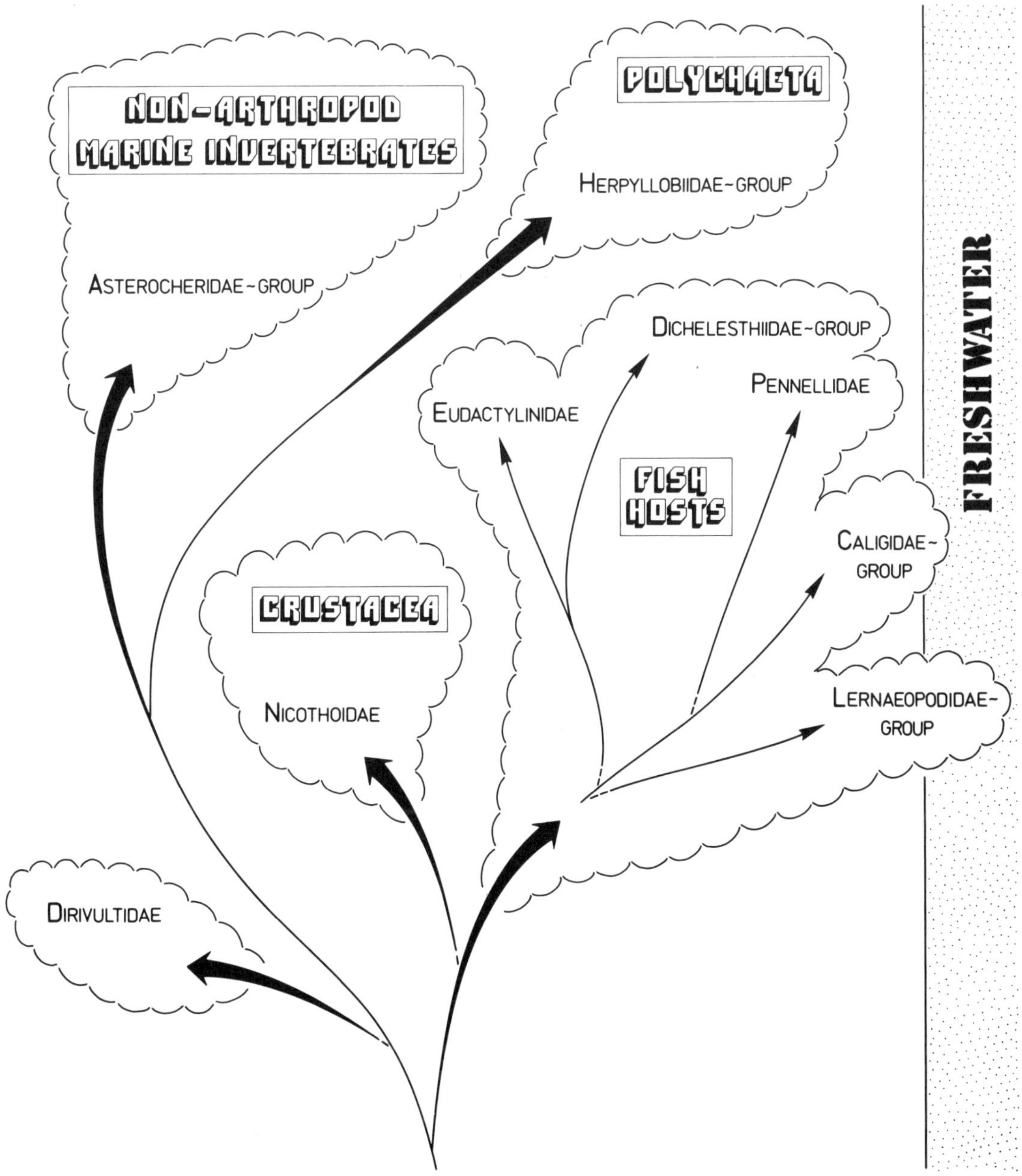

Figure 4.4.3 The ecological radiation of the Siphonostomatoida, showing the main habitats (host groups) utilised and an indication of the family groups or families found in each.

the plesiomorphic families, such as the Dirivultidae and Ecbathyriontidae, occur in the deep-sea which may have served as a refuge for these ancient forms. The Asterocheridae and its relatives have exploited a wide range of invertebrate phyla as hosts. These siphonostomatoids occupy a variety of microhabitats on the host; asterocherids associated with sponges, for example, typically inhabit the internal canal system of the sponge. Those associated with sea urchins typically move freely over the external surface of the host, between the protective spines, although some (e.g. *Codoba* Heegaard) are found within cysts inside the echinoderm host. The Nicothoidae are external parasites of other crustaceans. Some are found on the outer surface of their hosts, others occur under the carapace fold or in the marsupium. A considerable number of these are approximately the same size and shape as the host's eggs and may well be egg mimics. The Nicothoidae is the only siphonostomatoid family found on invertebrate hosts to have a frontal filament attaching the larva to its host. Some siphonostomatoids are found free in marine plankton in shallow water, such as *Pontoeciella* Giesbrecht, or in the deep sea, such as *Hyalopontius* (Boxshall, 1979). These forms probably attach temporarily to planktonic hosts to feed and then drop off after feeding.

The Herpyllobiidae is a small family of highly transformed parasites found on marine polychaete hosts. The adult female body comprises two unsegmented parts, an endosoma which is embedded in the host, and an ectosoma which protrudes outside the host and bears the genital apertures. Herpyllobiids have no appendages in the adult female and are amongst the most highly derived of all copepods.

Monstrilloida: The monstrilloids have endoparasitic larval stages and free-living, non-feeding adults. The known hosts include polychaete worms and prosobranch molluscs. The order comprises a single family, all exhibiting a similar life cycle. They presumably evolved from an ancestral form that had creeping nauplii which were associated with the surface of marine invertebrates.

Summary: The long and intricate evolutionary history of the Copepoda is summarised in figure 4.4.4. This portrays the phylogenetic relationships between the orders against a background of their habitat exploitation. Every order had its origin in the marine epibenthic environment, providing further evidence that the ancestral copepod lived there. The Calanoida exploited the pelagic environment to the full but became so well adapted for that mode of life that it became an evolutionary cul-de-sac. The Misophrioida-Cyclopoida-Gelyelloida lineage exploits a range of habitats but its greatest success is represented by the radiation of the cyclopoids in fresh water. The nearest the Misophrioida got to terrestrial and freshwater habitats is the anchialine caves which they have successfully colonised. The Gelyelloida are restricted to the subterranean freshwater habitat. The Mormonilloida-Harpacticoida-Poecilostomatoida-Siphonostomatoida-Monstrilloida lineage is the dominant podoplean group both in terms of diversity and range of habitats utilised. It culminates in the explosive radiation of the Poecilostomatoida-Siphonostomatoida-Monstrilloida clade into parasitic and associated lifestyles. This clade may well be the most diverse and successful of all the copepod groups.

4.5 NEW CLASSIFICATION OF THE COPEPODA

a. Perspectives

We hope that the ideas on copepod evolution proposed here represent an advance on existing schemes. The most important take-home message of this book is the reminder of the central position of homology in phylogenetic studies. Without accurate determination of the homology of character states the construction of a character matrix on which further analysis is based is impossible. The rush to generate phylogenies using parsimony based techniques has resulted in neglect of the concept of homology. In particular, there have been few attempts to extend the concept of homology to include developmental processes (Ferrari, 1988b; Boxshall & Huys, 1989). We have attempted to apply a strict criterion to the characters used in this study of copepod phylogeny: if we were unable to make a positive statement on the homology of characters or character states then these were discarded from subsequent analysis. This rigorous approach to homology should be applied to all taxa not just to copepods. Despite this increased attention to the determination of the homology of all characters states used in the matrix we were still unable

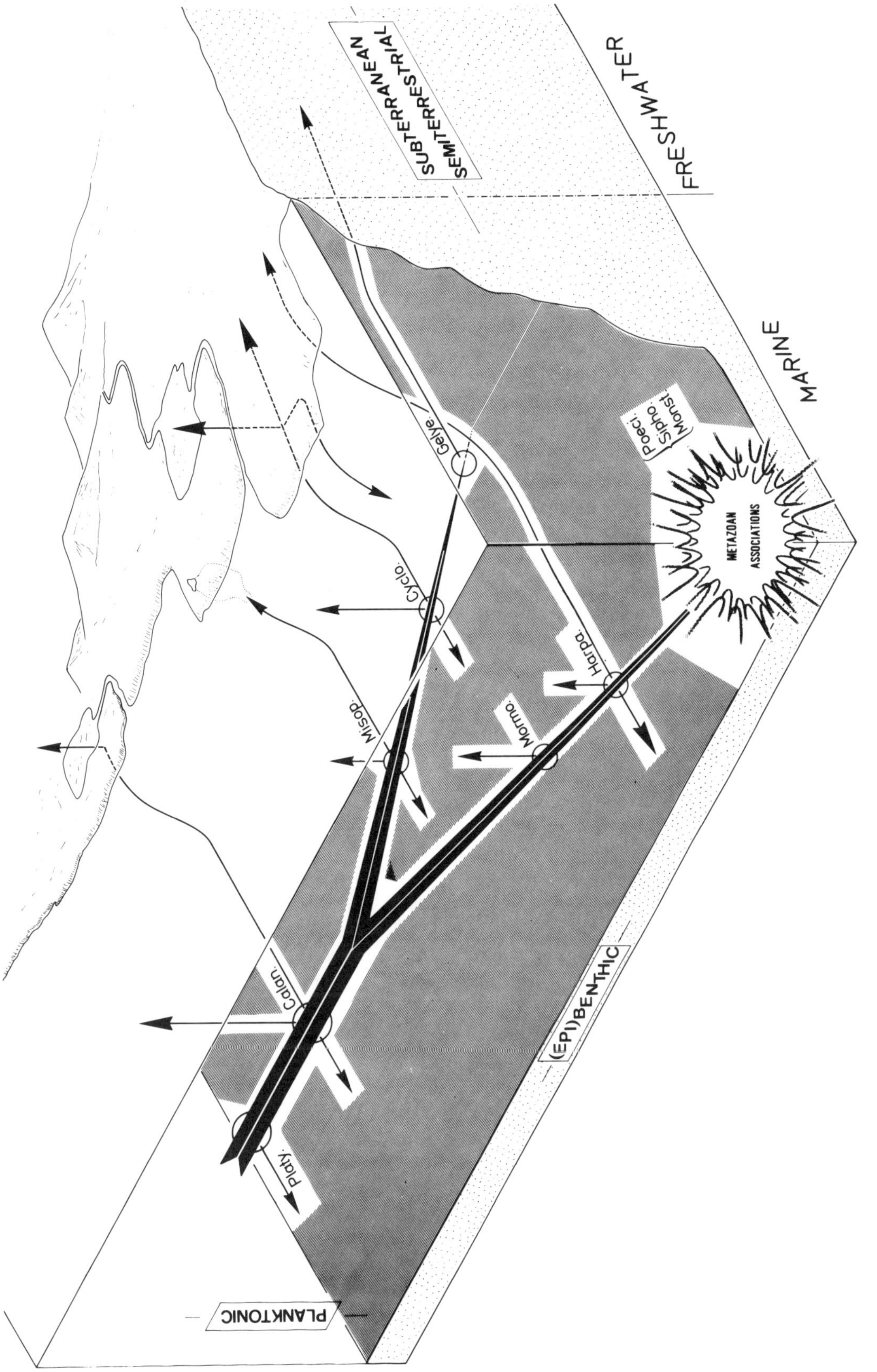

Figure 4.4.4. Schematic representation of the evolutionary history of habitat exploitation by copepods. The horizontal plane represents the ancestral epibenthic habitat that is retained in at least some representatives of most orders. The vertical arrows indicate independent colonisations of the water column and pelagic environment, in both marine and freshwater habitats.

to generate a parsimony based phylogenetic scheme that, in our opinion, accurately reflected the subtleties of the evolutionary history of the group. This failure of parsimony based analysis may well be a consequence of our exclusion of numerous characters for which there was insufficient data to enable the accurate assessment of their homology. We do not, however, consider that merely presenting the PAUP generated cladograms (figure 4.3.1A-D) represents the best estimate of relationships with the data available. Accepting any one of these cladograms forces us to accept changes in character states and into making assumptions for which there is no morphological evidence. This would be misleading and in no way represents our view on copepod evolution, so we have presented a new scheme of relationships (figure 4.3.2) based on our subjective consideration of the characters involved. This represents our current working hypothesis.

Focusing attention on the determination of homology will greatly improve the quality of character sets used in phylogenetic analysis. The raw data of any phylogenetic analysis are the setal and segment counts in taxonomic descriptions. These must be based on accurate observation and attention to fine detail is an essential part of this process. Taxonomic descriptions can serve a number of purposes and we consider the comments made by von Vaupel Klein in the 21st issue of Monoculus, the newsletter of the World Association of Copepodologists, very pertinent here. He suggested that descriptions of the type species of genera should be as detailed and comprehensive as possible, so that they may then be used for wider phylogenetic studies, but recognised that descriptions separating congeners could be constructed on an essentially comparative basis.

We urge everyone involved in copepod taxonomy to try to identify the segmental homologies of the limbs they are describing rather than just presenting simple segment counts, and to invest similar care in their enumeration of setation patterns. If this is done the full phylogenetic significance of their work will be more apparent. Similarly the adoption of the standard terminology of the limbs, limb segments and setation formulae presented in chapter 1.5 will greatly facilitate comparative studies both within the Copepoda and between copepods and other crustacean taxa. We recognise that the reduction of the limbs in the parasitic groups, particularly the Poecilostomatoida and Siphonostomatoida, can present a problem in establishing segmental homologies so we have illustrated and compared basic mouthpart structure in these two orders (figure 4.5.1).

Future studies of copepod phylogeny will undoubtedly centre around the problem of assessing homology. The ultimate goal will be to develop criteria for the identification of each and every seta or spine on every segment of all limbs. These will have to be given unambiguous names. The key to this difficult task lies in studies of ontogeny. Tracking individual setation elements through successive moults ensures that homology can be determined vertically through the life cycle stages and would help considerably with the determination of homology horizontally, between different taxa. Observations made on individuals in the process of moulting are particularly valuable here because novel elements, without a precursor at the preceding stage, can readily be identified. It is also important to compare males and females since female morphology can often be helpful in elucidating the homologies of male secondary sexual characters.

There are many gaps in our knowledge of copepods, especially their biology, mating behaviour and larval development. Studies of functional morphology will also help to identify linked suites of characters and in delimiting the boundaries between characters. In conjunction with behavioural studies they provide some understanding of the significance of particular characters in the life of the copepod. Many novel copepods have been found in recent years and it is possible to identify certain hot spots on the surface of the planet, such as hydrothermal vents and cold seeps in the deep sea, anchialine caves and the hyperbenthic environment in the deep sea, all of which probably still hold many surprises. New developments in technology may enable these difficult sites to be sampled more easily in future and we eagerly await further discoveries of new forms from these habitats. Future studies of copepod relationships using the techniques of molecular biology are also awaited with great interest as they hold out the prospect of testing our ideas on evolution with a very different data set.

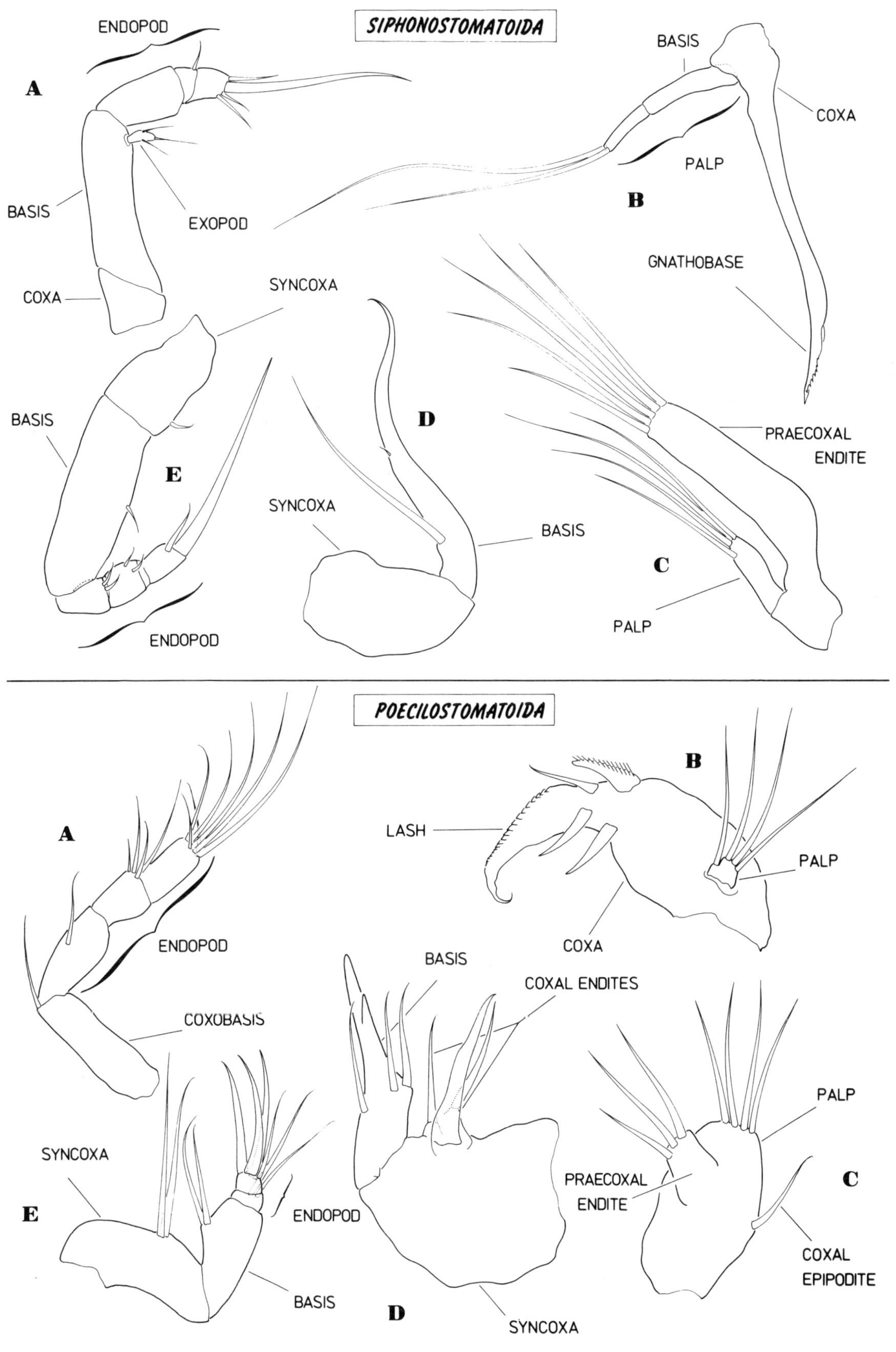

Figure 4.5.1 A comparison of the mouthparts of siphonostomatoids and poecilostomatoids showing the homologies of the various parts of each limb. [A = antenna, B = mandible, C = maxillule, D = maxilla and E = maxilliped.]

b. Key to Orders

1. Body showing gymnoplean tagmosis, with prosome-urosome boundary between fifth pedigerous and genital somites 2
Body showing podoplean tagmosis, with prosome-urosome boundary between fourth and fifth pedigerous somites.. 3

2. Swimming legs 2 and 3 with 2 spines on outer margin of first exopodal segment; maxillule with lobate exite bearing 2 setae on outer margin of basis...................... **PLATYCOPIOIDA**
Swimming legs 2 and 3 with at most 1 spine on outer margin of first exopodal segment; maxillule with at most 1 seta on outer margin of basis .... **CALANOIDA**

3. Adult female carrying eggs on ovigerous spines associated with median ventral genital aperture; cephalothorax lacking appendages from antennae to maxillipeds .... **MONSTRILLOIDA**
Adult female without ovigerous spines, typically carrying eggs in paired egg sacs; antennae to maxillipeds present 4

4. Antennary exopod 9-segmented in male, 8-segmented in female with 2,1,1,1,1,1,1,3 setal formula .... **MORMONILLOIDA**
Antennary exopod with 8 segments or less in either sex, with maximum setation of 1,1,1,1,1,1,1,4 5

5. Swimming legs 1 to 3 lacking intercoxal sclerites but with coxae fused in midline; legs 4 and 5 absent.. **GELYELLOIDA**
Swimming legs 1 to 3 with intercoxal sclerites, or with legs 1 to 3 absent; legs 4 and 5 present or absent 6

6. Antennary exopod at most 1-segmented; fifth legs with at most 1 seta representing baseoendopod.. 7
Antennary exopod usually with 2 or more segments, rarely 1-segmented or absent, in which case baseoendopod of fifth leg with 2 or more setae 9

7. Oral cone present, formed by labrum and labium (derived by medial fusion of paragnaths); mandible with stylet-like coxal gnathobase passing medially into oral cone.. **SIPHONOSTOMATOIDA**
Oral cone absent, paragnaths separate; mandibular gnathobase not stylet-like................. 8

8. Male antennules typically geniculate; female antennules up to 26-segmented; maxillipeds usually similar in both sexes; female genital somite with single midventral copulatory pore (except in Oithonidae) .... **CYCLOPOIDA**
Male antennules non-geniculate; female antennules at most 7-segmented; maxillipeds always sexually dimorphic; female genital somite with copulatory pores located within dorsolateral genital apertures (except in Erebonasteridae).. **POECILOSTOMATOIDA**

9. Antennules at least 16-segmented.. **MISOPHRIOIDA**
Antennules at most 14-segmented in male, 9-segmented in female .... **HARPACTICOIDA**

c. Full Classification of the Copepoda to Family Level

Subclass COPEPODA Milne Edwards 1840
- Infraclass PROGYMNOPLEA Lang 1948
  - Order PLATYCOPIOIDA Fosshagen 1985
    - Family Platycopiidae Sars 1911
- Infraclass NEOCOPEPODA nov.
  - Superorder GYMNOPLEA Giesbrecht 1882
    - Order CALANOIDA Sars 1903
      - Family Acartiidae Sars 1903
      - Family Aetideidae Giesbrecht 1892
      - Family Arietellidae Sars 1902
      - Family Augaptilidae Sars 1905
      - Family Bathypontiidae Brodsky 1950
      - Family Boholinidae Fosshagen 1990
      - Family Calanidae Dana 1849
      - Family Calocalanidae Bernard 1958
      - Family Candaciidae Giesbrecht 1892
      - Family Centropagidae Giesbrecht 1892
      - Family Clausocalanidae Giesbrecht 1892
      - Family Diaixidae Sars 1902
      - Family Diaptomidae Baird 1850
      - Family Discoidae Gordejeva 1975
      - Family Epacteriscidae Fosshagen 1973
      - Family Eucalanidae Giesbrecht 1892
      - Family Euchaetidae Giesbrecht 1892
      - Family Heterorhabdidae Sars 1902
      - Family Lucicutiidae Sars 1902
      - Family Mecynoceridae Andronov 1973
      - Family Megacalanidae Sewell 1947
      - Family Mesaiokeratidae Matthews 1961
      - Family Metridinidae Sars 1902
      - Family Paracalanidae Giesbrecht 1892
      - Family Parapontellidae Giesbrecht 1892
      - Family Phaennidae Sars 1902
      - Family Phyllopodidae Brodsky 1950
      - Family Pontellidae Dana 1853
      - Family Pseudocyclopidae Giesbrecht 1893
      - Family Pseudocyclopiidae Sars 1902
      - Family Pseudodiaptomidae Sars 1902
      - Family Ridgewayiidae Wilson 1958
      - Family Ryocalanidae Andronov 1974
      - Family Scolecithricidae Giesbrecht 1892
      - Family Spinocalanidae Vervoort 1951
      - Family Stephidae Sars 1902
      - Family Sulcanidae Nicholls 1945
      - Family Temoridae Giesbrecht 1892
      - Family Tharybidae Sars 1902
      - Family Tortanidae Sars 1902
  - Superorder PODOPLEA Giesbrecht 1882
    - Order MISOPHRIOIDA Gurney 1933
      - Family Misophriidae Brady 1878
    - Order CYCLOPOIDA Burmeister 1834
      - Family Archinotodelphyidae Lang 1949
      - Family Ascidicolidae Thorell 1859
      - Family Chordeumiidae Boxshall 1988

Family Cucumaricolidae Bouligand & Delamare-Deboutteville 1959
Family Cyclopidae Dana 1853
Family Cyclopinidae Sars 1913
Family Lernaeidae Cobbold 1879
Family Mantridae Leigh-Sharpe 1934
Family Notodelphyidae Dana 1853
Family Oithonidae Dana 1853
Family Ozmanidae Ho & Thatcher 1989
Family Thespesiopsyllidae Wilson 1924
Order GELYELLOIDA Huys 1988
Family Gelyellidae Rouch & Lescher-Moutoué 1977
Order MORMONILLOIDA Boxshall 1979
Family Mormonillidae Giesbrecht 1892
Order HARPACTICOIDA Sars 1903
Family Adenopleurellidae Huys 1990
Family Aegisthidae Giesbrecht 1892
Family Ambunguipedidae Huys 1990
Family Ameiridae Monard 1927
Family Ancorabolidae Sars 1909
Family Argestidae Por 1986
Family Balaenophilidae Sars 1910
Family Cancrincolidae Fiers 1990
Family Canthocamptidae Brady 1880
Family Canuellidae Lang 1944
Family Cerviniidae Sars 1903
Family Chappuisiidae Chappuis 1940
Family Cletodidae Scott 1904
Family Clytemnestridae Scott 1909
Family Cristacoxidae Huys 1990
Family Cylindropsyllidae Sars 1909
Family Darcythompsoniidae Lang 1936
Family Diosaccidae Sars 1906
Family Ectinosomatidae Sars 1903
Family Hamondiidae Huys 1990
Family Harpacticidae Dana 1846
Family Huntemanniidae Por 1986
Family Laophontidae Scott 1904
Family Laophontopsidae Huys & Willems 1989
Family Latiremidae Božić 1969
Family Longipediidae Brady 1880
Family Louriniidae Monard 1927
Family Metidae Boeck 1872
Family Miraciidae Dana 1846
Family Neobradyidae Oloffson 1917
Family Orthopsyllidae Huys 1991
Family Paramesochridae Lang 1944
Family Paranannopidae Por 1986
Family Parastenheliidae Lang 1936
Family Parastenocarididae Chappuis 1933
Family Peltidiidae Claus 1860
Family Phyllognathopodidae Gurney 1932
Family Porcellidiidae Brady 1880
Family Rhizothricidae Por 1986
Family Rotundiclipeidae Huys 1988
Family Superornatiremidae Huys, in prep.
Family Tachidiidae Boeck 1864

Family Tegastidae Sars 1904
Family Tetragonicipitidae Lang 1944
Family Thalestridae Sars 1905
Family Thompsonulidae Lang 1944
Family Tisbidae Stebbing 1910

Order POECILOSTOMATOIDA Thorell 1859

Family Anomoclausiidae Gotto 1964
Family Anomopsyllidae Sars 1921
Family Antheacheridae Sars 1870
Family Anthessiidae Humes 1986
Family Bomolochidae Sumpf 1871
Family Catiniidae Bocquet & Stock 1957
Family Chondracanthidae Milne Edwards 1840
Family Clausidiidae Embleton 1901
Family Clausiidae Giesbrecht 1895
Family Corallovexiidae Stock 1975
Family Corycaeidae Dana 1852
Family Echiurophilidae Delamare-Deboutteville & Nunes-Ruivo 1955
Family Erebonasteridae Humes 1987
Family Ergasilidae Nordmann 1832
Family Eunicicolidae Sars 1918
Family Gastrodelphyidae List 1890
Family Lamippidae Joliet 1882
Family Lichomolgidae Kossmann 1877
Family Mesoglicolidae de Zulueta 1911
Family Myicolidae Yamaguti 1936
Family Mytilicolidae Bocquet & Stock 1957
Family Nereicolidae Claus 1875
Family Oncaeidae Giesbrecht 1892
Family Paralubbockiidae Boxshall & Huys 1990
Family Pharodidae Illg 1948
Family Philichthyidae Vogt 1877
Family Philoblennidae Izawa 1976
Family Phyllodicolidae Delamare-Deboutteville & Laubier 1961
Family Pseudanthessiidae Humes & Stock 1972
Family Rhynchomolgidae Humes & Stock 1972
Family Sabelliphilidae Gurney 1927
Family Sapphirinidae Thorell 1859
Family Serpulidicolidae Stock 1979
Family Shiinoidae Cressey 1975
Family Spiophanicolidae Ho 1984
Family Splanchnotrophidae Norman & Scott 1906
Family Synaptiphilidae Bocquet 1953
Family Taeniacanthidae Wilson 1911
Family Tegobomolochidae Avdeev 1978
Family Telsidae Ho 1967
Family Tuccidae Vervoort 1962
Family Urocopiidae Humes & Stock 1972
Family Vahiniidae Humes 1967
Family Vaigamidae Thatcher & Robertson 1984
Family Ventriculinidae Leigh-Sharpe 1934
Family Xarifiidae Humes 1960

Order SIPHONOSTOMATOIDA Thorell 1859

Family Artotrogidae Brady 1880
Family Asterocheridae Giesbrecht 1899
Family Brychiopontiidae Humes 1974

Family Caligidae Burmeister 1835
Family Calverocheridae Stock 1968
Family Cancerillidae Giesbrecht 1897
Family Cecropidae Dana 1852
Family Dichelesthiidae Dana 1853
Family Dinopontiidae Murnane 1967
Family Dirivultidae Humes & Dojiri 1980
Family Dissonidae Yamaguti 1963
Family Ecbathyriontidae Humes 1987
Family Entomolepidae Brady 1899
Family Eudactylinidae Yamaguti 1963
Family Euryphoridae Wilson 1905
Family Hatschekiidae Kabata 1979
Family Herpyllobiidae Hansen 1892
Family Hyponeoidae Heegaard 1962
Family Kroyeriidae Kabata 1979
Family Lernaeopodidae Olsson 1869
Family Lernanthropidae Kabata 1979
Family Megapontiidae Heptner 1968
Family Micropontiidae Gooding 1957
Family Nanaspididae Humes & Cressey 1959
Family Nicothoidae Dana 1852
Family Pandaridae Milne Edwards 1840
Family Pennellidae Burmeister 1835
Family Pontoeciellidae Giesbrecht 1895
Family Pseudocycnidae Wilson 1922
Family Rataniidae Giesbrecht 1897
Family Sphyriidae Wilson 1919
Family Sponginticolidae Topsent 1928
Family Spongiocnizontidae Stock & Kleeton 1964
Family Stellicomitidae Humes & Cressey 1958
Family Tanypleuridae Kabata 1969
Family Trebiidae Wilson 1905
Family Xenocoelomatidae Bresciani & Lützen 1966

Order MONSTRILLOIDA Sars 1903

Family Monstrillidae Giesbrecht 1892

BIBLIOGRAPHY

Abdelhalim, A.I. **1990**. Morphology and epidemiology of some parasitic copepods (Poecilostomatoida: Ergasilidae) from British freshwater fish. 279 pp. Unpubl. Ph.D. Thesis, University of London.

Abele, L.G., **Kim**, W. & **Felgenhauer**, B.E. **1990**. Molecular evidence for inclusion of the phylum Pentastomida in the Crustacea. *Mol. Biol. Evol.* **6**: 685-691.

Alvarez, M.P.J. **1985**. A new species of misophrioid copepod from the near-bottom waters off Brazil. *J. nat. Hist.* **19**: 953-959.

Alvarez, M.P.J. **1988**. A new siphonostomatoid copepod, *Rhynchomyzon compactum* n. sp., from the Brazilian continental shelf. *Crustaceana* **55**: 88-92.

Andronov, V.N. **1974**. Phylogenetic relations of large taxa within the suborder Calanoida (Crustacea, Copepoda). *Zool. Zh.* **53**: 1002-1012. [In Russian, English summary.]

Andronov, V.N. **1985**. Benthic Copepoda in the area of Cape Blanc (Islamic Republic of Mauritania). 1. The family Platycopiidae. *Zool. Zh.* **64**: 1735-1739. [In Russian, English summary.]

Anstensrud, M. **1989**. A vital stain for studies of behaviour and ecology of the parasitic copepod *Lernaeocera branchialis* (Pennellidae). *Mar. Ecol. Prog. Ser.* **53**: 47-50.

Avdeev, G.V. **1982**. New species of harpacticoid copepods, parasites of octopuses in the north-western Pacific. *Parazitologiya* **16**: 107-116. [In Russian, English summary.]

Avdeev, G.V. **1983**. New harpacticoid copepods (Tisbidae), parasites of octopuses in the Ross Sea. *Zool. Zh.* **62**: 1775-1785. [In Russian, English summary.]

Avdeev, G.V. **1986**. New harpacticoid copepods associated with Pacific cephalopods. *Crustaceana* **51**: 49-65.

Avdeev, G.V., **Tzimbaljuk**, E.M. & **Lukomskaya**, O.G. **1986**. *Philoblenna littorina* sp. n., a parasitic copepod (Philoblennidae, Poecilostomatoida) from gastropods of the genus *Littorina* from the Gulf of Peter the Great (Sea of Japan). *Parazitologiya* **20** (1): 78-81. [In Russian, English summary.]

Baird, W. **1850**. *The natural history of the British Entomostraca*: i-viii, 1-364, pls 1-36. The Ray Society, London.

Barber, V.C. & **Emerson**, C.J. **1979**. Cupula-receptor cell relationships with evidence provided by SEM microdissection. *Scanning Electron Microscopy* **III**: 939-968.

Barnett, B.E. **1980**. A physico-chemical method for the extraction of marine and estuarine benthos from clay and resistant muds. *J. mar. Biol. Ass. U.K.* **60**: 255.

Bell, S.S., **Walters**, K. & **Kern**, J.C. **1984**. Meiofauna from seagrass habitats: a review and prospectus for future research. In: R.J. Orth, K.L. Heck & M.P. Weinstein [Eds], *Faunal relationships in seagrass and marsh ecosystems - Estuaries* **7**: 331-338.

Björnberg, T.K.S. **1972**. Developmental stages of some tropical and subtropical planktonic marine copepods. *Stud. Fauna Curaçao* **40**: 1-185.

Björnberg, T.K.S. **1986**. Aspects of the appendages in development. *Syllogeus* **58**: 51-66.

Blades, P.I. **1977**. Mating behavior of *Centropages typicus* (Copepoda: Calanoida). *Mar. Biol. Berlin* **40**: 57-64.

Blades, P.I. & **Youngbluth**, M.J. **1979**. Mating behavior of *Labidocera aestiva* (Copepoda: Calanoida). *Mar. Biol. Berlin* **51**: 339-355.

Bliss, L.C., **Courtin**, G.M., **Pattie**, D.L., **Riewe**, R.R., **Whitfield**, D.W.A. & **Widden**, P. **1973**. Arctic Tundra ecosystems. *A. Rev. Ecol. Syst.* **4**: 359-399.

Bocquet, C. & **Stock**, J.H. **1963**. Some recent trends in work on parasitic copepods. *Oceanography mar. Biol.* **1**: 289-300.

Bodin, Ph. **1968**. Copépodes Harpacticoides des étages bathyal et abyssal du Golfe de Gascogne. *Mém. Mus. natn. Hist. nat. Paris* (A) **55** (1): 1-107.

Bowman, T.E. **1971**. The case of the nonubiquitous telson and the fraudulent furca. *Crustaceana* **21**: 165-175.

Bowman, T.E. & **Gonzalez**, J.G. **1961**. Four new species of *Pseudocyclops* (Copepoda: Calanoida) from Puerto Rico. *Proc. U.S. natn. Mus.* **113**: 37-59.

Boxshall, G.A. **1974a**. Infections with parasitic copepods in North Sea marine fishes. *J. mar. biol. Ass. U.K.* **54**: 355-372.

Boxshall, G.A. **1974b**. The population dynamics of *Lepeophtheirus pectoralis* (Müller): seasonal variation in abundance and age structure. *Parasitology, Cambridge* **69**: 373-390.

Boxshall, G.A. **1977**. The planktonic copepods of the northeastern Atlantic Ocean: some taxonomic observations on the Oncaeidae (Cyclopoida). *Bull. Br. Mus. nat. Hist.* (Zoology) **31**: 103-155.

Boxshall, G.A. **1979**. The planktonic copepods of the northeastern Atlantic Ocean: Harpacticoida, Siphonostomatoida and Mormonilloida. *Bull. Br. Mus. nat. Hist.* (Zoology) **35**: 201-264.

Boxshall, G.A. **1982**. On the anatomy of the misophrioid copepods, with special reference to *Benthomisophria palliata* Sars. *Phil. Trans. R. Soc.* (B) **297**: 125-181.

Boxshall, G.A. **1983**. Three new genera of misophrioid copepods from the near-bottom plankton community in the North Atlantic Ocean. *Bull. Br. Mus. nat. Hist.* (Zoology) **44**: 103-124.

Boxshall, G.A. **1984**. The functional morphology of *Benthomisophria palliata* Sars, with a consideration of the evolution of the Misophrioida. *Crustaceana* (Supplement 7): 32-46.

Boxshall, G.A. **1985**. The comparative anatomy of two copepods, a predatory calanoid and a particle feeding mormonilloid. *Phil. Trans. R. Soc.* (B) **311**: 303-377.

Boxshall, G.A. **1986a**. The comparative anatomy of the feeding apparatus of representatives of four orders of copepods. *Syllogeus* **58**: 158-169.

Boxshall, G.A. **1986b**. Phylogeny of Mormonilloida and Siphonostomatoida. *Syllogeus* **58**: 173-176.

Boxshall, G.A. **1986c**. Panel discussion on copepod phylogeny. [Edited by Z. Kabata.] *Syllogeus* **58**: 197-208.

Boxshall, G.A. **1988**. A review of the copepod endoparasites of brittlestars (Ophiuroida). *Bull. Br. Mus. nat. Hist.* (Zoology) **54**: 261-270.

Boxshall, G.A. **1989**. Colonization of inland marine caves by misophrioid copepods. *J. Zool., Lond.* **219**: 521-526.

Boxshall, G.A. **1990a**. The skeletomusculature of siphonostomatoid copepods, with an analysis of adaptive radiation in structure of the oral cone. *Phil. Trans. R. Soc.* (B) **328**: 167-212.

Boxshall, G.A. **1990b**. Siphonostome copepods associated with sponges from Hong Kong. In: B.S.Morton [Ed.], *Proceedings of the Second International Marine Biological Workshop. The Marine Flora and Fauna of Hong Kong and Southern China*: 523-547. Hong Kong University Press.

Boxshall, G.A. **1990c**. Precopulatory mate guarding in copepods. *Bijdr. Dierk.* **60** (3-4): 209-213.

Boxshall, G.A., **Ferrari**, F. & **Tiemann**, H. **1984**. The ancestral copepod: towards a consensus of opinion at the First International Conference on Copepoda 1981. *Crustaceana* (Supplement 7): 68-84.

Boxshall, G.A. & **Huys**, R. **1988-1989**. New family of deep-sea planktonic copepods, the Paralubbockiidae, (Copepoda: Poecilostomatoida). *Biol. Oceanogr.* **6** (2): 163-173.

Boxshall, G.A. & **Huys**, R. **1989**. A new tantulocarid, *Stygotantulus stocki*, parasitic on harpacticoid copepods, with an analysis of the phylogenetic relationships within the Maxillopoda. *J. crust. Biol.* **9**: 126-140.

Boxshall, G.A. & **Iliffe**, T.M. **1986**. New cave-dwelling misophrioids (Crustacea: Copepoda) from Bermuda. *Sarsia* **71**: 55-64.

Boxshall, G.A. & **Iliffe**, T.M. **1987**. Three new genera and five new species of misophrioid copepods (Crustacea) from anchihaline caves on Indo-West Pacific and North Atlantic Islands. *Zool. J. Linn. Soc.* **91**: 223-252.

Boxshall, G.A. & **Iliffe**, T.M. **1990**. Three new species of misophrioid copepods from oceanic islands. *J. nat. Hist.* **24**: 595-613.

Boxshall, G.A. & **Lincoln**, R.J. **1987**. The life cycle of the Tantulocarida (Crustacea). *Phil. Trans. R. Soc.* (B) **315**: 267-303.

Boxshall, G.A. & **Roe**, H.S.J. **1980**. The life history and ecology of the aberrant bathypelagic genus *Benthomisophria* Sars, 1909 (Copepoda: Misophrioida). *Bull. Br. Mus. nat. Hist.* (Zoology) **38** (1): 9-41.

Boxshall, G.A., **Stock**, J.H. & **Sanchez**, E. **1990**. A new species of *Stephos* Scott, 1892 (Copepoda: Calanoida) from an anchihaline lava pool on Lanzarote, Canary Islands. *Stygologia* **5** (1): 33-41.

Brady, G.S. **1878**. *A monograph of the free and semi-parasitic Copepoda of the British Islands*. **1**: 1-148, pls 1-33. The Ray Society, London.

Brady, G.S. **1880a**. *A monograph of the free and semi-parasitic Copepoda of the British Islands*. **2**: 1-182, pls 34-82. The Ray Society, London.

Brady, G.S. **1880b**. *A monograph of the free and semi-parasitic Copepoda of the British Islands*. **3**: 1-83, pls 83-93. The Ray Society, London.

Brehm, V. **1927**. Ordnung der Crustacea Entomostraca: Copepoda. In: Kükenthal, W. & Krumbach, T. *Handbuch der Zoologie* **3** (1): 435-496.

Burmeister, H. **1835**. Beschreibung einiger neuen oder weniger bekannten Schmarotzerkrebse, nebst allgemeine Betrachtungen über die Gruppe, welcher sie angehören. *Nova Acta physico-med.* **17**: 269-336.

Burton, H. & **Hamond**, R. **1981**. Harpacticoid copepods from a saline lake in the Vestfold Hills, Antarctica. *Aust. J. mar. Freshwat. Res.* **32**: 465-468.

Buskey, E.J., **Mann**, C.G. & **Swift**, E. **1986**. The shadow response of the estuarine copepod *Acartia tonsa* (Dana). *J. exp. mar. Biol. Ecol.* **106**: 65-75.

Calman, W.T. **1909**. Crustacea. In: R. Lankester [Ed.], *A treatise on Zoology* VII (Appendiculata) (Fascicule 3): i-viii, 1-346. [Copepoda - Chapter 4: 71-105.]

Canu, E. **1892**. Les Copépodes du Boulonnais: morphologie, embryologie, taxonomie. *Trav. Inst. zool. Lille* **6**: 1-292, pls 1-30.

Carton, Y. **1970**. Description de *Paranicothoe* n. gen. un nouveau réprésentant de la famille des Nicothoidae. *Galathea Rep.* **11**: 239-246.

Caullery, M. & **Mesnil**, F. **1914**. Sur deux Monstrillides parasites d'Annélides (*Polydora giardi* Mesn. et *Syllis gracilis* Gr.). *Bull. scient. Fr. Belg.* **48**: 15-29.

Cedhagen, T. **1989**. A method for disaggregating clay concretions and eliminating formalin smell in the processing of sediment samples. *Sarsia* **74**: 221-222.

Claus, C. **1857**. Das Genus *Cyclops* und seine einheimischen Arten. *Arch. Naturgesch.* **23**: 1-40.

Claus, C. **1862**. Untersuchungen über die Organisation und Verwandtschaft der Copepoden. *Verh. phys.-med. Ges. Wurzb.* **3**: 51-103.

Claus, C. **1863**. Die frei lebenden Copepoden mit besonderer Berücksichtigung der Fauna Deutschlands, der Nordsee und des Mittelmeeres: i-x, 1-230, pls 1-37. Leipzig.

Coineau, Y. & **Coineau**, H. **1979**. Une nouvelle technique d'observation des animaux interstitiels: les modeles de réseaux intertitiels microscopiques transparents. *Mikroskopie* **35**: 319-329.

Coull, B.C. **1977**. Marine Flora and Fauna of the Northeastern United States. Copepoda Harpacticoida. *NOAA Technical Report. NMFS Circular* **399**: 1-47.

Cressey, R.F. & **Boxshall**, G.A. **1989**. *Kabatarina pattersoni*, a fossil parasitic copepod from a Lower Cretaceous fish, *Cladocyclus gardneri* Agassiz. *Micropaleontology* **35**: 150-167.

Cressey, R.F. & **Collette**, B.B. **1970**. Copepods and needlefishes: a study in host-parasite relationships. *Fishery Bull. Fish Wildl. Serv. U.S.* **68** (3): 347-432.

Cressey, R.F. & **Patterson**, C. **1973**. Fossil parasitic copepods from a Lower Cretaceous fish. *Science* **180**: 1283-1285.

Dahms, H.-U. **1988**. Development of functional adaptation to clasping behaviour in harpacticoid copepods (Copepoda, Harpacticoida). In: Boxshall, G.A. & Schminke, H.K. [Eds], *Biology of Copepods*: 505-513. Kluwer Academic Publishers, Dordrecht.

Dahms, H.-U. **1989a**. Antennule development during copepodite phase of some representatives of Harpacticoida (Copepoda, Crustacea). *Bijdr. Dierk.* **59**: 159-189.

Dahms, H.-U. **1989b**. First record of a lecithotrophic nauplius in Harpacticoida (Crustacea, Copepoda) collected from the Weddell sea (Antarctica). *Polar Biol.* **10**: 221-224.

Dahms, H.-U. **1991**. Naupliar development of Harpacticoida (Crustacea, Copepoda) and its significance for phylogenetic systematics. *Mikrofauna Mar.* **6**: 169-272.

Damkaer, D.M. **1975**. Calanoid copepods of the genera *Spinocalanus* and *Mimocalanus* from the Central Arctic Ocean, with a review of the Spinocalanidae. *NOAA tech. Rep. NMFS CIRC* No. 391: 1-88.

Dana, J.D. **1846**. Notice of some genera of Cyclopacea. *Ann. Mag. nat. Hist.* **18**: 181-185; *Am. J. Sci.* (2) **1**: 225-230.

Dana, J.D. **1848**. Conspectus crustaceorum, in orbis terrarum circumnavigatione, C. Wilkes e classe reipublicae faederatae duce, collectorum auctore. I. *Proc. Am. Acad. Arts Sci.* **1**: 149-155.

Dana, J.D. **1852**. Conspectus crustaceorum quae orbis terrarum circumnavigatione, Carolo Wilkes e classe reipublicae faederatae duce, lexit et descripsit. II. *Proc. Am. Acad. Arts Sci.* **2**: 9-61.

Dana, J.D. **[1853] 1852**. United States Exploring Expedition during the during the years 1838, 1839, 1840, 1841, 1842 under command of Charles Wilkes, U.S.N. **13** Crustacea. Part II: 686-1618. [Atlas of 96 plates published in 1855.]

Davis, C.C. & **Green**, J.M. **1974**. Three monstrillides (Copepoda: Monstrilloida) from the Arctic. *Int. Revue ges. Hydrobiol.* **59**: 57-63.

Deets, G.B. & **Ho**, J.-S. **1988**. Phylogenetic analysis of the Eudactylinidae (Crustacea: Copepoda: Siphonostomatoida), with descriptions of the two new genera. *Proc. biol. Soc. Wash.* **101** (2): 317-339.

Desmarest, A.G. **1825**. *Considérations générales sur la classe des Crustacés et description des espèces de ces animaux, qui vivent dans la mer, sur les côtes, ou dans les eaux douces de la France*: i-xix, 1-446, pls 1-56, tables 1-5. Paris.

Do, T.T., **Kajihara**, T. & **Ho**, J.-S. **1984**. The life history of *Pseudomyicola spinosus* (Raffaele & Monticelli, 1885) from the blue mussel, *Mytilus edulis galloprovincialis* in Tokyo Bay, Japan, with notes on the production of atypical male. *Bull. Ocean res. Inst.* **17**: 1-65.

Dojiri, M. & **Cressey**, R.F. **1988**. Revision of the Taeniacanthidae (Copepoda: Poecilostomatoida) parasitic on fishes and sea urchins. *Smithson. Contr. Zool.* No. 447: 1-250.

Dressel, D.M., **Heinle**, D.R. & **Grote**, M.C. **1972**. Vital staining to sort dead and live copepods. *Chesapeake Sci.* **13**: 156-159.

Dudley, P.L. **1966**. Development and systematics of some Pacific marine symbiotic copepods. A study of the biology of the Notodelphyidae, associates of ascidians. *Univ. Wash. Publs Biol.* **21**: 1-282.

Dumont, H.J. & **Maas**, S. **1988**. Five new species of leaf litter harpacticoids (Crustacea, Copepoda) from Nepal. *Zoologica Scr.* **17**: 55-68.

Dussart, B.H. **1984**. A propos du répertoire mondial des Calanoides des eaux continentales. *Crustaceana* (Supplement 7): 25-31.

Dussart, B.H. & **Defaye**, D. **1983**. *Répertoire mondial des Copépodes I. Calanoides*: 1-224. Centre National de la Recherche Scientifique. Paris.

Dussart, B.H. & **Defaye**, D. **1985**. *Répertoire mondial des Copépodes Cyclopoides*: 1-236. Centre National de la Recherche Scientifique. Paris.

Ellis, J.E. **1981**. Some type specimens of Isopoda (Flabellifera) in the British Museum (Natural History), and the isopods in the Linnean collection. *Bull. Br. Mus. nat. Hist.* (Zoology) **40**: 121-128.

Fahrenbach, W.H. **1962**. The biology of a harpacticoid copepod. *Cellule* **62**: 302-376.

Fanta, E.S. **1973**. Anatomy of the nauplii of *Euterpina acutifrons* (Dana) (Copepoda, Harpacticoida). *Crustaceana* **23**: 165-181.

Fanta, E.S. **1976**. Anatomy of the nauplii of *Oithona ovalis* Herbst (Copepoda, Cyclopoida). *Bolm Zool.* **1**: 205-238.

Ferrari, F.D. **1984**. Pleiotropy and *Pleuromamma*, the looking glass copepods (Calanoida). *Crustaceana* (Supplement 7): 166-181.

Ferrari, F.D. **1985**. Postnaupliar development of a looking-glass copepod, *Pleuromamma xiphias* (Giesbrecht, 1889), with analyses of distributions of sex and asymmetry. *Smithson. Contr. Zool.* No. 420: 1-55.

Ferrari, F.D. **1988a**. Evolutionary transformations and Dollo's law. *J. crust. Biol.* **8**: 618-619.

Ferrari, F.D. **1988b**. Developmental patterns in numbers of ramal segments of copepod post-maxillipedal legs. *Crustaceana* **54**: 256-293.

Ferrari, F.D. & **Bowman**, T.E. **1980**. Pelagic copepods of the family Oithonidae (Cyclopoida) from the east coasts of Central and South America. *Smithson. Contr. Zool.* No. 312: 1-27.

Fiers, F. **1982**. New Canuellidae from the northern coast of Papua New Guinea (Copepoda: Harpacticoida). *Bull. Inst. r. Sci. nat. Belg.* (Biologie) **54**: 1-32.

Fiers, F. **1984**. A new record of *Ellucana longicauda* Sewell, with the description of the male (Copepoda: Harpacticoida: Canuellidae). *Indo-Malayan Zool.* **2**: 177-185.

Fiers, F. **1986**. New and interesting copepods (Crustacea, Copepoda) from brackish waters of Laing Island (Northern Papua, New Guinea). *Bull. Inst. r. Sci. nat. Belg.* (Biologie) **56**: 99-120.

Fiers, F. **1987**. *Enhydrosoma vervoorti* spec. nov., a new harpacticoid copepod from India (Harpacticoida: Cletodidae). *Zool. Meded., Leiden* **61**: 295-302.

Fiers, F. **1990**. *Abscondicola humesi* n. gen. n. sp. from the gill chambers of land crabs and the definition of Cancrincolidae n. fam. (Copepoda, Harpacticoida). *Bull. Inst. r. Sci. nat. Belg.* (Biologie) **60**: 69-103.

Fiers, F. & **van de Velde**, I. **1984**. Morphology of the antenna and its importance in the systematics of the Cyclopidae. *Crustaceana* (Supplement 7): 182-199.

Fleminger, A. **1988**. *Parastephos esterlyi*, a new species of copepod (Stephidae: Calanoida: Crustacea) from San Diego Bay, California. *Proc. biol. Soc. Wash.* **101**: 309-313.

Fosshagen, A. **1968**. Marine biological investigations in the Bahamas. 4. Pseudocyclopidae (Copepoda, Calanoida) from the Bahamas. *Sarsia* **32**: 39-62.

Fosshagen, A. **1970**. Marine biological investigations in the Bahamas. 15. *Ridgewayia* (Copepoda, Calanoida) and two new genera of calanoids from the Bahamas. *Sarsia* **44**: 25-58.

Fosshagen, A. **1972**. Marine biological investigations in the Bahamas. 17. Platycopiidae (Copepoda, Calanoida) from the Bahamas. *Sarsia* **48**: 51-60.

Fosshagen, A. & **Iliffe**, T.M. **1985**. Two new genera of Calanoida and a new order of Copepoda, Platycopioida, from marine caves on Bermuda. *Sarsia* **70**: 345-358.

Fosshagen, A. & **Iliffe**, T.M. **1988**. A new genus of Platycopioida (Copepoda) from a marine cave on Bermuda. In: Boxshall, G.A. & Schminke, H.K. [Eds], *Biology of Copepods*: 357-361. Kluwer Academic Publishers, Dordrecht.

Frost, B. & **Fleminger**, A. **1968**. A revision of the genus *Clausocalanus* (Copepoda: Calanoida) with remarks on distributional patterns in diagnostic characters. *Bull. Scripps Instn Oceanogr. tech. Ser.* **12**: 1-235.

Fryer, G. **1957**. The feeding mechanism of some freshwater cyclopoid copepods. *Proc. zool. Soc. Lond.* **129**: 1-25.

Gannon, J.E. & **Gannon**, S.A. **1975**. Observations on the narcotization of crustacean zooplankton. *Crustaceana* **28**: 220-224.

Gee, M. **1989**. An ecological and economic review of meiofauna as food for fish. *Zool. J. Linn. Soc.* **96**: 243-261.

George, J.D. **1975**. The culture of benthic polychaetes and harpacticoid copepods on Agar. *10th. Europ. Symp. Mar. Biol.* **1**: 143-159.

Gerstaecker, C.A.E. **1866-1879**. Spaltfüssler: Copepoda. In: H.G. Bronn, *Klassen und Ordnungen des Tierreiches* **5** (Abt. 1) (Crustacea) (1): 590-806.

Giere, O. & **Welberts**, H. **1985**. An artificial 'sand system' and its application for studies on interstitial fauna. *J. exp. mar. Biol. Ecol.* **88**: 83-89.

Giesbrecht, W. **1882**. Die freilebenden Copepoden der Kieler Foehrde. *Ber. Comm. wiss. Untersuch. dt. Meere* VI (1877-1881) (Abt. 1): 87-168.

Giesbrecht, W. **1892**. Systematik und Faunistik der pelagischen Copepoden des Golfes von Neapel und der angrenzenden Meeres-Abschnitte. *Fauna Flora Golf. Neapel* **19**: 1-831.

Giesbrecht, W. **1899**. Die Asterocheriden des Golfes von Neapel und der angrenzenden Meeres-Abschnitte. *Fauna Flora Golf. Neapel* **25**: 1-217.

Glatzel, T. **1988**. The genital fields of *Canuella perplexa* and *C. furcigera* (Copepoda, Harpacticoida) - Comparative morphology and functional aspects. *Bijdr. Dierk.* **58**: 105-113.

Gophen, M. **1979**. Mating process in *Mesocyclops leuckarti* (Crustacea: Copepoda). *Israel J. Zool.* **28**: 163-166.

Gotto, R.V. **1979**. The association of copepods with marine invertebrates. *Adv. mar. Biol.* **16**: 1-109.

Gresty, K.A. **1990**. The feeding biology of *Mytilicola intestinalis* Steuer in the mussel host *Mytilus edulis* L., and the host-parasite relationships. 196 pp. Unpubl. Ph.D. Thesis, University of Exeter.

Grobben, C. **1892**. Zur Kenntnis des Stammbaumes und des Systems der Crustaceen. *Sber. Akad. Wiss. Wien* (Abt. 1) **101**: 237-274.

Grygier, M.J. **1983**. Ascothoracida and the unity of the Maxillopoda. In: F.R.Schram [Ed.], *Crustacean Phylogeny*: 73-104. A.A.Balkema, Rotterdam.

Grygier, M.J. **1987**. New records, external and internal anatomy, and systematic position of Hansen's y-larvae (Crustacea: Maxillopoda: Facetotecta). *Sarsia* **72**: 261-278.

Gurney, R. **1931**. *British freshwater Copepoda* **1**: i-lii, 1-238. The Ray Society, London.

Gurney, R. **1933a**. Notes on some Copepoda from Plymouth. *J. mar. biol. Ass. U.K.* (N.S.) **19**: 299-304.

Gurney, R. **1933b**. *British freshwater Copepoda* **3**: i-xxix, 1-384. The Ray Society, London.

Gurney, R. **1945**. Some notes on the development and classification of parasitic Copepoda. *Ann. Mag. nat. Hist.* (11)**12**: 121-127.

Hamner, W.M. & **Carleton**, J.H. **1979**. Copepod swarms: attributes and role in coral reef ecosystems. *Limnol. Oceanogr.* **24**: 1-14.

Hamond, R. **1969**. Methods of studying the copepods. *J. Quekett microsc. Club.* **31**: 137-149.

Harding, J.P. **1956**. A rare estuarine copepod crustacean, *Enhydrosoma gariensis*, found in the Holocene of Kent. *Nature, Lond.* **178**: 1127-1128.

Hardy, A. **1970**. *The Open Sea. The World of Plankton.* 335 pp. Collins, London.

Hartmann, O. **1961**. A new monstrillid copepod parasitic in capitellid polychaetes in southern California. *Zool. Anz.* **167**: 325-334.

Heegaard, P.E. **1940**. Some new parasitic copepods (Chondracanthidae and Lernaeopodidae) from western Australia. *Vidensk. Meddr dansk naturh. Foren.* **104**: 87-101.

Heegaard, P.E. **1947**. Contribution to the phylogeny of the arthropods. *Spolia zool. Mus. haun.* **8**: 1-236.

Herbst, H.V. **1964**. Cyclopoida Gnathostoma (Crustacea Copepoda) aus dem Litoral und Küstengrundwasser des Roten Meeres. *Kieler Meeresforsch.* **2** (Sonderheft): 155-169.

Heron, G.A. & **Damkaer**, D.M. **1969**. Five species of deep-water cyclopoid copepods from the plankton of the Gulf of Alaska. *Smithson. Contr. Zool.* **20**: 1-24.

Hessler, R.R. & **Newman**, W.A. **1975**. A trilobitomorph origin for the Crustacea. *Fossils Strata* **4**: 437-459.

Hicks, G.R.F. **1988**. Systematics of the Donsiellinae Lang (Copepoda, Harpacticoida). *J. nat. Hist.* **22**: 639-684.

Hicks, G.R.F. & **Coull**, B.C. **1983**. The ecology of marine meiobenthic harpacticoid copepods. *Oceanography mar. Biol.* **21**: 67-175.

Higgins, R.P. **1983**. Atlantic Barrier Reef ecosystem at Carrie Bow Cay, Belize, II. Kinorhyncha. *Smithson. Contr. mar. Sci.* **18**: 1-131.

Hill, L. & **Coker**, R. **1930**. Observations on mating habits in *Cyclops*. *J. Elisha Mitchell scient. Soc.* **45**: 206-220.

Ho, J.-S. **1984a**. New family of poecilostomatoid copepods (Spiophanicolidae) parasitic on polychaetes from southern California, with a phylogenetic analysis of nereicoliform families. *J. crust. Biol.* **4**: 134-146.

Ho, J.-S. **1984b**. Accessory antennule and the origin of the Chondracanthidae (Poecilostomatoida). *Crustaceana* (Supplement 7): 242-248.

Ho, J.-S. **1986**. Phylogeny of Cyclopoida. *Syllogeus* **58**: 177-183.

Ho, J.-S. **1988**. Cladistics of *Sunaristes*, a genus of harpacticoid copepods associated with hermit crabs. In: Boxshall, G.A. & Schminke, H.K. [Eds], *Biology of Copepods*: 555-560. Kluwer Academic Publishers, Dordrecht.

Ho, J.-S. **1990**. Phylogenetic analysis of copepod orders. *J. crust. Biol.* **10** (3): 528-536.

Ho, J.-S. & **Hong**, J.-S. **1988**. Harpacticoid copepods (Thalestridae) infesting the cultivated Wakame (Brown alga, *Undaria pinnatifida*) in Korea. *J. nat. Hist.* **22**: 1623-1637.

Ho, J.-S. & **Thatcher**, V.E. **1989**. A new family of cyclopoid copepods (Ozmanidae) parasitic in the hemocoel of a snail from the Brazilian Amazon. *J. nat. Hist.* **23**: 903-911.

Hockin, D.C. **1981**. Gurr's neutral mounting medium: a suitable mountant for the Harpacticoida (Copepoda). *Crustaceana* **40**: 222-223.

Hulings, N.C. & **Gray**, J.S. **1971**. A manual for the study of meiofauna. *Smithson. Contr. Zool.* **78**: 1-vii, 1-83.

Humes, A.G. **1965**. New species of *Hemicyclops* (Copepoda, Cyclopoida) from Madagascar. *Bull. Mus. comp. Zool. Harv.* **134**: 159-260.

Humes, A.G. **1973**. Cyclopoid copepods associated with the ophiuroid *Astroboa nuda* in Madagascar. *Beaufortia* **21**: 25-35.

Humes, A.G. **1975**. Cyclopoid copepods (Nanaspididae and Sabelliphilidae) associated with holothurians in New Caledonia. *Smithson. Contr. Zool.* No. **202**: 1-41.

Humes, A.G. **1977**. Pseudanthessiid copepods (Cyclopoida) associated with Crinoids and Echinoids (Echinodermata) in the tropical western Pacific Ocean. *Smithson. Contr. Zool.* No. **243**: 1-43.

Humes, A.G. **1980a**. A review of the copepods associated with holothurians, including new species from the Indo-Pacific. *Beaufortia* **30**: 31-123.

Humes, A.G. **1980b**. Copepoda (Cyclopoida, Lichomolgidae) associated with the Alcyonacean *Nephthea* in the Molluccas. *Hydrobiologia* **68**: 49-71.

Humes, A.G. **1987**. Copepoda from deep-sea hydrothermal vents. *Bull. mar. Sci.* **41**: 645-788.

Humes, A.G. **1988**. Copepoda from deep-sea hydrothermal vents and cold seeps. In: Boxshall, G.A. & Schminke, H.K. [Eds], *Biology of Copepods*: 549-554. Kluwer Academic Publishers, Dordrecht.

Humes, A.G. **1990**. *Aphotopontius probolus*, sp. nov., and records of other siphonostomatoid copepods from deep-sea vents in the eastern Pacific. *Scient. Mar.* **54**: 145-154.

Humes, A.G. & **Dojiri**, M. **1983**. Copepoda (Xarifiidae) parasitic in scleractinian corals from the Indo-Pacific. *J. nat. Hist.* **17**: 257-307.

Humes, A.G. & **Gooding**, R.U. **1964**. A method for studying the external anatomy of copepods. *Crustaceana* **6**: 238-240.

Humes, A.G. & **Smith**, W.L. **1974**. *Ridgewayia fosshageni* n. sp. (Copepoda; Calanoida) associated with an actiniarian in Panama, with observations on the nature of the association. *Caribb. J. Sci.* **14**: 125-139.

Humes, A.G. & **Stock**, J.H. **1973**. A revision of the family Lichomolgidae Kossmann, 1877, cyclopoid copepods mainly associated with marine invertebrates. *Smithson. Contr. Zool.* **127**: 1-368.

Huys, R. **1987a**. Some morphological observations on the Neobradyidae Oloffson, 1917 (Copepoda, Harpacticoida) including the redescription of *Antarcticobradya tenuis* (Brady, 1910) comb. nov. *Bull. Inst. r. Sci. nat. Belg.* (Biologie) **57**: 133-148.

Huys, R. **1987b**. Studies on the Cylindropsyllidae (Copepoda, Harpacticoida). 1. The status of *Leptastacus laticaudatus* Nicholls. *Zoologica Scr.* **16**: 155-166.

Huys, R. **1988a**. Gelyelloida, a new order of stygobiont copepods from European karstic systems. In: Boxshall, G.A. & Schminke, H.K. [Eds], *Biology of Copepods*: 485-495. Kluwer Academic Publishers, Dordrecht.

Huys, R. **1988b**. *Boxshallia bulbantennulata* gen. et spec. nov. (Copepoda: Misophrioida) from an anchihaline lava pool on Lanzarote, Canary Islands. *Stygologia* **4**: 138-154.

Huys, R. **1988c**. A redescription of the presumed associated *Caligopsyllus primus* Kunz, 1975 (Harpacticoida, Paramesochridae) with emphasis on its phylogenetic affinity with *Apodopsyllus* Kunz, 1962. *Hydrobiologia* **162**: 3-19.

Huys, R. **1988d**. Rotundiclipeidae fam. nov. (Copepoda, Harpacticoida) from anchihaline caves on Tenerife, Canary Islands. *Stygologia* **4**: 42-63.

Huys, R. **1988e**. Sexual dimorphism in Aegisthid cephalosomic appendages (Copepoda, Harpacticoida): A reappraisal. *Bijdr. Dierk.* **58**: 114-136.

Huys, R. **1990a**. A new harpacticoid copepod family collected from Australian sponges and the status of the subfamily Rhynchothalestrinae Lang. *Zool. J. Linn. Soc.* **99**: 51-115.

Huys, R. **1990b**. A new family of harpacticoid copepods and an analysis of the phylogenetic relationships within the Laophontidea T. Scott. *Bijdr. Dierk.* **60** (2): 79-120.

Huys, R. **1990c**. Allocation of the Mantridae Leigh-Sharpe to the Cyclopoida (Crustacea: Copepoda) with notes on *Nearchinotodelphys* Ummerkutty. *Bijdr. Dierk.* **60** (3-4): 283-291.

Huys, R. **1990d**. *Pholenota spatulifera* Vervoort (Copepoda: Harpacticoida): aberrant laophontid or specialized diosaccid. *J. nat. Hist.* **24**: 635-646.

Huys, R. **[In press.]** A new species of Erebonasteridae (Copepoda: Poecilostomatoida) from New Caledonian deep waters. Resultats de la Campagne MUSORSTOM IV. Nouvelle-Caledonie. *Mém. Mus. natn. Hist. nat. Paris*.

Huys, R. & **Boxshall**, G.A. **1990a**. The rediscovery of *Cyclopicina longifurcata* (Scott) in deep water in the North Atlantic, with a key to genera of the subfamily Cyclopininae. *Sarsia* **75**: 17-32.

Huys, R. & **Boxshall**, G.A. **1990b**. Discovery of *Centobnaster humesi* gen. et spec. nov. (Erebonasteridae), the most primitive poecilostomatoid copepod known, in New Caledonian deep waters. *J. crust. Biol.* **10** (3): 504-519.

Huys, R., **Boxshall**, G.A. & **Böttger-Schnack**, R. **[In press.]** On the discovery of the male of *Mormonilla* Giesbrecht 1892 (Copepoda: Mormonilloida). *Bull. Br. Mus. nat. Hist.* (Zoology).

Huys, R. & **Gee**, J.M. **1990**. A revision of the Thompsonulidae Lang, 1944 (Copepoda: Harpacticoida). *Zool. J. Linn. Soc.* **90**: 1-49.

Huys, R. & **Gee**, J.M. **[In press]**. A revision *Danielssenia perezi* Monard, *D. paraperezi* Soyer, *D. eastwardae* Coull (Harpacticoida, Paranannopidae) and their removal to a new genus. *Zool. J. Linn. Soc.*

Huys, R. & **Kunz**, H. **1988**. On the generic boundaries within the marine interstitial Latiremidae (Copepoda: Harpacticoida). *Stygologia* **4** (3): 292-305.

Illg, P.L. & **Dudley**, P.L. **1980**. The family Ascidicolidae and its subfamilies (Copepoda, Cyclopoida), with descriptions of new species. *Mém. Mus. natn. Hist. nat. Paris* (A) (Zool.) **117**: 1-192.

Isaac, M.J. **1974a**. Copepoda Monstrilloida from south-west Britain including six new species. *J. mar. biol. Ass. U.K.* **54**: 127-140.

Isaac, M.J. **1974b**. Monstrilloid copepods in the Zoological Museum, Berlin. *Mitt. zool. Mus. Berl.* **50**: 131-135.

Itô, T. **1980**. Two species of the genus *Longipedia* Claus from Japan with reference to the taxonomic status of *L. weberi* previously reported from Amakusa, southern Japan (Copepoda: Harpacticoida). *J. nat. Hist.* **14**: 17-32.

Itô, T. **1982a**. The origin of 'biramous' copepod legs. *J. nat. Hist.* **16**: 715-726.

Itô, T. **1982b**. Harpacticoid copepods from the Pacific abyssal off Mindanao. I. Cerviniidae. *J. Fac. Sci. Hokkaido Univ.* (Zoology) **23** (1): 63-127.

Itô, T & **Burton**, J.J.S. **1980**. A new genus and species of the family Canthocamptidae (Copepoda Harpacticoida) from a hot spring at Dusun Tua, Selangor, Malaysia. *Zool. Jb.* (Systematik) **107**: 1-31.

Izawa, K. **1986**. On the development of parasitic Copepoda. IV. Ten species of poecilostome cyclopoids, belonging to Taeniacanthidae, Tegobomolochidae, Lichomolgidae, Philoblennidae, Myicolidae, and Chondracanthidae. *Publs Seto mar. biol. Lab.* **31**: 81-162.

Izawa, K. **1987**. Studies on the phylogenetic implications of ontogenetic features in the poecilostome nauplii (Copepoda: Cyclopoida). *Publs Seto mar. biol. Lab.* **32**: 151-217.

Jeppesen, P.C. **1988**. Use of vacuum in rehydration of biological tissue, with a review of liquids used. *Crustaceana* **55**: 268-273.

Jones, J.B. **1980**. New Notodelphyidae (Copepoda: Cyclopoida) from New Zealand solitary ascidians. *N.Z. Jl mar. freshw. Res.* **13**: 533-544.

Jonge, V.N.de & **Bouwman**, L.A. **1977**. A simple density separation technique for quantitative isolation of meiobenthos using the colloidal silica Ludox-TM. *Mar. Biol. Berlin* **42**: 143-148.

Kabata, Z. **1958**. *Lernaeocera obtusa* n.sp.: Its biology and its effect on the haddock. *Mar. Res.* **1958** (3): 1-26.

Kabata, Z. **1979**. *Parasitic Copepoda of British Fishes.* **152**: i-xii, 1-468, figs 1-2031. The Ray Society, London.

Kabata, Z. **1981**. Copepoda (Crustacea) parasitic on fishes: problems and perspectives. *Adv. Parasitol.* **19**: 1-71.

Kabata, Z. **1985**. *Parasites and diseases of fish cultured in the tropics.* i-xi, 1-318. Taylor & Francis, London & Philadelphia.

Kabata, Z. & **Cousens**, B. **1973**. Life cycle of *Salmincola californiensis* (Dana, 1852) (Copepoda: Lernaeopodidae). *J. Fish. Res. Bd Can.* **30**: 881-903.

Kern, J.C. & **Carey**, A.G. Jr **1983**. The faunal assemblage inhabiting seasonal sea ice in the nearshore Arctic Ocean with emphasis on copepods. *Mar. Ecol. Progr. Ser.* **10**: 159-167.

Kim, W. & **Abele**, L.G. **1990**. Molecular phylogeny of selected decapod crustaceans based on 18S mRNA nucleotide sequences. *J. crust. Biol.* **10**: 1-13.

Klie, W. **1949**. Harpacticoida (Copepoda) aus dem Bereich von Helgoland und der Kieler Bucht. 1. *Kieler Meeresforsch.* **6**: 90-128.

Lamarck, J.B.P.A. de **1818**. Les Crustacés (Crustacea). In: *Histoire naturelle des animaux sans vertèbres* **5**: 109-273. Paris.

Land, M.R. **1984**. Crustacea. In: M.A. Ali [Ed.], *Photoreception and Vision in Invertebrates*: 401-438. Plenum Press, New York & London.

Lang, K. **1934**. Marine Harpacticiden von der Campbell-Insel und einigen anderen südlichen Inseln. *Acta Univ. lund.* (N.S.) (Avd. 2) **30** (14): 1-56.

Lang, K. **1948a**. *Monographie der Harpacticiden*: **I**: 1-896; **II**: 897-1682. Håkan Ohlsson Booksellers, Lund.

Lang, K. **1948b**. Copepoda 'Notodelphyoida' from the Swedish west-coast with an outline on the systematics of the Copepods. *Ark. Zool.* **40A** (14): 1-36.

Lang, K. **1949**. On a new copepod family related to Notodelphyidae and on two new copepod species from South-Georgia. *Ark. Zool.* **42B** (4): 1-7.

Lang, K. **1965**. Copepoda Harpacticoidea from the Californian Pacific coast. *K. svenska VetenskAkad. Handl.* (4) **10** (2): 1-560.

Latreille, P.A. **1802**. *Histoire naturelle générale et particulière des Crustacés et des Insectes*. Paris.

Latreille, P.A. **1817**. In: G. Cuvier, *Le règne animal distribué d'après son organisation.* [Ed. 1] **3** (contenant les Crustacés).

Latreille, P.A. **1829**. In: G. Cuvier, *Le règne animal distribué d'après son organisation.* [Ed. 2] **4** (contenant les Crustacés).

Leigh-Sharpe, W.H. **1934**. The Copepoda of the Siboga Expedition. Part II. Commensal and parasitic Copepoda. *Siboga Exped.* **29b** (123): i-vii, 1-43.

Lescher-Moutoué, F. **1974a.** Sur la biologie et l'écologie des Copépodes Cyclopides hypogés (Crustacés). *Annls Spéléol.* **28** (3): 429-502.

Lescher-Moutoué, F. **1974b.** Sur la biologie et l'écologie des Copépodes Cyclopides hypogés (Crustacés). *Annls Spéléol.* **28** (4): 581-674.

Lincoln, R.J. & **Boxshall**, G.A. **1983**. Deep-sea asellote isopods of the north-east Atlantic: the family Dendrotionidae and some new ectoparasitic copepods. *Zool. J. Linn. Soc.* **79**: 297-318.

Löffler, H. **1968**. Zur Harpacticidenfauna der östlichen Nepal mit besonderer Berücksichtigung der Gattung *Maraenobiotus*. *Arch. Hydrobiol.* **65**: 1-24.

Lowe, E. **1935**. On the anatomy of a marine copepod, *Calanus finmarchicus* (Gunnerus). *Trans. R. Soc. Edinb.* **58**: 561-603.

Lowndes, A.G. **1928**. Freshwater Copepoda from the New Hebrides. *Ann. Mag. nat. Hist.* (10) **1**: 704-712.

Lowndes, A.G. **1931**. Some fresh-water Entomostraca of the Birmingham district. *Ann. Mag. nat. Hist.* (10) **8**: 561-577.

Malaquin, A. **1901**. Le parasitisme évolutif des Monstrillides (Crustacés Copépodes). *Archs Zool. exp. gén.* (3) **9**: 81-232.

Malt, S.J. **1986**. Developmental stages of *Oncaea media* Giesbrecht, 1891 and *Oncaea subtilis* Giesbrecht, 1892. *Bull. Br. Mus. nat. Hist.* (Zoology) **43**: 129-151.

Mann, H. **1951**. Qualitätsverminderung des Fleisches der Miesmuscheln durch den Befall mit *Mytilicola intestinalis*. *Fischereiwelt* (3) (8): 121-122.

Mann, H. **1953**. *Lernaeocera branchialis* (Copepoda parasitica) und seine Schadwirkung bei einigen Gadiden. *Arch. FischWiss.* **4**: 133-144.

Manton, S.M. **1977**. *The Arthropoda. Habits, functional morphology and evolution*: 527 pp. Clarendon Press, Oxford.

Marcotte, B.M. **1977**. An introduction to the architecture and kinematics of harpacticoid (Copepoda) feeding: *Tisbe furcata* (Baird, 1837). *Mikrofauna Meeresbodens* **61**: 183-196.

Marcotte, B.M. **1982**. Evolution within the Crustacea. Part 2. Copepoda. In: Abele, L.G. [Ed.], *The Biology of Crustacea. 1. Systematics, the Fossil Record and Biogeography*: 185-197. Academic Press, New York & London.

Marcotte, B.M. **1986**. Phylogeny of the Copepoda Harpacticoida. *Syllogeus* **58**: 186-190.

McKay, C.R. & **Hartzband**, D.J. **1970**. Propylene phenoxetol: narcotic agent for unsorted benthic invertebrates. *Trans. Am. microsc. Soc.* **89**: 53-54.

Mielke, W. **1984**. Interstitielle Fauna von Galapagos XXXI. Paramesochridae (Harpacticoida). *Mikrofauna Mar.* **1**: 63-147.

Milne Edwards, H. **1840**. Ordre des Copépodes. In: *Histoire naturelle des Crustacés, comprenant l'anatomie, la physiologie et la classification de ces animaux* **3**: 411-529.

Moeschler, P. & **Rouch**, R. **1988**. Découverte d'un nouveau représentant de la famille des Gelyellidae (Copepoda, Harpacticoida) dans les eaux souterraines de Suisse. *Crustaceana* **55**: 1-16.

Monod, T. & **Dollfus**, R. **1932**. Les Copépodes parasites de mollusques. *Annls Parasit. hum. comp.* **10** (2): 129-204.

Moore, R.C. & **McCormick**, L. **1969**. General features of Crustacea. In: *Treatise on Invertebrate Paleontology.* Part R. Arthropoda 4. Crustacea (except Ostracoda), Myriapoda-Hexapoda: R57-R119.

Müller, K. & **Walossek**, D. **1988**. External morphology and larval development of the Upper Cambrian maxillopod *Bredocaris admirabilis*. *Fossils Strata* **23**: 1-70.

Nagasawa, K., **Bresciani**, J. & **Lützen**, J. **1988**. Morphology of *Pectenophilus ornatus*, new genus, new species, a copepod parasite of Japanese scallop *Patinopecten yessoensis*. *J. crust. Biol.* **8**: 31-42.

Nicholls, A.G. **1935**. Copepods from the interstitial fauna of a sandy beach. *J. mar. biol. Ass. U.K.* **20**: 379-405.

Nicholls, A.G. **1944**. Littoral Copepoda of South Australia (II) Calanoida, Cyclopoida, Notodelphyoida, Monstrilloida and Caligoida. *Rec. S. Aust. Mus.* **8** (1): 1-62.

Nishida, S. **1985**. Taxonomy and distribution of the family Oithonidae (Copepoda, Cyclopoida) in the Pacific and Indian Oceans. *Bull. Ocean res. Inst.* **20**: 1-167.

Oakley, C.L. **1930**. The Chondracanthidae (Crustacea: Copepoda); with a description of five new genera and one new species. *Parasitology, Cambridge* **22**: 182-201.

Ohtsuka, S. & **Mitsuzumi**, C. **1990**. A new asymmetrical near-bottom calanoid copepod, *Paramisophria platysoma*, with observations of its integumental organs, behavior and in-situ feeding habit. *Bull. Plankton Soc. Jap.* **36** (2): 87-101.

Ooishi, S. & **Illg**, P.L. **1977**. Haplostominae (Copepoda, Cyclopoida) associated with compound ascidians from the San Juan Archipelago and vicinity. *Spec. Publs Seto mar. biol. Lab.* Series V: 1-154.

Ooishi, S. & **Illg**, P.L. **1988**. Two morpho-types of *Botryllophilus* (Cyclopoida, Ascidicolidae). In: Boxshall, G.A. & Schminke, H.K. [Eds], *Biology of Copepods*: 561-566. Kluwer Academic Publishers, Dordrecht.

Oshel, P.E. **1985**. Paraffin-carving: a preparation technique for scanning electron microscopy of crustaceans. *J. crust. Biol.* **5**: 327-329.

Pallares, R.E. **1979**. Copepodos harpacticoides marinos de Tierra del Fuego (Argentina). Isla de los Estados III. *Contrnes cient. Centro Invest. Biol. mar. Buenos Aires* No. 142: 1-22.

Palmer, A.R. **1960**. Miocene copepods from the Mojave Desert, California. *J. Paleont.* **34**: 447-452.

Palmer, A.R. **1969**. Copepoda. In: *Treatise on Invertebrate Paleontology*. Part R. Arthropoda 4. Crustacea (except Ostracoda), Myriapoda-Hexapoda: R200-203.

Park, T. **1965**. The biology of a calanoid copepod *Epilabidocera amphitrites* McMurrich. *Cellule* **66**: 129-251.

Park, T. **1986**. Phylogeny of Calanoid Copepods. *Syllogeus* **58**: 191-196.

Pelseneer, P. **1914**. Ethologie de quelques *Odostomia* et un Monstrillide parasite de l'un d'eux. *Bull. scient. Fr. Belg.* (7) **48**: 1-14.

Perkins, E.J. **1956**. Preparation of copepod mounts for taxonomic work and for permanent collections. *Nature*, London **178**: 1075-1076.

Perryman, J.C. **1961**. The functional morphology of the skeletomusculature system of the larval and adult stages of the copepod *Calanus*, together with an account of the changes undergone by this system during larval development. Unpubl. Ph.D. Thesis, University of London.

Petkovski, T.K. **1955**. IV. Beitrag zur Kenntnis der Copepoden. *Acta Mus. maced. Sci. nat.* **3** (3) (25): 71-104.

Petkovski, T. **1977**. *Cubanocleta noodti* n. gen., n. sp., ein neuer Harpacticoide (Crustacea, Copepoda) aus dem hyporheal Kubas. *Fragm. balcan.* **10** (7) (227): 57-68.

Pfannkuche, O. & **Thiel**, H. **1988**. 9. Sample Processing. In: R.P.Higgins & H. Thiel [Eds], *Introduction to the study of meiofauna*: 134-145. Smithsonian Institution Press, Washington, D.C.

Por, F.D. **1983**. A note on two new species of Canuellidae (Copepoda, Harpacticoida) from the Red Sea. *Crustaceana* **44**: 187-197.

Por, F.D. **1984a**. Notes on the benthic Copepoda of the mangal ecosystem. *Developments Hydrobiol.* **20**: 67-70.

Por, F.D. **1984b**. Canuellidae Lang (Harpacticoida, Polyarthra) and the ancestry of the Copepoda. *Crustaceana* (Supplement 7): 1 24.

Pugh, P.R. & **Boxshall**, G.A. **1984**. The small scale distribution of plankton at a shelf station off the northwest African coast. *Continental Shelf Res.* **4**: 399-423.

Pulsifer, J. **1975**. Some techniques for mounting copepods for examination in a scanning electron microscope. *Crustaceana* **28**: 101-105.

Reid, J. **1986**. Some usually overlooked cryptic copepod habitats. *Syllogeus* **58**: 594-598.

Richman, S., **Loya**, Y. & **Slobodkin**, L.B. **1975**. The rate of mucus production by corals and its assimilation by the coral reef copepod *Acartia negligens*. *Limnol. Oceanogr.* **20**: 918-923.

Rouch, R. & **Lescher-Moutoué**, F. **1977**. *Gelyella droguei* n. g. n. sp., curieux Harpacticide des eaux souterraines continentales de la nouvelle famille des Gelyellidae. *Annls Limnologie* **13**: 1-14.

Sars, G.O. **1901-1903**. *An account of the Crustacea of Norway. IV. Copepoda Calanoida*: 171 pp., 109 pls. Bergen Museum.

Sars, G.O. **1903-1911**. *An account of the Crustacea of Norway. V. Copepoda Harpacticoida*: 449 pp., 284 pls. Bergen Museum.

Sars, G.O. **1911**. *Platycopia perplexa* n. gen. and sp., a remarkable new type of deep-water Calanoida from the Norwegian coast. *Arch. Math. Naturv.* (B) **31** (7): 1-16, pls 1-2.

Sars, G.O. **1913-1918**. *An account of the Crustacea of Norway. VI. Copepoda Cyclopoida*: 225 pp., 118 pls. Bergen Museum.

Sars, G.O. **1919-1921**. *An account of the Crustacea of Norway. VII. Copepoda Supplement*: 121 pp., 74 pls. Bergen Museum.

Sars, G.O. **1921**. *An account of the Crustacea of Norway. VIII. Copepoda Monstrilloida & Notodelphyioida*: 90 pp., 37 pls. Bergen Museum.

Sars, G.O. **1924**. Copépodes particulièrement bathypélagiques provenant des campagnes scientifiques du Prince Albert Ier de Monaco. *Résult. Camp. scient. Prince Albert I* **69**: pls 1-127.

Sars, G.O. **1925**. Copépodes particulièrement bathypélagiques provenant des campagnes scientifiques du Prince Albert Ier de Monaco. *Résult. Camp. scient. Prince Albert I* **69**: 1-408.

Schellenberg, A. **1922**. Neue Notodelphyiden des Berliner und Hamburger Museums mit einer Uebersicht der Ascidienbewohnenden Gattungen und Arten. *Mitt. zool. Mus. Berl.* **10**: 217-298.

Schminke, H.K. **1976**. The ubiquitous telson and the deceptive furca. *Crustaceana* **30**: 292-300.

Schram, F.R. **1986**. *Crustacea*. 606 pp. Oxford University Press, New York & London.

Schwinghamer, P. **1981**. Extraction of living meiofauna from marine sediments by centrifugation in a silica sol-sorbitol mixture. *Can. J. Fish. Aqua. Sci.* **38**: 476-478.

Scott, A. **1909**. The Copepoda of the Siboga Expedition. Part 1. Free-swimming, littoral and semi-parasitic Copepoda. *Siboga Exped.* **29a**: 1-323, pls 1-69.

Scott, T. **1894**. Additions to the fauna of the Firth of Forth. *Rep. Fishery Bd Scotl.* **12** (3): 231-271, pls 5-10.

Scott, T. **1901**. Notes on gatherings of Crustacea, collected for the most part by the fishery steamer *Garland* and the steam trawler *St Andrew* of Aberdeen, and examined during the year 1900. *Rep. Fishery Bd Scotl.* **19** (3): 235-281, pls 17-18.

Scourfield, D.J. **1946**. Preserving Entomostraca. *J. Quekett microsc. Club.* (4)**2**: 98.

Sekiguchi, H. **1974**. Relation between ontogenetic vertical migration and the mandibular gnathobase in pelagic copepods. *Bull. Fac. Fish. Mie Univ.* **1**: 1-10.

Sewell, R.B. Seymour **1940**. Copepoda, Harpacticoida. *Scient. Rep. John Murray Exped.* **7** (2): 117-382, 1 chart.

Sewell, R.B. Seymour **1947**. The free swimming planktonic Copepoda. Systematic account. *Scient. Rep. John Murray Exped.* **8** (1): 1-303.

Sewell, R.B. Seymour **1949**. The littoral and semi parasitic Cyclopoida, the Monstrilloida and Notodelphyoida. *Scient. Rep. John Murray Exped.* **9** (2): 17-199.

Sinderman, C.J. **1970**. *Principal diseases of marine fish and shellfish.* 399 pp. Academic Press, New York.

Smirnov, S. **1933**. Notiz über *Limnocletodes behningi* Borutzky. *Zool. Anz.* **102**: 118-129.

Starobogatov, Ya.I. **1986**. Systematics of Crustacea. *Zool. Zh.* **65**: 1769-1781. [In Russian].

Starobogatov, Ya.I. **1988**. Systematics of Crustacea. *J. crust. Biol.* **8**: 300-311. [English translation of Starobogatov (1986) by M.J. Grygier.]

Steedman, H.F. **1976**. *Zooplankton fixation and preservation.* 1-350 pp. UNESCO Press, Paris.

Stock, J.H. **1965**. Copépodes associés aux invertébrés des côtes du Roussillon. V. Cyclopoides siphonostomes spongicoles rares et nouveaux. *Vie Milieu* (A) **16**: 295-324.

Stock, J.H. **1967**. Copépodes associés aux invertébrés des côtes du Roussillon. VI. Sur deux espèces nouvelles de la famille des Spongiocnizontidae. *Vie Milieu* (A) **18**: 189-201.

Stock, J.H. **1981**. Book Review. *Crustaceana* **40**: 110-112.

Stock, J.H. **1982**. Description de *Cotylemyzon vervoorti* gen. et sp. nov., un Copépode Cyclopoide très original, parasite d'un Polychète d'Amboine. *Neth. J. Zool.* **32** (3): 364-373.

Stock, J.H. **1986**. Phylogeny of Poecilostomatoida. *Syllogeus* **58**: 184-185.

Stock, J.H. **1989**. Copepoda Siphonostomatoidea associated with West Indian hermatypic corals, 2. Associates of Scleractinia, Monastreinae and Trochosoniliidae. *Uitg. natuurw. StudKring Suriname* No. 123: 145-169.

Strickler, J.R. **1974**. Swimming of planktonic *Cyclops* species (Copepoda, Crustacea): pattern, movements and their control. In: T.Y.T. Wu, C.J. Broklaw & C. Brennen [Eds], *Swimming and Flying in Nature*, **2**: 599-613.

Strickler, J.R. **1985**. Feeding currents in calanoid copepods: two new hypotheses. In: M.S. Laverack [Ed.], *Physiological adaptations of marine animals*: 459-485. The Company of Biologists, Inc., Cambridge MA.

Thiel, H., **Thistle**, D. & **Wilson**, G.D. **1975**. Ultrasonic treatment of sediment samples for more efficient sorting of meiofauna. *Limnol. Oceanogr.* **20**: 472-473.

Thompson, J.R., **Thompson**, M.H. & **Drummond**, S. **1966**. A method for restoring dried crustacean specimens to taxonomically usable condition. *Crustaceana* **10**: 109.

Thorell, T. **1859**. Till Kännedomen om vissa parasitiskt lefvande Entomostraceer. *Öfvers. K. VetenskAkad. Förh. Stockh.* **16** (8): 355-362.

Tiemann, H. **1984**. Is the taxon Harpacticoida a monophyletic one? *Crustaceana* (Supplement 7): 47-59.

Toda, T., **Suh**, H.-L. & **Nemoto**, T. **1989**. Dry fracturing: a simple technique for scanning electron microscopy of small crustaceans and its application to internal observations of copepods. *J. crust. Biol.* **9**: 409-413.

Toohey, M.K., **Prakash**, G., **Goettel**, M.S. & **Pillai**, J.S. **1982**. *Elaphoidella taroi*: the intermediate copepod host in Fiji for the mosquito pathogenic fungus *Coelomomyces*. *J. Invert. Path.* **40**: 378-382.

Vancleave, H.J. & **Ross**, J.A. **1947**. A method for reclaiming dried zoological specimens. *Science* **105**: 318.

Vaupel Klein, J.C. von. **1982**. A taxonomic review of the genus *Euchirella* Giesbrecht, 1888 (Copepoda, Calanoida). II. The type-species, *Euchirella messinensis* (Claus, 1863). A. The female of f. typica. *Zool.Verh. Leiden* **198**: 1-131.

Vaupel Klein, J.C. von. **1984**. An aberrant P2 in *Euchirella messinensis* (Copepoda, Calanoida) and the original number of segments in the calanoid swimming leg. *Crustaceana* **46**: 110-112.

Vervoort, W. & **Tranter**, D. **1961**. *Balaenophilus unisetus* P.O.C. Aurivillius (Copepoda Harpacticoida) from the southern Hemisphere. *Crustaceana* **3**: 70-84.

Volkmann, B. **1979**. A revision of the genus *Tisbe* (Copepoda, Harpacticoida). Part 1. *Archo Oceanogr. Limnol.* **19**: 121-284.

Vuorinen, I., **Rajasilta**, M. & **Salo**, J. **1983**. Selective predation and habitat shift in a copepod species - support for predation hypothesis. *Oecologia* **59**: 62-64.

Webb, D.G. & **Weaver**, A.J. **1988**. Predation and the evolution of free spawning in marine calanoid copepods. *Oikos* **51**: 189-192.

Wells, J.B.J. **1967**. The littoral Copepoda (Crustacea) of Inhaca Island, Mozambique. *Trans. R. Soc. Edinb.* **67** (7): 189-358.

Wells, J.B.J. **1988**. 37. Copepoda. In: R.P.Higgins & H.Thiel [Eds] *Introduction to the study of meiofauna*: 380-388. Smithsonian Institution Press, Washington, D.C.

Westheide, W. & **Purschke**, G. **1988**. 10. Organism Processing. In: R.P.Higgins & H.Thiel [Eds] *Introduction to the study of meiofauna*: 146-160. Smithsonian Institution Press, Washington, D.C.

Whisler, H.C., **Zebold**, S.L. & **Shemanchuk**, J.A. **1974**. Alternate host for mosquito parasite *Coelomomyces*. *Nature, Lond.* **251**: 715-716.

Whisler, H.C., **Zebold**, S.L. & **Shemanchuk**, J.A. **1975**. Life history of *Coelomomyces psorophorae*. *Proc. natn. Acad. Sci. U.S.A.* **72**: 693-696.

Wilson, C.B. **1910**. The classification of the copepods. *Zool. Anz.* **35**: 609-620.

Wilson, C.B. **1917**. North American parasitic copepods belonging to the Lernaeidae with a revision of the entire family. *Proc. U.S. natn. Mus.* **53** (2194): 1-150, pls 1-21.

Wilson, C.B. **1932**. The copepods of the Woods Hole region, Massachusetts. *Bull. U.S. natn. Mus.* **158**: 1-635, pls 1-41.

Wilson, M.S. **1946**. The species of *Platycopia* Sars (Copepoda, Calanoida). *Smithson. misc. Collns* **106** (9): 1-16.

Wolff, T. **1960**. The hadal community: an introduction. *Deep-Sea Res.* **6**: 96-124.

Yager, J. **1981**. Remipedia. A new class of Crustacea from a marine cave in the Bahamas. *J. crust. Biol.* **1**: 328-333.

Yamaguti, S. **1963**. *Parasitic Copepoda and Branchiura of fishes*: i-x, 1-1104. Interscience Publishers, New York.

Yeatman, H.C. **1983**. Copepods from microhabitats in Fiji, Western Samoa, and Tonga. *Micronesia* **19**: 57-90.

Zenker, W. **1854**. System der Crustaceen. *Arch. Naturgesch.* **20** (1): 108-117.

APPENDIX 1

LIST OF MATERIAL EXAMINED

PLATYCOPIOIDA

Antrisocopia prehensilis Fosshagen 1985. Holotype ♂, Bermuda: Roadside Cave, Hamilton Parish, depth 0.1-1.5 m, 27 August 1982 [AMNH 11316]; 2 ♀♀ paratypes (dissected) and 1♂ (dissected) [AMNH 11317].

Platycopia inornata Fosshagen 1972. 2 ♀♀, Bahamas: Eleuthera, NW of Poison Point, 24°51'08"N 76°13'40"W, depth 3 m, sand/*Thalassia*, 25 April 1967 [A Fosshagen]; 1 ♂, Bahamas: Little San Salvador, West Bay, 24°34'40"N 75°57'30"W, depth 5-6 m, sand, 27 April 1967 [A Fosshagen].

Platycopia perplexa Sars 1911. 5 ♀♀, 2 ♂♂, Norway: Korshavn, depth 60 fthms, coarse muddy sand (Sars collection) [ZM Oslo F20688]; 4 ♀♀, 2 ♂♂, Norway: Frierfjord/Langesundfjord, depth 99 m, deep mud, spring 1985 [R Huys].

CALANOIDA

Acartia clausi Giesbrecht 1892. Numerous specimens, The Netherlands: Vlissingen, West Schelde estuary, in plankton, 28 July 1986 [R Huys].

Amallophora altera Farran 1929. 2 ♀♀ paratypes, *Terra Nova* Expedition 1910, Stns 267 and 282 [BNMH 1930.1.1.700-701].

Anomalocera patersoni Templeton 1837. 6 ♀♀, 21 ♂♂, 3 copepodids, England: Plymouth [BMNH 1908.12.17.61-70].

Augaptilina scopifera Sars 1920. Holotype ♀ (dissected), Golfe de Gascogne: Stn 2983, 1910 (Sars collection) [ZM Oslo F5382-F5383].

Calanus finmarchicus (Gunnerus 1770). Numerous ♀♀, Canada: Ungava Bay, M/V *Calanus*, Stns 13 and 18, 13 and 17 July 1947 (*M Fontaine*) [BMNH 1956.12.10.1-2]; 10 ♂♂, locality data not specified [BMNH 1972.11.13.3].

Candacia norvegica Boeck 1864. 2 ♀♀, 2 ♂♂, Norway: Christiana Fjord (Norman collection, from Sars collection) [BMNH 1911.11.8.40154-40157].

Centraugaptilus horridus (Farran 1909). Numerous specimens, Arabian Sea: *John Murray* Expedition 1933-34 [BMNH 1949.12.31.458].

Centropages typicus Krøyer 1848. 1 ♀, 22 ♂♂, 5 copepodids, Shetland (Norman collection) [BMNH 1900.3.29.217].

Disseta palumboi Giesbrecht 1892. Numerous ♀♀ and ♂♂, *John Murray* Expedition 1933-34, Stns 76, 96, 131D and 172 [BMNH 1949.12.31.415-418].

Enantiosis cavernicola Barr 1984. Holotype ♂ [USNM 195388], allotype ♀ [USNM 195389], 6 ♀♀ and 2 ♂♂ paratypes [USNM 195390], Bahamas: Lighthouse Cave, San Salvador Island, 5 June 1982.

Epacteriscus rapax Fosshagen 1973. Holotype ♀ (dissected), Florida: Broad Creek, N of Key Largo. 25°20'30"N 80°14'50"W, depth 3 m, 7 June 1971 [USNM 14720]; 4 ♀♀, Bermuda: Cherry Pit Cave, 26 January 1982 (*TM Iliffe*) [A Fosshagen].

Erebonectes nesioticus Fosshagen 1985. Holotype ♂ (dissected), Bermuda: Christie's Cave, Hamilton Parish, depth 4 m, 30 August 1984 [AMNH 11312]; paratype ♀ (dissected), same locality, 24 November 1982 [AMNH 11313].

Eucalanus attenuatus (Dana 1849). Numerous specimens, *John Murray* Expedition 1933-34 [BMNH 1949.12.31.32-52].

Eurytemora velox (Lilljeborg 1853). Scotland: SW coast of Little Cumbrae, brackish pool in splash zone, 7 August 1984 [BMNH 1984.283].

Exumella polyarthra Fosshagen 1970. 1 ♀, 2 ♂♂, Bahamas: off Harvey Cay Light, Exuma Cays, 24°09'20"N 76°31'30"W, depth 6-7 m, sand/algae, 1 May 1967 [A Fosshagen].

Haloptilus oxycephalus (Giesbrecht 1889). Several ♀♀, *Terra Nova* Expedition 1910. [BMNH 1930.1.1.1017-1020].

Labidocera trispinosa Esterly 1906. 5 ♀♀, 4 ♂♂, Pacific Ocean: 32°38'N 117°14'W, 9 March 1964 (*R Lasker*) [BMNH 1964.9.5.4].

Mesaiokeras nanseni Matthews 1961. 3 ♀♀, 2 ♂♂, 5 copepodids, Norway: Raunefjorden, near Skogsvåg, 60°16'N 05°08'E, depth 240 m, muddy substrate, 3 March 1961 [A Fosshagen].

Paracyclopia naessi Fosshagen 1985. 2 ♀♀, 3 ♂♂, Bermuda: Devonshire Cave, Devonshire Parish, depth 0.5 m, 12 September 1984 [A Fosshagen].

Paramisophria cluthae T Scott 1897. 1 ♀, Norway: Christiansund (Sars collection) [ZM Oslo F20537].

Paramisophria sp. 4 ♀♀, Japan: off Zazami Island, 26°15.9'N 127°21.4'E, depth 120 m, sandy bottom, 23 May 1989 [S Ohtsuka].

Placocalanus insularis Fosshagen 1970. 1 ♀, Bahamas: eastern side of Hogsty Reef, 21°41'30"N 73°47'00"W, depth 5-8 m, *Thalassia*, 11 March 1968 [A Fosshagen].

Pleuromamma xiphias (Giesbrecht 1889). 2 ♀♀, 2♂♂, Sargasso Sea: 24°46.3'N-24°44.7'N 70°24.6'W-70°26.4'W, depth 280 m, 17 February 1983 [Smithsonian Oceanographic Sorting Center].

Pseudocyclops bahamensis Fosshagen 1968. 4 ♀♀, 3 ♂♂, 6 copepodids, Bahamas: Exuma Cays, Great Guana Cay, bay between White Point and Black Point, 24°04'25"N 76°23'45"W, 3-4 m depth, sand, 30 April 1967 [A Fosshagen].

Pseudocyclops spp. 5 ♀♀, Belize: from washings of coral boulders in lagoons around Carrie Bow Cay (*GA Boxshall*) [BMNH 1991.58-62].

Rhincalanus nasutus Giesbrecht 1892. 6 ♀♀, 3 copepodids, *Terra Nova* Expedition 1910, Stns 80-120 [BMNH 1930.1.1.182-186].

Ridgewayia wilsoni Fosshagen 1970. 1 ♀, 2 ♂♂, 1 copepodid, Bahamas: Exuma Cays, Great Guana Cay, 1.5 miles S of White Point, 24°01'30"N 76°21'40"W, depth 3-4 m, sand, 29 April 1967 [A Fosshagen].

Scaphocalanus magnus (T Scott 1894). 3 ♀♀, *Investigator*, Stn 670 (Zoological Survey of India) [BMNH 1925.1.31.100-102].

Stephos canariensis Boxshall, Stock & Sanchez 1990. Paratypes, Canary Islands: anchialine lava pool at Playa de Montaña Bermeja, Lanzarote, 3 November 1988 (*GA Boxshall, JH Stock & E Sanchez*) [BMNH 1989.504-514].

Stephos lucayensis Fosshagen 1970. 3 ♀♀, 2 ♂♂, Bahamas: Little San Salvador, western side of lagoon, 24°34'40"N 75°56'40"W, coarse sand/dead *Thalassia*, 26 April 1967 [A Fosshagen].

Tropodiaptomus sp. 7♀♀, 5♂♂, Nigeria: pond near Molai, Borno State [BMNH 1991.46-57].

MISOPHRIOIDA

Archimisophria discoveryi Boxshall 1983. 1 paratype ♀ [BMNH 1982.129] and 3 paratype ♂♂

[BMNH 1982.130-132], North Atlantic Ocean: SW of Azores, *Discovery* Stn 10379#37, 34°57'N 32°55'W, depth 3000 m.

Archimisophria squamosa Alvarez 1985. 5 ♀♀, BALGIM expedition, R/V *Cryos*, Stn DW16, depth 1280 m, 30 May 1984 [CENTOB].

Benthomisophria cornuta Hulsemann & Grice 1964. 10 ♀♀, 6 ♂♂, North Atlantic Ocean: *Discovery* Stn 9541, 20°N 21°W, depth 3839 m, April 1977 and Stn 9131, 20°N 21°W, depth 3865-4036 m, November 1976 [BMNH 1979.71-86].

Benthomisophria palliata Sars 1909. 203 ♀♀, 117 ♂♂, North Atlantic Ocean: *Discovery* Stn 9541, 20°N 21°W, depth 3839-4105 m, April 1977 and Stn 9131, 20°N 21°W, depth 3865-4036 m, November 1976 [BMNH 1979.1-20].

Boxshallia bulbantennulata Huys 1988. Holotype ♀ (dissected), paratype ♂ (dissected), Canary Islands: Lanzarote, Playa de Montaña Bermeja, anchialine lava pool, 14 May 1987 (*JH Stock*) [ZMA Co.102.811a-b].

Expansophria galapagensis Boxshall & Iliffe 1990. 28 ♀♀ paratypes, 3 ♂♂ paratypes, Galapagos Islands: Santa Cruz Island, near Tortuga Bay, depth 9-10 m, 18 June 1987 (*TM Iliffe*) [BMNH 1989.937-950].

Misophria pallida Boeck 1864. Scotland, 1897 (Norman collection) [BMNH 1911.11.8.42443-42447]; England: Plymouth, 1903 (Norman collection) [BMNH 1911.11.8.42450-42452]; Norway (Sars collection) [ZM Oslo F20793-F20794]; 5 ♀♀, Norway: Frierfjord/Langesundfjord, depth 99 m, deep mud, spring 1985 [R Huys].

Misophriopsis dichotoma Boxshall 1983. Holotype ♀, North Atlantic Ocean: SW of Azores, *Discovery* Stn 10379#37, 34°57'N 32°55'W, depth 3000 m [BMNH 1982.139].

Misophriopsis sp. Numerous specimens, Greenland: Norwegian Arctic Expedition, *Fram*, 1898-1902 (Sars collection) [ZM Oslo 21161]; 4 ♀♀, 2 ♂♂, 2 copepodids, Norway: Voring plateau, 66°58.8'N 4°10.2'E [A Fosshagen]; 2 ♂♂, Norway: Frierfjord/Langesundfjord, depth 99 m, deep mud, spring 1985 [R Huys].

Speleophria bivexilla Boxshall & Iliffe 1986. Holotype ♀ [BMNH 1991.116], 14 ♀♀ paratypes [BMNH 1991.117-126], Bermuda: Roadside Cave, 12 November 1982, 28 August 1984, 22 September 1984 and 27 September 1984 (*TM Iliffe*).

Speleophria scottodicarloi Boxshall & Iliffe 1990. Holotype ♀ (dissected), Bermuda: Chalk Cave, Smith's Parish, depth 0-1.5 m, 31 August 1982 (*TM Iliffe*) [BMNH 1989.963].

HARPACTICOIDA

Alteutha oblonga (Goodsir 1864). Numerous specimens, Scilly Isles: BM(NH) and University of London Sub-Aqua Expedition 1966 [BMNH 1967.10.31.18].

Ambunguipes rufocincta (Brady 1880). 9 ♀♀, 6 ♂♂, England: Norfolk, West Runton, in washings of algae, 29 August 1988 [R Hamond].

Apodopsyllus sp. 45 ♀♀, 23 ♂♂, The Netherlands: SW coast, depth 6.5 m, sand, 17 October 1984 (*R Huys*) [R Huys].

Bathyidia remota Farran 1926. 3 ♀♀, 1 ♂, Arabian Sea: *Meteor*, 1450-1650 m [R Böttger-Schnack].

Caligopsyllus primus Kunz 1975. Holotype ♀, paratype ♂, South Africa: shell gravel from tidal pools of reef, mouth of Gonubie River, E of East London (*H Kunz*) [ZM Hamburg K30370].

Cancrincola abbreviata Humes. Numerous specimens, Middle Congo: shore of Songolo river near Pointe-Noire, from gill chambers of land crab *Sesarma huzardi* (*AG Humes*) [USNM]

Canuella perplexa T & A Scott 1893. Numerous specimens, England: Norfolk, Brancaster, 0.5

km N of golf club, low-water/spring tide, 9 October 1987 [R Hamond]; numerous specimens (SEM), England: West Sussex, Worthing, beach (*H Platt*) [BMNH 1991.63-72].

Canuellina insignis Gurney 1927. 4 ♀♀, Suez Canal: Port Said, Cambridge Suez Canal Expedition 1924 [BMNH 1970.5.15.3].

Carribula elongata (Gee 1988). 2 ♂♂ paratypes, 2 ♀♀ and 2 ♂♂ paratypes (dissected), Gulf of Mexico: off Louisiana coast, 29°50'N 90°30'W, depth 20 m (*M Murrell*) [ZM Oslo F20936].

Chappuisius inopinus Kiefer 1938. 3 ♀♀, 2 ♂♂, Germany: Aschaffenburg, 1938 (*F Kiefer*) [NR Stockholm 86].

Cletodes sp. Numerous specimens, Australia: Great Barrier Reef, about 1 km from Yonge Reef, depth 35 m, coralline sand, 28 September 1967 (*A Coomans*) [R Huys].

Cristacoxa petkovskii Huys 1990. 1 ♂, West Indies: Bonaire, 12°05'53"N 68°14'02"W, 11 June 1984 (*JH Stock*) [JH Stock].

Cylindropsyllus laevis Brady 1880. 1 ♀, 3 ♂♂, Sweden: Bonden, Bohuslän, depth 20 m, *Amphioxus*/ sand, 19 August 1974 (*H Kunz*) [H Kunz].

Ellucana longicauda (Sewell 1940). 1 ♀ and 1 ♂ (dissected), Papua New Guinea: Laing Island, Hansa Bay, Madang Province, lagoon, depth 6 m, coral debris/ mud (*J van Goethem*) [KIN Brussels P2144 and P2427].

Geeopsis incisipes (Klie 1913). 3 ♀♀, 2 ♂♂, England: Norfolk, Reedham (*R Gurney*) [BMNH 1930.8.28.2].

Hamondia superba Huys 1990. Holotype ♀ [NMV Melbourne J17367] and paratype ♂ [NMV Melbourne J17369], Australia: washings of unidentified sponges from vertical rock face, Pope's Eye, Port Philip, depth 15-18 m, 30 May 1976 (*JE Watson*).

Intermedopsyllus intermedius (T & A Scott 1895). 17 ♀♀, 2 ♂♂, The Netherlands: SW coast, depth 6.5 m, medium sand, 17 October 1984 (*R Huys*) [R Huys].

Laophonte cornuta Philippi 1840. 12 ♀♀, 7 ♂♂, Corsica: Bay of Calvi, 4 m depth, in washings of *Posidonia*, May 1985 (*C Heip & L Thielemans*) [R Huys].

Laophontodes bicornis A Scott 1896. 2 ovigerous ♀♀, Italy: Gulf of Naples, N coast of Ischia, near Punta Vico, on *Posidonia oceanica*, spring 1981 [R Novak].

Laophontopsis borealis Huys & Willems 1989. 3 ♀♀, England: Norfolk, Blakeney Harbour, amongst *Laminaria saccharina*, 18 December 1956 (*R Hamond*) [R Hamond]; 1 ♀ and 1 ♂, The Netherlands: East Schelde, Dortsman, 51°33'25"N 04°02'02"E, 9 September 1981 (*KA Willems*) [KA Willems]; 2 ♀♀, Norway: Christiania Fjord, Hvalør (Sars collection) [ZM Oslo F20286].

Leptastacus sp. 2 ♀♀, Corsica: Bay of Calvi, depth 3 m, in coarse sand between *Posidonia oceanica*, May 1985 (*C Heip & L Thielemans*) [R Huys].

Leptopontia sp. 1 ovigerous ♀, The Netherlands: SW coast, depth 5 m, medium sand, 1 November 1984 (*R Huys*) [R Huys].

Limnocletodes secundus Sewell 1934. 5 ♀♀, 5 ♂♂, India: Andra Pradesh, Lake Kolleru and reservoir at Nagarjuna University (*Y Ranga Reddy & Y Radhakrishna*) [BMNH 1980.387-396].

Longipedia coronata Claus 1863. 2 ♀♀, 1 ♂, Norway: Frierfjord/Langesundfjord, depth 99 m, deep mud, spring 1985 [R Huys].

Longipedia helgolandica Klie 1949. Numerous females, England: Norfolk [R Hamond].

Longipedia minor T & A Scott 1893. Numerous specimens, Norway: west coast (Sars collection) [ZM Oslo F17781].

Longipedia scotti Sars 1903. 3 ♀♀, 2 ♂♂, Australia: Great Barrier Reef, 1 km from Yonge Reef, depth 35 m, coralline sand, 28 September 1967 (*A Coomans*) [R Huys].

Mesochra lilljeborgi Boeck 1864. Numerous specimens, England: Norfolk: various localities (*R Hamond*) [R Hamond].

Namakosiramia californiensis Ho & Perkins 1977. 4 ♀♀, California: near large rock 600 m N of Pt. Vincente, off Palos Verdes, from washings of *Stichopus parvimensis* [J-S Ho].

Nannopus palustris Brady 1880. Numerous specimens, The Netherlands: West Schelde, Saaftingen, 51°21'11"N 04°07'07"E, 14 December 1978 (*KA Willems*) [KA Willems].

Neobradya pectinifera T Scott 1892. 1 ♀, Scotland: Firth of Clyde (*T Scott*) (Norman collection) [BMNH 1911.11.8.44496]; 1 ♂ (dissected), Sweden: Isle of Bonden, Bohuslän (*H Kunz*) [KIN Brussels].

Neoechinophora fosshageni Huys 1991. 2 ♀♀, 1 ♂, Bermuda: Roadside Cave, 18 September 1984 (*A Fosshagen*) [A Fosshagen].

Noodtorthopsyllus psammophilus (Noodt 1955). 1 ♂, Canary Islands: Tenerife, Pozo Playa, San Marcos, 24 April 1987 (*JH Stock & E Sanchez*) [R Huys]; 1 ♀, Canary Islands: Hierro, Pozo La Bonanza, 27 April 1987 (*JH Stock*) [R Huys].

Orthopsyllus bahamensis Huys 1991. 3 ♀♀, 4 ♂♂, Bahamas: Great Inagua, off Matthew Town, 20°57'00"N 73°41'00"W, depth 5 m, sand/*Thalassia*, 10 March 1968 (*A Fosshagen*).

Orthopsyllus sp. Numerous adults and copepodids I-V, Australia: Great Barrier Reef, 1 km from Yonge Reef, depth 35 m, coralline sand, 28 September 1967 (*A Coomans*) [R Huys].

Paramesochra mielkei Huys 1987. Numerous specimens, The Netherlands: SW coast, 51°36'04"N 03°35'47"E, depth 12 m, sand, 6 September 1984 (*R Huys*) [R Huys].

Parastenhelia spinosa (Fischer 1860). Numerous specimens, Norway: western coast (*GO Sars*) (Sars collection) [ZM Oslo F20205].

Pholenota spatulifera Vervoort 1964. Holotype ♀ (dissected), Caroline Islands: Ifaluk Atoll, Falarik, 17 October 1953 (*FM Bayer*) [USNM 00109761].

Phyllothalestris mysis (Claus, 1863). Numerous specimens, England: mouth of river Yealm, Devon (Norman Collection) [BMNH 1911.11.8.45971-45990].

Porcellidium sp. Numerous ♀♀ and ♂♂, Kenya: Mombasa, Tudor Creek, washings of seagrasses, 4 August 1988 (*R Huys*) [R Huys].

Rhynchothalestris helgolandica (Claus 1863). 1♀, 1 ♂, Norway: Bog Fjord (Norman collection) [BMNH 1911.11.8.46140-46149].

Rotundiclipeus canariensis Huys 1988. Holotype ♀, 2 paratypes ♂♂, Canary Islands: Tenerife, Cueva del Agua, El Balayo, shallow cave above high water mark, 14 May 1987 (*JH Stock & E Sanchez*) [ZMA Co.102.807a-c].

Sacodiscus littoralis (Sars 1904). Numerous specimens, Scilly Isles: Great Britain Rock, BM(NH) and University of London Sub-Aqua Expedition 1966 [BMNH 1967.10.31.26].

Sarsocletodes typicus (Sars 1920). 1 ♀, Norway: Fanafjorden, 60°14'27"N 05°17'03"E, depth 155 m, silt, 21 November 1966 (*Marine Biological Station, Espegrend*) [ZM Bergen 53203]; 1 ♂, Norway: Korsfjorden, depth 690 m, mud, 19 December 1962 (*Marine Biological Station, Espegrend*) [ZM Bergen 53281].

Scottopsyllus langi Mielke 1984. 2 ♀♀, Galapagos: Isla Santa Cruz, in front of marine laboratory of Bahia Academy, 18 February 1988 (*A Coomans*) [R Huys].

Sunaristes dardani Humes & Ho 1969. 6 ♂♂, 1 ♀, New Caledonia: Noumea, Ricaudy Reef, intertidal, from *Dardanus megistos* [BMNH 1972.11.9.7].

Superornatiremis mysticus Huys 1991. 5 ♀♀, 2 ♂♂, Bermuda: Walsingham Cave, 1 October 1984 [JH Stock].

Tachidiopsis bozici Bodin 1968. Allotype ♂ (dissected), R/V *Job-ha-Zelian*, 46°32'N 04°55'W (Bay of Biscay), depth 1200 m, muddy bottom, 11 August 1963 [P Bodin CXLIV].

Tachidiopsis cyclopoides Sars 1911. 15 ♀♀, Norway: Korshavn, depth 20 fthms (*GO Sars*) (Sars collection) [ZM Oslo F20350].

Tetragoniceps bergensis Por 1968. Holotype ♂, Norway: Raunefjorden, Skogsvågdypet, depth 240 m, muddy bottom, 18 December 1962 [ZM Bergen 47973].

Thompsonula curticauda CB Wilson 1932. 8 ♀♀ syntypes, 41 ♂♂ syntypes, Massachusetts: Woods Hole, Buzzards Bay, beach sand washings, 20 July 1927 (*CB Wilson*) [USNM 00063870].

Thompsonula hyaenae (Thompson 1889). 20 ♀♀, 3 ♂♂, England: Cornwall, Whitsand Bay, 31 August 1903 (*AM Norman & T Scott*) (Norman collection) [BMNH 1911.11.8.43566-43585].

Tigriopus japonicus Mori 1938. Numerous specimens, Hong Kong: Cape d'Aguilar, in front of Swire Marine Laboratory, hypersaline rock pools, 13 September 1990 (*R Huys*) [R Huys].

Undescribed **new family** from Great Barrier Reef. 1 ♀, 1 ♂, Australia: Great Barrier Reef, 1 km from Yonge Reef, depth 35 m, coralline sand, 28 September 1967 (*A Coomans*) [R Huys].

MONSTRILLOIDA

Monstrilla grandis Giesbrecht 1891. Several ♂♂ and ♀♀, England: Norfolk, in plankton (*R Hamond*) [BMNH 1954.9.30.1].

Monstrilla helgolandica Claus 1863. 1♀, England: Sussex, Brighton, seawater intake of power station [BMNH 1965.6.8.1]; 1 ♂ (labelled *M. serricornis*), Norway: Stavanger Fjord, Bukken (*GO Sars*) (Sars collection) [ZM Oslo unregistered]; 3 ♀♀, Norway: Christiansund (*GO Sars*) (Sars collection) [ZM Oslo unregistered].

Monstrilla longicornis Thompson 1890. 11 ♀♀, 5 ♂♂, Norway: Risør, Bukken and Skutesnaes (*GO Sars*) (Sars collection) [ZM Oslo unregistered].

Monstrilla longiremis Giesbrecht 1892. 4 ♀♀, 7 ♂♂, Norway: Hvalør and Bukken (*GO Sars*) (Sars collection) [ZM Oslo unregistered].

Monstrilla nasuta Davis & Green 1974. Holotype ♀, Canada: North West Territories, Cornwallis Island, in plankton from beneath ice cover at Resolute Bay, 20 December 1972 (*JM Green*) [NMC C-1984-1125].

Monstrilla sp. Numerous specimens, Japan: Okinawa, off pier at Sesoko Marine Science Center, in plankton (*M Grygier*).

Monstrillopsis dubia (T Scott 1904). 1 ♂, Norway: Raunefjorden, depth 120 m (*GA Boxshall & RJ Lincoln*) [BMNH 1985.377-380].

Monstrillopsis sp. Numerous specimens, Japan: Okinawa, off pier at Sesoko Marine Science Center, in plankton (*M Grygier*).

Thaumaleus longispinosus (Bourne 1890). 3 ♂♂, S.A.S. *Le Prince Albert I de Monaco* (Sars collection) [ZM Oslo F6103-F6105].

Copepodid V stage of unidentified monstrillid, France: Morlaix Bay, in gut of *Serpula vermicularis*, depth 25 m, 28 September 1955 [ZMA Co.100.670].

MORMONILLOIDA

Mormonilla minor Giesbrecht 1891. Numerous ♀♀, Cape Verde Islands: *Discovery* Stn 7089, 18°N 25°W, depth 410-1250 m [BMNH 1977.282-291].

Mormonilla phasma Giesbrecht 1891. Numerous ♀♀, Cape Verde Islands: *Discovery* Stn 7089,

18°N 25°W, depth 410-1250 m [BMNH 1977.272-281]; 1 ♂, Arabian Sea: *Meteor* Stn 347, 20°44'N 59°40'E, depth 1450-1650 m, (*R Böttger-Schnack*) [BMNH 1991.73].

GELYELLOIDA

Gelyella droguei Rouch & Lescher-Moutoué 1977. 3 ♀♀, 2 ♂♂, France: in subterranean water of karstic system near Saint-Gély-du-Fesc, Hérault, depth 60 m (*F Lescher-Moutoué*) [R Rouch].

CYCLOPOIDA

Archinotodelphys polynesiensis Monniot 1988. 1 ♀, Philippines: from *Molguloides vitrea* [C Monniot].

Archinotodelphys profundus Monniot 1986. Holotype ♀ (dissected), allotype ♂ (dissected), *Atlantis II* expedition, 38°46'N 70°06'W, depth 2996 m, in *Cnemidocarpa digonas* [C Monniot].

Archinotodelphys typicus Lang 1949. 4 ♀♀, South Georgia: Islas Orcadas, 54°00.1'S 37°40.6'W, depth 68-80 m, from *Molgula pulchra* [C Monniot].

Ascidicola rosea Thorell 1859. 1 ♀, England: Essex, Burnham-on-Crouch, from *Ciona intestinalis*, 1 December 1976 (*GA Boxshall*) [BMNH 1976.1376-1379].

Cryptocyclops bicolor (Sars 1863). 2 ♀♀ (dissected), Germany: Flachmoor, near Karlsruhe, 1935 (*F Kiefer*) [F Kiefer].

Cyclopicina longifurcata (T Scott 1901). 1 ♀, North Atlantic Ocean: SW of Azores, *Discovery* Stn 10379, 35°N 33°W, depth 2980 m (50 m off bottom) [BMNH 1989.473].

Cyclopina gracilis Claus 1863. Numerous specimens, Scotland: Isle of Cumbrae, washings of *Amphipholis squamata* (*GA Boxshall*) [BMNH 1986.377]; 5 ♀♀, 2 ♂♂, Norway: Skutesnaes (*GO Sars*) (Sars collection) [ZM Oslo F20409].

Cyclopina schneideri T Scott 1903. 2 ♀♀, Canada: Ungava Bay, Quebec [BMNH 1955.10.4.1].

Cyclopinodes elegans (T Scott 1894). 3 ♀♀, 3 ♂♂, Norway: Farsund, depth 20 fthms, sand (*GO Sars*) (Sars collection) [ZM Oslo F20418].

Cyclopinoides longicornis (Boeck 1872). 13 ♀♀, 12 ♂♂, Norway: Farsund and Risør (*GO Sars*) (Sars collection) [ZM Oslo F20414-F20415].

Cyclopinoides schulzi Herbst 1964. 1 ♀, 1 ♂, Red Sea: Al Ghardaqa, littoral zone, fine and muddy sand, 23 and 29 March 1956 (*A Remane & E Schulz*) [H-V Herbst].

Cyclops strenuus Fischer 1851. Numerous specimens, Belgium: (*S Maas*) [R Huys].

Cyclops vicinus Ulianine 1875. Numerous specimens, England: London, Regent's Park lake (*GA Boxshall*) [BMNH 1991.74-83].

Enterocola fulgens van Beneden 1860. 1 ♀, England: Devon, Salcombe, from *Botryllus* (*AM Norman*) (Norman collection) [BMNH 1911.11.8.42406-42410].

Euryte robusta Giesbrecht 1900. 1 ♀, 1 ♂, Norway: Raunefjorden, dredged off shell gravel bottom, depth 40 m (*GA Boxshall*) [BMNH 1986.358].

Herbstina exigua (Herbst 1974). 5 ♂♂ paratypes, Germany: Isle of Sylt, List, littoral zone, sand (*W Mielke*) [H-V Herbst].

Lamproglena monodi Capart 1944. 5 ♀♀, Uganda: River Semliki, from *Haplochromis bloyetti* [BMNH 1974.215-219].

Lamproglena pulchella von Nordmann 1832. 2 ♀♀, Bohemia (*A Fric*) (Norman collection) [BMNH 1911.11.8.48353-48355].

Macrocyclops albidus (Jurine 1820). 2 ♀♀, 1 ♂ (dissected), Germany: Bodensee, 1936 (*F Kiefer*) [F Kiefer].

Mantra speciosa Leigh-Sharpe 1934. Holotype ♀ (dissected), locality unknown: Dutch Siboga Expedition, *Chama* sp. [ZMA Co.102.604].

Mesocyclops rarus Kiefer 1981. 1 ♂, Tanzania: Muheza estate, small pond (*J Pell*) [BMNH 1986.651-660].

Metacyclopina harpacticoidea Klie 1949 sensu Kunz 1981. 1 ♀, 1 ♂, Germany: Helgoland, shell gravel (*H Kunz*) [ZM Kiel Cop.2146].

Notodelphys allmani Thorell 1859. Numerous ♀♀, England: Essex, Burnham-on-Crouch, in *Ciona intestinalis* (*GA Boxshall*) [BMNH 1976.1380-1385]; 1 ♀ syntype, Scandinavia (*T Thorell* via *GS Brady*) [BMNH 1951.8.10.759].

Notodelphys elegans Thorell 1859. 1 ♂, Scotland: Millport, in *Ascidiella aspersa* (*GA Boxshall*) [BMNH 1984.235].

Oithona helgolandica Claus 1863. England: off Yorkshire coast at Whitby, depth 0.5 m, (*GA Boxshall*) [BMNH 1976.625-629].

Oithona nana Giesbrecht 1892. Numerous specimens, continental shelf off Mauritania: *Discovery* Stn 9529, 21°09'N 17°18'W, depth 10 m (bottom depth 60 m) [BMNH unregistered].

Oithona robusta Giesbrecht 1891. Numerous ♀♀, Cape Verde Islands: *Discovery* Stn 7089, 18°N 25°W, November 1969 [BMNH 1976.771-780].

Oithona setigera (Dana 1849). 2 ♀♀, 2 ♂♂, Cape Verde Islands: *Discovery* Stn 7089, 18°N 25°W, November 1969 [BMNH 1976.781-790].

Oithona sp. 2 ♀♀, Cape Verde Islands: *Discovery* Stn 7089, 18°N 25°W, November 1969 [ex BMNH 1976.781-790].

Ozmana haemophila Ho & Thatcher 1989. 1 ♀, 1 ♂, Brazil: Amazon river basin, Manaus, in blood of mesogastropod snail *Pomacea maculata* [J-S Ho].

Parachordeumium amphiurae (Hérouard 1906). 1 copepodid, England: Langerstone Point, Devon, exposed rocky shore, in brittlestar *Amphipholis squamata* (*M Fahd*) [BMNH 1991.84-87].

Pterinopsyllus insignis (Brady 1878). 4 ♀♀, 2 ♂♂, Scotland: Loch Etive, 17 September 1901 [BMNH 1956.9.25.67].

Pterinopsyllus sp. Bahamas: Great Inagua, Matthew Town, 20°57'00"N 73°41'00"W, depth 5 m, sand/*Thalassia*, 10 March 1968 [A Fosshagen].

Thespesiopsyllus paradoxus (GO Sars 1913). 1 ♀, 1 ♂, Norway: Raunefjorden, Skogsvågdypet, depth 240 m, 25 February 1965 (*A Fosshagen*) [ZM Bergen 50462-50463].

Undescribed **new genus** of interstitial cyclopinid. 5 ♀♀, 7 ♂♂, 3 copepodids, The Netherlands: SW coast, depth 6.5 m, 17 October 1984 (*R Huys*) [R Huys].

SIPHONOSTOMATOIDA

Acontiophorus scutatus (Brady & Robertson 1873). 1 ♀ (dissected), Scilly Isles: BM(NH) and University of London Sub-Aqua Expedition 1966 (*MH Thurston*) [BMNH 1968.1.30.8].

Asterocheres reginae Boxshall & Huys 1991. Holotype ♀ [BMNH 1991.88], 13 paratypes [BMNH 1991.89-101], Belize: Carrie Bow Cay, shallow water, from *Agelas clathrodes* (*GA Boxshall*).

Australomyzon typicus Nicholls 1944. 1 ♀ syntype, 2 ♂♂ syntypes, Australia: Sellick Beach, low tide, 31 January 1937 and 25 March 1939 (*HM Hale*) [SAM Tc10884-10886].

Bariaka alopiae Cressey 1966. 7 ♀♀, Southern Californian Bight: 3 miles SW of Point Dume, from *Alopias superciliosus*, 23 October 1980 (*G Deets*) [BMNH 1991.39-45].

Brychiopontius falcatus Humes 1974. 4 ♀♀, 3 ♂♂, SW of Ireland: 50°04.7'N 15°44.8'W, R/V *Chain*, Cruise 106, Stn 328, depth 4426-4435 m, washings from *Oneirophanta mutabilis*, 23 August 1972 [USNM 142984].

Chasmatopontius thescalus Humes 1990. 10 ♂♂, 10 ♀♀, Mariana Back-Arc Basin: DSRV *Alvin*, dive 1845, 18°12.6-8'N 144°42.4'E, depths 3640 m and 3595 m, from washings of tubes of *Paralvinella hessleri* [MNHN Cp372].

Collocheres comanthiphilus Humes 1987. 4 ♀♀, 4 ♂♂, Moluccas: Banda Island, SW shore of Goenoeng Api, depth 4 m, from *Comanthus bennetti*, 28 April 1975 (*AG Humes*) [AG Humes].

Dermatomyzon nigripes Brady & Robertson 1876. 1 ♀, 6 ♂♂, Hong Kong: New Territories, Peng Chau, depth 5 m, from dark green branching sponge, 15 April 1986 (*GA Boxshall*) [BMNH 1987.99-106].

Ecbathyrion prolixicauda Humes 1987. 104 ♀♀ paratypes, 12 ♂♂ paratypes, Galapagos Rift: DSRV *Alvin*, dive 983, 00°48.0'N 86°13.0'W, depth 2457 m, November 1979 [USNM 233513].

Entomopsyllus adriae (Eiselt 1959). Numerous specimens, France: Banyuls-sur-Mer, washings from sponges (*GA Boxshall*) [BMNH 1991.141-150].

Eudactylinella alba CB Wilson 1932. 2 ♂♂, Florida: Lemon Bay, from killifish (*R Bere*) [USNM 79138]; 4 ♀♀ paratypes, Massachusetts: Woods Hole [USNM 56667].

Fissuricola caritus Humes 1987. 5 ♀♀ paratypes, East Pacific Ridge: DSRV *Alvin*, dive 1226, 20°50.0'N 109°06.0'W, depth 2616 m, 10 May 1982 [USNM 233510].

Hammatimyzon dimorphum Stock 1981. Holotype ♀, allotype ♂, New Hebrides: Api Island, 16°45'S 168°07'E, depth 115-128 m, in gall of *Stylaster sanguineus*, 18 August 1874 [ZMA Co.102666a-b].

Hermacheres montastreae Stock 1989. Holotype ♀, allotype ♂ (dissected), 21 ♀♀ paratypes, Curacao: 500 m west of Piscadera Bay, depth 5-6 m, from *Montastrea cavernosa*, 18 December 1973 [ZMA Co.102746a-c].

Hyalopontius typicus GO Sars 1909. Numerous specimens, North Atlantic Ocean: *Discovery* Stn 8509, 44°N 12°W [BMNH 1978.312-318].

Kabatarina pattersoni Cressey & Boxshall 1989. 8 fragments, Brazil: Ceara, Sierra do Araripe, from gills of fossil teleost fish, *Cladocyclus gardneri*, in calcareous nodules in the Santana Formation [BMNH IN.63466-63470 and IN.63625-63627].

Lepeophtheirus pectoralis (OF Müller 1776). Numerous specimens, England: Yorkshire, Robin Hood's Bay, from *Pleuronectes platessa*, August 1973 (*GA Boxshall*) [BMNH 1975.443-453].

Lepeophtheirus salmonis (Krøyer, 1838). Numerous specimens, England: Yorkshire, off Robin Hood's Bay, from body surface of sea trout *Salmo trutta* (*GA Boxshall*) [BMNH 1975.524-534].

Lernaeocera sp. Larva, England: Yorkshire, 2 miles off Whitby, depth 0.5 m, 29 March 1976 (*GA Boxshall*) [BMNH 1976.692].

Lernaeocera branchialis (L. 1767). Numerous premetamorphic adults and larvae, Greenland: from gills of *Myxocephalus scorpius* [BMNH 1991.102-106].

Lernanthropus kroyeri van Beneden 1851. 1 ♀, England: Yorkshire, Robin Hood's Bay, on *Dicentrarchus labrax* (*GA Boxshall*) [BMNH 1975.666].

Nicothoe astaci Audouin & Milne Edwards 1826. 2 ♀♀ (dissected), locality data unknown, July 1924 (*MGL Perkins*) [BMNH 1949.9.13.22-23].

Paranicothoe cladocera Carton 1970. Lectotype ♂ (dissected), South Africa: Natal, *Galathea*

Expedition, 25°20'S 35°17'E, depth 590 m, from brood pouch of *Orbione* sp. found in branchial cavity of *Hymenopenaeus triarthrus*, 21 February 1951 [ZM Copenhagen].

Pontoeciella abyssicola (T Scott 1894). Numerous specimens, North Atlantic Ocean: *Discovery* Stn 9541, 20°N 21°W [BMNH 1977.250-263].

Protodactylina pamelae Laubier 1966. California: San Francisco Bay, from *Notorhynchus maculatus* (*G Deets*) [BMNH 1991.197-201].

Rhynchomyzon compactum Alvarez 1988. Holotype ♀ (dissected), paratype ♀, South Atlantic Ocean: off coast of Brazil, 23°25'S 43°00'W [MZU São Paulo].

Scotoecetes introrsus Humes 1987. 23 ♀♀, 6 ♂♂, Pacific Ocean: off Mexico, 12°48.8'N 103°56.8'W, DSRV *Cyana*, dive 84-38, depth 2635 m, 15 March 1984 [USNM 231988].

Scottocheres elongatus T & A Scott 1894. 10 ♀♀, 4 ♂♂, Jamaica: on *Madracis* (*P Snelgrove*) [BMNH 1991.107-120].

Spongiocnizon vermiformis Stock 1967. 9 ♀♀, 1 ♂, France: Mediterranean coast, between St Cyprien and Le Racou, from washings of sponge, *Lophon hyndmani* var. *funis*, muddy bottom, 12 August 1965 (*JH Stock*) [ZMA Co.101.003].

Stellicomes supplicans Humes 1971. 1050 paratypes, Madagascar: SW of Isles Mitsio, 13°02.5'S 48°21.5'E to 13°00.5'W 48°22.5'E, trawl depth 59-45 m, from *Asterodiscus elegans*, 19 June 1967 [USNM 137433].

Stygiopontius cinctiger Humes 1987. 3 ♀♀, East Pacific Ridge: DSRV *Alvin*, dive 1226, 20°50.0'N 109°06.0'W, depth 2616 m, 10 May 1982 [AG Humes].

Stygiopontius quadrispinosus Humes 1987. 8 mating pairs, Gorda Ridge: 41°00'N 127°29.3'W, 6 June 1988 [AG Humes].

Stygiopontius stabilitus Humes 1990. 2 ♀♀, Mariana Back-Arc Basin: DSRV *Alvin*, dive 1845, 18°12.6-8'N 144°42.4'E, depths 3640 m and 3595 m, washings of tubes of *Paralvinella* sp., 6 May 1987 [BMNH 1989.692-701].

Tuphacheres micropus Stock 1965. Holotype ♀, allotype ♂, 4 ♀♀ and 4 ♂♂ paratypes, France: Mediterranean coast, Cap Béar, depth 70 m, from *Dysidea tupha*, 14 September 1964, (*JH Stock*) [ZMA Co.100.913].

POECILOSTOMATOIDA

Amphicrossus pacificus Huys 1991. Holotype ♀ (dissected), New Caledonia: Grand Passage zone, 19°07.6'S 163°22.7'E, depth 155 m, coarse sandy bottom, 14 September 1985 [MNHN Cp577].

Boylea longispica Cressey 1977. 3 ♀♀ paratypes, Gulf of Thailand, Palau Islands and Caroline Islands, from nasal sinus of *Elegatus bipinnulatus* [USNM 168188-168190].

Centobnaster humesi Huys & Boxshall 1990. Holotype ♀ (dissected), New Caledonia: NE of Thio, 21°32.84'S 166°23.85'E, depth 500 m, 12 April 1987 [MNHN Cp558].

Chauliolobion bulbosum Humes 1975. 1 ♂, 1 ♀, New Caledonia: Nouméa, N of Isle Maître, 22°19'30"S 166°24'35"E, depth 3 m, from *Actinopyga obesa palauensis*, 13 July 1971 (*AG Humes*) [AG Humes].

Clausidium vancouverense (Haddon 1912). 5 ♀♀ topotypes, 4 ♂♂ topotypes, Canada: Vancouver Island, Hammond Bay, from body surface and gill chambers of *Callianassa californiensis*, 28 June 1957 (*R Gooding*) [ZMA Co.100.399].

Cotylemyzon vervoorti Stock 1982. Holotype ♀ (dissected), Indonesia: anchorage of Amboina, in *Eupolyodontes amboinensis*, depth 40 m, coralline sand, 14-18 November 1899 [ZMA Co.102.692a-b].

Erebonaster protentipes Humes 1987. 48 ♀♀ paratypes, 95 ♂♂ paratypes, Gulf of California: Guayamas Basin, 27°01.0'N 111°25.0'W, DSRV *Alvin*, dive 1176, depth 2022 m, from box cores, 19 January 1982 [BMNH 1989.1016-1020].

Ergasilus sieboldi von Nordmann 1832. Numerous specimens, England: Woking, Cobetts Lake, from gills of tench (*AI Abdelhalim*) [BMNH 1990.1269-1278].

Farranula gibbula (Giesbrecht 1891). 1 ♂, *John Murray* Expedition, Stn 61A, surface [BMNH 1963.6.28.419]; 1 ♀, *John Murray* Expedition, Stn 61D, surface [BMNH 1963.6.28.432].

Hemicyclops carinifer Humes 1965. 1 ♀ paratype, 1 ♂ paratype, Madagascar: Pte Ambarionaomby, Nosy Kamba, from burrows [BMNH 1965.4.21.3].

Hemicyclops purpureus Boeck 1873. 1 ♀, 1 copepodid, Norway: Oslo Fjord, Moss (*GO Sars*) (Sars collection) [ZM Oslo F7736-F7737].

Lamippe concinna Humes 1957. 3 ♀♀ paratypes, Sierra Leone: Freetown, off Kissy, from *Virgularia* sp., 1955 (*AR Longhurst*) [BMNH 1958.10.9.1-3].

Lichomolgus forficula Thorell 1859. Scotland: Firth of Clyde, Rubha na Croiche, 55°56.3'N 5°11.0'W, depth 17 m, from *Ascidia mentula*, (*GA Boxshall*) [BMNH 1984.237].

Lubbockia extenuata Boxshall 1977. 1 ♀ paratype, 1 ♂ paratype, Cape Verde Islands: *Discovery* Stn 7089, 18°N 25°W, depth 300-500 m, November 1969 [BMNH 1976.64-65].

Nemerthessius nemertophilus (Gallien 1936). 3 ♀♀ topotypes, 3 ♂♂ topotypes, Straits of Dover: Wimereux, Fort Croy, intertidal zone, from *Lineus longissimus*, 10 September 1955 (*JH Stock*) [ZMA Co.102.716].

Oncaea media f. **minor**. Sewell 1947. Numerous specimens, continental shelf off Mauritania: *Discovery* Stn 9529, 21°09'N 17°18'W, depth 10 m (bottom depth 60 m) [BMNH 1991.121-130].

Oncaea venusta Philippi 1843. Numerous specimens, North Atlantic Ocean: *Discovery* cruise 82, 20°N 21°W, depth 0-2 m [BMNH 1991.131-140].

Paraergasilus minutus (Fryer 1956). 1 ♀, 1 ♀ (dissected), Nigeria: Al-lainsi, from *Sierriathrisa* sp., 2 July 1971 (*R Shotter*) [BMNH 1975.1182-1187].

Paralubbockia longipedia Boxshall 1977. Holotype ♀, 1 ♂ paratype, 5 ♀♀ paratypes, Cape Verde Islands: *Discovery* Stn 7089, 18°N 25°W, November 1969 [BMNH 1976.8-13].

Serpulidicola placostegi Southward 1963. Allotype ♂ (dissected), continental slope between British Isles and France: 48°27'N 10°15'W, R/V *Sarsia*, depth 450-760 m, on *Placostegus tridentatus*, 29 November 1958 [BMNH 1963.2.7.5].

Stellicola flexilis Humes 1976. Holotype ♂ and 7 ♂♂ paratypes, Moluccas: western Ceram, Marsegoe Island, 2°59'30"S 128°03'30"E, depth 4 m, from *Linckia guildingi*, 15 May 1975 [ZMA].

Taeniacanthus wilsoni A Scott 1929. 3 ♀♀, England: Yorkshire, off coast at Whitby, on gills of *Raja naevus* [BMNH 1973.863-865].

Tychidion guyanense Humes 1973. Holotype ♀, paratype ♀ (dissected), 3 copepodids, continental slope off Guyana: 8°01'N 57°24'W, depth 500 m, from *Lamellibranchia* sp., 4 September 1970 [RNH Leiden F795-F796].

Zazaranus fungicolus Humes & Dojiri 1983. 11 ♂♂ paratypes, 1 preadult ♀ paratype, Madagascar: S of Nosy Bé, Banc du Touareg, depth 15 m, from *Fungia* sp., 1 September 1967 (*AG Humes*) [USNM 210428].

APPENDIX 2

METHODS USED IN STUDY OF COPEPODS

1. EXTRACTION TECHNIQUES

1.1 Sediment-inhabiting copepods

Copepods are relatively easy to extract from sediments. Pfannkuche & Thiel (1988) gave a detailed account of the most common extraction techniques for meiofauna including copepods. The optimum method depends on the median grain size of the sediment and whether the samples are preserved or fresh. An adequate method for extracting copepods from muddy samples contaminated with a high amount of detritus is based on the flotation-centrifugation technique employing the colloidal silica polymer LUDOX (see Jonge & Bouwman, 1977). Distilled water must be used here because LUDOX precipitates immediately on contact with seawater. Schwinghamer (1981) suggested a method involving a flotation medium to extract living organisms from mud. It is based on the use of a 'Percoll'-sorbitol mixture which, in contrast to LUDOX, is non-toxic to meiofaunal organisms.

Even the best extraction techniques can fail to remove all the detritus from a sample residue. Ultrasonic treatment as described by Thiel et al. (1975) can be used to disperse clay concretions very effectively but causes damage to a significant percentage of the specimens. Similarly, Barnett's (1980) method for the dispersion of clay by freezing destroys many fragile copepods. Cedhagen (1989) recommended mixing the fixed sample with a solution of the alkaline detergent AJAX (Colgate-Palmolive). After leaving the sample for 20-40 minutes at 80-90°C, subsequent sorting is facilitated as the detergent breaks down clay concretions and faecal pellets but keeps even fragile copepods clean and unaffected.

The extraction of tiny copepods from samples and their transfer to preservation vials or observation dishes can be done with hooked needles, which work especially well for elongate animals, or with fine loops of thin stainless steel (Irwin loops). Pipettes can also be used but are not recommended because specimens can stick inside. Coating the pipette by dipping it into hot silicone reduces this problem.

1.2 Phytal copepods

Copepods on seaweed can be collected by placing a plastic bag over the fronds and removing the whole seaweed from the substrate. In the laboratory, repeatedly turning a bright light (positioned to one side of the sorting dish) on and off can help to concentrate 90-95% of the (phototactic) species. In general, seaweed-dwelling species can be extracted by shaking them in water followed by decantation. Extraction efficiency is enhanced by the addition of an anaesthetic, or by using tapwater instead of seawater. It is not advisable to fix macrophyte samples in formalin as this causes many copepods to cling more tightly to the fronds, thereby reducing extraction efficiency. Large algae, such as fucoids and laminarians, produce large amounts of mucus, hindering the efficient collection of clean specimens. However, copepods are generally more abundant on smaller filamentous and tufty seaweeds which produce hardly any mucus.

1.3 Planktonic copepods

Details of collection and suitable extraction techniques for planktonic copepods are given in the UNESCO handbook edited by Steedman (1976).

1.4 Associated copepods

Most copepods associated with invertebrate hosts can be extracted by placing their hosts in seawater containing 5% ethanol (95%) and leaving them overnight. The copepods leave their hosts and accumulate in the sediment on the floor of the container. They are collected by filtering the wash water through a fine mesh net. Rapid washing of the marine invertebrate hosts in 5% ethanol in seawater produces few, if any copepods. Maceration of the host by mechanical means obscures any associated copepods in the resulting mass of debris and mucus. For some endoparasites it is necessary to dissolve the host's tissues with aggressive chemicals. Extraction of mesoparasitic copepods, which attach to their hosts via an embedded anchor process, can be achieved by cutting out a 'steak' of the fish large enough to contain all the anchor. This is left in saturated potassium hydroxide overnight at 20 °C. The tissues of the fish host dissolve, as do the internal tissues of the copepod, leaving the intact exoskeleton of the copepod showing the undamaged form of the anchor.

Kabata (1985) provided a useful overview of how to recover copepod parasites from dead fish. The fish host is examined according to a set procedure, working through the fish beginning with the outer tissues and proceeding gradually inwards. In this way each tissue is observed intact *in situ* before it is disturbed by dissection.

2. MICROSCOPIC METHODS

A stereomicroscope with swinging arm stands is recommended for dissection as it minimises disturbance. In order to reveal structural details and external coloration, it is necessary to study large calanoids and most fish parasites with inclined incident light. Incident light can heat up the dissection dish when ordinary lamps or low voltage lamps are used so cold light sources are recommended. These offer the greatest brightness and best focusing capacity for observations under high power. Sorting and dissection of small copepods is best achieved with transmitted light using a total magnification of at least 40x but up to 240x is desirable. A compound microscope (bright-field) with a set of objectives including a 100x oil immersion objective is necessary for routine analysis of preparations on glass slides. However, the use of interference contrast illumination is recommended for descriptive purposes. Interference contrast illumination produces a conspicuous 3-dimensional image of all unstained, transparent objects, including the finest details and the images are free from halos.

Minute linear structures which scatter light are often visible under dark-field illumination, even if their thickness is below the resolving power of the objective. However the objects might not be represented with absolute accuracy.

Inverted microscopes for transmitted light are highly recommended for observation of living material in chambers, petri dishes, etc., and for identification without dissection. The advantages are the large working distance which allows the use of tall culture dishes, and the retention of image sharpness at high magnifications.

Linear measurements of copepods and their limbs are made using an eyepiece micrometer whose scale division appears together with the image of the object to be measured. Calibration is performed against a stage micrometer which is usually a glass slide with an engraved scale, 1 or 2 mm in length and divided into 100 or 200 intervals respectively. When drawing with the aid of a camera lucida a scale should be added to the drawing using a stage micrometer at the same objective/eyepiece combination as used for tracing.

3. LIVE OBSERVATIONS

3.1 Mounting

Short-term observations can be made on specimens placed on an ordinary slide in a drop of water, preferably from the same habitat, and covered with a coverslip. Water may be gradually removed with a small piece of filter paper until the animal is immobilised. For larger and soft-bodied animals the edges of the coverslip should be supported by small flecks of wax or by fragments of coverslip. Long-term studies of behaviour using cinematography or video-recordings are typically performed in special observation chambers which reduce evaporation (see Westheide & Purschke, 1988 for different types).

Artificial sand systems have been used to study the behaviour of meiofaunal copepods. These are designed to simulate the natural conditions. Coineau & Coineau (1979) constructed a transparent model based on small resin casts made from moulds which in turn were prepared from blocks commonly used in the printing industry. A similar but more natural model was designed by Giere & Welberts (1985) by photographic transfer of the normal sand grains to a plastic mould using modern block-generating techniques. Micro-agar plates are also useful for culturing and making live observations on copepods (George, 1975).

3.2 Narcotisation

Freshly collected copepods that are preserved with formalin typically exhibit severe reactions to the preservative before they die. These reactions are often expressed in violent movements that cause ejection of gut contents and dropping of egg sacs, rendering such samples almost useless for analysis of food habits and measurements of secondary productivity. Narcotisation before preservation is therefore recommended. Many of the narcotisation methods may be used for temporarily anaesthetising copepods and allowing their subsequent recovery after observations have been made. Preferably, the animals should not be transferred directly into the narcotising solution because the amount necessary for relaxation depends on the species involved. The anaesthetic should be added drop by drop, gradually replacing the original fluid until the copepods are immobilised.

Gannon & Gannon (1975) recommended carbonated water, chloroform and methyl alcohol as the best agents to narcotise freshwater crustacean zooplankton. Carbonated water (1 volume to 20 volumes of lake water) is preferred because it is cheap, readily accessible everywhere, and easy to use in the field. Both McKay & Hartzband (1970) and Hulings & Gray (1971) preferred propylene phenoxetol for meiofaunal copepods. One volume of a 1.5% stock solution should be mixed to ten volumes of seawater and poured over the sample. The induction time is about 30 minutes. In general, a magnesium chloride solution isotonic to seawater (about 7.5 g $MgCl_2.6H_2O$ dissolved in 100 ml distilled water) is suitable for marine species; the specimens must remain for 10 to 15 minutes before being transferred into fixative.

3.3 Vital staining

Copepods are small organisms and their erratic swimming makes them difficult to observe alive. Vital staining increases their visibility and is useful in making behavioural observations. Various water soluble dyes are available but the basic dyes Neutral red and Methylene Blue are preferred because they are the least harmful to the copepods. *Intra vitam* staining (Dressel et al., 1972) with Neutral Red vividly stains live copepods, providing a rapid technique for sorting dead copepods from live ones. Copepods are placed into fresh or seawater containing the vital stain and only live individuals take up the stain. Copepod eggs are inconsistently stained by this technique. Anstensrud (1989) used Neutral Red to mark particular developmental stages or individuals and, unless the specimens were overexposed, found that the stain had negligible or no effect on the survival and behaviour of the parasitic copepods.

3.4 High-speed cinematography

Studies using high-speed, high-magnification microcinematography allow direct observations of food capture and handling by tethered animals and the analysis of swimming and foraging patterns of freely swimming copepods. A detailed description of the optical pathways employed to observe swimming calanoids and their feeding behaviour is presented by Strickler (1985).

4. FIXATION AND PRESERVATION

In practice it is advisable to use two separate fluids, one for fixation and another for preservation.

Most fixatives are designed for rapid effects on tissues but lead to excessive hardening when used as a preservative over long periods. Furthermore, most fixatives are not suitable for open-dish use because they are corrosive or toxic.

Formalin: Copepods are most conveniently fixed and preserved in 5% buffered formalin solution. This low concentration reduces the tendency of formalin to make copepods brittle. This effect is significant when using higher concentrations but can be ameliorated by adding glycol (2 to 5% propylene glycol) which has the capacity for maintaining flexibility of tissues and joints in arthropods. It is also a powerful inhibitor of fungal growth and appears to assist in the penetration of formaldehyde as a fixative (Steedman, 1976). It is vital to buffer the formalin solution at a minimum pH of 8.2. Suitable buffers for commercial formalin are borax (sodium tetraborate) or hexamethylene tetramine which are added in an amount of 200 $g.l^{-1}$.

Ethanol: Alcohol, although frequently used for museum collections, is less appropriate for preservation because it leads to brittleness, destroys the colour, and leaches the tannins out of cork stoppers and transfers them to the animals, turning them brown or black. The yellow colour of alcohol solutions containing planktonic copepods is generally due to dissolved oils and fat. Transferring such solutions to formalin may result in the deposition of a thin, slimy film on the specimens. Ethanol also produces a milky precipitate with sea water, its dissolved salts being thrown out of solution and often deposited on the specimens obscuring minute morphological details. When diluted with water it becomes too weak to kill bacteria and loses its preservative power. A further disadvantage is that it evaporates rapidly under the stereomicroscope thereby creating currents which make the specimens whirl around uncontrollably during open-dish sorting. There are advantages occasionally in fixing in formaldehyde and then transferring to 75% ethanol.

Preservative for zooplankton: Steedman (1976) recommends a solution made up of propylene phenoxetol (0.5 ml), propylene glycol (4.5 ml) and distilled water or sea water (95 ml) and may easily replace old formaldehyde solutions.

Other preservatives: Many authors claim that the use of glycerine in preservative recipes is advantageous. In general, glycerine can be used to help retaining colours. Volkmann (1979) used aqueous glycerine (2 volumes of glycerine + 1 volume of distilled water) in order to retain the natural colour patterns of *Tisbe* species. Adding a branch of fresh red algae and storing the specimens in the dark might also help (Hamond, pers. comm.). Glycerine also acts as a safeguard against drying up should the vial be imperfectly sealed. Hamond (1969) recommended a preservative made up by 40% formalin (1 part), glycerol (2 parts) and distilled water (15 parts). Scourfield (1946) suggested the following recipe as the best preservative for freshwater cladocerans and copepods; 100% formalin (1 part), absolute alcohol (2 parts), glycerine (1 part), distilled water (12 parts) and a trace of glacial acetic acid.

5. RESTORING DRIED-OUT SPECIMENS

Specimens can dry out as a result of a cracked lid of a vial, bad packing for shipment, or any of a number of other reasons. In order to allow restorative chemicals to penetrate the body tissues air must be expelled from the specimen. Ellis (1981) recommended either direct immersion into 80% IMS (industrial methylated spirit), or, when the specimen fails to sink, the application of gentle heat until the solution reaches boiling point, immediately after which the container should be allowed to cool. Following this procedure the specimen is placed into distilled water and relaxed using different chemical treatments (see Ellis, 1981: 122 for more information). Jeppesen (1988) satisfactorily rehydrated various crustaceans by placing them in a solution of Decon 90 or dioctyl sodium sulfosuccinate ($C_{20}H_{37}NaO_7S$), subjecting them to repeated application of vacuum/equalisation at room temperature for 24 hours, rinsing in water and finally transferring to the desired preservative.

A restorative solution which has proved to be extremely effective for small crustaceans where little swelling is required, is trisodium phosphate ($Na_3PO_4.12H_2O$). Van Cleave & Ross (1947) used a 0.25-0.5% solution, briefly heated the specimens and left them to stand for about 1 hour whilst cooling. Harding (1956) preferred a 2% solution which generally is sufficient to break down clinging organic matter. Thompson et al. (1966) obtained fairly good results using a mixture of equal volumes of distilled water and ethylene glycol. Dried specimens were completely restored in 12 to 24 hours. Specimens were transferred from the ethylene glycol solution to 50% and then to 70% ethanol. Lactic acid, potassium hydroxide (KOH), sodium carbonate (Na_2CO_3) and a mixture of glycerine and water are also frequently used but seem to cause deterioration of the tissues.

6. SLIDE PREPARATIONS

6.1 Clearing

Prior to dissection the specimen must be cleaned of any attached detritus. This can be achieved by repeatedly sucking up and discharging the specimen into a vial or watch glass, half-filled with water, using a pasteur micropipette, or by vigorous shaking in a small vial two thirds full of water.

Dissection is best achieved on cavity slides with the specimens immersed in a viscous fluid that also serves to clear the specimen. Glycerol and propylene glycol are widely used but lactic acid is a better clearing agent. Lactic acid renders the cuticle more supple and may be used as a temporary clearing agent. Over an extended period it will soften most tissues to a point at which they disintegrate. Most clearing media are hypertonic and specimens have to be protected from collapsing by sudden loss of internal fluids. This can be achieved by penetrating the exoskeleton with a dissection needle, or by soaking in a 50% aqueous solution of the medium before transfer to the undiluted mountant.

Examination of integumental structures is considerably facilitated by removal of internal tissues. This can be done by carefully warming the specimens in 10% KOH by weight in distilled water at about 90°C for 1-2 hours. After rinsing the exoskeleton in distilled water and subsequent staining in an aqueous Chlorazol Black E (1%) solution for about 10-20 seconds, the specimen can be transferred to glycerol for examination. Pepsin can be used to dissolve soft tissues but usually does not work on formalin-fixed animals.

6.2 Staining

Staining with Rose Bengal, Lignin Pink or Chlorazol Black E may facilitate sorting of copepods from sediments or extraction residues and may give some benefit under bright field microscopy, but it is preferable not to stain when using Nomarski interference contrast microscopy. Rose Bengal can be employed either at the time of preservation or on samples already partly processed. Formalin fixed samples can be stained with 10 ml of 1% Rose Bengal solution (1 g Rose Bengal in 1 l of 10% formalin). Rose Bengal stains best at a pH of 4-5, however it obscures natural colour patterns and fine structural detail. Borax carmine stains all crustaceans and other small zooplankton red and facilitates their recognition in plankton samples (Nichols in Steedman, 1976). This method is particularly useful for the identification, staging and enumeration of nauplii and early copepodid stages, since they are virtually transparent even after fixation.

According to English & Heron (in Steedman, 1976) Solophenol blue 2RL (= Chlorantine fast blue 2RLL) can stain some copepod structures slowly and selectively to a pale mauve shade, this contrasts with most dyes (e.g. Chlorazol Black E, Ligin pink) which penetrate the chitin so quickly and stain so intensely that morphological details may be obscured. Specimens are gradually immersed and briefly soaked in a few drops of a mixture of about 10 mg Solophenol blue 2RL per ml lactic acid.

6.3 Mounting and sealing media

Alcohol-soluble mounting media: Euparal is an excellent mounting medium for stained sections and whole mounts. Even old preparations can be dissolved in 95% ethanol for remounting.

Hydrocarbon-soluble mounting media: Canada balsam dissolved in xylene, benzene or chloroform is particularly useful for whole mounts because of its high solids content. A disadvantage is that Canada balsam mounts darken with time, eventually assuming a dark amber colour.

Water-soluble mounting media: Suitable media are Hoyer's or Faure's medium, 10% glycerin in 95% ethanol and Zeis W15. The latter is recommended because of its unusually high refractive index of 1.515. The original recipe of Hoyer's medium contains 200 g chloral hydrate but Higgins' (1983) modification reduced this amount to 100-125 g to prevent overclearing of specimens. Higgins further recommends the addition of 2 g iodine crystals and 1 g potassium iodide.

Lactic acid & Berlese's fluid: These media should not be used as mountants because of their strong clearing properties.

Gurr's Neutral Mounting Medium: Hockin (1980) proposed using Gurr's neutral mounting medium as an alternative to acidic mounting media such as Canada balsam and Polyvinyl Lactophenol. It is a slow-drying medium so that the specimens can be positioned and arranged precisely. It is recommended for some interstitial copepods which are sensitive to other mountants.

Polyvinyl lactophenol: This is widely used but is not recommended for type collections since it overclears the preparation within about ten years. The mountant is also gradually replaced by rosettes of long thin crystals and often dries out if not sealed.

Lactophenol: This is by far the best medium for microscopic preparations. It does not have a strong clearing effect and allows the preparation to be remounted in a more suitable orientation, even after a long period. It consists of melted phenol crystals (30 ml), lactic acid (10 ml), glycerol (20 ml) and distilled water (10 ml). Preparations have to be sealed. Many commercial sealants such as Araldite, Murrayite, Bioseal, and Glyceel are available.

6.4 Dissection

The dissection medium depends on the mountant used. Both Reyne's and Hoyer's media are aqueous based and therefore the specimen has to be dissected in water. For lactophenol and polyvinyl lactophenol the dissection is done in lactic acid. Dissection is performed using two dissecting needles made from ca. 0.2 mm diameter tungsten wire projecting about 2-3 cm from a holder (pin vice or glass capillary tube). The tip of the needle can be sharpened by electrolysis using a 6-volt supply (a stereo microscope lamp transformer is suitable), where the needle is dipped in a saturated solution of potassium hydroxide. The immersed part of the needle must be dipped repeatedly and gently in and out to give the desired shape of the point.

Another method for sharpening needles is based on anhydrous sodium nitrite (Wells, 1988) but is not recommended here as it can be dangerous. Crystals of $NaNO_2$ are carefully melted in a crucible to give a deep yellow liquid. When the end of a thin wire is dipped into this, a ball of incandescence forms at once on the tip below the liquid surface and migrates rapidly up the wire into the open air, where it vanishes, leaving the end of the wire eroded to a fine point.

The following dissection technique is recommended for routine identification work:

1. Dissection is carried out under maximum magnification (at least 40x) and entails using one needle to hold the specimen steady on its side, while using the other needle to cut laterally through the body somites.

2. First hold the prosome and cut away the urosome, then proceed anteriorly to divide the prosome into the individual pedigerous somites together with their respective appendages and finally tease off the first swimming legs from the cephalothorax.

3. The head appendages should then be separated from the cephalic shield. In practice it might be possible to dissect all the mouthparts when dealing with large species, however in smaller animals only the antennules, antennae and maxillipeds might be successfully removed.

4. Place a streak of polyvinyl lactophenol (or Reyne's mountant) transversely across the centre of the slide.

5. Transfer each part as it is dissected, to the mountant on the point of a dissecting needle to its equivalent position in the streak. The urosome should be mounted ventral face up (in podopleans the fifth leg can be separated at this stage). It is crucial that the swimming legs are mounted in the correct order (particularly the second to fourth swimming legs which are often very similar) and anterior face upwards.

6. In order to avoid the dissected parts floating around when the coverslip is placed on top, allow the mounting medium to become tacky. Place a cross of mountant on a coverslip or a drop of mountant on top of the streak and gently lower the coverslip into position.

7. Note the positions of the dissected parts on an adhesive label.

An alternative method is to mount each element in one of six drops of polyvinyl lactophenol, placed within a 15x15 mm area and cover all the drops with a small coverslip. Using this method there is little risk of transposing the limbs but it is inconvenient for examination, especially under oil immersion. Here, the position of each element can be labeled on the underside of the slide with a fine indelible pen.

For detailed taxonomic studies it is necessary to dissect out all the cephalothorax appendages, to separate the fifth leg from the urosome (in podopleans) and to ensure that the legs are mounted anterior face upwards. It is recommended that each of the dissected parts is mounted on a separate slide, or, in the case of minute species, that the head appendages are mounted separate from the swimming legs, and the latter from the urosome. Alternative dissection strategies are described by Hamond (1969) and Coull (1973).

6.6 Mounting

The Cobb metal slide frame preparation holds a double coverglass mounted preparation and allows the microscopic examination of copepod from either of the two surfaces. This technique was introduced for harpacticoids by Perkins (1956) and was also used by Humes & Gooding (1964). A recent variation of the Cobb slide is the Higgins-Shirayama slide which consists of two standard microslide-sized pieces of plastic fused into a single unit the same thickness of a standard slide. It allows for a more precise centering of the specimen at a level equidistant between the upper and lower surface of the finished preparation.

The open-mount technique described by Humes & Gooding (1964) offers the advantage that a single specimen can provide a full set of observations, since dissection can be stopped at any point and the results examined or drawn under the compound microscope even with oil immersion. With the slide upside down the dissected parts are placed in a small drop of lactic acid on the exposed surface of the coverslip. The animal may then be examined under the compound microscope by inverting the slide. The dissected parts are thus hanging in a drop of fluid and are not exposed to any compression. For permanent preparations the dissections can be covered with Hoyer's medium and a smaller cover slip which allows the mounted specimen to be examined from both sides.

The mounting procedure we have used in the course of this study is extremely simple. The specimen or the dissected part is mounted in lactophenol in a 'sandwich slide', i.e. the coverslip is supported on both sides or on one side, by fragments of broken coverslip or by complete coverslips. The number of supporting coverslips required can be adjusted according to the thickness of the specimen. The art of making a sandwich slide is to pinch the specimen just enough to hold it in position without squashing it out of shape. The pressure of the coverslip can be regulated by sliding the supporting coverslips in or out rather than by the addition or subtraction of lactophenol. It is extremely important in the analysis of segmentation patterns that limbs are viewed in their natural shape and configuration. Ordinary mounting techniques inevitably result in squashing of the dissected parts, thereby distorting length:width ratios and the 3-dimensional structure. Folds and depressions are heavily accentuated in squashed preparations and can be misinterpreted as genuine segmentary boundaries such as the alleged praecoxa-coxa boundary in the maxilliped of the Oithonidae. A second advantage of this technique is that it allows the specimen or the limb to be re-orientated by manipulation of the top coverslip so that it can be viewed from virtually any angle. This is particularly helpful for the examination of complex structures such as the chirocer antennules of harpacticoids or the maxillulary arthrite. When examination of the preparation is finished it can be orientated in any position desired for permanent mounting prior to sliding out the supporting coverslips.

7. ANATOMICAL AND HISTOLOGICAL PROCESSING - TEM

There is an extensive volume of literature on fixatives and methods used in transmission electron microscopy. We will give here only one possible way of preparing specimens for TEM (Blades & Youngbluth, 1979), which is highly recommended. Specimens are placed in Beem capsules, fixed in 5% glutaraldehyde in 0.4 M Millonig's phosphate buffer, and post-fixed at 7°C for 45 minutes in 1% osmium tetroxide in 0.4 M Millonig's buffer. The animals were then rapidly dehydrated in ascending concentrations of ethanol to 100%, exchanged in propylene oxide, and embedded in Epon. Thin sections were cut on a ultramicrotome with a diamond knife and stained with saturated uranyl acetate, followed by lead citrate.

8. SCANNING ELECTRON MICROSCOPY - SEM

8.1 Fixation and postfixation

Specimens should be selected carefully for SEM preparation using the cleanest specimens with the least physical distortion. Transparent gelatinous material, not detectable under the stereomicroscope, might cover the body or limbs and can agglutinate during dehydration. Rinsing in a potassium hydroxide (KOH) aqueous solution or ultrasonic treatment in a freon medium fails to remove all adhering dirt particles, but heating the specimens to 93°C in 25% aqueous solutions of hydrochloric acid (HCl) can be effective for removing debris from the body surface.

Specimens are fixed in formalin or glutaraldehyde and postfixed for 24 hours in unbuffered 2% osmium tetroxide before dehydration. The specimens are then washed in several changes of distilled water and left in distilled water overnight. Postfixation in osmium tetroxide has been shown to reduce specimen shrinkage and collapse. OsO_4 also darkens the cuticle which makes tiny specimens more visible after critical point-drying.

8.2 Dehydration and critical point-drying

Specimens are dehydrated in graded ethanol; 30%, 50%, 70%, 80%, 95% and 100%. Dehydration can also be accomplished using graded acetone which sometimes gives better results for tiny animals. Large specimens should be transferred into a porous capsule with a cap, or into a capsule covered with nylon net on both ends. To avoid loss, small animals such as nauplii and early copepodids, and dissected parts can be attached to a coverslip which was cleaned ultrasonically and heated in a Bunsen burner until the flame becomes coloured. The cooled coverslip is transferred to a 1% aqueous solution of poly-L-lysine and used within 10 minutes of drying. Specimens are released in a small drop of buffer from a Pasteur pipette onto the coverslip where they should be left for 2 minutes. The same amount of 5% glutaraldehyde solution is then added. After washing and dehydration the coverslip with the specimens attached is placed in the critical point-drying apparatus.

Either liquid CO_2 or freon 13 can be used for critical point-drying. As an alternative specimens can be freeze-dried using liquid nitrogen as a coolant (Cohen et al., 1968).

8.3 Mounting

After drying the copepods are extremely lightweight and highly subject to static electricity which causes them to cling to the sides of the working surface or to the forceps. Another effect of static electricity is that dust particles adhere to the specimen. Handling specimens after critical point-drying should therefore be kept to a minimum. Using a stereomicroscope and incident illumination, the animals can be mounted on stubs in a particular orientation with a dissection needle so that the desired surface is accessible for the electron beam. Tilting or rotating the stub allows examination of various aspects of the same specimen. If sufficient material is available, it is advisable to have a series of specimens mounted in dorsal, right and left lateral, and in ventral aspect, but care should be taken to leave sufficient space between them. Best results in the scanning electron microscope are obtained if the stub angle to the electron beam is 45°. Specimens should therefore be mounted in a particular orientation; this may be facilitated by using a plexiglass stub holder for holding stubs at 45° (Pulsifer, 1975). Mounted stubs should be protected from dust before and after they are sputter coated in a vacuum with gold or a gold-palladium alloy.

8.4 Dry fracturing

Toda et al. (1989) developed a new technique for examining internal structures of copepods. Following critical point-drying, specimens are mounted on a stub with double-sided adhesive tape and pressed with a similar stub. The two stubs are then pulled apart so that the specimen is separated into two halves. Both can be observed with SEM and is possible to make observations of internal surfaces of digestive tracts, or gut contents, or endoparasites. The technique was successfully used to observe developing nauplii inside an egg sac. Dry fracturing tends to produce randomly broken specimens and has a low probability of showing the desired structures. An alternative technique is paraffin-carving (Oshel, 1985) which offers a means of revealing internal structures *in situ* in a controlled fashion. After embedding in paraffin wax, the excess paraffin wax is first removed and the unwanted portions of the specimen are carved away under a dissecting microscope (and cool illumination) with a sharp razor blade or microscalpel. After carving the specimen is de-embedded from the block and returned to absolute ethanol. It is then processed for SEM as usual. More details about SEM microdissection of crustaceans are given by Barber & Emerson (1979).

8.5 Preservation

For permanent storage stubs can be mounted in covered plastic boxes kept in a desiccator above silica gel or P_4O_{10}, as moisture is detrimental to the thin metal coating. Re-coating the stub is recommended when specimens have been stored for a long period. Prior to re-coating, limbs or other parts of the body can be removed with a dissection needle in order to examine specific morphological details or underlying structures.

9. RNA NUCLEOTIDE SEQUENCING

The application of molecular biological techniques to the study of copepods is in its infancy but will undoubtedly be one of the most important areas for future work. The small-subunit rRNA macromolecules have proven to be quite useful in phylogenetic analyses because of a number of advantages: they are (1) universal, (2) conservative, (3) of a size that provides sufficient data for analysis, (4) functionally constant, and (5) relatively simple to sequence (Kim & Abele, 1990). For a detailed protocol of the technique as used on crustacean material, we refer to Abele et al. (1989) and Kim & Abele (1990).

APPENDIX 3

GLOSSARY

abdomen - The postgenital region of the trunk; primitively comprising 3 free somites and the telson (= anal somite).
accessory antennule - The offset terminal segment of the antennary endopod, found in some members of the family Chondracanthidae (Poecilostomatoida).
aesthetasc - A simple, tubular, sensory filament, typically found on the antennules, rarely found on other mouthparts; *aesthete, aesthetask.*
alae - Wing-like expansions of a body somite; *elytra*
allobasis - A compound segment formed by fusion of the basis and first endopodal segment, typically found on the antenna (*antennary allobasis*), but also on the maxilla (*maxillary allobasis*).
anal somite - The terminal 'segment' of the body, bearing the anus either terminally or dorsally; represents the telson or a somitic complex incorporating abdominal somite(s) and telson.
anchialine - Used of an inland marine habitat with no direct surface connection with the sea.
antenna - The second cephalic appendage.
antennule - The first cephalic appendage.
apodeme - An infolding of the exoskeleton, serving as an attachment site for muscles.
apomorphic - Derived; used of a character state different from the ancestral type.
armature - The spines and setae present on a segment or appendage.
arthrite - A movable endite; used for the praecoxal endite of the maxillule.
arthrodial membrane - The flexible membrane connecting body somites and limb segments.
associate - A copepod that lives in any kind of symbiotic relationship with a host organism, including for example parasites and commensals.
baseoendopod - The proximal part of the fifth leg formed by fusion of basis and endopod.
basipod 1 - The proximal segment of a 2-segmented protopod: see *coxa.*
basipod 2 - The distal segment of the protopod: see *basis.*
basipodite - see *basis.*
basis - The distal segment of the protopod, bearing the rami.
biramous - Two-branched, having an exopod and an endopod.
brachium - The distal segment of the maxilla of some siphonostomatoid copepods, representing the basis plus basal endite.
canna - A specialised armature element on the apex of the basal endite of the maxilla of some siphonostomatoid copepods.
calamus - A specialised armature element on the apex of the basal endite of the maxilla of some siphonostomatoid copepods.
caudal rami - The paired, setiferous appendages on the posterior surface of the anal somite.
cephalic shield - The dorsal covering of the cephalosome or cephalothorax, formed by fusion of the tergites of the incorporated somites.
cephalon - The anterior region of the body, comprising the first five somites (antennulary to maxillary somites).
cephalosome - The anterior 6 somites of the body covered by the dorsal cephalic shield; comprising 5 cephalic somites and the first thoracic (=maxilliped-bearing) somite.
cephalothorax - The anterior 7 or more somites of the body covered by the dorsal cephalic shield; comprising 5 cephalic plus at least the first and second thoracic somites (those bearing the maxillipeds and first swimming legs respectively).
chirocer - The condition of a male antennule with the geniculation located between a very swollen, thick-walled, subapical segment and the apical segment; *chirocerate.*
copepodid - The postnaupliar stage in copepod development; there are typically 5 copepodid stages in the life cycle prior to the adult; designated copepodid I to V (CI - CV).
copepodite - An alternative to copepodid.
copulation - The transfer of spermatophores from male to female.

copulatory duct - The duct leading from the copulatory pore to the seminal receptacle.
copulatory pore - The opening or pair of openings of the duct leading into the seminal receptacles of the female, into which the spermatophores discharge.
corpus - The massive proximal part of the subchelate maxilliped in some parasitic copepods; representing either the basis or the fused basis plus syncoxa; *corpus maxillipedis.*
coxa - The middle segment of the 3-segmented protopod of postnaupliar limbs, the proximal segment of the 2-segmented protopod of naupliar limbs; *coxopodite.*
coxobasis - A compound segment derived by fusion of coxa and basis.
coxopodite - see *coxa.*
coupler - see *intercoxal sclerite.*
digeniculate - Used of an antennule with two geniculations, with the distal one located between ancestral segments XX and XXI.
dolichoplean - Used of podoplean copepods, particularly harpacticoids, in which there is little differentiation between prosome and urosome.
ectosoma - The part of a herpyllobiid that is outside its host.
elytra - Flattened, wing-like expansions of the dorsal or dorsolateral surface of postcephalic trunk somites in some parasitic siphonostomatoids.
egg sac - A clutch of one or more eggs contained within a sac-like membrane that emerges from the genital aperture.
egg mass - Mass of eggs attached to body of female copepod but not enclosed within common outer membrane.
endite - A medially directed process on a protopodal segment of an appendage.
endobenthic - Living within the sediment; burrowing through sediment.
endopod - The inner ramus of an appendage; *endopodite.*
endopodite - see *endopod.*
endopodital lobe - The inner lobe of the baseoendopod of the fifth leg, derived from the endopod.
endosoma - The part of a herpyllobiid that is inside the host.
epibenthic - Living at the surface of the sea bed or lake bottom; inhabiting the sediment-water interface.
epimera - The lateral projection of a tergite of a free pedigerous somite.
epipodite - An outer lobe (exite) on the coxa.
exite - A lateral process on the outer margin of a protopodal segment of an appendage.
exopod - The outer ramus of an appendage; *exopodite.*
exopodite - see *exopod.*
first antenna - see *antennule.*
first maxilla - see *maxillule.*
free - not fused.
furcal rami - see *caudal rami.*
geniculate - Knee-like; used of male antennules with a well developed articulation between proximal and distal regions; also used of armature elements with a well defined flexure zone.
genital antrum - The internal chamber into which the eggs are released from the oviducts to be fertilised by spermatozoa entering via the receptacle ducts from the seminal receptacles.
genital aperture - The opening of the reproductive system; in the female the genital aperture is the external opening of the genital antrum which primitively contains both the oviduct opening (the gonopore) and the copulatory pore; typically paired but sometimes medially fused to form a common genital aperture.
genital complex - A compound body region formed by fusion of fifth pedigerous and genital double somites.
genital double somite - The double somite resulting from fusion of the genital and first abdominal somites in females.
genital field - The structures associated with the female genital apertures on the ventral surface of the double somite; this term has been used collectively for both internal and external structures present in the area and has led to much confusion, it is best avoided.
genital operculum - The plate derived from the sixth legs that closes off the genital aperture or the gonopore.
genital somite - The somite bearing the genital apertures; the seventh thoracic somite.

genital trunk - A region of the body comprising the fused pedigerous and genital somites.
genitoabdomen - A posterior body region formed by fusion the genital and abdominal somites.
gnathobase - The coxal endite of the mandible, bearing the toothed cutting edge distally.
gonopore - The opening of the oviduct in the female and of the vas deferens in the male.
gymnoplean tagmosis - The body plan in which prosome and urosome are divided by a specialised hinge joint lying between the fifth pedigerous and genital somites.
haplocer - The condition of the male antennule in which the middle segments are only slightly modified and there are a number of segments distal to these; *haplocerate*.
head - see *cephalon*.
heart - A contractile vessel located in a pericardial sinus situated dorsally in the mid-prosomal region of copepods, typically with anterior and posterior ostia.
heterochrony - An evolutionary change in the onset or timing of a feature relative to the appearance or rate of development of the same feature in the ontogeny of an ancestor.
hyaline frill - A transparent, membranous extension of the posterior margin of a body somite or the distal margin of an appendage segment, that covers the arthrodial membrane of the joint.
intercoxal sclerite - A flat plate connecting the coxae of a pair of the swimming legs.
interpodal bar - see *intercoxal sclerite*.
interstitial - Living within the pore spaces between sediment particles.
labium - A median plate or lobe forming the posterior border of the oral opening; derived by fusion of the paragnaths.
labrum - A posteroventrally directed, muscular lobe forming the anterior margin of the oral opening.
lacertus - The proximal segment (representing the syncoxa) of the maxilla of siphonostomatoid copepods.
lacinia mobilis - A small toothed process articulated with the incisor process of a mandible; not found in copepods.
lash - A slender, toothed, whip-like structure, probably representing an elaboration of the middle blade on the gnathobase of the mandible of poecilostomatoid copepods.
lecithotrophic - Used of developmental stages that are rich in yolk and, typically, are non-feeding.
lunule - A small sucker-like structure located ventrally on the plates at the frontal margin of the cephalothorax of some caligiform copepods.
mandible - The third cephalic appendage.
mandibular palp - That part of the mandible distal to the coxa, comprising basis, exopod and endopod.
mandibular stylet - The slender, modified gnathobase of siphonostomatoid copepods.
mate guarding - The clasping by an adult male of a juvenile female (copepodid I to V inclusive) until the final moult of the female after which copulation can take place.
maxilla - The fifth and last pair of cephalic appendages.
maxillary glands - The paired excretory organs of most adult copepods, opening on the protopod of the maxilla.
maxilliped - The first pair of thoracic appendages; carried on last somite of cephalosome; uniramous and typically modified as feeding appendages.
maxillule - The fourth cephalic appendage.
meiobenthos - Small benthic organisms that pass through a 1 mm mesh sieve but are retained by a 0.1 mm mesh.
metanauplius - A naupliar stage with more than 3 pairs of functional appendages.
metasome - The part of the prosome comprising the free pedigerous somites; a locomotory tagma.
monophyletic - Derived from a common ancestral taxon not shared by any other taxon; used of a group sharing the same common ancestor.
myxal surface - The medial surface of the corpus of the maxilliped in siphonostomatoids; often produced into myxal processes.
naupliar limb - Any of the 3 pairs of appendages present in the nauplius stage i.e. antennules, antennae and mandibles.
nauplius - The first larval stage of a copepod; there is a maximum of 6 nauplius stages (denoted NI - NVI) before the metamorphic moult into the first copepodid.

nauplius eye - The tripartite eye, consisting of 1 ventral and 2 dorsal ocelli, found in the copepod nauplius and retained in the adult.
neocopepodan geniculation - The specialised joint primitively located between ancestral segments XX and XXI of the antennules of male calanoids and podopleans.
operculum - A posteriorly directed extension of the dorsal surface of the anal somite, covering the anus at least in part.
oral cone - The conical structure formed around the mouth by the labrum and labium in siphonostomatoid copepods.
oral opening - The mouth.
ornamentation - The surface sculpturing, and superficial rows or patches of fine spinules, denticles or pinnules formed by the epicuticular layer of the integument of the body and appendages. Ornamentation is used of surface structures that do not penetrate the integument.
ovigerous spines - The long, egg-bearing spinous processes on the ventral surface of the genital double somite of female monstrilloid copepods.
palp - The part of a mandible or maxillule distal to the main coxal gnathobase or praecoxal arthrite respectively.
paragnath - A small lobe lying on ventral surface of cephalosome, either side of midline between bases of mandibles and maxillules.
paraphyletic - Used of a group of taxa descended from a single ancestral taxon but which does not contain all the descendants of the most recent common ancestor; based on common possession of plesiomorphic characters.
pedestal - An outgrowth of the ventral surface of the cephalosome upon which an appendage is inserted. The maxillipeds of siphonostomatoids are often located on a pedestal.
pediger - see *pedigerous somite*.
pedigerous somite - A thoracic somite bearing a pair of swimming legs.
pereopod - see *swimming leg*.
phytal - Living on or in plants.
planktotrophic - Used of developmental stages that feed on planktonic organisms, rather than depending on yolk.
plesiomorphic - Used of the ancestral or original state of a character.
podoplean tagmosis - The body plan in which prosome and urosome are divided by a specialised hinge joint lying between the fourth and fifth pedigerous somites.
polyphyletic - Derived from two or more different lineages; used of a group comprising taxa descended from two or more different ancestors.
postantennal process - A tapering, spinous process located on the ventral surface of the cephalothorax in some siphonostomatoids (e.g. Caligidae) and some poecilostomatoids (e.g. Taeniacanthidae); derived by elaboration of a ventral cephalic sclerite.
post-displacement - Used of a character that appears later in the ontogeny of a descendant taxon than in its ancestor.
praecoxa - The proximalmost segment of the three-segmented protopod of a postmandibular appendage.
precoxa - see *praecoxa*.
prehensile - Raptorial; used of an appendage modified for grasping.
prosome - The region of the body lying anterior to the major articulation.
prosomite - A somite of the prosome.
protopod - The common basal part of an appendage, typically comprising coxa and basis in the naupliar limbs, or praecoxa, coxa and basis, in the postmandibular limbs. The basis bears the ramus or rami; *protopodite*.
protopodite - see *protopod*.
pseudoperculum - A dorsal outgrowth of the posterior margin of the preanal somite, extending over the anus.
pseudorostrum - An median process, lying between the antennules and articulating with the dorsal cephalic shield but which does not carry the rostral sensory complex of paired frontal sensilla and median pore.
quadrithek - The armature of an antennulary segment consisting of 2 setae and 2 aesthetascs; found in males of some calanoid copepods.

ramus - A branch of an appendage, either the exopod or the endopod.
receptaculum seminis - see *seminal receptacle.*
reversal - The reappearance of an ancestral character state in a taxon whose immediate ancestor displayed a derived state of the same character.
rostrum - A median extension, between the antennules, of the anterior margin of the dorsal cephalic shield that carries the rostral sensory complex of paired frontal sensilla and a median pore.
second antenna - see *antenna.*
second maxilla - see *maxilla.*
seminal receptacle - The storage chambers of the female reproductive system where spermatozoa are stored after insemination.
seta - A tapering, flexible armature element which has a hollow central core, and is inserted into a hole passing through the integument.
setule - A small, slender ornamentation element, which is borne in a hollow on the surface of the integument.
sexual dimorphism - A difference in the state of any structure between the sexes.
somite - A segment of the body.
spermatophore - A small, oval vesicle in which spermatozoa are transferred from the male to the female.
spermatophore tubule - The exit tube of the spermatophore through which the spermatozoa are discharged.
spine - A rigid armature element which has a hollow central core and is inserted into a hole passing through the integument.
spinule - A small rigid ornamentation element which is borne in a hollow on the surface of the integument.
sternal furca - A typically forked structure on the ventral surface of the cephalothorax, derived as an elaboration of the median intersomitic sclerite lying between the maxillipedal and first pedigerous somites in some siphonostomatoids.
subchela - The distal, movable part of an appendage that opposes the unmodified flat surface of the proximal segment.
subchirocer - The condition of a male antennule in which the middle segments proximal to the geniculation are markedly swollen and there are 2 segments distal to the geniculation.
symplesiomorphy - A shared ancestral character state.
sympod - A double segment comprising fused coxa and basis, used for the swimming legs of parasitic copepods.
synapomorphy - A shared derived character state.
syncoxa - A double segment derived from fusion of praecoxa and coxa.
tagma - A major region of the body defined by a common function.
tagmosis - The division of the body into functional regions (tagmata).
telson - The terminal part of the body having its mesoderm derived directly from the teloblasts after budding of the metameres has ceased.
tergite - The dorsal plate of a somite; *terga.*
thoracopod - A thoracic limb; used in copepods for the first to fifth swimming legs which are the second to sixth thoracic limbs.
thorax - The middle region of the body, comprising the seven postcephalic trunk somites from the maxillipedal to the genital.
trithek - The typical armature of an antennulary segment, consisting of 2 setae and 1 aesthetasc.
trunk - The postcephalosomic region of the body.
tube pore - A flexible, cylindrical extension around the exit pore of a somitic or secretory integumental gland.
uniramous - Having a single ramus.
uropod - see *caudal ramus.*
urosome - The region of the body posterior to the major articulation.
urosomite - A somite of the urosome.

INDEX

(Illustrations in bold)